P9-BIF-217

Introduction to
Japan

For a country that lived in self-imposed isolation until 150 years ago, Japan has not hesitated in making up for lost time since the world came calling. Anyone who's eaten sushi or used a Sony Walkman feels they know something about this slinky archipelago of some 6800 volcanic islands and yet, from the moment of arrival in this oddly familiar, quintessentially oriental land it's almost as if you've touched down on another planet.

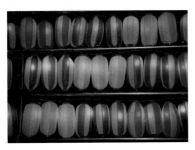

Japan is a place of ancient gods and customs, but is also the cutting edge of cool modernity. High-speed trains whisk you from one end of the country to another with frightening punctuality. You can catch sight of a farmer tending his paddy field, then turn the corner and find yourself next to a neon-festooned electronic games parlour in the suburb of a sprawling metropolis. One day you could be picking through the fashions in the biggest department store on earth, the next relaxing in an outdoor hot-spring pool, watching cherry blossom or snowflakes fall, depending on the season.

Few other countries have, in the space of a few generations, experienced so much or made such an impact. Industrialized at lightning speed, Japan shed its feudal trappings to become the most powerful and outwardly aggressive country in Asia in a matter of decades. After defeat in World War

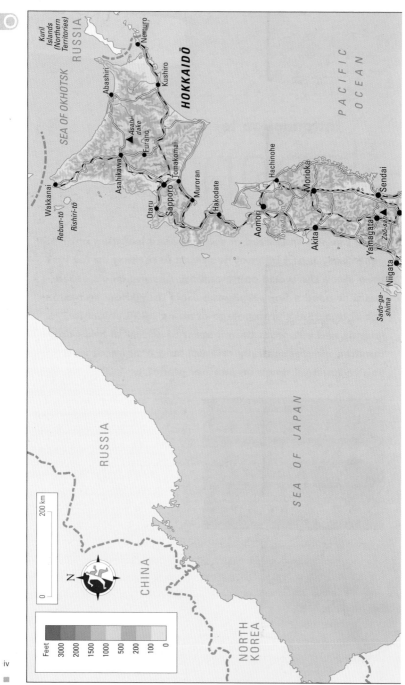

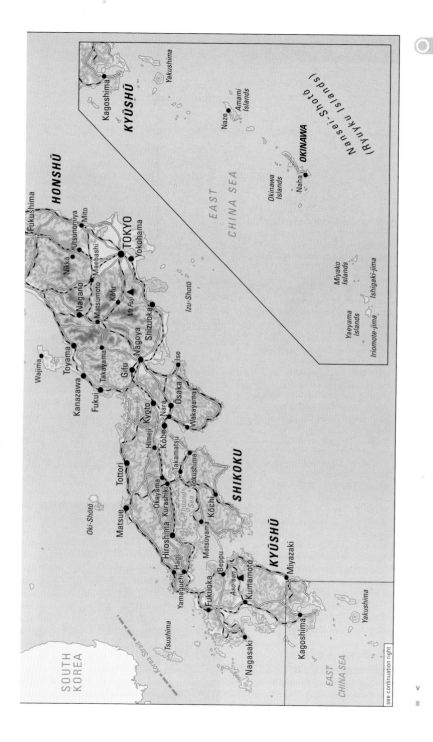

see continuation right

v

Fact file

● Japan is made up of around 6800 **islands**, the main five being (in descending order of size) Honshū, Hokkaidō, Kyūshū, Shikoku and Okinawa. Travelling from Sōya Misaki, Japan's northernmost point, to Haterumajima, the southernmost island in Okinawa, you'll cover over 3000km. Despite many Japanese telling you what a small country they live in, Japan is in fact twice the size of the UK. This sense of smallness is due to the fact that much of the country is covered by forested mountains, with the result that some 127 million people are squished into the flat quarter of the country, making the southern coastal plain of Honshū from Tokyo down to Ōsaka one of the most densely populated areas in the world.

● Amongst this population, Japanese predominate, making this one of the world's most **ethnically homogeneous** societies. Japan's 650,000 resident Koreans are the most significant non-Japanese group, although you'd be hard pressed to notice this practically invisible minority. Indigenous people such as the Ainu, mainly concentrated in Hokkaidō, account for no more than 77,000 people. Japan is also a rapidly ageing society, with a very low birth rate and long life expectancy.

● Although not the **economic powerhouse** it once was, Japan's economy still has a very respectable GDP of US$4 trillion. Manufacturing drives the economy, with the electronics, machine tools and automobile industries dominating. The country has long been experiencing price deflation and unemployment is around five percent.

● The head of state is the **emperor**, still greatly respected, even if he is no longer considered a living god.

II, it transformed itself from atom bomb victim to wonder economy, the envy of the globe. Currently facing up to recession and rising unemployment after years of conspicuous consumption, Japan still remains fabulously wealthy and intent on reinvention for the twenty-first century.

The vast majority of the 127 million population live on the crowded coastal plains of the main island of **Honshū**. The three other main islands, running north to south, are **Hokkaidō**, **Shikoku** and **Kyūshū**, and all are linked to Honshū by bridges and tunnels that are part of one of Japan's modern wonders – its super-efficient transport network of trains and highways. In the **cities** you'll first be struck by the mass of people. These hyperactive metropolises are the place to catch the latest trend, the hippest fashions and technologies, the most cutting-edge cuisine before they hit the rest of the world. It's not all about modernity, however: cities like Tokyo and Ōsaka also provide the best opportunities to view traditional performance arts,

△ Shinjuku, Tokyo

such as Kabuki and Nō plays, or track down the wealth of Japanese visual arts in the major museums. **Outside the cities** there's a vast range of travel options, from the wide open spaces and deep volcanic lakes of Hokkaidō to the balmy subtropical islands of Okinawa, and you'll seldom have to go far to catch sight of a lofty castle, ancient temple or shrine, or locals celebrating at a colourful street festival.

It's not all perfect. The Japanese are experts at focusing on detail (the exquisite wrapping of gifts and the tantalizing presentation of food are just two examples) but often miss the broader picture. Rampant development and sometimes appalling pollution are difficult to square with a country also renowned for cleanliness and appreciation of nature. Part of the problem is that natural cataclysms, such as earthquakes and typhoons, regularly hit Japan, so few people expect things to last for long anyway. There's also a blindness to the pernicious impact of mass tourism, with ranks of gift shops, ugly hotels and crowds often ruining potentially idyllic spots. And yet, time and again, Japan redeems itself with unexpectedly beautiful landscapes, charmingly courteous people, and its tangible sense of history and cherished traditions. Most intriguing of all is the opaqueness at the heart of this mysterious "hidden" culture that stems from a blurring of traditional boundaries between East and West – Japan is neither wholly one nor the other.

Japan is never going to be a cheap place to travel, but there's no reason

vii

△ Rice paddy, Iwate, Honshū

why it should be wildly expensive either. Some of the most atmospheric and traditionally Japanese places to stay and eat are often those that are the best value. There's been significant price-cutting in some areas in recent years, particularly airline tickets which now rival the famed bargain rail passes as a means to get to far-flung corners of the country.

Where to go

Two weeks is the minimum needed to skim the surface of what Japan can offer. The capital Tokyo, and the former imperial city and thriving cultural centre of Kyoto, will be top of most visitors' itineraries, and deservedly so, but you could avoid the cities entirely and head to the mountains or smaller islands to discover an alternative side of the country, away from the most heavily beaten tourist tracks.

You could spend two weeks just in **Tokyo**. The metropolis is home to some of the world's most ambitious architecture, stylish shops and outrageous restaurants and bars – as well as glimpses of traditional Japan at scores of temples, shrines and imperial gardens. Consider also taking in a couple of the city's surrounding attractions, in particular the historic towns of **Nikkō**, home to the amazing Tōshō-gū shrine complex, and **Kamakura**, with its giant Buddha statue and tranquil woodland walks.

Northern Honshū sees surprisingly few visitors, but its sleepy villages and nicely laid-back cities deserve to be better known. The Golden Hall

△ Lanterns and cherry blossom, Tokyo

The trouble with sumo

In a neat reversal of Japan's appropriation of baseball and export of professional players to the US league, four of sumo's most revered stars of recent years were born abroad. Both the top-ranked *yokuzuna* Konishiki (a.k.a. the "dump truck") and Akebono, who retired in 1998 and 2001 respectively, were born in Hawaii; the 237kg Musashimaru, a *yokuzuna* since 1999, hails from American Samoa; while Asashoryu – a relative lightweight at 137kg, who became the 68th *yokuzuna* in February 2003 – was born Dolgorsuren Dagvadorj in Ulan Bator, Mongolia.

The success of the foreign wrestlers is just one of the factors that is said to be turning Japanese off the 1500-year-old sport. At recent bouts there have been large chunks of unsold seats – unthinkable in the past – and even TV viewing figures are down as younger Japanese tune into soccer instead. The Japan Sumo Association finds itself in a bind. On the one hand they have tried to limit the number of foreign wrestlers to help preserve the sport's Japanese character. On the other, they are acutely aware that fewer young Japanese wish to submit to the punishing regime needed to become a top sumo wrestler. And so the keen young foreigners may just prove to be sumo's saviours.

Finding enough people to fight is only one of the Sumo Association's problems. The other is dealing with wrestlers like Asashoryu who flout the game's strict code of behaviour. The Mongolian *yokuzuna* has been known to show his emotions on winning or losing a bout – very much a no-no – and his out-of-the-ring antics keep Japan's scandal rags very happy. Given sumo's slipping profile, however, this may be just the sort of publicity the sport needs to keep it in the public's increasingly unappreciative eye.

Living dolls

Arthur Golden's *Memoirs of a Geisha* and similar books have awakened curiosity about the centuries-old institution of the geisha. Often mistakenly considered to be high-class prostitutes, geisha (which means "practitioner of the arts") are in fact refined women who entertain men of ample means with their various accomplishments, such as singing, dancing, playing a traditional instrument and conversation.

The world of the geisha is a shrinking one, however: from a pre-World War II peak of eighty thousand there are now reckoned to be no more than a few thousand geisha left, the majority concentrated in Kyoto, the bastion of the tradition. It takes five years for an apprentice geisha, known as *maiko*, to master their art, training like Olympic athletes in the various arts and living according to a strict code of dress and deportment, almost like living dolls. Not surprisingly, few women are tempted to sign up as apprentices. Not that becoming a geisha isn't popular, though. As the geisha teahouses die out, Kyoto has a new industry: the instant geisha make-over. There are now some fifty make-over studios in the Kyoto region offering allcomers the chance to don the distinctive white make-up, lacquered hairdos and fabulously expensive kimono that constitute the epitome of geisha beauty.

of **Hiraizumi** more than justifies the journey, and can easily be combined with the islet-sprinkled **Matsushima Bay** or rural **Tōno**. The region is also known for its vibrant **summer festivals**, notably those at Sendai, Aomori, Hirosaki and Akita, and for its sacred mountains including **Dewa-sanzan**, home to a sect of ascetic mountain priests, and the eerie, remote wastelands of **Osore-zan**.

Further north across the Tsugaru Straits, **Hokkaidō** is Japan's final frontier, with many national parks including the outstanding **Daisetsu-zan National Park**, offering excellent hiking trails over mountain peaks and through soaring rock gorges. The lovely far northern islands of **Rebun-tō** and **Rishiri-tō** are ideal summer escapes. Hokkaidō's most historic city is **Hakodate**, with its late nineteenth-century wooden houses and churches built by expat traders. Hokkaidō's modern capital, **Sapporo**, is home to the raging nightlife centre of Suskino and the original Sapporo Brewery. Winter is also a fantastic time to visit and catch Sapporo's amazing Snow Festival and go skiing at some of Japan's best resorts.

△ Zen garden, Daitoku-ji, Kyoto

Skiing, mountaineering and soaking in hot springs are part of the culture of **Central Honshū** (Chubu), an area dominated by the magnificent Japan Alps. Either the old castle town of **Matsumoto** or **Nagano**, with its atmospheric temple of pilgrimage, Zenkō-ji, can be used as a starting point for exploring the region. Highlights include the tiny mountain resort of **Kamikōchi** and the immaculately preserved Edo-era villages of **Tsumago** and **Magome**, linked by a short hike along the remains of a three-hundred-year-old stone-paved road. **Takayama** deservedly draws many visitors to its handsome streets lined with merchant houses and temples built by genera-tions of skilled carpenters. In the remote neighbouring valleys you'll find the rare thatched hous-es of **Ogimachi**, **Suganuma** and **Ainokura**, remnants of a fast dis-appearing rural Japan. On the Sea of Japan coast, the historic city of **Kanazawa** is home to Kenroku-en, one of Japan's best gardens, and is also the departure point for the charming fishing villages along the wild coastline of the **Noto-hantō** peninsula. On the heavily industrialized southern coast the major city of **Nagoya**, location of Expo 2005, has a few minor points of interest, includ-ing the Tokugawa Art Museum. From here it's a short hop to the pretty cas-tle towns of **Inuyama** and **Gifu**, which holds summer displays of the ancient skill of *ukai*, or cormorant fishing.

> In the cities you'll first be struck by the mass of people. These hyperactive metropolises are the place to catch the latest trend, the hippest fashions and technologies, the most cutting-edge cuisine before they hit the rest of the world

South of the Japan Alps, the **Kansai** plains are scattered with ancient temples, shrines and the remnants of imperial cities. **Kyoto**, Japan's premier cultural centre, is home to its most refined cuisine, classy ryokan, magnificent temples and palaces, and glorious gardens. Nearby **Nara** is a more manageable size but no slouch when it comes to venerable monuments, notably the great bronze Buddha of Tōdai-ji and Hōryū-ji's unrivalled collection of early Japanese statuary. The surrounding region contains a number of still-thriving religious foundations, such as the highly atmospheric temples of **Hiei-zan** and **Kōya-san**. Over on the east coast is Japan's most revered Shinto shrine, the austere **Ise-jingū**. Not all Kansai is so rarefied, though. The slightly unconventional metropolis of **Ōsaka** has an easy-going atmosphere and boisterous nightlife, plus several interesting sights. Further west, the port of **Kōbe** offers a gentler cosmopolitan atmosphere, while **Himeji** is home to Japan's most fabulous castle, as well as some impressive modern gardens and buildings.

> Outside the cities, you'll seldom have to go far to catch sight of a lofty castle, ancient temple or shrine

▽ Torii gates, Fushumi Inari Taisha, Kyoto

For obvious reasons **Hiroshima** is the most visited location in **Western Honshū**. On the way there pause at **Okayama** to stroll around one of Japan's top three gardens, Kōraku-en, and the appealingly preserved Edo-era town of **Kurashiki**. The beauty of the Inland Sea, dotted with thousands of islands, is best appreciated from the idyllic fishing village of **Tomonoura**, the port of **Onomichi** and the relaxed islands of **Naoshima, Ikuchi-jima** and **Miyajima**.

Crossing to the San-in coast, the castle town of **Hagi** retains some handsome samurai houses and atmospheric temples, only surpassed by the even more enchanting **Tsuwano**, further inland. One of Japan's most venerable shrines, **Izumo Taisha**, lies roughly midway along the coast, near the watery capital of **Matsue**, which has the region's only original castle. At the far eastern end of the region lies the pine-forested sand spit at **Amanohashidate**, one of Japan's top scenic spots.

You don't need to visit all 88 temples on Japan's most famous pilgrimage to enjoy the best of **Shikoku**, the country's fourth largest island. Apart from dramatic scenery in the Iya valley and along the often rugged coastline, the places to aim for are **Matsuyama**, with its imperious castle and splendidly ornate Dōgo Onsen Honkan – one of Japan's best hot springs; the lovely garden Ritsurin-kōen in **Takamatsu**; and the ancient shrine at **Kotohira**, one of the most important in the Shinto religion.

The southernmost of Japan's four main islands, **Kyūshū** is probably best known as the target for the second atomic bomb, which exploded over **Nagasaki** in 1945. This surprisingly attractive and cosmopolitan city is rightly Kyūshū's prime tourist attraction, while hikers and onsen enthusiasts should head up into the central highlands, where **Aso-san**'s smouldering peak dominates the world's largest volcanic crater, or to the more southerly meadows of **Ebino Kōgen**. So much hot water gushes out of the ground in **Beppu**, on the east coast, that it's known as Japan's hotspring capital, complete with jungle baths and sand baths. **Fukuoka** takes pride in its innovative modern architecture and an exceptionally lively entertainment district.

△ Chinatown, Yokohama

Average daily temperatures and monthly rainfall

	Jan	Feb	Mar	Apr	May	June	July	Aug	Sept	Oct	Nov	Dec
Akita												
max °C	2	3	6	13	18	23	26	28	24	18	11	4
min °C	-5	-5	-2	4	8	14	18	19	15	8	3	-2
rainfall mm	142	104	104	105	112	127	198	188	211	188	191	178
Kōchi												
max °C	12	12	15	19	22	24	28	29	28	23	19	14
min °C	4	4	7	12	17	19	24	25	22	17	12	7
rainfall mm	64	142	160	188	244	323	257	213	323	279	175	107
Nagasaki												
max °C	9	10	14	19	23	26	29	31	27	22	17	12
min °C	2	2	5	10	14	18	23	23	20	14	9	4
rainfall mm	71	84	125	185	170	312	257	175	249	114	94	81
Sapporo												
max °C	2	2	6	13	18	21	24	26	22	17	11	5
min °C	-10	-10	-7	-1	3	10	16	18	12	6	-1	-6
rainfall mm	25	43	61	84	102	160	188	155	160	147	56	38
Tokyo												
max °C	10	10	13	18	23	25	29	31	27	21	17	12
min °C	1	1	4	10	15	18	22	24	20	14	8	3
rainfall mm	110	155	228	254	244	305	254	203	279	228	162	96

Okinawa comprises more than a hundred smaller islands stretching in a great arc from southern Kyūshū to within sight of Taiwan. The islands formed an independent kingdom until the early seventeenth century, and traces of their distinctive culture still survive. The beautifully reconstructed former royal palace dominates the capital city, **Naha**, but to really appreciate the region you need to make for the remoter islands. Though not undiscovered, this is where you'll find Japan's most stunning white-sand beaches and its best diving, particularly around the subtropical islands of **Ishigaki** and **Iriomote**.

When to go

Average temperature and weather patterns vary enormously across Japan. The main influences on the climate on Honshū are the mountains and surrounding warm seas, bringing plenty of rain and snow. **Winter** weather differs greatly, however, between the western Sea of Japan and the Pacific coasts, the former suffering cold winds and heavy snow while the latter tends towards dry, clear winter days. Regular heavy snowfalls in the mountains provide ideal conditions for skiers.

Despite frequent showers, **spring** is one of the most pleasant times to visit Japan, when the weather reports chart the steady progress of the cherry blossom from warm Kyūshū in March to colder Hokkaidō around May. A rainy season (*tsuyu*) during June ushers in the swamp-like heat of **summer**; if you don't like tropical conditions, head for the cooler hills or the northern reaches of the country. A bout of typhoons and more rain in September precede **autumn**, which lasts from October through to late November and is Japan's most spectacular season, when the maple trees explode into a range of brilliant colours.

Also worth bearing in mind when planning your visit are Japan's **national holidays**. During such periods as the days around New Year, the "Golden Week" break of April 29 to May 5 and the Obon holiday of mid-August the nation is on the move, making it difficult to secure last-minute transport and hotel bookings. Avoid travelling during these dates, or make your arrangements well in advance.

36

things not to miss

*It's not possible to see everything Japan has to offer in one trip —
and we don't suggest you try. What follows is a selective taste of
the country's highlights: stunning traditional and contemporary
architecture, dramatic landscapes, fabulous festivals and tempting
food. They're arranged in five colour-coded categories to help you
find the very best things to see, do, eat and experience. All
highlights have a page reference to take you straight into the
guide, where you can find out more.*

01 Yakushima Page **861** • Commune with thousand-year-old cedar trees in the World Heritage-listed Kirishima-Yaku National Park.

02 Obuse Page **427** • Surrounded by orchards, this charming town is famous for its excellent sake and chestnut confections.

03 Skiing Page **78** • Hit the slopes and enjoy the perfect powder snow at Niseko in Hokkaidō or the great runs and charming atmosphere of Nagano's Nozawa Onsen.

05 Dewa-sanzon Page **332** • Join white-clothed pilgrims on the arduous but scenic climb up the sacred mountain of Dewa-sanzan in northern Honshū.

07 Kabuki Page **184** • Tokyo's venerable Kabuki-za theatre is the place to catch this most dramatic of traditional Japanese performing arts.

04 New Year Page **68** • Head to a temple or shrine to welcome in the New Year – Tokyo's Meiji-jingū draws crowds in their millions.

06 Omotesandō, Tokyo Page **149** • Tokyo's leafy shopping boulevard and the surrounding streets of Harajuku are the country's prime hunting ground for the latest in cool consumables.

08 Nebuta and Neputa Matsuri Pages **311 & 321–322** • Aomori and Hirosaki's Obon festivals feature lively parades with fabulous giant lanterns and paper-covered figures.

ACTIVITIES | CONSUME | EVENTS | NATURE | SIGHTS |

xvii

09 **Nara** Page **574** • The ancient former capital of Nara is home to the monumental bronze Buddha of Tōdai-ji and fine collections of religious art.

10 **Ogimachi** Page **453** • Quaint village filled with distinctive *gasshō-zukuri* houses, whose steep-sided thatched roofs are said to recall two hands joined in prayer.

11 **Himeji** Page **614** • Relive the days of the samurai at the magnificent donjon of Himeji-jō, a prime example of a feudal-era fortress.

12 **Climb Mount Fuji** Page **220** • Make the tough but rewarding hike up Japan's tallest peak, a long-dormant volcano of classic symmetrical beauty.

13 **Yuki Matsuri** Page **365** • Gawp at mammoth snow and ice sculptures in Sapporo, Hokkaidō, every February.

14 Awa Odori Page **736** • Dance the night away at the country's biggest Obon bash, held in Tokushima, Shikoku.

16 Adachi Museum of Art Page **696** • Interesting contemporary art museum – although the real attraction is the stunning surrounding gardens which envelop the galleries and steal attention at every turn.

15 Fukuoka Page **790** • Kyūshū's most happening city, energetic Fukuoka boasts striking modern architecture, vibrant nightlife and an interesting culture.

ACTIVITIES | CONSUME | EVENTS | NATURE | SIGHTS |

xix

17 Kamikōchi Page **438** • The busy but beautiful mountain village of Kamikōchi preserves a Shangri-La atmosphere and serves as the gateway to the magnificent Northern Alps.

19 Taketomi-jima, Okinawa Page **923** • Unwind on this tiny island graced with a charming village of buildings roofed with terracotta tiles and surrounded by beautiful flower gardens.

18 Hiroshima Page **651** • Pay your respects to the A-bomb's victims at the Peace Memorial Park and Museum in the city of Hiroshima, now amazingly reborn from the ashes of World War II.

20 Onsen Page **773** • Take a dip at a top onsen resort town, such as Dōgo, with its magnificent bathhouse, or experience the exquisite warmth of a rotemburo (outdoor bath) as the snow falls.

21 The Inland Sea Page **621** • Stretching between Honshū and Shikoku, the waters of the Inland Sea are sprinkled with myriad islands including beautiful Naoshima, and Miyajima, with its famous red shrine gate rising straight out of the sea.

22 Nikkō Page **196** • Set amidst splendid mountains north of Tokyo, the pilgrim town of Nikkō is home to the fabulously over-the-top Tōsho-gū shrine, one of Japan's most sumptuous buildings.

23 Roppongi Hills Page **126** • Tokyo's hippest neighbourhood is home to the new Mori Art Museum and a plethora of restaurants and top-class boutiques.

24 Fireworks Page **660** • Spectacular displays are held every July and August across the country, including at the famous torii at Miya-jima in Western Honshū.

ACTIVITIES | CONSUME | EVENTS | NATURE | SIGHTS |

25 Gion Matsuri Page **556** • Watch geishas perform en masse at Kyoto's biggest spectacle, held every July.

26 Tsukiji Page **158** • This hyperactive Tokyo fish and produce market is the place to go for an early breakfast and the freshest sashimi and sushi in Japan.

27 Kyoto Page **512** • The capital of Japan for a thousand years, endowed with an almost overwhelming legacy of temples, palaces and gardens, and also home to the country's richest traditional culture and most refined cuisine.

28 Earth Celebration Page **349** • Vibrant international world music festival, hosted by the drumming group Kodô on the lovely island of Sado-ga-shima.

29 Nagasaki Page **807** • One of Japan's most picturesque cities, whose long and cosmopolitan history is reflected in Western colonial-style buildings and an exuberantly colourful Confucian shrine.

30 Chūzenji-ko Page **204** • This serene, mountain-bound lake is a wonderful place to see the changing colours of the autumn leaves.

31 Kenroku-en Page **461** • Nature has been tamed and primped to its most beautiful at Kanazawa's star attraction, one of the country's top traditional gardens.

32 The Kiso Valley Page **442** • The three-hour hike from Tsumago to Magome in Nagano takes you through gorgeous countryside between two lovingly preserved Edo-era post towns.

33 **Sumo** Page **76** • Visit a major sumo tournament and see the titanic, ritualized clashes of Japan's sporting giants.

34 **Koya-san** Page **590** • Mingle with monks and pilgrims on one of Japan's holiest mountains, home to over a hundred monasteries.

35 **Kaiseki-ryōri** Page **55** • Indulge yourself with a meal of *kaiseki-ryōri*, Japan's haute cuisine, comprising a selection of beautifully prepared morsels made from the finest seasonal ingredients.

36 **Iriomote-jima** Page **925** • This wild island at the far southern end of Okinawa-ken boasts perfect sandy beaches and forest hikes to picturesque waterfalls.

Contents

Using this Rough Guide

We've tried to make this Rough Guide a good read and easy to use. The book is divided into five main sections, and you should be able to find whatever you want in one of them.

Colour section

The front colour section offers a quick tour of Japan. The **introduction** aims to give you a feel for the place, with suggestions on where to go and information about the weather. Next, our authors round up their favourite aspects of Japan in the **things not to miss** section – whether it's amazing sights, great food or a special festival. Right after this comes a full **contents** list.

Basics

The Basics section covers all the **pre-departure** nitty-gritty to help you plan your trip. This is where to find out which airlines fly to Japan, what paperwork you'll need, what to do about money and insurance, Internet access, food, security, public transport, car rental – in fact just about every piece of **general practical information** you might need.

Guide

This is the heart of the book, divided into user-friendly chapters, each of which covers a specific region. Every chapter starts with a list of **highlights** and an **introduction** to help you to decide where to go. Likewise, introductions to the various towns and regions within each chapter should help you plan your itinerary. We start most town accounts with information

on accommodation, followed by a tour of the sights, and finally reviews of places to eat and drink, and details of nightlife. Longer accounts also have a directory of practical listings. Each chapter concludes with **public transport** details for that region..

Contexts

Read Contexts to get a deeper understanding of what makes Japan tick. We include a brief **history**, along with articles about Japanese **religion**, **film**, **music**, **art**, **environmental issues** and **pop culture**, plus a detailed further reading section that reviews dozens of **books** relating to the country.

Language

The Language section gives useful guidance for speaking Japanese and pulls together all the vocabulary you might need on your trip, including a comprehensive **menu reader**, plus a **glossary** of words and terms peculiar to the country.

small print and Index

As well as a **full index**, this section covers publishing information, credits and acknowledgements, and also has our contact details in case you want to send in updates and corrections to the book – or suggestions as to how we might improve it.

Chapter list and map

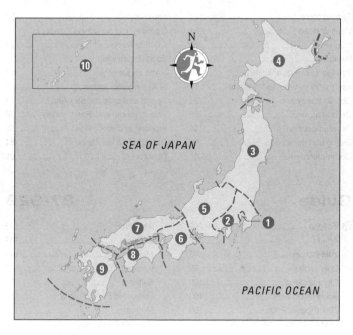

CONTENTS

Contents

4

Contexts

931–1022

Language

1023–1039

small print and Index

1041–1056

Basics

Basics

Getting there

Most people travelling to Japan fly into either Tokyo or Ōsaka, although several Asian airlines have services to regional airports such as Sapporo, Nagoya and Fukuoka. A more adventurous route to Japan is by ferry from Korea, Taiwan and China, or even by a combination of ferry and Trans-Siberian train from Russia.

Airfares always depend on the **season**, with the highest being around the Japanese holiday periods of Golden Week at the beginning of May, and the O-bon festival period in mid-August; as well as at Christmas and New Year, when seats are at a premium; prices drop during the "shoulder" **seasons** – April through June and September through October – and you'll get the best deals in the low season, January through March and November through December (excluding Christmas and New Year when prices are hiked up).

You can often cut costs by going through a **specialist flight agent** – either a consolidator, who buys up blocks of tickets from the airlines and sells them at a discount, or a **discount agent**, who in addition to dealing with discounted flights may also offer special student and youth fares and a range of other travel-related services such as travel insurance, rail passes, car rentals, tours and the like. Another possibility is to see if you can arrange a courier flight, although you'll need a flexible schedule, and preferably be travelling alone with very little luggage. In return for shepherding a parcel through customs, you can expect to get a deeply discounted ticket. You'll probably also be restricted in the duration of your stay.

If Japan is only one stop on a longer journey, you might want to consider buying a Round the World (RTW) ticket. Some travel agents can sell you an "off-the-shelf" RTW ticket that will have you touching down in about half a dozen cities (Tokyo is on some itineraries); others will have to assemble one for you, which can be tailored to your needs but is apt to be more expensive. Figure on £800/US$2500/A$3800 upwards for an RTW ticket including Japan.

Booking flights online

Many airlines and discount travel websites offer you the opportunity to book your tickets, hotels and holiday packages online, cutting out the costs of agents and middlemen; these are worth going for, as long as you don't mind the inflexibility of non-refundable, non-changeable deals. There are some bargains to be had on auction sites too. Almost all airlines have their own websites, offering flight tickets that can sometimes be just as cheap, and are often more flexible.

Online booking agents and general travel sites

Ⓦ **www.cheapflights.co.uk** (in the UK & Ireland), Ⓦ **www.cheapflights.com** (in the US), Ⓦ **www.cheapflights.ca** (in Canada), Ⓦ **www.cheapflights.com.au** (in Australia). Flight deals, travel agents, plus links to other travel sites.
Ⓦ **www.cheaptickets.com** Discount flight specialists (US only). Also ☎1-888/922-8849.
Ⓦ **www.ebookers.com** Efficient, easy to use flight bookings, with competitive fares.
Ⓦ **www.etn.nl/discount** A hub of consolidator and discount agent links, maintained by the nonprofit European Travel Network.
Ⓦ **www.expedia.co.uk** (in the UK), Ⓦ **www.expedia.com** (in the US), Ⓦ **www.expedia.ca** (in Canada). Discount airfares, all-airline search engine and daily deals.
Ⓦ **www.flyaow.com** "Airlines of the Web" – online air travel info and reservations.
Ⓦ **www.gaytravel.com** US gay travel agent, offering accommodation, cruises, tours and more. Also at ☎1-800/GAY-TRAVEL.
Ⓦ **www.geocities.com/thavery2000** An extensive list of airline websites and US toll-free numbers.
Ⓦ **www.hotwire.com** Bookings from the US only. Last-minute savings of up to forty percent on

11

regular published fares. Travellers must be at least 18 and there are no refunds, transfers or changes allowed. Log-in required.

Ⓦ **www.kelkoo.co.uk** Useful UK-only price-comparison site, checking several sources of low-cost flights (and other goods & services) according to specific criteria.

Ⓦ **www.lastminute.com** (in the UK),

Ⓦ **www.lastminute.com.au** (in Australia),

Ⓦ **www.lastminute.co.nz** (in New Zealand),

Ⓦ **www.site59.com** (in the US). Good last-minute holiday package and flight-only deals.

Ⓦ **www.opodo.co.uk** Popular and reliable source of low UK airfares. Owned by, and run in conjunction with, nine major European airlines.

Ⓦ **www.orbitz.com** Comprehensive web travel source, with the usual flight, car hire and hotel deals but also great follow-up customer service.

Ⓦ **www.priceline.co.uk** (in the UK),

Ⓦ **www.priceline.com** (in the US). Name-your-own-price website that has deals at around forty percent off standard fares.

Ⓦ **www.skyauction.com** Bookings from the US only. Auctions tickets and travel packages to destinations worldwide.

Ⓦ **www.travelocity.co.uk** (in the UK),

Ⓦ **www.travelocity.com** (in the US),

Ⓦ **www.travelocity.ca** (in Canada),

Ⓦ **www.zuji.com.au** (in Australia). Destination guides, hot fares and great deals for car rental, accommodation and lodging.

Ⓦ **www.travelshop.com.au** Australian site offering discounted flights, packages, insurance, and online bookings. Also on ☎1-800/108 108.

Ⓦ **www.travel.yahoo.com** Incorporates some Rough Guides material in its coverage of destination countries and cities across the world, with information about places to eat and sleep.

Ⓦ **www.travelzoo.com** Great resource for news on the latest airline sales, cruise discounts and hotel deals. Links bring you directly to the carrier's site.

Flights from the UK and Ireland

Japan's two main international air gateways from Britain are Tokyo and Ōsaka. Four airlines (All Nippon Airways, British Airways, Japan Airlines and Virgin) fly nonstop from London into New Tokyo International airport (better known as Narita), while JAL also fly daily, nonstop to Kansai International airport, built on an artificial island in Ōsaka Bay. There are plenty of airlines with indirect flights to Narita and Kansai – some also offer connecting services to major regional airports, such

as Nagoya and Fukuoka. Direct flights from London take around twelve hours.

There are no direct flights **from Ireland** – you'll need to stop over in Europe en route, with the cheapest deals usually being via London (Ryan Air fly daily from Dublin to London for around €50).

To find out the best deals on **fares** to Japan, contact a flight agent – see the list below for a list of dependable ones. You could also check the ads in the travel pages of the weekend newspapers, regional listings magazines, Teletext and Ceefax and **Web sites** such as Ⓦ www.ebookers.com, Ⓦ www.travelocity.co.uk, Ⓦ www.expedia .co.uk and Ⓦ www.deckchair.com for special deals and the latest prices. Whoever you buy your ticket through, check that the agency belongs to the travel industry bodies ABTA or IATA, so that you'll be covered if they go bust before you receive your ticket. **Students** and **under-26s** can often get discounts through specialist agents such as USIT in Ireland or STA (see box on p.14).

Seasons differ from airline to airline, but generally July, August and December are the costliest months to travel. If you're not tied to particular dates, check the changeover dates between seasons; you might make a substantial saving by travelling a few days sooner or later. **Fares** to Tokyo from London start from around £500. However, you can find occasional special deals from as low as £300, so it pays to shop around.

Stopovers, open-jaws and round-the-world tickets

If you have time, you might think about breaking your journey with a **stopover** en route to Japan. Not all airlines charge extra for this option, and with some you'll have to stop over anyway while waiting for a connecting flight. It's also worth noting that some bargain fares to Australia from London can include stopovers in Tokyo or Ōsaka.

Another way to cut the cost of a flight – although you'll be limited on your luggage – is to apply for a **courier flight**, where in exchange for a lower fare you have to carry documents or parcels from airport to airport. Courier flights start at around £200 return. For details, contact the **International**

Association of Air Travel Couriers (UK ☎0800/074 6481 or 01291/625 656, www.aircourier.co.uk), who act as agents for lots of companies.

On airlines that serve more than one international airport in Japan, it's possible to buy **open-jaw tickets**, usually at no extra cost, making it possible, say, to fly into Tokyo and out of Ōsaka. These tickets are well worth considering as a way of saving the time and money involved in backtracking on a journey around the country. Both JAL and ANA offer open-jaw tickets for the same price as a simple return.

A further option is a **round-the-world** (RTW) ticket, although you may have to hunt around flight agents for those who include Tokyo on their global itineraries. Prices start at around £800 for a one-year open ticket.

Japan isn't a difficult country for the independent traveller to negotiate, nor need it be horrendously expensive. However, if you're worried about the cost or the potential language problems, a **package tour** is worth considering. Packages tend to come into their own if you want to stay in upmarket hotels – these usually offer cheaper rates for group bookings. All tours use scheduled airline flights, so it's usually no problem extending your stay beyond the basic package. If you want to venture off the beaten track, however, package tours will not be for you.

For a return flight, five nights' accommodation at a three- to four-star hotel, airport transfers and a sightseeing tour, prices begin around £600, based on double occupancy. You'll pay more if you're on a package that combines Tokyo with other areas of Japan or a specialized tour. All the tour prices quoted include flights unless otherwise stated.

Airlines

Aeroflot ☎020/7355 2233, ⓦwww.aeroflot.co.uk Direct flights from Heathrow to Tokyo twice a week, and via Moscow four times a week.
Air France ☎0845/084 5111, ⓦwww.airfrance.com Flights from eight UK cities daily to Tokyo and Ōsaka via Paris.
Alitalia ☎0870/544 8259, Republic of Ireland ☎01/677 5171, ⓦwww.alitalia.co.uk. Daily departures from Heathrow to Tokyo and three times a week to Ōsaka, all via Milan or Rome.
All Nippon Airways (ANA) ☎020/7224 8866,

ⓦwww.anaskyweb.com Daily direct services from Heathrow to Tokyo. You can also book discounted domestic flights when booking from abroad (restrictions apply).
British Airways ☎0870/850 9850, ⓦwww.britishairways.com Direct flights from Heathrow to Tokyo daily.
Cathay Pacific ☎020/8834 8888, ⓦwww.cathaypacific.com/uk. Flights from Heathrow daily to Ōsaka, Nagoya, Tokyo, Sapporo and Fukuoka, all via Hong Kong.
Finnair ☎020/7408 1222, ⓦwww.finnair.com. From Heathrow twice weekly, and from Manchester weekly, to Tokyo via Helsinki.
Japan Airlines (JAL) ☎0845/774 7700, Republic of Ireland ☎01/408 3757, ⓦwww.jal -europe.com. Daily direct flights from Heathrow to Tokyo or Ōsaka.
KLM Royal Dutch Airlines ☎0870/507 4074, ⓦwww.klm.com. Flights from fifteen UK cities via Amsterdam to Tokyo and Ōsaka daily.
Korean Air International toll-free ☎00800/0656 2001, Republic of Ireland ☎01/799 7990, ⓦwww.koreanair.eu.com. Five flights weekly from Heathrow to Tokyo, Fukuoka, Nagoya and Ōsaka, all via Seoul.
Lufthansa German Airlines ☎0870/837 7747, ⓦwww.lufthansa.co.uk. Daily flights from Heathrow to Tokyo via Frankfurt.
Malaysia Airlines ☎0870/607 9090, ⓦwww.malaysiaairlines.com. Daily flights from Heathrow to Tokyo and Ōsaka, and three times a week to Nagoya, all via Kuala Lumpur.
Ryan Air UK ☎0871/246 0000, Republic of Ireland ☎0818/30 30 30, ⓦwww.ryanair.com. Daily flights from Dublin to Gatwick, Stansted or Luton, for connecting flights to Japan.
SAS Scandinavian Airlines ☎0870 6072 7727, Republic of Ireland ☎01/844 5440, ⓦwww.scandanavian.net. Daily flights from Heathrow and Manchester to Tokyo, via Copenhagen.
Singapore Airlines ☎0870/608 8886, Republic of Ireland ☎01/671 0722, ⓦwww.singaporeair.com. From Heathrow and Manchester daily to Tokyo, Ōsaka and Nagoya, and five times a week to Fukuoka, all via Singapore.
Swiss UK ☎0845/601 0956, Republic of Ireland ☎1890/200 515, ⓦwww.swiss.com. Daily flights from Heathrow to Tokyo via Zurich.
Thai Airways ☎0870/606 0911, ⓦwww.thaiair.com. From Heathrow daily to Tokyo and Ōsaka, and five times weekly to Fukuoka and Nagoya, all via Bangkok.
Virgin Atlantic Airways ☎08705/747 747, ⓦwww.virgin-atlantic.com. Daily flights from Heathrow to Tokyo.

Discount travel agents

Aran Travel First Choice Republic of Ireland
ⓣ091/562595, ⓦwww.firstchoicetravel.ie.
Worldwide flight agent offering deals to Japan.
AWL Travel UK ⓣ020/7222 1144,
ⓦwww.awlt.com. Specialists in travel to Japan,
offering bargain airfares and Japan Rail passes.
Bridge the World UK ⓣ0870/443 2399,
ⓦwww.bridgetheworld.com. Specialists in long-
haul travel, with good-value flight deals, RTW tickets
and tailor-made packages, all aimed at the
backpacker market.
Dial-a-Flight UK ⓣ0870/333 4488,
ⓦwww.dialaflight.com. Telephone sales of
scheduled flights; the website is useful for tracking
down bargains.
Emerald Travel UK ⓣ020/7312 1700,
ⓦwww.etours-online.com. Discount flight agent.
North-South Travel UK ⓣ01245/608291,
ⓦwww.northsouthtravel.co.uk. Friendly and
competitive travel agency offering discount fares
worldwide; profits are used to support projects in the
developing world, especially the promotion of
sustainable tourism.
Quest Travel UK ⓣ020/8481 4000,
ⓦwww.questtravel.com. Specialists in RTW and
discount fares to Asia.
STA Travel UK ⓣ0870/160 0599,
ⓦwww.statravel.co.uk. Worldwide specialists in
low-cost flights, overland and holiday deals. Good
discounts for students and under-26s.
Trailfinders UK ⓣ020/7938 3939,
ⓦwww.trailfinders.com; Republic of Ireland
ⓣ01/677 7888, ⓦwww.trailfinders.ie. One of the
best-informed and most efficient agents for
independent travellers; they produce a very useful
quarterly magazine worth scrutinizing for round-the-
world routes (ring for a free copy).
USIT Northern Ireland ⓣ028/9032 7111,
ⓦwww.usitnow.com; Republic of Ireland
ⓣ0818/200 020, ⓦwww.usit.ie. Specialists in
student, youth and independent travel – flights,
trains, study tours, TEFL, visas and more.

Tour operators

Asia Fare ⓣ020/7038 3940, ⓦwww.asia
-fare.co.uk. Customized itineraries.
Carrick Travel Ltd ⓣ01926/311 415. Flight
agent and specialist tour operator who can put
together tailor-made packages to Japan.
Explore Worldwide ⓣ01252/760 000,
ⓦwww.exploreworldwide.com (in the Republic of
Ireland contact Maxwells Travel ⓣ01/679 3948).

Offers a "Shogun Trail" two-week guided tour of
Japan, flying into Tokyo and out of Fukuoka. From
£1899, including flights and accommodation.
Far East Gateways (The Cheshire Travel Centre)
ⓣ0161/437 4371. Offers escorted sightseeing tours
and accommodation packages, promoting multi-
country trips. The "Classical Japan Escorted Tour"
comprises a seven-day trip (including Kyoto) for
£1329, including flights.
The Imaginative Traveller ⓣ01473/667337,
ⓦwww.adventurebound.co.uk. This flight agent
and tour operator offers two tours of Japan, including
the fifteen-day "Empire of the Sun" tour which
includes a night on Mount Fuji and a day in the
Peace Park in Hiroshima. Prices start at £1295 (not
including international flights).
Jaltour ⓣ020/7462 5577, ⓦwww.jaltour.co.uk.
Japanese specialists – they're the tour arm of Japan
Airlines. Can arrange flights, tours, city breaks, rail
passes and accommodation packages. Four nights in
Kyoto from £579, including flights and
accommodation.
Japan Travel Centre ⓣ020/7255 8283. Offers
flights to Japan, accommodation packages, Japan
Rail passes and guided tours of Japan. Four nights in
Tokyo from £579, including flights and
accommodation.
The Oriental Caravan ⓣ020/7582 0716,
ⓦwww.theorientalcaravan.com Offer small guided
group tours, one taking in west Japan and Kyūshū,
the other the northern Tōhoku region. From £1595,
excluding airfares.

Flights from the US and Canada

A number of airlines serve Tokyo International
airport (Narita) and – less often – other
Japanese international airports nonstop from
North America, with connections from virtually everywhere in Canada and the US. Many
flights are offered at up to half-price, so keep
an eye out for special offers. It's also possible
to reach Japan via Europe, though this is
likely to be a lot more expensive.

Barring special offers, the cheapest of the
airlines' published fares is usually an **Apex**
ticket, although this will carry certain restrictions: you have to book – and pay – at least
21 days before departure, spend at least
seven days abroad (maximum stay three
months), and you tend to get penalized if
you change your schedule. Some airlines
also issue **Special Apex** tickets to people
younger than 24, often extending the maxi-

mum stay to a year. Many airlines offer youth or student fares to **under-26s**, though these tickets are subject to availability and can have eccentric booking conditions. It's worth remembering that most cheap return fares involve spending at least one Saturday night away and that many will only give a percentage refund if you need to cancel or alter your journey, so make sure you check the restrictions carefully before buying a ticket.

You can normally cut costs further by going through a **specialist flight agent** – either a consolidator or a discount agent. Bear in mind, though, that penalties for changing your plans can be stiff. Remember too that these companies make their money by dealing in bulk – don't expect them to answer a lot of questions. If you travel a lot, **discount travel clubs** are another option – the annual membership fee may be worth it for benefits such as cut-price air tickets and car rental. The **Internet** is a useful resource; check out: ⓦwww.cheaptickets.com, ⓦwww.travelocity.com and ⓦwww.last-minute.com to compare prices.

Don't automatically assume that tickets purchased through a travel specialist will be cheapest – once you get a quote, check with the airlines and you may turn up an even better deal. Be advised also that the pool of travel companies is swimming with sharks – exercise caution, and never deal with a company that demands cash up front or refuses to accept payment by credit card.

Airlines running **direct nonstop** flights from North America to Narita and Ōsaka's Kansai airport include All Nippon, American, Delta, Korean, Northwest and United. Flying time is fifteen hours from New York, thirteen hours from Chicago and ten hours from Los Angeles and Seattle. Returning to North America from Japan takes an hour less due to favourable wind currents. Many European and Asian airlines, such as Air France, Cathay Pacific and Malaysia Airlines, offer **indirect** flights (often with a stopover in their home city included in the price) to Narita and Kansai, as well as to Fukuoka, Hiroshima, Nagoya, Okinawa, Sapporo and Sendai. It's also possible to get to other points in Japan by flying via Narita, though you should bear in mind that most domestic flights leave Tokyo from Haneda air-

port, over one hour by train or bus from Narita.

Fares are highest in July and August, and at Christmas and New Year; prices drop April through June and September through October; you'll get the best deals in low season (Jan–March & Nov to mid-Dec). The fares quoted below give a rough idea of what you can expect to pay for a round-trip ticket to Tokyo bought direct from the airlines exclusive of airport tax, which is an extra $20. From Chicago tickets cost $930–1600 (midweek in low season to weekend in high season); from Los Angeles, $675–1600; from Vancouver, CAN$900–1400; from New York, $960–1800; from San Francisco, $675–1450; from Seattle, $830–1400; and from Toronto, CAN$1215–1650. However, unless you need to travel at very short notice, you are likely to get a much better deal through a specialist flight agent or consolidator (see box on p.16).

Round-the-world tickets, Circle Pacific deals and courier flights

If Japan is only one stop on a longer journey, you might want to buy a **round-the-world** (RTW) ticket. Some travel agents can sell you an "off the shelf" RTW ticket to five or six destinations, including Tokyo; others will have to tailor-make one for you, which can prove more expensive. Prices can be anything from $2500 to $5000 for an RTW ticket including Japan. It may also be worth checking out the **Circle Pacific** deals offered by many of the major airlines; these allow four stopovers at no extra charge if tickets are bought fourteen to thirty days in advance of travel.

A further possibility is to see if you can arrange a **courier flight**, although the hit-or-miss nature of these makes them most suitable for the single traveller who travels light and has a very flexible schedule. You're likely also to be restricted in your length of stay. Details of courier-flight brokers – the Air Courier Association, International Association of Air Travel Couriers and Now Voyager – are listed in the box on p.16.

A number of **tour operators** in the US and Canada offer tours in Japan. Most focus on Tokyo, Kyoto or trekking in the Japan Alps, but there are several tours available of the traditional countryside as well as a few specializing in cultural aspects, such as traditional cuisine and folk art. Before booking, confirm exactly what expenses are included, what class of hotel you'll be offered and how large a group you'll be joining.

Airlines

Air Canada US & Canada ☎ 1-888/247-2262, ⓦ www.aircanada.ca. Daily nonstop to Ōsaka's Kansai airport from Vancouver (with connections from Montreal, Winnipeg and Calgary), and daily nonstop to Tokyo's Narita airport from Toronto.

Air France US ☎ 1-800/237-2747, Canada ☎ 1-800/667-2747, ⓦ www.airfrance.com. Flights from several US cities, as well as Montreal and Toronto, to Narita via Paris.

All Nippon Airways (ANA) ☎ 1-800/235-9262, ⓦ www.anaskyweb.com. Daily nonstop flights to Narita from New York, Los Angeles and Washington DC.

American Airlines ☎ 1-800/433-7300, ⓦ www.americanairlines.com. Nonstop daily flights to Narita from New York, Los Angeles, Chicago, Dallas and San José.

Asiana Airlines ☎ 1-800/227-4262, ⓦ www.flyasiana.com. Flights from New York, Los Angeles, San Francisco and Seattle – all via Seoul – to Fukuoka, Hiroshima, Kansai, Nagoya, Narita, Okinawa and Sendai.

British Airways US ☎ 1-800/247-9297, Canada ☎ 1-800/668-1059, ⓦ www.britishairways.com. Flights to Tokyo's Narita airport from several US and Canadian cities, via London. Best value of the routes via Europe.

Cathay Pacific ☎ 1-800/233-2742, ⓦ www.cathay-usa.com. Daily flights from New York, Los Angeles, San Francisco, Vancouver and Toronto to Fukuoka, Kansai, Nagoya, Narita and Sapporo, all with stopovers. Also sells the good-value All Asia Pass ($999–1499, register online to get this fare), valid for a round-trip flight to any Asian city they serve from North America.

Continental Airlines ☎ 1-800/231-0856, ⓦ www.continental.com. Daily East and West Coast flights to Fukuoka, Kansai, Nagoya, Narita, Sapporo and Sendai via Honolulu and Guam.

Delta Airlines ☎ 1-800/241-4141, ⓦ www.delta.com. Daily nonstop flights to Narita from Atlanta, with connections across the US.

Japan Airlines (JAL) ☎ 1-800/525-3663, ⓦ www.japanair.com. Daily nonstop flights to Narita from New York, Chicago, Los Angeles and San Francisco, as well as nonstop flights to Ōsaka from Los Angeles. Departures to Tokyo from Vancouver

five times a week.

Korean Airlines ☎ 1-800/438-5000, ⓦ www.koreanair.com. Daily nonstop flights to Narita from Los Angeles. Flights to Narita via Seoul from New York (daily), from San Francisco, Atlanta and Chicago (5 weekly).

Malaysia Airlines ☎ 1-800/552-9264, ⓦ www.malaysia-airlines.com. Flights to Narita and Ōsaka's Kansai airport from Los Angeles via Kuala Lumpur five times weekly, and to Nagoya via Kuala Lumpur three times weekly.

Northwest Airlines ☎ 1-800/447-4747, ⓦ www.nwa.com. Daily nonstop flights to Narita airport from Chicago, Los Angeles, San Francisco, Seattle and Honolulu, with extensive connections from other American cities.

Singapore Airlines US ☎ 1-800/742-3333, Canada ☎ 1-800/387-8039 or 663-3046, ⓦ www.singaporeair.com. Daily nonstop flights to Narita from Los Angeles.

United Airlines ☎ 1-800/538-2929, ⓦ www.united.com. Daily nonstop flights to Ōsaka's Kansai airport and Narita from Los Angeles and San Francisco, with numerous connections from other American cities.

Discount flight agents

Air Brokers International ☎ 1-800/883-3273, ⓦ www.airbrokers.com. Consolidator and specialist in RTW and Circle Pacific tickets.

Air Courier Association ☎ 1-800/280-5973, ⓦ www.aircourier.org. Courier flight broker. Membership (US$35 for a year) also entitles you to twenty percent discount on travel insurance and name-your-own-price non-courier flights.

Cheap Tickets, Inc. ☎ 1-888/922-8849, ⓦ www.cheaptickets.com. Consolidator.

Discount Airfares Worldwide On-Line ⓦ www.etn.nl/discount.htm. A hub of consolidator and discount-agent Web links, maintained by the non-profit European Travel Network.

Dr Cheaps ☎ 1-800/731-5086, ⓦ www.drcheaps.com. Consolidator.

Education Travel Center ☎ 1-800/747-5551, ⓦ www.edtravel.com. Student/youth and consolidator fares.

High Adventure Travel ☎ 1-800/350-0612 or 1-415/977-7100, ⓦ www.highadv.com. Specialists in RTW and Circle Pacific tickets.

International Association of Air Travel Couriers ☎ 308/632-3273, ⓦ www.courier.org. Courier flights; annual membership $45.

Now Voyager ☎ 212/459-1616, ⓦ www.nowvoyagertravel.com. Gay- and lesbian-run courier flight broker and consolidator.

Skylink ℡1-800/AIR-ONLY or 212/573-8980, with branches in Chicago, Los Angeles, Montreal, Toronto and Washington, DC. Consolidator.
STA Travel US ℡1-800/781-4040, Canada ℡1-888/427-5639, ⓦwww.statravel.com. Worldwide discount travel firm specializing in student/youth fares; also student IDs, travel insurance, car rental and so on.
Student Flights ℡1-800/255-8000 or 480/951-1177, ⓦwww.isecard.com. Student/youth fares and student IDs.
Travel Avenue ℡1-800/333-3335, ⓦwww.travelavenue.com. Full-service travel agent that offers discounts in the form of rebates.
Travel Cuts Canada ℡1-866/246-9762 or US ℡1-800/592-CUTS, ⓦwww.travelcuts.com. Branches all over Canada. Student fares, IDs and other travel services.
Travelocity ⓦwww.travelocity.com. Online consolidator.

Tour operators

Abercrombie & Kent ℡1-800/554-7016 or 630/954-2944, ⓦwww.abercrombiekent.com. High-end tailor-made tours, including transfers and sightseeing with private local guides.
Adventure Center ℡1-800/228-8747 or 510/654-1879, ⓦwww.adventurecenter.com. Fifteen-day tour starting in Tokyo, with visits to temples and traditional villages, cities and hot-springs on the islands of Honshū and Kyūshū.
Asia Transpacific Journeys ℡1-800/642-2742 or 303/443-6789, ⓦwww.asiatranspacific.com. Upmarket tours and customized trips.
Cross-Culture ℡1-800/491-1148 or 413/256-6303, ⓦwww.crosscultureinc.com. Cultural tours of cities and countryside.
General Tours ℡1-800/221-2216, ⓦwww.generaltours.com. Wide selection of tours and authorized Japan Rail pass agent.
Geographic Expeditions ℡1-800/777-8183 or 415/922-0448, ⓦwww.geoex.com. City, village and walking tours, plus one focusing on Japanese cuisine and arts.
Guides for All Seasons ℡1-800/457-4574 or 916/994-3613. Japan specialists with two trekking expeditions, cultural walking tours and meetings with Kyoto's traditional artisans.
Japan Travel Bureau ℡1-800/235-3523 or ℡212/698-4900, ⓦwww.jtbusa.com. Day-trips across the country, including Tokyo, Tokyo Disneyland, Kyoto, Kamakura, Nikkō and Mount Fuji.
Journeys East ℡1-800/527-2612 or 707/987-4531, ⓦwww.journeyseast.com. Tours focusing on art and architecture.

Kintetsu International Express ℡1-212/259-9600, ⓦwww.kintetsu.com. Package and day-tour operator.
Northwest World Vacation Northwest Airlines ℡1-800/800-1504, ⓦwww.nwaworldvacations.com. Standard package tours.
Orient Flexi-Pax Tours ℡1-800/223-7460, ⓦwww.orientflexipax.com. Run a six-night tour of Tokyo, Takayama and Kyoto. From $2585, including flights and accommodation.
Pacific Holidays ℡1-800/355-8025 or 212/629-3888, ⓦwww.pacificholidaysinc.com. Solid package-tour operator.
Pleasant Holidays ℡1-800/742-9244, ⓦwww.pleasantholidays.com. Several "modules" from which to select and combine, including Tokyo, Mount Fuji and Hakone, and a tea ceremony experience.
Tour East ℡1-800/667-3951 or 416/929-0888, ⓦwww.toureast.ca. Cultural tours combining modern and traditional Japan.
Vantage Travel ℡1-800/322-6677, ⓦwww.vantagetravel.com. Tours of Asia, including Japan, for over-55s.
Worldwide Adventures ℡1-800/387-1483, ⓦwww.worldwidequest.com. Operator focusing on mountain trekking, with a culture tour as well.

Flights from Australia and New Zealand

There are few **direct flights** to Japan from Australia and New Zealand, and most of these go to Tokyo (Narita airport) or Ōsaka (Kansai International airport). You can also reach Japan from either Australia or New Zealand via a whole range of other destinations in Southeast Asia.

Fares for services from **eastern Australia** (Sydney, Brisbane and Cairns) to Tokyo and Ōsaka are generally the cheapest, kicking off at around A$1400 return. There are a few direct flights each week to Tokyo from **Melbourne** with prices around A$2100 return. From **western Australia**, Qantas fly direct from Perth to Tokyo for around A$1700. All the fares quoted below are for travel during low or shoulder seasons, and exclude airport taxes; flying at peak times (primarily mid-Dec to mid-Jan) can add substantially to these prices. Call one of the **discount flight agents** listed on p.18 to find out about the latest fares and any special offers. If you're a **student** or **under 26**, you may be able to undercut some of the prices given here; STA is a good place to start. Return fares with Garuda, Korean and Malaysia airlines can be as low as A$1100, but these generally restrict stays to ninety days or less and involve longer flight times and stops en route. Tickets valid for stays of up to a year cost around A$2000, though special fares are sometimes available to holders of working holiday visas which can bring prices down nearer the A$1400 mark. For an **open-jaw ticket**, which enables you to fly into one Japanese city and out of another, saves on backtracking and doesn't add hugely to the cost – count on around A$2000 out of Sydney, flying with JAL or Qantas.

From **New Zealand**, Air New Zealand, Garuda, Qantas and Singapore Airlines (among others) operate regular or code-share services to Tokyo, with fares starting at NZ$1400, though the most direct routings will cost at least NZ$1600. Air New Zealand also has services to Nagoya and Ōsaka.

If you can only manage a short visit and are happy to base yourself in one city or region, **package deals** can be an economical and hassle-free way of getting a taste for Japan. Five-night packages in Tokyo or Kyoto from eastern Australia start at around A$1700, including return airfare, transfers, twin-share accommodation and breakfast – a good deal considering the cost of airfares alone. A few **specialist tour operators**, such as Jalpak and Japan Experience (and others listed below), offer more comprehensive tours; most can also arrange Japan Rail passes and book accommodation in regional Japan – either in business-style hotels or at more traditional minshuku and ryokan through consortia such as the Japanese Inn Group.

Airlines

Air New Zealand Australia ☎13 24 76, New Zealand ☎0800/737 000, ⊛www.airnz.com.
Asiana Airlines Australia ☎1300 767 234, ⊛www.flyasiana.com.
Cathay Pacific Airways Australia ☎13 17 47, New Zealand ☎09/379 0861, ⊛www.cathaypacific.com.
Garuda Australia ☎02/9334 9944, New Zealand

☎09/366 1862, ⊛www.garuda-indonesia.com.
JAL (Japan Airlines) Australia ☎02/9272 1111, New Zealand ☎09/379 9906, ⊛www.jal.co.jp.
Korean Air Australia ☎02/9262 6000, New Zealand ☎09/307 3687, ⊛www.koreanair.com.
Malaysian Airlines Australia ☎13 26 27, New Zealand ☎09/373 2741, ⊛www.mas.com.my.
Philippine Airlines Australia ☎02/9279 2020, ⊛www.philippineair.com.
Qantas Australia ☎13 13 13, New Zealand ☎09/661 901, ⊛www.qantas.com.au.
Singapore Airlines Australia ☎13 10 11, New Zealand ☎09/303 2129, ⊛www.singaporeair.com.

Discount flight agents

Anywhere Travel 345 Anzac Parade, Kingsford, Sydney ☎02/9663 0411, ⓔanywhere@ozemail.com.au. Bargain airfare retailer.
Budget Travel 16 Fort St, Auckland, plus branches around the city ☎09/366 0061 or 0800/808 040, ⊛www.budgettravel.co.nz.
Destinations Unlimited 3 Milford Rd, Auckland ☎09/373 4033.
Flight Centres Australia ☎13 31 33, New Zealand ☎09/358 4310, ⊛www.flightcentre.com.au.
Northern Gateway 22 Cavenagh St, Darwin ☎08/8941 1394, ⊛www.northerngateway.com.au.
STA Travel Australia ☎1300/733 035, ⊛www.statravel.com.au, New Zealand ☎0508/782 872, ⊛www.statravel.co.nz.
Student Uni Travel 92 Pitt St, Sydney ☎02/9232 8444, ⓔaustralia@backpackers.net.
Trailfinders 8 Spring St, Sydney ☎02/9247 7666, ⊛www.trailfinders.com.au.
Travel.Com.Au 76–80 Clarence St, Sydney ☎02/9249 5444, ⊛www.travel.com.au.

Specialist tour operators

Active Travel 1st Floor, Garema Centre, Canberra ☎1800 634 157, ⊛www.activetravel.com.au. Agent offering some unusual itineraries, including hiking trips and tours themed around food and Japanese gardens.
Adventure World ☎02/8913 0755, www.adventureworld.com.au, New Zealand ☎09/524 5118, ⊛www.adventureworld.co.nz. Agents for Explore Worldwide's Shogun Trail train tour from Tokyo to Fukuoka.
Deep Powder Tours PO Box 317, Caringbah, NSW 2229 ☎02/9525 9774,

Ⓦwww.skijapan.com.au. Long-running tour company specializing in ski trips to Niseko and Rusutsu ski resorts in Hokkaidō.

Jalpak Travel Sydney ℡02/9285 6600. Sells Jaltour packages and can put together personalized itineraries.

Japan Experience Tours Australia Square Tower, Sydney ℡02/9247 3086. Contact them to find out about Price Travel Service, who have 21 years' experience in running tours in Japan, including two-week language programmes.

Japan Travel Bureau Level 24, 1 Market St, Sydney ℡02/9510 0100. Head office for Jaltour packages, with a good range of hotel options around Japan and specialist tours.

Nippon Travel Agency Level 9, 135 King St, Sydney ℡02/9338 2333; 25/151 Queen St, Auckland ℡09/309 5750. The local office of this giant Japanese travel agency, offering standard and bespoke tours.

SnoWave 46 Pittwater Rd, Manly, Sydney ℡02/9977 7488, Ⓦwww.snowave.com. Ski specialist for Niseko in Hokkaidō. Also run tours to the Sapporo Snow Festival.

Getting to Japan by train and ferry

Adventurous travellers can take advantage of a number of alternative routes to Japan from Europe and Asia combining **train and ferry** transport. There are three long-distance train rides – the Trans-Siberian, Trans-Mongolian and Trans-Manchurian – all of which will put you on the right side of Asia for a hop across to Japan. The shortest ferry route is on the hydrofoil between Pusan in South Korea and Fukuoka (Hakata port) on Japan's southern island of Kyūshū. Advance reservations are recommended for all ferries.

The Trans-Siberian train and ferries from Russia

The classic overland adventure route to or from Japan is via the **Trans-Siberian** train, a seven-night journey from Moscow to Vladivostok on Russia's far eastern coast. The cost of a one-way ticket in a four-berth sleeper compartment plus a couple of nights' accommodation in Moscow and Vladivostok is around £630/US$1015/A$1530; tickets can be booked through travel agents in the UK (see p.14), Australia (see p.18), the US

(see p.17) and Japan (see p.20). The same agents can arrange tickets on the **Trans-Manchurian** train, which heads from Moscow down through northern China and terminates in Beijing, and the Trans-Mongolian, which runs from Moscow via Mongolia to Beijing. You can then take a train to Shanghai and pick up a ferry to Japan. Although purists will want to do the whole train journey at one stretch, you might want to stop off for a break in Irkutsk, the jumping-off point for Lake Baikal, which contains around one fifth of the world's freshwater supplies.

Vladivostok Air has **flights** departing three times a week from Vladivostok to Niigata (around US$270 one-way) and, less regularly, to Ōsaka (US$380) and Toyama (US$300). Alternatively, Bizens Intur Servis in Vladivostok (℡7-4232/49 73 91, Ⓦwww.bisintour.com) handles bookings on the fairly regular **ferries** that run most of the year to the Japanese port of Fushiki, near Toyama (see p.456). This takes 42 hours and the cheapest ticket is around US$200 including a basic berth and all meals.

Although it is possible, making your own travel arrangements for this route in Russia can be a big hassle, which makes booking a package well worth considering. For those planning to return to Europe from Japan, it's worth noting that if you can afford to wait two weeks and have all the correct paperwork, arranging a **visa** for Russia at the Russian Embassy in Tokyo (2-1-1 Azabudai, Minato-ku, Tokyo 106 ℡03/3583-5982), or the consulate (1-2-2 Nishimidorigaoka, Toyonaka-shi, Ōsaka ℡06/6848-3452) is a simpler and cheaper process than in the UK. Visas cost ¥1000 if issued in a month, or ¥5000 if issued within one week.

The shortest journey from Russia to Japan is on the weekly service (May to October) from **Korsakov** on the Siberian island of Sakhalin to Wakkanai in Hokkaidō, taking six hours and thirty minutes and costing US$150 one-way. To get to Korsakov you either have to fly to Sakhalin or take a ferry from Vanino in the Russian Far East.

Ferries from China and Taiwan

If you want to take the slow boat **from China** to Japan, you can board a ferry from

Shanghai to Ōsaka or Kōbe, and Tanggu to Kōbe. The Japan China International Ferry Company (☏06/6536-6541, ⊛www.fune.co .jp/chinjif/index.html) sails from Shanghai to Kōbe and Ōsaka, while the Shanghai Ferry Company (☏06/6243-6345 in Japan, ☏021-6537 5111 in China, ⊛www.shang-hai-ferry.co.jp) sails from Shanghai to Ōsaka. The frequency of services varies with the seasons, but there are usually a couple of departures a week, taking 48 hours and costing around ¥20,000. Conditions on board are good, the berths are clean and comfortable, and facilities include swimming pools, restaurants, and even discos. Similar services, run by China Express Line (☏078/321-5791 in Japan, ☏022-2420 5777 in China, ⊛www2.celkobe.co.jp), leave Tanggu, the port 50km east of Tianjin, for Kōbe once a week. The journey takes 51 hours and costs around ¥25,000.

You can reach Japan's southern islands of Okinawa in twenty hours from the port of Keelung in **Taiwan**. This is a great way to arrive or leave Japan, as the ferry stops at the Miyako and Ishigaki islands en route. There are weekly sailings to Shin-kō port in Naha, Okinawa's main town, with prices starting from around ¥15,600. Tickets are available from Yeong An Maritime Co in Taipei (☏02/771-5911) and Keelung (☏02/424-8151). In Naha, tickets can be bought from the ferry company Arimura Sangyō (see p.898) and it's also possible to arrange onward connections from here to Ōsaka by ferry for around ¥16,000.

Ferries from South Korea

The most popular and fastest sea route to Japan is from the South Korean port of **Pusan**, some 200km north of Kyūshū, across the Korea Strait. There are daily serv-ices from Pusan to Fukuoka in Kyūshū and Shimonoseki at the western tip of Honshū.

From Pusan to Fukuoka there's a choice of two services. The daily hydrofoil *Beetle 2*, operated by JR Kyūshū, takes about three hours. The fare is ¥13,000 one way. Reservations can be made in Pusan (☏051/465-6111) through major travel agencies in Japan such as JTB, or in

Fukuoka (☏092/281-2315). The slower (15hr 40min) and cheaper daily service is on the ferry *Camellia*. The cheapest fare is ¥9000 for a tatami room, rising to ¥12,000 for a first-class berth in a two- to three-per-son cabin. Reservations can be made in Fukuoka (☏092/262-2323) or in Pusan (☏051/466-7799).

Ferries from Pusan to Shimonoseki, oper-ated by Kampu Ferry Co (see below), leave daily in the early evening and arrive in Shimonoseki at around 8am the next day. The lowest regular fare is ¥8500, rising to ¥18,000 for a first-class berth in a two-per-son cabin, with an extra ¥600 charge to pay at Shimonoseki. If you are doing a return trip from Shimonoseki, it's cheaper to buy sepa-rate one-way tickets rather than a return from Japan, since the fares in Pusan are cheaper.

Ferry and tour agents in Japan

Arimura Sangyō Co Echo Kyōbashi Building, 3-12-1 Kyōbashi, Chūō-ku, Tokyo ☏03/3562-2091; New Okazakibashi Building, 2-5-19 Nishimoto-chō, Nishi-ku, Ōsaka ☏06/6531-9267; Naha ☏098/860-1980. Main agent for ferry tickets from Okinawa to Taiwan, via the Miyako and Ishigaki islands.

Euras Tours 1-26-8 Higashi Azabu, Minato-ku, Tokyo ☏03/5562-3381, ⓔeuras-tyo@ma.neweb.ne.jp. Can arrange rail journeys across Russia to Europe and ferry tickets to Russia from Japan.

Fushiki Kairiku Unsu Co 5-1 Fushiki-minato-machi, Takaoka-shi, Toyama ☏0766/45-1175. Agent for the Fushiki–Vladivostok ferry.

Japan–China International Ferry Co (JIFCO) 10–14 Sarugakuchō, Shibuya-ku, Tokyo 150 ☏03/5489-4800; Sa-ai Building, 1-18-6, Shinmachi, Nishi-ku, Ōsaka ☏06/6536-6541. Booking agent for ferry services from Ōsaka, Kōbe and Shanghai.

Kampu Ferry Co. 1-10-60 Higashi-yamatochō, Shimonoseki, Yamaguchi-ken ☏0832/24-3000. Agent for the Shimonoseki–Pusan ferry.

MO Tourist CIS Russian Centre 2F Kandatsukasa-chō Bldg, 2-2-12 Kandatsukasa-chō, Chiyoda-ku, Tokyo ☏03/5296-5783, ⊛www.motcis.com. Arranges Trans-Siberian tours from Japan.

United Orient Shipping Agency 3-10-2 Ningyōchō, Chūō-ku, Tokyo ☏03/3249-4415. General agent for Fushiki–Vladivostok ferry tickets.

Visas and red tape

All visitors to Japan must have a valid passport for the duration of their stay, but only residents of certain countries need apply for a visa in advance. Citizens of Ireland, the UK and certain other European countries can stay in Japan for up to ninety days without a visa provided they are visiting for tourism or business purposes. This stay can be extended for another three months (see below).

Citizens of Australia, Canada, New Zealand, and the US can also stay for up to ninety days without a visa, though this is unextendable and you are required to be in possession of a return airline ticket. Anyone wishing to stay longer will have to leave the country then re-enter.

Citizens of certain other countries must apply for a visa in advance in their own country – if in doubt, check with your nearest embassy or consulate. These are usually free, though in certain circumstances you may be charged a fee of around ¥3000 for a single-entry visa. The rules on visas do change from time to time, so check first with your embassy or consulate, or on the Japanese Foreign Ministry website (Ⓦ www.mofa.go.jp/j_info/visit/visa/index.html), for the current situation.

To get a **visa extension** you'll need to fill in two copies of an Application for Extension of Stay, available from local immigration bureaux (see the Listings sections of major city accounts in the guide). These must be returned along with passport photos, a letter explaining your reasons for wanting to extend your stay, and a processing fee of ¥4000. In addition, you may be asked to show proof of sufficient funds, and a valid onward ticket out of the country. If you're not a national of one of the few countries with six-month reciprocal visa exemptions (these include Ireland and the UK), expect a thorough grilling from the immigration officials. An easier option – and the only alternative available to nationals of those countries who are not eligible for an extension – may be a short trip out of the country, say to South Korea or Hong Kong, though you'll still have to run the gauntlet of immigration officials on your return.

Citizens of Australia, Britain, Canada and New Zealand aged between 18 and 30 can apply for a **working holiday visa**, which grants a six-month stay and one possible six-month extension. This entitles the holder to work for a maximum of twenty hours a week. You need to apply at least three weeks before leaving your home country, and must be able to show evidence of sufficient funds, which effectively means a return ticket (or money to buy one) plus around US$2000 or the equivalent to live on while you look for work. Contact your local embassy or consulate to check the current details of the scheme.

British nationals are also eligible for the **volunteer visa** scheme, which allows holders to undertake voluntary work for charitable organizations in Japan for up to one year. Your application must include a letter from the host organization confirming details of the voluntary work to be undertaken and the treatment the volunteer will receive (pocket money and board and lodging is allowed, but more formal remuneration is not). You must also be able to show evidence of sufficient funds for your stay in Japan, such as a return ticket (or money to buy one) plus money to live on if you're not receiving full board and lodging from your host institution. Contact your local embassy or consulate to check the current details of the scheme.

If you enter Japan on a working holiday or volunteer visa you must apply for an Alien Registration card (see box on p.82) within ninety days of arrival. In addition, if you're on any sort of working visa and you leave Japan temporarily, you must get a **re-entry visa** before you leave, if you wish to return and continue working. Re-entry visas are available from local immigration bureaux.

The **duty-free allowance** for bringing goods into Japan is 400 cigarettes or 100 cigars or 500 grams of tobacco; three 760cc bottles of alcohol; two ounces of perfume; and gifts and souvenirs up to a value of ¥200,000. As well as firearms and drugs, Japanese customs officials are particularly strict about the import of pornographic material, which will be confiscated if your bags are searched.

On the plane you'll be given an immigration form and a **customs declaration** to fill out; if you're within the allowances outlined above, you can ignore the customs form. If you're arriving from a developing country you'll also have to fill out a yellow health form, detailing any illness you may have suffered in the previous fourteen days. If you've been well, you can ignore this form, too.

There is no limit on the amount of foreign or Japanese **currency** that you can bring into the country, but ¥5 million is the maximum that you can take out of Japan.

Japanese embassies and consulates

You'll find addresses for other embassies and consulates on the Ministry of Foreign Affairs **website** (ⓦwww.mofa.go.jp/j_info/ visit/visa/index.html), and links to many of them from the UK Embassy site (ⓦwww.uk .emb-japan.go.jp/en/webjapan/links.html). **Australia** 112 Empire Circuit, Yarralumla, Canberra ACT 2600 ⓣ02/6273 3244, ⓦwww.japan.org.au; 17th Floor, Comalco Place, 12 Creek St, Brisbane, Queensland 4000 ⓣ07/3221-5188; Level 15, Cairns Corporate Tower, 15 Lake St, Cairns, Queensland 4870, ⓣ07/4051 5177; 45th Floor, Melbourne Central Tower, 360 Elizabeth St, Melbourne, Victoria 3000 ⓣ03/9639-3244; 21st Floor, The Forrest Centre, 221 St George Terrace, Perth, WA 6000 Australia ⓣ08/9321 7816; Level 34, Colonial Centre, 52 Martin Place, Sydney, NSW 2000 ⓣ02/9231-3455. **Canada** 255 Sussex Drive, Ottawa, ON KIN 9E6 ⓣ613/241-8541, ⓦwww.ca.emb-japan.go.jp; 2480 ManuLife Place, 10180-101 St, Edmonton, AB T5J 3S4 ⓣ780/422-3752; 600 Rue de la Gauchetière Ouest, Suite 2120, Montreal, PQ, H3B 4L8 ⓣ514/866-3429; Suite 3300, Royal Trust Tower, 77 King St W, PO Box 10, Toronto-Dominion Centre, Toronto, ON, M5K 1A1 ⓣ416/363-7038; 800-1177 West Hastings St, Vancouver, BC V6E 2K9 ⓣ604/684-5868.

China 7 Ri Tan Rd, Jian Guo Men Wai, Beijing ⓣ10/6532-2361, ⓦwww.cn.emb-japan.go.jp; 46–47th Floors, One Exchange Square, 8 Connaught Place, Central, Hong Kong ⓣ2522 1184, www.hk.emb-japan.go.jp. **Ireland** Nutley Building, Merrion Centre, Nutley Lane, Dublin 4 ⓣ01/202-8300, ⓦwww.ie.emb-japan.go.jp. **New Zealand** Level 18, Majestic Centre, 100 Willis St, Wellington 1 ⓣ04/473-1540, ⓦwww.nz.emb-japan.go.jp; Level 12, ASB Bank Centre, 135 Albert St, Auckland 1 ⓣ09/303-4106; Level 5, Forsyth Barr House, 764 Colombo St, Christchurch 1 ⓣ03/366-5680. **Singapore** 16 Nassim Rd, Singapore, 258390 ⓣ6235-8855, www.sg.emb-japan.go.jp. **South Korea** 18-11 Jhoonghak-dong, Jhongro-gu, Seoul, Republic of Korea ⓣ02/2170-5200, ⓦwww.kr.emb-japan.go.jp. **Thailand** 1674 New Petchaburi Rd, Bangkok 10320 ⓣ02/252-6151, ⓦwww.embjp-th.org. **UK** 101–104 Piccadilly, London W1J 7JT ⓣ020/7465-6500, ⓦwww.uk.emb-japan.go.jp; 2 Melville Crescent, Edinburgh EH3 7HW ⓣ0131/225-4777, ⓦwww.edinburgh.uk .emb-japan.go.jp.

US 2520 Massachusetts Ave NW, Washington, DC 20008-2869 ⓣ202/238-6700, ⓦwww.us.emb-japan.go.jp; Alliance Center Suite 1600, 3500 Lenox Road, Atlanta, Georgia 30326 ⓣ404/240-4300; Federal Reserve Plaza, 14th Floor, 600 Atlantic Ave, Boston, MA 02210 ⓣ617/973-9772; Olympia Center, Suite 1100, 737 North Michigan Ave, Chicago, IL 60611 ⓣ312/280-0400; 400 Renaissance Center, Suite 1600, Detroit, MI 48243 ⓣ313/567-0120; 1742 Nuuanu Ave, Honolulu, HI 96817-3201 ⓣ808/543-3111; Wells Fargo Plaza Suite 2300, 1000 Louisiana St, Houston, TX 77002 ⓣ713/652-2977; 350 South Grand Ave, Suite 1700, Los Angeles, CA 90071 ⓣ213/617-6700; Brickell Bay View Center, Suite 3200, 80 SW 8th St, Miami, FL 33130 ⓣ305/530-9090; Suite 2050, 639 Loyola Ave, New Orleans, LA 70113 ⓣ504/529-2101; 299 Park Ave, New York, NY 10171 ⓣ212/371-8222; 50 Fremont St, Suite 2300, San Francisco, CA 94105 ⓣ415/777-3533; 601 Union St, Suite 500, Seattle, WA 98101 ⓣ206/682-9107.

Insurance

It's essential to take out a good travel insurance policy, particularly one with comprehensive medical coverage, due to the high cost of hospital treatment in Japan. A typical travel insurance policy should also provide cover for the loss of baggage, tickets and – up to a certain limit – cash or cheques, as well as cancellation or curtailment of your journey. Most policies exclude so-called dangerous sports unless an extra premium is paid: in Japan this can mean scuba-diving, whitewater rafting and bungee jumping, skiing and mountaineering. Read the small print and benefits tables of prospective policies carefully, as coverage can vary wildly for roughly similar premiums.

With many policies you can exclude coverage you don't need, but for Japan you should definitely take **medical coverage** that includes both hospital treatment and medical evacuation; be sure to ask for the 24-hour medical emergency number. Keep all medical bills and, if possible, contact the insurance company before making any major outlay. Very few insurers will arrange on-the-spot payments in the event of a major expense – you'll usually be reimbursed only after going home.

When securing **baggage cover**, make sure that the per-article limit – typically under £500 equivalent – will cover your most valuable possession. If you have anything stolen, get a copy of the **police report**; otherwise you won't be able to claim. Always make a note of the policy details and leave them with someone at home in case you lose the original.

Before buying a policy, check that you're not already covered. Your **home insurance policy** may cover your possessions against loss or theft even when overseas, or you can extend cover through your household contents insurer. Many **bank** and **charge accounts** include some form of travel cover, and insurance is also sometimes included if you pay for your trip with a **credit card** (though it usually only provides medical or accident cover).

In **North America**, Canadian provincial health plans usually provide some overseas medical coverage, although they are unlikely to pick up the full tab in the event of a mishap. Holders of official student/teacher/ youth cards are entitled to meagre accident coverage and hospital in-patient benefits. Students will often find that their student health coverage extends during the vacations and for one term beyond the date of last enrolment.

Rough Guide travel insurance

Rough Guides Ltd offers a low-cost travel insurance policy, especially customized for our statistically low-risk readers by a leading British broker, provided by the American International Group (AIG) and registered with the British regulatory body, GISC (the General Insurance Standards Council). There are five main Rough Guides insurance plans: **No Frills** for the bare minimum for secure travel; **Essential**, which provides decent all-round cover; **Premier** for comprehensive cover with a wide range of benefits; **Extended Stay** for cover lasting four months to a year; and **Annual Multi-Trip**, a cost-effective way of getting Premier cover if you travel more than once a year. Premier, Annual Multi-Trip and Extended Stay policies can be supplemented by a "Hazardous Pursuits Extension" if you plan to indulge in sports considered dangerous, such as scuba-diving or trekking. For a **policy quote**, call the Rough Guide Insurance Line: toll-free in the UK ☏0800/015 0906 or ☏+44 1392 314 665 from elsewhere. Alternatively, get an online quote at www.roughguides.com/insurance.

Health

Japan has high standards of health and hygiene, and there are no significant diseases worth worrying about. Nor are any compulsory immunizations or health certificates needed to enter the country.

Medical treatment and drugs are of a high quality, but can be expensive – if possible you should bring any medicines you might need with you, especially prescription drugs. Also bring a copy of your prescription and make sure you know what the generic name of the drug is, rather than its brand name. Some common drugs widely available throughout the US and Europe are generally not available in Japan. The contraceptive pill is available, but only on prescription.

Although mosquitoes buzz across Japan in the warmer months, **malaria** is not endemic, so there's no need to take any tablets. It's a good idea to pack mosquito repellent, however, and to burn coils in your room at night, or to use a plug-in repellent.

Tap **water** is safe to drink throughout Japan, but you should avoid drinking directly from streams or rivers. It's also not a good idea to walk barefoot through flooded paddy fields, due to the danger of water-borne parasites. Food-wise, you should have no fears about eating raw seafood or seafish, including the notorious *fugu* (globe fish). However, raw meat and river fish are best avoided.

In the case of an **emergency**, the first port of call should be to ask your hotel to phone for a doctor or ambulance. You could also head for, or call, the nearest tourist information office or international centre (in major cities only), which should be able to provide a list of local doctors and hospitals with English-speaking staff. Alternatively, you could call the toll-free 24-hour *Jhelp.com* (☎0570-000911) or, in a last resort, contact the Prefecture's Foreign Advisory Service (see "Emergencies" in individual city listings in the guide).

If you need to call an **ambulance** on your own, dial ☎119 and speak slowly when you're asked to give an address. Ambulance staff are not trained paramedics, but will take you to the nearest appropriate hospital. Unless you're dangerously ill when you go to hospital, you'll have to wait your turn in a clinic before you see a doctor, and you'll need to be persistent if you want to get full details of your condition: some doctors are notorious for withholding information from patients.

For minor ailments and advice, you can go to a **pharmacy**, which you'll find in most shopping areas. There are also numerous smaller private **clinics**, where you'll pay in the region of ¥10,000 to see a doctor. You could also try **Asian medical remedies**, such as acupuncture (*hari*) and pressure point massage (*shiatsu*), though it's worth trying to get a personal recommendation to find a reputable practitioner.

Medical resources for travellers

UK

British Airways Travel Clinics 213 Piccadilly, London W1 (Mon–Fri 9.30am–6pm, Sat 10am–4pm, no appointment necessary; ☎0845/600 2236); 101 Cheapside, London EC2 (Mon–Fri 9am–4.45pm, appointment required; ☎0845/600 2236); ⊛www.britishairways.com/travel/healthclinintro. Vaccinations, tailored advice from an online database and a complete range of travel healthcare products.
Hospital for Tropical Diseases Travel Clinic 2nd Floor, Mortimer Market Centre, off Capper Street, London WC1E 6AU (Mon–Fri 9am–5pm, by appointment only; ☎020/7388 9600, www.thehtd.org; a consultation costs £15, which is waived if you have your injections here). A recorded Health Line (☎0906/133 7733; 50p per min) gives hints on hygiene and illness prevention as well as listing appropriate immunizations.
MASTA (Medical Advisory Service for Travellers Abroad) London School of Hygiene and Tropical Medicine (⊛www.masta.org). Regional clinics around the UK (call ☎0870/606

2782 for the nearest). Also operates a pre-recorded 24-hour Travellers' Health Line (☎0906/822 4100; 60p per min), giving written information tailored to your journey by return of post.

North America

Centers for Disease Control 1600 Clifton Rd NE, Atlanta, GA 30333 ☎ 1-800/311-3435 or 404/639-3534, ⓦwww.cdc.gov. Publishes outbreak warnings, suggested inoculations, precautions and other background information for travellers. Useful website plus International Travelers Hotline on ☎1-877/FYI-TRIP.

International Association for Medical Assistance to Travellers (IAMAT) 417 Center St, Lewiston, NY 14092 ☎716/754-4883, ⓦwww.iamat.org and 1287 St. Clair Avenue West, Suite #1, Toronto, Ontario M6E 1B8 ☎416/652-0137. A non-profit organization supported by donations, it can provide a list of English-speaking doctors in Japan, climate charts and leaflets on various diseases and inoculations.

Travel Medicine 351 Pleasant St, Suite 312, Northampton, MA 01060 ☎1-800/872-8633, ⓦwww.travmed.com. Sells first-aid kits, mosquito netting, water filters and other health-related travel products online.

Australia and New Zealand

Travellers' Medical and Vaccination Centres 27–29 Gilbert Place, Adelaide, SA 5000 ☎08/8212 7522; 1/170 Queen St, Auckland ☎09/373 3531; 5/247 Adelaide St, Brisbane, Qld 4000 ☎07/3221 9066; 5/8–10 Hobart Place, Canberra, ACT 2600 ☎02/6257 7156; 270 Sandy Bay Rd, Sandy Bay Tas, Hobart 7005 ☎03/6223 7577; 2/393 Little Bourke St, Melbourne, Vic 3000 ☎03/9602 5788; Level 7, Dymocks Bldg, 428 George St, Sydney, NSW 2000 ☎02/9221 7133; Shop 15, Grand Arcade, 14–16 Willis St, Wellington ☎04/473 0991. The website www.tmvc.com.au has a list of all the Travellers' Medical and Vaccination Centres throughout Australia, New Zealand and Southeast Asia, as well as general information on travel health.

Travellers with disabilities

Though the situation is improving, Japan is not an easy place to travel around for anyone using a wheelchair, or for those who find it difficult to negotiate stairs or walk long distances. Most train and subway stations have seemingly endless corridors, and few have escalators or lifts; the sheer crush of people can also be a problem at times. It's usually possible to organize assistance at stations, but you'll need a Japanese-speaker to make the arrangements. Shinkansen trains and a few other services, such as the Narita Express from Narita International airport into Tokyo, have spaces for wheelchair users, but you'll need to make reservations well in advance. For travelling short distances, taxis are an obvious solution, though few drivers will offer help getting in or out of the car.

When it comes to **accommodation**, the international chains or modern Western-style hotels, as well as some of the newer youth hostels, are most likely to provide facilities such as fully adapted rooms and lifts. Similarly, most modern shopping complexes, museums and other public buildings are equipped with ramps, wide doors and accessible toilets. For further information, including links to other resources, take a look at the Global Access website (ⓦwww.geocities.com/Paris/1502/index .html) or contact the organizations listed on p.26.

Disability has always been something of an uncomfortable topic in Japan, with disabled people often hidden away from public view. In recent years, however, there has been a certain shift in public opinion, particularly following the publication in 1998 of Ototake

Hirotada's *No One's Perfect* (Kodansha International), the upbeat, forthright autobiography of a 23-year-old student born with truncated limbs. An instant bestseller, the book looks set to shake up Japanese perceptions of disability.

Contacts for travellers with disabilities

Britain and Ireland

Disability Action Group Portside Business Park, 189 Airport Rd West, Belfast BT3 9ED ☎028/9029 7880, ⓦwww.disabilityaction.org. Can provide general information about holidays and accommodation suitable for disabled travellers, as well as a wide range of useful publications.
Holiday Care 2nd Floor, Imperial Building, Victoria Rd, Horley, Surrey RH6 7PZ ☎0845/124 9971 or ☎0208/760 0072, ⓦwww.holidaycare.org.uk. Provides various information sheets, including one on financial help for holidays.
Tripscope Alexandra House, Albany Road, Brentford, Middlesex TW8 0NE ☎ 08457/585 641 or ☎0117/93907782, ⓦwww.tripscope.org.uk. This registered charity provides a national telephone information service offering free advice on UK and international transport for those with a mobility problem.

North America

Directions Unlimited 123 Green Lane, Bedford Hills, NY 10507 ☎1-800/533-5343 or 914/241-1700. Tour operator specializing in custom-made tours for people with disabilities.
Mobility International USA PO Box 10767,

Eugene, OR 97440 ☎541/343-1284 (Voice and TDD), ⓦwww.miusa.org. Information and referral services, access guides, tours and exchange programmes. Annual membership $35 (includes quarterly newsletter).
Society for Accessible Travel & Hospitality (SATH) 347 Fifth Ave, New York, NY 10016 ☎212/447-7284, ⓦwww.sath.org. Non-profit educational organization that has actively represented travellers with disabilities since 1976. Annual membership $45; $30 for students and seniors.
Travel Information Service Moss Rehabilitation Hospital, 1200 West Tabor Rd, Philadelphia, PA 19141 ☎215/456-9600. Telephone information and referral service.
Twin Peaks Press Box 129, Vancouver, BC 98666 ☎360/694-2462 or 1-800/637-2256, ⓦhttp://home.pacifier.com/~twinpeak. Publisher of the *Directory of Travel Agencies for the Disabled*, listing more than 370 agencies worldwide; *Travel for the Disabled* ($19.95); the *Directory of Accessible Van Rentals* ($12.95); and *Wheelchair Vagabond* ($19.95), loaded with personal tips. Available on the Amazon website, www.amazon.com.

Australia and New Zealand

ACROD (Australian Council for Rehabilitation of the Disabled), PO Box 60, Curtin, ACT 2605 ☎02/6282 4333, ⓦwww.acrod.org.au. Provides lists of useful organizations, as well as offering information and advice on specialist travel agencies and tour operators.
Disabled Persons Assembly 4/173–175 Victoria St, Wellington ☎04/801 9100, ⓦwww.dpa.org.nz. Referral organization dealing with access and mobility for the disabled overseas.

Information, maps and websites

The Japan National Tourist Organization (JNTO) maintains a number of overseas offices (see p.28), which are stocked with a wealth of free maps and leaflets, varying from general tips on Japanese culture to detailed area guides, lists of accommodation and practical information about local transport. You'll find a selection of the same material on the JNTO websites; see p.28 for details of these and other recommended information sources on the Internet.

Within Japan, JNTO operate a couple of **Tourist Information Centres (TIC)**, both of which have English-speaking staff. These offices are located in central Tokyo and at Tokyo's Narita airport (see p.98 & p.96) and provide a similar range of information as JNTO's overseas offices, covering the whole of Japan as well as their local area. The Narita office provides accommodation booking services (no commission), while the Tokyo

TIC is located next door to the Welcome Inn Reservation Centre (see p.104 for details). Though staff will help sort out routes and timetables, they can't make travel reservations, nor usually sell tickets to theatres, cinemas and so on; instead, they'll direct you to the nearest appropriate outlet. It's worth noting that much of their printed English-language information isn't always available in the regions, so stock up while you can.

Japanese addresses

Japanese **addresses** are described by a hierarchy of areas, rather than numbers running consecutively along named roads. A typical address starts with the largest administrative district, the *ken* (prefecture), accompanied by a seven-digit postcode – for example, Nagasaki-ken 850-0072. However, there are four exceptions: Tokyo-*to* (metropolis), Kyoto-*fu* and Ōsaka-*fu* (urban prefectures), and Hokkaidō are all independent administrative areas at the same level as the *ken*, also followed by a seven-digit code. Next comes the *shi* (city) or, in the country, the *gun* (county) or *mura* (village). The largest cities are then subdivided into *ku* (wards), followed by *chō* (districts), then *chōme* (local neighbourhoods), blocks and, finally, individual buildings.

Japanese addresses are therefore written in reverse order from the Western system. However, when written in English, they usually follow the Western order; this is the system we adopt in the guide. For example, the address 2-12-7 Kitano-chō, Chūō-ku, Kōbe-shi identifies building number 7, somewhere on block 12 of number 2 *chōme* in Kitano district, in Chūō ward of Kōbe city. Most buildings bear a small metal tag with their number (eg 2-12-7, or just 12-7), while lampposts often have a bigger plaque with the district name in *kanji* and the block reference (eg 2-12). Note that the same address can also be written 12-7 Kitano-chō 2-chōme, Chūō-ku.

Though the system's not too difficult in theory, actually **locating an address** on the ground can be frustrating. The consolation is that even Japanese people find it tough. The best strategy is to have the address written down, preferably in Japanese, and then get to the nearest train or bus station. Once in the neighbourhood, start asking; local police boxes (*kōban*) are a good bet and have detailed maps of their own areas. If all else fails, don't be afraid to phone – often someone will come to meet you. And fairly soon technology should come to the rescue with hand-held personal navigation systems, much like those for cars, which are currently under development.

Local tourist offices with English-speaking staff are called **"i" centres** – you'll find these in all major towns and cities, usually located in or close to the main train station. In practice, the amount of English information available – whether written or spoken – is a bit hit or miss, but at least the staff should be able to assist with local maps, hotel reservations (some charge a small commission) and simple queries. At the next level down are the ordinary tourist information offices: practically every town (and many villages) have these. Though there's little chance of getting English-language assistance, they can usually supply maps, transport information, and sometimes help with accommodation.

Another useful source of English-language information is the **Goodwill Guides**, groups of volunteer guides located in nearly thirty cities mostly in central and western Japan. The guides' services are free – although you're expected to pay for their transport, entry tickets and any meals you have together – and the language ability obviously varies. But they provide a great opportunity to learn more about Japanese culture and to visit local restaurants, shops and so forth with a Japanese speaker. The TICs have a list of groups and their contact details, or the local information office should be able to help with arrangements; try and give at least two days' notice.

Japan National Tourist Organization

Australia Level 18, Australia Square Tower, 264 George St, Sydney, NSW 2000 ☎02/9251-3024, ✉jntosyd@tokyonet.com.au.
Canada 165 University Ave, Toronto, ON, M5H 3B8 ☎416/366-7140, ✉jnto@interlog.com.
China 6F, Chang Fu Gong Office Building, 26 Jianguomenwai Dajie, Chaoyang-qu, Beijing 100022 ☎010/6513-9023; Suite 3704-05, 37F, Dorset House, Taikoo Place, Quarry Bay, Hong Kong ☎2968-5688.
South Korea 10F, Press Centre Offices, 25 Taepyongno 1-ga, Chung-gu, Seoul ☎02/732-7525.
Thailand 19F, Ramaland Building, 952 Rama 4 Rd, Bangrak District, Bangkok 10500 ☎02/233-5108.
UK Heathcoat House, 20 Savile Row, London W1X 1AE ☎020/7734 9638, ⓦwww.jnto.go.jp.

US One Rockefeller Plaza, Suite 1250, New York, NY 10020 ☎212/757-5640, ✉info@jntonyc.org; 360 Post St, Suite 601, San Francisco, CA 94108 ☎415/989-7140, ✉sfjnto@webjapan.com; 515 Figueroa St, Suite 1470, Los Angeles, CA 90071 ☎213/623-1952, ✉info@jnto-lax.org.

Maps

The Japan National Tourist Organization publishes four tourist **maps** covering Japan, Tokyo, Kansai and Kyoto. These are available free at JNTO offices abroad and at the TICs in Japan, and are perfectly adequate for most purposes. Tourist offices in other areas usually provide local maps, which are of varying quality, and often only in Japanese, but generally adequate. If you need anything more detailed, most bookshops sell maps, though you'll only find English-language maps in the big cities (see individual city Listings for details). By far the most useful are the **bilingual maps** published by Kodansha or Shōbunsha, which are available from specialist shops outside Japan (see below for suggested outlets). Kodansha's *Tokyo City Atlas* and *Kyoto–Ōsaka Bilingual Atlas* are a must for anyone spending more than a few days in these cities, while Shōbunsha's *Japan Road Atlas* is the best available map for exploring by car. If you're **hiking**, an excellent guide is the relevant *Area Map*, published by Shōbunsha in Japanese only.

Note that **maps on signboards** in Japan, such as a map of footpaths in a national park, are usually oriented the way you are facing. So, if you're facing southeast, for example, as you look at the map, the top will be southeast and the bottom northwest.

Specialist map suppliers

UK and Ireland

Stanfords 12–14 Long Acre, London WC2E 9LP ☎020/7836 1321, ⓦwww.stanfords.co.uk. Other branches at 39 Spring Gardens, Manchester ☎0161/831 0250, and 29 Corn St, Bristol ☎0117/929 9966. One of the best travel bookshops in the world, with a global catalogue, expert knowledge and worldwide mail order.
Blackwell's Map and Travel Shop 50 Broad St, Oxford OX1 3BQ ☎01865/793 550, ⓦwww.blackwell.bookshop.co.uk. Branches in

Bristol, Cambridge, Cardiff, Leeds, Liverpool, Newcastle, Reading and Sheffield.

Daunt Books 83 Marylebone High St, London W1U 4QW ⓣ020/7224 2295, ⓕ7224 6893; 193 Haverstock Hill, London NW3 4QL ⓣ020/7794 4006.

Easons Bookshop 40/42 Lower O'Connell St, Dublin 1 ⓣ01/873 3811.

Fred Hanna's Bookshop 27–29 Nassau St, Dublin 2 ⓣ01/677 1255, ⓦwww.hannas.ie.

Heffers Map and Travel 20 Trinity St, Cambridge CB2 1TY ⓣ01223/568 568, ⓦwww.heffers.co.uk.

John Smith and Sons Glasgow Caledonian University, 70 Cowcaddens Road, Glasgow G4 0BA ⓣ0141/332 8177, ⓕ332 5717, www.johnsmith.co.uk.

The Map Shop 30a Belvoir St, Leicester LE1 6QH ⓣ0116/247 1400, ⓦwww.mapshopleicester.co.uk.

National Map Centre 22–24 Caxton St, London SW1H 0QU ⓣ020/7222 2466, www.mapsnmc.co.uk.

Newcastle Map Centre 55 Grey St, Newcastle upon Tyne NE1 6EF ⓣ0191/261 5622, www.newtraveller.com.

Ottakar's Unit 69, Eastgate Centre, Inverness IV2 3PB ⓣ01463/233500, ⓦwww.ottakars.co.uk.

The Travel Bookshop 13–15 Blenheim Crescent, London W11 2EE ⓣ020/7229 5260, ⓦwww.thetravelbookshop.co.uk.

Waterstone's 91 Deansgate, Manchester M3 2BW ⓣ0161/837 3000, ⓕ839 1789, www.waterstonesbooks.co.uk.

North America

110 North Latitude US ⓣ336/369-4171, www.110nlatitude.com.

Book Passage 51 Tamal Vista Blvd, Corte Madera, CA 94925 and in the historic San Francisco Ferry Building ⓣ1-800/999-7909 or ⓣ415/927-0960, ⓦwww.bookpassage.com.

Distant Lands 56 S Raymond Ave, Pasadena, CA 91105 ⓣ1-800/310-3220, ⓦwww.distantlands.com.

Globe Corner Bookstore 28 Church St, Cambridge, MA 02138 ⓣ1-800/358-6013, ⓦwww.globecorner.com.

Longitude Books 115 W 30th St #1206, New York, NY 10001 ⓣ1-800/342-2164, ⓦwww.longitudebooks.com.

Map Town 400 5 Ave SW #100, Calgary, AB, T2P 0L6 ⓣ1-877/921-6277 or ⓣ403/266-2241, ⓦwww.maptown.com.

Travel Bug Bookstore 3065 W Broadway, Vancouver, BC, V6K 2G9 ⓣ604/737-1122, ⓦwww.travelbugbooks.ca.

World of Maps 1235 Wellington St, Ottawa, ON, K1Y 3A3 ⓣ1-800/214-8524 or ⓣ613/724-6776, ⓦwww.worldofmaps.com.

Australia and New Zealand

Mapland 372 Little Bourke St, Melbourne ⓣ03/9670 4383, ⓦwww.mapland.com.au.

The Map Shop 6–10 Peel St, Adelaide ⓣ08/8231 2033, www.mapshop.net.au.

Mapworld 173 Gloucester St, Christchurch ⓣ0800/627 967 or 03/374 5399, ⓕ374 5633, ⓦwww.mapworld.co.nz.

Perth Map Centre 1/884 Hay St, Perth ⓣ08/9322 5733.

Specialty Maps 46 Albert St, Auckland ⓣ09/307 2217.

Travel Bookshop Shop 3, 175 Liverpool St, Sydney ⓣ02/9261 8200.

Worldwide Maps and Guides 187 George St, Brisbane ⓣ07/3221 4330.

Websites

There is a massive number of **websites** in both English and Japanese on Japan. Yahoo's directory (ⓦwww.yahoo.com) is a good jumping-off point for a general overview of Japan-related sites – a few of the more useful are detailed below. See p.45 for online accommodation resources; p.34 for transport information; p.98 for useful sites with information on Tokyo; and p.63 for information about getting online while in Japan.

Airports ⓦwww.narita-airport.or.jp and ⓦwww.kansai-airport.or.jp/english/index.htm. Both Narita and Kansai International airports run their own homepages, complete with flight information, floor plans and the lowdown on local access.

Being A Broad ⓦwww.being-a-broad.com. Tons of useful info on life in Japan from a female perspective.

Big Daikon ⓦwww.bigdaikon.com. Lets you find out what JETs (see p.83) past, present and future think about Japan.

Japan Reference Forum ⓦwww.jref.com/forum. For anything Japanese you wish to chat or ask questions about.

Japan Travel Updates ⓦwww.jnto.go.jp. Though no longer as comprehensive as it was, JNTO's is still the best single place to start looking for general travel-related information. The databases are most immediately useful, particularly the train and flight timetables, as well as links to accommodation resources.

Kateigaho ⓦwww.kateigaho.com/int. Leading Japanese glossy magazine on culture and the arts –

it now has a great English edition, details of which are available on the website.

Kabuki for Everyone
Ⓦ www.fix.co.jp/kabuki/kabuki.html. Good introduction to Kabuki, with video and sound clips, play summaries and so forth.

Kids Web Japan
Ⓦ www.jinjapan.org/kidsweb/index.html. Anyone travelling with children should take a look at this site. In addition to simple background information, folk legends and general cultural titbits, it offers an insight into what's currently cool at school in Japan.

Links Ⓦ http://jguide.stanford.edu, Ⓦ www.jinjapan.org and Ⓦ http://jin.jcic.or.jp/navi/index.html (Japan Web Navigator) Stanford University's *Jguide* has a vast, well-organized list of sites. The *Japan Information Network* comprises a number of useful and interesting sites, among them the *Japan Web Navigator*, with a more manageable array of links.

News Ⓦ mdn.mainichi.co.jp, Ⓦ www.japantimes.co.jp and Ⓦ www.japantoday.com. Among the online English-language newspapers, the *Mainichi Daily News* is the pick of the bunch, while the digital *Japan Times* has the advantage of searchable archives. *Japan Today* features all the latest news in English from Japan and around the region, including business news, features and commentary.

Outdoor Japan Ⓦ www.outdoorjapan.com. The best resource for information on all outdoor activities across the country, plus lots of travel advice for off-the-beaten-track destinations.

Prices Ⓦ www.pricechecktokyo.com. Lists prices for a whole range of items, from café latte to a tube of toothpaste. If it's not there, they'll find the price for you.

Trends in Japan Ⓦ www.jinjapan.org/trends. Covers arts and entertainment, as well as business, sports, fashion and much more.

Costs, money and banks

Japan's ongoing economic recession is good news for travellers: there are now more discount deals available and, in certain cases, yen prices have remained stable or even fallen slightly. Unfortunately, such advantages have largely been wiped out by the recent strength of the yen, meaning that your foreign currency buys you that much less. However, with careful planning Japan is still a manageable destination even for those on a modest budget. The key is to do what the majority of Japanese do: eat in local restaurants, stay in Japanese-style inns and take advantage of any available discounts. That said, choosing the wrong bar or taking a longish taxi ride can blow your budget.

The **Japanese currency** is the yen (¥), of which there are no subdivisions. Notes are available in denominations of ¥1000, ¥2000, ¥5000 and ¥10,000, while coins come in values of ¥1, ¥5, ¥10, ¥50, ¥100 and ¥500. Apart from the ¥5 piece, a copper-coloured coin with a hole in the centre, all other notes and coins indicate their value in Western numerals. Note that not all ticket, change and vending machines have been upgraded to accept the new ¥2000 notes and ¥500 coins (although the older, more silvery ¥500

Money and information

bank	ginkō	銀行
foreign exchange desk	Gaikoku kawase mado-guchi/ryōgae jo	外国為替窓口／両替所
yen	en	円
tourist information office	kankō annaijo	観光案内所

coins do work). At the time of writing the **exchange rate** was approximately ¥183 to £1, ¥108 to US$1, and ¥76 to A$1. Japan is currently experiencing negative inflation at a rate hovering between zero and minus one percent.

Costs

By far your biggest outlays are likely to be on accommodation and transport. In the case of **accommodation**, you can keep costs down by staying in hostels or cheap Japanese inns and by sharing a room (see "Accommodation" on p.44 for details). As an approximate guide, the average price of staying in a youth hostel dorm is ¥3000 (£16/US$28); for a double room in a basic Japanese inn, expect to pay from around ¥5000 (£27/US$46) per person; while a similar room in a moderately comfortable business hotel will set you back upwards of ¥6000 per person (£33/US$55).

As regards **transport**, the best strategy for most travellers is to buy a Japan Rail Pass before departure, though it's also worth investigating special deals on internal flights. Within the country, all sorts of discount fares and excursion tickets are available, while overnight ferries and buses are an economical, if not always comfortable, way of getting around; see "Getting Around" on p.33 for more details. There's almost invariably an **admission charge** to museums and other tourist sights; school-age children and students usually get reduced rates, which may be up to half the adult price.

By staying in youth hostels and eating in the cheapest local restaurants, the absolute minimum **daily budget** for food and accommodation is ¥5000 (£27/US$46). By the time you've added in some transport costs, a few entry tickets, meals in better-class restaurants and one or two nights in a ryokan or business hotel, you'll be reaching a more realistic expenditure of at least ¥10,000 (approximately £54/US$92) per day.

Holders of **international student cards** are eligible for discounts on transport and some admission fees. If you're planning to stay in hostels, it's worth buying a **Hostelling International card** in your home

country; not only does the card qualify you for slight reductions at some hostels (see p.50), but you can also take advantage of discount tour packages offered by the Japan Youth Hostel Association (see p.50 for details). Before setting off, it's also worth checking JNTO's website for tips on how to save money. Also check if there are any "**Welcome Card**" schemes operating in the areas you intend visiting. At the time of writing, there were schemes in Aomori-ken, Narita, the GRUTT museum card for Tokyo, Mt Fuji, covering the Fuji/Hakone/Izu regions, the Tokai area, covering Aichi, Gifu, Mie and Shizuoka prefectures, Kagawa-ken, the Seto Inland Sea, Kita-kyūshū, and Fukuoka.

Changing money

Though credit cards are gaining in popularity, Japan is still very much a **cash society**; even in major cities you'll be settling most bills in ready money. Thanks to the country's low crime levels and a surprisingly undeveloped banking system, most Japanese carry around relatively large amounts of yen, and it's fine for you to follow suit. That said, it's always safest to carry the bulk of your money in **travellers' cheques**, with the added advantage that in Japan they attract a slightly better exchange rate than notes. The most widely accepted cheques are American Express, Visa and Thomas Cook. You'll have no problem changing dollar or sterling travellers' cheques in major towns and cities, but be wise to carry an emergency reserve of yen travellers' cheques or dollars cash if you plan to visit more remote areas.

When exchanging either cash or travellers' cheques, **banks** usually offer the best rates, with little variation between them and no commission fees; look for banks announcing "Foreign Exchange Bank" in English outside

Banking hours

Banks open Monday to Friday 9am to 3pm, though some don't open their exchange desks until 10.30am or 11am. All Japanese banks close on Saturdays, Sundays and national holidays.

the front door. Remember to take your passport along in case it's needed, and allow plenty of time, since even a simple transaction can take twenty minutes or more. Note that, while all authorized foreign exchange banks accept dollars and the vast majority will take sterling, other currencies can be a problem even in Tokyo; if you're stuck, Tokyo Mitsubishi Bank handles the widest range of currencies and has branches in most large cities.

Main **post offices** often have an exchange counter where you can change cash or travellers' cheques in eight major currencies, including American, Canadian and Australian dollars, sterling and the euro; their rates are usually close to the banks' and they have slightly longer opening hours (Mon–Fri 9am–4pm).

If you need to change money at any other time, big **department stores** often have an exchange desk, though most only handle dollars or a limited range of currencies and might charge a small fee. **Hotels** are only supposed to change money for their guests, but some might be persuaded to help in an emergency. In rural areas, however, you'll be lucky to find a bank or anywhere else offering exchange services, so make sure you've got plenty of cash before heading into the sticks. Finally, when changing money, ask for a few ¥10,000 notes to be broken into lower denominations; these come in handy for ticket machines and small purchases.

Credit cards and wiring money

Credit and debit cards are far more widely accepted in Japan than they were a few years ago. The most useful cards to carry are Visa and American Express, followed closely by Mastercard, then Diners Club, which you should be able to use in those hotels, restaurants, shops and travel agen-

cies where they're used to serving foreigners. However, many retailers only accept locally issued cards, so it's never safe to assume you'll be able to use your foreign plastic.

Making **cash withdrawals** using plastic is becoming easier. Citibank have teamed up with the Post Office to operate ATMs accepting foreign-issued credit and debit cards in thousands of post offices – and a few other handy locations such as Citibank offices, department stores and public buildings – throughout the country. The machines are identified with a sticker saying "International ATM Service" and you can opt for instructions in English. They handle cards from nine networks, including Visa, PLUS, Mastercard, Cirrus, American Express and Diners Club; you'll need your PIN to make a withdrawal, which can be anywhere between ¥1000 and ¥999,000, depending on the issuer and your individual credit limit; if the machine doesn't allow you money in the first instance, try again with a smaller amount. The card must be inserted face up and with the strip to the right. In major post offices the ATMs are accessible at weekends and after the counters have closed, though none is open 24 hours, and sometimes they just don't work for whatever reason, so it's best not to be totally reliant on your card.

In addition, Visa and Mastercard now have a fairly good spread of international ATMs in major cities, while Citibank operates a number of its own ATM corners in Tokyo and a few other cities. JNTO (see p.28) can provide lists of locations, or consult the relevant website: ⓦwww.visa.com, ⓦwww.mastercard.com and ⓦwww.citibank.co.jp. Most of these machines are accessible outside normal banking hours and some are open 24 hours. The minimum withdrawal is normally ¥10,000. If you're having problems, pick up the phone beside the ATM and ask to speak to someone in English.

In an emergency, **wiring money** is the quickest option. You'll need to contact one of the major Japanese banks to check exactly how they handle these transfers and what charges they levy, then call on a reliable friend to make the arrangements at the other end. The whole process can take several

24-hour credit card emergency numbers

If you lose a credit or debit card, call the following toll-free numbers:
American Express ℡0120-020120 (general enquiries ℡0120-020666; Mon–Fri 9am–7pm).
Mastercard ℡00531/11-3886 (also handles general enquiries).
Visa International ℡0120-133173 (also handles general enquiries).

days, and hefty charges are made at both ends (in Japan, typically around ¥2500 for yen transfers, while charges for other currencies are generally built into the exchange rate employed). Alternatively, you can use MoneyGram (ⓦ www.moneygram.com), whereby you receive the transfer via a MoneyGram agent; charges vary according to the amount, but can be up to ten percent.

Getting around

Birthplace of the Shinkansen, or "Bullet Train", Japan is one of the world's great railway countries, though you shouldn't automatically assume that the train is always the best way to get around the country. Although tunnels and bridges now link all four of the main islands, to reach hundreds of others you have no choice but to board a ferry or a plane. The length of the country also makes flying – say, from Tokyo to Sapporo in the north or Kagoshima in the south – well worth considering, especially since the difference in cost compared to the fastest trains is negligible. It's also worth considering flying into one airport and home from another (see p.12 & 18).

The time of year is an important factor to consider when arranging your transport around Japan. **Peak travelling seasons** are the few days either side of New Year, the Golden Week holidays of late April and early May, and the mid-August Obon holidays (see p.65 for further details of national holidays). During these times the whole of Japan can seem on the move, with trains, planes and ferries packed to the gills and roads clogged with traffic. If you want to be assured of a seat, book well in advance and be prepared to pay higher fares on flights, as all discounts are suspended during peak periods.

The main domestic **travel agencies** – JTB and NTA (see relevant city Listings sections for details) – can handle bookings for all types of transport and are also useful sources for checking travel schedules. The staff in these agencies have access to the

jikokuhyō timetable, an incredible source of information, updated monthly, on virtually every form of public transport in Japan. There's always a *jikokuhyō* available for consultation at stations, and most accommodation has a copy too. If you're going to travel around Japan a lot, and especially if you're planning an adventurous trek through rural areas, having your own timetable can be invaluable. Pocket versions are available cheaply from most bookstores, and train stations often give out free mini train timetables for the areas they serve. Although they're all in Japanese, once you've decoded the relevant *kanji* characters they're simple to use. Easiest of all, especially if you have a rail pass, is to get hold of a JR English timetable for all the Shinkansen and many major express train services, available from JNTO offices in Japan and abroad.

33

Useful travel phrases

Shinkansen	*Shinkansen*	新幹線
Limited express train	*tokkyū*	特急
Express train	*kyūkō*	急行
Rapid train	*kaisoku*	快速
Ordinary train	*futsū*	普通
Reserved seat	*shitei-seki*	指定席
Unreserved seat	*jiyū-seki*	自由席
Non-smoking seat	*kin'en-seki*	禁煙席
Green car	*guriin-sha*	グリーン車

Tickets

One-way	*katamichi*	片道
Return	*ōfuku*	往復
Seishun Jūhachi-kippu	*Seishun Jūhachi-kippu*	青春十八切符
shūyūken	*shūyūken*	周遊券
Multiple purchase ticket	*kaisūken*	回数券
Discount ticket shop	*kinken shoppu*	金券ショップ

Online travel resources

There are several useful travel websites in English to help you plan your journey around Japan.

Japan Rail (JR) Ⓦ www.japanrail.com and Ⓦ www.world.eki-net.com. Information on rail passes, train and ferry schedules and some fares. The World Eki-net site allows you to book Shinkansen tickets online. For online details about Japan Rail Passes, see p.37.

Kancycling & Adventure Cyclists Club Ⓦ www.kancycling.com and Ⓦ www.t3.rim.or.jp. Two English-language sites that will help those planning a biking tour of Japan.

Online Odakyu Ⓦ www.odakyu-group.co.jp /english. Details of Odakyū Railway Company's tours, discount tickets and service centre in Tokyo's Shinjuku Station. Also has information on sightseeing around the Odakyū network, which covers Hakone and Kamakura.

The Subway Page and Subway Navigator Ⓦ www.reed.edu/~reyn/transport.html and Ⓦ www.subwaynavigator.com. Info on subway maps around the world. In Japan, you'll find maps for Tokyo, Ōsaka, Nagoya, Sapporo and Kyoto. Subway Navigator even tells you how much time it will take from one stop to another.

By train

Japan has the world's most efficient and frequent **trains**, with services running to all regions of the country and varying from high-speed Shinkansen to chugging steam locomotives maintained as tourist attractions. The vast majority of services are operated by **JR** (Japan Railways), which was split into seven regional networks when it was priva-

Eating and drinking on trains and at stations

Buffet cars are an increasingly rare feature of Japanese trains, but there'll almost always be a **trolley** laden with overpriced drinks and snacks being pushed down the aisle. You're generally better off both financially and in culinary terms packing your own picnic for the train, but useful fallbacks are the station **noodle stands** and the **ekiben**, a contraction of *eki* (station) and bentō (boxed meal). At the station noodle stalls, you can get warming bowls of freshly made hot noodles, usually soba or the thicker udon, for under ¥500; they can be slurped up in minutes. *Ekiben*, often featuring local speciality foods, are sold both on and off the trains and come in a wide range of permutations. Although some *ekiben* are famous for their quality, few are worth the ¥1000-plus often charged; if you have time, pop into a convenience or department store close to the station for better quality and a more keenly priced selection of bentō.

Sunrise Tours

If you only plan to visit a couple of places in Japan, there are a couple of great-value deals offered by Sunrise Tours, a division of the Japan Travel Bureau (these deals are only available to overseas visitors on tourist visas). For ¥19,000, Sunrise offers a two-day, one-night unaccompanied trip to Kyoto with reserved seats on the Shinkansen and a night's accommodation at a reasonable tourist hotel in Kyoto – for slightly more you can upgrade your hotel and go on the faster Nozomi trains. Not only is this actually cheaper than the cost of a return Shinkansen ticket to Kyoto alone, but the package is also flexible: you can stay longer in Kyoto than one night and return on any train you like (on the specified day) as long as you cancel your return seat reservation and take your chances in the unreserved section of the train (see box, p.36). Sunrise offer similar train and accommodation deals to Hiroshima from ¥29,000 and Hakone from ¥9900 – check out latest details on ⓦ www.jtb.co.jp/sunrisetour.

tized in 1987 but still runs as a single company as far as buying tickets is concerned. In addition, there are fourteen smaller rail companies, including Hankyū, Odakyū and Tōbu, which are based in the major cities and surrounding areas, but in the vast majority of Japan it's JR services that you'll be using.

Individual **tickets** are expensive, especially for the fastest trains, but there is a range of discount tickets and **rail passes** available to cut the cost. Japan Rail Passes provide the best overall deal (see p.37), while a couple of tours by the Japan Travel Bureau's Sunrise Tours arm (see box above) are also excellent value. If you have lots of time, and are travelling during the main student holiday periods, the **Seishun Jūhachi-kippu** (see p.38) is also an excellent buy.

Shinkansen

The Shinkansen speeding past snow-capped Mount Fuji is one of the most famous images of Japan, and for many a trip on the **Bullet Train** (so-called because of the smooth, rounded design of the earliest locomotives) is an eagerly anticipated part of a trip to the country. So smooth-running are these trains that you'll barely notice the speed, which on the top-of-the-range *Nozomi*-503 averages 261.8kph, making it the fastest train in the world. They are also frighteningly punctual – ten seconds late on the platform and you'll be waving goodbye to the back end of the train – and reliable: only the severest

weather conditions or earthquakes stop the Shinkansen.

There are six Shinkansen lines, all starting at either Tokyo or Ueno stations in Tokyo. The busiest route is the **Tōkaidō-Sanyō** line, which runs south along the coast of Honshū through Nagoya, Kyoto, Ōsaka and Hiroshima, terminating at Hakata Station in Fukuoka. (The Tōkaidō line runs from Tokyo to Shin-Ōsaka Station, while the Sanyō line continues from there to Fukuoka.) There are plans to extend this line to Kagoshima and part of the track has already been completed.

The **Tōhoku line** is the main northern route, passing through Sendai and terminating at Hachinohe. The fastest service, stopping only at major stations, is the *MAX Yamabiko*, for which you don't have to pay extra. The **Akita line** runs from Tokyo to Akita on the north coast, while the **Yamagata line** to Shinjō, in the middle of the Tōhoku region, splits off west from the Tōhoku line at Fukushima.

The **Jōetsu line** heads north from Tokyo, tunnelling through the mountains to Niigata along the Sea of Japan coast, with the **Nagano line** (also known as the Hokuriku line), built for the 1998 Winter Olympics, branching off west at Takasaki to end at Nagano. There are plans to extend this line from Nagano to Kanazawa and along the Sea of Japan coast.

Three types of Shinkansen services are available: the *Kodama*, which stops at all stations; the *Hikari*, which stops only at major stations; and the *Nozomi* (available on

Train classes and reservations

On Shinkasen trains and on JR *tokkyū* (limited express) and *kyūkō* (express) services, there's a choice of **ordinary** (*futsū-sha*) carriages or more expensive first-class **Green Car** (*guriin-sha*) carriages (where seats are two abreast either side of the aisle, as opposed to three) – the extra legroom and plusher seats of the Green Car aren't worth the extra money. You also have a choice between smoking and non-smoking cars. On *Nozomi* Shinkansen it's also possible to buy standing-only tickets, but these only get you a small discount.

Each train also has both reserved (*shitei-seki*) and unreserved (*jiyū-seki*) sections. Seat reservations cost ¥510 (free if you have a rail pass) and are always worth making, particularly if you plan to travel at peak times. You cannot sit in the reserved section of a train without a reservation, even if it's empty and the unreserved section full, although you can buy a reservation ticket from the train conductor.

If you don't have a reservation, aim to get to the station with thirty minutes to spare, locate your platform and stand in line at the marked section for the unreserved carriages; ask the platform attendants for *jiyū-seki*, and they'll point the way. If you have a reservation, platform signs will also direct you where to stand, so that you're beside the right door when the train pulls in.

the Tokaido–Sanyo line only), the fastest service, for which you'll have to pay an extra fee (and which you're not allowed to take if you're travelling on most types of rail pass). If you're travelling from Tokyo to Fukuoka, the *Nozomi* shaves an hour off the six-hour journey on the *Hikari*, but for shorter hops to Nagoya, Kyoto or Ōsaka the time saved isn't generally worth the extra expense of the ticket.

To travel by Shinkansen you'll pay a hefty **surcharge** on top of the basic fare. On the train there are announcements and electronic signs in English telling you which stations are coming up. Get to the door in good time before the train arrives, as you'll generally only have a few seconds in which to disembark before the train shoots off again. A range of **refreshments** (see box on p.34) is always available from the attendants who regularly hawk their wares up and down the aisles. Very few trains have dining cars, and when they do they're nothing special. The newer Shinkansen have telephones and vending machines for drinks.

Other trains

Aside from the Shinkansen, the fastest services are **limited express** (*tokkyū*) trains, so-called because they make a limited number of stops. Like Shinkansen, you have to pay a surcharge to travel on *tokkyū* and there are separate classes of reserved and non-

reserved seats (see box above). Less common are the **express** (*kyūkō*) trains, which also only stop at larger stations but carry a lower surcharge. Despite their name, the **rapid** (*kaisoku*) trains are slower still, making more stops than a *kyūkō*, but with no surcharge. Finally, the **ordinary** (*futsū*) trains are local services stopping at all stations and usually limited to routes under 100km.

The above categories of train and surcharges apply to all JR services, and to some, but not all, private rail routes. To further confuse matters, you may find that if you're travelling on a JR train on one of the more remote branch lines, you may be charged an additional fare due to part of the old JR network having been sold off to another operating company.

For long-distance journeys between major cities, such as from Tokyo to Sapporo or from Ōsaka to Nagasaki and Kyoto, you can catch an overnight **sleeper train**, which will be either *tokkyū* or *kyūkō*. If you have a Japan Rail Pass (see opposite) and want a berth for the night, you'll have to pay the berth charge, plus the surcharge for the express or limited express service. Some overnight trains have reclining seats or carriages without seats where you can sleep on the floor. These don't carry a surcharge, though it's a good idea to make a reservation.

Even though JR last ran a regular **steam train** service in the mid-1970s, the old locomotives enjoy an enthusiastic following and there are now seven SL (for "steam locomotive") services across the country which run from spring through to autumn, mainly on weekends and holidays. These leisurely trains, with lovingly restored engines and carriages, have proved a huge hit with tourists and you'd be well advised to book in advance. Among the more popular routes are the Yamaguchi line between Ogōri and Tsuwano in Western Honshū, and the Mōka line from Shimodate to Motegi via Mashiko in Tochigi-ken.

Buying tickets

JR tickets can be bought at any JR station and at many travel agencies, though agents may charge a handling fee. At most stations there are both **ticket counters** and **vending machines**; you can use the latter to buy all local (*futsū*) and some *kyūkō* train tickets. Only at major city stations will there be a fare map in English beside the vending machine, and you'll probably feel more comfortable going to the ticket counter. It's a good idea to have written down on a piece of paper the date and time you wish to travel, your destination, the number of tickets you want and whether you'll need smoking or non-smoking seats. This will hopefully overcome any language difficulties you may have with the station staff. If you're still not sure, just buy the minimum fare ticket from the vending machine, and pay any surcharges on the train.

To make **advance reservations** for *tokkyū* and Shinkansen trains, or to buy special types of tickets, you'll generally need to go to the green window (*midori-no-madoguchi*) sales counters, marked by a green logo. In order to swap your exchange voucher for a Japan Rail Pass (see below), you'll have to go to one of the much less common JR Travel Service Centres (see p.38). It's worth noting that few train stations accept credit cards, and if you wish to pay this way you should buy your ticket from a major travel agent, most of which accept cards.

Japan Rail passes

If you plan to make just one long-distance train journey, such as Tokyo to Kyoto one-way, a **Japan Rail Pass** (⑩www.japanrailpass

Travel information service

JR East Infoline (Mon–Fri 10am–6pm; ☎03/3423-0111) is an English-language information service dealing with all train enquiries nationwide.

.net/eng/en01.shtml) will not be good value. In all other cases it will be and you should invest in one before you arrive, since, with a few exceptions, the passes can only be bought *outside* Japan. If you want unfettered flexibility, then the comprehensive Japan Rail Pass is the only way to go. If you want to concentrate on a particular area of the country, the regional Japan Rail Passes (of which there are four) are good deals. All five types of Japan Rail Pass are available in ordinary or the more expensive Green Car versions; all the prices quoted below are for the ordinary version.

The traditional **Japan Rail Pass** allows travel on virtually all JR services throughout Japan, including buses and ferries, and is valid for seven (¥28,300), fourteen (¥45,100) or twenty-one (¥57,700) consecutive days. The major service for which it is not valid is the *Nozomi* Shinkansen; if you're caught on one of these, even unwittingly, you'll be liable for the full Shinkansen fare for the trip. This pass is the best if you plan, say, to fly into Tokyo and head down to Kyūshū by train, stopping off along the way. As with all JR tickets, children between 6 and 11 inclusive pay half-price, while those under 6 travel free.

If you plan to explore a less extensive area of Japan, the regional versions of the pass are likely to be better buys. The **JR East Pass** is valid on all services operated by JR East, including the Shinkansen, and covers the northern half of Honshū from Nagano-ken up to Aomori-ken. This pass is particularly good value if you're aged between 12 and 25. For five days' consecutive use, the price is ¥20,000 (¥16,000 for 12- to 25-year-olds), while a ten-day pass is ¥32,000 (¥25,000 for 12- to 25-year-olds). Even better value is the flexible four-day pass (¥20,000/¥16,000), which is valid for any four days within a month from the date when the pass is issued. This pass can be bought abroad and in Japan at specific JR East tick-

et offices (see their website ⓦwww.jreast.co
.jp/eastpass/index.htm) as long as you are
travelling on a tourist visa.

In a similar vein, the **JR-West Rail Pass**
can be used for trips along both the San'yō
Shinkansen and regular lines running west
from Ōsaka to Fukuoka in Kyūshū, as well
as on the super-fast *Nozomi* Shinkansen.
It's valid for four (¥20,000) or eight
(¥30,000) consecutive days, and children
aged 6 to 11 inclusive travel for half- price,
though there's no youth fare. The pass also
gives a discount on car rental at Eki Rent-
a-Car offices (see Listings sections of relevant city accounts). This pass can also be
bought in Japan from Green Ticket windows in JR-West Stations, TIS travel
agents in JR stations, or from other travel
agents such as JTB or NTA. See
ⓦwww.westjr.co.jp/english/english/index.ht
ml for more details.

The **JR Hokkaidō Rail Pass** is valid on all
JR Hokkaidō trains for three days and costs
¥14,000. It can be bought in Japan; see
ⓦwww.jrhokkaido.co.jp/global/railpass1.htm
l for more details.

Like the full JR Rail Pass, the **JR-Kyūshū
Rail Pass** can only be bought outside of
Japan. It's valid on all JR trains (except the
Shinkansen) within Japan's southern island
of Kyūshū, and costs ¥15,000 for five days
and ¥20,000 for seven days. It also gives a
discount on car rental with Eki Rent-a-Car.
See ⓦwww.jrkyushu.co.jp/english/f_rail-
pass1.html for more details.

The cost of all these passes in your own
currency will depend on the exchange rate
at the time of purchase – you can also save
money by **shopping around** between
agents offering the pass, because they
don't all use the same exchange rate. To
check on the agents who offer the pass,
ask at the nearest JNTO office (see p.28).
When you buy any of the passes, you'll be
given an exchange voucher which must be
swapped for a pass in Japan **within three
months**. Once issued, the dates on the
pass cannot be changed. Exchanges can
only be made at **JR Travel Service
Centres** at major stations; you'll be issued
with a list of locations when you buy your
pass. It's important also to note that passes
can only be issued if you're travelling on a

temporary visitor visa; JR are very strict
about this and you'll be asked to show your
passport when you present your exchange
voucher for the pass. Also, if you lose your
pass, it will not be replaced, so take good
care of it.

Finally, it's worth noting that rail-pass holders can get a discount, sometimes quite
substantial, at all JR Group Hotels; check
the list in the information booklet provided
when you buy your pass.

Other discount tickets

If you don't have a JR Rail Pass, you can still
get a wide range of discount tickets and other
rail passes. It's also worth hunting out some
of the specialist discount agencies (see opposite) for cheaper Shinkansen tickets.

At the budget end of the range is the
Seishun Jūhachi-kippu (Youth 18 ticket),
available to everyone regardless of age, but
only valid during school vacations. These
are roughly March 1 to April 10, July 20 to
September 10 and December 10 to
January 20; tickets go on sale ten days
prior to the validity period and stop ten
days before the end. For ¥11,500 you get
five day-tickets that can be used to travel
anywhere in Japan as long as you take only
the slow *futsū* and *kaisoku* trains. The tickets can also be split and used by up to four
other people. If you're not in a hurry, this
ticket can be the biggest bargain on the
whole of Japan's rail system, allowing you,
for example, to go from Tokyo to Hiroshima
for ¥2300, as long as you don't mind being
on a slow train all day and much of the
night. The tickets are also handy for touring
a local area in a day, since you can get on
and off trains as many times as you wish
within twenty-four hours.

If two or more of you are travelling together,
you should check out the **kaisūken** (multiple
purchase ticket) deal. *Kaisūken* are usually
four or more one-way tickets to the same
destination. These work out substantially
cheaper than buying the tickets individually
and, among other places, are available on
the limited express services from Tokyo to
Matsumoto and Nagano-ken.

There are also many types of **shūyūken**
and **furii kippu** (excursion tickets) available for

various areas of Japan, which combine return travel – typically by Shinkansen – with unlimited use of local transport for a specified period of time. **Waido** (wide) **shūyūken**, for example, are available for Hokkaidō and Kyūshū; the latter is especially worth considering since it allows you to travel part or all of one way by ferry. Despite their name, *furii kippu* (meaning "free ticket") always cost money, but allow unlimited travel within a certain area over a set amount of time. One of the best value is the **Hakone Furii Pass**, offered by the Odakyū railway company, which covers routes from Tokyo to the lakeland area of Hakone. If you plan to travel in one area, it's always worth asking the JR Infoline or the tourist information offices if there are any other special tickets that could be of use.

Married couples whose combined ages total at least 88 are eligible for the **Full Moon Pass** (¥80,500 for 5 days, ¥99,900 for 7 days and ¥124,400 for 12 days). These prices cover both people for travel in Green Cars on all trains (except the *Nozomi*), including sleeper trains. Although this pass is very pricey, it may be worth considering if you're planning a lot of travel and want to do it in comfort. If one spouse is aged 70 or over, there's a ¥5000 discount.

If you're thinking of renting a car (see p.41), it's worth looking into the **Eki Rent-a-Car-kippu** tickets, which you can buy if your total journey is more than 200km. These provide a twenty percent discount on the cost of the train fare and car rental.

By air

Since the deregulation of the airline industry in 1996, **domestic flights** in Japan have come down in price. **Skymark** (🌐 www.sky-

mark.co.jp), modelled after no-frills European services such as Go and Easyjet, has led the way with price slashing on its Tokyo–Fukuoka, Tokyo–Tokushima, Tokyo–Aomori and Ōsaka–Fukuoka routes. Air Do (🌐 www.airdo21.com) is another newcomer (it has a cute teddy bear as a mascot), operating on the Tokyo–Sapporo route, the busiest in the world, with eight million passengers a year.

The big two domestic airlines – All Nippon Airways (ANA) and Japan Airlines (JAL), which now includes Japan Air System (JAS) – have responded with price initiatives of their own. JAL, for example, offers an eighteen percent discount for bookings over the Net, while ANA has had campaigns offering all domestic fares at ¥10,000 on certain days. The majors are also planning to launch cut-price subsidiary carriers, but they still have the market pretty much carved up between them and, busiest routes apart, there remains little competition as far as prices and quality of service are concerned – choose whichever airline offers the most convenient flight time. Of the smaller domestic airlines, Air Nippon (ANK) and Japan TransOcean Air (JTA) offer the widest choice of routes.

If you **book in advance**, you can make substantial savings on the regular fares with all the major airlines. Tickets booked two months to 28 days in advance qualify for a 45–50 percent discount; if you book 21 days in advance, you can get a 30 percent discount, and fourteen days in advance gives a 20 percent reduction. There's also sometimes 35–40 percent off early-morning (generally before 7am) departures. If you're not using a rail pass (see p.37), discounted

Contacting the airlines

ANA, JAL and JAS all have English-speaking reservation agents who can be contacted on the toll-free numbers below from anywhere in Japan. They also all have English-language websites, of which JAS and ANA's are the most useful, offering flight schedules, seat availability, fares and airport access information.

ANA ☎0120-029222, ⓦwww.ana.co.jp
JAL ☎0120-255971, ⓦwww.jal.co.jp
JAS ☎0120-511283, ⓦwww.jas.co.jp

plane fares are well worth considering in comparison to train fares. For example, to travel by train to Sapporo from Tokyo costs ¥22,780 and takes the better part of a day, compared to a discounted plane fare which can fall as low as ¥9000 from Tokyo to Shin-Chitose airport, near Sapporo, a journey of ninety minutes. Note that discounts are generally not available during the peak travelling season of the April/May Golden Week holidays (see p.66), most of August and over New Year.

If you plan to fly long distances in Japan or want to make several plane trips, it's worth considering JAL's **Welcome to Japan** or ANA's **Visit Japan** fare systems. You don't need to fly with either airline to Japan to take advantage of these tickets, which offer a minimum of two flights anywhere in the country for ¥25,200, three flights for ¥37,800, four for ¥50,400 and five (maximum) for ¥63,000. This fare is excellent value if you plan to visit far-flung destinations, such as the islands of Okinawa, where standard one-way fares are ¥34,500. There are a few conditions, but the main one to keep in mind is that these tickets are not available during peak travelling seasons (Aug 1–25) and the New Year holidays.

By bus

Japan has a comprehensive system of long-distance **buses** (*chōkyori basu*), including night buses between major cities such as Tokyo, Kyoto and Ōsaka. Fares are always cheaper than on the train, but the buses are much slower and can get caught up in traffic, even on the expressways, Japan's fastest roads, especially during peak travel periods. Most bus journeys start and finish next to or near the main train station. For journeys over two hours, there is usually at least one rest stop along the way.

There's little pleasant scenery along the highways, so if you have a long journey to make, it's worth considering a **night bus** (*yakō basu*), where available. You'll save on a night's accommodation, and the seats recline (unlike those on overnight trains), making sleep possible. To compare costs, the overnight bus from Tokyo to Kyoto, for example, costs ¥8180 and takes eight hours, while the Shinkansen costs ¥13,220 and takes two hours and forty minutes. There are hundreds of small bus companies operating different routes, so for full details of current services, timetables and costs make enquiries with local tourist information offices.

In all Japan's major cities and tourist areas you'll find escorted **bus tours**, though these are generally expensive and, outside of Tokyo and Kyoto, you're unlikely to find any with English-speaking guides.

By ferry

One of the most pleasant ways of travelling around the island nation of Japan is by **ferry**. If you have the time, the overnight journeys to and from Honshū to Hokkaidō in the north, and Kyūshū and Shikoku in the south, are highly recommended. A particularly good-value service connects Niigata on Honshū and Otaru on Hokkaidō, a relaxing eighteen-hour cruise costing as little as ¥5250. Also memorable are the cruises across the beautiful Inland Sea, or from Kyūshū to the Southwest Islands and Okinawa. If you only have a little time, try a short hop, say to one of the islands of the Inland Sea, or from Niigata to Sado-ga-shima.

There's little reason to shell out extra for the first-class sections of ferries, which provide more luxurious accommodation and facilities, as second class is fine. On the

overnight ferries in particular, the cheapest fares, which entitle you to a sleeping space on the floor of a large room with up to a hundred other passengers, are a bargain compared to train and plane fares to the same destinations. For example, the overnight ferry fare from Ōarai, two hours north of Tokyo, to Tomakomai, around an hour south of Sapporo on Hokkaidō, can be as low as ¥6500. Even if you pay extra for a bed in a shared or private berth, it's still cheaper than the train and you'll have a very comfortable cruise into the bargain. Ferries are also an excellent way of transporting a bicycle or motorbike (though you'll pay a small supplement for these) and many also take cars.

Ferry **schedules** are subject to seasonal changes and also vary according to the weather, so for current details of times and prices it's best to consult the local tourist information office. The Japan Long Distance Ferry Association, Lino Building, 2-1-1 Uchisaiwaichō Chiyoda-ku, Tokyo (☎03/3501-0806), also publishes a free annual English-language brochure, detailing current schedules and fares.

By car

While it would be foolhardy to rent a car to get around Japan's cities, **driving** is often the best way to tour the country's less populated and off-the-beaten-track areas, such as Hokkaidō or the San-in coast of Western Honshū. Japanese roads are generally of a good standard, with the vast majority of signs on main routes being in rōmaji as well as Japanese script. Although you'll have to pay pricey tolls to travel on the expressways, many other perfectly good roads are free and petrol is cheaper than in Europe, aver-

aging ¥90 a litre. If you team up with a group of people, renting a car to tour a rural area over a couple of days can work out much better value than taking infrequent and expensive buses. It's often possible to rent cars for less than a day, too, for short trips.

There are **car rental** counters at all the major airports and train stations in cities and towns, with the main local companies being Nippon Rent-a-Car, Toyota Rent-a-Car, Mazda Rent-a-Car, Japaren (which has a tie-up with Avis) and the JR-run Eki Rent-a-Car. Budget and Hertz also have rental operations across Japan (although not as widely spread). For car rental firms' contact numbers, see the Listings sections in the relevant city accounts. Rates, which vary little between companies and usually include unlimited mileage, start from around ¥6500 for the first 24 hours for the smallest type of car (a subcompact Minica, seating four people), plus ¥1000 insurance. During the peak seasons of Golden Week, Obon and New Year, rates for all cars tend to increase.

Most cars come with a **GPS** (Global Positioning Satellite) navigation system. It's sometimes possible to get an English-version CD to work with the GPS – make sure you ask for this when you book. A very handy feature is that you can input the telephone number for a location (say the number of the hotel you're staying at or a museum you want to visit) and the GPS system will plot the course for you.

Since you're unlikely to want to drive in any of the cities, the best rental **deals** are often through Eki Rent-a-Car, who give a discounted rate by combining the rental with a train ticket to the most convenient station for the area you wish to explore (see p.39). With any rental company, it's also worth thinking about making a return trip, since one-way charges are high.

To rent a car you must have an **international driver's licence** as well as your national licence; if you've been in Japan for more than six months you'll need to apply for a Japanese licence. Driving is on the left, the same as in Britain, Ireland, Australia and most of Southeast Asia, and international traffic signals are used. It's a good idea to buy a copy of the bilingual *Japan Road Atlas* (¥2890) published by Shōbunsha, which

Cable cars and ropeways

It's worth noting a linguistic distinction that applies to the transport at several of Japan's mountain resorts. What is known as a cable car in the West (a capsule suspended from a cable going up a mountain) is called a **ropeway** in Japan, while the term **"cable car"** is used to refer to what we know as a funicular or rack and pinion railway.

includes many helpful notes, such as the dates when some roads close during winter. If you're a member of an automobile association at home, the chances are that you'll qualify for reciprocal rights with the Japan Auto Federation, 3-5-8 Shiba-kōen, Minato-ku, Tokyo 105 (℡03/3436-2811), which publishes the English-language *Rules of the Road* book, detailing Japan's driving code.

The top **speed limit** in Japan is 80kph, which applies only on expressways, though drivers frequently exceed this and are rarely stopped by police. In cities, the limit is 40kph, but you'll usually be lucky to be travelling at anything close to this rate, let alone speeding. To use the expressways you have to pay a **toll**, typically around ¥30 per kilometre, which can add up and make the overall cost more expensive than taking a bus or train. On the Tokyo–Ōsaka route, for example, you'll shell out around ¥10,000 in tolls; for ¥3500 extra you could take the Shinkansen instead.

You shouldn't forget **parking** charges for towns and cities, either, where free roadside parking is virtually unheard of. There are always car parks close to main train stations; at some your vehicle will be loaded onto a rotating conveyor belt and whisked off to its parking spot. Reckon on ¥500 per hour for a central city car park and ¥300 per hour elsewhere. If you manage to locate a parking meter, take great care not to overstay the time paid for (usually around ¥300 per hour); some have mechanisms to trap cars, which will only be released once the fine has been paid directly into the meter. In rural areas, parking is not so much of a problem and rarely attracts a charge.

If you've drunk any **alcohol** at all, even the smallest amount, don't drive – it's illegal and if you're stopped by the police and breathalyzed you'll be in big trouble.

Pre-booking car rental

You may find it more convenient to pre-book your car rental before you leave home. If you do this from the UK, you should expect to pay around £50 a day, or £200 a week. From the US, rates are $60–80 for a day, $400–450 for a week, while in Australia you should expect to pay in the region of A$90–110 per day (depending on the duration of the rental) for the smallest vehicle, inclusive of insurance and unlimited kilometres.

Australia and New Zealand

Budget Australia ℡13 2727, ⓦwww.budget.com.au; New Zealand ℡09/375 2222, ⓦwww.budget.co.nz

UK and Ireland

Budget UK ℡0800/181181, ⓦwww.budgetrentacar.com; Ireland ℡09/0662 7711, ⓦwww.budget-ireland.com
Hertz UK ℡0870/844 8844, ⓦwww.hertz.com
National UK ℡01895/233, 300 ⓦwww.nationalcar.com

In North America

Budget US ℡1-800/527-0700, ⓦwww.budget.com
Hertz Canada ℡1-800/263-0600, ⓦwww.hertz.com; US ℡1-800/654-3001, ⓦwww.hertz.com
National US ℡1-800/227-3876, ⓦwww.nationalcar.com

By bike

Although you're unlikely to want to **cycle** around the grimy, traffic-clogged streets of Japan's main cities, in the smaller towns and countryside a bike is a great way to get from A to B while seeing plenty en route. Outside of the main island, Honshū, cycle touring is a very popular activity over the long summer vacation with students. Hokkaidō, in particular, is a cyclist's dream, with excellent roads through often stunning scenery and a network of basic but ultra-cheap cyclists' accommodation.

In many tourist towns you can **rent bikes** from outlets beside or near the train station; some towns even have free bikes – enquire at the tourist office. Youth hostels often rent out bikes too, usually at the most competitive rates. You can buy a brand-new bike in Japan for under ¥20,000 but you wouldn't want to use it for anything more than getting around town; for sturdy touring and mountain bikes, hunt out a specialist bike shop or bring your own. Although repair shops can be found nationwide, for foreign models it's best to bring essential spare parts with you. And despite Japan's low crime rate, a small but significant section of the Japanese public treats bikes as common property; if you don't want to lose it, make sure your bike is well chained whenever you leave it.

If you plan to take your bike on a train or bus, ensure you have a bike bag in which to parcel it up; on trains you're also supposed pay a special **bike transport supplement** of ¥270 (ask for a *temawarihin kippu*), although ticket inspectors may not always check.

If you're planning a serious cycling tour, an excellent investment is *Cycling Japan* (¥2200; Kodansha), a handy practical guide detailing many touring routes around the country. The book is edited by Brian Harrell, who also edits the *Oikaze* cycling newsletter, available from 2-24-3 Tomigaya, Shibuya-ku, Tokyo. There's also some useful cycling information on ⓦ www.outdoorjapan.com.

Hitching

There's always a risk associated with **hitching**. That said, Japan is one of the safest and easiest places in the world to hitch a ride, and in some rural areas it's just about the only way of getting around without your own transport. It's also a fantastic way to meet locals, who are often only too happy to go kilometres out of their way to give you a lift just for the novelty value (impecunious students apart, hitching is very rare in Japan), or the opportunity it provides to practise English.

As long as you don't look too scruffy you'll seldom stand around long waiting for a ride. It's a good idea to write your intended destination in large *kanji* characters on a piece of card to hold up. Also carry a stock of small gifts you can leave as thank yous; postcards, sweets and small cuddly toys are usually popular. Will Ferguson's entertaining travel narrative *Hokkaidō Highway Blues* (see p.1016) is also a useful reference.

City transport

All Japanese cities are served by buses and trains, but only the largest have subway systems. Some towns and cities have retained their trams, although in Tokyo, Ōsaka and Sapporo they've all but disappeared. Taxis are always a useful standby and needn't be too pricey if used over short distances or by a group of people.

Subways and trains

The easiest and fastest way of getting around the major cities is to use the efficient **subways** and local **trains**. Stations almost always have English signs and trains are often colour-coded to match the transport maps.

You need to buy a ticket before getting on an overground or subway train, usually from a ticket machine. Some machines take yen bills and all will give change if you don't have the exact fare. If you're not sure what the fare is, buy the cheapest ticket and sort out the difference either on the train or with the guard at the ticket gate when you get off. You can also buy **stored value cards**, which work out slightly cheaper than buying individual tickets. Another deal to look out for is **kaisūken** tickets, a carnet-type deal of, say, eleven ¥200 tickets for ¥2000. Generally, to make it worth buying any of the unlimited-use day tickets (available, for example, in Tokyo, Ōsaka and Sapporo), you'll have to travel long distances on the trains and subways and get on and off frequently.

If you don't relish being squashed in a tight spot, avoid travelling on subways and trains during the morning rush hour, which generally lasts between 8am and 9.30am. The evening rush hour is not so much of a problem since workers tend to go home at different times, but it's worth remembering that virtually all public transport systems close down shortly after midnight and don't restart until around 5am.

Buses and trams

Buses tend not to be that useful for non-Japanese speakers, since their signs are seldom translated into English. However, you may need to use them for getting about towns or parts of the cities not covered by subways or trains. On some city buses you'll pay a flat fare on entering the bus; if you don't have the correct change, there's always a machine to convert large coins and ¥1000 bills (but nothing larger) beside the slot where you deposit the fare. If you pay the fare on leaving the bus, you'll need to pick up a small ticket with a zone number on when you enter the bus – if in doubt, watch what the other passengers do. There will be a fare chart at the front of the bus which tells you how much to pay according to where you got on.

It's generally the smaller, more characterful cities, such as Matsuyama, Kōchi, Nagasaki and Hakodate, that have retained extensive **tram** systems, although you'll find the odd route still in Tokyo and Ōsaka. Unlike the buses, it's fairly easy to work out where you're going on a tram by looking at local transport maps, even if the signs are written in Japanese. Fares usually work in a similar way to the buses, with payment of either a flat fee, or different amounts depending on where you got on.

Taxis

Taxis can be flagged down on the streets of all towns and cities; even in quiet country villages you'll probably find one hanging around outside the train station. However, because of the cost, you are only likely to take a taxi on very short journeys. They work out a better deal if shared by a group of people, but it's worth noting that there's a limit of four people in most taxis.

The minimum **rate**, posted on the driver's window, is generally around ¥600 for the first 2km, rising by around ¥100 per 350m thereafter. If you get stuck in traffic you'll pay a time charge, and rates also rise by about twenty percent between 11pm and 5am. Tipping is not expected.

An empty taxi will show a red light. There's never any need to open or close the passenger doors since they are operated automatically by the taxi driver. It's also a good idea to have the name and address of your destination clearly written on a piece of paper to hand to the driver. Don't expect the driver to know where he's going, either; a stop at a local policebox may be necessary to locate the exact address.

Accommodation

There's no escaping the fact that accommodation in Japan will take a large portion of your budget, though with a bit of planning it's possible to keep costs within reasonable limits. While some places offer a mix of rooms, accommodation tends to divide broadly into various permutations of Western-style hotels and Japanese ryokan, or the more downmarket minshuku. In all cases rooms are likely to be small but, as a general rule, Japanese tatami rooms represent slightly better value for money – they at least feel more spacious. Youth hostels still offer some of the cheapest accommodation options, particularly for people travelling alone, but minshuku aren't always that much more expensive, particularly if you include the meals. Though not always particularly cheap, camping is a possibility in certain areas. Throughout the text of this guide, language boxes give the English, rōmaji (for pronunciation) and Japanese characters for accommodation establishments; see p.1025 for more on the language boxes.

Before arriving in Japan, it's wise to **reserve** at least your first few nights' accommodation, especially in Tokyo and Kyoto, where budget places are particularly scarce. During peak holiday seasons, however, reservations are essential throughout the country as rooms get booked up months in advance. You can get lists of accommodation from JNTO offices abroad (see p.28) and make your own arrangements or, alternatively, ask your travel agent to help. Both the Welcome Inn Group and Japanese Inn Group (see p.48) offer inexpensive accommodation which can be booked before departure, while some of the bigger hotel chains, such as Tōkyū, Prince, New Ōtani and ANA hotels, have overseas offices and may offer discounts on bookings made outside Japan. You can also find details of a limited range of accommodation, and make reservations, on the Web (see below). If you do arrive without a reservation, make use of the free accommodation booking services in Narita and Kansai International airports (see p.95 and p.494).

Within Japan, it pays to book one or two days ahead to ensure that you're not left having to stay somewhere expensive. Outside the peak season, however, you'll rarely be stuck for accommodation. The best bet is to head for the nearest **train station**, where there's usually a clutch of cheap business hotels and a **tourist information desk** – most will make a booking for you, or at least provide a list of phone numbers.

Most large- and medium-sized hotels in big cities have English-speaking receptionists who'll take a booking over the phone. The cheaper and more rural the place, however, the more likely you are to have to speak in Japanese, or a mix of Japanese and English. Don't be put off: armed with the right phrases (see "Language", p.1033), and speaking slowly and clearly, you should be able to make yourself understood – many of the terms you'll need are actually English words pronounced in a Japanese way. If time allows, booking by fax or email is another option, with the advantage that written English is easier for people to understand. Otherwise, ask the local tourist information office or the staff at your current accommodation for help.

Almost without exception, **security** is not a problem, though it's never sensible to leave valuables lying around in your room. In youth hostels it's advisable to use the lockers, if provided, or leave important items at the reception desk. Standards of **service** and **cleanliness** vary according to the type of establishment, but are usually more than adequate. When **checking in**, the registration form won't necessarily be in English but the details are fairly obvious: name, age, passport number, dates of arrival and departure. Check-in is generally between 4pm and 7pm, and check-out by 10am.

While credit cards are becoming more widely accepted, in the majority of cases **payment** will be expected in cash. In youth hostels and many cheaper business hotels you'll be expected to pay when you check in. It's always worth asking beforehand whether the advertised rates include **tax** (see box on p.31) and **service charges**, as these can bump up your bill considerably. In general, only top- and middle-range hotels or ryokan levy a service charge, typically between ten and twenty percent. In hot-spring resorts, there's a small **onsen tax** (usually ¥150), though again this may already be included in the rates. Note that **tipping** is not necessary, nor expected, in Japan.

Online accommodation resources

An increasing number of hotels and ryokan have their own websites, as listed in the guide chapters. In addition, there are a number of sites run by associations, of which the two major online resources are the Japanese Inn Group (𝕨 members.aol.com/jinngroup) and JNTO's Welcome Inn reservation service (𝕨 www.itcj.or.jp/indexwel.html); see p.48 for more on these two groups. Below we list the best of the rest, all of which offer online reservation in some form.

Japan City Hotel Association

𝕨 www.cha.yadojozu.ne.jp/english/index.htm. Has a smaller, less widespread group of hotels than other association websites, but at more modest prices. The site gives plenty of detail, including interior photos and access maps.

Japan Hotel Association 𝕨 www.j-hotel.or.jp/welcome-e.html. The biggest and most comprehensive of the associations, with over 400 hotels covering nearly all prefectures, though they tend to be big, expensive chain hotels. Lots of information provided.

Japan E-Hotel 𝕨 www.e-hoteljapan.com. The online version of the *Japan Hotel Guide*, covering mostly mid- and top-range hotels in eight cities from Tokyo to Fukuoka. No interior views, but links to the hotels' own sites, lots of detail and good area maps.

Japanese Guest Houses

𝕨 www.japaneseguesthouses.com. Booking service for scores of decent ryokan – from humble to grand – across the country. Also runs "Meet a Geisha" tours in Kyoto.

Accommodation price codes

All accommodation in this book has been graded according to the following **price codes**, which refer to the cheapest double or twin room available except in periods of unusually high demand such as New Year, and include taxes. Note that rates may increase during peak holiday periods, in particular around Christmas and New Year, the Golden Week (April 29–May 5) and Obon (the week around August 15), when accommodation is very difficult to get without an advance reservation. In the case of hostels providing **dormitory accommodation**, we've given the price per person. Most hotels have **single rates**, which can be anything from half to three quarters the double rate. Accommodation at some business hotels consists mainly of single rooms; at these places, we've also given the single rate, as well as a price code.

- ❶ under ¥3000
- ❷ ¥3000–5000
- ❸ ¥5000–7000
- ❹ ¥7000–10,000
- ❺ ¥10,000–15,000
- ❻ ¥15,000–20,000
- ❼ ¥20,000–30,000
- ❽ ¥30,000–40,000
- ❾ over ¥40,000

Japan Ryokan Association

ⓦ www.ryokan.or.jp. Another booking service for ryokan nationwide.

Hotels

Most Western-style **hotel** rooms in Japan come with en-suite bathrooms, TV, phone and air conditioning as standard – as well as a numbing lack of character, though things are beginning to improve at the upper end of the market. **Rates** for a double or twin room range from an average of ¥30,000 at a top-flight hotel, to ¥15,000–20,000 for a smartish establishment, probably with its own restaurant, room service and other refinements. At the lowest level, a room in a basic hotel with minimal amenities will cost ¥7000–10,000. Charges are almost always on a per-room basis and usually exclude meals, though breakfast may occasionally be provided, and note that it's always worth asking if they have any special deals, usually referred to as "plans". **Single rooms** are widely available at business hotels; rates are usually from a half to three-quarters the price of a double.

Top hotels provide the full range of services – a choice of restaurants and bars, a swimming pool or fitness centre, shopping arcade, business centre, non-smoking rooms and so forth. However, most visitors to Japan are likely to be staying in the more modest **business hotels** that constitute the middle and lower price brackets. As the name suggests, these places are primarily designed for travelling businessmen (rarely women, though most are happy to accept women) and are usually clustered around train stations. They are generally clean, efficient, offer a minimum level of service and are perfect if all you want is a place to crash out. The majority of business hotel rooms are single, but most places have a few twins, doubles or "semi-doubles" – a large single bed which takes two at a squeeze. They're functional and perfectly adequate, though at the cheapest places you may find smoky boxes with tiny beds, a desk and a chair squeezed into the smallest possible space. Squeeze is also the operative word for the aptly named "unit baths", which business hotels specialize in; these moulded plastic units contain a shower, bathtub, toilet and washbasin but leave little room for manoeuvre. That said, some business hotels are relatively smart and there are a number of reliable chains. One of the best and cheapest is Toyoko Inn (ⓦ www.toyoko-inn.com/eng), which has some forty hotels across the country, many offering a simple breakfast and free Internet connections in their room rates. Slightly more upmarket are Washington hotels, Sunroute, Tōkyū Inn and Dai-ichi Inn, while the Green, Alpha and Hokke Club hotels are cheap and usually very basic. Look out, too, for the Hyper chain, offering budget rooms at a decent standard for the price.

Japan's unique contribution to the hotel scene is the **capsule hotel**, which originated in the early 1970s to cater for office workers who had missed their last train home – you'll find them mostly near major stations. Inside, ranks of plastic or fibreglass cubicles, roughly 2m by 1m, contain everything the stranded, often inebriated, salaryman could want: bedding, *yukata* (a cotton dressing gown), towel, phone, alarm and TV with porn pay-channels. Each cubicle is "sealed" with a flimsy curtain, so noisy neighbours can be a problem, and they are definitely not designed for claustrophics. However, they're relatively cheap (averaging around ¥3800 per night) and fun to try at least once, though the majority are for men only. You can't stay in the hotel during the day – not that you'd want to – but you can leave luggage in their lockers. Check-in usually starts at 4pm to 5pm and often involves buying a ticket from a vending machine in the lobby.

Love hotels (see Contexts, p.1005) are another wonderful hybrid which can be a source of cheap accommodation for the adventurous. Generally located in entertainment districts, they are immediately recognizable from their ornate exteriors, incorporating cupids, crenellations or, most incongruously, the Statue of Liberty, and a sign quoting prices for "rest" or "stay". They're not as sleazy as they might sound and the main market is young people or married couples taking a break from crowded apart-ments. You usually choose your room from a back-lit display indicating those still available – the best contain moving beds, lurid murals and even swimming pools – and then negotiate with a cashier lurking behind a tiny window. Though daytime rates are high (from about ¥4000 for 2hr), the price of an overnight stay costs a little less than a basic business hotel (roughly ¥5000–7000). The main drawback is that you can't check in until around 10pm.

Japanese-style accommodation

A night in a traditional Japanese inn, or **ryokan**, is one of the highlights of a visit to Japan. The best can be shockingly expensive, but there are plenty where you can enjoy the full experience at affordable prices. At the cheaper end, ryokan merge into **min-shuku**, family-run guesthouses, and the larger government-owned **kokuminshukusha** (People's Lodges) located in national parks and resort areas. In addition, some temples and shrines offer simple accommodation, or you can arrange to stay with a Japanese family through the **homestay** programme.

Staying in Japanese-style accommodation

Whenever you're staying in Japanese-style accommodation, you'll be expected to check in early – between 4pm and 6pm – and to follow local custom from the moment you arrive.

Just inside the front door, there's usually a row of **slippers** for you to change into, but remember to slip them off when walking on the tatami (see p.70 for more on footwear). The **bedding** is stored behind sliding doors during the day and only laid out in the evening. In top-class ryokan this is done for you, but elsewhere be prepared to tackle your own. There'll be a mattress (which goes straight on the tatami) with a sheet to put over it, a soft quilt to sleep under and a pillow stuffed with rice husks.

Most places provide a **yukata**, a loose cotton robe tied with a belt, and a short jacket (*tanzen*) in cold weather. The *yukata* can be worn in bed, during meals, when going to the bathroom and even outside – in resort areas many Japanese holidaymakers take an evening stroll in their *yukata* and wooden sandals (*geta*), also supplied by the ryokan. Whether male or female, you should always wrap the left side of the *yukata* over the right; the opposite is used to dress the dead.

The traditional Japanese **bath** (*furo*) is a luxurious experience with its own set of rules (see p.70). In ryokan there are usually separate bathrooms for men and women, but elsewhere there will either be designated times for males and females, or guests take it in turns – it's perfectly acceptable for couples and families to bathe together, though there's not usually a lot of space.

Evening **meals** tend to be early, at 6pm or 7pm. Smarter ryokan generally serve meals in your room, while communal dining is the norm in cheaper places. **At night**, the doors are locked pretty early, so check before going out – they may let you have a key.

Unlike at hotels, it's advisable to **reserve** at least a day ahead if you want to stay in Japanese-style accommodation, and essential if you want to eat in. Though a few don't take foreigners, mainly through fear of language problems and cultural faux pas, you'll find plenty that do listed in the guide chapters. JNTO also publishes useful lists of ryokan and distributes brochures for the two following organizations, which specialize in inexpensive, foreigner-friendly accommodation.

The government-run **Welcome Inn Group** (main office at the Tokyo TIC, see p.98) has over 700 members, and covers a wide range of mostly Japanese-style accommodation, as well as hotels, pensions and youth hostels. You can make up to three reservations from abroad using their free, centralized booking system, as long as you apply several weeks before departure – at least three in the case of postal applications, or two for fax and email (reservations by phone are not accepted). Once in Japan, it's possible to make further bookings in person at their Tokyo office, the Kyoto Tourist Information Centre and in Narita and Kansai airports. Note that rates may be slightly higher if you contact the establishments direct rather than using the central reservation service.

The **Japanese Inn Group** (c/o Ryokan Shigetsu, 1-31-11 Asakusa, Taitō-ku, Tokyo 111; or Kyoto Liaison Office, c/o Hiraiwa Ryokan, 314 Hayao-chō, Kaminokuchi-agaru, Ninomiyachō-dōri, Kyoto 600; @members.aol.com/jinngroup for both) is a private association of about eighty budget ryokan and minshuku, with rates varying between ¥4000 and ¥10,000 per person excluding meals. Most also belong to the Welcome Inn Group, but tend to be the smaller, more homely places. If they're not part of the Welcome Inn system, you can book direct with each member by mail, phone, fax or email as appropriate. Some may ask for a deposit, but all take either American Express or Visa cards (often both), while many also accept Mastercard. Once in Japan, one member will help make onward reservations for the cost of the phone call.

Alternatively, you can contact the **Japan Minshuku Centre**, B1, Kōtsū Kaikan, 2-10-

1 Yūrakuchō, Tokyo 100 (Mon–Sat 10am–7pm; ℡03/3216-6556, ⓦwww.min-shuku.co.jp), which claims more than three thousand members throughout Japan. They don't issue lists of minshuku, but will make reservations on your behalf. If you book from abroad they charge a ¥2500 handling fee plus ¥700 per reservation and a deposit of up to fifty percent. Once in Japan, however, you can make reservations in person at the Centre's Tokyo office (¥300–500 commission per reservation), or ask local tourist offices for recommendations in their area.

Ryokan

Accommodation in a typical **ryokan** consists of a bare room, with just a low table sitting on pale-green tatami (rice-straw matting) and a hanging scroll – nowadays joined by a TV and phone – decorating the alcove (*tokonoma*) on one wall. Though you'll increasingly find a toilet and washbasin in the room, baths are generally communal. The rules of ryokan etiquette (see box on p.47) can seem daunting at first, but they're really not complicated, and, once you've got the hang of it, these are great places to stay.

Room rates vary according to the season, the grade of room, the quality of meal you opt for and the number of people in a room; prices almost always include breakfast and an evening meal. Rates are usually quoted per person and calculated on the basis of two people sharing. One person staying in a room will pay slightly more than the advertised per-person price; three people sharing a room, slightly less. On average, a night in a basic ryokan will cost between ¥8000 and ¥10,000 per head, while a more classy establishment, perhaps with meals served in the room, will set you back between ¥10,000 and ¥20,000. If money is no object, a top-class ryokan with exquisite meals and the most attentive service imaginable can be upwards of ¥50,000 per person.

At cheaper ryokan it's possible to ask for a room without **meals**, though this is frowned on at the more traditional places and, anyway, the meals are often very good value. If you're offered the choice of Japanese or Western food, Japanese meals are invariably better. However, many Westerners find miso soup, cold fish and rice a bit hard to tackle in the morning, so you might want to opt for a Western breakfast, if available.

Minshuku and kokuminshukusha

There's a fine line between the cheapest ryokan and a **minshuku**, the mainstay of accommodation outside big cities. In general, minshuku are smaller and less formal than ryokan: more like staying in a private home, with varying degrees of comfort and cleanliness. All rooms will be Japanese-style, with communal bathrooms and dining areas, and few minshuku provide towels or *yukata*. At the most basic level, a night in a minshuku will cost from ¥4000 per person excluding meals, or between ¥6000 and ¥10,000 with two meals; rates are calculated in the same way as for ryokan.

In the national parks, onsen resorts and other popular tourist spots, minshuku are supplemented by large, government-run **kokuminshukusha** (People's Lodges), which cater to family groups and tour parties. They're often quite isolated and difficult to get to without your own transport. The average cost of a night's accommodation is around ¥6500 per person, including two meals.

In country areas and popular resorts, you'll also find homely guesthouses called **pensions** – a word borrowed from the French. Though the accommodation and meals are Western-style, these are really minshuku in disguise. They're family-run – generally by young couples escaping city life – and specialize in hearty home-cooking. Pensions seem to appeal mostly to young Japanese and can be pretty remote, though someone will usually collect you from the nearest station. Rates average around ¥8000 per head, including dinner and breakfast.

Temples and shrines

Traditionally reserved for pilgrims, a number of Buddhist **temples** and Shinto **shrines** now take in regular guests for a small fee, and some belong to the Japanese Inn Group (see opposite) or the Japan Youth Hostels association (see p.50). By far the best places to experience temple life are at the Buddhist retreat of Kōya-san (p.590) and in Kyoto's temple lodges (see p.520).

Homestay programmes

Homestay programmes are a wonderful way of getting to know Japan – contact any of the local tourism associations and international exchange foundations listed in this book to see if any programmes are operating in the area you plan to visit.

A couple of international organizations can also help you stay with a Japanese family. **EIL** (the Experiment in International Living; ⓦwww.experiment.org) can help set up homestays with a Japanese family for between one and four weeks. At £334 per person for one week (and up to £663 for four weeks), it's not particularly cheap, but it is one of the best ways to get a real feel for the country. Details are available from the EIL office in Britain at 287 Worcester Rd, Malvern WR14 1AB ☎01684/ 562577, ⓦwww.eiluk.org; the website lists membership organizations in 23 other countries, including Australia, Canada and the US. Applications take at least two months to process.

It's also possible to arrange to stay at one of fifty organic farms around Japan through **WWOOF** (Willing Workers on Organic Farms). Bed and board is provided for free in return for work on the farm; see Working and studying in Japan, p.82, for more details. This is a great way to really get in touch with how country folk in Japan live and to get away from the big cities and beaten tourist path. For more details check ⓦwww.wwoof.org or contact them at PO Box 2675, Lewes BN7 1RB, UK. Contact details for the Japanese branch are: WWOOF Japan, Kita 16-jo, Higashi 16-chome, 3-22, Higashi-ku, Sapporo, 065-0016, ⓦwww.wwoofjapan.com/index_e .shtml. To download the list of participating farms from their website will cost you AUS$50, US$40, or ¥4000.

Though the accommodation is inevitably basic, the food can be superb, especially in temple lodgings (*shukubō*), where the monks serve up delicious vegetarian cuisine (*shōjin ryōri*). In many temples you'll also be welcome to attend the early-morning prayer ceremonies. Prices vary between ¥3500 and ¥10,000 per person, with no meals or perhaps just breakfast at lower rates.

Youth hostels

Japan has around 350 **youth hostels** spread throughout the country, offering some of the cheapest accommodation, especially for people travelling alone. There's no upper age limit (although children under 5 years aren't accepted). Once you've included meals, however, a night at a hostel may work out only slightly less expensive than staying at an ordinary minshuku. With some notable exceptions, the majority of hostels are well-run, clean and welcoming. The best are housed in wonderful old farmhouses or temples, often in great locations, while you'll also find hostels in most big cities. The main drawbacks are a raft of regulations, an evening curfew and a maximum stay of three nights.

The average **price** of hostel accommodation is ¥3000 per person, with meals (optional) costing around ¥600 for breakfast and ¥1000 for dinner; occasionally a five percent consumption tax (see p.31) is added to the bill. Rates at some hostels increase during peak holiday periods, while many charge up to ¥1000 per night more to those without membership cards (see below).

Hostels are either run by the government or by Japan Youth Hostels (JYH; ⓦwww.jyh.or.jp), which is affiliated to Hostelling International (HI; ⓦwww.iyhf.org), or are privately owned. **Membership** cards are not required at government hostels, though they will want ID, but all other hostels ask for a current Youth Hostel card. It's easiest and cheapest to get one at home, provided your national Youth Hostel Association is a full member of HI. Alternatively, you can buy a Hostelling International card (¥2800) in Tokyo at the main JYH office (Mon–Sat 10am–5pm, closed every other Sat; see box on p.51 for details). Otherwise, non-members have to buy a "welcome stamp" (¥600)

each time they stay at a JYH or private hostel; six stamps within a twelve-month period entitles you to the Hostelling International card. Note that a few hostels only accept people with a fully paid-up card.

JNTO offices stock copies of the free **map** giving contact details of all youth hostels, but it's also worth investing in the *Youth Hostel Handbook* (¥580). Though nearly all in Japanese, it gives useful location maps (by no means to scale, so beware) for each hostel, together with an English-language key; with a bit of patience it's possible to work out the essentials. The handbook comes free when you take out JYH/Hostelling International membership within Japan, or you can buy it at JYH in Tokyo or from larger hostels.

It's essential to make **reservations** well in advance for the big-city hostels and anywhere during school vacations: namely, New Year, March, around Golden Week (late April through mid-May), and in July and August. At other times, it's a good idea to book ahead, since hostels in prime tourist spots are always busy, and some close for a day or two off-season (others for the whole winter). If you want an evening meal, you also need to let them know a day in advance. The simplest way to make a reservation is via the JYHA website (ⓦwww.jyh.or.jp). You can also reserve by phone – staff often speak a little English and will help you make onward bookings.

Hostel accommodation normally consists of either dormitory bunks or shared Japanese-style tatami rooms, with communal bathrooms and dining areas. A few also have private or family rooms, but these tend to fill up quickly. **Bedding** is provided, though in some hostels you have to pay an extra ¥100 or so for sheets; since many hostels only issue one sheet, you may want to carry a sheet sleeping bag. The majority of hostels have **laundry** facilities.

Though hostel **meals** vary in quality, they are often pretty good value. Dinner will generally be Japanese-style, while breakfast frequently includes bread, jam and coffee, sometimes as part of a buffet. Some hostels have a basic "members' kitchen" which you can use for a small fee, or you can picnic in the dining room. Note that one or two hostels don't provide evening meals and there may not be any restaurants close by, so ask when you book.

Check-in is generally between 3pm and 8pm (by 6pm if you're having the evening meal), and you have to vacate the building during the day (usually by 10am). In the evening, they lock up around 9.30pm or 10pm – maybe as late as 10.30pm if you're lucky – while loudspeakers announce when it's time to bath, eat, turn the lights out and get up; there's even an approved way to fold hostel blankets. Some people find this boarding-school atmosphere totally off-putting, but you'll come across plenty of hostels with a more laid-back attitude. And you won't be expected to do any chores, beyond clearing the table after meals and taking your sheets down to reception when you leave.

Hostel managers, tellingly known as "parents", traditionally hold an **evening meeting** to talk about the area and encourage people to mix. Nowadays it's likely to be a fairly informal gathering and, though not compulsory, your participation will be appreciated.

Youth hostel associations

Australia and New Zealand

Australian Youth Hostels Association Level 3, 10 Mallett Street, Camperdown, New South Wales 2050 ☏02/9565 1699, ⓦwww.yha.org.au.
Youth Hostels Association of New Zealand PO Box 436, Christchurch 1 ☏03/379 9970, ⓦwww.yha.org.nz.

Britain and Ireland

Youth Hostel Association (YHA) Trevelyan House, 8 St Stephen's Hill, St Albans, Herts AL1 2DY ☏0870/8708 808, ⓦwww.yha.org.uk. London membership desk and booking office: 14 Southampton St, London WC2 7HY ☏020/7836 8541. Annual membership £12 (£6 for under-18s).
Youth Hostel Association of Northern Ireland 22 Donegal Rd, Belfast BT12 5JN ☏028/9031 5435, ⓦwww.hini.org.uk. Annual membership £8.
An Oige 61 Mountjoy St, Dublin 7 ☏01/830 4555, ⓦwww.irelandyha.org. Annual membership €13.
Scottish Youth Hostel Association 7 Glebe Crescent, Stirling FK8 2JA ☏01786/891400, ⓦwww.syha.org.uk. Annual membership £6.

Japan

Japan Youth Hostels Suidōbashi Nishiguchi Kaikan, 2-20-7 Misaki-chō, Chiyoda-ku, Tokyo 101 ☏03/3288-1417, ⓦwww.jyh.or.jp.

US and Canada

Hostelling International-American Youth Hostels (HI-AYH) 733 15th St NW, Suite 840, Washington, DC 20005 ☏1-800/444-6111, ⓦwww.hiayh.org.
Hostelling International Canada Suite 400, 205 Catherine St, Ottawa, ON K2P 1C3 ☏613/237-7884, ⓦwww.hostellingintl.ca.

Camping and mountain huts

There are nearly three thousand **campsites** (*kyampu-jō*) scattered throughout Japan, with prices ranging from nothing up to ¥4000 or more to pitch a tent. In some places you'll also pay an entry fee of a few hundred yen per person, plus charges for water and cooking gas, making it a fairly pricey option. In general, facilities are pretty basic compared to American or European sites; many have no hot water, for example, and the camp shop may stock nothing but pot-noodles. Most sites only open during the summer months, when they're packed out with students and school parties.

JNTO publishes lists of selected campsites, or ask at local tourist offices. If you haven't got your own tent, you can often hire everything on-site or rent simple cabins from around ¥2500 – check before you get there. Camping is a better prospect if you've got your own transport, since the best sites are in national parks and can be both time-consuming and costly to get to. You're not supposed to sleep rough in national parks, but elsewhere in the countryside **camping wild** is tolerated. However, it's advisable to choose an inconspicuous spot – don't put your tent up till dusk, and leave early in the morning.

In the main hiking areas, you'll find a good network of **mountain huts**. These range from basic shelters to much fancier places with wardens and meals. Again, the huts get pretty crowded in summer and during student holidays, and aren't particularly cheap; count on at least ¥5000 per head, including two meals. You can get information about mountain huts from local tourist offices or, if you're going to be spending a lot of time in the mountains, invest in Lonely Planet's *Hiking in Japan* or Kodansha's older *Hiking in Japan*, both of which include details of accommodation along recommended hiking trails.

Long-term accommodation

Finding reasonably priced **long-term accommodation** is a perennial problem for foreigners (*gaijin*) working in Japan. Not only is it prohibitively expensive, but many landlords simply won't rent apartments to non-Japanese. If possible, make sure accommodation is covered in your contract, or be prepared for a long haul.

Unless they're on some expat package, most newcomers start off in what are known as **gaijin houses**. Located in Tokyo, Kyoto and other cities with large foreign populations, these privately owned houses or apartments consist of shared and private rooms with communal cooking and washing facilities. They're usually rented by the month, though if there's space, weekly or even nightly rates may be available. Many are not entirely legal and are very unhygienic, while the best ones are nearly always full. But ask around and scan the English-language press or notice boards and you may be lucky. Monthly rates start from ¥30,000–40,000 per person for a shared room and ¥50,000 for a single (a deposit may be required), while a night's accommodation costs from around ¥2000 per person.

To find your own **apartment**, it helps enormously to have a Japanese friend or colleague to act as an intermediary; alternatively, you could try a housing agent. Once you've found somewhere, you'll have to fork out for "key money" (one to two months' rent), a refundable deposit (one to three months' rent), and the first month's rent in advance, plus a month's rent in commission for the agent. Rentals in Tokyo start at ¥50,000–60,000 per month for a one-room box. After all that, the "management fee", normally a few thousand yen a month, hardly seems worth mentioning.

Eating and drinking

One of the great pleasures of a trip to Japan is exploring the full and exotic range of Japanese food. Whilst dishes such as sushi and tempura are well known the world over these days, there are hundreds of other types of local cuisine that will be new discoveries to all but the most sophisticated of Western palates. Many Japanese recipes embody a subtlety of flavour and mixture of texture rarely found in Western cuisine, and the presentation is often so exquisite that it feels an insult to the chef to eat what has been so beautifully crafted. Throughout this Guide, language boxes give the English, rōmaji (for pronunciation) and Japanese characters for the names of restaurants and bars, unless they are clearly signed in English or rōmaji.

Picking at delicate morsels with chopsticks is only one small part of the dining experience, though. Robust and cheap dishes such as hearty bowls of **ramen noodles** or the comforting concoction **karē raisu** (curry rice) are staples of the Japanese diet, along with burgers and fried chicken from ubiqui-tous Western-style fast-food outlets. All the major cities have an extensive range of restaurants serving Western and other Asian dishes, with Tokyo and Ōsaka in particular being major-league destinations for foodies. In addition, each region has its own distinctive culinary traditions – boxes at the beginning of each guide chapter give the low-down on what dishes to look out for locally.

With a little planning, eating out needn't cost the earth. Lunch is always the best-value meal of the day, seldom costing more than ¥2000. If you fuel up earlier in the day, a cheap bowl of noodles for dinner could carry you through the night.

Meals

Breakfast is generally served early (from around 7am to 9am) at most hotels, ryokan and minshuku, with a traditional meal con-sisting of a gut-busting combination of miso soup, fish, pickles and rice. Western-style breakfasts, when available, seldom resemble what you might eat at home, and usually involve wedges of thick white tasteless bread, and some form of eggs and salad. Away from home and hotels, many Japanese prefer a quick *kōhii* and *tōsuto* (coffee and toast) to start the day, which is served at most cafés on the "morning-service" menu.

Restaurants generally open for **lunch** around 11.30am and finish serving at 2pm. Try to avoid the rush hour from noon to 1pm, when most office workers eat. Lacklustre sandwiches are best passed over in favour of a full meal at a restaurant, all of which offer **set menus** (called *teishoku*), usually around ¥1000 for a couple of courses, plus a drink, and rarely topping ¥2000 per person. At any time of day you can snack in stand-up noo-dle bars – often found around train stations – and beside the revolving conveyor belts at cheap sushi shops.

Dinner, the main meal of the day, can be eaten as early as 6pm, with many places tak-ing last orders around 9pm. The major cities are about the only option for late-night dining. In a traditional Japanese meal (see pp.55–57 for a description of the main dishes), you'll usually be served all your courses at the same time, but at more formal places, rice and soup are always served last. Heavy **puddings** are almost unheard of in traditional Japanese restaurants, and you are most likely to finish your meal with a piece of seasonal **fruit**, such as melon, orange, persimmon or *nashi* (a crisp type of pear), or an ice cream (if it's green, it will be flavoured with *matcha* tea).

At **tea ceremonies** (see p.50), small, intensely sweet *wagashi* cakes are served – these prettily decorated sweetmeats are usually made of pounded rice, red azuki beans or chestnuts. *Wagashi* can also be bought from specialist shops and depart-ment stores and make lovely gifts. Western-style cakes available in *kissaten* are often disappointingly synthetic, although there are pastry shops across Japan that specialize in tasty nibbles.

Where to eat and drink

One of the most common types of Japanese restaurant is the **shokudō** (eating place), which serves a range of traditional and gen-erally inexpensive dishes. Usually found near train and subway stations and in busy shop-ping districts, *shokudō* can be identified by the displays of plastic meals in their win-dows. Other restaurants (*resutoran*) usually serve just one type of food, for example sushi and sashimi (*sushi-ya*), or yakitori (*yaki-tori-ya*), or specialize in a particular style of cooking, such as *kaiseki* (haute cuisine) or *teppan'yaki*, where food is prepared on a steel griddle, either by yourself or a chef.

Bentō: the Japanese packed lunch

Every day millions of Japanese trot off to school or work with a bentō stashed in their satchel or briefcase. Bentō are boxed lunches which can be made at home or bought from shops all over Japan. Traditional bentō include rice, pickles, grilled fish or meat and vegetables. There are thousands of permutations depending on the season and the location in Japan (see box on railway food, p.34), with some of the best being available from department stores – there's always a model or picture to show you what's inside the box. At their most elaborate, bentō served in classy Japanese restaurants will come in beautiful multilayered lacquered boxes, each compartment containing some exquisite culinary creation.

It's worth searching out empty bentō boxes in the household section of department stores, since they make unusual souvenirs.

All over Japan, but particularly in city suburbs, you'll find bright and breezy **family restaurants**, such as *Royal Host* and *Denny's*, American-style operations specifically geared to family dining and serving Western and Japanese dishes – the food can be on the bland side, but is invariably keenly priced. They also have menus illustrated with photographs to make ordering easy. If you can't decide what to eat, head for the restaurant floors of major **department stores**, where you'll find a collection of Japanese and Western operations, often outlets of reputable local restaurants. Many will have plastic food displays in their front windows and daily special menus.

Western and other ethnic food restaurants proliferate in the cities, and it's seldom a problem finding popular **foreign cuisines** such as Italian (*Itaria-ryōri*), French (*Furansu-ryōri*), Korean (*Kankoku-ryōri*), Chinese (*Chūgoku-* or *Chūka-ryōri*) or Thai (*Tai-ryōri*) food. However, the recipes are often adapted to suit Japanese tastes, so be prepared for the dishes to be less spicy than you may be used to.

Coffee shops (*kissaten*) are something of an institution in Japan, often designed to act as an alternative lounge or business meeting place for patrons starved of space at home or the office. Others have weird designs or specialize in, say, jazz or comic books. For this reason, in many of the old-style *kissaten* a speciality coffee or tea will usually set you back a pricey ¥500 or more. In recent years a caffeine-fuelled revolution has taken place, with cheap and cheerful operations like *Doutor* and *Mister Donuts* springing up across the country, serving drinks and nibbles at reasonable prices; search these places out for a cheap breakfast or snack.

The best-value and liveliest places to **drink** are the **izakaya** pub-type restaurants, which also serve an extensive menu of small dishes. The major breweries run reliable *izakaya* chains, such as Sapporo's *Lions Beer Hall* and Kirin's *Kirin City*, which are generally large with a boozy atmosphere. The traditional *izakaya* are rather rustic-looking, although in the cities you'll come across more modern, trendy operations aimed at the youth market. One type of traditional *izakaya* is an *aka-chōchin*, named after the red

lanterns hanging outside, with another variation being the *robatayaki*, which serves food grilled over charcoal. Most *izakaya* open around 6pm and shut down around midnight. From mid-June to late August, outdoor **beer gardens** flourish across Japan's main cities and towns; look out for the fairy lights on the roofs of buildings, or in street-level gardens and plazas.

Regular bars, or **nomiya**, often consist of little more than a short counter and a table, and are usually run by a *mama-san* (or sometimes a *papa-san*), a unique breed who both charm and terrorize their customers. Prices at *nomiya* are high and, although you're less likely to be ripped off if you speak some Japanese, it's no guarantee. All such bars operate a **bottle keep** system for regulars to stash a bottle of drink with their name on it behind the bar. It's generally best to go to such bars with a regular, since they tend to operate like mini-clubs, with non-regulars being given the cold shoulder. *Nomiya* will stay open to the early hours, provided there are customers.

If there's live music in a bar you'll pay for it through higher drinks prices or a **cover charge**. Some regular bars also have cover charges, although there's plenty of choice among those that don't, so always check before buying your drink. Bars specializing in **karaoke** (see "Pop Culture", p.1004) aren't difficult to spot; if you decide to join in, there's usually a small fee to pay and at least a couple of songs with English lyrics to choose from, typically *Yesterday* and *My Way*.

Ordering and etiquette

On walking into most restaurants in Japan you'll be greeted by the word *Irasshaimase* ("welcome"), often shouted out with brio by the entire staff. In response, you should indicate with your fingers how many places are needed. After being seated you'll be handed an *oshibori*, a damp, folded hand towel, usually steaming-hot, but sometimes offered refreshingly cold in summer. A chilled glass of water (*mizu*) will also usually be brought automatically.

The most daunting aspect of eating out in Japan comes next – deciphering the menu. There's a basic glossary of essential

Kaiseki-ryōri: Japanese haute cuisine

At the top end of the eating spectrum is Japan's finest and most expensive style of cooking, **kaiseki-ryōri**, comprising a series of small, carefully balanced and expertly presented dishes. Though never cheap, it's a dining experience that shouldn't be missed while in Japan.

This style of cooking began as an accompaniment to the tea ceremony and still retains the meticulous design of that elegant ritual. At the best *kaiseki-ryōri* restaurants the atmosphere of the room in which the meal is served is just as important as the food, which invariably will reflect the best of the season's produce; you'll sit on tatami, a scroll decorated with calligraphy will hang in the *tokonoma* (alcove) and a waitress in kimono will serve each course on beautiful china and lacquerware. For such a sublime experience you should expect to pay ¥10,000 or more for dinner, although a lunchtime *kaiseki* bentō (see box on p.53) is a more affordable option.

words and phrases on p.1038; for more detail, try *Japanese: A Rough Guide Phrasebook*, or the comprehensive *What's What in Japanese Restaurants* by Robb Satterwhite (¥1200; Kodansha). In addition, it's always worth asking if an English menu is available (*eigo no menyū ga arimasu-ka*). If a restaurant has a plastic-food window display, use it to point to what you want. If all else fails, look round at what your fellow diners are eating and point out what you fancy. Remember that the *teishoku* (set meal) or *kōsu* (course) meals offer the best value, and look out for the word "Viking" (*Baikingu*), which means a help-yourself buffet.

Chopsticks (*hashi*) come with their own etiquette; don't stick them upright in your rice – an allusion to death. If you're taking food from a shared plate, turn the chopsticks round and use the other end to pick up the food. Also never cross your chopsticks when you put them on the table or use them to point at things. When it comes to eating soupy noodles, you can relax and enjoy a good slurp; it's also fine to bring the bowl to your lips and drink directly from it.

When you want the **bill**, say *okanjō kudasai*; the usual form is to pay at the till on the way out, not to leave the money on the table. There's no need to leave a tip, but it's polite to say *gochisō-sama deshita* ("That was delicious!") to the waiter or chef. Only the most upmarket Western restaurants and top hotels will add a service charge (typically ten percent).

Sushi, sashimi and seafood

Many *gaijin* falsely assume that all **sushi** is fish, but the name actually refers to the way the rice is prepared with vinegar, and you can also get sushi dishes with egg or vegetables. Fish and seafood are, of course, essential and traditional elements of Japanese cuisine, and range from the seaweed used in *miso-shiru* (soup) to the slices of tuna, salmon and squid laid across the slabs of sushi rice. Slices of raw fish and seafood on their own are generally called **sashimi**.

In a traditional **sushi-ya** each plate is freshly made by a team of chefs working in full view of the customers. If you're not sure of the different types to order, point at the trays on show in the glass chiller cabinets at the counter, or go for the *nigiri-zushi moriawase*, six or seven different types of fish and seafood on fingers of sushi rice. Other types of sushi include *maki-zushi*, rolled in a sheet of crisp seaweed, and *chirashi-zushi*, a layer of rice topped with fish, vegetables and cooked egg.

While a meal at a *sushi-ya* averages ¥5000 (or much more at a high-class joint), at **kaiten-zushi** shops, where you choose whatever sushi dish you want from the continually replenished conveyor belt, the bill will rarely stretch beyond ¥1500 per person. In *kaiten-zushi*, plates are colour-coded according to how much each one costs, and are totted up at the end for the total cost of the meal. If you can't see what you want, you can ask the chefs to make it for you. Green tea is free, and you can usually order beer or sake.

If you want to try the infamous **fugu**, or blowfish, you'll generally need to go to a specialist fish restaurant, which can be easily identified by the picture or model of a balloon-like fish outside. *Fugu*'s reputation derives from its potentially fatally poisonous nature rather than its bland, rubbery taste. The actual risk of dropping dead at the counter is virtually nil – at least from *fugu* poisoning – and you're more likely to keel over at the bill, which (cheaper cultivated *fugu* apart) will be in the ¥10,000 per-person bracket.

A more affordable and tasty seafood speciality is **unagi**, or eel, typically basted with a thick sauce of soy and sake, sizzled over charcoal and served on a bed of rice. This dish is particularly popular in summer, when it's believed to provide strength in the face of sweltering heat. Restaurants specializing in **crab** (*kani*) dishes are also popular and are easily identified by the models of giant crabs with wiggling pincers over the doorways.

Noodles

One of Japan's most popular and best-value meals is a bowl of **noodles**, the three main types being soba, udon and ramen. **Soba** are thin noodles made of brown buckwheat flour and are particularly ubiquitous in the central Honshū prefectures of Gifu and Nagano, though available all over Japan. If the noodles are green, they've been made with green tea powder.

There are two main styles of serving soba: hot and cold. *Kake-soba* is served in a clear hot broth, often with added ingredients such as tofu, vegetables and chicken. Cold noodles piled on a bamboo screen bed, with a cold sauce for dipping (which can be flavoured with chopped spring onions, seaweed flakes and *wasabi* – grated green horseradish paste) is called *zaru-soba* or *mori-soba*. In more traditional restaurants you'll also be served a flask of the hot water (*soba-yu*) to cook the noodles, which is added to the dipping sauce to make a soup drink once you've finished the soba.

In most soba restaurants, **udon** will also be on the menu. These chunkier noodles are made with plain wheat flour and are served in the same hot or cold styles as soba. In Nagoya, a variation on udon is *kishimen*, flattened white noodles, while the Shikoku and Okayama-ken version is known as *sanuki-udon*. In **yakisoba** and **yakiudon** dishes the noodles are fried, often in a thick soy sauce, along with seaweed flakes, meat and other vegetables.

Ramen, or stringy yellow noodles, were originally imported from China but have now become part and parcel of Japanese cuisine. They're usually served in big bowls in a steaming oily soup, which typically comes in three varieties: *miso* (flavoured with fermented bean paste); *shio* (a salty soup); or *shōyu* (a broth made with soy sauce). A range of garnishes, including seaweed, bamboo shoots, pink and white swirls of fish paste, and pork slices, often finishes off the dish, which you can spice up with added garlic or a red pepper mixture. As with the other types of noodle, many regions of Japan have their own local versions of the dish, such as Sapporo, which specializes in the rich *miso* and *batā-kōn* (butter- and corn-flavoured) ramen. Wherever you eat ramen, you can also usually get **gyōza**, fried half-moon-shaped dumplings filled with pork or seafood, to accompany them.

Rice dishes

Although fluffy, white (and frequently tasteless) bread is becoming more and more popular in Japan, it will never replace the ever-present bowl of **rice** as the staple food. Rice also forms the basis of both the alcoholic drink sake and **mochi**, a chewy dough made from pounded glutinous rice, usually prepared and eaten during festivals such as New Year.

A traditional meal isn't considered finished until a bowl of rice has been eaten, and the grain is an integral part of several cheap snack-type dishes. **Onigiri** are palm-sized triangles of rice with a filling of soy, tuna, salmon roe, or sour *umeboshi* (pickled plum), all wrapped up in a sheet of crisp *nori* (seaweed). They can be bought at convenience stores for around ¥150 each and are ingeniously packaged so that the *nori* stays crisp until the *onigiri* is unwrapped. **Donburi** is a bowl of rice with various toppings, such as chicken and egg (*oyako-don*, literally "parent and child"), strips of stewed beef (*gyū-don*) or *katsu-don*, which come with a *tonkatsu* (see below) pork cutlet.

Finally, the Japanese equivalent of beans on toast is **curry rice** (*karē raisu* in rōmaji). This bears little relation to the Indian dish: what goes into the sludgy brown sauce that makes up the curry is a mystery, and you'll probably search in vain for evidence of any beef or chicken in the so-called *biifu karē* and *chikin karē*. However, the dish definitely qualifies as a top comfort food and cheap snack.

Meat dishes

Meat is alien to traditional Japanese cuisine, but in the last century dishes using beef, pork and chicken have become a major part of the national diet, and burger and fried chicken (*kara-age*) fast-food outlets are just as common these days as noodle bars. The more expensive steak restaurants serving up dishes like **sukiyaki** (thin beef slices cooked in a soy, sugar and sake broth) and **shabu-shabu** (beef and vegetable slices cooked at the table in a light broth and dipped in various sauces) are popular treats.

Like *sukiyaki* and *shabu-shabu*, **nabe** (the name refers to the cooking pot) stews are prepared at the table over a gas or charcoal burner by diners who throw a range of raw ingredients (meat or fish along with vegetables) into the pot to cook. As things cook they're fished out, and the last thing to be immersed is usually some type of noodle. *Chanko-nabe* is the famous chuck-it-all-in stew used to beef up sumo wrestlers.

Other popular meat dishes include: **tonkatsu**, breadcrumb-covered slabs of pork, crisply fried and usually served on a bed of shredded cabbage with a brown, semi-sweet sauce; and **yakitori**, delicious skewers of grilled chicken (and sometimes other meats and vegetables). At the cheapest *yakitori-ya*, you'll pay for each skewer individually. **Kushiage** is a combination of *tonkatsu* and *yakitori* dishes, where skewers of meat, seafood and vegetables are coated in breadcrumbs and deep-fried.

Vegetarian dishes

Despite being the home of macrobiotic cooking, **vegetarianism** isn't a widely practised or fully understood concept in Japan.

You might ask for a vegetarian (*saishoku*) dish in a restaurant and still be served something with meat or fish in it. If you're a committed vegetarian, things to watch out for include *dashi* stock, which contains bonito (dried tuna), and most breads and cakes, which can contain lard. Omelettes, too, can often contain chicken stock. To get a truly vegetarian meal you will have to be patient and be prepared to spell out exactly what you do and do not eat when you order. The Tokyo Veg website (W www.tokyoveg.com) has some useful general information in English, plus a few restaurant recommendations on its info board section.

If you're willing to turn a blind eye to occasionally eating meat, fish or animal fats by mistake, then tuck in because Japan has bequeathed some marvellous vegetarian foods to the world. Top of the list is **tofu**, compacted cakes of soya-bean curd, which comes in two main varieties, *momengoshi-dōfu* (cotton tofu), so-called because of its fluffy texture, and the smoother, more fragile *kinugoshi-dōfu* (silk tofu). Buddhist cuisine, *shōjin-ryōri*, concocts whole menus based around different types of tofu dishes; although they can be expensive it's worth searching out the specialist restaurants serving this type of food, particularly in major temple cities, such as Kyoto, Nara and Nagano. Note, though, that the most popular tofu dish you'll come across in restaurants – *hiya yakko*, a small slab of chilled tofu topped with grated ginger, spring onions and soy sauce – is usually sprinkled with bonito flakes.

Miso (fermented bean paste) is another crucial ingredient of Japanese cooking, used in virtually every meal, if only in the soup *miso-shiru*. It often serves as a flavouring in vegetable dishes and comes in two main varieties, the light *shiro-miso* and the darker, stronger-tasting *aka-miso*. One of the most delicious ways of eating the gooey paste is *hōba miso*, where the miso is mixed with vegetables, roasted over a charcoal brazier, and served on a large magnolia leaf. This dish is a speciality of Takayama, where vegetarians should also sample the *sansai* (mountain vegetable) dishes.

One question all foreigners in Japan are asked is "can you eat **nattō**?". This sticky, stringy fermented bean paste has a strong taste and unfamiliar texture, which can be off-putting to Western palates. It's worth trying at least once, though, and is usually served in little tubs at breakfast, to be mixed with mustard and soy sauce and eaten with rice.

Other cuisines

Said to have been introduced to Japan in the sixteenth century by Portuguese traders, **tempura** are lightly battered pieces of seafood and vegetables. Best eaten piping hot from the fryer, tempura are dipped in a bowl of light sauce (*ten-tsuyu*) mixed with grated *daikon* radish and sometimes ginger. At specialist tempura restaurants, you'll generally order the *teishoku* set meal, which includes whole prawns, squid, aubergines, mushrooms and the aromatic leaf *shiso*.

Oden is a warming dish, usually served in winter but available at other times too – it tastes much more delicious than it looks. Large chunks of food, usually on skewers, are simmered in a thin broth, and often served from portable carts (*yatai*) on street corners or in convenience stores from beside the till. The main ingredients are blocks of tofu, *daikon* (a giant radish), *konnyaku* (a hard jelly made from a root vegetable), *konbu* (seaweed), hard-boiled eggs and fish cakes. All are best eaten with a smear of fiery English-style mustard.

Japan's equivalent of the pizza is **okonomiyaki**, a fun, cheap meal which you can often assemble yourself. A pancake batter is used to bind shredded cabbage and other vegetables, with either seafood or meat. If it's a DIY restaurant, you'll mix the individual ingredients and cook them on a griddle in the middle of the table. Otherwise, you can sit at the kitchen counter watching the chefs at work. Once cooked, *okonomiyaki* is coated in a sweet brown sauce and/or mayonnaise and dusted off with dried seaweed and flakes of bonito fish, which twist and curl in the rising heat. At most *okonomiyaki* restaurants you can also get fried noodles (*yakisoba*). In addition, *okonomiyaki*, along with its near-cousin **takoyaki** (battered balls of octopus), are often served from *yatai* carts at street festivals.

Authentic Western restaurants are now commonplace across Japan, but there is also a hybrid style of cooking known as **yōshoku** (Western food) that developed during the Meiji era at the turn of the century. Often served in *shokudō*, *yōshoku* dishes include omelettes with rice (*omu-raisu*), deep-fried potato croquettes (*korokke*) and hamburger steaks doused in a thick sauce (*hanbāgu*). The contemporary version of *yōshoku* is **mukokuseki** or "no-nationality" cuisine, a mishmash of world cooking styles usually found in trendy *izakaya*.

Drinks

The Japanese are enthusiastic social drinkers, several shared bottles of beer or flasks of sake being the preferred way for salarymen and -women to wind down after work. It's not uncommon to see totally inebriated people slumped in the street, though on the whole drunkenness rarely leads to violence.

If you want a **non-alcoholic** drink, you'll never be far from a coffee shop (*kissaten*) or a *jidō hambaiki* (vending machine), where you can get a vast range of canned soft drinks, teas and coffees, both hot and cold, though canned tea and coffee is often very sweet. Cans from machines typically cost ¥110 and hot drinks are identified by a red stripe under the display. It's worth noting that vending machines selling beer, sake and other alcoholic drinks shut down at 11pm, the same time as liquor stores. A few 24-hour convenience stores may sell alcohol after this time; look for the *kanji* for sake outside.

Sake

Legend has it that the ancient deities brewed **sake** – Japan's most famous alcoholic beverage – from the first rice of the new year. Although the twentieth-century newcomer, beer, is now Japan's most popular tipple, thousands of different brands of the clean-tasting rice wine are still produced throughout the country in sweet (*amakuchi*) and dry (*karakuchi*) varieties. Some 2500 local sake breweries make *ji-zaké* (regional sake); these can be identified by the ball of cedar leaves hanging over the shop door.

Although sake is graded as *tokkyū* (superior), *ikkyū* (first) and *nikyū* (second), this is mainly for tax purposes; if you're after the best quality, connoisseurs recommend going for *ginjō-zukuri* (or *ginjō-zō*), the most expensive and rare of the *junmai-shu* pure rice sake. Some types of sake are cloudier and less refined than others, and there's also the very sweet, milky *amazaké*, often served at temple festivals and at shrines over New Year.

In restaurants and *izakaya*, you'll have a choice of drinking your sake warm (*atsukan*) in a small flask (*tokkuri*), or cold (*reishu*). Sometimes it might be served in a small wooden box with a smidgen of salt on the rim to counter the sweet taste; in other places the cup will be in a saucer that catches the overflow of the sake since the glass is filled to the brim. Cups are generally small because, at 15–16.5 percent alcohol content (or more), sake is a strong drink, which goes to your head even more quickly if drunk warm. For more on sake check out the books and informative website of long-time resident *gaijin* expert John Gautner, ⓦ www.sake-world.

Beer

When **beer** was first brewed in Japan in Sapporo during the late nineteenth-century colonization period of Hokkaidō, the locals had to be bribed to drink it. These days, they need no such encouragement, knocking back a whopping seven million litres a year. Beer in Japan generally means lager, produced by the big four brewers Asahi, Kirin, Sapporo and Suntory, who also turn out a range of ale-type beers (often called black beer), as well as half-and-half concoctions, which are a mixture of the two. The current bestseller is Asahi Superdry, a dry-tasting lager.

Standard-size cans of beer cost around ¥200 from a shop or from vending machine, while bottles (*bin-biiru*) served in restaurants and bars usually start at ¥500. Draught beer (*nama-biiru*) is also sometimes available and, in beer halls, will be served in a *jokki*, which comes in three different sizes: *dai* (big), *chū* (medium) and *shō* (small).

In recent years, the big four breweries have seen their monopoly on domestic sales eroded by cheap foreign imports and deregulation of the industry, which has encouraged local **microbreweries** to expand their operations. In Japanese, the new brews are called *ji-biiru* (regional beer), and although few have got their act together to produce really fine beers, their drinks are always worth sampling as an alternative to the bland brews of the big four.

Other alcoholic drinks

Much stronger and cheaper than sake is the distilled grain alcohol, **shōchū**, usually mixed with a soft drink into a *sawā* (as in lemonsour) or a *chūhai* highball cocktail. At best, *shōchū* is like vodka, and very drinkable; at worst it tastes like diesel and is reputed to leave the worst hangovers in Japan.

The Japanese love **whisky**, with the top brewers producing several respectable brands, often served with water and ice and called *mizu-wari*. In contrast, Japanese **wine** (*wain*), often very sweet, is a less successful product, at least to Western palates. Imported wines, however, are available and are becoming cheaper in both shops and restaurants.

Tea, coffee and soft drinks

Other than in the relatively new coffee shops, such as *Doutor* and *Pronto*, **coffee**

Drinking etiquette

If you're out **drinking** with Japanese friends, always pour your colleagues' drinks, but never your own; they'll take care of that. In fact, you'll find your glass being topped up after every couple of sips, making it difficult to judge how much you've imbibed.

In many bars you'll be served a small snack or a plate of nuts (*otōshi*) with your first drink, whether you've asked for it or not; this is often a flimsy excuse for a cover charge to be added to the bill. It's fine to get blinding drunk and misbehave with your colleagues at night, but it's very bad form to talk about it in the cold light of day. The usual way to make a **toast** in Japanese is "*kampai*".

tends to be expensive in Japan, averaging ¥400–500 a cup. Most of the time you'll be served blend (*burendo*), a medium-strength coffee which is generally black and comes in a choice of hot (*hotto*) or iced (*aisu*). American coffee is a weaker version. If you want milk, ask for *miruku-kōhii* (milky coffee) or *kafe-ōre* (café au lait). Treat cappuccino on the menu with caution; whilst some *kissaten* take great care over their gourmet coffees, on the whole a really frothy cup is a rarity (although you can be sure of fine coffee at the *Starbucks* and *Segafredo Zanetti* café chains in metropolitan areas).

You can also get regular **black tea** in all coffee shops, served either with milk, lemon or iced. If you want the slightly bitter Japanese **green tea**, *ocha* ("honourable tea"), you'll usually have to go to a traditional teahouse, or be invited into a Japanese home. Green teas, which are always served in small cups and drunk plain, are graded according to their quality. *Bancha*, the cheapest, is for everyday drinking and, in its roasted form, is used to make the smoky *hōjicha*, or mixed with popped brown rice for the nutty *gen-maicha*. Medium-grade *sencha* is served in upmarket restaurants or to favoured guests, while top-ranking, slightly sweet *gyokuro* (dewdrop) is reserved for special occasions. Other types of tea you may come across are *ūron-cha*, a refreshing Chinese-style tea, and *mugicha*, made from roasted barley.

As well as the international brand-name **soft drinks** and fruit juices, there are sports or isotonic drinks that are unique to Japan. You'll probably want to try *Pocari Sweat*, *Post Water* or *Calpis* for the name on the can alone.

The tea ceremony

Tea was introduced to Japan from China in the ninth century and was popularized by Zen Buddhist monks, who appreciated its caffeine kick during their long meditation sessions. Gradually, tea-drinking developed into a formal ritual known as *cha-no-yu*, the **tea ceremony**, whose purpose is to heighten the senses within a contemplative atmosphere. In its simplest form the ceremony takes place in a tatami room, undecorated save for a hanging scroll or display of *ikebana* (traditional flower arrangement). Using beautifully crafted utensils of bamboo, iron and rustic pottery, your host will whisk *matcha* (powdered green tea) into a thick, frothy brew and present it to each guest in turn. Take the bowl in both hands, turn it clockwise 8cm or so and drink it down in three slow sips. It's then customary to admire the bowl while nibbling on a dainty sweetmeat (*wagashi*), which counteracts the tea's bitter taste.

Communications

For a supposedly high-tech nation, Japan's communications infrastructure can at times seem rather old-fashioned – it's not unusual, for example, to see post office staff counting on an abacus. And although public telephones are available in the most unlikely of places – including on top of Mount Fuji – few allow you to make international calls, while Internet cafés are thin on the ground outside the main urban centres.

Mail

Japan's **mail** service is highly efficient and fast, with post offices (*yūbin-kyoku*) all over the country, easily identified by their red-and-white signs of a T with a parallel bar across the top, the same symbol that you'll find on the red letterboxes. Letters posted within Japan should get to their destination in one to two days, and all post can be addressed in Western script (*rōmaji*) provided it's clearly printed.

Inside urban post offices there are separate counters, with English signs, for postal and banking services; in central post offices you can also exchange money, at rates comparable to those in banks. Within Japan, a stamp (*kitte*) for a letter up to 25g costs ¥80, and for a postcard (*hagaki*) ¥50. For **overseas post** to anywhere in the world, it costs ¥70 to send a postcard and ¥90 for an aerogram. Letters up to 25g cost ¥110 to North America, Australasia and Europe. Stamps are also sold at convenience stores, shops displaying the post office sign, and at larger hotels.

If you need to send bulkier items or **parcels** back home, all post offices sell reasonably priced special envelopes and boxes for packaging, with the maximum weight for an overseas parcel being 20kg. A good compromise between expensive air mail and lengthy sea mail is Surface Air Lifted (SAL) mail, which takes around three weeks to reach most destinations, and costs somewhere between the two.

Central **post offices** generally open Monday to Friday 9am to 7pm, Saturday 9am to 5pm and Sunday 9am to 12.30pm, with most other branches opening Monday to Friday 9am to 5pm only. A few larger branches may also open on a Saturday from 9am to 3pm, and may operate after-hours services for parcels and express mail. The Tokyo International Post Office, next to Tokyo Station, is open daily 24 hours for both domestic and international mail (see p.191).

Poste restante (*tomeoki* or *kyoku dome yūbin*) is available at the larger central post offices in the big cities, but mail will only be held for thirty days before being returned. The same goes for American Express offices (which only accepts mail for card holders), unless it's marked "please hold for arrival". American Express has offices in Tokyo (see p.189 for details).

For sending parcels and baggage around Japan, take advantage of the excellent, inexpensive *takuhaibin* (or *takkyūbin*, as it's more commonly known after the successful trade name of one of the courier companies) or **courier delivery services**, which can be arranged at most convenience stores, hotels and some youth hostels. These services – which typically cost under ¥2000 – are especially handy if you want to send luggage (usually up to 20kg) on to places where you'll be staying later in your journey or to the airport to be picked up prior to your departure.

Phones

You're rarely far from a payphone in Japan, but only at certain ones – usually grey or metallic silver and bronze colour, with a sign in English – can you make **international calls**. It's sometimes difficult to find one of these phones – try a major hotel or international centre.

Mail and telephone glossary

Post	*yūbin*	郵便
Post office	*yūbin-kyoku*	郵便局
Stamp	*kitte*	切手
Postcard	*hagaki*	はがき
Courier delivery service	*takkyūbin*	宅急便
Poste restante	*tomeoki yūbin/kyoku dome yūbin*	留め置き/留置郵便

Telephones

Telephone	*denwa*	電話
Mobile phone	*keitai-denwa*	携帯電話
Phonecard	*terefon kādo*	テレフォンカード

In some restaurants and coffee shops you'll find antique dial phones that only accept ¥10 coins (worth sixty seconds of local talk time), but the vast majority of payphones take both coins (¥10 and ¥100) and **phonecards** (*terefon kādo*). The latter come in ¥500 (50-unit) and ¥1000 (105-unit) versions and can be bought in department and convenience stores and at station kiosks. Virtually every tourist attraction sells specially decorated phonecards, which come in a vast range of designs, though you'll pay a premium for these, with a ¥1000 card only giving ¥500 worth of calls.

Payphones don't give change, but do return unused coins, so for local calls use ¥10 rather than ¥100 coins. For international calls, it's best to use a phonecard and to call between 7pm and 8am Monday to Friday, or at any time on weekends or holidays, when rates are cheaper. Alternatively, use a pre-paid calling card, such as Brastel (advertised in all the Tokyo English-language media), to undercut the local rates altogether. All toll-free numbers begin with either ☎0120 or 0088; for operator assistance for overseas calls, dial ☎0051.

Mobile phones

Mobile phones (*keitai-denwa*, sometimes just shortened to *keitai*) are ubiquitous in Japan. Nowadays, nearly everyone seems to have a camera phone, and phones are also used to surf the Net and send emails. The advance technology systems that make all this possible also mean that, with a few hi-tech exceptions, you cannot bring your mobile phone to Japan and expect it to work. The solution is to **hire** a Japan-compatible mobile phone or buy a pre-paid one once you're in the country (go to any big electronics store where a phone plus calls should cost in the region of ¥10,000–15,000). Phones can be hired both abroad and in Japan. In the UK, Adam Phones rents phones for £1 a day; contact them on ☎08000-321200. In Japan, try Tokyobay Communication Co (☻www.tokyobay.co .jp/worldphone), who rent phones for ¥3500 for three days or ¥15,000 a month; you can pick up their phones at Narita or Kansai International airports when you fly into the

country. For the latest info on Japan's cell phone system check the website of the biggest operator NTT DoCoMo, ☻www.nttdocomo.com.

Phoning Japan from abroad

To **call Japan** from abroad, dial your international access code (UK and Ireland ☎00; US ☎011; Canada ☎011; Australia ☎0011; New Zealand ☎00), plus the country code (☎81), plus the area code minus the initial zero, plus the number.

Phoning abroad from Japan

The main companies in Japan offering **international phone calls** are KDDI (☎010), Japan Telecom (☎0041), Cable & Wireless IDC (☎0061) and NTT (☎0033). If you want to call abroad from Japan, choose a company (there's little to choose between them all as far as rates are concerned) and dial the relevant number, then the country code (UK ☎44; US ☎1; Canada ☎1; Australia ☎61; New Zealand ☎64), plus the area code minus the initial zero, plus the number. If you're resident in Japan, you can also register with one or several telephone companies, in which case all you need dial is ☎010, plus the country code and so on. To do this, contact Myline Information Centre (☻www.myline.org).

You can make **international operator-assisted calls** by using the Home Country Direct Call service to speak with an operator in your home country (UK ☎0039/441; US ☎005-39111; Canada ☎0039/161; Australia ☎0039-611; New Zealand ☎0039/641).

Alternatively, you could use a **charge card or calling card** (see below) which will automatically debit the cost of any calls from your domestic phone account or credit card. To use these, dial the relevant access code (see above), followed by your account and PIN number, then the number you want to call. Discount calling cards in Japan, such as Brastel, can be bought at Japanese convenience stores.

Charge card operators

UK BT ☎00/3100 4410; Cable & Wireless Calling ☎00/665 5444 (☎0039/444 for calls to the UK).

US and Canada AT&T ☎0039/111; MCI ☎0039/121; Sprint ☎0039/131.

Australia and New Zealand Optus Calling Card ☎0039/612; New Zealand Telecom's Calling Card ☎0039/641; Telstra Telecard ☎00539/611.

Phoning within Japan

Everywhere in Japan has an **area code**, which must be dialled in full if you're making a long-distance call and is omitted if the call is a local one. Area codes are given for all telephone numbers throughout the book.

Faxes, email and the Internet

Most hotels and youth hostels will allow you to send a **fax** for a small charge, while receiving a fax is usually free if you're a guest. Alternatively, most central post office or convenience stores (often open 24hr) have public fax machines.

Cybercafés can be found across Japan – often as part of a 24-hour computer game and manga (Japanese comic) centre. Free access is sometimes available (usually in cultural exchange centres, or regular cafés looking to boost business); otherwise, expect to pay around ¥300–500 per hour. Cybercafés come and go fairly swiftly, although the copy-shop Kinko's is pretty reliable and has branches in most major cities. Check the

Listings sections of town and city accounts in the guide chapters for Internet availability.

Emails can be received through an account with a Web-based email service, such as Hotmail (🔘www.hotmail.com) or Yahoo! Mail (🔘www.yahoo.com). Alternatively, arrange a POP3 email account with your Internet Service Provider (ISP), which allows you to access your account from any computer on the Internet.

If you're travelling with **your own computer**, ask your ISP for details of any associated providers in Japan; AOL has a local node, and another popular provider is Global Online Japan (GOL) (☎03/5334-1720, 🔘http://home.gol.com/cgi-bin/start/ startjump.cgi?jt&LANGUAGE=english). Japanese phones use the standard American RJ11 plug, and you can access the phone system in your hotel or via your own cellphone. Many hotels now have **broadband Internet** access in every room, often offered free or for a small daily fee (typically ¥1000 per day). For this you'll need to have a LAN (local area network) cable; if the hotel doesn't provide one, they can be bought in all electronic shops for around ¥500. It's also possible to plug your laptop into the increasingly widespread grey international public phones – they have a display screen and are fitted with both analog and ISDN jacks, but only permit local access.

The media

If you read Japanese, Japan is a news-junkie heaven, with 166 daily national and local newspaper companies printing some seventy million papers a day, more than triple the amount for the UK and even topping the US and China, despite having a much smaller population than both those countries. Japan's top paper, the *Yomiuri Shimbun*, sells over ten million copies daily, making it the most widely read newspaper in the world. Lagging behind by about two million copies a day is the *The Asahi Shimbun*, seen as the intellectual's paper, with the other three national dailies, the *Mainichi Shimbun*, the right-wing *Sankei Shimbun* and the business paper the *Nihon Keizai Shimbun*, also selling respectable numbers.

The most widely available **English-language** daily throughout Japan is the independent, but far from sparkling, *Japan Times* (¥160). It carries comprehensive coverage of national and international news, and a major "situations vacant" section every Monday, as well as occasionally interesting features, some culled from the world's media. A far better read and almost as widely available is *The International Herald Tribune* (¥150), published in conjunction with the English-language version of the *Asahi Shimbun*.

Doing a reasonable job on the features front is the *Daily Yomiuri* (¥120), with specially compiled sections from the *Los Angeles Times* on Saturdays and Britain's *Independent* newspaper on Sundays, as well as a decent arts and entertainment supplement on Thursdays. Also worth a look is the Japan edition of the *Financial Times*. Outside of the major cities, however, you'll be hard pushed to find anything but the *Japan Times*, if that. The best places to hunt out copies are the main stations and local international centres, which often have reference copies of foreign newspapers.

The most widely available English-language **magazines** are *Time* and *Newsweek*. Bookstores such as Kinokuniya and Maruzen stock extensive (and expensive) ranges of imported and local magazines; in Tokyo and Ōsaka, Tower Records is the cheapest place to buy magazines. Local titles to look out for include the weekly *Metropolis* (free), the monthly *Kansai Time Out* (¥300) and the quarterly *Tokyo Journal* (¥600). *Japanzine*, a free monthly published out of Nagoya, is also worth searching out for its irreverent but informative take on Japan.

If you're studying Japanese, or even just trying to pick up a bit of the language during your vacation, the bilingual magazines *Nihongo Journal* and *Hiragana Times* are good. *AERA* is one of Japan's most respected weekly magazines, while *Pia* and the Walker series (*Tokyo Walker, Kansai Walker*) are the best Japanese listings magazines.

Television

Japanese **television**'s notorious reputation for silly game shows and *samurai* dramas is well earned. If you don't speak Japanese, you're likely to find all TV shows, bar the frequent weather forecasts, totally baffling – and only a little less so once you have picked up the lingo. However, watching some TV during your stay is recommended if only because of the fascinating insight it gives into Japanese society.

NHK, the main state broadcaster, has two channels (in Tokyo, NHK on channel one and NHK Educational on channel three), which are roughly equal to BBC1 and BBC2 in the UK, although much less adventurous. If you have access to a bilingual TV, it's possible to tune into the English-language commentary for NHK's nightly 7pm news. Films and imported TV shows on both NHK and the commercial channels are also sometimes broadcast with an alternative English soundtrack. In Tokyo, the other main channels are Nihon TV (four), TBS (six), Fuji TV (eight), TV Asahi (ten) and TV Tokyo (twelve), all flagship channels of the nationwide networks, with little to choose between them.

The one bright spark on Japan's TV horizon is the increasing inroads made by **satellite** and **cable** channels. As well as the ubiquitous CNN and MTV, BBC World is now available in most major cities and is often part of the room package at the top-end hotels. Perfect TV is a satellite operation offering a wide range of channels, including several devoted to sport and movies.

Radio is nowhere near as popular in Japan as TV, with most young people preferring to listen to CDs and tapes. In Tokyo the main FM stations broadcasting bilingual programmes are J-WAVE (81.3MHz) and Inter FM (76.1MHz), although both tend towards the bland end of the music spectrum. You can check out Inter FM on the Web at ⓦwww.interfm.co.jp. In the Kansai area, bilingual broadcasts are available on CO-CO-LO (76.5MHz). In other areas of the country the only alternative is likely to be the American Forces Network (AFN), worth enduring just once for its bizarre public-service announcements.

Opening hours, national holidays and festivals

Business hours are generally Monday to Friday 9am to 5pm, though private companies often close much later in the evening and may also open on Saturday mornings. Department stores and bigger shops tend to open around 10am and shut at 7pm or 8pm, with no break for lunch. Local shops, however, will generally stay open later, while many convenience stores stay open 24 hours. Most shops take one day off a week, not necessarily on a Sunday.

Banks open on weekdays from 9am to 3pm, and close on Saturdays, Sundays and national holidays. **Post offices** tend to work 9am to 5pm on weekdays, closing at weekends and also on national holidays, though a few open on Saturdays from 9am to 3pm. Central post offices, on the other hand, open till 7pm in the evening and on Saturdays from 9am to 5pm and Sundays and holidays from 9am to 12.30pm. Larger offices are also likely to operate an after-hours service for parcels and express mail, sometimes up to 24 hours at major post offices.

The majority of **museums** close on a Monday, but stay open on Sundays and national holidays; last entry is normally thirty minutes before closing. While most museums and department stores stay open on **national holidays**, they usually take the following day off instead. However, during the New Year festival (January 1–3), Golden Week (April 29–May 5) and Obon (the week around August 15), almost everything shuts down. Around these periods all transport and accommodation is booked out weeks in advance, and all major tourist spots get overrun.

Festivals

Festivals (*matsuri*) still play a central role in many Japanese communities. Most are Shinto in origin and mark important occasions in the agricultural cycle, re-enact historic events or honour elements of the local economy, such as sewing needles or silkworms. Since every shrine and temple observes its own festivals, in addition to national celebrations, the chances are you'll stumble across a *matsuri* at some stage during your visit. However, if you get the chance,

it's worth trying to take in one of the major festivals, some of which are described below.

Matsuri (meaning both "festival" and "worship") can take many forms, from stately processions in period costume to sacred dances, fire rituals, archery contests, phallus worship or poetry-writing competitions. The best are riotous occasions where *mikoshi* (portable shrines) are shouldered by a seething, chanting crowd, usually fortified with quantities of sake and driven on by resonating drums. Don't stand back – anyone prepared to enter into the spirit of things will be welcome. However, if you are heading for any of the famous festivals, make sure you've got your transport and accommodation sorted out well in advance.

Though not such a lively affair, by far the most important event in the Japanese festive calendar is the **New Year** festival of renewal, *Oshōgatsu* (see p.68). It's mainly a time for family reunions, and most of the country – bar public transport – closes down for at least the first three days of the year, with many people taking the whole week off work (roughly December 29 to January 3). Whilst Japanese traditionally celebrated the lunar New Year, since the Meiji government adopted the Western calendar in 1873, the festivities have been moved to January 1. According to the Japanese system of numbering years, starting afresh with each change of emperor, 2001 is the thirteenth year of Heisei – Heisei being the official name of Emperor Akihito's reign.

In recent years, several **non-Japanese festivals** have been catching on, with a few adaptations for local tastes. Only women give men gifts on **Valentine's Day** (February 14), usually chocolates, while on **White Day**

(March 14) men get their turn to give their loved ones more chocolates (white, of course), perfume or racy underwear. Another import is **Christmas**, celebrated in Japan as an almost totally commercial event, with carols, plastic holly and tinsel in profusion. Christmas Eve, rather than New Year, is *the* time to party and a big occasion for romance – you'll be hard-pressed to find a table at any restaurant or a room in the top hotels.

Major festivals and national holidays

Note: if any of the following national holidays fall on a Sunday, then the following Monday is also a holiday.

January

Ganjitsu (or *Gantan*) January 1. On the first day of the year everyone heads for the shrines and temples to pray for good fortune (national holiday).
Yamayaki January 15. The slopes of Wakakusa-yama, Nara, are set alight during a grass-burning ceremony.
Seijin-no-hi (Adults' Day) Second Monday in January. Twenty-year-olds celebrate their entry into adulthood by visiting their local shrine. Many women dress in sumptuous kimono (national holiday).

February

Setsubun February 3 or 4. On the last day of winter (by the lunar calendar), people scatter lucky beans round their homes and at shrines or temples to drive out evil and welcome in the year's good luck.
Yuki Matsuri February 5–11. Sapporo's famous snow festival features giant snow sculptures.
National Foundation Day February 11 (national holiday).

March

Hina Matsuri (Doll Festival) March 3. Families with young girls display sets of fifteen dolls (*hina ningyō*) representing the Emperor, Empress and their courtiers dressed in ancient costume. Department stores, hotels and museums put on special exhibitions of antique dolls.
Spring Equinox March 20 or 21 (national holiday).
Cherry-Blossom festivals Late March to early May. With the arrival of spring in late March, a pink tide of cherry blossom washes north from Kyūshū, travels up Honshū during the month of April and peters out in Hokkaidō in early May. There are cherry-blossom festivals, and the sake flows at

blossom-viewing parties. Though every area has its own favoured cherry-blossom spots, the most celebrated are the mountains around Yoshino (near Kyoto), Tokyo's Ueno Kōen and Hirosaki on the tip of northern Honshū.

April

Hana Matsuri April 8. Buddha's birthday is celebrated at all temples with parades, and a small statue of Buddha is sprinkled with sweet tea.
Takayama Matsuri April 14–15. Parade of ornate festival floats (*yatai*), some with acrobatic marionettes.
Greenery Day April 29 (national holiday).

May

Constitution Memorial Day May 3 (national holiday).
Kokumin no Shukujitsu May 4 (national holiday).
Kodomo-no-hi (Children's Day) May 5. The original Boys' Day now includes all children as families fly carp banners, symbolizing strength and perseverance, outside their homes (national holiday).
Aoi Matsuri (Hollyhock Festival) May 15. Costume parade through the streets of Kyoto, with ceremonies to ward off storms and earthquakes.
Tōshō-gū Grand Matsuri May 17. Nikkō's most important festival, featuring a parade of over a thousand costumed participants and horseback archery to commemorate the burial of Shogun Tokugawa Ieyasu in 1617. There's a smaller-scale repeat performance on October 17.
Sanja Matsuri Around May 18. Tokyo's biggest festival takes place in Asakusa. Over a hundred *mikoshi* are jostled through the streets, accompanied by lion dancers, geisha and musicians.

July

Hakata Yamagasa July 1–15. Fukuoka's main festival culminates in a five-kilometre race, with participants carrying or pulling heavy *mikoshi*, while spectators douse them with water.
Tanabata Matsuri (Star Festival) July 7. According to legend, the only day in the year when the astral lovers, Vega and Altair, can meet across the Milky Way. Poems and prayers are hung on bamboo poles outside houses.
Gion Matsuri July 17. Kyoto's month-long festival focuses around a parade of huge floats hung with rich silks and paper lanterns.
Marine Day Third Monday of the month (national holiday).
Hanabi Taikai Last Saturday in July. The most spectacular of the many summer firework displays takes place in Tokyo, on the Sumida River near Asakusa. There

other firework displays in early August too.

August

Nebuta and Neputa Matsuri August 1–7. Aomori and Hirosaki hold competing summer festivals, with parades of illuminated paper-covered figures, like huge lanterns.

Tanabata Matsuri August 6–8. Sendai holds its famous Star Festival a month after everyone else, so the lovers get another chance.

Obon (Festival of Souls) August 13–15, or July 13–15 in some areas. Families gather around the ancestral graves to welcome back the spirits of the dead and honour them with special *Bon-odori* dances on the final night.

Awa Odori August 12–15. The most famous *Bon odori* takes place in Tokushima, when up to eighty thousand dancers take to the streets.

September

Respect-for-the-Aged Day Third Monday of September (national holiday).

Autumn Equinox: September 23 or 24 (national holiday).

October

Okunchi Matsuri October 7–9. Shinto rites mingle with Chinese- and European-inspired festivities to create Nagasaki's premier celebration, incorporating dragon dances and floats in the shape of Chinese and Dutch ships.

Sports Day Second Monday in October (national holiday).

Kawagoe's Grand Matsuri October 14 and 15. One of the most lively festivals in the Tokyo area, involving some twenty-five ornate floats and hundreds of costumed revellers.

Jidai Matsuri October 22. Kyoto's famous, if rather sedate, costume parade vies with the more exciting Kurama Matsuri, a night-time fire festival which takes place in a village near Kyoto.

November

Culture Day November 3 (national holiday).

Shichi-go-san (Seven-five-three) November 15. Children of the appropriate ages don mini-kimono and *hakama* (loose trousers) to visit their local shrine.

Labour Thanksgiving Day November 23 (national holiday).

December

Emperor's Birthday December 23 (national holiday).

Ōmisoka December 31. Just before midnight on the last day of the year, temple bells ring out 108 times to cast out each of man's earthly desires and start the year afresh.

Rock and pop music festivals

Late July and August in Japan is the time for **rock and popular music festivals**. One of the best is the **Earth Celebration** on Sado-ga-shima (see box, p.349), where the famed Kodo drummers collaborate with guests from the world music scene. If you want to catch up on the latest in Japanese rock then schedule your visit to coincide with **Rock in Japan** (ⓦ www.rijfes.co.jp), a three-day event held at Kokuei Hitachi Kaihin-kōen, Hitachinaka, Ibaraki-ken. Headline acts at the 2003 festival included Dragon Ash, Kick The Can Crew and the Tokyo Ska Paradise Orchestra. Tickets cost ¥9500 (one day), ¥18,000 (two day) and ¥24,000 (three day).

The most established event as far as foreign bands is concerned is **Fuji Rock** (ⓦ www.fujirockfestival.com). Going since 1997, this huge three-day event is Japan's equivalent of the UK's Glastonbury Festival (and it can get just as muddy), with a wide range of acts covering musical genres from dance and electronica to jazz and blues. It takes place in the mountains of Niigata Prefecture at Naeba Ski Resort, with multiple stages, top-name acts and plenty of other things going on. It's possible to camp here or stay in the hotels that usual cater to the winter ski crowd. One-day tickets cost ¥14,500, two-day ¥29,000 and three-day ¥38,000.

Even bigger in terms of crowds (it attracts an audience of well over 100,000) and easier to get to is **Summer Sonic** (ⓦ www.summersonic.com), a two-day event held both in Chiba, just across the Edogawa river from Tokyo, and Ōsaka. This festival showcases a good mix of both local and overseas bands and has both indoor and outdoor performances. The organizers like to compare it to the UK's Reading Music Festival, with a more aggressive, harder line-up of rock acts. Tickets go for ¥13,000 (one-day) and ¥23,000 (two-day).

Oshōgatsu

In the days leading up to New Year, generally known as **Oshōgatsu**, Japan succumbs to a frenzy of cleaning as the previous year's bad luck is swept away. People decorate their rooms, doorways and even car radiators with bamboo and pine sprigs, and visit temple fairs to buy lucky charms such as rakes, arrows and **daruma dolls** – the chubby little red fellow with staring white eyes; the idea is to make a wish while drawing in one eye and complete the other when it comes true. Shops also do well, as everyone gets a new haircut or a new kimono, buys bundles of the obligatory New Year cards and generally lays in food to tide them over the coming festivities – fortunately, traditional year-end bonuses help cover the costs. There are the interminable rounds of aptly named "forget the year" parties (*bōnen-kai*) when groups of colleagues, club members and friends consume enough alcohol to wipe out any bad memories or ill luck from the previous year.

By the time **New Year's Eve** (*ōmisoka*) arrives, everyone's exhausted. So nowadays, at around 7pm, the whole nation flops down to watch a three-hour plus TV extravaganza of the best – and worst – pop groups from the previous year. Those with only mild hangovers might slurp a bowl of *toshi-koshi soba*, extra-long noodles symbolizing longevity, which traditionally form the last meal of the year, and then hurry off to the nearest shrine or temple to join the crowds waiting to make their first offerings of the New Year. Temple bells ring out 108 times to cast out the 108 human frailties; the last chime heralds the New Year and a clean slate.

The first shrine visit (*hatsu-mōde*), the first meal, the first drive – each activity in the new year must be performed properly and safely to ensure good luck. On the first day, families share a **celebratory meal** (*o-sechi ryōri*), prepared earlier since no-one's supposed to work for the first three days, consisting of symbolic foods. It starts with a toast of sweet sake mixed with medicinal herbs designed to confer long-life, followed by a feast including herring roe (prosperity and fertility), black beans (good health), chestnuts (success) and *mochi*. These sticky-rice cakes are usually served with vegetables in a special soup (*ozōni*); they may not look – or taste – like much, but *mochi* are said to ensure strength, stamina and, again, longevity.

The traditional **New Year's greeting** is *akemashite omedetō gozaimasu*, and it's customary for adults to give the children of friends and family envelopes containing several thousand yen in crisp notes.

Social conventions and etiquette

Japan is famous for its complex web of social conventions and rules of behaviour, which only someone who has grown up in the society could hope to master. Fortunately, allowances are made for befuddled foreigners, but it will be greatly appreciated – and even draw gasps of astonishment – if you show a grasp of the basic principles. The two main danger areas are shoes and bathing, which, if you get them wrong, can cause great offence.

The Japanese treat most foreigners with incredible, even embarrassing, kindness. There are endless stories of people going out of their way to help, or paying for drinks or even meals after the briefest of encounters. That said, foreigners will always remain "outsiders" (*gaijin*), no matter how long they've lived in Japan or how proficient they are in the language and social niceties. On the positive side this can be wonderfully liberating; you're expected to make mistakes, so don't get too hung up about it. The important thing is to be seen to be trying. As a general rule, when in doubt simply follow what everyone else is doing.

Meetings and greetings

Some visitors to Japan complain that it's difficult to meet local people, and it's certainly true that many Japanese are shy of foreigners, mainly through a fear of being unable to communicate. A few words of Japanese will help enormously, and there are various opportunities for fairly formal contact, such as through the Home Visit System and Goodwill Guides (see p.28). Otherwise, youth hostels are great places to meet people of all ages, or try popping into a local bar, a *yakitori* joint or suchlike; emboldened by alcohol, the chances are someone will strike up a conversation.

Japanese people tend to **dress** smartly, especially in cities. Though as a tourist you don't have to go overboard, you'll be better received if you look neat and tidy, and for anyone hoping to do business in Japan, a snappy suit is *de rigueur*. It's also important to be punctual for social and business **appointments**.

Whenever Japanese meet, express thanks or say goodbye, there's a flurry of **bowing**. The precise depth of the bow and the length of time it's held for depend on the relative status of the two individuals – receptionists are sent on courses to learn the precise angles required. Again, foreigners aren't expected to bow, but it's terribly infectious and you'll soon find yourself bobbing with the best of them. The usual compromise is a slight nod or a quick half-bow. Japanese more familiar with Western customs might offer you a hand to shake, in which case treat it gently – they won't be expecting a firm grip.

Japanese **names** are traditionally written with the family name first, followed by a given name, which is the practice used throughout this book (except where the Western version has become famous, such as Issey Miyake). When dealing with foreigners, however, they may well write their name the other way round. Check if you're not sure because, when **addressing people**, it's normal to use the family name plus -*san*; for example, Suzuki-san. *San* is an honorific term used in the same way as Mr or Mrs, so remember not to use it when introducing yourself, or talking about your friends or family. As a foreigner, you can choose whichever of your names you feel comfortable with; inevitably they'll tack a -*san* on the end. You'll also often hear -*chan* as a form of address; this is a diminutive reserved for very good friends, young children and pets.

An essential part of any business meeting is the swapping of *meishi*, or **name cards**. Always carry a copious supply, since you'll be expected to exchange a card with everyone present. It's useful to have them printed in Japanese as well as English; if necessary, you can get this done at major hotels. *Meishi* are offered with both hands, facing so that the recipient can read the writing. It's polite to read the card and then place it on the table beside you, face up. Never write on a *meishi*, at least not in the owner's presence, and never shove it in a pocket – put it in your wallet or somewhere suitably respectful. Business meetings invariably go on much longer than you'd expect and rarely result in decisions. They are partly for building up the all-important feeling of trust between the two parties, as is the after-hours entertainment in a restaurant or karaoke bar.

Hospitality, gifts and tips

Entertaining, whether it's business or purely social, usually takes place in bars and restaurants. The host generally orders and, if it's a Japanese-style meal, will keep passing you different things to try. You'll also find your glass continually topped up. It's polite to return the gesture, but if you don't drink, or don't want any more, leave it full. See p.54 and p.59 for more on eating and drinking etiquette.

It's a rare honour to be invited to someone's home in Japan and you should always take a small **gift**. Fruit, flowers, chocolates or alcohol (wine, whisky or brandy) are safe bets, as is anything from your home country, especially if it's a famous brand name. The gift should always be wrapped, using plenty of fancy paper and ribbon if possible. If you buy something locally, most shops giftwrap purchases automatically and anything swathed in paper from Mitsukoshi or one of the other big department stores has extra cachet.

Japanese people love giving gifts, and you should never refuse one if offered, though it's good manners to protest at their generosity first. Again it's polite to give and receive with both hands, and to belittle your humble donation while giving profuse thanks for the gift you receive. However, it's not the custom to open gifts in front of the donor, thus avoiding potential embarrassment.

If you're fortunate enough to be invited to a **wedding**, it's normal to give money to the happy couple. This helps defray the costs, including, somewhat bizarrely, the present you'll receive at the end of the meal. How much you give depends on your relationship with the couple, so ask a mutual friend what would be appropriate. Make sure to get crisp new notes and put them in a special red envelope available at stationers. Write your name clearly on the front and hand it over as you enter the reception.

Tipping is not expected in Japan, and if you press money on a taxi driver, porter or bellboy it can cause offence. If someone's been particularly helpful, the best approach is to give a small gift, or present the money discreetly in an envelope.

Shoes and slippers

It's customary to change into **slippers** when entering a Japanese home or a ryokan, and not uncommon in traditional restaurants, temples or, occasionally, in museums and art galleries. In general, if you come across a slightly raised floor and a row of slippers, then use them; either leave your shoes on the lower floor (the *genkan*) or on the shelves (sometimes lockers) provided. Slip-on shoes are much easier to cope with than lace-ups and, tricky though it is, try not to step on the *genkan* with bare or stockinged feet.

Once inside, remove your slippers before stepping onto tatami, the rice-straw flooring, and remember to change into the special **toilet slippers** lurking inside the bathroom door when you go to the toilet. (See below for more on toilet etiquette.)

Bathing

Taking a traditional Japanese **bath**, whether in a ryokan, hot spring (onsen), or public bathhouse (*sentō*), is a ritual that's definitely worth mastering. Nowadays most baths are segregated, so memorize the *kanji* for male and female (see the box below). It's customary to bathe in the evening, and in small ryokan or family homes there may well be only one bathroom. In this case you'll either be given a designated time or simply have to wait till it's vacant.

Key points to remember are that everyone uses the same water and the bathtub is only for soaking. It's therefore essential to wash and rinse the soap off thoroughly – showers and bowls are provided, as well as soap and shampoo in many cases – *before* stepping into the bath. Ryokan and the more upmarket public bathhouses provide small towels, though no one minds full nudity. Lastly, the bath in a ryokan and family home is filled once each evening, so never pull the plug out.

Toilets

Traditional Japanese **toilets** (*toire* or *otearai*) are of the Asian squat variety. Though these are still quite common in homes, old-style restaurants and many public buildings, Western toilets are gradually becoming the norm. Look out for nifty enhancements such as a heated seat – glorious in winter – and those that flush automatically as you walk away. Another handy device plays the sound of flushing water to cover embarrassing noises. These are either automatic or are activated with a button and were invented because so much water was wasted by constant flushing. In some places toilets are still communal, so don't be alarmed to see a urinal in what you thought was the women's room, and note that public toilets rarely provide paper. If you can't find a public lavatory on the street (there are lots of them around), then dive into the nearest department store or big shop, all of which have bathroom facilities for general use.

Toilet	toire/otearai	トイレ／お手洗い
Male	otoko	男
Female	onna	女

Increasingly, you'll be confronted by a high-tech Western model, known as a **Washlet**, with a control panel to one side. It's usually impossible to find the flush button, and instead you'll hit the temperature control, hot-air dryer or, worst of all, the bidet nozzle, resulting in a long metal arm extending out of the toilet bowl and spraying you with warm water.

Some general pointers

It's quite normal to see men urinating in the streets in Japan, but **blowing your nose** in public is considered extremely rude – just keep sniffing until you find somewhere private. In this very male, strictly hierarchical society, men always take precedence over women, so ladies shouldn't expect **doors** to be held open or **seats** vacated. Although meticulously polite within their own social group, the Japanese relish **pushing and shoving** on trains or buses. Never respond by getting angry or showing **aggression**, as this is considered a complete loss of face.

By the same token, don't voice your **opinions** too forcefully or contradict people outright; it's more polite to say "maybe" than a direct "no".

The meaning of "yes" and "no" can in themselves be a problem, particularly when **asking questions**. For example, if you say "Don't you like it?", a positive answer means "Yes, I agree with you, I don't like it", and "No" means "No, I don't agree with you, I *do* like it". To avoid confusion, try not to ask negative questions – stick to "Do you like it?". And if someone seems to be giving vague answers, don't push too hard unless it's important. There's a good chance they don't want to offend you by disagreeing or revealing a problem.

Finally, you'll be excused for not **sitting** on your knees, Japan-style, on the tatami mats. It's agony for people who aren't used to it, and many young Japanese now find it uncomfortable. If you're wearing trousers, sitting cross-legged is fine; otherwise, tuck your legs to one side.

Shopping and souvenirs

Even if you're not an inveterate shopper, cruising Japan's gargantuan department stores or rummaging around its vibrant discount outlets is an integral part of local life that shouldn't be missed. Japan also has some of the most enticing souvenirs in the world, from lacquered chopsticks and luxurious, handmade paper to a wealth of wacky electronic gadgets.

Historically, the epicentre of commercial frenzy is Tokyo's Ginza, to such an extent that the name has become synonymous with shopping street; you'll find "little Ginzas" all over Japan. However, the mechanics of shopping are the same throughout: all prices are fixed, except in flea markets and some discount electrical stores where bargaining is acceptable. Few shops take **credit cards** and fewer still accept cards issued abroad, so make sure you have plenty of cash. All except the smallest purchases will be meticulously wrapped.

In general, shop **opening hours** are from 10am to 7pm or 8pm. Most shops close one day a week, not always on Sunday, and smaller places tend to shut on national holidays. Nearly all shops close for at least three days over New Year. If you need anything **after hours**, you'll find 24-hour convenience stores in most towns and cities, often near the train station. These sell a basic range of toiletries, stationery and foodstuffs, at slightly inflated prices: Lawson, Family Mart, AM/PM and Seven-Eleven are the most common.

Automated shopping

Japan boasts an estimated 5.4 million **vending machines** – roughly one for every twenty people. Nearly all essentials, and many non-essentials, can be bought from a machine: pot noodles, drinks, films, batteries, shampoo, razors, CDs, flowers and so on. Some of them are getting pretty crafty, too. Some cold drinks machines, for example, are equipped with wireless modems so that the price can be adjusted according to the prevailing temperature, while Coca-Cola has been experimenting with "intelligent" machines that automatically raise their prices in hot weather.

Their prime attraction of vending machines is obviously convenience, but they also allow people in this highly self-conscious society to buy things surreptitiously – condoms, sex aids and alcohol are obvious examples; Japanese law prohibits the sale of alcohol to anyone under 20 years old. But since mid-2000, concern over rising levels of alcoholism and under-age drinking has led to a voluntary restriction by alcohol vendors – it's estimated that around seventy percent of machines have been taken out of action or restocked with soft drinks.

Taxes, duty-free and discount stores

A five-percent **consumption tax** is levied on virtually all goods sold in Japan. Sometimes this tax will be included in the advertised price, and sometimes it will be added at the time of payment, so you should check first for large purchases.

Foreigners can buy **duty-free** items (that is, without consumption tax), but only in certain tourist shops and the larger department stores. Perishable goods, such as food, drinks, tobacco, cosmetics and film, are exempt from the scheme, and most stores only offer duty-free if the total bill exceeds ¥10,000. The shop will either give you a duty-free price immediately or, in department stores especially, you pay the full price first and then apply for a refund at their "tax-exemption" counter. The shop will attach a copy of the customs document (*wariin*) to your passport, to be removed by customs officers when you leave Japan. Note that regulations vary for foreign residents, and also that you can often find the same goods elsewhere at a better price, including tax, so shop around first.

Some of the best places to look for cut-price goods are the **discount stores**, which have mushroomed since the Japanese economy began to falter. You'll find them mainly around train stations selling mostly household items and unusual souvenirs (the "¥100" shops, where everything costs just that, are easy to spot). But perhaps the most interesting discount stores are those offering electrical goods and cameras (see p.74), which you'll find in nearly all major cities.

Department stores

Japan's most prestigious **department stores** are Mitsukoshi and Takashimaya, followed by the cheaper, more workaday Matsuya, Matsuzakaya, Seibu and Tōbu. All these big names have branches throughout Japan, and sell almost everything, from impressive food halls through fashion, crafts and household items, to stationery and toys. One floor is usually devoted to restaurants, and somewhere near the top of the store you'll generally find a section specializing in discount items. Bigger stores may also have an art gallery, travel bureau, ticket agent and a currency-exchange desk, as well as English-speaking staff and a duty-free service. It's also worth looking out for the excellent bargain sales in January, July and August. Thanks to a trend towards discount outlets and bargain-hunting, Japan's department stores have been hit particularly hard by the economic recession. One of the most prominent failures has been Sogō, which was forced to close its landmark Yūrakuchō store, amongst others, and undergo financial restructuring in the wake of a ¥180 billion debt – largely the result of massive overexpansion in the heady 1980s.

Art, crafts and souvenirs

Japan is famous for its wealth of **arts** and **crafts**, many dating back thousands of years, and handed down from generation to generation (see Contexts, p.962, for more on the arts). Though the best are phenomenally expensive, there are plenty at more manageable prices which make wonderful **souvenirs**. Most department stores have a reasonable crafts section, but it's far more enjoyable to trawl Japan's specialist shops, even if you do pay a little extra for the pleasure. Kyoto is renowned for its traditional crafts, and even in Tokyo you'll find a number of artisans still plying their trade, while most regions have a vibrant local crafts industry turning out products for the tourists.

Tokyo and Kyoto are also well known for their regular **flea markets**, usually held at shrines and temples (see individual city accounts for details). You need to get there early for the best deals, but you might come across some gorgeous secondhand kimono, satin-smooth lacquerware or rustic pottery, among a good deal of tat. Keep an eye out, too, for unusual items in the discount stores, which can yield amazing gizmos for next to nothing.

Japan's most famous craft is its **ceramics** (*tōjiki*). Of several distinct regional styles, Imari-ware (from Arita in Kyūshū) is best known for its colourful, ornate designs, while the iron-brown unglazed Bizen-ware (from near Okayama) and Mashiko's simple folk-pottery are satisfyingly rustic. Other famous names include Satsuma-yaki (from Kagoshima), Kasama-yaki (from Ibaraki) and Kyoto's Kyō-yaki. Any decent department store will stock a full range of styles, or you can visit local showrooms. Traditional tea bowls, sake sets and vases make popular souvenirs.

Originally devised as a means of making everyday utensils more durable, **lacquerware** (*shikki* or *urushi*) has developed over the centuries into a unique artform. Items such as trays, tables, boxes, chopsticks and bowls are typically covered with reddish-brown or black lacquer and either left plain or decorated with paintings, carvings, sprinkled with eggshell or given a dusting of gold or silver leaf. Though top-quality lacquer can be hideously expensive, you'll find a whole range of lesser pieces at more reasonable prices. Lacquer needs a humid atmosphere, especially the cheaper pieces which are made on a base of low-quality wood which cracks in dry conditions, though inexpensive plastic bases won't be affected. Wajima is one of the most famous places for lacquerware in Japan.

Some of Japan's most beautiful traditional products stem from **folk crafts** (*mingei*), ranging from elegant, inexpensive **bamboo-ware** to **wood-carvings**, **toys**, **masks**, **kites** and a whole host of delightful **dolls** (*ningyō*). Peg-shaped *kokeshi* dolls from northern Honshū are among the most appealing, with their bright colours and sweet, simple faces. Look out, too, for the rotund, round-eyed *daruma* dolls, made of papier-mâché, and fine, clay *Hakata-ningyō* dolls from Kyūshū.

Traditional Japanese **paper** (*washi*), made from mulberry or other natural fibres, is fashioned into any number of tempting souvenirs. You can buy purses, boxes, fans, oiled umbrellas, lightshades and toys all made from paper, as well as wonderful stationery. Indeed, some *washi* is so beautifully patterned and textured that a few sheets alone make a great gift.

Original **woodblock prints**, *ukiyo-e*, by world-famous artists such as Utamaro, Hokusai and Hiroshige, have long been collectors' items fetching thousands of pounds. However, you can buy copies of these "pictures of the floating world", often depicting Mount Fuji, willowy geisha or lusty heroes of the Kabuki stage, at tourist shops for more modest sums. Alternatively, some art shops specialize in originals, both modern and antique.

Japan has a long history of making attractive **textiles**, particularly the silks used in kimono (see box, p.74). Other interesting uses of textiles include **noren**, a split curtain hanging in the entrance to a restaurant or bar; cotton **tenugui** (small hand towels), decorated with cute designs; and the large, square, versatile wrapping cloth, **furoshiki**.

Whilst the chunky iron kettles from Morioka in northern Honshū are rather unwieldy mementos, the area also produces delicate *fūrin*, or **wind chimes**, in a variety of designs. **Damascene** is also more portable, though a bit fussy for some tastes. This metal inlay-work, with gold and silver threads on black steel, was originally

The comeback of the kimono

Few visitors to Japan will fail to be impressed by the beauty and variety of **kimono** available for both women and men. This most traditional form of Japanese dress is still commonly worn for special occasions, such as weddings and festival visits to a shrine. Over the last few years it has also made something of a comeback in the fashion stakes, particularly amongst young women, who sometimes wear kimono like a coat over Western clothes or who coordinate their kimono with coloured rather than white *tabi* (traditional split-toed socks).

The kimono boom has been helped by several kimono makers offering their services over the Internet and fashion designers turning to kimono fabrics and styles for contemporary creations. Every department store has a corner devoted to ready-made or tailored kimono. None is particularly cheap: the ready-made versions can easily cost ¥100,000, while a ¥1 million for the best made-to-measure kimono is not uncommon.

Given such price tags, it's a good idea to buy the much more affordable secondhand or antique versions at tourist shops, flea markets or in the kimono sales held by department stores, usually in spring and autumn. Prices can start as low as ¥1000, but you'll pay more for the sumptuous, highly decorated wedding kimono which make striking wall hangings, as well as the most beautifully patterned **obi**, the broad silk sash worn with a kimono.

A cheaper, more practical alternative is the light cotton kimono, **yukata**, which are popular as dressing gowns; you'll find them in all department stores and many speciality stores. To complete the outfit, you could pick up a pair of *zōri*, traditional straw **sandals**, or their wooden counterpart, *geta*.

---

used to fix the family crest on sword hilts and helmets, though nowadays you can buy all sorts of jewellery and trinket boxes decorated with birds, flowers and other intricate designs. **Pearls**, however, are undoubtedly Japan's most famous jewellery item, ever since Mikimoto Kōkichi first succeeded in growing cultured pearls in Toba in 1893. Toba is still the centre of production, though you'll find specialist shops in all major cities selling pearls at fairly competitive prices.

Finally, there are a host of **edible souvenirs**. Items that might tempt you include **rice-crackers** (*sembei*), vacuum-packed bags of **pickles** (*tsukemono*), and Japanese **sweets** (*okashi*) such as the eye-catching *wagashi*. Made of sweet, red-bean paste in various colours and designs, *wagashi* are the traditional accompaniment to the tea ceremony. **Tea** itself (*ocha*) comes in a variety of grades, often in attractive canisters, while **sake** is another inexpensive gift option, and occasionally comes in interesting-shaped bottles.

Electrical goods and cameras

Japan is a well-known producer of high-quality and innovative **electrical** and **elec-** tronic goods. New designs are tested on the local market before going into export production, so this is the best place to check out the latest technological advances. The majority of high-tech goods are sold in discount stores, where prices may be up to forty percent cheaper than at a conventional store. Akihabara, in central Tokyo, is the country's foremost area for discount electronic goods, but in every major city you can buy audio equipment, computers, software and any number of wacky gadgets at competitive prices.

If you're keen to buy, check the best deals you can get at home before leaving, since the item may not be much cheaper in Japan thanks to the strong yen. It's also important to make sure that the goods are compatible with your domestic electricity system; the Japanese power supply is 100V, but export items usually have a voltage switch that can adapt the appliance to your own system. If English-language instructions, after-sales service and guarantees are important, stick to export models, which are sold mostly in stores' duty-free sections. It's worth shopping around first and, though you may not get it, always ask for a discount.

Similarly, Japanese **cameras** and other photographic equipment are among the best in the world. Shinjuku, in Tokyo, is the main centre, where you can pick up the latest models and find discontinued and second-hand cameras at decent prices.

Books and music

Imported foreign-language **books** are expensive in Japan, and only available in major cities. However, some locally produced English-language books are cheaper here than at home, if you can find them at all outside Japan. The best bookstores are Kinokuniya, Tower Books (part of Tower Records), Maruzen and Yūrindō, all of which stock imported newspapers and magazines as well as a variable selection of foreign-language books. Alternatively, most top-class hotels have a small bookstore with a range of titles on Japan and a limited choice of imported fiction and journals.

Foreign-label **CDs** are generally slightly cheaper than their local counterparts, and may well cost less than you would pay at home; in addition, Japanese versions of some CDs often contain extra tracks or other specials such as a DVD. Major record stores such as Tower Records, HMV and Virgin Megastore have a tremendous selection – everything from Japanese classical and folk music to world music, rock and the latest club hits.

Clothes

All Japan's big department stores have several floors devoted to **fashion**, from haute couture to more modest items at affordable prices. Elsewhere, you'll find trendy **boutiques** – many of them stacked in multi-storey "fashion stores" – catering to a younger, less affluent crowd, selling cut-price clothes and the latest in recycled grunge gear. **Factory outlet stores** and low-price retailers, such as UniQlo and Comme ça du Mode, have recently made an appearance, as have **foreign chains** led by Gap. The centre of high fashion, on the other hand, is Tokyo's Omotesandō, where you'll find the likes of Issey Miyake, Hanae Mori, Comme des Garçons and Yohji Yamamoto, as well as premium foreign brands like Louis Vuitton, Chanel and Benetton, whose showrooms make for great window-shopping, even if you don't have money to burn.

Finding clothes that fit is becoming easier as young Japanese are, on average, substantially bigger-built than their parents, and foreign chains tend to carry larger sizes. **Shoes**, however, are more of a problem. Some stores do stock bigger sizes, and Washington shoe shops are usually a good bet, though the women's selection is pretty limited. You'll also find outlets, such as Tokyo's ABC Mart, specializing in more casual imported brands, but you'll be hard-pressed to find anything over a size 10.

Sports and outdoor activities

Big believers in team spirit, the Japanese embrace many sports with almost religious fervour. It's not uncommon for parts of the country to come to a complete standstill during crucial moments of major baseball matches and sumo basho (tournaments), as fans gather round television screens in homes, offices, shops, bars, and even on the street. Baseball is actually more popular than the home-grown sumo, and hot on the heels of both sports is soccer, which since the launch of the professional J-League in 1993 has enjoyed phenomenal popularity.

Martial arts, such as aikido, judo and karate, all traditionally associated with Japan, have a much lower profile than you might expect. Tokyo, with its many *dōjō* (practice halls), is the best place in the country in which to view or learn these ancient sports. Tokyo's TICs (see p.98) have a full list of *dōjō* that allow visitors to watch practice sessions for free.

If you're interested in attending any sporting event, check the local media, such as the *Japan Times* and *Metropolis*, for details. To get tickets it's best, in the first instance, to approach one of the major ticket agencies: Ticket Pia, for example, can be found in most big cities, and their Tokyo office has an English-language telephone booking line (℡03/5237-9999). Major games and events sell out quickly, so a second approach is to go directly to the venue on the day and see if you can get a ticket from the box office or a tout outside; expect to pay well over the odds, though, if it's a popular game.

In terms of participatory sports, **golf** is the most popular, with some fourteen million golfers in Japan, and more courses and driving ranges than you can swing a club at. The recession has taken the shine off the sport, and the golf course is now less frequently used as the venue for business meetings, but fees for playing a round still remain out of the reach of all but the most dedicated visiting golf fan.

More accessible outdoor activities are **skiing** during the winter and **hiking** and **mountain climbing** during the summer. If you're interested, it's worth getting in touch with the Tokyo-based **International Adventurers Club** (IAC; ⊛www.iac-tokyo.org) or its sister club for the Kansai region, the **International Outdoor Club** (IOC; ⊛www.geocities.com/ioc-kansai), both of which provide informal opportunities to explore the Japanese countryside and mountains in the company of like-minded people. The websites ⊛www.skijapanguide.com and ⊛www.outdoorjapan.com are also mines of useful information.

Baseball

Baseball first came to Japan in the 1870s, but it wasn't until 1934 that the first professional teams were formed. Now Japan is *yakyū* (baseball) crazy, and if you're in the country from April to the end of October during the baseball season, think about taking in a professional match. Even if you're not a fan, the buzzing atmosphere and audience enthusiasm can be infectious.

In addition to the two professional leagues, Central and Pacific, each with six teams, there's the equally (if not more) popular All-Japan High School Baseball Championship. You might be able to catch one of the local play-offs before the main tournament, which is held each summer at Kōshien Stadium near Ōsaka; check with the tourist office for details.

In the professional leagues, the teams are sponsored by big businesses, a fact immediately apparent from their names, such as the Yakult (a food company) Swallows and Yomiuri (a newspaper conglomerate) Giants. The victors from the Central and Pacific leagues go on to battle it out for the supreme title in the seven-match Japan Series every autumn. **Tickets** for all games are available from the stadia or at advance ticket booths. They start at ¥1000 and go on sale on the Friday two weeks prior to a game. For more information on Japan's pro-baseball leagues, check out ⊛www.npb.or.jp.

Sumo

There's something fascinating about Japan's national sport **sumo**, even though the titanic clashes between the enormous, near-naked wrestlers can be blindingly brief. The age-old pomp and ceremony that surrounds sumo – from the design of the *dohyō* (the ring in which bouts take place) to the wrestler's slicked back topknot – give the sport a gravitas completely absent from Western wrestling. The sport's aura is enhanced by the majestic size of the wrestlers themselves: the average weight is 136kg, but they can be much larger – Konishiki, for example, weighed 272kg.

Accounts of sumo bouts (*basho*) are related in Japan's oldest annals of history when it was a Shinto rite connected with praying for a good harvest. By the Edo period, sumo had developed into a spectator sport and really hit its stride in the post-World War II period when *basho* started to be televised.

The old religious trappings remain, though: the *gyōji* (referee) wears robes not dissimilar to those of a Shinto priest and above the *dohyō* hangs a thatched roof like those found at shrines.

At the start of a bout the two *rikishi* wade into the ring, wearing only *mawashi* aprons, which look like giant nappies. Salt is tossed to purify the ring, the *rikishi* hunker down and indulge in the time-honoured ritual of psyching each other out with menacing stares. When ready, each *rikishi* attempts to throw his opponent to the ground or out of the ring using one or more of 82 legitimate techniques. The first to touch the ground with any part of his body other than his feet, or to step out of the *dohyō*, loses.

Despite their formidable girth, top *rikishi* (wrestlers) enjoy the media status of supermodels. When not fighting in tournaments, groups of *rikishi* live and train together at their *heya* (stables), the youngest wrestlers acting pretty much as the menial slaves of their older, more experienced colleagues. If you make an advance appointment, it's possible to visit some *heya* to observe the early-morning practice sessions; contact the Tokyo TIC (see p.98) for details. For all you could want to know and more on the current scene, plus how to buy tickets, check out the official website of sumo's governing body, Nihon Sumo Kyōkai, at ⓦwww.sumo.or.jp/eng/index.php. Also see the boxed text, "The trouble with sumo", on p.ix, and "Religion, belief and ritual" on p.959.

Soccer

Soccer was introduced to Japan in 1873 by an Englishman, Lieutenant Commander Douglas of the Royal Navy, but it wasn't until the **J-League**, Japan's first professional soccer league, was launched amid a multi-billion-yen promotional drive in 1993 that the sport captured the public's imagination. Following on from the success of the World Cup 2002, hosted jointly by Japan and Korea, the game is now a huge crowd puller.

Games are played between March and October, with a summer break. The J-League's original ten teams have now grown to two leagues with a total of 28 teams. Sixteen clubs play in the J1 league, twelve in the J2; all participate in the JL Yamazaki Nabisco Cup and there are a host of other cups and contests including the JOMO Cup, in which fans pick their dream teams from among all the J-League players. For full details of the J-League in English, including match reports, check out the website at ⓦwww.j-league.or.jp/english/index.html.

The annual sumo tournaments

The must-see **Annual Sumo Tournaments** are held at the following locations, always starting on the Sunday closest to the tenth of the month and lasting for two weeks: **Tokyo**, at Kokugikan Hall in January, May and September; **Ōsaka**, at Ōsaka Furitsu Taiiku Kaikan in March; **Nagoya**, at Aichi-kenTaiiku-kan in July; and in **Fukuoka**, at Fukuoka Kokusai Centre in November.

Despite sumo's declining popularity (see "The trouble with sumo" box on p.ix), it's still very difficult to book the prime ringside **seats**, but quite feasible to bag reserved seats in the balconies (they cost around ¥7000, for which you'll also get a bag of souvenirs) or the cheapest unreserved seats (¥2100), which go on sale on the door on the day of the tournament at 9am. To be assured of a ticket you'll need to line up well before that, especially towards the end of a *basho*. Matches start for the lower-ranked wrestlers at 10am and at this time it's OK to sneak into any vacant ringside seats to watch the action close up; when the rightful owners turn up, just return to your own seat. The sumo superstars come on around 4pm and tournaments finish at around 6pm.

Apart from the sumo association's website (see ⓦwww.sumo.or.jp/eng/index.html), you can buy tickets at any branch of the Lawson convenience store. If you can't get a ticket, NHK televises each *basho* daily from 3.30pm, and you can tune into FEN on 810 KHz for a simultaneous English commentary.

Aikido

Half sport, half religion, **aikido** translates as "the way of harmonious spirit" and blends elements of judo, karate and kendo into a form of non-body-contact self-defence. It's one of the newer martial arts, having only been created in Japan in the twentieth century, and, as a rule, is performed without weapons.

The **International Aikido Federation**, 17-18 Wakamatsu-chō, Shinjuku-ku ☎03/3203-9236; ⓦwww.aikikai.or.jp, is around ten minutes by bus from the west exit of Shinjuku Station in Tokyo. The *Aikikai Hombu Dōjō* (same address and telephone number) welcomes visitors who want to watch practice sessions.

Judo

Probably the martial art most closely associated with Japan, **judo** is a self-defence technique that developed out of the Edo-era fighting schools of Jūjutsu. All judo activities in Japan are controlled by the **All-Japan Judo Federation**, at the Kōdōkan Dōjō, 1-16-30 Kasuga, Bunkyō-ku ☎03/3818-4199; ⓦwww.judo.or.jp, reached from either Kasuga or Kōrakuen subway stations in Tokyo. The *dōjō* has a spectators' gallery open to visitors free of charge (Mon–Fri 6–7.30pm, Sat 4–5.30pm). There's also a hostel here where you can stay if you have an introduction from an authorized judo body or an approved Japanese sponsor. Judo is also taught at the Nippon Budōkan Budō Gakuen, 2-3 Kitanomaru-kōen, Chiyoda-ku ☎03/3216-5143, near Kudanshita subway station in Tokyo.

Karate

Karate has its roots in China and was only introduced into Japan via the southern islands of Okinawa in 1922. Since then the sport has developed many different styles, all with governing bodies and federations based in Tokyo. One of the main overseeing bodies, the **Japan Karate Association**, 4F, Sanshin Building, 29–33 Sakuragaoka-chō, Shibuya-ku ☎03/5459 6226, has classes which are open to spectators (usually Mon–Sat 10.30–11.30am & 5–8pm), but it's best to call first. To reach the *dōjō*, take Exit 2A from Takanawadai Station, turn left and walk along the main street for five minutes.

The umbrella organization, **Japan Karatedō Federation**, 6F, 2 Nippon Zaidan Building, 1-11-2 Toranomon, Minato-ku, Tokyo ☎03/3503-6640; ⓦwww.karatedo.co.jp (Mon–Fri 9am–5pm), can advise on the main styles of karate and where you can best see practice sessions or take lessons. The closest subway station is Toranomon.

Kendo

Meaning "the way of the sword", **kendo** is Japanese fencing using either a long bamboo weapon, the *shinai*, or a lethal metal *katana* blade. This martial art has the longest pedigree in Japan, dating from the Muromachi period (1392–1573). It developed as a sport during the Edo period and is now watched over by the **All-Japan Kendo Federation**, Nippon Budōkan, 2–3 Kitanomaru-kōen, Chiyoda-ku, Tokyo ☎03/3211-5804, ⓦwww.kendo.or.jp, near Kudanshita subway station. Practice sessions are not generally open to the public, but you might be fortunate enough to catch the All-Japan Championships held in Tokyo each December at the Budōkan.

Skiing

Every winter so many Japanese head for the slopes to perfect their **ski** technique, or just to hang out in the latest designer gear, that you'll feel left out if you don't join them. It's easy enough to arrange a ski day-trip, especially since many of the major resorts on Honshū are within a couple of hours' train ride of Tokyo, Nagoya or Ōsaka. Serious skiers will want to take more time to head to the northern island of Hokkaidō, which has some of the country's best ski resorts.

The **cost** of a ski trip needn't be too expensive. Lift passes are typically ¥4000 per day, or less if you ski for several days in a row; equipment rental averages around ¥4000 for the skis, boots and poles; whilst accommodation at a family-run minshuku compares favourably to that of many European and American resorts.

Transport to the slopes is fast and efficient; at one resort (Gala Yuzawa in Niigata) you can step straight off the Shinkansen onto the ski lifts. Ski maps and signs are often in English, and you're sure to find some English-speakers and, at the major resorts, *gaijin* staff, if you run into difficulties.

The main drawback of skiing in Japan is that top resorts can get very crowded, especially at weekends and holidays; if you don't want to ski in rush-hour conditions, plan your trip for midweek. In addition, the runs are, on the whole, much shorter than in Europe and the US. Compensating factors, however, are fast ski lifts, beautiful scenery – especially in the Japan Alps area of Nagano – and the opportunity to soak in onsen hot springs at night. **Snowboarding** is very fashionable, especially among younger skiers, and is allowed at most major resorts, although it's best to check with local tourist offices first.

Recommended resorts for beginners include **Gala Yuzawa** and trendy **Naeba**, both reached in under two hours from Tokyo by Shinkansen. **Nozawa Onsen** also has good beginners' runs, but its off-the-beaten-track location makes it a better bet for more experienced skiers. **Appi Kōgen** and **Zaō** in northern Honshū and **Hakuba** in Nagano are considered the Holy Trinity of Japanese ski resorts. **Shiga Kōgen** is another mammoth resort in Nagano, parts of which were used for competitions during the 1998 Winter Olympics. If you're after the best powder-snow skiing without the crowds, head north to Hokkaidō, to the world-class resorts of **Furano** and **Niseko**. There are also many slopes easily accessible on a day-trip from Sapporo.

All the major travel agents offer **ski packages**, which are worth looking into – Tokyo's Beltop Travel (☎03/3211-6555, ⓦwww.beltop.com) and the Hakuba-based Ski Japan Holiday (ⓦwww.japanspecialists.com) both have plenty of experience setting up deals for the expat community. **Youth hostels** near to ski areas often have excellent-value packages, too, including accommodation, meals and lift passes, and can arrange competitive equipment rental; see Furano and Niseko in Hokkaidō and Togakushi, and Norikura Kōgen Onsen in Nagano-ken.

There are several comprehensive annual **guides** in Japanese listing all resorts, providing detailed maps of the runs and lists of all the facilities; one of the best is *Ski Mapple*, published by Shōbunsha. For English-language information, invest in the spot-on *Ski Japan!* by T.R. Reid (¥2300; Kodansha). On the Web, check out ⓦwww.skijapan-guide.com.

Mountaineering and hiking

Until the twentieth century few Japanese would have considered climbing one of their often sacred mountains for anything other than religious reasons. These days, prime highland beauty spots such as Kamikōchi are widely popular with day **hikers** and serious **mountaineers**, so much so that they run the risk of being overrun. In addition, there are 28 national parks (see Contexts, p.986) and exploring these and other picturesque areas of the countryside on foot is one of the great pleasures of a trip to Japan. Nevertheless, it's as well to bear in mind that those areas close to cities can get very busy at weekends and holidays. If you can, go midweek or out of season when the trails are less crowded.

Hiking trails, especially in the national parks, are well marked. Campsites and mountain huts open during the climbing season, which runs from June to the end of August. The efficient train network means that even from sprawling conurbations like Tokyo you can be in beautiful countryside in just over an hour. Top hiking destinations from the capital include the lakes, mountains and rugged coastline of the Fuji-Hakone-Izu National Park to the southwest and Nikkō to the north. Also west of the capital is the Chichibu-Tama National Park and the sacred mountain Takao-san, particularly lovely when the leaves change colour each autumn; for details of hiking in these areas and 31 others across Japan, pick up a copy of *Hiking in Japan* by Paul Hunt (¥2000; Kodansha), or Lonely Planet's more recent *Hiking in Japan*.

The website ⓦwww.outdoorjapan.com also has useful ideas and information if you plan to go hiking or camping in Japan.

Beaches, surfing and diving

Given that Japan is an archipelago, you'd be forgiven for thinking that it would be blessed with some pleasant beaches. The truth is that industrialization has blighted much of the coastline and that many of the country's beaches are covered with litter and/or polluted. The best **beaches** are those furthest away from the main island of Honshū, which means those on the islands of Okinawa, or the Izu and Ogasawara islands south of Tokyo.

Incredibly, Japan's market for surf goods is the world's largest, and when the surfers aren't hauling their boards off to Hawaii and Australia, they can be found braving the waves at various home locations. Top spots include the southern coasts of Shikoku and Kyūshū. Closer to Tokyo, pros head for the rocky east Kujūkuri coast of the Chiba peninsula, while the beaches around Shōnan, near Kamakura, are fine for perfecting your style and hanging out with the trendiest surfers. Check out ⓦwww.outdoorjapan.com for more information on surfing locations around Japan.

Diving in Japan is expensive. The best places to head for are Okinawa (see p.909 for more details); around the island of Sado-ga-shima, near Niigata; and off the Izu Peninsula, close to Tokyo.

Police, trouble and emergencies

Japan boasts one of the lowest crime rates in the world, and personal safety is rarely a worry. On the whole, the Japanese are honest and law-abiding, there's little theft, and drug-related crimes are relatively rare. The main exception is bicycle theft, which is rife, so make sure yours is securely locked whenever you leave it. In addition, it always pays to be careful in crowded areas and to keep money and important documents stowed in an inside pocket or money belt, or in your hotel safe.

In theory, you should carry your **passport** or ID at all times; the police have the right to arrest anyone who fails to do so. In practice, however, they rarely stop foreigners, though car drivers are more likely to be checked. If you're found without your ID, the usual procedure is to escort you back to your hotel or apartment to collect it. Anyone found **taking drugs** will be treated less leniently; if you're lucky, you'll simply be fined and deported, rather than sent to prison.

The presence of **police boxes** (*kōban*) in every neighbourhood helps discourage petty crime, and the local police seem to spend the majority of their time dealing with stolen bikes and helping bemused visitors – Japanese and foreigners – find addresses. This benevolent image is misleading, however, as the Japanese police are notorious for forcing confessions and holding suspects for weeks without access to a lawyer, and recent Amnesty International reports have criticized Japan for its brutal treatment of illegal immigrants and other foreigners held in jail.

Racial discrimination can be a problem in Japan, especially for non-whites, though it is mainly directed at immigrant workers rather than tourists. **Sexual discrimination** is widespread, and foreign women working in Japan can find the predominantly male business culture hard-going. The generally low status of women is reflected in the amount of groping that goes on in crowded commuter trains – there are even pornographic films and comics aimed at gropers. If you do have the misfortune to be groped, the best solution is to grab the offending hand, yank it high in the air and embarrass the guy as much as possible. Fortunately, more violent **sexual abuse** is rare, though rape is seriously under-reported and may be up to ten times higher than the current statistics suggest (under 2000 cases per year). Women working in hostess clubs are particularly at risk, as the murder of Lucie Blackman in 2000 sadly goes to prove. In the wake of the publicity, several other women came forward to make accusations of sexual abuse, including cases where the victims had been drugged.

If you need **emergency help**, phone ☎110 for the police or ☎119 for an ambulance or fire engine. You can call free from any public phone by pressing the red button before dialling, though with the old-style pink or red phones you need to put a coin in first to get the dialling tone. Better still, ask someone to call for you, since few police speak English. If you get really stuck, Tokyo Metropolitan Police operates an English-language hotline on ☎03/3501-0110 (Mon–Fri 8.30am–5.15pm). Each prefecture also has a Foreign Advisory Service, with a variety of foreign-language speakers on call who can be contacted as a last resort (see individual city Listings sections for details).

Earthquakes

Earthquakes are a part of life in Japan, with at least one quake recorded every day somewhere in the country, though fortunately, the vast majority consist of minor tremors which you probably won't even notice. The country is home to one-tenth of the world's active volcanoes and the site of one-tenth of its major earthquakes (over magnitude 7 on the Richter scale). The most recent major

quake occurred at Kōbe in January 1995, when more than 6000 people died, many of them in fires that raged through the old wooden houses, though most of the newer structures – built since the 1980s, when tighter regulations were introduced – survived.

Prior to Kōbe, the last really big quake was the Great Kantō Earthquake, which devastated Tokyo in 1923, killing an estimated 140,000 people. There's a sequence of major quakes in Tokyo every seventy-odd years, and everyone's been talking about the next "Big One" for at least a decade. Whilst scientists argue about the likelihood of another serious earthquake, Tokyo is equipped with some of the world's most sophisticated sensors, which are monitored round the clock, and architects employ mind-boggling techniques to try to ensure the city's new high-rises remain upright.

Nevertheless, earthquakes are notoriously difficult to predict and it's worth taking note of a few basic **safety procedures** (see box below). You should beware of aftershocks, which may go on for a long time, and can topple structures that are already weakened, and note that most casualties are caused by fire and traffic accidents, rather than collapsing buildings. In the aftermath of a major earthquake, it may be impossible to contact friends and relatives for a while, since the phone lines are likely to be down or reserved for emergency services.

Earthquake safety procedures

- Extinguish any fires and turn off electrical appliances (TV, air conditioners, kettles and so on).
- Open any doors leading out of the room, as they often get jammed shut, blocking your exit later.
- Stay away from windows because of splintering glass. If you have time, draw the curtains to contain the glass.
- Don't rush outside (many people are injured by falling masonry), but get under something solid, such as a ground-floor doorway, or a desk.
- If the earthquake occurs at night, make sure you've got a torch (all hotels, ryokan, etc provide torches in the rooms).
- When the tremors have died down, go to the nearest park, playing field or open space, taking your documents and other valuables with you. It's also a good idea to take a cushion or pillow to protect your head against falling glass.
- Eventually, make your way to the designated neighbourhood emergency centre for information, food and shelter.
- Ultimately, get in touch with your embassy.

Working and studying in Japan

Since the Japanese economy took a nosedive, the days of *gaijin* flying into Japan and immediately being hired on a lucrative salary for a few hours' work (typically teaching English) are well and truly over. With the exception of the government-sponsored JET programme (see opposite), employment opportunities for foreigners have shrunk, while the number of well-qualified, Japanese-speaking *gaijin* in Japan has increased. That said, finding employment is far from impossible, especially if you have the right qualifications (a degree is essential) and appropriate visa.

Australian, British, Canadian, French, New Zealand and South Korean citizens aged between 18 and 30 can apply for a working holiday visa (see p.21). All other foreigners working in Japan must apply for a **work visa** *outside* the country, for which the proper sponsorship papers from your prospective employer will be necessary. A few employers may be willing to hire you in Japan before the proper papers are sorted, but you shouldn't rely on this, and if you arrive in the country without a job make sure you have plenty of funds to live on until you find one. Working visas do not need to be obtained in your home country, so if you do get offered a job in Japan, it's possible to sort out the paperwork in South Korea, for example.

Apart from some specific websites (see opposite), the main places to look for job adverts are Monday's edition of the *Japan Times*, the free weekly magazines *Metropolis* and *Tokyo Notice Board* and, in the Kansai area, *Kansai Time Out*. The most common job available to foreigners is **teaching English**. The big employers are the national school chains, such as Berlitz, Shane, GEOS, ECC and NOVA. Some have recruit-

ing drives abroad (look in your local media under "teaching opportunities" or "overseas work"), so you can try and arrange a job before arriving. However, some of the conversation schools are far from professional operations (and even the biggies get lots of complaints), so before signing any contract it's a good idea to attend a class and find out what will be expected of you. If you have a professional teaching qualification, plus experience, your chances of getting one of the better jobs will be higher, as will they if you also speak another language such as French or Italian. Susan Griffith's book *Vacation Work's Teaching English Abroad* is recommended as a good source of general information.

A much more limited job option for *gaijin* is rewriting or editing translations of Japanese for technical documents, manuals, magazines and so on, so that they make grammatical sense and read well in English. For such jobs, it will be a great help if you have at least a little Japanese. Other options include modelling, for which it will be an asset to have a professional portfolio of photographs, and bar work and hostessing,

Certificate of alien registration

Whether you're on holiday, working or studying, if you stay in Japan for over three months, you must apply for a **certificate of alien registration** from the local government office closest to the area in which you live. This small identification card (usually referred to as a *gaijin* card) includes your photograph and must be carried at all times; if you're stopped by the police on the street (even for innocuous activities such as riding a bike late at night through the city), you'll have to produce this card, or your passport. If you have neither, expect a trip to the local police station to do some explaining.

although the dangers of this type of work have been exposed by the Lucie Blackman case (see p.81). Whatever work you're looking for – or if you're doing any sort of business in Japan – a smart set of clothes will give you an advantage, as will following other general rules of social etiquette (see p.68).

Online employment resources

The following **websites** should help you if you want to find out more about working or studying in Japan.

Work in Japan Ⓦ www.daijob.com/wij. Japan's largest bilingual jobs website.

Japan Association for Working Holiday Makers and **Jobs in Japan** Ⓦ www.jawhm.or.jp and Ⓦ www.jobsinjapan.com. Classified job ads.

Metropolis Ⓦ metropolis.japantoday.com. Tokyo's main English-language magazine has jobs listings each week.

Association of International Education in Japan Ⓦ www.aiej.or.jp/index.html. Information on studying in Japan.

Ski Japan Ⓦ www.skijapanguide.com. Information about working on the ski slopes.

WWOOF (Willing Workers on Organic Farms) Ⓦ www.wwoofjapan.com/index_e.shtml. Opportunities to work and live on organic farms across Japan.

The JET programme

One of the best ways to work in Japan is to get a place on the **Japan Exchange and Teaching (JET) programme** (Ⓦ www.jetprogramme.org), started by the government in 1987 in an attempt to improve foreign-language teaching in schools and promote international understanding. The benefits, which include a generous salary and help with accommodation, return air travel to Japan and paid holidays, have led to the programme being a huge success, and there are now more than 5800 graduates taking part each year from some 37 different countries. The scheme is only open to those aged between 18 and 35, though in certain circumstances people over the age limit will be considered.

Around ninety percent of applicants are employed as Assistant Language Teachers (ALTs) in secondary schools, their duties being primarily to team-teach with Japanese instructors of English and other foreign languages, and also to act as ambassadors for their country. Other applicants opt for one of the local government posts as Coordinator for International Relations (CIRs), though a functional command of Japanese is essential for this work. CIR duties include assisting in a range of international exchange projects and tasks, such as interpreting, editing and producing bilingual pamphlets and receiving guests from abroad.

Applying for the JET programme is a lengthy process for which you need to be well prepared. Application forms for the following year's quota are available from late September, with the deadline for submission being early December. Interviews are held in January and February, with decisions made in March. After health checks and orientation meetings, ALTs and CIRs head off to their posts in Japan in late July on year-long contracts. These contracts can be renewed for up to two more years by mutual consent.

For further details of the scheme and **application forms**, UK citizens should contact the JET Programme Desk, Council on International Educational Exchange, 52 Poland St, London W1V 4QJ ☎0171/478 2010, whilst residents of the US and Canada should ring ☎1-800/INFO-JET, consult Ⓦ www.jetprogramme.org online or, along with residents of Australia and New Zealand, contact their nearest Japanese consulate or embassy (see p.22).

Studying Japanese language and culture

If you're thinking about **studying Japanese** in Japan, consider picking a school away from the main urban centres. Regional cities such as Sapporo and Kanazawa are cheaper places to live and you're much more likely to find yourself having to use Japanese on an everyday basis than you would be in Tokyo or Ōsaka. That said, the range of courses and institutions on offer in the big cities is much wider.

As well as the language, there are opportunities to study other aspects of Japanese culture, from pottery to playing the *shakuhachi* (a traditional flute). In order to get a **cultural visa**, you'll need documents from the institutions where you plan to study, including one stating that all tuition fees have been paid, and a letter of guarantee from a private sponsor, preferably Japanese. Full-time courses are expensive, but once you have your visa you may be allowed to undertake paid work to support yourself.

Japan's Ministry of Education, Culture, Sports, Science and Technology (Mombu Kagaku-shō) offers three types of annual **scholarships** to foreign students. These are available to those who wish to further their knowledge of Japanese or Japanese studies, undertake an undergraduate degree, or become a research student at a Japanese university. The scholarships include return airfare, tuition fees and a generous monthly allowance. For more details, contact the nearest Japanese embassy or consulate.

The monthly bilingual language magazines *Nihongo Journal* and *Hiragana Times*, and the listings magazines *Metropolis*, *Tokyo Journal* and *Kansai Time Out* all carry adverts for Japanese language schools. Also check out the Association of International Education Japan, 4-5-29 Komaba, Meguro-ku, Tokyo 153 ☏03/5454-5216, fax 5454-5236, ⓦwww.aiej.or.jp, whose website lists details of accredited institutions and has other useful information for those considering studying in Japan.

Gay and lesbian Japan

Despite there being an honourable tradition of male homosexuality in Japan, with some ancient Buddhist sects believing that love among men was preferable to love between the sexes, modern gay life in Japan is very low-key compared to that in similar industrialized countries. There is still a huge amount of pressure put on men and women to marry, this being an almost essential step along the career ladder at many corporations. Such expectations keep many Japanese gays in the closet and, outside of the main cities such as Tokyo and Ōsaka, the gay scene is all but invisible.

This is not to say that nothing is happening. On the contrary: if you know where to look, the Japanese gay and lesbian scene is very much alive. To get an idea of the scale of the scene check out the magazine *Badi*, gay Japan's premier publication; you'll find it in the bookshops of Shinjuku Ni-chōme in Tokyo. There are gay parades across the country, although they have been sporadic; for details of Tokyo's check out ⓦwww.tlgp.org/eng.

In recent times homosexuality has come to be seen as trendy, particularly in the major cities and among the all-important, cash-rich group of young working women known as "office ladies", or OLs. Comic books and movies with homosexual characters have been a huge success with OLs, who swoon over the gay romances. Gay and transvestite celebrities are the in thing on TV and there are even bars in Tokyo staffed by cross-dressing women, who flatter and fawn over their female customers in only a slightly more macho way than bona fide hostesses do over salarymen (see p.180 for gay bars in Tokyo).

Whilst you're highly unlikely to encounter any problems as a gay traveller in Japan, you may find it difficult to break into any local gay scene without having some contacts: the following list of gay information sources is a good start.

Gay information sources

International Gay Friends is a networking group for gays which organizes support groups for men and women. To contact them, write to **if/Passport,**

CPO 180, Tokyo 100-91, or call ☏03/5693-4569. **GayNet Japan** (ⓦ www.gnj.or.jp) has some discussion groups that you may find useful. For details of the lesbian scene contact **OCCUR** (Japan Association for the Lesbian and Gay Movement), Ishikawa-Building, 2nd Floor, 6-12-11 Honcho Nakano, Tokyo 164 Japan ☏03/3383-

5556, ⓕ3229-7880, a grassroots gay activist organization and sponsor of the annual Tokyo Gay and Lesbian Film/Video Festival (ⓦ lgffweb.www21.wnj.je/e/). **Utopia Asia** ⓦ www.utopia-asia.com/tipsjapn.htm. Covers gay life in Japan and lists bars and clubs around the country.

Directory

CHILDREN The Japanese love children and, with standards of health and hygiene so high, there is no real reason not to bring your kids here. All the products you need – such as nappies and baby food – are easily available at shops and department stores, though taking a pram on subways and trains is problematic, since there are often no elevators at stations. Children under 6 ride free on trains, subways and buses, while those aged 6 to 11 pay half fare (this applies to the Japan Rail Pass too). On domestic flights, children under 3 fly free but have to share a parent's seat, while kids aged 3 to 11 are charged half-price. Unless they're very young, reduced accommodation rates for children are rare, although the large Western chain hotels, such as the *Hilton* and *Holiday Inn*, don't charge extra if children share rooms with their parents. Only at upmarket hotels will you be able to arrange babysitting. Virtually all tourist attractions have a set of reduced charges for children, depending on their age.

CIGARETTES One of Japan's bargain buys, cigarettes are available in a vast range of brands – usually from vending machines – at around ¥250 a pack.

CONTRACEPTIVES The Pill is available only on prescription and costs around ¥3000 a packet; it's better to bring them with you. The "morning-after" pill is also available on prescription, but it's more difficult to find a clinic offering it. Local-brand condoms are widely sold in pharmacies and vending machines.

ELECTRICITY The electrical current is 100v, 50Hz AC in eastern Japan including Tokyo, and 100v, 60Hz AC in western Japan including Nagoya, Kyoto and Ōsaka. Japanese plugs have two flat pins and, although they are identical to North American plugs, you'll need a transformer to use any foreign appliances safely.

EMERGENCIES In order to get a quick response from the national police emergency number (☏110) or the ambulance and fire services (☏119), you'll need to speak some Japanese. Tokyo English Lifeline (TELL; ☏03/3968-4099) is open for calls daily 9am–4pm and 7–11pm; they can give advice and put you in touch with the right people. In the last resort, contact the Prefecture's Foreign Advisory Service (see individual Listings for details).

JAPANESE CALENDAR Although Japan uses the Western system of dates for months and days, for years it more commonly uses its own Imperial system. This calculates the number of the year from the accession of the last emperor. Each emperor is assigned a special name. For example, Hirohito's reign (1926–89) is called Shōwa. The current Emperor Akihito began counting his reign, called Heisei, in 1989, so 2004 is Heisei 16.

LAUNDRIES A laundry service is available in all types of accommodation, with most cheaper hotels and hostels having coin-operated washing machines and dryers. All Japanese neighbourhoods also have coin laundries (*koin randorii*), often open long hours, which charge between ¥200 and ¥300 per wash and ¥100 for around ten minutes of drying time. Virtually all Japanese washing machines use cold water.

LEFT LUGGAGE You'll usually only find left-luggage offices at the largest train stations in big cities, though all train stations, many subway stations and some department stores and shopping centres have coin lockers where you can stash your luggage. These come in a range of sizes, charging from ¥300 to ¥600 for a day's storage.

PHOTOGRAPHY All major brands of film are available across Japan at relatively cheap prices, especially if bought in bulk from the discount camera shops in the big cities. If you want special types of film, it's best to stock up here, too, before setting off to Japan's more remote areas, where the choice is more limited. Worth considering are disposable cameras, which come in a vast range of sizes and types (with or without flash; panoramic; sepia-tinted or black-and-white images; advance photo system). These cost from as little as ¥700 and make great presents.

PUBLIC TOILETS All trains and subway stations, parks, department stores and large hotels have public lavatories; ask for the *otearai* or *toire*, pronounced "toy-ray". Note that, hotels and department stores excepted, there is rarely toilet paper, so carry around some tissues; the small packs carry-ing advertising that are dished out free at busy stations and shopping districts are ideal. See p.70 for more on toilets.

STUDENT CARDS It's a good idea to bring along an International Student Identity Card (ISIC), since many museums and other tourist facilities charge lower prices for students.

TAMPONS While you won't find foreign brands such as Tampax in Japan, larger chemists sell locally produced tampons and pads.

TIME ZONES The whole of Japan is nine hours ahead of Greenwich Mean Time, so at noon in London it's 9pm in Tokyo. Japan is fourteen hours ahead of Eastern Standard Time in the US. There is no daylight saving, so during British Summer Time, for example, the difference drops to eight hours.

TIPS Tipping is not a Japanese custom and nobody expects it. The only exception is at high-class Japanese inns, where it's good form to leave ¥2000 for the room attendant, but only if the money is put in an envelope and handed over discreetly.

WEIGHTS AND MEASURES The only exception to Japan's use of the metric system is its measurement of rooms, usually quoted in *jō*, the size of one tatami. It's worth noting that tatami size varies around the country, Tokyo having the smallest size at 1.76m by 0.88m.

Guide

Guide

Tokyo

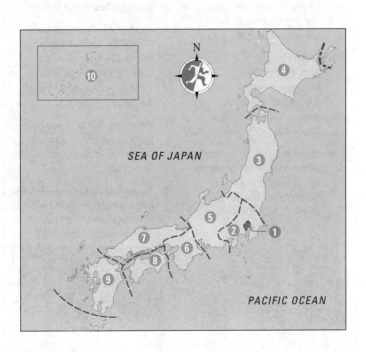

CHAPTER 1 # Highlights

✳ **Roppongi Hills** Explore the city's hippest neighbourhood, home to the new Mori Art Museum and a plethora of restaurants and top-class boutiques. **See p.126**

✳ **Asakusa** The city's most colourful and evocative district, full of old craft shops, traditional inns, restaurants and the bustling Sensō-ji temple. **See p.128**

✳ **Ueno** Home to a famous park and the Tokyo National Museum, the best place for a comprehensive overview of Japanese cultural history. **See p.132**

✳ **Shinjuku** Tokyo in a microcosm, from the bright lights of Kabukichō to the Gotham-city-like Tokyo Metropolitan Government Building. **See p.141**

✳ **Meiji-jingū** Escape the clamour of the city amid the verdant grounds of Tokyo's most venerable Shinto shrine. **See p.146**

✳ **Harajuku** Stroll past the lively shops of tree-lined Omotesandō boulevard towards the stunning Prada building. **See p.149**

✳ **Japan Folk Crafts Museum** One of the country's most impressive collections of crafts, from giant pots to exquisitely designed kimono. **See p.153**

✳ **Happōen** One of Tokyo's loveliest traditional gardens, with a delightful teahouse. **See p.156**

✳ **Tsukiji** Get up early to see the nation's top fish market in full flight and to enjoy a fresh sushi breakfast. **See p.158**

△Giant lantern, Sensō-ji

Tokyo

Perplexing and beguiling, **TOKYO** is a city that confounds simple translation. Gaudily hung about with eyeball-searing neon and messy overhead cables, plagued by seemingly incessant noise, often clogged with bumper-to-bumper traffic and packed with twelve million people squashed into minute apartments, it seems like the stereotypical urban nightmare. Yet step back from the frenetic main roads and chances are you'll find yourself in a world of tranquil backstreets, where wooden houses are fronted by neatly clipped bonsai trees; wander beyond the high-tech emporia, and you'll find ancient temples and shrines. Lively neighbourhood festivals are held virtually every day of the year, people regularly visit their local shrine or temple and scrupulously observe the passing seasons. And at the centre of it all lies the mysterious **Imperial Palace** – the inviolate home of the emperor and a tangible link to the past.

In many ways Tokyo is also something of a modern-day utopia. Trains run on time; the crime rate is hardly worth worrying about; shops and vending machines provide everything you could need (and many things you never thought you needed) 24 hours a day; the people wear the coolest fashions, eat in fabulous restaurants and party in the hippest clubs. First-time visitors should be prepared for a massive assault on the senses – just walking the streets of this hyperactive city can be an energizing experience. You'll also be surprised by how affordable many things are. Cheap-and-cheerful *izakaya* (bars that serve food) and noodle shacks far outnumber the swanky restaurants and high-class *ryōtei*, while day-tickets for a sumo tournament or a Kabuki play can be bought for the price of a few drinks. Many of the city's highlights are even free: a stroll through the evocative **Shitamachi** (low city) area around Asakusa and the major Buddhist temple **Senso-ji**; a visit to the tranquil wooded grounds of **Meiji-jingū**, the city's most venerable Shinto shrine, and the nearby teenage shopping mecca of **Harajuku**; the frenetic fish market at **Tsukiji**; the crackling, neon-saturated atmosphere of the mini-city **Shinjuku** – you don't need to part with lots of cash to explore this city.

Even if you don't arrive in Tokyo, chances are you will end up here or pass through on your way to other parts of Japan, since the capital is the major **transport hub**. Every day, scores of Shinkansen (bullet trains) speed up to the far north of Honshū or south to Kyūshū, while flights, buses and ferries connect Tokyo to the far-flung corners and islands of the Japanese archipelago.

The only time Tokyo is best avoided is during the steamy height of summer in August and early September, when the city's humidity sees its citizens scurrying from one air-conditioned haven to another. October and November, by contrast, are great months to take in the spectacular fireburst of autumn leaves

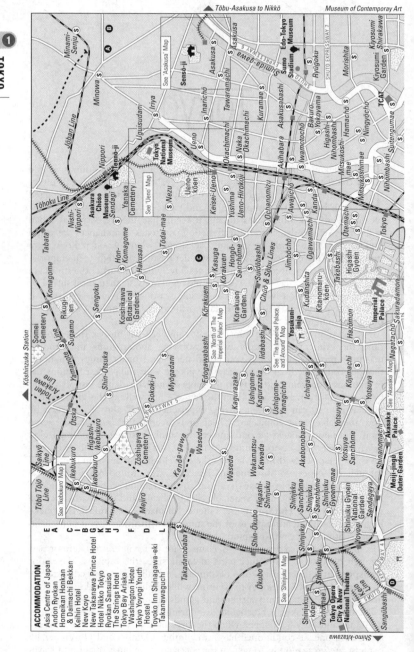

TOKYO

ACCOMMODATION

- Asia Centre of Japan — E
- Andon Ryokan — A
- Homeikan Honkan & Daimachi Bekkan — I
- Keihin Hotel — C
- New Koyo — B
- New Takanawa Prince Hotel — G
- Hotel Nikko Tokyo — K
- Ryokan Sansuiso — H
- The Strings Hotel — J
- Tokyo Bay Ariake — F
- Washington Hotel — D
- Tokyo Yoyogi Youth Hostel — L
- Toyoko Inn Shinagawa-eki Takanawaguchi

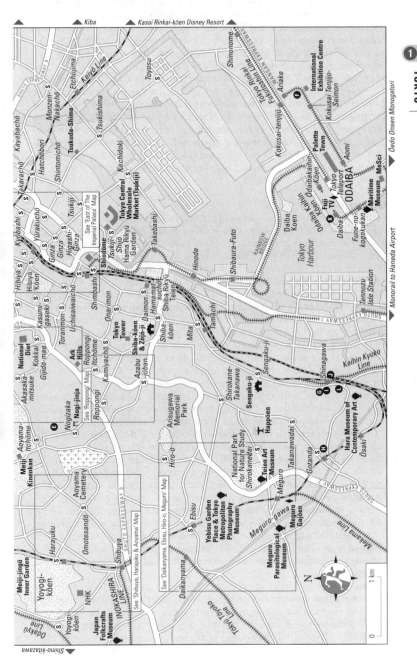

Kiba ▲   Kasai Rinkai-kōen Disney Resort ▲

Ōedo Onsen Monogatari ▶

Monorail to Haneda Airport ▶

Shimo-kitazawa ▶

Keiyō Line

Etchūjima
Monzen-Nakachō
Kayabachō
Takaracho
Hatchōbori
Shintomichō
Tsukishima
Tsukuda-Shima
Toyosu

Shinonome
Tōkyō Rinkai Fukutoshin
Ariake
International Exhibition Centre
Kokusai Tenjijō-Seimon

Kachidoki
Kokusai-tenjū
Palette Town
Aomi

Kyōbashi
Yūrakuchō
Ginza
Ginza
Higashi-Ginza
Tsukiji

See 'East of The Imperial Palace' Map

Tokyo Central Wholesale Market (Tsukiji)

Shiodome
Tsukiji Shijō
Hama Rikyū Garden

Odaibakaihin-kōen
Fuji TV
Odaiba-kaihin-kōen
ODAIBA
Tōkyō Teleport

Daiba Kōen
Daiba
Maritime Museum
Fune-no-kagakukan
MeSci

Hibiya
Hibiya Kōen
Kasumigaseki

Shimbashi
Hamamatsuchō
Daimon
Onarimon
Uchisaiwaichō

Takebashi
Hinode
Shibaura-Futo

RAINBOW BRIDGE

Tokyo Harbour

National Diet
Kokkai-Gijidō-mae
Akasaka-mitsuke

Ark Hills
Roppongi
Toranomon
Tokyo Tower
Shiba-kōen & Zōjō-ji
Shiba-kōen

Shiba Rikyū Teien
Hamamatsuchō

Tamachi
Tennōzu Isle Station

Meiji Kinenkan
Aoyama-itchōme
Nogizaka
Nogi-jinja
Azabu-jūban
Roppongi
Kamiyachō

See 'Roppongi' Map

Arisugawa Memorial Park

Shirokane-Takanawa
Sengaku-ji
Sengaku-ji

Mita
Shinagawa

Keihin Kyūkō Line

Hara Museum of Contemporary Art

Aoyama Cemetery

Hiro-o
National Park for Nature Study Shirokanedai
Teien Art Museum
Happoen

Takanawadai
Gotanda
Ōsaki

Harajuku
Omotesandō
Shibuya
Meijingū Inner Garden

Meiji-jingū Inner Garden
Yoyogi-kōen
NHK

INOKASHIRA LINE

See 'Shibuya, Harajuku & Aoyama' Map

See 'Daikanyama, Ebisu, Hiro-o, Meguro' Map

Daikanyama
Ebisu
Yebisu Garden Place & Tokyo Metropolitan Photography Museum
Meguro Parasitological Museum
Meguro
Meguro Gajōen

Meguro-gawa

Takanawadai
Mikawa Line

SHUTO EXPRESSWAY 2

Japan Folkcrafts Museum
Yoyogi-kōen

Ōdakyū Line

Tōkyū Tōyoko Line

N

0   1 km

in Tokyo's parks and gardens. Temperatures dip to freezing in the winter months, though the crisp blue skies are rarely disturbed by rain or snow showers. April is the month when Tokyoites love to party beneath the flurries of falling cherry blossoms – one of the best months to visit the capital. Carrying an umbrella is a good idea during tsuyu, the rainy season in June and September, when typhoons occasionally strike the coast.

Legend says that a giant catfish sleeps beneath Tokyo Bay, and its wriggling can be felt in the hundreds of small tremors that rumble the capital each year. Around every seventy years, the catfish awakes, resulting in the kind of major earthquake seen in 1995 in Kōbe. There is a long-running, half-hearted debate about moving the Diet and main government offices out of Tokyo, away from danger. Yet, despite the fact that the city is well overdue for the Big One, talk of relocating the capital always comes to nothing. Now, more than ever before, Tokyo is the centre of Japan, and nobody wants to leave and miss any of the action.

Some history

Today's restless metropolis sprawling along the western shores of Tokyo Bay began life as a humble fishing village called **Edo** ("Mouth of the Estuary") beside the marshy Sumida-gawa. The city's founding date is usually given as 1457, when minor lord Ōta Dōkan built his castle on a bluff overlooking the river. However, a far more significant event occurred in 1590, when the feudal lord **Tokugawa Ieyasu** (see "History", p.937) chose this obscure castle-town for his power base. In little over a decade Ieyasu had conquered all rivals, taken the title of "shogun" and established the **Tokugawa clan** as the effective rulers of Japan for the next two and a half centuries. Though the emperor continued to hold court in Kyoto, Japan's real centre of power lay in Edo.

The Tokugawa set about creating a city befitting their new status. By 1640 **Edo Castle** was the most imposing in all Japan, complete with a five-storey central keep, a double moat and a spiralling network of canals. Instead of perimeter walls, however, there were simple barrier gates and a bewildering warren of narrow, tortuous lanes, sudden dead ends and unbridged canals to snare unwelcome intruders. Drainage work began on the surrounding marshes, and embankments were raised to guard the nascent city against floods.

The shogun protected himself further by requiring the *daimyō* to split the year between Edo, where their families were kept as virtual hostages, and their provincial feudal holdings. This left them with neither the time nor the money to raise a serious threat, though they were compensated with large plots on the higher ground to the west of the castle, an area that became known as **Yamanote**. Artisans, merchants and others at the bottom of the pile were confined to **Shitamachi**, a low-lying, overcrowded region to the east. By the mid-eighteenth century, Edo's population was well over one million, making it the world's largest city, of whom roughly half were squeezed into Shitamachi at an astonishing 70,000 people per square kilometre. Though growing less distinct, this division between the "high" and "low" city is still apparent today.

During the long period of peace, the shogunate and its beneficiaries grew ever more conservative, but life down in the Shitamachi buzzed with a wealthy merchant class and a vigorous, often bawdy, subculture. This is the world most closely associated with Edo, the world of geisha and Kabuki, of summer days on the Sumida-gawa, moon-viewing parties and picnics under the spring blossom – fleeting moments captured in *ukiyo-e*, pictures of the floating world. Inevitably, there was also squalor, poverty and violence, as well as frequent fires;

in January 1657, the **Fire of the Long Sleeves** laid waste to three-quarters of the city's buildings and killed an estimated 100,000 people.

A year after the **Meiji Restoration** in 1868 (see p.940), the emperor took up permanent residence in the city, now renamed **Tokyo** (Eastern Capital) in recognition of its proper status. As Meiji Japan embraced the new, Western technologies, the face of Tokyo gradually changed: the castle lost its outer gates and much of its grounds; canals were filled in or built over; the commercial focus shifted south into Ginza, and Shitamachi's wealthier merchants decamped to more desirable Yamanote. However, the city was still disaster-prone; the **Great Kantō Earthquake** of 1923 devastated half of Tokyo, and another 100,000 people lost their lives.

More trauma was to come during **World War II**. In just three days of sustained incendiary bombing in March 1945, hundreds of thousands were killed and great swathes of the city burnt down, including Meiji-jingū, Sensō-ji, Edo Castle and most of Shitamachi. From a prewar population of nearly seven million, Tokyo was reduced to around three million people in a state of near-starvation. This time regeneration was fuelled by an influx of American dollars and food aid under the Allied Occupation, and a manufacturing boom sparked by the Korean War in 1950.

By the time Emperor Hirohito opened the Tokyo **Olympic Games** in October 1964, Tokyo was truly back on its feet and visitors were wowed by the stunning new Shinkansen trains running west to Ōsaka. The economy boomed well into the late **1980s** and Tokyo land prices reached dizzying heights, matched by excesses of every conceivable sort, from gold-wrapped sushi to mink toilet-seat covers. The heady optimism was reflected in the building projects of the time – the Metropolitan Government offices in Shinjuku, the Odaiba reclamation and the vast new development of Makuhari Messe. Then, in 1991, the bubble burst. This, along with revelations of political corruption, financial mismanagement and the release of deadly Sarin gas on Tokyo commuter trains by the AUM cult in 1995 (see p.947) – a particularly shocking event in what is one of the world's safest cities – led to a more sober Tokyo in the late 1990s.

While the **new millennium** has brought the glimmerings of an economic recovery, they are tempered by a growing list of spectacular business failures, higher unemployment and a general sense of unease – not that you'll notice this much on the streets. New buildings continue to go up at a dizzying speed, teen fashions get wilder and funkier every year, and the Tokyo buzz is as addictive as ever.

Arrival, information and orientation

If you're **arriving** in Tokyo from abroad, you'll almost certainly touch down at New Tokyo International Airport. If you're coming to the capital from elsewhere in Japan, you'll arrive at one of the main train stations (Tokyo, Ueno, Shinagawa or Shinjuku), the ferry port at Ariake on Tokyo Bay, or the long-distance bus terminals, mainly at Tokyo and Shinjuku stations.

By plane

Some 66km east of the city centre, **New Tokyo International Airport** (better known as Narita) has two terminals; which one you arrive at depends on the airline you fly. Flight arrival and departure information is available on ☎0476/34-5000 and ⊛www.tokyo-airport-bldg.co.jp. Be prepared for immigration delays and baggage searches. There are **cash machines** which accept foreign credit and debit cards and a **bureau de change** at both terminals (Terminal One: 6.30am–11pm; Terminal Two: 7am–1pm), which offer the same rates as city banks. The main **tourist information centre** (daily 9am–8pm; ☎0476/34-6251) is at the newer Terminal Two; staff here can provide maps and leaflets for across Japan. The neighbouring Welcome Inn counter can make hotel bookings free of charge. Terminal One has a smaller information centre (daily 9am–8pm), providing much the same service. If you have a Japan Rail Pass exchange order, you can arrange to use your pass either immediately or at a later date at the JR travel agencies (not the ticket offices) in the basement; English signs indicate where these are.

Transport between the city and airports

The fastest way into Tokyo **from Narita** is on one of the frequent JR or Keisei **trains** that depart from the basements of both terminals. Keisei, located on the left side of the basements, offers the cheapest connection into town: the no-frills *tokkyū* (limited express) service, which costs ¥1000 to Ueno (every 30min; 1hr 10min). This service also stops at Nippori, a few minutes north of Ueno, where it's easy to transfer to the Yamanote or the Keihin Tōhoku lines. If you're staying around Ueno, or you're not carrying much luggage, this – or the slightly faster and fancier Skyliner (¥1920) – is the best option.

JR, who operate on the right-hand side of the basements, run the more luxurious red and silver **Narita Express** (N'EX) to several city stations. The cheapest fare is ¥2940 to Tokyo Station (every 30min; 1hr), and there are frequent direct N'EX services to Shinjuku (hourly; 1hr 20min) for ¥3110. The N'EX services to Ikebukuro (¥3110) and Yokohama (¥4180) are much less frequent – you're better off going to Shinjuku and changing onto the Yamanote line for Ikebukuro, while there are plenty of trains to Yokohama from Tokyo Station. Cheaper than the N'EX are JR's kaisoku (rapid) trains, which, despite their name, chug slowly into Tokyo Station (hourly; 1hr 20min) for ¥1280.

Limousine buses are useful if you're weighed down by luggage but are prone to delays in traffic. Although the tickets are pricier than the train, once you factor in the cost of a taxi from one of the train stations to your hotel, these buses are probably a better deal. You buy tickets from the limousine bus counters in each of the arrival lobbies; the buses depart directly outside (check which platform you need) and stop at a wide range of places around the city, including all the major hotels and train stations. The journey to hotels in Shinjuku and Ikebukuro costs around ¥3000 and takes a minimum of ninety minutes. **Taxis** to the city centre can be caught from stand 9 outside the arrivals hall of Terminal One and stand 30 outside the arrivals hall of Terminal Two; the journey will set you back around ¥20,000, and is no faster than going by bus.

From **Haneda Airport** it's a twenty-minute monorail journey to Hamamatsuchō Station on the Yamanote line (daily 5.20am–11.15pm; every 5–10min) for ¥460. A **taxi** from Haneda to central Tokyo costs ¥6000, while a **limousine bus** to Tokyo Station is ¥900.

If you're **leaving** Tokyo from Narita airport, it's important to set off around four hours before your flight, though you can skip the queues to some extent by checking in and completing immigration formalities (8am–6pm) at the Tokyo City Air Terminal (TCAT; ☎03/3665-7111), located above Suitengūmae Station at the end of the Hibiya line. Not all airlines have desks at TCAT, so check first. The onward journey is then by limousine bus – allow at least one hour – with departures every ten minutes (¥2900). If you went through immigration at TCAT, you'll have been given a special card that allows you to scoot through the "crew line" at passport control in Narita. Nevertheless, during peak holiday periods, queues at the baggage check-in and immigration desks at both Narita and TCAT are lengthy. **International departure tax** from Narita is included in the price of your ticket.

Tokyo: arrival

Haneda Airport	*Haneda Kūkō*	羽田空港
New Tokyo International Airport (Narita)	*Shin-Tōkyō Kokusai Kūkō (Narita)*	新東京国際空港（成田）

Bus, ferry and train stations

Ikebukuro	*Ikebukuro-eki*	池袋駅
Shibuya	*Shibuya-eki*	渋谷駅
Shinagawa	*Shinagawa-eki*	品川駅
Shinjuku	*Shinjuku-eki*	新宿駅
Tokyo	*Tōkyō-eki*	東京駅
Tokyo Ferry Port	*Tōkyō Ferii Noriba*	東京フェリー乗り場
Ueno	*Ueno-eki*	上野駅

Located on a spit of land jutting into Tokyo Bay 20km south of the Imperial Palace, **Haneda Airport** is where most domestic flights touch down (flight information ☏03/5757-8111); the only international connection at Haneda is provided by Taiwan's China Airlines. There's a small branch of the **Tokyo Tourist Information Centre** (☏03/5757-9345; daily 9am–10pm), and the airport information desk can provide you with an English-language map of Tokyo. There are direct bus and train connections from Narita to Haneda; the bus (1hr 20min; ¥3000) is more frequent than the train (1hr 10min; ¥1580).

By train

If you're coming into Tokyo by Shinkansen **JR train** from Ōsaka, Kyoto and other points west, you'll pull in to **Tokyo Station**, close to the Imperial Palace, or **Shinagawa Station**, around 6km southwest. Most Shinkansen services from the north (the Hokuriku line from Nagano, the Jōetsu line from Niigata and the Tōhoku lines from Akita, Hachinoe and Yamagata) arrive at Tokyo Station, though a few services only go as far as **Ueno**, some 4km northeast of the Imperial Palace. Tokyo, Shinagawa and Ueno stations are all on the Yamanote line and are connected to several subway lines, putting them in reach of most of the capital. Other long-distance JR train services stop at Tokyo and Ueno stations, Shinjuku Station on Tokyo's west side and Ikebukuro Station in the city's northwest corner.

Non-JR trains terminate at different stations: the Tōkyū Tōyoko line from Yokohama ends at Shibuya Station, southwest of the Imperial Palace; the Tōbu Nikkō line runs from Nikkō to Asakusa Station, east of Ueno; and the Odakyū line from Hakone finishes at Shinjuku Station, which is also the terminus for the Seibu Shinjuku line from Kawagoe – all these stations have subway connections and (apart from Asakusa) are on the Yamanote rail line.

By bus

Long-distance buses pull in at several major stations around the city, making transport connections straightforward. The main overnight services from Kyoto and Ōsaka arrive at the bus station beside the eastern Yaesu exit of Tokyo Station – other arrival stations for buses are Ikebukuro, Shibuya, Shinagawa and Shinjuku.

By boat

The most memorable way to arrive in the capital is by long-distance **ferry**, sailing past the suspended roads and monorail on the Rainbow Bridge and the harbour wharves to dock at **Tokyo Ferry Port** at Ariake, on the man-made island of Odaiba (see p.160) in Tokyo Bay. There are ferry connections to Tokyo from Kita-Kyūshū in Kyūshū, Kōchi and Tokushima on Shikoku, and Naha on Okinawa-Hontō. Buses run from the port to Shin-Kiba Station both on the subway and the JR Keiyō line and ten minutes' ride from Tokyo Station. A taxi from the port to central Tokyo shouldn't cost more than ¥2000.

Information

Tokyo has several sources of English-language information, and it's best to take advantage of them before heading off to other regions. **JNTO's main office** (Mon–Fri 9am–5pm, Sat 9am–noon; ℡03/3201-3331) has information on all Japan – it's on the tenth floor of Tokyo Kotsu Kaikan, immediately east of Yūrakuchō Station. There are multilingual staff here, a Welcome Inn booking desk for accommodation across Japan and a noticeboard with some information on upcoming events. A more comprehensive monthly list of festivals is available on request.

More useful for purely Tokyo information is the **Tokyo Tourist Information Centre**, 1st floor, Tokyo Metropolitan Government No 1. Bldg, 2-8-1 Nishi-Shinjuku; (daily 9.30am–6.30pm; ℡03/5321-3077); the closest subway station is Tochō-mae. There are also small branches at Haneda Airport (℡03/5757-9345; daily 9am–10pm) and in the Kesei line station at Ueno (℡03/3836-3471; daily 9.30am–6.30pm).

You can pick up free **maps** of the city from any of the tourist centres; look out for the handy "Welcome to Tokyo" map of central Tokyo (within the Yamanote line), with detailed area maps on the back. If you plan to be here for more than just a few days or want to wander off the beaten track, it's well worth investing in Kodansha's bilingual *Tokyo City Atlas* (¥2100), which gives more detail and, importantly, includes *chōme* and block numbers to help pin down addresses (see box, p.27).

The best overall **English-language magazine** is the free weekly *Metropolis*, which is packed with ads, reviews, features and listings for film and music events. *Tokyo Notice Board* (ⓦwww.tokyonoticeboard.co.jp) is another free weekly devoted almost entirely to classifieds. Also worth a look are a couple more freesheets: the irreverent national monthly magazine *Japanzine* (ⓦwww.japan-zine.com), which has a Tokyo listings and review section; and *Tokyo Weekender* (ⓦwww.weekender.co.jp), which caters to the expat and

---

Tokyo on the Web

The following are all worth checking out for up-to-the-minute city info.

Yes! Tokyo ⓦwww.tcvb.or.jp. Put together by the Tokyo Convention and Visitors' Bureau, this is one of the most comprehensive guides around.

Metropolis ⓦwww.metropolis.japantoday.com. Read the weekly English-language freesheet (see above) online and trawl its back issues for everything from celebrity interviews to personal ads.

Superfuture ⓦwww.superfuture.com. Tells you where to head for the coolest shops and bars.

Tokyo Q ⓦwww.club.nokia.co.jp/tokyoq. Long-running online weekly magazine with a fun, authoritative and quirky take on the city, including a good clubbing guide.

Tokyo Food Page ⓦwww.bento.com. Lists scores of restaurants, cafés and bars around the city.

Tokyo Toursim Info ⓦwww.tourism.metro.tokyo.jp. The official site of the Tokyo Government, with details of events around the city, including local festivals, plus a wide range of self-guided walking tours.

diplomatic scene. You might also find the quarterly *Tokyo Journal* (¥600; ⓦ www.tokyo.to) of interest. You'll find all these at the Tokyo Tourist Information Centre, larger hotels, foreign-language bookstores and bars or restaurants frequented by *gaijin*.

Orientation

Think of Tokyo not as one city with a central heart but as several mini-cities, linked by the arteries of the railway and the veins of the subway system. It's a vast place, spreading from the mountains in the north and west to tropical islands some 1300km to the south, but as a visitor you're unlikely to stray beyond its most central wards. The most useful reference point is the **Yamanote line**, an elongated overland train loop that connects and encloses central Tokyo and virtually everything of interest to visitors. Sightseeing destinations that fall outside of the loop are mainly within what was once called Shitamachi, or the "low city", east of the Imperial Palace, including Asakusa and Ryōgoku, and on Tokyo Bay to the south, including the nascent 21st-century metropolis of Odaiba.

Get your bearings by tracing the Yamanote route on a map, starting at the mini-city of **Shinjuku**, on the west side of Tokyo, where a cluster of sky-scrapers provides a permanent directional marker wherever you are in the city. From Shinjuku, the line heads north towards the mini-city of **Ikebukuro**, where the sixty-storey Sunshine Building, east of the station, is another landmark. The Yamanote then veers east towards **Ueno**, the jumping-off point for the park and national museums. Further east of Ueno, at Asakusa, is **Sensō-ji**, Tokyo's major Buddhist temple.

From Ueno the Yamanote runs south to **Akihabara**, the electronic discount shop district. From Akihabara Station, the **Sōbu line** heads directly westwards, providing – together with the **Chūō line** from Tokyo Station – the shortest rail route back to Shinjuku. Handy stations along these two lines include Suidōbashi for Tokyo Dome and Kōrakuen garden; Iidabashi for the Tokyo International Youth Hostel; and Sendagaya for the Metropolitan Gymnasium and the gardens of Shinjuku Gyoen. East of Akihabara, on the other hand, the Sōbu line runs across the Sumida-gawa to the sumo centre of Ryōgoku.

From Akihabara the Yamanote continues south through **Tokyo Station**, immediately east of the Imperial Palace and business districts of Ōtemachi and Marunouchi. Further south lie the entertainment districts of **Ginza** (closest stop Yūrakuchō) and **Shimbashi**, after which the line passes **Hamamatsuchō** (connected by monorail to Haneda airport), where you'll be able to see, to the east, the gardens of Hama Rikyū, next to the market at Tsukiji, on the edge of Tokyo Bay. On the west side is Tokyo Tower, just beyond which is the party district of **Roppongi**, marked by the colossal Mori Tower, heart of the new Roppongi Hills development.

The Rainbow Bridge across to the man-made island of **Odaiba** is clearly visible as the Yamanote veers down to **Shinagawa**, a hub of upmarket hotels, with rail connections through to Kawasaki, Yokohama and beyond. From here, the line turns sharply north and heads up towards fashionable **Shibuya**, another mini-city. On the western flank of **Harajuku**, the next stop after Shibuya, are the wooded grounds of Meiji-jingū, the city's most important shrine, and Yoyogi Park. **Yoyogi**, the station after Harajuku, is also on the Chūō line, and is just one stop from the start of your journey at Shinjuku.

City transport

The whole of Tokyo's public transport system is efficient, clean and safe, but as a visitor you'll probably find the **trains and subways** the best way of getting around: the simple colour-coding on trains and maps, as well as clear signposts (many in English) and directional arrows, make this by far the most *gaijin*-friendly form of transport. And while during rush hour (7.30–9am & 5.30–7.30pm) you may find yourself crushed between someone's armpit and another person's back, only rarely do the infamous white-gloved platform attendants shove commuters into carriages.

The lack of any signs in English makes the **bus system** a lot more challenging. However, once you've got a feel for the city, buses can be a good way of cutting across the few areas of Tokyo not served by a subway or train line and, as long as you have a map, fellow passengers should be able to help you get to where you want to be. For short, cross-town journeys, **taxis** are handy and, if shared by a group of people, not that expensive.

Once you've chosen the area you wish to explore, **walking** is the best way to get yourself from one sight to another, and you're almost guaranteed to see something interesting on the way. **Cycling**, if you stick to the quiet backstreets, can also be a good way of zipping around (see Listings, p.190, for rental places).

Given the excellent public transport facilities, the often appalling road traffic, the high cost of parking (if you're lucky enough to find a space) and Tokyo's confusing street layout, you'd need a very good reason to want to **rent a car** to get around the city, but we've listed some rental companies on p.190.

The subway

Its colourful map may look like a messy plate of noodles, but Tokyo's **subway** is relatively easy to negotiate. There are two systems, the nine-line **Tokyo Metro** (formerly known as the Eidan; @www.tokyometro.jp/e/top.html), and the four-line **Toei** (@www.kotsu.metro.tokyo.jp), run by the city authority, which also manages the buses and the tram line. The systems share some of the same stations, but unless you buy a special ticket from the vending machines that specifies your route from one system to the other, you cannot switch mid-journey between the two sets of lines without paying extra at the ticket barrier. Subways have connecting passageways to overland train lines, such as the Yamanote. See the back of the book for a colour **map** of the Tokyo subway system.

You'll generally pay for your **ticket** at the vending machines beside the electronic ticket gates – apart from major stations (marked with a triangle on the subway map), there are no ticket sales windows. If fazed by the wide range of price buttons you can choose from, buy the cheapest ticket and sort out the difference with the gatekeeper at the other end. You must always buy separate tickets for subways and overland trains, unless you're using an SF Metro or Pasunetto card (see opposite).

Trains run daily from around 5am to just after midnight, and during peak daytime hours as frequently as every five minutes. Leaving a station can be complicated by the number of exits (sixty in Shinjuku, for example), but there are maps close to the ticket barriers and on the platforms indicating where the exits emerge, and strips of yellow tiles on the floor mark the routes to the ticket barriers.

The cheapest subway ticket is ¥160 and, since most journeys across central Tokyo cost no more than ¥190, few of the **travel passes** on offer are good value for short-stay visitors. However, if you're going to be travelling around a lot, it makes sense to buy kaisūken, carnet-type tickets where you get eleven tickets for the price of ten – look for the special buttons on the automated ticket machines at the stations. Off-peak tickets give you twelve tickets for the price of ten, but can only be used 10am to 4pm weekdays, while Saturday/holiday tickets give you fourteen tickets for the price of ten. Handiest of all is the **SF Metro Card**, or **Pasunetto Card**, which saves you no money, but can be used on both Tokyo Metro and Toei subways and on all the private railways (but not JR) in the Tokyo area. As you go through a ticket barrier, the appropriate fare is deducted from the card's stored value (¥1000, ¥3000 or ¥5000); these cards can be bought from ticket offices and machines, and also used in machines to pay for tickets. If you're here for a month or more and will be travelling the same route most days, you might buy a *teiki* season ticket, which runs for one, three or six months, and covers your specified route and stations in between.

Trains

Spend any length of time in Tokyo and you'll become very familiar with the JR **Yamanote train line** that loops around the city centre (see p.99 for a summary of its route). Other useful JR train routes include the **Chūō line** (orange), which starts at Tokyo Station and runs west to Shinjuku and the suburbs beyond to terminate beside the mountains at Takao – the rapid services (look for the red *kanji* characters on the side of the train) miss out on some stations. The yellow **Sōbu line** goes from Chiba in the east to Mitaka in the west, and runs parallel to the Chūō line in the centre of Tokyo, doubling as a local service, stopping at all stations. The **Keihin Tōhoku line**, with blue trains, runs from Ōmiya in the north, through Tokyo Station, to Yokohama and beyond. It's fine to transfer between JR lines on the same ticket, but you must buy a new ticket if you transfer to a subway line.

As on the subway, **tickets** are bought from vending machines. The lowest fare on JR lines is ¥130. Like the subways, JR offers pre-paid cards and *kaisūken* (carnet) deals on tickets. One of the handiest is the **Suica**, a stored-value card similar to the SF Metro Card (see above) which is available from ticket machines in all JR stations.

Buses

Although Tokyo's **buses** are handy for crossing the few areas without convenient subway and train stations, only a small number of the buses or routes are labelled in English, so you'll have to get used to recognizing the *kanji* names of places or memorizing the numbers of useful bus routes. The final destination is on the front of the bus, along with the route number. You pay on entry, by dropping the flat rate of ¥200 into the fare box by the driver. There is a machine in the box for changing notes. A recorded voice announces the next stop in advance, as well as issuing constant warnings about not forgetting your belongings when you get off the bus. If you're not sure when your stop is, ask your fellow passengers. The Transport Bureau of Tokyo Metropolitan Government issues a useful English pamphlet and map of all the bus routes; pick one up from one of the tourist information centres (see p.98).

Ferries

The Tokyo Cruise Ship Company (www.suijobus.co.jp) runs several ferry services, known as *suijō basu* (water buses), in and around Tokyo Bay. The most popular is the double-decker service plying the 35-minute route between the Sumidagawa River Cruise stations at Asakusa, northeast of the city centre, and Hinode Sanbashi, on Tokyo Bay (daily every 40min until 6.15pm; ¥660). The large picture windows, which give a completely different view of the city from the one you'll get on the streets, are reason enough for hopping aboard, especially if you want to visit both Asakusa and the gardens at Hama Rikyū on the same day, and then walk into Ginza. The ferries stop at the gardens en route, and you can buy a combination ticket for the ferry and park entrance for around ¥720.

Hinode Sanbashi (close by Hinode Station on the Yurikamome monorail line or a ten-minute walk from Hamamatsuchō Station on the Yamanote line) is also the jumping-off point for several good daily **cruises** around Tokyo Bay and to various points around the island of Odaiba (see p.160; one way ¥500, return ¥900), or across to Kasai Rinkai-kōen (see p.162; one way ¥800, return ¥900) on the east side of the bay. In bad weather the ferries and cruises are best avoided, especially if you're prone to seasickness.

Taxis

For short hops around the centre of Tokyo, **taxis** are often the best option, though heavy traffic can slow them down. The basic rate is ¥660 for the first 2km, after which the meter racks up ¥80 every 274m, plus a time charge when the taxi is moving at less than 10km per hour. Between 11pm and 5am, rates are about twenty percent higher.

Tokyo accommodation

Akasaka Yōkō Hotel	Akasaka Yōkō Hoteru	赤坂陽光ホテル
Andon Ryokan	Andon Ryokan	行燈旅館
Arimax Hotel	Arimakkusu Hoteru	アリマックスホテル
Asakusa Central Hotel	Asakusa Sentoraru Hoteru	浅草セントラルホテル
Asakusa View Hotel	Asakusa Byū Hoteru	浅草ビューホテル
Asia Center of Japan	Hoteru Ajia Kaikan	ホテルアジア会館
Capsule Hotel Riverside	Kapuseru Hoteru Ribasaido	カプセルホテルリバーサイド
Capsule Land Shibuya	Kapuserurando Shibuya	カプセルランド渋谷
Central Hotel Shinjuku	Sentoraru Hoteru Shinjuku	セントラルホテル新宿
Hotel Century Southern Tower	Hoteru Senchurii Sazantawā	ホテルセンチュリーサザンタワー
Cerulean Tower Tōkyū Hotel	Serurian Tawā Tōkyū Hoteru	セルリアンタワー東急ホテル
Hotel Clarion	Hoteru Kurerion	ホテルクレリオン
Dai-ichi Inn Ikebukuro	Dai-ichi In Ikebukuro	第一イン池袋
Daimachi Bekkan	Daimachi Bekkan	大町別館
Hotel Excellent	Hoteru Ekuserento	ホテルエクセレント
Hotel Floracian	Hoteru Furorashion	ホテルフロラシオン
Fontaine Akasaka	Fontēnu Akasaka	フォンテーヌ赤坂
Four Seasons Hotel Tokyo at Marunouchi	Fuoru Shisonzu Tōkyō Maronouchi	フォルシソンズ東京丸の内
Ginza Tōbu Hotel	Ginza Tōbu Hoteru	銀座東武ホテル
Grand Hyatt Tokyo	Gurando Haiatto Tōkyō	グランドハイアット東京
Green Plaza Shinjuku	Guriin Puraza Shinjuku	グリインプラザ新宿
Hōmeikan Honkan	Hōmeikan Honkan	鳳名館本館
Hotel Ibis	Hoteru Aibisu	ホテルアイビス
Keihin Hotel	Keihin Hoteru	京浜ホテル
Kimi Ryokan	Kimi Ryokan	貴美旅館
Hotel Metropolitan	Hoteru Metoroporitan	ホテルメトロポリタン
New Kōyō	Nyū Kōyō	ニュー紅陽
New Ōtani	Nyū Ōtani	ニューオータニ
New Takanawa Prince Hotel	Shin Takanawa Purinsu Hoteru	新高輪プリンスホテル

Taxis can be flagged down on most roads – a red light next to the driver means the cab is free; green means it's occupied. There are designated stands in the busiest parts of town, but after the trains stop at night, be prepared for long queues, especially in areas such as Roppongi and Shinjuku. For more about taxis see p.44 in Basics.

Accommodation

Tokyo offers a wide range of **places to stay**, from first-class hotels to budget dormitory bunks. The main difficulty is finding somewhere affordable, since rates are governed more by square-footage than by quality of service. We've concentrated on hotels in the middle and lower price categories but also include here a representative sample at the higher end – for more extensive listings see *The Rough Guide to Tokyo*. At all levels, security and cleanliness are top-notch, and you'll nearly always find someone who speaks some English.

Hotel Nikkō Tokyo	*Hoteru Nikkō Tōkyō*	ホテル日光東京
Hotel Ōkura	*Hoteru Ōkura*	ホテルオークラ
Hotel Villa Fontaine Roppongi	*Hoteru Virā Fontēnu Roppongi*	ホテルヴィラフォンテーヌ六本木
Park Hotel Tokyo	*Pāku Hoteru Tōkyō*	パークホテル東京
Park Hyatt Tokyo	*Pāku Haiatto Tōkyō*	パークハイアット東京
Hotel Pine Hill	*Hoteru Pain Hiru*	ホテルパインヒル
Ryokan Katsutarō	*Ryokan Katsutarō*	旅館勝太郎
Ryokan Sansuisō	*Ryokan Sansuisō*	旅館山水荘
Ryokan Shigetsu	*Ryokan Shigetsu*	旅館指月
Sakura Hotel	*Sakura Hoteru*	サクラホテル
Sawanoya Ryokan	*Sawanoya Ryokan*	澤の屋旅館
Shibuya Tōbu Hotel	*Shibuya Tōbu Hoteru*	渋谷東武ホテル
Shibuya Business Hotel	*Shibuya Bijinesu Hoteru*	渋谷ビジネスホテル
Shibuya Excel Hotel Tōkyū	*Shibuya Ekuseru Hoteru Tōkyū*	渋谷エクセルホテル東急
Shinjuku Washington Hotel	*Shinjuku Washinton Hoteru*	新宿ワシントンホテル
Sofitel Tokyo	*Sofiteru Tōkyō*	ソフィテル東京
Suigetsu Hotel Ohgaisō	*Suigetsu Hoteru Ohgaisō*	水月ホテル鴎外荘
Taitō Ryokan	*Taitō Ryokan*	対十旅館
The Strings Hotel	*Za Sutoringusu Hoteru*	ザストリングスホテル
Tokyo Bay Ariake Washington Hotel	*Tōkyō Bei Ariake Washinton Hoteru*	東京ベイ有明ワシントンホテル
Tokyo International Youth Hostel	*Tōkyō Kokusai Yūsu Hosuteru*	東京国際ユースホステル
Tokyo Yoyogi Youth Hostel	*Tōkyō Yoyogi Yūsu Hosuteru*	東京代々木ユースホステル
Tōyoko Inn Shinagawa-eki Takanawaguchi	*Tōyoko In Shinagawa-eki Takanawaguchi*	東横イン品川駅高輪口
Hotel Watson	*Hoteru Watoson*	ホテルワトソン
Yaesu Terminal Hotel	*Yaesu Tāminaru Hoteru*	八重洲ターミナルホテル
YMCA Asia Youth Centre	*YMCA Ajia Yūsu Sentā*	ＹＭＣＡアジアユースセンター

Most **hotels** are Western-style and seriously lacking in character; you'll find better value and a more authentic atmosphere at the family-run **ryokan** and **minshuku** in Tokyo's less central districts. Moving down the scale, there's a clutch of cheap **hostels** catering largely to foreigners, while the relatively inexpensive **capsule hotels**, clustered around major train stations, are fun to try at least once. Otherwise, the only alternatives for budget travellers are Tokyo's two city-centre **youth hostels**, which have the usual proviso of a three-day maximum stay and an evening curfew. Wherever you stay, bear in mind that trains stop running around midnight; if you're a night animal, opt for somewhere within walking distance of one of the entertainment districts to avoid mounting taxi fares.

If you're staying in Tokyo for more than a week and need to keep costs down, you'll probably have to start looking at the so-called **gaijin houses**. These provide cheap, rented rooms for foreigners (*gaijin*) in a shared house or apartment, and usually operate on a weekly or monthly basis, though some offer daily rates. They are privately owned and not always legal; the best are often full and the worst are the stuff of nightmares. We suggest one or two of the more central and reliable ones below. For other long-term options, check the English press, particularly *Metropolis* (see p.98), or contact the Kimi Information Centre, 8F, Oscar Building, 2-42-3 Ikebukuro (☎03/3986-1604, ⓦwww.kimiwillbe.com), which runs a useful letting agency.

Whatever your budget, it's wise to **reserve** your first few nights' accommodation before arrival. This is especially true of the cheaper places, which tend to fill up quickly, particularly over national holidays and in late February, when thousands of students descend on Tokyo for the university entrance exams. If you do arrive without a reservation, head for Narita airport's tourist information desk, which handles hotel bookings (see "Arrival", p.96), or the Welcome Inn Reservation Centre (Mon–Fri 9.15–11.30am & 1–4.45pm; ☎03/3211-4201, ⓦwww.jnto.go.jp), at the Tokyo Tourist Information Centre (see p.97).

There are various additional **taxes** to look out for when paying for accommodation in Tokyo (as throughout the rest of the country). Top-end hotels levy a service charge of ten to fifteen percent, while if your room costs over ¥15,000 per night (including service charges), an extra three percent will be added. In addition, if your room costs over ¥10,000 per night, the Tokyo Metropolitan Government charges an additional ¥100 per night (or ¥200 per night if your room costs over ¥15,000).

Akasaka

The following hotels are marked on the map on p.124.

Akasaka Yōkō Hotel 6-14-12 Akasaka, Minato-ku ☎03/3586-4050, ⓦwww.yokohotel.co.jp. Pleasant mid-range hotel in a red-brick building with a smart marble lobby and simple rooms. Reasonable single rates for the area. Akasaka Station. ❺

Asia Centre of Japan 8-10-32 Akasaka, Minato-ku ☎03/3402-6111, ⓦwww.asiacenter.or.jp. Recently upgraded and a bargain for this area, so it fills up quickly. The small, neat rooms are Western style, and cheaper if you forgo en-suite bathrooms. Also has an inexpensive café and good single rates. Aoyama Itchōme or Nogizaka stations. ❸–❺

Fontaine Akasaka 4-3-5 Akasaka, Minato-ku ☎03/3583-6554. One of the more expensive capsule hotels, but a touch more respectable than most, and takes both men and women. Rates are ¥4800 (¥4500 for women) with check-in from 5pm. Akasaka-Mitsuke Station. ❷

New Ōtani 4-1 Kioichō, Chiyoda-ku ☎03/3265-1111, ⓦwww.newotanihotels.com. Mammoth hotel which is a tourist attraction in its own right (see p.125) for its traditional gardens. It also sports a staggering 36 restaurants and bars, a tea ceremony room, art gallery, swimming pools, tennis courts, and much more. Some rooms have been gaudily refurbished, but all are comfortable and most have great views. Akasaka Mitsuke Station. ⑦–⑧

Hotel Ōkura 2-10-4 Toranomon, Minato-ku
☎03/3582-0111, ⓦwww.hotelokura.co.jp/tokyo.
One of Tokyo's most prestigious hotels, with a

classic 1950s-style lobby with low chairs and garden view, although the room decor lags behind
that of Tokyo's top contemporary design-conscious
hotels. Kamiyachō Station. ⑦–⑧

Asakusa and around

The following hotels are marked on the map on p.129.

Andon Ryokan 2-34-10 Nihonzutsumi, Taitō-ku
☎03/3873-8611, ⓦwww.andon.co.jp. Tokyo's
first real designer ryokan, this is a special place.
The ultra-modern building, in a traditional area five
minutes' walk from Minowa Station, glows invit-
ingly like a lantern. The tatami rooms are small,
and all share common bathrooms, but come
equipped with DVD players, and there's also a
Jacuzzi spa you can book for private dips, free
Internet access and super-friendly English-speaking staff. Minowa Station. ④

Asakusa Central Hotel 1-5-3 Asakusa, Taitō-ku
☎03/3847-2222, ⓦwww.pelican.co.jp. Modest
business hotel that's a cut above the competition
for its convenient location on Asakusa's main
street, English-speaking staff and its small but
well-appointed rooms, all with TV and telephone.
Singles start at ¥7800. Asakusa Station. ⑤

Asakusa View Hotel 3-17-1 Nishi-Asakusa,
Taitō-ku ☎03/3847-1111,
ⓦwww.viewhotels.co.jp/asakusa. Asakusa's
grandest hotel, all sparkling marble and chandeliers. The rooms are more ordinary, but have great
views from the higher floors. There's a top-floor
bar, which also does a reasonable buffet lunch,
plus a shopping arcade and swimming pool (a
pricey ¥3000). Tawaramachi Station. ⑦

Capsule Hotel Riverside 2-20-4 Kaminarimon
☎03/3844-1155, ⓕ3841-6566. One of the
cheapest capsule deals in Tokyo. It's mainly for
men (there are just fifteen capsules for women on

a separate floor). Basic English spoken. Asakusa
Station. ②

New Kōyō 2-26-13 Nihonzutsumi, Taitō-ku
☎03/3873-0343, ⓦwww.newkoyo.com. This former day labourers' flop house is well off the beat-
en track but popular among budget travellers and
job-hunters for its ultra-cheap singles (¥2500; no
doubles). It's worth paying ¥200 extra for a four-
mat room, though even these are pretty cell-like.
There are reasonably clean communal baths, toilets and kitchen, plus coin laundry, Internet access
and bike rental. Minami-Senju Station.

Ryokan Shigetsu 1-31-11 Asakusa, Taitō-ku
☎03/3843-2345, ⓦwww.shigetsu.com. Just off
bustling Nakamise-dōri, this elegant ryokan is definitely the place to stay in Asakusa. Inside is a
world of kimono-clad receptionists and tinkling
shamisen music, but it's surprisingly affordable,
with a choice of small Western- or Japanese-style
rooms, all en suite. There's also a Japanese bath
on the top floor with views over temple roofs.
Asakusa Station. ⑤–⑥

Taitō Ryokan 2-1-4 Nishi-Asakusa ☎03/3843-
2822, ⓦwww.libertyhouse.gr.jp. This atmospheric,
if somewhat dilapidated, wooden ryokan is turning
into a quasi-*gaijin* house, thanks to its central
location, cheap prices (¥3000 per person) and
enthusiastic English-speaking owner. There are
only seven tatami rooms (none en suite), so you'll
need to book ahead. No smoking. Tawaramachi
Station. ③

Ginza and around

The following hotels are marked on the map on p.115.

Four Seasons Hotel Tokyo at Marunouchi
Pacific Century Place Marunouchi, 1-11-1
Marunouchi, Chiyoda-ku ☎03/5222-7222,
ⓦwww.fourseasons.com. Chic interior design and
a very handy location slap against Tokyo Station
are two pluses. But it's the little things – like asking when you'd like your room cleaned, giving you
a choice of newspaper or having free bikes on
hand – that make this intimate, 57-room hotel a
top choice. Tokyo Station. ⑨

Ginza Tōbu Hotel 6-14-10 Ginza ☎03/3546-
0111, ⓦwww.tobuhotel.co.jp/ginza. Top-of-the-
range business hotel which preserves a personal
touch. Rooms are a decent size, well-furnished

and reasonably priced, and there's a business
centre, bar and restaurants. Higashi-Ginza
Station. ⑥

Park Hotel Tokyo Shiodome Media Tower, 1-7-1
Higashi-Shinbashi, Minato-ku ☎03/6252-1111,
ⓦwww.parkhoteltokyo.com. Classy new place
with a soaring atrium and wow views on all sides.
The standard rooms are a little on the small size
but fairly priced for what you get. The lobby is on
the 25th floor; take the lifts to the right as you
enter the building. Shiodome Station. ⑦

Yaesu Terminal Hotel 1-5-14 Yaesu, Chūō-ku
☎03/3281-3771, ⓕ3281-3089. Welcoming business hotel offering good rates for such a central

location, though cheaper rooms are cramped. It's also situated in an appealing area, tucked among

lively backstreets just northeast of Tokyo Station. Nihombashi Station.

Ikebukuro

The following hotels are marked on the map on p.139.

Hotel Clarion 2-3-1 Ikebukuro, Toshima-ku ☏03/5396-0111, ⓦwww.clariontokyo.com. International-class hotel in a good location on the west side of Ikebukuro Station. It's well priced and has more character than its local rivals. Ikebukuro Station. ⓻

Dai-ichi Inn Ikebukuro 1-42-8 Higashi-Ikebukuro ☏03/3986-1221, ⓦwww.daiich-hotels.co.jp. This mid-range business hotel offers mainly single and twin rooms. Prices are reasonable, with a discount if you book online. Ikebukuro Station. ⓺

Kimi Ryokan 2-36-8 Ikebukuro, Toshima-ku ☏03/3971-3766, ⓦwww.kimi-ryokan.jp. With doubles from ¥6500 and singles at ¥4500, this is

a great-value institution on Tokyo's budget scene and a good place to meet fellow travellers – but you'll need to book well ahead. It's tricky to find, in the backstreets of west Ikebukuro. 1am curfew. Ikebukuro Station.

Hotel Metropolitan 1-6-1 Nishi-Ikebukuro, Toshima-ku ☏03/3980-1111, ⓦwww.itbc.co.jp/hotel. Also known as the *Crowne Plaza Metropolitan Tokyo*, Ikebukuro's plushest hotel has all the facilities you'd expect, including limousine bus connections to Narita Airport. The rooms are comfortable and well priced, and it's located on the more interesting west side of Ikebukuro. Ikebukuro Station. ⓻

Meguro, Shinagawa and Tokyo Bay

The following hotels are marked on the maps on p.92 & p.154.

Hotel Excellent 1-9-5 Ebisu-nishi, Shibuya-ku ☏03/5458-0087, ⓕ5458-8787. Standard business hotel – nothing flash, but reasonably priced for such a handy location. Singles go for ¥8700. Ebisu Station. ⓹

Keihin Hotel 4-10-20 Takanawa, Minato-ku ☏03/3449-5711, ⓦwww.keihin-hotel.co.jp. Small, old-fashioned hotel directly opposite the station. There are some Japanese-style rooms (starting at ¥12,000) which are good value if shared. Shinagawa Station. ⓹

New Takanawa Prince Hotel 3-13-1 Takanawa, Minato-ku ☏03/3442-1111, ⓦwww.princehotels .co.jp/english/index1.html. The best of the three Prince hotels in Shinagawa. The sedate lobby overlooks the elegant gardens created for Prince Takeda and there's a swimming pool in summer. Shinagawa Station. ⓼

Hotel Nikkō Tokyo 1-9-1 Daiba, Minato-ku ☏03/5500-5500, ⓦwww.hnt.co.jp. Modern works of art adorn the walls, and there are great views of the Rainbow Bridge and the city across Tokyo Bay. Rooms are spacious and have small balconies. Daiba Station. ⓼

Ryokan Sansuisō 2-9-5 Higashi-Gotanda, Shinagawa-ku ☏03/3441-7475, ⓕ3449-1944. Homely and spotless ryokan. Only a few of the tatami rooms have en-suite bath, and no meals are available. It's a five-minute walk from the station, near the Gotanda Bowling Centre. Good-value singles (from ¥4900). Gotanda Station. ⓸

The Strings Hotel Shinagawa East One Tower, 2-16-1 Konan, Minato-ku ☏03/4562-1111, ⓦwww.stringshotel.com. Super-smart hotel hidden away on the 26th floor upwards of one of Shinagawa's new brace of towers. The airy atrium lobby with its water, wood and stone combination evokes Japan, but in a thoroughly modern way. If you're not staying, afternoon tea (¥2500) at either of its restaurants is a good way to soak up the atmosphere. Shinagawa Station. ⓼

Tokyo Bay Ariake Washington Hotel 3-1 Ariake, Minato-ku ☏03/5564-0111, ⓦwww.ariake -wh.com. Best value for the Odaiba area, this upmarket chain hotel has decent-sized rooms. Also home to *Georgetown*, a good buffet restaurant and *ji-biru* bar. Kokusai-tenjijō Seimon Station. ⓺

Tōyoko Inn Shinagawa-eki Takanawaguchi 4-32-2 Takanawa ☏03/3280-1045, ⓦwww.toyoko -inn.co.jp. Handy branch of this bargain business hotel chain that doesn't stint on room features (including trouser press and LAN sockets for free Internet access). Rates include a continental breakfast and there are free Internet terminals in the lobby. Singles cost ¥7140. Shinagawa Station. ⓸

Hotel Watson 2-26-5 Kami-Ōsaki, Shinagawa-ku ☏03/3490-5566. Sleek business hotel with friendly English-speaking management and decent-sized rooms with TV and minibar. Meguro Station. ⓺

North of the Imperial Palace

The following hotels are marked on the map on p.120.

Hōmeikan Honkan and Daimachi Bekkan 5-10-5 Hongo, Bunkyo-ku ☎03/3811-1187, ⓦwww1.odn.ne.jp/homeikan. This elegant Meiji-era *Hōmeikan Honkan* is the only inn in the city that's a listed cultural property, but it's the sister establishment across the road, *Daimachi Bekkan*, that's the real looker, with its ancient carpentry and ryokan design. There are no en-suite bathrooms, but all rooms have tatami mats and some have window-cased balconies overlooking an exquisite Japanese garden. Singles start at around ¥7000. Kasuga Station ⑤

Sakura Hotel 2-21-4 Kanda-Jimbōchō ☎03/3261-3939, ⓦwww.sakura-hotel.co.jp. Cherry-pink building a couple of blocks south of Yasukuni-dōri. The rooms are boxy and all share common bathrooms, but they're spotless and good value for such a central location. Choose between singles (around ¥7000), bunk-bed twins (¥8400) and dormitory bunks (¥3800 per person). Also has a cheap café. Jimbōchō Station. ④

Tokyo International Youth Hostel 18F, Central Plaza Building, 1-1 Kagurazaka, Shinjuku-ku ☎03/3235-1107, ⓦwww.tokyo-yh.jp/eng/e_top.html. On a clear winter's day you can see Mount Fuji from this smart hostel above Iidabashi Station. Each bunk (¥3500 per night) has its own curtains and locker, and there are international phones, a members' kitchen and laundry facilities. Reception is open 3pm to 9.30pm and there's a 10.30pm curfew. Exit B2b from the subway brings you straight up into the lift lobby; alternatively, from the JR station's west exit, turn right into the Ramla Centre and keep straight ahead to find the lift. Iidabashi Station. ❷

YMCA Asia Youth Centre 2-5-5 Sarugakuchō, Chiyoda-ku ☎03/3233-0611, ✉ayc@ymca-japan.org/ayc/jp. Tucked away in the backstreets, and open to both men and women. The rooms, mostly single, are a bit worn and gloomy, but all come with bathroom and TV. Weekend rates start at around ¥5000 for a single, rising to ¥6300 on weekdays; there's a small discount for YMCA members. Suidōbashi Station. ④–❺

Roppongi

The following hotels are marked on the map on p.127.

Grand Hyatt Tokyo 6-10-3 Roppongi, Minato-ku ☎03/4333-1234, ⓦwww.grandhyatttokyo.com. The most glamorous of the clutch of recently opened swanky hotels in Tokyo. The standout design of the rooms uses wood and natural fabrics and the latest in technology, including flat-screen TVs. The Beckhams stayed here – the modern equivalent of an imperial endorsement. Roppongi Station. ❾

Hotel Ibis 7-4-4 Roppongi, Minato-ku ☎03/3403-4411, ⓦwww.ibis-hotel.com. A stone's throw from Roppongi crossing; the lobby is on the fifth floor, where there's also Internet access. The cheapest doubles are small but bright and have TV and fridge – one of the best deals in the area – and there are friendly English-speaking staff. Roppongi Station. ❺–❼

Hotel Villa Fontaine Roppongi 1-6-2 Roppongi, Minato-ku ☎03/3560-1110, ⓦwww.villa-fontaine.co.jp. Very stylish business hotel tucked into a corner of the Izumi Garden development directly above the subway station. The larger-than-average rooms are pleasantly decorated and have free LAN Internet connections; rates include a buffet breakfast. Roppongi-Itchome Station. ❻

Shibuya and Harajuku

The following hotels are marked on the map on p.152.

Arimax Hotel 11-15 Kamiyama-chō, Shibuya-ku ☎03/5454-1122, ⓦwww.arimaxhotelshibuya.co.jp. There's a classic European feel to this elegant boutique hotel a short walk from the action in Shibuya. English is spoken and it's all very professional. The suites come with their own cosy sauna. Shibuya Station. ❼

Capsule Land Shibuya 1-19-14 Dōgenzaka, Shibuya-ku ☎03/3464-1777, ⓦwww.capsule-land.com. Easy-to-find men-only capsule hotel at the top of the Dōgenzaka. Also has "semi-double" rooms for singles (including women) and couples, but they're very cramped. Shibuya Station. ❷

Cerulean Tower Tōkyū Hotel 26-1 Sakuragaoka-chō, Shibuya-ku ☎03/3476-3000, ⓦwww.ceruleantower-hotel.com. Stylish new addition to Tōkyū's clutch of hotels in this area. Some rooms have bathrooms with a glittering view of the city, and there's a pool and gym (free to guests on the executive floor, otherwise ¥2000), several restaurants, a jazz club plus a nō theatre in the basement. Shibuya Station. ❼–❽

Hotel Floracian 4-17-58 Minami-Aoyama, Minato-ku ⊤03/3403-1541, ⓦ www.floracian-aoyama.com. In a quiet residential area, with high-standard Western-style rooms and a convenient location, handy for the designer end of Omotesandō. Omotesandō Station. ❺

Shibuya Tōbu Hotel 3-1 Udagawachō, Shibuya-ku ⊤03/3476-0111, ⓦ www.tobuhotel.co.jp/shibuya. Pleasant chain hotel, well located near Shibuya's department stores, with friendly service and a good range of restaurants. Shibuya Station. ❻

Shibuya Business Hotel 1-12-5 Shibuya ⊤03/3409-9300, ⓕ 3409-9378. Apart from a capsule hotel, the cheapest deal you'll find in this pricey but happening part of town – meaning it often gets booked up. Set in a quiet location behind the post office. Singles are ¥8285. Shibuya Station. ❺

Shibuya Excel Hotel Tōkyū 1-12-2 Dōgenzaka, Shibuya-ku ⊤03/5457-0109, ⓦ www.tokyuho-tels.co.jp. High-tech fixtures and contemporary furnishings complement this new skyscraper hotel, atop the Shibuya Mark City complex. Better value than the nearby *Shibuya Tōkyū Inn*, and women get a floor to themselves. Shibuya Station. ❼

Shinjuku

The following hotels are marked on the map on p.142.

Central Hotel Shinjuku 3-34-7 Shinjuku, Shinjuku-ku ⊤03/3354-6611, ⓕ 3355-4245. The elegant lobby sets the tone at this classy boutique-style hotel, in an ultra-convenient location. Also has non-smoking rooms. Shinjuku Station. ❻

Hotel Century Southern Tower 2-2-1 Yoyogi, Shinjuku-ku ⊤03/5354-0111, ⓕ 5354-0100, ⓦ www.southerntower.co.jp. Part of the new Odakyū Southern Tower complex, this smart, stylish hotel has better-value room rates than many of its older rivals in Nishi-Shinjuku. They don't charge extra for broadband Internet access in their rooms. Shinjuku Station. ❼

Green Plaza Shinjuku 1-29-2 Kabukichō, Shinjuku-ku ⊤03/3207-4923. The lobby is on the fourth floor of this large men-only capsule hotel (has room for 660), with friendly staff and a good fitness and sauna area. The roof-top spa baths cost extra. Shinjuku Station. ❷

Park Hyatt Tokyo 3-7-1-2 Nishi-Shinjuku, Shinjuku-ku ⊤03/5322-1234, ⓦ www.parkhyatt-tokyo.com. The best of Nishi-Shinjuku's luxury hotels; the huge rooms and decor are the epitome of sophistication. The restaurants and spa, pool and fitness centre, all occupying the pinnacles of Tange Kenzō's tower, have breathtaking views on all sides. Tochō-mae Station. ❾

Shinjuku Washington Hotel 3-2-9 Nishi-Shinjuku, Shinjuku-ku ⊤03/3343-3111, ⓦ www.shinjuku-wh.com. Business hotel in the building with the port-hole windows. The lobby is on the third floor, where there are automated check-in machines (as well as humans) dishing out the electronic key cards for the compact, good-value rooms. You may also find yourself in the nearby Annex building. Tochō-mae Station. ❻

Tokyo Yoyogi Youth Hostel 3-1 Kamizonochō, Shibuya-ku ⊤03/3467-9163, ⓦ www.tokyo-yh.jp/eng. Comfortable, single rooms only at this modern hostel which is part of the Olympic Youth Centre, and in a complex of buildings at the top of the hill. Guests must be out between 9am and 4pm, and there's a vague 10pm curfew. Book well in advance. Sangūbashi Station. ❷

Ueno and around

The following hotels are marked on the map on p.133.

Hotel Pine Hill 2-3-4 Ueno, Taitō-ku ⊤03/3836-5111, ⓕ 3837-0080. Best value among the clutch of ordinary, mid-range business hotels in central Ueno. Rooms are small but adequate. Ueno-Hirokōji Station. ❻

Ryokan Katsutarō 4-16-8 Ikenohata, Taitō-ku ⊤03/3821-9808, ⓦ www.katsutaro.com. A good alternative if *Sawanoya* (see below) is full, handily located within walking distance of Ueno Park. It's a homely place with just seven slightly faded tatami rooms, some with bath, and laundry facilities. Nezu Station. ❹

Sawanoya Ryokan 2-3-11 Yanaka, Taitō-ku ⊤03/3822-2251, ⓦ www.sawanoya.com. Welcoming ryokan with good-value, traditional tatami rooms (around ¥5000 per person), all with washbasin, TV, telephone and air conditioning, though only two are en suite. The owner, Sawa-san, is something of a local character, and his son performs lion dances for guests. The surrounding streets are worth exploring and Ueno Park is within walking distance. Nezu Station. ❹

Sofitel Tokyo 2-1-48 Ikenohata, Taitō-ku ⊤03/5685-7111, ⓦ www.sofiteltokyo.com. Unmissable landmark tower – the one that looks like a kid's lego project – that's a darn sight more

attractive on the inside. Recently renovated rooms are all tastefully done out in sepia tones and there are some lovely views of the park. Yushima Station. **⑦**
Suigetsu Hotel Ohgaisō 3-3-21 Ikenohata, Taitō-ku ☎03/3822-4611, ⓦwww.ohgai.co.jp. One of

very few mid-range hotels with a Japanese atmosphere. Its three wings, containing a mix of Western and tatami rooms, are built around the Meiji-period house and traditional garden of novelist Mori Ōgai. Nezu Station. **④–⑤**

Central Tokyo

A vast chunk of **central Tokyo** is occupied by a swathe of green, at the core of which sits the **Imperial Palace**, inaccessible and wrapped round with moats and broad avenues. The surrounding public gardens, however, provide a gentle introduction to the city, with a glance back to its origins as a castle town. More recent history continues to stir debate at Yasukuni-jinja, north of the palace, where the nation's war dead are remembered at a solemn shrine.

East of the palace, the city really gets into its stride. The districts of **Yūrakuchō**, **Ginza** and **Nihombashi** may be lacking in aesthetic appeal, but they form the heart of downtown Tokyo, with the city's biggest concentration of department stores, theatres and cinemas, its financial centre and major train station, plus enough bars and restaurants to last a lifetime. The best approach is simply to wander, but there are several specific sights, notably a clutch of **art museums**, the **Tokyo International Forum**, with its soaring glass atrium, and the new skyscraper district of **Shiodome**.

North of the palace, **Kanda**'s historic shrines, the nearby bookshop district of **Jimbōchō** and the gardens of **Suidōbashi** won't be on anyone's must-see list, though they merit a quick look in passing. Neighbouring **Akihabara**, dubbed Tokyo's silicon city, is a much livelier place, crammed with cut-price electronic goodies, while from Akihabara it's a short hop east across the Sumida-gawa to **Ryōgoku**, the Mecca of sumo and home to the ultra-modern **Edo–Tokyo Museum**, which celebrates the city's history since the seventeenth century.

After a hard day's work, the bureaucrats and politicians from Kasumigaseki and Nagatachō head for **Akasaka**, the glitzy entertainment district south of the Imperial Palace, and home to many of Tokyo's luxury hotels, while a younger generation of Japanese and *gaijin* party down in **Roppongi**, to the west. The views from atop the Mori Tower at the heart of the phenomenally popular **Roppongi Hills** development take in **Tokyo Tower**, the area's retro landmark. Nearby **Zōjō-ji**, once the temple of the Tokugawa clan, has a long history, as does Akasaka's premier shrine **Hie-jinja**, with its attractive avenue of red *torii*.

The Imperial Palace and around

The natural place to start exploring Tokyo is the **Imperial Palace**, home to the emperor and his family, and the city's geographical and spiritual heart. Well hidden behind the old castle's massive stone ramparts and a wall of trees, the palace itself is off limits, but parts of its grounds have been hived off as public parks, providing a green lung for the city centre. Most attractive of these is **Higashi Gyoen**, site of the castle's main keep, while to its north, **Kitanomaru-kōen** has a mixed collection of museums and makes a pleasant approach to Japan's most controversial shrine, **Yasukuni-jinja**.

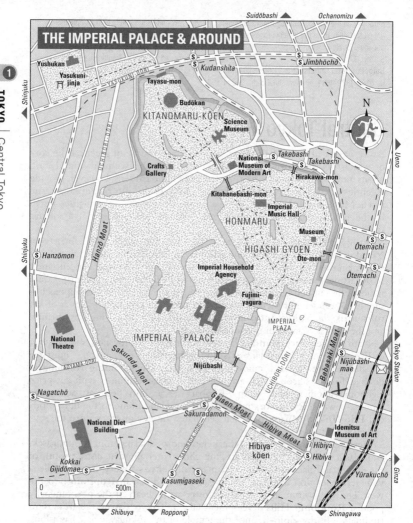

THE IMPERIAL PALACE & AROUND

The Imperial Plaza

Huge and windswept, the **Imperial Plaza** forms a protective island in front of
the modern royal palace. In earlier times the shogunate's most trusted followers
were allowed to build their mansions here, but after 1899 these were razed to
make way for today's austere expanse of spruce lawns and manicured pine trees.
The primary reason to follow the groups of local tourists straggling across the
broad avenues is to view one of the palace's most photogenic corners,
Nijūbashi, where two bridges span the moat and a jaunty little watchtower
perches on its grey stone pedestal beyond. Though this double bridge is a late
nineteenth-century embellishment, the tower dates back to the seventeenth century and is one of the castle's few original structures. The present palace is a long,
sleek, 1960s structure, built to replace the Meiji palace burnt down in the 1945

bombing raids. The imperial residences themselves are tucked away out of sight beyond another moat in the thickly wooded westernmost Fukiage Garden.

Twice a year (on December 23, the emperor's birthday, and on January 2) thousands of well-wishers file across Nijūbashi to greet the royal family, lined up behind bullet-proof glass, with a rousing cheer of *"Banzai"* ("May you live 10,000 years"). Apart from these two days, the general public is only admitted to the palace grounds on pre-arranged **official tours**, conducted in Japanese. The tours are a bit of a hassle to get on, but there is a certain fascination in taking a peek inside this secret world, and the pre-tour video shows tantalizing glimpses of vast function rooms and esoteric court rituals. Phone the Imperial Household Agency (☎03/3213-1111 ext 485; Mon–Fri 9am–4.30pm) several days in advance to make a reservation, then go to their office inside the palace grounds at least one day before the appointed day to collect a permit, taking along your passport. Tours take place twice daily on weekdays (10am & 1.30pm) and last about ninety minutes; there are no tours from July 21 to August 31.

Higashi Gyoen

The finest of Edo Castle's remaining watchtowers, three-tiered **Fujimi-yagura**, stands clear above the trees to the north of the Imperial Plaza. Built in 1659 to protect the main citadel's southern flank, these days it ornaments what is known as **Higashi Gyoen**, or the East Garden (daily except Mon & Fri 9am–4.30pm; also closed occasionally for court functions; free). Hemmed round with moats, the garden was opened to the public in 1968 to commemorate the completion of the new Imperial Palace. It's a good place for a stroll, though there's little to evoke the former glory of the shogunate's castle beyond several formidable gates and the towering granite walls.

Around the Imperial Palace, Ginza and Nihombashi		
Imperial Palace	*Kōkyo*	皇居
Higashi Gyoen	*Higashi Gyoen*	東御苑
Kitanomaru-kōen	*Kitanomaru-kōen*	北の丸公園
National Museum of Modern Art	*Kokuritsu Kindai Bijutsukan*	国立近代美術館
Yasukuni-jinja	*Yasukuni-jinja*	靖国神社
Hibiya	*Hibiya*	日比谷
Yūrakuchō	*Yūrakuchō*	有楽町
Marunouchi	*Marunouchi*	丸の内
Idemitsu Museum of Arts	*Idemitsu Bijutsukan*	出光美術館
Tokyo International Forum	*Tōkyō Kokusai Fōramu*	東京国際フォーラム
Ginza	*Ginza*	銀座
Bridgestone Museum of Art	*Burijisuton Bijutsukan*	ブリヂストン美術館
Kabuki-za	*Kabuki-za*	歌舞伎座
Kite Museum	*Tako no Hakubutsukan*	凧の博物館
Sony Building	*Sonii Biru*	ソニービル
Nihombashi	*Nihombashi*	日本橋
Mitsukoshi	*Mitsukoshi*	三越
Shiodome	*Shiodome*	汐留

Descendants of the Sun Goddess

Japan's **imperial family** is the world's longest reigning dynasty. According to traditionalists Emperor Akihito, the 125th incumbent of the Chrysanthemum Throne, traces his ancestry back to 660 BC and Emperor Jimmu, great-great-grandson of the Sun Goddess Amaterasu (see "Religion" p.949). Until the twentieth century, emperors were regarded as living deities whom ordinary folk were forbidden to set eyes on, or even hear. But on August 15, 1945, a stunned nation listened to the radio as Emperor Hirohito's quavering voice announced Japan's surrender to the allies, and a few months later he declared that emperors no longer held divine status.

Today the emperor is a symbolic figure, a head of state with no governmental power, and the family is gradually abandoning its cloistered existence. Emperor Akihito was the first to benefit: as crown prince, he had an American tutor and studied at Tokyo's elite Gakushūin University, followed by a stint at Oxford University. In 1959 he broke further with tradition by marrying a commoner he supposedly met on the tennis court. His children have continued the modernizing trend without denting the public's deep respect for the imperial family, though polls reveal a growing indifference, and the more radical papers are becoming bolder in their criticism – Akihito's daughter in law, Crown Princess Masako, has been the subject of unusually severe censure for impudently walking in front of her husband and for speaking too much at a press conference. Pretty tame stuff, but the feeling is that there's a power struggle going on behind the scenes, and that the royal wives are bearing the brunt of a conservative backlash against the, albeit very gentle, moves to modernize Japan's imperial institution.

All this has become more pertinent since December 2001, when Crown Princess Masako gave birth to a baby girl, Aiko. Despite current laws forbidding female succession, there's growing support for the move to make Princess Aiko heir to the Chrysanthemum Throne. And with reforming Prime Minister Koizumi himself in favour of such a change, it may just come to pass that Japan one day has an empress as its head of state.

The main gate to the garden – and formerly to Edo Castle itself – is **Ōtemon**; on entry you'll be given a numbered token to hand in again as you leave. The first building ahead on the right is a small **museum** (☎03/3213-1111, ⓦwww.kunaicho.go.jp; free), exhibiting a tiny fraction of the eight thousand artworks in the imperial collection, though it's still worth a quick look. Just beyond the museum is a shop where you can pick up a useful **map** of the garden (¥150).

From here a path winds gently up, beneath the walls of the main citadel, and then climbs more steeply towards **Shiomizaka**, the Tide-Viewing Slope, from where it was once possible to gaze out over Edo Bay rather than the concrete blocks of Ōtemachi. You emerge on a flat grassy area, empty apart from the stone foundations of **Honmaru** (the "inner citadel"), with fine views from the top, and a scattering of modern edifices, among them the bizarre, mosaic-clad **Imperial Music Hall**. Designed by Imai Kenji, the hall commemorates the sixtieth birthday of the (then) empress in 1963, and is used for occasional performances of court music.

Kitanomaru-kōen

The northern citadel of Edo Castle is now occupied by the park of **Kitanomaru-kōen**, home to a couple of interesting museums. The main one to head for, immediately to the right as you emerge from the Higashi Gyoen through the Kitahanebashi-mon gate, is the **National Museum of Modern Art** (Tues–Sun 10am–5pm, Fri until 8pm; ¥420; ☎03/5777-8600,

Ⓦ www.momat.go.jp), which reopened in 2002 following a ¥7.8 billion reno-
vation. The museum's excellent collection features Japanese works, including
Gyokudo Kawa's magnificent screen painting *Parting Spring* and works by
Kishida Ryusei and Fujita Tsuguharu, as well as foreign artists such as Picasso,
Juan Gris, Kandinsky and Francis Bacon. The renovation has also added a pleas-
ant café with a terrace overlooking the Imperial Palace.

A short walk away on the west side of Kitanomaru-kōen, the **Crafts Gallery**
(Tues–Sun 10am–5pm, Fri until 8pm; ¥420) exhibits a selection of top-quality traditional Japanese crafts, many of them by modern masters. Erected in
1910 as the headquarters of the Imperial Guards, this Neo-Gothic red-brick
pile is one of very few Tokyo buildings dating from before the Great
Earthquake of 1923.

Back beside the entrance to Kitanomaru-kōen, a white concrete latticework
building houses the **Science Museum** (daily 9.30am–4.50pm; ¥600;
Ⓣ 03/5777-8600, Ⓦ www.jsf.or.jp). Aimed at kids, it's often inundated with
school parties, but some of the interactive displays are great fun, and worth
exploring. Start on the fifth floor and work your way down, stopping to step
inside an Escher room, "listen" to the earth's magnetic field or get a bug's-eye
view of life.

The park's last major building is the **Budōkan** martial arts hall, built in 1964
to host Olympic judo events. The design, with its graceful, curving roof and
gold topknot, pays homage to a famous octagonal hall in Nara's Hōryū-ji temple, though the shape is also supposedly inspired by that of Mount Fuji. Today
the huge arena is used for sports meetings, graduation ceremonies and, most
famously, big-name rock concerts.

Yasukuni-jinja

Across the road from Kitanomaru-kōen an oversized, grey steel *torii*, claiming to
be Japan's tallest, marks the entrance to **Yasukuni-jinja**. This shrine, whose
name means "for the repose of the country", was founded in 1869 to worship
supporters of the emperor killed in the run-up to the Meiji Restoration. Since
then it has expanded to include the legions sacrificed in subsequent wars, in
total nearly 2.5 million souls, of whom some two million died in the Pacific War
alone; the parting words of kamikaze pilots (see p.861) were said to be "see you
at Yasukuni".

Not surprisingly, all sorts of tensions and protests revolve around Yasukuni-
jinja. To start with, its foundation was part of a Shinto revival promoting the
new emperor and so it became a natural focus for the increasingly aggressive
nationalism that ultimately took Japan to war in 1941. Then, in 1978, General
Tōjō and a number of other Class A war criminals were enshrined here, to
be honoured along with all the other military dead. Equally controversial are
the visits made to Yasukuni by cabinet ministers on the anniversary of Japan's
defeat (August 15) in World War II. Because Japan's postwar constitution
requires the separation of State and religion, ministers have usually maintained they attend as private individuals, but in 1985 Nakasone, in typically
uncompromising mood, caused an uproar when he signed the visitors' book
as "Prime Minister".

For many ordinary Japanese, Yasukuni is simply a place to remember family
and friends who died in the last, troubled century. Its surprisingly unassuming
Inner Shrine stands at the end of a long avenue lined with cherry and ginkgo
trees, and through a simple wooden gate. The architecture is classic Shinto
styling, solid and unadorned except for two gold imperial chrysanthemums
embossed on the main doors.

To the right of the Inner Shrine you'll find the fascinating **Yushukan** (daily: March–Oct 9am–5pm; Nov–Feb 9am–4.30pm; ¥800; ☎03/3261-8326, ⓦwww.yasukuni.or.jp), a military museum established in 1882 but recently fully renovated with the addition of a new gallery. Most exhibits consist of sad personal possessions: bloodstained uniforms, letters and faded photographs from conflicts stretching back to the Sino-Japanese war (see p.941) of 1894. The most disturbing displays concern the kamikaze pilots and other suicide squads active during the Pacific War. It's hard to miss them: the museum's central hall is dominated by a replica glider, its nose elongated to carry a 1200-kilo bomb, while a spine-chilling, black *kaiten* (manned torpedo) lours to one side.

As an antidote, take a walk through the little Japanese **garden** lying behind the shrine buildings. Just beyond, the sunken enclosure is the venue for a sumo tournament during the shrine's spring festival, when top wrestlers perform under trees laden with cherry blossom. It's also well worth visiting in early July during the shrine's lively summer *matsuri* when its precincts are illumated by thousands of paper lanterns and there's nightly dancing, parades and music.

East of the Imperial Palace

Walk east from the Imperial Palace, across Babasaki Moat, and you're plunged straight into the hurly-burly of **downtown Tokyo**, among grey-faced office blocks, swanky department stores and streets full of rush-hour crowds, transformed at dusk into neon-lit canyons. It's a compact district, with no dramatic sights, but one where you can happily spend an hour exploring a single high-rise stacked with boutiques and cafés, or rummaging in the backstreets. Even the most anonymous building can yield a speciality store or avant-garde gallery, while some wonderfully atmospheric eating and drinking places lurk under the train tracks that split the area from north to south.

West of the tracks, **Yūrakuchō**, **Marunouchi** and **Hibiya** are theatre-land, and also where you'll find lots of airline offices, major banks and corporate headquarters – Marunouchi is enjoying something of a revival with the recent opening of the 36-storey Marunouchi Building. From here it's a short walk east into **Ginza**, home to some of Tokyo's most exclusive shops and restaurants. Ginza spills northwards along Chūō-dōri, merging with the high-finance district of **Nihombashi**, once the heart of boisterous, low-town Edo but now the preserve of blue-suited bankers. On Ginza's southern flank is the new suburb of **Shiodome**, where a brace of sparkling skyscrapers house hotels, restaurants, and a few tourist sights.

Yūrakuchō, Marunouchi and Hibiya

Within the first few days of arriving in Tokyo most people find themselves at the JR Station in **Yūrakuchō**, heading for the nearby TIC (see p.98). Once you've done there, head over to the nearby **Tokyo International Forum** (ⓦwww.t-i-forum.co.jp), the stunning creation of American architect Raphael Viñoly: the boat-shaped main hall is a sixty-metre-high atrium sheathed in 2600 sheets of "earthquake-resistant" glass, with a ceiling ribbed like a ship's hull – it looks magical at night. The forum hosts concerts and conventions, plus the Oedo Antique Fair (third Sunday of the month, except Nov).

Immediately north of here the business-focused Marunouchi district is currently being given a makeover to make it more attractive to pedestrians and shoppers; check out the street sculptures and new shops along Marunouchi Naka-dōri as you stroll towards the glass tower of the **Marunouchi Building**

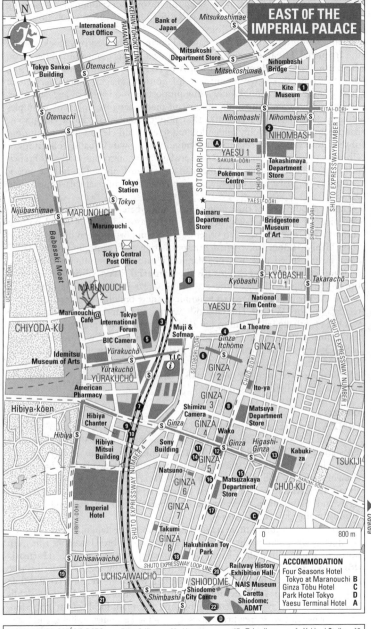

EAST OF THE
IMPERIAL PALACE

▲ Ueno   TCAT & Asakusa ▲

TOKYO | Central Tokyo

1

International Post Office ✉
Tokyo Sankei Building
Ōtemachi
S Ōtemachi
S

Bank of Japan
Mitsukoshimae S
Mitsukoshi Department Store S
Mitsukoshimae

Nihombashi Bridge
Kite Museum ➊

Nihombashi   Nihombashi ➋   NIHOMBASHI
Maruzen
A YAESU 1
SAKURA-DŌRI
Pokémon Centre
Takashimaya Department Store
EITAI-DŌRI

Imperial Palace ▲
Nijūbashimae ▲
MARUNOUCHI
Tokyo S Tokyo
Tokyo Station

Babasaki Moat
UCHIBORI-DŌRI
Marunouchi ↑

Tokyo Central Post Office ✉
MARUNOUCHI 2

Daimaru Department Store
Bridgestone Museum of Art

B

S KYŌBASHI
Kyōbashi   Takarachō
YAESU 2

National Film Centre

CHIYODA-KU
Marunouchi @ Café
Tokyo International Forum
BIC Camera
Idemitsu Museum of Arts
Yūrakuchō
Muji & Sofmap ➌
Le Theatre ➍
GINZA 1
➎
Ginza Itchōme
➏
GINZA 2
Ito-ya

T.I.C. ℹ
American Pharmacy
Yūrakuchō
YŪRAKUCHŌ
➐

GINZA 3 ➑
Shimizu Camera
Matsuya Department Store

Hibiya-kōen
Hibiya Chanter ➒
Hibiya S
Hibiya Mitsui Building
➓
Ginza GINZA 4
Wako
Ginza
Higashi-Ginza
Kabuki-za ⓭
TSUKIJI

Sony Building
⓫ ⓬
GINZA 5
⓮
Natsuno
⓰
GINZA 6
Matsuzakaya Department Store ⓯
CHŪŌ-KU
HARUMI-DŌRI

Imperial Hotel
GINZA 7
⓱

Takumi
GINZA 8
Hakuhinkan Toy Park
⓲

S Uchisaiwaichō
⓳
UCHISAIWAICHŌ
Railway History Exhibition Hall
⓴
SHIODOME
NAIS Museum
Caretta Shiodome; ADMT
C

⓴ ㉑
Shimbashi S
Shiodome City Centre
㉒

▲ Odaiba

SHUTO EXPRESSWAY NUMBER 1
SHUTO EXPRESSWAY NUMBER 2
SHUTO EXPRESSWAY LOOP LINE
KEIHIN-TŌHOKU LINE
YAMANOTE LINE
SOTOBORI-DŌRI
CHŪŌ-DŌRI
SHOWA-DŌRI
YAESU-DŌRI
HIBIYA-DŌRI

0   800 m

ACCOMMODATION
Four Seasons Hotel
 Tokyo at Maranouchi   **B**
Ginza Tōbu Hotel   **C**
Park Hotel Tokyo   **D**
Yaesu Terminal Hotel   **A**

RESTAURANTS, CAFÉS & BARS					
300 Bar	**15**	Farm Grill	**20**	Lion	
Afternoon Tea		Cha Ginza	**14**	G-Zone	**4**	Nair's	
Baker and Diner	**6**	Daidaiya	**18**	Kagaya	**21**	Nataraj	**16**
Aroyna Tabeta	**3**	En	**22**	Le Doutor Café		Robata Honten	**9**
				Expresso	**12**	Shin Hi No Moto	**7**

Taimeiken	**17**	Yakitori Stalls	**10**
Takara	**13**	Yamamotoyama	**2**
Tenmaru	**16**		
Torigin Honten	**11**		
Town Cryer	**19**		

D

115

(Ⓦwww.marubiru.jp), the area's latest multistorey development, combining offices and all manner of restaurants and cafés. There are great views from here of the handsome entrance to Tokyo Station.

From the south exit of the International Forum, head west two blocks to find the **Imperial Theatre**, which hosts big-budget Western musicals. Above it, on the ninth floor, the **Idemitsu Museum of Arts** (Tues–Sun 10am–5pm; ¥800; Ⓣ03/5777-8600, Ⓦwww.idemitsu.co.jp) houses a magnificent collection of mostly Japanese art, though only a tiny proportion is on show at any one time. This includes many historically important pieces, ranging from fine examples of early Jōmon (10,000 BC–300 BC) pottery to Zen Buddhist calligraphy, hand-painted scrolls, richly gilded folding screens and elegant *ukiyo-e* paintings of the late seventeenth century. The museum also owns valuable collections of Chinese and Korean ceramics, as well as slightly incongruous works by French painter Georges Rouault and American artist Sam Francis. The lounge area is a comfortable place for a break, with views over the Imperial Palace moats and gardens.

The area southwest of the museum (and immediately south of the castle) was occupied by the Tokugawa shogunate's less-favoured *daimyō*. The land was cleared after 1868, but was too waterlogged to support modern buildings, so in 1903 **Hibiya-kōen**, Tokyo's first European-style park, came into being. These days the tree-filled park is a popular lunchtime spot for office workers and courting couples. Across the road is the **Imperial**, Tokyo's first Western-style **hotel**. On August 31, 1923, the eve of the Great Earthquake, the hotel celebrated the formal opening of its magnificent new building by American architect Frank Lloyd Wright. This famously withstood both the earthquake and the war but eventually fell victim to the 1960s property development boom. Today, just a hint of Wright's style exists in the *Old Imperial Bar*, with some old tiles and furniture; the original facade and main lobby have been reconstructed in Meiji Mura, near Nagoya (see p.479).

Walk from here onto the main road, Harumi-dōri, and you're immediately into the bright lights of Ginza.

Ginza

GINZA, the "place where silver is minted", took its name after Shogun Tokugawa Ieyasu started making coins here in the early 1600s. It was a happy association – Ginza's Chūō-dōri grew to become Tokyo's most stylish shopping street. Though some of its shine has faded and cutting-edge fashion has moved elsewhere, Ginza still retains much of its elegance and its undoubted snob appeal. Here you'll find the greatest concentration of exclusive shops, art galleries and restaurants in the city, the most theatres and cinemas, and branches of most major department stores.

Ginza is packed into a mere half-square-kilometre rectangular grid of streets completely enclosed by the Shuto expressway. Three broad avenues run from north to south, Chūō-dōri being the main shopping street, while **Harumi-dōri** cuts across the centre from the east. This unusually regular pattern is due to British architect Thomas Waters, whose task was to create a less combustible city after a fire in 1872 destroyed virtually all of old, wooden Ginza. His "Bricktown", as it was soon known, became an instant local tourist attraction, with its rows of two-storey brick houses, tree-lined avenues, gaslights and brick pavements. But since the airless buildings were totally unsuited to Tokyo's hot, humid climate, people were reluctant to settle until the government offered peppercorn rents. Most of the first businesses here dealt in foreign wares, and in no time Ginza had become the centre of all that was modern, Western and therefore fashionable – Western dress and hairstyles, watches, cafés and beer halls. Bricktown itself didn't survive the Great Earthquake, but Ginza's status was by then well established. The height of sophistication in the 1930s was simply to stroll around Ginza, and the practice still continues, particularly on Sunday afternoons, when Chūō-dōri is closed to traffic and everyone turns out for a spot of window-shopping.

In the west, Ginza proper begins at the Sukiyabashi crossing, where Sotobori-dōri and Harumi-dōri intersect. The **Sony Building** (daily 11am–7pm; free; ☎03/3573-2371, ⓦ www.sonybuilding.jp), occupying the crossing's southeast corner, is a must for techno-freaks, with six of its eleven storeys showcasing the latest Sony gadgets. Continuing east along Harumi-dōri, you'll reach the intersection with Chūō-dōri known as **Ginza Yon-chōme crossing**, which marks the heart of Ginza. Awesome at rush hour, this spot often features in films and documentaries as the epitome of this overcrowded yet totally efficient city. A number of venerable emporia cluster round the junction. **Wakō**, now an exclusive department store, started life roughly a century ago as the stall of a young, enterprising watchmaker who developed a line called Seikō (meaning "precision"); its clock tower, built in 1894, is one of Ginza's most enduring landmarks. Immediately north of Wakō on Chūō-dōri, **Kimuraya bakery** was founded in 1874, while **Mikimoto Pearl** opened next door a couple of decades later. South of the crossing, just beyond the cylindrical, glass San'ai Building, **Kyūkyodō** has been selling traditional paper, calligraphy brushes and inkstones since 1800, and is filled with the dusty smell of *sumi-e* ink.

Heading on east down Harumi-dōri, **Kabuki-za** has been the city's principal Kabuki theatre since its inauguration in 1889. Up until then Kabuki had belonged firmly to the lowbrow world of Edo's Shitamachi, but under Meiji it was cleaned up and relocated to this more respectable district. The original, European-style Kabuki-za made way in 1925 for a Japanese design, of which the present building is a 1950s replica. See p.184 for details of performances.

Shiodome

Following the railway tracks south from Ginza you'll reach the new commercial centre of **Shiodome**, a clutch of ultra-modern skyscrapers built on the site of Japan Railways' old freight terminal. The towers that have opened are already home to some of Japan's top companies, including ad agency Dentsu, Nippon TV and Kyodo News, and it's estimated that by 2005 some 60,000 people will be living and working here. Shiodome has less of an integrated and pedestrian-friendly feel than the rival mega-development of Roppongi Hills (see p.126) – the way the development fits into the existing streets and the connections between and around the various buildings are poorly thought out, creating a slightly alienating concrete environment with none of the softening landscaping and street art that make Roppongi Hills so successful in comparison. There are a few attractions worth checking out, however, as well as many restaurants and four major hotels. The most interesting sight is the high-tech Advertising Museum Tokyo, or **ADMT** (Tues–Fri 11am–6.30pm, Sat 11am–4.30pm; free; ☎03/6218-2500, ⓦ www.admt.jp), which can be found on the B1 and B2 floors of **Caretta Shiodome** skyscraper, the sleek headquarters of the Dentsu ad agency. In the small permanent exhibition a montage of ads provides a fascinating flick through some of the twentieth century's most arresting commercial images, and it's fun to watch videos of past TV commercials; you can also peruse some 100,000 images on Dentsu's computerized database. Afterwards, zip up to the top of the Caretta Shiodome building in the glass-fronted elevators to the restaurants on the 46th and 47th floors for a free panoramic view across Tokyo Bay and the nearby Hama Rikyū Teien traditional garden (p.159).

Immediately west of Caretta Shiodome (and linked to it by a pedestrian deck) is Shiodome's second major tower complex, **Shiodome City Centre**. Back in 1872, this was the site of the original Shimbashi Station, the terminus of Japan's first railway line. A faithful reproduction of the station building, designed by American architect R.P. Bridgens, now rests incongruously at the foot of the tower and contains the passably interesting **Railway History Exhibition Hall** (Tues–Sun 11am–6pm; free; ☎303/3572-1872, ⓦwww.ejrcf.or.jp), as well as the fancy *Grand Café Shimbashi Mikuni*. Part of the foundations of the original building, uncovered during excavations on the site, have been preserved, and you can also see some fascinating woodblock prints and old photographs of how the area once looked.

Of more minor interest is the **NAIS Museum** (Tues–Sun 10am–5.30pm; ¥500; ☎03/6218-0078, ⓦwww.shiodome.nais.jp), a small gallery with changing exhibitions alongside a permanent display on the French religious artist Georges Rouault. It's housed in the showroom of **Matsushita Electric Works**, where you can also see the latest in kitchen and bathroom technology, including the newest hi-tech electronic toilets.

From Shiodome you can also pick up the monorail to **Odaiba** (p.160).

Nihombashi and around

North of Ginza, on the northern fringes of central Tokyo, **Nihombashi** (Bridge of Japan) grew from a cluster of riverside markets in the early seventeenth century to become the city's chief financial district. Once the heart of Edo's teeming Shitamachi (see p.94), the earlier warehouses and moneylenders have evolved into the banks, brokers and trading companies that line the streets today.

Since 1603, the centre of Nihombashi, and effectively of all Japan, was an arched red lacquer-coated **bridge** – a favourite of *ukiyo-e* artists – which marked the start of the Tōkaidō, the great road running between Edo and Kyoto. The original wooden structure has long gone, but distances from Tokyo are still measured from a bronze marker at the halfway point of the present stone bridge, erected in 1911. Although it's now smothered by the Shuto Expressway, it's still worth swinging by here to see the fabulous bronze statues of dragons and wrought-iron lamps that decorate the bridge.

A little further north on Chūō-dōri is the most traditional of Japan's department stores, **Mitsukoshi**. The shop traces its ancestry back to a dry-goods store opened in 1673 by Mitsui Takatoshi, who revolutionized retailing in Edo and went on to found the Mitsui empire. This was the first store in Japan to offer a delivery service, the first to sell imported goods, and the first with an escalator, though until 1923 customers were still required to take off their shoes and don Mitsukoshi slippers. The most interesting part of today's store is the north building, which dates from 1914 and whose main atrium is dominated by a weird and wonderful statue, carved from 500-year-old Japanese cypress, of Magokoro, the Goddess of Sincerity.

Crossing Nihombashi and heading south along Chūō-dōri, duck immediately to the left into the side streets to locate the cluttered little **Kite Museum** (Mon–Sat 11am–5pm; ¥200; ☎03/3275-2704, ⓦwww.tako.gr.jp/eng/index_e.html); there's no English sign, but it's on the fifth floor above *Taimeiken* restaurant. Since 1977 the restaurant's former owner has amassed over four hundred kites of every conceivable shape and size, from no bigger than a postage stamp to a monster 8m square.

Returning to Chūō-dōri, a row of cheerful red awnings on the left-hand side announces another of Tokyo's grand old stores, **Takashimaya**, which dates back to a seventeenth-century kimono shop and is worth popping into for its fabulous old-fashioned lifts. Across the street, **Maruzen** bookstore is a relative upstart, founded in 1869 to import Western texts as part of Japan's drive to modernize and still a good source of foreign-language books.

Further south on Chūō-dōri, across Yaesū-dōri, is the **Bridgestone Museum of Art** (Tues–Sun 10am–6pm; entrance from Yaesu-dōri; ¥700; ℡03/3563-0241, ⓦwww.bridgestone-museum.gr.jp). This superb collection focuses on the Impressionists and continues through all the great names of early twentieth-century European art, plus a highly rated sampler of Meiji-era, Japanese paintings in Western style. It's not an extensive display, but offers a rare opportunity to enjoy works by artists such as Renoir, Picasso and Van Gogh in an (often) almost deserted gallery.

In front of the museum, Yaesu-dōri heads west towards Daimaru department store and the east entrance to **Tokyo Station**, known as the Yaesu entrance. Here you'll find the main entrance to the Shinkansen tracks, as well as the desk for exchanging Japan Rail Passes, the Express Bus ticket office and left-luggage room. Limousine buses for Narita and Haneda airports stop across the road outside Daiwa Bank.

North of the Imperial Palace

Kanda, the region immediately north and west of Nihombashi, straddles Tokyo's crowded eastern lowlands – the former Shitamachi – and the more expansive western hills. The area's scattered sights reflect these contrasting styles, kicking off at **Ochanomizu** with historic Kanda Myōjin, a lively Shinto shrine, and an austere monument to Confucius at Yushima Seidō. Below them lie the frenetic, neon-lit streets of **Akihabara**, the "Electric City", dedicated to technological wizardry. Akihabara is also the jumping-off point for **Ryōgoku**, over on the east bank of the Sumida-gawa, which is the heartland of sumo and home to one of the city's most enjoyable museums. Heading back westwards, **Suidōbashi** has a couple of minor attractions in the form of Tokyo's foremost baseball stadium and a classic seventeenth-century garden, while a studious hush prevails among the secondhand bookshops of **Jimbōchō**, just to the south.

North of the Imperial Palace		
Akihabara	*Akihabara*	秋葉原
Edo–Tokyo Museum	*Edo–Tōkyō Hakubutsukan*	江戸東京博物館
Jimbōchō	*Jimbōchō*	神保町
Kanda	*Kanda*	神田
Kanda Myōjin	*Kanda Myōjin*	神田明神
Koishikawa-Kōrakuen	*Koishikawa-Kōrakuen*	小石川後楽園
National Sumo Stadium	*Kokugikan*	国技館
Nikolai Cathedral	*Nikorai-dō*	ニコライ堂
Ochanomizu	*Ochanomizu*	御茶ノ水
Ryōgoku	*Ryōgoku*	両国
Suidōbashi	*Suidōbashi*	水道橋
Tokyo Dome	*Tōkyō Dōmu*	東京ドーム
Yushima Seidō	*Yushima Seidō*	湯島聖堂

▲ *National Sumo Museum (see inset)*

NORTH OF THE IMPERIAL PALACE

▲ A & B

RESTAURANTS, CAFES & BARS
Tomoegata 2
Yabu Soba 1

ACCOMMODATION
Daimachi Bekkan B
Homeikan Honkan A
Sakura E
Tokyo International Youth Hostel C
YMCA Asia Youth Centre D

Koishikawa Kōrakuen

Tokyo Dome

LaQua Amusement Park

KASUGA-DORI

Ⓢ Hongo-Sanchome

Ⓢ Yushima

Naka-Okachimachi Ⓢ

SHOWA-DORI

SOBU LINE

Ⓢ Akihabara

Akihabara

YAMANOTE LINE

Ⓢ Suehirochō

CHUO-DORI

Kanda Myōjin ⛩

Yushima Seidō ⛩

Ⓢ Ochanomizu

Laox

Radio Depāto

Transportation Museum

Ⓢ Awajichō

Kanda Ⓢ

Kanda

CHUO-DORI

SOTOBORI-DORI

Nikolai Cathedral ⛩

Ⓢ Ogawamachi

HONGO-DORI

YASUKUNI-DORI

Kodemmachō Ⓢ

SHOWA-DORI

Kanda-gawa

HONGO-DORI

SOTOBORI-DORI

Ⓢ Suidōbashi

Suidōbashi

D

HAKUSAN-DORI

Sanseido

Ⓢ Jimbōchō

Kitazawa E

YASUKUNI-DORI

SHUTO EXPRESSWAY 5

Japan Youth Hostels H.Q.

Ⓢ Kudanshita

Ⓢ Iidabashi

500 m
0

CHUO LINE

C

N

RYŌGOKU

Asakusabashi

Sumida-gawa

SHUTO EXPRESSWAY 6

National Sumo Stadium

Edo-Tokyo Museum

Ⓢ Ryōgoku

2

Ochanomizu to Akihabara

Kanda's two great shrines lie on the north bank of the Kanda-gawa river and are within easy reach of either **Ochanomizu**'s JR or Marunouchi line stations. If you're here in the afternoon, take a quick detour south along Hongō-dōri, to visit the Russian Orthodox **Nikolai Cathedral** (Tues–Fri 1–3pm; free). It's not a large building but its Byzantine flourishes stand out well against the surrounding characterless blocks and the refurbished altarpiece positively glows in the soft light. Founded by Archbishop Nikolai Kasatkin, who came to Japan in 1861 as chaplain to the Russian consulate in Hokkaidō, the cathedral took seven years to complete (1884–91); the plans were sent from Russia but the British architect Josiah Conder supervised the project and gets most of the credit.

Back at the river, some woods on the north bank hide the distinctive shrine of **Yushima Seidō** (daily 9.30am–5pm, Nov–April until 4pm; free), dedicated to the Chinese sage Confucius. The Seidō (Sacred Hall) was founded in 1632 as an academy for the study of the ancient classics at a time when the Tokugawa were promoting Confucianism as the State's ethical foundation. In 1691 the hall was moved to its present location, where it became an elite school for the sons of samurai and high-ranking officials, though most of these buildings were lost in the fires of 1923. Today, the quiet compound contains an eighteenth-century wooden gate and, at the top of broad steps, the Taisen-den, or "Hall of Accomplishments", where the shrine to Confucius is located. This imposing, black-lacquered building was rebuilt in 1935 to the original design; look up to see four panther-like guardians poised on the roof tiles.

Follow the road round to the north of Yushima Seidō to find a large copper *torii* and a traditional wooden shop, Amanoya, selling sweet, ginger-laced sake (*amazaké*). Beyond, a vermilion gate marks the entrance to **Kanda Myōjin** (9am–4.30pm; free), one of the city's oldest shrines and host to one of its top three festivals, the **Kanda Matsuri**, which takes place in mid-May every odd-numbered year (see p.183). Founded in 730 AD, the shrine originally stood in front of Edo Castle, where it was dedicated to the gods of farming and fishing (Daikoku and Ebisu). Later, the tenth-century rebel Taira no Masakado – who was beheaded after declaring himself emperor – was also enshrined here; according to legend, his head "flew" to Edo, where he was honoured as something of a local hero. When Shogun Tokugawa Ieyasu was strengthening the castle's fortifications in 1616, he took the opportunity to move the shrine, but mollified Masakado's supporters by declaring him a guardian deity of the city.

Some 500m southeast of Kanda Myōjin, following Yushima-zaka as it drops steeply downhill, a blaze of adverts and a cacophony of competing audio systems announce **Akihabara**. This is Tokyo's foremost discount shopping area for electrical and electronic goods of all kinds, from computers and DVDs to mobile phones and "washlets" – electronically controlled toilet-cum-bidets with an optional medical analysis function. Today's high-tech stores are direct descendants of a postwar black market in radios and radio parts that took place beneath the train tracks around Akihabara Station. You can recapture some of the atmosphere in the narrow passages under the tracks just west of the station, or among the tiny stalls of **Tokyo Radio Depāto** – four floors stuffed with plugs, wires, boards and tools for making or repairing radios; follow the Sōbu line tracks west from Akihabara Station to find the store just off Chūō-dōri.

Ryōgoku

From Akihabara, hop on a Sōbu-line train two stops west across the Sumida-gawa to **Ryōgoku**, a sort of sumo town where shops selling outsize clothes and restaurants serve flavourful tureens of *chanko-nabe*, the wrestlers' traditional body-building stew. Three times each year major sumo tournaments fill the **National Sumo Stadium**, outside Ryōgoku Station's west exit, with a two-week pageant of thigh-slapping, foot-stamping and arcane ritual (see p.76 for more on sumo). The one-room historical **museum** (Mon–Fri 10am–4.30pm; closed during tournaments; free) beside the stadium is one for die-hard fans only; better to simply wander the streets immediately south of the train tracks. Until recently, this area housed many of the major "stables" where wrestlers lived and trained, but rising land prices have forced most of them out. Nevertheless, there's still a good chance of bumping into some junior wrestlers, in their *yukata* and wooden *geta* with slicked-back hair, popping out to a store or for a quick snack of *chanko-nabe*. If you're feeling peckish yourself, one of the best places to sample this traditional sumo hotpot packed with tofu and vegetables is *Tomoegata* restaurant (see p.169 for details).

You'll need plenty of stamina for the next stop, the **Edo-Tokyo Museum** (Tues–Sun 9.30am–5.30pm; Thurs & Fri open until 8pm; ¥600; ☎03/3626 9974, ⓦwww.edo-tokyo-museum.or.jp), housed in a colossal building behind the Sumo Stadium; the ticket lasts a whole day, so you can come and go. The museum tells the history of Tokyo from the days of the Tokugawa shogunate to postwar reconstruction, using life-size replicas, models and holograms, as well as more conventional screen paintings, ancient maps and documents, with plenty of information in English. The museum starts on the sixth floor, where a bridge (a replica of the original Nihombashi; see p.118) takes you over the roofs of famous Edo landmarks – a Kabuki theatre, *daimyō* residence and Western-style office – on the main exhibition floor below. The displays then run roughly chronologically; they are particularly strong on life in Edo's Shitamachi, with its pleasure quarters, festivals and vibrant popular culture, and on the giddy days after 1868, when Japan opened up to the outside world.

Suidōbashi

Take the Sōbu line back into central Tokyo, past Akihabara to **Suidōbashi**, where the stadium and thrill rides of **Tokyo Dome City** (ⓦwww.tokyo-dome.co.jp) punctuate the skyline. The centrepiece is the plump, white-roofed **Tokyo Dome**, popularly known as the "Big Egg", Tokyo's major baseball venue and home ground of the Yomiuri Giants (see p.191). The Dome's **Baseball Hall of Fame and Museum** (March–Sept Tues–Sun 10am–6pm; Oct–April open until 5pm; ¥400; ⓦwww.baseball-museum.or.jp) is for die-hard fans only, who'll appreciate the footage of early games and all sorts of baseball memorabilia, including one of Babe Ruth's jackets.

On the west side of the site is the recently upgraded **LaQua** amusement park (daily 10am–10pm; ⓦwww.laqua.jp). The highlight is Thunder Dolphin (¥1000), a high-tech rollercoaster guaranteed to get you screaming. If you haven't got the stomach for it the world's first spokeless ferris wheel (¥800) provides a gentler ride and plenty of time to take a photo of the passing view. The hokey 13 Doors (¥800), a Japanese house of horrors, also provides some goulish laughs. A one-day passport (¥4000; or ¥2800 after 5pm) gets you access to all the park's rides. Alternatively, skip the rides and soak away your stress at the excellent **Spa LaQua** (see box opposite)

Immediately to the west of Tokyo Dome is **Koishikawa-Kōrakuen** (daily 9am–5pm; ¥300) a fine example of an early-seventeenth-century **stroll-garden**. Winding paths take you past waterfalls, ponds and stone lanterns down to the shores of a small lake draped with gnarled pines and over daintily humped bridges, where each view replicates a famous beauty spot. Zhu Shun Shui, a refugee scholar from Ming China, advised on the design, so Chinese as well as

Japanese landscapes feature, the most obvious being Small Lu-shan, represented by rounded hills of bamboo grass. The garden attracts few visitors, though intrusive announcements from Tokyo Dome, looming over the trees, mean it's not always totally peaceful. The main entrance gate lies in the garden's southwest corner, midway between Suidōbashi and Iidabashi stations; there's another entrance close by Tokyo Dome.

Tokyo onsens and spas

Until just a few decades ago, when people began installing bathrooms at home, life in Tokyo's residential neighbourhoods focused round the **sentō**, the public bath. Though you no longer find them every few blocks, a surprising number of bathhouses survive, of which we've given a sampler below. Take along your own soap, shampoo and a towel – or buy them at the door. See p.70 for tips on bathing etiquette.

The sentō have been recently joined by a couple of mega **onsen** (hot spring) complexes: Spa LaQua in Suidōbashi and Oedo Onsen Monogatari in Odaiba. Both are much more expensive than a traditional sentō, but offer extensive bathing facilities, a range of places to eat and relaxation areas with very comfortable reclining chairs.

Asakusa Kannon Onsen 2-7-26 Asakusa, Taitō-ku ☎03/3844-4141. This big old ivy-covered bathhouse isn't the cheapest sentō around, but it's right next to Sensō-ji and uses real onsen water. The clientele ranges from yakuza to grannies – very Asakusa. Daily 6.30am–6pm; ¥700. Asakusa Station.

Azabu-Jūban Onsen 1-5-22 Azabu-Jūban, Minato-ku ☎03/3404-2610. Of the two options here, the casual ground-floor baths offer better value (3–11pm; ¥400) while upstairs is a much classier affair (11am–9pm; ¥1260, or ¥940 after 6pm). Either way, the brown, mineral-rich onsen water is scalding hot. Closed Tues. Azabu-Jūban Station.

Jakotsu-yu 1-11-11 Asakusa, Taitō-ku ☎03/3841-8641. Spruce bathhouse down a back alley just south of Rox department store – one bath is designed to give you a mild but stimulating electric shock. Each section has a small rock garden and a handy coin laundry in the changing room. Daily except Tues 1pm–midnight. ¥400. Tawaramachi Station.

Ōedo Onsen Monogatari 2-57 Omi, Koto-ku ☎03/5500-1126, ⓦwww.ooedoonsen .jp. More of a theme park than a bathhouse, this newly developed onsen on the southwestern edge of Odaiba goes in for nostalgic kitsch in a big way. Admission includes a colourful yukata and towels. There's an outdoor bath and various street performers keep the atmosphere jolly. Daily 11am–9am; ¥2872, after 6pm ¥1987. Telecom Centre Station.

Rokuryū 3-4-20 Ikenohata, Bunkyō-ku ☎03/3821-3826. Another real onsen bath boasting a lovely traditional-style frontage. The interior is more ordinary, but clean and spacious. Tues–Sun 3.30–11pm. ¥400. Nezu Station.

Spa LaQua 1-1-1 Kasuga, Bunkyō-ku ☎03/3817-4173, ⓦwww.laqua.jp. By far the most sophisticated of Tokyo's bathing complexes, this new place spread over five floors (the entrance is on the 6th floor) uses real onsen water pumped from 1700m underground. Admission includes towels and loose pyjamas to wear around the complex. Access to the Healing Baden set of special therapeutic saunas costs ¥300 extra. It's also a great place to pass the time if you miss the last train home and don't want to fork out for a capsule or cheap business hotel. Daily 11am–9am. ¥2300. Suidōbashi Station.

Onsens and spas

Asakusa Kannon Onsen	*Asakusa Kannon Onsen*	浅草観音温泉
Azabu-Jūban Onsen	*Azabu-Jūban Onsen*	麻布十番温泉
Jakotsu-yu	*Jakotsu-yu*	蛇骨湯
Ōedo Onsen Monogatari	*Ōedo Onsen Monogatari*	大江戸温泉物語
Rokuryū-kōsen	*Rokuryū-kōsen*	六龍鉱泉
Spa LaQua	*Supa Rakuwa*	スパラクワ

Jimbōchō

From Suidōbashi hop on the Toei Mita subway one stop, or walk 1km south down Hakusan-dōri to **Jimbōchō**, a lively student centre which is also home to dozens of secondhand **bookshops** around the intersection of Yasukuni-dōri and Hakusan-dōri. You'll find the best ones along the south side of Yasukuni-dōri, in the blocks either side of Jimbōchō subway station, where racks of dog-eared novels and textbooks sit outside shops stacked high with dusty tomes. Most of these are in Japanese, but some dealers specialize in English-language books – both new and old – while a bit of rooting around might turn up a volume of old photographs or cartoons in one of the more upmarket anti-quarian dealers. Note that many shops close on either Sunday or Monday.

South and west of the Imperial Palace

To the southwest of the Imperial Palace, beside the government areas of Kasumigaseki and Nagatachō, is **Akasaka**. This was once an agricultural area (*akane*, plants that produce a red dye, were farmed here, hence the area's name, which means "red slope"), but subsequently developed as an entertainment

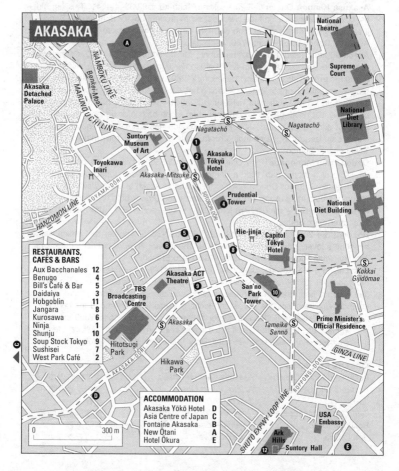

district in the late nineteenth century, when *ryōtei* restaurants, complete with performing geisha, started opening to cater for the modern breed of politicians and bureaucrats. The area still has its fair share of exclusive establishments, shielded from the hoi polloi by high walls and even higher prices. Their presence, along with the headquarters of the TBS TV station and some of Tokyo's top hotels, lends Akasaka a certain cachet, though prices at many of the restaurants and bars are no worse than elsewhere in Tokyo.

The main thoroughfare of Akasaka is **Sotobori-dōri**. At its southern end stands a huge stone *torii* gate, beyond which is a picturesque avenue of red *torii* leading up the hill to the **Hie-jinja**, a shrine dedicated to the god Ōyamakui-no-kami, who is believed to protect against evil. Although the ferro-concrete buildings date from 1967, Hie-jinja's history stretches back to 830 AD, when it was first established on the outskirts of what would become Edo. The shrine's location shifted a couple more times before Shogun Tokugawa Ietsuna placed it here in the seventeenth century as a source of protection for his castle (now the site of the Imperial Palace). Today, Hie-jinja hosts the **Sannō Matsuri** (June 10–16), one of Tokyo's most important festivals. The highlight is a parade on June 15 involving four hundred participants dressed in Heian period costume and carrying fifty sacred *mikoshi* (portable shrines) – there's a festival every year, but the *mikoshi* parade only takes place every other year (in even-numbered years). The front entrance to the shrine is actually through the large stone *torii* on the east side of the hill, beside the *Capitol Tōkyū Hotel*. Fifty-one steps lead up to a spacious enclosed courtyard, in which roosters roam freely and salarymen bunk off work to idle on benches. To the left of the main shrine, look for the carving of a female monkey cradling its baby, a symbol that has come to signify protection for pregnant women.

Heading north from the shrine along Sotobori-dōri and across Benkei-bashi, the bridge that spans what was once the outer moat of the shogun's castle, you'll soon reach the **New Ōtani** hotel. Within its grounds is a beautiful traditional Japanese **garden**, originally designed for the *daimyō* Katō Kiyomasa, lord of Kumamoto in Kyūshū, over four hundred years ago. You can stroll freely through the garden or admire it while sipping tea in the New Ōtani's lounge. The hotel also has its own small **art gallery** (Tues–Sun 10am–6pm; ¥500, free to guests), with works from Japanese and European artists, including Chagall and Modigliani, and a tea-ceremony room, where tea (¥1050) is served in the traditional way from Thursday to Saturday between 11am and 4pm.

Returning across the Benkei-bashi to the Akasaka Mitsuke intersection brings you to the Suntory Building, which houses the elegant **Suntory Museum of Art** on the eleventh floor (Tues–Sun 10am–5pm, Fri until 7pm; ¥500, or more depending on the exhibition; ☏03/3470-1073, ⓦwww.suntory.co.jp/sma). As

South and west of the Imperial Palace		
Akasaka	*Akasaka*	赤坂
Akasaka Detached Palace	*Geihinkan*	迎賓館
Ark Hills	*Āku Hiruzu*	アークヒルズ
Hie-jinja	*Hie-jinja*	日枝神社
Suntory Museum of Art	*Santorii Bijutsukan*	サントリー美術館
Toyokawa Inari shrine	*Toyokawa Inari-jinja*	豊川稲荷神社
Roppongi	*Roppongi*	六本木
Nogi-jinja	*Nogi-jinja*	乃木神社
Roppongi Hills	*Roppongi Hiruzu*	六本木ヒルズ
Tokyo Tower	*Tōkyō Tawā*	東京タワー
Zōjō-ji	*Zōjō-ji*	増上寺

well as changing exhibitions of ceramics, lacquerware, paintings and textiles, the museum has a traditional tea-ceremony room, where tea and sweets are served for around ¥300.

Walking southwest from the museum along Aoyama-dōri, you'll soon encounter the colourful **Toyokawa Inari** (also known as Myōgon-ji), an example of a combined temple and shrine which was much more common across Japan before the Meiji government forcibly separated Shinto and Buddhist places of worship. The temple's compact precincts are decked with red lanterns and banners and the main hall is guarded by statues of pointy-eared foxes wearing red bibs – the messengers of the Shinto god Inari, found at all Inari shrines. Toyokawa Inari borders the extensive grounds of the grand, European-style **Akasaka Detached Palace** (Geihinkan), which serves as the official State Guest House and is off limits to humble visitors.

Returning to Sotobori-dōri and heading southeast past Hei-jinja will bring you to Roppongi-dōri. Turn south along this road to reach the **Ark Hills** complex, housing the *ANA Hotel* and the classical music venue **Suntory Hall**. Behind Ark Hills and next to the *Hotel Ōkura* is the **Ōkura Shūkokan** art museum (Tues–Sun 10am–4.30pm; ¥500, free to hotel guests), established in 1917 by the self-styled Baron Ōkura Tsuruhiko and housing an intriguing collection of Oriental ceramics, paintings, prints and sculptures from a collection of over 1700 traditional works of art.

Roppongi

Around a kilometre south of Akasaka is **Roppongi**, favourite haunt of young Japanese and expats out for a night on the tiles. The district, which had grown somewhat seedy, has been given a huge kick up the pants with the opening of the swish **Roppongi Hills** development (Ⓦwww.roppongihills.com), a phenomenal success story and indication that there's plenty of life yet in Japan's supposedly moribund economy. It took seventeen years for local property magnate Mori Minoru to realize his dream of an "Urban New Deal" for Tokyo, and since its opening in April 2003, this ¥280-billion complex of offices, shops, residences and entertainment venues has been a phenomenal success, clocking up one million visitors in its first three days alone.

A large part of the development's popularity is down to its design, whose apparently muddled mix of conflicting architectural styles gives the complex a natural feel, as if it had evolved over time. Added to this is the use of open space and greenery; with a Japanese garden and pond, an open-air arena for free performances, several roof gardens and even a rice paddy on the roof of the Keyakizaka Complex, above the state-of-the-art Virgin Cinema multiplex. The overhead utility cables that plague the rest of Tokyo have been banished, and funky street sculptures have been liberally applied, including Louise Bourgeois' **Maman**, an iconic giant bronze, stainless steel and marble spider, squatting at the base of the 54-storey, Kohn Pederson Fox-designed Mori Tower. If you approach Roppongi Hills through the main Metro Hat entrance from Roppongi Station you'll see the spider at the top of the escalators.

Directly ahead of the spider is the "Museum Cone", a glass structure enclosing a swirling staircase which forms the entrance to Roppongi Hill's highlight, the **Mori Art Museum** (MAM; daily 10am–10pm; Tues until 5pm, Fri & Sat until midnight; ¥1500; ☎03/6406-6100, Ⓦwww.mori.art.museum). In line with Mori Minoru's philosophy of combining culture with commercialism in what he fancifully calls an "artelligent city", the prime top floors of the Mori Tower have been given over to the museum. MAM doesn't have its own collection but puts on exhibitions of works gathered from around Japan and

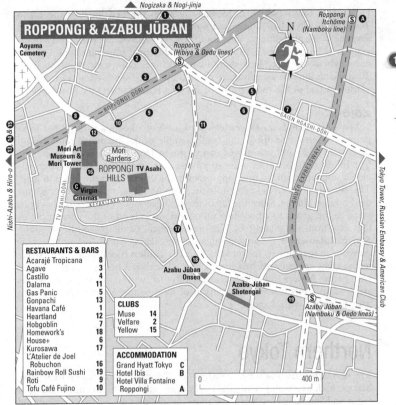

ROPPONGI & AZABU JŪBAN

Aoyama
Cemetery

① *Roppongi*
Itchōme Ⓢ Ⓐ
(Namboku line)

N

Roppongi
Ⓑ *(Hibiya & Oedo lines)*
Ⓢ

ROPPONGI-DORI

GAIEN HGASHI-DORI

SHUTO EXPRESSWAY

Mori Art
Museum &
Mori Tower

Mori
Gardens

⑯ ROPPONGI
HILLS

TV Asahi

TV ASAHI-DORI

Ⓒ Virgin
Cinemas

KEYAKIZAKA-DORI

Azabu Jūban
Onsen

Azabu-Jūban
Shotengai

Azabu Jūban
(Namboku & Oedo lines) Ⓢ

RESTAURANTS & BARS

Acarajé Tropicana	8
Agave	3
Castillo	4
Dalarna	11
Gas Panic	5
Gonpachi	13
Havana Café	1
Heartland	12
Hobgoblin	7
Homework's	18
House+	6
Kurosawa	17
L'Atelier de Joel Robuchon	16
Rainbow Roll Sushi	19
Roti	9
Tofu Café Fujino	10

CLUBS

Muse	14
Velfare	2
Yellow	15

ACCOMMODATION

Grand Hyatt Tokyo	C
Hotel Ibis	B
Hotel Villa Fontaine Roppongi	A

0   400 m

---

abroad, with a particular focus on the best contemporary art and design, and on Asian artists. The museum also includes the **Tokyo City View** observation deck, Tokyo's highest viewpoint (daily 9am–1am; included in entrance to MAM, otherwise ¥1500; for an extra ¥500 you can go up onto the 270-metre-high roof, though it's only open when the weather is good).

In comparison to all this, Roppongi's other attractions seem rather pale. Beside the Roppongi exit of the Nogizaka subway station is **Nogi-jinja**, a small shrine honouring the Meiji-era **General Nogi Maresuke**, a hero in both the Sino-Japanese and Russo-Japanese wars. When the emperor Meiji died, Nogi and his wife followed the samurai tradition and committed suicide in his house within the shrine grounds. On the second Sunday of every month, there's a good antique flea market in the shrine grounds.

Heading back to Roppongi crossing and sticking on Gaien-higashi-dōri for around 1km will eventually bring you to **Tokyo Tower** (daily 9am–10pm; main observatory ¥820, top observatory ¥1420; ☏03/3433-5111, ⓦwww.tokyotower.co.jp). Built during an era when Japan was becoming famous for producing cheap copies of foreign goods, this 333-metre red and white copy of the Eiffel Tower, opened in 1958, manages to top its Parisian role model by several metres. The uppermost observation deck, at 250m, has been surplanted as the highest viewpoint in Tokyo by the roof deck of Roppongi

Hills' Mori Tower (which incidentally provides the best view of the Tokyo Tower, especially when illuminated at night). More attractions have been added over the years, including an aquarium (¥1000), a waxworks (¥870) and a holographic "Mystery Zone" (¥400), as well as the usual souvenir shops – to the point where the place feels more like an amusement arcade than the Eiffel Tower. Unless it's an exceptionally clear day, you'd be wise saving your cash for a drink at one of the rooftop bars of any of a host of other city skyscrapers.

Zōjō-ji

Tokyo Tower stands on the eastern flank of Shiba-kōen, a park whose main point of interest is **Zōjō-ji**, the family temple of the Tokugawa clan. Zōjō-ji dates from 1393 and was moved to this site in 1598 by Tokugawa Ieyasu (the first Tokugawa shogun) in order to protect southeast Edo spiritually and provide a waystation for pilgrims approaching the capital from the Tōkaidō road. This was once the city's largest holy site, with 48 sub-temples and over a hundred other buildings. Since the fall of the Tokugawa, however, Zōjō-ji has been razed to the ground by fire three times, and virtually all of the current buildings date from the mid-1970s. The main remnant of the past is the imposing **San-gadatsu-mon**, a 21-metre-high gateway dating from 1612 and the oldest wooden structure in Tokyo. Ahead lies the **Taiden** (Great Main Hall), while to the right are ranks of Jizō statues, capped with red bonnets and decorated with plastic flowers and colourful windmills that twirl in the breeze. Amid this army of mini-guardians lie the remains of six shogun, behind a wrought-iron gate decorated with dragons.

Northern Tokyo

The northern districts of Tokyo are where you'll find the city at its most traditional, harking back to a world before the bright lights and high-tech commercialism of Ginza and Shinjuku. Nowhere is this more obvious than among the craftshops and neighbourhood restaurants of **Asakusa**, a must on any visit to Tokyo, and in the constant festival atmosphere around its magnificent temple, **Sensō-ji**.

West of Asakusa, **Ueno** is best known for its park and museums, including the flagship **Tokyo National Museum**, offering a comprehensive romp through Japanese art history. The Yamanote line loops west from Ueno past **Rikugi-en**, a serene classical garden, before grinding into **Ikebukuro**, whose huge department stores and entertainment district are like a downmarket version of Shinjuku and Shibuya, though it's worth exploring for its relatively cheap accommodation (see p.106) and discount shops.

Asakusa

Last stop on the Ginza line heading north, **Asakusa** is best known as the site of Tokyo's most venerable Buddhist temple, **Sensō-ji**, whose towering worship hall is filled with a continual throng of petitioners and holidaymakers. Stalls before the temple cater to the crowds, peddling trinkets and keepsakes as they have done for centuries, while old-fashioned craftshops display exquisite hair combs, paper fans and calligraphy brushes, and all around is the inevitable array of restaurants, drinking places and fast-food stands. It's this infectious carnival atmosphere that makes Asakusa so appealing: this is the area of Tokyo where you'll find the most vivid reminders of Edo's Shitamachi and the popular culture it spawned – one which seems to be constantly in the throes of some cel-

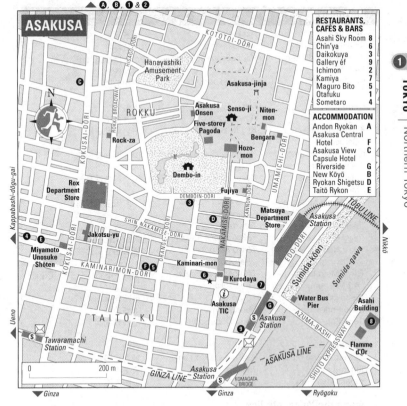

ASAKUSA

KOTOTOI-DŌRI

HISARI-DŌRI

Hanayashiki
Amusement
Park

Asakusa-jinja

ⓒ

N

ROKKU

ROKU BROADWAY

Asakusa
Onsen

Senso-ji

Niten-
mon

Five-storey
Pagoda

Bengara

Rock-za

Hozo-
mon

KOKUSAI-DŌRI

UMAMICHI-DŌRI

Dembo-in

Kappabashi-dōgu-gai

Rox
Department
Store

Fujiya

DEMBOIN-DŌRI

❸

SHIN NAKAMISE-DŌRI

ⓓ

Matsuya
Department
Store

Asakusa
Station

TOBU LINE

Jakotsu-yu

ORANGE-DŌRI

NAKAMISE-DŌRI

KANNON-DŌRI

EDO-DŌRI

Nikkō

❹ ⓔ

Miyamoto
Unosuke
Shōten

KOKUSAI-DŌRI

KAMINARIMON-DŌRI

❶❺

Kaminari-mon

Sumida-kōen

Sumida-gawa

Ueno

❻ ★

Kurodaya

❼

TAITŌ-KU

ⓘ
Asakusa
TIC

Water Bus
Pier

Asahi
Building

ⓖ

AZUMA-BASHI

❽

Ⓢ Asakusa
Station

❾

Tawaramachi
Station

Ⓢ

ASAKUSA LINE

Flamme
d'Or

SHUTO EXPRESSWAY 6

0   200 m

GINZA LINE

Asakusa
Station

Ⓢ KOMAGATA
BRIDGE

▼ Ginza

▼ Ginza

▼ Ryōgoku

**RESTAURANTS,
CAFÉS & BARS**
Asahi Sky Room 8
Chin'ya 6
Daikokuya 3
Gallery éf 9
Ichimon 2
Kamiya 7
Maguro Bito 5
Otafuku 1
Sometaro 4

ACCOMMODATION
Andon Ryokan A
Asakusa Central
  Hotel F
Asakusa View C
Capsule Hotel
  Riverside G
New Kōyō B
Ryokan Shigetsu D
Taitō Ryokan E

❶

TOKYO | Northern Tokyo

---

ebration or other. The biggest bash is the Sanja Matsuri (see p.131), but there are numerous smaller festivals, so it's worth asking at Tourist Information Centres (see p.98) if there's anything in the offing.

One of the best ways to get to Asakusa is by **riverboat**, following the Sumida-gawa north from Hama Rikyū Teien or Hinode Pier (see p.101 for details) to dock under Azuma Bridge, across the river from Philippe Starck's eye-catching Asahi Brewery Building – though its rooftop flame looks, according to local opinion, more like a golden turd.

Sensō-ji

Walking west from the river or the Ginza line subway station, you can't miss the solid, red-lacquer gate with its monstrous paper lantern that marks the southern entrance to **Sensō-ji**. This magnificent temple, also known as Asakusa Kannon, was founded in the mid-seventh century to enshrine a tiny golden image of Kannon, the Goddess of Mercy, which had turned up in the nets of two local fishermen. Though most of the present buildings are postwar concrete reconstructions, there's a great sense of atmosphere as you draw near the main hall with its sweeping, tiled roofs. Before heading into the temple grounds, cross over to the helpful **Asakusa Information Centre** (daily 10am–8pm; ☏03/3842-5566) to see if there are any special events going on; they also offer Sunday afternoon walking tours of the area in English (1.30pm & 3pm; free).

Northern Tokyo

Asakusa	*Asakusa*	浅草
Asakusa-jinja	*Asakusa-jinja*	浅草神社
Kappabashi-dōgu-gai	*Kappabashi-dōgu-gai*	かっぱ橋道具街
Sensō-ji	*Sensō-ji*	浅草寺
Sumida-kōen	*Sumida-kōen*	隅田公園
Ueno	*Ueno*	上野
Ameyoko-chō	*Ameyoko-chō*	アメ横丁
Kyū Iwasaki-tei Gardens	*Kyū Iwasaki-tei Tei-en*	旧岩崎邸庭園
National Museum of Western Art	*Kokuritsu Seiyō Bijutsukan*	国立西洋美術館
National Science Museum	*Kokuritsu Kagaku Hakubutsukan*	国立科学博物館
Shitamachi Museum	*Shitamachi Fūzoku Shiryōkan*	下町風俗資料館
Tokudai-ji	*Tokudai-ji*	徳大寺
Tokyo Bunka Kaikan	*Tōkyō Bunka Kaikan*	東京文化会館
Tokyo National Museum	*Tōkyō Kokuritsu Hakubutsukan*	東京国立博物館
Tokyo Metropolitan Art Museum	*TōkyōMetoroporitan Bijutsukan*	東京メトロポリタン美術館
Tōshō-gū	*Tōshō-gū*	東照宮
Ueno Park	*Ueno-kōen*	上野公園
Ueno Zoo	*Ueno Dōbutsuen*	上野動物園
Yanaka	*Yanaka*	谷中
Asakura Chōso Museum	*Asakura Chōso-ken*	朝倉彫塑
Tennō-ji	*Tennō-ji*	天王寺
Yanaka Cemetery	*Yanaka Reien*	谷中霊園
Along the Yamanote line		
Kōgan-ji	*Kōgan-ji*	
Kōshinzuka Station	*Kōshinzuka-eki*	高岩寺
Rikugi-en	*Rikugi-en*	庚申塚駅
Sugamo	*Sugamo*	六義園
Toden Arakawa Line	*Toden Arakawa-sen*	巣鴨
		都電荒川線
Ikebukuro	*Ikebukuro*	
Japan Traditional Crafts Centre	*Zenkoku Dentōteki Kōgeihin Sentā*	池袋 全国伝統的工芸品センター
Metropolitan Art Space	*Tōkyō Geijutsu Gekijō*	
Rikkyō University	*Rikkyō Daigaku*	東京芸術劇場 立教大学

The main approach starts under the great **Kaminari-mon**, or "Thunder Gate", named for its two vigorous guardian gods of Thunder and Wind (Raijin and Fūjin), and proceeds along Nakamise-dōri, a colourful parade of small shops packed with gaudy souvenirs, tiny traditional dolls, kimono accessories and sweet-scented piles of *sembei* rice crackers. A double-storeyed treasure gate, **Hōzō-mon**, stands astride the entrance to the main temple complex; the treasures, fourteenth-century Chinese sutras, are locked away on the upper floor. Its two protective gods – *Niō*, the traditional guardians of Buddhist temples – are even more imposing than those at Kaminari-mon; look out for their enormous rice-straw sandals slung on the gate's rear wall.

Beyond, there's a constant crowd clustered around a large, bronze incense bowl where people waft the pungent smoke – breath of the gods – over themselves for its supposed curative powers. There's nothing much to see inside the temple itself, since the little Kannon – said to be just 7.5cm tall – is a *hibutsu*, a hidden image considered too holy to be on view. The hall, however, is full of life, with the rattle of coins being tossed into a huge wooden coffer, the swirling plumes of incense smoke and the constant bustle of people coming to pray, buy charms and fortune papers or to attend a service. Three times a day (6am, 10am & 2pm) drums echo through the hall into the courtyard as priests chant sutras beneath the altar's gilded canopy.

Like many Buddhist temples, Sensō-ji accommodates Shinto shrines in its grounds, the most important being **Asakusa-jinja**, dedicated to the two fishermen brothers who netted the Kannon image, and their overlord. The shrine was founded in the mid-seventeenth century by Tokugawa Iemitsu and this is the original building, though it's hard to tell under all the restored paintwork. More popularly known as Sanja-sama, "Shrine of the Three Guardians", this is the focus of the tumultuous **Sanja Matsuri**, Tokyo's biggest festival, which takes place every year on the third weekend in May. The climax comes on the second day, when over one hundred *mikoshi* (portable shrines) are manhandled through the streets of Asakusa by a seething crowd, among them the three *mikoshi* of Asakusa-jinja, each weighing around 1000kg and carried by at least seventy men.

Sensō-ji's eastern entrance is guarded by the attractively aged **Niten-mon**. Originally built in 1618, this gate is all that remains of a shrine honouring Tokugawa Ieyasu which was relocated to Ueno in 1651 after a series of fires. Niten-mon has since been rededicated and now houses two seventeenth-century Buddhist guardians of the south and east. The road heading east leads to a narrow strip of park, **Sumida-kōen**; the river here provides the stage for one of the city's great summer firework displays (*hanabi taikai*), held on the last Saturday of July.

West of Sensō-ji

When Kabuki and Bunraku were banished from central Edo in the 1840s they settled in the area known as **Rokku** (Block 6), between Sensō-ji and today's Kokusai-dōri. Over the next century almost every fad and fashion in popular entertainment started life here, from cinema to cabaret and striptease. Today a handful of the old venues survives, most famously **Rock-za**, with its nightly strip-show, and there are loads of cinemas, pachinko parlours, gambling halls and drinking dives. It's not all lowbrow, though: theatres just down from Rock-za still stage *rakugo*, a centuries-old form of comic monologue where familiar jokes and stories are mixed with modern satire.

A wide avenue called Kokusai-dōri forms the western boundary of Rokku. Near its southerly junction with Kaminarimon-dōri, across from the Rox department store, **Miyamoto Unosuke Shōten** (daily except Tues 9am–6pm; ☏03/3842-5622, ⊛www.miyamoto-unosuke.co.jp) is easily identifiable from the elaborate *mikoshi* in the window. The shop is an Aladdin's cave of traditional Japanese percussion instruments and festival paraphernalia: masks, *happi* coats (shortened kimono-style jackets), flutes, cymbals and, of course, all kinds of *mikoshi*, the largest with a price tag over ¥3 million. Since 1861, however, the family passion has been drums, resulting in an impressive collection from around the world which now fills the fourth-floor **Drum Museum** (Wed–Sun 10am–5pm; ¥300). There's every type of percussion material and, best of all, you are allowed to have a go on some. A red dot on the name card indicates those not to be touched; blue dots mean you can tap lightly, just with your hands; and the rest have the appropriate drumsticks ready waiting.

Continuing westwards from this corner, after a few blocks you hit another main road, Kappabashi-dōgu-gai. Locally known as **"Kitchenware Town"**, this is the best-known of several wholesale markets in northeast Tokyo, where you can kit out a whole restaurant. You don't have to be a bulk-buyer, however, and this is a great place to pick up unusual souvenirs, such as the plastic food displayed outside restaurants to tempt the customer. This practice dates from the nineteenth century, originally using wax, but came into its own about thirty years ago when foreign foods were being introduced to a puzzled Japanese market. The best examples are absolutely realistic; try Maizuru or Tokyo Biken for a particularly mouthwatering show. These are both open daily 9am–6pm, but note that many shops along here close on Sunday.

Ueno

Most people visit **Ueno** for its **park** (*kōen*), which is one of Tokyo's largest open spaces and also contains a host of museums, including the prestigious **Tokyo National Museum**, plus a few relics from a vast temple complex that once occupied this hilltop. But Ueno also has proletarian, Shitamachi roots, and much of its eastern district has a rough-and-ready feel, especially around the station and the raucous markets extending south beside the tracks.

Ueno Kōen

Cut through with wide avenues where families come to feed the pigeons at weekends, **Ueno Kōen** is where all Tokyo seems to flock during the spring cherry-blossom season. From Ueno Station there are two routes into the park: "Park Exit" takes you to the main, west gate where you'll also find an **information desk** (daily 9am–5pm); the "Shinobazu Exit" brings you out closer to the southern entrance, above Keisei-Ueno Station, where trains depart for Narita Airport. On the southerly option, at the top of the steps leading up to the park from the street, stands a bronze statue of **Saigō Takamori**, out walking his dog. Despite his casual appearance, this is the "Great Saigō", leader of the Restoration army, who helped bring Emperor Meiji to power but then committed ritual suicide in 1877 after his ill-fated Satsuma Rebellion (see p.850). General Saigō's popularity was such, however, that he was rehabilitated in 1891 and his statue unveiled a few years later, though a military uniform was deemed inappropriate.

Following the main path northwards, the red-lacquered **Kiyomizu Kannon-dō** comes into view on the left. Built out over the hillside, this temple is a smaller, less impressive version of Kyoto's Kiyomizu-dera (see p.535), but it has the rare distinction of being one of Kan'ei-ji's few existing remnants, dating from 1631. The temple is dedicated to **Senju Kannon** (the 1000-armed Kannon), whose image is displayed only in February, although the second-rank **Kosodate Kannon** receives more visitors as the Bodhisattva in charge of conception. Hopeful women leave dolls at the altar during the year, following which they're all burnt at a rather sad memorial service on September 25.

The temple faces westwards over a broad avenue lined with ancient cherry trees towards **Shinobazu Pond**. Once an inlet of Tokyo Bay, the pond is now a wildlife protection area and, unlikely as it may seem in the midst of a city, hosts a permanent colony of wild black cormorants as well as temporary populations of migrating waterfowl. A causeway leads out across its reeds and lotus beds to a small, leafy island occupied by an octagonal-roofed temple, **Benten-**

dō, dedicated to the goddess of good fortune, water and music among other things. Inside the half-lit worship hall, you can just make out Benten's eight arms, each clutching a holy weapon, while the ceiling sports a snarling dragon.

Head back into the park on the tree-lined avenue which marks the approach to Tokugawa Ieyasu's shrine, **Tōshō-gū**. Ieyasu died in 1616 and is buried in Nikkō (see p.196), but this was his main shrine in the city, founded in 1627, rebuilt on a grander scale in 1651 and now listed as a National Treasure. For once it's possible to penetrate beyond the screened entrance and enclosing walls to take a closer look inside (daily 9am–4.30pm or 5pm, July & Aug until 6pm; ¥200). A path leads from the ticket gate clockwise round the polychrome halls and into the worship hall, whose faded decorative work contrasts sharply

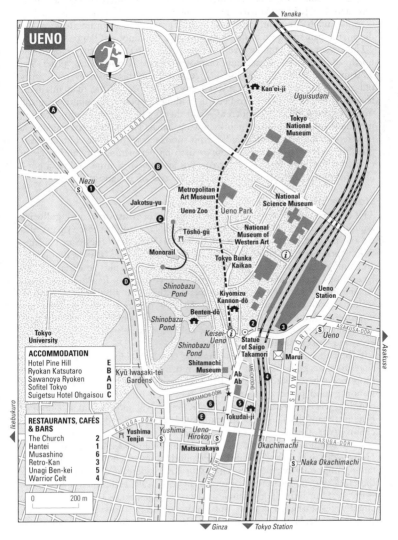

UENO

Yanaka

Kan'ei-ji

Uguisudani

Tokyo National Museum

Nezu

Metropolitan Art Museum

Jakotsu-yu

Ueno Zoo

Ueno Park

National Science Museum

Tōshō-gū

National Museum of Western Art

Monorail

Tokyo Bunka Kaikan

Shinobazu Pond

Kiyomizu Kannon-dō

Benten-dō

Ueno Station

Shinobazu Pond

Keisei-Ueno

Statue of Saigo Takamori

Ueno

ASAKUSA-DŌRI

Tokyo University

Shinobazu Pond

Shitamachi Museum

Marui

Kyū Iwasaki-tei Gardens

ACCOMMODATION

Hotel Pine Hill	E
Ryokan Katsutaro	B
Sawanoya Ryoken	A
Sofitel Tokyo	D
Suigetsu Hotel Ohgaisou	C

NAKAMACHI-DŌRI

Tokudai-ji

RESTAURANTS, CAFÉS & BARS

The Church	2
Hantei	1
Musashino	6
Retro-Kan	3
Unagi Ben-kei	5
Warrior Celt	4

Yushima Tenjin

Yushima

Ueno-Hirokoji

Matsuzakaya

Okachimachi

Naka Okachimachi

0   200 m

Ikebukuro

Ginza   Tokyo Station

Asakusa

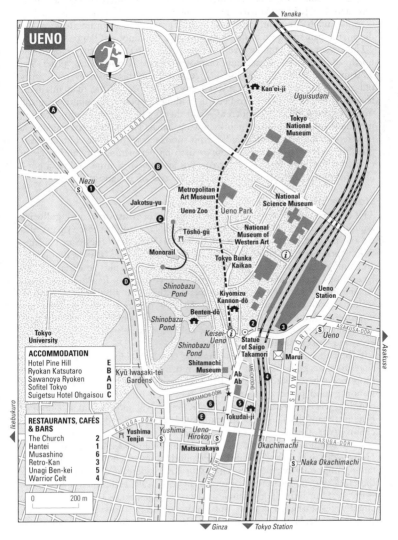

The GRUTT Pass

If you're planning on visiting several museums and galleries in Tokyo it's well worth investing in the **GRUTT Pass**. The pass costs ¥2000, is valid for two months from the date of first use and gets you into 44 public, national and private institutions including all Tokyo's major museums; it also gives you discounts on special exhibitions at the museums. The ticket can be bought at the counters of most participating museums or from Ticket PIA outlets (see Listings, p.191).

with the burnished black and gold of Ieyasu's shrine room behind. Before leaving, take a look at the ornate, Chinese-style front gate, where two golden dragons carved in 1651 by Hidari Jingorō – he of Nikkō's sleeping cat (see p.202) – attract much attention; so realistic is the carving that, according to local tradition, the pair sneak off at midnight to drink in Shinobazu Pond.

The seventeenth-century, five-storey pagoda rising above the trees to the north of Tōshō-gū is actually marooned inside **Ueno Zoo** (Tues–Sun 9.30am–5pm; ¥600; ☎03/3828-5171). Considering this zoo is over a century old and in the middle of a crowded city, it's less depressing than might be feared. In recent years they've been upgrading the pens – though they're still small and predominantly concrete – and there's plenty of vegetation around, including some magnificent, corkscrewing lianas. The main attractions are a new reptile house and the pandas, who snooze away on their concrete platform, blithely unaware they're supposed to be performing for the hordes of excited school children. As ever, weekends are the worst time, and it's a good idea to bring a picnic since prices inside the zoo are expensive.

Ueno's museums

The best reason to visit Ueno is for its wealth of **museums and galleries** around the north and eastern edges of the park. First stop has to be Japan's oldest and most important, the **Tokyo National Museum** (Tues–Sun 9.30am–5pm, April–Sept Fri until 8pm; ¥420; ☎03/3822-1111, ⓦwww.tnm.go.jp), containing the world's largest collection of Japanese art, plus an extensive collection of Oriental antiquities. Displays are rotated every few months from a collection of 89,000 pieces, and the special exhibitions are usually also worth seeing if you can stand the crowds. Though the new galleries are a vast improvement, the museum style tends towards old-fashioned reverential dryness. Nevertheless, among such a vast collection there's something to excite everyone's imagination.

It's best to start with the **Hon-kan**, the central building, where you'll find English-language booklets at the lobby information desk and a good museum shop in the basement. The Hon-kan presents the sweep of Japanese art, from Jōmon-period pottery (pre-fourth century BC) to early twentieth-century painting, via theatrical costume for Kabuki, Nō and Bunraku, colourful Buddhist mandalas, *ukiyo-e* prints, exquisite lacquerware and even seventeenth-century Christian art from southern Japan.

In the building's northwest corner look out for a passage leading to the new **Heisei-kan**, where you'll find the splendid Japanese Archeology Gallery containing important recent finds. Though it covers some of the same ground as the Hon-kan, modern presentation and lighting really bring the objects to life – the best are refreshingly simple and burst with energy. Highlights are the chunky, flame-shaped Jōmon pots and a collection of super-heated Sue stoneware, a technique introduced from Korea in the fifth century. Look out, too, for the bug-eyed, curvaceous clay figures (*dogū*) of the Jōmon period, and the funerary *haniwa* from the fourth to sixth centuries AD – these terracotta representations of houses, animals, musicians and stocky little warriors were placed on burial mounds to protect the deceased lord in the afterlife.

In the southwest corner of the compound, behind the copper-domed Hyōkei-kan, built in 1908 and now an Important Cultural Property in its own right, lurks the **Hōryū-ji Hōmotsu-kan**. This sleek new gallery contains a selection of priceless treasures donated over the centuries to Nara's Hōryū-ji temple (see p.585). The most eye-catching display comprises 48 gilt-bronze Buddhist statues in various poses, each an island of light in the inky darkness, while there's also an eighth-century Chinese zither and an inkstand said to have been used by Prince Shōtoku (see p.934) when annotating the lotus sutra.

The museum's final gallery is the **Tōyō-kan**, on the opposite side of the compound, housing a delightful hotchpotch of Oriental antiquities where Javanese textiles and nineteenth-century Indian prints rub shoulders with Egyptian mummies and a wonderful collection of Southeast Asian bronze Buddhas. The Chinese and, particularly, Korean collections are also interesting for their obvious parallels with the Japanese art seen earlier. If you've got the energy, it's well worth taking a quick walk through, though there's frustratingly little English labelling.

There are sometimes interesting temporary exhibitions at the **Tokyo Metropolitan Art Museum** (Mon–Sun 9am–5pm; closed first and third Monday of the month; admission varies; ☎03/3823-6921; ⓦwww.tobikan.jp), in a partly underground brick building immediately southwest of the Tokyo National Museum. In the park's northeast corner, the **National Science Museum** (Tues–Sun 9am–4.30pm; ¥420; ☎03/3822-0111, ⓦwww.kahaku.go .jp/english/index.htm) is easily identified by a life-size statue of a romping blue whale outside. Compared with Tokyo's other science museum (see p.113), this one has fewer interactive exhibits but a great deal more information, some of it in English, covering natural history as well as science and technology. Best is the "Science Discovery Plaza", in the new building at the back, where pendulums, magnets, mirrors and hand-powered generators provide entertainment for the mainly school-age audience.

South of here is the **National Museum of Western Art** (Tues–Sun 9.30am–5pm, Fri until 8pm; ¥420; ☎03/3828-5131, ⓦwww.nmwa.go.jp), instantly recognizable from the Rodin statues populating the forecourt. The museum, designed by Le Corbusier, was erected in 1959 to house the mostly French Impressionist paintings left to the nation by Kawasaki shipping magnate Matsukata Kōjirō. Since then, works by Rubens, Tintoretto, Max Ernst and Jackson Pollock have broadened the scope of this impressive collection.

At the southern end of the park, the **Shitamachi Museum** (Tues–Sun 9.30am–4.30pm; ¥300; ☎03/3823-7451) is set in a distinctive, partly traditional-style building beside Shinobazu Pond. The museum opened in 1980 to preserve something of the Shitamachi while it was still within living memory. A reconstructed merchant's shop-house and a 1920s tenement row, complete with sweet shop and coppersmith's workroom, fill the ground floor. The upper floor is devoted to rotating exhibitions focusing on articles of daily life – old photos, toys, advertisements and artisans' tools. All the museum's exhibits have been donated by local residents; you can take your shoes off to explore the shop interiors and can handle most items. There's plenty of information in English, plus a well-produced museum booklet (¥400).

South of Ueno Park

Ueno town centre lies to the south of the park and is a lively mix of discount outlets, market streets, drinking clubs, a sprinkling of upmarket stores and craft shops, "soaplands" (a euphemism for brothels), love hotels and restaurants. While it's not strong on sophistication or culture, there's a greater sense of raw vitality here than you'll find elsewhere in Tokyo.

The biggest draw for both bargain-hunters and sightseers is the bustling **market** area south of Ueno Station, **Ameyoko-chō**, which extends nearly half a kilometre along the west side of the elevated JR train lines down to Okachimachi Station, spilling down side-alleys and under the tracks. The name is an abbreviation of "Ameya Yokochō", or "candy sellers' alley", dating from the immediate postwar days when sweets were a luxury and hundreds of stalls here peddled mostly sweet potatoes coated in sugar syrup. Since rationing was in force, black-marketeers joined the candy sellers, dealing in rice and other foodstuffs, household goods, personal possessions – whatever was available. Later, American imports also found their way from army stores onto the streets here, especially during the early 1950s Korean War. By then the market had been legalized, and over the years the worst crime has been cleaned up, but Ameyoko-chō still retains a flavour of those early days: gruff men with sand-paper voices shout out their wares; stalls selling bulk tea and coffee, cheap shoes, ready-peeled fruit, jewellery and fish are all jumbled up, cheek by jowl; and under the arches a clutch of *yakitori* bars still tempts the market crowds. In the thick of all this it's not surprising to stumble across a **temple**, **Tokudai-ji**, dedicated to a goddess offering prosperity and abundant harvests. Look out for the temple's colourful banners, up on the second floor two blocks before the southern limit of Ameyoko-chō.

The west side of central Ueno is dominated by seedy love hotels and dubi-ous bars. A short walk past Yushima Station, however, you'll discover a remark-able remnant of a much more genteel past. The **Kyū Iwasaki-tei Gardens** (daily 9am–5pm; ¥400; ☎03/3823-8340, ⓦwww.tokyo-park.or.jp) date from 1896 and surround an elegant **house**, designed by British architect Josiah Condor, which combines a café au lait, Western-style two-storey mansion with a traditional single-storey Japanese residence. The wooden Jacobean and Moorish-style arabesque interiors of the Western-style mansion are in fantas-tic condition; the severely faded screen paintings of the Japanese section are in stark comparison. The lack of furniture in both houses makes them a little life-less, but it's nonetheless an impressive artefact in a city where such buildings are increasingly rare. You can take tea in the Japanese section (¥500) or sit out-side and admire the tranquil gardens, which also combine Eastern and Western influences.

West along the Yamanote line

Travelling **west** from Ueno to Ikebukuro on the Yamanote line there are a couple of sights worth making time for. Nippori station is the place to hop off and explore **Yanaka**, one of Tokyo's most delightful areas, packed with charm-ing old buildings and temples scattered around the large and picturesque Yanaka cemetery. Further west, Komagome Station is close by **Rikugi-en**, one of the city's most attractive Edo-period gardens. The next station west is **Sugamo**, a popular gathering spot for Tokyo's old folk, who flock here to visit the local temple **Kōgan-ji** where they seek relief from the gods for their phys-ical ailments. From here it's a short walk to Kōshinzuka Station on the Toden Arakawa line (see box, p.138), Tokyo's last tram service.

Yanaka

After the Long Sleeves Fire of 1657, many temples relocated to the higher ground of Yanaka, where they remain today, alongside old wooden buildings that seem to have miraculously escaped the ensuing centuries' various calamities. It's a charming area to explore on foot, and you could spend many hours rambling through its narrow, quiet streets, discovering small temples and traditional craft shops. If you only have a short amount of time, the obvious place to start is **Yanaka Cemetery** immediately west of Nippori Station. A five-minute walk south of the Nippori entrance to the cemetery, you'll find one of the area's most attractive temples, **Tennō-ji**, within the grounds of which is a large copper Buddha dating from 1690. Head southwest down the main cemetery avenue from here to reach the graveyard offices (daily 8.30am–5pm), where you can pick up a Japanese map of the plots locating various notables such as author Natsume Sōseki (see "Contexts", p.1019); the last Tokugawa shogun, Yoshinobu; and, in a separate fenced off area, Archbishop Nikolai Kasatkin, founder of the Russian Orthodox Nikolai Cathedral (see p.121).

Return to the Nippori entrance to the cemetery, turn west and walk a few hundred metres to reach another of Yanaka's many hidden gems, the **Asakura Chōso Museum** (Tues–Thurs, Sat & Sun 9.30am–4.30pm; ¥400; ☎03/3821-4549), the former home and studio of sculptor **Asakura Fumio** (1883–1964) – it's very well preserved, almost as if the artist had just nipped out for a quick stroll around Yanaka himself. Completed in 1935, the house successfully combines a modernist concrete building, used by the artist as his studio, with a wood-and-bamboo Japanese-style home. In the centre is a lovely Japanese garden, while on the roof of the studio is an equally delightful Western-style garden with great views across the area. Many of Asakura's works are on display, including some incredibly lifelike sculptures of his beloved cats.

Rikugi-en

Rikugi-en is Tokyo's best surviving example of a classical, Edo-period stroll-garden (daily 9am–5pm; ¥300), and it's also large enough to be relatively undisturbed by surrounding buildings and traffic noise. The entrance lies five minutes' walk south of Komagome Station on Hongō-dōri, taking a right turn one block before the next major junction.

In 1695 the fifth shogun granted one of his high-ranking feudal lords, **Yanagisawa Yoshiyasu**, a tract of farmland to the north of Edo. Yanagisawa was both a perfectionist and a literary scholar: he took seven years to design his celebrated garden – with its 88 allusions to famous scenes, real or imaginary, from ancient Japanese poetry – and then named it Rikugi-en, "garden of the six principles of poetry", in reference to the rules for composing *waka* (poems of 31 syllables). After Yanagisawa's death, Rikugi-en fell into disrepair until Iwasaki Yatarō, founder of Mitsubishi, bought the land in 1877 and restored it as part of his luxury villa. The family donated the garden to the Tokyo city authorities in 1938, since when it has been a public park.

Not surprisingly, few of the 88 landscapes have survived – the guide map issued at the entrance identifies a mere eighteen. Nevertheless, Rikugi-en still retains its rhythm and beauty, kicking off with an ancient, spreading cherry tree, then slowly unfolding along paths that meander past secluded arbours and around the indented shoreline of an islet-speckled lake. In contrast, there are also areas of more natural woodland and a hillock from which to admire the whole scene.

Tokyo's last tramline

Early twentieth-century Tokyo boasted a number of tram lines, of which only the twelve-kilometre **Toden Arakawa line** remains, running north from Waseda to Minowa-bashi. The most interesting section lies along a short stretch from **Kōshinzuka Station**, a fifteen-minute walk northwest of Sugamo station, from where the line heads southwest towards Higashi-Ikebukuro, rocking and rolling along narrow streets and through Tokyo backyards. Most of the original tram lines were private enterprises – the Arakawa line was built purely to take people to the spring blossoms in Asukayama Park – and have gradually been replaced with subways. Now the last of the *chin chin densha* ("ding ding trains"), as they're known from the sound of their bells, the Arakawa line will probably survive for its nostalgia value if nothing else. All tickets cost ¥160, however far you go; you pay as you enter. Station signs and announcements are in English.

Ikebukuro

Marsh and farmland until a hundred years ago, **Ikebukuro** is a product of the train age. Its first station was completed in 1903 and now six lines connect the area with central Tokyo and the low-cost dormitory suburbs to the north and east. Cheap accommodation and good transport have attracted an increasing number of resident expatriates, typically Chinese and Taiwanese, but including a broad sweep of other nationalities, which lends Ikebukuro a faintly cosmopolitan air.

The decidedly un-hip district is dominated by two vast department stores – Tobu and Seibu – glaring at each other from opposite sides of its confusing station. The area west of the train tracks, **Nishi-Ikebukuro**, is the more interesting to explore, particularly the wedge of streets spreading out towards the attractive Rikkyō University campus, if only for its plethora of bars and restaurants. Across the tracks, **Higashi-Ikebukuro** is the main shopping centre and has good discount stores, with cameras and electronic goods at prices rivalling Akihabara (see p.121). Apart from a pretty tacky entertainment district, Higashi-Ikebukuro's only other draw is the **Sunshine City** complex, home to the monstrous, sixty-storey Sunshine 60 building and the Ancient Orient Museum.

West Ikebukuro

Ikebukuro Station handles around one million passengers per day – second only to Shinjuku – and its warren of connecting passages, shopping arcades and countless exits is notoriously difficult to negotiate. It's even worse on the west side, when the helpfully colour-coded signs mutate to blue, indicating you are now in Tōbu territory. **Tōbu** is Japan's largest department store, with over 80,000 square metres of floor space in three interconnected buildings, including the glass-fronted Metropolitan Plaza, where you'll find the excellent **Japan Traditional Crafts Centre** (daily 11am–7pm; until 5pm every other Tues, and occasionally closed Wed; free; ☎03/5954-6066, ⓦ www.kougei.or.jp/english/center.html). This has an extensive display of arts and crafts from all over the country, including lacquerware, ceramics, dolls and handmade paper, and many of the items are for sale. There's an information desk where the staff speak English, and a small library with English-language books on traditional arts.

Both the nearby *Hotel Metropolitan* and **Metropolitan Art Space** belong to the Tōbu empire. The latter, facing Tōbu store across an open square, hosts regular concerts and theatre performances, plus occasionally rewarding

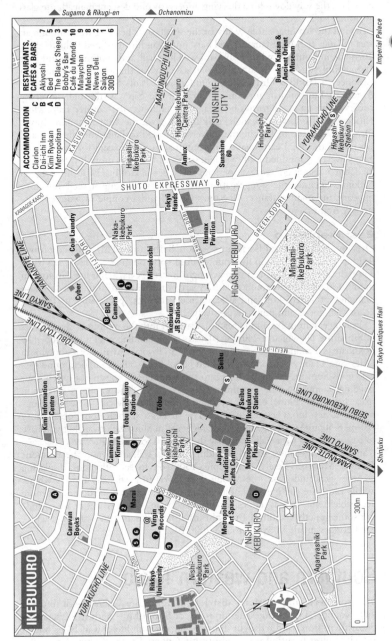

IKEBUKURO

▲ Sugamo & Rikugi-en　　▲ Ochanomizu

▶ Imperial Palace

▶ Tokyo Antiques Hall

▶ Shinjuku

ACCOMMODATION	
Clarion	C
Dai-ichi Inn	B
Kimi Ryokan	A
Metropolitan	D

RESTAURANTS, CAFÉS & BARS	
Akiyoshi	7
Bed	5
The Black Sheep	3
Bobby's Bar	4
Café du Monde	8
Malaychan	9
Mekong	2
News Deli	1
Saigon	6
300B	

MARUNOUCHI LINE

YURAKUCHO LINE

Higashi-Ikebukuro Central Park

SUNSHINE CITY

Bunka Kaikan & Ancient Orient Museum

Hindechō Park

Higashi-Ikebukuro Station

KASUGA-DŌRI

Higashi-Ikebukuro Park

Amlux

Sunshine 60

SHUTO EXPRESSWAY 6

KAWAGOE-KAIDO

Tōkyū Hands

Naka-Ikebukuro Park

Mitsukoshi

MEIJI-DŌRI

SUNSHINE 60-DORI

Humax Pavilion

HIGASHI-IKEBUKURO

GREEN-DŌRI

Minami-Ikebukuro Park

Coin Laundry

Cyber

BIC Camera

SAIKYO LINE

YAMANOTE LINE

TŌBU TŌJŌ LINE

Kimi Information Centre

TOKIWA-DŌRI

Ikebukuro JR Station

Seibu

MEIJI-DŌRI

Tōbu

Tōbu Ikebukuro Station

Seibu

Seibu Ikebukuro Station

SEIBU IKEBUKURO LINE

YURAKUCHO LINE

Camera no Kimura

Ikebukuro Nishiguchi Park

Japan Traditional Crafts Centre

Metropolitan Plaza

SAIKYO LINE

YAMANOTE LINE

Caravan Books

Marui

NISHIGUCHI KAISAN-DORI

Metropolitan Art Space

NISHI-IKEBUKURO

Virgin Records

Nishi-Ikebukuro Park

RIKKYO-DŌRI

Rikkyō University

Agariyashiki Park

300m

N

139

exhibitions. Its main claim to fame, though, is its long **escalator**, best experienced on the way down for a dizzying, ninety-second descent beneath the glass atrium.

Behind the Art Space, follow any of the small roads heading west through an area of lanes rich in restaurants and bars, until you hit tree-lined Rikkyō-dōri. Turn left, in front of a white clapboard wedding hall, and continue for just over 100m until you see a square, red-brick gateway on the left. This is the main entrance to **Rikkyō University**, founded as St Paul's School in 1874 by an American Episcopalian missionary. Through the gateway, the old university courtyard has an incongruous Ivy League touch in its vine-covered halls, white windows and grassy quadrangle, making it a favourite venue for film crews. Originally located in Tsukiji, the university moved to Ikebukuro in 1918 and weathered the 1923 earthquake with minimal damage except for one toppled gate tower; the lopsided look was left, so it's said, as a memorial to those who died, but a deciding factor was perhaps the sheer lack of bricks. Other original buildings include the congregation hall, now a nicotine-stained refectory opposite the main entrance, All Saint's Chapel and a couple of wooden missionary houses.

East Ikebukuro

Over on the east side of Ikebukuro Station, **Seibu** rules. This is the company's flagship store, the largest in the country until Tōbu outgrew it a few years back. Though the group has been retrenching in recent years, Seibu has a history of innovation and spotting new trends. Apart from the main store, there are also branches of Parco, Loft and Wave, Seibu offshoots specializing in fashion, household goods and music respectively.

Heading east from Ikebukuro Station, you can't miss the monstrous sixty storeys of **Sunshine 60**, which at 240m was Japan's tallest building until it was pipped by Yokohama's Landmark Tower. Just in front is Toyota's **Amlux** car showroom (Tues–Sun 11am–8pm), one for die-hard petrol-heads only; an underground passage leads from the basement here into the Sunshine 60 tower, just one of four buildings comprising the **Sunshine City** complex of shops, offices, exhibition space, hotel and cultural centres – though compared to the city's newer developments, it all looks rather dowdy. The tower's sixtieth-floor observatory (10am–8.30pm; ¥620) may be a shade higher than Shinjuku's rivals, but you have to pay, and unless it's a really clear day there's not a lot to see anyway.

Sunshine City's most easterly building, Bunka Kaikan, houses the **Ancient Orient Museum** (daily 10am–5pm; ¥500) on its seventh floor, displaying archeological finds from the Middle East (Syria in particular) and elsewhere. While there are the inevitable bits of old pot, the collection focuses on more accessible items such as statues, jewellery, icons and other works of art, including some superb Gandhara Buddhist art from Pakistan and a smiling, wide-eyed goddess made in Syria around 2000 BC.

Southern and western Tokyo

The **southern and western districts** of Tokyo are where you'll find the city's younger, hipper side. The mini-city of **Shinjuku** – with its skyscrapers, department stores and red-light district – buzzes with life, and includes one of the city's most beautiful parks, **Shinjuku Gyoen**. South of Shinjuku are the ritzy residential, shopping and entertainment districts of **Aoyama** and

Harajuku, a collective showcase of contemporary Tokyo fashion and style. Consumer culture is not the only thing on offer, however; the verdant grounds of the city's most venerable shrine, **Meiji-jingū**, stretch from Aoyama to Harajuku, where you'll also find the stadiums of **Yoyogi-kōen**, the focus of the 1964 Olympics. There's plenty of cosmopolitan atmosphere at the designer shops and cafés along the super-chic **Omotesandō**, a tree-lined boulevard often referred to as Tokyo's Champs Elysées, while the transport hub of **Shibuya**, further south, is another youth-orientated commercial enclave, with trendsetting shops and restaurants, plus a handful of museums.

Further south, **Ebisu** and **Daikenyama** are also fertile hunting grounds for dining and drinking. Ebisu is also home to the excellent **Tokyo Metropolitan Photography Museum**, while neighbouring **Meguro** has a couple of interesting museums, as well as the tranquil **National Park for Nature Study** and **Happōen** traditional garden and teahouse. It's a short walk east from here to the temple **Sengaku-ji**, a key location in one of the city's bloodiest true-life samurai sagas, and the Tokyo Bayside transport and hotel hub of **Shinagawa**, one of the original checkpoints for entry to the old capital of Edo.

Shinjuku

Some 4km due west of the Imperial Palace, **Shinjuku** is the modern heart of Tokyo. The district has a long history of pandering to the more basic of human desires, and a day and an evening spent in the area will show you Tokyo at its best and worst – from the love hotels and hostess bars of Kabukichō to the no-frills bars of Shomben Yokochō (Piss Alley) and the shop-till-you-drop department stores and high-tech towers.

Shinjuku is split in two by a thick band of train tracks. The western half, **Nishi-Shinjuku**, with its soaring skyscrapers, is a showcase for contemporary architecture; the raunchier eastern side, **Higashi-Shinjuku**, is a nonstop red-light and shopping district, and the inspiration for Ridley Scott's *Blade Runner*. Also on the east is one of Tokyo's most attractive parks, **Shinjuku Gyoen**.

Shinjuku Station is a messy combination of three terminals (the main JR station, plus the Keiō and Odakyū stations beside their respective department stores on the west side) and connecting subway lines. There's also the separate **Seibu Shinjuku Station**, northeast of the JR station. At least two million commuters are fed into these stations every day and spun out of sixty exits. The rivers of people constantly flowing along the station's many underground passages only add

Shinjuku		
Shinjuku	*Shinjuku*	新宿
Golden Gai	*Gōruden Gai*	ゴールデン街
Hanazono shrine	*Hanazono-jinja*	花園神社
Kabukichō	*Kabukichō*	歌舞伎町
Kinokuniya	*Kinokuniya*	紀伊国屋
New National Theatre	*Shin Kokuritsu Gekijō*	新国立劇場
Piss Alley	*Shomben Yokochō*	しょんべん横丁
Shinjuku Gyoen	*Shinjuku Gyoen*	新宿御苑
Shinjuku-Nichōme	*Shinjuku-Nichōme*	新宿二丁目
Shinjuku Park Tower	*Shinjuku Pāku Tawā*	新宿パークタワー
Taisō-ji	*Taisō-ji*	大宗寺
Tokyo Metropolitan Government Building	*Tōkyō Tochō*	東京都庁
Tokyo Opera City	*Tōkyō Opera Shitii*	東京オペラシティー

SHINJUKU

ACCOMMODATION

Central Hotel Shinjuku	B
Hotel Century Southern Tower	D
Green Plaza Shinjuku	A
Park Hyatt Tokyo	E
Shinjuku Washington Hotel	C
Tokyo Yoyogi Youth Hostel	F

RESTAURANTS, CAFÉS & BARS

Angkor Wat	24	New York Bar	24
Ban Thai	5	New York Grill	5
Ben's Café	1	Rendezvous	1
Café Comme Ça	11	Rolling Stone	11
Clubhouse	6	Seiryūmon	15
Jetée	8	Shion	6
Kakiden	18	Shun Kan	18
The Dubliners	14	-roku	10
Tōhō-kenbun	23	Tsunahachi	17
		Vagabond	7

CLUBS

Ace	19
Advocates	16
Arty Farty	21
Code	4
Dragon	21
Fuji Bar	21
GB	21
Kinswomyn	12
Liquid Room	3

Map labels:

Akebonobashi & Tokyo YWCA Sadohara — Yotsuya

MEIJI-DORI · GYOEN-DORI · YASUKUNI-DORI · TOEI SHINJUKU LINE · MARUNOUCHI LINE

SHINJUKU NICHOME · Shinjuku Gyoen · Shinjuku-mon (Main gate to Park)

Golden Gai · Hanazono-jinja · Isetan Department Store · SHIN-NO MICHI PROMENADE

KABUKI-CHŌ · Koma Theatre · SHINJUKU-KU · Shinjuku Sanchome · Shinjuku-Sanchome

Marui Department Store · Mitsukoshi Department Store · Kinokuniya Bookstore · Studio Alta

Shinjuku Station · East Exit · Shin-Minami Entrance to Shinjuku Station · Takashimaya Times Square · Kinokuniya Bookstore (Main Building) · Tenryū-ji

SEIBU SHINJUKU LINE · Seibu Shinjuku Station · YAMANOTE LINE · SAIKYO LINE · CHŪŌ + SOBU LINES

Takadanobaba, 1 & 2 · Idabashi · Shinjuku-Nishiguchi Subway Station · Shomben Yokochō (Piss Alley) · Odakyu Department Store West Exit · Odakyu Station (Shinjuku) · Keiō-Shinjuku

ODAKYU LINE · KEIO LINE · KEIO SHIN-SEN LINE · Roppongi · Yoyogi

Jōen-in · Jōsen-in · KOSHŪ KAIDO · Yasuda Kasai Kaijō

Shinjuku Nomura Building · (Pentax Forum) Shinjuku Mitsui Building · Shinjuku Sumitomo Building · Tokyo Medical College Hospital · Nishi-Shinjuku Station · ŌME KAIDO · CHŌ-DŌRI

NISHI-SHINJUKU · Keiō Plaza Hotel · PLAZA-DORI · Keiō Department Store · Highway Bus Terminal · Yodobashi Camera · Sakuraya Camera · Shinjuku · KDDI Building · Shinjuku NS Building · Metropolitan Assembly Hall · HIGASHI-DORI · GINZŌ-DORI

Shinjuku Park Tower & Living Design Ozone · Tokyo Metropolitan Government Building · TOCHO-DORI · Tochōmae · MINAMI-DORI · KITA-DORI · KŌEN-DŌRI · Shinjuku Chūō-Kōen

Nakano · Nerima · ŌEDO LINE · Tokyo Opera City, NTT Intercommunications Centre (ICC) & The New National Theatre

N · 300 m

to the confusion and it's easy to get hopelessly lost. If this happens, head immediately for street level and get your bearings from the skyscrapers to the west.

Nishi-Shinjuku

If there's one area of Tokyo in which you can fully appreciate Japan's monumental wealth and economic power, it is among the soaring skyscrapers of
Nishi-Shinjuku (West Shinjuku). In themselves, few of these towers of glass,
concrete and steel are worth spending much time exploring, though most of
them have free observation rooms on their upper floors, and a wide selection
of restaurants and bars with good views. Collectively, however, their impact is
striking, mainly because their scale, coupled with the spaciousness of their surroundings, is so unusual for Tokyo – this is still predominantly a low-rise city.
To reach Nishi-Shinjuku, either head for the west exit at Shinjuku Station and
then go through the pedestrian tunnel beyond the two fountains in the sunken
plaza in front of the Odakyū department store, or hop out of the subway at
Tochōmae Station, on the Ōedo line.

On the left-hand side of Chūō-dōri as you emerge at the end of the tunnel
is the monumental **Tokyo Metropolitan Government Building** (TMGB),
a 400,000-square-metre complex designed by top Tokyo architect Tange
Kenzō. Thirteen thousand city bureaucrats go to work each day at the TMGB,
and the entire complex – which includes twin 48-storey towers, an adjacent
tower block, the Metropolitan Assembly Hall (where the city's councillors
meet) and a sweeping, statue-lined and colonnaded plaza – feels like Gotham
City. Tange was actually aiming to evoke Paris's Notre Dame, and there's certainly something of that cathedral's design in the shape of the twin towers. But
the building's real triumph is that it is unmistakably Japanese; the dense criss-
cross pattern of its glass and granite facade is reminiscent of both traditional
architecture and the circuitry of an enormous computer chip. Both the twin
towers have identical free observation rooms on their 45th floors (Mon–Fri
9.30am–10pm, Sat & Sun 9.30am–7pm), and it's worth timing your visit for
dusk, so you can see the multicoloured lights of Shinjuku spark and fizzle into
action as the setting sun turns the sky a deep photochemical orange. The
TMGB also has inexpensive cafés on the 32nd floor and the ground floor of
the Metropolitan Assembly Hall. Free **tours** are available in English (Mon–Fri
10am–3pm) from the Tokyo Information Centre on the ground floor of
Tower 1.

Just behind the TMGB is Shinjuku Chūō-kōen, a dusty park on the south
side of which is **Shinjuku Park Tower**, another building across which Tange's
modernist signature is confidently written. The style credentials of this complex of three linked towers, all topped with glass pyramids, are vouched for by
the presence of the luxurious *Park Hyatt Hotel* (which occupies the building's
loftiest floors), the Conran Shop, and the **Living Design Centre Ozone**
(daily except Wed 10.30am–6.30pm; entrance fee varies with exhibition;
T03/5322 6500, Wwww.ozone.co.jp), a spacious museum specializing in interior design, with interesting, regularly changing exhibitions by both Japanese
and Western designers. A regular free shuttle bus runs from opposite the
Odakyū department store to the south side of the tower.

A ten-minute walk west of the tower, and connected to Hatsudai Station on
the Keiō line, is **Tokyo Opera City**, with 54 floors of offices, shops and restaurants. The 234-metre-high tower also has a state-of-the-art concert hall and, on
the fourth floor, the **NTT Intercommunication Centre** (ICC; Tues–Sun
10am–6pm, Fri until 9pm; ¥800; T0120-144199, Wwww.ntticc.or.jp), the most
innovative interactive exhibition space in Tokyo. There's usually something

interesting to see here; past displays of "high-tech art" have included a sound-proof room where you listen to your own heartbeat and light-sensitive robots you can control with your brain waves. Directly behind Tokyo Opera City is the **New National Theatre**, an ambitious complex of three performing arts auditoria (see "Nightlife and entertainment", p.185).

Modern architecture in Tokyo

From the swirling rooftop of the National Yoyogi Stadium to the seemingly bubble-wrapped Prada building on Omotesandō, Tokyo has an astonishing array of **modern architecture**. Japan's top postwar architect, **Tange Kenzō**, has done more than most to define Tokyo's eclectic style – his monumental Tokyo Metropolitan Government Building (see p.143) in Shinjuku has been described as the last great edifice of postmodernism, though some would argue that he has gone one step further with the other-worldly Fuji TV building in Odaiba (see p.162). Other works by Tange in Tokyo include the 1964 Olympic Stadium in Yoyogi (see p.149) and the United Nations University on Aoyama-dōri.

Tange is one of three Japanese architects to have received architecture's most prestigious international award, the Pritzker Prize. Another is **Andō Tadao**, former boxer and self-taught architect. His Collezione building, at the far east end of Omotesandō in Harajuku (see p.149), is a good example of his liking for rough concrete and bold structural forms. He has also been commissioned to design the complex of shops and apartments replacing the now demolished Donjunkai Aoyama apartments in the middle of Omotesandō. For now, though, his best work, such as Ōsaka's Church of Light, the Literature Museum in Himeji (see p.614), and the contemporary art museum, Benesse House, on Naoshima (see p.726), can be seen around his hometown of Ōsaka.

Maki Fumihiko is Japan's third Pritzker Prize winner. His work includes the futuristic Tokyo Metropolitan Gymnasium in Sendagaya, the Spiral Building near Omotesandō, with its deliberately fragmented facade, and the ambitious Hillside Terrace in ritzy Daikan'yama, a complex of homes, offices and shops developed over a 23-year period. Among other prominent Japanese architects, **Isozaki Arata**'s Ochanomizu Square Building, just north of the Imperial Palace, is a good example of how old and new architecture can be successfully combined. Visibly taking its inspiration from traditional Japanese art – in this case, paintings of overlapping mountains fading into the mists – is **Rokkaku Kijō**'s Tokyo Budōkan, the martial arts mecca.

Many top foreign architects have used Tokyo as a canvas on which to work out their most extravagant designs. In Asakusa, look for **Philippe Starck**'s Super Dry Hall, with its enigmatic "golden turd" on the roof; and **Sir Norman Foster**'s Century Tower at Ochanomizu, which incorporates the vernacular design of the *torii*, ten of which appear to be piled on top of each other on the building's facade. Light floods into the soaring glass hall of **Rafael Viñoly**'s Tokyo International Forum in Yūrakuchō, while **Sir Richard Rogers**' Kabukichō Building, swathed in a framework of stainless-steel rods, is hidden on a Shinjuku side street. Most recently in 2003 **Jacques Herzog** and **Pierre de Meuron** of Switzerland (the team responsible for London's Tate Modern) unveiled their stunning Prada building, a jewel-like edifice of rhomboid crystals, cuddled on one side by a velvety, moss-covered wall.

If you want to take a quick tour of Tokyo's modern architectural highlights, walk from Sendagaya Station along Gaien-nishi-dōri to Aoyama-dōri, turn right and continue to the crossing with Omotesandō. From here you can either continue down to Shibuya, past the Spiral Hall and the UN building, or turn left to reach the Prada Building and La Collezione. Either way, you'll have passed many of the best examples of modern Tokyo architecture. Although it misses out on some of the past decade's additions to the city's skyline, Tajima Noriyuki's illustrated, pocket-sized *Tokyo: A Guide to Recent Architecture* is still the best around.

Returning to the east side of Shinjuku Station, squashed up against the train tracks running north from the Odakyū department store, are the narrow alleyways of the **Shomben Yokochō**, also known as Omoide Yokochō. The name of this cramped, four-block neighbourhood of ramshackle mini-bars and restaurants translates as "Piss Alley", but don't be put off exploring this atmospheric quarter – you're less likely to be ripped off for a drink here than in the similar Golden Gai district of Kabukichō. A pedestrian tunnel at the southern end of the alleys, just to the right of the cheap clothes outlets, provides a short cut to the east side of Shinjuku Station and Studio Alta.

Higashi-Shinjuku

Some days it seems as if all of Tokyo is waiting at Shinjuku's favourite meeting spot, beneath the huge TV screen on the **Studio Alta** building on the east (*higashi*) side of the JR station. It's worth bearing this in mind if you arrange to meet anyone there – a generally less crowded option is at the plaza opposite Studio Alta, from where you can soak up the supercharged atmosphere, especially at night, when the district is ablaze with neon. To the southeast of here is **Shinjuku-dōri**, along which you'll find some of the classier department stores and shops, such as Mitsukoshi and **Isetan**, which has excellent food halls in its basement, a good range of restaurants on the top floor and an art gallery that frequently holds notable exhibitions (check local English-language newspapers and magazines for details). In addition, beneath the pounding feet of pedestrians on Yasakuni-dōri lies an extensive subterranean shopping complex, **Shinjuku Subnade**, while a tunnel with exits to all the major shops runs the length of Shinjuku-dōri from the main JR station to the Shinjuku-Sanchōme subway station.

Directly to the north of Studio Alta, across the wide boulevard of Yasakuni-dōri, lies the red-light district **Kabukichō**, at the heart of which is the Koma Theatre, where modern musicals and samurai dramas are performed. The tatty plaza in front of the theatre is lined with cinemas, many showing the latest Hollywood blockbusters, and the streets radiating around it contain a wide range of bars and restaurants. Stray a block or so further north and you're in the raunchier side of Kabukichō, with soaplands, hostess bars and girly shows lining the narrow streets. You stand a good chance of spotting members of the *yakuza* crime syndicates at work (the tight-perm hairdos and 1970s-style clobber are giveaway signs) around here, but the overall atmosphere is not unlike London's Soho, where the porn industry and illicit goings-on nestle unthreateningly beside less salacious entertainment.

Local shopkeepers come to pray for business success at Kabukichō's attractive **Hanazono-jinja**. This shrine predates the founding of Edo by the Tokugawa, but the current granite and vermilion buildings are modern recreations. It's worth paying a visit at night, when spotlights give the shrine a special ambience. From here, you're well poised to take a stroll through the **Golden Gai**, the low-rent drinking quarter where intellectuals and artists have rubbed shoulders with Kabukichō's demi-monde since the war. In this compact grid of streets there are around two hundred bars, no larger than broom cupboards and presided over by no-nonsense *mama-sans* and *masters*. Unless you speak good Japanese, you probably won't want to stop for a drink; at most bars only regulars are welcome, while the others will fleece you rotten.

By contrast, the city's squeaky-clean future is on display at **Takashimaya Times Square**, close by the Shin-Minami ("New South") entrance to Shinjuku Station, which is shifting Shinjuku's focus away from Kabukichō. The sleek new shopping and entertainment complex is connected to the southern

(Shin-Minami) entrance of Shinjuku Station by a broad wooden promenade, and includes branches of the Takashimaya department store, interior design and handicrafts superstore Tōkyū Hands, and the vast seven-floor **Kinokuniya** bookstore. Inside the mall are also **Shinjuku Joypolis** (daily 10am–11.15pm; ¥300), a high-tech amusement park of virtual-reality rides produced by Sega, and the **Tokyo IMAX Theatre** (¥1300), which screens 3-D films on its six-storey-high cinema screen – both good places to keep the kids occupied if you want to go shopping.

Shinjuku Gyoen and around

Five minutes' walk east of Takashimaya Times Square, close by the Shinjuku-Gyoen-mae subway station, is the main entrance to **Shinjuku Gyoen** (Tues–Sun 9am–4.30pm, last entry 4pm; ¥200), the largest and possibly most beautiful gardens in Tokyo. The grounds, which once held the mansion of Lord Naitō, the *daimyō* of Tsuruga on the Sea of Japan coast, became the property of the Imperial Household in 1868. After World War II, the 150-acre park was opened to the public. Apart from their spaciousness, the gardens' main feature is their variety of design. The southern half is traditionally Japanese, with winding paths, stone lanterns, artificial hills, islands in ponds linked by zigzag bridges and *Rakuutei*, a pleasant **teahouse** (10am–4pm; ¥700). At the northern end of the park are formal, French-style gardens, with neat rows of tall birch trees and hedge-lined flowerbeds. Clipped, broad lawns dominate the middle of the park, modelled on English landscape design. On the eastern flank next to the large greenhouse (daily 11am–3.30pm), packed with subtropical vegetation and particularly cosy on a chilly winter's day, an imperial wooden **villa** from 1869 has been reconstructed (second and fourth Sat of month, 10am–3pm). In spring, the whole park bursts with pink and white cherry blossoms, while in early November kaleidoscopic chrysanthemum displays and golden autumn leaves are the main attractions. There are several cafés within the gardens where you can grab a reasonable lunch for around ¥900, but it's much nicer to bring a picnic and relax in the tranquil surroundings. An alternative entrance to the gardens is through the western gate, a five-minute walk under and alongside the train tracks from Sendagaya Station.

Walking back towards Shinjuku Station will take you past the **gay district** of **Shinjuku Nichōme**. During the day the area is inconspicuous, but come nightfall the numerous bars spring into action, catering to every imaginable sexual orientation. Close by is **Taisō-ji**, a temple founded in 1668, which has the city's largest wooden statue of Yama, the King of Hell. The statue is in the temple building next to a large copper Buddha dressed in a red bib and cap. You have to press a button to illuminate the 5.5-metre Yama, whose fearsome expression is difficult to take seriously once you've spotted the offerings at his feet – a couple of tins of fruit are the norm.

Meiji-jingū

Covering parts of both Aoyama and Harajuku, the areas immediately south of Shinjuku, is **Meiji-jingū**, Tokyo's premier Shinto shrine, a memorial to Emperor Meiji, who died in 1912, and his empress Shōken, who died in 1914. The shrine is split into two sections: the **Outer Garden**, between Sendagaya and Shinanomachi stations, contains the Meiji Memorial Picture Gallery and several sporting arenas, including the National Stadium and Jingū Baseball Stadium; the more important **Inner Garden**, beside Harajuku Station, includes the emperor's shrine, the empress's iris gardens, the imperial couple's Treasure House and extensive wooded grounds.

Together with the neighbouring shrines to General Nogi and Admiral Tōgō

△ Tokyo Tower

(see p.150), Meiji-jingū was created as a symbol of imperial power and Japanese racial superiority. Rebuilt in 1958 after being destroyed during World War II, the shrine remains the focus of several **festivals** during the year. The most important of these, **Hatsu–mōde** (first visit of the year to a shrine), is held on January 1 and attracts three million visitors – traffic lights have to be operated within the shrine grounds to control the crowds on the day. More entertaining is **Seijin-no-hi** (Adults' Day) on the second Monday in January. On this day, 20-year-olds attend the shrine, the women often dressed in elaborate long-sleeved kimono, fur stoles wrapped around their necks, while Meiji-jingū's gravel approach is lined with ice sculptures and there's a colourful display of traditional *momoteshiki* archery by costumed archers. On April 29 to May 3 and November 1 to 3, *bugaku* (court music and dances) are performed on a stage erected in the shrine's main courtyard, while *Shichi-go-san-no-hi* (Seven-Five-Three Day), on November 15, provides an opportunity to see children of these ages dressed in delightful mini-kimono. Apart from the festivals, Meiji-jingū is best visited midweek, when its calm serenity can be appreciated without the crowds.

The Outer Garden and around

The closest subway to the entrance to Meiji-jingū's Outer Garden is Aoyama Itchōme. The **Meiji Memorial Picture Gallery** (daily 9am–5pm; ¥500; ☏03/3401-5179, ⓦwww.meijijingu.or.jp/gaien/01.htm) lies at the northern end of a long, ginkgo tree-lined approach road, which runs beside the rugby and baseball stadiums northwest of the subway, and has a stern, European-style exterior and a marble-clad entrance hall which soars up to a central dome. On either side are halls containing forty paintings which tell the life story of the Emperor Meiji – more interesting for their depiction of Japan emerging from its feudal past than for their artistic merits.

Next to the gallery looms the 75,000-seater **National Stadium**, Japan's largest sporting arena, built for the 1964 Olympics. On the western side of the stadium – and best viewed from outside Sendagaya Station – is the outer garden's most striking feature: the **Tokyo Metropolitan Gymnasium**, designed by Maki Fumihiko (see box on p.144). At first glance the building looks like a giant alien spacecraft, but on closer examination it becomes obvious that the inspiration is a traditional samurai helmet. The corrugated stainless-steel-roofed building houses the main arena, while in the block to the right, crowned with a glass pyramid roof, are public swimming pools and a subterranean gym (entry ¥450).

Following the railway line and road west will lead you to a sign pointing to the **National Nō Theatre**, set back from the street in a walled compound. Only built in 1983, the theatre incorporates traditional Japanese architectural motifs, particularly in the design of its slightly sloping roofs. Although Nō, Japan's oldest and most stylized form of theatre, is something of an acquired taste, this is one of the best places in which to see a production. Return to the main road and follow the raised expressway as it crosses over the railway lines. You'll go under the tracks and veer off left up the hill to Meiji-jingū's Inner Garden eastern entrance.

The Inner Garden

The most impressive way to approach the **Inner Garden** is through the southern gate next to Jingū-bashi, the bridge across from Harajuku's toy-town station building, complete with mock-Tudor clock tower. If you visit here on Sunday, your progress into the shrine will almost certainly be halted by the strange fashion parade of the **cosu-play-zoku**, a tourist attraction in its own bizarre right. Most of the participants – mainly girls, but some boys – are Japanese teenagers, but among the crowd you may also spot the odd *gaijin* getting in on the fun by dressing up as their favourite rock star from bands such as Psycho Le Lemu or Dir Engrey. Some of the costumes, incorporating Nazi regalia or the kind of garments more regularly seen in a porn video than on some 13-year-old on the street, are confronting to say the least, but most will blow you away with their creativity and downright weirdness.

From the gateway a wide gravel path runs through densely forested grounds to the twelve-metre-high **Ō-torii**, the largest Myōjin-style gate in Japan, made from 1500-year-old cypress pine trees from Taiwan. Just before the gate, on the right, is the **Bunkakan**, a new complex housing a restaurant, café, gift shop and the generally uninteresting annexe of the **Treasure House** (daily: April–Nov 8.30am–4pm; Jan–March & Dec 9.30am–3.30pm; ¥500 entry to both buildings); this is where you'll alight from your bus if you visit on an organized tour. To left of the Ō-torii is the entrance to the **Jingū Naien** (daily 8.30am–5pm; ¥500), a traditional garden – said to have been designed by the emperor Meiji for his wife – which is at its most beautiful (and most crowded) in June, when over one hundred varieties of **irises**, the empress's favourite flowers, pepper the lush greenery with their purple and white blooms.

Returning to the garden's entrance, the gravel path turns right and passes through a second wooden *torii*, **Kita-mon** (north gate), leading to the impressive **honden** (central hall). With their Japanese cypress wood and green copper roofs, the buildings are a fine example of how Shinto architecture can blend seamlessly with nature. There are exits from the courtyard on its eastern and western flanks; follow either of the paths northwards through the woods to arrive at the pleasant grassy slopes and pond before the main **Treasure House** (same hours as annexe). Don't bother going in – the contents of the museum are no more thrilling than the lumpen grey concrete building that houses them.

Harajuku

Apart from the wooded grounds of Meiji-jingū, **Harajuku** is also blessed with Tokyo's largest park, **Yoyogi-kōen**, a favourite spot for joggers and bonneted groups of kindergarten kids with their minders. Once an imperial army training ground, the park was dubbed "Washington Heights" after World War II, when it was used to house US military personnel. In 1964 the land was used for the Olympic athletes' village, after which it became Yoyogi-kōen. Two of the stadia, built for the Olympics, remain the area's most famous architectural features. The main building of Tange Kenzō's **Yoyogi National Stadium** is a dead ringer for Noah's ark, and its steel suspension roof was a structural engineering marvel at the time. Inside are a swimming pool and skating rink (Mon–Sat noon–8pm, Sun 10am–6pm; ¥900). The smaller stadium, used for basketball, is like the sharp end of a giant swirling seashell.

Omotesandō and around

Harajuku's most elegant boulevard, lined with *zelkova* trees, **Omotesandō**, leads from the entrance to Meiji-jingū to the cluster of contemporary designer boutiques on the other side of Aoyama-dōri. On either side are dense networks of streets, packed with funky little shops, restaurants and bars. One of the most famous roads is **Takeshita-dōri**, whose hungry mouth gobbles up teenage fashion victims as they swarm out of the north exit of Harajuku Station and spits them out the other end on Meiji-dōri minus their cash. The shops sell every kind of tat imaginable, are hugely enjoyable to root around, and provide a window on Japanese teen fashion. On Sundays the crush of bodies on the street is akin to that on the Yamanote line at rush hour.

Aoyama, Harajuku and Shibuya

Aoyama	*Aoyama*	青山
Aoyama Cemetery	*Aoyama Reien*	青山霊園
Harajuku	*Harajuku*	原宿
Meiji-jingū	*Meiji-jingū*	明治神宮
Meiji Memorial Picture Gallery	*Meiji Kaigakan*	明治絵画館
National Nō Theatre	*Kokuritsu Nō Gekijō*	国立能劇場
Nezu Museum of Art	*Nezu Bijutsukan*	根津美術館
Omotesandō	*Omotesandō*	表参道
Ōta Memorial Museum of Art	*Ōta Kinen Bijutsukan*	太田記念美術館
Takeshita-dōri	*Takeshita-dōri*	竹下通り
Tōgō-jinja	*Tōgō-jinja*	東郷神社
Yoyogi-kōen	*Yoyogi-kōen*	代々木公園
Shibuya	*Shibuya*	渋谷
Dōgenzaka	*Dōgenzaka*	道玄坂
Hachikō	*Hachikō*	ハチ公
Japan Folk Crafts Museum	*Mingeikan*	民芸館
TEPCO Electric Energy Museum	*TEPCO Denryokukan*	TEPCO電力館
Tobacco and Salt Museum	*Tabako-to-Shio-no-Hakubutsukan*	たばこと塩の博物館
Toguri Museum of Art	*Toguri Bijutsukan*	戸栗美術館
Tokyo Metropolitan Children's Hall	*Tōkyō-to Jidō Kaikan*	東京都児童会館

Serious bargain hunters never miss out on the outdoor antiques market held on the first and fourth Sundays of each month in the precincts of the neighbouring **Tōgō-jinja**. The market sells everything from fine *tansu* (traditional Japanese chests) to old kimono and crockery. You'll need to know what you're looking for to avoid being ripped off, but it's also possible to snag bargains if you come at the end of the day when the stalls are packing up and the sellers are prepared to haggle. The **shrine** itself is dedicated to Admiral Tōgō Heihachirō, who led the victorious Japanese fleet against the Russians in the Russo–Japanese War of 1904–5, and has a pretty pond and garden fronting onto Meiji-dōri.

Walking back towards the crossing with Omotesandō, look out for Laforet, a trendy boutique complex, behind which is the excellent **Ōta Memorial Museum of Art** (Tues–Sun 10.30am–5pm; ¥500; ☎03/3403-0880, ⓦwww.ukiyoe-ota-muse.jp), well worth investigating. You'll have to leave your shoes in the lockers and put on slippers to wander the small galleries on two levels featuring *ukiyo-e* paintings and prints from the private collection of the late Ōta Seizō, the former chairman of the Tōhō Life Insurance Company. The art displayed comes from a collection of 12,000 pieces, including masterpieces by Utamaro, Hokusai and Hiroshige.

In complete contrast to all this is the **Design Festa Gallery** (daily 11am–8pm; free; ☎03/3479-1442, ⓦwww.designfesta.com), a joyfully anarchic art space sprouting out of the funky backstreets of Harajuku like some bargain basement Pompidou Centre. The gallery is an offshoot of Design Festa, Japan's biggest art and design event, held twice yearly at Tokyo Big Site (see p.160). It's hard to believe that beneath the day-glo paintings, graffiti, mad scaffolding and traffic cones, swarming over the building's front like some alien metal creeper, lies a block of ordinary apartments. Inside, the art is no less eclectic, ranging from sculpture to video installations – even the toilet is plastered from floor to ceiling with artworks. Behind it is a good *okonomiyaki* café and bar (see p.171). To find the gallery, take the street directly opposite the eastern Meiji-dōri end of Takeshita-dōri, then turn north at the second junction on your left.

Returning to Omotesandō and heading east, you'll pass Mori Building's latest project, the redevelopment of the **Dojunkai Aoyama Apartments** site, due to finish in 2006. Andō Tadao (see p.144), who has been charged with designing this new complex of shops and homes, plans to keep the complex low-rise, and also intends to reconstruct one of the original 1927 ivy-clad multi-family housing blocks that were a much-loved part of Omotesandō before being demolished in 2003.

As it crosses Aoyama-dōri, Omotesandō narrows and becomes lined with top designer-label boutiques including **Prada**, which occupies an incredible glass-bubble building which is a tourist attraction in its own right (see "Modern architecture" box on p.144). At the T-junction, just beyond the Andō Tadao-designed Collezione building, turn right for the entrances to the **Nezu Museum of Art** (Tues–Sun 9.30am–4.30pm; ¥1000; ☎03/3400-2536, ⓦwww.nezu-muse.or.jp). The rather steep entrance charge makes this small museum a bit of a luxury, but it does have a classy collection of Oriental arts, including many national treasures. The best time to visit is the ten-day period at the end of April and beginning of May, when Ōgata Kōrin's exquisite screen paintings of irises are displayed. Otherwise, the museum's nicest feature is its garden, which slopes gently away around an ornamental pond and features several traditional teahouses.

Turning left at the end of Omotesandō, the road leads round into Tokyo's most important graveyard, officially entitled Aoyama Reien, but generally known as **Aoyama Bochi**. Everyone who was anyone, including Hachikō the faithful dog (see p.153), is buried here, and the graves, many decorated with elaborate calligraphy, are interesting in their own right. Look out for the section where foreigners are buried; their tombstones provide a history of early *gaijin* involvement in Japan. Despite it being a cemetery, many locals enjoy partying here during the *hanami* season under the candy-floss bunches of pink cherry blossoms.

An alternative route leads southwest from the Aoyama-dōri crossing with Omotesandō to pass (on your left) the **Spiral Building**, which includes a gallery, a couple of restaurants and a trendy card shop. The interior, with its sweeping, seemingly freestanding ramp walkway, is worth a look. Closer to Shibuya is the funky **National Children's Castle** (Tues–Fri 12.30–5.30pm, Sat & Sun 10am–5pm; ¥500; ☎03/3797-5666, ⓦwww.kodomo-shiro.or.jp), a large kids' playground featuring a real hotel and a swimming pool (¥300 extra).

Shibuya

Immediately south of Harajuku is **Shibuya**, birthplace of a million-and-one consumer crazes, where teens and twenty-somethings throng Centre Gai, the shopping precinct that splits the district's rival department-store groups: **Tōkyū**, who own the prime station site, the Mark City complex and the Bunkamura arts hall; and **Seibu**, whose outlets include the fashionable, youth-orientated Loft and Parco stores. Frenetic as it is in daytime, Shibuya is primarily an after-dark destination, when the neon signs of scores of restaurants, bars and cinemas battle it out with five-storey-tall TV screens for the attention of passers-by.

In a plaza on the west side of the station is the famous waiting spot of **Hachikō the dog** (see p.153), and the best place from which to take in the evening buzz. Head into the adjacent Shibuya Mark City, a restaurant and hotel complex, for a bird's-eye view. Opposite, to the west, the 109 Building stands at the apex of Dōgenzaka and Bunkamura-dōri, the former leading up to one of Tokyo's most famous love-hotel districts.

If you walk through Dōgenzaka, over the crest of the hill and past the On Air live music venues, you'll end up next to the main entrance to the **Bunkamura** (ⓦ www.bunkamura.co.jp), an arts complex with an excellent gallery (showing temporary exhibitions of mainly Western art), a couple of cinemas, the 2000-seater Orchard Hall, home of the Tokyo Philharmonic Orchestra, and the Theatre Cocoon, which hosts some of the city's more avant-garde productions. The ticket counter is on the first floor (daily 10am–7.30pm; ⓣ03/3477-3244 for programme information).

Walk a few minutes uphill behind the Bunkamura to reach the **Toguri Museum of Art** (Tues–Sun 9.30am–5.30pm; ¥1030; ⓣ03/3465-0070, ⓦ www.toguri-museum.or.jp), which displays Edo-era and Chinese Ming dynasty (1368–1644) ceramics. Although it's not to everyone's taste (and entrance is pricey), this small but exquisitely displayed exhibition, comprising selections from a collection of some six thousand pieces, is worth the expense if you're interested in pottery.

ACCOMMODATION		RESTAURANTS, CAFÉS & BARS						CLUBS	
Arimax Hotel	B	Andersens	14	Koots Green Tea	11	Oh! God	9	Club Asia	33
Capsule Land Shibuya	F	Bape Café!?	21	Las Chicas	16	Pariya	17	La Fabrique	27
Cerulean Tower		Cantina	15	Lion	32	Pink Cow	24	Maniac Love	23
Tōkyū Hotel	G	Christon Café	35	Maisen	8	Rojak	28	Mix	12
Hotel Floracian	A	Chung King Lo	13	Miyoko	26	Sakuratei	3	The Ruby Room	30
Shibuya Business		Coins Bar 300	25	Mominoki House	1	Soho's	5	Womb	34
Hotel	D	Le Faubourg	20	Montoak	7	Soul	18		
Shibuya Excel Hotel		Fujimamas	6	Moph	22	Suzuki	2		
Tōkyū	E	Heirokuzushi	10	Nobu Tokyo	31	Xanadu	29		
Shibuya Tōbu Hotel	C	Immigrant's Café	19	Office & Sign	4				

Hachikō: a dog's life

The story of **Hachikō** the dog proves that fame in Japan comes to those who wait. Every morning, the Akita pup faithfully accompanied his master Ueda Eisaburō, a professor in the Department of Agriculture at the Imperial University, to Shibuya Station, and would be back at the station in the evening to greet him. In May 1925, Professor Ueda died while at work, but Hachikō continued to turn up every day at the station. By 1934, Hachikō had waited patiently for nine years, and locals were so touched by the dog's devotion that a bronze statue was cast of him.

In 1935, Hachikō was finally united in death with his master and was buried with Ueda in Aoyama cemetery. The stuffed skin of a second dog was used to create a doppelgänger Hachikō, which can be viewed at the National Science Museum (see p.135). During World War II, the original Hachikō statue was melted down for weapons, but a replacement was reinstated beside the station in 1948. Today, this is the most famous rendezvous in all of Tokyo, though the throngs of people around the small statue and the rats that rummage through the rubbish in the surrounding bushes do not make it a particularly convivial place to hang out in.

Back down the hill, on the upper slope of Kōen-dōri, is the altogether quirkier **Tobacco and Salt Museum** (Tues–Sun 10am–5.30pm; ¥100; ☎03/3476-2041). Take the lift to the fourth floor, which has temporary exhibitions, and work your way down past displays on the third, which focus on the harvesting of salt from the sea and other sources of sodium. The second floor has the tobacco exhibits, including two thousand packets from around the world, and dioramas showing how the leaves were prepared for smoking in the past. It's all in Japanese, and only on the ground floor are you allowed to light up a fag.

If you've got kids in tow, there are a couple of places worth searching out back down the hill from NHK. On Fire Street, the **TEPCO Electric Energy Museum** (daily except Wed 10am–6pm; free; ☎03/3477-1191, ⓦwww.den-ryokukan.com) has seven floors of exhibits relating to electricity. The English brochure says "Let's make friends with electricity", and TEPCO, Tokyo's power company, goes out of its way to convince you that this is possible, even to the extent of hosting free showings of Hollywood movies on Mondays. Look out for the laser that can etch your profile and name (in Japanese characters) onto a credit-card-sized piece of card. Nip under the train tracks and across Meiji-dōri to reach **Tokyo Metropolitan Children's Hall** (daily 9am–5pm; free; ☎03/3409-6361, ⓦwww.jidokaikan.metro.tokyo.jp), an excellent government-sponsored facility for kids, including a rooftop playground, library, music room and craft-making activities.

Finally, just two stops from Shibuya on the Keiō Inokashira line to Komaba-Tōdaimae Station, or a twenty-minute walk west of Dōgenzaka to Komaba-kōen, lies the very impressive **Japan Folk Crafts Museum** (or *Mingeikan*; Tues–Sun 10am–5pm; ¥1000; ☎03/3467-4527, ⓦwww.mingeikan.or.jp), set in a handsome stone-and-stucco building and boasting an excellent collection of pottery, textiles and lacquerware. The gift shop is a fine source of souvenirs, and an annual new work competition and sale is held between November 23 and December 3. Opposite the museum stands a nineteenth-century **nagaya-mon** (long gate house), brought here from Tochigi-ken by the museum's founder, Yanagi Sōetsu (see "Contexts", p.969).

Ebisu and Daikan'yama

Although not quite so trendy as it once was, **Ebisu**, just south of Shibuya, still has a buzz. Above Ebisu Station you'll find the **Atre** shopping mall, which has a good range of restaurants on its sixth floor, but the main focus of the area is **Yebisu Garden Place**, a huge shopping, office and entertainment complex, connected to the station by a long moving walkway, built on the site of the nineteenth-century Sapporo brewery that was once the source of the area's fortunes. Here you'll find a couple of interesting museums, the best of which is the **Tokyo Metropolitan Photography Museum** (Tues–Sun 10am–6pm, Thurs & Fri until 8pm; admission charges vary; ⓣ03/3280-0031, ⓦwww.tokyo-photo-museum.or.jp), on the west side of the complex. This has excellent changing exhibitions of shots by major Japanese and Western photographers, along with study rooms and an experimental photography and imaging room. The museum's policy of concentrating on one photographer at a time in its frequently changing exhibitions allows you to see the artist's work develop and gain an understanding of the motivations behind it.

On the western side of the complex, behind the Mitsukoshi department store, the history of beer in Japan – and of the brewery that used to be here – is detailed at the lively **Yebisu Beer Museum** (Tues–Sun 10am–6pm; free; ⓣ03/5423-7255, ⓦwww.sapporobeer.jp/brewery/ebisu). Look out for the touchscreen video displays and a computer simulation, where one of the people taking part in the tour is chosen to be the leader of a virtual-reality tour around different aspects of the brewing process. There's also an opportunity to sample some of Sapporo's beers, at ¥200 for a small glass. If you have time, head for the restaurants on the 38th and 39th floors of the **Yebisu Tower**, next to the photography museum; you don't need to eat or drink here to enjoy the spectacular free views of the city.

Daikan'yama, Ebisu, Meguro and Shinagawa

Ebisu	*Ebisu*	恵比寿
Tokyo Metropolitan Photography Museum	*Tōkyō-to Shashin Bijutsukan*	東京都写真美術館
Yebisu Garden Place	*Ebisu Gāden Pureisu*	恵比寿ガーデンプレイス
Daikan'yama	*Daikan'yama*	代官山
Meguro	*Meguro*	目黒
Happōen	*Happōen*	八芳園
Meguro Gajoen	*Meguro Gajoen*	目黒雅叙園
Meguro Parasitological Museum	*Meguro Kiseichū-kan*	目黒寄生虫館
National Park for Nature Study	*Kokuritsu Shizen Kyōikuen*	国立自然教育園
Tokyo Metropolitan Teien Art Museum	*Tōkyō-to Teien Bijutsukan*	東京都庭園美術館
Shinagawa	*Shinagawa*	品川
Hara Museum of Contemporary Art	*Hara Bijutsukan*	原美術館
Sengaku-ji	*Sengaku-ji*	泉岳寺

A ten-minute stroll west along Komazawa-dōri from Ebisu Station, or one stop from Shibuya on the Tōku Tōyoko line, is **Daikan'yama**, home to some of the city's classiest homes, shops and watering holes – the village-like area's laid-back vibe is a refreshing break from the frenzy of nearby Shibuya. Daikan'yama's contemporary style has been defined by the smart **Hillside Terrace** complex, designed by Maki Fumihiko (see box on p.144). Strung along leafy Kyū-yamate-dōri, the various stages of Hillside Terrace were developed over nearly a quarter century; the **Hillside Gallery** (Tues–Sun, 10am–5pm; free), opposite the Danish Embassy, has interesting modern art exhibitions. Closer to the station are the smart **Daikan'yama Address** and **La Fuente** complexes where you'll find more groovy boutiques and ritzy restaurants and cafés.

Meguro and around

South of Ebisu, stylish **Meguro** is mainly a residential area, but there are some sightseeing surprises to be found here. A five-minute walk downhill, west of Meguro Station, the towering complex of **Meguro Gajoen** (☎03/5434-3920, ⓦwww.megurogajoen.co.jp) replaced the original wedding hall, built at the end of the nineteenth century and known as Ryūgū-jō (Fairytale Dragon Palace). Something of its fantastic nature remains in the many restored painted wooden carvings (huge *ukiyo-e*-style panoramas of kimonoed ladies and samurai warriors) and lacquer and mother-of-pearl inlaid scenes of flowers and birds, culled from the old building, which now decorate the enormous interior – big enough to host some twenty-odd weddings simultaneously. Visit on a weekend and the place buzzes with bridal parties. The complex has a hotel and several pricey restaurants, including a thatched farmhouse surrounded by a lush garden.

Return to Meguro-dōri and walk a few blocks further west across the Meguro-gawa and up the hill just beyond Yamate-dōri to reach the quirky **Meguro Parasitological Museum** (Tues–Sun 10am–5pm; free; ☎03/3716-1264). Any ideas you had of Japan being a healthy place to live in will be quickly dispelled by these two floors of exhibits on parasites, which emphasize the dangers of creepy crawlies in uncooked food. Record-breaking tapeworms (one 8.8m long) are on display, pickled in jars, along with some gruesome photographs of past victims, including one poor fellow whose swollen testicles scrape the ground.

Heading east from Meguro Station along Meguro-dōri, past the raised Shuto Expressway, brings you to the elegant **Tokyo Metropolitan Teien Art Museum** (10am–6pm; closed second and fourth Wed of the month; entrance fee depends on the exhibition; ☏03/3443-0201, ⊛www.teien-art-museum.ne.jp). This Art Deco building is the former home of Prince Asaka Yasuhiko, Emperor Hirohito's uncle, who lived in Paris for three years during the 1920s, where he developed a taste for the European style. It's worth popping into for the gorgeous interior decoration and landscaped grounds with Japanese gardens, pond and tea-ceremony house (entry to gardens only is ¥200).

Next to the museum's grounds is the **National Park for Nature Study** (Tues–Sun 9am–4pm; May–Aug until 5pm; ¥200; ☏03/3441-7176, ⊛www.ins.kahaku.go.jp). Covering about 200,000 square metres, the park is an attempt to preserve the original natural features of the countryside before Edo was settled and developed into Tokyo. It partially succeeds – among the 8000 trees in the park there are some that have been growing for 500 years; frogs can be heard croaking amid the grass beside the marshy ponds; and the whole place is a bird-spotter's paradise. The best thing about the park is that entry at any one time is limited to 300 people, making it one of the few public areas in Tokyo where you can really escape the crowds.

An alternative access point for the park is Shirokanedai Station, on the Namboku and Toei Mita subway lines. This station is also the handiest for the lovely **Happōen** (daily 10am–5pm; free). The garden's name means "beautiful from any angle" and, despite the addition of a modern wedding hall on one side, this is still true. A renowned adviser to the shogunate, Hikozaemon Okubo, lived here during the early seventeenth century, although most of the garden's design dates from the early twentieth century when a business tycoon bought up the land, built a classical Japanese villa (still standing by the garden's entrance) and gave it the name Happōen. Take a turn through its twisting pathways and you'll pass 200-year-old bonsai trees, a stone lantern said to have been carved 800 years ago by the Heike warrior Taira-no Munekiyo, and a central pond. Nestling amid the trees is the delightful **teahouse** (daily 11am–5pm; ¥800), where ladies in kimono will serve you *matcha* and *okashi*. Again, at the weekend, the whole scene is enlivened by many smartly dressed wedding parties, lining up for group photos against the verdant backdrop.

Shinagawa and around

The location of one of the original checkpoints on the Tōkaidō, the major highway into Edo during the reign of the shoguns, **Shinagawa**, remains a major Tokyo transport and hotel hub. The opening of a new Shinkansen station here in 2003 is revitalizing the area, mainly east of the tracks, where a clutch of modern towers reaches for the sky. None is particularly interesting to visit, though, and apart from the traditional gardens sandwiched between the *Takanawa Prince* and the *New Takanawa Prince* hotels (see "Accommodation", p.106) on the west side of Shinagawa, which are the former grounds and mansion of a member of the imperial family, the area's principal sights lie north and south of the station.

The 47 rōnin

Celebrated in Kabuki and Bunraku plays, as well as on film, *Chūshingura* is a true story of honour, revenge and loyalty. In 1701, a young *daimyō*, Asano Takumi, became embroiled in a fatal argument in the shogun's court with his teacher and fellow lord Kira Yoshinaka. Asano had lost face in his performance of court rituals and, blaming his mentor for his lax tuition, drew his sword within the castle walls and attacked Kira. Although Kira survived, the shogun, on hearing of this breach of etiquette, ordered Asano to commit *seppuku*, the traditional form of suicide, which he did.

Their lord having been disgraced, Asano's loyal retainers, the **rōnin** – or masterless samurai – vowed revenge. On December 14, 1702, the 47 *rōnin*, lead by **Ōishi Kuranosuke**, stormed Kira's villa (the remains of which are in Ryōgoku), cut off his head and paraded it through Edo in triumph before placing it on Asano's grave in Sengaku-ji. Although their actions were in line with the samurai creed, the shogun had no option but to order the *rōnin*'s deaths. All 47 committed *seppuku* on February 14, 1703, including Ōishi's 15-year-old son. They were buried with Asano in Sengaku-ji, and today their graves are still wreathed in the smoke from the bundles of incense placed by their gravestones.

Sengaku-ji, the famous temple which houses the graves of **Asano Takumi** and his **47 rōnin** (see box above), is around 1km north of Shinagawa; the closest station is Sengaku-ji on the Toei Asakusa Line. Most of the temple was destroyed during the war and has since been rebuilt, but a striking gate dating from 1836 and decorated with a metalwork dragon remains. The statue and grave of **Ōishi Kuranosuke**, the avenging leader of the 47 *rōnin*, are in the temple grounds. A **museum** (daily 9am–4pm; ¥200; ☏03/3441-5560, ⓦwww.sengakuji.or.jp) to the left of the main building contains the personal belongings of the *rōnin* and their master Asano, as well as a receipt for the severed head of Kira.

Tucked into a quiet residential area south of Shinagawa you'll find the 1938 Bauhaus-style house that now contains the interesting **Hara Museum of Contemporary Art** (Tues & Thurs–Sun 11am–5pm, Wed 11am–8pm; ¥1000; ☏03/3445-0651, ⓦwww.haramuseum.or.jp). Their small permanent collection includes some funky installations, such as *Rondo*, by Morimura Yasumasa, whose self-portrait occupies the downstairs toilet. The building itself, designed by Watanabe Jin, the architect responsible for Ueno's Tokyo National Museum and the Wako department store in Ginza, is worth a look, as are the tranquil sculpture gardens overlooked by the museum's pleasant café. Check their website for details of their annex **Hara Museum ARC** in Shibukawa, Gunmaken; bus trips are sometimes run there by the museum.

Bayside Tokyo

It comes as something of a shock to many visitors (and some residents) that Tokyo is actually beside the sea. Yet many of the *ukiyo-e* masterpieces of Hokusai and Hiroshige depict waterside scenes of **Tokyo Bay**, and several of the city's prime attractions are to be found here. The teeming fish market of **Tsukiji** provides a rowdy early-morning antidote to the serenity of the nearby traditional gardens, **Hama Rikyū Teien**. East of the market is **Tsukudashima**, a pocket of traditional wooden homes and shops dating from the Edo period, while to the south, across the Rainbow Bridge, lie the modern waterfront city and pleasure parks of **Odaiba**, built on vast islands of reclaimed land.

Bayside Tokyo

Tokyo Bay	*Tōkyō-wan*	東京湾
Central Wholesale Market	*Chūō Oroshiuri Ichiba*	中央卸売市場
Decks Tokyo Beach	*Dekkusu Tōkyō Biichi*	デックス東京ビーチ
Hama Rikyū garden	*Hama Rikyū Teien*	浜離宮庭園
Kasai Rinkai-kōen	*Kasai Rinkai-kōen*	葛西臨海公園
Museum of Maritime Science	*Fune no Kagakukan*	船の科学館
Odaiba Seaside Park	*Odaiba Kaihin-kōen*	お台場海浜公園
Sumiyoshi-jinja	*Sumiyoshi-jinja*	住吉神社
Tokyo Disneyland	*Tōkyō Dizuniirando*	東京ディズニーランド
Tsukiji Hongan-ji	*Tsukiji Hongan-ji*	築地本願寺
Tsukudashima	*Tsukudashima*	佃島

Beyond Odaiba on the north side of Tokyo Bay, some of the city's older recreational facilities still pull the crowds. The open spaces of **Kasai Rinkai-kōen** are a good place to catch the sea breeze, but the park's greatest attraction is its aquarium and particularly the doughnut-shaped tuna tank, where silver shoals race round you at dizzying speeds. From the park, the Cinderella spires of **Tokyo Disneyland** are clearly visible to the west. Though not everyone's cup of tea, this little bit of America can make a hugely entertaining day out, even if you're not travelling with kids.

Tsukiji

A dawn visit to the vast **Tokyo Central Wholesale Market**, on the edge of Tokyo Bay, some 2km southeast of the Imperial Palace, is one of the highlights of any trip to Tokyo and is a must for raw-fish fans, who can breakfast afterwards on the freshest slices of sashimi and sushi. Covering 56 acres of reclaimed land south of Ginza, the market is popularly known as **Tsukiji** (Reclaimed Land), and has been here since 1923. The area it stands on was created in the wake of the disastrous Furisode (Long Sleeves) Fire of 1657. Tokugawa Ieyasu had the debris shovelled into the marshes at the edge of Ginza, thus providing his lords with space for their mansions and gardens. In the early years of the Meiji era, after the *daimyō* had been kicked out of the city, the city authorities built a special residential area for Western expats here. The market relocated to this area from Nihombashi after the 1923 earthquake. There's talk of another move around 2015; the ward office Chūō-ku is not in favour of this plan, but Tokyo Metropolitan Government is, and various locations across the bay are being debated.

Emerging from Tsukiji subway, you'll first notice the **Tsukiji Hongan-ji**, one of the largest and most Indian-looking of Tokyo's Buddhist temples. Pop inside to see the intricately carved golden altar and cavernous interior with room for a thousand worshippers. From the temple, the most direct route to the **market** is to continue along Shin-Ōhashi-dōri, crossing Harumi-dōri (the route from Ginza) and past the row of grocers and noodle bars. On the next block lies the sprawling bulk of the market. Every day, bar Sundays and public holidays, 2300 tonnes of fish are delivered here from far-flung corners of the earth. Over four hundred different types of seafood come under the hammer, including eels from Taiwan, salmon from Santiago and tuna from Tasmania. But, as its official title indicates, fish is not the only item on sale at Tsukiji, which also deals in meat, fruit and vegetables.

The auctions, held at the back of the market, aren't officially open to the public, but no one will stop you slipping in quietly to watch the buyers and sellers gesticulating wildly over polystyrene crates of squid, sea urchins, crab and the like. The highlight is the sale of rock-solid frozen tuna, looking like steel torpedoes, all labelled with yellow stickers indicating their weight and country of origin. Depending on their quality, each tuna sells for between ¥600,000 to ¥1 million. At around 7am, Tokyo's restaurateurs and food retailers pick their way through the day's catch on sale at 1600 different wholesalers' stalls under the crescent-shaped hangar's roof.

Sloshing through the water-cleansed pathways, dodging the mini-forklift trucks that shift the produce around, and being surrounded by piled crates of seafood – some of it still alive – is what a visit to Tsukiji is all about. If you get peckish, head for the outer market area (Jōgai Ichiba), which is crammed with sushi stalls and noodle bars servicing the 60,000 people who pass through here each day. Good choices include *Daiwa Zushi* and *Sushi-bun*, both open from 5.30am, and actually within the market, while *Tatsuzushi* and the more expensive *Sushisei* are in the block of shops between the market and Tsukiji Hongan-ji. Expect to pay around ¥2000 for a set course.

The closest **subway station** to the market is Tsukiji (on the Hibiya line), but if you want to witness the frantic auctions that start at 5am you'll have to catch a taxi or walk to the market. If you can't make it that early, it's still worth coming here; the action in the outer markets continues through to midday.

Hama Rikyū Teien and Tsukudashima

The contrast between bustling Tsukiji and the traditional garden of **Hama Rikyū Teien** (Tues–Sun 9am–4.30pm; ¥300), less than a ten-minute walk east, couldn't be more acute. This beautifully designed park once belonged to the shogunate, who hunted ducks here. These days the ducks, protected inside the garden's nature reserve, are no longer used for target practice and only have to watch out for the large number of cats that wander the idly twisting pathways. There are three ponds, the largest spanned by a trellis-covered bridge that leads to a floating teahouse, *Nakajima-no-Chaya* (¥500 for tea). Next to the entrance is a sprawling, three-hundred-year-old pine tree and a manicured lawn dotted with sculpted, stunted trees. One of the best times of year to come here is in early spring, when lilac wisteria hangs in fluffy bunches from trellises around the central pond. From the Tokyo Bay side of the garden, you'll get a view across to the Rainbow Bridge, and can see the floodgate which regulates how much sea water flows in and out of this pond with the tides. By far the nicest way of approaching the gardens is to take a ferry from Asakusa, down the Sumida-gawa (see p.101 for details).

Another rewarding diversion from Tsukiji, across the Sumida-gawa, is **Tsukudashima**, a tiny enclave of Edo-period houses and shops, clustered around a backwater spanned by a dinky red bridge. Sheltering in the shadow of the modern River City 21 tower blocks, the area has a history stretching back to 1613, when a group of Ōsaka fishermen were settled on the island by the shogun. In addition to providing food for the castle, the fishermen were expected to report on any suspicious comings and goings in the bay. For their spiritual protection, they built themselves the delightful **Sumiyoshi-jinja**, dedicated to the god of the sea, like the related shrine in Ōsaka (see p.503). The water well beside the shrine's *torii* has a roof with eaves decorated with exquisite carvings of scenes from the fishermen's lives. Every three years, on the first weekend in August, the shrine hosts the Sumiyoshi Matsuri **festival**, during which a special *mikoshi* (portable shrine) is dowsed in water as it is paraded through the streets; this is symbolic of the real dunking it would once have had in the river.

The Tsukudashima community is also famous for **tsukudani**, delicious morsels of seaweed and fish preserved in a mixture of soy sauce, salt or sugar. You'll find eighteen different types of this speciality served up at *Ten'yasu Honten* (daily 9am–6pm; ℡03/3531-2351), a weather-worn wooden shop typical of the area, outside of which hangs a tattered *noren* (cloth shop sign). Ask nicely and the white-aproned ladies, who sit cross-legged on the tatami platform from which customers are served, will allow you to take a peep behind the scenes to see how this delicacy is made. A wooden box set of six types of *tsukudani* costs from ¥2000.

To reach Tsukudashima on foot, head for the Tsukuda-Ōhashi bridge, a ten-minute walk from Tsukiji subway station, past St Luke's Hospital. The area is easily spotted on the left side of the island as you leave the bridge and should-n't take more than thirty minutes to explore. The closest **subway station** is Tsukishima, on the Yūrakuchō and Ōedo line.

Odaiba

Returning to Tsukiji and heading west towards the raised Shuto Expressway will bring you to Shimbashi Station and the start of the Yurikamome monorail line out to an **island** of reclaimed land in Tokyo Bay. Popularly known as **Odaiba**, the island takes its name from the cannon emplacements set up in the bay by the shogun in 1853 to protect the city from Commodore Perry's threat-ening Black Ships (see p.939). The remains of the two cannon emplacements are now dwarfed by the huge landfill site – Rinkai Fukutoshin, of which Odaiba is a part – on which the Metropolitan Government set about constructing a 21st-century city in 1988. The economic slump and spiralling development costs slowed the project down and, when the Rainbow Bridge linking Odaiba to the city opened in 1993, the area was still a series of empty lots.

A decade on, Odaiba is yet to reach its full potential, but is still worth visit-ing; futuristic buildings linked by the zippy monorail, a man-made beach, parks and architectural wonders have turned the island into such a local hit that on weekends the monorail and shopping plazas are swamped with day-trippers. For overseas visitors its principal highlights are a couple of excellent museums and a raucous new onsen complex (see box, p.123). At night, the illuminated Rainbow Bridge, giant technicolour ferris wheel and twinkling towers of the Tokyo skyline make Odaiba a romantic spot – you'll see plenty of canoodling couples staring wistfully at the glittering panorama.

The easiest way of reaching Odaiba is on the **Yurikamome monorail**, which arcs up to the Rainbow Bridge on a splendid circular line and stops at all the area's major sites, terminating at Ariake Station. A one-day ticket (¥800) is best if you intend to see all the island – walking across Odaiba is a long slog. In addition, **trains** on the Rinkai Line, linked with the JR Saikyo line, run to the central Tokyo-Teleport Station on Odaiba. **Buses** from Shinagawa Station, southwest of the bay, cross the Rainbow Bridge and run as far as the Maritime Museum, stopping at Odaiba Kaihin-kōen on the way. Alternatively, you can take a **ferry** from Hinode Sanbashi to either Ariake or the Maritime Museum via Harumi and Odaiba Kaihin-kōen – a journey that costs no more than ¥520, doubling as a quick, cut-price cruise of Tokyo Bay.

The following description of sights starts at the far south side of Odaiba and ends with a walk back across the Rainbow Bridge – easily the highlight of any trip out to this ultra-modern world.

Tokyo Big Sight and Palette Town

One stop from the monorail terminus at Ariake is the enormous and striking Tokyo International Exhibition Centre, better known as the **Tokyo Big Sight**

(☎03/5530-1111, ⊛www.bigsight.jp). Its entrance is composed of four huge inverted pyramids, and in front stands a 15.5-metre sculpture of a red-handled saw, sticking out of the ground as if left behind by some absent-minded giant. This is one of Japan's largest venues for business fairs and exhibitions; check their website for details of events, which include huge antique fairs and the twice-yearly Design Festa (see p.160).

Aomi Station is the stop for the vast **Palette Town** shopping and entertainment complex (⊛www.palette-town.com), which offers something for almost everyone. On the east side is potentially the most interesting piece of the package, the **Toyota City Showcase** (daily 11am–9pm; free), displaying all of Toyota's range of cars. Enthusiasts will enjoy just strolling around this huge showroom, but anyone with a faint interest in cars will also be able to take part in the fuel-injected fun by signing up for the various activities, such as designing your own car using CAD technology, taking a ride in an electric vehicle (¥200) or a virtual-reality drive (¥500), or even selecting any of Toyota's models and taking it for a test drive (¥300). Given the crowds, for some of these activities it's best making advance bookings (☎0070-800-☎849-000, ⊛www.megaweb.gr.jp). Just behind the showroom are some more high-tech diversions, the best of which is the 115-metre-diameter **Wonder Wheel** (daily 10am–10pm; ¥900), a candy-coloured ferris wheel that takes sixteen minutes to make a full circuit.

The upper floor on the west side of Palette Town is dominated by **Venus Fort**, described as a "theme park for ladies", but basically a shopping mall, designed as a mock Italian city, complete with piazza, fountains and Roman-style statues – even the ceiling is painted and lit to resemble a perfect Mediterranean sky from dawn to dusk. Most of the theme-style restaurants and shops here are totally bland (the exception is the Lab Labo area, where young designers offer their interior design and accessory creations), but the complex is worth swinging through if only to gawk at the sheer lunacy of it all. Downstairs is Sun Walk, a more restrained shopping mall, at the back of which you'll find the **History Garage** (daily 11am–10pm; free), displaying a good range of classic cars and including a gallery with around three thousand miniature cars and an extensive range of car-related books.

MeSci and around

West of Palette Town is a fat finger of reclaimed land partly covered by Tokyo's container port and overlooked by the **Telecom Centre**, a wannabe clone of Paris's Grande Arche at La Défense. The centre has a viewing platform on its 21st floor (¥600), but this can safely be skipped in favour of Tokyo's best science museum, the National Museum of Emerging Science and Innovation or **MeSci** (daily except Tues 10am–5pm; ¥500; ☎03/3570-9151, ⊛www .miraikan.jst.go.jp), which is chock-full of fascinating high-tech displays. Here you can learn about the latest in robot technology, superconductivity (including maglev trains), the environment, space and much more. Check out the weather around the world by looking up at the giant sphere covered with one million light-emitting diodes and showing the globe as it appears from space that day. All displays have English explanations and there are also plenty of English-speaking volunteer guides on hand.

Directly south of MeSci is the new spa complex, **Oedo Onsen Monogatari** (see p.123 for details).

Museum of Maritime Science

From MeSci it's a short walk to the excellent **Museum of Maritime Science** (Mon–Fri 10am–5pm, Sat & Sun 10am–6pm; ☎03/5550-1111,

Ⓦ www.funenokagakukan.or.jp), housed in a concrete reproduction of a 60,000-tonne cruise ship. The exhibits include many detailed model boats and the engines of a giant ship. Docked outside are a couple of real boats: the *Sōya*, which undertook scientific missions to the South Pole, and the *Yōtei Marine*, a ferry refitted as an exhibition space. Admission to the two ships only is ¥600; for the museum and the Yotei Marine ¥700; for everything, ¥1000. Within the museum grounds you'll also find a couple of lighthouses, submarines, a flying boat and two open-air swimming pools (open July 18–Aug 31; ¥2800 including admission to the museum).

Head around the waterfront from the museum, past the curiously shaped triangular tower (an air vent for the road tunnel that goes under Tokyo Bay) to reach a park, **Odaiba Kaihin-kōen**. Across the bay, the lines of red cranes at the container port look like giraffes at feeding time.

The beach and around

As you turn the corner of the island and the Rainbow Bridge comes into view, Odaiba's man-made **beach** begins. As Japanese beaches go, it's not bad, but you'd be wise to avoid it on sunny weekends, when you'll see more raw flesh than sand. Fronting onto the beach are the **Aqua City** and **Decks Tokyo Beach** shopping malls. Apart from trendy shops and restaurants, the former includes the Mediage multiplex cinema, while the latter has its own brewery and **Joypolis** (daily 10am–11.30pm; ¥500 admission only), a multistorey arcade filled with Sega's interactive entertainment technology.

Next to the mall, a surreal aura hangs over Tange Kenzō's **Fuji TV Building**, a futuristic block with a huge metal sphere suspended in its middle – it looks like it has been made from a giant Meccano set. You can pay to head up to the 25th-floor **viewing platform** (Tues–Sun 10am–8pm; ¥500), or you can do the sensible thing and put the cash towards a cocktail in the Sky Lounge at the top of the neighbouring *Meridien Grand Pacific Hotel*, and have the view thrown in for free.

From the Sunset Beach row of restaurants beside the Decks Mall, you can walk across onto one of the shogun's gun emplacement islands, now a public park, or continue for an exhilarating walk along the **Rainbow Bridge**. This 918-metre-long single-span suspension bridge has two levels, the lower for the waterfront road and the monorail, and the upper for the Metropolitan Expressway. On both sides is a pedestrian promenade linking the **observation rooms** (daily: April–Oct 10am–9pm; Jan–March, Nov & Dec 10am–6pm; ¥300) in the anchorages at either end of the bridge. The walk along the bridge takes about forty minutes and provides magnificent views across the bay, even as far as Mount Fuji, if the sky is clear. One minute's walk from the exit from the shoreside observation room is the station for the monorail back to Shimbashi.

Beyond Odaiba

West of Odaiba, older blocks of reclaimed land sporting dormitory towns, golf links and other recreational facilities jut out into Tokyo Bay. The prime attractions are **Kasai Rinkai-kōen**, a seaside park boasting one of Tokyo's biggest aquariums and a birdwatching centre, and the enormously popular **Tokyo Disneyland**. Though you probably won't have time to visit both in one day, these places are at adjacent stops on the JR Keiyō line from Tokyo Station. Coming from Odaiba, you can pick up the Keiyō line at Shin-Kiba Station.

Kasai Rinkai-kōen

Lying between its JR station and the sea, the flat expanse of **Kasai Rinkai-kōen** (open 24hr; free) isn't the most attractive of landscapes, but there's more to it than first appears. For many Tokyo families this is a favourite weekend spot – for picnicking, cycling or summer swimming from its small, crescent-shaped beach – while bird enthusiasts ogle waterbirds and waders in the well-designed bird sanctuary. The park's biggest draw, however, is its large aquarium, **Tokyo Sea Life Park** (Tues–Sun 9.30am–5pm, last entry 4pm; ¥800), under a glass-and-steel dome overlooking the sea. The first things you meet coming down the escalators are two vast tanks of tuna and sharks, the aquarium's highlight; go down again and you stand in the middle of this fishy world, surrounded by 2200 tonnes of water. Smaller tanks showcase sea life from around the world, from flashy tropical butterfly fish and paper-thin seahorses to the lumpy mudskippers of Tokyo Bay. Not everyone is here to admire the beauty of the fish – as you walk round, listen out for murmurs of *oishii* (the Japanese equivalent of "delicious!"). The short videos on show in the 3-D theatre are in Japanese only, but worth catching for the visuals.

If you're heading back into central Tokyo from here, one of the nicest ways is to hop on to a **ferry** for the 55-minute ride (¥800) via Ariake to Hinode Sanbashi near Hamamatsuchō. Boats leave hourly from the park's western pier, with the last departure at 5pm. See p.101 for further details.

Tokyo Disney Resort

The big daddy of Tokyo's theme parks, **Tokyo Disney Resort** (ⓦ www.tokyodisneyresort.co.jp) comprises two separate but adjacent attractions: **Tokyo Disneyland**, a pretty close copy of the Californian original, and the new **DisneySea Park**, a water- and world travel-themed area. The parks are plonked in commuter land a fifteen-minute train ride east of the city centre, and both follow the well-honed Disney formula of theme lands, parades and zany extravaganzas. Few people seem to have a good word for the DisneySea Park, but whatever your preconceptions, it's pretty hard not to have a good time overall.

You'll probably want to devote a whole day to each park to get your money's worth; a one-day "**passport**" for either costs ¥5500; a two-day passport to both parks is ¥9800; there are also a couple of discount passports available for Disneyland only if you enter later in the day. The resort is generally open from 8am or 9am to 10pm, but hours may vary and the park is occasionally closed for special events, so it's best to check beforehand by phone. The best option is to visit the **Tokyo Disney Resort Ticket Centre** (daily 10am–7pm; ☎03/3595-1777) in Yūrakuchō, where you can pick up an English leaflet and buy your tickets at the same time; the office is in the Hibiya Mitsui Building near Hibiya subway station (see map on p.115).

The gates to Disneyland sit right in front of Maihama Station (on the JR Keiyō line). Inside, you'll find World Bazaar, with its shops and general services (pushchair rentals, bank, lockers and information), followed by the central plaza in front of Cinderella's castle, from where the six theme lands radiate. Tomorrowland's Star Tours and Space Mountain offer the most heart-stopping rides. Next door, DisneySea Park offers an additional 23 water-based attractions spread across seven zones and a grand European-style *Hotel MiraCosta*. A monorail encircles the two sites, stopping near Maihama Station at a shopping complex which is also home to the Art Deco *Disney Ambassador Hotel*, where real addicts can collect complimentary Mickey toiletries before breakfasting with the mouse himself. Expect long queues: Disneyland attracts over 30,000 visitors per day on average, and many more over weekends and holidays.

Tokyo for kids

Tokyo is a fantastic city for kids. There's Disneyland, of course (see p.163), and the thrill rides at Big Egg City (see p.122), as well as the wonderful Ghibli Museum, Mitaka (see p.217) a short train ride from Shinjuku. If your children are young, the facilities at the National Children's Castle (see p.151) and the Tokyo Metropolitan Children's Hall (see p.153) will keep them occupied for many an hour. There's a whole bag of educational **museums**, the best ones being Ueno's National Science Museum (see p.135) and Odaiba's MeSci (see p.161), plus Ueno's zoo (see p.134) and the fabulous aquarium at Kasai Seaside Park (see p.162). For **toy shops** featuring the latest hit toys and Japanese crazes, visit Omotesandō's Kiddyland (6-1-9 Jingūmae, Shibuya-ku; ☎03/3409-3431), Hakuhinkan Toy Park (8-8-1 Ginza, Chūō-ku; ☎03/3571-8008) and the Pokémon Centre (3-2-5 Nihonbashi, Chūō-ku; ☎03/5200-0707) – though they'll probably end up making a big dent in your wallet. For more information, the English-language website ⊛www.tokyowithkids.com is an excellent resource.

Eating

Deciding what to **eat** in Tokyo can be a bewildering experience. Besides the problem of working out what's on the menu (or even on your plate), you're also swamped with choice – there are around 300,000 places to eat in the city, from simple street food vendors to classy restaurants. Choose any country, from Belarus to Vietnam, and you're likely to find their cuisine somewhere in the city. And, of course, there are endless renditions and permutations of Japanese favourites such as sushi, ramen, tempura and *yakitori*.

Fast-food city

Too much to do in Tokyo and too little time to do it? No need to hang about eating – do as Tokyoites do and grab some fast food or food to go. Round-the-clock **convenience stores** such as Seven-Eleven, AM/PM and Lawson sell a wide range of snacks and meals which can be heated up in the shop's microwave or reconstituted with hot water. For more upmarket goodies, make your way to the basement food halls of the major department stores, where you'll also find good **bentō** (set boxes of food). For Japanese **fast food**, head for *Yoshinoya*, which serves reasonably tasty *gyūdon* (stewed strips of beef on rice), and *Tenya*, which offers a similar low-cost deal for tempura and rice dishes. You'll find plenty of *McDonald's* and *KFC*s around town; a good local chain is *Mos Burger*, serving up rice burgers, carrot juice and green *konnyaku* jelly (a root vegetable).

The latest fast-food hits include **soup** and decent Western-style **sandwiches** – something Tokyo's been lacking for a while. *Soup Stock Tokyo* (⊛www.soup-stock-tokyo.com) serves steaming mugs of hearty broths; their main branch is in Akasaka, and you'll also find them in Ueno station, Roppongi Hills (B2F Hollywood Plaza), and the Maru Building in Marunouchi, among other locations. Upmarket sandwiches are available from *Benugo* (⊛www.benugo.co.jp), in Yebisu Garden Place, Akasaka and Shiodome, as well as from the UK chain *Pret A Manger* (⊛www.pretamanger.com), in Akasaka, Hamamatsuchō, Kamiyachō and Shinjuku. For a Hawaiian twist on the sandwich and burger genre try the very tasty offerings at *Kua 'Aian* (⊛www.four-seeds.co.jp), currently one of the most popular places in the city: you'll find them on the corner of Aoyama-dōri and Koto-dōri in Aoyama, and in the Maru Building, Marunouchi, among other places.

With so many options, there's no need to panic about prices. Tokyo has a plethora of ever-reliable noodle bars, *shokudō* and chain restaurants, where the Japanese go when they need to fill up without fear of the cost; many cluster around and inside train stations. There's also an abundance of fast-food options (see box opposite) and a wide variety of chain cafés (see box on p.173) offering light meals. Many of the pubs (*izakaya*) and live music venues listed on pp.175–179 and pp.181–182 – such as Ebisu's *What the Dickens!* and Hibya's *Town Cryer* – serve fine food, too.

Restaurants

With so much competition in the food stakes, it's perhaps not surprising that many Tokyo restaurants are concentrating on decor to give them the wow-factor edge. On the one hand you have contemporary design stunners like *Daidaiya* and *Shunjū*; on the other, themed dining fantasies such as *Seiryūmon*, *Ninja* and *Christon Café*. If you're not bothered about design, Tokyo has several unpretentious **restaurant chains** worth checking out. For **Indian** food, *Moti*, with outlets in Roppongi and Akasaka, and *Samarat*, in Roppongi, Shibuya, Shinjuku and Ueno, are long-time local favourites. For good **Italian** dishes, head for *Capricciosa*, with branches all over the city – its sign is in elongated *katakana* on a green, red and white background. The casual American-style *News Deli* (ⓦ www.sunrisejapan.com/restaurants) is also all over the city; find them in Aoyama, Daikan'yama, Ikebukuro and Shinjuku.

Among the **Japanese chains** to look out for are *Sushisei*, a classy sushi restaurant with branches in Tsukiji, Akasaka and Roppongi; *Kushinobō*, the folk craft-decorated *kushikatsu* (deep-fried morsels on skewers) restaurants; and *Tsunahachi*, which is *the* place for tempura. The *Gonpachi*, *La Bohème*, *Monsoon* and *Zest* chains (branches in Ginza, Harajuku, Shibuya, Nishi–Azabu and Daikan'yama) are all run by the same company (ⓦ www.global -dining.com) and can be relied on for value and late-night dining in chic settings.

If you can't decide what to go for, make your way to the restaurant floors of the major **department stores** and **shopping malls**, such as Ebisu's Yebisu Garden City, Shiodome, My City in Shinjuku and Roppongi Hills, where there are enough options to keep you well fed for weeks. At such places you'll find a wide choice of cuisines and dining atmospheres under one roof, often with plastic food displays in the windows and daily specials. Also, don't overlook the good-value **family restaurants**, such as *Royal Host* (in Shinjuku, Shinagawa and Takodanobaba, among other locations) and *Jonathan's* (Shinjuku, Harajuku, Asakusa), which serve both Western and Japanese dishes and have easy-to-choose-from picture menus; most are open 24 hours, too.

Restaurant prices

Restaurants in Tokyo have been graded as **inexpensive** (under ¥1000 for a meal without alcohol); **moderate** (¥1000–4000); **expensive** (¥4000–6000); and **very expensive** (over ¥6000). The cheapest time to eat out is lunchtime, when even the priciest places offer good-value set meals, and you'd be hard pressed to spend over ¥2000. **Tipping** is not expected, but **consumption tax** (five percent) can push up the total cost. Some restaurants and bars serving food, especially those in hotels, add on a **service charge** (typically ten percent). Make sure you have cash to hand; payment by **credit card** is becoming more common, but is generally restricted to upmarket restaurants and hotels.

Tokyo restaurants and tea houses

Akiyoshi	*Akiyoshi*	秋吉
Atariya	*Atariya*	当リヤ
Cha Ginza	*Cha Ginza*	茶銀座
Chin'ya	*Chin'ya*	ちんや
Daikokuya	*Daikokuya*	大黒屋
En	*En*	えん
Gonpachi	*Gonpachi*	権八
Hantei	*Hantei*	はん亭
Heirokuzushi	*Heirokuzushi*	平禄寿司
Jangara	*Jangara*	じゃんがら
Kurosawa	*Kurosawa*	黒澤
Kushinobō	*Kushinobō*	串の坊
Maguro Bito	*Maguro Bito*	まぐろ人
Maisen	*Maisen*	マイ泉
Myōkō	*Myōkō*	妙高
Mominoki House	*Mominoki Hausu*	モミノキハウス
Musashino	*Musashino*	武蔵野
Ninnikuya	*Ninnikuya*	ニンニク屋
Ōtafuku	*Ōtafuku*	大多福
Robata Honten	*Robata Honten*	爐端本店
Sakuratei	*Sakuratei*	さくら亭
Seiryūmon	*Seiryūmon*	青龍門
Shion	*Shion*	しおん
Shunjū	*Shunjū*	春秋
Sometarō	*Sometarō*	染太郎
Sushisei	*Sushisei*	寿司清
Suzuki	*Suzuki*	寿々木
Taimeiken	*Taimeiken*	たいめいけん
Tenmaru	*Tenmaru*	天マル
Tonki	*Tonki*	とんき
Torigin Honten	*Torigin Honten*	鳥ぎん本店
Tomoegata	*Tomoegata*	巴潟
Tsunahachi	*Tsunahachi*	つな八
Unagi Ben-kei	*Unagi Ben-kei*	鰻弁慶
Yabu Soba	*Yabu Soba*	やぶそば
Yamamotoyama	*Yamamotoyama*	山本山

For more information on Tokyo's restaurants, check out the free weekly magazine *Metropolis* or some of the websites listed in the box on p.98. The *Zagat Survey of Tokyo Restaurants* (¥1500) is the most up-to-date guidebook; you can also read their listings at Ⓦwww.zagat.com. In the listings below we give the closest subway or train station to the restaurant and the telephone number in case you get lost; bookings are advisable for many places, especially on Friday, Saturday and Sunday nights. For more on Japanese cuisines, see p.52 in Basics.

Akasaka

The following restaurants are marked on the map on p.124.

Aux Bacchanales 2F Ark Mori Bldg, 1-12-32 Akasaka, Minato-ku ☎03/3582-2225. Tucked away in the Ark Hills complex, opposite Suntory Hall, this is one of Tokyo's most authentic Parisian-style brasseries – their *steak frite* is the real thing

and it's a pleasant spot to hang out sipping coffee or red wine. Roppongi-Itchōme Station. Moderate. **Jangara** Sotobori-dōri, near the entrance to the Hie-jinja. Funky noodle bar serving up large bowls of Kyūshū-style ramen (Chinese noodles) in three types of soup: fish, mild and light, and greasy garlic, from ¥550, with beer at ¥450. Also has branches in Akihabara, Ginza and two in Harajuku, both close by Omotesandō. Akasaka Station. Inexpensive.

Kurosawa 2-7-9 Nagatachō, Chiyoda-ku ☎03/3580-9638. Slightly pricey but very tasty *soba* noodles and pork *sukiyaki* dishes are served at this atmospheric restaurant, whose design was inspired by the sets from Akira Kurosawa's movies *Yojimbo* and *Red Beard*. They also have a cute restaurant specializing in *udon* noodles near Roppongi Hills (☎03/3403-9638). Tamekei-Sannō Station. Moderate.

Ninja 1F Akasaka Tokyū Bldg, 2-14-31 Nagatachō, Chiyoda-ku ☎03/5157-3936. Dark, twisting corridors, waiters who jump out of secret doorways, a magician who does amazing tricks at your table – all this and more makes up the fun dining experience at this upmarket *ninja* (see box, p.427) themed *izakaya*. The modern Japanese cuisine is in small but tasty portions. Open evenings only. Akasaka-Mitsuke Station. Moderate to expensive.

Shunjū 27th floor, San'nō Park Tower, 2-11-1 Nagatachō, Chiyoda-ku ☎03/3592-5288. You've perhaps read their cook book, now try the real thing. This is the modern Japanese dining experience *par excellence*, matching stylish contemporary interior design with food made from the freshest seasonal ingredients. Courses kick off at ¥6000, and note the extra twenty percent in service and taxes on the bill. There are also a couple of branches in Shibuya and the more casual *Kitchen Shunjū* (☎03/5369-0377) in Shinjuku's My City department store (see below). Tamekei-Sannō. Expensive to very expensive.

Sushisei 3-11-4 Akasaka, Minato-ku ☎03/3582-9503. One of the city's best sushi restaurant chains, which means you may have to wait to be served at peak times. Per-piece charges start at ¥100, much less than at similar à la carte *sushi-ya*. There are also branches in Tsukiji, close to the market, and Roppongi on TV Asahi-dōri. Closed Sun. Akasaka Station. Moderate.

West Park Café 2F Akasaka Tōkyū Plaza, 2-14-3 Nagatachō, Chiyoda-ku ☎03/3580-9090. Relaxed American-style deli-café, with an outdoor terrace and an airy interior. Good for light meals, and for their weekend brunch. There are other branches a five-minute walk west of Yoyogi-kōen at 23-11 Moto-Yoyogichō, and on the firth floor of the Maru Building, Marunouchi. Akasaka Mitsuke Station. Moderate.

Asakusa

The following restaurants are marked on the map on p.129.

Chin'ya 1-3-4 Asakusa, Taitō-ku ☎03/3841-0010. Founded in 1880, this famous, traditional *shabu-shabu* and *sukiyaki* restaurant offers basic menus from ¥3000. It occupies seven floors, with cheaper, more casual dining in the basement. Closed Wed. Asakusa Station. Moderate to expensive.

Daikokuya 1-38-10 Asakusa, Taitō-ku ☎03/3844-1111. Meiji-era tempura restaurant in an attractive old building opposite Dembō-in garden. The speciality is *tendon*, a satisfying bowl of shrimp, fish and prawn fritters on a bed of rice (from ¥1400). The tatami room upstairs tends to be less hectic, but it's best not to visit during peak lunchtime hours. Closed Thurs. Asakusa Station. Moderate.

Maguro Bito 1-5 Asakusa, Taitō-ku ☎03/3844-8736. Fuji-TV viewers voted this the top *kaiten-zushi* shop in Japan, and it's easy to see why: the quality of fish and other ingredients is excellent, the turnover fast and the decor on the ritzy side. Expect a queue, but it moves fast. Electronically price-coded plates range from ¥130 to ¥400.

There's also a stand-up/take-away branch opposite Kaminari-mon. Asakusa Station. Inexpensive.

Ōtafuku 1-6-2 Senzoku, Taitō-ku ☎03/3871-2521. Customers have been coming to this charming restaurant for over eighty years for *oden* – not surprising since their selection is delicious and includes rarities such as shark, both flesh and bone. Wash it all down with a beaker of pine-scented *tarozake* (sake). Some Japanese would help here, but the staff are very friendly and you can sit at the counter and point at what you want in the bubbling brass vats. Open evenings only; closed Mon April–Sept. Iriya Station. Moderate to expensive.

Sometarō 2-2-2 Nishi-Asakusa, Taitō-ku ☎03/3844-9502. Homely restaurant specializing in *okonomiyaki*, cheap and filling savoury pancakes cooked on a hotplate. One good-sized bowl costs from ¥400, depending on your ingredients. There's a book of English instructions and plenty of people to offer advice. To find it look for a bamboo-fenced garden and lantern halfway up the street. Tawaramachi Station. Inexpensive.

Ebisu, Hiro-o and Meguro

The following restaurants are marked on the map on p.154.

Cardenas Charcole Grill 1-12-14 Ebisu Nishi, Shibuya-ku ☎03/5428-0779. Dramatic, multi-level basement space showcases some of Tokyo's best contemporary fusion cuisine – the fishcakes in *uni* sauce look like spiky sea urchins and taste fantastic. Steaks are expensive, but the other grilled dishes needn't break the bank. For something less formal, try the same company's relaxed *Fummy's Grill* (2-1-5 Ebisu ☎03/3473-9629). Ebisu Station. Moderate to expensive.

Ebisu Tower Yebisu Garden City. Two floors of restaurants with great views across the city. Try *Yebisu* (☎03/5420-1161), on the 39th floor, a classy *yakitori-ya* with sets for around ¥1000; or *Chibo* (☎03/5424-1011), a fun Ōsaka-style *okonomiyaki* restaurant on the 38th. Ebisu Station. Moderate.

Good Honest Grub 1-11-11 Ebisu Minami, Shibuya-ku ☎03/3710-0400. Relaxed, brightly decorated place that serves up just what the name says: chunky sandwiches, big salads and sizeable plates of pasta. The fruit shakes and slurpies are good, and they also have organic wine. Ebisu Station. Inexpensive to moderate.

Homework's 5-1-20 Hiro-o, Shibuya-ku ☎03/3440-4560. Decent burgers – the chunky home-made variety – at this popular pitstop at the end of Hiro-o's main shopping street. The French fries are well up to scratch, too. There are also branches at 1-5-8 Azabu-Jūban, Minato-ku (☎03/3405-9884). Hiro-o Station. Moderate.

Kushinobō 6F Atre, 1-5-5 Ebisu, Shibuya-ku ☎03/5475-8415. This *kushiage* restaurant has a cosy, folk-craft ambience and does great-value lunch sets from under ¥1000, as well as lots of interesting deep-fried nibbles on skewers. There are other branches around the city, including at Roppongi (2F, 7&7 Building, 7-14-18 Roppongi), which specializes in *fugu*; Shibuya (5F, J&R Building, 33-12 Udagawachō); and Shinjuku (1-10-5 Kabukichō). Ebisu Station. Moderate.

Ninnikuya 1-26-12 Ebisu, Shibuya-ku ☎03/3446-5887. Tokyo's original garlic restaurant, and still one of the best. Virtually everything on the menu is cooked with the pungent bulb, and the buzzing atmosphere in the long dining room with large shared wooden tables can't be beaten. Ebisu Station. Open evenings only; closed Mon. Moderate to expensive.

Tonki 1-1-2 Shimo-Meguro, Meguro-ku ☎03/3491-9928. Tokyo's most famous *tonkatsu* restaurant, where a seemingly telepathic team makes order out of chaos. You'll need to queue up outside the main branch, west of the station, which is only open from 4pm; for lunch, go to *Tonki Annex* on the east side of the station, across the plaza on the second floor of the corner building. Closed Tues. Meguro Station. Moderate.

Ginza and Shiodome

There's plenty to choose from dining wise in the new Shiodome complex, while the more adventurous will want to muck in with the locals at the numerous *yakitori* bars nestling under the railway tracks between Yūrakuchō and Shimbashi stations. All the following restaurants are marked on the map on p.115.

Afternoon Tea Baker and Diner 2-3-6 Ginza, Chūō-ku ☎03/5159-1635. Department store restaurant set up with the help of Jamie Oliver – his grub kicks off at ¥3500 for three courses at lunch, ¥5000 for four courses at dinner. Daily 11.30am–2.00pm & 5.30–9pm. Ginza-Itchōme Station. Moderate to expensive.

Aroyna Tabeta 3-7-11 Marunouchi, Chiyoda-ku ☎03/5219-6099. Note the big ¥500 sign – that's the price you'll pay for all food, including set lunches, at this basic Thai eatery under the tracks. The cooking is heavy on the chilli (a surprise in Tokyo) but tasty, and great value for what you get. Open daily 24 hours. Yūrakuchō Station. Inexpensive.

Atariya 3-5-17 Ginza, Chūō-ku ☎03/3564-0045. One of the more reasonable places to eat in Ginza, this small, workaday restaurant, marked by a big red lantern, has an English menu and is a good introduction to *yakitori* bars. Mon–Sat 4.30–11pm. Ginza Station. Moderate.

Daidaiya 2F Ginza Nine Bldg, 8-5 Ginza-nishi ☎03/5537-3566. In a city of stunning restaurant interiors, this one really knocks your socks off. The food is "nouvelle Japonaise", with items such as foie gras on lotus root cakes, as well as a good sushi and *tempura* selection. There are other spectacular branches in Shinjuku (☎03/5362-7173) and Akasaka's Belle Vie complex (☎03/3588-5087). Open evenings only. Shimbashi Station. Expensive.

En 42nd Floor, Shiodome City Centre, 1-5-2 Higashi Shimbashi, Minato-ku ☎03/5537-2096. This upmarket Japanese *izakaya* has rustic stylings, a menu with a wide range of vegetable and fish dishes and killer views across to Hama Rikyū Teien (see p.159) and the bay. Shiodome Station. Moderate.

Farm Grill 2F, Ginza Nine, 3-8-6 Ginza, Chūō-ku ☎03/5568-6156. Pay as you enter for this popular California-style buffet located under the expressway. It's ¥1000 at lunch or ¥2500 for dinner, and there's a 2hr time limit. Drinks are not included, but in the evening you can opt for a ¥3800 *nomi-hodai* (drink as much as you like) which includes wine, whisky, coffee and a choice of fifty cocktails. Shimbashi Station. Moderate.

G-Zone 1-2-3 Ginza, Chūō-ku. The Global Dining group has gathered together all its concept restaurants at this complex beneath the Shuto Expressway – from ye olde Japanese-style *Gonpachi* (☎03/5524-3641) at one end to the faux-European *La Bohème* (☎03/5524-3616) at the other, with the Mexican *Zest Cantina* (☎03/5524-3621) and Southeast Asian *Monsoon Café* (☎03/5524-3631) in the middle. Ginza-Itchōme Station. Moderate to expensive.

Nair's 4-10-7 Ginza, Chūō-ku ☎03/3541-8246. The decor is on the Bollywood tacky side but this Tokyo institution has been going since 1949, and offers decent Kerala home-cooking. It's maybe not the best Indian around, but the food's tasty and reasonably cheap for Ginza. Closed Tues. Higashi-Ginza Station. Moderate.

Nataraj 7-9F Ginza Kosaka Bldg, 6-9-4 Ginza ☎03/5537-1515 Vegetarians will want to check out this quite classy Indian chain restaurant, which does a fine range of veggie curries and *naan* breads. Ginza Station. Moderate.

Robata Honten 1-3-8 Yūrakuchō, Chiyoda-ku ☎03/3591-1905. The delicious food at this rustic *izakaya* (look for the basket of veggies outside) is laid out in big plates for you to see – order what you fancy and the genial, kimono-clad owner will whisk it off to be prepared. Open evenings only. Hibiya Station. Moderate

Taimeiken 1-12-10 Nihombashi, Chūō-ku. One of Tokyo's original Western-style restaurants, whose *omu-raisu* (rice-stuffed omelette) was featured in the movie *Tampopo* (see p.999). Downstairs is a cheap and cheerful cafeteria serving large portions of curry rice, *tonkatsu* and noodles, with a more expensive restaurant above. Closed Sun. Nihombashi Station. Inexpensive to moderate.

Tenmaru 6-9-2 Ginza, Chūō-ku ☎03/3289-1010. Consistently good tempura restaurant in a basement just off Chūō-dōri. Expect to spend at least ¥2000 a head. English menu available. Ginza Station. Moderate.

Torigin Honten B1, 5-5-7 Ginza, Chūō-ku ☎03/3571-3333. Bright, popular restaurant serving *yakitori* and *kamameshi* (kettle-cooked rice with a choice of toppings), tucked down an alley two blocks east of Ginza's Sony Building among a clutch of cheeky copycat rivals. Good for a snack or a full meal, particularly if you opt for *kamameshi* or a weekday lunch set, both from around ¥800. The English menu makes it a lot easier. Ginza Station. Inexpensive to moderate.

Ikebukuro

The following restaurants are marked on the map on p.139.

Akiyoshi 3-30-4 Nishi-Ikebukuro, Toshima-ku ☎03/3982-0601. Unusually large *yakitori* bar with a good atmosphere and a helpful picture menu. You might have to queue at peak times for the tables, but there's generally space at the counter. Open evenings only. Ikebukuro Station. Inexpensive.

Malaychan 3-22-6 Nishi-Ikebukuro, Toshima-ku ☎03/5391-7638. Unpretentious Malay restaurant dishing up decent food, from grilled fish on banana leaf and *mee goreng* to winter steam boats. The beer pitchers are good value, or throw in a Singapore Sling and you can still eat well for around ¥2000. Weekday lunch menus from ¥800. Ikebukuro Station. Inexpensive to moderate.

Mekong B1, 3-26-5 Nishi-Ikebukuro, Toshima-ku ☎03/3988-5688. The decor may not be much to rave about, but the tastes and aromas will take you straight back to Thailand. The lunchtime buffet is a steal at ¥1050; at other times you can eat well for around ¥2000 a head from their picture menu. Closed Tues lunchtime. Ikebukuro Station. Moderate.

Saigon 3F, 1-7-10 Higashi-Ikebukuro, Toshima-ku ☎03/3989-0255. Friendly, unpretentious place serving authentic Vietnamese food, even down to the *333* beer. *Banh xeo* (sizzling pancake with a spicy sauce) or *bunh bo* (beef noodle soup) are recommended, with a side dish of *nem* (spring rolls) if you're really hungry. Weekday lunchtime sets are excellent value at ¥750. Ikebukuro Station. Inexpensive to moderate.

Kanda and Ryōgoku

The following restaurants are marked on the map on p.120.

Tomoegata 2-17-6 Ryōgoku, Sumida-ku ☎03/3632-5600. In the heart of sumo territory, this is one of the best places to sample the wrestlers' protein-packed stew, *chanko-nabe*. For

¥2800 you can have the full-blown meal cooked at your table, though most people will find the smaller, ready-made version (¥840; lunch only) more than enough. It's two blocks south of the station, and easy to spot from its parade of colourful flags; there's a new annexe on the north side of the street. Ryōgoku Station. Closed Mon. Inexpensive to moderate.

Yabu Soba 2-10 Kanda-Awajichō, Chiyoda-ku ☏03/3251-0287. Connoisseurs travel a long way to slurp the noodles here and to listen to the cheerful waiting staff's distinctive singsong cries. You might have to wait at busy times, but it doesn't take long, and there's an attractive garden to look out on. Prices start at around ¥600. Awajichō Station. Inexpensive to moderate.

Roppongi, Nishi-Azabu and Azabu-Juban

The following restaurants are marked on the map on p.127.

Dalarna 5-9-19 Roppongi, Minato-ku ☏03/3478-4690. This intimate Swedish restaurant offers yummy meatballs with lingonberry jam, gravlax and other Scandinavian dishes. There are good lunch deals and the set dinner is ¥3500. Roppongi Station. Moderate.

Gonpachi 1-13-11 Nishi-Azabu, Minato-ku ☏03/5771 0170. That monumental *kura* (storehouse) at Nishi-Azabu crossing looks as if it's somehow survived since the Edo period, but it's actually one of the newest on the block. Inside, take your pick between soba and grilled items on the ground and second floor, while on the third it's sushi. President Bush ate here, but don't let that put you off – it has a wonderful Samurai drama atmosphere. Roppongi Station. Moderate.

Havana Café 4-12-2 Roppongi, Minato-ku ☏03/3423-3500. There's more of a Tex-Mex than a Cuban lilt to the menu at this brightly decorated café away from the main Roppongi drag. The portions are large, the prices reasonable and there's a happy hour from 5pm to 7pm. Roppongi Station. Moderate.

L'Atelier de Joel Robuchon 2F Roppongi Hills Hillside, 6-10-1 Roppongi, Minato-ku ☏03/5772-7500. Of all the many, many restaurants in

Roppongi Hills, this is the one that has created the biggest buzz – and the longest queues, since they have a no-bookings policy. Be patient or lucky and you'll eventually get a seat at the long counter facing onto the open kitchen and be able to see what all the fuss is about, as black-garbed chefs create mini-culinary masterpieces before your very eyes. The six-course menu is ¥6000, but it's possible to treat yourself to a couple of the degustation-size dishes for less. Roppongi Station. Expensive to very expensive.

Rainbow Roll Sushi 2F Monteplaza, 1-10-3 Azabu-Juban ☏03/5572-7689. Sushi gets a contemporary makeover at this sleekly designed restaurant where fish is often the last thing you'll find in your California-style roll. They do great cocktails too. Azabu-Juban Station. Moderate.

Roti 1F Piramide Bldg, 6-6-9 Roppongi, Minato-ku ☏03/5785 3671. You'd better be hungry before dining at this "modern American brasserie" because the portions are huge. You could easily share their speciality – rotisserie chicken, flavoursome birds from Kyushu well worth ¥2000 – or any of their other grilled meat dishes. Also serves fine microbrew beers and a tempting range of desserts. Roppongi Station. Moderate.

Shibuya, Harajuku and Aoyama

The following restaurants are marked on the map on p.152.

Christon Café B1F, 2-10-7 Dogenzaka, Shibuya-ku ☏03/5728-2225. This basement restaurant could be the set for a Hammer horror movie set in a Gothic cathedral, though the nicely presented Asian fusion food won't scare you. There's also a branch in Shinjuku (☏03/5287-2426). Open evenings only. Shibuya Station. Moderate.

Chung King Lo 3-14-17 Minami-Aoyama, Minato-ku ☏03/5771-0338. Modern Chinese café and bar, part of the Idée design group, tucked away in the backstreets at the designer end of Omotesandō. Given that it's oh so stylish, it's actually not bad value, and the food is fine. Good for a quiet drink too. Omotesandō Station. Moderate.

Fujimamas 6-3-2 Jingūmae, Shibuya-ku

☏03/5485-2262. There's a bit more style than substance to the East–West fusion food at this popular place, but it's generally good value and the menu (desserts are headed "Oh, I just couldn't . . . but I will!") is a hoot. Meiji-jingūmae Station. Moderate.

Heirokuzushi 5-8-5 Jingūmae, Shibuya-ku. Perennially popular *kaitenzushi* (conveyor-belt sushi) restaurant in a prime position on Omotesandō. Plates range from ¥120 to ¥240. Meiji-jingūmae Station. Inexpensive.

Immigrant's Café 5-9-15 Minami-Aoyama, Minato-ku ☏03/5766-8995. In the basement of the building next to Max Mara, this friendly and casual restaurant has a suitably international vibe for a menu that offers inexpensive dishes from around the world. Omotesandō Station. Inexpensive to moderate.

Las Chicas 5-47-6 Jingūmae, Shibuya-ku ☎03/3407-6865. There are few nicer places to dine on a summer's night than in the enchanting courtyard here, and there's also a spacious indoor restaurant and a lively bar (with Internet terminals). Food is Italian-fusion, supported by some fine Antipodean wines. Omotesandō Station. Moderate.

Maisen 4-8-5 Jingūmae, Shibuya-ku ☎03/3470-0071. Set in an old bathhouse, this long-running *tonkatsu* restaurant serves up great-value set meals. Omotesandō Station. Moderate.

Myōkō 1-17-2 Shibuya, Shibuya-ku ☎03/3499-3450. You really can't go wrong with the hearty metal bowls of *Yamanashi-ken* flat udon noodles in a rich *nabe* stew – just the ticket on a chilly day. Or try the cold noodle dishes in summer. Look for the water wheel outside. Closed Sun. Shibuya Station. Moderate.

Mominoki House 2-18-5 Jingūmae, Shibuya-ku ☎03/3405-9144. Lots of natural ingredients are used at this macrobiotic restaurant on the quiet side of Harajuku. Plants, paintings and jazz add to the atmosphere, and a good lunch can be had for around ¥1500. Closed Sun. Meiji-jingūmae Station. Moderate.

Nobu Tokyo 6-10-17 Minami-Aoyama, Minato-ku ☎03/5467-0022. Japanese–Peruvian fusion cuisine by superstar chef Nobu Matsuhisa – try the signature black cod with miso – served in what looks like a luxurious family diner, with big pink rose prints, expensive black leather seats and an open kitchen with chefs in baseball caps. The lunch set for ¥3000 is a bargain. Omotesandō Station. Closed Sat & Sun lunchtime. Expensive.

Pariya 3-12-14 Kita Aoyama, Minato-ku, just off Aoyama-dōri ☎03/3486-1316. Three Bapa Papas greet you at this fun eatery where you can mix 'n' match your own choice of meat and fish ingredients. The English menu explains the options, or you could come for lunch when there's a good-value spread of modern Japanese food. Omotesandō Station. Moderate.

Rojak 6-3-14 Minami-Aoyama, Minato-ku ☎03/3409-6764. Tucked away down a cul-de-sac near the *Blue Note Tokyo* jazz club, this place does appealing and reasonably priced Asian/organic food and has a very cosy library-style bar with sofas. There's also a new branch in Roppongi Hills. Omotesandō Station. Moderate to expensive.

Sakuratei 3-20-1 Jingūmae, Shibuya-ku ☎03/3479-0039. Funky cook-your-own *okonomiyaki* and *yakisoba* joint behind the weird and wonderful Design Festa gallery (see p.150). From 11.30am to 3pm daily you've got ninety minutes to eat as much as you like for ¥980, and it's just as good value at night. Daily 11.30am–11pm. Meiji-jingūmae Station. Inexpensive.

Shinjuku and around

All the following restaurants are marked on the map on p.142.

Angkor Wat 1-38-13 Yoyogi, Shibuya-ku ☎03/3370-3019. Tokyo's best Cambodian restaurant. Tell the waiters your price limit and let them bring you a selection of dishes (¥3000 per head is more than enough). The sweetly spicy salads, soups and vegetable rolls are all excellent. It's a five-minute walk west of Yoyogi Station; look for the pottery elephant outside the entrance on a side street. Yoyogi Station. Moderate.

Ban Thai 1-23-14 Kabukichō, Shinjuku-ku ☎03/3207-0068. Shinjuku's most famous Thai restaurant, serving authentic dishes at moderate prices. On the third floor of a building surrounded by the screaming neon strip joints of Kabukichō. Shinjuku Station. Moderate.

Kakiden 8F Yasuyo Building, 3-37-11 Shinjuku, Shinjuku-ku ☎03/3352-5121. One of the best places in Tokyo to sample *kaiseki-ryōri*, Japanese haute cuisine. There's a lunch for ¥4000, but you won't regret investing in the eighteen-course dinner for ¥8000. From 6pm to 8pm there are live performances on the thirteen-stringed *koto*. Shinjuku Station. Very expensive.

New York Grill Park Hyatt Tower, 3-7-1-2 Nishi-Shinjuku ☎03/5323-3458. Stylish 52nd-floor restaurant where great views, huge portions and a bustling vibe make for a truly memorable eating experience. The ¥4400 lunch is worth splurging on. Booking essential. Shinjuku Station. Expensive.

Rendezvous B1 Yanagiya Bldg, 2-18-6 Takadanobaba, Shinjuku-ku ☎03/5285-0128. Small, friendly café serving the most authentic Burmese food among the cluster of places catering to the area's expat Burmese community. Try the *lape-toh* (fermented tea leaf salad) or *mohinga* (noodles in a spicy, thick broth). The slightly fancier café *Nagani* in the same location is also worth a look. Takadanobaba Station. Moderate.

Seiryūmon 3/4F Shinjuku Remina Building, 3-17-4 Shinjuku, Shinjuku-ku ☎03/3355-0717. One of Tokyo's first theme restaurants, and still going strong: this branch of the Chinese/Taiwanese chain is Shanghai opium den circa 1840. You dine inside cages and there's a mock secret entrance to the restaurant. Shinjuku Station. Moderate to expensive.

Shion 1-25 Kabukichō. Round the corner from *Kirin City* on the west side of Shinjuku, this is one of the area's cheapest conveyor-belt sushi operations. There's often a queue, but it moves quickly. Plates are ¥100 or ¥200 each, and you can order beer and sake. Shinjuku Station. Inexpensive.

Shun Kan 7th and 8th floors, My City, 3-38-1 Shinjuku. This department store has given its restaurant floors a super-snazzy makeover, worth seeing in itself. The more populist 7th floor has walls decorated with an ingenious range of items – from old video recorders to flattened cardboard boxes; the 8th floor is all zen coolness. Among the wide range of restaurants it's worth checking out

Kowloon Ten Shin (☎03/5360-8191) for an all-you-can-eat Chinese and dim sum buffet (lunch/dinner ¥1800/2800), *Kitchen Shunjū* (see review above), the Okinawan *Nabbie and Kamado* (☎03/5379-1070) and the Korean *Saikaho*. Shinjuku Station. Moderate.

Tsunahachi 3-31-8 Shinjuku ☎03/3352-1012. The main branch of the famous tempura restaurant almost always has a queue outside. You're likely to sit down quickly if you settle for the upstairs rooms away from the frying action. Everything is freshly made, and even with the ¥1100 set (including soup, rice and pickles) you'll be full. Shinjuku Station. Moderate.

Ueno

All the following restaurants are marked on the map on p.133.

Hantei 2-12-15 Nezu, Bunkyō-ku ☎03/3828-1440. Stylish dining in a beautiful, three-storey wooden house. There's only one dish, *kushiage* – deep-fried skewers of crunchy seafood, meat and vegetables with special dipping sauces – served in combination plates, six at a time: ¥2700 for the first plate; ¥1300 thereafter, until you say stop. Nezu Station. Moderate to expensive.

Musashino 2-8-11 Ueno, Bunkyō-ku ☎03/3831-1672. Ueno is famed for its *tonkatsu* (breaded pork cutlets), worth trying at this traditional restaurant behind bamboo screens and pot plants, where prices for a big thick slab that melts in the mouth are reasonable. Choose between standard *rōsu* or fillet, at around ¥1500 including soup, rice and pickles. They also serve fried prawns (*ebi-fry*). Ueno-Hirokōji Station. Moderate.

Retro-kan Ueno Station. Handy if you're waiting for a train, this recently renovated restaurant mall attached to Ueno Station is home to some stylish places. *Coca* on the first floor has an eclectic world cuisine menu, while the neighbouring *Tsuki-no-Shizuku* serves handmade tofu, among other Japanese dishes. There are also branches of *Hard Rock Café* and the British chain pub *Rose & Crown*. Ueno Station. Moderate.

Unagi Ben-kei 4-5-10 Ueno, Bunkyō-ku ☎03/3831-2283. Eel (*unagi*) is the order of the day at this informal, traditional restaurant on three floors – try their *unagi donburi* lunchtime set for a taster (¥1050; Mon–Sat). They also do well-priced *sukiyaki* and *shabu shabu* meals (from ¥1260 for lunch), as well as tempura, sashimi and so forth. English menu available. Closed third Mon of the month. Ueno Station. Moderate.

Cafés and teahouses

Tokyo's **café scene** was revolutionized in the early 1990s with the advent of the cheap chain coffee shop (see box opposite), a process that has only been accelerated by the mass colonization of Tokyo by the Seattle-based *Starbucks*. For all the convenience of these operations, you shouldn't miss sampling at least one of Tokyo's old-style **kissaten**, where the emphasis is on service and creating an interesting, relaxing space. You'll pay more, but many of these places, such as Shibuya's *Lion*, have become institutions. If you want to mingle with the beautiful people, cafés in Omotesandō and Daikan'yama are still the places to hang out. Just remember to take your time, since you've rented the table rather than paid for a quick pick-me-up.

Teahouses are much thinner on the ground, and your only real chance of attending a traditional Japanese tea ceremony will be at the *New Ōtani* and the *Ōkura* hotels (see p.104 and p.105). For pretty settings, try the teahouses in Shinjuku Gyoen (see p.146), Happōen (see p.156) and the Kyū Iwasaki-tei Gardens (see p.136). It's worth noting that while cafés often keep late hours, teahouses are strictly a daytime affair. The listings below give the nearest subway or train station.

Tokyo's chain cafés

Of the many **chain cafés** now liberally spread around the city, *Renoir* and *Almond*, with its famous branch at Roppongi crossing, are the oldest survivors. However, with their stuck-in-the-1970s decor, such places are now overshadowed by bright upstarts such as *Café Veloce*, *Doutor*, *Mister Donuts* and *Tully's*. These serve straightforward "blend" (medium-strength) coffee and tea from as little as ¥180, and offer a decent range of pastries, sandwiches and other snacks – particularly *Mister Donuts*, one of the few places to offer free coffee refills; they're ideal for breakfast or a quick snack. The chain cafés *Giraffe* and *Pronto* also transform into bars in the evening, serving reasonably priced alcoholic drinks and nibbles.

From just one outlet in 1996, *Starbucks* now seems to be everywhere; for sheer location power, check out the branch overlooking the crossing at Shibuya Station. Unlike other branches, this one only serves the more expensive, large-size coffees. For a less mercenary approach, nip across to another recent foreign import, *Segafredo Zanetti*, in the Shibuya Mark City complex (there are others in Hiro-o, Shinagawa and Shinjuku). This famous Italian-brand coffee shop has more Euro-chic and serves decent *panini*, beer and pear schnapps. Not to be outdone, the local biggie, *Doutor*, has very stylish branches in Shibuya, just north of Tower Records, and at *Le Café Doutor Espresso*, at the main Ginza crossing opposite the department store Wako.

Cafés

Andersen 5-1-26 Aoyama, Minato-ku. This Tokyo outpost of Hiroshima's famed Swedish-style bakery (see p.659) has an excellent range of pastries and sandwiches and a reasonably priced sit-down café, a good option for breakfast and lunch. Omotesandō Station.

Bape Café!? B1F, 5-3-18 Minami-Aoyama, Minato-ku ☎03/5778-9726. Part of the booming *A Bathing Ape* empire of trendy streetware (see "Shopping", p.187), this design-driven café-bar is a fun and surprisingly good-value place for a drink, with everything at ¥500. Their lunch sets for ¥1000 are also great. Omotesandō Station.

Ben's Café 1-29-21 Takadanobaba, Shinjuku-ku ☎03/3202-2445, ⓦwww.benscafé.com. Any time is a good time to visit this laid-back New York-style café with its fine range of coffees, drinks and snacks. Also has an Internet terminal. Takadanobaba Station.

Café du Monde Spice 2 Building, 1-10-10 Nishi-Ikebukuro, Toshima-ku. Bright, modern New Orleans coffee shop specializing in authentic chicory coffee and *beignets* (doughnuts fried in cotton-seed oil) with various dipping sauces. Ikebukuro Station.

Café Comme Ça 3-26 Shinjuku, Shinjuku-ku. In the trendy Five Foxes Store and serving delicious cakes. Stark concrete surfaces are enlivened by paintings of Buddhist deities and piles of coloured powder as bright as the clothes downstairs. Shinjuku Station.

Cantina B1 Shibuya Homes Bldg, 2-1 Udagawa-chō, Shibuya-ku ☎03/5489-2433. Kids will like this café-diner combining drinks and Western-style food with movie tie-in toys (some of them for sale). There's lots of movie memorabilia, plus monitors screening videos, while a Harrison Ford waxwork props up the bar. Shibuya Station.

Gallery éf 2-19-18 Kaminarimon, Taito-ku ☎03/3841-9079. It's worth popping in here if only for the miraculous survival of the *kura* (traditional storehouse) hidden at the back, which now houses a very eclectic gallery. The café also does decent lunch sets for around ¥900. Closed Mon. Asakusa Station.

Lion 2-19-13 Dōgenzaka, Shibuya-ku ☎03/3461-6858. Not a place for animated conversations, this Addam's Family-style institution amid the love hotels of Dōgenzaka is where salarymen and pensioners come to quietly appreciate classical music with their coffee – hardly strong stuff, since many of the clients seem to be asleep. Seats are arranged to face a pair of enormous speakers. Shibuya Station.

Montook 6-1-9 Jingūmae, Shibuya-ku ☎03/5468-5928. Snooty but stylish watering hole, the Omotesandō café of the moment. Its glass facade faces onto Harajuku's famous shopping street. DJs create a suitably loungy vibe, and there's sometimes live music at weekends. Meiji-Jingūmae Station.

Moph 1F Sibuya Parco Part-1, 15-1 Udagawa-chō, Shibuya-ku ☎03/5456-8244. Shibuya-ku. Trendy self-service café where you can get a good set of three types of tasty tapas-like nibbles plus a drink for ¥680. Shibuya Station.

Tofu Café Fujino 1F Hollywood Beauty Plaza 6-4-1 Roppongi, Minato-ku ☎03/5771-0102. Cute bunnies are the mascot at this fun modern café where soy milk is used in all drinks and you can enjoy a variety of other tofu-based desserts. Their lunch box for ¥900 is good value, or you could go for a black sesame soy milk smoothie (¥600). Roppongi Station.

Teahouses

Café Artifagose 20-23 Daikan'yama, Shibuya-ku ☎03/5489-1133. The "concept" is bread, cheese and, er, tea. Still, this café has a prime al fresco spot in the heart of ritzy Daikan'yama and offers a wide range of fine Darjeeling and other teas, plus excellent cheese. Daikan'yama Station.

Cha Ginza 5-5-6 Ginza, Chiyoda-ku ☎03/3571-1211. A recent spin-off from a tea merchant in business in Tsukiji for over 70 years, this tea shop offers a pleasing new take on the business of sipping *sencha*; ¥500 gets you two cups of the refreshing green stuff, plus sweet and sour nibbles and a taste of beer or wine first to allow you to taste the contrast. Iron walls add a contemporary touch and the rooftop area, open in clement weather, is the place to hang out with those Tokyo ladies who make shopping a career. Ginza Station.

Koots Green Tea 6-27-4 Jingūmae, Shibuya-ku ☎03/5469-3300. First of two branches (the other's in Kamiyachō) of a new chain of green tea cafés borrowing an awful lot of the *Starbucks* concept – hence *macha* and *sencha* in multiple hot and cold combos. Their snack foods – *onigiri*, salads and a few sweets – are also traditional. In a quiet location just off Meiji-dōri. Meiji-jingūmae Station.

Suzuki 1-15-4 Jingūmae, Shibuya-ku ☎03/3404-8007. Tucked behind teeming Takeshita-dōri, but a million miles away in atmosphere, this shop specializing in *okashi* sweets has tatami rooms, *fusuma* screens and manicured gardens to gaze upon. A frothy *macha* (powdered green tea) and one pick from the sweets costs ¥900. Harajuku Station.

Yamamotoyama 2-5-2 Nihonbashi, Chūō-ku ☎03/3281-0010. You can sip all grades of green tea at the back of this venerable and very traditional tea merchant's shop. The tea comes either with a sweet rice cake (¥600) or rice cracker (¥400). Nihombashi Station.

Nightlife and entertainment

Tokyo's **nightlife** and **entertainment** options run the full gamut, from grand Kabuki theatres and cinemas to broom-cupboard bars and live music venues (known as "live houses"). The distinction between restaurants, **bars and clubs** in the city's *sakariba* (lively places), such as Ginza, Shibuya or Shinjuku, is a hazy one, with many places offering a range of entertainment depending on the evening or customers' spirits.

On the cultural side, you can sample all Japan's major **performing arts** in Tokyo, from stately **Nō**, the oldest in its theatrical repertoire, to **Butō**, the country's unique contribution to contemporary dance. However, if you only have the energy, or budget, for one such cultural experience, then save it for **Kabuki**, with its larger-than-life heroes, flamboyant costumes and dramatic finales. Information about these and other performances is available in the English-language press, and from Tokyo TIC (see p.98). Tickets are available from theatres and ticket agencies (see "Listings", p.191).

Bars and izakaya

The authentic Japanese **bar** – smoky, cramped, exclusively male and always expensive – is the **nomiya**, often containing nothing more than a short counter bar, generally run by a *mama-san*, a unique breed who both charm and terrorize their customers, and who are less likely to rip you off if you speak some Japanese (but that's no guarantee). If you're game, try the *nomiya* under the tracks at Yūrakuchō, along Shinjuku's Shomben Yokochō (Piss Alley) and

Bars and izakaya

Ichimon	*Ichimon*	一文
Jetée	*Jute*	ジュテ
Kagaya	*Kagaya*	かがや
Kamiya	*Kamiya*	神谷
Mukashiya	*Mukashiya*	昔屋
Shin Hi No Moto	*Shin Hi No Moto*	新日の基
Soul	*Sōru*	ソウル
Takara	*Takara*	たから
Tōhōkenbunroku	*Tōhōkenbunroku*	東方見聞録

Golden Gai, and on Nonbei Yokochō, the alley running alongside the train tracks just north of Shibuya Station.

The major breweries have their own reliable chains of **izakaya** (Japanese pubs), which are generally quite large, serve a good range of drinks and bar snacks and often have a lively atmosphere. Ones to look out for include *Kirin City*, in Ginza, Harajuku and Shinjuku; the *Hub* in Ueno, Ikebukuro, Shibuya and Shinjuku; Sapporo's *Lions Beer Hall* in Ebisu, Ginza, Ikebukuro and Shinjuku; the identikit Oirish bar *The Dubliners* in Akasaka, Ikebukuro and Shinjuku; and the faux-Victorian British pub *Rose & Crown* at Yūrakuchō, Shinbashi and Shinjuku. These *izakaya* open at around 6pm and shut down around midnight, while the *nomiya* stay open to the early hours, as long as there are customers.

Roppongi easily has Tokyo's greatest concentration of foreigner-friendly *gaijin* bars, but note that many are closed on Sunday. If there's live music anywhere you'll often be paying for it through higher drinks prices or a cover charge. Some regular bars also have cover charges (and *izakaya* almost always do, though you'll usually get a small snack served with your first drink), but there's plenty of choice among those that don't, so always check the deal before buying your drink.

For **bars with a view**, the major hotels are hard to beat, though you'll need to dress up in order not to feel out of place amid the gold-card crowd. Try the top-floor bars in the *New Ōtani*, the *Park Hyatt* and the *Cerulean Tower Tōkyū Hotel* for views across the centre of the city, the *Park Hotel Tokyo* and *Nikkō* for panoramas of Tokyo Bay and the Rainbow Bridge. From mid-June through to late August, **outdoor beer gardens** sprout around Tokyo – look for the red lanterns and fairy lights on the roofs of buildings or in street-level gardens and plazas; two of the nicest – in real gardens – are *Hanezawa Gardens*, 3-12-15 Hiro-o, Shibuya-ku (℡03/3400-2013), and *Sekirei* at the Meiji Kinenkan building, 2-2-23 Moto-Akasaka, Minato-ku (℡03/3746-7723).

Akasaka and Roppongi

The following places are marked on the maps on p.124 and p.127.

Acarajé Tropicana B2F Edge Building, 1-1-1 Nishi-Azabu, Minato-ku ℡03/3479-4690, ⓦwww.tropicana.co.jp. Join the all-night Brazilian line-dancing sessions at this popular Latin American-style basement bar-restaurant just off Roppongi-dōri. Closed Mon. Roppongi Station. **Agave** B1F Clover Bldg, 7-15-10 Roppongi, Minato-ku ℡03/3497-0229. One for the tequila- and cigar-lovers among us, this atmospheric base-

ment bar packs an authentic Latin American tang, with 400 varieties of the Mexican tipple on their shelves and a humidor bulging with stogies. Roppongi Station.
Bill's Café & Bar 3-16-11 Akasaka, Minato-ku ℡03/3586-8018. Super-spacious bar (for Akasaka) with a few outdoor tables, making it a pleasant place to drop by on a warm evening. Akasaka-Mitsuke Station.

Castillo 6-1-8 Roppongi, Minato-ku ℡03/3475-1629. If you never got over the disco craze of the 1970s and 1980s, this cosy bar, around the corner from Roppongi Crossing, is the place for a boogie. They also run a *gaijin*-house guesthouse. Roppongi Station.

Gas Panic 50 Togensha Building, 3-15-24 Roppongi, Minato-ku ℡03/3405-0633, ⓦwww.gaspanic.co.jp. Popular and grungy bar, and although it's just about the last word in sleaze (drunken *gaijin* males groping scantily clad Japanese girls), virtually everyone passes through here at least once. There's also a branch in Shibuya, at the station end of Centre Gai (℡03/3462-9042). Roppongi Station.

Heartland 1F Roppongi Hills West Walk, 6-10-1 Roppongi, Minato-ku ℡03/5772-7600. There's usually standing room only at this über-trendy but friendly bar in the northwest corner of Roppongi Hills. Sink one of their trademark green bottled beers and watch arty videos on the panoramic plasma screen behind the bar. Roppongi Station.

Hobgoblin Aoba Roppongi Bldg, 3-16-33 Roppongi, Minato-ku ℡03/3568-1280. British microbrewery Wychwood serves up its fine ales at this spacious bar that's fast become a Roppongi classic – which means you'll be part of a very boozy, noisy crowd of *gaijin* at weekends and on nights when there are major football matches and other sporting events on their big-screen TVs. There's also homely and very comforting pub-style food. They also run the Costa-del-Roppongi like *Vodka Bar* in the same building, and there's a smaller *Hobgoblin* in Akasaka (B1 Tamondo Bldg, 2-13-19 Akasaka, Minato-ku ℡03/6229-2636). Roppongi Station.

House+ 12F Roi Bldg, 5-5-1 Roppongi, Minato-ku ℡03/3402-2871. High above Roppongi's more dubious bars lies this curious mix of contemporary *izakaya*, secondhand clothes store and CD listening space – the brightly coloured Scandinavian-style furnishings give it the feel of an iza-ikea. There's also a shower should you feel the need to freshen up. Roppongi Station.

Asakusa

The following places are marked on the map on p.129.

Asahi Super Dry Hall 1-23-1 Azumabashi, Taitō-ku ℡03/5608-5381. Modernist beer hall located on the first and second floors of the Flamme d'Or building. Daily 10am–9pm. Asakusa Station.

Ichimon 3-12-6 Asakusa, Taitō-ku ℡03/3875-6800. This traditional *izakaya* has a cosy, rustic atmosphere and specializes in various types of sake and dishes made with a range of unusual meats including ostrich, turtle, crocodile and whale. Payment is by wooden tokens which you purchase on entering. Tawaramachi Station.

Kamiya 1-1-1 Asakusa, Taitō-ku ℡03/3841-5400. A feature of Asakusa since 1880, this was Tokyo's first Western-style bar and the haunt of famed Japanese literary figures. It's also famous for its Denkibran ("electric brandy"), first brewed in 1883 when electricity was all the rage and made up of a small shot of gin, wine, Curaçao and brandy – it's a potent tipple, though they also make a weaker version. The ground floor's the liveliest and most informal; pay at the cash desk as you enter for your first round of food and drinks. Closed Tues. Asakusa Station.

Daikan'yama, Ebisu and Hiro-o

The following places are marked on the map on p.154.

Enjoy House! 2F Daikan'yama Techno Bldg, 2-9-9 Ebisu-Nishi, Shibuya-ku ℡03/5489-1591. The unique look here is zebra prints, low velour sofas, red lace curtains and tons of shiny disco balls. The master wears shorts and Jackie Onassis-style sunglasses. Busy at weekends with a suitably young and attitude-free crowd. Ebisu Station.

Footnik 1F Asahi Bldg, 1-11-2 Ebisu, Shibuya-ku ℡03/5795-0144. Located a short walk east of Ebisu station, this is Tokyo's only bar devoted to soccer. There's a game or two on the big screen every night, but for popular matches you'll have to pay an entry charge. Japanese movies with subtitles are also screened occasionally, and there's reasonable food. Takadanobaba Station.

Kotobuki Diner 5-3 Hiro-o, Shibuya-ku ℡03/3473-5463. Lively, modern *izakaya* on two floors, popular with expats, and with a ground-floor bar open to the street in the summer. There's an English menu running the gamut from Mexican-style taco rice to crab pasta. Hiro-o Station.

Smash Hits B1, M2 Hiro-o Building, 5-2-26 Hiro-o, Shibuya-ku ℡03/3444-0432. Karaoke for exhibitionists in this basement bar designed as a mini-amphitheatre. With 12,000 English songs to choose from, plus many in other languages, you'll never be stuck for a tune. Costs ¥3000 including two drinks. Closed third Monday of month. Hiro-o Station.

Symposion 17-16 Sarugakuchō, Shibuya-ku

☎03/5458-6324. Pure *belle époque* restaurant and bar – you almost expect Toulouse-Lautrec and a troupe of girls to come high-kicking through the Art Nouveau doors. Very expensive. Daikan'yama Station.

Yebisu Beer Station Yebisu Garden Place, Ebisu, Shibuya-ku. Several bars and *izakaya* spread across Sapporo's office and shopping development, and including a spacious beer garden. Ebisu Station.

Ginza and around

The following places are marked on the map on p.115.

300 Bar B1F Fazenda Bldg, 5-9-11 Ginza, Chūō-ku ☎03/3572-6300. This is the new, bargain-basement face of Ginza – a standing-only bar where all the drinks are ¥300. Ginza Station.
Kagaya B1F Hanasada Bldg, 2-5-12 Shinbashi, Minato-ku ☎03/3591-2347, ⓦwww1.ocn.ne.jp/~kagayayy. English-speaking crazy guy Mark runs this simple basement bar as if he's hosting an 8-year-old's birthday party with alcohol. We're not going to give too much away since it would spoil the fun – which you will certainly have. Around ¥3000 will get you plenty of drink, food and side-splittingly silly games. Bookings recommended. Shinbashi Station.
Lion 7-9-20 Ginza, Chūō-ku ☎03/3571-2590. Opened in 1934, this baronial beer hall, flagship of the Sapporo chain, harks back to the days of Lloyd Wright (see the *Imperial Hotel*, p.116), with its dark tiles and mock wood panelling. There are Germanic-style snacks on offer, and a restaurant upstairs. Ginza Station.

Shin Hi No Moto 1-chōme Yūrakuchō, Chiyoda-ku ☎03/3214-8012. Lively traditional *izakaya* under the tracks just south of Yūrakuchō Station. One of the few places to try the excellent Sapporo Red Star beer, or cheap, strong *shōchū* (grain liquor). The manager's English, so tell him what you'd like to eat and your budget. The fish comes fresh from Tsukiji. Yūrakuchō or Hibiya stations.
Takara B1F Tokyo International Forum, 3-5-1 Marunouchi, Chiyoda-ku ☎03/5223-9888. John Gautner, Tokyo's *gaijin* sake guru, holds seminars on *nihonshu* here. There's a full English menu and the food is quite decent. Yūrakuchō Station.
Town Cryer B1 Hibiya Central Building, 1-2-9 Nishi-Shinbashi, Minato-ku ☎03/3519-6690. "Genuine British pub" (well, it's got beams and horse brasses) run by the team behind Ebisu's *What the Dickens!*, which means the hearty meals can be relied on. Closed Sat & Sun. Ōtemachi Station.

Shibuya, Harajuku and Aoyama

The following places are marked on the map on p.152.

Coins Bar 300 B1 Noa Shibuya Bldg, 36-2 Udagawa-chō, Shibuya-ku ☎03/3463-3039. The choice at this convivial basement bar is simple: ¥300 for any drink or plate of food, or ¥2500 for as much as you like of either over two and a half hours. Given how cheap it is, it's surprisingly stylish. Top choice if you're on a budget. Shibuya Station.
Office 2-7-18 Kita-Aoyama, Minato-ku ☎03/5788-1052. This trendy fifth-floor bar is for those who, when they leave the office, don't really want to leave the office. Huddle round the photocopier, squat at childishly low tables and knock back the booze without the boss raising an eye. On the ground level of the same building, *Sign* has a DJ to keep punters grooving along nicely. Gaienmae Station.
Oh! God 6-7-18 Jingūmae, Shibuya-ku ☎03/3406-3206. Basement bar in the same complex as the *La Bohème* and *Zest* restaurants. The real attraction is the free movies screened nightly, although you won't see anything up to date. Drinks start at around ¥700 and there are two pool

tables. It's a good post-club venue, since it's open till around 6am. Meiji-jingūmae Station.
Pink Cow Villa Moderna, 1-3-18 Shibuya, Shibuya-ku ☎03/3406-5597, ⓦwww.thepinkcow.com. Now in a new and easier-to-find location, this funky haven for local artists and writers has a good range of imported wines and also runs a Friday- and Saturday-night home-cooked buffet for ¥2500. Call for details of other regular events such as DJ nights. Shibuya Station.
Soho's 4F V28 Bldg, 6-31-17 Jingūmae, Shibuya-ku ☎03/5468-0411. There are killer views from this upmarket bar and restaurant in a modernist curved building overlooking the Omotesandō-Meiji-dōri crossing. Worth dropping by for a quiet drink during the day, too. Meiji-Jingūmae Station.
Soul 3-12-3 Kita-Aoyama, Minato-ku ☎03/5466-1877. Popular *izakaya* on the road beside the Kinokuniya supermarket. The menu is in Japanese, but you can point to the large plates of food on the counter. Dishes tend to be spicy, so order lots of beer. Closed Sun. Omotesandō Station.
Xanadu B1 F Hontis Building, 2-23-12

Dōgenzaka, Shibuya-ku ☎03/5489-3750. Kublai Khan's pleasure dome it certainly ain't, but to most of the up-for-it *gaijin* and young Japanese crowd such things hardly matter. The place keeps going all night long at weekends, when the cover charge is at least ¥1000 (includes a drink).

Ikebukuro

The following places are marked on the map on p.139.

The Black Sheep B1, 1-7-12 Higashi-Ikebukuro, Toshima-ku ☎03/3987-2289. Tiny, lively, friendly bar down a dark alleyway – the perfect place for a low-brow, high-fun night on the Ikebukuro tiles. Ikebukuro Station.

Bobby's Bar 3F Milano Bldg, 1-18-10 Nishi-Ikebukuro, Toshima-ku ☎03/3980-8875. Nothing too radical or offensive at this *gaijin*-friendly bar run by the eponymous Bobby, and their home-made samosas get the thumbs up. Ikebukuro Station.

300B (also known as *Sanbyaku B*) 3-29 Nishi-Ikebukuro. Big, bubbling *izakaya*, popular with a young crowd for the cheap prices and good food. There are two *300B*s on opposite sides of the road – this is the one (no.1) with the dried whale's penis hanging in the entrance. Ikebukuro Station.

Shinjuku and around

The following places are marked on the map on p.142.

Clubhouse 3F Marunaka Building, 3-7-3 Shinjuku, Shinjuku-ku ☎03/3359-7785. Sports bar that's big on space and atmosphere and has a policy of being cheaper than the Roppongi competition. Does fine fish 'n' chips (¥800) and has a good selection of vegetarian dishes. Closed Mon. Shinjuku-Sanchōme Station.

The Dubliners 2F, Shinjuku Lion Hall, 3-28-9 Shinjuku, Shinjuku-ku ☎03/3352-6606. Popular branch of Irish bar chain, with Guinness and Kilkenny bitter on tap and Irish stew on the menu. Good for a quiet lunch or coffee as well as a rowdy night's drinking. Shinjuku Station.

Jetée 2F, 1-1-8, Kabukichō, Shinjuku-ku ☎03/3208-9645. Run by Kawai-san, a Francophile *mama-san* whose passion for films and jazz is combined in this quintessential tiny Golden Gai bar – but don't bother turning up during May, when she decamps to the Cannes Film Festival. Cover charge ¥1000. Closed Sun. Shinjuku-Sanchōme Station.

New York Bar *Park Hyatt Hotel*, 3-7-1-2 Nishi-Shinjuku, Shinjuku-ku ☎03/5323-3458. Top-class live jazz music plus the glittering night view of Shinjuku are the not-inconsiderable attractions of this sophisticated bar attached to the *Park Hyatt*'s *New York Grill*. Tochōmae Station.

Rolling Stone B1, Ebichu Building, 3-2-7 Shinjuku, Shinjuku-ku ☎03/3354-7347. Conversation is out, ear-splitting rock music in at this long-running rock 'n' roll bar. Every weekend it becomes a sweaty hell hole for those who can't think of anything better to do than mosh their way to the bar. The table charge is at least ¥300; on Friday and Saturday expect to pay ¥2000 entry including two drinks. Shinjuku-Sanchōme Station.

Tōhō-kenbun-roku 3-6-7 Shinjuku, Shinjuku-ku ☎03/5367-3188. Ultra-stylish chain *izakaya*, on the fourth floor above a pachinko parlour, with cosy wood and tatami booths around a radioactively green glass pond. The speciality is *yakitori*. If you order cold sake, it will come in a large pottery cup overflowing into a saucer. ¥300 cover charge. There are two other branches in Shinjuku, plus ones in Ginza and Shibuya. Shinjuku-Sanchōme Station.

Vagabond 1-4-20 Nishi-Shinjuku, Shinjuku-ku ☎03/3348-9109. Shinjuku institution where Matsuoka-san plays the genial host, greeting guests and sometimes accompanying the jazz pianists who play every night. There's a ¥500 cover charge, but the drinks are good value and the atmosphere is priceless. Also has a downstairs bar, without live music. Shinjuku Station.

Tokyo Bay

The following places are marked on the map on p.92.

Sunset Beach Brewing Company 1-6-1 Decks Tokyo Beach, Odaiba. The beer is actually made within the mall. You can either sample a couple of glasses at the stand-up bar or venture inside for a so-so all-you-can-eat buffet. The real attraction is the view across Tokyo Bay of the Rainbow Bridge.

Odaiba Kaihin-kōen Station.

T.Y. Harbor Brewery Bond St, 2-1-3 Higashi-Shinagawa, Shinagawa-ku ☎03/5479-4555. There have been rave reviews for the beer at this microbrewery, in a converted Bayside warehouse, which also has an outdoor deck and a less-fêted

Californian-cuisine restaurant. The real ales include amber ale, porter, wheat beer and

California pale ale. Take the monorail from Hamamatsuchō to Tennoz Isle Station.

Ueno

The following places are marked on the map on p.133.

The Church B1, 1-57 Ueno-kōen, Ueno, Taitō-ku ☎03/5807-1957, ⓦwww.tokyo-church.com. Basement space hard by the station with a vaguely ecclesiastical theme and a reasonable range of British ales, mostly bottled, plus pub-style food. They often have Japanese and overseas bands and solo musicians performing. Ueno Station.

The Warrior Celt 3F, Ito Building, 6-9-22 Ueno ☎03/3841-5400. Things can get pretty raucous at this good-time bar in the thick of Ueno. Prime ingredients are a fine range of beers, a nightly happy hour (5–7pm), live bands on Fri and Sat (from 8.30pm) and, last but not least, Ladies' Night on Thurs (all drinks ¥500). Add fish 'n' chips – or a mean hummus – and you're away. Ueno Station.

Clubs and discos

The chameleon-like nature of the city's nightlife, fuelled by an insatiable appetite for new trends, means that Tokyo is one of the most exciting, but also most unpredictable, places in the world to party. While some **clubs** weather the vagaries of fashion, it pays to check the media before heading out. Check the websites listed in the box on p.98 as well as that of the Club Information Agency (ⓦwww.ciajapan.com) and look for their free monthly booklet of discount flyers at clubs and shops, such as Tower Records. Most major clubs also have their own website detailing their monthly schedules.

At all clubs, there'll be a **cover charge**, typically ¥2500–3000, which usually includes tickets for your first couple of drinks. You can often save a small amount if you pick up a flyer for the club from one of the record shops or boutiques around town. With the exception of *Velfare* (see p.180), most clubs don't really get going until after 11pm, especially at weekends, and most stay open until around 4am. There's also a growing scene of **recovery parties** (again see *Velfare*), kicking off at 6am.

Ageha Studio Coast, 2-2-10 Shin-kiba, Kōtō-ku ☎03/5534-2525, ⓦwww.ageha.com. Ultra-cool mega-club with a sound system guaranteed to send your whole body shimmering, and a rosta of high-profile events. The only problem is its remote location way across Tokyo Bay. There's a free shuttle bus to and from the east side of Shibuya Station – check the website for details and make sure you turn up a least half an hour before you want to depart to get a ticket to board the bus. Shin-Kiba Station.

Bed B1 Fukuri Bldg, 3-29-9 Nishi-Ikebukuro ☎03/3981-5300, ⓦwww.ikebukurobed.com. About as hip as nightlife gets in Ikebukuro. A mix of hip hop, reggae, R&B, and the occasional drum 'n' bass keeps things jumping until 5am. Also stages live shows. Ikebukuro Station.

Club Asia 1-8 Maruyamachō, Shibuya-ku ☎03/5458-1996, ⓦwww.clubasia.co.jp. Long-running techno/trance club in the heart of the Dōgenzaka love-hotel district, with several dance floors and an attached alfresco Asian restaurant. Popular place for special events such as visiting

DJs and special club nights. Shibuya Station.

Code 4F Shinjuku Toho Kaikan, 1-19-9 Kabukichō, Shinjuku-ku ☎03/3209-0702, ⓦwww.clubcomplexcode.com. One of Japan's biggest clubs, with three dance floors and room for two thousand people. Hosts gay nights last Fri of every month. Shinjuku Station.

La Fabrique B1F Zero Gate, 16-9 Udagawa-chō, Shibuya-ku ☎03/5428-5100. Although you can come here for dinner (their speciality is *flammekueche*, wafer-thin pizza from Alsace), the main selling point is their French house nights (Fri & Sat; entrance ¥3000, smart, a bit snooty and oh so Parisian. A similar recipe is offered at the sister establishment, *Le Faubourg*, in Aoyama (5-8-1 Minami-Aoyama, ☎03/5468-3636). Shibuya Station.

Liquid Room 7F Shinjuku HUMAX Pavilion, 1-20-1 Kabukichō, Shinjuku-ku ☎03/3200-6831, ⓦwww.liquidroom.net. There are all kinds of music genres on the decks at this trendy live house and club in the heart of Shinjuku. Also a favourite spot for various gay club nights. Check local media and flyers for details. Shinjuku Station.

Maniac Love B1, 5-10-6 Minami-Aoyama, Minato-ku ☎03/3406-1066, ⓦ www.maniaclove.com. Small but happening basement club just off Kotto-dōri, playing everything from ambient and acid jazz to hard house and garage. Hardcore clubbers adore its sound system, lighting and early-morning raves. Omotesandō Station.

Muse 1-13-3 Nishi-Azabu, Minato-ku ☎03/5467-1188. A pick-up joint, but a very imaginatively designed one, with lots of interesting little rooms to explore or canoodle in. There's a groovy dance area at the back which picks up at the weekends. Roppongi Station.

Mix 3-6-19 Kita-Aoyama, Minato-ku ☎03/3797-0551, ⓦ www.at-mix.com. This long narrow basement space on Aoyama-dōri hosts an arty crowd at weekends who don't seem to mind being squashed in like sardines. Perhaps it's got something to do with the music, an infectious mix of soul and reggae. ¥3000 including two drinks. Omotesandō Station.

The Ruby Room 2-25-17 Dogenzaka, Shibuya-ku ☎03/3462-7766. Upstairs from the casual California diner *Sonoma*; eat in the diner and you'll get into this groovy little club without having to pay the cover charge. Shibuya Station.

Velfare 7-14-22 Roppongi, Minato-ku ☎03/3402-8000, ⓦ http://velfarre.avex.co.jp. Monolithic club, which cost its sponsors ¥4 billion. Often packed by 9pm, since it shuts at no later than 1am. Hosts recovery parties on Sunday from 6am. Roppongi Station.

Womb 2-16 Maruyama-chō, Shibuya-ku ☎03/5459-0039; ⓦ www.womb.co.jp. For central Tokyo this counts as a big club, with a spacious dance floor, enormous glitterball and a pleasant chill-out space. Top DJs work the decks, but be warned that at big events it can get dangerously crowded. Shibuya Station.

Yellow 1-10-11 Nishi-Azabu, Minato-ku ☎03/3479-0690, ⓦ www.space-lab-yellow.com. Look for the blank yellow neon sign and go down to the basement to discover one of Tokyo's most enduring clubs, offering a range of music on different nights. Mainly techno and house at the weekends. Roppongi Station.

Gay bars and clubs

The **gay and lesbian** scene in Tokyo is relatively open compared to the rest of Japan; elsewhere, even in big cities like Ōsaka, things are a lot more cliquey and closeted. The **Shinjuku-Nichōme** area is the epicentre of Tokyo's gay world and is packed with hundreds of small bars and clubs, is as cruisey as it gets for Japan and can be a fun place for people of any sexual persuasion to hang out in. Even so, compared to London, San Francisco or Sydney, Tokyo's scene is a low-key affair. The annual gay pride march (first held in Tokyo only in 1995) was called off in 2003 but hopefully should be back in August 2004. August's annual **Tokyo International Lesbian and Gay Video and Film Festival**, based in Aoyama's Spiral Hall (see p.151), is a more permanent fixture on the calendar.

Apart from the venues listed below, all in Nichōme (the closest subway station is Shinjuku-Sanchōme), there are several gay events held at clubs around the city, including *Ageha*, *Code* and *Liquid Room* – see the club listings on p.179. Unless otherwise mentioned, these bars are for men only.

All the following places are marked on the Shinjuku map on p.142.

Ace B2 Dai-ni Hayakawaya Building, 2-14-6 Shinjuku, Shinjuku-ku ☎03/3352-6297. House and garage rule at this basement club just next to the cruising park in Nichōme.

Advocates 7th Tenka Bldg, 2-18-1 Shinjuku, Shinjuku-ku ☎03/3358-3988. The actual bar itself is barely big enough for ten people, which is why scores of other patrons, both male and female, hang out on the street corner outside. This is *the* place to see and be seen around here, with the most casual vibe in Nichōme. Downstairs round the corner is the easily confusable *Advocates Bar*,

where there's often a hefty cover charge for the drag show.

Arty Farty 2F Dai 33 Kyutei Bldg, 2-11-7 Shinjuku, Shinjuku-ku ☎03/5362-9720. New Mexico adobe chic meets Christmas grotto bar. The clientele are still on the young side.

Dragon B1F Accord, 2-12-4 Shinjuku, Shinjuku-ku ☎03/3341-0606. The music can be on the dodgy side of happy-clappy house, but it can still get hot and sweaty on weekend nights down in this unpretentious club opposite *GB*. Admission ¥1000 men, ¥2000 women, including one drink.

Fuji Bar 2-12-16 Shinjuku ☎03/3354-2707. This cosy karaoke bar (¥100 per song) in the basement of a building around the corner from *GB* has a wide selection of English songs, in case you're in the singing mood, and attracts a mixed crowd.

GB B1 Business Hotel T Building, 2-12-3 Shinjuku ☎03/3352-8972. Only for the boys, this basement bar is a long-standing pick-up joint for Japanese

and foreigners. Most *gaijin* come here first before exploring the more exotic corners of Nichōme.

Kinswomyn 3F Dai-ichi Tenka Building, 2-15-10 Shinjuku ☎03/3354-8720. Tokyo's top women-only bar, which has a more relaxed ambience (and lower prices) than many of Nichōme's other lesbian haunts. Drinks are ¥700 and there's no cover charge.

Live music, film and cultural events

There's always plenty going on culturally in Tokyo, though language can be a problem when it comes to performance arts. Colourful extravaganzas like **Takarazuka** or the more traditional **Kabuki** are the easiest to enjoy, but even the notoriously difficult **Nō** or **Butō** are worth seeing once. Tokyo may not seem the obvious place to seek out a classical concert or Shakespeare play, but major international **orchestras** and **theatre** groups often pass through on their tours, and the city now boasts several top-class performance halls – though tickets are expensive and often hard to get hold of.

Live music

Tokyo has a wide range of **live-music venues** offering everything from the most mellow jazz to the hardest of rock and indie pop. "Live houses" are little more than a pub with a small stage, but the city also has several prestigious venues, such as the Tokyo Dome (affectionately known as the "Big Egg"), where the likes of U2 and Madonna play when they're in town. Check the websites listed below for performance schedules.

Blue Note 6-3-16 Minami-Aoyama, Minato-ku ☎03/5485-0088, ⓦwww.bluenote.co.jp. Tokyo's premier live jazz venue, part of the international chain, attracts world-class performers at top ticket prices. Shows at 7pm and 9.30pm. Closed Sun. Entry from ¥6000 (including one drink) depending on the acts. Omotesandō Station.

Blues Alley Japan B1 *Hotel Wing International Meguro*, 1-3-14 Meguro, Meguro-ku ☎03/5496-4381, ⓦwww.bluesalley.co.jp. This offshoot of the Washington DC blues and jazz club occupies a small basement space near the station. Admission cost depends on the acts; sets kick off at 7.30pm. Meguro Station.

Club Citta 4-1-26 Ogawachō, Kawasaki ☎044/246-8888; ⓦclubcitta.co.jp. One of Tokyo's major live music venues, in the suburb-city of Kawasaki, hosting a variety of rock bands. Varying ticket prices. 5min walk south of Kawasaki Station.

Club Quattro 5F Quattro Building, 32-13 Udagawa-chō, Shibuya-ku ☎03/3477-8750, ⓦwww.net-flyer.com. Intimate rock-music venue in a loft-like space, which hosts both well-known local and international acts. Tends to showcase up-and-coming bands and artists. Shibuya Station.

Crocodile 6-18-8 Jingūmae, Shibuya-ku ☎03/3499-5205, ⓦwww.music.co.jp/~croco. You'll find everything from samba to blues and

reggae at this long-running basement space on Meiji-dōri between Harajuku and Shibuya. Also broadcasts gigs live on the Internet. Shows start at around 8pm. Cover charge ¥2000–3000. Meiji-jingūmae Station.

Cyber B1, 1-43-14 Higashi-Ikebukuro ☎03/3985-5844, ⓦwww.explosionworks.net/cyber. Dark, throbbing rock dive among the soaplands and love hotels north of Ikebukuro Station – the bands are variable, though you might strike lucky. Concerts start around 5.30pm. Entry ¥2000 and up, depending on the act. Ikebukuro Station.

The Fiddler B1F, 2-1-2 Takadanababa, Shinjuku-ku ☎03/3204-2698, ⓦwww.thefiddler.com. British pub (aka *The Mean Fiddler*) with rock and blues bands playing most nights and occasional English comedy nights. Also serves fish 'n' chips and shepherd's pie, while pints of Guinness and Bass go for ¥900. At the intersection of Waseda-dōri and Meiji-dōri. No cover charge. Takadanababa Station.

JZ Brat 2F *Cerulean Tower Tōkyū Hotel*, 26-1 Sakuragaoka-chō, Shibuya-ku ☎03/5728-0168, ⓦwww.jzbrat.com. Swanky new jazz club in Shibuya's top hotel, with a spacious contemporary design and a respectable line-up of artists. Sets at 7.30pm and 9.30pm. Music charge from ¥3000. Shibuya Station.

Milk B1 Roob 6 Building, 1-13-3 Ebisu-Nishi, Shibuya-ku ☎03/5458-2826, ⓦwww.milk-tokyo.com. Live house and club which packs in a lively crowd – If you get bored of the live thrash rock bands, check out the dildos and other sex toys in the cabinet in the kitchen. ¥3000–3500 entrance charge Fri & Sat including two drinks. Ebisu Station.

On Air East & West 2-3 Maruyamachō, Shibuya-ku ☎03/5458-4646, ⓦwww.onair-web.co.jp/hall. These two pop concert venues in the middle of Shibuya's love-hotel district often attract top international acts. Shibuya Station.

Shinjuku Pit Inn B1 Accord Shinjuku Building, 2-12-4 Shinjuku, Shinjuku-ku ☎03/3354-2024, ⓦwww.pit-inn.com. Serious, long-standing jazz club which has been the launch platform for many top Japanese performers. Also attracts overseas acts. Shinjuku Station.

What the Dickens! 4F, Roob 6 Building, 1-13-3 Ebisu-Nishi, Shibuya-ku ☎03/3780-2099, ⓦwww.ookawara-kikaku.com/dickens. There's live music nightly at this olde English pub complete with beams and candle-lit nooks, with draught Guinness and Bass pale ale (¥950 a pint, ¥600 a half). The food – a range of hearty pies served with potatoes, veggies and bread – is also worth coming for. Ebisu Station.

Cinema

Cinemas aren't cheap: average ticket prices are around ¥1800 (¥2500 for *shitei-seki* – reserved seats). You can cut the cost by buying discount tickets in advance from a **ticket agency**, such as Ticket Saison and Pia (see "Listings", p.191). On "Cinema Day", generally the first Wednesday of the month, tickets at all cinemas cost only ¥1000. Hollywood blockbusters predominate, and movies are generally subtitled in Japanese, not dubbed. The last show is usually at 7pm. Listings are published on Thursday in the *Daily Yomiuri* and every Friday in *Metropolis*, which also has reviews as well as maps locating all the major cinemas.

Major releases are shown at the following state-of-the-art multiplexes: Mediage, Aqua City Odaiba (☎03/5531-7878, ⓦwww.cinema-mediage.com); Shinagawa Prince Cinema at the *Shinagawa Prince Hotel* (☎03/5421-1113); and Virgin Cinemas Roppongi Hills (☎03/5775-6090, ⓦwww.virgincinemas.co.jp/roppongi/index.html) which has all-night screenings every weekend and shows Japanese and foreign art-house films, often with English subtitles.

For **art-house and independent** releases head for Iwanami Hall (☎03/3262-5252) in Jimbochō and Theatre Ikebukuro (☎03/3987-4311), which showcases films from Asia, Africa and Latin America. The Hibiya Chanter (☎03/3591-1551), near Yūrakuchō Station, and Cinema Rise (☎03/3464-0052), at the top of Spain-zaka in Shibuya, carve up between themselves most of the independent movies coming out of Europe and the USA. Cine Saison Shibuya (☎03/3770-1721), in the Prime Building in Shibuya, also screens a good range of films, including classic revivals. Shibuya's Bunkamura (☎03/3477-9111) has two screens and provides one of the few opportunities you'll have to see Japanese films with English subtitles at the **Tokyo International Film Festival** (ⓦwww.tiff-jp.net), held each November at these and other local cinemas. Shin-Bungei-za (☎03/3971-9422), in Ikebukuro, shows old films and has matinée double bills.

The National Film Centre (☎03/3272-8600, ⓦwww.momat.go.jp), near Kyōbashi Subway Station, is a real treasure trove for film lovers, with a gallery showing film-related exhibitions (¥300) and two small cinemas screening retrospectives from their 17,000 archived movies (mostly Japanese classics).

Contemporary theatre

Tokyo has a flourishing contemporary **theatre** scene, and though most performances are in Japanese, the more accessible forms are definitely worth checking out. Perhaps the most famous is **Takarazuka**, the all-singing, all-dancing, all-female revue which originated near Ōsaka in the early 1910s (see p.510). It's a great spectacle in which mostly Hollywood musicals are sugar-coated and punched out by a huge cast in fabulous costumes in front of an audience comprised mainly of middle-aged housewives and star-struck teenage girls. Regular performances alternate with ordinary dramas in the Takarazuka Theatre (☎03/5251-2001; ⓦhttp://kageki.hankyu.co.jp/english/index.html), opposite the *Imperial Hotel* (see p.116); ask at the theatre or look in the English-language press for details of the current schedule.

Major Tokyo festivals

Whenever you visit Tokyo, the chances are there'll be a **festival** (*matsuri*) taking place somewhere in the city. The TIC (see p.98) has comprehensive lists of events in and around Tokyo, or check in the English press for what's on. Below is a review of the city's biggest festivals (see p.66 for more about nationwide celebrations). Note that dates may change, so be sure to double-check before setting out.

Jan 1: Ganjitsu (or Gantan) The first shrine visit of the year (Hatsu-mōde) draws the crowds to Meiji-jingū, Hie-jinja, Kanda Myōjin and other city shrines. Performances of traditional dance and music take place at Yasukuni-jinja.

Jan 6: Dezomeshiki Tokyo firemen in Edo-period costume pull off dazzling stunts atop long bamboo ladders. Held at Harumi, Tokyo Bay.

Second Monday in Jan: Momoteshiki Archery ritual at Meiji-jingū to celebrate "Coming-of-Age Day". A good time to spot colourful kimono, here and at other shrines.

Feb 3 or 4: Setsubun The last day of winter is celebrated with a bean-scattering ceremony to drive away evil. The liveliest festivities take place at Sensō-ji, Kanda Myōjin, Zōjō-ji and Hie-jinja.

Early April: Hanami Cherry blossom-viewing parties get into their stride. The best displays are at Chidorigafuchi Park and nearby Yasukuni-jinja, Aoyoma Cemetery, Ueno-kōen and Sumida-kōen.

Mid-May: Kanda Matsuri One of Tokyo's top three festivals, held in odd-numbered years at Kanda Myōjin, during which people in Heian-period costume escort eighty gilded *mikoshi* through the streets.

Third weekend in May: Sanja Matsuri Tokyo's most rumbustious annual bash, centred on Asakusa-jinja, with music, dance and a costume parade featuring over one hundred *mikoshi*.

June 13–20: Sannō Matsuri The last of the big three festivals takes place in even-numbered years at Hie-jinja, with fifty *mikoshi* taken in a parade through Akasaka.

Early July: Yasakuni Matsuri The four-night summer festival at Tokyo's most controversial shrine is well worth attending for its jovial parades, *obon* dances and festoons of lanterns.

Late July & Aug: Hanabi Taikai The summer skies explode with thousands of fireworks, harking back to traditional "river-opening" ceremonies. The Sumida-gawa display is the most spectacular (view it from riverboats or Asakusa's Sumida-kōen), but those in Edogawa, Tamagawa, Arakawa and Harumi come close.

Mid-Aug: Fukagawa Matsuri Every three years Tomioka Hachiman-gū (Monzennakachō Station) hosts the city's wettest festival, during which spectators throw buckets of water over 54 *mikoshi* as they're carried through the streets. The next event is in 2005.

Nov: Tori-no-ichi Fairs selling *kumade*, bamboo rakes decorated with lucky charms, are held at shrines on "rooster days", according to the zodiacal calendar. The main fair is at Ōtori-jinja (Iriya Station).

Nov 15: Shichi-go-san Kids aged 7, 5 and 3 in traditional garb, and their doting grandparents, come out in force at Meiji-jingū, Yasukuni, Hie-jinja and other shrines to celebrate their health and pray for future happiness.

Dec 17–19: Hagoita-ichi The build-up to New Year begins with a battledore fair outside Asakusa's Sensō-ji (see p.129).

Keep an eye out as well for **Butō** performances. This unique, highly expressive dance form developed in the early 1950s, inspired by contemporary American dance, and until recently was more popular abroad than in Japan (see p.972 for more). It's not to everyone's taste – minimalist, introspective, and often violent or sexually explicit – but shouldn't be missed if you're interested in Japanese performing arts. The most active venue is Terpsichore, 3-49-15 Nakano (℡03/3383-3719), a tiny theatre under the tracks just west of Nakano Station. You'll find some performances listed in the English-language press, or ask at the TIC (see p.98).

Both Takarazuka and Butō have entered the mainstream arts world, but there's plenty happening on the fringes as well, as a glance at *Metropolis*'s listings will confirm. Prime places to catch the most accessible of Tokyo's **avant-garde theatre** include Tiny Alice (℡03/3354-7307), near Shinjuku-Sanchōme Station, Setagaya Public Theatre (℡03/5432-1526) near Sangenjaya Station, and Akasaka's Japan Foundation Forum (℡03/5562-3892). All are known for hosting collaborative works featuring Japanese and international – mostly Asian – groups. For **English-language theatre**, apart from visiting international troupes (see opposite) there are productions put on by the long-running amateur group Tokyo International Players (ⓦwww.tokyoplayers.org), usually staged at the American Club in Kamiyachō (℡03/3224-3670) and by the new semi-pro Intrigue Theatre (ⓦwww.intriguetheatre.com).

Traditional theatre

Of the traditional performance arts, **Kabuki** is by far the most accessible for both Japanese and foreign spectators: it's dramatic, colourful and the plots are easy to follow even if you don't understand a word of Japanese, while shouts of appreciation from the audience add to the sense of occasion. The one drawback is that performances tend to be lengthy, often lasting three or four hours. However, these days you can buy single-act tickets for the **Kabuki-za** (℡03/5565-6000, ⓦwww.shochiku.co.jp/play/kabukiza/theatre), the main theatre in Ginza (see p.117), where they hold performances during the first three weeks of every month. There are two daily programmes, starting at around 11am and 4.30pm, for which you can buy tickets at the theatre or an agency. Prices start at around ¥2500 for the full programme, while one-act tickets usually cost under ¥1000, depending on the length – note that one-act tickets are only on sale at the theatre itself. The theatre produces a brief English summary of the programme (free at the TIC and hotels), or you can rent an earphone guide (¥650, plus ¥1000 deposit) for background information about Kabuki, as well as the plot. Bring binoculars if you have them – all the cheapest seats are way up at the back.

The other main venue for Kabuki is **Kokuritsu Gekijō** (℡03/3230-3000, ⓦwww.ntj.jac.go.jp/english/index.html), the National Theatre west of the Imperial Palace near Hanzōmon Station, which holds a varied programme of traditional theatre and music. There are also performances here three or four times a year of **Bunraku**, a form of puppet theatre which predates Kabuki, but shares many of the same plots. The puppets need three people to manipulate them, and their artistry is astounding. Again, English-language programmes and earphones are available, and tickets start at ¥1500 for Kabuki and ¥4400 for Bunraku.

Nō is Japan's oldest and least accessible form of theatre. Even most Japanese find it unfathomable, and its esoteric, highly stylized, painfully slow movements and ancient form of language certainly don't make for a rip-roaring theatrical experience. That said, it's not all tedious: during the intervals *kyōgen*, short satirical plays with an earthy humour and simple plots, provide light relief. There are several schools of Nō in Tokyo, each with their own theatre, including Shibuya's **Kanze Nō-gakudō** (℡03/3469-5241) and the **National Nō Theatre** (℡03/3423-1331, ⓦwww.ntj.jac.go.jp/english/index.html), five minutes' walk from Sendagaya Station (see p.148). Tickets cost upwards of ¥2000 and can be bought from agencies or the theatre itself. It's also worth asking at the TIC (see p.98) about free performances by amateur groups.

International performance arts

Tokyo is on the circuit for many international **theatre companies**, who usually get a tremendous reception, with seats selling out months in advance, though a few are often reserved for sale on the day. The New National Theatre (℡03/5352-9999, ⓦwww.nntt.jac.go.jp) in Shinjuku hosts high-profile theatre, opera, dance and classical music troupes. Le Theatre Ginza (℡03/3535-5151), a luxury theatre next to the equally plush *Hotel Seiyō*, is another popular venue for international groups.

There are usually at least one or two concerts of **Western classical music** on every week, performed either by one of Tokyo's several resident orchestras (notably the Tokyo Philharmonic or Japan Philharmonic) or a visiting group, as well as occasional performances of opera and ballet. Major performance halls include Tokyo Opera City (℡03/5353-9999, ⓦwww.operacity.jp/en/index2 .html) and the New National Theatre (see above), both in Shinjuku, and another four halls in Yūrakuchō's Tokyo International Forum (℡03/5221-9000; ⓦwww.t-i-forum.co.jp/english/index.html). Among the older auditoria, Suntory Hall (℡03/505-1001, ⓦwww.suntory.co.jp/suntoryhall), in Akasaka's Ark Hills, NHK Hall (℡03/3465-1751), south of Meiji-kōen, and the Orchard Hall (03/3477-9111, ⓦwww.bunkamura.co.jp), in Shibuya's Bunkamura, are the main venues. Tickets, which tend to be expensive (¥3000 and above), are available from the box offices or a ticket agency.

Shopping

Tokyo has shops to suit every taste and budget, from swanky **department stores** to ragbag **flea markets**. The city is a prime hunting ground for the latest electronic gadgets, electrical equipment and cameras. CDs may be slightly less expensive than at home, and the selection of world music, jazz and techno in particular takes some beating. Foreign-language books and magazines are less well represented and very pricey, though Tokyo is the place to stock up before heading off to other regions. There are also some wonderful crafts shops (though perhaps not quite up to Kyoto standards), and a visit to the regular flea markets might turn up unusual souvenirs, while the city's fashion boutiques carry the latest in post-millennial chic.

Ginza remains the preserve of the city's conservative elegance, and is still regarded as Tokyo's traditional shopping centre, although it's been overshadowed by the ritzy emporia of **Roppongi Hills** of late. **Shinjuku** has long put up a strong challenge, with an abundance of department stores and malls offering everything under one roof. Young and funky, **Shibuya** and **Harajuku** are probably the most enjoyable places to shop: even if you don't want to buy, the passing fashion parade doesn't get much better. The haute couture boutiques of nearby **Omotesandō** and **Aoyama** provide a more rarefied shopping experience, while, of the northern districts, only **Asakusa** figures highly for its crafts shops, while **Ikebukuro** is best known for its plethora of discount stores. For toyshops see the recommendations in the box on p.164.

Tokyo also has a number of wholesale districts that can be fun to poke around. The most famous are **Tsukiji fish market** (see p.158), **Kappabashi** "Kitchenware Town" (see p.132), the bookshops of **Jimbōchō** (see p.124) and **Akihabara**'s electrical emporia (see p.189). North of Asakusabashi Station, **Edo-dōri** and its backstreets specialize in traditional Japanese dolls, while further north again the area called **Kuramae** is "Toy Town", where shops sell fireworks, fancy goods and decorations, as well as toys of every description. Between Ueno's mainline station and the Shuto Expressway, slick-haired guys in leathers stalk the rows of sleek machines in **"Motorbike Town"**.

Department stores

The most obvious place to start shopping is in one of Tokyo's massive **department stores**: they're convenient, usually have English-speaking staff and are more likely to accept foreign credit cards or offer duty-free prices. You could spend a whole day exploring just one store, from its basement food hall, through fashion and furnishings to the rooftop garden centre, eat on the restaurant floor and then see what's on at the in-store art gallery. The main drawbacks are the sheer size of these places (grab a floor guide on the way in) and the fact that they also tend to be more expensive than the competition. However, they often hold excellent bargain sales several times a year – the kimono sales are most famous – which you'll find advertised in the English-language press, and most stores have an area among their top floors offering a variety of discount items.

Chūō-dōri, heading north from Ginza, is the epicentre of Tokyo's department stores and where you'll find the city's most prestigious establishments: **Mitsukoshi**, represented by its flagship Nihombashi store (℡03/3241-3311; see p.118; other branches in Shinjuku, Ikebukuro and Ebisu), and nearby **Takashimaya** (℡03/3211-4111) – which also has an enormous branch in Shinjuku. Elegant and spacious, these two stores are renowned for their quality, and also stock a good range of traditional household items, as well as kimono, *obi* and other accessories. **Matsuya** (℡03/3567-1211; Ginza and Asakusa) and **Matsuzakaya** (℡03/3572-1111; Ginza and Ueno) are more workaday places which appeal to similarly conservative tastes but at lower prices.

For younger fashion, head for Shibuya, where **Parco** and **Loft** (℡03/3462-0111) are the famous trendsetters, not only in designer clothes but also general merchandise, and their racks and shelves groan with state-of-the-art ephemera. These two stores belong to the **Seibu** group, whose sprawling Ikebukuro headquarters competes with neighbouring **Tōbu** to be Tokyo's most confusing store – it's better to shop in Seibu's smaller outlet in Shibuya. Seibu is also the group behind the phenomenally successful **Muji**; their best Tokyo store is at Yūrakuchō (℡03/5208-8241).

Also worth checking out are the main **Tōkyū** department store in Shibuya and the fantastic **Tōkyū Hands**, specializing in DIY and craft products, also in Shibuya (℡03/5489-5111; other branches in Ikebukuro and Shinjuku). **Isetan** (℡03/3225-2514) is Higashi-Shinjuku's top department store, offering well-designed local produce at reasonable prices, while the two branches of **Marui** (℡03/3354-0101), in Shibuya and Ikebukuro, consist of several self-explanatory buildings called "Fashion", "Young" and "Men's".

Clothes and fashion stores

Cruising Tokyo's **boutiques** and **fashion stores** toting a couple of designer-label carrier bags is such a part of Tokyo life that it's hard not to get caught up in the general enthusiasm. Once you've cut your teeth on the department stores above, it's time to hit the streets. There are plenty of familiar names – Gap, Zara and Timberland all have Tokyo outlets nowadays, alongside internationally famous Japanese brands such as Yoji Yamamoto, Comme des Garçons, Issey Miyake and Hanae Mori. Most have an outlet along **Omotesandō**, the epicentre of Japanese style, where the designer showrooms make for great window-shopping even if you don't have money to burn. The long-running Hysteric Glamour (6-23-2 Jingūmae, Shibuya-ku; ⓣ03/3409-7227) is one of Harajuku's top boutiques, with the pop stars' favourite A Bathing Ape (4-28-22 Jingūmae, Shibuya-ku; ⓣ03/5474-0204) hot on its heels. For used clothes and old kimono a good place to head for is Chicago (6-31-21 Jingūmae, Shibuya-ku; ⓣ03/3409-5017).

At the other extreme, nearby **Takeshita-dōri** swarms with hordes of high-school students, who descend to rummage through stalls selling the latest in recycled grunge gear, while Centre Gai in nearby Shibuya is just as manic, packed with fashion-victim teens and twenty-somethings. For more mainstream clothes at reasonable prices, look out for two local chains: UniQlo, with stores in all major centres including Ueno, Shibuya, Shinjuku and Ikebukuro; and Comme Ça Du Mode. The latter's main outlet in Shinjuku's Five Foxes' Store (ⓣ03/3409-7227) has the benefit of a stylish café (see p.173), while their Harajuku branch resides on the ground floor of the splendidly named Touch Your All building, opposite Harajuku Station.

For a somewhat more relaxed shopping experience, head out to one of the residential neighbourhoods such as **Daikan'yama** and **Shimo-Kitazawa**, both a short train ride from Shibuya. Daikan'yama is the smarter and more expensive of the two, but its village atmosphere is appealing, and it's a good place to check out up-and-coming Japanese designers; see p.153 for more on the area. Shimo-Kitazawa, on the other hand, has a studenty, bohemian air. There are any number of funky boutiques, some selling secondhand clothes where you can scoop big-name labels at bargain prices, and keep an eye open too for creations by local art and design students. To get there, take the Keiō-Inokashira Line four stops from Shibuya, or the Odakyū Line six stops from Shinjuku.

Arts, crafts and souvenirs

While most department stores have a fair selection of **arts and crafts**, it's more enjoyable to rummage around Tokyo's specialist shops. Asakusa offers the largest concentration of traditional crafts among all its touristy souvenirs, as well as the most attractive environment. A few beautiful Edo-era shops still survive in the thick of Ginza and Nihombashi, while, if money is no object, arcades in the big hotels, such as the *Imperial*, *Ōkura* and *New Ōtani*, provide luxury gifts from Mikimoto pearls to Arita porcelain. Also worth checking out are the shops attached to major museums; in particular, head to the Japan Folk Crafts Museum (see p.153) near Shibuya for the best of traditional souvenirs, and Roppongi Hills' MAM (see p.126) for great contemporary design goods and fun throwaway stuff. Listed below are a few of the more interesting places to head for.

Bengara 2-35-11 Asakusa, Taitō-ku. West of Sensō-ji, this is *the* place to look for *noren*, the split curtains which hang outside every traditional shop or restaurant. There's a whole range of patterns, sizes and prices, or you can order your own design. Closed Thurs. Asakusa Station.

Beniya 4-20-19 Minami-Aoyama, Minato-ku ⓣ03/3403-8115. One of Tokyo's best range of folk-crafts (*mingei*) from around the country. They also have craft exhibitions from time to time. Omotesandō Station.

Fuji-Torii 6-1-10 Jingūmae, Shibuya-ku

03/3400-2777. Omotesandō shop specializing in *ukiyo-e*, plus other works of art and antiques. Closed Tues and third Mon of the month. Meiji-jingūmae Station.

Fujiya 2-2-15 Asakusa, Taitō-ku ℡03/3841-2283. Hand-printed cotton towels, *tenugui*, make a packable souvenir, and you won't find a better selection than this. Some Fujiya towels are now collectors' items. Closed Thurs. Asakusa Station.

Itō-ya 2-7-15 Ginza, Chūō-ku ℡03/3561-8311. This wonderful stationery store, with nine floors and two annexes, is great for a whole range of lightweight souvenirs. *Itō-ya 3* specializes in traditional *washi* paper, calligraphy brushes, inks and so on. Other branches in Shibuya and Ikebukuro. Ginza Station.

Kurodaya 1-2-5 Asakusa, Taitō-ku ℡03/3844-7511. For over one hundred years Kurodaya has been selling handmade *washi* paper and anything

that can be made from it – boxes, fans, kites and all types of stationery, as well as wood-block prints and wrapping papers. Closed Mon. Asakusa Station.

Natsuno 6-7-4 Ginza, Chūō-ku ℡03/3569-0952. An incredible collection of over a thousand types of chopsticks, plus chopstick rests and rice bowls; prices range from ¥200 up to ¥60,000 for a pair made from ivory. Also check out their store just off Omotesandō (4-2-17 Jingūmae, Shibuya-ku; ℡03/3403-6033). Ginza Station.

Oriental Bazaar 5-9-13 Jingū-mae, Shibuya-ku ℡03/3400-3933. Popular, one-stop souvenir emporium, selling everything from secondhand kimono to origami paper, all at reasonable prices. Closed Thurs. Meiji-jingūmae Station.

Takumi 8-4-2 Ginza, Chūō-ku. Folk-craft shop chock-a-block with bags, baskets, pots, toys and fabrics. Closed Sun. Shimbashi Station.

Antique and flea markets

There's at least one **flea market** in Tokyo every weekend, though you'll need to arrive early to find any bargains. Among the regular markets, weather permitting, stalls at Hanazono-jinja (see p.145) spring into life every Sunday, while Tōgō-jinja (see p.150) hosts a market on the first and fourth Sundays of the month and Yasakuni-jinja on the third Sunday.

Alternatively, try one of the two upmarket **antique halls**, which are permanent fixtures consisting of several dealers gathered under one roof. Among a good deal of tat, you'll come across original *ukiyo-e*, magnificent painted screens, or samurai armour – but don't expect any particular bargains. Antique Gallery Meguro, 2F, 2-24-18 Kami-ōsaki, has around fifty stalls, while the Tokyo Antiques Hall, 3-9-5 Minami-Ikebukuro (℡03/3980-8228; closed Thurs), and the Antique Market, in the basement of the Hanae Mori Building, 3-6-1 Kita-Aoyama (11am–8pm; some shops close on Thurs), are slightly smaller.

Several times a year about two hundred dealers get together for the **Heiwajima Antiques Fair**, held over three days at the Ryūtsū Centre (10am–6pm), one stop on the monorail from Hamamatsuchō to Haneda. If you're in town, it's well worth the journey. Tokyo TIC (see p.98) can give you the current schedule for this and all the other markets and fairs around Tokyo.

Books and music

Tokyo's best selection of new foreign-language **books and magazines** can be found in Shinjuku's seven-storey Kinokuniya (℡03/3354-0131) behind Takashimaya Times Square; there's also a good selection at Tower Records (℡03/3496-3661) in Shibuya, where the prices are cheaper for imported journals and newspapers. In Nihombashi, Maruzen (℡03/3273-3313) stocks a wide range of imported and locally produced books, with a strong showing in art and design. The best selections of **secondhand books** are at Ebisu's excellent Good Day Books (℡03/5421-0957, ⓦwww.gooddaybooks.com), next to the bar *Footnik* (see p.176), and at Ikebukuro's Caravan Books (℡03/5951-6404, ⓦwww.booksatcaravan.com), tucked away in the backstreets on the west side of the station.

Shibuya's Tower Records is currently the biggest **music** store in Tokyo, with six floors of CDs, records and related paraphernalia, including videos and games. Prices tend to be slightly lower and the selection better at HMV, which has signs spattered over central Tokyo; their main store is at 24 Udagawachō (☎03/5458-3411), opposite the Loft and Seibu department stores. Virgin has a large outlet in Shinjuku (3-1-13 Shinjuku; ☎03/3353-0056) and a smaller outlet in Marui's Ikebukuro store. For secondhand records and CDs, Recofan and Disk Union are two names to look out for. Both have branches in Shibuya, Shinjuku and Shimo-Kitazawa (see p.187), amongst other places.

Cameras and electronic equipment

Shinjuku is Tokyo's prime centre for **cameras**. Yodobashi Camera (☎03/3346-1010) in Nishi-Shinjuku claims to be the world's largest camera shop and usually offers decent reductions and stocks the broadest range; they have a smaller branch in Ueno. Sakuraya (☎03/3354-3636) gets plenty of recommendations. There's another branch of Sakuraya in Ikebukuro as well, but the market here is dominated by BIC Camera (☎03/3988-0002), which is renowned for its cheap prices and has branches scattered all over Higashi-Ikebukuro; their main outlet lies immediately north of the station on Meiji-dōri. They also now occupy the old Sogo department store at Yūrakuchō (☎03/5221-1111) – practically any electronic goods you want can be found here, plus (strangely enough) discount wine and liquor. Professional photographers, meanwhile, swear by Shimizu Camera (☎03/3564-1008) in the backstreets of Ginza, northeast of the Sukiyabashi crossing.

Akihabara boasts Tokyo's biggest concentration of stores selling **electronic goods**. It can be bewildering at first, with the big stores split into several outlets – each one a megastore of up to seven floors apiece – selling overlapping product ranges. Fortunately, they're mostly concentrated along a small stretch of Chūō-dōri and its side streets, all within walking distance of Akihabara Station. Of the big stores, Laox (1-2-9 Soto-Kanda, Chiyoda-ku; ☎03/3253-7111) is the best place to start: prices are reasonable, they have a well-established duty-free section with English-speaking staff, and their nine stores sell everything from pocket calculators to plasma-vision TVs. Nowadays you'll also find plenty of discount stores in Shinjuku, Shibuya and Ikebukuro offering competitive, sometimes even cheaper prices, so it's important to shop around and, though you might not get it, always ask for a discount.

Listings

Airlines Aeroflot ☎03/3343-9671; Air Canada ☎03/5404-8800; Air China ☎03/5251-0711; Air France ☎03/3475-1511; Air India ☎03/3214-1981; Air New Zealand ☎03/3287-6311; Air Nippon ☎03/5435-0707; Air Pacific ☎03/5208-5171; Alitalia ☎03/3580-2181; All Nippon Airways ☎0120-029333; American Airlines ☎03/3214-2111; Asiana Airlines ☎03/3582-6600; British Airways ☎03/3593-8811; Cathay Pacific ☎03/3504-1531; China Airlines ☎03/3436-1661; Delta Airlines ☎03/5275-7000; Dragonair ☎03/3506-8361; Garuda Indonesia ☎03/3240-6161; Japan Airlines International ☎0120-255931; Japan Air System International ☎0120-711283; KLM ☎03/3216-0771; Korean Air ☎03/5443- 3311; Lufthansa ☎03/3699-5551; Malaysian Airlines ☎03/3503-5961; Northwest Airlines ☎03/3533-6000; Philippine Airlines ☎03/3593-2421; Qantas ☎03/3593-7000; Singapore Airlines ☎03/3213-3431; South African Airways ☎03/3470-1901; Thai Airways International ☎03/3503-3311; United Airlines ☎0120-114466; Varig ☎03/3211-6751; Vietnam Airlines ☎03/3508-1481; Virgin Atlantic ☎03/3499-8811.

Airport information Haneda ☎03/5757-8111; Narita ☎0476/34-5000; Tokyo City Air Terminal (TCAT) ☎03/3665-7111.

American Express 4-30-16 Ogikubo, Suginami-ku ☎03/3220-6000; travel service centre (Mon–Fri 9am–7pm).

Banks and exchange You'll find dozens of authorized "Foreign Exchange Banks" all over central Tokyo; Tokyo Mitsubishi Bank generally handles the broadest range of currencies. If you need money outside banking hours (see p.32), the major department stores often have exchange desks, though most handle a very restricted range of currencies. You can make credit card withdrawals from "international ATMs" at the post office (see opposite for more) and at cash corners run by Visa (☏0120-133173), Mastercard (☏00531/11-3886) and Citibank (☏0120-504189); call their 24hr toll-free English-language helplines to find the machine nearest you – some are accessible 24hr. The American Express office in Ōgikubo (see p.189) also has a 24hr ATM (American Express cards only). Visa and Mastercard holders can make over-the-counter cash withdrawals from Tokyo Mitsubishi Bank's head office (2-7-1 Marunouchi), while major branches of Mitsui Sumitomo handle Visa card withdrawals only.

Bike rental Try Rental Acom at 1-1-8 Shinjuku, Shinjuku-ku (☏03/3350-5081) and 3-11-1 Shimbashi, Minato-ku (☏03/5401-0800). Both branches are open daily from 10am to 7pm and also rent out just about anything else you could need. An ordinary bike is ¥2100 per day and a mountain bike ¥4200 (minimum 2-day hire). You'll need to present your passport and make an advance booking in Japanese.

Car rental The main rental companies are: Avis ☏03/5550-1015; Hertz ☏0120-489882, ⓦwww.hertz-car.co.jp; Nippon ☏03/3468-7126; Nissan ☏03/5424-4111; Orix ☏03/3779-0543; and Toyota ☏0070/8000-10000. All have branches around the city and at Narita and Haneda airports, and English-speaking staff. Prices start at around ¥6500 per day for the smallest car, plus ¥1000 insurance.

Credit cards For lost credit cards call the relevant toll-free 24hr number: American Express ☏0120-020120; Mastercard ☏0031/11-3886; Visa ☏0120-133173.

Embassies Australia, 2-1-14 Mita, Minato-ku ☏03/5232-4111; Canada, 7-3-58 Akasaka, Minato-ku ☏03/5412-6200; China, 3-4-33 Moto-Azabu, Minato-ku ☏03/3403-3380; Ireland, 2-10-7 Kōjimachi, Chiyoda-ku ☏03/3263-0695; New Zealand, 20-40 Kamiyamachō, Shibuya-ku ☏03/3467-2271; Russian Federation, 2-1-1 Azabudai, Minato-ku ☏03/3583-4291; South Africa 2-7-9 Hirakawachō, Chiyoda-ku ☏03/3265-3366; UK, 1 Ichibanchō, Chiyoda-ku ☏03/5211-1100; US, 1-10-5 Akasaka, Minato-ku ☏03/3224-5000.

Emergencies Phone the English-language helpline of Tokyo Metropolitan Police on ☏03/3501-0110 (Mon–Fri 8.30am–5.15pm). Tokyo English Life Line (TELL; ☏03/5774-0992; ⓦwww.teljp.com) provides telephone counselling on their helpline (daily 9am–4pm & 7–11pm). Numbers for the emergency services are listed in Basics on p.85.

Hospitals and clinics To find an English-speaking doctor and the hospital or clinic best suited to your needs, phone the Tokyo Medical Information Service (☏03/5285-8181; Mon–Fri 9am–8pm); they can also provide emergency medical translation services. Otherwise, two major hospitals with English-speaking doctors are St Luke's International Hospital, 9-1 Akashichō, Chūō-ku (☏03/3541-5151), and Tokyo Adventist Hospital, 3-17-3 Amanuma, Suginami-ku (☏03/3392-6151); their reception desks are open Mon–Fri 8.30–11am for non-emergency cases. Among several private clinics with English-speaking staff, try Tokyo Medical and Surgical Clinic, 32 Mori Building, 3-4-30 Shiba-kōen, Minato-ku (☏03/3436-3028, by appointment only), or the International Clinic, 1-5-9 Azabudai, Minato-ku (☏03/3583-7831).

Immigration To renew your tourist or student visa, apply to the Tokyo Regional Immigration Bureau, T5-5-30 Konan, Minato-ku (☏03/5796-7112, ⓦwww.moj.go.jp/ENGLISH/IB/ib-18.html; open Mon–Fri 9am–noon & 1–4pm). To reach it, take the Konan exit from Shinagawa Station and then bus #99 from bus stop 8. Go early in the day since the process takes forever.

Internet access For details on how to connect your own computer to the LANs at major hotels see Basics, p.63. Otherwise, at the time of writing the following places were offering free or cheap (for the cost of a cup of coffee) Internet connections: Marunouchi Café (closed Sun), 3-2-3 Marunouchi, where you can also plug in your own computer; Sofmap's store in Yūrakuchō, beside the JR station; Virgin record stores in Shinjuku and Ikebukuro; Yahoo Café Omotesandō, 5-11-2 Jingūmae, Shibuya-ku, connected to a Starbucks in a side street behind the Chanel store on Omotesandō. In all the main areas of the city you'll find 24hr manga and computer games parlours where you can also access the Web. One of the best is Gera Gera (B1 Remina Bldg, 3-17-4 Shinjuku, Shinjuku-ku; ☏03/3350-5692). Pay ¥380 for one hour (then ¥50 every extra 10 mins) and you can surf the Web, play video games, watch DVDs or leaf through over 50,000 comics. Drink all you want for an extra ¥180. They also have comfy double-seat sofas – good if you fancy chilling out whilst watching a movie or crashing after the clubs but before the trains start up again. Kinkos, the 24hr one-stop office service centre, has branches scattered all over Tokyo; call their toll-free number (☏0120-001966) to find the one nearest you.

Left luggage Most hotels will keep luggage for a few days. If not, the baggage room at Tokyo Station takes bags for up to fifteen days, at a daily rate of ¥410 for the first five days and ¥820 per day thereafter; you'll find it at the far southeast end of the station, beyond the Express Bus ticket office. Note that coin lockers can only be used for a maximum of three days.

Lost property If you've lost something, try the local police box (*kōban*). Alternatively, ask your hotel to call the following Japanese-speaking offices to reclaim lost property: Taxis ☏03/3648-0300; JR Tokyo Station ☏03/3231-1880; Tokyo Metro subways ☏03/3834-5577; and Toei buses and subways ☏03/3812-2011. If all else fails, contact the Metropolitan Police Lost and Found Office ☏03/3814-4151.

Pharmacies The American Pharmacy, Hibiya Park Building, 1-8-1 Yūrakuchō (☏03/3271-4034; Mon–Sat 9.30am–8pm, Sun 10am–6.30pm), has English-speaking pharmacists and a good range of drugs and general medical supplies. Alternatively, try the National Azabu Pharmacy (☏03/3442-3495), above the National Azabu supermarket (nearest subway station is Hiro-o). Major hotels usually stock a limited array of common medicines.

Post offices The Tokyo Central Post Office is on the west side of Tokyo Station (☏03/3284-9500; Mon–Fri 9am–7pm, Sat 9am–5pm, Sun 9am–12.30pm; 24hr service for stamps and parcels). The International Post Office, 2-3-3 Ōtemachi (☏03/3241-4891; same times) is a bit less convenient, but usually quieter. For English-language information about postal services, call ☏03/5472-5851 (Mon–Fri 9.30am–4.30pm). Poste restante can be collected from the basement counter of the Tokyo Central Post Office (Mon–Fri 8am–8pm, Sat 8am–5pm, Sun 9am–12.30pm); take your passport. The postal address is 2-7-2 Marunouchi, Chiyoda-ku, Tokyo 100.

Sports The baseball season runs from April to the end of October. The Yomiuri Giants play at Tokyo Dome (☏03/3811-2111, ⓦwww.tokyo-dome.co.jp/dome) in Suidōbashi, while the Yakult Swallows are based at Jingū Stadium (☏03/3404-8999) near Gaienmae Station. Tickets start from ¥1000. If you're keen to see some martial arts action, the TIC at Yūrakuchō (see p.98) has a full list of *dōjō* that allow visitors to watch practice sessions for free. For soccer, you can catch FC

Tokyo or FC Verdi playing at the Ajinomoto Stadium (☏03/0424/40-0555, ⓦwww.ajinomotostadium.com) in Chōfu; take the Keiō Line from Shinjuku. Tickets vary from ¥1200 to ¥6000. If you want to watch one of the tournaments at the National Sumo Stadium (see p.122), go to a ticket agency (see below) or, better still, line up early – before 9am – outside the stadium box office for one of the unreserved tickets sold on the day (¥2100); note that tickets are particularly hard to come by on the first and last days. Dates of tournaments, amongst other useful information, are posted on the Nihon Sumō Kyōkai website (ⓦwww.sumo.or.jp).

Taxis The major taxi firms are Daiwa ☏03/3503-8421; Hinomaru Limousine ☏03/3212-0505, ⓦwww.hinomaru.co.jp; Kokusai ☏03/3452-5931; and Nippon Kōtsū ☏03/3799-9220 (24hr English answering service).

Ticket agencies To get tickets for theatre performances, films, concerts and sporting events, it's best, in the first instance, to approach one of the major advance ticket agencies. Ticket Pia (☏03/5237-9999) can be found in the main city areas, such as Ginza, Ikebukuro, Shibuya and Shinjuku, or try phoning Lawson (☏03/3569-9900) or CN Playguide (☏03/5802-9999). Major events sell out quickly. You can go directly to the venue on the day and see if you can get a ticket from the box office or a tout outside, but expect to pay well over the odds.

Tours Japan Travel Bureau (Sunrise Tours; ☏03/5620-9500, ⓦwww.jtb.co.jp/sunrisetour/) and Japan Gray Line (☏03/0800-080810, ⓦwww.jgi.co.jp/inbound/index.htm) offer all-inclusive bus tours of Tokyo and nearby attractions, including Kamakura, Nikkō and Hakone, with English-speaking guides. Prices start at around ¥3300 for a half-day tour of the main sights, to ¥9000 for a full day including lunch or dinner – well over double what a similar DIY tour would cost. Tours can be booked at the TIC in Yūrakuchō (see p.98) and at all major hotels.

Trains For English-language information on JR's services, including train times and ticket prices, call the JR East-Infoline (☏03/3423-0111; Mon–Fri 10am–6pm).

Travel agents For international tickets, try one of the following English-speaking agents: No.1 Travel (Shinjuku; ☏03/3205-6073, ⓦwww.no1-travel.com; other branches in Shibuya and Ikebukuro); A'cross Traveller's Bureau (Shinjuku; ☏03/3340-6749, ⓦwww.across-travel.com; other branches in Shibuya and Ikebukuro); and Hit Travel (Ebisu; ☏03/3473-9040). The main domestic travel agents are Japan Travel Bureau (JTB;

03/5620-9500, www.jtb.co.jp), which has dozens of branches all over Tokyo; Nippon Travel Agency (03/3572-8744); and Kinki Nippon

Tourist (03/3263-5522) – the contact numbers take you to their foreign tourist departments.

Travel details

Trains

Tokyo Station to: Fukuoka (Hakata Station) (16 daily; 4hr 40min–6hr 10min); Hiroshima (29 daily; 4–5hr); Kamakura (every 10–20min; 55min); Karuizawa (23 daily; 1hr 20min); Kyoto (every 15–30min; 2hr 15min–4hr); Morioka (16 daily; 2hr–3hr 20min); Nagano (every 30min–1hr; 1hr 40min–2hr); Nagoya (every 15–30min; 1hr 40min–3hr); Niigata (every 30min–1hr; 2hr); Okayama (every 30min–1hr; 3hr 15min–4hr); Sendai (every 30min–1hr; 1hr 40min–2hr); Shimoda (hourly; 2hr 40min–3hr); Shin-Kōbe (every 30min–1hr; 3hr 15min); Shin-Ōsaka (every 15–30 min; 2hr 30min–4hr 10min); Yokohama (every 15min; 30–40min).
Asakusa Station to: Nikkō (14 daily; 1hr 55min).
Shinjuku Station to: Hakone (23 daily; 1hr 30min); Kōfu (27 daily; 1hr 30min); Matsumoto (18 daily; 2hr 38min).

Buses

Tokyo Station to: Aomori (1 daily; 9hr 30min); Fukui (1 daily; 8hr); Hiroshima (1 daily; 12hr); Kōbe (1 daily; 8hr 45min); Kōchi (1 daily; 11hr 35min); Kyoto (2 daily; 8hr); Matsuyama (2 daily; 11hr 55min); Morioka (1 daily; 7hr 30min); Nagoya (16 daily; 5hr 20min); Nara (1 daily; 9hr 30min); Ōsaka (3 daily; 8hr 20min); Sendai (2 daily; 5hr 30min); Shimonoseki (2 daily; 14hr 20min); Takamatsu (1 daily; 10hr 15min); Yamagata (2 daily; 5hr 15min).
Ikebukuro Station to: Ise (3 daily; 8hr); Kanazawa (4 daily; 7hr 30min); Nagano (4 daily; 4hr 10min); Niigata (6 daily; 5hr); Ōsaka (1 daily; 8hr); Toyama (3 daily; 6hr 50min).
Shibuya Station to: Himeji (daily; 9hr); Kōbe (daily; 8hr 40min).
Shinagawa Station to: Hirosaki (1 daily; 9hr 15min); Imabari (1 daily; 12hr 10min); Kurashiki (1 daily; 11hr); Tokushima (daily; 9hr 20min).
Shinjuku Station to: Akita (1 daily; 8hr 30min);

Fuji Yoshida (14 daily; 1hr 50min); Fukuoka (Hakata Station) (1 daily; 14hr 20min); Hakone-Tōgendai (14 daily; 2hr 11min); Kawaguchi-ko (at least 14 daily; 1hr 45min); Kurashiki (2 daily; 11hr); Matsumoto (16 daily; 3hr 10min); Nagano (4 daily; 3hr 40min); Nagoya (2 daily; 7hr 10min); Okayama (2 daily; 10hr 30min); Ōsaka (4 daily; 7hr 40min); Sendai (3 daily; 5hr 30min); Takayama (2 daily; 5hr 30min).

Ferries

There are regular **ferry** connections between Tokyo Ferry Port, at Ariake on the area of reclaimed land in Tokyo Bay to Kōchi and Tokushima on Shikoku, and Naha in Okinawa. From Shin-Kiba subway and train station on the east side of Tokyo Bay, you can take a bus to the ferry port.
Tokyo Ferry Terminal to: Kōchi (1 daily; 21hr 30min); Naha (1–2 weekly; 45hr); Tokushima (1 daily; 18hr 40min).

Flights

Haneda to: Akita (6 daily; 1hr); Asahikawa (7 daily; 1hr 35min); Fukuoka (hourly; 1hr 45min); Hakodate (8 daily; 1hr 15min); Hiroshima (10 daily; 1hr 25min); Kagoshima (10 daily; 1hr 50min); Kansai International (9 daily; 1hr 15min); Kōchi (5 daily; 1hr 50min); Komatsu (for Kanazawa) (8 daily; 1hr); Kumamoto (8 daily; 1hr 50min); Kushiro (5 daily; 1hr 35min); Matsuyama (8 daily; 1hr 25min); Misawa (4 daily; 1hr 10min); Miyazaki (9 daily; 1hr 45min); Nagasaki (9 daily; 1hr 55min); Obihiro (4 daily; 1hr 35min); Ōita (8 daily; 1hr 30min); Okayama (4 daily; 1hr 20min); Okinawa (Naha) (10 daily; 2hr 30min); Ōsaka (Itami) (9 daily; 1hr); Sapporo (Chitose) (hourly; 1hr 30min); Takamatsu (7 daily; 1hr 10min); Tokushima (6 daily; 1hr 15min); Toyama (6 daily; 1hr); Yamagata (3 daily; 55min).
Narita to: Nagoya (1 daily; 1hr).

2

Around Tokyo

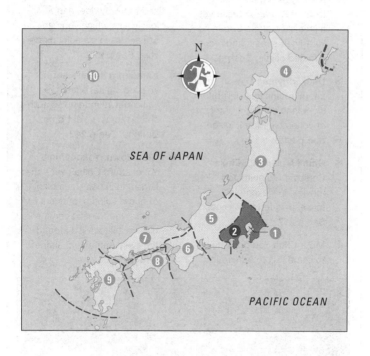

CHAPTER 2   # Highlights

△ Shin-kyō bridge, Nikkō

2

Around Tokyo

Tokyo is hemmed into its coastal location on the Kantō plain by a ring of mountains and volcanoes, featuring temples, parks and a couple of bustling towns and cities. It doesn't take long to get out of the capital – two hours at most – and it's well worth the effort. The single best reason for venturing out lies to the north, at **Nikkō**, where the incredible shrine complex of **Tōshō-gū**, built to deify the Tokugawa shoguns, offers a riotous feast for the senses. Even if you dislike the shrine's ostentatiousness, you won't regret making the journey to see it, since the surrounding mountains are beautiful throughout the year – particularly when decked out in autumn colours – and hold some fantastic walking country. If you can, make time to check out the spectacular waterfalls nearby, up at the lakes by Chūzenji and Yumoto, another excellent area for walking and cross-country skiing.

The temple complex of **Naritasan Shinshō-ji**, with its lovely pagoda, extensive gardens, woods and ornamental ponds, is the highlight of the pilgrim town of **Narita**, some 60km northeast of Tokyo. Ceramics lovers shouldn't miss out on **Mashiko**, north of Tokyo in Tochigi-ken, a pottery town associated with the famed craftsman Hamada Shōji and British potter Bernard Leach. East of Mashiko lies the town of **Mito**, home to Kairakuen, one of Japan's top three traditional landscaped gardens.

Some 40km north of Tokyo in Saitama-ken is **Kawagoe**, known as "Little Edo", a great place to wander through nostalgic nineteenth-century streetscapes, poke around ancient temples and shrines, and indulge in some serious souvenir shopping.

Sacred **Mount Takao**, just an hour west of the capital, provides a more verdant escape for the casual walker and is the starting point for serious hikes northwest to the **Chichibu-Tama National Park**. Closer to the city, pause at **Mitaka** to meet up with the cute animated characters that call the **Ghibli Museum** home.

Looming to the west of Tokyo is Japan's most famous landmark, the venerable **Mount Fuji**, where you can either make the tough ascent up the volcano or simply relax in the surrounding countryside. Nearby, the inviting landscapes of the Fuji-Hakone-Izu National Park, particularly around **Hakone** and south through **Izu Hantō**, warrant a day's exploration.

Closer to Tokyo, the deceptively unassuming town of **Kamakura** is one of Japan's major historical sights, home to several imposing Zen temples and the country's second largest bronze Buddha, the magnificent **Daibutsu**. There are also hiking trails through the surrounding hills, and an enjoyable train ride further along the coast to the sacred island of Enoshima. Just north of Kamakura you're back into the urban sprawl where Tokyo merges with **Yokohama**, Japan's second largest and most cosmopolitan city, with a smattering of attractions, not least the gourmet restaurants of Chinatown.

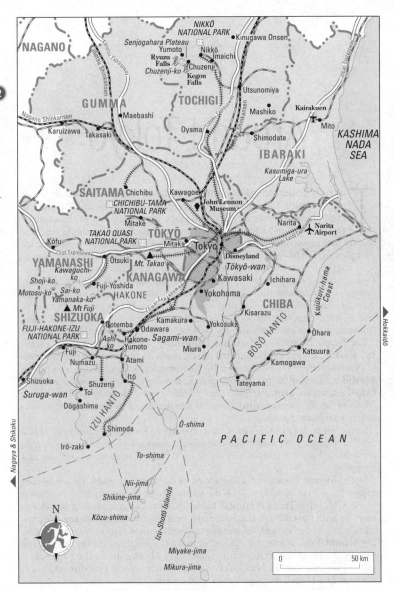

Nikkō and around

If you make one trip from Tokyo, it should be to the pilgrim town of **NIKKŌ**, 128km north of the capital, where the World Heritage-listed **Tōshō-gū** shrine complex sits amid splendid mountains criss-crossed by outstanding hiking trails. The antithesis of the usually austere Shinto shrines – and often considered overbearingly gaudy – Tōshō-gū (appropriately enough, the name means "sunlight") attracts masses of Japanese tourists year round, who tramp dutifully around the shrine and the surrounding holy buildings, which include the **Futarasan-jinja** shrine and the Buddhist temple of **Rinnō-ji**. After you've done the same, it's worth investigating the **Nikkō Tōshō-gū Museum of Art**, in the woods behind Tōshō-gū, and then escaping the crowds by crossing the Daiya-gawa River to explore the dramatically named **Ganman-ga-fuchi abyss**, which is in fact a tranquil riverside walk. If it's the great outdoors you're

Nikkō and around

Nikkō	*Nikkō*	日光
Futarasan-jinja	*Futarasan-jinja*	二荒山神社
Ganman-ga-fuchi abyss	*Ganman-ga-fuchi*	含満ヶ淵
Kosugi Hōan Museum of Art	*Kosugi Hōan Bijutsukan*	小杉放庵美術館
Nikkō Tōshō-gu Museum of Art	*Nikkō Tōshō-gū Bijutsukan*	日光東照宮美術館
Rinnō-ji	*Rinnō-ji*	輪王寺
Shin-kyō bridge	*Shin-kyō*	神橋
Taiyūin-byō	*Taiyūin-byō*	大猷院廟
Tōshō-gū	*Tōshō-gū*	東照宮

Around Nikko

Chūzenji-ko Lake	*Chūzenji*	中禅寺湖
Kegon Falls	*Kegon-no-taki*	華厳の滝
Nikkō Edo Village	*Nikkō Edo-mura*	日光江戸村
Yumoto	*Yumoto*	湯元

Accommodation

Chūzenji Kanaya Hotel	*Chūzenji Kanaya Hoteru*	中禅寺金谷ホテル
Hotori-an	*Hotori-an*	ほとり庵
Narusawa Lodge	*Narusawa Rojji*	鳴沢ロッジ
Nikkō Daiyagawa Youth Hostel	*Nikkō Daiyagawa Yūsu Hosuteru*	日光大谷川ユースホステル
Nikkō Kanaya Hotel	*Nikkō Kanaya Hoteru*	日光金谷ホテル
Nikkō Lakeside Hotel	*Nikkō Rēkusaido Hoteru*	日光レークサイドホテル
Nikkō-shi Kōryū Sokushin Centre	*Nikkō-shi Kōryū Sokushin Sentā*	日光市交流促進センター
Pension Green Age Inn	*Penshon Guriin Eiji In*	ペンショングリーンエイジイン
Petit Pension Friendly	*Puchi Penshon Furendorii*	プチペンションフレンドリー
Turtle Inn Nikkō	*Tātoru In Nikkō*	タートルイン日光
Yumoto Hillside Inn	*Yumoto Hirusaido In*	湯元ヒルサイドイン
Yunoka	*Yunoka*	ゆの香

Eating

Hippari Dako	*Hippari Dako*	ひっぱり凧
Inoha	*Inoha*	いのは
Kikou	*Kikō*	希光
Meiji-no-Yakata	*Meiji-no-Yakata*	明治の館
Milky House	*Mirukii House*	ミルキーハウス
Steak House Mihashi	*Sutēki Hausu Mihashi*	ステーキハウスみはし
Suzuya	*Suzuya*	鈴家
Tsugaya	*Tsugaya*	つがや
Yumoto Rest House	*Yumoto Resuto Hausu*	湯元レストハウス

after, don't miss out on the most beautiful part of the Nikkō National Park around **Chūzenji-ko**, some 17km from Nikkō, or the quieter and less touristy resort of **Yumoto**, higher in the mountains.

Although with an early start it's possible to see both Tōshō-gū and Chūzenji-ko in a long day-trip from Tokyo, it's better to stay overnight in or around Nikkō. Cramming both places into one day during the peak summer and autumn seasons is impossible – it's far better to concentrate on Nikkō alone. A final tip: pack some warm clothes, since Nikkō is cooler than lowland Tokyo, and in winter you can expect plenty of snow.

Some history

Although Nikkō has been a holy place in both the Buddhist and Shinto religions for over a thousand years – a hermitage was built here in the eighth century – its fortunes only took off with the death of **Tokugawa Ieyasu** in 1616. In his will, the shogun requested that a shrine be built here in his honour, which was duly done and finished in 1617. The structure, however, was deemed not nearly impressive enough by Ieyasu's grandson, **Tokugawa Iemitsu**, who ordered work to begin on the elaborate decorative mausoleum seen today.

Iemitsu's dazzling vision was driven by practical as well as aesthetic considerations. The shogun wanted to stop rival lords amassing money of their own, so he ordered the *daimyō* to supply the materials for the shrine, and to pay the thousands of craftsmen. The mausoleum, Tōshō-gū, was completed in 1634 and the jury has been out on its over-the-top design ever since. Whatever you make of it, Tōshō-gū – along with the slightly more restrained Taiyūin-byō mausoleum of Iemitsu – is entirely successful at conveying the immense power and wealth of the Tokugawa dynasty. Every year, on May 18, the **Grand Festival** re-stages the spectacular interment of Ieyasu at Tōshō-gū, with a cast of over one thousand costumed priests and warriors in a colourful procession through the shrine grounds topped off with horseback archery. It's well worth attending, as is the smaller-scale festival on October 17 – this doesn't have the archery and only lasts half a day, but does coincide with "Light Up Nikkō" (Oct 16–20), during which the major temple buildings are illuminated at night to great effect.

Arrival and city transport

The cheapest and easiest way of reaching Nikkō is to take a Tōbu-Nikkō **train** from Asakusa in Tokyo (the station is in the basement of the Matsuya department store and connected by tunnel to Asakusa subway station). *Kaisoku* (rapid) trains make the journey in around two hours and twenty minutes and cost ¥1320 one way. The marginally faster "Spacia" *tokkyū* (limited express) takes just under two hours, and costs ¥2740. On some trains you'll need to change at Shimo-Imaichi. Nikkō is also served by JR trains, but this route, which takes longer and costs more than the Tōbu line, only makes sense if you have a JR pass. The fastest route is by Shinkansen from either Tokyo or Ueno stations to Utsunomiya Station, a journey of fifty minutes, where you must change to the JR Nikkō line for a local train taking 45 minutes to reach the Nikkō terminus, a minute's walk east of the Tōbu station.

The Tōbu railway offers various **travel passes**, known as "free passes", for travel to and around the Nikkō area from Tokyo. These tickets, which can only be bought at Tokyo's Tōbu stations, include the train fare from Asakusa to Nikkō (express train surcharges still apply), unlimited use of local buses, and discounts on entrance charges at many of the area's attractions, including the

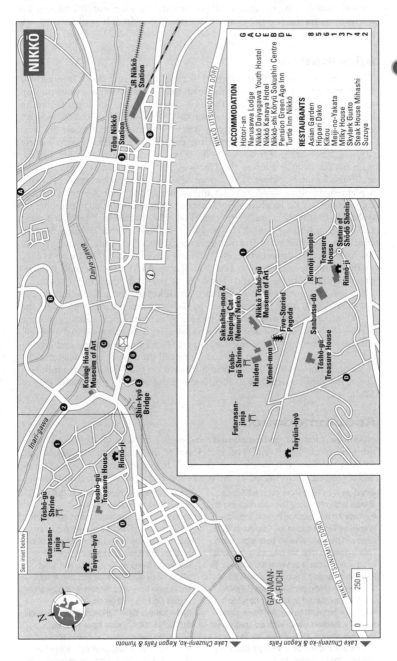

NIKKŌ

See inset below

Toshō-gū Shrine
Futarasan-jinja
Taiyūin-byō
Rinnō-ji
Toshō-gū Treasure House

Inari-gawa
Daiya-gawa

Kosugi Hōan Museum of Art
Shin-kyō Bridge

JR Nikkō Station
Tōbu Nikkō Station

NIKKŌ UTSUNOMIYA DŌRO

GANMAN-GA-FUCHI

NIKKŌ UTSUNOMIYA DŌRO

0   250 m

ACCOMMODATION	
Hotori-an	G
Narusawa Lodge	A
Nikkō Daiyagawa Youth Hostel	C
Nikkō Kanaya Hotel	E
Nikkō-shi Kōryū Sokushin Centre	B
Pension Green Age Inn	D
Turtle Inn Nikkō	F

RESTAURANTS	
Asian Garden	8
Hippari Dako	5
Kikou	6
Meiji-no-Yakata	1
Milky House	3
Skylark Gusto	7
Steak House Mihashi	4
Suzuya	2

Futarasan-jinja
Toshō-gū Shrine
Haiden
Yōmei-mon
Sakashita-mon & Sleeping Cat (Nemuri Neko)
Nikko Toshō-gū Museum of Art
Five-Storied Pagoda
Sanbutsu-dō
Toshō-gū Treasure House
Rinnōji Temple
Treasure House
Rinnō-ji
Statue of Shōdō Shōnin
Taiyūin-byō

▲ Lake Chuzenji-ko & Kegon Falls & Yumoto   ▲ Lake Chuzenji-ko & Kegon Falls cable cars and boat trips at Chūzenji-ko. If you only intend to visit Tōshō-gū, it's not worth buying the pass, but if you're planning a trip out to Chūzenji-ko the most useful ticket is the Nikkō Mini Free Pass, which is valid for two days and costs ¥4940.

Information

The **Tōbu Nikkō Station**, designed like a giant Swiss chalet, is fronted by a square surrounded by gift shops; the main road in the western corner runs up to Tōshō-gū. Inside the station there's a cloakroom for left luggage and an **information desk** (daily 8.30am–5pm; ☏0288/53-4511), where the assistant speaks some English and can provide you with maps and leaflets on the area. The town's main **tourist information centre** is the Nikkō Kyōdo Centre (daily 8.30am–5pm; ☏0288/54-2496, ⓦwww.city.nikko.tochigi.jp), on the main road from the station to the Tōshō-gū complex; assistants here can make accommodation bookings. The centre also has an attached **gallery** (daily 8.30am–5pm) showcasing local art and showing short videos – with English commentaries – on local attractions, history and culture. If you're planning on **walking** in the area, pick up copies of the excellent English-language *Guidebook for Walking Trails* (¥150) and the free *Tourist Guide of Nikkō*, both of which feature good maps and pictures of local flora and fauna. The centre also has coin-operated **Internet** access (¥100 per 30min). Note that the post office on the main approach road to Tōshō-gū has an **ATM** which accepts foreign-issued cards; otherwise, it's near impossible to use credit cards in the town.

You can save money if you buy the right **ticket** for the temples and shrines in Nikkō. If you intend to see Rinnō-ji, Tōshō-gū and Futarasan-jinja, buy the ¥1000 *nisha-ichiji* **combination ticket**, which includes entrance to the Taiyūin-byō mausoleum and the roaring dragon hall (*Honji-dō*) in Tōshō-gū, but not the area containing the sleeping cat (*Nemuri neko*) carving and Ieyasu's tomb at Tōshō-gū (these last two can be tacked on to your combination ticket for an additional ¥520). The combination ticket can be bought from booths beside the Sanbutsu-dō hall in Rinnō-ji and outside the Omote-mon gate to Tōshō-gū.

Accommodation

Nikkō has plenty of **accommodation**, ranging from youth hostels and pensions to plush hotels and ryokan. However, in peak holiday seasons and autumn, advance reservations are essential. Rates at virtually all places are slightly higher from August 21 to November 3, and during major holidays.

Hotori-an 8-28 Takumi-chō ☏0288/53-3663, ⓦwww.turtle-nikko.com. The modern annexe to the *Turtle Inn* (see opposite) is set in a tranquil location beside the path to the Ganman-ga-fuchi abyss and has good-value en-suite tatami rooms. There's a pottery shop and café, and a bath with forest views. Dinner is served at the *Turtle Inn*. ⑤

Narusawa Lodge 1 Tokorono ☏ & ⓕ0288/54-1630, ⓦwww.nikko-narusawa.com. Delightful *minshuku*, surrounded by flowers and set well away from the tourist throng. The tatami rooms are lovely, the shared bathrooms are spotless and the family who run it are very friendly and speak a little English. Prices drop by ¥300 per person if you stay more than one night. ④

Nikkō Daiyagawa Youth Hostel 1075 Naka-Hatsuishi-machi ☏0288/54-1974, ⓦwww.jyh.or.jp. From either station, take the first left after you've passed the NTT building on the main road and follow the English signposts that point the way down a narrow back path to this cosy hostel facing the river. Run by a very hospitable family and deservedly gets rave reviews. Dorms have bunk beds. Dinner (¥840; book ahead) is good. Dorms ¥2730 per person.

Nikkō Kanaya Hotel 1300 Kami-Hatsuishi-machi ☏0288/54-0001, ⓦwww.kanayahotel.co.jp. Nikkō's top Western-style hotel harks back to the glamorous days of early twentieth-century travel. Most rooms are pricey – and rates skyrocket dur-

ing peak holiday seasons – though there are some cheaper rooms with en-suite shower or just a toilet (the hotel has a communal bath). ⑤–⑦
Nikkō-shi Kōryū Sokushin Centre 2854 Tokorono ☏0288/54-1013, ⓦ www.city.nikko.tochigi.jp/nyh. On the far side of the Daiya-gawa from the town, this hostel/hotel has a secluded location behind the high school. The en-suite tatami rooms are excellent and have lovely views of the town, and there are also Western-style rooms, a laundry and a small kitchen for self-caterers. There's a 10pm curfew. ④
Pension Green Age Inn 10-9 Nishi-sandō ☏0288/53-3636, ⓦ www.nikko-pension.jp.

Eccentric decorations (including an organ, stained-glass windows and mock-Tudor facade) enliven this small Western-style hotel close by Tōshō-gū. The rooms are comfy and excellent value, and there's also French-influenced cooking and an onsen bath. ⑤
Turtle Inn Nikkō 2-16 Takumi-chō ☏0288/53-3168, ⓦ www.turtle-nikko.com. Popular pension run by an English-speaking family in a quiet location next to the Daiya-gawa River, close to the main shrines, with small, plain tatami rooms, common bathrooms and a cosy lounge. The ¥2000 evening meal is a good deal, but breakfast is pricey. ④

The Town

First impressions of Nikkō as you come out of either train station aren't great – the uphill approach to the shrine is lined with run-down shops and houses. However, frequent buses head towards the main approach to Tōshō-gū and the walk along the town's main street only takes fifteen minutes. At the top of the gently sloping road you'll pass one of Nikkō's most famous landmarks, the red-lacquered **Shin-kyō bridge**. Legend has it that when the Buddhist priest Shōdō Shōnin visited Nikkō in the eighth century he was helped across the Daiya-gawa River at this very spot by the timely appearance of two snakes, who formed a bridge and then vanished. The original arched wooden structure first went up in 1636, but has been reconstructed many times since – the bridge was being completely rebuilt at the time of writing and is due to reopen in March 2005.

If you have time, it's worth turning right at the bridge and walking up to the modern, terracotta-coloured **Kosugi Hōan Museum of Art** (Tues–Sun 9.30am–4.30pm; ¥700), which displays the dreamily beautiful figurative and landscape paintings of local artist Hōan (1920–64). Concerts are sometimes held here in the evenings – ask at tourist information. The main shrine and temple complex are in the opposite direction; take the left-hand path uphill across from the bridge and you'll emerge in front of the main compound of **Rinnō-ji** (April–Oct 8am–4.30pm; Nov–March 8am–3.30pm), a Tendai Buddhist temple founded in 766 by Shōdō Shōnin, whose statue stands on a rock at the entrance. The large, red-painted hall, **Sanbutsu-dō**, houses three giant gilded statues: the thousand-handed Kannon, the Amida Buddha and the fearsome horse-headed Kannon. It's worth paying to view these awe-inspiring figures from directly beneath their lotus-flower perches – entry is included in the combination ticket (see opposite), which you can buy at the booth outside. Rinnō-ji's **Treasure House** (daily 8am–5pm; ¥300), opposite the Sanbutsu-dō, has some interesting items on display, but its nicest feature is the attached Shōyō-en, an elegant garden with a strolling route around a small pond.

Tōshō-gūe and Nikkō Tōshō-gū Museum of Art

The broad, tree-lined Omotesan-dō leads up to the main entrance to **Tōshō-gū** (daily April–Oct 8am–4.30pm; Nov–March 8am–3.30pm), just to the east of Rinnō-ji. You'll pass under a giant stone *torii* gate (one of the few remaining features of the original 1617 shrine), while on the left is an impressive red and green five-storey pagoda, an 1819 reconstruction of a 1650 original, which burned down. Ahead is the Omote-mon gate, the entrance to the main shrine precincts, where you'll need to hand over a section of your combination ticket or Tōshō-gū and sleeping cat-only ticket (¥1300), either of which can be bought from the booth in front of the gate.

Inside the precincts, turn left to reach the **Three Sacred Storehouses** (*Sanjinko*) on the right and the **Sacred Stables** (*Shinkyūsha*) on the left. There's usually a crowd of amateur photographers in front of the stables jostling to capture one of Tōshō-gū's many famous painted wood-carvings – the "hear no evil, see no evil, speak no evil" **monkeys**, which represent the three major principles of Tendai Buddhism. The route leads to the steps up to the dazzling **Yōmei-mon** (Sun Blaze Gate), with wildly ornate carvings, gilt and intricate decoration. Impressive as it is, the gate has less dramatic impact than the detailed panels on the flanking walls, which are adorned with fantastic flowers and birds. A belfry and drum tower stand alone amid pools of pebbles in front of the gate. Behind the drum tower is the **Honji-dō** (¥50). This small hall is part of Rinnō-ji temple and contains a ceiling painting of a "roaring dragon"; a priest will demonstrate how to make the dragon roar by standing beneath its head and clapping to create an echo.

It's better to pay the small charge to see the roaring dragon rather than fork out ¥520 for the less impressive **sleeping cat** (*Nemuri neko*), just above the Sakashita-mon gate to the right of the inner precinct beyond the Yōmei-mon – you'd easily miss this minute carving if it wasn't for the gawping crowd. Two hundred stone steps lead uphill from the gate to the surprisingly unostentatious **tomb of Ieyasu**, amid a glade of pines, and about the only corner of the shrine where the crowds are generally absent.

Directly in front of the Yōmei-mon is the serene white and gold gate of **Kara-mon**, beyond which is the **Haiden**, or hall of worship. The side entrance to the hall is to the right of the gate and you'll need to remove your shoes and stop taking photographs. Inside, you can walk down into the Honden, the shrine's central hall, still decorated with its beautiful original paintwork. On the way back out through the Yōmei-mon, you'll pass the Jinyōsha, a building where the *mikoshi* (portable shrines) used during Tōshō-gū's spring and autumn festivals are hidden away.

Before rushing off, don't miss the **Nikkō Tōshō-gū Museum of Art** (daily 8am–4pm, April–Oct until 5pm; ¥800), at the back of the shrine complex, to the left as you walk out of the Omote-mon gate. The traditional, impressively simple wooden mansion which the museum is set in dates from 1928 and is the former head office of the shrine. Inside, the sliding doors and screens were decorated by the top Japanese painters of the day and together constitute one of the most beautiful collections of this type of art that you'll see anywhere in the country.

Not far east of here are the grounds of **Meiji-no-Yakata**, the early twentieth-century holiday home of the American trade representative F.W. Horne. The various houses amid the trees are now fancy restaurants (see opposite), but it's worth wandering around even if you don't eat here to take in the pretty gardens and sylvan setting.

Futarasan-jinja, Taiyūin-byō and the Ganman-ga-fuchi abyss

A trip around Tōshō-gū is likely to leave you visually (if not physically) exhausted, but it's worth pressing on to some of the other temples and shrines in the surrounding woods. At the end of the right-hand path next to Tōshō-gū's pagoda, the simple red colour scheme of the **Futarasan-jinja** comes as a relief to the senses. This shrine, originally established by the priest Shōdō Shōnin in 782, is the main one dedicated to the deity of Nantai-san, the volcano whose eruption created nearby Chūzenji-ko. The middle shrine is beside the lake and the innermost shrine stands on the top of the mountain. There are some good paintings of animals and birds on votive plaques in the shrine's main hall, while the attached garden (¥200) offers a quiet retreat with a small teahouse serving *macha* green tea and sweets for ¥350. You can also inspect the *bakemono tōrō*, a "phantom lantern" made of bronze in 1292 and said to be possessed by demons.

Just beyond Futarasan-jinja, and bypassed by the tourist mêlée, is the charming **Taiyūin-byō** (¥550), which contains the mausoleum of the third shogun, Tokugawa Iemitsu, who died in 1651. This complex – part of Rinnō-ji and hidden away on a hillside, surrounded by lofty pines – was deliberately designed to be less ostentatious than Tōshō-gū. Look out for the green god of wind and the red god of thunder in the alcoves behind the Niten-mon gate, and the beautiful Kara-mon (Chinese-style gate) and fence surrounding the gold and black lacquer inner precincts.

If the relative peacefulness of Taiyūin-byō has left you wary of Nikkō's ever-present tourist scrum, make for another nearby tranquil escape. From the temple area, head for the Nishi-sandō main road (where the bus to and from Nikkō's stations stops), cross over and continue down to the Daiya-gawa River – five minutes' walk west is the Ganman-bashi, a small bridge across from which begins the riverside pathway through the **Ganman-ga-fuchi abyss**. Part of this restful walk, along the attractive and rocky river valley, is lined by the *Narabi-jizō*, some fifty decaying stone statues of Jizō, the Buddhist saint of travellers and children.

Eating

Avoid the bland tourist restaurants clustered around Nikkō's train and bus stations and chances are you'll **eat** pretty well. This area's speciality is *yuba-ryōri* – thin, tasty strips of tofu made from soya beans, usually rolled into tubes and cooked in various stews. You're likely to be served this at your hotel or pension, the best place to eat if you stay overnight, since most restaurants shut around 8pm.

Asian Garden Indian restaurant with a good vegetarian set menu (¥950) and reasonably priced meat-based meals. Daily 10am–10pm.

Hippari Dako Inexpensive *yakitori* and noodle café – look for the giant kite outside – popular with just about every *gaijin* who has ever set foot in Nikkō, as the written recommendations and *meishi* that plaster the walls testify. The menu has plenty of vegetarian options, plus beer and sake.

Kikou Just before *Hippari Dako* as you come from the station. A small Korean restaurant with tatami mat seating and hearty set meals under ¥1000. Open till midnight.

Meiji-no-Yakata ☎0288/53-3751. The smartest restaurant in this collection of eateries beyond the Tōshō-gū car park is the cheapest, if you go for à la carte and don't mind shelling out ¥1500 for curry rice. Best to dig deeper and sample the exquisite *shojin-ryōri* vegetarian course (¥3500) in the traditional *Gyoshintei*, where the waitresses wear kimono and you can gaze out on a lovely garden. The Art Nouveau *Fujimoto* is very elegant, French-influenced and expensive.

Milky House 2-2-3 Inari-machi. Convivial coffee shop, serving inexpensive snacky meals and beer; also has Internet access (¥300 for 30min). Closed Wed.

Nikkō Kanaya Hotel 1300 Kami-Hatsuishi-machi. A meal in this hotel's elegant second-floor dining room will set you back at least ¥3500 for lunch and ¥6000 for dinner. The first-floor *Maple Leaf* coffee shop is cheaper, but less glamorous. Your best bet is the *Yashio* Japanese restaurant, behind the coffee shop, which has set lunches for under ¥2000.

Skylark Gusto Stylish family restaurant with good-value meals from a wide menu of Western and Japanese favourites. It also qualifies as Nikkō's only late nightspot, since it closes late (2am) and serves beer.

Steak House Mihashi Set steak meals – fairly good value at ¥2800 per person.

Suzuya Stand-alone restaurant just before you cross over the bridge up the slope from the Kosugi Hōan Museum of Art. This is a good place to sample *yuba-ryōri*; the set lunch costs ¥1300 and includes tempura, rice, noodles and rolled tofu. Daily except Thurs 11am–3pm.

Chūzenji-ko and the Kegon Falls

Some 10km west of Nikkō lie **Chūzenji-ko** and the dramatic **Kegon Falls** that flow from it. Local buses (¥1100 each way without a pass) usually take less than an hour to get here, running east along Route 120 and up the twisting, one-way road to reach Chūzenji, the lakeside resort, though travelling times can easily be doubled – or even tripled – during kōyō in mid-October, the prime time for viewing the changing autumn leaves, when it's bumper-to-bumper traffic.

Both the lake and waterfalls were created thousands of years ago, when nearby Mount Nantai erupted, its lava plugging the valley. The best way of seeing the evidence of this geological event is to hop off the bus at Akechi-daira, the stop before Chūzenji, where a **cable car** (daily 9am–4pm; ¥390 one way, ¥710 return) will whisk you up to a viewing platform. From here it's a 1.5-kilometre walk uphill and across the Chanoki-daira plateau, where there are sweeping views of Chūzenji-ko, Mount Nantai and the famous waterfalls. An even better view of the falls can be had from the viewing platform at their base (daily: May–Sept 7.30am–6pm; Oct 7.30am–5pm; March, April & Nov 8am–5pm; Jan, Feb & Dec 9am–4.30pm; ¥530). The lift to this vantage point lies east across the car park behind the Chūzenji bus station; don't be put off by the queues of tour groups – a shorter line is reserved for independent travellers. The lift drops 100m through the rock to the base of the falls, where you can see over a tonne of water per second cascading from the Ojiri River, which flows from the lake.

Walking west along the shore for around 1km will bring you to the second **Futarasan-jinja** of the Nikkō area. This colourful shrine, which once bore the name Chūzenji now adopted by the town, has a pretty view of the lake, but is nothing extraordinary. There's also a third Futarasan-jinja, on the actual summit of the volcano; to reach it you'll have to pay ¥500 to climb the sacred volcano of Nantai-san, which is owned by the shrine. The hike up to the 2484-metre peak takes around four hours and should only be attempted in good weather.

Practicalities

Chūzenji's **hotels** and tourist facilities are clustered around the northeastern corner of the lake. The most luxurious place to stay is the *Chūzenji Kanaya*, 2482 Chugushi (T0288/51-0001, Wwww.kanayahotel.co.jp; **⑦**), en route to the Ryūzu falls (see opposite), and specially designed to blend in with its woodland surroundings. Set back from the lake near the bus station, the *Nikkō Lakeside Hotel*, 2482 Chūzenji (T0288/55-0321, F55-0771; **⑧** including two meals), offers Western-style rooms at reasonable prices and has a couple of restaurants. For a more homely feel, head for *Petit Pension Friendly*, Chūzenji (T0288/55-0027, F55-0549; **⑥–⑦** including two meals), overlooking the lake five minutes' walk from the bus station. This family-run hotel and café has both Western and Japanese-style rooms, the cheaper ones without en suite.

As far as **eating** goes, a good choice is the elegant, European-style *Chez Hoshino*, on the main row of hotels and giftshops facing Chūzenji-ko (a three-course set lunch costs around ¥2500) – the restaurant has a real log fire in winter and an English menu. The cheap and cheerful *Inoha* (daily 9am–5am) has udon from ¥600 and lunch sets from ¥1000; it's on the second floor above the souvenir shop on the corner opposite the National Science Museum (which can be safely missed as all the displays are in Japanese). For light lunches and snacks like burgers and tacos, head for the *Coffee House Yukon* (closed Jan–March & Dec), a log house next to the *Chūzenji Kanaya Hotel*, where you must order at the counter before sitting down (give your table number).

Yumoto

Before exploring Chūzenji, a rewarding day can be spent by continuing on the bus to the end of the line and getting off at the onsen village of **YUMO-TO**, which nestles cosily at the base of the mountains on the northern shore of lake **Yuno-ko**. Five minutes' walk from the bus terminal at the back of the village is the **Yu-no-daira**, a field where bubbling water breaks through the ground – this is the source of the sulphur smell that hangs so pungently in the air. Nearby is **Onsen-ji**, a small temple notable for its onsen bath, which you can bathe in.

You can rent rowing boats (50min; ¥1000) at the *Yumoto Rest House* from May to the end of October – a lovely way to take in the surrounding scenery. Alternatively, you could walk around the lake in about an hour. If you're feeling energetic, it's worth embarking on the easy and enjoyable ten-kilometre hike from Yumoto across the **Senjōgahara marshland plateau**, past two spectacular waterfalls and back to Chūzenji-ko. First, follow the west bank of Yuno-ko around to the steps down to the picturesque Yudaki Falls, where you could stop off at the lodge serving delicious grilled fish and rice cakes (*mochi*) dipped in sweet miso paste. The trail continues along the Yu-gawa through shady woods before emerging beside the Izumiyado, a large pond and the start of a two-hour tramp across the raised walkways above the Senjōgahara marshland, which blooms with many wild flowers during the summer.

Roughly one hour further on, at the Akanuma junction, you can branch off back to the main road or continue along the riverside path for thirty minutes to the main road and bridge overlooking the spectacular **Ryūzu Falls**, with clear views of Chūzenji-ko. At the base of the falls you'll find several giftshops and noodle bars, one of which is superbly located, overlooking the water as it gushes into the lake. A lakeside path continues back to Chūzenji, finally emerging on the main road around 1km before Furatasan-jinja. A more relaxing way of completing this last section is to board a boat at Shobugahama, the jetty near the base of the Ryūzu Falls, and cruise for twenty minutes back to Chūzenji.

Practicalities

One of the most attractive **places to stay** in Yumoto is the *Yumoto Hillside Inn* (☎0288/62-2434, ℉62-2519; ❼ including two meals), a Western-style hotel in a wooden chalet with an outdoor deck, English-speaking owners, a small heated swimming pool and indoor and outdoor onsen. Also good is the nearby *Yunoka* (☎0288/62-2326, ✉yunoka@d4.dion.ne.jp; ❼ including two meals), a small minshuku above a giftshop a few minutes' walk east of the bus terminus, which offers tatami and Western-style rooms. The *Yumoto Rest House*, set beside Yuno-ko and with a lovely view of the lake, is a large **café** with a good selection of set meals from around ¥850 per person; pay first at the cash desk, where a photo menu will help you choose your food.

Nikkō Edo Village

There are several onsen resorts dotted along the Kinugawa River, which flows through the mountains northeast of Nikkō. Avoid the touristy Kinugawa Onsen, where multistorey concrete hotels line the riverbank, and head instead for **Nikkō Edo Village** (daily: April–Nov 9am–5pm; Jan–March & Dec 9.30am–4pm; ¥4500), a fantasy recreation of eighteenth-century life complete with bewigged samurai guides and entertaining shows, many of which are great for kids. Light-hearted Japanese costume dramas are played out year round at this theme park, where you can easily spend half a day, though to get the jokes in the geisha and comedy shows you'll need to know some Japanese. The live ninja aerial-action display is a real hoot, as is "Hell Temple", a Buddhist take on a house of horrors. To get here from Tōbu Nikkō Station, go one stop to Tōbu Shimo-Imaichi, and change to a train on the Tōbu Kinugawa line (¥290), getting off at Shin-Takatoku station (a five-minute walk from Western Village, a cowboy theme park) and crossing the road to catch the shuttle bus to Nikkō Edo Village, five minutes' ride away.

Mashiko

Some 30km south of Nikkō, the village of **MASHIKO** is home to a major pottery museum, numerous pottery shops and over three hundred working kilns spread out around the surrounding paddy fields. **Mashiko-yaki**, the distinctive country-style earthenware pottery, has been made in this area since the Nara period (710–784), although the village only achieved nation-wide fame in the 1930s, when the potter and "living national treasure" Hamada Shōji built a kiln here and promoted Mashiko-yaki pottery throughout Japan. Hamada's former residence has since been restored and relocated – along with his traditional-style kiln – to the impressive **Tōgei Messe** complex (daily except Wed 9am–4pm; ¥600). The building contains a pottery studio where you can take lessons for around ¥1200 for two hours (bookings essential on ☎0285/72-7555) and a **museum** featuring works by Hamada and Bernard Leach, the renowned English potter who lived for a short time in this village. To reach the complex, walk from Mashiko Station along the main street, Jōnaizaka, which takes roughly twenty minutes – or longer if you browse the many pottery shops along the way. Alternatively, hop on a bus from Utsunomiya or Mashiko stations (see below); an announce-ment in English will let you know when to get off for the complex, which is a ten-minute walk to the east of the bus stop.

Practicalities

The easiest way to get to Mashiko is to take the **Shinkansen** (50min; ¥4290) from Tokyo to Utsunomiya, where you'll need to transfer to a **bus** (1hr; ¥1100); this leaves from bus stop 14, to the left of the Miyano-hashi, the bridge on the west side of the station. Taking a **train** is marginally cheaper: first take the JR Tōhoku line to Oyama (1hr), then change to the Mito line and change again at Shimodate to the private Mōka line, from where it's a forty-minute journey to Mashiko. On weekends and holidays between March and December you can travel for ¥500 extra on a restored **steam train** on the Mōka line – tickets can be booked at JR stations (ask for a ticket on the "SL"). English maps and leaflets on Mashiko are available at the **tourist information booths** in Utsunomiya Station (daily 8.30am–8pm; ☎028/636-2177) and next to Mashiko Station (daily 8.30am–5pm; ☎0285/72-8846, @info@mta.mashiko.tochigi.jp), though the staff don't speak English. If you want to tour around the kilns, you'll need to rent a car, since they're spread over a wide area; try Eki Rent-a-Car in Utsunomiya (☎028/625-6629). There are several ryokan and minshuku around the village, but once you've checked out the pottery there's little reason to stay.

Narita and around

The rambling temple complex of **Naritasan Shinshō-ji** is the main attraction at the pilgrim town of **NARITA**, some 60km northeast of Tokyo, and an interesting stopoff on your way to or from Narita Airport. Every year, millions of people visit this thousand-year-old temple, which is an important landmark in the Shingon sect of Buddhism, but it's such a vast place that, as long as you're not here on one of the main festival days (New Year, and Setsubun on February 3 or 4), you won't notice the crowds.

To get to **Naritasan Shinshō-ji**, follow the central shopping street, Omotesandō, which is to the left from the plaza in front of the station. Head north for ten minutes, turning downhill when it forks beside a small triangular paved island and you'll reach the souvenir stalls lining the approach to the temple's ornate Niō-mon gate. Many of the buildings inside the complex are modern reproductions, but the colourful three-storey pagoda in front of the Great Main Hall dates from the eighteenth century and is decorated with fearsome gilded dragon heads snarling from under brightly painted rafters. Behind the main hall, the temple's gardens include small forests and ornamental ponds and rivers.

While you're in this area, it's worth checking out the **National Museum of Japanese History** (Tues–Sun 9.30am–4.30/5pm; ¥420) in **Sakura**, four stops before Narita on the Keisei line. Set in wooded grounds a ten-minute walk east from Keisei Sakura Station, this huge museum houses a great collection of Japanese arts and crafts, including 10,000 BC Jōmon pottery figurines (which look as though they could be sculptures by Picasso), detailed models of temples, towns and settlements through the ages, and an extensive range of colourful cultural artefacts. An English pamphlet and taped commentary will help guide you around.

Narita, Mashiko and Mito

Narita	*Narita*	成田
Keisei Sakura Station	*Keisei Sakura-eki*	京成佐倉駅
Naritasan Shinshō-ji	*Naritasan Shinshō-ji*	成田山新勝寺
National Museum of Japanese History	*Kokuritsu Rekishi Minzoku Hakubutsukan*	国立歴史民族博物館
Accommodation		
ANA Hotel Narita	*Narita Zennikkū Hotel*	成田全日空ホテル
Holiday Inn Tōbu Narita	*Horidei In Tōbu Narita*	ホリデイ・イン東武成田
Kirinoya Ryokan	*Kirinoya Ryokan*	桐之家旅館
Ohgiya Ryokan	*Ōgiya Ryokan*	扇屋旅館
Skycourt Narita Youth Guest House	*Sukaikōto Narita Yūsu Gesuto Hausu*	スカイコート成田ユースゲストハウス
Mashiko	*Mashiko*	益子
Tōgei Messe	*Tōgei Messe*	陶芸メッセ
Utsunomiya Station	*Utsunomiya-eki*	宇都宮駅
Mito	*Mito*	水戸
Kairakuen	*Kairakuen*	偕楽園
Kōbuntei	*Kōbuntei*	好文亭
Kōdōkan	*Kōdōkan*	弘道館
Tokugawa Museum	*Tokugawa Hakubutsukan*	徳川博物館

Practicalities

Frequent JR **trains** go to Narita from Tokyo Station, leaving from underground platforms 2, 3 and 4. Keisei trains depart from Ueno and Nishi Nippori stations: the journey takes around an hour and fifteen minutes. From the airport, both JR and Keisei trains take less than ten minutes to reach the town, pulling in at separate stations on Omotesandō.

The **tourist information** desks at Narita Airport (see p.96) are the places to head for maps, pamphlets and hotel bookings if you're just arriving in the country. Make sure you also ask for the **Narita Welcome Card**, which comes with a useful information pack and offers discounts at a range of local tourist attractions, restaurants and accommodation. You can also get the card from the TIC in Tokyo (see p.98) and the **Narita Tourist Pavilion** (Tues–Sun: June–Sept 10am–6pm; Jan–May & Oct–Dec 9am–5pm, ⓦwww.nitma.jp), on Omotesandō in Narita.

The town has plenty of **accommodation** to cater for the groups of pilgrims. Upmarket choices include the *ANA* (☎0476/33-1311, ⓦwww.anahotels.com; ❼) and *Holiday Inn Tobu Narita* (☎0476/32-1234, ⓦwww.holidayinntobunarita.com/eng/index.html; ❻), both of which have free shuttle buses from the airport, as does the rather swanky *Skycourt Narita Youth Guest House* (☎0478/73-6211, ⓔnarita@skyc.jp; ❹) – more of a cheap business hotel than hostel. While fine for late-night arrivals at the airport, none of these is convenient for sightseeing in the town.

If you want to stay in central Narita, there are good-value tatami rooms at the friendly *Ohgiya Ryokan* (☎0476/22-1161, ⓦwww.naritakanko.jp/ohgiya; ❺). Meals and en-suite rooms cost extra, but you pay nothing more for the rooms overlooking the lovely garden with a carp pond. The ryokan is a ten-minute walk from the station towards the temple; take the left-hand turn where the road forks at the traffic island. The best budget option is *Kirinoya Ryokan* (☎0476/22-0724, ⓦwww.root.or.jp/kirinoya; ❹), five minutes east of the main entrance to Naritasan Shinshō-ji. This spotless if somewhat worn Japanese-style establishment is described by its English-speaking owner Katsumata-san as a "museum hotel", and is crammed with his samurai family's heirlooms, including gold-plated suits of armour, swords, muskets, and even a palanquin. There's also a café and a small carp pond to gaze at from the communal bathroom.

You'll find plenty of decent **restaurants**, particularly along Omotesandō. *Kikuya*, immediately downhill across the road from the Tourist Pavilion, is reasonably priced and has an English menu, as does *World Cook*, an Indian restaurant that is closer to the stations and has plenty of vegetarian options. *The Barge Inn*, also on Omotesandō, is a British-style pub popular with local expats and visiting flight crews.

Mito

An hour's train ride northeast of Tokyo, the sleepy town of **MITO** was once home to the Mito clan, one the three main families of the Tokugawa Shogunate that ruled Japan from 1603 to 1867 – although you'd hardly guess the town's former importance from its nondescript central district, dominated by an ugly train and bus terminal complex. Most of the town's surviving attractions were the work of the ninth lord of Mito, **Nariaki Tokugawa** (1800–1860), who in 1841 created the sprawling **Kairakuen** (6am–7pm; free), now officially classified as one of the nation's top three gardens. The best time to visit Mito is from early February to late March, when the garden's innumerable plum trees are in blossom, but the town still has enough sights to make a pleasant day-trip from Tokyo at any time of the year.

Kairakuen lies several kilometres outside the town. Coming into Mito on the train from Tokyo, you'll pass right through it; although there's a station in the park, it's only opened during the peak plum blossom season. To reach the gardens from Mito Station, take a bus (15min; ¥230 each way) from stand 4 outside the north exit to the terminal below the park: a steep set of stairs leads up the hill to the main gates. There's a small **museum** containing a few minor artworks and historical exhibits, but it's so tiny you can poke your head in the door and have a look around before the attendants have time to ask you to pay for admission. Save your money and head instead into the garden proper: Kairakuen was planted with some three thousand plum trees for the enjoyment of Nariaki's vassals (the garden's name means "to share pleasure"). At the centre of the main section of plum-tree plantings stands **Kōbuntei** (daily 9am–4pm; ¥190), a two-storey house that was used by Mito clan members as a retreat and as a venue for poetry readings. The original structure was destroyed by fire-bombing in World War II: the impressive replica, completed in 1958, manages to look as if it has been standing for much longer, while the second-floor observation room affords sweeping views of the garden and nearby lake. From here it's a brisk twenty-minute walk to the **Tokugawa Museum** (daily 10am–4.30pm, Sat & Sun until 5pm; ¥600), housing artefacts once owned by various Tokugawa feudal lords and their families, with a focus on clan family portraits and samurai armour and weaponry. To reach the museum from the main garden of Kairakuen, take the overhead walkway across the train lines, turn right, follow the path parallel to the tracks until you come to the main road, then turn left and walk five minutes up the hill.

Returning to Mito station, take the first right on the left-hand side of the Livin' department store and walk uphill, bearing right, for a couple of minutes until you reach the well-preserved **Kōdōkan** (daily 9am–4pm, ¥190), the Mito clan's school of calligraphy and swordsmanship, built by Nariaki in the same year as Kairakuen. You can explore the connected, low-set school buildings, strolling through a series of classrooms with tatami mat flooring. The rooms are rather gloomily lit but have enough visual displays, paintings and artefacts to offer an insight into the lives of those privileged enough to receive the rigorous academic training provided here.

Practicalities

Mito is on the Jōban line between Tokyo and Hitachi. The easiest way to get there is to take the frequent express **train** departing from Ueno Station (65min; ¥4200 one way). Mito's **tourist information centre** (daily 9.30am–4pm; ☎0292/21-6456) is a desk in the View Plaza on your left as you exit the turnstiles. The solitary staff member on duty should speak some English, and they have plenty of English-language material to help you on your way. Mito is known for its "old style" ramen – coarser than usual, and in a plainer soup unsullied by Korean culinary influences. The tourist information centre dishes out walking maps showing the best-known ramen restaurants. The town is also known for its *nattō* dishes, a strong-smelling fermented soy bean product in a mucus-like substance. The *Kairakuen Rest House*, outside the east gate of the garden opposite the main temple, offers a ¥2500 set meal featuring *nattō* tempura, *nattō* soup, and even *nattō* ice cream. If for some reason that doesn't appeal, try the decent selection of restaurants on the sixth floor of the Excel department store adjoining the station complex.

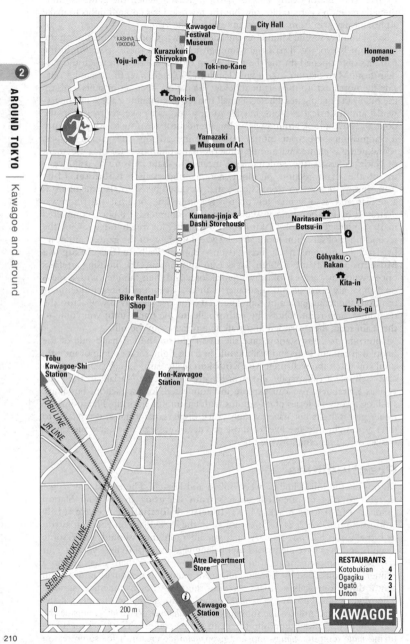

2

AROUND TOKYO | Kawagoe and around

City Hall

Kawagoe Festival Museum

KASHIYA YOKOCHŌ

Honmanu-goten

Kurazukuri Shiryokan ❶

Yoju-in

Toki-no-Kane

Choki-in

N

Yamazaki Museum of Art

❷   ❸

Kumano-jinja & Dashi Storehouse

Naritasan Betsu-in

❹

Gōhyaku Rakan

Kita-in

Bike Rental Shop

Tōshō-gū

CHUO-DORI

Tōbu Kawagoe-Shi Station

Hon-Kawagoe Station

TŌBU LINE

JR LINE

SEIBU SHINJUKU LINE

Atre Department Store

0   200 m

ℹ

Kawagoe Station

RESTAURANTS

Kotobukian	4
Ogagiku	2
Ogatō	3
Unton	1

KAWAGOE

Kawagoe and around

Saitama-ken, immediately northeast of the capital, comes in for a lot of stick as an achingly dull place. This is a gross generalization and, if anything, the prefecture should be high on your list of places to visit because it's home to the old castle town of **KAWAGOE**, an interesting and highly enjoyable day-trip, only 40km north of Tokyo. Although it doesn't look promising on arrival, Kawagoe's compact area of sights, around 1km north of the main station, is aptly described as a "Little Edo", and can easily be toured in a few hours, although once you've browsed the many traditional craft shops and paused to sample the town's culinary delights you'll probably find the day has flown by. This would certainly be the case on the third Saturday and Sunday of October, when Kawagoe's grand **matsuri** is held, one of the most lively festivals in the Tokyo area, involving some 25 ornate floats (called *dashi*) and hundreds of costumed revellers.

Kawagoe's fortunes owe everything to its strategic position on the Shingashi River and Kawagoe-kaidō, the ancient highway to the capital. If you wanted to get goods to Tokyo, then called Edo, they more than likely had to go via Kawagoe, and the town's merchants prospered as a result, accumulating the cash to build fireproof **kurazukuri**, the black, two-storey shop-houses the town is now famous for. At one time there were over 200 of these houses, but their earthenware walls didn't prove quite so effective against fire as hoped (nor were they much use in the face of Japan's headlong rush to modernization). Even so, some thirty still remain, with sixteen prime examples clustered together along Chūō-dōri, around 1km north of the JR and Tōbu stations.

Along Chūō-dōri, around 200m before the main enclave of *kurazukuri*, you'll pass a small shrine, **Kumano-jinja**, beside which is a tall storehouse containing a magnificent *dashi* float; this is your only chance to inspect one up close outside of the annual festival. At the next major crossroads, on the left-hand side, is the old Kameya *okashi* (sweet) shop, warehouse and factory. These buildings now house the **Yamazaki Museum of Art** (daily except Thurs and the last two days of the month; 9.30am–5pm; ¥500), dedicated to the works of Meiji-era artist Gaho Hashimoto. Some of his elegant screen paintings hang in the main gallery, while there are artistic examples of the sugary confections once made here in the converted *kura* (storehouses); entry includes a cup of tea and *okashi*.

Heading up Chūō-dōri, you'll pass several craft shops, including *Machikan*, which specializes in knives and swords (costing anything from ¥20,000 to ¥800,000), and *Sōbiki Atelier*, which sells woodwork. On the left, take a moment to duck into **Choki-in**, a temple with a statue of an emaciated Gandara-style Buddha in its grounds along with a pretty lily pond and sculpted bushes and trees. Back on the main street, the **Kurazukuri Shiryōkan** museum (Tues–Sun 9am–5pm; ¥100) is housed inside an old tobacco wholesaler's, one of the first *kurazukuri* to be rebuilt after the great fire of 1893. In the living quarters you can squeeze around the tiny twisting staircase that leads from the upper to the ground level, and one of the *kura* contains early twentieth-century firefighting uniforms and woodblock prints of the fires that ravaged the town. Just north of here on the main road is the new **Kawagoe Festival Museum** (daily except second and fourth Wed of the month; 9.30am–4.30/5pm; ¥500) which houses two magnificent *dashi* floats along with videos of past festivals and various displays, though there are no English descriptions.

Kawagoe

Kawagoe	*Kawagoe*	川越
Chōki-in	*Chōki-in*	長喜院
Honmaru-goten	*Honmaru-goten*	本丸御殿
John Lennon Museum	*Jon Renon Myūjiamu*	ジョンレノンミュージアム
Kashiya Yokochō	*Kashiya Yokochō*	菓子屋横町
Kita-in	*Kita-in*	喜多院
Kumano-jinja	*Kumano-jinja*	熊野神社
Kurazukuri Shiryōkan	*Kurazukuri Shiryōkan*	蔵造り資料館
Naritasan Betsu-in	*Naritasan Betsu-in*	成田山別院
Saitama Shintoshin	*Saitama Shintoshin*	さいたま新都心
Toki-no-kane	*Toki-no-kane*	時の鐘
Yamazaki Museum of Art	*Yamazaki Bijutsukan*	山崎美術館
Yoju-in	*Yoju-in*	養寿院
Eating		
Kotobukian	*Kotobukian*	寿庵
Ogagiku	*Ogagiku*	小川菊
Ogatō	*Ogatō*	小川藤
Unton	*Unton*	うんとん

Opposite the Kurazukuri Shiryōkan, you won't miss the **Toki-no-Kane**, the wooden bell tower, rebuilt in 1894, that was used to raise the alarm when fires broke out. An electric motor now powers the bell, which is rung four times daily. Take the turning on the left after the bell tower and follow it down until you reach **Yoju-in**, another handsomely wrought temple with pleasant grounds. Just north of here is the **Kashiya Yokochō**, or confectioners' alley, a picturesque pedestrian street still lined with several colourful sweet and toy shops – another great place to browse for souvenirs.

It's a 500-metre hike east of the Kurazukuri Shiryōkan, along the main road, to reach the scant remains of **Kawagoe Castle**, now mainly parkland and the grounds of the senior high school, but still containing the vast **Honmaru-goten**, the former residence of the *daimyō*. There's a museum inside (Tues–Sun 9am–5pm; ¥100) containing mainly archeological artefacts, but it's the building itself, dating from 1848, that is the main attraction, with its Chinese-style gabled roof, spacious tatami rooms and gorgeous painted screens.

Heading south from the castle grounds you'll soon reach **Naritasan Betsu-in**, an otherwise unremarkable shrine that comes to life on the 28th of each month, when it hosts a busy flea market.

Kita-in

Some 500m southeast of the *kurazukuri* lies **Kita-in**, the main temple complex of the Tendai Buddhist sect and one of Kawagoe's highlights. There's been a temple on these grounds since 830 AD, and it gained fame when the first Tōkugawa Shogun Ieyasu declared the head priest Tenkai Sōjō a "living Buddha". Such was the reverence in which the priests here were held that, when the temple burnt down in 1638, the third Shogun, Iemitsu, donated a secondary palace from Edo Castle (on the site of Tokyo's present-day Imperial Palace) as a replacement building. This was dismantled and moved here piece by piece, and is now the only remaining structure from Edo Castle which survives anywhere.

You have to pay an entry fee (¥400) to view the palace part of the temple, but it's well worth it. The room with a painted floral ceiling is believed to be where Iemitsu was born. Serene gardens surround the palace and a covered wooden bridge leads across into the temple's inner sanctum, decorated with a dazzling golden chandelier. The entry fee also includes access to the **Gōhyaku Rakan**, a remarkable grove of stone statues. Although the name translates as "500 Rakans", there are actually 540 of these enigmatic dwarf disciples of Buddha, and no two are alike. It's also fun to search for the statue which bears the Chinese symbols of your birth year. Kita-in also has its own mini **Tōshō-gū**. Like its famous cousin in Nikkō, this enshrines the spirit of Tokugawa Ieyasu and is decorated with bright colours and elaborate carvings.

Practicalities

Of the choice of three **train lines** to Kawagoe, the fastest service is the express on the Tōbu line from Ikebukuro (32min; ¥450); you can either get off at Kawagoe Station (which is also on the slower JR Saikyō line) or at Tōbu Kawagoe-shi, which is marginally closer to Chūō-dōri. Seibu Shinjuku line trains run from Shinjuku to Hon-Kawagoe Station (43min; ¥480), which is the most convenient of the lot for the *kurazukuri*. Immediately northwest of the main square in front of the Seibu line terminus is the Shimo bicycle store (closed Wed and second Thurs of the month; some English spoken), where you can rent **bicycles** (¥700 per day) – handy if you plan to see all of Kawagoe's somewhat scattered sights. Note that there's an unrelated bicycle repair shop (which doesn't hire out bikes) confusingly close to the Shimo store.

The staff at the **tourist information office** (daily 9am–4.30pm; ℡0492/ 22-5556, ⓦwww.sainokuni-kanko.jp/english/index.html) at Kawagoe Station don't speak English but can provide you with a map of the town and an English pamphlet on the sights. They can also recommend local accommodation, but the town is so close to Tokyo that there's no need to stay the night. It is, however, worth lingering in Kawagoe for its fine range of **eating** options. The local speciality is *unagi* (eel); a couple of good rustic places to try this rich dish are *Ogatō* and *Ogagiku*, both a short walk southeast of the *kurazukuri*. *Kotobukian*, beside Kita-in, is renowned for its *soba* (buckwheat noodles) and eel. For udon, try the popular *Unton*, behind the soy-sauce store Kinbue on Chūō-dōri, opposite the Kawagoe Festival Museum.

Around Kawagoe: the John Lennon Museum

Around 23km from Kawagoe lies the absorbing **John Lennon Museum** (daily except Tues 11am-6pm; ¥1500; ℡048-601-0009, ⓦwww.taisei.co.jp/museum). It's easy to be cynical about this blatant cash grab: the semi-governmental body in charge of the museum was looking to draw in the crowds when it splurged £12.7m on building it and, so far, their investment has been well justified by the museum's popularity. Overall, however, the museum makes a genuine attempt to honour one of the twentieth century's most iconic pop artists, despite the tendency to idealize Lennon and Yoko Ono's life (Ono was instrumental in helping establish the museum, gifting it many personal items), and anyone with even a casual interest in pop culture will enjoy seeing Lennon's original sketches, scribbled lyrics, instruments and much more. Keep an eye too on Yoko Ono's art exhibit "Telephone Peace": if this white telephone rings when you pass it, pick it up and you'll find yourself chatting with the artist – apparently Ono calls from time to time to find out how things are going.

The closest **train** station is Saitama Shintoshin on the Keihin Tōhoku, Utsunomiya and Takasaki train lines from Ueno in Tokyo (around 35min); the museum is a five-minute walk from the station. Kita-yono station, on the Saikyo line from Shinjuku and Ikebukuro, is also close by.

Mt Takao and around

Heading west from Shinjuku Station along the Chūō line there are several pleasant day-trip opportunities, the best of which is a visit to **Mount Takao**, crowned by a picturesque temple, **Yakuo–in**, which hosts a spectacular fire-walking festival annually. The rest of the year, pilgrims are joined by multitudes of hikers who meander along the many trails around the 600-metre mountain; several paths lead further afield to Chichibu-Tama National Park to the northwest. If you're heading directly to the park, **Mitake** is a main gateway. As at Takao, the nearby Mount Mitake (930m) is home to an ancient, picturesque shrine.

Closer to Tokyo (and not to be confused with Mitake) is Mitaka, where those with kids or anyone interested in animation should consider dropping by the charming **Ghibli Museum, Mitaka**, where you can see the wonderful work of Oscar-winning animator Miyazaki Hayao (see p.995). Finally, between Mitake and Takao at Musashi Koganei, is the **Edo-Tokyo Open Air Architectural Museum**, an annexe of the Edo-Tokyo Museum (see p.122) and a convenient, if somewhat sterile, place to view prime examples of vernacular architecture from the mid-nineteenth century onwards saved from the wrecking ball.

Mount Takao

Only an hour west of Shinjuku, **MOUNT TAKAO**, also referred to as Takao-san, is a popular hiking area – so much so that you'd be well advised to avoid it at the weekend, when the main trails are clogged with day-trippers and picnic parties cover the slopes of the mountain. This said, Takao-san, surrounded by a quasi-national park and also home to the attractive and venerable **Yakuo-in** temple, is a particularly pleasant place midweek for a quick escape from Tokyo, and a starting point for longer trails into the mountains.

Mt Takao and around

Mount Takao	*Takao-san*	高尾山
Mount Kobotoke Shiroyama	*Mount Kobotoke Shiroyama*	小仏城山
Ukai Toriyama	*Ukai Toriyama*	うかい鳥山
Yakuo-in	*Yakuo-in*	薬王院
Mitake	*Mitake*	御岳
Chichibu-Tama National Park	*Chichibu-Tama Kokuritsu-kōen*	秩父多摩国立公園
Gyokudō Art Museum	*Gyokudō Bijutsukan*	玉堂美術館
Mitake-jinja	*Mitake-jinja*	御嶽神社
Mitake Youth Hostel	*Mitake Yūsu Hosuteru*	御嶽ユースホステル
Momiji-ya	*Momiji-ya*	紅葉屋
Edo-Tokyo Open Air Architectural Museum	*Edo-Tōkyō Tatemono-kōen*	江戸東京建物公園
Ghibli Museum, Mitaka	*Jiburi Myūjiamu, Mitaka*	ジブリミュージアム三鷹
Inokashira Park	*Inokashira-kōen*	井の頭公園

The Keiō line from Shinjuku provides the simplest and cheapest way of reaching the terminus of Takao-san-guchi (1hr; ¥370). If you take the slightly slower and more expensive JR Chūō line, you'll need to change to the Keiō line at Takao to go one last stop to Takao-san-guchi. It comes as something of a relief to arrive here, as the unremitting city sprawl is brought to a halt by the verdant slopes of the Takao Quasi National Park.

There are seven marked trails on the mountain, of various lengths and difficulty, with the longest three starting from Takao-san-guchi; all are detailed on a map (in Japanese) provided by the Keiō train company, or in English from the TICs in Tokyo (see p.98) or the Takao Visitor Centre at the top of the mountain. To reach the start of these trails turn right outside the station and follow the riverside path for 100m past the noodle restaurants to the **cable car and chairlifts** (both ¥470 one way, ¥900 return). If you take these, you'll save a kilometre or so of slogging up the main no. 1 trail.

Rejoin the no. 1 trail at the top of the cable-car station, pass the undistinguished **Wild Grass and Monkey Park** (daily 9.30am–4.30pm; ¥500), home to scores of Japanese macaques, and continue to the ranks of red-painted lanterns leading up to **Yakuo-in**. This temple was founded in the eighth century and is notable for the ornate polychromatic carvings which decorate its main hall, very reminiscent of those in Nikkō. In front of the hall and dotted around the temple grounds are striking statues of Tengu, the winged, Pinocchio-nosed deity of the mountains. Just before climbing the stairs to the main hall, pause to sample the *okashi* (sweets) and nuts offered at a temple stall – good hiking snacks for later in the day. Yakuo-in also has a small temple beside the Biwataki falls on the no. 6 trail (see below) and hosts a spectacular **fire ritual** annually on the second Sunday in March back in Takao-san-guchi, where you can watch priests and pilgrims march across hot coals – and even follow them yourself.

It doesn't take very long from the temple to reach Takao's summit, where you'll find a cluster of *soba* stalls and the **visitor centre** (Tues–Sun 10am–4pm; ☎0426/64-6157), which has some nature displays, though all the information is in Japanese. On a fine day there are good views back towards the city and, in the opposite direction, if you're really lucky, of Mount Fuji. However, those hoping for a real hiking workout would be forgiven for feeling somewhat shortchanged. If you want to continue, take the path down the hill behind the visitor centre and pick up the undulating trail to **Mount Kobotoke Shiroyama** (670m), another 45 minutes away, where the panoramic views of Lake Sagami make up for the ugly telecommunications tower. This route is also part of the seven-stage, 74-kilometre **Kantō Fureai-no-michi** hike from Takao-san-guchi to Kamihinata in the Chichibu-Tama-Kai National Park; pick up a topographical map from the visitor centre if you plan to follow this trail.

Of the several routes back from the visitor centre to Takao-san-guchi, no. 6 trail is particularly attractive, passing through a range of forest habitats and then hugging the side of a stream (and at one point running down its rocky centre). On the way you'll pass the **Biwataki**, a freezing waterfall under which religious ascetics take a shower. This route remains within the trees; if you want some more countryside views, follow the Inariyama trail. Neither route should take more than ninety minutes at a steady pace.

While there are plenty of places to **eat** along the trails and at Takao-san-guchi, with rustic cafés dishing up soba and udon noodles, there's little to choose between them and they tend to be overpriced and undistinguished. The exception is the delightful *Ukai Toriyama* (☎0426/61-0739), a traditional restaurant in a sylvan setting specializing in charcoal-broiled chicken and Hida beef; meals are served by kimono-clad waitresses in small tatami rooms. Set-course menus start at ¥4500.

Mitake

The mountains in the 126,259-hectare **Chichibu-Tama National Park** provide the headwaters for several fast flowing rivers including the Tama-gawa. The attractively rocky gorge that this river flows through as it passes **MITAKE** is what sets this sleepy town apart from nearby Takao; there are also several places to stay on Mount Mitake, including a pleasant youth hostel in an old thatched building. Otherwise, Mitake shares many similar features with Takao: a cable car up a sacred mountain, an attractive temple and plenty of easy to follow hiking trails which get crowded on weekends and holidays. A midweek day-trip from Tokyo is best if you want to avoid the weekend crowds.

Heading here from Shinjuku Station, you'll again need to take the JR Chūō line, then branch off at Hajima Station onto the Ome line. This runs alongside the Tama-gawa, providing fine views of the river and **gorge**; to get up close, alight at Ikusabata or Sawai station and follow the riverside walk to Mitake Station, where you'll find the **Mitake Information Centre** (☎0428/78-8836; Tues–Sun 8am–4pm) which has maps of the area. The assistants are unlikely to speak English, but they will point out the stop across the road at which you can catch a bus (¥270) heading to the cable car up Mount Mitake. The buses are fairly frequent, but if you have time to kill it's worth crossing the bridge over to the river's south side and visiting the **Gyokudō Art Museum** (☎0428/78-8335; ¥500; Tues–Sun 10am–5pm), home to some fine paintings by Gyokudo Kawai (1873-1957) and a serene Zen rock garden.

The **cable car** (¥570 one-way) will deposit you near the summit of the 929-metre sacred mountain, about twenty minutes' walk from the 1250-year-old **Mitake-jinja**. The statue in front of this picturesque shrine is of the Kamakura-era hero Hatakeyama Shigetada; his armour is on display in the shrine's treasure house (daily 9.30am-4.30pm; ¥300), but it's not that interesting that you'd really want to pay to see it. On the way to the shrine from the cable car you'll pass another **visitor centre** (Tues–Sun 9am–4.30pm; ☎0428/78-9363). The assistants here have more maps and can help you find a good hiking route or accommodation on the mountain at one of several attractively thatched traditional houses. These include the reasonable *Mitake Youth Hostel* (☎0428/78-8774; ⓦwww.jyh.or.jp; ❶), a quiet place to hang out for a day or two. If you're hungry, try a traditional dish of noodles at *Momiji-ya*, a simple café by the approach to the shrine.

Edo-Tokyo Open Air Architectural Museum

A kind of retirement home for old Tokyo buildings which have proved surplus to requirements in modern times, the **Edo-Tokyo Open Air Architectural Museum** is worth swinging by on your way to or from Takao or Mitake if you don't have the time to visit similar (and better) museums around the country, such as Meiji-Mura near Nagoya (see p.479) or the Historical Village of Hokkaidō near Sapporo (see p.369). The museum was the inspiration for the abandoned theme park in Studio Ghibli's Oscar-winning *Spirited Away* (see p.999).

The museum (Tues–Sun: April–Sept 9.30am–5.30pm; Oct–March 9.30am–4.30pm; ¥400) is set within the parkland of Koganei-kōen, a twenty-minute walk north of Musashi Koganei Station or a five-minute bus ride (¥170). Some 35 buildings of varying degrees of interest are gathered here, plus an exhibition hall with archeological artefacts and folk crafts. You can enter most of the buildings (taking your shoes off first), whose interiors have also been faithfully preserved or recreated. On the west side of the sprawling complex, the most engaging structure is the very grand Mitsue residence, an 1852 mansion moved from Kyoto and furnished with painted screens, lacquered shrines and chandeliers. There are also several thatched farmhouses. On the east side a Shitamachi (Tokyo downtown) street of houses and shops has been reconstructed, including a tailor's shop and stationer's, plus kitchenware and flower stores. The highlight is a public bathhouse, a veritable palace of ablutions with magnificent Chinese-style gables and a lakeside view of Fuji painted on the tiled wall inside. Also look out for the House of Uemura, its copper cladding pocked by shrapnel from World War II bombings.

Ghibli Museum, Mitaka

Less than thirty minutes out of Shinjuku along the Chūō line is **MITAKA**, near where you'll find the charmingly inventive **Ghibli Museum, Mitaka** (daily except Tues 10am–6pm; ¥1000, reductions for children; ☎0570/055777, Ⓦwww.ghibli-museum.jp), located at the southwest corner of leafy Inokashira Park. The museum celebrates the work of the Ghibli animation studio, responsible for some of Japan's biggest ever movies, including *My Neighbour Totoro*, *Princess Mononoke* and the Oscar-winning *Spirited Away* (see p.999). Beautifully designed throughout, the museum gives visitors an insight not only into Ghibli's films but also the animator's art in general. There's also a small movie theatre where original short animated features, exclusive to the museum, are screened. Kids will love it, and it's a guaranteed fun day out that will probably have you scurrying to the video shop later.

In order to keep the museum free of crowds, only 2400 entry **tickets** are available daily; all must be purchased in advance and are for a specified time. The museum's website lists details in English of how to apply for tickets overseas. This is much easier than applying for tickets in Japan itself, where you'll first have to make a reservation by phone (☎0570/00-0403, if your Japanese is up to it), then go to one of the country's 7600 Lawson convenience stores within three days to pick up your ticket; you'll need to specify the date and time (10am, noon, 2pm or 4pm) you would like to visit. Given the massive popularity of Ghibli's movies, the museum can be booked out for weeks at a time, particularly during school holidays and over weekends.

The museum is a short walk or bus ride from the south exit of Mitaka Station on the JR Chūō line. Follow the canal for about fifteen minutes towards Inokashira Park (there are signs) or take the regular bus (¥200). It's a good idea to combine a visit here with a stroll around **Inokashira Park**, which has a pleasant carp-filled lake, tree-shaded walks and a small zoo. Long a favourite haunt of courting couples, during *hanami* season the park is a profusion of pink blossoms.

Fuji Five Lakes

The best reason for heading 100km west from Tokyo towards the area known as **Fuji Five Lakes** is to climb **Mount Fuji**, Japan's most sacred volcano and, at 3776m, its highest mountain. Fuji-san, as it's respectfully known by the Japanese, has long been worshipped for its latent power (it last erupted in 1707) and near-perfect symmetry; it is most beautiful from October to May, when the summit is crowned with snow. The climbing season (see box, p.220) runs from July to September, but even if you don't fancy making the rather daunting ascent, just getting up close to Japan's most famous national symbol is a memorable experience.

Fuji Five Lakes		
Fuji Five Lakes	*Fuji Go-ko*	富士五湖
Fujikyū Highland	*Fujikyū Hairando*	富士急ハイランド
Fuji Sengen-jinja	*Fuji Sengen-jinja*	富士浅間神社
Fuji-Yoshida	*Fuji-Yoshida*	富士吉田
Kawaguchi-ko	*Kawaguchi-ko*	河口湖
Kubota Itchiku Art Museum	*Kubota Itchiku Bijutsukan*	久保田一竹美術館
Motosu-ko	*Motosu-ko*	本栖湖
Mount Fuji	*Fuji-san*	富士山
Sai-ko	*Sai-ko*	西湖
Shōji-ko	*Shōji-ko*	精進湖
Yamanaka-ko	*Yamanaka-ko*	山中湖

Accommodation and eating

Fuji-Yoshida Youth Hostel	*Fuji-Yoshida Yūsu Hosuteru*	富士吉田ユースホステル
Hanaya	*Hanaya*	花屋
Kawaguchi-ko Youth Hostel	*Kawaguchi-ko Yūsu Hosuteru*	河口湖ユースホステル
Petit Hotel Ebisuya	*Puchi Hoteru Ebisuya*	プチホテルエビスヤ
Taikoku-ya	*Taikoku-ya*	大国屋

Apart from Fuji-san, the single most interesting place to head for is the area's transport hub of **Fuji-Yoshida**, with its wonderfully atmospheric shrine, **Fuji Sengen-jinja**, and nearby state-of-the-art amusement park. During the summer, the **five lakes** – the large Yamanaka-ko, south of Fuji-Yoshida, touristy Kawaguchi-ko to the west, and the smaller lakes of Sai-ko, Shōji-ko and Motosu-ko – are packed with urbanites fleeing the dust and grime of Tokyo. The best lake to head for is **Kawaguchi-ko**: as well as being a popular starting point for climbing Mount Fuji, it features a kimono museum and the easily climbable Mount Tenjō, with its outstanding views of Fuji-san and the surrounding lakes.

Fuji-Yoshida, Kawaguchi-ko and around

FUJI-YOSHIDA, some 100km west of Tokyo, lies so close to Mount Fuji that when the dormant volcano eventually blows her top the local residents will be toast. For the time being, however, this small, prosperous town acts as an efficient transport hub for the area, as well as the traditional departure point for journeys up the volcano, with frequent buses leaving for Fuji-san's fifth station (see box on p.220) from outside the train station.

The volcano aside, the town's main attraction is its Shinto shrine. To reach it, head southwest from the station uphill along the main street, Honchō-dōri, which will take you past several ornate **pilgrims' inns** (*oshi-no-ie*). These old lodging houses, where pilgrims used to stay before climbing Mount Fuji, are set back from the road, their entrances marked by narrow stone pillars. Some of the inns still operate as minshuku today (see "Accommodation", p.221). Where the road hits a junction, turn left and after a couple of hundred metres you'll see a giant *torii* and a broad gravel pathway lined with stone lanterns leading to **Fuji Sengen-jinja**, a large, colourful shrine set in a small forest. Sengen shrines, dedicated to the worship of volcanoes, encircle Fuji, but this is the most important, dating right back to 788. The beautiful main shrine (*honden*) was built in 1615. Look around the back for the jolly, brightly painted wooden carvings of the deities Ebisu the fisherman and Daikoku, the god of wealth, good humour and happiness, who appears content to let a rat nibble at the bales of rice he squats upon.

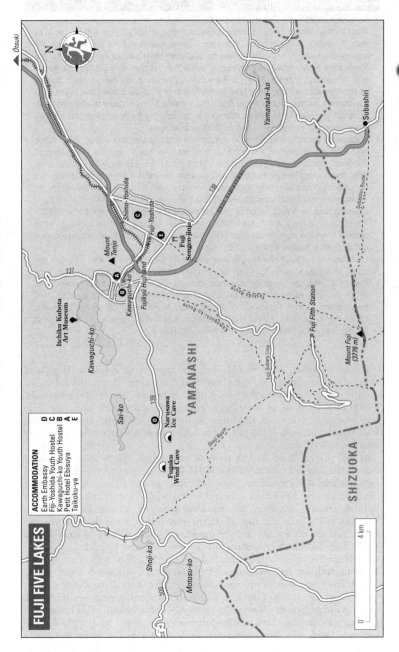

FUJI FIVE LAKES

ACCOMMODATION
Earth Embassy   D
Fiji-Yoshida Youth Hostel   C
Kawaguchi-ko Youth Hostel   B
Petit Hotel Ebisuya   A
Taikoku-ya   E

N

▲ Ōtsuki

Yamanaka-ko

● Subashiri

Fuji Expressway

138

Subashiri Route

Shimo-Yoshida

Mount Tenjo ▲

Fuji-Yoshida

Fuji Sengen-jinja

Yoshida Route

137

Fujikyu Highland

Kawaguchi-ko

Itchiku Kubota Art Museum ◆

Kawaguchi-ko Route

Fuji Fifth Station

Kawaguchi-ko

Sai-ko

Fuji Subaru Line

Mount Fuji (3776 m) ▲

YAMANASHI

139

● Narusawa Ice Cave

Shoji Route

■ Fugaku Wind Cave

SHIZUOKA

Shoji-ko

300

Matosu-ko

0   4 km

Climbing Mount Fuji

"A wise man climbs Fuji once. A fool climbs it twice," says the Japanese proverb – don't let the sight of children and grannies trudging up lull you into a false sense of security: this is a tough climb. There are several **routes** up the volcano, with the ascent divided into sections known as **stations**. Most people take a bus to the Kawaguchi-ko fifth station (*go-gōme*), where a Swiss chalet-style giftshop marks the end of the road about halfway up the volcano. The traditional hike, though, begins at Fuji-Yoshida; walking from here to the fifth station takes around five hours, and it's another six hours before you reach the summit. Many choose to climb at night to reach the summit by dawn; during the season, the lights of climbers' torches resemble a line of fireflies trailing up the volcanic scree.

Essential items to carry include at least one litre of water and some food, a torch and batteries, a raincoat and extra clothes; however hot it might be at the start of the climb, the closer you get to the summit the colder it becomes, with temperatures dropping to well below freezing, and sudden rain and lightning strikes are not uncommon. You can rest en route at any of seventeen **huts**, most of which provide dorm accommodation from around ¥5000 per night for just a bed (no need for a sleeping bag), and ¥7000 with dinner. It's essential to book in advance (℡0555/22-1948). Once at the summit, it will take you around an hour to make a circuit of the crater. Otherwise you can take part in the time-honoured tradition of making a phone call or mailing a letter from the post office.

Mount Fuji's official **climbing season**, when all the facilities on the mountain are open, including lodging huts and pay phones at the summit, runs from July 1 to August 27. You can climb outside these dates, but don't expect all, or indeed any, of the facilities to be in operation, and be prepared for snow and extreme cold towards the summit. For more details, pick up a free copy of the *Mt Fuji Climber's Guide Book*, published by the Fuji-Yoshida city hall and available at the local tourist information office (see opposite) and Tokyo TIC (see p.98).

These fun-loving gods would certainly approve of **Fujikyū Highland** (Mon–Fri 9am–5pm, Sat 9am–7pm, Sun 9am–6pm; closed third Tues of month, except Aug, when the park is open daily 8am–9pm; ¥1200 entry only, ¥4500 one-day pass), an appealingly ramshackle amusement park, one train stop west of Fuji-Yoshida, and featuring the terrifying Fujiyama rollercoaster. It's a popular place, so avoid coming at weekends or holidays unless you enjoy standing in long queues.

At first glance, there doesn't seem to be a whole lot to recommend the shabby lakeside resort of **KAWAGUCHI-KO**, a couple of kilometres west of Fuji-Yoshida. With its dolphin-shaped cruise boats and crass souvenir shops, this is the tourist hub of the area and is often choked with traffic during the holiday season. However, the fabulous view of Mount Fuji and lake Kawaguchi-ko from the top of **Tenjō-zan** makes a trip here worth the effort. You can either take a three-minute cable-car ride up to the lookout (daily 9am–5.20pm; ¥700 return), or get some exercise by hiking up, which takes around 45 minutes. Kawaguchi-ko's other highlight is the Gaudí-esque **Kubota Itchiku Art Museum** (April–Nov daily 9.30am–5.30pm; Jan & Feb daily except Tues 10am–5pm; March & Dec daily 10am–5pm; ¥1300), on the northern shore of the lake. This small museum, approached through a striking Indian gateway, houses the work of Kubota Itchiku, who has refined the traditional *tsujigahana* textile-patterning technique and applied it to kimono. Inside the pyramid-shaped building are pieces from the artist's *Symphony of Light* series, a continuous mountain landscape through the seasons, formed when the kimono are placed side by side. The museum is some

4km west of the town and can be reached by bus from both Fuji–Yoshida and Kawaguchi-ko.

The smallest of the other four lakes, horseshoe-shaped **Shōji-ko**, 2km west of Kawaguchi-ko, is by far the prettiest. The largest lake, **Yamanaka**, south of Fuji–Yoshida, is just as developed as Kawaguchi-ko and has fewer attractions, while **Motosu-ko** and **Sai-ko** are marginally less touristy, but not worth the trouble of visiting.

Practicalities

The easiest way to reach the Fuji Five Lakes area is to take the **bus** (¥1700) from the Shinjuku bus terminal in Tokyo, on the west side of the train station; in good traffic, the trip takes around one hour and 45 minutes, and during the climbing season there are frequent services, including at least three a day that run directly to the fifth station. The **train** journey from Shinjuku Station involves transferring from the JR Chūō line to the Fuji Kyūkō line at Ōtsuki, from where a local train chugs first to Fuji–Yoshida and then on to Kawaguchi-ko. On Sundays and public holidays, an early-morning train from Shinjuku does the trip in just over two hours.

The best place for **information** is the Fuji–Yoshida Tourist Information Service (daily 9am–5.30pm; ℡0555/22-7000, ⒲www.city.fujiyoshida .yamanashi.jp), to the left as you exit Fuji–Yoshida Station. The helpful English-speaking staff will shower you with leaflets and can help with accommodation. Similar services are provided at the Kawaguchi-ko Tourist Information Centre (daily 9am–4.30pm; ℡0555/72-6700), outside Kawaguchi-ko Station, and the Fuji Information Centre (daily 8am–6pm; ℡0555/72-2121), five minutes' walk west of the station on the way to the youth hostel.

A comprehensive system of buses will help you **get around** once you've arrived at either Fuji–Yoshida or Kawaguchi-ko. Individual bus fares are high, so if you're going to be touring the area it's worth buying the Yutari Fuji Isshu Free Pass (¥3500) at Shinjuku or as soon as you arrive at Ōtsuki – this is valid for three days and covers all rail travel and buses around the five lakes, plus tickets for the cable car and lake cruise at Kawaguchi-ko.

Accommodation

Fuji–Yoshida and Kawaguchi-ko have plenty of good **places to stay**, including youth hostels and hotels. Fuji climbers could consider overnighting in one of the mountain huts (see box opposite), but the claustrophobic should stick to the roomier accommodation at the base of the mountain. There are also several campsites around the lakes.

Earth Embassy and Solar Café Narusawa-mura 8529-74 ℡0555/85-2576, ⒲www.earthembassy .org. This organic café and farm is run by volunteers who love cooking and farming workshops as well as provide basic dorm accommodation (¥2500 per person) and camping space (¥2000 per person, or ¥1500 per person if you bring your own tent). Reservations strongly advised. Add ¥2000 for a vegetarian dinner and breakfast. Take the local (not express) Motosuko bus from Kawaguchi-ko Station (last bus 7:23pm) and get off at the Koyodai Entrance bus stop. The Embassy is on Route 139, 300m past the bus stop on the right.

Fuji-Yoshida Youth Hostel 2-339 Shimo Yoshida Hon-chō, Fuji-Yoshida-shi ℡0555/22-0533, ⒲www.jyh.or.jp. Small, basic hostel in a family home twenty minutes' walk from Fuji-Yoshida Station, or a shorter walk from Shimo-Yoshida, the preceding station. English is spoken and you can also get meals. Dorm beds ¥2700 per person.
Kawaguchi-ko Youth Hostel 2128 Funatsu, Kawaguchi-ko-machi ℡0555/72-1431, ⒲www.jyh.or.jp. Run by a friendly manager who speaks a little English, this large hostel, a five-minute walk southwest of Kawaguchi-ko Station, has tatami rooms and bunks, and bikes for rent (¥800 per day). Dorm beds ¥2900 per person.

Petit Hotel Ebisuya 3647 Funatsu, Kawaguchi-ko-machi ☎0555/72-0165, ℻72-1165. Though it's not much to look at from the outside, this family-run hotel is conveniently located to the right of the concourse as you come out of Kawaguchi-ko Station and has splendid views of Mount Fuji from some of its tatami rooms. The café downstairs serves hearty set meals. ❺

Taikoku-ya Honchō-dōri, Fuji-Yoshida ☎0555/22-3778. This original pilgrim's inn on the main road still takes guests in its very traditional and beautifully decorated tatami rooms from May to September. Note that the owner prefers not to accept guests who can't make themselves understood in Japanese. ❺, including two meals.

Eating

The best place to **eat** is Fuji-Yoshida, renowned for its thick *teuchi udon* (handmade) noodles, prepared and served in people's homes at lunchtime only – the tourist information office can provide a list and map of the best places (in Japanese). One of the easiest to locate is the convivial *Hanaya*, towards the top of Honchō-dōri, which serves just three types of dishes: *yumori*, noodles in a soup; *zaru*, cold noodles, and *sara*, warm noodles dipped in hot soup – simple stuff, but manna from heaven compared to the dreary, overpriced tourist cafés in **Kawaguchi-ko**, where the best option is a picnic lunch from the lakeside 7-Eleven convenience store. During the climbing season you can buy snacks and stamina-building dishes, such as curry rice, from the huts on Mount Fuji – but the prices, needless to say, are high.

Hakone

South of Mount Fuji and 90km west of Tokyo is the lakeland and mountain area known as **HAKONE**. There aren't any must-see sights here, but a visit to the region is enjoyable, especially if you follow the well-established day-trip route, which combines rides on several trains or buses, a funicular, cable car and pirate ship. You can also take in the lake, **Ashino-ko**, numerous **onsen**, some excellent walks, several art museums, and – weather permitting – great views of nearby Mount Fuji. There's so much to do that an overnight stop is best, especially if you want to unwind at one of Hakone's top-notch hotels and ryokan, all with their own hot-spring baths. The region is always busy on weekends and holidays, however; if you want to avoid the crowds, come during the week. Excellent transport links mean that you can stay pretty much anywhere and go where you want within the day.

Getting around

The traditional day-trip route through Hakone runs anticlockwise in a series of madcap rides from Shinjuku Odakyū Station (on the west side of Shinjuku Station in Tokyo), to Hakone-Yumoto, gateway to the Fuji-Hakone-Izu National Park, then over Mount Sōun, across the length of Ashino-ko lake to Moto-Hakone and back to the start. Approaching Hakone from the west, you can follow a similar route clockwise from Hakone-machi on the southern shore of Ashino-ko to Hakone-Yumoto.

If you plan to follow the traditional route, it's well worth buying either the three-day **Hakone Free Pass** (¥5500) or the two-day **Hakone Weekday Pass** (¥4700), valid Monday to Thursday, not including public holidays. Both are available from Odakyū stations and cover a return journey on the Odakyū line from Shinjuku to Odawara, and unlimited use of the Hakone-Tōzan line, Hakone-Tōzan funicular railway, cable car, pirate boat across the lake and most local buses. The passes save you money on the total cost of all these trips and

HAKONE

FUJI-HAKONE-IZU
NATIONAL PARK

ACCOMMODATION

Chōraku	C
Fuji Hakone Guest House	A
Fujiya	E
Hakone Lake Villa Youth Hostel	G
Hakone Prince	F
Hakone Sengokuhara Youth Hostel	B
Moto-Hakone Guest House	H
Motonamikan	D

RESTAURANTS

| Gyōza Centre | 1 |
| Kodanaki | 2 |

Tokyo

ODAKYŪ LINE

Shinjuku

Odawara

Nagoya & Ōsaka

JR TOKAIDO LINE

TOKAIDO SHINKANSEN

Hakone Itabashi

Kazamatsuri

Iriuda

HAKONE-TOZAN LINE

Kappa
Tengoku
Notemburo

Hakone-Yumoto

Tenzan
Notemburo

Tonosawa

Ōhiradai

Miyanoshita

Mt Sengen
(804 m)

Kōwakudani

Hakone Open-Air Museum

Gora

Hakone
Museum
of Art

Sōunzan

Ōwakudani

Ōwakudani
Natural Science

Ubako

Sengokuhara

Gotemba & Mt Fuji

Gotemba

Ashi-no-ko
Camping
Ground

Tōgendai

Ashi-ko

Sightseeing Boats

Mt Komaga-take
(1357 m)

Hakone
Shrine

Moto-Hakone

Hakone Detached
Palace Garden

Amazake-jaya
Teahouse

Stone-paved
section of
Tōkaidō

Avenue of
Cryptomeria

Hakone
Barrier

Hakone-machi

Hatajuku

Hamamatsu & Nagoya

Atami

Ashi-no-ko Skyline Driveway

138

N

2 km

0

Hakone

Hakone	Hakone	箱根
Amazake-jaya Teahouse	Amazake-jaya	甘酒茶屋
Ashino-ko	Ashino-ko	芦の湖
Gōra	Gōra	強羅
Hakone Barrier	Hakone Sekisho	箱根関所
Hakone-machi	Hakone-machi	箱根町
Hakone Museum of Art	Hakone Bijutsukan	箱根美術館
Hakone Open-Air Museum	Chōkoku-no-Mori Bijutsukan	彫刻の森美術館
Hakone Gongen	Hakone Gongen	箱根権現
Hakone-Yumoto	Hakone-Yumoto	箱根湯元
Hatajuku	Hatajuku	畑宿
Kappa Tengoku Notemburo	Kappa Tengoku Notemburo	かっぱ天国野天風呂
Kōen-ue	Kōen-ue	公園上
Komaga-take	Komaga-take	駒ヶ岳
Miyanoshita	Miyanoshita	宮/下
Moto-Hakone	Moto-Hakone	元箱根
Odawara	Odawara	小田原
Ōwakudani	Ōwakudani	大湧谷
Ōwakudani Natural History Museum	Ōwakudani Shizen Kagakukan	大湧谷自然科学館
Tenzan Notemburo	Tenzan Notemburo	天山野天風呂

Accommodation

Chōraku	Chōraku	長楽
Fuji Hakone Guest House	Fuji Hakone Gesuto Hausu	富士箱根ゲストハウス
Fujiya Hotel	Fujiya Hoteru	富士屋ホテル
Hakone Lake Villa Youth Hostel	Hakone Reiku Vira Yūsu Hosuteru	箱根レイクヴィラユースホステル
Hakone Prince Hotel	Hakone Purinsu Hoteru	箱根プリンスホテル
Hakone Sengokuhara Youth Hostel	Hakone Sengokuhara Yūsu Hosuteru	箱根仙石原ユースホステル
Moto-Hakone Guest House	Moto-Hakone Gesuto Hausu	元箱根ゲストハウス
Motonamikan	Motonamikan	元波館

get you discounts at many of Hakone's attractions. For ¥870 extra one way, you can take the more comfortable "Romance Car", which goes directly through to Hakone-Yumoto in ninety minutes, around 25 minutes faster than the regular express train. With a JR pass, the fastest route is to take a Shinkansen to Odawara, from where you can catch either an Odakyū train or bus into the national park area (Odakyū transport passes from Odawara cost ¥4130 and ¥3410 respectively: there's also a ¥2000 one-day ticket that doesn't cover the cable car or the boat). If you don't fancy hopping on and off trains, take the Odakyū express **bus** (¥1950) from Shinjuku bus terminal – this will get you to Ashino-ko in a couple of hours.

Odawara and Hakone-Yumoto

Travelling from Tokyo to Hakone, you'll pass through the historic castle town of **ODAWARA**, some 75km west of the capital. The castle (daily 9am–4.30pm; ¥600) looks pretty impressive, especially in spring, when the cherry trees in the grounds explode in pink blossom, but it's a recent reconstruction and a visit here is soured by the appalling conditions of the zoo just next door.

It's better to press on to **HAKONE-YUMOTO**, the small town nestling in the valley at the gateway to the national park. Despite being marred by scores of concrete-block hotels and *bessō* (vacation lodges for company workers), not to mention the usual cacophony of souvenir shops, the town has some good **onsen**, ideal for unwinding after a day's sightseeing around the park. You can also pick up a **map** of the area at the Hakone Tourist Information Office (daily 9.30am–5.30pm, Ⓦwww.kankou.hakone.kanagawa.jp/index_e.html), across the street from the Hakone-Yumoto Station, in the buildings at the bus terminal. Up the hill from the station is the **Kappa Tengoku Notemburo** (daily 10am–10pm; ¥750), a small, traditional outdoor onsen, which can get crowded. More stylish is **Tenzan Notemburo** (daily 9am–11pm; ¥900), a luxurious public onsen complex at Oku-Yumoto, 2km southwest of town. The main building has separate male and female outdoor baths, including waterfalls and Jacuzzi baths, in a series of rocky pools. Men also have a clay-hut sauna, and for ¥200 extra on weekdays (¥900 on weekends) both men and women can use the wooden baths in the building across the car park. A free shuttle bus runs to the baths from the bridge just north of Hakone-Yumoto Station.

While you probably won't want to stay in Hakone-Yumoto, it's a good place **to eat**, with plenty of places to get a nourishing serving of noodles. *Yama Soba* is on the main road between the station and the tourist information office and serves up soba sets from ¥1100, while across the road is *Chikuzen*, the best of the town's udon restaurants. There are also three good-value restaurants at the Tenzan Notemburo, serving rice, *shabu-shabu* (sautéed beef) and *yakiniku* (grilled meat) dishes.

Miyanoshita and around

Rising up into the mountains, the Hakone-Tōzan switchback railway zigzags for nearly 9km alongside a ravine from Hakone-Yumoto to the village of Gōra (see p.226). There are small traditional inns and temples at several of the stations along the way, but the single best place to alight – and even stay overnight – is the village onsen resort of **MIYANOSHITA**. As well as hot springs, the village has decent antique shops along its main road, and several hiking routes up 804-metre **Mount Sengen** on the eastern flank of the railway – one path begins just beside the station. At the top, you'll get a great view of the gorge below.

Miyanoshita's real draw is its handful of splendid **hotels**. Worth popping into – if only for a peek at the handsome wooden interior – is the *Fujiya Hotel* (Ⓣ0460/2-2211, Ⓦwww.fujiyahotel.co.jp; ❻–❼), which opened for business in 1878 and is a living monument to a more glamorous era of travel. Despite being the first Western-style hotel in Japan, the *Fujiya* has lots of Japanese touches, including traditional gardens and temple-like decorative gables. The plush, 1950s-style decor is retro-chic and the rooms are good value, especially from Sunday to Friday, when foreign guests qualify for a cheaper rate. There's also the delightful, European-style *Motonamikan* (formerly the *Pension Yamaguchi*; Ⓣ0460/2-3158, Ⓔmotonami@jt5.so-net.ne.jp; ❼), a five-minute walk downhill from the train station, and tucked away off the main road behind the post office – the rates here include meals.

As far as **eating** goes, the *Fujiya*'s Orchid Lounge is great for afternoon tea, while its ornate French restaurant is an excellent, if pricey, choice for lunch or dinner. The *Picot Bakery* on the main road outside the *Fujiya* is a good place to pick up bread and cakes for breakfast or lunch. Opposite Miyanoshita's singularly unhelpful tourist information centre is *An*, a small, cheerful café with an English menu that features reasonably priced spaghetti and curry-rice dishes.

Around Miyanoshita

Moving on, two more stops on the Hakone-Tōzan railway bring you to Chōkoku-no-Mori Station, where the nearby **Hakone Open-Air Museum** (daily 9am–4pm, March–Nov until 5pm; ¥1600) is well worth making time for. This wide-ranging museum is packed with sculptures, with works from Rodin and Giacometti to Michelangelo reproductions and bizarre modern formations scattered across the landscaped grounds, which have lovely views across the mountains to the sea. There's an enclave of 26 pieces by Henry Moore, a "Picasso Pavilion", which houses 230 paintings, lithographs, ceramics and sculptures by the Spanish artist, and four galleries featuring works by Chagall, Miró and Renoir, plus works by modern Japanese artists such as Umehara Ryuzaburo and Takeshi Hayashi. You can rest between galleries at several restaurants or cafés – there's also a traditional Japanese teahouse.

A short walk downhill from the museum is a reasonably inexpensive **accommodation** option, *Chōraku* (☎0460/2-2192, ⓕ2-4533; ❺). This modern ryokan has simple tatami rooms, onsen baths and a friendly manager who speaks a little English.

Gōra, Kōen-ue and Ōwakudani

There's little reason to stop at **GŌRA** except to have lunch (see below) or to transfer from the Hakone Tōzan railway to a funicular tram (¥410), which takes only ten minutes to cover the short but steep distance to **Sōunzan**, the start of the cable car across Mount Sōun. On the way, you might want to stop at **KŌEN-UE**, a couple of stops from Gōra. Here the **Hakone Museum of Art** (daily except Thurs 9am–4/4.30pm; ¥900) and its collection of ancient ceramics is likely to appeal to experts only, but the delicate moss gardens and the view from the traditional teahouse across the verdant hills is captivating.

From Sōunzan, the **cable car** (¥1330 one way) floats like a balloon on its thirty-minute journey high above the mountain to the Tōgendai terminal, beside the lake, Ashino-ko, stopping at a couple of points along the way. The first stop, **ŌWAKUDANI**, is the site of a constantly bubbling and steaming valley formed by a volcanic eruption three thousand years ago. You can learn more about this at the informative **Ōwakudani Natural History Museum** (daily 9am–4pm; ¥400), downhill from the cable-car station, with an entertaining diorama model of a volcano that flashes, rumbles and glows red at the point of eruption. To see the real thing, hike up the valley through the lava formations to the bubbling pools, where eggs are boiled until they are black and scoffed religiously by every Japanese tourist, for no better reason than it's the done thing to do when visiting Ōwakudani.

There are a couple of good **places to stay** on this side of Hakone. The quiet *Fuji-Hakone Guest House* (☎0460/4-6577, ⓦwww.remix.ne.jp/~hakone; ❺), in Sengokuhara (best reached by bus #4 from the east exit of Odawara Station), is run by the friendly, English-speaking Takahashi-san, and has tatami rooms and onsen water piped into a communal bath – only breakfast is available. Directly behind, in a lovely wooden building, is the *Hakone Sengokuhara Youth Hostel* (☎0460/4-8966, ⓦwww.jyh.or.jp; dorms ¥2950 per person, rooms ❺), run by the same family and offering accommodation in dorms or Japanese-style rooms.

You shouldn't miss out on the *Gyōza Centre* (daily except Thurs, 11.30am–3pm & 5–8pm) on the main road between Gōra and the Hakone Open-Air Museum. This two-floor **restaurant** usually has a long line of customers waiting to sample the thirteen types of delicious home-made dumplings (*gyōza*), including ones stuffed with prawns (*ebi*) and fermented beans (*nattō*). A set meal with rice and soup costs ¥1155. At Ōwakudani the best eating choice is one of the noodle bars beside the entrance to the volcanic area. Also good for lunch is the café downstairs at the Tōgendai cable-car terminal, which is reasonably priced and has pleasant views across the lake.

Ashino-ko and around

Emerging from the cable car at Tōgendai, you'll find yourself at the northern end of the bone-shaped lake, **Ashino-ko**, from where, weather permitting, you'll get fantastic views of **Mount Fuji**. If it's cloudy you'll have to make do with the less impressive 1357-metre **Komaga-take** on the eastern shore. A walk around the shoreline trails along the western side of the lake to the small resort of Hakone-machi, some 8km south, takes around three hours. It's more fun to board one of the colourful, cartoon-like "pirate ships" (¥840) that regularly sail the length of the lake in around thirty minutes. This area of Hakone, part of the *Prince* empire of hotels and resorts, is not covered by the Hakone Free Pass and so is somewhat marginalized from the rest of the national park's attractions – and all the more peaceful for it. Boats run from Tōgendai to the *Prince* hotel resort at Hakone-en, midway down the east side of the lake, where there's also a large outdoor skating rink and a cable car up to Komaga-take's summit, from where there's a fabulous view. The summit can also be reached by bus from the tourist village of Moto-Hakane.

A cluster of upmarket hotels and ryokan can be found at **HAKONE-MACHI**, where the "pirate ships" dock. This is also the location of the **Hakone Barrier** (daily 9am–4.30pm; ¥200) through which all traffic on the Tōkaidō, the ancient road linking Kyoto and Edo, once had to pass (see box on p.228). What stands here today is a reproduction, enlivened by waxwork displays which provide the historical background. There's nothing much to keep you here, though; instead, stroll north of the barrier around the wooded promontory, past the bland reconstruction of the emperor Meiji's Hakone Detached Palace, and take in the views of the lake.

Running for around 1km beside the road leading from the Hakone Barrier to the lakeside village of **MOTO-HAKONE** is part of the Tōkaidō road, shaded by 420 lofty cryptomeria trees, planted in 1618 and now designated "Natural Treasures". Across the lake, you'll spot a vermilion *torii* gate, standing in the water just north of Moto-Hakone – a scene celebrated in many a *ukiyo-e* print and modern postcard. The gate belongs to the **Hakone Gongen** and is the best thing about this small Shinto **shrine**, set back in the trees, where samurai once came to pray.

Though it's fairly touristy, you'll find some decent **accommodation** at Moto-Hakone. At the bottom of the price range is the *Hakone Lake Villa Youth Hostel* (☎0460/3-1610, ⓦwww.jyh.or.jp; dorms ¥3300 per person), in a secluded spot above Ashino-ko lake. The hostel has tatami and Western-style dorms, a lounge with a large outdoor deck surrounded by woods, a bath filled with onsen water, and good-value meals. A lot more upmarket is the *Hakone Prince Hotel* (☎0460/3-1111, ⓦwww.princehotels.co.jp/hakone-e/index.html; ❼), with a prime location on the Komaga-take side of Ashino-ko and a multitude of facilities – the nicest rooms are in the Japanese-style annexes. A short bus ride (get off at Ashinokoen-mae) or stiff ten-minute walk uphill from the village lies the *Moto-Hakone Guest House* (☎0460/3-7880, ⓦwww.remix.ne .jp/~hakone; ❺), offering spotless, Japanese-style rooms, though the only meal available is breakfast (¥800).

The Hakone Barrier

In 1618, the second shogun, Tokugawa Hidetada, put up the **Hakone Barrier** (Sekisho) – actually more of a large compound than a single gate – which stood at Hakone-machi until 1869. The shogun decreed that all his lords' wives and their families live in Edo (now Tokyo) and the lords themselves make expensive formal visits to the capital every other year, a strategy designed to ensure no one attempted a rebellion. The Tōkaidō, on which the barrier stands, was one of the major routes in and out of the capital, and it was here that travellers were carefully checked to see how many guns they were taking into the Edo area and that the lords' hostage families were stopped from escaping. Any man caught trying to dodge the barrier was crucified and then beheaded, while accompanying women had their heads shaved and were, according to contemporary statute, "given to anyone who wants them".

Back to Hakone-Yumoto

From either Moto-Hakone or Hakone-machi you can take a **bus** back to Hakone-Yumoto or Odawara. Far more rewarding, however, is the eleven-kilometre **hike** along part of the Tōkaidō road, which after the first couple of kilometres is all downhill and takes around four hours. The route begins five minutes up the hill from the Hakone Tōzan bus station in Moto-Hakone, where large paving stones are laid through the shady forests. When the path comes out of the trees and hits the main road, you'll see the **Amazake-jaya Teahouse**, where you can rest, just as travellers did hundreds of years ago, and sip a restorative cup of the milky, sweet and alcoholic rice drink *amazake*, with some pickles, for ¥400.

From the teahouse, the path shadows the main road to the small village of **HATAJUKU**, where since the ninth century craftsmen have perfected the art of *yosegi-zaiku*, or marquetry. The wooden boxes, toys and other objects inlaid with elaborate mosaic patterns make great souvenirs and there are workshops throughout the village, including one right where the path emerges onto the main road. Hatajuku is a good place to pick up the bus for the rest of the way to Hakone-Yumoto if you don't fancy hiking any further. From here the path descends to the **Sukumo-gawa** and past several old temples, as well as the Tenzan Notemburo (see p.225), before ending up in the centre of **Hakone-Yumoto**.

Izu Hantō

Formed by Mount Fuji's ancient lava flows, **Izu Hantō** protrudes like an arrowhead into the ocean west of Tokyo, a mountainous spine whose tortured coastline features some superb scenery and a couple of decent beaches. It takes at least two days to make a complete circuit of this region, taking in some intriguing historical sights and stopping at a few of the peninsula's estimated 2300 hot springs.

Direct train services from Tokyo run down Izu's more developed east coast, passing through **Atami**, with its stylish art museum, to the harbour town of **Shimoda**, one of the places Commodore Perry parked his "Black Ships" in 1854 and the site of Japan's first American consulate. Shimoda makes a good base for exploring southern Izu, including the Rendaiji hot spring and the striking coastal scenery around Irō-zaki at its most southerly tip.

Over on west Izu, **Dōgashima** is another famous beauty spot, with a crop of picturesque islands set in clear, tropical-blue water. Most of this coast still belongs to traditional fishing communities and the central uplands are also sparsely populated, with only a few roads cutting through the maple and beech forests to give sweeping views over the peninsula and north to Fuji. The only settlement of any size in central Izu is **Shuzenji**, whose nearby **onsen** resort has long been associated with novelists such as Kawabata and Natsume Sōseki (see p.1019). Local history also inspired a popular Kabuki play based on the twelfth-century murder of a former Kamakura Shogun. The town's few sights revolve around these events and it's a good place to stay before taking the train north out of Izu.

Izu's mild climate makes it a possible excursion even in winter, though it's close enough to Tokyo to be crowded at weekends, and is best avoided during

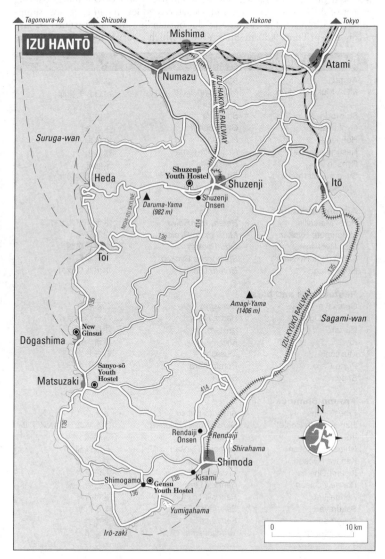

the summer holidays. If you haven't got a JR pass and want to explore the whole peninsula, check out the various discount tickets available, such as the four-day "Izu Free Q Kippu" (¥13,190), which covers the Shinkansen from Tokyo as well as local transport by train and bus. Renting a car is a good idea, as public transport is slow and only really covers the main coastal settlements; you'll find rental companies in Atami (Eki Rent-a-Car; ☎0557/82-1382), Shimoda and Shuzenji (see p.235 and p.242 for details).

Atami

Situated on the Shinkansen line between Tokyo and Ōsaka, the hot-spring resort of **ATAMI** serves as the eastern gateway to Izu. It's an expensive, sometimes garish, place, but is home to the outstanding **MOA Museum of Art** (daily except Thurs 9.30am–5pm; ¥1600), which is carved into a hillside above

Atami and Shimoda		
Atami	*Atami*	熱海
MOA Museum of Art	*MOA Bijutsukan*	ＭＯＡ美術館
Shimoda	*Shimoda*	下田
Gyokusen-ji	*Gyokusen-ji*	玉泉寺
Hōfuku-ji	*Hōfuku-ji*	宝福寺
Nesugata-yama	*Nesugata-yama*	寝姿山
Ryōsen-ji	*Ryōsen-ji*	了仙寺
Shimoda Memorial Museum	*Shimoda Kaikoku Hakubutskan*	下田開国博物館
Accommodation		
Hotel Marseille	*Hoteru Maruseiyu*	ホテルマルセイユ
Matsumoto Ryokan	*Matsumoto Ryokan*	松本旅館
Ōizu Ryokan	*Ōizu Ryokan*	大伊豆旅館
Shimodaya Ryokan	*Shimodaya Ryokan*	下田屋旅館
Hotel Uraga	*Hoteru Uraga*	ホテルウラガ
Restaurants and bars		
Gorosaya	*Gorosaya*	ごろさや
Harbour Light	*Harbā Raito*	ハーバーライト
Izu-tarō	*Izu-tarō*	伊豆太郎
Kiyū	*Kiyū*	亀遊
Musashi	*Musashi*	むさし
Porto Caro	*Poreto Kāro*	ポルトカーロ
Shōya	*Shōya*	しょうや
Around Shimoda		
Ernest House	*Ānesuto Hausu*	アーネストハウス
Gensu Youth Hostel	*Gensu Yūsu Hosuteru*	げんすユースホステル
Irō-zaki	*Irō-zaki*	石廊崎
Ishibashi Ryokan	*Ishibashi Ryokan*	石橋旅館
Kanaya Ryokan	*Kanaya Ryokan*	金谷旅館
Kisami-Ōhama	*Kisami-Ōhama*	吉佐美大浜
Rendaiji Onsen	*Rendaiji Onsen*	蓮台寺温泉
Rendaiji-sō	*Rendaiji-sō*	蓮台寺荘
Sakuraya	*Sakuraya*	さくらや
Seiryū-sō	*Seiryū-sō*	清流荘
Yumigahama	*Yumigahama*	弓ヶ浜

Will Adams

In 1600, before Japan closed its doors to the world, a Dutch ship washed up on east Kyūshū. It was the lone survivor of five vessels that had set sail from Europe two years previously; three-quarters of the crew had perished from starvation and the remaining twenty-five were close to death.

One of those rescued by Japanese fishermen was the navigator, an Englishman called **Will Adams** (1564–1620). He was summoned by Tokugawa Ieyasu, the future shogun, who quizzed Adams about European affairs, religion and various scientific matters. Ieyasu liked what he heard – at the time there was growing distrust of merchants from Catholic countries (see "History", p.939) – and made Adams his personal adviser on mathematics, navigation and guns. Adams, known locally as Anjin (meaning "pilot"), later served as the shogun's interpreter and as a diplomat, brokering trade treaties with both Holland and Britain. In return he was granted samurai status, the first and last foreigner to be so honoured, along with a Japanese wife and an estate near Yokosuka on the Miura Peninsula.

Adams' main task, however, was to oversee the construction of Japan's first Western-style sailing ships. In 1605 he set up a shipyard at **Itō**, on the east coast of Izu, where he built at least two ocean-going vessels over the next five years. One of these apparently made it to Mexico, while Adams himself took to the seas on diplomatic missions to the Philippines and China.

By the end of his career, the government had grown increasingly opposed to foreign intervention, and after Ieyasu died in 1616 Adams retired to his Miura estate, where he was buried in 1620. His fascinating life story forms the basis for James Clavell's novel, *Shogun* (see "Books", p.1021), and he is still remembered in Itō each August with his own festival, the Anjin Matsuri.

the town. Though the steep admission charge is off-putting, the museum's remarkable architecture and collection of mostly ancient oriental art justify a visit. Note that you can buy slightly reduced tickets (¥1400) at the **tourist information desk** (Mon–Sat 9.30am–5.30pm; ℡0557/81-5297) inside Atami Station before hopping on a bus from the station concourse up to the museum (5min; ¥160). Buses drop you outside the museum's lower entrance, from where you ride four escalators cut through the rock to the main exhibition halls. Each room contains just a few pieces, of which the most famous, only put on show in February of each year, is a dramatic folding screen entitled *Red and White Plum Blossoms* by the innovative Ogata Kōrin (1658–1716). The most eye-catching exhibit is a full-size replica of a golden tearoom, lined with gold leaf and equipped with utensils made of gold, built in 1586 when the warlord Toyotomi Hideyoshi invited Emperor Ogimachi over for a cuppa. The museum's well-tended gardens contain teahouses serving *macha* and sweet cakes (¥630).

Shimoda

At Atami trains peel off down the east coast of Izu, cutting through craggy headlands and running high above bays ringed with fishing villages or resort hotels. Nearly halfway down the peninsula, **ITŌ** port was where Will Adams launched Japan's first Western-style sailing ships (see box above), but there's nothing really to stop for until you reach **SHIMODA**. Off season, this small, amiable town, with its attractive scenery and sprinkling of temples and museums, makes a good base for a couple of days' exploring. Its sights revolve around Shimoda's moment of glory, when Commodore Perry sailed his Black Ships (*Kurofune*) into the harbour in 1854, and it became one of Japan's first

SHIMODA

ACCOMMODATION
Hotel Marseille	A
Matsumoto Ryokan	C
Ōizu Ryokan	D
Shimodaya Ryokan	B
Hotel Uraga	E

RESTAURANTS, CAFÉS & BARS
Gorosaya	4
Harbour Light	8
Izu-tarō	2
Jazz Port	7
Kiyū	6
Musashi	3
Porto Caro	9
Shōya	1
Tiny Bee	5

Izu Station

Ropeway
Nesugata-yama

Bike Rental

NTT

Hōfuku-ji

Tourist Wharf

Gyokusen-ji

Irō-zaki

Shimoda Memorial Museum

Ryōsen-ji

PERRY ROAD

Shimoda Harbour

N

0   200 m

Shimoda-kōen

▼ Headland Walk   ▼ Headland Walk

ports to open to foreign trade. Shimoda people are immensely proud of their part in Japanese history and you'll find Black Ships everywhere, from a replica outside the train station to a customized tourist bus; there's even a **Black Ships Festival** (around the third Saturday in May), when American and Japanese naval bands parade through the streets, followed by the inevitable fireworks.

JR express trains, known as *Odoriko* (The Dancing Girl), after Kawabata's novel (see p.1019), run direct from Tokyo Station to Shimoda several times a day; there's also the daily *Super View Odoriko* from Ikebukuro and Shinjuku to Shimoda and back, which has extra-wide windows to take in the spectacular coastal views; you'll need to make an obligatory reservation to use this service. Some regular *Odoriko* trains divide at Atami for Shuzenji, so check you're on the right section; note too that JR Passes are only valid for the journey as far as Itō; beyond Itō it's a private line down to Shimoda.

Some history

Following his first, brief sally into Tokyo Bay in 1853, American **Commodore Perry** returned the next year to begin the negotiations which ultimately prized Japan out of its isolation (see "History", p.939). Having signed an initial treaty in Yokohama, which granted America trading rights in Shimoda and Hakodate (on Hokkaidō) and consular representation, Perry sailed his Black Ships down to Izu. Here, in Shimoda's Ryōsen-ji temple, he concluded a supplementary "**Treaty of Friendship**" in 1854. Russian, British and Dutch merchants were granted similar rights soon after, and in 1856 **Townsend Harris** arrived in Shimoda as the first American Consul – a controversial figure, thanks to his relationship with his Japanese servant, Okichi (see box below). By now, however, it was obvious that Shimoda was too isolated as a trading post and Harris began negotiating for a revised treaty, which was eventually signed (again in Shimoda) in July 1858. According to this new agreement, Kanagawa replaced Shimoda as an open port, so the burgeoning foreign community decamped north to Yokohama.

The Town

Central Shimoda lies on the northwestern shore of a well-sheltered harbour, surrounded by steep hills. Most of its sights are in the older, southerly district, where you'll find a number of attractive grey-and-white latticed walls near the original fishing harbour; this style of architecture (known as *namako-kabe*), found throughout Izu, is resistant to fire, earthquakes and corrosive sea air. Your first stop should be **Ryōsen-ji**, the temple where Perry signed the Treaty of Friendship in May 1854, though this small but elaborate temple, founded in 1635, is less interesting than its attached **museum** (daily 8.30am–5pm; ¥500), which is full of fascinating historical documents from the 1850s. Delightful portraits of Perry and his devilish crew, penned by Japanese artists, contrast with the European view of Japan – embellished with Chinese touches – from contemporary editions of the *Illustrated London News*. Many exhibits relate to the tragic Okichi, the servant of Consul Harris (see box below), while a second room downstairs contains an odd display of sex in religious art – including some beautiful pieces from India, Nepal and Japan's Shinto shrines.

From Ryōsen-ji, **Perry Road** leads along a small river lined with picturesque old houses and willows east to **Shimoda-kōen**. This extensive hilltop park has good views over the town and harbour but little else to recommend it outside the hydrangea season (June), when over one million blooms colour the slopes. Instead, walk back past Ryōsen-ji to the nearby **Shimoda Memorial Museum** (daily 8.30am–5.30pm; ¥1000), housed in two traditional latticework buildings. Alongside caricatures of big-nosed foreigners, Harris and Okichi are again much in evidence – exhibits include Harris's kimono, decorated with the American eagle, and a portrait of a beautiful young woman which is commonly held to be Okichi. The museum also has information, much of it in English, about local life, including the area's distinctive architecture and festivals.

Tōjin Okichi and Townsend Harris

In 1854, local officials ordered the 17-year-old **Tōjin Okichi** to abandon her fiancé, Tsurumatsu, and to work for the American consul, Townsend Harris, a puritanical bachelor in his mid-50s who suffered from stomach ulcers. Whether Okichi was sent as a concubine, perhaps at Harris's request, or simply as a nurse or maidservant, is unclear, but her beauty fuelled endless gossip. Whatever the truth, Okichi was tainted by association with a foreigner. After Harris was posted back to America, where he died in New York in 1878, she wandered aimlessly until she bumped into Tsurumatsu in Yokohama. The two settled for a while, but by now she had started drinking and eventually he divorced her. Okichi then returned to Shimoda, where she opened a restaurant, but it wasn't a success, and before long she was forced to sell. Soon after, aged 47, she was partially paralyzed by an alcohol-induced stroke but survived another three years before finally drowning herself in a local river in 1890. A festival in Shimoda on March 27 celebrates this tragic figure.

Heading north again, the last sight in central Shimoda is **Okichi's grave**. When Okichi died in 1890, none of her family came forward to claim her body, so it was left to a local priest to bring her back to the family temple for burial. She now lies behind the otherwise unremarkable **Hōfuku-ji**, where there's another small museum (daily 8am–5pm; ¥300) dedicated to her memory. The exhibits are much the same, though this time it's the original, sepia-tinted photo of Okichi on display alongside stills from some of the many films made about her.

The east side of Shimoda is dominated by the 200-metre peak of **Nesugata-yama**. On a clear day it's worth taking the ropeway (daily 9am–5pm, departures every 10–15min; ¥1000 return ticket) from beside the train station up to the summit for dramatic views of the harbour and out to the Izu islands on the eastern horizon. Nesugata-yama's south face drops steeply to the harbour, where there's a string of resort hotels and a tourist wharf from where a "Black Ship" makes short, expensive **harbour cruises** (20min; ¥920).

On the far, eastern side of the bay, **Gyokusen-ji** is where Townsend Harris established Japan's first American consulate in 1856 – it's a bit of a hike but an interesting diversion if time allows. A monument in front of the temple records Harris's misgivings, noted later in his diary, as he raised the flag here at 2.30pm on September 4: "Grave reflections. Ominous of change. Undoubted beginning of the end. Query, – if for the real good of Japan?" Nearby, a black-stone slab scrawled with US President Carter's signature commemorates his visit in 1979, while across the courtyard there's a strange memorial donated by Tokyo butchers; it supposedly marks where the first cow was slaughtered in Japan for human consumption, at Harris's request.

Townsend Harris lived and worked in Gyokusen-ji for about fifteen months, accompanied by his Dutch interpreter, Chinese servants and, possibly, Okichi. On entering the **Townsend Harris Memorial Hall** (daily 8am–5pm; ¥300), to the right of the temple, you're greeted by a startling, life-size model of Harris, complete with splendid handlebar moustache, relaxing in his rocking chair in full evening dress while Okichi offers him a glass of milk. Other exhibits include a few of Harris's rather battered possessions, a host of memorial plaques and photos of various visiting dignitaries, from Emperor Hirohito to Jimmy Carter. As you leave, turn left immediately outside the hall and follow the path uphill to find the graves of three Russians who died off Shimoda in 1854 when their ship was wrecked by a tidal wave. On the opposite side of the temple, in the main part of the cemetery, five Americans are also buried, including three of Perry's young sailors. To reach Gyokusen-ji, take a bus from Shimoda Station (see below) to Kakizaki (4min; ¥160), from where it's a two-minute walk; alternatively, it's a rather tedious hike along the busy main road.

A much more pleasant **walk** is to retrace your steps to Shimoda-kōen and follow the coast road south around the headland. When you reach the aquarium – not really worth the hefty ¥1700 entry fee – walk through the car park, keeping the dolphin pools on your left, and you'll come out on the next bay. A cycle track leads along a quieter stretch of coast, with refreshingly little concrete in sight, though not entirely unspoiled thanks to a large resort hotel, and then take a right turn when you meet the road to return to Perry Road. The whole circuit takes roughly one hour.

Practicalities

Shimoda's **train station** lies on the north side of town. There's an **information** desk inside the front exit (daily 9am–5.30pm; ☎0558/22-3200), or try the helpful Shimoda Tourist Association (daily 10am–5pm; ☎0558/22-1531), to the left of the station in a traditional-style building beside the main cross-roads. Both places can help with town maps and accommodation; the latter sometimes has the advantage of an English-speaking member of staff.

Local **buses** depart from in front of the station: Shimoda Bus operates within the town boundaries, including Rendaiji (see p.236), while Tōkai Bus (marked TB) serves the long-distance routes to Dōgashima and Irō-zaki (see p.239 and p.237). If you're exploring the local area, it's worth buying Tōkai Bus's two-day "Minami Izu Free Pass" (¥2790); you'll make a saving on these two day-trips alone, and their buses also serve Gyokusen-ji (see opposite) and Rendaiji. Passes are available from the Tōkai Bus office on the other side of the bus terminal from the station. You can **rent bikes** at Noguchi Rentacycle (daily 9.30am–6pm; ¥500 per hour, ¥2000 per day), one block south of the station; take along a copy of your passport. Alternatively, **car rental** is available from Nippon Rent-a-Car (☎0558/22-5711) inside the station, or across the main road at Nissan (☎0558/22-7401) and Toyota (☎0558/27-0100).

Accommodation

Although the town's accommodation is dominated by pricey resort **hotels** on the harbourfront, Shimoda's most appealing options are around the station and among the older streets to the south. Other possibilities in the area include Rendaiji's more upmarket ryokan, the beach-side hotels at Kisami-Ōhama and an HI youth hostel at Shimogamo (see p.237).

Hotel Marseille 1-1-5 Higashi-Hongo ☎0558/23-8000, ℉23-8001. Well-kept business hotel beside the station with a cheerful French theme. The single rooms (around ¥8000) are small but the doubles and twins (from around ¥15,000) are a decent size; all are nicely decorated and come with TV, phone and en-suite bathrooms. ❺

Matsumoto Ryokan 2-9-19 Shimoda-shi ☎0558/22-0023. One of Shimoda's more atmospheric places to stay, with its cross-hatched walls and tiny entrance garden. It's all a bit dilapidated and none of the tatami rooms is en suite, but there's an onsen bath and prices are reasonable at ¥5000 per person. No meals. ❺

Ōizu Ryokan Shimoda-shi ☎0558/22-0123. Round the corner from the *Harbour Light* karaoke bar, this simple and somewhat gloomy – but authentic – ryokan is one of Shimoda's cheapest options. ❹

Shimodaya Ryokan 2-13-31 Shimoda-shi ☎0558/22-0446. Smarter but less characterful version of the *Matsumoto Ryokan*, although it has the advantage of providing meals (count on ¥3000 per person for two meals). ❺

Hotel Uraga 3-3-10 Shimoda-shi ☎0558/23-6600, ℉23-6603. Clean, bright business hotel in the south part of town. It's worth paying a little extra for the larger, twin rooms (❺), but all the rooms are comfortable, with TV, phone and bathroom, and the coffee shop serves Japanese and Western breakfasts (from ¥700). Some English spoken. ❹

Eating and drinking

Shimoda has a number of affordable *izakaya* and sushi **restaurants**, as well as straightforward soba joints, and several places serving *yakiniku*. There are a few cheap **coffee shops** around the station and fancier places along Perry Road, some of which double as antiques showrooms.

Gorosaya 1-5-25 Shimoda-shi ☎0120-155638. Relaxed and popular fish restaurant (best to book ahead). Prices are surprisingly reasonable if you keep to the set meals – their standard *teishoku* (¥1500) includes a choice of sashimi, tempura or fried fish (*yaki-sakana*). English menu. Closed Thurs.

Harbour Light 2F, 3-3-4 Shimoda-shi. If you're looking for some action, head for this small, retro karaoke bar with a friendly, English-speaking owner and a decent song-list. Closed Sun.

Izu-tarō 1-2-1 Higashi-Hongo. Popular *kaiten-zushi* near the station. Plates are priced at ¥110–310, and they also offer soup, fruits and desserts. Daily until 8pm.

Jazz Port 4-5-16 Shizuoka. You can't miss this jazz café-bar behind the Shimoda Memorial Museum, its entrance littered with artful junk. Inside it's even more of an old curiosity shop – worth dropping by just for the ambience. Daily except Wed until 9pm.

Kiyū 1-10-18 Shimoda-shi ⓣ0558/22-8698. There's a warm welcome at this lively fish restaurant with a choice of well-priced set meals from around ¥1600. Closed one day a week – call to check. **Musashi** 1-13-1 Shin-shi. Casual, welcoming soba restaurant with wooden tables. Its extensive menu also offers sashimi and standard rice dishes, such as *tendon* (rice with tempura) and *katsudon* (with breaded pork fillet), all for ¥1000 or less. Daily except Tues until 8pm.

Porto Caro 2F, 3-3-7 Shimoda-shi ⓣ0558/22-5514. This cute Mediterranean restaurant turns out pretty authentic-tasting pizza, pasta and paella, among other dishes. The lunchtime deals are good value at around ¥1000; in the evening count on at least ¥2000 per head. English menu. Closed Wed.

Shōya 2F, 1-8-7 Higashi-Hongo ⓣ0558/22-2989. One of Shimoda's top *yakiniku* restaurants (best to reserve) though it's not cheap – expect to pay at least ¥3000 per person. Selective English menu. Evenings only; closed Mon.

Tiny Bee 1-18-12 Shimoda-shi. Indulge in home-made cakes, muffins and open sandwiches at this spick-and-span coffee shop. More substantial lunches are also available. English menu. Daily except Tues until 7pm.

Around Shimoda

Though Shimoda is a popular hot-spring resort, onsen connoisseurs will find better bathing a little further north at **Rendaiji Onsen**. This village, accessible by train or bus, has a collection of classy ryokan, several of which open their *rotemburo* to the public. Heading in the opposite direction, south Izu's rocky, indented coastline shelters some of the peninsula's best **beaches** and has stretches of dramatic scenery around **Irō-zaki**, its southernmost tip. Though a car is the ideal way of getting around, all the places mentioned below are covered by local buses; if you're travelling by bus and combining this area with Dōgashima (see p.239), it's worth investing in a "Minami Izu Free Pass" (see "Practicalities", p.234, for more about transport around Shimoda).

Rendaiji Onsen

Set in a narrow valley just west of National Highway 414, this quiet, one-street village consists mostly of exclusive ryokan which tap into the area's abundant supply of hot water. It's these onsen baths that make **RENDAIJI ONSEN** worth a visit, though there are also a few meandering back lanes to explore, and you might want to splash out on a night of luxury. Two or three **trains** an hour (3–4min; ¥160) run between Shimoda – roughly 3km to the south – and Rendaiji Station, from where it's a short walk west across the river and highway to the village. Local **buses** are slightly less frequent, but most drop you right on the main street; both Shimoda and Tōkai buses ply this route (10min; ¥250).

The most appealing of Rendaiji's **onsen** is the big wooden public bath (¥1000) at *Kanaya Ryokan* (ⓣ0558/22-0325, ⓕ23-6078; ❺–❻), a traditional place with several pools, including a rotemburo, where many of your fellow bathers will be local families. They even have an observatory for stargazing and a tea ceremony room. You'll find the ryokan on the main highway, just north of the village turning; there's a bus stop right outside or it's a couple of minutes' walk to the station. Walking south, peek in at the immaculate entrance to *Seiryū-sō* (ⓣ0558/22-1361, Ⓦwww.seiryuso.co.jp; ❾) on the left before the bridge; this elegant ryokan is where President Carter stayed in 1979 when he visited Gyokusen-ji (see p.234) – unfortunately, the baths here are for residents only.

Opposite *Seiryū-sō*, a road heads west into Rendaiji proper. Here you'll find one of the town's more affordable accommodation options, *Sakuraya* (ⓣ0552/22-1966, ⓕ22-1967; ❺–❼), 200m along on the left and close to the bus stop. When it comes to public baths, the beautiful old *Ishibashi Ryokan*, also known as the *Kur Hotel* (ⓣ0558/22-2222, ⓕ22-2121; ❼–❽), has the best facilities, with rotemburo, Jacuzzi and sauna (¥1000). It's tucked under a small hill on the right as you walk from the highway. Continue past it for a few minutes until, almost opposite *Sakuraya*, you come to a neat bamboo fence belonging to *Rendaiji-sō* (T 0558/22-3501, F 23-0373; ⑥–⑧), a rambling ryokan whose jungle baths (¥1000; 8am–8pm) – one hosting a 25-year-old hibiscus – provide a steamy finale.

South to Irō-zaki

In summer, Izu's beaches are packed with surfers and sun-worshippers, but out of season they're usually fairly deserted. The major resort is just north of Shimoda, at Shirahama, but there are a couple of smaller, more attractive bays southwest of the town on the Tōkai Bus route to Izu's southern cape, **Irō-zaki**. From Shimoda Station **buses** depart for Irō-zaki roughly every thirty minutes, but check before boarding as some buses skip certain stops. If you want to continue round the coast, hop on one of the four daily buses which leave from Irō-zaki for the picturesque ride to Matsuzaki (see p.238), from where you can loop back to Shimoda, or continue to Dōgashima; alternatively, take one of the **tourist boats** which ply between Irō-zaki port and Shimoda for the return journey (see below).

Around 4km southwest of Shimoda, Highway 136 passes through the village of **KISAMI**, where a road forks left across a river towards the coast. **Ōhama**, the name of Kisami's sandy bay, is one of south Izu's more attractive beaches – marred slightly by a factory on the far horizon – and a popular surfing spot. Along the road there's a handful of small **hotels**, the nicest of which is *Ernest House* (T 0558/22-5880, W www.artfarm.co.jp/ernesthouse/index_e.html; ⑤–⑥); its fresh, bright rooms get booked up at weekends and in season, so it pays to phone ahead. They offer **meals** – including great picnic breakfasts; otherwise try one of the laid-back cafés closer to the beach; *Marley Café* is particularly recommended. If you're travelling by bus, ask the driver to drop you on the main road at Ōhama-iriguchi, from where it's a ten-minute walk.

A little further along the coast, **YUMIGAHAMA** is a larger, more developed resort but has the advantage that buses from here take you all the way down to the wide horseshoe bay, ringed with pines and casuarina. The beach is about ten minutes' bike ride from *Gensu Youth Hostel* (T 0558/62-0035; dorms ¥3500 per person), an HI **youth hostel** in the town of **SHIMOGAMO**, about 25 minutes by bus from Shimoda (¥630); ask for the Yakuba-mae stop. You'll need to be a Hostelling International member to stay here (they're pretty strict) and evening meals are not provided, but there are shops and restaurants close by.

Continuing round the coast from Yumigahama, the road climbs through lush vegetation to emerge in an expanse of car parks that cap the headland. Fortunately, **IRŌ-ZAKI** improves dramatically as you walk out along the promontory for about 500m, past souvenir shops and lighthouse, to a minuscule **shrine** balanced on the cliff edge. The views here are superb: on either side the sea has cut deep-blue gashes into the coastline, leaving behind a sprinkling of rocky islets between which colourful **tourist boats** bob and weave. The boats leave from Irō-zaki port – a tiny fishing village sheltering in the northern bay; from the headland it's a pleasant, five-minute stroll downhill, or get off the bus at Irōzaki-kō *iriguchi* on the main highway, a short walk from the village. Depending on the weather and the season, there are one or two trips per hour around the headland (¥1120 for 25min), or three daily sailings all the way back to Shimoda (40min; ¥1530).

West Izu

Despite its rugged coastal scenery and occasionally spectacular views of Mount Fuji, **west Izu** remains far less developed than the eastern side – with the

West Izu and Shuzenji

Dōgashima	*Dōgashima*	堂ヶ島
Minshuku Koharu-sō	*Minshuku Koharu-sō*	民宿小春荘
NEW Ginsui	*NEW Ginsui*	NEW銀水荘
Sebama-zushi	*Sebama-zushi*	瀬浜寿し
Matsuzaki	*Matsuzaki*	松崎
Hamamiya	*Hamamiya*	浜宮
Izu-Matsuzaki-sō	*Izu-Matsuzaki-sō*	伊豆まつざき荘
Mingei Sabō Fumoto	*Mingei Sabō Fumoto*	民芸砂防ふもと
San'yo-sō Youth Hostel	*San'yo-sō Yūsu Hosuteru*	山余荘ユースホステル
Sunset Hill Matsuzaki	*Sansetto Hiru Matsuzaki*	サンセットヒル松崎
Tontsū	*Tontsū*	とん通
Shuzenji	*Shuzenji*	修善寺
Shuzenji Onsen	*Shuzenji Onsen*	修善寺温泉
Fukui	*Minshuku Fukui*	民宿福井
Goyōkan	*Goyōkan*	五葉館
Hako-yu	*Hako-yu*	はこゆ
Kikuya	*Kikuya*	菊屋
Nanaban	*Nanaban*	なな番
Shigetsu-den	*Shigetsu-den*	指月殿
Shūzen-ji Temple	*Shuzen-ji*	修善寺
Shuzenji Youth Hostel	*Shuzenji Yūsu Hosuteru*	修善寺ユースホステル
Yu-no-sato-mura	*Yu-no-sato-mura*	湯の里村
Toi	*Toi*	土肥
Heda	*Heda*	戸田

exception of **Dōgashima**, whose pitted, pine-tufted islands draw the coach parties in droves. This lack of development is largely due to the difficulties of access, since public transport is limited to slow bus routes between the main settlements and infrequent ferry services. If you've got time to spare, it's worth taking a couple of days to meander between the traditional fishing ports that punctuate the journey north.

Matsuzaki

Travelling from Shimoda, the main road cuts across Izu's upland spine to **MATSUZAKI** on the west coast. Though spoiled by the high-rise *Prince Hotel* plonked in its midst, this modest town hides some attractive streets of traditional latticework buildings along the riverfront and down by its busy harbour. Along the river a clock tower stands in front of the **Nakasetei** (daily 9am–5pm; ¥100), an old kimono merchant's shop and residence that's worth a quick look.

Matsuzaki is also an onsen resort, but its main attraction is good-value **accommodation**. For budget travellers, there's the appealingly aged *San'yo-sō Youth Hostel* (☎ & ℉0558/42-0408; ¥3500 per person), set in a traditional garden among rice fields 3km east of town; Shimoda–Matsuzaki buses stop right outside and you can rent bikes to explore the surrounding area. Alternatively, there's *Izu-Matsuzaki-sō* (☎0558/42-0450, ℉42-0796; ❹–❺), at the north end of Matsuzaki's rather grey beach, which offers a choice of comfortable Western or Japanese rooms and communal onsen baths, but no private bathrooms. Finally, *Sunset Hill Matsuzaki* (☎0558/42-1515, ℉42-2688; ❺) sits perched on a hill at the north end of town, ten minutes' walk from the bus station, or phone for a free shuttle bus. This is another onsen hotel, with great views over the bay from its large rotemburo (¥1000 for non-guests).

All the above places serve food, but if you're looking for somewhere to **eat** in Matsuzaki, head south round the bay to the port, where *Mingei Sabō Fumoto* (daily 7.30am–7.30pm) doubles as a fishmonger and folksy restaurant, serving *teishoku* from around ¥1000. Back along the beach, behind a small pine grove, *Hamamiya* (closed Wed) is a more upmarket fish place, or try *Tontsū*, a homely *tonkatsu* restaurant three blocks further inland, for something more modest.

Dōgashima

Just 5km up the road from Matsuzaki, **DŌGASHIMA** is West Izu's prime tourist trap, with hotels, souvenir shops and cafeterias catering to a steady stream of punters. The focus of all this activity is a collection of picturesque limestone outcrops lying serenely offshore. You can admire these islands from various viewpoints around the bay or, better still, from one of the **tour boats** which putter among their caves and tunnels; boats depart every five to ten minutes (daily 8.15am–4.30/5pm; ¥920) from a jetty in front of the main car park. The highlight of the twenty-minute ride is a cave with a large cavity in its roof; afterwards, walk up onto the hill immediately north of the jetty to watch the boats sail through from above.

The old part of Dōgashima, a traditional fishing village known as **Sawada**, occupies the bay's south side. It's sheltered by a rocky promontory with a **rotemburo** (¥500, or ¥300 if you're staying in Dōgashima; closed Tues) in a spectacular location halfway up the cliff-face on the seaward side; skippers on the tourist boats take pleasure in sailing slowly by the apparently unconcerned bathers. This area is also the best place for affordable accommodation, but otherwise there's no reason to linger.

With an hour to spare, Dōgashima's **Orchid Sanctuary** (daily 8.30am–5pm; ¥1300) is surprisingly interesting, though a little expensive; walk inland from the boat jetty to find the ticket gate. The sanctuary grows more than eight thousand types of orchid, from cosseted miniatures to hardier varieties growing wild in the woods. A well-marked route leads through the extensive park to lookout points over the bay, and then out through the inevitable souvenir shop.

The centre of Dōgashima is a large car park which also doubles as the **bus terminal**. The **information office** (Mon–Sat 8.30am–5pm, July–Aug also Sun 8.30am–5pm; ☎0558/52-1268) lies across the main road, north of the tourist jetty, and can help with local maps (in Japanese only) and hotel bookings; if they're closed, try the Tōkai Bus office, opposite. Both these places provide information about **onward transport**. There are hourly buses northeast through Toi to Shuzenji, or ferries which hop up the lovely coast via Toi and Heda to Numazu on the JR Tōkaidō line.

Dōgashima is dominated by big, expensive resort **hotels**, most of which have stunning views and luxurious onsen baths. Pick of the bunch is the *NEW Ginsui* (☎0558/52-2211, ℱ52-1210; ❾), located on its own beach, five minutes' drive north of town. Prices are more affordable in Sawada fishing village at the southern end of Dōgashima, where you'll find dozens of minshuku, such as the cheerful *Koharu-sō* (☎ & ℱ0558/52-0181; ❻), one block in from the main road. There's no shortage of **places to eat** if you don't mind the cafeteria-style dining rooms of the souvenir shops. For somewhere less hectic – despite its location on the central car park – *Sebama-zushi* serves sushi sets from around ¥1300, as well as soba and other staples.

△ Daibutsu, Kamakura

Inland to Shuzenji Onsen

Travelling north from Dōgashima the road hugs the coast, climbing over headlands and then zigzagging down to fishing villages squeezed into sheltered bays. At **TOI**, the largest settlement in west Izu, the main road turns inland, but a few buses continue on up the coast to **HEDA**, a very picturesque village, with onward bus connections to Shuzenji; these buses are few and far between, so check the timetables before setting off. Both Toi and Heda lie on the ferry route from Dōgashima to Numazu, while Toi also has regular sailings to Tagonoura-kō (near Shin-Fuji Station on the Shinkansen line) on the north coast of Suruga Bay.

Beyond Toi, Highway 136 climbs eastward through pine-clad mountains before dropping down into the wide valley of **SHUZENJI**. The modern town holds no interest beyond its transport connections, but the original settlement of **SHUZENJI ONSEN**, some 3km southeast, has a couple of historical sights that are worth exploring. To get there, you can take a bus from outside Shuzenji Station to a tiny terminal east of the village centre (every 15–20min; ¥210).

Shuzenji Onsen consists of little more than one road and a string of riverside hotels and souvenir shops along a narrow valley. Follow the main street west and you'll soon reach an open area with some pleasing older buildings and a succession of red-lacquered bridges over the tumbling Katsura-gawa. Here, on a rocky outcrop beside the river, a very skimpy, see-through palisade surrounds Shuzenji's first and most famous **onsen**, *Tokko-no-yu* (24hr; free; unsegregated). According to legend, the onsen was "created" in 807 AD, by Kōbō Daishi, the founder of Shingon Buddhism (see p.954), when he found a boy washing his ailing father in the river; the priest struck the rock with his *tokko* (the short, metal rod carried by Shingon priests) and out gushed hot water with curative powers.

Kōbō Daishi is also credited with founding the nearby **temple**, **Shūzen-ji**, from which the town gets its name. Standing at the top of the steps on the river's north bank, the present temple was rebuilt roughly a century ago and its now quiet halls belie a violent history. During the Kamakura period (1185–1333), Shūzen-ji was a favourite place of exile for the shoguns' potential rivals. In 1193 Minamoto Noriyori, the younger brother of Shogun Yoritomo, committed suicide – some say he was murdered – after being banished here on suspicion of treason. A more famous death occurred soon after when **Minamoto Yoriie** was murdered in the bath. Yoriie was the son of Yoritomo and succeeded to the title of Shogun in 1199, aged only 18. Four years later his mother, Hōjō Masako, and grandfather seized power and sent Yoriie packing to Shūzen-ji, where he started planning his revenge. The plot was discovered, however, in 1204 and not long after Yoriie was found dead, supposedly killed by bathing in poisoned water. Opposite the temple office you'll find a small **museum** (daily 8.30am–4/4.30pm; ¥300) full of temple treasures, including possessions allegedly belonging to Kōbō Daishi. But its main interest is the wealth of information in English about Shūzen-ji's eventful history.

Minamoto Yoriie's grave lies on the hillside directly across the valley from Shūzen-ji, beside a smaller temple, **Shigetsu-den**, which a repentant Hōjō Masako built to appease the soul of her son. Though not a dramatic building, it's the oldest in Shuzenji and has some fine Buddhist statues inside.

Returning to the bridge beside *Tokko-no-yu*, the old-style building with a watchtower offers more secluded soaking in its lovely cedar-wood **onsen bath**, *Hako-yu* (noon–9pm; ¥350). Alternatively, follow the path west along the river, meandering across pretty bridges and through bamboo groves, and you'll eventually emerge near a modern bathhouse, *Yu-no-sato-mura* (daily 9am–10pm; ¥1000 for 3hr), complete with both rotemburo and sauna. The bathhouse marks the western outskirts of Shuzenji village; turn right and you're back on the main street.

Practicalities

Travelling to Shuzenji from Tokyo, the best option is an *Odoriko-gō* Limited Express **train** direct from Tokyo Station; the trains divide at Atami, so make sure you're in the right carriage. Alternatively, hop on any of the regular JR services to Mishima, from where the private Izu-Hakone Railway runs south to Shuzenji (¥500). There's an **information desk** inside the station (daily 5am–11.30pm; ⓣ & ⓕ0558/72-0667), while **buses** for Shuzenji Onsen, Dōgashima and other destinations around Izu depart from a terminal outside. If you want to **rent a car**, you could try Nissan (ⓣ0558/72-2332) or Toyota (ⓣ0558/74-0100) – both have branches near Shuzenji Station.

It's best to **stay** in Shuzenji Onsen, where one of the nicest options – patronized most famously by the writer Natsume Sōseki (see p.1019) – is the elegant ryokan *Kikuya* (ⓣ0558/72-2000, ⓕ72-2002; ⓦwww.kikuya-spa .co.jp/; ⓮), under a high-peaked roof immediately opposite the bus terminal. A few doors down the road to the east, behind a latticework facade, *Goyōkan* (ⓣ0558/72-ⓣ2066, ⓕ72-8212; ⓭) is a comfortable ryokan whose lack of en-suite facilities and evening meals is compensated for by large onsen baths and English-speaking owner. Prices get cheaper as you walk away from the river. Among a group of minshuku on the far northern hillside, *Fukui* (ⓣ0558/72-0558, ⓕ72-3529; ⓬–⓭) is one of the few that welcomes non-Japanese speakers – none of the rooms has its own bathroom, but it's got a small rotemburo with views across the valley. The well-run HI **Shuzenji Youth Hostel** (ⓣ0558/72-1222, ⓕ72-1771; closed Jan 18–22 & May 30–June 3; ¥3000 per person) is on the west side of town in the hills above Shuzenji Onsen; take a bus bound for "New Town" from Shuzenji Station and get off fifteen minutes later at "New Town *iriguchi*" (¥260), from where the hostel is signed a three-minute walk uphill. Note that the last bus departs from the station at 5.30pm and there are no restaurants nearby, but the hostel meals are excellent value.

When it comes to **eating**, you'll find plenty of atmosphere at *Nanaban* (10am–4.30pm; closed Thurs; ⓣ0558/72-0007), a rustic soba restaurant east of Shuzenji Onsen's bus terminal. Though they serve reasonably priced rice and noodle dishes, their speciality is *Zen-dera* soba, in which you dip cold soba in an eye-watering, do-it-yourself sauce of sesame and freshly grated horse-radish – it's said to bring you the blessings of Buddha, so is surely a bargain at ¥1260.

Kamakura and around

An hour's train ride south of Tokyo lies the small, relaxed town of **KAMAKU-RA**, trapped between the sea and a circle of wooded hills. Kamakura is steeped in history, and many of its 65 temples and 19 shrines date back some eight centuries, when, for a brief and tumultuous period, this was Japan's political and military centre. Its most famous sight is the **Daibutsu**, a glorious bronze Buddha surrounded by trees, but the town's ancient **Zen temples** are equally compelling.

Kamakura	*Kamakura*	鎌倉
Daibutsu	*Daibutsu*	大仏
Daibutsu Hiking Course	*Daibutsu Haikingu Kōsu*	大仏ハイキングコース
Engaku-ji	*Engaku-ji*	円覚寺
Ennō-ji	*Ennō-ji*	円応寺
Hase	*Hase*	長谷
Hase-dera	*Hase-dera*	長谷寺
Hōkoku-ji	*Hōkoku-ji*	報国寺
Jōchi-ji	*Jōchi-ji*	浄智寺
Kakuon-ji	*Kakuon-ji*	覚園寺
Kamakura-gū	*Kamakura-gū*	鎌倉宮
Kamakura National Treasure Hall	*Kamakura Kokuhō-kan*	鎌倉国宝館
Kenchō-ji	*Kenchō-ji*	健長寺
Kita-Kamakura	*Kita-Kamakura*	北鎌倉
Sugimoto-dera	*Sugimoto-dera*	杉本寺
Ten'en Hiking Course	*Ten'en Haikingu Kōsu*	天園ハイキングコース
Tōkei-ji	*Tōkei-ji*	東慶寺
Tsurugaoka Hachiman-gū	*Tsurugaoka Hachiman-gū*	鶴岡八幡宮
Zeniarai Benten	*Zeniarai Benten*	銭洗弁天
Zuisen-ji	*Zuisen-ji*	瑞泉寺
Accommodation		
Kamakura Kagetsuen Youth Hostel	*Kamakura Kagetsuen Yūsu Hosuteru*	鎌倉花月園ユースホステル
Hotel Kamakura Mori	*Hoteru Kamakura Mori*	ホテル鎌倉モリ
Shangrila Tsuruoka	*Shangurira Tsuruoka*	シャングリラ鶴岡
Hotel Tsurugaoka Kaikan	*Hoteru Tsurugaoka Kaikan*	ホテル鶴岡会館
Restaurants		
Chaya-kado	*Chaya-kado*	茶屋かど
Fudō-jaya	*Fudō-jaya*	不動茶屋
Hachi-no-ki Honten	*Hachi-no-ki Honten*	鉢の木本店
Ōishi	*Ōishi*	大石
Raitei	*Raitei*	檑亭
Sometarō	*Sometarō*	染太郎
Tsukui	*Tsukui*	津久井
Enoshima	*Enoshima*	江の島

Kamakura's prime sights can be covered on a day-trip from Tokyo, starting with the temples of **Kita-Kamakura**, the town's northern suburb, and then walking south to the sights of **central Kamakura**, before finishing up at the Great Buddha in **Hase** on its western outskirts. If you can only spare a day, make sure you get an early start: most sights close early (generally 4.30pm in winter and only a little later in summer). However, the town more than justifies a two-day visit, allowing you time to explore the enchanting temples of **east Kamakura**, to follow one of the gentle "hiking courses" up into the hills, or to ride the Enoden line west to tiny **Enoshima** island. If at all possible, avoid weekends and national holidays, when both Kamakura and Enoshima are swamped with tourists.

Kamakura's biggest **festivals** take place in early April and mid-September, including displays of horseback archery and costume parades, though the hour-long summer fireworks display (second Tues in Aug) over Sugami Bay is its most spectacular event. The town is also well known for its spring blossoms and autumn colours, while many temple gardens are famous for a particular flower – for example, Japanese apricot at Zuisen-ji and Tōkei-ji (February) and hydrangea at Meigetsu-in (mid-June).

The easiest way of **getting to Kamakura** is on the JR Yokosuka line from Tokyo Station (¥890) via Yokohama (¥330). Trains stop in Kita-Kamakura before pulling into the main Kamakura Station three minutes later; make sure you board a Yokosuka- or Kurihama-bound train to avoid changing at Ōfuna. For a two-day outing, it's worth considering the Kamakura–Enoshima Free Kippu (¥1970), a discount ticket covering both the Yokosuka and Enoden lines.

Some history

When the epic power struggle between the Taira and Minamoto clans (see "History", p.935) ended in 1185, the warlord **Minamoto Yoritomo** became the first permanent shogun and the effective ruler of Japan. Seven years later he established his military government – known as the *Bakufu*, or "tent government" – in Kamakura. Over the next century, dozens of grand monuments were built here, notably the great Zen temples founded by monks fleeing Song-dynasty China. Zen Buddhism flourished under the patronage of a warrior class who shared similar ideals of single-minded devotion to duty and rigorous self-discipline.

The Minamoto rule was brief and violent. Almost immediately, Yoritomo turned against his valiant younger brother, Yoshitsune, who had led the clan's armies, and hounded him until Yoshitsune committed ritual suicide – a favourite tale of Kabuki theatre. Both the second and third Minamoto shoguns were murdered, and in 1219 power passed to the Hōjō clan, who ruled as fairly able regents behind puppet shoguns. Their downfall followed the Mongol invasions in the late thirteenth century, and in 1333 Emperor Go-Daigo wrested power back to Kyoto; as the imperial armies approached Kamakura, the last Hōjō regent and an estimated eight hundred retainers committed *seppuku*. Kamakura remained an important military centre before fading into obscurity in the late fifteenth century. Its temples, however, continued to attract religious pilgrims until Kamakura was "rediscovered" at the beginning of the twentieth century as a tourist destination and a desirable residential area within commuting distance of Tokyo.

Arrival, information and getting around

Trains from Tokyo pass through Kita-Kamakura before terminating at the central **Kamakura Station**. On the west side of the station you'll find ticket machines and platforms for the private Enoden line to Hase (see p.250) and Enoshima (see p.252), with trains running from roughly 6am to 11pm. Outside the station's main, eastern exit, and immediately to the right, there's a small **tourist information** window (daily 9am–5/6pm; ☎0467/22-3350, ⓦwww.kcn-net.org/kamakura) with English-speaking staff. There are no free maps here; a simple one costs ¥200 or a small guidebook ¥800 – check with a tourist information centre in Tokyo before heading out here if you want free maps or pamphlets.

Local **buses** depart from the main station concourse. Given the narrow roads and amount of traffic, however, it's usually quicker to use the trains as far as possible and then walk. The only time a bus might come in handy is for the more

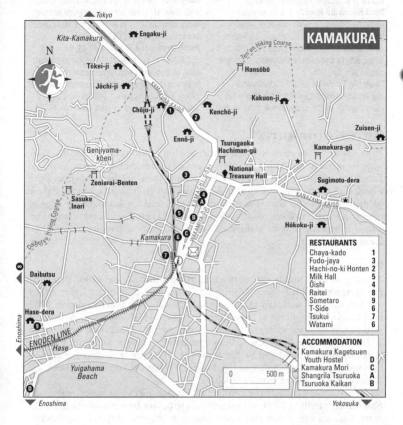

far-flung restaurants or the eastern sights; in the latter case you want bus #23, #24 or #36 from stand 5 (¥170 minimum fare). A better, but more expensive, option is to rent a **bike** from the outfit (daily 8.30am–5pm; ☎0467/24-2319) up the slope beyond the tourist office; rates are on a sliding scale from ¥500 for the first hour to ¥1500 for a day. Note that prices increase by ¥100 on weekends and national holidays, when you'll need to get there early.

Accommodation

Central Kamakura offers little budget **accommodation**, but a fair choice of mid-range hotels. Many places charge higher rates at weekends and during peak holiday periods – generally over New Year, Golden Week (April 29–May 5) and the summer months of July and August – when it's hard to get a room in any case.

Kamakura Kagetsuen Youth Hostel 27-9 Sakanoshita ☎0467/25-1238. Small hostel with rather aged bunk-bed dormitories in a hotel on the seafront ten minutes' walk from Hase Station.

Reception is open from 3.30pm to 8pm, and there's an 11pm curfew. Neither evening meals nor a members' kitchen is available, but there are convenience stores close by and restaurants

around Hase Station. ¥3000 per person.
Hotel Kamakura Mori 3F, 1-5-21 Komachi
ⓣ0467/22-5868, ⓦwww1.ocn.ne.jp/~hotelkm/.
Round the corner from the station on Dankazura,
offering bright, clean, decent-sized twin or triple
rooms with TV and en-suite bathrooms. Expensive
single rates. ❻
Shangrila Tsuruoka 3F, 1-9-29 Yukinoshita
ⓣ0467/25-6363, ⓕ25-6456. If the *Mori* is full, or
too expensive, try this small, friendly hotel hidden

away on the third floor of a shopping mall. Though
a bit fussy, the rooms are light, well kept and perfectly adequate. They're all twins, but single rates
are a reasonable ¥8400. ❺
Hotel Tsurugaoka Kaikan 2-12-27 Komachi
ⓣ0467/24-1111, ⓕ24-1115. Big, old-fashioned
hotel on Dankazura with glitzy chandeliers and
expanses of floral wallpaper. The comfortable
rooms are more restrained, with Western beds, a
tatami sitting area and en-suite bathroom. ❼

Kita-Kamakura

As the Tokyo train nears Kita-Kamakura Station, urban sprawl gradually gives
way to gentle, forested hills which provide the backdrop for some of
Kamakura's greatest Zen temples. Chief among these are **Kenchō-ji** and the
wonderfully atmospheric **Engaku-ji**. It takes over an hour to cover the prime
sights, walking south along the main road, the Kamakura-kaidō, to the edge of
central Kamakura. With more time, follow the Daibutsu Hiking Course up
into the western hills to wash your yen at an alluring temple dedicated to
Zeniarai Benten.

Engaku-ji

The second most important but most satisfying of Kamakura's major Zen temples, **Engaku-ji** (daily 8am–4/5pm; ¥200) lies buried among ancient cedars
just two minutes' walk east of Kita-Kamakura Station. It was founded in 1282
by a Chinese Zen monk, at the request of Regent Hōjō Tokumine, to honour
victims (on both sides) of the ultimately unsuccessful Mongolian invasions in
1274 and 1281 (see "History", p.936). The layout follows a traditional Chinese
Zen formula – a pond and bridge (now cut off by the train tracks), followed
by a succession of somewhat austere buildings – but the encroaching trees and
secretive gardens add a gentler touch.

The first building inside the compound, Engaku-ji's two-storeyed main gate,
San-mon, rebuilt in 1783, is a magnificent structure, beneath which the well-
worn flagstones bear witness to generations of pilgrims. Beyond, the modern
Butsu–den (Buddha Hall) houses the temple's primary Buddha image, haloed
in soft light, while behind it the charming **Shari-den** lies tucked off to the left
past an oblong pond. This small reliquary, usually closed to visitors, is said to
contain a tooth of the Buddha brought here from China in the early thirteenth
century. It's also considered Japan's finest example of Song-dynasty Zen architecture, albeit a sixteenth-century replica. The main path continues gently
uphill to another pretty thatched building, **Butsunichi-an** (¥100), where
regent Hōjō Tokimune was buried in 1284; in fine weather they serve green
tea (¥500 including entrance) in its attractive garden. Finally, tiny **Ōbai-in**
enshrines a pale-yellow Kannon statue but its best attribute is a nicely informal garden with a grove of February-flowering Japanese apricot.

On the way out, follow signs up a steep flight of steps to the left of San-mon
to find Kamakura's biggest bell, **Ōgane**, forged in 1301 and an impressive 2.5m
tall. From its wooden platform you get a fine view across the valley to Tōkei-
ji, the next stop.

Tōkei-ji and Jōchi-ji

Two minutes' walk along the main road from Engaku-ji, **Tōkei-ji** (daily
8.30am–4/5pm; ¥100) was founded as a nunnery in 1285 by the young widow

of Hōjō Tokimune. It's an intimate temple, with a pleasing cluster of buildings and a profusion of flowers at almost any time of year: Japanese apricot in February, magnolia and peach in late March, followed by peonies and then irises in early June; September is the season for cascades of bush clover.

Tōkei-ji is more popularly known as the "Divorce Temple". Up until the mid-nineteenth century, when women were given the legal right to seek divorce, this was one of the few places where wives could escape domestic ill-treatment. If they reached the sanctuary, which many didn't, they automatically received a divorce after three years, according to traditional temple law. Husbands could be summoned to resolve the dispute or, ultimately, sign the divorce papers. Some of these documents are preserved, along with other temple treasures, in the Treasure House (¥300), including two books detailing the women's reasons for seeking sanctuary – unfortunately, not translated. At the back of the temple, take a walk round the peaceful, mossy cemetery hidden among stately cryptomeria trees where many famous and forgotten nuns lie buried.

Continuing along the main valley almost as far as the train tracks, a sign to the right indicates **Jōchi-ji** (daily 9am–4.30pm; ¥150). The fourth most important of Kamakura's great Zen temples, founded by the nephew of Hōjō Tokumine in 1283, Jōchi-ji was almost completely levelled by the 1923 earthquake. Nevertheless, it's worth walking up the lane to see its beautifully proportioned Chinese-style gate which doubles as a bell tower. The small worship hall contains a trinity of Buddhas, while, at the back, there's another graveyard, this time sheltered by a bamboo grove.

Zeniarai Benten and the Daibutsu Hiking Course

Follow the lane running north beside Jōchi-ji and you'll find the steps which mark the start of the **Daibutsu Hiking Course**. This meandering ridge-path (2.2km) makes an enjoyable approach to Hase's Great Buddha (see p.250), but in any case it's well worth taking a diversion as far as the captivating cave-shrine dedicated to the goddess **Zeniarai Benten** (Money-Washing Benten). From Jōchi-ji, follow signs for Genjiyama-kōen along a trail heading southeast through the park to a road junction, where the main trail turns right. Here, take the steps straight ahead and duck under the shrine's tunnel-entrance to emerge in a natural amphitheatre filled with a forest of *torii* wreathed in incense and candle smoke.

Despite being so hidden, a constant stream of hopeful punters comes to test the goddess's powers. According to tradition, money washed in the spring, gushing out of a cave on the opposite side from the entrance, is guaranteed to double at the very least, though not immediately. It's worth a shot – your notes won't dissolve, but let the money dry naturally, to retain the beneficial effects.

If you're following the hiking trail **to Hase**, rather than retracing your steps, take the path heading south under a tunnel of tightly packed *torii*, zigzagging down to the valley bottom, then turn right at a T-junction to find another avenue of vermilion *torii* leading deep into the cryptomeria forest. At the end lies a simple shrine, **Sasuke Inari**, dating from before the twelfth century, which is dedicated to the god of harvests. His messenger is the fox; as you head up the steep path behind, climbing over tangled roots, you'll find fox statues of all shapes and sizes peering out of the surrounding gloom. At the top, turn right and then left at a white sign board to pick up the hiking course for the final kilometre to the Daibutsu.

South to Kenchō-ji and Ennō-ji

Back at the main road near Jōchi-ji, walk southwest for another five minutes to find the greatest of Kamakura's Zen temples, **Kenchō-ji** (8.30am–4.30pm;

¥300). Headquarters of the Rinzai sect and Japan's oldest Zen training
monastery, Kenchō-ji is more formal than Engaku-ji and a lot busier, partly
because of the neighbouring high school and some major construction work.
It contains several important buildings, most of which have been relocated here
from Tokyo and Kyoto to replace those lost since the temple's foundation in
1253. Again, the design of the layout shows a strong Chinese influence; the
founding abbot was another Song Chinese émigré, in this case working under
the patronage of Hōjō Tokiyori, the devout fifth Regent and father of Engaku-
ji's Tokumine.

The main complex begins with the towering, copper-roofed **San-mon**, an
eighteenth-century reconstruction, to the right of which hangs the original
temple **bell**, cast in 1255 and considered one of Japan's most beautiful. Beyond
San-mon, a grove of gnarled and twisted juniper trees hides the dainty, nicely
dilapidated **Butsu-den**. The main image is, unusually, of Jizō seated on a lotus
throne, his bright, half-closed eyes piercing the gloom. Behind is the **Hattō**, or
lecture hall, one of Japan's largest wooden Buddhist buildings. The curvaceous
Chinese-style gate, **Kara-mon**, and the **Hōjō** hall beyond are much more
attractive structures. Walk round the latter's balcony to find a **pond-garden**
generally attributed to a thirteenth-century monk, making it Japan's oldest-surviving Zen garden, though it's recently been spruced up considerably.

Behind the Hōjō, a path heads up steep steps past **Hansōbō**, a shrine guarded by statues of long-nosed, mythical *tengu*. This is the start of the **Ten'en
Hiking Course**: it takes roughly two and a half hours to complete the five-
kilometre trail from Kenchō-ji, which loops round the town's northeast outskirts to Zuisen-ji (see p.250); for a shorter walk (2.5km), you can cut down
earlier to Kamakura-gū (see p.250).

Sticking to the main road, though, from Kenchō-ji there's one last temple to
visit before you hit central Kamakura. **Ennō-ji** (daily 9am–3.30/4pm; ¥200)
looks fairly insignificant, but inside its hall reside the red-faced King of Hell,
Enma, and his ten cohorts. This ferocious crew are charged with deciding the
appropriate level of reincarnation in your next life and their wonderfully realistic expressions are meant to scare you into better ways. The statues are actually reproductions – the originals are in safekeeping in the National Treasure
Hall, but usually only one is displayed there, whereas here you get to see the
whole gang.

From Ennō-ji it's only another five minutes through the tunnel and downhill to the side entrance of Tsurugaoka Hachiman-gū (see opposite).

Central Kamakura

Modern Kamakura revolves around its central **train station** and a couple of touristy streets leading to the town's most important shrine, Tsurugaoka Hachiman-gū. The traditional approach to this grand edifice lies along **Wakamiya-ōji** (also known as Dankazura-dōri), at its northern end, which runs straight from the sea to the shrine entrance. Shops here peddle a motley collection of souvenirs and crafts, the most famous of which is *kamakura-bori*, an 800-year-old method of laying lacquer over carved wood. More popular, however, is *hato*, a pigeon-shaped French-style biscuit first made by Toshimaya bakers a century ago – follow the trail of yellow and white bags to find their main shop (daily except Wed 9am–7pm) halfway up Dankazura-dōri. Shadowing Wakamiya-ōji to the west, **Komachi-dōri** is a narrow, pedestrian-only shopping street, packed with more souvenir shops, restaurants and expensive boutiques.

Tsurugaoka Hachiman-gū

A majestic, vermilion-lacquered *torii* marks the front entrance to **Tsurugaoka Hachiman-gū**, the Minamoto clan's guardian shrine since 1063. Hachiman-gē, as it's popularly known, was moved to its present site in 1191, since when it has witnessed some of the more unsavoury episodes of Kamakura history. Most of the present buildings date from the early nineteenth century, and their striking red paintwork, combined with the parade of souvenir stalls and the constant bustle of people, creates a festive atmosphere in sharp contrast to Kamakura's more secluded Zen temples.

Three humpback bridges lead into the shrine compound between two connected ponds known as **Genpei-ike**. These were designed by Minamoto Yoritomo's wife, Hōjō Masako, and are full of heavy, complicated symbolism, anticipating the longed-for victory of her husband's clan over their bitter enemies, the Taira (see p.935 for the history of this feud); strangely, the bloodthirsty Masako was of Taira stock. Moving hurriedly on, the **Mai-den**, an open-sided stage at the end of a broad avenue, was the scene of another unhappy event in 1186, when Yoritomo forced his brother's mistress to dance for the assembled samurai. Yoritomo wanted his popular brother, Yoshitsune, killed and was holding Shizuka prisoner in the hope of discovering his whereabouts; instead, she made a defiant declaration of love and only narrowly escaped death herself, though her newborn son was murdered soon after. Her bravery is commemorated with classical dances and Nō plays during the shrine **festival** (Sept 14–16), which also features demonstrations of horseback archery.

Beyond the Mai-den, a long flight of steps leads up beside a knobbly, ancient ginkgo tree, reputedly one thousand years old and scene of the third shogun's murder by his vengeful nephew, to the **main shrine**. It's an attractive collection of buildings set among trees, though, like all Shinto shrines, you can only peer in. Appropriately, the principal deity, Hachiman, is the God of War.

The **Hōmotsu-den** (daily 8.30am–4.15pm; ¥100), in a corridor immediately left of the shrine, contains a missable exhibition of shrine treasures – although its ticket desk sells informative maps of Hachiman-gē (¥100). Instead, head back down the steps and turn left to find the beautifully restrained, black-lacquered **Shirahata-jinja**, dedicated to the first and third Kamakura shoguns, then take the path south to the modern **Kamakura National Treasure Hall** (Tues–Sun 9am–4pm; ¥300; English-language leaflet ¥250). This one-room museum is noted for its collection of Kamakura- and Muromachi-period art (1192–1573), mostly gathered from local Zen temples. Unfortunately, only a few of the priceless pieces are on display at any one time.

East Kamakura

The eastern side of Kamakura contains a scattering of less-visited shrines and temples, including two of the town's most enchanting corners. Though it's possible to cover the area on foot in a half-day, or less if you hop on a bus for the return journey, by far the best way to explore these scattered locations is to rent a bicycle (see pp.244–5 for information on buses and bikes).

From Hachiman-gē work your way eastwards through a quiet suburban area north of the main highway, the Kanazawa-kaidō, until you find signs indicating an optional left turn for **Kamakura-gū**. Mainly of interest for its history and torchlight Nō dramas in early October (tickets allocated by postal lottery in early Sept), this shrine was founded by Emperor Meiji in 1869 to encourage support for his new imperial regime. It is dedicated to Prince Morinaga, a forgotten fourteenth-century hero who helped restore his father, Emperor Go-Daigo, briefly to the throne. The prince was soon denounced, however, by power-hungry rivals and held for nine months in a Kamakura cave before being executed. The small cave and a desultory treasure house (daily 9.30am–4.30pm; ¥300) lie to the rear of the classically styled shrine, but don't really justify the entry fee.

A road heading north from Kamakura-gū marks the beginning – or end – of the short cut to the Ten'en Hiking Course (see p.248), though the main trail starts 900m further east, near **Zuisen-ji** (daily 9am–5pm; ¥100). The temple's fourteenth-century Zen garden, to the rear of the main building, is rather dilapidated, but the quiet, wooded location and luxuriant gardens in front of the temple make it an attractive spot.

From Kamakura-gū you have to join the main road for the last short stretch to Kamakura's oldest temple, **Sugimoto-dera** (daily 8am–4.30pm; ¥200), at the top of a steep, foot-worn staircase lined with fluttering white flags. Standing in a woodland clearing, the small, thatched temple, founded in 734, exudes a real sense of history. Inside its smoke-blackened hall, spattered with pilgrims' prayer stickers, you can slip off your shoes and take a look behind the altar at the three wooden statues of Jūichimen Kannon, the eleven-faced Goddess of Mercy. The images were carved at different times by famous monks, but all three are at least one thousand years old. According to legend, they survived a devastating fire in 1189 by taking shelter – all by themselves – behind a giant tree; since then the temple has been known as *Sugimoto* ("Under the Cedar").

Just a few minutes further east along Kanazawa-kaidō, turn right over a small bridge to reach the entrance to **Hōkoku-ji** (daily 9am–4pm; ¥200), or *Take-dera*, the "Bamboo Temple". The well-tended gardens and simple wooden buildings are attractive in themselves, but the temple is best known for a grove of evergreen bamboo protected by the encircling cliffs. This dappled forest of thick, gently curved stems, where tinkling water spouts and the soft creaking of the wind-rocked canes muffles the outside world, would seem the perfect place for the monks' meditation. Too soon, though, the path emerges beside the manicured rear garden, which was created by the temple's founding priest in the thirteenth century.

To return to central Kamakura, you can catch a bus for the two-kilometre ride from opposite Sugimoto-dera. Alternatively, take the small lane left in front of Hōkoku-ji and follow it west through an attractive residential area, which cuts off at least a chunk of the highway.

Hase-dera and the Daibutsu

The west side of Kamakura, an area known as **Hase**, is home to the town's most famous sight, the Daibutsu (Great Buddha), cast in bronze nearly 750 years ago. On the way, it's worth visiting Hase-dera to see an image of Kannon, the Goddess of Mercy, which predates the Daibutsu by at least five hundred years and is said to be Japan's largest wooden statue. Both these sights are within walking distance of Hase Station, three stops from Kamakura Station (¥190) on the private Enoden line.

Hase-dera (daily March–Sept 8am–5pm; Oct–Feb 8am–4.30pm; ¥300) stands high on the hillside a few minutes' walk north of Hase Station, with good views of Kamakura and across Yuigahama beach to the Miura peninsula beyond. Though the temple's present layout dates from the mid-thirteenth century, according to legend it was founded in 736, when a wooden eleven-faced Kannon washed ashore nearby. The statue is supposedly one of a pair carved from a single camphor tree in 721 by a monk in the original Hase, near Nara; he placed one Kannon in a local temple and pushed the other out to sea.

Nowadays the **Kamakura Kannon** – just over 9m tall and gleaming with gold leaf, a fourteenth-century embellishment – resides in an attractive, chocolate-brown and cream building at the top of the temple steps. This central hall is flanked by two smaller buildings: the right hall houses a large Amidha Buddha carved in 1189 for Minamoto Yoritomo's 42nd birthday to ward off the bad luck traditionally associated with that age; on the left is a small **treasure hall** (daily 9am–4pm), whose most prized exhibits are the original temple bell, cast in 1264, and an early fifteenth-century statue of Daikoku-ten, the cheerful God of Wealth. Beside the viewing platform, the Sutra Repository contains a revolving drum with a complete set of Buddhist scriptures inside – one turn of the wheel is equivalent to reading the whole lot. Ranks of Jizō statues are a common sight in Hase-dera, some clutching sweets or "windmills" and wrapped in tiny, woollen mufflers; these sad little figures commemorate stillborn or aborted children.

From Hase-dera, turn left at the main road and follow the crowds north for a few hundred metres to find the **Daibutsu** (daily 7am–5.30/6pm; ¥200), in the grounds of Kōtoku-in temple. After all the hype, the Great Buddha can seem a little disappointing, but as you approach, and his serene, rather aloof face comes into view, the magic begins to take hold. He sits on a stone pedestal, a broad-shouldered figure lost in deep meditation, with his head slightly bowed, his face and robes streaked grey-green by centuries of sun, wind and rain.

The eleven-metre-tall image represents Amida Nyorai, the future Buddha who receives souls into the Western Paradise, and was built under the orders of Minamoto Yoritomo to rival the larger Nara Buddha (see p.581). Completed in 1252, the statue is constructed of bronze plates bolted together around a hollow frame – you can climb inside for ¥20 – and evidence suggests that, at some time, it was covered in gold leaf. Amazingly, it has withstood fires, typhoons, tidal waves and even the Great Earthquake of 1923. Its predecessor, however, was less successful: the wooden statue was unveiled in 1243, only to be destroyed in a violent storm just five years later. And various attempts to build a shelter suffered similar fates until, happily, they gave up after 1498 and left the Daibutsu framed by trees and an expanse of sky.

Eating and drinking

Kamakura is famous for its beautifully presented vegetarian cuisine, known as **shōjin ryōri**, though there's plenty more affordable food on offer at local **restaurants**. To eat in a temple and sample the traditional vegetarian food eaten by monks, call **Chōju-ji** (☏0467/22-2149) and make a reservation at least a day in advance. For a **picnic**, Kinokuniya has a good food hall on the west side of Kamakura Station, or try Union Store on Dankazura.

Chaya-kado 1518 Yamanouchi. This homely soba restaurant, on the opposite side of the main road just north of Kenchō-ji, makes a good pit stop on the temple trail. Try *chikara udon* with a couple of filling *mochi* (steamed rice cakes). Prices start at ¥700 for a meal. Daily 10am–5pm.

Fudō-jaya 2-2-21 Yukinoshita. Delightfully quirky restaurant next to a tiny cave-shrine; recommended for its ambience rather than its food, which comprises a limited selection of noodle dishes from around ¥700. It's also well off the main tourist trail, down a lane of picturesque houses to the west of Hachiman-gū. Daily except Thurs 11am–5pm.

Hachi-no-ki Honten 7 Yamanouchi ☎0120-22-8719. Reservations are recommended for this famous *shōjin ryōri* restaurant beside the entrance to Kenchō-ji, though it's easier to get a table at their newer Kita-Kamakura branch (☎0120-23-3722) opposite Tōkei-ji. Whichever you opt for, prices start at around ¥3500 for a set course.

Milk Hall 2-3-8 Komachi. Relaxed, jazz-playing coffee-house-cum-antique-shop buried in the backstreets west of Komachi-dōri. Best for a coffee and cake, or an evening beer, rather than a place to eat.

Ōishi 2F, 1-9-14 Yukinoshita. Locals swear by this small, discreet tempura restaurant; the lunchtime deals offer best value, such as *tendon teishoku* at ¥1400. Closed Wed.

Raitei Takasago ☎0467/32-5656. Atmospheric restaurant in an old farmhouse set in gardens among the hills west of Kamakura, with views to

Fuji if you're lucky. Basic soba dishes start at around ¥900 and there's a choice of beautifully presented *bentō* from ¥3700 up; the garden entry fee (¥500) is discounted from your bill. Though a bit off the beaten track, it's worth the effort; take bus #4 or #6 from stand 6 outside Kamakura Station to the Takasago stop (2–3 hourly; 20min; ¥230). Daily 11am–dusk.

Sometaro 2F, 3-12-11 Hase. Traditional *okonomiyaki* (do-it-yourself savoury pancakes) restaurant in front of Hase-dera. It costs around ¥900 for a bowl of ingredients, or try the more expensive *teppanyaki*.

T-Side 2F 1-6-2 Komachi ☎0467/24-9572. No-nonsense Indian restaurant serving a wide variety of tasty dishes, generally with a Bollywood movie for background music. The portions aren't huge, but you can still eat for under ¥2000 per head in the evening, while on weekdays they serve excellent-value lunch sets from ¥900.

Tsukui 11-7 Onarimachi. Another cheap, friendly and relaxed *okonomiyaki* and *yakisoba* joint in the centre of Kamakura. Find it on the west side of Kamakura Station and right, down a stone-paved alley at the north end of Onari-dōri. English menu. Closed Tues.

Watami 3F, 1-6-17 Komachi. Lively, modern *izakaya* – you'll need to arrive early to get a seat. Their huge picture menu offers everything from fried potatoes to *sashimi* and from sake to cocktails. Most dishes are under ¥400 and you can feast for ¥1500–2000 per head excluding drinks, though even those are well priced.

Around Kamakura

With so much to see in Kamakura, there's little time left for exploring the surrounding area. However, one possibility is the tiny, sacred island of **ENOSHIMA**, twenty minutes west of Kamakura Station on the private Enoden line (¥250). Tied to the mainland by a six-hundred-metre-long bridge, Enoshima has a few sights – some shrines, a botanical garden and a missable cave – but its prime attraction is as a pleasant place to walk away from motor traffic. The island's best appreciated on weekdays in the off season; during summer and on holiday weekends, it seems liable to sink under the weight of visitors. If you do happen to be here in July or August, there's solace to be had in the funky wooden bars lining the beaches from Kamakura to Enoshima and in the spectacular summer firework displays – Enoshima's (July 25) lasts a staggering ninety minutes. This Shōnan coast, as it's known, is also a favourite spot for windsurfers.

As the Enoden-line train rattles into Enoshima Station from Kamakura, look out on the right for the copper-clad roofs of **Ryūkō-ji**. This temple was built on the spot where the monk Nichiren, founder of the eponymous Buddhist sect (see p.954), was nearly beheaded in 1271 for his persistent criticisms of the government and rival sects. According to legend, as the executioner's sword was about to fall, a fortuitous bolt of lightning split the blade in two, just in time for the shogun's messenger to arrive with a reprieve. Ryūkō-ji was founded a few years later and the main hall, its Buddha image surrounded by a sea of gold, is a good example of the sect's striking decorative style. To the left of the hall there's a statue of Nichiren in the cave where he was imprisoned and a staircase leading up to a smaller temple. Turn right here and follow the path round to where a magnificent five-storey pagoda, erected in 1910, seems part of the surrounding forest.

From Enoshima Station it's roughly fifteen minutes' walk southwest to the island via a bridge constructed over the original sand-spit. Enoshima's eastern side shelters a yacht harbour and car parks, but otherwise the knuckle of rock – less than 1km from end to end – is largely covered with woods and a network of well-marked paths. Where the bridge ends, walk straight ahead under the bronze *torii* and uphill past restaurants and souvenir shops (the first on the left stocks informative English maps), to where the steps begin; though the climb's easy enough, there are three escalators tunnelled through the hillside (¥330, or pay for each separately).

Enoshima is mostly famous for a naked **statue of Benten**, the Goddess of Fortune and the Arts, which is housed in an octagonal hall (daily 9am–5pm; ¥150) halfway up the hill. Though the pale-skinned, purple-haired beauty strumming her lute is said to be 600 years old and is ranked among Japan's top three Benten images, it's a little hard to see what all the fuss is about. Continuing uphill you'll pass several other shrine buildings belonging to Enoshima-jinja, founded in the thirteenth century and dedicated to the guardian of sailors and fisherfolk, before emerging beside a nicely laid-out **botanical garden** (daily 9am–5pm; ¥200). If it's clear, you'll get good views south to Ōshima's smoking volcano and west to Fuji from the lighthouse (an extra ¥280) inside the garden. The path then drops down steeply to the island's rocky west shore and two caves known as **Iwaya** (daily 9am–4pm, 5pm in summer; ¥500). Though it's an attractive walk, you might want to give these very artificial grottoes, with their piped music and roaring dragons, a miss.

If you're heading back **to central Tokyo** from Enoshima, the easiest route is the Odakyū-Enoshima line direct to Shinjuku, though note that these trains depart from a different station; from the island causeway, turn left across the river to find Katase-Enoshima Station, with its distinctive Chinese-style facade. Alternatively, walk back to Enoshima Station and take the Enoden line west to its terminal in Fujisawa, where you have to change stations for Tōkaidō-line trains to Tokyo Station via Yokohama and Shinagawa.

Yokohama and around

YOKOHAMA feels far more spacious and airy than neighbouring Tokyo, thanks to its open harbour frontage and generally low-rise skyline. Locals are proud of their city's international heritage, and there's definitely a cosmopolitan flavour to the place, with its scattering of Western-style buildings, Chinese temples and world cuisines, and its sizeable foreign community.

Though it can't claim any outstanding sights, Japan's second most populous city (home to 3.5 million people) has enough of interest to justify a day's outing from Tokyo. It might seem strange to come all this way to look at nineteenth-century European-style buildings, but the upmarket suburb of **Yamate** is one of the city's highlights, an area of handsome residences, church spires and bijou teashops. Yamate's "exotic" attractions still draw Japanese tourists in large

Yokohama and around

Yokohama	*Yokohama*	横浜
Chinatown	*Chūka-gai*	中華街
Doll Museum	*Ningyō no Ie*	人形の家
Foreigners' Cemetery	*Gaikokujin Bochi*	外国人墓地
Ishikawachō	*Ishikawachō*	石川町
Kannai	*Kannai*	関内
Kantei-byō	*Kantei-byō*	関帝廟
Minato Mirai	*Minato Mirai*	みなとみらい
Mitsubishi Minato Mirai Industrial Museum	*Mitsubishi Minato Mirai Gijutsukan*	三菱みなとみらい技術館
Motomachi	*Motomachi*	元町
Sakuragichō	*Sakuragichō*	桜木町
Sambō Centre	*Sambō Sentā*	サンボーセンター
Silk Museum	*Shiruku Hakubutsukan*	シルク博物館
Yamate	*Yamate*	山手
Yokohama Archives of History	*Yokohama Kaikō Shiryōkan*	横浜開港資料館
Yokohama Daisekai	*Yokohama Daisekai*	横浜大世界
Yokohama Museum of Art	*Yokohama Bijutsukan*	横浜美術館

Accommodation

Echigoya Ryokan	*Echigoya Ryokan*	エチゴヤ旅館
Kanagawa Youth Hostel	*Kanagawa Yūsu Hosuteru*	神奈川ユースホステル
Navios Yokohama	*Nabiosu Yokohama*	ナビオス横浜
Hotel New Grand	*Hoteru Nyū Gurando*	ホテルニューグランド
Royal Park Hotel Nikkō	*Roiyaru Pāku Hoteru Nikkō*	ロイヤルパークホテルニッコー
Sakuragichō Washington Hotel	*Sakuragi Wasington Hoteru*	桜木町ワシントンホテル
San'ai Yokohama Hotel	*San'ai Yokohama Hoteru*	三愛ヨコハマホテル
Star Hotel	*Sutā Hoteru*	スターホテル
Tōyoko Inn Yokohama Sakuragi-chō	*Tōyoko In Yokohama Sakuragi-chō*	東横イン桜木町
Yokohama Plaza Hotel	*Yokohama Puraza Hoteru*	横浜プラザホテル

Restaurants

Capricciosa	*Kapurichōza*	カプリチョーザ
Edosei	*Edosei*	江戸清
Heichinrō	*Heichinrō*	萬珍樓
Manchinrō	*Manchinrō*	萬珍樓
Meikōkaku	*Meikōkaku*	茗香閣
Peking Hanten	*Pekin Hanten*	北京飯店
Rikyūan	*Rikyūan*	利久庵
Shei Shei	*Shei Shei*	謝謝
Shōfukumon	*Shōfukumon*	招福門
Suro Saikan Honkan	*Suro Saikan Honkan*	四五六菜館本館
Yamate Jūbankan	*Yamate Jūbankan*	山手十番館

Negishi	*Negishi*	根岸
Rāmen Museum	*Rāmen Hakubutsukan*	ラーメン博物
Sankei-en	*Sankei-en*	三渓園
Shin-Yokohama	*Shin-Yokohama*	新横浜

numbers, as do the vibrant alleys and speciality restaurants of nearby **Chinatown**. There's a clutch of assorted **museums** along the seafront, and north to where **Kannai** boasts a few grand old Western edifices, in complete contrast to **Minato Mirai 21**'s high-tech skyscrapers in the distance. This "harbour-city of the 21st century" forms the focus of Yokohama's ambitious plans to grab some of the initiative away from Tokyo.

A tour of these central sights will easily fill a day, but with a little extra time **Sankei-en**, just south of Yokohama, makes a good half-day excursion. This extensive Japanese garden provides a perfect backdrop for its collection of picturesque temples and other ancient buildings. If modern culture's more your thing, don't miss Shin-Yokohama's **Ramen Museum** en route back to Tokyo, which celebrates Japan's answer to the hamburger.

Some history

When Commodore Perry sailed his "Black Ships" into Tokyo Bay in 1853 (see p.939), Yokohama was a mere fishing village of some eighty houses on the distant shore. But it was this harbour, well out of harm's way as far as the Japanese were concerned, that the shogun designated one of the five **treaty ports** open to foreign trade in 1858. At first, foreign merchants were limited to a small, semi-restricted compound in today's Kannai – allegedly for their protection from anti-foreign sentiment – but eventually they moved up onto the more favourable southern hills.

From the early 1860s until the first decades of the twentieth century, Yokohama flourished on the back of raw silk exports, a trade dominated by British merchants. During this period the city provided the main conduit for new ideas and inventions into Japan: the first bakery, photographers, ice-cream shop, brewery and – perhaps most importantly – the first railway line, which linked today's Sakuragichō with Shimbashi in central Tokyo in 1872. Soon established as Japan's major international port, Yokohama held pole position until the **Great Earthquake** levelled the city in 1923, killing more than 40,000 people. It was eventually rebuilt, only to be devastated again in air raids at the end of World War II. By this time Kōbe was in the ascendancy and, though Yokohama still figures among the world's largest ports, it never regained its hold over Japanese trade.

Orientation, arrival and getting around

With the harbour bounding its east side, hills to the south and a couple of useful landmark towers, Yokohama is an easy enough place to get your bearings. On the northwest side of town, **Yokohama Station** functions as the city's main transport hub, offering train, subway, bus and even ferry connections, and featuring several gargantuan department stores. From here the JR Negishi line, part of the Keihin-Tōhoku line, runs south through central Yokohama, passing the majority of sights and tourist facilities which lie scattered between the train tracks and the harbour. **Kannai**, two stops down the line, is the traditional downtown area and a focus for banks and offices.

Arrival

The best way to get to Yokohama **from central Tokyo** is on a Tōkyū-Tōyoko-line **train** from Shibuya Station (every 5min; 40min; ¥270), which calls at Yokohama Station before heading off underground to Minato Mirai and terminating at the Motomachi, Chukagai, Yamashita Kōen station. Coming from Tokyo Station, there's a choice between the Tōkaidō line and Yokosuka line (both every 5–10min; 30min; ¥450) or the Keihin-Tōhoku line (every

YOKOHAMA

RESTAURANTS, CAFÉS & BARS

Alte Liebe	6	Pure	12
Beer Next	2	Rikyuan	21
Cape Cod	19	Shei Shei	16
Capricciosa	9	Shofukumon	7
Chano-ma	2	Suro Saikan	2
Colombo	17	Honkan	11
Edosei	8	The Tavern	4
Enokitei	18	Windjammer	20
Gas Panic	1	World Food	
Heichinrou	10	Court	3
Manchinrou	13	Yamate	
Meikoukaku	15	Jūbankan	14
Motion Blue	2	Yokohama Curry	
Peking Hanten	5	Museum	22

ACCOMMODATION

Echigoya Ryokan	J
Kanagawa Youth Hostel	H
Navios Yokohama	B
New Grand	C
Royal Park Nikkō	E
Sakuragicho	G
Washington Hotel	I
San'ai Yokohama	D
Star	
Toyoko Inn Yokohama	F
Sakuragichō	
Yokohama Plaza Hotel	A

▲ Yokohama Bay Bridge

▲ Tokyo

◀ Shin-Yokohama & Tokyo

Negishi & Sankei-en ▶

Harbour View Park

Motomachi-kōen

Foreigners' Cemetery

Yamate Museum

Christ Church

YAMATE

Motomachi-kōen

Chūkagai & Yamashita-kōen

MOTOMACHI

METROPOLITAN EXPRESSWAY

Doll Museum

Marine Tower

Sea Bass Pier

CHINATOWN

Kanteibyō

Daisekai

Yokohama

Ishikawachō

Hikawa-maru

Yamashita-kōen

Sanbo Centre & Silk Museum

HON-ODŌRI

Yokohama Archives of History

NIHON ODŌRI

Customs House

Royal Wing Cruise Terminal

Yokohama Passenger Terminal

Yokohama International Passenger Terminal

Akarenga

SHINKŌ-CHŌ

World Porters

Cosmo Clock 21

Nippon-maru

Yokohama Maritime Museum

Kanagawa Government Offices

Port Opening Memorial Hall

Kanagawa Prefectural Museum

Bashamichi

MINATO ODŌRI

Yokohama Stadium

KANNAI

Kannai

KANNAI ODŌRI

BASHAMICHI

METROPOLITAN EXPRESSWAY

ISEZAKICHŌ

Hinodechō

Tobe

Takashimachō

JR NEGISHI LINE

Sakuragichō

Sakuragichō

Landmark Tower

Landmark Plaza

Queen's Square

Minato Mirai

MINATO MIRAI 21 (MM21)

Mitsubishi Minato Mirai Industrial Museum

Yokohama Museum of Art

Media Tower

Convention Hall

Pacifico Yokohama Exhibition Hall

Minato Mirai Pukari-sanbashi

Jackmall Yokohama

Shin-Takashima

METROPOLITAN EXPRESSWAY

Takashima

YCAT

Luminé Department Store

Sogō Department Store

Sea Bass Pier

Yokohama

N

0   500 m

5–10min; 40min; ¥450). All three are JR lines; the first two terminate at Yokohama Station, while the latter is more convenient if you're continuing to Sakuragichō, Kannai or beyond.

Arriving straight **from Narita Airport**, services on JR's **Narita Express** (N'EX) depart roughly every hour for Yokohama Station and take ninety minutes (¥4180); note that not all N'EX trains go to Yokohama and some divide at Tokyo Station, so check before you get on. Otherwise, get on the cheaper rapid train (JR, "Airport Narita"), which takes two hours to reach Yokohama Station (¥1890). From **Haneda Airport**, a limousine bus is the best option, with frequent departures and only a thirty-minute ride into town (¥560); the bus drops you at **YCAT** (Yokohama City Air Terminal), in the Sky Building just east of Yokohama Station. Alternatively, take the Airport line to Keikyū-Kamata Station, then change onto a Keihin-Kyūkō train for Yokohama, a total journey time of forty minutes (¥470).

Shinkansen trains from Kyoto, Ōsaka and points south pause briefly at **Shin-Yokohama**, 5km north of the centre. From here there's a subway link to the main Yokohama Station (¥230), Sakuragichō and Kannai, but it's cheaper and usually quicker to get the first passing JR Yokohama-line train and change at Higashi-Kanagawa Station onto the Keihin-Tōhoku line (¥160).

Information

Yokohama's plethora of "i" **information** centres with English-speaking staff puts Tokyo to shame. You'll find them in the underground concourse outside the east exit of **Yokohama Station** (daily 10am–6pm; ℡045/441-7300); in the booth immediately outside **Sakuragichō Station**'s east entrance (daily 9am–6pm, Aug until 8pm; ℡045/211-0111); and at the harbourfront **Sambō Centre** east of Kannai Station (Mon–Fri 9am–5pm; ℡045/641-4759). A block west you'll find the **Kanagawa Prefectural Tourist Association** (Mon–Sat 9am–5.30pm, ℡045/681-0077, ⓦwww.kanagawa-kankou.or.jp/index-e.html). There's also a small office in **Shin-Yokohama Station** under the Shinkansen tracks on the northwest side of the main concourse (daily 10am–1pm & 2–6pm; ℡045/473-2895). All these places provide free **city maps** and brochures and can help with hotel reservations. While there's no official information desk at **YCAT**, some staff there speak English and will help with basic enquiries. The city's website is ⓦwww.city.yokohama.jp.

Getting around

Getting around central Yokohama is best done on either the Tōkyū-Tōyoko line or the JR Negishi line (the local name for Keihin-Tōhoku trains); trains on both lines run every five minutes. A single **subway** line connects Kannai and stations north to Shin-Yokohama, but it's more expensive and usually slower than regular trains; services run every five to fifteen minutes and the minimum fare is ¥200. The most enjoyable way of getting about the city and sightseeing at the same time is on one of the *Sea Bass* **ferries** that shuttle between Yokohama Station (from beside Sogō department store) and southerly Yamashita-kōen via Minato Mirai. There are departures every fifteen minutes (10am–7pm), with one-way tickets costing ¥600 for the full fifteen-minute journey, or ¥340 to Minato Mirai. From Yamashita-kōen you can also join the *Marine Shuttle* for a variety of **sightseeing cruises** round the harbour; prices start at ¥900 for forty minutes. In addition, the **Royal Wing** cruise ship (℡045/662-6125, ⓦwww.royalwing.co.jp) departs from the new Yokohama International Port Terminal for lunch, tea or dinner cruises (1hr 45 min). The cost of the cruise is ¥2000 plus anything from ¥2000 to ¥25,000 depending on what you eat.

Accommodation

Yokohama's new luxury **hotels**, all located in MM21, are a tourist attraction in their own right. You'll need a reservation at the weekend (when premium rates also usually apply), though weekdays shouldn't be a problem. Lower down the scale, there are a few reasonable business hotels scattered round the city centre, particularly the *Toyoko Inn* chain, but very little in the way of budget accommodation.

Echigoya Ryokan 2F, 1-14 Ishikawachō, Naka-ku ☏045/641-4700, ⓦ www.ny.airnet.ne.jp/i~mall/4 -10html. One of the few budget places in central Yokohama, conveniently located on the chic Motomachi shopping street, one minute's walk east of Ishikawachō Station. The tatami rooms are basic and a bit worn, and none is en suite, but it's a relaxed, friendly place and the landlord can speak a little English. Look out for a sign next to *Vie de France* bakery. No meals are served and there's a midnight curfew. ❹

Kanagawa Youth Hostel 1 Momijigaoka, Nishi-ku ☏045/241-6503, ⓦ yokohama@xf6.so-net.ne.jp. Aged and overpriced, this isn't the most appealing youth hostel, but its dormitory beds are the cheapest option in town. From the west exit of Sakuragichō Station, walk north along the tracks, beside a graffiti-spattered wall, and take the first left after the Jomo gas stand, over a small bridge and uphill. Reception open 5am–8pm. ¥3000 per person.

Navios Yokohama Sinkō-chō, Naka-ku ☏045/633-6000, ⓦ www.navios-yokohama-com. The light, spacious rooms and reasonable rates make this one of the best-value options in Yokohama. Ask for a room facing Landmark Tower for the best night-time views. Facilities include a restaurant, coffee shop and the International Seamen's Club bar. ❼

Hotel New Grand 10 Yamashitachō, Naka-ku ☏045/681-1841, ⓦ www.hotel-newgrand.co.jp. Built in the late 1920s in European style, the main building retains some of its original elegance, while rooms are slightly cheaper than in the new tower. All come with satellite TV and en-suite bath, and many have harbour views. There's also a choice of three restaurants. ❽

Royal Park Hotel Nikkō 2-2-1-3 Minato Mirai, Nishi-ku ☏045/221-1111, ⓦ www.yrph.com/index-e.html. The gargantuan Landmark Tower houses the *Nikkō's* guestrooms on its 52nd to 67th floors, so spectacular views are guaranteed. The rooms are spacious and elegant, with a separate bath and shower cubicle. As well as a fitness club (¥5000) and swimming pool on the 49th floor, facilities include a tea ceremony room (¥1100), *Sky Lounge* bar, and French, Chinese and Japanese restaurants. Ask about special weekday rates. ❾

Sakuragichō Washington Hotel 1-1-67 Sakuragichō, Naka-ku ☏045/683-3111, ⓦ www.yokohama-s-wh.com. Huge addition to the *Washington* chain, right next to Sakuragichō Station, with relatively spacious rooms above the Cross Gate shopping mall, which has a good range of dining options. ❻

San'ai Yokohama Hotel 3-95 Hanasakichō, Naka-ku ☏045/242-4411, ⒻAX242-7485. One of the cheaper business hotels in central Yokohama. The rooms – in Japanese or Western style – are uninspiring but a decent size, and all come with en-suite bathrooms. English spoken. ❺

Star Hotel 11 Yamashitachō, Naka-ku ☏045/651-3111, ⒻAX651-3119, ⓦ www.starhotel.co.jp. Right on the seafront, this popular hotel offers reasonable value for money in Yokohama terms. The bright, fresh decor compensates for smallish rooms at the cheaper end, though all have bathrooms, fridge, TV and phone. Upgrade for extra space and harbour views. ❻

Tōyoko Inn Yokohama Sakuragichō 6-55 Honchō, Naka-ku ☏045-671 1045, ⓦ www.toyoko-inn.co.jp. One of several Yokohama branches of this Japan-wide chain of budget business hotels, with good-value rooms (including non-smoking rooms), free Internet access and breakfast. There's another branch beside Yokohama Stadium (☏045/664-1045, ⒻAX664–1046), convenient for Chinatown. ❹

Yokohama Plaza Hotel 2-12-12 Takashima, Nishi-ku ☏045/461-1771, ⓦ www.yokohamaplazahotel.co.jp. If you need somewhere to stay near Yokohama Station, this mid-range business hotel outside the east exit is a good option. The rooms are simple but brighter and better maintained than the competition. Some English spoken. ❻

The City

Though much of Yokohama was destroyed in the 1923 earthquake and again in bombing raids during World War II, it retains a few European-style buildings from its days as a treaty port, some of which lie scattered around **Kannai**, the traditional city centre. For a more evocative atmosphere, climb up to **Yamate** (also known as "the Bluff"), a genteel residential area of clapboard houses, tennis clubs and church spires on the southern hills. **Chinatown**, back down on the levels, makes for a lively contrast, with its hoards of colourful trinket shops and bustling restaurants. From here it's a short stroll down to the **harbourfront** Marine Tower and a couple of nearby museums, or a train ride north to where the aptly named **Landmark Tower**, Japan's tallest building, pinpoints the futuristic **Minato Mirai 21** (MM21) development. Among its gleaming hotels, shopping malls and conference centres, there are a couple of specific sights, notably a modern art museum and an incongruous four-masted barque, the **Nippon-maru**. All these central sights can be covered in an easy day's outing; the account below starts with Yokohama's southern districts and heads north.

Motomachi and Yamate
Southeast of central Yokohama, the JR Negishi line stops at **Ishikawachō Station** before plunging into a series of tunnels beneath Yamate hill. Take the station's southeastern exit to find **Motomachi**, a fashionable shopping street from prewar days, which used to serve the city's expatriate community and still exudes a faint European flavour. Today this narrow lane of small shops, selling foreign brand names and exotic foodstuffs, continues to draw the punters, particularly on Sundays and holidays, when it's turned over to pedestrians; note that many stores close on Monday or Thursday.

At the east end of Motomachi, a wooded promontory marks the beginning of **Harbour View Park**; take any of the paths going uphill to find the lookout point where the British and French barracks once stood – the panoramic view of the harbour and its graceful Bay Bridge is particularly beautiful at night. Turning inland and walking through the park will bring you to the **Foreigners' Cemetery** on the western hillside. Over 4500 people from more than forty countries are buried here, the vast majority either British or American. Wandering among the crosses and sculpted angels, look out for Edward Morel, chief engineer on the Yokohama–Tokyo railway, who died of TB at the age of 30, and Charles Richardson, a British merchant whose murder in 1862 provoked a war between Britain and the Shimazu clan (see p.848–850). You'll also find more modern tombstones – an average of twenty foreigners a year are still buried on Yamate.

Heading south along the cemetery's eastern perimeter, you'll pass a handsome row of houses, including the turreted *Yamate Jūbankan* – now a French restaurant (see p.264) – and, next door to it, the city's oldest wooden building. The latter, erected in 1909 for a wealthy Japanese family, now houses the **Yamate Museum** (daily 11am–4pm; ¥200), most interesting for its collection of cartoons from *Japan Punch*, a satirical magazine published in Yokohama for a while in the late nineteenth century. Just beyond, the square tower of **Christ Church**, founded in 1862 but rebuilt most recently in 1947, adds a village-green touch to the neighbourhood, which is still the most popular residential district for Yokohama's wealthy expatriates.

Down to the harbour
From the cemetery, drop down through Motomachi-kōen and cross Motomachi shopping street to find one of the several entrance gates to **Chinatown**. Founded in 1863, Yokohama's Chinatown is the largest in Japan; its streets contain roughly two hundred restaurants and over 300 shops, while some eighteen million tourists pass through its narrow byways every year to

browse among stores peddling Chinese herbs or cooking utensils, and grocers, silk shops and jewellers with windows full of flashy gold. Few leave without tasting what's on offer, from steaming savoury dumplings to a full-blown meal in one of the famous speciality restaurants (see "Eating", p.263).

The fortunes of the Chinese community based here (around two thousand ethnic Chinese) have followed the vagaries of mainland history: during the late nineteenth and early twentieth centuries hundreds of radicals (most famously, Sun Yat-sen and Chiang Kai-shek) sought refuge here, while Communist and Nationalist factions polarized Chinatown in the 1940s and later during the Cultural Revolution. The focus of community life is **Kantei-byō** (daily 10am–8pm; free), a shrine dedicated to Guan Yu, a former warlord and guardian deity of Chinatown. The building is a bit cramped, but impressive nonetheless, with a colourful ornamental gateway and writhing dragons wherever you look. Inside, a long-haired Guan Yu sits on the main altar, gazing over the heads of supplicants petitioning for health and prosperity. The best times to visit are during the major festivities surrounding Chinese New Year (late Jan or early Feb) and Chinese National Day (Oct 1). A few hundred metres northeast of Kantei-byō at 97 Yamashita-chō is the new **Yokohama Daisekai** (¥500; daily 10am–10pm), a Disneyesque China Museum that aims to recreate Shanghai in the roaring 1920s. About the only thing possibly worth spending the entrance fee on here are Chinese dance shows – the food courts that take up the majority of floors are decidedly passé.

From the eastern edge of Chinatown it's a short hop down to the harbour – aim for the pink-grey **Marine Tower** (daily: Feb–Nov 10am–9pm; Jan & Dec 10am–7pm; ¥700; joint ticket with Hikawa-maru ¥1300, or ¥1550 including the Doll Museum). This 106-metre-high tower, built in 1961 to celebrate the port's centenary, is supposedly the world's tallest lighthouse, but it's better to save your money for the Landmark's much higher observation deck. In front of the tower, **Yamashita-kōen** is a pleasant seafront park created as a memorial to victims of the Great Earthquake. Here you can pick up a *Sea Bass* ferry (see p.257) or take a harbour cruise from the pier beside the **Hikawa-maru** (mid-June to mid-Sept daily 9.30am–9/9.30pm; mid-Sept to mid-June Mon–Fri 9.30am–7.30pm, Sat & Sun 9.30am–9pm; ¥800), a retired passenger liner. The vessel, also known as the *Queen of the Pacific*, was built in 1930 for the NYK line Yokohama–Seattle service, though it was commandeered as a hospital ship during the war. It now serves as a "floating amusement ship" whose best feature is a small museum full of nostalgic memorabilia from the days of the great ocean-going liners.

At the south end of Yamashita-kōen, the **Doll Museum** (Tues–Sun 10am–5pm; July & Aug 10am–7pm; ¥300) offers a more diverting display of dolls from around the world. Unfortunately there's little information in English, but the vast collection of Japanese folk and classical dolls is worth a look. Don't miss the exquisite, ceremonial *hina* dolls, traditionally displayed on March 3 during the Hina Matsuri (Doll Festival).

On the southwestern flank of Chinatown outside Kannai Station is **Yokohama International Stadium** (℡045/477-5006, ⓦwww.hamaspo .com/stadium), venue for the 2002 soccer World Cup final. If you wish to relive the drama of that match or just take a look around the 70,000 capacity stadium, one of Japan's largest, there are tours (¥500) four times daily except when there's an event on.

North to Sakuragichō

Yokohama's rapid growth in the late nineteenth century was underpinned by a flourishing export trade in raw silk. You can check out the practical aspects of silk production, from mulberry leaves to gorgeously coloured kimono, at the **Silk Museum**, at the north end of Yamashita-kōen (Tues–Sun 9am–4.30pm; ¥500).

Continuing north across a leafy square, you'll come to a modern, windowless building which houses the **Yokohama Archives of History** (Tues–Sun 9.30am–5pm; ¥200). This is the best of the city's historical museums, thanks to an unusual amount of English translation. The museum itself details the opening of Yokohama (and Japan), after 1853, through an impressive collection of photos, artefacts and documents, including contemporary newspaper reports from London.

You're now in the thick of Yokohama's administrative district, where several European-style facades still survive. Kanagawa government offices occupy the next block north, while the biscuit-coloured **Customs House**, opposite, is a more attractive structure, topped by a distinguished, copper-clad dome. Or follow the road heading inland, Minato Ōdori, to find the graceful **Port Opening Memorial Hall**; erected in 1918, this red-brick Neo-Renaissance building now serves as public function rooms. In front of the hall, turn north again, onto Honchō-dōri, to reach the last and most ornate of Yokohama's Western-style facades. The building was completed in 1904 as the headquarters of a Yokohama bank, and then later converted into the **Kanagawa Prefectural Museum** (Tues–Sun 9.30am–4.30pm; ¥300). The exhibition itself is a missable affair, dealing primarily with local archeology and natural history.

The museum sits near the junction of Honchō-dōri and **Bashamichi** – this tree-lined shopping street, once the showcase of Yokohama and much vaunted in the tourist literature for its old-fashioned street lamps and red-brick paving, is somewhat disappointing. Bashamichi heads west across the train tracks near Kannai Station and then continues as a pedestrianized shopping mall called **Isezakichō**. For now, though, follow Honchō-dōri north over a bridge for 500m to **Sakuragichō Station**.

Minato Mirai 21 (MM21)

In a bid to beat Tokyo at its own game, Yokohama now boasts Japan's tallest building and is in the process of creating a nonstop, high-tech international 21st-century city: **Minato Mirai 21** – or **MM21** as the development is better known. This mini-city of hotels, apartment blocks, offices and cultural facilities is rapidly changing the face of Yokohama, and will eventually occupy over two square kilometres of reclaimed land and disused dockyards, with its own subway line and state-of-the-art waste disposal and heating systems. The bulk of the hotels, conference facilities, shopping malls and museums is already in place. Next will come the office blocks, exhibition halls and waterfront parks to fill the empty plots behind.

MM21 can be accessed from either the Minato Mirai station on the Tōkyū-Tōyoko-line or Sakuragichō train and subway station, from where a covered moving walkway whisks you towards the awesome, 296-metre-tall **Landmark Tower**. Inside, take the world's fastest lift for an ear-popping, forty-second ride up to the 69th-floor **Sky Garden** (July–Aug daily and Sat all year 10am–10pm; Sept–June daily 10am–9pm; ¥1000). On clear days, when Fuji is flaunting her beauty, superb views more than justify the observatory's steep entry fee. Alternatively, if you don't mind missing the thrill of the elevator, you can enjoy a coffee for about the same price in the opulent *Sirius Sky Lounge* on the seventieth floor of the *Nikkō Hotel*, or splash out on an early-evening cocktail as the city lights spread their magic.

Next door, the **Landmark Plaza** consists of a swanky shopping mall set around a five-storey-high atrium. Here you'll find flash boutiques, Yurindo bookstore on the fifth floor – with an excellent foreign-language section – and plenty of restaurants, bars and coffee shops, some of which are built into the stone walls of an old dry dock.

Another water-filled dock in front of Landmark Tower is now home to the sleek **Nippon-maru** sail training ship, part of the enjoyable **Yokohama Maritime Museum** (Tues–Sun 10am–4.30/5pm; July & Aug 10am–6.30pm; ¥600). The *Nippon-maru* was built in 1930 and served up until 1984, during which time she sailed the equivalent of 45 times round the world; when her pristine white sails are hoisted twice monthly, it's clear why she's more familiarly known as the *Swan of the Pacific*. You can explore the entire vessel, from the engine room to the captain's wood-panelled cabin. There's copious English labelling and alternating Japanese and English commentary over the loudspeakers. The museum's main exhibition rooms occupy a purpose-built underground hall beside the ship. In addition to well-designed coverage of Yokohama's historical development, there's also a lot about the modern port and the technical side of sailing, though little in English. Nevertheless, you can still test your navigational skills at a mock-up bridge with a simulator, or have a bash at unloading a container vessel.

Landmark Tower stands in the extreme southern corner of MM21. Off to the east, the stepped towers of **Queen's Square** – another vast complex of shops, offices, a concert hall and the sail-shaped *Intercontinental Hotel* – fill the skyline. More inviting is the slowly revolving **Cosmo Clock 21** (daily: mid-March to Nov 11am–9/10pm; Dec to mid-March 11am–8/9pm; ¥700), standing on the adjacent island of **Shinkō-chō**, which was reclaimed about a hundred years ago as part of Yokohama's then state-of-the-art port facilities. With a capacity of 480 passengers, this 112-metre ferris wheel claims to be the world's largest; one circuit takes around fifteen minutes, allowing plenty of time to admire the view. A short walk east of here past Yokohama World Porters, yet another shopping centre, are the **Akarenga**, two handsome red-brick warehouses dating from 1911 which reopened in 2002 as a smart shopping, dining and entertainment complex.

MM21's two major museums are to be found in the blocks immediately north of Landmark Tower. Head first for the splendid **Yokohama Museum of Art** (Mon–Wed, Sat & Sun 10am–6pm, Fri 10am–8pm; ¥500; varying prices for special exhibitions), in which mostly twentieth-century Japanese and Western art is set off to fine effect by designer Tange Kenzō's cool, grey space. In fact, the architecture – particularly the magnificent central atrium – grabs your attention as much as the exhibits. The photography galleries are always worth checking out, while the Art Library contains a wealth of international art and design publications.

Kids will be in their element at the **Mitsubishi Minato Mirai Industrial Museum** (Tues–Sun 10am–5.30pm; ¥500; @ www.mhi.co.jp/museum) in the neighbouring block. The museum's six well-laid-out zones illustrate technological developments, from today's power generators, oil platforms and deep-sea probes to the space stations of tomorrow. There are plenty of models and interactive displays, with English-speaking staff on hand if needed, but the biggest draw is the "Sky-Walk Adventure" up on the second floor. At one time kids were queuing round the block to have a ride in this helicopter simulator, though it's now usually pretty clear. After a two-minute flying lesson, you get to take the "real" chopper swooping and soaring over Fuji or down into the Grand Canyon for a stomach-wrenching fifteen-minute ride.

Around Yokohama Station

Apart from one small but important art museum, there's not a great deal to see around **Yokohama Station**. However, this is the city's prime centre for department stores: Mitsukoshi, Takashimaya and Joinus vie for shoppers on the station's west side, above a warren of underground arcades known as "The Diamond"; over to the east, on the other hand, the Sogō, Marui and Luminè stores lord it over "Porta" underground mall. This east side is also home to the city's Central Post Office, the long-distance bus terminal and to Yokohama City Air Terminal (YCAT), while *Sea Bass* ferries for Minato Mirai and Yamashita-kōen depart from a pier behind Sogō (see p.257 for details).

If you're not here to shop or catch onward transport, the area's only real attraction is located on Sogō's sixth floor. The two-room **Hiraki Ukiyo-e Museum** (daily except Tues 10am–7/7.30pm; ¥500) houses one of Japan's most highly rated collections of woodblock prints. Unfortunately, only a small portion of the museum's 8000 *ukiyo-e* can be displayed during each month-long exhibition. Nevertheless, all the great woodblock artists are represented and there's usually something to capture the imagination of any art enthusiast.

Eating

One of Yokohama's highlights is its great choice of cuisines. Most visitors head straight for **Chinatown**, but there's also a huge variety of other options, including plenty of Japanese restaurants, of course. Shopping malls such as Landmark Plaza, Queen's Square and Shinkō-chō's World Porters and Akarenga are the best hunting grounds for other places to eat.

Chinatown

Edosei 185 Yamashitachō. Mega-size steamed dumplings are this shop's speciality, stuffed with interesting ingredients including black bean and walnut, onion and seafood, and shrimp and chilli, as well as the usual barbecued pork. Daily 9am–8pm.
Heichinrō 149 Yamashitachō ☎ 045/681-3001. Large, popular Cantonese institution with dark, intimate booths. Food includes dim sum from around ¥800 per plate (until 4.30pm), while evening menus start at ¥3500. Get there early or be prepared to queue, especially at weekends.
Manchinrō 153 Yamashitachō ☎ 045/681-4004. Another famous old name, this time serving Guangdong cuisine. Choose carefully and eating here needn't break the bank, with noodle and fried-rice dishes starting at around ¥1100 and lunch sets at ¥2700, though evening-course menus (from ¥4600) are less affordable. The branch behind serves a full range of dim sum. English spoken. Daily 11am–10pm.
Meikōkaku 220 Yamashitachō ☎ 045/201-4188. Simple, stylish Chinese teashop with some thirty types of tea on the menu from ¥800 for a pot

serving up to six small cups. Daily 11.30am–8pm.
Peking Hanten 79 Yamashitachō. Right beside Chinatown's eastern gate, this highly decorated Beijing restaurant is unmissable. It's fairly low-key inside, however, and has well-priced lunchtime menus from around ¥1000. Their late opening hours (until 2am) and English menu are also plus points.
Shei Shei 138 Yamashitachō. Casual Szechuan restaurant serving an excellent-value set lunch on weekdays (¥500), or choose from their picture menu. There are only a handful of tables, so at busy times you'll be asked to share. Daily until 8.30pm.
Shōfukumon 81-3 Yamashitachō ☎ 045/664-4181. Multistorey restaurant offering eat-all-you-can dim sum deals for ¥2500 – worth considering if you've worked up a healthy appetite.
Suro Saikan Honkan 190 Yamashitachō. Decorated with gorgeous mosaics, this place is popular for its reliable Shanghai cuisine. Weekday lunch sets start at under ¥700 and courses from around ¥3000, but count on at least ¥4000 in the evening.

The rest of the city

Alte Liebe 11 Nihon-dōri, Naka-ku ☎ 045/222-3346. Pretty authentic-looking Viennese style café-restaurant on the corner of one of Yokohama's

grand old buildings, now partly modernized to include the Japan Newspaper Museum.
Capricciosa 2F, 1-31 Motomachi ☎ 045/664-

1733. Lively outlet of this cheap-and-cheerful pasta and pizza chain, which continues to be popular for its generous portions – you'll eat well for less than ¥2000 per person.

Chano-ma 3F Akarenga 2, 1-1-2 Shinkō, Naka-ku ☎045/650-8228. Sit back with a cocktail and nibble interesting modern Japanese dishes at this relaxed restaurant with a very contemporary vibe.

Colombo 2F, 2-88-1 Motomachi ☎045/664-3777. Watch the world go by from this breezy, café-style Sri Lankan restaurant on Motomachi shopping street. Weekday lunches at under ¥1000 represent the best deal; otherwise, reckon on at least ¥2000 per head for a good feast.

Enokitei 89-6 Yamatechō ☎045/623-2288. Set in a venerable Yamate home, this cute English-style café serves dainty sandwiches and home-made cakes, and you can sit in the front garden and watch the world pass by.

Rikyuan 2-17 Masagochō ☎045/662-2857. Traditional soba joint tucked down a backstreet, two blocks east of JR Kannai Station. The menu includes *donburi* as well as various soba dishes; prices start at around ¥850. Mon–Sat 11am–8.30pm.

World Food Court 1F, World Porters, 11 Shinkō-chō. A selection of self-service fast-food restaurants – burgers, pizzas, salads, curry and Chinese – around a central seating area. It's better than it sounds, and perfect for a group with different tastes. If none of those appeals, there are several proper restaurants in the complex.

Yamate Jūbankan 247 Yamatechō ☎045/621-4466. Pleasant French restaurant in a pretty clapboard house opposite the Foreigners' Cemetery. There's a restaurant upstairs and a less formal dining area on the ground floor, where you can snack on a sandwich or croque. Set lunches cost around ¥3000. In July and August they run a popular beer garden.

Yokohama Curry Museum 1-2-3 Isezaki-chō, Naka-ku ☎045/250-0833. On the seventh and eighth floors above a pachinko parlour and bearing as much relation to a museum as Japanese curry does to Indian. Still, this collection of some eleven different curry outlets is a fun and colourful place to wander around and sample a few regional Japanese specialties, as well as more common items like spicy curry ice cream – just don't expect to discover much about curry.

Bars and nightlife

Though it's generally less boisterous than Tokyo, Yokohama still has no shortage of lively drinking holes. The west side of Yokohama Station comprises the main **nightlife** area, but the area around Chinatown and across to Kannai Station also has a sprinkling of bars. Summer brings the **beer gardens**: both the Luminè department store (near Yokohama Station) and the *Star Hotel* (see "Accommodation" p.258) sport the rooftop variety, or there's a real garden next to *Yamate Jūbankan* (see above).

Beer Next 3F Akarenga No 2, 1-1-2 Shinkō, Naka-ku ☎045/226-1961. Stylish beer hall and restaurant in this warehouse conversion. Their own-brew Spring Valley beer (¥480) is refreshing, and they also have Guinness on tap.

Cape Cod 2F, 1-4-2 Tokiwachō ☎045/661-0700. Above the *Star Diner*, this relaxed, spit-and-sawdust bar has reasonable prices and draws an international crowd. They can rustle up cheapish bar snacks and there's also a dartboard. Closed Sun.

Gas Panic Jackmall East, 4-8-1 Minato Mirai ☎045/680-0291. Yokohama branch of Roppongi's grungiest but ever-popular nightclub. The music is the standard, crowd-pleasing mix of techno, hip-hop, pop and good old rock'n'roll. No cover charge; drinks cost ¥300 all night on Thursdays and from 6pm to 9.30pm other nights.

Motion Blue Akarenga 2, 1-1-2 Shinkō, Naka-ku ☎045/226-1919, ⓦwww.motionblue.co.jp. Cool jazz club in the renovated Akarenga buildings attracting top acts – for which you'll pay top prices. There's no cost though for parking yourself at the attached *Bar Tune*'s long counter and soaking up the ambience with a drink.

Pure 1 Ōtamachi ☎045/663-8485, ⓦwww.clubpure.com. The happening club of the moment amongst Yokohama's *gaijin*, with all-you-can-drink nights (men/women ¥3500/2500) on Fridays and Saturdays.

The Tavern B1, 2-14 Minami Saiwai-chō. This British-style pub, popular with local expats, is a good place to kick off an evening in the nightlife district west of Yokohama Station; turn left out of the station to find it opposite the Daiei store. There's live music on Tuesdays, half-price drinks for women on weekdays (6–7pm) and the sort of bar food that will appeal to homesick Brits.

Windjammer 215 Yamashitachō ☎045/662-3966. Another expat haunt, somewhere between a cocktail lounge and a jazz bar, with live bands nightly (music charge Mon–Fri & Sun ¥300, Sat ¥500).

Listings

Banks and exchange The area east of Kannai Station is where you'll find branches of major banks with foreign-exchange facilities; try along Kannai Ōdōri and Honchō-dōri. The World Currency Shop (daily except Tues 10am–7pm) can change travellers' cheques and cash outside normal banking hours; it's in B2 of Sōgō department store, near the exit to Yokohama Station. For credit-card advances, Citibank's ATM on the west side of Yokohama Station (follow the walkway to find it next to the *Sheraton Hotel*) offers 24hr access. Otherwise, there are international ATMs in the two main post offices (see below).

Bike rental The outlet under the Marine Tower charges from ¥300 for 2hr, rising to ¥900 per day (10am–6pm).

Buses JR long-distance and night buses leave from bus terminals on the east side of Yokohama Station; Sotetsu and Kintetsu buses from the west side. Nearby, YCAT is the departure point for limousine buses for Haneda and Narita airports.

Cinemas The eight-screen MyCal Cinema (☏045/222-2500), on the fifth floor of World Porters, shows the latest Hollywood releases, often in English. Tickets normally cost ¥1800, but look out for special deals.

Emergencies Kaga-chō police station (203 Yamashita-chō, Naka-ku; ☏045/641-0110), a ten-minute walk from JR Kannai Station, has interpreters on call 24hr. For information about emergency medical care, call the 24hr helpline on ☏045/201-1199, but have a Japanese speaker on hand. If all else fails, try contacting the Foreign Advisory Service on ☏045/671-7209. For more advice on what to do in an emergency, see Basics, p.80.

Festivals The lunar new year (late Jan or early Feb) and China's National Day (Oct 1) are celebrated in style with lion dances around the streets of Chinatown. On July 20 the city puts on a dramatic firework display (*hanabi taikai*) over the harbour, while jazz fills the air for a week in early October.

Internet access Try Kinko's, towards the northeast end of Honchō-dōri at 4-36 Honchō (open 24hr; ¥210 per 20min).

Post offices The city's Central Post Office is located on the east side of Yokohama Station. However, the main office for international mail, including a poste restante service, is Yokohama Port Post Office at 5-3 Nihon-Ōdōri, Naka-ku, near Kannai Station. Both have 24hr mail counters.

Shopping After cutting their teeth on MM21's World Porters, Landmark Plaza and Queen's Square, shopaholics should make a pilgrimage – on a weekday if at all possible – to one of Japan's largest factory-outlet malls, Bayside Marina, to the south of Yokohama. It's built to resemble Nantucket town, which at least means it's low-rise, and there are some pleasant waterfront restaurants. The Factory Outlet Zone boasts over fifty shops selling cut-price goods, including brands such as Timberland, Lacoste and Reebok.

Around Yokohama

A short bus ride south from Yokohama will bring you to Negishi and the traditionally Japanese lakes and winding pathways of **Sankei-en**. It's well worth devoting half a day to exploring this large stroll-garden with its historic tea arbours, aristocratic residences and farmhouses. Heading north towards Tokyo, make time for **Shin-Yokohama**, with its delightfully quirky museum dedicated to noodles.

Sankei-en

In the late nineteenth century a wealthy silk merchant, Hara Tomitaro, established his residence in sculptured parkland on Yokohama's southern hills and filled it with rare and beautiful buildings from Kamakura and the Kansai region. Today **Sankei-en** (daily: outer garden 9am–5pm, inner garden 9am–4.30pm; ¥300 each; @ www.sankeien.or.jp) is divided into an outer garden and a smaller inner core, where most of the famous structures are located. To reach Sankei-en, take bus #8 from Yokohama or Sakuragichō stations to Honmoku Sankeien-mae, from where the garden is a three-minute walk, or hop on a JR Negishi-line train to Negishi Station and then a bus as far as the Honmoku stop, 600m north of the main gate.

From the gate, follow the well-marked route to the **inner garden**, where **Rinshunkaku** – an elegant, lakeside mansion built for one of the Tokugawa lords in 1649 – is the only structure of its kind still in existence. Another Tokugawa legacy, dating from 1623, sits beside a picturesque stream a few minutes further on; named **Choshukaku**, it originally served as a tea ceremony house in the grounds of Kyoto's Nijō Castle (see p.528). **Tenju-in** may not be as famous, but it's worth walking up beside the stream to see its fine carving. This little seventeenth-century temple dedicated to Jizō, the guardian deity of children, hails from Kamakura.

In the less formal **outer garden**, thatched farm roofs blend with bamboo thickets and groves of twisted plum trees, above which rises a graceful three-tiered pagoda. The most interesting building here is **Old Yanohara House** (¥100), the former home of a wealthy farmer, where you can take a close look at the vast roof built in *gassho* style – no nails but plenty of rope. Don't bother climbing up the hill to Shofukaku: the concrete viewing platform has great views of billowing chimney stacks and industrial dockyards.

Shin-Yokohama

Even if you're not a noodle fan, it's worth making the trek to **Shin-Yokohama** – on the subway or JR Yokohama line – to visit the **Rāmen Museum** (daily except Tues 11am–11pm; restaurants open until 9.45pm; ¥300). This well-designed museum-cum-restaurant is devoted to Japan's most popular fast food, in its most basic form a noodle soup garnished with roast pork, bamboo shoots and dried seaweed. It's five minutes' walk northeast of Shin-Yokohama Station; walk straight ahead, to the left of the NTT Building, to the second set of traffic lights, then turn right and first left.

The museum's first-floor hall delves into the roots of ramen, tracing them back to southern China, and then chronicles the moment in 1958 when instant ramen – chicken-flavoured – was launched on the world, followed in 1971 by cup noodles. There are some mind-boggling statistics: as a taster, in 1993 the world consumed an estimated 22.1 billion bowls of ramen.

Once you've digested all of that, head for the basement, where you're transported into 1950s downtown Japan. Below you lies a city square at dusk: lights are coming on in the shops and *pachinko* parlours, as vendors call out their wares under grimy film posters. Walk round the mezzanine's dingy alley, complete with bars and an old-fashioned sweet shop, before heading down into the courtyard, where each storefront hides a restaurant from Japan's most famous ramen regions. The local variety is available in the Beauty Salon, while other stalls specialize in ramen from Fukuoka, Sapporo, Kumamoto or Tokyo; buy a ticket (from around ¥900, or ¥500 for a half-portion) at the machine – ask for help, as it's all in Japanese – and then join the slurping throng at tables in the courtyard. Note that there's no smoking except in the bars on the mezzanine floor, and it's best to avoid the crowds at lunchtimes and weekends.

Travel details

Trains

The trains between the major cities listed below are the fastest, direct services. There are also frequent slower services, run by JR and several private companies, covering the same destinations. It is usually possible, especially on long-distance routes, to get there faster by changing between services.

Atami to: Kyoto (16 daily; 3hr 20min); Shimoda (every 30min; 1hr–1hr 25min); Tokyo (at least every 10min; 35min–2hr 10min).
Enoshima to: Tokyo (Shinjuku Station) (8–10 daily; 1hr).
Kamakura to: Enoshima (every 10–15min; 25min); Tokyo (every 10–20min; 55min).

Mito to: Tokyo (Ueno Station) (14 daily; 65min).
Narita to: Tokyo (every 30min; 1hr); Ueno (every 30min; 1hr).
Shimoda to: Rendaiji (every 20–30min; 3–4min); Tokyo (hourly; 2hr 40min–3hr).
Shuzenji to: Mishima (every 10–15min; 25–30min); Tokyo (3 daily; 2hr 10min).
Yokohama to: Kamakura (every 10–20min; 25min); Tokyo (every 5–10min; 30–40min); Tokyo (Shibuya Station) (every 5min; 40min).

Buses

The buses listed below are mainly long-distance services – often travelling overnight – between the major cities, and local services where there is no alternative means of transport. For shorter journeys, however, trains are almost invariably quicker and often no more expensive.

Dōgashima to: Irō-zaki (3 daily; 1hr 20min–1hr 45min); Matsuzaki (every 15–20min; 6–10min), Shuzenji (1–2 hourly; 1hr 30min); Toi (1–2 hourly; 40min).
Heda to: Shuzenji (5 daily; 50min).
Shimoda to: Dōgashima (hourly; 1hr); Irō-zaki (every 30min; 40min); Matsuzaki (every 40min; 50min); Shuzenji (1 daily; 2hr).
Toi to: Heda (5 daily; 35min); Shuzenji (1–2 hourly; 50min).
Yokohama to: Hirosaki (1 daily; 9hr); Hiroshima (1 daily; 12hr); Kyoto (1 daily; 8hr); **Nagoya** (1 daily; 6hr 30min); Nara (1 daily; 6hr 30min); Ōsaka (1 daily; 8hr).

Ferries

Dōgashima to: Numazu (4–6 daily; 1hr–1hr 20min).
Toi to: Tagonoura-ko (4–5 daily; 55min).

Northern Honshū

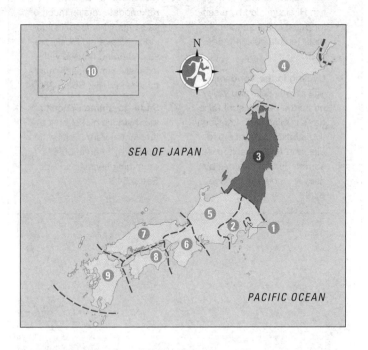

CHAPTER 3 **Highlights**

❋ **Kinkazan** Roam the steeply wooded slopes of the island of Kinkazan, with its views, framed by wind-whipped pines, of Matsushima Bay and Oshika Hantō. **See p.293**

❋ **Zazen at Mōtsū-ji** Take part in an early morning *zazen* meditation session at Mōtsū-ji in Hiraizumi, led by a senior priest in the spectacular main temple building. **See p.297**

❋ **Cycling in the Tōno valley** The mostly flat Tōno valley offers the perfect spot for a day's cycling, with its evocative landscape of rice paddies and traditional houses, surrounded on all sides by heavily wooded hills. **See p.298**

❋ **Ja-ja men** *Ja-ja men* – udon-like noodles served with a generous dollop of brown miso paste – are one of the north's most distinctive culinary flavours. Try them at the *Pairong* restaurant in Morioka. **See p.308**

❋ **Kakunodate** The town of Kakunodate retains much of its samurai heritage, including streets of gloriously preserved grand houses with extensive, impeccably maintained gardens. **See p.330**

❋ **Sado-ga-shima** Dance to the rhythmic global beat at the annual Earth Celebration hosted by international drumming sensation Kodo. **See p.342**

△ Matsushima

3

Northern Honshū

W hen the famous poet Matsuo Bashō set out on his travels along the "narrow road to the deep north" in 1689, he commented, somewhat despondently, "I might as well be going to the ends of the earth." Even today, many urban Japanese regard the harsh, mountainous provinces of **NORTHERN HONSHŪ** as irredeemably backward. Not that it's all thatched farmhouses and timeless agricultural vistas, but certainly the rural traditions have survived here longer than in most other parts of the country. However, it doesn't take long to discover the region's particularly vibrant **crafts** industry and huge array of **festivals**. Nor do you have to delve much deeper to find the rich heritage of folk tales and evidence of ancient religious practices which give parts of north Honshū a deliciously mysterious tang.

Northern Honshū, or Tōhoku as it's often called, was the last part of Japan's main island to be brought under central control. As such, it boasts more in the way of military sights – ruined castles, samurai towns and aristocratic tombs – than great temples or religious foundations. The one glorious exception is north of **Sendai** at the seemingly insignificant town **Hiraizumi**, whose opulent Golden Hall (Konjiki-dō) is the highlight of any tour of the region. By way of contrast, the archetypal north-country town lies not far away at **Tōno**, often referred to as the birthplace of Japanese folklore, where goblin-like *kappa* inhabit local rivers and fairy children scamper through old farmhouses. Much of this is now heavily commercialized, but it's still worth exploring Tōno's more secretive shrines, with their references to primitive cults. Darker forces are also at work much further north where souls in purgatory haunt **Osore-zan**'s volcanic wasteland on the hammer-head Shimokita Hantō. In summer, pilgrims come here to consult blind mediums, while over on the west coast the holy mountain of **Dewa-sanzan** is home to *yamabushi*, ascetic priests endowed with mystical powers.

The region is also characterized by its splendid scenery, ranging from prolific rice fields and cosseted orchards to wild, rugged coastlines and the pine-crusted islands of **Matsushima Bay**. The central spine of magnificent mountains provides excellent opportunities for hiking and skiing, notably around the volcano of **Bandai-san** in the south and the more northerly **Towada–Hachimantai** area. Both are noted for their flora and fauna, including black bears in remoter districts, while **Towada-ko** itself is a massive crater lake accessed via the picturesque **Oirase valley**. The World Heritage-listed **Shirakami-Sanchi** mountains, on the border between Aomori and Akita prefectures, are equally beautiful, and remote enough to remain undeveloped. In **Sado-ga-shima**, a large island lying off Niigata, dramatic mountain and coastal scenery provides the backdrop for a surprisingly rich culture – a legacy of its isolation and a number of famous, or infamous, characters who were exiled to the island.

Although there are good **transport** links between the main cities, you'll need to allow plenty of time to explore the more remote corners of northern Honshū – this is one place where car rental is definitely worth considering. Public buses can be sporadic at the best of times, with many services stopping

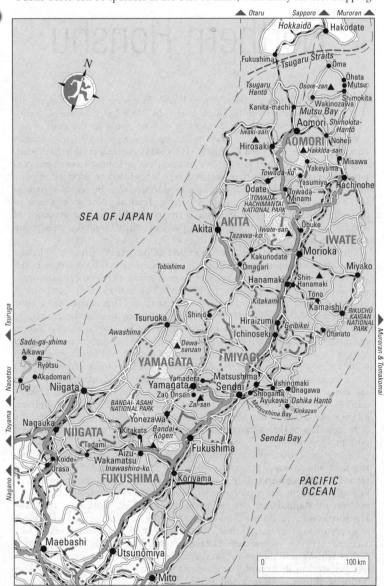

Northern Honshū cuisine

Fresh **seafood** is abundant along northern Honshū's heavily populated Pacific Ocean and the Sea of Japan coastlines, and dishes based on fish, scallops, squids and crabs are legion, while oysters from Matsushima Bay and Mutsu are particularly prized. Away from the sea, you'll encounter plenty of towns claiming that **noodles** of one variety or the other are a speciality to their region. Seemingly every inland town in northern Honshū boasts that they have the best ramen in all of Japan, with towns like Kitakata making their collection of ramen restaurants a tourist attraction. Speciality **soba** (buckwheat noodle) dishes also abound. Morioka is famous for its *wanko-soba*, small bowls of thin, flat buckwheat noodles often consumed in eating contests, while the farming valley of Tōno is known for its *hitsuko soba*, small bowls of rough, handmade noodles eaten with a mix of chicken, raw egg, onion and mushrooms. During the blazingly hot summers, chilled noodle dishes are popular, including *reimen*, cold, semi-transparent, slightly chewy egg noodles eaten with spicy Korean *kimchi*, and *sōmen*, delicate *soba*-style noodles served floating in water studded with ice cubes. Other **regional specialities** worth seeking out include Akita's *kiritampo*, a stew of chicken, mushrooms, onions, glass noodles, seasonal vegetables and *mochi* (rice cakes); *gyū-tan* (broiled, smoked or salted calf's tongue), which can be had at countless restaurants in Sendai; and the Yamagata speciality *imoni*, a slightly sweet winter stew of taro, meat, *konnyaku* (devil's tongue) and onions.

completely in winter, when **heavy snowfalls** close the mountain roads. In general, the **best time to visit** is either spring or autumn, before it gets too busy and while the scenery is at its finest, though the uplands also provide welcome relief from summer's sweltering heat. Note, however, that early August brings thousands of people flocking to Tōhoku's big four **festivals** in Sendai, Aomori, Hirosaki and Akita. If you're travelling at this time, make sure you've got your transport and accommodation sorted out well in advance. Apart from ski resorts, many tourist facilities outside the major cities shut down from early November to late April.

JR offers a variety of **special rail tickets** covering the Tōhoku district. JR East operates three schemes similar to the regular JR Pass (see p.37 for details). Their four-day, five-day and ten-day passes are valid on all JR trains, including the Shinkansen, from Izu and Nagano to the northern tip of Honshū. Of these, the four-day pass is the most useful, since it's valid for any four days within a month, rather than a consecutive period, so you can save it to cover longer train journeys within the region. Note that these passes are only available to those on a "temporary visitor" visa and must be purchased outside Japan. The ten-day Tōhoku Wide Pass can be bought in Japan and covers all JR trains and buses within the Tōhoku region, including travel from Tokyo but excluding Shinkansen trains. However, the ten days must run consecutively, and to get your money's worth you'll have to take a number of long journeys within this period.

Aizu-Wakamatsu and around

The small, relaxed but rather featureless city of **AIZU-WAKAMATSU** sits in a wide valley near one of Japan's largest lakes, some two-and-a-half hours' train ride north of Tokyo. An important castle town on what was once the main trunk road north from Edo (now Tokyo), the area's major sights revolve around its warrior past, including a reconstructed castle keep, an attractive samurai house and the graves of nineteen young heroes of the Boshin War (see opposite).

The surrounding area, with its mountain climate and abundant supplies of pure water, is famous for its high-quality **sake**. The centre of production is **Kitakata**, a sprawling town north of Aizu-Wakamatsu, where a collection of traditional sake storehouses, *kura*, attest to its former wealth. In winter, the area is popular for **skiing**, especially around **Bandai Kōgen**, a plateau rising to the northeast which also offers great summer hiking and a dramatic bus ride across to Fukushima.

The City

Central Aizu-Wakamatsu consists of a rectangular grid of streets with the main **train station** on its northwest corner. Chūō-dōri, the main shopping street, runs south from the station for 3km to the castle and surrounding sights, while Byakko-dōri heads east to the town's most famous attraction, the **Iimori-yama**, where a band of young soldiers committed *seppuku* (ritual suicide) in a useless but heroic gesture during one of the last battles of the Meiji Restoration. After a brief visit to their graves, head for the southern district where you'll find a beautiful replica of a samurai house, **Buké-yashiki**, and the reconstructed castle keep, **Tsuruga-jō**. Nearby, there's also a herb garden, an old sake brewery and a moderately interesting museum. Though it's possible to cover all these sights on foot in a long day, it's worth taking a few bus rides or renting a bike (see p.277).

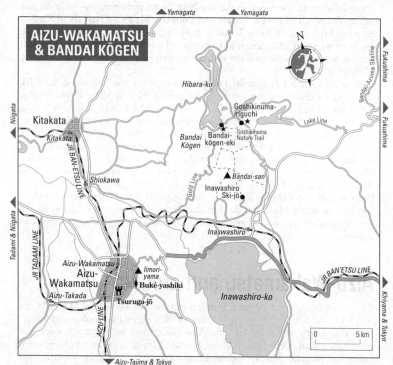

Aizu-Wakamatsu	Aizu-Wakamatsu	会津若松
Aizu Sake History Museum	Aizu Shuzō Rekishikan	会津酒造歴史館
Buké-yashiki	Buké-yashiki	武家屋敷
Fukushima Museum	Fukushima Kenritsu Hakubutsukan	福島県立博物館
Iimori-yama	Iimori-yama	飯盛山
Oyaku-en	Oyaku-en	御薬園
Sazae-dō	Sazae-dō	さざえ堂
Tsuruga-jō	Tsuruga-jō	鶴ヶ城

Accommodation and restaurants

Aizu-no-sato Youth Hostel	Aizu-no-sato Yūsu Hosuteru	会津の里ユースホステル
Aizuno Youth Hostel	Aizuno Yūsu Hosuteru	会津野ユースホステル
Hotel Alpha One	Hoteru Arufā Wan	ホテルアルファーワン
Fuji Grand Hotel	Fuji Gurando Hoteru	フジグランドホテル
Green Hotel Aizu	Guriin Hoteru Aizu	グリーンホテル会津
Sasa-no-an	Sasa-no-an	笹乃庵
Takino	Takino	田季野
Washington Hotel	Washinton Hoteru	ワシントンホテル

Kitakata	Kitakata	喜多方
Makoto Shokudō	Makoto Shokudō	誠食堂
Sasaya Ryokan	Sasaya Ryokan	笹屋旅館
Yamatogawa Sake Brewing Museum	Yamatogawa Shuzō Kitakata Fūdokan	大和川酒造北方風土館

Bandai Kōgen	Bandai Kōgen	磐梯高原
Bandai-kōgen-eki	Bandai-kōgen-eki	磐梯高原駅
Goshikinuma-iriguchi	Goshikinuma-iriguchi	五色沼入口
Hotel Goshiki-sō	Hoteru Goshiki-sō	ホテル五色荘
Inawashiro	Inawashiro	猪苗代
Inawashiro Ski-jō	Inawashiro Sukii-jō	猪苗代スキー場
Resort Inn Shiki	Rezōto In Shiki	レゾートイン四季
Urabandai Royal Hotel	Urabandai Roiyaru Hoteru	裏磐梯ロイヤルホテル
Urabandai Youth Hostel	Urabandai Yūsu Hosuteru	裏磐梯ユースホステル

Iimori-yama

A quick climb up **Iimori-yama** is a good way to get your bearings, taking in views of the town as you scale the hill's steep staircases or ride the handy escalator (March–Nov daily 8am–5pm; ¥250). At the top, an imperial eagle – a gift of the Italian Fascist Party in 1928 – dominates the small clearing and underlines some of the more disturbing aspects of local history, whose main focus is the line of **Byakkotai graves** over to the left. During the **Boshin War**, a series of skirmishes surrounding the Meiji Restoration in 1868, the warriors of Aizu-Wakamatsu were among the few clans to put up serious opposition to the imperial armies. The Byakkotai (White Tigers) were one of several bands of young fanatics who joined the fighting and, in one of the final battles, a group of twenty Byakkotai, aged 16 and 17, were cut off from their comrades. Trying to reach the safety of the castle, they climbed Iimori-yama, only to see Tsuruga-jō apparently in flames. Assuming the battle was lost, they did what all good samurai should do and killed themselves by ritual disembowelment, though one boy was saved before he bled to death. Although the castle was not burning and the boys' deaths were completely unnecessary, the Byakkotai are revered as heroic role models. Twice a year (April 24 and Sept 24) proud parents watch as local schoolboys of the same age re-enact the suicides.

Further down the hill, **Sazae-dō** (daily 8.15am to sunset; ¥400) is an attractive antidote. This elegant, octagonal building, erected in 1796 as part of a larger temple complex, is a unique structure, containing two ramps spiralling round a central pillar. Sealed inside the pillar are 33 statues of Kannon, the Goddess of Mercy. At the bottom of the hill, turn left and you'll find a distinctive white building housing the **Byakkotai Memorial Hall** (daily: April–Nov 8am–5pm; Jan–March & Dec 8.30am–4.30pm; ¥400), of interest mostly for its portraits of the young soldiers and videos of related television dramas and documentaries.

Buké-yashiki, Oyaku-en and Tsuruga-jō

From Iimori-yama, follow the bypass south for 2km and then turn left for **Buké-yashiki** (daily: April–Nov 8.30am–5pm; Jan–March & Dec 9am–4.30pm; ¥850), a magnificent reproduction of a nineteenth-century samurai residence belonging to Saigō Tanomo, a chief retainer of the Aizu clan. Its 38 rooms range from a sand-box toilet and cypress bathtub to a "classy reception room" reserved for the Lord of Aizu. In 1868, Saigō went off to fight in the Boshin War, leaving his wife and daughters, aged between 2 and 16 years, at home. As the imperial army closed in, the family decided to commit suicide rather than be taken prisoner; the 16-year-old failed to die immediately but was killed soon after by an enemy soldier, and the house was set on fire. The complex also includes a number of original buildings, such as a rice mill and thatched shrine brought from surrounding villages.

Two kilometres west of Buké-yashiki lie the imposing walls of Aizu's castle, but on the way it's worth taking a stroll round **Oyaku-en** (daily 8.30am–5pm; closed first weeks of July & Dec; ¥310), famed for its medicinal herbs. Oyaku-en was laid out in 1670 by one of the Aizu lords as a tea-ceremony garden, with rustic arbours and a shallow lake patrolled by ducks and slow fat carp. Unusually, he devoted a part of the garden to neat rows of around three hundred different herbs, such as angelica, lycoris and gentian. You can buy dried herbs and remedies in the garden's giftshop, or take a cup of *macha* (¥500) in the teahouse.

The north gate of **Tsuruga-jō** stands fifteen minutes' walk southwest of Oyaku-en. Its imposing entrance lies over a moat, between massive stone ramparts, inside which the dainty white keep (daily 8.30am–4.30pm; closed first weeks of July & Dec; ¥500) seems rather dwarfed. Originally built in 1384, the castle was besieged by Meiji troops for several months in 1868, before the Aizu clan finally surrendered. After the new government ordered it to be demolished, it lay in ruins until 1965, when the central keep was rebuilt – it now houses an uninteresting local history museum – and the gardens were landscaped. The castle is the focus of the city's main **festival** (Sept 22–24), which includes a procession of samurai and ceremonies for the Byakkotai (see p.275).

Outside Tsuruga-jō's east gate lies the ultra-modern **Fukushima Museum** (Tues–Sun 9.30am–5pm; ¥500), covering local history from mock-ups of Jōmon-period huts (2000 BC) to a charcoal-driven bus from the 1930s. The displays are well presented, with sufficient English to get the gist of what's going on. Equally interesting is the **Aizu Sake History Museum** (daily: mid-March to mid-Dec 8.30am–5pm; mid-Dec to mid-March 9am–4.30pm;

¥300), five minutes' walk north of the castle gates, in an old wooden building where the Yamaguchi family has been brewing sake for 350 years.

Practicalities

From Tokyo, the quickest way to reach Aizu-Wakamatsu is to take a Shinkansen on the Tōhoku line from either Tokyo or Ueno stations as far as Kōriyama, where you change onto the JR Ban'etsu line. It's a pleasant ride up from Kōriyama, but if you have time a more attractive approach is via the private Tōbu and Aizu lines from Asakusa Station, changing trains at Aizu-Tajima; this route has the added advantage of allowing you to visit Nikkō (see p.196) on the way. If you're coming **from Niigata**, or heading onto the west coast, you have a choice of direct JR Ban'etsu line services, or very slow local trains on the JR Tadami line via Koide and Urasa. This latter option is especially recommended in October, when the autumn colours are at their peak.

Aizu-Wakamatsu has two helpful **tourist information centres**, one in the train station (daily 10am–5/6pm; ☎0242/32-0688, ⓔinfo@aizukanko.com) and the other inside the castle's north gate (daily 8.30am–5.30pm; ☎0242/27-4005, ⓔinfo@tsurugajo.com). Some English is spoken at both. **City buses** depart from outside the train station every twenty minutes for Buké-yashiki (stand 4), or you can catch loop-line buses (clockwise or anticlockwise) from stand 6 to Tsuruga-jō, Buké-yashiki and Iimori-yama. **Bike rental** is available at Eki Rent-a-Car (daily 8.40am–7pm; ☎0242/24-5171; ¥1500 per day), which occupies the left-hand corner of the station building as you exit the station; alternatively, for much cheaper rates (and free Internet access while you're there), head south along the road directly outside the station (parallel to Chūō-dōri) to Aizu-machikata Folklore Museum (daily March–Nov 9am–4pm, closed first Mon–Thurs of July; ☎0242/22-8686, or book in advance by ☎0242/27-4102; ¥500 a day). If you want to **rent a car**, try Eki Rent-a-Car (see above) or Nissan (☎0242/25-4123), near the station. You'll find foreign exchange facilities at **banks** on Chūō-dōri, including Fukushima Bank, located about halfway down.

Accommodation

Aizu-no-sato Youth Hostel 36 Kofune-hatakata, Aizu-Shiokawa-chō ☎ 0241/27-2054, ⓦwww.jyh.or.jp. Homely, well-worn youth hostel, run by a genial English-speaking owner, with two floors of shared tatami rooms. It's at Shiokawa Station, the third stop on the JR Ban'etsu line towards Kitakata (10min from Aizu-Wakamatsu Station). From the station, walk up to the first set of lights, turn left and keep walking for about ten minutes. The hostel is on the left straight after the bridge. *Okonomi-yaki* dinners served. ¥2100 per person.

Aizuno Youth Hostel 88 Kakiyashiki, Terasaki Aizu-Takada-chō ☎0242/55-1020, ⓦwww.jyh.or.jp. Small, spick-and-span hostel set among rice fields, offering bunk beds in shared rooms, good food and bike rental. It's a twenty-minute walk northwest of Aizu-Takada Station, on the JR Tadami line (20min from Aizu-Wakamatsu Station); walk straight ahead from the station, take the second right and keep going (note that services on this line are infrequent). ¥3200 per person. ❺

Hotel Alpha One 5-8 Ekimae-machi ☎0242/32-6868, ⓕ32-6822. Smartish business hotel near the station (behind the *Fuji Grand*), offering reasonable-size rooms with TV, phone and mini-bathroom. ❺

Fuji Grand Hotel 5-25 Ekimae-machi ☎0242/24-1111, ⓔinfo@fujigrandhotel.co.jp. Big, busy business hotel. The older rooms are a bit worn, but a touch cheaper than the *Alpha One*. Located right outside the station. ❹

Green Hotel Aizu 3-7-23 Chūō ☎0242/24-5181, ⓕ24-5182. This small, spruce hotel has a choice of Western or (better-value) tatami rooms. It's in the backstreets, just south of the *Washington Hotel*. ❹–❺

Washington Hotel 201 Byakko-machi ☎0242/22-6111, ⓦwww.wh-rsv.com/english/aizu/index.html. New hotel on Byakko-dōri, a few minutes' walk east of the station and offering all the standard *Washington Hotel* chain services, including a coffee lounge, bar and restaurants.

Eating

Aizu-Wakamatsu is not that well off for **restaurants**. The best area to head for is along Chūō-dōri and Nanokomachi-dōri, which cuts across it halfway down, or try *Takino*, tucked into the backstreets southeast of this junction. It's a little tricky to find, but worth it for the beautiful old building and tasty food. The house speciality is *wappa-meshi*, a wooden box of steamed rice with various toppings such as flowering fern (*zenmai*), fish or mushrooms (*kinoko*) depending on the season (from ¥1350, including pickles and soup). Closer to the station, on the same road as the Aizu-machikata Folklore Museum, the cheerful *Sasa-no-an* (Tues–Sat 11.30am–2pm & 5.30–8pm, Sun 11.30–2pm) serves some of Aizu-Wakamatsu's renowned handmade soba noodles and a great vegetable tempura.

Around Aizu-Wakamatsu

Twenty kilometres north of Aizu-Wakamatsu, the town of **Kitakata** is famed for its sake and more than two thousand *kura* (traditional storehouses), built in a variety of styles. Some of these once housed a sake brewery, which is now a museum. Further afield, the lake-spattered plateau of **Bandai Kōgen** is worth exploring, for its gentle nature strolls or a more strenuous hike up Bandai-san, its highest peak.

Kitakata

In contrast to Aizu-Wakamatsu, **KITAKATA** was always an important commercial centre, producing sake, miso paste, rice and charcoal. At some point, a craze for building **kura** swept through the town until almost everyone had one of these fireproof storehouses encased in thick mud walls. Later, they started building brick versions, and today even the post office and other public offices hide behind *kura* facades. It's best to concentrate on the central district, where you can visit a **sake brewery** and take in several *kura* en route, but there's no need to devote more than a couple of hours to Kitakata, since the storehouses are now swamped by an otherwise uninteresting sprawling town.

Trains from Aizu-Wakamatsu (on the JR Ban'etsu line) arrive on the south side of Kitakata, from where it's a twenty-minute walk to the central shopping street, **Chūō-dōri**, where you'll see your first *kura*. Two blocks beyond the *Sasaya Ryokan* (see opposite), a left turn at the Lion d'Or supermarket leads to the **Yamatogawa Sake Brewing Museum** (daily 9am–4.30pm; free). The museum occupies an attractive collection of seven *kura* where sake was made from 1790 to 1990, before production moved to a new automated plant. You'll be given a guided tour – a brief English pamphlet should be available – and the opportunity to taste a few samples, though there's no obligation to buy. As you go round, note the globe of cedar fronds hanging in the entrance hall. Traditionally, breweries hang a green cedar ball outside in March, when the freshly brewed sake is put in vats to age; by September the browned fronds indicate that it's ready to drink.

Practicalities

You can pick up English-language **maps** of Kitakata at the **tourist office** (daily 8.30am–5.15pm; ℡0241/24-2633, ℮info@kitakata-kanko.jp) outside the train station, though the staff don't speak English. **Bike rental** (daily 8am–6pm) is available at the laundry on the northeast side of the station concourse (¥250 per hour, ¥1000 per day), and Yoshida Rent-a-Cycle (℡0241/22-2583; ¥1200 per day), about 70m before the first set of lights on the main road leading from the station into town. Alternatively, in summer you can take a relaxed **tour** of the town in a *kura*-shaped horse-drawn cart which leaves every couple of hours from outside the station (April–Nov daily 10am–2.30pm; ¥1300).

You're unlikely to want **to stay** in Kitakata, but, if you need to, head for the newly renovated *Sasaya Ryokan* on Chūō-dōri (☎0241/22-0008, ℱ22-0238; ❻), in a beautiful old Meiji-era building with its own *kura*. As for food, Kitakata is known for its ramen, with nearly one hundred **ramen restaurants** to choose from. *Makoto Shokudō*, in the backstreets east of Chūō-dōri (daily 7.30am–7pm), has atmospheric old tatami rooms and also serves other, inexpensive dishes; take a right turn at the Brewery Museum junction as you come from the station.

Bandai Kōgen

Northeast of Aizu-Wakamatsu, **Bandai-san** (1819m) rises steeply above Lake Inawashiro, its wooded flanks shaved here and there for **ski slopes**. In 1888 this previously dormant volcano erupted, blowing a huge hole in its north face and triggering mudflows that dammed the local rivers. In the process, the plateau now known as **Bandai Kōgen** was created. This beautiful area of some three hundred lakes and marshes scattered among beech forests is an easy day-trip by bus or car from Aizu-Wakamatsu or makes a pleasant stop on the spectacular Bandai-Azuma Skyline road (see below) north to Fukushima.

The most popular walk on Bandai Kōgen is the 3.7-kilometre-long **Goshikinuma Nature Trail**, an easy woodland romp past a series of lakes tinged various shades of cobalt blue, white and red according to their mineral content. The trail starts at **Goshikinuma-iriguchi** bus stop, where you can buy maps (¥200) at the **visitor centre** (daily except Tues 8.40am–4pm; ☎0241/32-2850), and then head roughly west to emerge about an hour later at the bus stop near **Bandai-kōgen-eki**. This hamlet – little more than a collection of hotels and restaurants – lies at the south end of the plateau's largest lake, **Hibara-ko**, and is the starting point for another recommended walk (3.2km) along the lake's eastern shore. It's also the jumping-off point for one of the longer routes up Bandai-san (allow around four hours to reach the summit, from where there are spectacular views as you skirt round the red lake that fills the still-steaming crater. In winter (mid-Dec to March), Bandai-san's deep snow cover provides some excellent **skiing**, and there are numerous resorts in the area. One of the more accessible is **Inawashiro Ski-jō** (☎0242/62-3800), perched above Inawashiro town, from where there's a regular bus service to Inawashiro Station (20min).

Several scenic toll roads cut across the Bandai plateau. You'll need your own transport to explore most of these, but between late April and early November public buses run northeast along the **Bandai-Azuma Skyline**. There are two to three buses a day from Bandai-kōgen-eki via Goshikinuma-iriguchi to Fukushima (3hr; ¥2780), and one tour bus from Aizu-Wakamatsu which makes a circuit of the sights and also includes a cruise on Hibara-ko (7hr 30min; ¥7970). From Bandai Kōgen the road climbs steeply through forests, giving stunning views back to Bandai-san or down to crinkle-cut lakes, before reaching **Jōdodaira**, a high, volcanic wasteland. The buses pause here for thirty minutes, allowing plenty of time to scramble up the tiny, perfect cone of Azuma-Kofuji (Little Fuji). Journey's end is **Fukushima**, from where you can catch a train back to Tokyo or head on north to Yamagata or Sendai.

Practicalities

From Aizu-Wakamatsu the quickest route to Bandai Kōgen is by **train** to Inawashiro Station and then over the road to pick up a **local bus** via Goshikinuma-iriguchi to Bandai-kōgen-eki. Note that the last departure from Inawashiro is 6pm, and the last bus down leaves Goshikinuma-iriguchi at around 7.30pm. After that, call ☎0242/32-2950 for a **taxi**.

If you decide to **stay** on the plateau, the best options are all located around Goshikinuma-iriguchi. The slightly dilapidated *Urabandai Youth Hostel* (T0241/32-2811, W www.jyh.or.jp; closed Dec–April; dorm beds ¥2940 without meals,¥3890 with meals) is nicely situated in woodland at the start of the nature trail; to find it, turn right by the Red Cross monument in the car park of the *Hotel Goshiki-sō* (see below). *Resort Inn Shiki* (T & F0241/32-2155; ❺ including meals) is another cheapish option; it's across from the visitor centre and bus depot, then 100m up the side road. Two smarter places, both with onsen-style baths, are the homely *Hotel Goshiki-sō* (T0241/32-2011, E goshikisou@msin.co.jp; ❼ including meals), overlooking the first Goshikinuma lake, and the more upmarket *Urabandai Royal* (T0241/32-3111, F 32-3130; ❼–❽), across the main road.

Yamagata and around

Few tourists make it to **YAMAGATA**, a large, workaday city ringed by high mountains, and those that do are usually just passing through. Apart from a couple of engaging museums, Yamagata's prime attraction is as a base for visiting the atmospheric temples of **Yamadera** and **Zaō Onsen**. The nearby mountain of Zaō-san provides excellent summer hiking, while winter transforms the area

Yamagata and around

Yamagata	*Yamagata*	山形
City Museum	*Kyōdokan*	郷土館
Kajō-kōen	*Kajō-kōen*	霞城公園
Prefectural Office	*Bunshōkan*	文翔館
Yamakō Building	*Yamakō Biru*	山交ビル

Accommodation and restaurants
Benibana-tei	*Benibana-tei*	べにばな亭
Hotel Castle	*Hoteru Kyassuru*	ホテルキャッスル
Green Hotel	*Guriin Hoteru*	グリーンホテル
Hotel Metropolitan	*Hoteru Metoroporitan*	ホテルメトロポリタン
Sagorō	*Sagorō*	佐五郎
Sakaeya	*Sakaeya*	栄屋
Shiraume	*Shiraume*	志ら梅
Hotel Tōyō	*Hoteru Tōyō*	ホテル東陽
Washington Hotel	*Washinton Hoteru*	ワシントンホテル
Yamashiroya Ryokan	*Yamashiroya Ryokan*	山城屋旅館

Hirashimizu	*Hirashimizu*	平清水
Bun'emon-gama	*Bun'emon-gama*	文右衛門窯
Heikichi-gama	*Heikichi-gama*	平吉窯
Seiryū-gama	*Seiryū-gama*	清竜堂
Shichiemon-gama	*Shichiemon-gama*	七右衛門窯

Yamadera	*Yamadera*	山寺
Yamadera Pension	*Yamadera Penshon*	山寺ペンション

Zaō Onsen	*Zaō Onsen*	蔵王温泉
Okama	*Okama*	お釜
Zaō Sanroku Ropeway	*Zaō Sanroku Rōpu-uei*	蔵王山麓ロープウェイ

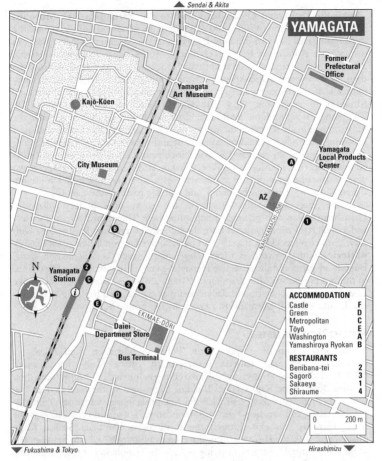

YAMAGATA

Former
Prefectural
Office

Yamagata
Art Museum

Kajō-Kōen

Yamagata
Local Products
Center

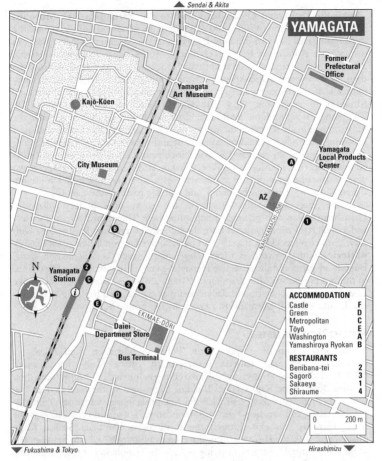

City Museum

AZ

N

Yamagata
Station

Daiei
Department Store

EKIMAE-DŌRI

Bus Terminal

ACCOMMODATION	
Castle	F
Green	D
Metropolitan	C
Tōyō	E
Washington	A
Yamashiroya Ryokan	B
RESTAURANTS	
Benibana-tei	2
Sagorō	3
Sakaeya	1
Shiraume	4

0   200 m

into one of Japan's top three skiing destinations, known for its deep snow and beguiling "snow monsters" – fir trees engulfed in wind-sculpted ice and snow. In early August (5–7), the city turns out for its major festival, the **Hanagasa Matsuri**, during which *yukata*-clad women wearing flowery hats perform a slow, graceful dance.

The City

Central Yamagata occupies a grid of streets lying northeast of the train station. Its southern boundary is Ekimae-dōri, a broad avenue leading straight from the station as far as the *Hotel Castle*, from where the main shopping street, Nanokamachi-dōri, strikes north to the former **Prefectural Office**, about twenty minutes' walk from the station. This imposing, European-style building of stone and ornate stucco dominates the north end of Nanokamachi-dōri. Originally built in 1911, the **interior** (Tues–Sun 9am–4.30pm; free) has been magnificently restored, particularly the third floor, with its parquet-floored dining room and elegant Assembly Hall. The ceilings are decorated with spectacular plasterwork, all handcrafted by one man at the rate of 15cm per day.

From the Prefectural Office, head west to the **Yamagata Art Museum** (Tues–Sun 10am–5pm; ¥500–1000 depending on what's on display) beside the castle walls. This modern museum boasts a small collection of major European names, such as Picasso, Chagall, Renoir and Monet, but unless there's a special exhibition of interest it's not really worth the entrance fee. Instead, cross the train tracks to enter **Kajō-kōen** by its beautifully restored East Gate, the only remnant of the former castle. Inside the park, turn left past the Prefectural Museum to reach the **City Museum** (Tues–Sun 9am–4.30pm; ¥200), occupying a delightful, multicoloured clapboard building. Erected in 1878, the museum originally served as the town's main hospital, and its exhibits include a fearsome array of early medical equipment and anatomical drawings, including a guide to pregnancy rendered as woodblock prints. There's also a room devoted to an Austrian, Dr Albert von Roretz, who came here in 1880 and spent two years instructing local doctors in the ways of Western medicine. When leaving the museum, it's easiest to backtrack and exit the park via the East Gate.

On the city's southeastern outskirts, the pretty little pottery village of **Hirashimizu** has a surprisingly rural atmosphere. There's just one main street and a small river running down from the hills, which provides local potters with their distinctive, speckled clay. If you poke about a bit, you'll find several family **potteries** with showrooms (daily 9am–5/6pm), such as Shichiemon-gama, Bun'emon-gama and the attractive Heikichi-gama, all of which offer the chance to throw a pot or two (daily 9am–3pm; ¥1800–2500). To reach Hirashimizu, take a bus from Yamagata Station (8 daily; 30min) or the Yamakō Building bus terminal (hourly; 20min). Alternatively, a taxi will cost around ¥2000 one way.

Practicalities

Yamagata is a stop on a spur of the Tōhoku Shinkansen from Tokyo via Fukushima. The main **tourist information office** (daily 9.30am–8pm; ☎0236/47-2333, ⒲www.yamagatakanko.com/english/index.html) is located on the first floor of the Kajō Central Building, right next to the train station. The office has English-speaking staff, plentiful English-language information, including city maps, and can help with accommodation. There's another office in the View Plaza as you exit through the turnstiles of Yamagata Station (daily 10am–6pm; ☎0236/31-7865). Limousine buses (40min; ¥700) run between the airport and central Yamagata, stopping outside the station and at the central **bus terminal** in the Yamakō Building, behind Ekimae-dōri's Daiei department store. All long-distance buses use this terminal, while most city buses depart from outside the station's east exit. If you'd rather be independent, there are several **car rental** companies clustered around the Kajō Central Building; try Eki Rent-a-Car (☎0236/46-6322) or Toyota (☎0236/25-0100).

To **change money**, there are branches of Yamagata Bank (marked by a cherry logo) and 77 Bank close to the station on Ekimae-dōri, and another branch of the Yamagata Bank next to the Yamagata Local Products Centre on Nanokamachi-dōri. Nanokamachi-dōri boasts a mixture of traditional **shops** and big stores such as AZ (pronounced "Azu"), while at its north end the Yamagata Local Products Centre (daily 9am–5.30pm; Nov & Dec closed Mon) sells a range of local souvenirs. The most famous Yamagata products are *sasanobori* (carvings made out of a single block of wood depicting hawks or roosters with flamboyant, curling tail feathers), cast-iron kettles and chunky, wooden Japanese chesspieces, *shōgi*.

Accommodation

Yamagata has a reasonable choice of **accommodation** within easy walking distance of the train station. At the cheaper end, *Yamashiroya Ryokan*

(℡0236/22-3007, ⓔinfo@e-yamashiroya.jp; ❹) has a few basic but perfectly adequate tatami rooms with shared washing facilities; it's located in the back-streets just to the north of the station. Ekimae-dōri boasts a number of more comfortable alternatives, such as the *Hotel Tōyō* (℡0236/42-2111, ⓕ42-2115; ❹), offering Western-style rooms with en-suite bathrooms. Further along Ekimae-dōri, about seven minutes' walk from the station, *Hotel Castle* (℡0236/31-3311, ⓦwww.hotelcastle.co.jp/main.htm; ❺) has a range of well-priced rooms and used to be the smartest place in town until the *Metropolitan* (℡0236/28-1111, ⓕ28-1166; ❻) opened above the station; it offers substantial discounts if you're travelling on a JR rail pass.

Eating

Yamagata's **speciality foods** include marbled Yonezawa beef, similar to the more famous Matsuzaka variety, and *imoni*, a warming winter stew of taro, meat, *konnyaku* (a jelly-like food made from the root of the devil's tongue plant) and onions served in slightly sweet sauce. If you fancy a splurge, *Sagorō* (℡0236/31-3560; closed Sun) is one of the city's best **restaurants** for beef, dished up as *sukiyaki*, *shabu-shabu* (from ¥4000) or straightforward steaks (from ¥7000); it's on the second floor above a butcher's shop on Ōtemon-dōri, to the north of Ekimae-dōri. Opposite *Sagorō*, locals fill the few tables of *Shiraume* (closed Sun), which has no menu as such but serves a range of well-priced seafood-based *teishoku* (from ¥700), as well as *imoni* in season (¥500). If you're looking for a pit stop near Nanokamachi-dōri, take the side street opposite the AZ store for the rustic *Sakaeya* (11.30am–7pm; closed Wed), serving an unusual selection of ramen in generous portions – in summer, you can even feast on cold ramen, served on a bed of ice with an attractive salad of corn, tomato, beef, shrimp and egg. Above the station, there's a small parade of restaurants accessed via a walkway at the north end of the second-floor Metro Plaza shopping mall (or look for the stairs directly outside the police box on the ground floor of the station). The cheap and friendly *Benibana-tei* (daily 11am–10pm) offers reasonable *izakaya*-style food and set meals.

Zaō Onsen

Roughly 20km southeast of Yamagata city, **ZAŌ ONSEN** is the main focus of activity in the Zaō Quasi National Park, an attractive region of volcanoes, crater lakes and hot springs. In winter (Dec to late March), the resort offers some of Japan's best **skiing**, with fourteen runs to choose from, night skiing and onsen baths to soak away the aches and pains. Non-skiers can enjoy the cable-car ride over **Juhyō Kōgen**, where a thick covering of snow and hoar frost transforms the plateau's fir trees into giant "snow monsters" (*juhyō*).

Buses run approximately every hour from Yamagata Station to the Zaō Onsen bus terminal (40min; ¥840), at the bottom of the village, where you'll also find the **tourist information office** (℡0236/94-9328). From here it's a ten-minute walk southeast to the **Zaō Sanroku Ropeway** (8am–5pm, every 15min; ¥1400 return), which whisks you up to Juhyō Kōgen. The snow monsters are at their best in February, though you can see photos of them at other times of year in the **Juhyō Museum** (daily 9am–4pm; free), located in the terminal building. A second ropeway (same times and ticket) then continues up to Zaō Jizo Sanchō Station at 1661m. This top station lies between Sampō Kōjin-san (1703m) and Jizō-san (1736m), just two of the peaks which make up the ragged profile of **Zaō-san**. In the summer hiking season (May–Oct) you can follow the right-hand (southeasterly) path over Jizō-san and Kumano-dake (1841m) for spectacular views and a fairly rugged hour's walk to the desolate, chemical-blue **Okama crater lake**.

Yamadera

The temple complex of Risshaku-ji, or **YAMADERA** as it's more popularly known, is one of Tōhoku's most holy places. It was founded in 860 AD by a Zen priest of the Tendai sect and reached its peak in the Kamakura period (1185–1333). Today around forty temple buildings still stand scattered among the ancient cedars on a steep, rocky hillside. The temple lies close by Yamadera Station on the JR Senzan line between Yamagata and Sendai.

From the station, follow the crowds across the river and right, past shops selling walking sticks, snacks and souvenirs, to where you can see the temple roofs on the slopes of Hōju-san. Ignore the first two flights of steps to your left and take the third staircase up to the temple's main hall, **Kompon Chūdō**. This impressive building, dating from 1356, shelters a flame brought from Enryaku-ji, the centre of Tendai Buddhism near Kyoto (see p.563), 1100 years ago and which has supposedly been burning ever since – as you peer inside, it's the left-hand one of the two hanging lanterns. Walking back west along the hillside, you pass a small shrine and a solemn statue of Bashō who, travelling before the days of coach parties, penned a characteristically pithy ode to Yamadera: "In the utter silence of a temple, a cicada's voice alone penetrates the rocks." He sits across from the modern **Hihōkan** (daily 8.30am–5pm; closed Dec to mid-April; ¥200), which houses a fine collection of temple treasures, including a beautiful 3-D mandala and a large painting of Buddha in repose sporting a tight perm.

A few steps further on, San-mon marks the entrance to the **mountain** (daily 6am–6pm; ¥300), from where over 1100 steps meander past moss-covered Jizō statues, lanterns and prayer wheels, and squeeze between rocks carved with prayers and pitted with caves. It takes about forty minutes to reach the highest temple, **Okuno-in**, where breathless pilgrims tie prayer papers round a mammoth lantern. Before setting off downhill, don't miss the views over Yamadera from the terrace of **Godai-dō** perched on the cliff-face just beyond the distinctive red **Nōkyō-dō** pavilion.

Yamadera village consists mainly of souvenir shops and expensive ryokan. However, if you need **accommodation**, *Yamadera Pension* (☎0236/95-2134, ⓔyamadera@mmy.ne.jp; ❻ including meals) is the most attractive option. It's in a half-timbered building right in front of the station, with a decent **restaurant** downstairs.

Sendai

The largest city in the Tōhoku region, **SENDAI** is a sprawling but pleasant place, with broad, tree-lined avenues and a lively downtown district. Though often just regarded as a staging post on the way to Matsushima Bay (see p.289), the city's **castle ruins**, with their local history museum, and the ornate mausoleum of Sendai's revered founder, the *daimyō* **Daté Masamune**, are worth a brief stop. During the **Tanabata Matsuri** (Star Festival; Aug 6–8), the city centre is awash with thousands of bamboo poles festooned with colourful paper tassels, poems and prayers, celebrating the only day in the year – weather permitting – when the two astral lovers, Vega the weaver and Altair the cowherd, can meet.

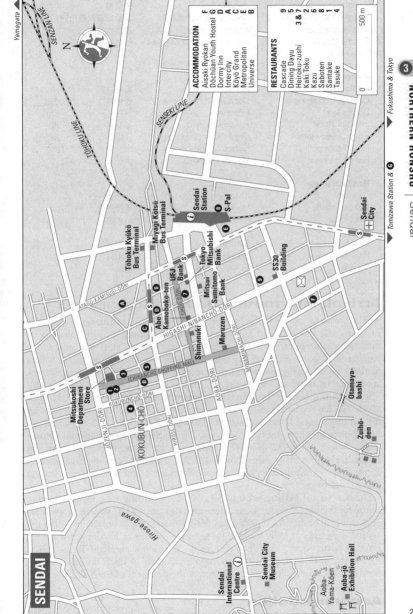

SENDAI

▲ Ichinoseki & Morioka   ▲ Sendai Port   ▲ Matsushima

Yamagata

SENZAN LINE

N

TŌHOKU LINE

SENSEKI LINE

▼ Fukushima & Tokyo

▼ Tomizawa Station & G

ACCOMMODATION	
Aisaki Ryokan	F
Dōchūan Youth Hostel	G
Dormy Inn	D
Intercity	A
Kōyō Grand	C
Metropolitan	E
Universe	B

RESTAURANTS	
Cascade	9
Dining Dayu	5
Heiroku-zushi	3 & 7
Kaki Toku	2
Kazu	6
Saboten	8
Santake	1
Tasuke	4

0 ————— 500 m

Sendai Station

S-Pal

8

Tōhoku Kyūkō Bus Terminal

Miyagi Kōtsū Bus Terminal

E

Sendai City

ATAGO-KAMISUGI-DŌRI

A

C

Abe D Kamoboko-ten

UFJ Bank

Tokyo Mitsubishi Bank

HIGASHI-NIBANCHŌ-DŌRI

Mitsui Sumitomo Bank

7

SS30 Building

9

Shimanuki

Maruzen

ICHIBANCHŌ SHOPPING MALL

6

B

MINAMIMACHI-DŌRI

AOBA-DŌRI

Mitsukoshi Department Store

KOKUBUNCHŌ-DŌRI

1 2

3

5

B

4

JŌZENJI-DŌRI

KOKUBUN-CHŌ

HIROSE-DŌRI

Hirose-gawa

Otamaya-bashi

Zuihō-den

Sendai International Centre

Sendai City Museum

Aoba-Yama-Kōen

Aoba-jō

Exhibition Hall

Sendai		
Sendai	*Sendai*	仙台
Aoba-jō	*Aoba-jō*	青葉城
Aoba-jō Exhibition Hall	*Aoba-jō Shiryōtenjikan*	青葉城資料展示館
Aobayama-kōen	*Aobayama-kōen*	青葉山公園
Sendai City Museum	*Sendai-shi Hakubutsukan*	仙台市博物館
Zuihō-den	*Zuihō-den*	瑞鳳殿
Accommodation		
Aisaki Ryokan	*Aisaki Ryokan*	相崎旅館
Dōchūan Youth Hostel	*Dōchūan Yūsu Hosuteru*	道中庵ユースホステル
Dormy Inn	*Dōmii In*	ドーミーイン
Intercity Hotel	*Intāshitii Hoteru*	インターシティーホテル
Kōyō Grand Hotel	*Kōyō Gurando Hoteru*	江陽グランドホテル
Hotel Metropolitan	*Hoteru Metoroporitan*	ホテルメトロポリタン
Hotel Universe	*Hoteru Yunibāsu*	ホテルユニバース
Restaurants		
Cascade	*Kasukēdo*	カスケード
Heiroku-zushi	*Heiroku-zushi*	平禄寿司
Kaki Toku	*Kaki Toku*	かき徳
Kazu	*Kazu*	和
Saboten	*Saboten*	サボテン
Santake	*Santake*	さん竹
Tasuke	*Tasuke*	太助

Arrival, information and getting around

The majority of visitors to Sendai arrive at the main JR **station** on the east side of town, near the local and long-distance **bus terminals**. The city also has an international **airport**, with flights from Seoul, Beijing, Honolulu and Hong Kong, as well as domestic services; limousine buses run from the airport to Sendai Station (40min; ¥910). **Ferries** from Nagoya and Hokkaidō (Tomakomai) dock at Sendai Port, northwest of the city, which is served by local buses (40min; ¥490).

Sendai's main **tourist information centre** (daily 8.30am–8pm; ☎022/222-4069, ⓦwww.siip.city.sendai.jp/kankokoryu/english/index.html) is located on the station's second floor; the English-speaking staff can help with city maps and hotel bookings. Alternatively, try the more relaxed **Sendai International Centre** (daily 9am–8pm; ☎022/265-2471), out near the castle, which also runs an **English Hotline** (daily 9am–8pm; ☎022/224-1919) and provides free Internet access. The municipal authorities run the reasonably useful Sendai Home Page at ⓦwww.sira.or.jp.

The best way of **getting around** Sendai is by **local bus** – ask the information centre for their list of useful routes. The minimum fare is ¥150, payable to the driver as you exit, or there's a one-day pass (¥620), though this is only valid within the central zone and not really worth it for most visitors. Sendai has one **subway** line, running north–south, which is useful for the *Dōchūan Youth Hostel*. The system is easy to use, with announcements and signs in English; to reach the subway from Sendai's JR station, follow the signs through the basement of the Seibu store.

Accommodation

Sendai has plenty of mid-range and expensive business **hotels** within walking distance of the station, but is less well provided with budget accommodation.

However, it does boast one of Japan's most attractive city youth hostels, which more than repays the trek out into Sendai's southern suburbs.

Aisaki Ryokan 5-6 Kitame-machi, Aoba-ku ☏022/264-0700, ✉sendai@aisakiryokan.com. One of the cheaper places in the city centre, a fifteen-minute walk southeast of the station – look for the red Coke sign in a back alley behind the central post office. The facilities are old and basic, with a choice between Western or tatami rooms, some en suite. ❹

Dōchūan Youth Hostel 31 Onoda-Kitayashiki, Taihaku-ku ☏022/247-0511, ⓦwww.jyh.or.jp. The best of three youth hostels in Sendai, built among trees in traditional farmhouse style. Accommodation is in cramped tatami dormitories with a TV and washbasin, while there's also a cedar bath and excellent food – the English-speaking warden grows his own rice and vegetables. The only downside is the hostel's out-of-the-way location: it's a ten-minute walk due east from Tomizawa Station or fifteen minutes by subway from central Sendai (¥290). ❸

Dormy Inn 2-10-17 Chūō, Aoba-ku ☏022/715-7077, Ⓕ 715-7078. This new budget business hotel has a range of boxy but adequate en-suite rooms, with satellite TV and minibar. It's about five minutes from the station, near Hirose-dōri subway station. ❺

Intercity Hotel 2-9-14 Hon-chō, Aoba-ku ☏022/221-3311, Ⓕ 222-5006. Across Hirose-dōri from the cheaper *Dormy Inn*, this small, welcoming hotel is nicely decorated and well priced. All rooms come with their own bathroom. ❺

Kōyo Grand Hotel 2-3-1 Hon-chō, Aoba-ku ☏022/267-5111, Ⓕ 265-2252. It's worth taking a walk through the lobby of this extraordinary hotel, decked out with "antique" French furniture, cupids, Versailles mirrors and stuffed antelope heads. The rooms are only slightly more restrained and, not surprisingly, a little on the pricey side. ❻

Hotel Metropolitan 1-1-1 Chūō, Aoba-ku ☏022/268-2525, ✉e-kikaku@s-metro.stbl.co.jp. Big swish hotel next door to Sendai Station, with a range of comfortable Western- and Japanese-style rooms. Facilities include a choice of restaurants, Sky Lounge bar, gym and indoor pool. ❻–❼

Hotel Universe 3F, 4-3-22 Ichiban-chō, Aoba-ku ☏022/261-7711, ✉sen@h-uni.com. Simple business hotel on Ichiban-chō shopping street. Rooms are a good size for the price, with their own bathroom, phone, TV and minibar, and there's free Internet access. ❹–❺

The City

Though central Sendai had to be rebuilt after World War II, its streets follow the original grid pattern laid out by Daté Masamune in the seventeenth century. The main downtown area, a high-rise district of offices, banks and shopping malls, lies on the east bank of the Hirose-gawa. Its principal thoroughfare, Aoba-dōri, runs west from the train station to the far side of the river, where the city's few sights are located. After an initial bus ride, the area is best tackled on foot.

The natural place to start exploring is the wooded hilltop park, **Aobayama-kōen**, which was once the site of the magnificent Sendai Castle, popularly known as **Aoba-jō**. Only a few stretches of wall and a reconstructed gateway remain, but the site is impeccable, protected by the river to the east and a deep ravine on its south side. Buses run from Sendai Station (stand 9) to Aobajōshi-mae, a twenty-minute journey, from where it's a short walk to the **statue of Masamune** astride his horse, surveying the city below. A fearsome warrior, Masamune was nicknamed the "One-Eyed Dragon", thanks to a childhood attack of smallpox. He had been granted the fiefdom in return for helping bring Tokugawa Ieyasu to power in 1603, and the Daté clan continued to rule Sendai for the next 270 years. Their castle was constructed in highly ornate Momoyama style, with painted ceilings and huge rooms divided by glorious screens, more like a luxurious palace than a fortress. Though it's a bit gimmicky, you can get an idea of its former glory in the small **Aoba-jō Exhibition Hall** (daily 9am–5pm; ¥700), located above the park's souvenir shops, where a short, computer-generated film takes you "inside" the castle; the red seats are equipped with foreign-language earphone sets.

Ten minutes' walk down the north side of the hill brings you to the more interesting **Sendai City Museum** (Tues–Sun 9am–4.45pm; ¥400, extra for special exhibitions).This modern, well-laid-out installation traces the city's history from the early Stone Age to the present day, though the main emphasis is on the glory days under Masamune and his successors. On the second floor you'll find displays of his armour, with the distinctive crescent moon on the helmet, his sword and various portraits – always with two eyes.

When Daté Masamune died in 1636, aged 70, he was buried in the **Zuihō-den** on a wooded hillside just along the river from Aoba-jō. Eventually his two successors joined him, and their three **mausoleums** (daily 9am–4.30pm;¥550) now stand at the top of broad, stone steps, all in the same opulent Momoyama style, their polychrome carvings glittering against the plain dark wood and overhanging eaves. In fact, the mausoleums are fairly recent reconstructions – during the five-year project the graves were opened and you can see the treasures they unearthed, as well as a fascinating video of the excavations, in a one-room **museum** beside the Zuihō-den.Though the mausoleums are only a short distance from Aoba-jō as the crow flies, getting here is either a good twenty-minute walk, or you have to take a bus back to Sendai Station and out again (stand 11) to the Otamaya-bashi stop.

Eating and drinking

Sendai's **speciality foods** include *gyū-tan* (broiled, smoked or salted calf's tongue) and, in winter (Dec–March), oysters from Matsushima Bay. *Sasa-kamaboko*, a leaf-shaped cake of rather rubbery white-fish paste, is a popular local snack, which you can sample in *Abe Kamaboko-ten*, a famous shop on the Chūō-dōri shopping mall. Chūō-dōri and the connecting Ichiban-chō arcades are good places to look for **restaurants and cafés**, while S-Pal, at the south end of Sendai Station, and the top two floors of the SS30 Building, also have a decent selection. **Kokubun-chō**, just west of the Ichiban-chō shopping mall, is Sendai's main entertainment district.

Cascade 4-6-1 Chūō. If you're looking for a break from Japanese food, try the eatery located on the basement floor of the *Sendai Kokusai Hotel*. Western-style breakfasts start at ¥1000, while lunches and dinners are ¥1500–2000.

Dayu Dining 2F, 4-2-13 Ichiban-chō. Casual restaurant on the Ichiban-chō arcade specializing in garlic cuisine and a variety of Indonesian, Thai and Italian foods. Prices are reasonable, though there's an annoying table charge. Open evenings only.

Heiroku-zushi Chūō-dōri & Ichiban-chō. Two spick-and-span sushi outlets on the shopping arcades, with a takeaway service or conveyor-belt counter. Dishes cost ¥100 and ¥200.

Kaki Toku 2F, 4-9-1 Ichiban-chō. Elegant oyster and seafood restaurant with a choice of tables or tatami seating. Set menus cost from ¥6000, though there are plenty of cheaper options, including rice and tempura dishes from ¥1000.

Kazu B1, 2-11-11 Chūō. Small, friendly *okonomiyaki* joint that's worth seeking out in the backstreets north of Chūō-dōri. They cook the pancake for you, from a choice of ingredients and regional styles. Closed Sun.

Saboten B1, S-Pal building. This well-rated, café-style *tonkatsu* restaurant is surprisingly good value, with individual dishes from ¥1000 and various set meals.

Santake 4-9-24 Ichiban-chō. Casual soba shop opposite Mitsukoshi department store on the Ichiban-chō arcade. Individual dishes from ¥600, or ¥1000 plus for a set meal. Tues–Sun 11am–8pm.

Tasuke 2-11-11, Kokubun-chō. One of Sendai's best-known *gyū-tan* (calf tongue) restaurants, where you can eat tongue in all its forms. If it's full, try the cheaper outlets in the alleys opposite. Closed Mon.

Listings

Airlines Air China ☎022/221-2025; ANA domestic ☎0120-029222, international ☎0120-029333;

Asiana Airlines ☎022/265-0022; Cathay Pacific/Dragon Air ☎022/227-8681; JAL domestic

☏0120-255971; international ☏0120-255931; Japan Air System domestic ☏0120-511283, international ☏0120-711283.

Airport information ☏022/382-0080.

Banks and exchange There are branches of major foreign exchange banks, such as Sanwa, Mitsubishi Sumitomo Bank, UFJ and Tokyo Mitsubishi, at the east end of Aoba-dōri, near Sendai Station.

Buses Long-distance JR Buses (☏022/256-6646) for Niigata and Tokyo (Shinjuku) leave from the east side of Sendai Station. Express buses go to Kyoto, Ōsaka, Nagoya and destinations around Tōhoku from outside the Miyagi Kōtsū (☏022/261-5333) office at the west end of Hirose-dōri, as does the JR bus to Akita. On the opposite side of the road, Tōhoku Kyūkō (☏022/262-7031) buses leave for Tokyo Station.

Car rental Central car rental outlets, all outside the east exit of Sendai station, include Eki Rent-a-Car (☏022/292-6501), Mazda (☏022/293-1021) and Nippon (☏022/297-1919).

Emergencies The main police station is at 1-25 4-chome, Ichibanchō Aoba-ku (☏022/222-7171). In an absolute emergency, contact the Foreign Advisory Service on ☏022/224-1919. For other emergency numbers, see Basics on p.81.

Ferries Taiheiyō Ferry (☏022/263-9877) runs overnight services daily to Nagoya and on alternate days to Hokkaidō (Tomakomai). Both services leave from Sendai Port, accessible by bus from Sendai Station (stand 34; 40min; ¥490). It's best to book ferries with the English-speaking staff of the JTB on Higashi-nichibanchō.

Hospitals Sendai City Hospital, 3-1 Shimizu-kōji (☏022/263-9900) has a 24hr emergency clinic; otherwise, ring the English Hotline (daily 10am–8pm; ☏022/224-1919) for advice on clinics with English-speaking doctors.

Internet The Multimedia and Information Centre (5F, AER Building, ☏022/724-1200) offers thirty minutes' Internet access free of charge from 9am to 8pm daily. The Sendai International Centre (see p.286) also offers free Internet access.

Immigration For visa and other immigration problems, contact the Immigration Bureau at 3-20 Gorin 1-chome, Miyagino-ku (☏022/256-6076).

Post office Sendai Central Post Office, 1-7 Kitame-machi, Aoba-ku, has a 24hr service for stamps and international mail (Mon–Sat), and also poste restante. There's a useful sub-post office inside Sendai Station.

Shopping The main shopping streets are the covered malls of Chūō-dōri and Ichiban-chō. For traditional crafts, try Shimanuki, towards the west end of Chūō-dōri, which sells a good range of *kokeshi* dolls, wooden toys, *ittōbori* carved birds, fabrics, ironware and lacquer goods. Maruzen is the best place in town for foreign-language books and magazines; you'll find it on the southern extension of Ichiban-chō, across Aoba-dōri.

Taxis Plenty of taxis cruise the streets of Sendai and wait outside the station. If you need to call one, the two biggest firms are Kankō (☏022/252-1385) and Nikkō (☏022/241-4181).

Matsushima Bay

The jumble of wooded islands dotting **Matsushima Bay**, a short train ride northeast of Sendai, is officially designated one of Japan's top three scenic areas, along with Miyajima and Amanohashidate. Roughly 12km by 14km, the bay contains over 260 islands of every conceivable shape and size. The smaller islets are cut through with tunnels and sculpted by wind and waves into fanciful likenesses of tortoises, whales, or even human profiles with a scraggy fringe of contorted pine trees – or so the guides would have you believe. In between, the shallower parts of the bay have been used for farming oysters for around three hundred years.

Bashō, travelling through in 1689, commented that "much praise had already been lavished upon the wonders of the islands of Matsushima", and many visitors today find the bay slightly disappointing. Nevertheless, a **boat trip** among the white, ribbed islands makes an enjoyable outing, though it's best to avoid weekends and holidays. **Matsushima town** has a couple of less-frequented picturesque spots, and a venerable temple, **Zuigan-ji**, with an impressive collection of art treasures. Most people visit Matsushima on a day-trip from Sendai, but there are some reasonable accommodation options in the area if you're heading on up the coast to Kinkazan (see p.293).

Matsushima Bay

Matsushima	*Matsushima*	松島
Century Hotel	*Senchurii Hoteru*	センチュリーホテル
Donjiki Chaya	*Donjiki Chaya*	どんじき茶屋
Folkloro Matsushima	*Forukurōro Matsushima*	フォルクローロ松島
Fukuura-jima	*Fukuura-jima*	福浦島
Godai-dō	*Godai-dō*	五大堂
Miyato-jima	*Miyato-jima*	宮戸島
Oku-Matsushima	*Oku-Matsushima*	奥松島
Oshima	*Oshima*	雄島
Saigyō Modoshi-no-matsu	*Saigyō Modoshi-no-matsu*	西行戻しの松
Santori Chaya	*Santori Chaya*	さんとり茶屋
Shintomi-yama	*Shintomi-yama*	新富山
Sōkanzan	*Sōkanzan*	双観山
Zuigan-ji	*Zuigan-ji*	瑞巌寺
Shiogama	*Shiogama*	塩釜
Hon-Shiogama	*Hon-Shiogama*	本塩釜
Marine Gate	*Marin Gēto*	マリンゲート
Nobiru	*Nobiru*	野蒜
Bōyō-sō	*Bōyō-sō*	望洋荘
Ōtakamori	*Ōtakamori*	大高森
Pi-La Matsushima Youth Hostel	*Pai-Ra Matsushima Yūsu Hosuteru*	パイラ松島ユースホステル

Touring the bay

The best approach to Matsushima is via **SHIOGAMA**, from where you can travel on across the bay **by boat**. A busy industrial and fishing port with a large tuna fleet, Shiogama lies on the JR Senseki line, which runs from the basement of Sendai Station through **Hon-Shiogama** (25–40min; ¥400) to Matsushima and beyond. The station's **tourist information office** (daily 10am–4pm) can give you timetables and point you to the **Marine Gate ferry pier**, ten minutes' walk to the east; turn right outside the station and right again under the train tracks, and you'll see the modern terminal building straight ahead. The Marine Gate pier is the departure point for both local **ferries** serving the inhabited islands and **tourist boats**, which take a leisurely trip through Matsushima Bay before dropping you in Matsushima town. In high season (April–Nov) boats run every thirty minutes (8am–4pm; 50min; ¥1420, or ¥2220 for the upper deck), and there's also the option of a longer voyage into the northern reaches of the bay (daily at 11.10am; 1hr 50min; ¥2950). From December through March, there are sailings every hour only on the shorter course.

It's also possible to take a cruise round the bay **from Matsushima** tourist pier (roughly every hour 8am–4pm; 45min; ¥1400), though they tend to be more crowded than the boats from Shiogama. Another more interesting route goes north from Matsushima to Miyato-jima (see p.292), with the possibility of catching a later boat back (May–Oct daily at 9am & noon; 1hr; ¥1220). Alternatively, you could rent your own four-person motorboat from Matsushima's two smaller piers; rates start at ¥4000 for a twenty-minute ride.

Matsushima

The modern town of **MATSUSHIMA** is little more than a strip of resort hotels and souvenir shops, but its origins go back to 828 AD, when Zen priests founded the temple of **Zuigan-ji** (daily 8am–3.30/4.30pm, April–Sept until 5pm; ¥700), overlooking the bay. The entrance to the temple is marked by a suitably grand grove of 400-year-old cedar trees halfway between (and a five-minute walk from) the central tourist pier, where boats from Shiogama dock, and the train station (Matsushima-kaigan). Zuigan-ji has been rebuilt many times since its foundation, but retains a compelling sense of history. Though deceptively plain from the outside, the **main hall** bears the unmistakeable stamp of Daté Masamune, the first lord of Sendai, who oversaw its reconstruction in the early seventeenth century. He employed the best craftsmen and the highest-quality materials to create a splendid monument of intricately carved doors and transoms, wood-panelled ceilings and gilded screens lavishly painted with hawks, chrysanthemums, peacocks and pines.

A number of these screens and other items on display are replicas, but you can see some of the originals in the modern **Seiryū-den** (included in the ticket), to the left as you exit Zuigan-ji's inner compound. Alongside the normal array of temple treasures, there are statues of the one-eyed Masamune, in full armour and in an uncompromising mood, and his angelic-looking wife and eldest daughter. Note that his daughter, dressed in black, is clutching a rosary; she was a firm Christian who refused to renounce her faith at a time when it was strictly prohibited in Japan.

In front of Zuigan-ji, just north of the ferry pier, two tiny islands are threaded together with arched vermilion bridges. No one knows why the bridges were built with precarious gaps between the planks, but one suggestion is that it kept women, in their awkward kimono, from despoiling the sacred ground. The object of their curiosity was the **Godai-dō**, a picturesque pavilion built by order of Masamune in the early 1600s. It houses statues of five Buddhist deities which can only be viewed every 33 years – so come back in 2006. Meanwhile, you'll have to make do with the charming carvings of the twelve animals of the zodiac decorating the eaves, starting with the rat on the north side.

If time allows, there are a couple of larger, less-frequented islands along the seafront, of which **Oshima**, five minutes' walk south, is the more interesting. On the way you'll pass **Karantei** (daily 8.30am–5pm; ¥200), a famous teahouse with a beautiful name – "place to view the ripples on the water" – but little else to recommend it. Instead, press on to where another red-lacquered bridge leads to Ōshima. Once a retreat for Buddhist priests, the island's soft rock is pocked with caves, tablets and monuments; from its east side you get attractive views of Matsushima Bay. The second island, **Fukuura-jima** (daily 8am–5pm; ¥200), lies north of Godai-dō across a 250-metre-long bridge. A natural botanical garden, it's home to more than 250 native plant species, and makes a good picnic spot.

The hills around Matsushima town provide plenty of opportunities for panoramic views of the bay. Of the four main lookout points, southerly **Sōkanzan** is reckoned to offer the best all-round views, including both Shiogama and Matsushima itself; take a taxi (¥2500 return fare) to avoid the thirty-minute climb on a busy road. Alternatively, **Saigyō Modoshi-no-matsu** is a more pleasant, fifteen-minute scramble west of the station, or allow a few minutes more for **Shintomi-yama**, on the northwest edge of town above Fukuura-jima.

Practicalities

You can travel to Matsushima by **boat** via Shiogama (see p.290) and by **train** directly to Matsushima from Sendai on the JR Senseki line (15–30min; ¥320), getting off at Matsushima-kaigan Station. There's a **tourist information office** outside the station (daily 9.30am–4pm; ☎022/354-2263) with English-speaking staff, and a second beside the boat pier (daily 8.30am–5pm; ☎022/354-2618, ⓦwww.matsushima-kanko.com).

Matsushima has a number of smart but expensive **hotels**; prices are more reasonable on weekdays and in winter (Dec to early April). If you're looking for budget accommodation, head on up the coast to Nobiru (see below). Right on the waterfront, the modern *Century Hotel* (☎022/354-4111, ⓔyoyaku@centuryhotel.co.jp1; ❺) has a choice of Western or tatami en-suite rooms, plus seafront balconies at the higher end and a huge onsen bath with picture windows over the bay. Alternatively, *Folkloro Matsushima* (☎022/353-3535, ⓕ353-3588; ❻ including breakfast) is a B&B-style hotel with small but clean and newish en-suite rooms. To reach it turn right from the station and follow the road leading under the tracks and up the hill about 700m.

Most of Matsushima's **restaurants** lining the main road cater to tour parties, but there are a couple of attractive alternatives. *Santori Chaya* (closed Wed), a small, simple place on the seafront north of the Godai-dō, serves a range of reasonable *teishoku* as well as sashimi, sushi and rice dishes; go upstairs for sea views over the kitchen roof. For a snack or light lunch, try the thatched *Donjiki Chaya*, surrounded by gardens in the woods south of Zuigan-ji, which offers soba, *dango* (rice dumplings) and drinks.

Oku-Matsushima

The eastern side of Matsushima Bay, known as **Oku-Matsushima**, is protected by a large, ragged island, **Miyato-jima**, linked to the mainland by a road bridge. Apart from a number of sandy beaches, the island's main draw is a low hill, **Ōtakamori**, from where you get more panoramic views over the bay.

The gateway to Oku-Matsushima is the small town of **NOBIRU**, fifteen minutes north on the JR Senseki line from Matsushima, which also provides some of the area's cheapest accommodation. The station **information office** (daily 8.30am–5.30pm; ☎0225/88-2611, ⓔkanko@okumatsushima-kanko.jp) provides maps and can help with reservations, though the staff don't speak English. One of the nicest **places to stay** around here is the smart *Pi-La Matsushima Youth Hostel* (☎0225/88-2220, ⓦwww.jyh.or.jp), with a choice of dormitories (¥3200 per person) or Western-style family rooms (¥3500 per person), and hearty meals. The hostel lies roughly fifteen minutes' walk from Nobiru Station; cross the bridge and keep heading south towards the sea until you find a right turn signed to the hostel. En route you'll pass *Bōyō-sō* (☎0225/88-2159; ❻ including two meals), the newest of several minshuku scattered in the pine woods south of Nobiru Station.

The pine trees stretch all along Nobiru beach, a wide expanse of dark sand which gets packed in summer, but there are better coves further south on Miyato-jima. The best way to explore the island is by **bicycle** – the youth hostel has bikes for rent (¥500 for 3hr, ¥800 per day) and the manager can advise on the best routes. It takes three to four hours to cycle round the whole island, plus an extra thirty minutes to walk up to the viewpoint on top of Ōtakamori.

Oshika Hantō

North of Sendai, Honshū's coastal plain gives way to a fractured shoreline of deep bays and knobbly peninsulas. The first of these is the **Oshika Hantō**, a

Ayukawa	*Ayukawa*	鮎川
Atami-sō	*Atami-sō*	あたみ荘
Caravan	*Kyaraban*	キャラバン
Minami-sō	*Minami-sō*	南荘
Misaki-ya	*Misaki-ya*	岬屋
Ojika Ryokan	*Ojika Ryokan*	おじか旅館
Oshika Whale Land	*Oshika Hoēru Rando*	おしかホエールランド
Ishinomaki	*Ishinomaki*	石巻
Kinkazan	*Kinkazan*	金華山
Ambe Ryokan	*Ambe Ryokan*	安部旅館
Koganeyama-jinja	*Koganeyama-jinja*	黄金山神社
Shiokaze	*Shiokaze*	潮風
Onagawa	*Onagawa*	女川

rugged spine on the eastern edge of Sendai Bay, whose broken tip forms the tiny island of **Kinkazan**. This has been a sacred place since ancient times, but its prime attractions these days are its isolation and hiking trails through forests inhabited by semi-wild deer and monkeys. The main gateway to the area is **Ishinomaki**, from where buses run down the peninsula to **Ayukawa**, a former whaling port with a moderately interesting museum and connecting ferries to Kinkazan. Many tourist facilities close in winter (Nov–March), so check the schedules first at the information offices in Sendai or Matsushima and ask them to help with booking accommodation.

Connections at Ishinomaki can be quite poor, with waits of up to an hour for a connecting bus or train. If you have time to kill and an interest in manga, follow the pointed arms of the life-size manga figures to the entertaining **Mangattan Museum** (9am–5/6pm, closed every third Tues; ¥800), housed in a flying saucer-style building across the river from the main shopping strip.

Kinkazan

The first inhabitants of **KINKAZAN** ("Mountain of the Gold Flowers"), a conical island lying 1km off the tip of Oshika Hantō, were gold prospectors. Though the seams were exhausted long ago, Kinkazan is still associated with wealth and good fortune, and its prime sight, the shrine of **Koganeyama-jinja**, is dedicated to the twin gods of prosperity, Ebisu and Daikoku. The shrine stands in a deer-cropped clearing on the west slope of Kinkazan, fifteen minutes' walk above the ferry pier – turn left from the pier and follow the road steeply uphill. From behind the shrine buildings a rough path leads on a stiff two-kilometre hike up Kinkazan (445m), where the effort is rewarded with truly magnificent views along the peninsula and west towards distant Matsushima.

Various other **hiking trails** are indicated on a small, green map you'll be given on the ferry or by Ayukawa tourist office (see p.294). However, be aware that the paths themselves are poorly signed and may well be overgrown, so check the route before setting out. Remember also to take plenty of food and water. If you do get lost, head down to the rough track circumnavigating the island; the whole place is less than 25km around, so you can't go too far wrong.

Practicalities

The best way of getting to Kinkazan is to take the JR Senseki line from Sendai (or Matsushima) to **Ishinomaki** and then hop on a bus for the scenic ride south to **Ayukawa** (1hr 30min; ¥1460). Buses depart from outside Ishinomaki Station, where there's also a small **tourist office** (daily 9.30am–5.30/6pm; Jan–March, Nov & Dec closed Mon; ☎0225/93-6448); **car rental** is available through Eki Rent-a-Car (☎0225/93-1665). There are hourly **ferries** from Ayukawa to Kinkazan from April to early November (12–25min; ¥900), and three boats per day during the rest of the year. Alternatively, high-speed catamarans depart for Kinkazan from **Onagawa**, at the end of the JR Ishinomaki line on the peninsula's northeast coast, but only in summer: reservations are advisable but not essential (30min; ¥1600 or ¥3040 for a same-day or next-day return; ☎0225/53-3121).

The most atmospheric **accommodation** on Kinkazan is the pilgrims' lodge at Koganeyama-jinja (☎0225/45-2264, ✉jkoganeyama@bea.hi-ho.ne.jp; dorm beds ¥9700 per person, including two meals), where you can attend the shrine's early-morning prayer sessions. Note that in the busiest season you may be sharing your – admittedly large – tatami dorm room with up to nine other guests. There are also two mangy minshuku a few hundred metres down the dirt road leading away from the right of the ferry pier: *Ambe Ryokan* (☎0225/45-3082; ⑤; closed Nov–May; ⑤, including two meals) and *Shiokaze* (☎0225/45-2666 daytime, ☎45-2244 evenings; ⑤, including two meals). Note that it's essential to book ahead and that there are no **restaurants** on the island, so bring something along to eat for lunch.

Ayukawa

The sleepy town of **AYUKAWA**, on the southwest tip of Oshika Hantō, makes an alternative base for Kinkazan. A thriving port until commercial **whaling** was banned in 1987, Ayukawa now depends on tourism and its only sight is a smart new whaling museum beside the ferry pier. Despite the moratorium, Japan still hunts whales for "scientific purposes" and the residents of Ayukawa continue to receive whale-meat rations. You can even eat whale (*kujira*) in local restaurants and buy whale products in the souvenir shops.

The well-designed **Oshika Whale Land** museum (daily 9am–6pm; Jan–March & Dec closed Tues; ¥700) pushes a more conservationist line while also tracing the history of Ayukawa's whaling fleet. The first exhibition hall takes you through the stylised ribcage of a whale, accompanied by recordings of their eerie underwater chatter. There are various films and interactive displays concerning the life of whales, many aimed at children, though you might want to miss the section full of pickled organs and embryos.

The museum, Kinkazan **ferry pier** and **bus terminal** are all grouped together at the south end of Ayukawa. You can buy ferry tickets in an office next to the bus stop (daily 8am–4.30/5pm; ☎0225/45-2181), while the **tourism bureau** (daily 8.30am–5pm; closed Jan–March, Nov & Dec; ☎0225/45-3456) is a few doors further north. Staff here can provide maps and make bookings for accommodation in both Ayukawa and Kinkazan.

If you're looking for **accommodation** in Ayukawa, the *Minami-sō* minshuku (☎0225/45-2501; ⑤) is close to the ferry pier and the place most likely to be open all year. It's in a grey iron building on the hill above the pier but, despite appearances, is perfectly adequate and turns out pretty good food. Smarter options are the new *Atami-sō* (☎0225/45-2227; ⑤), on the main road coming into town, or the more upmarket *Ojika Ryokan* (☎0225/45-3068; ⑤–⑥), in the backstreets two minutes' walk north of the pier.

A cluster of **restaurants** along the road behind the information office sells ultra-fresh seafood. Try *Misaki-ya* (closed Thurs), on the crossroads towards Whale Land, which serves moderately priced sushi, sashimi and a range of standard dishes, or the soba joint next door. Most places close at 5pm in the off season, but at the north end of town the *Caravan* coffee shop (closed Thurs) serves curry rice, spaghetti and other Western dishes until 8pm. Opposite *Caravan*, you'll find Ayukawa **post office**, while the **bank** on the main road in the middle of town has a foreign exchange desk.

Hiraizumi and around

For a brief period in the eleventh century the temples of **Hiraizumi**, now a quiet backwater around 120km north of Sendai, rivalled even Kyoto in their magnificence. Though the majority of monasteries and palaces have since been lost, the gloriously extravagant **Konjiki-dō**, the "Golden Hall", and the other treasures of **Chūson-ji** temple bear witness to the area's former wealth and level of artistic accomplishment. Hiraizumi's **Mōtsū-ji** also boasts one of Japan's best-preserved Heian-period gardens, while a boat ride along the nearby Satetsu-gawa, between the towering cliffs of **Geibikei gorge**, provides a scenic constrast.

Travelling north **to Hiraizumi** by train – whether on the Tōhoku Shinkansen or the Tōhoku main line – it's necessary to change at **ICHINOSEKI**, a small town 8km further south. From Ichinoseki you can either hop on the next stopping train or pick up one of the more frequent local buses, which depart from outside the station, though note that the last Hiraizumi bus leaves at around 7pm (6.30pm Sun). Ichinoseki is also the terminal for Geibikei trains, and you might find it more convenient to visit the gorge (see p.298) before travelling on to Hiraizumi. In Ichinoseki it's worth visiting the useful **information office** (daily 9am–5.00/5.30pm; ☎0191/23-2350, ✉info@i-kanko.com) right outside the gate to the platform as you exit Ichinoseki Station. There are also a couple of **car rental** outlets nearby: Eki Rent-a-Car (☎0191/21-5570), Toyota (☎0191/23-0100) and Mazda (☎0191/26-0828) – and several reasonable business **hotels**, notably the *City Hotel* (☎0191/23-7799, ⊜23-2299; ❺) and the more upmarket *Hotel Sunroute* (☎0191/26-4311, ⊜26-4317; ❺–❻).

Hiraizumi and around		
Hiraizumi	*Hiraizumi*	平泉
Chūson-ji	*Chūson-ji*	中尊寺
Geibikei Gorge	*Geibikei*	猊鼻渓
Gokusui-tei	*Gokusui-tei*	曲水亭
Izumiya	*Izumiya*	泉屋
Konjiki-dō	*Konjiki-dō*	金色堂
Mōtsū-ji	*Mōtsū-ji*	毛越寺
Mōtsū-ji Youth Hostel	*Mōtsū-ji Yūsu Hosuteru*	毛越寺ユースホステル
Sankōzō	*Sankōzō*	讃衡蔵
Seoul Shokudō	*Seoul Shokudō*	ソウル食堂
Shirayama Ryokan	*Shirayama Ryokan*	志羅山旅館
Ichinoseki	*Ichinoseki*	一関
City Hotel	*Shiti Hoteru*	シティホテル
Hotel Sunroute	*Hoteru Sanrūto*	ホテルサンルート

Hiraizumi

Nowadays it's hard to imagine **HIRAIZUMI** as the resplendent capital of the **Fujiwara** clan, who chose this spot on the banks of the Kitakami-gawa for their "paradise on earth". At first sight it's a rather dull little town on a busy main road, but the low western hills conceal one of the most important sights in northern Honshū, the gilded **Konjiki-dō**, which has somehow survived war, fire and natural decay for nearly nine hundred years. You can easily cover this and the nearby gardens of **Mōtsū-ji** in a day, with the option of staying in Hiraizumi itself or Ichinoseki.

In the early twelfth century, Fujiwara Kiyohira, the clan's first lord, began building a vast complex of Buddhist temples and palaces, lavishly decorated with gold from the local mines, in what is now Hiraizumi. Eventually, the Fujiwara's wealth and military might started to worry the southern warlord **Minamoto Yoritomo** (see p.935), who was in the throes of establishing the Kamakura shogunate. Earlier, Yoritomo's valiant brother, **Yoshitsune**, had trained with the warrior monks of Hiraizumi, so when Yoritomo turned against him (see p.244), Yoshitsune fled north. Though at first he was protected by the Fujiwara, they soon betrayed him on the promise of a sizeable reward, and in 1189 Yoshitsune committed suicide (although according to one legend he escaped to Mongolia, where he resurfaced as Genghis Khan). Meanwhile, Yoritomo attacked the Fujiwara, destroying their temples and leaving the town to crumble into ruin. Bashō, passing through Hiraizumi five hundred years after Yoshitsune's death, caught the mood in one of his famous haiku: "The summer grass, 'tis all that's left of ancient warriors' dreams."

The flight of Yoshitsune to Hiraizumi is commemorated with a costume parade during the town's main spring **festival** (May 1–5), which also features open-air Nō performances at Chūson-ji. Other important events include an ancient sacred dance, Ennen-no-Mai, held by torchlight at Mōtsū-ji on January 20, May 5 and during the autumn festival (Nov 1–3).

Chūson-ji

The Fujiwara's first building projects concentrated on **Chūson-ji** (daily: April–Oct 8am–5pm; Jan–March, Nov & Dec 8.30am–4.30pm; ¥800 including Konjiki-dō, Kyōzō and the Sankōzō), which had been founded by a Tendai priest from Kyoto in the mid-ninth century. Of the temple's original forty buildings, only two remain: Konjiki-dō (the Golden Hall) and the nearby sutra repository, Kyōzō. They sit on a forested hilltop, alongside a number of more recent structures, on the main bus route north from Ichinoseki and Hiraizumi stations (20min and 4min respectively).

From the main road, a broad avenue leads uphill past minor temples sheltering under towering cryptomeria trees, until you reach the first building of any size, the Hon-dō, at the top on the right-hand side. A few minutes further on, set back on the left, a concrete hall shelters Chūson-ji's greatest treasure. The **Konjiki-dō** is tiny – only 5.5 square metres – and protected behind plate glass, but it's still an extraordinary sight. The whole structure, bar the roof tiles, gleams with thick gold leaf, while the altar inside is smothered in mother-of-pearl inlay and delicate, gilded copper friezes set against dark, burnished lacquer. The altar's central image is of Amida Nyorai, flanked by a host of Buddhas, Bodhisattvas and guardian kings, all swathed in gold. This extravagant gesture of faith and power took fifteen years to complete and was unveiled in 1124; later, the mummified bodies of the four Fujiwara lords were buried under its altar.

Behind the Konjiki-dō, the second of Chūson-ji's original buildings, the **Kyōzō**, is not nearly so dramatic. This small, plain hall, erected in 1108, used to house more than five thousand Buddhist sutras written in gold or silver characters on rich, indigo paper. The next-door hall was built in 1288 to shelter the Konjiki-dō – you can still see the old foundation stones – while, across the way, there's a much more recent Nō stage where outdoor performances are held in summer by firelight (Aug 14), and during Hiraizumi's two major spring and autumn festivals. Finally, the road beside the entrance to the Konjiki-dō leads to the modern **Sankōzō**, a museum containing what remains of Chūson-ji's treasures. The most valuable items are a statue of the Senju Kannon (Thousand-Armed Goddess of Mercy), a number of sutra scrolls and a unique collection of lacy metalwork decorations (*kalavinkas*) that originally hung in the Konjiki-dō.

Mōtsū-ji

Hiraizumi's other main sight, the Heian-period gardens of **Mōtsū-ji** (daily 8.30am–4.30/5pm;¥500), lie eight minutes' walk west from Hiraizumi Station. In the twelfth century the Fujiwara added to this temple, originally founded in 850, until it was the largest in northern Honshū. Nothing remains now save a few foundation stones and Japan's best-preserved Heian garden, the **Jōdo-teien**. The garden's main feature is a large lake, speckled with symbolic "islands", in the midst of velvet lawns. There are a few simple buildings among the trees and ancient foundation stones, but otherwise the garden is simply a pleasant place to stroll. You'll find flowers in bloom at almost every season, including cherry, lotus, bush clover and azaleas, but the most spectacular display is in late June, when thirty thousand irises burst into colour. As you leave the temple gate, pop into the small **museum** on the left, which is most of interest for its photos of Mōtsū-ji's colourful festivals, including the sacred Ennen-no-Mai dance (see p.296) and a poetry-writing contest in Heian-period dress, which takes place on the last Sunday in May.

Practicalities

Hiraizumi has its own **information booth** (daily 8.30am–4.30/5pm; ℡0191/46-2110), to the right as you exit the station. Buses for Chūson-ji and Ichinoseki also depart from this concourse, and you can **rent bikes** (April–Nov daily 8am–5pm; ¥1000 per day) from beside the information office. Despite its size, Hiraizumi merits both a **post office** and foreign exchange **bank**, both located in the backstreets to the west of the station.

The best place to **stay** in Hiraizumi is *Mōtsū-ji Youth Hostel* (℡0191/46-2331, ⓦwww.jyh.or.jp; dorm ¥2800 per person, rooms ❹), in the grounds of Mōtsū-ji temple and run by the monks. Note that only breakfast is served here; you'll have to go into town for dinner or bring something to eat. In summer (July 20 to Sept 10) the hostel also doubles as a *shukubō* (temple lodging), with private tatami rooms overlooking the gardens, though all washing facilities are shared. You can attend prayers in the temple (daily 6.30–7am) at any time of year, and there are also free **zazen meditation sessions**. These are one of the only times you will be granted access to the gloriously gaudy inner chambers of a Japanese temple, so even if you're not particularly interested in Buddhism it's worth taking part, and the sense of calmness radiating from your instructor priest in the early-morning quiet is also impressive. Another possibility is the clean and comfortable *Shirayama Ryokan* (℡0191/46-2883, ⓕ46-3914; ❻ including meals), located in the side streets west of the station. You'll need to call ahead to let them know when you plan to arrive, as the family that runs the ryokan sometimes leave the building unattended for lengthy periods.

Hiraizumi has a couple of small **restaurants** lining the road from the station to Mōtsū-ji temple, including *Seoul Shokudō* (evenings only, closed Monday; ☎0191/46-5199) a *yakiniku* restaurant that has very cheap set meals, an English menu and the best range of vegetarian choices in town. Just before Seoul Shokudō on the same side of the road is the much more upmarket *Gokusui-tei* (noon–3pm, 5–9pm, closed Wed), which serves up traditional, rather expensive Japanese meals. On the north side of the station concourse, just before the crossroads, *Izumiya* (daily 9am–5.30pm) serves up good-value *soba teishoku*. If you fancy a picnic, there's a supermarket on the road to Mōtsū-ji.

Around Hiraizumi

The Hiraizumi area boasts two river **gorges** with confusingly similar names. **Geibikei** (as opposed to Gembikei) is the more impressive of the two, a narrow defile best viewed by boat, which lies some 20km east of Hiraizumi. Unless you've got your own transport, however, the easiest way to get there is by train from Ichinoseki Station. It's an attractive ride on the JR Ōfunato line to Geibikei Station (30min), marred at the end by a huge cement works. From the station, turn right and walk along the lane for five minutes, then follow the road under the tracks to find the boat dock.

Though not cheap, the Geibikei **boat trip** (hourly 8.30/9am–3/4.30pm; 90min; ¥1500) is a lot of fun. Despite poling fairly sizeable wooden punts upstream for 2km, the boatmen still find breath to regale their passengers with local legends, details of the passing flora and endless statistics about the gorge. It's all in Japanese, of course, but the general mirth is infectious and, on the way downstream, he'll break into song – getting a great echo off the hundred-metre-high cliffs. At the halfway point, everyone gets out on a shingle beach to throw stones into a small hollow in the opposite cliff, for luck, and to buy bags of fish food for the river's huge, brightly coloured carp.

The Tōno valley

The town of **Tōno** is set in a bowl of low mountains in the heart of one of Japan's poorest regions, surrounded by the flat **Tōno valley**. The people of Tōno and the farmers of the valley take pride in their living legacy of farming and folk traditions, embodied by the district's **magariya** – large, L-shaped farmhouses – and a number of museums devoted to the old ways. But the area is perhaps most famous for its wealth of **folk tales**, known as *Tōno Monogatari* (see box, p.301), and there are references to these legends all around the valley, alongside ancient shrines, rock carvings and traces of primitive cults, which help give Tōno its slightly mysterious undercurrent.

Today Tōno is connected to the modern world by train, an attractive journey east on the JR Kamaishi line from Hanamaki, or Shin-Hanamaki for the Shinkansen. Once in Tōno, it's best to rent a bike or taxi to explore the valley's far-flung sights, though in summer there are also tour buses (see p.300). Allow at least two days to do the area justice.

Tōno

TŌNO itself is a small town set among flat rice-lands, with orchards and pine forests clothing the surrounding hills. Although it's mainly of interest for its hotels, banks and other facilities, there are a couple of museums to see before

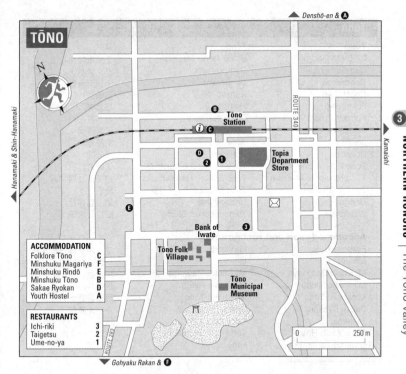

TŌNO

N

◀ Hanamaki & Shin-Hanamaki

ROUTE 340

▶ Kamaishi

Ⓑ Tōno Station

ⓘ Ⓒ

Ⓓ Ⓐ

❷ ❶

Topia Department Store

Ⓔ

✉

Bank of Iwate

❸

Tōno Folk Village

Tōno Municipal Museum

⛩

0   250 m

ROUTE 283

ACCOMMODATION
Folklore Tōno	C
Minshuku Magariya	F
Minshuku Rindō	E
Minshuku Tōno	B
Sakae Ryokan	D
Youth Hostel	A

RESTAURANTS
Ichi-riki	3
Taigetsu	2
Ume-no-ya	1

▼ Gohyaku Rakan & Ⓕ

setting off round the valley. From Tōno Station it's an eight-minute walk straight across town and over the river to the **Tōno Municipal Museum** (daily 9am–5pm; May–Oct closed last day of the month; Jan–April, Nov & Dec also closed Mon, Nov 24–30 & March 1–4; ¥310, or ¥520 combined entrance with Tōno Folk Village), at the back of a red-brick building which doubles as the library. This entertaining museum gives a good overview of life in Tōno – its festivals, crafts and agricultural traditions – and you can watch beautifully presented cartoon versions of the most famous legends which, though narrated in Japanese, are simple and easy to follow.

Walking back towards the station, turn left just across the river for **Tōno Folk Village** (daily 9am–5pm; ¥310, or ¥520 combined entrance with Tōno Municipal Museum). The "village" consists of several buildings, including the ryokan where Yanagita Kunio (see p.301) stayed while researching his legends and an old storehouse containing more dramatizations of the stories. While at the village, look out for the translations of Japanese fairy tales by Lafcadio Hearn (see p.693), compiled in the late nineteenth century; his interest in these stories helped keep them alive.

Practicalities

Tōno's **information office** (daily 8am–5.30/6pm; ☎0198/62-1333, ⓕ62-4244, ⓔtonocity@tonotv.com) is on the right as you exit the station. Though the staff don't speak English, they have English-language maps and brochures, and a larger-scale Japanese map which is useful for navigating around the valley. The attached shop stocks copies of *The Legends of Tōno* (¥2000); you might also find it at the Municipal Museum or Denshō-en (see p.303).

Tōno

Tōno	Tōno	遠野
Chiba Magariya	Chiba-ke no Magariya	千葉家の曲り屋
Dan-no-hana	Dan-no-hana	ダンノハナ
Denderano	Denderano	デンデラ野
Denshō-en	Denshō-en	伝承園
Fukusen-ji	Fukusen-ji	福泉寺
Furusato-mura	Furusato-mura	ふるさと村
Gohyaku Rakan	Gohyaku Rakan	五百羅漢
Jōken-ji	Jōken-ji	常堅寺
Sui-kōen	Sui-kōen	水公園
Tōno Folk Village	Tōno Mukashi Banashi Mura	遠野昔話村
Tōno Municipal Museum	Tōno Shiritsu Hakubutsukan	遠野市立博物館
Tsuzuki Stone	Tsuzuki-ishi	続石
Unedori-jinja	Unedori-jinja	卯子酉神社
Watermill	Yamaguchi no Suisha	山口の水車

Accommodation and restaurants

Folklore Tōno	Forukurōro Tōno	フォルクローロ遠野
Ichi-riki	Ichi-riki	一カ
Minshuku Magariya	Minshuku Magariya	民宿曲り屋
Minshuku Rindō	Minshuku Rindō	民宿りんどう
Minshuku Tōno	Minshuku Tōno	民宿遠野
Sakae Ryokan	Sakae Ryokan	さかえ旅館
Taigetsu	Taigetsu	待月
Tōno Youth Hostel	Tōno Yūsu Hosuteru	遠野ユースホステル
Ume-no-ya	Ume-no-ya	梅ノ家

Getting around

To make the most of the Tōno valley you really need your own transport.
There's a **car rental** place inside the station, Tōno Kankō Rent-a-Car
(☎0198/62-1375), and an Eki Rent-a-Car (☎0198/62-3200) nearby.
However, most people opt to cycle. You can **rent bikes** from the information
office and other outlets on the station concourse (¥1000 per day), or from *Tōno
Youth Hostel* (see opposite) for ¥800. Tōno maps show three recommended
cycling routes (also possible by car), of around four hours each, which cover
the main sights – they're reasonably well signposted, though not always in
English. You can also rent **taxis** outside Tōno Station: Tōno Kōtsū Taxi
(☎0198/62-3355), for example, offers a range of tours from ¥5350 for an hour.

In addition there are **organized tours**, the most comprehensive of which are
run by JR Bus (☎0198/62-2829), who operate two tours daily on weekends
from late April to late October, and daily throughout August; unfortunately, rail
passes aren't valid on these. The longer "A-course" tour (¥5000; departs Tōno
station at 10.30am, returns at 2.50pm) includes Tōno's two museums, Fukusen-
ji, Denshō-en, the Chiba Magariya and Gohyaku Rakan, while the "B-course"
(¥4400; departs Tōno station at 12.01pm, returns at 2.50pm) omits the two
museums. Both tours depart from outside the station and include lunch.
Alternatively, both Tōno Kōtsū Taxi (☎0198/62-3355) and Maruki Taxi
(☎0198/62-0123) offer tourist "courses": two-hour jaunts around Tōno start
from ¥10,730, while four-hour trips start from ¥20,590.

Local buses also stop outside the station, but the only really useful routes are
those heading northeast to Denshō-en and Furusato-mura (see p.303 for
details). These buses also stop near *Tōno Youth Hostel* (see opposite).

Accommodation

Tōno has a reasonable selection of **accommodation** within walking distance of the station. If you want more atmosphere, however, you can stay in a real *magariya* farmhouse on the west side of town, while Tōno's excellent youth hostel is located about 4km northeast.

Folklore Tōno 5-7 Shinkoku-chō ℡0198/62-0700, ℻62-0800. A JR-owned hotel inside the station building. Its rooms are Western-style, with TV, phone and bathroom, and the price includes a simple breakfast. ❺

Minshuku Magariya 30-58-3 Niisato, Ayaori-chō ℡0198/62-4564. This traditional farmhouse is located 3km southwest of the station (around ¥1000 by taxi). The rooms are all Japanese-style, with shared facilities, and excellent meals are served round a big open hearth. On the downside, it's a little inconvenient to get to, no one speaks English and they don't accept children. ❼

Minshuku Rindō 2-34 Daiku-chō ℡0198/62-5726, ℮rindou@crocus.ocn.ne.jp. Simple, homely minshuku on an attractive street, roughly five minutes' walk west from the station. The owner speaks a little English, and offers rooms with or without meals. ❺

Minshuku Tōno 2-17 Zaimoku-chō ℡ & ℻0198/62-4395. Small, friendly minshuku with an English-speaking owner, on the north side of the tracks. Rates with or without meals. ❺

Sakae Ryokan 3-14 Shinkoku-chō ℡0198/62-2407, ℻62-0483. More refined ryokan opposite the station, with nine well-kept tatami rooms, though none with en-suite facilities. Rooms available with or without meals. ❺

Tōno Youth Hostel 13-39-5 Tsuchibuchi-chō ℡0198/62-8736, ⓦwww.jyh.or.jp. Delightful modern hostel with dorms and family rooms, laundry facilities and excellent-value meals. It's set among rice fields about fifteen minutes' walk from the Denshō-en or Ashiarai-gawa bus stops (see p.303). The genial manager speaks a little English and can advise on local cycling routes. Bike rental available. ❸

The legends of Tōno

When the far-sighted folklorist **Yanagita Kunio** visited Tōno in 1909, he found a world still populated with the shadowy figures of demons and other usually malevolent spirits which the farmers strove to placate using ancient rituals. The following year he published **Tōno Monogatari** (published in English as *The Legends of Tōno*), the first book to tap the rich oral traditions of rural Japan. The 118 tales were told to him by Kyōseki Sasaki (or Kizen), the educated son of a Tōno peasant, to whom goblins, ghosts and gods were part of everyday life.

People in Tōno still talk about **Zashiki Warashi**, a mischievous child spirit (either male or female) who can be heard running at night, or who might put your pillow under your feet while you sleep, but also brings prosperity to the household. Another popular tale tells of a farmer's beautiful daughter who fell in love with their horse. When the farmer heard that his child had married the horse, he hung it from a mulberry tree, but his grieving daughter was whisked off to heaven clinging to her lover.

Probably the most popular character from the legends, however, is the **kappa**, an ugly water creature that isn't unique to Tōno but seems to exist here in large numbers. You'll find *kappa* images everywhere in town – on postboxes, outside the station, and even the police box is *kappa*-esque. The "real" *kappa* has long skinny limbs, webbed hands and feet, a sharp beak, and a hollow on the top of his head which must be kept full of water. He's usually green, sometimes with a red face, and his main pastime seems to be pulling young children into ponds and rivers – though many malformed babies were attributed to being fathered by a *kappa*. In the legends, one local *kappa* got a fright when he grabbed a horse's tail, hoping to drag it into the river, but was carried back to the stable instead. He hid under a bucket until he was discovered, and was then sent packing after promising never to cause trouble again. If you do meet a *kappa*, remember to bow – on returning your bow, the water will run out of the hollow on his head and he'll have to hurry off to replenish it.

Eating

Local **speciality foods** include *hitsuko soba*, small bowls of rough, handmade noodles eaten with a mix of chicken, raw egg, onion and mushrooms, and the regional dish, *nambu hitssumi* (or *suiton*), a soup laced with seasonal vegetables and dumplings. You can sample these and other local delicacies, such as *ayu* (river fish) and *jingisukan* (barbecued lamb), at the folk-village **restaurants**, or try one of the following places in central Tōno.

For a coffee or quick **snack**, walk down the main road from the station to where *Taigetsu* (daily 10am–11pm) serves good cake and coffee along with staples such as cheese toast, curry-rice and ramen dishes till relatively late. On the opposite side of the road, *Ume-no-ya* (daily except Tues 11.30am–8pm) is another simple place, offering good portions of curry-rice, *ebi*-fry, omelettes from ¥500 and set meals from ¥950. *Ichi-riki* (daily 11am–8pm), down towards the river on the last side street off the main road, is an attractive place with good fresh fish, tempura, warming winter stews and an excellent *tonkatsu* set dinner – great value at ¥1000.

If you plan to spend the day cycling around the valley, you can stock up on **picnic** supplies at the Topia shopping mall a block from the station. The ground floor of the mall has a well-stocked supermarket as well as a farmer's market selling very fresh and very cheap fruit and vegetables, complete with biographical notes and photographs of the farmers (and their families) who brought the produce to market.

West of Tōno

West of Tōno the main valley narrows, funnelling the road and railway along beside the Sarugaishi-gawa. The wooded southern hillside hides some unusual shrines and an appealing group of Buddha images, which make one of the best short trips out of Tōno. Further up the valley, an imposing *magariya* farmhouse attracts a lot of attention, but it's better to save your energy for more accessible examples on the east side of town.

Heading out of Tōno on the south side of the river (on the old Route 283), look out after 2.5km for a stone staircase on the left. At the bottom of the steps, past the house, you'll find a tree festooned with red and white ribbons and, behind it, **Unedori-jinja**. This little shrine is dedicated to the god in charge of matrimonial affairs; if you want to get married, tie a red ribbon onto the tree with your left hand. Having wowed the god with your skill, go back and climb the stone steps, cross a lane and follow the path into a narrow, wooded valley filled with mossy stones. Keep looking closely at these stones: at first you won't see anything, but gradually faint outlines appear, then full faces and rounded bodies, until you're seeing little figures everywhere. Known as the **Gohyaku Rakan**, there are supposed to be five hundred of these Buddhist "disciples", which were carved by a local monk in the late eighteenth century to commemorate victims of a terrible famine in 1754.

Before heading back down to the main road, turn right (east) along the lane and continue for 700m until you come to a *torii* on the right and a steep path leading up through the pine woods. At the top of a short, stiff climb there's a larger shrine building (usually locked) and two small shrines with a collection of phallic and female symbols made of stone or wood. Though rather dilapidated nowadays, this is one of the few remaining shrines dedicated to **Konsei-sama**, the local God of Fertility, and an interesting vestige of an ancient cult.

The thatch-roofed **Chiba Magariya** (daily: April–Oct 8.30am–5pm; Jan–March, Nov & Dec 9am–4pm; ¥350) stands high above the valley some

11km west of Tōno, north of the main valley up a steep sideroad. This two-hundred-year-old farmhouse was selected for restoration as an important example of a *magariya*, an L-shaped building with the stables in the shorter wing. It once housed the Chiba family plus fifteen labourers and twenty horses, but today it's rather empty and neglected. If you do venture out this way, take a look at the **Tsuzuki Stone**, 500m before the farmhouse and set back in the woods. Though it's said to be natural, the enormous, rounded boulder balanced on a smaller stone looks like a dolmen.

Northeast of Tōno

The broad valley northeast of Tōno is home to a number of somewhat touristy "folk villages" aimed at preserving the old crafts. It's worth visiting one of these, of which the new **Furusato-mura** is probably the best, though the smaller **Denshō-en** and **Sui-kōen** are slightly more accessible. Other sights to aim for include a *kappa* pool, an old watermill and a temple housing Japan's tallest Kannon statue. However, the area's chief highlight is its scenery, dotted with the occasional thatched farmhouse – it's best to get a bike and just follow the country lanes.

Denshō-en and Jōken-ji

The main road northeast of Tōno (Route 340) leads past **Denshō-en** (daily 9am–5pm;¥300), about 4km out of town. This village museum contains various buildings relocated from around Tōno, including a waterwheel, storehouses and a *magariya*, where local folk demonstrate weaving, rope-making and other crafts. Inside the *magariya*, follow the narrow corridor at the back to reach a small shrine room filled with brightly dressed dolls. These are images of **Oshira-sama**, an agricultural deity worshipped throughout northern Honshū. They're stick-like figures, their faces either drawn on or simply carved, and are made from mulberry – according to the legends, Tōno's original Oshira-sama came from the same tree on which the horse-husband died (see box, p.301). The deities, often used by blind mediums, are also supposed to predict the future – hence all the prayer papers tied around the shrine. Denshō-en is one of the few places which it's feasible to reach by local bus. Services depart every hour or so from Tōno Station and drop you either at the village or 100m further back at the Ashiarai-gawa stop (15–20min;¥290).

A short distance east along the main road from Denshō-en, a signposted right turn leads to **Jōken-ji**. Founded in 1490, the temple is mainly of interest for its statue of **Obinzuru-sama**, a little figure in a cloak and hat with a very shiny anatomy – the deity is supposed to cure illnesses if rubbed in the appropriate place. Behind the temple there's a **kappa pool**, with a particularly helpful *kappa* who is credited with dousing a fire in Jōken-ji. An eccentric local has built a small shrine to himself beside the pool and may well regale you with incomprehensible but good-natured stories.

Fukusen-ji and Furusato-mura

Just before Denshō-en, a road branches north, following the main valley for another 2km to **Fukusen-ji** (April–Nov daily 8am–5pm; closed Jan–March & Dec;¥300). This fairly modern temple, founded in 1912, is famous for its seventeen-metre-tall image of **Kannon**, the Goddess of Mercy. The slender, gilded statue with a blue hairdo is carved from a single tree trunk and took the craftsman twelve years before it was finally unveiled in 1963. It stands in an attractive temple at the top of the hill, where the artist's tools and photos of the huge tree being brought to Tōno by train are also on display. Get to the temple early in the day if you can, before the tour buses start rolling in.

Continue on this road another 3km and you'll reach **Furusato-mura** (daily 9am–5pm, last entry 4pm; ¥520). The biggest and most attractive of Tōno's folk museums, Furusato-mura resembles a working village, with its own rice fields, vegetable plots and duck ponds. There are five refurbished *magariya* on the hillside, where pensioners sit beside smoking hearths, busily making souvenirs such as straw slippers, wooden *kappa* and bamboo baskets – if you want to have a go, they'll be only too pleased to show you. You can buy their handiwork in the museum shop, where there's also a small **restaurant** with some good-value lunch sets. Some Denshō-en buses continue up the valley to Furusato-mura, though they're fairly sporadic (every 1–2hr; 25min; ¥500).

East of Denshō-en: Sui-kōen

The most beautiful part of the Tōno valley lies **east of Denshō-en**, though to appreciate it you'll have to get off onto the sideroads. One attractive ride takes you out to an old watermill and then loops back past the third folk-village. To find the turning, follow Route 340 for 3km east from Denshō-en and then fork right immediately after crossing a red-lacquered bridge. The lane climbs gently uphill, past a number of old farms to a small, thatched **watermill**. On the way you pass the **house of Kyōseki Sasaki** (of Tōno Legends fame; see p.301), opposite which there's a path signed to "**Dan-no-hana**". Again, there's not a great deal to see, but the small hill of Dan-no-hana is another of Tōno's slightly eerie places. In the not-so-distant past, old people were sent to places called Dan-no-hana to die; however, in this case the old folk got bored waiting, so they came down to work the fields during the day and returned to their hill at night.

Heading back down to the main road, look out on the left for a turning signed to "Denderano". Follow this lane west for nearly 2km and you'll come to the last of the folk-villages, **Sui-kōen** (daily 10am–5pm; ¥200), with a *magariya*, a *kappa* pool and displays of antique farm implements. From here you can drop down to the main road, or continue west along country lanes.

Morioka and around

A former castle town on the confluence of three rivers, the small, congenial city of **MORIOKA** has no outstanding sights, but the attractive setting, range of accommodation and interesting local cuisine make it a good overnight stop on the journey through northern Honshū, and, with a couple of hours to spare, you could stretch your legs around the castle ruins and some of the older neighbourhoods, or take a bus out to a rather bizarre art museum. Additionally, Morioka is one of the main access points for hikes around the nearby **Hachimantai plateau**.

The city has two major summer festivals. At the end of the rice-planting season the **Chagu–Chagu Umakko** (second Saturday in June) features a fifteen-kilometre procession of richly caparisoned horses, ending at the city's Hachiman-gū shrine. Then, in early August (1–3), thousands of dancers parade through town during the **Sansa Odori**, accompanied by flutes and drums and followed by a general knees-up.

Morioka and around

Morioka	Morioka	盛岡
Gozaku	Gozaku	ござ九
Hashimoto Art Museum	Hashimoto Bijutsukan	橋本美術館
Ishiwari-sakura	Ishiwari-sakura	石割桜
Iwate-kōen	Iwate-kōen	岩手公園
Kami-no-hashi	Kami-no-hashi	上ノ橋
Kōgensha	Kōgensha	高原社
Naka-no-hashi	Naka-no-hashi	中ノ橋

Accommodation and restaurants

Hotel Ace	Hoteru Ēsu	ホテルエース
Azuma-ya	Azuma-ya	東家
Chokurian	Chokurian	直利庵
Issaryō	Issaryō	一茶寮
Kumagai Ryokan	Kumagai Ryokan	熊ヶ井旅館
Morioka Youth Hostel	Morioka Yūsu Hosuteru	盛岡ユースホステル
Nanbu Doburokuya	Nanbu Doburokuya	南部どぶろく家
Pairong	Pairon	白龍
Hotel Ruiz	Hoteru Ruizu	ホテルルイズ
Seirōkaku	Seirōkaku	盛楼閣
Shokudōkan	Shokudōkan	食道館

Hachimantai	Hachimantai	八幡平
Iwate-san	Iwate-san	岩手山

Information and tours

Morioka's excellent **"i" information centre** (daily 9am–5.30pm; ☎019/625-2090, ✉kankou@city.morioka.iwate.jp) is located on the train station's second floor, near the southern entrance to the Shinkansen tracks. The English-speaking staff can provide maps and information about the region, and there's also a JR information desk next door. For news of local **events**, look out for *Hakuchō*, the International Association's newsletter (see "Listings", p.309).

Local and long-distance **buses** depart from the east side of Morioka Station (note that many bus services only operate from late April to late November), with services running to Tokyo, the Hachimantai plateau and Towada-ko. Apart from the Hashimoto Art Museum, central Morioka can easily be covered on foot, but from May to late November there's also the option of city **bus tours**, with a half-day tour starting at ¥4500, including lunch (or ¥2300 without lunch); ask at the information centre for details.

Accommodation

The cheapest **accommodation** in town is the friendly *Morioka Youth Hostel* (☎019/662-2220, ⓦwww.jyh.or.jp; ¥2900 per person), though it's rather inconveniently located in the northwestern suburbs. To get there, take a bus from Morioka Station to Takamatsu-no-ikeguchi (20min; ¥210) then walk a few metres back the way you came to reach a T-junction and the post office. Turn left at this intersection and take the side road 50m to the lake – the hostel is on the lower road to the right – the final sign to the hostel, at the stairs

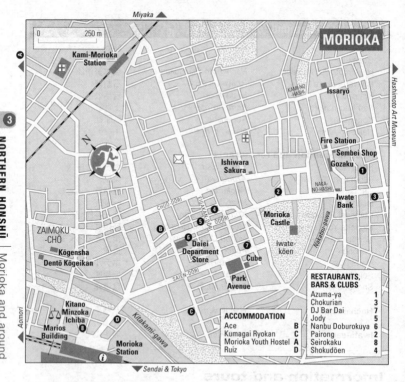

Map labels:

Miyaka ▲

MORIOKA

0   250 m

Kami-Morioka Station

KAMI-NO-HASHI

Issaryō

Hashimoto Art Museum

N

Fire Station
Sembei Shop
Gozaku ❶

Ishiwara Sakura

NAKA-NO-HASHI

Iwate Bank ❸

CHŪŌ-DŌRI

❷

EIKAN-DŌRI

ŌDŌRI

❹

❺

Morioka Castle

Nakatsu-gawa

ZAIMOKU-CHŌ

❽

Daiei Department Store

❻

Iwate-kōen

Kōgensha
Dentō Kōgeikan

❼

Cube

SAIEN-DŌRI

Park Avenue

RESTAURANTS, BARS & CLUBS
Azuma-ya 1
Chokurian 3
DJ Bar Dai 7
Jody 5
Nanbu Doborokuya 6
Pairong 2
Seirokaku 8
Shokudōen 4

Kitano Minzoka Ichiba

Marios Building ❽

Kitakami-gawa

ACCOMMODATION
Ace .... B
Kumagai Ryokan C
Morioka Youth Hostel .... A
Ruiz .... D

❶

Morioka Station

ⓘ

Aomori

▼ Sendai & Tokyo

NORTHERN HONSHŪ | Morioka and around

---

leading to the entrance, is difficult to spot at night because of the glare of two vending machines. Closer to the centre, the best option is the welcoming *Kumagai Ryokan* (☎019/651-3020, ☏626-0096, ⊛www.jpinn.com; ❹), south of Saien-dōri and about eight minutes' walk from the station in a lane leading off the side street right after the Christian centre; the owners speak a little English. In front of the station, *Hotel Ruiz* (☎019/625-2611, ✉info@hotel-ruiz.co.jp; ❺) is a standard, mid-range business hotel with a choice of Western-or Japanese-style rooms and in-house restaurants. If you'd rather be in the downtown area, *Hotel Ace* (☎019/654-3811, ☏654-3815; ❺), just north of Ōdōri, also has English-speaking staff and comfortable rooms, though it's worth paying a little extra to stay in the new wing.

The City

From the station, located on the far west side of town, it takes about twenty minutes to walk along Saien-dōri, one of Morioka's two major shopping streets, straight to **Morioka castle**. Once the seat of the Nambu lords, it took 36 years to complete (1597–1633), only to be destroyed in the battles of the Meiji Restoration. If you turn right in front of the castle park, **Iwate-kōen**, and walk down to the Nakatsu-gawa, you can pick up a pleasant riverside path to the east of the old walls. Alternatively, head east along **Ōdōri**, the city's fore-most shopping street, and across the river via the **Naka-no-hashi** bridge, to reach a remnant of the older city.

Immediately over the river, you can't miss the ornate red-brick and grey-slate facade of **Iwate Bank**, which dates from 1911. Inside, clerks still bustle around the original banking hall with its high plastered ceiling, elaborate woodwork and stone-flagged floor. Turn left beside the bank and you'll come to a row of traditional Meiji-era buildings known as **Gozaku**, whose centrepiece is a shop selling brushes, straw and wicker goods. Stores opposite specialize in the region's most famous **crafts** – heavy iron kettles and eye-catching cotton textiles dyed with intricate patterns – while appetizing odours greet you at the top of the street where a *sembei* shop turns out local-style rice crackers sprinkled with sesame seeds or nuts; walk round the side and you can see the bakers hard at work. The pale-blue clapboard building with a slender watch tower across the road from the bakery was built at the beginning of the nineteenth century and still functions as a **fire station**.

Continue north to the next T-junction where you'll find an old blackened **kura** (traditional storehouse) on your right. Turn left to reach the renowned seventeenth-century bridge, **Kami-no-hashi**, although you'd be forgiven for missing the bridge's most important feature: eighteen bronze, bulb-shaped topknots forged in the early 1600s which ornament the railings.

Heading south along the river from Kami-no-hashi, the next major avenue is Chūō-dōri, lined with civic offices. About 400m west of the river, a 300-year-old cherry tree bulges out of a fifteen-centimetre-wide fissure in a rounded granite boulder. Known as the **ishiwari-sakura**, or "rock-splitting cherry", no one knows whether the tree really split the rock, but it's a startling sight. If you follow Chūō-dōri west to the Kitakami-gawa, you'll reach a small neighbourhood known as **Zaimoku-chō**, whose main feature is a traditional shopping street running parallel to the river. Among smart modern boutiques there are a number of craftshops, notably **Kōgensha** (daily 10am–6pm), with two outlets on opposite sides of the street; they sell a good range of modern and more traditional ironware, paper and bamboo designs. Besides Kōgensha, the best selection and prices are found at **Dentō Kōgeikan** (daily 10am–6.30pm), a few minutes' walk to the west of Kōgensha.

Between Zaimoku-chō and the station, check out the **Kitano Minzoku Ichiba** (Wed & Fri 2–6.30pm), a vegetable and fish market. Take a left from the JR station, walk underneath the overpass and turn right on the main road. After about a minute, you'll see stairs leading down to what looks like a subway station but is in fact a basement walk-through to the other side of the main road. The farmers are stationed under the street selling cheap fresh fruit.

The last of Morioka's sights is the rather eccentric **Hashimoto Art Museum** (daily 10am–5pm; ¥700) on the town's eastern outskirts. Hashimoto Yaoji (1903–79), who designed the museum, was a man of eclectic tastes: works by Courbet and Daubigny are followed by local artists and Hashimoto's own bold, dark canvases. Other nooks and crannies are stuffed with priceless ceramics, folk art, antique Western furniture, festival gear and a wonderful collection of Nambu ironware kettles. And, to cap it all, there's a complete traditional *magariya* farmhouse perched on the roof. You'll need to catch a bus (4–7 daily; 22min; ¥270; mid-March to Nov only) to reach the museum; these depart from Morioka Station but don't run in winter and are infrequent at the best of times, though they are at least timed to give you about an hour in the museum.

Eating, drinking and entertainment

Morioka's famous speciality food is named **wanko-soba**, after the small bowls that these thin, flat buckwheat noodles are served in. They're now usually eaten as a contest, during which diners don an apron and shovel down as many bowls as possible while a waitress relentlessly dishes up more; to stop, you have to get the top on to your emptied bowl – easier said than done. It's not the most relaxed dining experience, but lots of fun with a large enough group. The meal includes side dishes, such as sashimi, chicken or mushrooms, but true *wanko-soba* eaters stick to the noodles; the record is a staggering 350 bowls or so. If you fancy having a go, the best-known **restaurant** is *Chokurian* (daily except Wed 11am–8pm), which has been open since 1884. Expect to pay ¥2500–¥3500 for *wanko-soba*, although they also serve standard noodle dishes in an adjoining room at reasonable prices. If that's full, try popping into *Azuma-ya* (daily 11am–8pm), across the street from the Daiei department store; *wanko* course menus start at ¥2500.

Another rather odd Morioka concoction, **reimen**, consists of a large bowl of cold, semi-transparent, slightly chewy egg noodles eaten with spicy Korean *kimchi*, and a variety of garnishes which might include boiled egg, sesame seeds and slices of apple or cold meat. This delight is only consumed in summer (May–Oct) and can be sampled at *Seirōkaku* (daily 11am–2am), opposite the station on the second floor above a *pachinko* parlour; they also serve more conventional *yakiniku* and other meat dishes (¥800–2500). Alternatively, try *Shokudōen* (11.30am–1am, closed first and third Tues of month), nestled in the backstreets of Morioka's drinking district, for *reimen* served to your required level of spiciness, plus *yakiniku* dishes that come with a bowl of raw egg and a single slice of *piman* (Japanese capsicum) for as little as ¥1050.

Locals also devour another unusual noodle dish, **ja-ja men**, a bowl of thick, white noodles (looking like udon) that comes with a few slices of cucumber, red pickles and a slab of brown miso paste. Many noodle shops serve *ja-ja men*, but the most popular – which means queues out front, especially during peak lunch and dinner hours – is *Pairong* (9am–8pm), which has two restaurants down an alley across Ōdōri from Iwate-kōen; walk under the big *torii* and turn right. Make sure you mix up the miso paste and noodles once you are served and, if you're still hungry, crack open and beat up one of the raw eggs on the table and hand it to your server, who will pour broth over it: the result is a bowl of rather bland soup, called *chii tantan*, designed to cleanse the palate. Portions are huge by Japanese standards, but cheap. There's no menu, and the large portions are so filling that the staff counsel new customers to try the regular (*futsū*) size (¥450) first. Taking up the egg soup option will set you back another ¥50.

In the town centre, **Ōdōri** and the **entertainment district** immediately to its north have a broad selection of more traditional eating and drinking places, from hamburger joints to top-class establishments. Folkish *Nanbu Doburokuya* (daily 5pm–2am) is a local favourite and serves up fish, meat, vegetables and horse sashimi for those who dare (¥800–2500). *Issaryō* is a relaxed and comfortable coffee shop in the old part of town. It's on the second floor of the building on the laneway behind the *kura* past the Meiji-era Gozaku buildings (see p.307).

Drinking and entertainment

Morioka has a surprisingly bustling **club scene**: *DJ Bar Dai* (Tues–Sun, 10pm until late) in the basement of the Toishita Building on Saien-dōri is the place to go for deep funk and hip-hop, with the cream of the region's DJs taking turns on the decks. Check ⓦwww.djbardai.com for a current schedule of events. For more traditional funk, R&B and soul, head over to *Jody* **bar** (daily 7.30pm–3am). This intimate bar is located in the basement of the Vent Vert Building on Eigakan-dōri, which runs north to Ōdōri. *Jody* owner and soul brother Sawada Akinobu will spin requests from the hundreds of records he has amassed over the past twenty years. Drinks start from ¥700, but the dance floor is free. Eigakan-dōri is home to a huge number of **cinemas**, which host various movie festivals throughout the year.

Listings

Banks Iwate Bank, Tōhoku Bank, Michinoku Bank and 77 Bank all have branches with foreign-exchange desks on Ōdōri. Iwate Bank also has a branch outside the train station.

Car rental Nippon Rent-a-Car (☏019/635-6605), Nissan (☏019/654-5825), Toyota (☏019/622-0100) and Eki Rent-a-Car (☏019/624-5212) all have offices in or near the station.

Hospitals The two main central hospitals are Iwate Medical University Hospital, 19-1 Uchi-maru (☏019/651-5111), and the Prefectural Hospital, 1-4-1 Ueda (☏019/653-1151).

Internet access The Iwate Multimedia Centre, 7F Marios (☏019/621-5150; Tues–Sun 10am–9am), offers one hour's free Internet access. The Marios tower building is directly outside the East-West Passage on the west exit of Morioka Station. The Internet and Comic Café, on the second floor of the building before the *Hotel Ruiz* as you come from the station, has plenty of terminals with a minimum charge of ¥400 for one hour, including all the soft drinks you can consume.

Iwate International Association 2-4-20 Ōsakawara ☏019/654-8900, ℱ654-8922. The local forum for international exchange; they can offer help and advice to any foreigner in difficulties.

Post office The Central Post Office, Morioka Chūō Yūbin-kyoku, Morioka-shi, just north of Chūō-dōri, has a poste restante service. There's also a more convenient sub-post office in the blocks in front of the station, as well as post kiosks in the station building, including one outside the tourist information office.

Shopping Nambu ironware, dyed cotton textiles and plain wooden *kokeshi* dolls are the representative crafts of this region. The best crafts shops are Kōgensha and Dentō Kōgeikan (see p.307), but you'll also find local souvenirs in the station's basement and in Park Avenue, Morioka's main department store on Saien-dōri. Or try the more modern Cube II, next door.

Taxi For a taxi, call the station's central booking office on ☏019/622-5240 (daily 9am–5am).

Around Morioka

Tōhoku's highest peak, **Iwate-san** (2041m), dominates Morioka's northern horizon and marks the eastern edge of the **Hachimantai plateau**, a beautiful area for hiking among marshes and pine forests. At present the volcanic peak is off limits, but you can spend a day walking around the plateau to the north of Iwate-san, from where it's an easy stroll to the less daunting summit of **Hachimantai** (1613m). From the Hachimantai Chōjō bus stop, a well-marked path leads to the summit (around forty minutes' walk), across Hachiman-numa marshes. Afterwards you can follow a variety of tracks wandering across the plateau with views south to the barren slopes of Iwate-san.

Buses from Morioka, or the slightly closer Ōbuke Station, run up to the plateau on the **Aspite line** toll road from late May to late October (5 daily; 1hr 25min–1hr 50min; ¥1320), after which these roads are closed by snow. Alternatively, you can combine this with a bus along the new **Jyukai line** road, which loops south through Matsukawa-onsen before joining the Aspite line at Hachimantai Chōjō bus stop. Since there are only three buses a day on this route (July & Aug only; 8.02am & 11.52am going up, 2.10pm on the return journey; 2hr 20min; ¥1350), it's best to travel up on the early-morning Jyukai line bus and return to Morioka on the Aspite line. There are also three buses daily from Hachimantai Chōjō for Towada-ko (see p.323), again in summer only.

Aomori and around

Honshū's most northerly city, **AOMORI**, sits at the bottom of Mutsu Bay, sheltered by the two claws of the Tsugaru and Shimokita peninsulas. It's a spacious but rather characterless city which has lost a good deal of its Hokkaidō-bound visitors now that trains run straight through to Hakodate via the Seikan

△Rowing boats, Tōhoku

Aomori

Aomori	Aomori	青森
Auga Building	Auga	アウガ
Keikokan	Keikokan	稽古館
Kyōdokan Museum	Kyōdokan	郷土館
Munakata Shikō Memorial Museum	Munakata Shiko Kinenkan	棟方志功記念館
Nebuta-no-sato	Nebuta-no-sato	ねぶたの里

Accommodation and restaurants

Aomori Moya Kōgen Youth Hostel	Aomori Moya Kōgen Yūsu Hosuteru	青森雲谷高原ユースホステル
Dai-ni Ryokan	Dai-ni Ryokan	大二旅館
Grand Hotel	Gurando Hoteru	グランドホテル
Hotel JAL City	Hoteru JAL Shitii	ホテルJALシティー
Jintako	Jintako	甚太古
Kakigen	Kakigen	柿源
Michinoku	Michinoku	みちのく
Nandaimon	Nandaimon	南大門
Nishi-mura	Nishi-mura	西村
Sakatsubo	Sakatsubo	酒壺
Hotel Sunroute	Hoteru Sanrūto	ホテルサンルート
Supage-tei Aomori	Supage-tei Aomori	すぱげ亭青森
Washington Hotel	Washinton Hoteru	ワシントンホテル

Tunnel (see box, p.376). However, the crowds still turn up for Aomori's **Nebuta Matsuri** (Aug 2–7), one of Japan's biggest and rowdiest festivals, featuring giant illuminated floats and energetic dancing. It takes less than a day to cover Aomori's main sights, of which the most appealing is a park displaying *nebuta* floats, followed by a couple of decent museums of history and folkcraft.

Southwest of Aomori, the small town of **Hirosaki** has a number of interesting historical sights around its once magnificent castle, which can be covered on a day-trip. Allow at least two days, however, to explore the **Shimokita Hantō**, the axe-head peninsula lowering over Aomori from the east. Shimokita is dominated by the sacred **Osore-zan**, an eerie wasteland where souls hover between life and death, but the region also has some excellent coastal scenery and a hardy wildlife population, including the world's most northerly population of wild monkeys.

Arrival, information and city transport

Aomori Station lies on the west side of the city centre, just inland from the Bay Bridge and **Aomori passenger terminal**, where **ferries** from Wakinosawa (on the Shimokita Hantō) dock. Arriving by boat from Hokkaidō's Hakodate or Muroran ports, you'll pull up at a wharf further west, from where it's a ten-minute taxi ride into the centre (around ¥1300). **Long-distance buses** terminate at Aomori Station, while limousine buses from the **airport** (40min; ¥560) drop you outside either the station or ASPAM.

The most useful **information centre** is the City Tourism Office (daily 8.30am–5.30pm; ☎0177/23-4670), located inside the JR Bus terminal on the left-hand side of the station concourse, which has English-speaking staff. Alternatively, there are information desks in the first-floor lobby of ASPAM (daily 9am–6pm; ☎0177/34-2500, ℻34-2501) and in Aomori Airport (daily 9am–6pm; ☎0177/39-4561).

Most of central Aomori is manageable on foot, but you'll need **local buses** to reach the southern sights. Both the green Shiei buses and the less frequent blue-and-white JR buses run out to Nebuta-no-sato from Aomori Station; rail passes are valid on these JR services.

Accommodation

It's a good idea to book **accommodation** in advance in Aomori at any time of year, but essential during the Nebuta Matsuri (Aug 2–7). Though there's a decent range of business hotels in the city centre, it's short on budget places – at this level you might consider staying in Hirosaki instead (see p.318).

Aomori Moya Kōgen Youth Hostel 9-5 Aza Yamabuki ōaza Moya ☎017/764-2888, ⓦwww.jyh.or.jp. Recently built youth hostel, nestled right at the foot of the Moya plateau a forty-minute bus ride from Aomori train station. You can't beat the clean shared tatami rooms, herbal tea and Guinness, although it gets a little cramped when busy. There's an onsen next door. Take the bus outside the JR Aomori Station going towards Moya Hills or the *Hotel Villa City Moya* (last bus 7.10pm) and get off at the Moya Kōgen stop; the hostel is one minute's walk down to the right. ¥3200 per person.

Dai-ni Ryokan 1-7-8 Furukawa ☎ & ⓕ0177/22-3037. Basic but well-kept tatami rooms (shared bathroom only) a couple of minutes' walk southeast of the station, behind the Sunfriend Building. No meals. ❸

Grand Hotel 1-1-23 Shin-machi ☎0120-23-1011, ⓕ34-0505. This smart, old-fashioned hotel on the main street offers a range of comfortable, well-furnished rooms, some with sea views. ❺

Hotel JAL City 2-4-12 Yasukata ☎0177/32-2580, ⓕ0177/35-2584. Popular new hotel with an upmarket feel. Rooms are nicely decorated and well priced, and there's an in-house restaurant. It's about six minutes' walk east from the station. ❻

Michinoku 1-2-15 Yasukata ☎0177/23-5173, ⓕ0177/23-1735. Slightly aged, bottom-end business hotel in a good location just northeast of the station. Western- and Japanese-style rooms available, some en suite. ❹

Hotel Sunroute 1-9-8 Shin-machi ☎0177/75-2321, ⓔinfo@sunroute-aomori.com. Good-value business hotel with largish, en-suite Western-style rooms with TV and minibar, and a choice of restaurants. ❺

Washington Hotel 2-1-26 Honchō ☎0177/75-7111, ⓦwww.wh-rsv.com/english/aomori/index.html. A member of the *Washington* chain, on the eastern edge of town. It's a fifteen-minute walk from the station but close to the airport limousine bus route (get off at Shin-machi 2-chōme). ❺

The City

The harbour-front **ASPAM** (Aomori Prefectural Centre for Tourism and Industry; daily 9am–6pm) building – a sleek glass pyramid about ten minutes' walk northeast of the station – is a good place to start exploring the city. There's usually a video of the Aomori Nebuta Matsuri playing in the entrance hall, but the highlight is a twenty-minute panoramic slide show of the region including its festivals and scenery (hourly 9.30/10am–5pm; ¥600). It's not really worth forking out for the top-floor observation lounge (daily 9am–10pm; ¥400, or

AOMORI

ACCOMMODATION
Aomori Moya	G
Youth Hostel	F
Dai-ni Ryokan	B
Grand	D
JAL City	A
Michinoku	C
Sunroute	C
Washington	E

RESTAURANTS
Jintako	1
Kakigen	6
Nandaimon	4
Nishi-mura	2
Sakatsubo	3
Supage-tei Aomori	5

▲ *Shimokita Hantō*

◀ *Wakinosawa*

Aomori Passenger Terminal

Pedestrian Bridge

Bay Bridge

ASPAM

Aomori Station

Bus Depot

Murata Kōgei

Auga

Kyōdōkan Museum

N

ROUTE 4

YANAGIMACHI-DŌRI

SHINMACHI-DŌRI

HAKKO-DŌRI

ASPAM-DŌRI

HEIWA-KŌEN-DŌRI

ROUTE 103

Tsutsumi-gawa

Munakata Shikō Memorial Museum

Aomori City

▼ *Hirosaki*

▼ *Sapporo*

▼ *Noheji & Morioka*

▼ *Nebuta-no-sato & Keikokan*

▼ *Moya Kōgen & G*

0   250 m

¥800 with the Panorama Theatre), but take a look at the fourth floor, where they occasionally have demonstrations of local crafts. The two streets right in front and parallel to the ASPAM have several kitsch antique shops.

Roughly fifteen minutes' walk southeast of ASPAM, the **Kyōdokan** Museum (Tues–Sun 9.30am–6pm; ¥250) takes a look at the region's history, culture and natural environment. Recent archeological digs have revealed evidence of human occupation since at least 3000 BC, and the museum kicks off with Jōmon-period earthenware pots, replica thatched huts and the beautiful, insect-eyed *dogū* figurines whose ritualistic purpose is still unclear. The most immediately interesting displays, however, are in the top-floor gallery devoted to local folk culture, where vine-woven baskets and rice-straw raincoats rub shoulders with fertility dolls and the distinctive agricultural deity Oshira-sama (see p.303).

From here you can return to Aomori Station along Aomori's main shopping street, **Shinmachi-dōri**, with its banks, craft shops and department stores as well as a plethora of trendy clothing stores on the side streets. At the west end, in front of the station, is the new **Auga Building** which has a good old-fashioned **food market** in the basement floor (Mon–Sat 5am–6.30pm). A large proportion of the stalls are loaded with iridescent fish, hairy crabs, scallops and squids, but among them you'll find neat pyramids of Aomori's other staple product: oversized, paper-wrapped apples.

Out of the centre

The city's remaining sights are all in the southern suburbs, of which by far the most rewarding is the exhibition of festival floats at **Nebuta-no-sato** (daily: June to mid-Sept 9am–8pm; mid-Sept to May 9am–5.30pm; June–Sept ¥630, Oct–May ¥420). JR and Shiei buses (1–2 hourly; 30min; ¥450) drop you on the main road, from where it's a short walk to the entrance. One of Japan's great summer festivals, the Nebuta Matsuri, is named after the gigantic bamboo-framed paper lanterns (*nebuta*) which take the form of Kabuki actors, samurai or even sumo wrestlers in dramatic poses. The features are painted by well-known local artists, and the lanterns – lit nowadays by electricity rather than candles – are mounted on wheeled carts and paraded through the night-time streets of Aomori. According to the most popular local legend, the lanterns originated in 800 AD, when local rebels were lured out of hiding by an imaginative general who had his men construct an eye-catching lantern and play festive music. You can see several of today's magnificent *nebuta* in a darkened hall on the hillside to the left as you walk through the park, alongside photos of early festivals and of the construction techniques. On the way out, take a look in a smaller hall, just before the river, which contains a fan-shaped float from the rival Hirosaki festival, known as the Neputa Matsuri (see pp.321–322).

On the way back into central Aomori, get off at the Kami-Tamagawa bus stop. This unpromising area of *pachinko* parlours and drive-ins is home to an interesting folk museum, the **Keikokan** (daily except Thurs & last day of the month 9am–4.30pm; free), dedicated to documenting the daily life of the "snow country" – Japan's mountainous interior. The museum has a valuable collection of local crafts, from fine lacquerware to heavily embroidered textiles and sturdy wooden furniture. If you're not going to Hokkaidō, the display of Ainu clothes and jewellery is also worth a look.

One of Aomori's most famous citizens, a woodblock artist inspired by Van Gogh, is honoured in the **Munakata Shikō Memorial Museum** (Tues–Sun 9.30am–5pm; ¥300). The small museum shows rotating exhibitions of Shikō's bold, almost abstract scenes of local festivals and Aomori people. Though best known for his black-and-white prints, Shikō also dabbled in oils, painted screens and calligraphy. To reach the museum, take a bus from Aomori Station bound for Koyanagi and get off at the Munakata Shikō Kinenkan-dōri-mae stop (15min; ¥190), from where it's a four-minute walk west to the museum, in front of the NTT building.

Eating, drinking and entertainment

Seafood, apples and apple products fill Aomori's food halls and souvenir shops. Among the more appetizing **speciality foods**, *hotate kai-yaki*, fresh scallops from Mutsu Bay grilled in their shells and served with a dash of miso sauce, and *jappa-jiru*, a winter cod-fish stew, are both worth a try. There are dozens of small eateries and sushi shops around the food market in the Auga Building, but it's best to stick to places with a price list to avoid being overcharged. Shinmachi-dōri, the main shopping street, and around the station, are good places to look for **restaurants**, and ASPAM also has a number of reasonable options.

Jintako 1-6 Yasukata ☎ 0177/22-7727. Cosy restaurant, and some of Aomori's famous *shamisen* (traditional stringed instrument) players give dinner concerts here in the evenings. Reservations are essential and it's not cheap (¥5000 or ¥6000 including food). Daily 6–11pm, closed first and third Sun of the month.

Kakigen Shin-machi 1-chōme. Small, casual restaurant specializing in *hotate* and other seafood, though also serving *tonkatsu, donburi* and noodle dishes at reasonable prices. Look for its moss-green *noren* (hanging curtain) just east of the *Hotel Sunroute* on Shinmachi-dōri. Daily 10.30am–8.30pm.

Nandaimon Shin-machi 1-chōme. This cheap and cheerful Chinese–Korean eatery serves good-value *yakiniku*, grilled *hotate* and other seafoods. Lunch sets start at ¥750. Daily 11am–10pm.

Nishi-mura 1-5 Yasukata ☎ 0177/73-2880.

Choose from a broad range of inexpensive local cuisine including *hotate* and *jappa-jiru* (winter cod-fish stew), or set meals from ¥1300. There's a picture menu and some staff speak a little English. Reservations recommended in the evening. Closed Sun.

Sakatsubo 2F, 1-8-1 Shin-machi, on the second floor above a Sunkus convenience store ☎ 017/722-7217. Incredible sashimi, grilled fish, tempura and other vegetables at very reasonable prices – try the set menu for around ¥1500. Also stocks quite a selection of regional sake, from ¥500. Mon–Sat 4.30–11pm.

Supage-tei Aomori 1-8-8 Shin-machi. A café-style spaghetti house in the basement next to *Kakigen*. Their handy English menu lists an unusual range of tasty pasta dishes – cod's roe, sea urchin, *kimchi* and ginger-flavoured soy sauce – mostly around ¥1000. Tues–Sun 11am–8.30pm.

Listings

Airlines Japan Air System ☎ 0120-511283; Korean Air ☎ 0177/29-0511; Skymark ☎ 0177/62-3767.

Airport information For flight information, phone ☎ 0177/73-2135.

Banks Dai-ichi Kangyō, Michinoku and Aomori banks are all located on Shinmachi-dōri, around the junction with ASPAM-dōri.

Bicycle rental You can rent fixed-gear bikes (May–Oct 9am–5pm) for ¥100 a day from the bicycle parking lot to the left of the station. You'll need to show photo ID.

Buses Limousine buses to Aomori airport (¥560) take forty minutes and leave every half hour from ASPAM, calling at the station en route. Long-distance buses for Tokyo, Sendai and Morioka depart from the station terminal.

Car rental Eki Rent-a-Car (☎ 0177/22-3930), Toyota (☎ 0177/34-0100), Nissan (☎ 0177/22-

2369) and Nissan (☎ 0177/22-4625) all have branches near the station.

Emergencies The main police station is at 2-15 Yasukata Aomori-shi (☎ 0177/23-0110). For other emergency numbers, see Basics on p.81.

Ferries Higashi-Nihon Ferry Co. (☎ 0177/82-3631) operates daily ferries and a high-speed *Unicorn* service to Hokkaidō (Hakodate and Murora) from the car ferry wharf, only accessible by taxi (¥1300). Passenger ferries for Wakinosawa and the coast of Shimokita Hantō (Shimokita Kisen; ☎ 0177/22-4545) leave from the passenger terminal beside Bay Bridge.

Hospital Aomori City Hospital, 1-14-20 Katsuda (☎ 0177/34-2171).

Internet access The Aomori municipal citizen's centre (daily 10am–9pm), on the fourth floor of the Auga building, offers an hour's free Internet access.

Post office Aomori Central Post Office has a poste

restante service but it's inconveniently located on the west side of town, at 1-7-24 Tsutsumi-machi. There's a more handy sub-post office in the Paruru Plaza Aomori building, on your right as you come out of the station building.

Shopping Apart from ASPAM's souvenir and craft-shops, browse along Shinmachi-dōri, where Murata Kōgei stocks a good range of local kites, embroidery, lacquerware, brightly painted horses and Tsugaru *kokeshi* dolls. Further east you'll also find Narita Books, with a small selection of English-language titles.

Taxis Aomori Taxi (℡0177/38-6000); Miyago Kankō Taxi (℡0177/43-0385).

Shimokita Hantō

The **Shimokita Hantō** protrudes into the ocean northeast of Aomori like a great axe-head. Its jagged blade is covered with low, forested peaks, of which the most notorious is **Osore-zan**, the "terrible mountain" where spirits of the dead are believed to linger on their way to a Buddhist paradise. Despite its growing commercialization, Osore-zan's bleak crater lake, surrounded by a sulphurous desert where pathetic statues huddle against the bitter winds, is a compelling, slightly spine-tingling place. On the way to or from Osore-zan it's worth visiting **Wakinosawa**, a port on the southwest tip with ferry connections to Aomori, and taking a boat trip along this wild coastline. With a bit of patience, you might also see some of Japan's hardy macaque monkeys or the sure-footed serow, a type of antelope, which still inhabit the forests north of Wakinosawa.

Osore-zan

The main focus of **Osore-zan**, an extinct volcano consisting of several peaks, lies about halfway up its eastern slopes, where **Osorezan-Bodaiji** (May–Oct daily 6am–6pm; ¥500) sits on the shore of a silvery crater lake. Though the temple was founded in the ninth century, Osore-zan was already revered in ancient folk religion as a place where dead souls gather, and it's easy to see why – the desolate volcanic landscape, with its yellow- and red-stained soil, multicoloured pools and bubbling, malodorous streams, makes for an unearthly scene. The temple also receives a steady trickle of non-spectral visitors, while during the summer **festival** (July 20–24) people arrive in force to contact their ancestors or the recently deceased through the mediation of *itako*, usually blind, elderly women who turn a profitable trade. During the open season (May–Oct) six **buses** a day run up to the temple from Mutsu (see opposite; May–Oct; 35min; ¥1500 return); the last bus leaves Osore-zan at 4.45pm.

Shimokita Hantō		
Mutsu	*Mutsu*	むつ
Masakari Plaza	*Masakari Puraza*	まさかりプラザ
Murai Ryokan	*Murai Ryokan*	むら井旅館
Nankō	*Nankō*	楠こう
Hotel New Green	*Hoteru Nyū Guriin*	ホテルニューグリーン
Noheji	*Noheji*	野辺地
Osore-zan	*Osore-zan*	恐山
Shimokita Station	*Shimokita-eki*	下北駅
Tanabu bus terminal	*Tanabu-eki*	田名部駅
Wakinosawa	*Wakinosawa*	脇野沢
Dome Minshuku	*Dōmu Minshuku*	民宿ドーム
Hotokegaura	*Hotokegaura*	仏ヶ浦
Sai-mura	*Sai-mura*	佐井村
Wakinosawa Youth Hostel	*Wakinosawa Yūsu Hosuteru*	脇野沢ユースホステル

From Mutsu, the road to Osorezan-Bodaiji winds through pine forests, past a succession of stone monuments and a spring where it's customary to stop for a sip of purifying water. At the top you emerge by a large lake beside which a small humped bridge represents the journey souls make between this world and the next; it's said that those who led an evil life will find it impossible to cross over. After a quick look round the temple, take any path leading over the hummock towards the lake's barren foreshore. The little heaps of stones all around are said to be the work of children who died before their parents. They have to wait here, building stupas, which demons gleefully knock over during the night – most people add a pebble or two in passing. **Jizō**, the guardian deity of children and the Bodhisattva charged with leading people to the Buddhist Western Paradise, also comes along to scare away the demons, though it seems with less success. Sad little statues, touchingly wrapped in towels and bibs, add an even more melancholy note to the scene. Many have offerings piled in front of them: bunches of flowers, furry toys – faded and rain-sodden at the end of summer – and plastic windmills whispering to each other in the wind.

Three times a day (6.30am, 11am & 2pm) the sound of chanting from **services** at Bodaiji echoes over the rocks, and the temple also offers expensive **accommodation** (℡0175/22-3826, ℱ22-3402; ❼ including meals). For most visitors, however, it's something of a relief to be heading back down to Mutsu, leaving Osore-zan to its wandering souls.

Mutsu

A workaday town on the southern edge of Shimokita Hantō, **MUTSU** is the main base for Osore-zan. The easiest **access** route is via JR train from Noheji, on the main Tōhoku line, to Shimokita Station in Mutsu's southern suburbs. **Local buses** to Osore-zan stop at Shimokita Station on their way to the central Mutsu bus terminal (which is on the main road leading away from the JR bus terminal, just past the Daiei department store), so you can go up to the mountain straight off the JR train and simply get off in the centre of Mutsu on the way back down if you plan to stay the night. Alternatively, blue-and-white JR buses (for which rail passes are valid) run from Ōminato Station, the last stop on the local JR line, to the JR bus terminal, which is confusingly called Tanabu "station", on the east side of Mutsu town centre (the bus terminal is next to a disused train station that served a defunct private railway). These buses also run down to Wakinosawa (see p.318) from the JR bus terminal via Ōminato Station.

Mutsu's **information desk** (daily 8.30am–5pm; ℡0175/22-0909) is in the ground-floor lobby of Masakari Plaza, a modern pink building immediately northwest of the JR bus terminal. Staff can provide English-language maps and bus timetables and can help with finding accommodation, though they don't speak English. One of the nicest **places to stay** in Mutsu is the *Murai Ryokan* (℡0175/22-4755, ℱ23-4572; ❹–❺ with meals, ❹ without), just in front of Masakari Plaza. None of the tatami rooms is en suite, but everything's spanking clean and the food is excellent value. A good alternative is the *Hotel New Green* (℡0175/22-6121, ℱ22-5180; ❹–❺), with a choice of Western- or Japanese-style rooms. It's about five minutes' walk from the JR bus terminal; follow the road straight ahead (west) past the Daiei department store and the private bus terminal, then left at the T-junction.

Though it's the smartest **restaurant** in town, prices at *Nankō* (daily 11.30am–9.30pm), located down the side street on the left just before the *Hotel New Green*, are surprisingly affordable. The best deals are their *teishoku* (from ¥1100), but you can also choose from a picture menu of seafood, steaks and stews for around ¥2000 per head. Alternatively, the second-floor restaurant in the Masakari Plaza (daily 10am–6pm) serves a decent range of Japanese-style set meals for around ¥1200, and noodle dishes for as little as ¥400.

Wakinosawa and around

Rather than backtracking to Noheji, you can leave the Shimokita Hantō by ferry from **WAKINOSAWA** direct to Aomori. Though it's possible to do this journey in a day, it's worth staying the night in Wakinosawa to take a boat trip along the attractive stretch of coast and see some of the local wildlife. The peninsula is home to an estimated four hundred macaques, the world's most northerly colony of wild monkeys, and a growing population of red-haired, goat-like serow, both of which are a protected species. There's more chance of seeing them in winter, when the animals move closer to human habitation in search of food, often within an hour's walk of the port.

Arriving **by bus** from Mutsu (1hr 35min; ¥1790) you'll come into Wakinosawa from the northeast. The first stop in the town sets you down on the road near the **ferry pier** and a red-roofed, octagonal building where you can get **information** and tickets for the ferry and boat trips (daily 7.30am–4.30pm; ℡0175/44-3371). **Ferries** run across Mutsu Bay to Aomori (sailings at 8.30am & 2pm daily; 50min; ¥2540), and there's also a car ferry to **Kanita-machi** on the Tsugaru Peninsula (1hr; ¥1120), where you can pick up JR trains for Aomori or Hokkaidō. The most interesting **boat trip** takes you north along the coast to Sai-mura (1hr 25min; ¥2640), past a small area of much-photographed, needle-shaped Hotokegaura cliffs; the 10.35am sailing from Wakinosawa will bring you back at noon. There's a more expensive, two-hour cruise (¥3800; departures at 10.45am and 2.45pm) which includes thirty minutes on shore at the Hotokegaura cliffs.

Wakinosawa has a small, homely **youth hostel** (℡0175/44-2341, ⓦwww.jyh.or.jp; ¥2850 per person), offering basic dormitory accommodation about five minutes' walk from the bus terminal on the west side of town; follow the road over a small headland and you'll find the hostel signed to the right. It's run by a friendly couple with a passion for the local wildlife – they'll recommend the most likely places to find anything and perhaps lend you maps and binoculars. If the hostel's full, try *Dome Minshuku* (℡0175/44-3216; ❺ including meals), in a three-storey building on the seafront.

Hirosaki

Behind its modern facade, **HIROSAKI**, former seat of the Tsugaru clan, still retains a few reminders of its feudal past. Most of its sights lie around **Hirosaki-kōen**, on the west side of the Tsuchibuchi-gawa, where one picturesque turret marks the site of Hirosaki-jō, the old city castle. Nearby you'll find **Fujita Kinen Teien**, a well-preserved Japanese garden, and a collection of Meiji-era Western-style buildings, contrasting with a street of traditional samurai houses on the north side of the castle grounds. Hirosaki's summer lantern festival, the **Neputa Matsuri** (Aug 1–7), has its own museum attached to a craft centre, and there's also a district of dignified **Zen temples** out on the west side of town. Though these sights can be covered in a full day's outing from Aomori, Hirosaki is a pleasant place to stay and is even worth considering as an alternative base for the area.

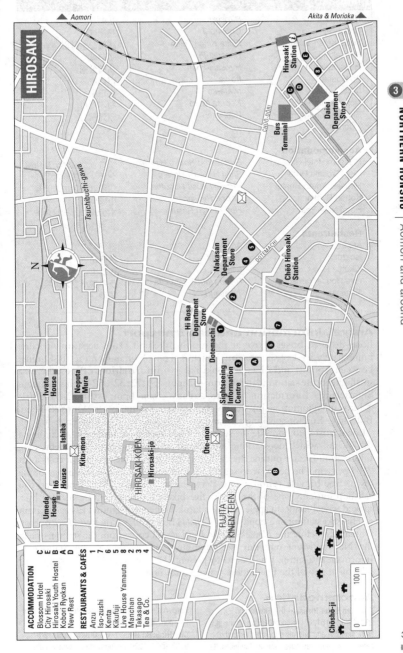

HIROSAKI

▲ Aomori

Akita & Morioka ▲

Tsuchibuchi-gawa

CHŌ-DŌRI

Hirosaki Station

Bus Terminal

Daiei Department Store

Ch**ō** Hirosaki Station

DOTEMACHI

Nakasan Department Store

Hi Rosa Department Store

Dotemachi

Neputa Mura

Iwata House

Ishiba

Itō House

Umeda House

Kita-mon

HIROSAKI-KŌEN

Hirosaki-jō

Ōte-mon

FUJITA KINEN TEIEN

Sightseeing Information Centre

Chōshō-ji

N

ACCOMMODATION
Blossom Hotel   C
City Hirosaki   E
Hirosaki Youth Hostel   B
Kobori Ryokan   A
New Rest   D

RESTAURANTS & CAFÉS
Anzu   1
Iso-zushi   7
Kenta   6
Kikufuji   5
Live House Yamauta   8
Manchan   2
Takasago   3
Tea & Co.   4

0   100 m

Hirosaki

Hirosaki	*Hirosaki*	弘前
Chōshō-ji	*Chōshō-ji*	長勝寺
Fujita Kinen Teien	*Fujita Kinen Teien*	藤田記念庭園
Hirosaki-jō	*Hirosaki-jō*	弘前城
Hirosaki-kōen	*Hirosaki-kōen*	弘前公園
Itō House	*Itō-ke*	伊藤家
Iwata House	*Iwata-ke*	岩田家
Neputa Mura	*Neputa Mura*	ねぷた村
Sightseeing Information Centre	*Kankōkan*	観光館

Accommodation		
Blossom Hotel Hirosaki	*Burossamu Hoteru Hirosaki*	ブロッサムホテル弘前
City Hirosaki Hotel	*Shitii Hirosaki Hoteru*	シティー弘前ホテル
Hirosaki Youth Hostel	*Hirosaki Yūsu Hosuteru*	弘前ユースホステル
Kobori Ryokan	*Kobori Ryokan*	小堀旅館
Hotel New Rest	*Hoteru Nyū Resuto*	ホテルニューレスト

Restaurants		
Anzu	*Anzu*	杏
Iso-zushi	*Iso-zushi*	磯寿司
Kikufuji	*Kikufuji*	菊富士
Live House Yamauta	*Raibu Hausu Yamauta*	ライブハウス山唄
Takasago	*Takasago*	高砂

Arrival, information and city transport

Long-distance **buses** arrive at the terminal behind Daiei department store, immediately west of the **station**, which is served by trains on the JR Ōu line between Aomori and Akita. Hirosaki has two **information offices**: there's a small one in the station (daily 8.45am–5/6pm; ☎0172/32-0524), plus the main Sightseeing Information Centre (daily 9am–6pm; ☎0172/37-5501, ⓔhirokan5@jomon.ne.jp) beside the southern entrance to Hirosaki-kōen. Both have English-speaking staff and can supply town guides in English.

Local buses stop outside the station for destinations around town, including a "¥100 bus" which does a long loop between the station and the Sightseeing Information Centre outside the castle grounds; as its name suggests, it costs a flat ¥100 per trip. The best way to see the sights, however, is to take advantage of the town's **free bicycle rental** system. Between 9am and 4pm (May/June–Oct) you can pop into any one of the town's five bike stations, which are marked by a spoked wheel inside an apple (there's a kiosk in the underground passage in front of Hirosaki station; one opposite *McDonald's* beyond the *New Rest Hotel*; one on Dotemachi before the *Hirosaki Grand Hotel* as you come from the station; one at the Neputa Mura museum (see opposite); and another at the Sightseeing Information Centre); you'll need to present ID to register. You can drop your bike off at any of the five stations when you're done.

Accommodation

Blossom Hotel Hirosaki 6-7 Ekimaechō ☎0712/32-4151, ⓔblossom@aioros.ocn.ne.jp. New, smallish and brightly decorated hotel that caters to women travelling alone and families. It's across the pedestrian mall from the *New Rest*

Hotel. A simple breakfast is included in the cost of the room. ⑤
City Hirosaki Hotel 1-1-2 Ōmachi ☎0172/37-0109, ⓕ37-1229. Big upmarket business hotel right outside the station with spacious, en-suite

rooms. There's also a choice of restaurants, a bar and a swimming pool (¥1575). ⑥
Hirosaki Youth Hostel 11 Mori-machi ⓣ & ⓕ0172/33-7066, ⓦ www.jyh.or.jp. Old but welcoming hostel in a prime location for exploring the castle area. Take a bus from the station to Daigaku Byōin-mae (20min; ¥170), from where it's a five-minute walk further west. ¥2900 per person.

Kobori Ryokan 89 Hon-chō ⓣ0172/32-5111, ⓕ34-8273. This old wooden ryokan near the castle offers a choice of smart tatami rooms, some with bath, as well as two Western-style rooms. ⑥–⑦ with meals, ⑤ without.
New Rest Hotel 14-2 Ekimae-chō ⓣ0172/33-5300, ⓕ33-2327. Basic business hotel opposite the train station, with bright, simple rooms. ④–⑤

The City

The older and more interesting part of Hirosaki lies around the park of Hirosaki-kōen, to the west of the modern town – take a bus from the station for the twenty-minute ride (¥170) to Shiyakusho-mae bus stop on the south side of the park. Before heading into Hirosaki-kōen, however, it's worth exploring the nearby **Fujita Kinen Teien** (mid-April to mid-Nov Tues–Sun 9am–5pm; ¥300), a beautiful and unusually varied Japanese garden designed in 1919 for a successful local businessman. The garden consists of three distinct sections flowing over a steep hillside. At the top, beside Fujita's elegant residence, dark pines frame the distant peak of Iwaki-san – a classic example of "borrowed scenery" – from where paths lead down, beside a tumbling waterfall and over a perfect, red-lacquer bridge, to another flat area of lawns and lakes at the bottom.

Back at the main park gates, the modern **Sightseeing Information Centre** (daily 9am–6pm), houses an information desk (see opposite), crafts displays and a **float pavilion** (same hours; free) in the hall behind. These floats, which mostly carry tableaux depicting historical scenes, originated in the late seventeenth century when merchants would parade them round the streets as part of a local shrine festival. Beyond the float pavilion, two colourful Western-style buildings stand out against the sleek concrete and steel. The **Former City Library** and **Missionaries' House** (daily 9am–4.30pm; ¥320) both date from the early 1900s and are nicely preserved, though there's no particular reason to go inside.

Ōte-mon, the main entrance to **Hirosaki-kōen**, lies across the road from the Sightseeing Centre. It takes ten minutes to walk from this gate, zigzagging between moats and walls, to reach the inner keep of **Hirosaki-jō**, where a tiny, three-storey tower (April to mid-Nov daily 9am–5pm; ¥300) guards the southern approach. There's nothing left of the original castle, constructed by the Tsugaru lords in 1611, but the tower was rebuilt in 1810 using traditional techniques. In late April the little white turret, floodlit and framed in pink blossom, is the focus of a **cherry-blossom festival** (April 23–May 5), as the park's five thousand trees signal the end of the harsh northern winter.

Leaving the park by its northern gate (Kita-mon), you emerge opposite the old **Ishiba** shop (daily 9am–5pm, closed first and third Sun of the month; ¥100), which was built 250 years ago to sell rice baskets and other household goods to the Tsugaru lords. Since the family (now selling sake), still live here, you only get a glimpse into the warehouse behind. However, there are several more houses from this era in a smart residential street behind the Ishiba shop – these open according to a complex rotation system, but at least one will be open on a given day (daily 10am–4pm; Jan–March & July–Oct closed Tues and Fri; Nov & Dec Sat & Sun only; free). At the west end of the street, the **Itō House** was once the home of the *daimyō*'s official doctor, while the next-door **Umeda House** was the residence of a minor samurai, as was the **Iwata House**, 500m further east.

Neputa Mura (daily 9am–4/5pm; ¥500), a museum focusing on Hirosaki's lantern festival, lies at the northeast corner of Hirosaki-kōen. The **Neputa**

Matsuri (Aug 1–7) is similar in style to Aomori's Nebuta festival (see p.311), but in this case the giant lanterns are fan-shaped and painted with scenes from ancient Chinese scrolls or with the faces of scowling samurai. Like the festival itself, the museum gets off to a rousing start with a demonstration of energetic drumming (you can try it yourself afterwards), after which you'll see a collection of floats, from a seven-metre-tall monster to child-size versions, followed by a display of local crafts – this is a good place to pick up souvenirs, such as ingenious spinning tops, cotton embroideries or stylish black-and-white Tsugaru pottery.

Hirosaki's final sight is a "temple town", around fifteen minutes' walk southwest of the castle park or twenty minutes by bus from the station – take bus #3 for Shigemori and get off at the Chōshō-ji Iriguchi stop. In the seventeenth century around thirty temples were relocated to this spot, of which the most interesting is **Chōshō-ji** (daily: April–Oct 8.30am–4.30pm; Jan–March, Nov & Dec 9am–4pm; ¥300). It stands at the end of a tree-lined road through a large, two-storey gate, dating from 1629, which barely contains the two guardian gods peering out of the gloom. Inside, ring the bell outside the thatched building on the right and someone will show you into the **main sanctuary** and the mortuary rooms behind. Chōshō-ji was the family temple and burial place of the Tsugaru clan; in 1954, excavations revealed the mummified body of Prince Tsugutomi, son of the eleventh lord, who had died about a century before – his death was variously blamed on assassination, poisoning or eating peaches with imported sugar. During the cherry-blossom festival (see p.321) the mummy is on display, but usually you'll have to make do with a photo in the mortuary room behind the main altar, where it's rather overshadowed by a life-like statue of Tsugaru Tamenobu, the founder of the clan. As you leave the building, take a closer look at the glass cabinets near the kitchen. These contain some of Prince Tsugutomi's prized possessions, including his telescope, watch and portraits of his favourite actresses.

Eating and entertainment

Like Aomori, Hirosaki has a fine tradition of folk **music**, played on the *Tsugaru Jamisen*, which has a thicker neck than the ordinary *shamisen* stringed instrument and is struck harder. You can hear dinner concerts at a couple of the **restaurants** listed below.

Anzu 1-44 Oyakata-machi ☎0172/32-6684. Named after an apricot, this cosy restaurant hosts evening *shamisen* concerts according to demand – it's best to reserve. Set meals range from ¥3000 to ¥5000. It's opposite the Asahi bowling alley, on a side street at the west end of Dotemachi. Mon–Sat 5–11pm.

Iso-zushi Wakaba Building, 11 Okeya-machi. Tiny, above-average sushi bar. There's a straightforward choice of three set meals (¥1100, ¥1600 and ¥2000), though non-Japanese speakers may find the owner a little unhelpful. Mon–Sat 6pm–4am.

Kenta 3 Okeya-chō ☎0172/35-9614. Cheap and popular *robatayaki* eatery on the edge of the city's bar zone; prices for individual dishes start at ¥500. Fills up quickly on the weekends – if you can't get a seat here, there's another branch around the corner. Daily 5pm–2am.

Kikufuji 1-1 Sakamoto-chō. A clean, bright restaurant with a good range of Japanese food, including well-priced sets (from ¥880 at lunchtime). Choose from their picture menu or window display. Daily 11am–10pm.

Live House Yamauta 2F, 1-2-7 Ōmachi ☎0172/36-1835. Well-known restaurant with inexpensive, *izakaya*-style food and live *shamisen* music most evenings. Reservations advised. Daily 5–11pm.

Manchan 36-6 Dotemachi ☎0172/35-4663. One of the oldest cafés in northern Honshū, with a pronounced apple theme – offerings include various delicious apple cakes, apple ice cream (around ¥800) and apple tea. Daily 9/9.30am–8pm; closed first and third Thurs of month.

Takasago 1-2 Oyakata-machi. Inexpensive soba restaurant in an old wooden house southeast of the castle grounds. The limited menu includes

tempura soba, *saru* soba and curry soba. Prices start at ¥650. Tues–Sun 11am–6pm.
Tea & Co Dotemachi. Relaxed coffee shop across the river from the Nakasan department store, with a great range of teas and coffees and some luscious home-made cakes. Daily 10am–8pm.

South to Towada-ko

Japan's third largest lake, **Towada-ko**, fills a three-hundred-metre-deep volcanic crater in the northern portion of the Towada-Hachimantai National Park. The steep-sided, crystal-clear lake rates as one of northern Honshū's top tourist attractions, but for many visitors the real highlight is the approach over high passes and along deep, wooded valleys. Though there are four main access roads, the most attractive route is south from Aomori via the Hakkōda mountains, Sukayu Onsen and the picturesque **Oirase valley**. For this last stretch it's the done thing to walk the final few kilometres beside the tumbling Oirase-gawa, and then hop on a cruise boat across to the lake's main tourist centre, **Yasumiya**.

Many roads around Towada-ko are closed in winter, and public **buses** only operate from April to November. During the season, however, there are regular services to the lake from Aomori, Morioka, Hachinohe, Hirosaki and (to the south) Towada-minami, a station on the line between Ōdate and Morioka. It's best to buy tickets in advance on all these routes, and reservations are obligatory on the JR buses from Aomori. Tickets can be bought at any JR green ticket window; rail passes are valid, but you still need to book.

Hakkōda-san and the Oirase valley

Leaving the dreary outskirts of Aomori behind, Route 103 climbs steeply onto the Kayano plateau and round the flanks of **Hakkōda-san**. Every winter, cold, wet winds dump snow up to 8m deep over these mountains, transforming the fir trees into "snow monsters" (see p.283) and maintaining a flourishing ski industry. This was also the site of the ill-fated "**snow march**" in January 1902, when Corporal Gotō and 210 soldiers on a training exercise in the run-up to the Russo-Japanese War (see "History", p.941) were caught in a blizzard. It

South to Towada-Ko

Towada-ko	*Towada-ko*	十和田湖
Hakkōda Ropeway	*Hakkōda Rōpu-uei*	八甲田ロープウェイ
Ishigedo	*Ishigedo*	石ヶ戸
Nenokuchi	*Nenokuchi*	子ノ口
Oirase Youth Hostel	*Oirase Yūsu Hosuteru*	おいらせユースホステル
Sukayu Onsen	*Sukayu Onsen*	酸ヶ湯温泉
Yakeyama	*Yakeyama*	焼山
Yasumiya	*Yasumiya*	休屋
Hakubutsukan Youth Hostel	*Hakubutsukan Yūsu Hosuteru*	博物館ユースホステル
Kuriyama	*Kuriyama*	栗山
Ōdate	*Ōdate*	大館
Oide Camp-jō	*Oide Kyampu-jō*	生出キャンプ場
Shuzan-sō	*Shuzan-sō*	春山荘
Towada-ko Grand Hotel	*Towada-ko Gurando Hoteru*	十和田湖グランドホテル
Towada-minami	*Towada-minami*	十和田南

took four days before rescuers found the half-frozen Corporal Gotō and only ten other survivors, most of whom lost at least one limb from frostbite.

In summer, however, it's a beautiful spot with excellent walking among Hakkōda-san's old volcanic peaks, of which the tallest is Ōdake (1584m). To ease the climb you can whisk to the top of nearby Tamoyachi-dake (1326m) on the **Hakkōda Ropeway** (daily 9am–4/4.45pm; closed for a few days mid-Nov; return ¥1800) and then walk down to **Sukayu Onsen**, both of which are stops on the bus route from Aomori to Towada-ko. The most famous of several onsen resorts in the area, Sukayu consists of just one **ryokan** (⊤0177/38-6400, ⓕ38-6677; ❻–❼ including breakfast), with a "thousand-person" cedar-wood bath (7am–7.30pm; ¥500). Sukayu's healing waters have been popular since the late seventeenth century and this is one of very few onsen left in Japan which is not segregated.

South of Sukayu the road crosses another pass and then starts descending through pretty, deciduous woodlands – spectacular in autumn – to **YAKEYA-MA** village, where you'll find the *Oirase Youth Hostel* (⊤0176/74-2031, ⓦwww.jyh.or.jp; dorm beds ¥2800 per person). Yakeyama is also the start of the **Oirase valley** walk, but it's better to join the path 5km further down the road at **ISHIGEDO**. From here it takes less than three hours to walk the 9km to Towada-ko following a well-trodden path running gently upstream, marred

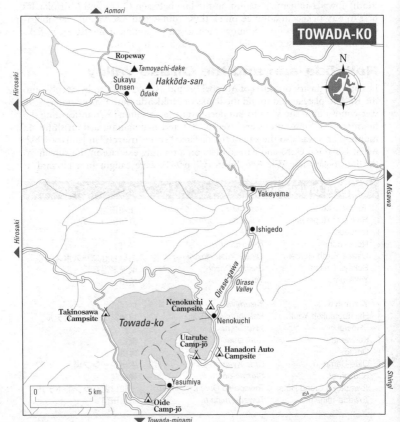

slightly by the fairly busy main road which you have to join for short stretches. But for the most part you're walking beside the Oirase-gawa as it tumbles among ferns and moss-covered rocks through a narrow, tree-filled valley punctuated by ice-white waterfalls. You emerge at lakeside **NENOKUCHI**, where you can either pick up a passing bus or take a scenic cruise across Towada-ko to Yasumiya (see below for details). Note that if you don't want to carry your bags there's a delivery service (May–Oct; ¥400 per piece) from either Ishigedo or Yakeyama to Nenokuchi.

Towada-ko

Two knobbly peninsulas break the regular outline of **Towada-ko**, a massive crater lake trapped in a rim of pine-forested hills within the Towada-Hachimantai National Park. The westerly protuberance shelters the lake's only major settlement, **YASUMIYA**, which is also known somewhat confusingly as Towada-ko. Roughly 44km in circumference, the lake is famous for its spectacularly clear water, with visibility down to 17m, best appreciated from one of several **boat trips** which run from early April to the end of January, though sailings are fairly limited in winter. The most interesting route is from Yasumiya to Nenokuchi (April to early Nov; 1hr; ¥1320); there's also a one-hour circuit between the two peninsulas from Yasumiya (Jan & mid-April to Nov; ¥1320). You can hire bicycles (¥630 for two hours) at Yasumiya and drop them off at Nenokuchi (or vice versa). Once you've navigated the lake, the only other thing to do in Towada-ko is pay a visit to the famous statue of the "**Maidens by the Lake**", which stands on the shore fifteen minutes' walk north of central Yasumiya. The two identical bronze women, roughcast and naked, seem to be circling each other with hands almost touching. They were created in 1953 by the poet and sculptor Takamura Kōtarō, then 70 years old, and are said to be of his wife, a native of Tōhoku, who suffered from schizophrenia and died tragically young.

About 20km east of Towada-ko along Route 454, the town of **SHINGŌ** is home to **Kirisuto No Haka** (Christ's Grave), a grave with a huge wooden cross which was built here in 1935 to commemorate an unusual local belief. Local devotees claim that it was actually Jesus's brother who was crucified, while Christ himself escaped and settled in Shingō, where he lived until the ripe old age of 106 – a small **museum** (daily except Wed 9am–5pm; ¥200) displays mysterious scripture which apparently proves their point. The site lies just west of the town centre and is signposted in English. Just a few minutes' walk west from Christ's Grave lie the **Ooishigami Pyramids**. According to ancient local writings, the Japanese built pyramids "tens and thousands" of years before the Egyptians and Mexicans. Both pyramids look a lot like a bunch of huge boulders, although the top of the second pyramid is a great spot for a packed lunch.

Practicalities

Though the small town of Yasumiya consists almost entirely of hotels and souvenir shops, its shady lakeside setting makes it a pleasant overnight stop. Its centre is dominated by two **bus terminals** opposite each other on a T-junction just inland from the boat pier; the more northerly one serves JR buses only. The **information office** (daily 8am–5pm; ☏0176/75-2909, ✉towadako01@net .pref.aomori.jp), in a separate building immediately right (north) of the JR bus terminal, has town maps and can help with **accommodation**. It's advisable to book rooms in advance from July through to October, when people come for the autumn leaves. The lakeside *Towada-ko Grand Hotel* (☏0176/75-1111,

Ⓕ78-1118; ❼), to the south of the ferry pier, offers a choice of Western or tata-mi rooms and also lets out some of its older rooms as the *Hakubutsukan Youth Hostel* (☎0176/75-2002, Ⓦwww.jyh.or.jp; dorm beds ¥3200 per person). Among a number of minshuku near the centre of Yasumiya, try the *Kuriyama* (☎ & Ⓕ0176/75-2932; ❻ including meals) or the older *Shuzan-sō* (☎0176/75-2607; ❺ including meals); both are a few minutes' walk inland from the pier. In summer, the patches of flat land around Towada-ko fill with tents; the closest **campsite** to Yasumiya is 4km southwest at *Oide Camp-jō* (☎0176/75-2079; late April to Oct).

Moving on from Yasumiya, buses to Towada-minami, Aomori and some Morioka services leave from the JR bus terminal, while other services for Morioka, Hirosaki and Hachimantai use the Towada-ko terminal, opposite. If you're heading to Akita, take a bus south to Towada-minami and then a local train to **Ōdate** on the main JR line between Aomori and Akita, or catch the daily bus (not JR) direct to Ōdate (April to early Nov 3.40pm).

Akita and around

One of the few big cities on the northwest coast of Japan, modern **AKITA** is an important port and industrial centre with access to some of the country's few domestic oil reserves. Though it was founded in the eighth century, almost nothing of the old city remains and Akita's few central sites – three contrasting museums – can easily be covered on foot in half a day. With its airport and Shinkansen services, however, Akita makes a convenient base for the region. The small town of **Kakunodate**, a short train ride to the east, preserves a street of two-hundred-year-old samurai houses, while nearby **Tazawa-ko**, Japan's deepest lake, offers boat rides and some attractive scenery, though it's not as striking as its northern rival, Towada-ko (see p.325) and it's better to press onto Nyūtō Onsen, a group of hot springs 10km northeast of the lake at the end of the Sendatsu-gawa valley.

The city of Akita is also home to the last of the great Tōhoku summer fes-tivals, the **Kantō Matsuri** (Aug 3–6) – though it's still a pleasantly low-key affair compared to events in Sendai (p.284) and Aomori (p.311). During the festival men parade through the streets balancing tall bamboo poles strung with paper lanterns, which they transfer from their hip, to head, hand or shoulder while somehow managing to keep the swaying, top-heavy structure upright.

The City

The centre of modern-day Akita is bounded to the east by its smart new train station, and to the north by the willow-lined moats of its former castle, **Kubota-jō**. This was Akita's second castle, founded in 1604 by the Satake clan who, unusually for northerners, backed the emperor rather than the shogun during the Meiji Restoration. Nevertheless, they still lost their castle after 1868 and the site is now a park, **Senshū-kōen**.

Walking straight ahead from Akita Station on the city's central avenue, Hiro-kōji, the **Atorion**'s twelfth-floor observatory is a good place to get the lie of the land. Atorion also houses a crafts hall, bookstore, concert hall and restau-rants around its classy atrium. A little further on, cross the moat into Senshū-kōen and you'll find the **Hirano Masakichi Art Museum** (Tues–Sun 10am–5/5.30pm; ¥610) on the second floor of the otherwise uninteresting

Prefectural Art Museum (entry is via the exterior stairway to the right of the main entrance). The Hirano museum has a valuable collection of work by Western artists, including Goya, Picasso, Rubens and Rembrandt, but it's more memorable for an enormous canvas (3.65m by 20.5m) by the local artist Fujita Tsuguhara (or Tsuguji; 1886–1968). The panel, entitled *Events in Akita*, depicts Akita's annual festivals and takes up one wall of the museum. It was completed in an incredible fifteen days in 1937, after which the wall of Tsuguhara's studio had to be knocked down to get it out.

You can learn more about local celebrations at the **Kantō Festival Centre** (daily 9.30am–4.30pm; ¥100, or ¥250 with Aka-renga Kyōdo-kan – see p.328), located to the west of Senshū-kōen and across a small river. There are videos of recent Kantō Matsuri and sample *kantō* to try out. The *kantō* is a bamboo pole, up to 10m tall and weighing perhaps 60kg, to which dozens of paper lanterns are attached on crossbars. During the festival (Aug 3–6), as many as two hundred poles are carried through the streets in celebration of the coming harvest, as teams of men and young boys show their skill in balancing and manipulating the hefty poles. The festival was originally a pre-harvest ritual and, as the line of *kantō* sway in the dark, the yellow lanterns look like so many heads of golden rice.

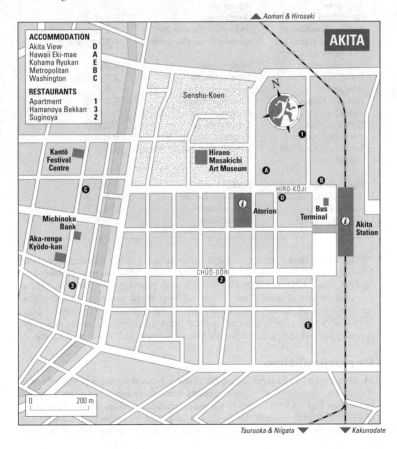

Akita	*Akita*	秋田
Aka-renga Kyōdo-kan	*Aka-renga Kyōdo-kan*	赤れんが郷土館
Atorion	*Atorion*	アトリオン
Hirano Masakichi Art Museum	*Hirano Masakichi Bijutsukan*	平野政吉美術館
Kantō Festival Centre	*Neburi-Nagashi-kan*	ねぶり流し館
Senshū-kōen	*Senshū-kōen*	千秋公園

Accommodation and restaurants		
Akita View Hotel	*Akita Byū Hoteru*	秋田ビューホテル
Hamanoya Bekkan	*Hamanoya Bekkan*	濱乃家別館
Hotel Hawaii Eki-mae	*Hoteru Hawai Eki-mae*	ホテルハワイ駅前
Kohama Ryokan	*Kohama Ryokan*	小浜旅館
Hotel Metropolitan	*Hoteru Metoroporitan*	ホテルメトロポリタン
Suginoya	*Suginoya*	杉のや
Washington Hotel	*Washinton Hoteru*	ワシントンホテル

Kakunodate	*Kakunodate*	角館
Aoyagi-ke	*Aoyagi-ke*	青柳家
Denshōkan	*Denshōkan*	伝承館
Folklore Kakunodate	*Forukurōro Kakunodate*	フォルクローロ角館
Hirafuku Memorial Art Museum	*Hirafuku Kinen Bijutsukan*	平福記念美術館
Hyakusui-en	*Hyakusui-en*	百穂苑
Inaho	*Shokudō Inaho*	食堂いなほ
Ishiguro-ke	*Ishiguro-ke*	石黒家
Ishikawa Ryokan	*Ishikawa Ryokan*	石川旅館
Murasaki	*Murasaki*	むら咲
Ōmiya Ryokan	*Ōmiya Ryokan*	大宮旅館
Takahashi Ryokan	*Takahashi Ryokan*	高橋旅館
Tamachi Bukeyashiki Hotel	*Tamachi Bukeyashiki Hoteru*	田町武家屋敷ホテル

Nyūtō Onsen	*Nyūtō Onsen*	乳頭温泉
Tsurunoyu Onsen	*Tsurunoyu Onsen*	鶴の湯温泉
Kaniba Onsen	*Kaniba Onsen*	蟹場温泉
Yamanoyado Inn	*Yamanoyado*	山の宿

From the Festival Centre, turn right and head south down this street for about 500m to the unmistakeable, red-and-white-brick **Aka-renga Kyōdo-kan** (daily 9.30am–4.30pm; ¥200). This Western-style building was erected in 1912 as the headquarters of Akita Bank, and its well-preserved banking hall and offices are worth a quick look. A modern extension behind houses a series of woodcuts by Katsuhira Tokushi, a self-taught local artist who won recognition for his appealingly bold, colourful portrayals of local farmers and scenes of rural life.

Practicalities

Most visitors to Akita arrive at the JR **station**, located on the east side of town, though the city also has its own **airport** some forty minutes to the south by limousine bus (¥890). The city's **information office** (daily 9am–7pm; ☎0188/32-7941) is inside the JR station, and there's a Prefectural Information Centre on the first floor of the Atorion Building (daily except Wed 9am–7pm;

ⓣ0188/36–7835); both stock English-language maps and other printed information, but in general the staff don't speak English.

Among a good choice of **accommodation**, *Kohama Ryokan* (ⓣ0188/32-5739, ⓦwww.itcj.or.jp; ❺) is recommended for local atmosphere, its kitsch collection of framed 1970s posters and knick-knacks, plus a friendly welcome from both the owner and her talkative pet parrot. None of the Japanese-style rooms is en suite, but everything's squeaky clean, the food's excellent and it's located just five minutes' walk south of the station. If they're full, try *Hotel Hawaii Eki-mae* (ⓣ & ⓕ0188/33-1111; ❸–❹), on Hiro-koji beside the southeast corner of Senshū-kōen; its rooms are small but spruce, though with only a washbasin in the cheaper rooms (there are another two similarly priced *Hotel Hawaii*s in the area: the staff at the *Eki-mae* hotel can direct you). Opposite the *Hawaii Eki-mae*, the *Akita View Hotel* (ⓣ0188/32-1111, ⓕ32-0037; ❻) offers the best rooms in town, plus a range of restaurants and even a pool (¥3500) in the fitness centre. For something more modest, try the *Hotel Metropolitan* (ⓣ0188/31-2222, ⓕ31-2290; ❻), immediately outside the station, or the lowlier *Washington Hotel* (ⓣ0188/65-7111, ⓦwww.wh-rsv.com/english/akita/index.html; ❺), at the far end of Hiro-koji, about fifteen minutes' walk away.

The region's most famous **speciality food** is *kiritampo*, a substantial stew of chicken, mushrooms, onions, glass noodles, seasonal vegetables and the key ingredient, *mochi* (rice cakes), made of pounded new rice and shaped round a cedar-wood stick before grilling over a charcoal fire. *Shottsuru* is more of an acquired taste – a strong-tasting stew made with a broth of fermented, salted fish. The most famous **restaurant** at which to sample these and other local dishes is *Hamanoya Bekkan*, 4-2-11 Ōmachi (ⓣ0188/62-6611; daily 11.30am–10pm), located one block southeast of the Aka-renga Kyōdo-kan museum in an amazingly well-preserved old house (there's also a branch in the *Hotel Metropolitan*); prices aren't too outrageous, but reservations are advisable on weekend evenings in the main restaurant. As ever, the station and surrounding streets provide a whole variety of eating choices, including *Suginoya*, 3F Topica Building, 7-1-2 Naka-dōri (daily 11am–9pm), which is less refined than *Hamanoya* but has a helpful window display and serves a wider range of foods at cheaper prices, including *kiritampo*, *shottsuru* and set meals from ¥1300. A few minutes' walk north of the station is the *Apartment* café-bar (Tues–Sun noon to midnight) – the coolest place to hang out in the whole of northern Japan. In a rickety two-storey building decked out with mismatching old armchairs, Shinobu, the owner and house DJ, flits between the turntables and a tiny kitchen/bar, serving up an eclectic range of cheap meals to go with the ¥500 mixed drinks and down-tempo/nu-jazz. From the station, take the first right after the *Hotel Metropolitan* and follow the road for 200m; *Apartment* is on the left just before the gaudy replica church.

Listings

Airlines ANA ⓣ0120-029222; JAL ⓣ0120-255971; JAS ⓣ0188/33-0271; Korean Air ⓣ0088-212001.
Airport information ⓣ0188/86-3366.
Banks and exchange For foreign exchange, try Akita Bank or Hokuto Bank on Chūō-dōri, running parallel to Hiro-koji two blocks further south, or the Michinoku Bank between the Akarenga-kan and *Washington Hotel*.
Buses Long-distance buses to Tokyo and Sendai

stop outside Akita Station.
Car rental Eki Rent-a-Car (ⓣ0188/33-9308), Nippon Rent-a-Car (ⓣ0188/32-5798) and Toyota Rentals (ⓣ0188/33-0100) are all located near Akita's JR station.
Emergencies The main police station is at 1-9 Meitoku-cho, Senshū Akita-shi (ⓣ0188/35-1111). In an absolute emergency contact the Akita International Association on ⓣ0188/64-1181. For other emergency numbers, see "Basics" on p.81.

Ferry Shin-nihonkai Ferry (☎0188/80-2600) sails
four times a week to Tomakomai (11hr 20min), the
main port on Hokkaidō and a gateway to Sapporo.
Hospitals The biggest central hospital is the Red
Cross Hospital, 222-1 Kamikitade Saruta-
nawashirusawa (☎0188/29-5000); alternatively,
try the University Hospital, 1-1-1 Hondō
(☎0881/34-1111), out on the east side of town.
Post office The central post office, at 5 Hodōno
Teppo-machi, Akita-shi, has a poste restante service.

Kakunodate

While Akita City has lost nearly all its historical relics, nearby **KAKUNO-DATE** still has the air of a feudal town, with its strictly delineated samurai and merchants' quarters. Kakunodate was established as a military outpost in 1620 by the lords of Akita, with a castle on a hill to the north, a samurai town of around eighty residences, and 350 merchants' homes in a cramped district to the south. This basic layout and a handful of the samurai houses have survived the years, as have several hundred of the weeping cherry trees brought from Kyoto three centuries ago. It's still an atmospheric place, and although you can visit on a day-trip from either Akita or Morioka, it merits an overnight stay.

Pick up a town map from the tourist information centre (see "Practicalities" below) before setting off for the samurai quarter, roughly fifteen minutes' walk northwest. You can't miss the division between the packed streets of the commercial town – now mostly modern and rather run-down – and the wide avenues where the samurai lived in their spacious mansions among neatly fenced gardens. The most interesting of the samurai houses is the **Aoyagi-ke** (daily: April–Nov 8.30am–4.30pm; Jan–March & Dec 9am–4pm; ¥500), a large, thatched house towards the north end of the samurai street, which is easily identified by an unusually grand entrance gate. Aoyagi-ke was lived in up to 1985, but now contains an odd mix of museums, including samurai armour, agricultural implements, memorabilia from the Sino-Japanese and Pacific wars, and a wonderful display of antique gramophones and cameras.

A little further up the street, the impressive **Ishiguro-ke** (daily 9am–5pm; ¥300) is one of the oldest of Kakunodate's samurai houses. Built in 1809 for the *daimyō*'s financial adviser, its main features are two large *kura*, fireproof warehouses used for storing rice, miso and other valuables. Despite its extraordinary green concrete exterior, the **Hirafuku Memorial Art Museum** (April–Nov daily 9am–5pm; Jan–March & Dec daily 9.30am–4.30pm; ¥300, or ¥510 with the Denshōkan), at the top end of the street, houses a small but decent collection of traditional Japanese art. Heading south again, the **Denshōkan** (daily 9am–4.30/5pm; ¥300, or ¥510 with the Hirafuku Memorial Art Museum) occupies a more attractive red-brick building. This museum of Satake-clan treasures also doubles as a training school for *kaba-zaiku*, the local craft in which boxes, tables and tea caddies are coated with a thin veneer of cherry bark. Developed in the late eighteenth century to supplement the income of impoverished samurai, *kaba-zaiku* is now Kakunodate's trademark souvenir. If you prefer your bark still on the trees, turn right outside the Denshōkan, where there's a two-kilometre tunnel of cherries along the Hinokinai-gawa embankment.

Practicalities

Kakunodate is best reached by train from either Akita or Morioka. The **station** lies on the southeast side of town, where you will also find the **tourist information centre** (daily 9am–5.30/6pm; ☎0187/54-2700, ℻54-1755) in a *kura*-style building to the right as you exit the station. If you're short of time, you can **rent bikes** at the Hanaba Taxi office directly opposite the station concourse on the road into town (¥300 per hour; 9am–4.30pm).

It's best to **stay** in one of Kakunodate's traditional ryokan. Most inns prefer you stay *sudomari*, or without meals, as part of the city's drive to have tourists eat out. Two possibilities are the simple but comfy *Ōmiya Ryokan* (☎0187/54-2040; ④) and *Takahashi Ryokan* (☎ & ℻0187/53-2659; ⑥ including meals), four blocks north of *Hyakusui-en* (see below). More upmarket is the *Ishikawa Ryokan* (☎0187/54-2030, ℻54-2031; ⑥ including meals), which offers comfortable tatami rooms, some en suite. The newly built *Tamachi Bukeyashiki Hotel* (☎0187/52-1700, ✉tbhotel@hana.or.jp; ⑦) is housed in a stunning Meiji-style building and provides both Western- and Japanese-style rooms; it's two blocks east of *Hyakusui-en* (see below). For Western-style accommodation, the recently built *Folklore Kakunodate* (☎0187/53-2070, ℻53-2118; ⑤) is right beside the station; rates include a basic breakfast.

In the samurai quarter, the Aoyagi house (see below) has a decent **restaurant** (daily 10.30am–4pm) serving *inaniwa udon*, long, slippery noodles in a thin soup of mushrooms, onion and bamboo shoots. Alternatively, try the noodles at *Kosendō* (daily 10.30am–4.30pm), set in an old schoolhouse also in the samurai quarter. In the centre of town, *Inaho* (Mon–Thurs & Sun 11.30am–4pm, Sat 11.30am–7pm) and the more casual *Murasaki* (daily 11am–2pm & 5–10pm) offer daily set menus at reasonable prices; they're both down a side street to the north of the main station road, one block before the Akita Bank – *Inaho* is upstairs in the corner building, while *Murasaki* is further down, around the bend in the street. The hundred-year-old *Hyakusui-en* (lunch daily 10.30am–4pm, dinner by appointment only; courses start from ¥6500) is popular for its English-speaking owner and hearty meals. The restaurant is ten minutes' walk from the station in the old merchants' quarter: head straight ahead from the station to the T-junction and turn left – it's in a black *kura* just past the post office.

Nyūtō Onsen

Northeast of Tazawa-ko, on the southeastern fringes of the Towada Hachimantai National Park, are numerous ski resorts and a hot-spring mecca, **Nyūtō Onsen**. This is made up of seven different onsen and adjoining ryokan, the most famous and quaint being the **Tsurunoyu Onsen** (☎0187/46-2139, ℻46-2761; ⑤–⑥ with two meals, or ¥400 just to take a bath), a 350-year-old establishment housing eight separate baths and three rotemburo, each fed by a different source; the basic tatami rooms come with a small *irori* or fire pit. There are more spacious rooms at Tsurunoyu's newish sister property, the *Yamanoyado Inn* (☎0187/46-2100; ⑦), a little further back down the road. It's a fifteen-minute walk from Nyūtō Onsen to **Kaniba Onsen** (☎0187/46-2021; ④–⑤, or ¥400 for bath only), whose rotemburo nestles quietly next to a small brook and forest – an ideal place to get rid of travelling stress – while the well-kept tatami rooms look out onto the surrounding woods, with some adjoining the wrap-around verandah.

The nearest train station for Nyūtō Onsen is Tazawako, 20km northeast of Kakunodate on the Shinkansen line between Morioka (29min; ¥1980) and Akita (56min; ¥3280). From the station, take a bus going towards the Tazawa Kōgen Ski-jō (every 70–90min) and get off at the Tazawa Kōgen Onsen bus stop, a journey of 50 minutes. Call *Tsurunoyu* or *Kaniba Onsen* beforehand, and someone will pick you up at the Tazawa Kōgen Onsen bus stop. If you're not staying for the night (most baths are open to the public 8am–6pm), take the bus to the Tsurunoyu-iriguchi stop and walk 5km to the onsen.

Dewa-sanzan and around

For more than one thousand years, pilgrims have been trekking up the slopes of **Dewa-sanzan** (or, simply, Dewa-san), one of Japan's most sacred mountains. It's an arduous rather than difficult climb, which takes in ancient cedar woods, alpine meadows and three intriguing shrines where *yamabushi* (mountain ascetics) continue to practise their secret rites. It's best to visit Dewa-san in summer (July to late Sept), when all three shrines are open, but at any time of year you'll find white-clothed pilgrims climbing the well-worn steps to the outer shrine on the summit of **Haguro-san**. From here the path follows the ridge to **Gassan**, the highest peak, before finally descending to the outer shrine, **Yudono-jinja**, an ochre-yellow rock washed by a hot spring. Though it's possible to complete the circuit in a long day, it's more enjoyable to spread it over two or three days and spend a couple of nights in the *shukubō* (temple lodgings) scattered over the mountain or in the village of **Haguro-machi**, the traditional start of the pilgrimage. Alternatively, **Tsuruoka** town, a short bus ride to the northwest, provides a convenient base and has a few moderately interesting historical sights of its own.

Dewa-sanzan and around

Dewa-sanzan	*Dewa-sanzan*	出羽三山
Chūren-ji	*Chūren-ji*	注蓮寺
Dainichibō	*Dainichibō*	大日坊
Gassan	*Gassan*	月山
Haguro Centre	*Haguro Sentā*	羽黒センター
Haguro-machi	*Haguro-machi*	羽黒町
Haguro-san	*Haguro-san*	羽黒山
Ideha Bunka Kinenkan	*Ideha Bunka Kinenkan*	いでは文化記念館
Ōami	*Ōami*	大網
Yudono-san	*Yudono-san*	湯殿神社
Yudono-jinja	*Yudono-jinja*	湯殿山

Accommodation		
Okuibō	*Okuibō*	奥井坊
Ōrimbō	*Ōrimbō*	桜林坊
Saikan	*Saikan*	斎館
Sankō-in	*Sankō-in*	三光院
Sanrōjo	*Sanrōjo*	参籠所

Tsuruoka	*Tsuruoka*	鶴岡
Chidō Hakubutsukan	*Chidō Hakubutsukan*	致道博物館
Chidō-kan	*Chidō-kan*	致道館
Togashi Rōsoku-ten	*Togashi Rōsoku-ten*	富樫ろうそく店
Tsuruoka-shi Bussan-kan	*Tsuruoka-shi Bussan-kan*	鶴岡市物産館

Accommodation and restaurants		
Dai-ichi Hotel	*Dai-ichi Hoteru*	第一ホテル
Narakan	*Narakan*	奈良館
Sanmai-an	*Sanmai-an*	山昧庵
Sannō Plaza	*Sannō Puraza*	山王プラザ
Takisui-tei	*Takisui-tei*	滝水亭
Tsuruoka Hotel	*Tsuruoka Hoteru*	鶴岡ホテル
Tsuruoka Youth Hostel	*Tsuruoka Youth Hostel*	つるおかユースホステル
Washington Hotel	*Washinton Hoteru*	ワシントンホテル

Tsuruoka

A former castle-town with a handful of attractive, willow-lined streets in its old centre, **TSURUOKA** is mainly useful as a staging post on the pilgrimage to Dewa-san. Its few sights are located in and around **Tsuruoka-kōen**, the site of the castle, and include an eclectic local museum and an unusual Edo-period school for samurai.

The old centre of Tsuruoka lies on the banks of the Uchi-gawa, some 2km southwest of the recently developed station, which is now surrounded by hotels, department stores and bus terminals. It takes about twenty minutes to walk from the station, along the river part of the way, to reach Tsuruoka-kōen. En route, look out for the virginal-white, wooden **Catholic church**, built by French missionaries in 1903; it houses a black Madonna and child as well as several faded stained-glass windows.

Tsuruoka's prime sight, the **Chidō Hakubutsukan** (Tues–Sun 9am–5pm; ¥700), lies on the southwest corner of the park in what was once a retirement home for lords of the ruling Sakai clan; buses from the station drop you right outside at the Chidō Hakubutsukan-mae stop. The compound now contains a number of striking buildings, kicking off with the **Nishitagawa District Office**, built in 1881 in Western style. The **Goinden**, the lords' residence, was constructed only two decades earlier but to a classic Japanese design, and now houses a few Sakai family heirlooms as well as a beautiful collection of bamboo fishing rods made by trainee samurai. Local folk culture is well represented in a massive thatched farmhouse and in a new building packed with old fishing tackle, sake barrels, lacquerware and huge wooden mortars. Look out, as well, for the intricate *bandori* backpacks used to cushion heavy loads; when worn, these woven, straw pads with their protruding shoulder straps are said to resemble flying squirrels (*bandori*).

Walking back along the south side of Tsuruoka-kōen, you'll pass another beautifully preserved Western-style building, the **Taishōkan**, built in 1915 as an assembly hall. It now houses a missable museum of local luminaries, but the **Chidō-kan** (Tues–Sun 9am–4.30pm; free), a little further along on the right-hand side, is worth a quick stop. This Confucian school was founded in 1805 by the ninth Sakai lord, who wanted to restore order among his restless clan and educate young samurai. They progressed to the next grade on merit alone; some students were 30 years old. Inside there are still a few of the original buildings, including a shrine to Confucius and the main auditorium, where you can see the old textbooks and printing blocks as well as some marvellous photos of the school when it was still in use.

In the next block east, the **Tsuruoka-shi Bussan-kan** shop (daily 9am–6pm) showcases a range of local produce, from aubergine pickles and Gas-san wine to painted candles and other crafts. You can see more of these somewhat expensive tapering candles on the way back to the station at **Togashi Rōsoku-ten** (closed first & third Sun each month), a 300-year-old shop. Alternatively, try painting one (¥1500) on the second floor of the **Shōnai Centre** opposite the station, where there's also a crafts centre and souvenir shops.

Practicalities

Tsuruoka's **train station** is located on the northeast side of town, while the Shōkō Mall **bus centre** lies a few minutes' walk west along the tracks under the *Dai-ichi Hotel*. Most buses also stop outside the station, including limousine buses serving the local **Shōnai Airport** (30min; ¥740). However, note that some long-distance buses start from outside the *Dai-ichi Hotel*. The town's **information office** (daily 9.30am–5/5.30pm; ☎0235/25-7678, ⓦwww.city .tsuruoka.yamagata.jp) is to the right as you exit the station building. You can pick up a **bicycle** for the day free of charge here. **Car rental** is available at Eki Rent-a-Car (☎0235/24-2670), next to the information office, or at the airport's Nissan Rentals (☎0234/92-3894).

For somewhere convenient to **stay** near the station, the *Washington Hotel* (☎0235/25-0111, ⓦwww.wh-rsv.com/english/tsuruoka/index.html; ❺), right opposite, has cheerful rooms with bathroom, TV and phone, though it fills up quickly with business travellers midweek. The friendly *Narakan* (☎0235/22-1202, ☏24-3548; ❺) has good-value tatami rooms and meals available on request; it's a five-minute walk south from the station along the main road, just after the second set of lights. If they're full, try the basic *Sannō Plaza* (☎0235/22-6501; ❹–❺), a white, seven-storey building tucked in the backstreets another five minutes further into town. Another possibility is the Meiji-era *Tsuruoka Hotel* (☎0235/22-1135, ☏23-1153; ❻ including two meals), a bit worn at the edges but offering lots of atmosphere; the hotel is near the Uchikawa-dōri bus stop, just across the river from Tsuruoka-kōen. The owner reads English much better than he speaks it, and so prefers requests for reservations by fax. The *Tsuruoka Youth Hostel* (☎ & ☏0235/73-3205, ⓦwww.jyh.or.jp, dorm beds ¥2500 per person) is a fifteen-minute walk from

Mirai Station, three stops out of town on the local line. It's off the beaten track, but if you're hanging out for some macrobiotic vegetarian fare, 1950s jazz and a day off from your travels, the young owner will be sure to welcome you. Ask for directions to the hostel (and a map) at the tourist office in Tsuruoka before you set out, as it can be hard to find, particularly at night. If you do stay at the hostel, be sure to visit the nearly overgrown temple complex immediately inland on the road back to the station.

For **places to eat** in Tsuruoka proper, try the decent udon restaurant, the *Sanmai-an*, beside the Chidō Hakubutsukan. Closer to the station, the *Takisui-tei*, on the second floor of the Shōnai Centre, is a simple place with a plastic-food display and a good range of meals from ¥1000. The restaurant's speciality, a simple but delicious cold buckwheat noodle dish called *mugikiri*, is highly recommended.

Dewa-sanzan

A lumpy extinct volcano, **Dewa-sanzan** faces the Sea of Japan across the famously prolific rice fields of the Shōnai plain. Many people take the road up its first peak, **Haguro-san** (414m), but it's well worth slogging up the 2446 stone steps, among venerable cedars, to reach the impressive, thatch-roofed **Gosaiden**, which enshrines the mountain's three deities. Dewa-san's middle shrine perches atop **Gas-san** (1984m), with spectacular views in clear weather, though otherwise it's the least interesting of the three. So if time is short, you might want to skip round by road to **Yudono-jinja**, visiting a couple of rather grisly mummified monks en route.

Today Dewa-san and its three shrines fall under the Shinto banner, but the mountain was originally home to one of the colourful offshoots of Esoteric Buddhism, later unified as **Shugendō** (see "Contexts", p.956). The worship of Dewa-san dates from the seventh century, when an imperial prince fled to this area following the death of his father. In a vision, a three-legged crow led him to Haguro-san (Black Wing Mountain), where he lived to the ripe old age of 90, developing his unique blend of Shinto, Buddhism and ancient folk religion. Later the **yamabushi**, the sect's itinerant mountain priests (literally "the ones who sleep in the mountains"), became famous for their mystic powers and their extreme asceticism – one route to enlightenment consisted of living in caves off a diet of nuts and wild garlic. Though once fairly widespread, the sect dwindled after the mid-nineteenth century, when Shinto reclaimed Japanese mountains for its own. Nevertheless, you'll still find a flourishing community of *yamabushi* around Dewa-san, kitted out in their natty checked jackets, white knickerbockers and tiny, black pillbox hats. They also carry a huge conch-shell horn whose haunting cry summons the gods.

The best time to see *yamabushi* in action is in Haguro-machi's *shukubō* (see p.336) and during the various **festivals**. The biggest annual bash is the Hassaku Matsuri (Aug 24–31), when pilgrims take part in a fire festival on Haguro-san to ensure a bountiful harvest. At New Year Haguro-san is also the venue for a festival of purification, known as the Shōreisai, which combines fire and acrobatic dancing with ascetic rituals.

Practicalities

There are various ways of tackling Dewa-san, depending on the time of year and how much walking you want to do. The recommended **route**, described on p.337, involves climbing Haguro-san on the first day and then continuing via Gas-san to Yudono-jinja on the second. From there you can either head straight back to Tsuruoka or overnight in a *shukubō* and visit the Ōami temples the next day. However, note that Gassan-jinja and Yudono-jinja are only open in summer (July to mid-Sept & May–Oct); the path itself stays open longer, depending on the weather.

Two **bus services** run from Tsuruoka: one via Haguro-machi to the Haguro-sanchō stop at the top of Haguro-san, with onward services to Gassan Hachigōme (see opposite) in summer only (July–Sept); the second operates between May and early November, looping round from Tsuruoka to Yudono-jinja. These services are few and far between, so make sure you pick up a map and timetable at Tsuruoka's **information centre** (see p.334 for details), where they can also help book accommodation. In Haguro-machi, the **Haguro Centre** (24hr; ☎0235/62-2260) is primarily a **taxi** service, but they also stock some English-language information and can assist in finding accommodation.

If possible, try to spend at least one night at a **shukubō** (temple lodgings) while visiting Dewa-san. There are at least thirty in Haguro-machi's Tōge district, including a number of traditional thatched-roof inns, each run by a *yamabushi*; you may well be invited to attend a prayer service, involving a lot of conch-blowing and a ritual fire. Prices don't vary much and they all serve the exquisite *shōjin-ryōri* (Buddhist vegetarian cuisine) favoured by *yamabushi*. In Haguro-machi, *Sankō-in* (☎0235/62-2302; ●) is a lovely old thatched place near the Haguro Centre, or try nearby *Ōrimbō* (☎0235/62-2322; ●), also thatched, or the newer *Okuibō* (☎0235/62-2283; ●), further down the road. If you have problems booking directly, the Haguro Town Office (☎0235/62-2111, ℱ62-3755) may be able to assist.

There are also a couple of useful *shukubō* on Haguro-san itself and near Yudono-jinja. The former, *Saikan* (☎0235/62-2357, ℱ62-2352; ● including meals), is an impressive old building with great views over the Shōnai plain, while the newer *Sanrōjo* (☎0235/54-6131, ℱ54-6134; ● including meals; June–Oct only) occupies a wonderful setting beside the Yudono-jinja bus terminal. Both these places also serve excellent vegetarian lunches to non residents (from ¥1500; reservations recommended).

Haguro-san

Regular buses from Tsuruoka (every 40min; 40min; ¥660) serve the village of **HAGURO-MACHI** at the beginning of the mountain trail; get off at the Haguro Centre stop, just where the road kinks left to the start of the path up the mountain. Before heading off along the track, **Ideha Bunka Kinenkan** (daily except Tues 8.30am–5pm; ¥400), a little further along the main road, is worth a look if you're interested in the *yamabushi*. This oddly high-tech museum contains examples of *yamabushi* clothes and foodstuffs, as well as holograms of various rituals. The Ideha centre also runs three-day taster courses (¥26,000) for would-be *yamabushi* in which you get to stand under waterfalls, leap over fires and take part in a pilgrimage – though not for the faint-hearted, these are a breeze compared to the genuine nine-day initiation.

A weather-beaten, red-lacquered gate marks the start of the **Haguro-san trail** (1.7km; roughly 1hr), which consists of three long staircases built by a monk in the early seventeenth century. The first stretch is a deceptively gentle amble beside a river, where pilgrims purify themselves, among stately cedar trees. Most of these cedars are between 300 and 500 years old but the oldest, a massive tree girded by a sacred rope, is reputed to be at least 1400 years old. After passing a magnificent five-storey pagoda, last rebuilt in the fourteenth century, it's uphill all the way, past a little **teashop** (late April to early Nov daily

8.30am–5pm) with superb views, until a large red *torii* indicates you've made it. If you're staying at the *Saikan shukubō* (see below), it's on the left at the end of a mossy path just before you duck under the *torii*.

The shrine compound contains a collection of unmistakeably Buddhist buildings. At the centre stands a monumental vermilion hall, the **Gosaiden**, where the mountain's three deities are enshrined behind gilded doors under an immaculate thatch. In front of the hall, the lily-covered **Kagami-ike** is said to mirror the spirits of the gods. However, it's probably more famous for its treasure trove of over five hundred antique polished-metal hand mirrors; in the days before women were allowed onto Dewa-san, their male relatives would consign one of their mirrors into the pond. The best of these are now on display in the shrine **museum** (daily 9am–4/4.30pm; ¥200). There's also a useful relief map of Dewa-san here.

Follow the paved road exiting the compound's south side and you'll find the Haguro-sanchō bus stop among restaurants and souvenir shops. Buses depart from here for Tsuruoka (6–12 daily; 50min) via Haguro-machi (10min), and also to Gas-san Hachigōme (see below); alternatively, it's a forty-minute walk further south – take the footpath rather than the road – to the Kyūka-mura stop beside Gas-san Visitor Centre, where you can also pick up buses to Gassan (see below).

Gas-san and Yudono-jinja

It's a long twenty-kilometre hike along the ridge from Haguro-san to **Gas-san**, so it really is worth taking a bus as far as the "Eighth Station", Gas-san Hachigōme. In summer (July–Sept) there are buses from Tsuruoka (2–3 daily; 1hr 30min) via Haguro-machi and Kyūka-mura, or you can take a bus from Haguro-sanchō (see opposite; 1–2 daily; 50min). Even from the Eighth Station it takes over two hours to cover the final 5km along the ridge to Gas-san (1900m), though it's a beautiful walk across the marshy Mida-ga-hara meadows, renowned for their profusion of rare alpine plants in late June.

The final few metres are a bit of a scramble onto the rocky peak, where **Gassan-jinja** (July to mid-Sept daily 6am–5pm; ¥500) huddles behind stout stone walls. There's not a lot to the shrine, but you need to be purified before venturing inside; bow your head while a priest waves his paper wand over you and chants a quick prayer; then rub the paper cut-out person (which he gives you) over your head and shoulders before placing it in the water.

From Gas-san, the trail drops more steeply to **Yudono-jinja** (May–Oct daily 6am–5pm; ¥500), located in a narrow valley on the mountain's west flank (9km). For the final descent you have to negotiate a series of iron ladders strapped to the valleyside where the path has been washed away. Once at the river it's only a short walk to the inner sanctum of Dewa-san, which occupies another walled area. Inside, take off your shoes and socks before receiving another purification, and then enter the second compound; note that photography is forbidden. Having bowed to the steaming orange boulder, you can then haul yourself over it using ropes to another little shrine on the far side. It's then just a ten-minute trot down the road to the Yudono-san bus stop, where the *Sanrōjo shukubō* (see opposite) occupies a black-and-white building beside the *torii*.

If you're arriving at Yudono-san by road, shuttle buses wait by the *torii* to take you up to Yudono-jinja (5min; ¥100), or it's a steepish, twenty-minute walk. From May to early November you can get here by local bus from Tsuruoka (2–4 daily; 1hr 20min; ¥1480).

Dainichibō and Chūren-ji

On the way back to Tsuruoka from Yudono-jinja, the hamlet of **ŌAMI** is worth a stop for its two "living Buddhas", the naturally mummified bodies of ascetic Buddhist monks who starved themselves to death. The mummies, or *miira*, are on display in two competing temples on either side of Ōami, each a few minutes' walk from where the bus drops you next to the village store; all buses from Yudono-san to Tsuruoka (see p.337) stop at Ōami (30min; ¥780).

Dainichibō (daily 8am–5pm; ¥500) is the more accessible of the two temples on the east side of the village; from the bus stop, follow red signs of a little bowing monk to take a left in front of the post office and past a school; you'll see the temple's colourful flags after about ten minutes. The temple was supposedly founded in 807 AD by Kōbō Daishi – after a brief purification ceremony and introductory talk, the head priest will show you the hard-working saint's staff, a handprint of Tokugawa Ieyasu and other temple treasures, before taking you to the mummy. The tiny figure sits slumped on an altar, dressed in rich, red brocades from which his hands and skull protrude, sheathed in a dark, glossy, parchment-thin layer of skin. He's said to have died in 1782 at the age of 96, which is quite extraordinary when you learn that he lived on a diet of nuts, seeds and water. As the end drew closer, the monk took himself off to a cave to meditate and eventually stopped eating all together. Finally he was buried alive with a breathing straw until he expired completely. Apparently this road to enlightenment was not uncommon prior to the nineteenth century, when the practice was banned.

Though it's a bit further to walk (2km), **Chūren-ji** (daily 8am–5pm; ¥500) is slightly less commercialized and more atmospheric. To reach the temple, head north from the bus stop on a country road. There are signs at every junction except one, where you need to take the left fork past a graveyard. Again, you receive a short talk and a purification ceremony, before entering the side hall, where the *miira* rests in a glass case. Another grimacing, walnut-brown figure swathed in red and gold, this little fellow reached Buddha-hood in 1829, aged 62 years.

Niigata

Most visitors to **NIIGATA**, the largest port-city on the Sea of Japan coast, are either on their way to Sado-ga-shima (see p.342 or making use of the ferry and air connections to Korea, China and Russia. It's a likeable but unexciting city, sitting on the banks of Shinano-gawa, with few specific sights beyond a well-presented local history museum. In 1964 a tidal wave devastated much of east Niigata, though the area on the west side of the river retains some attractive streets of older houses.

If you're travelling by Shinkansen from Tokyo, make sure you appreciate the journey. Completed in only 1982, this line took eleven years to build at a cost of ¥1.7 trillion – a staggering ¥6 billion per kilometre – making it the most expensive track in the world and throwing the whole of Japan's national railways into debt. More than one-third of the journey is through tunnels and the train takes a most bizarre route, stopping in one-horse villages where the station is the biggest thing around. All this was thanks to Tanaka Kakuei, the MP for Niigata who served briefly as prime minister (1972–74) and who almost single-handedly transformed Niigata from a backwater into a major industrial city – while also garnering a few votes and a substantial personal fortune along the way. For more about the notorious Tanaka and his role in Japanese politics, read *Shadow Shoguns* (see "Books", p.1013).

Arrival, information and city transport

Limousine buses connect the city's **airport** with the bus terminal at Niigata Station (1–2 hourly; 30min; ¥350), while ferries dock at one of three **ferry terminals** on the east bank of the Shinano-gawa. All three terminals are linked by local bus (15–30min; ¥180) to Niigata Station; alternatively, a taxi will cost around ¥1300. Most **express buses** use the Bandai City Bus Centre, about 500m northwest of Niigata Station, though some also stop outside the station. **Local buses** depart from the station terminal and may stop outside Bandai City depending on the route. Within the central district there's a flat fare of ¥170, which you pay on exit; on most buses you need to take a ticket as you enter.

Niigata is well provided with English-language maps and information, which you can pick up at the **"i" information centre** (daily 8.30am–5.15pm; ☎025/241-7914) outside the station's central (Bandai) exit. The English-speaking staff can also help with hotel reservations and ferry tickets to Sado. If you have more complicated language problems, the International Friendship Centre, 6-1211-5 Kamiōkawamae-dōri (☎025/225-2777), should be able to assist; they're located three blocks west of the Bandai Bridge.

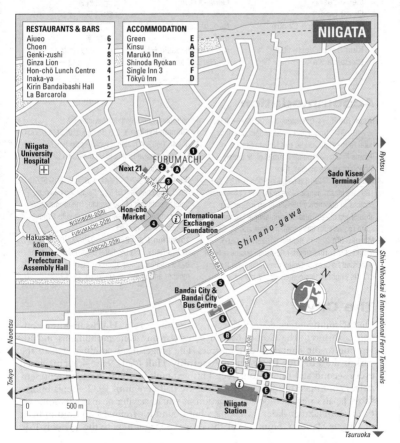

RESTAURANTS & BARS

Aiueo	6
Choen	7
Genki-zushi	8
Ginza Lion	3
Hon-chō Lunch Centre	4
Inaka-ya	1
Kirin Bandaibashi Hall	5
La Barcarola	2

ACCOMMODATION

Green	E
Kinsu	A
Marukō Inn	B
Shinoda Ryokan	C
Single Inn 3	F
Tōkyū Inn	D

NIIGATA

Niigata	*Niigata*	新潟
Furumachi	*Furumachi*	古町
Hakusan-kōen	*Hakusan-kōen*	白山公園
Hon-chō Market	*Hon-chō Ichiba*	本町市場
Northern Cultural Museum	*Kitakata Bunka Hakubutsukan*	北方文化博物館
Accommodation		
Green Hotel	*Guriin Hoteru*	グリーンホテル
Hotel Kinsu	*Hoteru Kinsu*	ホテル金寿
Marukō Inn	*Marukō In*	マルコーイン
Shinoda Ryokan	*Shinoda Ryokan*	篠田旅館
Single Inn 3	*Shinguru In 3*	シングルイン3
Tōkyū Inn	*Tōkyū In*	東急イン
Restaurants		
Aiueo	*Aiueo*	あいうえお
Chōen	*Chōen*	張園
Genki-zushi	*Genki-zushi*	元気寿司
Ginza Lion	*Ginza Raion*	銀座ライオン
Hon-chō Lunch Centre	*Ranchi Sentā Hon-chō*	ランチセンター本町
Inaka-ya	*Inaka-ya*	田舎家
Kirin Bandaibashi Hall	*Kirin Bandaibashi Hōru*	キリン万代橋ホール
La Barcarola	*Ra Barukarōra*	ラバルカローラ

Accommodation

Green Hotel 1-4-9 Hanazono ☎025/246-0341, ⨎246-0345. Bright and clean budget business hotel to the right as you exit Niigata Station. Rooms in the new building are slightly better, though most are singles. ❹

Hotel Kinsu 1429-8 Higashibori-dōri ☎025/229-1695, ✉kinsu@niigata-inet.or.jp. One of the best choices in downtown Niigata, in an interesting area of old streets and offering simple but fair-sized rooms with bathroom, minibar and TV. ❺

Marukō Inn 2-3-35 Benten ☎025/247-0505, ⨎243-3341. This smart, mid-range business hotel is located halfway between the station and Bandai City. Its bright rooms come with TV, phone and bathroom, some with kitchenette. ❺

Shinoda Ryokan 1-2-8 Benten ☎025/245-5501, ⨎244-0902. A nice old ryokan past the *Tōkyū Inn*. More expensive rooms have their own bathroom. ❻ including two meals.

Single Inn 3 2-2-23 Hanazono ☎ & ⨎025/243-3900. The cheapest of four *Single Inn* business hotels northwest of the station. The rooms are boxy but nicely done, and all come with TV and en-suite bathroom. ❹

Tōkyū Inn 1-2-4 Benten ☎025/243-0109, ⨎243-0401. This big hotel opposite the station has a range of good-sized en-suite rooms, with TV, minibar and phone as standard. ❺–❻

The City

On the southwestern edge of the city centre, the park of **Hakusan-kōen** contains a shrine to the God of Marriage and various stone monuments, including one to the happiness of pine trees. The gingerbread building next to the park is the **Former Prefectural Assembly Hall** (daily 9am–4.30pm, closed every second and third Mon; free). This was built in 1883, and local representatives continued to meet in the impressive hall here until 1932 – sepia photos show Japan's new democracy in action. If you're staying near the station, you can reach Hakusan-kōen by taking a bus bound for Irefune-chō from in front of Niigata Station (15min; ¥170); this drops you right next to the assembly hall.

From the assembly hall, either get back on a passing Irefune-chō bus or walk northwest along Nishibori-dōri for 1km to reach the landmark **Next 21** building; head up to the nineteenth-floor observation lounge for a free view of the city. Despite competition from Bandai City, this area, known as **Furumachi**, remains Niigata's foremost shopping district, though you'll still find some older buildings hidden away in the backstreets. Another relic of the past is the bustling **Hon-chō Market** (daily 10am–5pm; closed three days a month, usually on Sun), which spreads over a few streets to the south of Masaya-kōji. This fresh-produce market, where you can still bargain, is a prime place to look for cheap places to eat (see below).

The fertile plains around Niigata supported a number of wealthy landowners who lived in considerable luxury until the Land Reform Act of 1946 forced them to sell all rice land above 7.5 acres per household. One such was the Itō family, whose superb mansion, now the centrepiece of the **Northern Cultural Museum** (daily 9am–4.30/5pm; ¥700), is the largest and most accessible of several such houses around Niigata. The huge house was erected in 1887 and comprises sixty rooms containing family heirlooms, but the classic garden steals the show – viewed from inside, it forms a magnificent frieze along one side of the principal guest room. The museum is located in Yokogoshi village, 12km southeast of the city centre, and can be reached by express bus from Bandai City or the Eki-mae terminal by Niigata Station (4 daily; ¥500 one way, or ¥1570 return including entry ticket); the last bus back leaves at 3.40pm.

Eating and drinking

Niigata is famous for its fresh fish and fragrant rice, which means excellent sushi. Glutinous rice is used to make *sasa-dango*, a sweet snack of bean paste and rice wrapped in bamboo leaves, while in wintertime *noppe* combines taro root, ginkgo nuts, salmon roe and vegetables in a colourful stew. There are numerous **restaurants** and bars in the streets near the station and around Furumachi.

Aiueo 4F, Bandai Ciné Mall, 1-3-1 Bandai. Popular, rustic *izakaya* where English speakers are usually on hand to help out with the menu. Reasonable prices. Daily 4.30pm–midnight (Sat until 2am).

Choen (also know as *Harbin*) 1-6-2 Higashi-ōdōri. Cheap and cheerful Chinese restaurant serving good-value lunch sets from ¥700 and menus from ¥2000. Closed third Mon of the month.

Genki-zushi Hanazono. This spick-and-span sushi bar has a picture menu and prices from ¥105 per plate (two pieces). Look for the scowling-face logo.

Ginza Lion NTT Plaza, 7-1017 Higashibori-dōri. A branch of the famous Tokyo beer hall serving standard bar food, including sausages, fries and salads.

Hon-chō Lunch Centre 5-248 Honchō-dōri. In the midst of the Hon-chō street market, this friendly little cafeteria offers a huge range of sta-

ple dishes, including sushi, curry-rice, ramen and soba dishes. Some English spoken. Mon–Fri open until 8pm, Sat & Sun until 4pm.

Inaka-ya 1457 9-chome, Furumachi-dōri. *Wappa-meshi* (steamed rice with various toppings) is the order of the day at this unpretentious locals' restaurant. From ¥600, or ¥1100 for set meals.

Kirin Bandaibashi Hall 2-4-28 Bandai. Be prepared to queue at this big and imaginatively designed beer hall overlooking the Bandai Bridge. Eclectic menu. Evenings only.

La Barcarola 7-920 Nishiborimae-dōri. It's hard to resist the smell of pizzas cooking at this relaxed Italian place in Furumachi. The excellent lunchtime deals (Mon–Sat 11.30am–1.30pm) include a choice of pasta, pizza or paella, salad and free coffee refills for ¥720. Closed Wed.

Listings

Airlines ANA ☎0120-029222; JAL ☎0120-255931; J Air ☎0120-255971; JAS ☎0120-511283; Korean Air ☎025/244-3311; Kyokushin Air ☎025/273-0312; New China Airlines ☎025/275-4352.

Airport information ☎025/275-2633, ⊛www.niigata-airport.gr.jp.
Banks and exchange You'll find foreign exchange banks near the station on Akashi-dōri and along Masaya-kōji on the west side of the river.

Bookshops Kinokuniya, on the second floor of the Alta department store in the Bandai City complex, has Niigata's best selection of foreign-language books.

Car rental Around the station, try Eki Rent-a-Car ☎025/245-4292; Nippon ☎025/245-3221; Nissan ☎025/243-5523; or Toyota ☎025/245-0100.

Ferries Sado Kisen (☎025/245-1234) operates ferries and jetfoil services to Ryōtsu (Sado) from the Sado Kisen Terminal, reached by local bus from Niigata Station (15min). Ferries to Otaru (Hokkaidō) are run by Shin-Nihonkai Ferry (☎025/273-2171) and leave from the Shin-Nihonkai Ferry Terminal; take a bus from the station for Rinkō Nichōme and get off at the Suehiro-

bashi stop (20min).

Hospitals The two largest city-centre hospitals are Niigata University Hospital, 1-754 Asahimachi-dōri (☎025/227-2662), and Niigata City General Hospital, 2-6-1 Shichikuyama (☎025/241-5151).

Internet access CD Garden, 2F, Garesso Building, to the right of the Bandai exit of the JR Niigata station, has a busy Internet corner among the CD stacks (daily 10am–9pm; ¥100 per 30min).

Post office Niigata Central Post Office, 2-6-26 Higashi-ōdōri, is located a few minutes' walk north of the station and has a poste restante service.

Taxis Fuji ☎025/244-5166; Hato ☎025/287-1121; Miyakō ☎025/222-0611; Tōshin Taxi ☎025/245-6131.

Sado-ga-shima

For centuries, the rugged, S-shaped island of **Sado-ga-shima** was a place of exile for criminals and political undesirables, and even today it has a unique atmosphere, born of its isolation and a distinct cultural heritage encompassing haunting folk songs, Nō theatre and puppetry, as well as the more recently established Kodô drummers. It's a deceptively large island, consisting of two parallel mountain chains linked by a fertile central plain which shelters most of Sado's historical relics. These include several important **temples**, such as Kompon-ji, founded by the exiled Buddhist monk Nichiren, and a couple of bizarre, high-tech **museums** where robots perform Nō plays and narrate local history. The Edo-period gold mines of **Aikawa**, on Sado's northwest coast, make another interesting excursion, but the island's greatest attractions are really its scenery and glimpses of an older Japan, free of *McDonald's*, the Internet and the other clutter of modern life. Travelling by public bus it takes at least three days to cover the main areas, so it's well worth considering car rental or an organized tour round the more inaccessible regions.

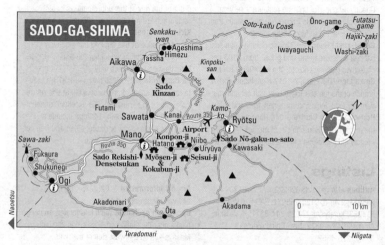

Sado-ga-shima	*Sado-ga-shima*	佐渡ヶ島
Ryōtsu	*Ryōtsu*	両津
Kagetsu Hotel	*Kagetsu Hoteru*	花月ホテル
Komozawa	*Komozawa*	こもざわ
Ryōtsu ferry terminal	*Ryōtsu futō*	両津埠頭
Sado Nō-gaku-no-sato	*Sado Nō-gaku-no-sato*	佐渡能楽の里
Sado Seaside Hotel	*Sado Shiisaido Hoteru*	佐渡シーサイドホテル
Tenkuni	*Tenkuni*	天国
Tōkyō-an	*Tōkyō-an*	東京庵
Yoshidaya	*Yoshidaya*	吉田家
Sawata	*Sawata*	佐和田
Green Village Youth Hostel	*Guriin Virejji Yūsu Hosuteru*	グリーンヴィレッヂユースホステル
Kokubun-ji	*Kokubun-ji*	国分寺
Kompon-ji	*Kompon-ji*	根本寺
Mano	*Mano*	真野
Myōsen-ji	*Myōsen-ji*	妙宣寺
Niibo	*Niibo*	新穂
Sado Rekishi-Densetsukan	*Sado Rekishi-Densetsukan*	佐渡歴史伝説館
Seisui-ji	*Seisui-ji*	清水寺
Silver Village	*Shirubā Birejji*	シルバービレッジ
Urashima Ryokan	*Urashima Ryokan*	浦島
Ogi	*Ogi*	小木
Gonzaya Ryokan	*Gonzaya Ryokan*	ごんざや旅館
Iwaya	*Iwaya*	岩屋
Hotel New Kihachiya	*Hoteru Nyū Kihachiya*	ホテルニュー喜八屋
Minshuku Sakaya	*Minshuku Sakaya*	民宿さかや
Ogi Sakuma-sō Youth Hostel	*Ogi Sakuma-sō Yūsu Hosuteru*	小木佐久間荘ユースホステル
Sakae-zushi	*Sakae-zushi*	栄寿司
Shukunegi	*Shukunegi*	宿根木
Shichiemon	*Sichiemon*	七右衛門
Aikawa	*Aikawa*	相川
Ageshima-yūen	*Ageshima-yūen*	揚島遊園
Dōyū Ryokan	*Dōyū Ryokan*	道遊旅館
Iwayaguchi	*Iwayaguchi*	岩谷口
Kokuminshukusha Senkaku-sō	*Kokuminshukusha Senkaku-sō*	国民宿舎尖閣荘
Hotel Ōsado	*Hoteru Ōsado*	ホテル大佐渡
Sado Belle Mer Youth Hostel	*Sado Beru Mēru Yūsu Hosuteru*	佐渡ベルメールユースホステル
Sado Fishers Hotel	*Sado Fisshâzu Hoteru*	佐渡フィッシャーズ
Sado Kinzan	*Sado Kinzan*	佐渡金山
Sado Royal Hotel Manchō	*Sado Roiyaru Hoteru Manchō*	佐渡ロイヤルホテル万長
Soto-kaifu Youth Hostel	*Soto-kaifu Yūsu Hosuteru*	外海府ユースホステル
Tassha	*Tassha*	達者
Akadomari	*Akadomari*	赤泊

Sado has a packed calendar of **festivals** from April to November. Many of these involve *okesa* folk songs and the devil-drumming known as *ondeko* (or *oni-daiko*), both of which are also performed nightly during the tourist season in Ogi and Aikawa. Throughout June, Nō groups perform in shrines around the central plain, while the island's biggest event nowadays is the Kodô drummers' international "Earth Celebration", held in Ogi (see box, p.349). Sports fans may also be interested in attending or taking part in the island's international triathlon (Ⓦwww.sado.gr.jp), which has been going for over fifteen years; it's generally held in early September.

If you're spending much time on the island, take a copy of Angus Waycott's affectionate and informative travelogue, *Sado: Japan's Island in Exile*. It's also worth picking up a copy of the annually updated English tourist map published by MIJ International (Ⓦwww.mijintl.com), available free from the island's tourist offices.

Some history

Since before the twelfth century, Sado was viewed as a suitably remote place for former emperors, outspoken monks and out-of-favour actors, as well as more ordinary criminals. The most illustrious exile was the ex-emperor Juntoku (reigned 1211–21), who tried to wrest power back from the Kamakura and spent the last twenty years of his life on Sado. A few decades later, Nichiren, the founder of the eponymous Buddhist sect (see p.954), found himself on the island for a couple of years after 1271, where he wasted no time in erecting temples and converting the local populace. Finally, Zeami, a famous actor and playwright credited with formalizing Nō theatre, died here in 1443 after eight years in exile; though he had certainly fallen out of favour at court, the exact reasons for his banishment aren't clear.

In 1601, rich seams of gold and silver were discovered in the mountains above Aikawa. From then on, criminals were sent to work in the mines, supplemented by "homeless" workers from Edo (Tokyo), who dug some 400km of tunnels down to 600m below sea level – all by hand. In 1896 Mitsubishi took the mines over from the imperial household and today they're owned by the Sado Gold Mining Co., who continued to extract small quantities of gold up until 1989.

Island practicalities

The main gateway to Sado is **Ryōtsu** town, on the east coast, which has ferry and air connections with Niigata. Sado Kisen (Niigata ℡025/245-1234, Ryōtsu ℡0259/27-5111) operates car **ferries** (6–8 daily; 2hr 20min; from ¥2060) and jet-foil services (3–11 daily; 1hr; ¥5960 one way, or ¥10,730 five-day return ticket) from Niigata's Sado Kisen Terminal (see p.342 for details). Reservations are required for the jetfoil and recommended for all crossings in the high summer season. Light **aeroplanes** operated by Kyokushin Air (Niigata ℡025/273-0312, Ryōtsu ℡0259/23-5005) make the crossing from Niigata to Ryōtsu airport in 25 minutes (2–5 daily; ¥7350 one way, or ¥11,020 seven-day return), from where buses shuttle to Ryōtsu's bus station (15min; ¥240), underneath the ferry terminal.

Sado Kisen ferries also operate between **Naoetsu port**, south of Niigata (20min by bus from Naoetsu Station), and **Ogi** on the island's south coast (2–7 daily; 2hr 30min; fares as for Ryōtsu). Jetfoils also ply this route from April to late November (2 daily; 1hr; fares as for Ryōtsu). There's also a ferry service from Teradomari to **Akadomari** on the island's southeast coast (2–3 daily except Jan 24–Feb 11; 2hr; from ¥1420).

You'll find maps, bus timetables and other **information** at each of the ferry terminals, though it's worth arriving in Ryōtsu to make the most of their well-provisioned office and English-speaking staff before heading into the wilds.

As long as you allow plenty of time, it's possible to get around most of the island by **bus**, although in winter some services only operate at weekends, while others stop completely. Even at the best of times, a number of routes have only two or three buses per day, so make sure you carry a copy of the island's bus timetable (available in English). If you're visiting over a weekend take advantage of the ¥2000 ticket which covers all transport over any two-day period. If you get stuck, Sado islanders have a good reputation for picking up hitchhikers.

An easier option is to take a tour – there's an array of **tour buses** around the island, varying according to the season and which port you arrive at. The most interesting route is probably the "Okesa Course" (April–Nov; ¥4500 for half-day trip, ¥7000 for full day), which takes you on a scenic toll road over the northern mountains from Ryōtsu. Tickets are available from travel agents, in the ferry terminals or at the relevant bus stations; in summer it's a good idea to buy tickets in advance.

By far the most flexible option for exploring Sado is to **rent a car**. You'll find Sado Kisen Rent-a-car (☎0259/27-5195) at all three ferry terminals, while Nippon Rent-a-car (☎0259/23-4020) and Watanabe Sanshō Rent-a-car (☎0259/27-5705) also have offices on the island. A day's rental costs around ¥6000 for the smallest vehicle, and prices go up roughly ten percent in July and August. Nakao Cycle (☎0259/27-2907) in Ryōtsu's main shopping street rents out bikes for ¥1500 per day. You can also rent bikes in Mano and at some youth hostels (see individual accounts for details).

Ryōtsu and around

Sitting on a huge horseshoe bay with the mountains of Sado rising behind, **RYŌTSU** is an appealing little place and makes a good base for a night. The town revolves around its modern ferry pier and bus terminal, at the south end, while there's still a flavour of the original fishing community in the older back-streets to the north, among the rickety wooden houses with their coiled nets and fishy odours. Much of the town occupies a thin strip of land between the sea and a large saltwater lake, **Kamo-ko**, which is now used for oyster farming.

The **Sado Nō-gaku-no-sato** museum (daily 8.30am–5pm; ¥800), on the south shore of Kamo-ko lake, celebrates Sado's long association with Nō. Unfortunately there's nothing in English, but the masks and costumes are enjoyable, as is the short performance by remarkably life-like robots who are admirably suited to Nō's studied movements. To reach the museum, take a bus on the Minami-sen route (line #2) for Sawata and get off after ten minutes at the Nō-gaku-no-sato-mae stop.

Once you've seen the museum, wandered the old streets and taken a look at the lake, there's not much else to do in Ryōtsu except plan your onward journey.

Practicalities

The main Sado-ga-shima **tourist office** (daily 8.30am–6/7pm, Jan–April, Nov & Dec closed Sat afternoon and Sun; ☎0259/23-3300, ⓦwww.ryotsu.sado.jp) is located in a row of shops opposite the ferry terminal building. Since this is the one place on Sado where you can obtain some English-language assistance, it's a good idea to check your planned route and bus timetables while you can. Local buses and tours depart from the bus terminal under the ferry building, where you'll also find car rental agencies and taxis. There's a **post office** on the north side of the channel leading from the lake, near the middle bridge, and foreign-exchange **banks** further along this high street.

Though Ryōtsu has plenty of expensive resort **hotels**, there's little in the way of more affordable accommodation. Your best bet is the friendly *Sado Seaside Hotel* (T0259/27-7211, F27-7213; ❺), which offers rather worn tatami rooms – some en suite – but a warm welcome, good food and an onsen bath. The hotel is located on a pebbly strip of beach at the very southern end of Ryōtsu, 1.6km from the pier; if you phone from Niigata, they'll meet you off the ferry. In the centre of Ryōtsu, about ten minutes' walk north from the pier, the *Kagetsu Hotel* (T0259/27-3131, F23-4446; ❺) is a much smarter place, with elegant tatami rooms and a garden running down to the lake. Alternatively, try the larger *Yoshidaya* (T0259/27-2151, F23-4488; ❼) nearby. All these places have English-speaking staff and offer full-board deals.

Ryōtsu has a better choice of **restaurants**. One of the nicest is *Komazawa* (T0259/27-2075), upstairs next to the tourist office; it serves fine sashimi *teishoku* and fried crab set meals for around ¥1500. The friendly *Tōkyō-an*, on the main street two blocks north of the river, specializes in handmade soba, while *Tenkuni* dishes up moderately priced sashimi, tempura and *donburi* dishes – it's south of the river on the main road, then down the right fork between a school and a temple.

Central Sado

Sado's **central plain** is the most heavily populated part of the island and home to a number of impressive temples, some dating back to the eighth century. Two routes cross this plain linking Ryōtsu to towns on the west coast: the main highway cuts north of Kamo-ko and Sado airport to **Sawata**, served by buses on the Hon-sen route (line #1), while the quieter, southerly route takes you through **Niibo**, **Hatano** and **Mano** along the Minami-sen bus route (line #2). The majority of historical sights lie scattered across this southern district – for many of them you'll need your own transport or be prepared to walk a fair distance. One solution is to **rent a bike** either in Mano's information office or at the *Green Village Youth Hostel* (see opposite).

Sado's most accessible and important temple, **Kompon-ji** (daily 8am–4/5.30pm; ¥300), is located a few kilometres south of Niibo village; buses from Ryōtsu run here fairly regularly during the day. Kompon-ji marks the spot where the exiled Nichiren lived in 1271, though the temple itself was founded some years later. If you can get there before the coach parties, it's a pleasant stroll round the mossy garden with its thatched temple buildings filled with elaborate gilded canopies, presided over by a statue of Nichiren in his characteristic monk's robes.

Backtracking a little way east from Kompon-ji along the main road, take the turning southeast signed to Onogawa Dam and follow the lane up a gentle valley. After about 2km you'll see, to your right, the crumbling steps of **Seisui-ji**. Founded in 808, this faded temple surrounded by cryptomeria trees and dancing dragonflies receives few visitors. Though it seems abandoned, its wooden terrace, built in imitation of Kyoto's famous Kiyomizu-dera (see p.535), has been repaired.

On the eastern outskirts of **MANO**, **Myōsen-ji** was founded by one of Nichiren's first disciples and includes a graceful five-storey pagoda. Nearby **Kokubun-ji** dates from 741, though the temple's present buildings were erected in the late seventeenth century. If you follow this sideroad south, skirting round the back of Mano town, you come to a simple shrine dedicated to Emperor Juntoku. He's actually buried about 800m further up the valley, but the next-door **Sado Rekishi-Densetsukan** (daily 8am–5.30pm; ¥700) is more interesting. Also known as Toki-no-sato, this museum is similar in style to Ryōtsu's Sado Nō-gaku-no-sato (see p.345), though in this case the robots and holograms represent Juntoku, Nichiren and other characters from local history or folk tales. Each scene only lasts a couple of minutes and, on the whole, they're easy enough to follow. The museum lies about thirty minutes' walk southeast from central Mano and about ten minutes from the nearest bus stop, Mano goryō-iriguchi, on the route from Sawata south to Ogi (line #10).

A few kilometres north along the coast from Mano, **SAWATA** now serves as Sado's main administrative centre, though there's no particular reason to stop unless you're changing buses or need accommodation. If you happen to be passing through around lunchtime, pop along to the **Silver Village** resort, on the town's northern outskirts, to catch the fifteen-minute display of *bun'ya*, a form of seventeenth-century puppetry performed by a couple of master puppeteers (April–Nov daily except Wed at noon, 12.45pm, 1.30pm & 3.30pm; ¥350). Afterwards you can inspect the displays of puppets, which seem to be in much better shape than the threadbare ones used in the performances themselves.

Practicalities

Sawata's bus terminal is located on the north side of town, not far from the *Silver Village*. You can rent **bikes** at *Silver Village* (daily 9am–6pm; ¥2000 per day), or in Mano's **tourist information office** (May–Oct daily 8.30am–5pm; Jan–April, Nov & Dec Mon–Fri 8.30am–5pm; ☎0259/55-3589) for only ¥1100 a day; the office is located a few doors south of the main junction between Route 350 and the Niibo road.

One of the nicest **places to stay** in central Sado is the homely *Green Village Youth Hostel*, 750-4 Uryūya (☎0259/22-2719, ℻22-3302; dorms ¥3000 per person), to the east of Niibo village – ask the bus driver to let you off at the turning. As well as good-value meals, they have bikes for rent and can suggest cycling routes. Sawata's *Silver Village* (☎0259/52-3961, ℻52-3963; ❺) has comfortable Western-style en-suite rooms with sea views. Opposite is the stylishly modern *Urashima Ryokan* (☎0259/57-3751, ⓦwww.r-urashima.com; ❻–❼), offering both Western-style en-suite rooms and tatami rooms using the rooftop common bathrooms. Nice as it is, the dazzlingly white design-magazine interiors are already looking a bit grubby in places.

Ogi and around

Sado's second port is tiny **OGI**, situated near the island's southern tip. This sleepy fishing town is best known for its tub boats, which now bob around in the harbour for tourists, and the annual "Earth Celebration" hosted by the locally based Kodô drummers (see box on p.349), during which the village's population of 3,800 balloons by several thousand. But the area's principal attraction is its picturesque indented coastline to the west of town. You can take boat trips round the headland or cycle over the top to **Shukunegi**, a traditional fishing village huddled behind a wooden palisade.

The **tub boats**, or *tarai-bune*, were originally used for collecting seaweed, abalone and other shellfish from the rocky coves. Today they're fibreglass but still resemble the cutaway wooden barrels from which they were traditionally made. If you fancy a shot at rowing one of these awkward vessels, go to the small jetty west of the ferry pier, where the women will take you out for a ten-minute spin round the harbour (daily 8/9am–4/5pm; ¥450 per person). The jetty is also the departure point for **sightseeing boats** (April–Nov, 6–18 daily; 40min; ¥1400 return trip) which sail along the coast past caves and dainty islets as far as Sawa-zaki lighthouse. Tickets for both the *tarai-bune* and tour boats are available from the Marine Terminal building beside the jetty.

Buses run west along the coast as far as Fukaura (5 daily; 20min), but the ideal way to explore the **headland** is to rent a bicycle (see "Practicalities", below). After a tough uphill pedal out of Ogi on the road to Shukunegi, turn right towards a concrete *jizō* standing above the trees. The statue itself isn't worth stopping for, but continue another 300m along this sideroad and you'll find a short flight of steps leading up to the **Iwaya cave** – the old trees and tiny, crumbling temple surrounded by *jizō* statues make a good place to catch your breath. Further along the Shukunegi road, next to a still-functioning boatyard, the **Sadokoku Ogi Folk Museum** (daily: March–Oct 8.30am–5pm; Jan, Feb, Nov & Dec closed Sat & Sun; ¥500) is worth a brief stop. It contains a delightful, dusty jumble of old photos, paper-cuts, tofu presses, straw raincoats and other remnants of local life. Behind, in a newer building, there's a relief map of the area and beautiful examples of the ingenious traps used by Ogi fisherfolk.

From here the road drops down steeply to **SHUKUNEGI** fishing village, tucked in a fold of the hills beside a little harbour full of jagged black rocks. The village itself is hardly visible behind its high wooden fence – protection against the fierce winds – where its old wooden houses are all jumbled together with odd-shaped corners and narrow, stone-flagged alleys. Two of the houses are open to the public (April–Oct daily 8.30am–5pm; ¥400, including village map), though they're not wildly interesting; tickets and refreshments are available at the soba restaurant (daily 8am–4/5pm, Jan–March & Oct–Dec closed Wed) beside the village car park.

Practicalities

Ogi is split in two by a small headland, with the original fishing harbour to the west and the new **ferry terminal** on its east side. **Tour buses** depart from the ferry building, while **local buses** use the station behind Ogi **post office**, just inland from the tourist-boat pier. The town's **information centre** (daily 9.30am–5/6pm; ☎0259/86-3200) occupies the ground floor of the Marine Plaza building, one block west of the post office, where you can get maps, book accommodation and arrange car rental. This building is also used for evening performances of *okesa odori* folk singing (April–Oct; ¥500). For **bike rental**, walk inland from the ferry terminal, in front of the *Hotel New Kihachiya* to the Seaside Villa shop, which has bikes for ¥1500 per day (daily 7am–7pm).

It's a good idea to book **accommodation** well ahead in summer, but during the rest of the year you shouldn't have any problem. The cheapest option is the basic *Ogi Sakuma-sō Youth Hostel* (☎0259/86-2565; ❷ closed Dec–March), located a good twenty minutes' walk uphill from the ferry; take the road heading west for Shukunegi, then turn right beside the Shell fuel station. For something more central, the seafront *Minshuku Sakaya* (☎0259/86-2535; ℱ86-2145; ❺ including meals) offers smart tatami rooms and tasty food. It's about five minutes' walk east of the ferry terminal – unfortunately its sea views are blocked by the harbour wall. During the Earth Celebration this is a very popular place – so no meals are served and you'll most likely end up sharing a room, depending on the size of your party. The more traditional *Gonzaya Ryokan* (☎0259/86-3161, ℱ86-3162; ❺–❻) has the option of rooms with en-suite facilities and without meals, and is located inland from the local bus terminal. Finally, the classiest place in town – despite its outward appearance – is the *Hotel New Kihachiya* (☎0259/86-3131, ⓦwww.kihachiya.com; ❼), which has Western and tatami rooms, some with harbour views.

For **food**, try *Sakae-zushi* in the block behind the Marine Plaza, where they serve sea-fresh sushi and sashimi at reasonable prices. Alternatively, head for *Shichiuemon*, at the top of the shopping street curving behind the western harbour, which dishes up just one variety of delicious, handmade soba (¥480).

Children of the drum

In the early 1970s a group of musicians came to the seclusion of Sado-ga-shima to pursue their study of traditional *taiko* drumming and to experiment with its potent music. A decade later the **Kodô Drummers** unleashed their primal rhythms on the world, since when they have continued to stun audiences with their electrifying performances. The name Kodô can mean both "heartbeat" and "children" – despite its crashing sound, the beat of their trademark giant *Ôdaiko* is said to resemble the heart heard from inside the womb.

The drummers are now based in Kodô Village, a few kilometres north of Ogi, where they have set up the **Kodô Cultural Foundation**. Apart from a two-year apprenticeship programme, the drummers hold occasional workshops (*Kodô juku*) which are open to anyone with a basic knowledge of Japanese. Each year, usually the third week of August, they also host the three-day "**Earth Celebration**" arts festival when percussionists from all over the world and a friendly multinational audience of several thousand stir up the sleepy air of Ogi. Details of Kodô's scheduled tours and the next Earth Celebration are posted on their website (Ⓦ www.kodo.or.jp), while their tour schedule also appears on the official Kodô site (Ⓦ www.kodo.com). Alternatively, you can contact them at Kodô Village, 148-1 Kaneta-shinden, Ogi (℡ 0259/86-3630, ℮ heartbeat@Kodô.or.jp).

North Sado

Sado's northern promontory contains the island's highest mountains and some of its best coastal scenery. **Aikawa**, the only settlement of any size in this area, was once a lively mining town whose gold and silver ores filled the shoguns' coffers. The mines are no longer working, but a section of tunnel has been converted into a museum, **Kinzan**, where yet more computerized robots show how things were done in olden times. North of Aikawa there's the rather overrated **Senkaku-wan**, a small stretch of picturesque cliffs; it's better to head on up the wild **Soto-kaifu** coast to Hajiki-zaki on the island's northern tip. Not surprisingly, this area isn't well served by public transport, particularly in winter, when snow blocks the mountain passes.

Aikawa

After gold and silver were discovered in 1601, the population of **AIKAWA** rocketed from a hamlet of just ten families to 100,000 people, including many who were convict labourers. Now a mere tenth of that size, there's nothing specific to see in Aikawa beyond the mine museum a few kilometres out of town. Nevertheless, it's not an unattractive place for an overnight stay once you get off the main road and delve among the temples, shrines and wooden houses pressed up against the hillside.

The road from Sawata enters Aikawa from the southeast beside the *Sado Royal Hotel Manchô* and then turns north along the seafront, past the bus terminal and skirts round the main town centre. Just beyond the municipal playing fields, at the north end of Aikawa, a right turn leads up a steep narrow valley to the old gold mines of **Sado Kinzan** (April–Oct 8am–5pm; Jan–March, Nov & Dec 8.30am–4.30pm; ¥700). The Sōdayū tunnel, one of the mine's richest veins, is now a museum showing working conditions during the Edo period, complete with sound effects and life-size mechanical models, followed by a small exhibition with equally imaginative dioramas of the miners at work. You can reach Sado Kinzan by local bus (line #21) from Ryōtsu (4 daily; 1hr 20min) and Aikawa (8 daily; 15min), though for most of the year these only run on weekends and national holidays. Alternatively, several tour buses include Kinzan on their itineraries, along with the "**Ōsado Skyline**" road, which climbs east to Kinpoku-san (1173m), from where there are fine views over the whole island.

Practicalities

Aikawa's **information office** (April–Oct daily except Tues 9am–5.30/6pm; ☎0259/74-3773) is located outside the bus terminal's seaward side, though the bus company staff can also provide maps and help with accommodation. From April to mid-November, evening **performances** of *okesa* are held in the Sado Kaikan (☎0259/74-3322), above the terminal building (¥800, or ¥700 if booked at your hotel).

If you're looking for somewhere to **stay** in Aikawa, head straight for *Dōyū Ryokan* (☎0259/74-3381, ℉74-3783; ❺), on a quiet street one block inland from the bus terminal. *Sado Royal Hotel Manchō* (☎0259/74-3221, ℉74-3738; ❻) is a less attractive possibility on the main road, while onsen addicts should walk south along the seafront to the large and luxurious *Hotel Ōsado* (☎0259/74-3300, ℉74-3219; ❽) to indulge in its glorious rotemburo.

The best place to look for somewhere to **eat** is in the main shopping street north of *Dōyū Ryokan*. For snacks, stock up on *dango*, *manjū* and other traditional sweets at the little *Kisuke Kashi-ten* bakery, on the main road northeast of town, opposite the turning for Sado Kinzan.

The northern cape

Five kilometres north of Aikawa the road skirts round the edge of a bay where jagged cliffs crumble away into clusters of little islands. You get a pretty good view of the bay of **Senkaku-wan** from the road itself or from the observatory in Ageshima-yūen (daily 8am–5pm; ¥400), a park on the bay's north side. If you want to get closer, a variety of **tour boats** set sail during the summer season from **Tassha** village, 2km further south. The choice is between glass-bottomed "shark" boats (April–Oct roughly every 30min according to demand; 30min; ¥850) and ordinary sightseeing (*yūransen*) boats (April to mid-Nov; 30min; ¥700). There are also four scheduled sailings every day from Tassha to Ageshima-yūen (April to mid-Nov; ¥720 one way, including entry to the park).

Echigo-Tsumari Art Triennial

Every three years the mountainous, rural and relatively unspoilt and untouristed Echigo-Tsumari region of Niigata-ken hosts a spectacular international art festival from mid-July to early September. The second **Echigo-Tsumari Art Triennial**, held in 2003 (the next will be in 2006) confirmed that this event is shaping up to be one of the best of its kind and well worth making a detour for. Artists from all over the world have been invited to exhibit their work, including Cai Guo Qiang from China, who reconstructed an old Chinese climbing kiln, and Serbian Marina Abramovic, in whose *Dream House* it was possible to stay overnight.

Even if you're not in Japan during the festival, a visit to this region is still a rewarding experience. The main places to head for are **Tokamachi**, **Matsudai** and **Matsunoyama**, all of which have fascinating permanent exhibition facilities built for the past triennials and plenty of sculptures and other interesting art works sited in paddy fields and on hillsides. Hiring a car to tour the region is ideal, although during the festival there are also free bikes available at all the main sites. Otherwise you can travel here by local train from either Eichigo-Yuzawa on the Niigata Shinkansen route or Saigata on the Joetsu line. For more details check out ⓦwww.echigo-tsumari.jp.

Tassha and Ageshima-yūen are both stops on the Kaifu-sen bus route (line #9) from Aikawa to Iwayaguchi, with services roughly every hour. On the hilltop near Ageshima-yūen, there's a good **youth hostel**, the *Sado Belle Mer* (☎0259/75-2011, ℱ75-2071; dorms ¥4000 per person), and the government-run *Kokuminshukusha Senkaku-sō* (☎0259/75-2226, ℱ75-2278; ❺ including meals). They're both a few minutes' walk from the Himezu bus stop.

Continuing north, the settlements gradually peter out and the scenery becomes wilder as you approach **Ōno-game**, a 167-metre rock rising up from the ocean. From here a pretty coastal pathway leads around to the island of **Futatsu-game**, linked to the mainland by a thin strip of black sand beach; along the path is an intriguing cave, **Sai-no-Kawara**, housing hundreds of *jizo* statues. In summer this area is popular for swimming and camping, but it's worth doing at any time of year for the journey alone. Returning to Ryōtsu down the east coast you're treated to further precariously twisting roads clinging to the base of the mountains as they plummet into the sea.

Between late April and early November it's possible to take a bus all the way round the peninsula from Aikawa to Ryōtsu (3hr 30min), with changes at Iwayaguchi, Ōno-game and Washi-zaki depending on the schedule. During the rest of the year services terminate at **Iwayaguchi**, where you'll find the *Sotokaifu Youth Hostel* (☎ & ℱ0259/78-2111; ❶ dorms ¥3000 per person), handy if you need somewhere to stay before heading back south. *Sado Fishers Hotel* (☎0259/26-2311, ⓦwww3.ocn.ne.jp/~sfht/; ❺–❼) offers standard tatami rooms overlooking Fatatsu-game, and you can also camp here (¥800 for a site; ¥4500 if you need to rent a tent).

Travel details

Trains

Aizu-Wakamatsu to: Aizu-Takada (8 daily; 20min); Inawashiro (hourly; 30min); Kitakata (16 daily; 15–25min); Koide (5 daily; 4hr); Koriyama (17 daily; 1hr–1hr 15min); Niigata (5 daily; 2hr 15min–3hr); Sendai (hourly; 2hr 30min); Shiokawa (16 daily; 10min); Tokyo via Koriyama (2hr 30min–3hr); Tokyo via Aizu-Tajima (12 daily; 4hr 15min–5hr); Yamagata (hourly; 3hr).

Akita to: Aomori (8 daily; 2hr 30min–3hr 40min); Kakunodate (12 daily; 45min); Morioka (hourly; 1hr 40min); Niigata (5 daily; 4hr); Tokyo (hourly; 4hr–4hr 30min); Tsuruoka (6 daily; 2hr).

Aomori to: Akita (9 daily; 2hr 30min–3hr 40min); Hakodate (hourly; 2hr–2hr 30min); Hirosaki (hourly; 30min–1hr); Morioka (1–2 hourly; 2hr–2hr 15min); Noheji (1–2 hourly; 30–45min); Sapporo (1 daily; 7hr 10min); Sendai (1–2 hourly; 4hr); Tokyo (2 daily; 9hr 30min).

Fukushima to: Sendai (every 10min; 25min–1hr 30min); Yamagata (1–2 hourly; 1hr–1hr 40min); Tokyo (every 10–20min; 1hr 25min–2hr).

Hiraizumi to: Hanamaki (hourly; 50min); Kitakami (hourly; 30min); Morioka (hourly; 1hr 20min);

Sendai (hourly; 45min–1hr).

Ichinoseki to: Geibikei (11 daily; 30min); Hiraizumi (hourly; 8min); Kogota (hourly; 50min); Morioka (hourly; 1hr 30min); Sendai (11 daily; 30min–45min); Shin-Hanamaki (1–2 hourly; 20–30min).

Ishinomaki to: Kogota (11 daily; 40min); Onogawa (12 daily; 55min–1hr 20min); Sendai (every 30min; 55min–1hr 20min).

Matsushima-kaigan to: Hon-Shiogama (every 30min; 10min); Ishinomaki (every 30min; 30–45min); Nobiru (every 30min; 12–18min); Sendai (every 30min; 25–35min).

Morioka to: Akita (hourly; 1hr 40min); Aomori (1–2 hourly; 2hr–2hr 15min); Hanamaki (every 30min; 20–35min); Kakunodate (hourly; 50min–2hr 25min); Kitakami (every 30min; 50min); Noheji (hourly; 1hr 45min); Shin-Hanamaki (1–2 hourly; 13min); Tazawako (4 daily; 46min); Tokyo (every 30min; 2hr 20min–3hr 30min); Towada-minami (7 daily; 1hr 45min–2hr 15min).

Niigata to: Aizu-Wakamatsu (6 daily; 2hr 15min–3hr); Kanazawa (3 daily; 3hr 40min); Kyoto (3 daily; 6hr); Nagano (2 daily; 3hr); Ōsaka (3 daily; 6hr 30min); Tokyo (1–3 hourly; 1hr 50min–5hr

30min); Tsuruoka (8 daily; 1hr 45min).
Noheji to: Aomori (1–2 hourly; 30–45min); Morioka (hourly; 1hr 45min); Shimokita (10 daily; 45min–1hr).
Sendai to: Fukushima (every 10min; 25min–1hr 30min); Hon-Shiogama (every 30min; 15–30min); Matsushima-kaigan (every 30min; 25–40min); Ichinoseki (hourly; 30min–45min); Ishinomaki (every 30min; 55min–1hr 20min); Morioka (1–3 hourly; 45min–1hr 20min); Tokyo (every 20min; 1hr 35min–2hr 30min); Yamadera (hourly; 50min–1hr 5min).
Tōno to: Hanamaki (12 daily; 50min–1hr 10min); Morioka (5 daily; 1hr 20min–2hr); Shin-Hanamaki (12 daily; 40min–1hr).
Towada-minami to: Morioka (7 daily; 1hr 45min–2hr 15min); Ōdate (10 daily; 30–40min).
Tsuruoka to: Akita (6 daily; 2hr); Niigata (8 daily; 1hr 45min).
Yamagata to: Sendai (hourly; 1hr 10min–1hr 30min); Tokyo (hourly; 2hr 30min–3hr); Yamadera (hourly; 20min).

Buses

Akita to: Sendai (7 daily; 3hr 30min); Tokyo (2 daily; 8hr 30min–9hr 30min).
Aomori to: Morioka (6 daily; 3hr 15min); Sendai (4 daily; 5hr); Tokyo (1 daily; 9hr 30min); Towada-ko (April to mid-Nov 4–8 daily; 3hr 10min).
Hirosaki to: Morioka (hourly; 2hr 20min); Sendai (6 daily; 4hr 20min); Tokyo (2 daily; 9hr); Towada-ko (April to late Oct 3–4 daily; 2hr 15min); Yokohama (1 daily; 9hr 45min).
Ichinoseki to: Chōson-ji (every 15–20min; 25min); Geibikei (9–11 daily; 30–40min); Hiraizumi (every 15–20min; 20min).
Inawashiro to: Bandai-kōgen-eki (hourly; 30min); Goshikinuma-iriguchi (hourly; 25min).
Ishinomaki to: Ayukawa (7 daily; 1hr 30min).
Morioka to: Aomori (6 daily; 3hr 15min); Hirosaki (hourly; 2hr 20min); Sendai (hourly; 2hr 40min); Tokyo (1 daily; 7hr 30min); Towada-ko (April to early Nov 5–6 daily; 2hr 15min).
Mutsu (Tanabu) to: Wakinosawa (8 daily; 1hr 35min).
Niigata to: Aizu-Wakamatsu (4 daily; 10hr); Kanazawa (2 daily; 4hr 40min); Kyoto (daily; 8hr 20min); Nagano (2 daily; 3hr 50min); Ōsaka (daily; 9hr 20min); Sendai (4 daily; 4hr–6hr 15min); Tokyo (6 daily; 5hr); Yamagata (2 daily; 3hr 45min).
Ryōtsu to: Aikawa (1–2 hourly; 1hr); Mano (1–2 hourly; 45min); Sawata (every 30min; 45min).
Sawata to: Aikawa (1–2 hourly; 20min); Ogi (hourly; 1hr 5min).
Sendai to: Akita (7 daily; 3hr 30min); Aomori (4

daily; 4hr 50min); Hirosaki (3 daily; 4hr 20min); Kyoto (1 daily; 10hr 40min); Morioka (hourly; 2hr 40min); Nagoya (1 daily; 10hr 30min); Niigata (4 daily; 4hr–6hr 15min); Ōsaka (1 daily; 12hr 20min); Tokyo (2 daily; 5hr 30min–8hr); Tokyo (Shinjuku) (3 daily; 5hr 30min); Tsuruoka (7 daily; 3hr); Yamagata (every 30min; 1hr).
Towada-ko to: Aomori (April to mid-Nov 4–8 daily; 3hr 10min); Hirosaki (April to late Oct 3–4 daily; 2hr 15min); Hachimantai (late-April to Nov 2 daily; 2hr 30min); Morioka (April to early Nov 5–6 daily; 2hr 15min); Ōdate (April to early Nov 1 daily; 1hr 30min); Towada-minami (April to early Nov 4 daily; 1hr).
Tsuruoka to: Sendai (7 daily; 3hr); Tokyo (2 daily; 8–9hr); Yamagata (10 daily; 2hr 15min).
Yamagata to: Niigata (2 daily; 3hr 45min); Sendai (every 30min; 1hr); Tokyo (2 daily; 5hr 40min–8hr 30min); Tsuruoka (10 daily; 2hr 15min).

Ferries

Akita to: Tomakomai (Hokkaidō) (4 weekly; 11hr 20min).
Aomori to: Hakodate (9–12 daily; 2hr–3hr 40min); Muroran (2 daily; 7hr); Wakinosawa (2 daily; 50min).
Kinkazan to: Ayukawa (3–10 daily; 25min); Onogawa (April to early Nov 4 daily; 30min).
Niigata to: Otaru (Hokkaidō) (1–2 daily; 17hr 30min); Ryōtsu (9–19 daily; 1hr–2hr 20min); Sado (16 daily; 1hr–2hr 20min).
Ogi to: Naoetsu (2–9 daily; 1hr 5min–2hr 30min).
Sendai to: Nagoya (1 weekly; 21hr); Tomakomai (Hokkaidō) (3–4 weekly; 15hr).
Wakinosawa to: Kanita-machi (2–3 daily; 1hr 10min); Sai-mura (1–2 daily; 1hr 25min).

Flights

From Northern Honshū there are some interesting international connections, mainly to Russia, Korea and China.
Akita to: Kansai International (daily; 1hr 30min); Nagoya (2 daily; 1hr 10min); Ōsaka (Itami) (2 daily; 1hr 20min); Sapporo (2 daily; 55min); Tokyo (7 daily; 1hr); Haneda (Tokyo) (daily; 1hr 30min).
Aomori to: Fukuoka (2 weekly; 2hr); Hiroshima (3 weekly; 1hr 35min); Khabarovsk (Russia) (2 weekly; 4hr 25min); Kansai International (daily; 1hr 35min); Nagoya (2–3 daily; 1hr 20min); Ōsaka (Itami) (2 daily; 1hr 30min); Sapporo (2–3 daily; 45min); Seoul (South Korea) (3 weekly; 2hr 50min); Tokyo (6 daily; 1hr 10min).
Niigata to: Fukuoka (3 daily; 1hr 40min); Hiroshima (1–2 daily; 1hr 15min); Khabarovsk, Russia (2 weekly; 1hr 55min); Kansai International

(3 daily; 1hr 30min); Nagoya (2 daily; 55min); Ōsaka (Itami) (6 daily; 1hr 10min); Ryōtsu (Sado) (2–5 daily; 25min); Sapporo (2–3 daily; 1hr 15min); Seoul, South Korea (4 weekly; 2hr); Shanghai (2 weekly; 3hr 45min); Vladivostok, Russia (2 weekly; 1hr 20min); Xi'an, China (2 weekly; 4hr 30min).

Sendai to: Beijing (China) (4 weekly; 5–7hr); Fukuoka (3 daily; 2hr); Hiroshima (1 daily; 1hr 35min); Hong Kong (4 weekly; 5hr 30min); Honolulu, Hawaii (6 weekly; 6hr 30min); Kansai International (1–2 daily; 1hr 40min); Nagoya (5 daily; 1hr 10min); Naha (Okinawa) (1 daily; 2hr 55min); Ōsaka (Itami) (6 daily; 1hr 20min); Sapporo (9 daily; 1hr 10min); Seoul, South Korea (7 weekly; 2hr 45min); Shanghai, China (2 weekly; 3hr 30min).

Tsuruoka (Shōnai) to: Kansai International (daily; 1hr 30min); Sapporo (daily; 1hr); Tokyo (3 daily; 1hr).

Yamagata to: Fukuoka (3 weekly; 1hr 55min); Kansai International (1 daily; 1hr 35min); Nagoya (1 daily; 1hr 5min); Ōsaka (Itami) (2 daily; 1hr 20min); Sapporo (2 daily; 1hr 5min); Tokyo (3 daily; 1hr).

Hokkaidō

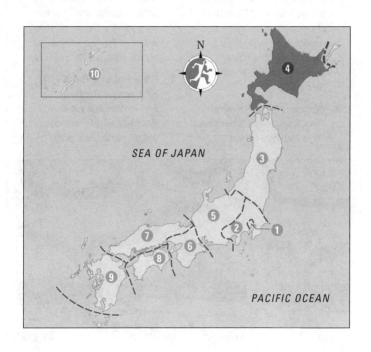

N

SEA OF JAPAN

PACIFIC OCEAN

CHAPTER 4   # Highlights

* **Susukino nightlife** Spend a night out in Sapporo's Susukino district, a raucous mix of busy restaurants and bars amid barely disguised massage parlours and sex cabarets. **See p.371**

* **Hakodate** Spend a day riding the engagingly rickety old trams around the pleasant port town of Hakodate, checking out the gentrified harbourside district and tucking into the city's famous seafood and beer. **See p.375**

* **Shikotsu-Tōya National Park** Explore the Shikotsu-Tōya National Park's expanse of volcanic crater lakes, heavily wooded mountains, spectacular scenery and bucolic towns and lakeside resorts. **See p.382**

* **Sōunkyō Gorge** Set at the base of the spectacular Sōunkyō Gorge, the tiny onsen town of Sōunkyō is a great place to soak travel-weary limbs before tackling a hike in the mountains above. **See p.393**

* **Rishiri-tō and Rebun-tō** Hike around the beautiful and remote islands of Rishiri-tō and Rebun-tō in the far north. **See p.397**

△Ainu fabric

Hokkaidō

M any Japanese see **HOKKAIDŌ** as an idyllic, unspoiled frontier – the perfect place to escape from industrialized Japan and get back in touch with nature. Although this vision is rose-tinted, Hokkaidō does retain a wild and remote quality and can feel worlds apart from the rest of the country – despite the fact that in many places you'll find the same ugly factories and buildings as on Honshū and that, far from being a hick town, **Sapporo**, the island's capital, is the fastest-growing city in Japan. Over seventy percent of the island is still covered by forest, and its enormous national parks, snow-covered slopes, rugged coastline and active volcanoes attract millions of nature lovers every summer. Fortunately, Hokkaidō can cope with such crowds; this is Japan's second largest island, yet a mere five percent of the country's population lives here.

With five national parks to explore, your main problem will be time. If you're here for a week, aim to see **Daisetsu-zan National Park** in central Hokkaidō, which features the island's highest mountain and many hiking trails and onsen resorts. In southern Hokkaidō, the **Shikotsu-Tōya National Park** has two beautiful lakes and a new-born volcano which was formed during an eruption in 1943. Highlights in the north include the lovely islands of **Rebun-tō** and **Rishiri-tō**, while at the western end of the island you'll find the dramatic **Shiretoko peninsula**, where you can bathe under thermally heated waterfalls and climb still-steaming volcanoes. In winter, Hokkaidō is Japan's prime **skiing** destination; the long and uncrowded slopes at **Niseko** in the south and **Furano** towards the centre of the island are among the best skiing spots in the country. Festivals are another highlight of this season – if you're here in February, don't miss Sapporo's fabulous snow and ice sculpture festival, the **Yuki Matsuri**.

Camping or hiking around the island may bring you into contact with some of Hokkaidō's unique **wildlife**, which includes the *tanchō* (a red-crowned crane), sable, Blakiston's fish-owl and the Hokkaidō brown bear (*ezo higuma*). There are believed to be around two thousand brown bears in the woods, and locals are careful to warn you about the potential dangers of an encounter with one – the bears can grow to a height of 2m and weigh up to 300kg.

Only colonized by the Japanese in the last 150 years, Hokkaidō is entirely devoid of ancient temples, shrines and historical monuments. What it does have is an intriguing cultural history, defined by its dwindling **Ainu** population (see box on p.361). This aboriginal group of uncertain origin nearly disappeared completely after Japan opened up to the West in 1868 and large-scale immigration to Hokkaidō started. Today the best way to explore their ancient traditions is to visit an Ainu museum or spend time in some rather touristy recreated villages.

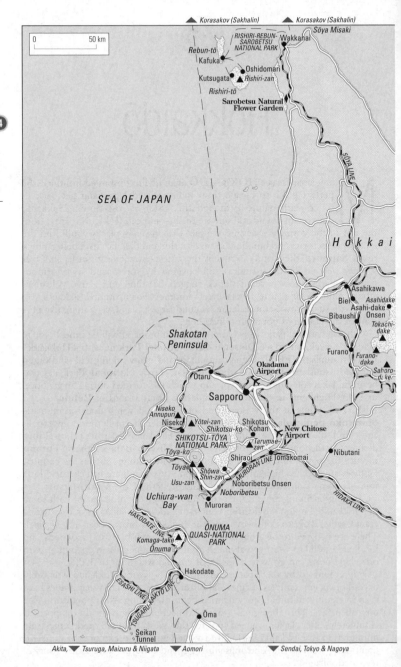

0   50 km

▲ Korasakov (Sakhalin)   ▲ Korasakov (Sakhalin)

Sōya Misaki

RISHIRI-REBUN-
SAROBETSU
NATIONAL PARK

Wakkanai

Rebun-tō
Kafuka

Oshidomari

Kutsugata   ▲ *Rishiri-zan*

Rishiri-tō

**Sarobetsu Natural
Flower Garden**

SŌYA LINE

SEA OF JAPAN

H o k k a i

Asahikawa

Biei   *Asahidake*
     Asahi-dake
Bibaushi   Onsen

*Shakotan
Peninsula*

        Tokachi-
        dake

Furano   *Furano-
       dake*

**Okadama
Airport**

      *Sahoro-
      dake*

Otaru

Sapporo

*Niseko
Annupuri* ▲

   Shikotsu
   Kohan

**New Chitose
Airport**

Niseko   ▲ *Yōtei-zan*
    Shikotsu-ko

*SHIKOTSU-TŌYA
NATIONAL PARK*

▲ *Tarumae-
  zan*

Tōya-ko

Shiraoi   Tomakomai

Nibutani

Tōya ▲▲
   *Shōwa
   Shin-zan*

MURORAN LINE

HIDAKA LINE

Usu-zan

Noboribetsu Onsen
   Noboribetsu

*Uchiura-wan
Bay*

Muroran

HAKODATE LINE

**ŌNUMA
QUASI-NATIONAL
PARK**

Komaga-take
Ōnuma

ESASHI LINE

TSUGARU-KAIKYŌ LINE

Hakodate

Ōma

Seikan
Tunnel

Akita, ▼ Tsuruga, Maizuru & Niigata   ▼ Aomori   ▼ Sendai, Tokyo & Nagoya

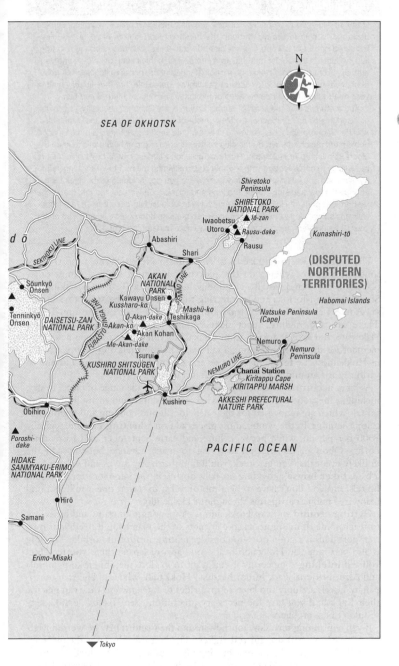

SEA OF OKHOTSK

Shiretoko
Peninsula

SHIRETOKO
NATIONAL PARK

Iwaobetsu   ▲ Iō-zan
Utoro   ●▲ Rausu-dake
              ●
              Rausu

Abashiri

Shari

Kunashiri-tō

(DISPUTED
NORTHERN
TERRITORIES)

AKAN
NATIONAL
PARK

Habomai Islands

Sōunkyō
Onsen

SEKIHOKU LINE

Kawayu Onsen
Kussharo-ko
Mashū-ko

Natsuke Peninsula
(Cape)

Tenninkyō
Onsen

DAISETSU-ZAN
NATIONAL PARK

Ō-Akan-dake Teshikaga
Akan-ko ▲
      ● Akan Kohan
Me-Akan-dake ▲

SENMO LINE

FURANO LINE

FURASTO LINE

Nemuro
Nemuro ●
Peninsula

Tsurui

KUSHIRO SHITSUGEN
NATIONAL PARK

NEMURO LINE

Chanai Station
Kiritappu Cape
KIRITAPPU MARSH

Obihiro

AKKESHI PREFECTURAL
NATURE PARK

Kushiro

PACIFIC OCEAN

▲
Poroshi-
dake

HIDAKE
SANMYAKU-ERIMO
NATIONAL PARK

● Hirō

Samani

Erimo-Misaki

▼ Tokyo

Hokkaidō cuisine

Many of Hokkaidō's signature dishes are fish-based soups – warming staples designed to help locals get through the harsh winters. *Ishikari-nabe*, a red-miso-flavoured hotpot of salmon and shellfish, daikon, leeks, Chinese cabbage and tofu, is a favourite in the colder months, as is *sampei jiru*, a thick soup of salmon and vegetables. From the Ainu, Hokkaidō's original inhabitants, come delicacies like *ruibe*, fresh, frozen salmon cut into slices of sashimi so wafer-thin that they literally melt in your mouth, and numerous varieties of marinated herring and fermented fish.

At the other end of the scale of sophistication is the Sapporo speciality, *jingisukan*, or "Genghis Khan" barbecue, a messy meal of flame-grilled lamb and vegetables. Another Sapporo speciality is ramen. One favourite version, *batā-kōn*, is ramen loaded up with the region's famed butter, plus seaweed, corn and plenty of garlic to keep the blood circulating. In Hakodate, Hokkaidō's second largest city, a bowl of ramen is more likely to come topped with a whole crab, reflecting the port town's fishing industry, although you'll find great seafood anywhere you go, including crabs (look for the abundant snow and king crabs), scallops and salmon. Be warned, though, that in the far-northern parts of Hokkaidō you may have trouble finding decent fresh fruit (especially in fishing villages, where vegetables can be quite dodgy, too), so stock up or eat your fill before venturing out into the more remote parts of the island.

The fastest route to Hokkaidō is by **plane** to New Chitose airport, 40km south of Sapporo, where you can pick up connecting flights to most other places on the island. You'll get good value out of a JR pass by taking the Shinkansen to Morioka and transferring to a limited express **train** to Sapporo, via Aomori and Hakodate, a total journey time of 11hr 30min from Tokyo. There are also nightly direct sleeper trains from Tokyo to Sapporo, via Hakodate, and several a week from Ōsaka, but you'll have to pay a hefty supplement for these if you're using a rail pass. The most relaxing way of arriving in Hokkaidō is by **ferry**: there are several overnight services from Honshū to various ports around the island (see "Travel details", p.412).

As far as **accommodation** goes, Hokkaidō has a wide range of places to stay, including the good-value Toho network of minshuku and many lively youth hostels which are renowned for their delicious home-cooking and nightly singalong sessions. In the winter, most places add on a **heating charge**, typically ¥300 per person, while between June and early September, and particularly during Obon in mid-August, it's vital to make advance bookings. In the unlikely event that you get stuck, you'll find that many towns and villages have a basic **biker house**, providing no-frills dorms, in the same locations as youth hostels, and you don't have to be a motorcyclist to stay at one. You'll also find many free public **campsites** throughout Hokkaidō.

Getting around most of Hokkaidō is easy enough on trains and buses, but to reach some of the more remote corners of the island you'll need your own transport. This is a good place to consider renting a car or motorbike – cycling is also very popular. Hokkaidō is also one area of Japan where you may find yourself **hitching** – especially if you want to explore the Shiretoko peninsula and Akan National Park in northeastern Hokkaidō, where public transport is patchy. Locals are only too keen to give rides to foreigners so they can practise their English; if you take the necessary precautions (see "Basics", p.80), safety shouldn't be a problem.

If you're planning on a slow journey around the island, it may be worth investing in one of several **special rail tickets**. The best value by far is the five one-day ticket package Seishun Jūhachi-kippu (see "Basics", p.38), which is valid on slow trains only from March 1 to April 10, from July 20 to September 10 and from December 10 to January 20 (¥11,500). This package can be great value, since it's possible to travel from one end of Hokkaidō to the other in a day, and the tickets can also be used on overnight services, as long as you don't go in the sleeping cars. There is also the Hokkaidō Free Kippu, which allows unlimited travel within Hokkaidō for three days (¥14,000) or seven days (¥23,750), and the Gururi Free Kippu, which is expensive at ¥33,500 for five days or ¥49,500 for ten days, but covers the Shinkansen Bullet Train or sleeping-car fare to Hokkaidō and back from Tokyo as well as travel within Hokkaidō over five or ten consecutive days. If you're travelling as a couple, you can take advantage of the Hokkaidō Pair Kippu, with gives you seven days' travel for two (note that you must travel together at all times) for ¥43,220. The staff of the JR East Infoline (☎03/3423-0111) can explain the options in detail.

The Ainu

> . . . they are uncivilizable and altogether irreclaimable savages, yet they are attractive and . . . I hope I shall never forget the music of their low sweet voices, the soft light of their mild, brown eyes and the wonderful sweetness of their smile.
>
> Isabella Bird, *Unbeaten Tracks in Japan*, 1880.

Victorian traveller Isabella Bird had some misconceived notions about the **Ainu**, but anyone who has ever listened to their hauntingly beautiful music will agree that they are a people not easily forgotten. The Ainu's roots are uncertain – some believe they come from Siberia or Central Asia, and they are thought to have lived on Hokkaidō and northern Honshū since the seventh century. The early Ainu were hairy, wide-eyed and lived a hunter-gatherer existence, but their culture – revolving around powerful animist beliefs – was sophisticated, as shown by their unique clothing and epic songs and stories in a language quite unlike Japanese.

Like Bird, the Japanese also considered the Ainu savages. As their control of the archipelago increased, the Ainu were forced to retreat to undeveloped Hokkaidō, then called Ezochi. But even here they were not safe once the Japanese began to fully colonize the island from the late 1860s. The new immigrants kicked them off their lands, cleared the forests where they used to hunt, brought new diseases and suppressed their culture. The Ainu had little choice but to assimilate, and their way of life went into seemingly terminal decline.

Today there are reckoned to be around 25,000 full- and part-blooded Ainu in Hokkaidō and in recent years there has been more interest in and sensitivity towards them. The United Nations Year of Indigenous People in 1993 helped promote the Ainu's cause, and Ainu activist Kayano Shigeru was elected to the House of Councillors – the second house of Japan's parliament – in 1994. A landmark legal verdict in 1997 recognized Ainu rights over the land (see p.387) and, although controversial, the New Ainu Law of 1997 aims to protect what is left of Ainu culture and ensure that it is passed on to generations to come.

There are several recreated **Ainu villages** around Hokkaidō, including Poroto Kotan in Shiraoi and Akan-kohan, but the best place to get an accurate idea of how the people live today is at **Nibutani** (see p.387), which has two excellent museums and is the only place in Japan where the Ainu form a majority of the community. Also worth seeking out for a broader understanding of the Ainu and their relationship to similar ethnic groups are the Museums of Northern Peoples in Hakodate (see p.379) and Abashiri (see p.402).

Despite her presumptions, Bird's account of the Ainu in *Unbeaten Tracks in Japan* (see "Books", p.1016) is still one of the best you can read, while, for an excellent insight into contemporary Ainu issues, have a look at *The Japan We Never Knew* by David Suzuki and Keibo Oiwa (see "Books", p.1016).

Sapporo and around

With a population of nearly two million, Hokkaidō's booming capital **SAP-PORO** is the fifth largest city in Japan. It's a pleasant and vibrant city despite its size and bustle, generously endowed with parks and gardens and laid out in an easy-to-follow grid plan – and as the transport hub of the island, you're almost bound to pass through. The city is dominated to the south by the mountains that served as the venue for the 1972 Winter Olympics, while it's also less than thirty minutes from the coast.

Sapporo is perhaps best known for its beer, which has been brewed here since 1891; a visit to the handsome, late-nineteenth-century **Sapporo Brewery** is a must, as is a stroll through the gardens and museums of the **Botanical Gardens**, which date from the same era. After dark, the bars and restaurants of **Susukino** (pronounced "suskino") spark to life and you'll be hard pressed to find a livelier nightlife district outside of Tokyo or Ōsaka.

Pleasantly cool temperatures tempt many visitors to Sapporo's **Summer Festival** (July 21–Aug 20), which features outdoor beer gardens and other events in **Ōdōri-kōen**, the swathe of parkland that cuts through the city centre. This park is also the focus of activity during the fabulous **Yuki Matsuri**, a "snow festival" held every February (see box, p.365), which draws over two million visitors to the city.

Sapporo and around

Sapporo	Sapporo	札幌
Botanical Gardens	Shokubutsu-en	植物園
Historical Village of Hokkaidō	Hokkaidō Kaitaku-no Mura	北海道開拓の村
Hokkaidō Museum of Modern Art	Hokkaidō Ritsu Kindai Bijutsukan	北海道立近代美術館
Moerenuma Park	Moerenuma-kōen	モエレ沼公園
Nakajima-kōen	Nakajima-kōen	中島公園
Ōdōri-kōen	Ōdōri-kōen	大通公園
Sapporo Beer Garden and Museum	Sapporo Biiru Hakubutsukan	サッポロビール博物館
Susukino	Susukino	すすきの

Accommodation

Hotel Clubby Sapporo	Hoteru Kurabii Sapporo	ホテルクラビーサッポロ
JR Tower Hotel Nikkō Sapporo	JR Tower Hotel Nikkō Sapporo	JRタワーホテル日航札幌
Keiō Plaza Hotel Sapporo	Keiō Puraza Hoteru Sapporo	京王プラザホテル札幌
Marks Inn Sapporo	Mākusu In Sapporo	マークスイン札幌
Nakamuraya Ryokan	Nakamuraya Ryokan	中村屋旅館
Hotel New Budget Sapporo	Hoteru Nyū Bajetto Sapporo	ホテルニューバジェット札幌
Hotel New Ōtani Sapporo	Hoteru Nyū Ōtani Sapporo	ホテルニューオータニ札幌
Safro Spa	Supa Safuro	スパサフロ
Sapporo House Youth Hostel	Sapporo Hausu Yūsu Hosuteru	札幌ハウスユースホステル
Sapporo Inn NADA	Sapporo In NADA	札幌インNADA
Sapporo International Youth Hostel	Sapporo Kokusai Yūsu Hosuteru	札幌国際ユースホステル
Sapporo Washington Hotel 1	Sapporo Dai-ichi Washinton Hoteru	札幌大1ワシントンホテル
Yūgiri Ryokan	Yūgiri Ryokan	夕霧旅館

There are some good day-trip possibilities around Sapporo. Top of the list is the **Historical Village of Hokkaidō**, a huge landscaped park featuring over sixty restored buildings from the island's frontier days, while **Moerenuma**, a park designed by the late Japanese–American sculptor Isamu Noguchi, also makes for a pleasant half-day trip. The nearby port of **Otaru**, one of the entry points into Hokkaidō, has some appealing nineteenth-century architecture and can be easily visited in half a day from the capital. Just about possible as a day-trip, but better experienced over a longer stay, are the ski slopes of **Niseko**, some 100km south of the city.

Sapporo's name comes from the Ainu word for the area, *Sari-poro-betsu*, meaning "a river which runs along a plain filled with reeds". The city's layout was designed in the 1870s by a team of European and American experts engaged by the government to advise on the development of the island. Statues of these advisers can be found around Sapporo; the most famous is the one of the American **Dr William S. Clark**, who set up Hokkaidō University and whose invocation to his students – "Boys, be ambitious!" – has been adopted as the city's motto.

Arrival, information and city transport

New Chitose Airport (☎0123/23-0111), 40km southeast of Sapporo, is the main gateway into Hokkaidō and the connecting point for flights to other

Eating

Aji-no-Tokeidai	*Aji-no-Tokeidai*	味の時計台
Aburiya	*Aburiya*	あぶりや
Daruma	*Daruma*	だるま
Kirin Beer Garden	*Kirin Biiru-en*	キリンビール園
Kitanofuji	*Kitanofuji*	北の富士
Rāmen Yokochō	*Rāmen Yokocho*	ラーメン横丁
Sapporo Bier Garten	*Sapporo Biiru-en*	サッポロビール園
Sapporo City Hall Shokudō	*Shiyakusho Shokudō*	市役所食堂
Taj Mahal	*Tāji Mahāru*	タージマハール

Around Sapporo

New Chitose airport	*Shin-Chitose Kūkō*	新千歳空港

Otaru

	Otaru	小樽
La Lulu	*Ra Ruru*	ラルル
Hotel Nord Otaru	*Hoteru Norudo Otaru*	ホテルノルド小樽
New Green Hotel	*Nyū Guriin Hoteru*	ニューグリーンホテル
Otaru Green Hotel	*Otaru Guriin Hoteru*	小樽グリーンホテル
Otaru Tengu-yama Youth Hostel	*Otaru Tengu-yama Yūsu Hosuteru*	小樽天狗山ユースホステル

Niseko

	Niseko	ニセコ
Niseko Annupuri Youth Hostel	*Niseko Annupuri Yūsu Hosuteru*	ニセコアンヌプリユースホステル
Niseko Kōgen Youth Hostel	*Niseko Kōgen Yūsu Hosuteru*	ニセコ高原ユースホステル
Niseko Prince Hotel	*Niseko Purinsu Higashiyama Hoteru*	ニセコ東山プリンスホテル
Pension Asauta	*Penshon Asauta*	ペンション愛彩譜・あさうた

HOKKAIDŌ | Sapporo and around

SAPPORO

0 ——— 200 m

N

Otaru & Hakodate

Kotoni Station

Hokkaidō Museum of Modern Art

Hokkaidō University Campus

Ⓐ

Ⓑ

Ⓓ

Daimaru Department Store

Sapporo

Ⓔ

Botanical Garden

Miyabe Hall

Ainu Museum

Ⓕ

Natural History Museum

Greenhouse

Old Hokkaidō Government Building

N6
N5
N4
N3
N2
N1
W10 W9 W8

NANBOKU LINE

Asabu Station

Sakaemachi Station & Moerenuma Park

ⓘ Sapporo Station ✉

Ⓒ

Sapporo Station Bus Terminal & Esta Department Store

Sapporo

Gobankan Seibu Department Store

TOHO LINE

Bus Stop for Sapporo Beer Garden, Museum & Sapporo Factory

American Express

Citibank

Sapporo International Communication Plaza

Ⓞ ⓘ

Tokeidai Clocktower

City Hall Ⓞ

Ⓖ

Ⓗ

Sapporo Beer Garden & Museum

Historical Village of Hokkaidō & Asahikawa

Sapporo Factory Shopping Mall

Chūō Bus Terminal

✉

Ōdōri Ⓢ

TV Tower

Shin-Sapporo Station &

Ōdōri Kōen
W7 W6 W5 W4 W3 W2 W1

TŌZAI LINE
S1

Ōdōri

TŌZAI LINE

S2

Ⓢ

Ⓢ

Ⓢ

Airs Cafe

@

Nishi-Yon-Chōme

Maruzen Books

S3

ICI Sports

Tanuki Koji Shopping Arcade

Ⓙ

S4

Ⓙ

Ⓖ

Ⓚ

S5

Ⓞ

Ⓛ

S6

S7

Ⓢ

Ⓢ

Ⓢ

Ⓢ

❸

❻

❺

❽

❿

⓫ ⓭

⓮

⓯ ⓰

❹

❼

Susukino

⓬

SUSUKINO

Hosui-Susukino

Ⓢ

⓱

Ⓜ

Nakajima-kōen

⓲

TŌZAI LINE

Shin-Sapporo Station &

Fukuzumi Station &

TOHO LINE

Ⓝ

⓳

Nakajima-kōen

Makomanai Station

ACCOMMODATION

Clubby Sapporo	G
Ino's Place	I
JR Tower Hotel Nikko	C
Keiō Plaza Hotel Sapporo	D
Marks Inn Sapporo	M
Nakamuraya Ryokan	F
New Budget Sapporo	J
New Ōtani Sapporo	H
Safro Spa Capsule Hotel	L
Sapporo House Youth Hostel	B
Sapporo Inn NADA	K
Sapporo International Youth Hostel	N
Sapporo Washington Hotel I	E
Yūgiri Ryokan	A

RESTAURANTS, CAFÉS & BARS

Aburiya	7	King Xhmu	
Daruma	13	Kirin Beer	
F45 Biru	10	Garden	3
Gaijin Bar	5	Kitanofuji	
Habana	6	Miss Jamaica	
Janbo	11	Mugishutei	9
Jazz Café		Sapporo City	
Bossa	8	Hall Shokudo	18
		Nights	14
Nuts Café			
Nuts Café NY	15		
Deli			
Rad Brothers 1	19		17
Ramen Yōkochō	16		12
Sapporo City			2
Taj Mahal			4
Aji-no-Tokeidai			1

4

364

The Yuki Matsuri

Sapporo's famous snow festival, the **Yuki Matsuri**, has its origins in the winter of 1950, when six small snow statues were created by high-school children in Ōdōri-kōen, the city's main park. The idea caught on and by 1955 the Japanese army was pitching in to help build the gigantic snow sculptures, which included intricately detailed copies of world landmarks such as the Taj Mahal.

Running from February 5 to 11 every year and spread across three sites (the Susukino entertainment district, Makomanai, south of the city centre, and Ōdōri-kōen), the festival now includes an international snow sculpture competition and many other events, such as coordinated ski jumping and nightly music performances in the park. Arrive one week in advance and you'll be able to see the statues being made, and even take part in the construction, since at least one giant statue in Ōdōri-kōen is a community effort – all you need do is turn up and offer your services. Be aware of the need to **book** transport and accommodation well ahead of time. With two million visitors flooding into Sapporo during the *matsuri*, finding last-minute accommodation in the city centre, and even arranging a flight or train to the city, can be very difficult.

destinations on the island. From the airport, the fastest way to Sapporo is on the frequent JR train (¥1040), which runs from Shin-Chitose Kūkō Station in the basement of the airport to Sapporo Station in around 35 minutes. The bus is cheaper (¥820) but takes at least twice as long to arrive at the **Chūō Bus Terminal**, one block north of the TV Tower at the eastern end of Ōdōri-kōen. **Okadama Airport** (☎011/781-4161), 8km northeast of Sapporo, is only for flights within Hokkaidō; a regular bus (¥310) runs from here to opposite the Chūō Bus Terminal.

Arriving by **train**, you'll pull in at busy Sapporo Station, six blocks north of Ōdōri-kōen. Long-distance **buses** terminate at the Chūō Bus Terminal and the Sapporo Station Bus Terminal on the south side of the train station beneath the Esta shopping complex. The closest port to Sapporo is Otaru, served by **ferries** from Honshū and also with a service to the Russian island of Sakhalin.

Finding your way around Sapporo is easy compared to many other Japanese cities because every address has a precise location within the city's **grid plan**. The city blocks are named and numbered according to the compass points, the apex being the TV Tower in **Ōdōri-kōen**, the **park** that bisects Sapporo from east to west – Sapporo Station, for example, is six blocks north of the TV Tower and three blocks west, so its address is North Six, West Three. *Nishi* is west; *minami* is south; *kita* is north; and *higashi* is east.

Information

Sapporo has several excellent tourist information facilities, all staffed by English-speakers. A useful first stop is the **International Information Corner** (daily 9am–5.30pm; ☎011/209-5030, ⊛www.welcome.city.sapporo.jp), inside the most western of the south entrances to Sapporo Station (opposite the Daimaru department store), which has an English pamphlet and map of the city, information on accommodation (though staff won't make bookings for you) and free Internet access (there's a randomly enforced ten-minute limit). More leaflets, along with camping, skiing and youth hostel guidebooks in English, are available at the **Sapporo International Communications Plaza "i"** (daily 9am–5.30pm; ☎011/211-3678), on the first floor of the MN Building, opposite the city's famous clock tower. There's also a good jobs and events noticeboard here, plus a lounge on the third floor where you can read

English newspapers and magazines, and may meet Japanese people eager to practise their English.

The free monthly English newsletter *What's on in Sapporo?* gives **listings** of the city's entertainment and events and is available from all tourist offices, as is the free bilingual magazine *Xene* (Ⓦ www.xene.net), which is also worth a browse, especially for **nightlife**.

City transport

Most of Sapporo's sights are within easy **walking** distance of each other, but the efficient network of subways and buses can be useful if you get tired. There are three **subway** lines: the green **Nanboku line** and the blue **Toho line** run from north to south through Sapporo Station, while the orange Tozai line intersects them both, running east to west under Ōdōri-kōen. The lowest fare is ¥200, which covers all the stops in the city centre. There's also one **tram** line (in purple on the tourist map), which for a flat fare of ¥170 runs from Nishi-Yon-Chōme, just south of Ōdōri-kōen, out to Mount Moiwa, south of the city, and back to Susukino. There are all-day passes for the subway (¥800) or a combined all-day pass covering the subway, tram and the city routes of the JR, Jotetsu and Chuo bus lines for ¥1000. If you're going to be in the city for a while, it's worth investing in the "Withyou" travel card, which gives ten percent extra travel for free and is valid on all types of transport.

City **buses** depart from various bus stops within a block of the station, while Jotetsu and Donan buses leave from a terminal in the basement of the Esta building (as does the bus for the Historical Village of Hokkaidō). The most useful service is the Factory bus (look for the word in stylish English lettering on the side of the white bus), which runs to the Sapporo Museum and Beer Garden via the Factory shopping centre. Bus fares start at ¥200.

Public transport stops running at around 11.30pm, after which you'll probably be glad of the many **taxis** that roam Sapporo's streets.

Accommodation

Even though Sapporo has plenty of **accommodation**, many places get booked up well in advance of the summer season and the Snow Festival in February. The bulk of the hotels are clustered around Sapporo Station, but if it's nightlife you're after you're better off staying in Susukino. If you can't find a room in town, consider staying at nearby Otaru, some 40km northwest of the capital (see p.373).

Hotel Clubby Sapporo Kita 2, Higashi 3 Ⓣ021/242-1111, Ⓔclubby@sapporo-factory.co.jp. This smart hotel is part of the Sapporo Factory redevelopment on the east side of the city. Leather and wood fittings lend an old-fashioned air to the lobby and restaurant, but the rooms are modern, spacious and elegantly decorated. ❼

JR Tower Hotel Nikko Sapporo Kita 5, Nishi 2 Ⓣ011/251-222, Ⓦwww.jrhotels.co.jp. This new luxury hotel occupies the top dozen floors of the JR Tower right on top of JR Sapporo station, with amazing views from the rooms and the 35th-floor bar and restaurant. ❼

Keiō Plaza Hotel Sapporo Kita 5, Nishi 7 Ⓣ011/271-0111, Ⓕ221-5450, Ⓦwww.keioplaza-sapporo.co.jp. Huge, upmarket hotel with conserv-

atively decorated rooms and a wide range of restaurants, plus a swimming pool, gym and sauna. Worth considering between Nov and April, when rates drop significantly. ❼

Marks Inn Sapporo Nishi 3, Minami 8 Ⓣ011/512-5001, Ⓔinfo@markshotels.co.jp. Business hotel conveniently located on the southern side of Susukino; the semi-doubles are a cosy bargain at ¥8500 for two people. Free toast and coffee included in rates. ❺

Nakamuraya Ryokan Nishi 7, Kita 3 Ⓣ011/241-2111, Ⓕ241-2118. Stylish Japanese inn in a modern block near the Botanical Gardens. The tatami rooms are spacious, the maids wear kimono, and there's a large communal bath and a pleasant café in the lobby. ❺

Hotel New Budget Sapporo Minami 3, Nishi 6, a few minutes' walk from Exit 2 of Susukino Station ℡011/261-4953, ℻261-4960. New, good-value business hotel offering en-suite non-smoking singles and twins. You can use the vending machines in the lobby to pay for your stay (no credit cards), and purchase prepaid cards for pay TV in your room or the laundry on the fifth floor. Simple continental breakfast included. ➍

Hotel New Ōtani Sapporo Kita 2, Nishi 1 ℡011/222-1111, ℻222-5521, Ⓦhttp://hrt.newotani.co.jp/sapporo/index-e.htm. One of Sapporo's most luxurious hotels, and within walking distance of both the JR station and Ōdōri-kōen. Rooms have all the conveniences you'd expect in this price range. Check out the striking fresco of Hokkaidō cranes by French artist Bernard Buffet in the ground-floor café. ➐

Ino's Place 6-5-3 4-chōme, Higashi-Sapporo, Shiroishi ℡011/832-1828, Ⓦwww.inos-place.com. Spruce and friendly new backpackers' hostel near Shiroishi subway station, five stops out from Sapporo Station on the Tozai line. The smaller dorms can be booked as private rooms (sleeping up to 4) for an additional fee. There's a clean, well-equipped kitchen and a pleasant lounge. The hostel is a bit hard to find: check their website for a detailed map and instructions. ¥3400–4800 per person.

Safro Spa (previously known as the *Hokuō Club*) Minami 6, Nishi 5 ℡011/531-2233, Ⓔinfo@safro.org. Amazingly luxurious and excellent-value capsule hotel in the heart of Susukino. Facilities include ornamental baths, a gym and a mini-cinema. There is also a floor of capsules for women. Check-in from 5pm. ➋

Sapporo House Youth Hostel Nishi 6, Kita 6 ℡011/726-4235, Ⓦwww.youthhostel.or.jp/English/menu2.htm. Spartan hostel with a strict timetable but an excellent location, a couple of minutes' walk west of Sapporo Station. ¥2670 per person.

Sapporo Inn NADA Minami 5, Nishi 9 ℡011/551-5882, Ⓔsapporoinnnada@jcom.home .ne.jp. Dorm accommodation in tatami rooms in a quiet neighbourhood ten minutes' walk west of Susukino. The atmosphere is relaxed, and there's no curfew, though the manager likes to be notified if you plan to check in after 6pm. Part of the Toho group. ¥3500 per person.

Sapporo International Youth Hostel Toyohira 6-6-5-35 ℡011/825-3120, Ⓦwww.youthhostel.or.jp/kokusai. Just east of Exit 2 of Toho-line Gakuen-Mae Station, this brand-new hostel has dorm rooms for single travellers, tatami rooms for families, and twins (➌) for married couples. English spoken. Dorms ¥3200 per person.

Sapporo Washington Hotel 1 Kita 4, Nishi 4 ℡011/251-3211, Ⓦwww.wh-rsv.com/english. The cheaper of the city's two *Washington* hotels. Rooms are bland but functional, and the singles are very small. ➏

Yūgiri Ryokan Kita 7, Nishi 5 ℡011/716-5482. Small and slightly shabby ryokan on the quieter north side of Sapporo Station. A cotton *yukata* and green tea are provided in the basic tatami rooms, but no meals are provided, and (despite the welcome sign in English outside) the management don't speak the language. However, it's very close to the station and quite cheap. ➍

The City

Although there isn't much to see in central Sapporo, it's a pleasant place simply to stroll around. The single best attraction is the compact and pretty **Botanical Gardens** (May–Sept Tues–Sun 9am–4pm; Oct Tues–Sun 9am–3.30pm; ¥400), a ten-minute walk southwest of Sapporo Station. Immediately to the right as you enter is the small but interesting **Ainu Museum**, known as the "Batchelor Kinenkan" in memory of the Reverend John Batchelor, a British priest and author of *The Ainu of Japan*, considered to be the definitive work on Hokkaidō's aborigines. The museum has a collection of around 2500 Ainu artefacts (though only a fraction is displayed at any time), ranging from clothes made of bird skins from the Kuril islands to a sacred altar for performing the ritual slaughter of a bear cub – there are English-language explanations. Following the red-gravel pathway around to the right of the museum leads you to **Miyabe Hall**, with intriguing displays of letters and journals belonging to Professor Miyabe Kingo, the first director of Hokkaidō University, who established the gardens in 1886. Miyabe's descriptions of his travels abroad, written in English and illustrated with photographs, make fascinating reading.

The gardens themselves are very attractive, with a long pond, a greenhouse, a rockery, shaded forest walks and neat flower gardens, including a collection which shows the plants and flowers used by the Ainu in their daily lives. In the centre of it all stands a **natural history museum**, housed in a pale-green wooden building dating from 1882. Inside you'll find a staggering collection of stuffed animals, paintings and other bizarre objects, including snarling wolves, huge sea lions, and a dog sled from Sakhalin.

On your way to or from the gardens, check out the **Old Hokkaidō Government Building**, at North Three, West Six. This palatial red-brick building is a fine example of the Sapporo-style of architecture that fused the late-nineteenth-century European and New World influences flooding into the country with Japanese traditions. You'll see the same style on the campus of Hokkaidō University at North Eight, West Seven, and at the Sapporo Brewery (see below). Directly in front of the Sapporo International Communication Plaza is the **Tokeidai**, a wooden clock tower that attracts hordes of Japanese tourists. You'd be right in thinking that this newly renovated building, which is a symbol of the city, would look more at home in somewhere like Boston, because that's where it was made in 1880. One block south lies Ōdōri-kōen and the contrasting 147-metre red steel **TV Tower**. There's no need to fork out ¥700 to go up to the viewing platform; the vista from the nineteenth floor of Sapporo City Hall opposite is free and just as good.

The neon-illuminated excess of **Susukino**, the largest area of bars, restaurants and nightclubs north of Tokyo, begins on the southern side of Ōdōri-kōen, and is best explored at night. If you've not yet had your fill of parks, **Nakajima-kōen**, at West Four, South Nine, is the third of central Sapporo's large-scale green spots and is only worth visiting to see the **Hasso-an**, an early Edo-period teahouse which is virtually the only traditional Japanese building in the city. Better to head to West Seventeen, North One, to the large, white **Hokkaidō Museum of Modern Art** (Tues–Sun 10am–5pm; ¥250 for permanent exhibition), which holds a modest but absorbing collection of paintings and sculptures, some by Japanese artists. The nearest subway station to the museum is Nishi Juhatchōme, on the Tozai line.

Sapporo Beer Garden and Museum

It was an American adviser to Hokkaidō who noted the hops growing locally and realized that with its abundant winter ice Sapporo was the ideal location for a commercial brewery. When the first brewery opened in 1876, locals didn't touch beer, so for years Sapporo exported to the foreign community in Tokyo. Things have changed somewhat since then, and today the Japanese knock back around seven million kilolitres a year.

The hugely popular **Sapporo Beer Garden and Museum** (daily 8.40/9am–4/5pm; free, reservations on ☎011/731-4368) stands just east of the city centre. Beer is still brewed in this grand red-brick building, which dates from 1891, but it's now the company's smallest brewery since much of the building has been turned over to a large, modern exhibition on the brewing process and the history of the company, not to mention several restaurants, pubs and souvenir shops. It's worth going on the free one-hour tour; you can pick up a recorded English-language commentary at the beginning, though this often gets drowned out by the guide's enthusiastic use of her mini-megaphone. The best tactic is to lag behind the tour group and catch up at the end, when free samples of the main product can be enjoyed. Look out for the ingenious combined model and video display where a fairy emerges from a glass of beer.

The beer garden (see p.371) and museum are roughly a twenty-minute walk east of Sapporo Station. The easiest way to get here is to hop on the Factory Bus, which departs every ten minutes or so from in front of the Seibu department store at West Three, North Four. The bus goes via the Sapporo Factory, the first of Sapporo's breweries in the city, converted in 1993 into a shopping and entertainment complex.

Historical Village of Hokkaidō

The brewery may pull the biggest crowds, but the best of the attractions around Sapporo – indeed, one of the most impressive sights on the entire island – is the **Historical Village of Hokkaidō** (Tues–Sun 9.30am–4.30/5pm; ¥610), some 14km east of the city centre. This impressive museum, laid out across a spacious park, gathers together some sixty buildings constructed around Hokkaidō between the mid-nineteenth and twentieth centuries, as large-scale immigration from Honshū cranked up. Wandering around the village's four main areas, representing town, farm, mountain and fishing communities, will give you a strong picture of what Hokkaidō looked like before prefabricated buildings and concrete expressways became the norm.

The buildings have been restored as beautifully inside as out and spruced up with displays related to their former use, be it a sweet shop, a silkworm house or a woodcutter's shanty. There are guides in some houses (explanations in Japanese only) and written English explanations in all. It's a good idea to wear slip-on shoes, as you'll be taking them off a lot to explore the interiors. In summer, you can hop aboard the horse-drawn trolley car (¥200) that plies the main street – in winter this is replaced by a sleigh. Some of the houses are shut from December to April, but the village is worth visiting even then for its special atmosphere when blanketed in snow.

To cover the whole site will take you a good half-day and it's a nice place to bring a picnic. Otherwise, there are a couple of inexpensive **restaurants** and refreshment stops within the village. You can extend your visit by exploring the neighbouring grounds of **Nopporo Forest Park**, created to commemorate Hokkaidō's centennial and containing the mildly interesting **Historical Museum of Hokkaidō** (Tues–Sun 9.30am–4.30pm; ¥300) and **Centennial Memorial Tower**, a 100-metre-tall metal spike which you can ascend for a free view of the city.

Three JR buses run directly to the Historical Village each morning from bus stop #3 at the Sapporo Station terminal, taking around an hour. There are more frequent buses from platform 10 at the terminus beneath Shin Sapporo Station, connected to the city centre by both train and subway. The bus journey from Shin Sapporo Station takes only fifteen minutes, but note that the last bus departs at 1.50pm (July 26–Aug 16 2.10pm). A taxi to or from the park to Shin Sapporo will cost you around ¥1000.

Moerenuma Park

A forty-minute subway and bus ride out of town is **Moerenuma Park**, part playground and part sculpture garden displaying the works of internationally renowned artist **Isamu Noguchi** (see box on p.370). Noguchi's large-scale works here include the *Play Mountain* (essentially a thirty-metre-high grassed pyramid), the *Tetra Mound* (a hollow, triangular stainless-steel pyramid), the *Music Shell* (two facing, solid hemispherical structures which double as a concert stage) and a giant glass pyramid, with observation decks and a library/lounge where you can peruse English-language books on the artist. With massed plantings of cherry trees, wide lawns and a shallow pebbled bathing beach, the park is popular with local families, making it a convivial spot for a picnic.

Isamu Noguchi

Born in Los Angeles in 1904 to an Irish–American teacher and a Japanese poet, **Isamu Noguchi** spent part of his childhood in Japan before returning to the States to continue his education. He trained in medicine at New York City's Columbia University before abandoning his studies to work full-time as a sculptor. Interests in Surrealism and abstract sculpture led to a Guggenheim Fellowship in Paris, where he worked with the great sculptor Constantin Brancusi, and to Mexico City, where he collaborated with the painter Diego Rivera. Noguchi returned to Japan after World War II, creating numerous site-specific pieces and working to bridge the cultural gap between Japan and the United States. Noguchi died in 1988, the year he completed the design of Moerenuma Park. He left behind a body of work that includes the Isamu Noguchi Garden Museum (New York City), and sculptures, fountains and gardens around the world.

To reach the park, take the Toho subway line from Sapporo Station to Kanjō-dōri station. From the bus terminal above the station take the #69 or #79 bus bound for Nakanuma Elementary School Street (¥320) and get off at Moere Koen Higashiguchi, from where it's a five-minute walk through the car park and over a bridge.

Eating

As you'd expect from a capital city, Sapporo has the best range of **restaurants** in Hokkaidō, and many of them are very good value, if not downright cheap. There are also plenty of cafés, including branches of the ever-reliable *Mr. Donut*, *Doutor* and *Starbucks*. The pick of the restaurants is clustered around the **Susukino** area, but there's also a good range of places above and beneath Sapporo Station, in the major department stores and at the Sapporo Factory shopping mall, east of the city centre.

Sapporo is renowned for its **ramen** noodles – try the version called *batā-kōn*, which is a noodle broth of butter and corn. A more expensive local speciality is the *jingisukan*, or "Genghis Khan" barbecue, a delicious feast of flame-grilled lamb and vegetables available at many restaurants and at all the city's beer gardens. At the beer gardens you'll be provided with a plastic bib to protect against dribbles from the dipping sauce, but it's still best to dress down, since the smell of sizzled mutton lingers long after you've left. At both the Sapporo and Kirin beer gardens you can pig out on as much barbecue and beer as you can get down you within one hundred minutes for a set price, but you'll find the quality of mutton much better at the smaller Susukino *jingisukan* joints.

It's best to book ahead at the restaurants below where we've given a telephone number.

Restaurants and cafés

Aburiya Minami 3, Nishi 2. Downstairs at the end of the Tanuki shopping arcade, this spacious and stylish *izakaya* specializes in fish dishes, which you can see being prepared at the open kitchen. There are other branches at Minami 2, Nishi 5 and Kita 4, Nishi 5 on the 16th floor of the Asty Building opposite Sapporo Station. Daily 5–11.30pm.

Aji-no-Tokeidai Kita 1, Nishi 3. One of a chain of lively noodle shops, serving large bowls of *batā-* *kōn* ramen for ¥1000. You'll be asked whether you want your soup flavoured with miso (fermented bean paste), *shōyu* (soy sauce) or *shio* (salt). You can sit at the bar downstairs and watch the white-aproned chefs at work.

Daruma Minami 5, Nishi 4. Run by a couple of crusty old ladies, this cosy *jingisukan* joint hides on a narrow street in the midst of Susukino; look for the red lantern and scowling bald Genghis on the sign outside. The cuts of meat are much juicier

than at the beer gardens, with one plate costing ¥700. Mon–Sat 5.30pm–2am, Sun 4.30pm–1am.
F45 Biru Minami 4, Nishi 5. Look for the giant cracked golden egg outside this fourteen-storey building in Susukino, housing a good range of restaurants and *izakaya*, as well as the popular *Ninikuya* (one of a chain of restaurants) in the basement, where everything is cooked with garlic. Most restaurants open daily 5.30pm–2am.
Kirin Beer Garden Minami 10, Nishi 1 ☏011/533-3000. The first floor houses the intimate *Bierhalle*, with regular acoustic live music, while the second and third floors form a vast, high-tech amphitheatre, called *Space Craft*. The all-you-can-eat-and-drink *jingisukan* and beer is ¥4000 per person for one hundred minutes.
Kitanofuji Minami 7, Nishi 4, in the Susukino Plaza Building. Atmospheric restaurant, complete with a mock sumo ring, serving a chuck-it-all-in stew dish used to fatten up sumo fighters. You can either sit on tatami or at tables, and meals start at around ¥2000 per person. Daily 4–11pm.
Nuts Café Nights Minami 6, Nishi 4. Open until 6am, with a full all-night menu (there's even a night-time "lunch" special for ¥750). For something light, try the dragon-noodle salad or "stick-za-vegetable" (sticks of carrots, celery and so on). Daily 5pm–6am.
Nuts Café NY Deli Minami 1, Nishi 4, on the 9th floor of the S1 building, next door to the ancient Steinway piano shop. This daytime sister restaurant to *Nuts Café Nights* offers a similarly eclectic menu and a great view of downtown. The "one coin lunch" (¥500) changes daily and might be a

herb chicken sandwich, chilled tomato pasta, an udon salad, or whatever the chef dreams up. The various "wrap sandwiches" are great. Daily 11.30am–1am.
Rāmen Yōkochō Minami 5, Nishi 3. This narrow alley in the heart of Susukino is crammed with scores of ramen joints and big on atmosphere. A huge bowl of freshly cooked noodles costs around ¥1000. Daily around 11am–2am.
Sapporo Bier Garten Kita 7, Higashi 9 ☏011/742-1531. There's a Germanic atmosphere in this airy restaurant in the old Sapporo Brewery (see p.368), with an outdoor area where you can down a cooling beer in the summer. The all-you-can-eat-and-drink deal is good value. Daily 11.30am–9pm.
Sapporo City Hall Shokudō Kita 1, Nishi 2. Around ¥600 gets you a decent lunch at this self-service canteen in the basement of Sapporo City Hall, and plastic food displays show what's on the menu. Pay for the appropriate ticket from the vending machine (look for a matching *kanji* label), present it at the counter, and then take your food and eat with the civil servants. Picture windows look out onto a pleasant ornamental garden, and there's a café and a good outdoor viewing platform on the nineteenth floor.
Taj Mahal Kita 2, Nishi 3. Part of a nationwide Indian chain, this second-floor restaurant serves hearty curries and freshly baked *nan*, and is a great place for vegetarians who are tired of *zaru soba*. Lunch sets cost from ¥720 and dinner sets from ¥1020. There's another branch in the Sapporo Factory shopping mall.

Drinking and nightlife

Apart from the beer gardens, the best place to head for a **drink** in Sapporo is bustling, neon-drenched **Susukino**. Susukino is notorious for its thinly disguised brothels, known as "soaplands", but people of all ages wander through the area at all hours on their way to reputable bars and restaurants, blithely ignoring the sleazy places. The **nightlife** here is as subject to the whims of fashion as any other of Japan's big cities. If only the hippest place will do, check first with the clued-up assistants at the International Communications Plaza "i" (see p.365) or leaf through the free bilingual info magazine *Xene* (ⓦwww.xene.net). Several of the bars listed below also serve good food.

Gaijin Bar Minami 2, Nishi 7. The sign outside translates as "nest of delinquent *gaijin*", but everyone knows this very casual second-floor joint by its shorter name. Serves a similar range of beers as *Mugishutei* (see p.372), but at cheaper prices and with no cover charge, and also has a ninety-minute all-you-can-drink deal for ¥1500. Closed Sun.
Habana Minami 3, Nishi 5, on the 2nd and 3rd floor above the Tanuki Arcade. Spicy chicken and

rice entrées and lively Latin American music, plus occasional salsa parties.
Janbo Minami 5, Nishi 4. Across the street from *Daruma* (see opposite), this tiny *yakitori* bar has a friendly, rock-loving owner who serves up succulent sticks of grilled chicken to nibble with your beer. Closed Sun.
Jazz Café Bossa Minami 3, Nishi 4, Gobangai Building, 3F. This small, slick, dimly lit bar with booth seating and walls lined with stacks of old

jazz records is the best place to chill out after a hectic night out.

King Xhmu Minami 7, Nishi 4. The exterior of this club (pronounced "King Mu") resembles a misplaced Mayan colossus, while the interior is a high-tech Indiana Jones adventure. Generally features thumping techno music; entry hovers around ¥4000, although it's only ¥1000 on Mon, Thurs and Fri if you're 23 or over. Entrance charge includes two drinks.

Miss Jamaica Minami 3, Nishi 6. Drinks are around ¥500 each at this funky Caribbean bar with a jukebox of rare gems and at least thirty different kinds of rum and tequila. The menu includes Jamaican curry and rice for ¥900.

Mugishutei Minami 9, Nishi 5, Onda Building, B1. Convivial basement bar at the quiet end of Susukino, decorated with 5000 beer cans and bottles from around the world. Over 250 different types of ale are served – plus food (including fish and chips). The owner, Phred, is a fixture of the Susukino scene who also owns the *Gaijin Bar*. Note that there's a substantial "charm charge" of ¥900. Daily 7pm–3am.

Rad Brothers 1 Minami 7, Nishi 3, Mitsuwa Building. Uncluttered bar on the corner of a block in Susukino with a young and rowdy clientele and beers for ¥500 each.

Listings

Airlines ANA & ANK, Kita 4, Nishi 4 ☎0120-029333; Cathay Pacific, Kita 4, Nishi 4 ☎0120-355747; JAL, Kita 2, Nishi 4 ☎0120-255971 (domestic flights), ☎0120-255931 (international); JAS, Kita 2, Nishi 4 ☎0120-511283; Korean Air, Kita 4, Nishi 5 ☎011/210-3311.

Banks Bank of Tokyo Mitsubishi, Ōdōri, Nishi 3, changes all major currencies, as does the Ōdōri post office, one block west, and the central post office east of Sapporo Station. Mitsukoshi, Marui and Gobankan Seibu department stores all have foreign-exchange counters, though only Mitsukoshi changes sterling, and the others only accept travellers' cheques.

Bookshops Maruzen, Minami 1, Nishi 4 (Tues–Sun 10am–7pm), with a wide range of English-language books and magazines on its fourth floor, has the edge over Kinokuniya (daily except Wed 10am–7pm), opposite the TV tower on Ōdōri, Nishi 1. For a good range of cheap secondhand books, head to the American-run New Day, 5F Arche Building, Minami 3, Nishi 4, on the corner of Tanuki Arcade and Ekimae-dōri (daily 10.30am–8pm).

Car rental Try Eki Rent-a-Car ☎011/241-0931; Nippon Rent-a-Car ☎011/746-0919; or Orix Rent-a-Car ☎011/241-0543.

Consulates Australia, Kita 1, Nishi 3 ☎011/242-4381; China, Minami 13, Nishi 23 ☎011/563-5563; Russia, Minami 14, Nishi 12 ☎011/561-3171; USA, Kita 1, Nishi 28 ☎011/641-1115.

Emergencies The main police station is at Kita 1, Nishi 5 ☎011/241-3201. In an absolute emergency, contact the Foreign Advisory Service on ☎011/211-2105. For other emergency numbers, see p.81.

Hospital Sapporo City General Hospital, Kita 11, Nishi 13 ☎011/726-2211.

Internet access You can check your email (quickly) inside the JR Sapporo station complex at the International Information Corner (10min limit). Alternatively, head to either Doutor, just inside the north exit (¥200 per 30min), or the Bon de Bon Café, behind the stairwell on the basement level of the Paseo shopping centre, entered opposite the east ticket gate (¥200 per 30min if you order food, or ¥900 for an hour, including a coffee and cake set). Another option is *Airs Café*, Minami 1, Nishi 4, 6F Create Building (opposite *Nuts Café NY*), a 24-hour Internet and comic café (¥100 per 15min including soft drinks).

Laundry Among the many 24-hour coin laundries about town are: Shirokuma, Minami 8, Nishi 6; Softer, Minami 9, Nishi 9; and Coin Laundry Tsudoi, Minami 9, Nishi 8.

Post office The central post office is at Kita 6, Higashi 1, two blocks east of the JR station (Mon–Fri 9am–7pm, Sat 9am–5pm, Sun 9am–12.30pm). There's also a branch in the Paseo shopping centre in the JR Sapporo station complex (Mon–Fri 10am–7pm, Sat & Sun 10am–5pm), and nearly a dozen more smaller post offices in the blocks between JR Sapporo station and the Susukino subway stations.

Shopping Sapporo has branches of all of Japan's top department stores, including Mitsukoshi, Seibu, Daimaru and Tōkyū. The huge Robinsons in Susukino is worth rooting around in, as is the Tanuki Koji, the covered shopping arcade that stretches for six blocks across Minami 3, which was once the city's main shopping street. If you are heading out for hiking or camping in Hokkaidō's national parks, ICI Sports (*Ishii Supotsu*), at Minami 2, Nishi 4 on Tanuki arcade, has outdoor gear, topographical maps and knowledgeable staff.

Taxis The main rank is at the south exit of Sapporo Station. To book a taxi (¥100 extra charge), call the Taxi Association on ☎011/892-6000; Japanese only.

Travel agency The main JTB office where you'll find English-speakers is in the Nissei Building at Kita 3, Nishi 4 ☎011/241-6201.

Otaru

One of the most relaxing ways of arriving at or leaving Hokkaidō is on a ferry
to or from the port of **OTARU**, some 40km northwest of Sapporo. Though
the town itself has no major attractions, save for an area of restored Meiji-era
buildings along a canal, and Mount Tengu, where there's skiing in winter, its
cluster of good-value **hotels** makes this a possible base if you can't find anywhere to stay in Sapporo.

To find the nineteenth-century canal quarter of Meiji-era buildings, head
towards the sea from Otaru Station down Chūō-dōri, the town's main street.
The canal is at its most attractive for a very short stretch to the right of Chūō-
dōri, especially at dusk, when the gas lamps flicker to life. Facing the canal to
the left of Chūō-dōri is the **Otaru Museum** (daily 9.30am–5pm; ¥100), with
an average collection of historical and nature displays in a converted 1893
warehouse. In one of the warehouses to the right of the main road you'll find
the **Otaru Biiru** *jibiiru* (microbrewery), where gleaming copper stills dominate
the wooden beer hall. The brewery serves three regular German-style **beers** (a
crisp Alt, the darker Dunkel and the cloudy, "banana-flavoured" Weissbier) at
¥500 a glass, as well as special seasonal beers and snacks. If they're around, the
German masterbrewer or his assistant can give you a tour of the brewery.

Limited express **trains** (¥620) from Sapporo take around thirty minutes to
reach Otaru – **buses** and local trains are slower and slightly cheaper. **Ferries**
from Niigata (see p.338) in northern Honshū and Maizuru and Tsuruga, both
north of Kyoto, dock at the ferry terminal, some 5km east of the train station.
Regular buses run between the ferry terminal and Otaru Station; a taxi will
cost around ¥1000. You can pick up an English map at the **tourist information office** inside the station (daily 9am–6pm; ☎0134/29-1333).

Of the cluster of **hotels** near Otaru Station, one of the cheapest is the *Otaru
Green Hotel* (☎0134/33-0333, ⓕ33-6741; ❹), five minutes' walk down Chūō-
dōri, offering a flat rate per person of under ¥4000. If that's full, try the nicer
but more expensive *New Green Hotel* (☎0134/33-6100, ⓕ33-6741; ❹) across
the road. *La Lulu* (☎0134/27-0866; ❷) is a youth hostel-style minshuku ten
minutes' walk north of Otaru Station with separate men's and women's dorms
(¥3500 per person). More upmarket is *Hotel Nord Otaru* (☎0134/24-0500,
ⓕ24-1085; ❼), with Western-style rooms in an elegant stone building overlooking the canal. The *Otaru Tengu-yama Youth Hostel* (☎0134/34-1474,
ⓦwww.tengu.co.jp/english/index.html; dorm beds ¥3000 per person, private
rooms ¥3200 per person) is 5km south of the station, near the cable car which
goes up Mount Tengu, and is convenient for the ski slope on the mountain. To
reach the hostel, take the bus from platform 3 outside the station.

Otaru is renowned for its **sushi** and **sashimi** restaurants, though none is cheap
– you'll find them at the end of the Sun Mall Ichiban-gai shopping arcade, to the
east of the station. A sushi assortment (*moriawase*) for one costs ¥2500–3000.

Niseko

Some 100km west of Sapporo, between the dormant volcano Mount Yōtei-san
(also known as the Ezo Fuji for its resemblance to its famous southern cousin)
and Mount Niseko Annupuri, lies **NISEKO**, one of the best **ski resorts** in
Japan. This widely spread-out town also lies within the Niseko-Shakotan-
Otaru Quasi National Park and makes a good summer base if you want to take
advantage of the many adventure sports activities on offer in the area.

The **ski slopes** are a couple of kilometres north of Niseko Station, at the
foot of Mount Niseko Annupuri. Ski lifts are run by three separate **resorts**:

Hirafu Kōgen, *Higashiyama* (part of the *Prince* hotel empire) and *Annupuri Kokusai*. You can buy individual lift tickets from each of the resorts, but the best deal is to go for the "Free Passport", which allows you to use all lifts, and thus ski the whole mountain. A one-day pass costs around ¥4500 and is issued as an electronic tag – you'll need to wave it at the barrier at each of the lifts. If you only buy a pass for one resort, take care not to ski beyond their lifts, otherwise you'll have to buy a single-ride ticket (*ikkaiken*) to get back up.

In summer the same mountain becomes the focus for **adventure sports**, including whitewater rafting, mountain biking and kayaking. The Niseko Adventure Centre (℡0136/23-2093, ⓦwww.nac-web.com), on Route 343 below the Hirafu ski fields, and the Niseko Outdoor Adventure Sports Club (℡0136/23-1688, ⓦwww.noasc.com), on the other side of the road, offer all these activities and more between mid-April and November; both companies employ a number of English-speaking guides and offer backcountry guiding, snowboarding, telemark skiing and ice climbing in winter.

Practicalities

Niseko is tricky to visit without your own car, except in winter, when **buses** run directly to the ski slopes from Sapporo and New Chitose Airport; the Chūō bus goes straight to Annupuri, while the Dōnan service stops first at Hirafu and Higashiyama. Buy your ticket from the booths on the second floor of the bus station under the Sogō department store, next to Sapporo Station. Alternatively, there are infrequent **trains** to Niseko Station, from where you'll have to take a bus or a taxi to the slopes. Combined lift-pass and bus or train-ticket packages will save you money; details are available from the tourist information centre in Sapporo (see p.365). **Ski maps** can be picked up at the accommodation places listed below and from the ticket offices at the three resorts. There are no information centres at the ski resorts, but there is a **tourist information office** next to the ticket window at Niseko station, and the English-speaking staff of the Niseko Outdoor Adventure Sports Club and Niseko Adventure Centre (see above) provide a wealth of information. Online, try ⓦwww.niseko.gr.jp/eigo.htm or ⓦwww.skijapanguide.com for details on Niseko and other areas.

With an early start it's possible to ski for most of the day at Niseko and return to Sapporo the same evening. If you stay overnight, you're best off **eating** breakfast or dinner at your pension or hostel, since there are few alternative options. There are plenty of places for lunch on the slopes – the *Rāmen Corner* hut at the Higashiyama resort is worth checking out, and there's a *KFC* at Hirafu. The Niseko Adventure Centre is home to *JOJO*'s café and bar, serving the best breakfast in the area.

Accommodation

Most of Niseko's **hotels** and **pensions** are at the Annupuri and Hirafu resorts – Higashiyama is the preserve of the *Prince Hotel* chain. Of the two youth hostels, the *Niseko Annupuri* is the most convenient for the slopes and has the nicest atmosphere.

Niseko Annupuri Youth Hostel 479-4 Niseko ℡0136/58-2084, ⓦwww.youthhostel.or.jp/English/menu2.htm. Charming European-style log-cabin pension with a roaring fire, a couple of minutes' walk from the Annupuri Kokusai resort. Mitsura-san, the friendly manager, can sort out ski rental, and he and his wife are excellent cooks. Dorm beds ¥3100 per person.

Niseko Kōgen Youth Hostel 336 Niseko ℡0136/44-1171, ℮kogenyh@rose.ocn.ne.jp. This former schoolhouse is rather isolated, but offers ski-break packages, and the managers will run you out to the slopes. Guests are entertained every night with an accordion concert. Dorm beds ¥3100 per person.

Niseko Prince Hotel Higashiyama ℡0136/44-

1111, ⓦ www.princehotels.co.jp/english /index.html. Upmarket hotel with comfortable rooms, several restaurants, an onsen bath and ski lifts close at hand. Has fantastic views of Mount Yōtei, especially from the newer Annex building. ⑧

Pension Asauta 35 Higashiyama ☏ 0136/44-2943, ⒺⒷⒾⒸⒿ daiko@itcj.or.jp. Excellent Western-style family-run accommodation in a pale-green wooden chalet close to the Higashiyama ski area at Niseko. The meals are delicious and Sato-san, the owner, speaks good English. ⑥

Hakodate and around

If you travel to Hokkaidō by train, the first major city you'll come to after emerging from the Seikan Tunnel (see box, p.376) is the attractive port of **HAKODATE**, 260km southwest of Sapporo. Along with Shimoda on the Izu Hantō (see p.231), this was one of the first **ports** to open to foreign traders following the Japan–US amity treaty of 1854. Over the next few years, ten countries including Britain, Russia and the USA established consulates in Hakodate, and foreigners built fancy wooden homes and elaborate churches on the steep hillsides, leaving the city with a legacy of European and American-style architecture.

Hakodate and around

Hakodate	Hakodate	函館
Goryōkaku fort	Goryōkaku	五稜郭
Hakodate City Museum of Northern Peoples	Hoppōminzoku Shiryōkan	北方民族資料館
Hakodate-yama	Hakodate-yama	函館山
Motomachi	Motomachi	元町
Seikan Tunnel	Seikan Tonneru	青函トンネル
Trappistine Convent	Torapisuchinu Shūdōin	トラピスチヌ修道院

Accommodation

Fitness Hotel 330 Hakodate	Fittonesu Hoteru 330 Hakodate	フィットネスホテル330函館
Hakodate Harbourview Hotel	Hakodate Hābābyū Hoteru	函館ハーバービューホテル
Hakodate Kokusai Hotel	Hakodate Kokusai Hoteru	函館国際ホテル
Hakodate Youth Guesthouse	Hakodate Yūsu Gesutohausu	函館ユースゲストハウス
Kokian	Kokian	古稀庵
Nagashima	Nagashima	長島
Niceday Inn	Naisudei In	ナイスディイン
Pension Hakodate-Mura	Penshon Hakodate-Mura	ペンションはこだて村
Tabiji	Tabiji	旅路

Eating

Aji-no-Ichiban	Aji-no-Ichiban	味の一番
Akachōchin	Akachōchin	あかちょうちん
Coyoacan Café	Koyoakan Café	コヨアカンカフェ
Hishii	Hishii	ひし伊
Nihombashi	Nihombashi	日本橋
Tonetsu	Ton'etsu	とん悦

Ōnuma

Ōnuma	Ōnuma	大沼
Chairoi-tori	Chairoi-tori	茶色い鳥
Ōnuma Kōen Youth Hostel	Ōnuma Kōen Yūsu Hosuteru	大沼公園ユースホステル

In 1868 the last of the Tokugawa shogun's forces was defeated in a siege of Hakodate's Goryōkaku fort, a victory celebrated each year in mid-May with a period costume parade through the town. A much larger parade is held during the Hakodate Port Festival, from August 1 to 5, when 20,000 people in cotton kimono and straw hats perform the "squid dance", an entertaining jig where hands are flapped and clapped in time to rhythmic drumming.

Despite the fishy aroma that sometimes hangs in the air, Hakodate has some compelling attractions. While you're here, be sure to check out the lively morning market of **Asa-ichi**, the early twentieth-century settlers' homes in the **Motomachi** area, and the outstanding exhibition on **Ainu** culture at the main museum. Finally, no self-respecting traveller should leave before taking in the "million-dollar" night view from the top of **Hakodate-yama**, the mountain in the middle of the hammerhead tip of the peninsula. In addition, the **Ōnuma Quasi National Park**, a beautiful lakeland and mountain area with good hiking trails, is within easy day-trip range of the city.

Arrival, information and city transport

Hakodate's **airport** (☎0138/57-8881) lies 8km north of the city; buses take roughly twenty minutes from here to reach Hakodate Station in the city centre on the eastern side of the harbour and cost around ¥300. **Trains** from Morioka and Aomori on Honshū, and Sapporo and New Chitose airport on Hokkaidō, also terminate at Hakodate Station – the **bus** terminal is in front of here. If you're arriving by **ferry** from Honshū, you'll dock at Hakodate-kō Port, some 4km north of Hakodate Station. Buses #1 and #19 leave from the Hokkudai-mae stop, seven minutes' walk south of the port, to the city centre; alternatively, take a taxi for around ¥2000.

For a map of the city, call in at the **Hakodate Tourist Information Office** (daily: April–Oct 9am–7pm; Jan–March, Nov & Dec 9am–5pm; ☎0138/23-5440, ⓦwww.city.hakodate.hokkaido.jp/kikaku/english), next to Hakodate Station, where the assistants speak English and can also make accommodation bookings.

Hakodate's sights are spread out, so you'll need to use public transport to get around. This is no hardship as the city has a good **tram** system with two lines, both starting at the onsen resort of Yunokawa east of the city and running past Goryōkaku and the train station before diverging at the Jūjigai stop in Motomachi. From here, tram #5 heads west to Hakodate Dokku-mae, while

---

The Seikan Tunnel

It took forty years to complete the mammoth **Seikan Tunnel**. Joining Honshū with Hokkaidō, the tunnel is 53.9km long, and over half its length is underwater, making it the world's longest submarine transport link. Travelling through Seikan isn't recommended for the claustrophobic: even the fastest train takes an hour to complete the underground portion of the journey, with the tunnel sinking to 240m beneath sea level at its deepest point. If you're comfortable with being this far down, however, you may want to go on a **tour** of the submarine facilities, which include a small exhibition area and a warren of passageways, one of which has its own cable-car link with the shore. For an extra ¥840 on top of your train fare, you can get off at one of the mid-tunnel stations (145m below sea level), where you'll be shown around by a Japanese-speaking guide. The tours must be booked in advance at JR ticket counters. Note that on all trains only the doors of carriage number 2 open at the tunnel station.

HAKODATE

▲ Goryūkaku, Yunokawa & Trappistine Convent

◄ Ōnuma Quasi National Park & Seikan Tunnel

◄ Hakodate dokku-mae

HOKKAIDŌ | Hakodate and around

Tsugaru-Kaikyō Strait

0   250 m

Train Station

Asa-ichi

Hakodate-eki-mae

Shiyakusho-mae

City Hall

Hakodate Harbour

Uoichiba-dōri

Jūjigai

Horai-chō

▶ Yachigashira

GOKOKU-JINJA SLAPE

Cable Car Station

MOTOMACHI

Hakodate City Museum of Northern Peoples

Suehiro-chō

Old British Consulate

Old Public Hall of Hakodate Ward

Motomachi-kōen

MOTOI-ZAKA SLAPE

Motomachi Roman Catholic

Russian Orthodox

Episcopal

Hakodate-yama

ACCOMMODATION	
Fitness Hotel 300	
Hakodate Harbourview	
Hakodate Kokusai	
Hakodate Youth Guesthouse	
Kokian	
Nagashima	
Niceday Inn	
Pension Hakodate-Mura	
Tabiji	

RESTAURANTS	
Aji-no-ichiban	1
Akachōchin	5
BAY Hakodate	3
Coyoacan Cafe	6
Hakodate Beer	2
Hishii	9
Lucky Pierrot	7
Nihombashi	4
Tonetsu	8

377

tram #2 continues further south to Yachigashira on the eastern side of Hakodate-yama. One-day (¥1000) and two-day passes (¥1700) can be bought from the tourist office for unlimited use of both the trams and city **buses** (but not Hakodate Bus Company buses). These passes, only worth buying if you plan to tour extensively around town, also cover the bus service up Hakodate-yama. The ¥600 all-day **tram** ticket is better value; individual tram trips cost ¥200–250.

Accommodation

There's a good range of **accommodation** in Hakodate, though the city gets crowded during the summer, when you'll need to book ahead. If you get stuck, head for the tourist office (see p.376), where staff can phone around to see what's available. The most interesting area to base yourself is **Motomachi**, the area of old residences and foreign consulates at the foot of Hakodate-yama. Another option is to stay 20km north of the city in the tranquil Ōnuma Quasi-National Park (see p.381), where there's a good youth hostel (see p.381).

Fitness Hotel 330 Hakodate 6-3 Wakamatsu-chō ☎0138/23-0330, Ⓔhako330@poppy.ocn.ne.jp. Keenly priced business hotel with very decent rooms, just across from the station. Guests can use the attached fitness club for an extra ¥600. ⑥

Hakodate Harbourview Hotel 14-10 Wakamatsu-chō ☎0138/22-0111, Ⓕ23-0154. Classy hotel next to the station, with smallish rooms but picturesque harbour views and a good range of restaurants. ⑥

Hakodate Kokusai Hotel 5-10 Ōtemachi ☎0138/23-5151, Ⓔkokusaihotel@hakodate.ne.jp. Hakodate's top hotel, set in a grungy warehouse area between the station and Motomachi. Rooms are spacious and comfortable, with harbour views, but the public areas lack sparkle – though the ninth-floor restaurants are glamorous and pricey. ⑦

Hakodate Youth Guesthouse 17-6 Horai-chō ☎0138/26-7892, Ⓦwww.youthhostel.or.jp/English/menu2.htm. Delightful guesthouse with Western-style rooms and a top-floor lounge with a view of Hakodate-yama. Coffee and bread for breakfast are included in the summer season, and free home-made ice cream is offered every night at 9pm to tempt people back before the 11pm curfew. Take the Yachigashira-bound streetcar to Horai-chō, from where it's a three-minute walk. Dorm beds ¥3800–4500.

Kokian 13-2 Suehiro-chō ☎0138/26-5753, Ⓔkokian@hakodate.or.jp. This nineteenth-century Motomachi wooden house has been smartly renovated into a hotel with a restaurant and bar. Rates include breakfast and dinner. ⑥

Nagashima 18-5 Hourai-machi ☎0138/26-2101, Ⓕ22-7298. Good-value, spotless minshuku near Hakodate-yama, offering mainly Western-style rooms, plus a couple of nice tatami ones for the same price. For two meals, add ¥2600 per person. ④

Niceday Inn 9-11 Ōtemachi ☎0138/22-5919. Friendly hostel conveniently located between the station and Motomachi. All the rooms have two bunk beds and are very small, but if it's quiet you may get one to yourself. The owners speak English and there's free tea and coffee. ③

Pension Hakodate-Mura 16-12 Suehiro-chō ☎0138/22-8105, Ⓦwww.hotweb.or.jp/p.h.mura/infor.english.htm. Friendly and tidy B&B in a handsome wooden building just off the waterfront at the start of Motomachi. Part of the Welcome Inn group. ④

Tabiji 8-12 Ōtemachi ☎0138/26-7652. Simple minshuku in a wooden building on a side road between the station and Motomachi, directly opposite the *Hakodate Kokusai Hotel*. The clean, Japanese-style rooms have TV but no air conditioning. For meals, add ¥2000 per person. ③

The City

Any tour of Hakodate should kick off at the atmospheric **Asa-ichi** (Morning Market; Mon–Sat 5am–noon) immediately to the west of the station. Even if you arrive at the relatively late hour of 9am, there's still plenty to see at the hundreds of tightly packed stalls in this waterside location. Old ladies in headscarves squat amid piles of vegetables and flowers at the back of the market, and huge, alien-like red crabs, squid and musk melons are the local specialities. Don't leave without trying one of the noodle stalls (see p.380).

A ten-minute walk west from the market leads to **Mount Hakodate** and the Motomachi district – alternatively, take the tramline running past the JR station and get off at Jūjigai. The 334-metre-high peak, crowned with television signal transmitters, is an excellent spot from which to soak up the town. On a clear day the view is spectacular, but best of all is the night-time panorama, when the twinkling lights of the port and the boats fishing for squid just off the coast create a magical scene – though be prepared for hordes of tourists hanging off the platform railings for a better view. The energetic can climb to the summit along various trails (May–Oct), but most people opt for the **cable car** (daily 10am–9/10pm; ¥640 one way, ¥1160 return), a seven-minute uphill walk from the Jūjigai tram stop. The cheaper alternative is to take the bus from Hakodate Station (April 25 to October 15 1.15pm–9pm; 30min; ¥360;); for drivers, the serpentine road up the mountain is open to private vehicles after 10pm. The viewing platforms are above the summit cable-car station, along with a couple of restaurants and gift shops.

Heading downhill, you'll find yourself in **Motomachi**, with its Western-style, late nineteenth-century architecture – it's easy when you're here to see why Hakodate is known as the San Francisco of Japan. The best thing to do is simply wander about, stopping to explore some of the churches, which are free (few of the other buildings merit their entrance charges). The most striking is the white **Russian Orthodox Church** of 1919, seven minutes uphill from Jūjigai tram stop, complete with green copper-clad onion domes and spires. Inside, the icon-festooned carved wood altarpiece is impressive and piped Russian choral music adds to the atmosphere. Nearby, the **Episcopal Church**, with its unusual modern architecture, is more interesting from the outside than in, while, slightly downhill, the Gothic-style **Motomachi Roman Catholic Church** is worth stepping into for its decoration based on the stations of the cross.

Walking west for a couple of hundred metres across the hillside streets will bring you to the extraordinary **Old Public Hall of Hakodate Ward** (daily 9am–5pm, April–Oct until 7pm; ¥300), a sky-blue and lemon confection with pillars, verandahs and fancy wrought-iron and plaster decoration. This replacement was completed in 1910 after a fire destroyed the original hall. In front of the hall is the small Motomachi Park, below which stands the rather twee **Old British Consulate**, which looked after the Empire's affairs in Hokkaidō from 1859 to 1934. The cream-and-blue building now houses a highly missable museum, a stuffy British tearoom and a giftshop.

Far more interesting is the **Hakodate City Museum of Northern Peoples** (daily 9am–5pm, April–Oct until 7pm; ¥300), in an old bank down the Motoi-zaka slope, which leads away from the consulate. The museum's superb collection of artefacts relating to the **Ainu** and other races across Eastern Siberian and Alaskan islands has good written English explanations and is well worth the entrance fee. Some of the clothes on display are amazing – look out for the Chinese silk robe embroidered with dragons, an example of the trade that existed between China, the islanders of Sakhalin and the Ainu.

Hakodate's other attractions include the heavily hyped remains of **Goryōkaku**, a Western-style fort some 3km northeast of the station and five minutes' walk north of the Goryōkaku-kōen-mae tram stop. Built in the late nineteenth century, the star-shaped fort was originally designed to protect Hokkaidō against attack from Russia. In the event, however, it was used by Tokugawa's naval forces in a last-ditch battle to uphold the shogun against the emperor in the short-lived civil war that ushered in the Meiji Restoration of 1869. What's left of the fort today – a leafy park, the moat and outer walls – looks best from the top of the rather ugly, sixty-metre-high **viewing tower** (daily 8am–6/7pm; ¥630) by the main entrance. It's best to visit here between late July to mid-August, when open-air plays about Hakodate's history are performed enthusiastically by five hundred amateur actors on Friday, Saturday and Sunday evenings.

Also rather disappointing is the **Trappistine Convent**, 10km southeast of Hakodate Station, established in 1868 by eight French nuns. You can't go inside – home-made cakes and biscuits are the real reason tour buses stop here. It takes at least one hour by public transport to reach the convent, either by an infrequent bus from Hakodate Station, or by tram to Yunokawa, then a bus.

On the way to the convent you'll pass the drab seaside suburb of **Yunokawa**, the oldest onsen resort in Hokkaidō and definitely looking it. A better (and cheaper) **onsen** option, closer to the town centre, is the huge public bath at **Yachigashira** (daily 6am–9.30pm; ¥340), a couple of minutes' walk from tram terminus #2 on the eastern side of Hakodate-yama.

Eating and drinking

Seafood is delivered fresh every day to the harbour, and the best places to feast on it are the sushi bars scattered around the morning market near Hakodate Station. Look out for the **local speciality**, a bowl of ramen topped with a whole crab and other seafood. You'll find a limited range of **restaurants** on the main shopping street near the station – for good value, head for *The Don*, part of a chain serving bowls of rice topped with fish or meat. For a splurge, Motomachi's smart restaurants by the seafront can be fun.

Goryōkaku is the city's main **drinking** area. More central are the converted warehouses in Motomachi that serve the local *ji-biiru* (microbrewery beer), Hakodate Beer; try the fairly touristy *Hakodate Beer*, just along from the *Kokusai Hotel*, towards Motomachi.

Aji-no-ichiban Noodle stall in the morning market serving up the local speciality for ¥1800, and plenty of cheaper dishes, plus delicious, freshly squeezed melon juice. Open daytime only.

Akachōchin 18-21 Wakamatsu-chō. The name means "red lantern" and there are plenty of these hanging inside this lively *robatayaki* (grilled food) restaurant, a couple of minutes' walk from the JR station. Expect to pay around ¥2500 per head.

BAY Hakodate 11-5 Toyakawa-chō. Stylish buffet-style restaurant in one of the converted warehouses by the waterfront in Motomachi. The menu features a wide range of Western dishes, with lunch at ¥1500 and dinner at ¥2500 per head – both are good value.

Coyoacan Café 23-22 Suehiro-chō. Small Mexican restaurant and bar with well-priced if not overly generous servings. Closed Tues.

Hishii 9-4 Horai-chō. Near the Horai-chō tram stop, this eighty-year-old wooden building, draped with ivy, houses an elegant teashop, bar and antique clothes shop. There's a tatami area on the second floor and the shop sells secondhand kimono from ¥5000.

Lucky Pierrot This hamburger and curry restaurant chain offers cheap, fast food Japanese-style, with eleven locations around town. The most interesting one is just west of the Jūjigai tram stop, towards the waterfront. The shop sign says "Santa Claus has come to Hakodate" and there are plenty of jolly red men decorating the front.

Nihombashi 7-9 Motomachi. Good-value Japanese restaurant serving huge set meals and bowls of noodles in a relaxing atmosphere.

Tonetsu Excellent tonkatsu restaurant with tatami seating and a good range of reasonably priced set meals from ¥1000, including free coffee.

Listings

Airlines ANA, 14-10 Wakamatsu-chō ☎0138/22-1166; JAL, 7-16 Wakamatsu-chō ☎0138/27-5711.

Banks The banks close to the JR station only change US dollar travellers' cheques, Mondays to Fridays only. For other currencies, go to the central post office (see opposite).

Bookshops A small selection of English-language paperbacks is available on the fifth floor of the

Boni Moriya department store annexe, opposite Hakodate Station.

Car rental Eki Rent-a-Car (☎0138/22-7864), next to Hakodate Station.

Hospitals Hakodate City Hospital, 1-10-1 Minato-chō ☎0138/43-2000.

Internet access HotWeb Café, 18-1 TMO Building, Wakamatsu-chō (daily except Tues 10am–10pm; ¥300 per hour including one soft drink) is a slick Internet café on the main road leading from Hakodate Station, one block beyond the Wako department store.

Laundry JUN coin laundry (open 24hr), a block past the fire station, close to the city hall.

Police The main police station is on the western side of Goryōkaku-kōen. Emergency numbers are listed in "Basics" on p.81.

Post office The central post office, 1-6 Shinkawa-chō, is a ten-minute walk east of Hakodate Station, near the Shinkawa-chō tram stop. Mon–Fri 9am–7pm, Sat, Sun 9am–5pm.

Taxis The main taxi rank sits outside Hakodate Station.

Travel agents The main JTB office is at 16-24 Yanagawa-chō (☎0138/56-1717), a five-minute walk west of the Goryōkaku-kōen-mae tram stop. There's a more conveniently located JTB office on the ground floor of the Wako department store opposite Hakodate Station.

Ōnuma Quasi National Park

The serene lakeland area of **Ōnuma Quasi National Park**, 20km north of Hakodate, can easily be visited in a day, but is worth considering as an overnight stop or even an alternative to staying in Hakodate itself. There are three **lakes** in the park – Ōnuma, Konuma and Junsai-numa. The largest and most beautiful, **Ōnuma**, lying just east of the main tourist village of the same name outside Ōnuma-kōen Station, is carpeted with water lilies and contains over one hundred tiny islands.

The nicest way to take in the scenery is to walk around the islands, which are joined by bridges. The view towards the 1133-metre jagged peak of the dormant volcano of **Komaga-take** is rightly considered to be one of the most breathtaking in Japan. Unsurprisingly, Ōnuma is popular with tour groups, but they are usually herded into the boats that depart every thirty minutes, leaving you to stroll in peace. **Cycling** is another good way of exploring – bikes can be rented for around ¥500 an hour or ¥1500 a day from numerous shops around the station. Avid **hikers** can also tackle the **volcano**, which has two main routes, both taking around two and a half hours to complete – one route starts near the woodland shrine on the northern shore of Ōnuma Lake, while the other starts to the west on Route 5.

Local **trains** from Hakodate to Ōnuma-kōen Station take around forty minutes, or you can do the journey in half the time on the less frequent and more expensive limited express trains. There are also five **buses** a day, taking around one hour. Apart from the **campsite** on the eastern shore of Ōnuma Lake, around 6km from the station, the cheapest **accommodation** is at the *Ōnuma Kōen Youth Hostel* (☎0138/67-4126, ⓦwww.youthhostel.or.jp/English/menu2.htm; dorm beds ¥2900 per person), 3km by taxi from Ōnuma-kōen Station, or three minutes' walk from Ikedaen Station. This is a friendly place with bunk-bed dorms, good breakfasts and dinners and a wide range of activities such as canoeing, cross-country skiing and ice fishing, depending on the season. A good alternative is *Chairo-tori* (☎0138/67-2231; ❺ including two meals), a homely minshuku opposite the station. There are several touristy **restaurants** around the station, but the best place for lunch or dinner is *Wald* (daily except Thurs 10am–9pm), the log house on the way to the youth hostel; the menu here is in English and includes hearty sandwiches with chips, salad and beer.

Shikotsu-Tōya National Park and around

Follow the coastal road or rail line around Uchiura-wan from Hakodate and you'll reach the eastern side of the **SHIKOTSU-TŌYA NATIONAL PARK**, one of Hokkaidō's prettiest lakeland and mountain areas, but also the most developed, thanks to its location within easy reach of Sapporo, some 80km to the north. It's difficult to say which of the park's two main caldera lakes – **Tōya-ko** to the east or **Shikotsu-ko** to the west – is the best to visit; both have gorgeous locations, are active volcanoes and are surrounded by excellent hiking trails. Shikotsu-ko is certainly less touristy than Tōya-ko, but the latter is only 2km from the geological wonder **Shōwa Shin-zan**, a volcano that only started sprouting in the 1940s. Between the two lakes is **Noboribetsu Onsen**, the largest hot-spring resort in Hokkaidō, worth visiting to soak up the otherworldly landscape of bubbling and steaming **Jigokudani** (Hell Valley). Between Noboribetsu and Shikotsu-ko, in the coastal town of Shiraoi, is **Poroto Kotan**, a recreated Ainu village that provides a rather nostalgic glimpse into the culture of Hokkaidō's original inhabitants. For an impression of how the Ainu live today, visit the real village of **Nibutani**, around 50km due east of Tomakomai, which has two fine museums and is the home of Japan's first Ainu MP, Kayano Shigeru.

Shikotsu-Tōya National Park	*Shikotsu-Tōya Kokuritsu-kōen*	支笏洞爺国立公園
Tōya-ko	*Tōya-ko*	洞爺湖
Shōwa Shin-zan	*Shōwa Shin-zan*	昭和新山
Usu-zan	*Usu-zan*	有珠山
Accommodation		
Ōno Pension	*Penshon Ōno*	ペンションおおの
Shōwa Shin-zan Youth Hostel	*Shōwa Shin-zan Yūsu Hosuteru*	昭和新山ユースホステル
Tōya Sun Palace Hotel	*Tōya San Paresu Hoteru*	洞爺サンパレスホテル
Noboribetsu Onsen	*Noboribetsu Onsen*	登別温泉
Jigokudani	*Jigokudani*	地獄谷
Accommodation		
Dai-ichi Takimoto-kan	*Dai-ichi Takimoto-kan*	第一滝本館
Hanaya	*Kashōtei Hanaya*	花鐘亭はなや
Kanefuku Youth Hostel	*Kanefuku Yūsu Hosuteru*	金福ユースホステル
Mahoroba	*Mahoroba*	まほろば
Muroran	*Muroran*	室蘭
Nibutani	*Nibutani*	二風谷
Poroto Kotan	*Poroto Kotan*	ポロトコタン
Shiraoi	*Shiraoi*	白老
Tomakomai	*Tomakomai*	苫小牧
Shikotsu-ko	*Shikotsu-ko*	支笏湖
Koke-no-dōmon	*Koke-no-dōmon*	コケの洞門
Poropinai	*Poropinai*	幌美内
Shikotsu Kohan	*Shikotsu Kohan*	支笏湖畔
Tarumae-zan	*Tarumae-zan*	樽前山
Accommodation		
Marukoma Onsen	*Marukoma Onsen*	丸駒温泉
Shikotsu-ko Youth Hostel	*Shikotsu-ko Yūsu Hosuteru*	支笏湖ユースホステル

4

HOKKAIDŌ | Shikotsu-Tōya National Park and around

Tōya-ko and Shōwa Shin-zan

The beautiful caldera lake of **Tōya-ko** is punctuated dead centre by the ice-cream-cone island of **Ōshima**, while its southern shore is home to the town of **Tōya-ko Onsen**, where you'll find accommodation and local transport connections. Hordes of visitors regularly descend on the area, especially between May and October, when a spectacular nightly firework display illuminates the lake. Pretty as it is, the best reason for visiting Tōya-ko is to see the nearby active volcano **Usu-zan**, some 2km south, and its steaming "parasite volcano" **Shōwa Shin-zan**, which started to sprout out of the ground as recently as 1944.

On December 28, 1943, severe earthquakes began shaking the area around Usu-zan and continued to do so until September 1945. In the intervening period a new lava dome rose out of the ground, sometimes at the rate of 1.5m

383

a day. By the time it had stopped growing, Shōwa Shin-zan, the "new mountain" named after the reigning emperor, stood 405m above sea level. The wartime authorities were desperate to hush up this extraordinary event for fear that the fledgling mountain would serve as a beacon for US bomber planes.

Fortunately, Shōwa Shin-zan's birth was carefully documented by local postmaster **Mimatsu Masao**, a 57-year-old amateur volcanologist who kept daily records of the mountain's growth. After the war, Mimatsu bought the land on which the mountain stood so it would be protected from the mining companies who were intent on digging up the rich mineral deposits beneath it. Despite tempting offers from the tourist industry (one rumoured to be ¥300 million), Mimatsu declared, "I purchased the volcano to continue my research uninterrupted. I did not buy it to make money. Nor did I buy it for tourists to gawk at." His efforts were rewarded in 1958 when Shōwa Shin-zan was made a Special Natural Treasure by the government.

Nevertheless, Mimatsu never turned away gawking tourists – but nor did he charge them admission, a practice still upheld by Shōwa Shin-zan's current owner Mimatsu Saburō, Masao's son-in-law, who can often be found in the **Mimatsu Masao Memorial Hall** (daily 8am–5pm; ¥300). This small museum is tucked behind the ghastly row of giftshops at the base of the volcano, and contains an interesting collection of exhibits on the history of the fledgling volcano.

Usu-zan, Shōwa Shin-zan's neighbouring parent volcano, is still frighteningly active; eruptions which began March 31, 2000 coated Tōya-ko Onsen with volcanic dust and forced a three-month evacuation. Townsfolk returned at the end of June, cleaned the place up and reopened businesses with lower prices, determined to win tourists back. The volcano still steams unpredictably, but it's safe enough for you to brave taking the **cable car** (daily 8.30am–5.30pm; ¥1450 return) up to a viewing platform 300m from the crater, for the stunning vistas over Shōwa Shin-zan, Tōya-ko and out to sea. The cable-car station is at the end of the row of tourist shops by Shōwa Shin-zan. From April to October, free buses run every hour from the Dōnan Bus Terminal in Tōya-ko Onsen to Shōwa Shin-zan.

The best way to enjoy the positive side of volcanic activity – onsen water – is to pop into the huge *Tōya Sun Palace*, the hotel beside the lake, home of the **Fantastic Large Hot Spring Bathhouse** (daily 10am–4pm; ¥1050), featuring two floors of over twenty different soaking pools, some with views across the lake, and a large swimming pool with artificial waves and a water slide.

Don't bother taking the kitsch yellow castle **ferry** *Espoir* (daily 8am–4.30pm, sailings every 30min; ¥1320) around Ōshima, the largest of the islands in the centre of Tōya-ko, unless you have a burning desire to glimpse Ezo deer grazing in the island's forests.

Practicalities

Trains from Hakodate and Sapporo run to Tōya Station, on the coast, from where you can get a bus (¥320) up the hill to Tōya-ko Onsen. There are daily **buses** to Tōya-ko Onsen from Sapporo and Hakodate, and from late April to October five buses a day run to Noboribetsu Onsen from Tōya-ko Onsen along a scenic mountain route, via the Orufure Pass. Buses pull in at the Dōnan Bus Terminal, five minutes' walk from the shore of Tōya-ko. Just down from the terminal is a tourist office where you can pick up an English **map** of the area.

Tōya-ko Onsen has plenty of top-notch **hotels**, which usually include two meals in their rates and offer substantial discounts outside the busy summer season. The *Tōya Sun Palace* (☎0142/75-4126, ℻75-2875; ❼) is a good upmarket option, or you can find cheaper places to stay outside of town, on the way to the volcanoes. The *Shōwa Shinzan Youth Hostel* (☎0142/75-2283, ⓦwww.youthhostel.or.jp/English/menu2.htm;¥3300 per person), at the turn-off to Shōwa Shin-zan, a ten-minute bus ride (¥220) from Tōya-ko Onsen, has bunk-bed dorms, shared tatami rooms and its own onsen, and rents out bikes (¥1000 per day). The *Ōno Pension* (☎0142/75-4128, ⓔp-ohno@lake.biglobe.ne.jp; ❻), nearer to Tōya-ko Onsen on the lakeside road, is a good-value mid-range hotel; two meals are included in the rates.

None of the **restaurants** at Tōya-ko Onsen or Shōwa Shin-zan makes much of an effort to provide anything beyond the usual noodle and rice dishes: most people eat in their ryokan or hotel and you'd be wise to do the same. Of the small cluster of cafés at the turn-off from the lake to the volcanoes, *Ōdera*, opposite the youth hostel, does good-value set meals, including sashimi, tempura and noodles, for ¥1500.

Noboribetsu Onsen and around

Some 18km east of Tōya-ko, nestling amid lush green mountain slopes ripped through by a bubbling wasteland of volcanic activity, lies **NOBORIBETSU ONSEN**. Although this small, purpose-built resort is Hokkaidō's top hot-spring destination (and has huge, unsightly hotels to prove it), the dramatic landscape of Jigokudani – the source of Noboribetsu's fame – is less touristy than a similar area in Beppu in Kyūshū (see p.841) and is definitely worth seeing. Afterwards, don't miss out on a wallow in the luxurious **baths** of the Dai-ichi Takimoto-kan.

A ten-minute walk from the bus stop up Gokuraku, Noboribetsu's main street, will bring you to a roadside **shrine** guarded by two brightly painted statues of demons. This is the entrance to **Jigokudani** (Hell Valley), a steaming, lunar-like valley created by an ancient volcanic eruption. It takes about thirty minutes to explore the area, wandering along wooden pathways through a landscape of rusty red rocks, streaked green and white by mineral deposits. Close to the start of the valley walkway you'll notice a tiny wooden shrine where you can sip a cup of the onsen water, which tastes a bit like diluted vinegar. Twenty minutes' walk further on, a well-signposted pathway leads to **Oyu-numa**, a malevolent-looking hot-water lake which looks exactly what you'd expect to find in somewhere called hell.

All the hotels draw water from Jigokudani (ten thousand tonnes of water are pumped out daily) and many have built elaborate **baths** so that guests and visitors can enjoy the water's therapeutic benefits. The nicest baths open to the public are at the back of the **Dai-ichi Takimoto-kan** (daily 9am–3pm; ¥2000), with 29 different kinds of tub, including several Jacuzzis, a rotemburo (outdoor pool), a cypress-wood bath and a swimming pool with a water slide (you'll need to take a bathing costume with you to use this, or rent one on the premises). The main onsen bath hall, supported by Roman pillars, has a sweeping view across Jigokudani.

You're unlikely to be tempted by Noboribetsu's other main attraction, a deplorable **Bear Park** (daily: April–Nov 7.30am–6/6.30pm; Jan–March & Dec 9am–4.30pm; closed Nov 20–Dec 20; entrance & cable car ¥2520) on the summit of Kuma-yama, the mountain that rises over the resort. Even if you find performing animals entertaining, the sight of scores of fully grown bears begging for snacks in spartan concrete bunkers is upsetting. The only pleasure to be had here is the panoramic view of the surrounding mountains you'll get from the cable car, which runs up to the park from the resort.

Returning from the onsen to Noboribetsu Station, the incongruous grey turrets of the red-brick Sea Fantasy Castle Nixe loom into view. This is the main attraction of **Marine Park Nixe** (daily 9am–5pm; ¥2300), a kitsch medley of a Hans Christian Andersen-style amusement park, multistorey aquarium and sea-lion and dolphin shows.

Practicalities

Noboribetsu Station is on the JR Muroran line and is served by **trains** from Hakodate and Sapporo; the onsen is a thirteen-minute bus ride from the station. There are also direct **buses** to Noboribetsu Onsen from Sapporo, Chitose Airport, and the nearby ports of Tomakomai to the north and Muroran to the south. If you're travelling between Tōya-ko Onsen and Noboribetsu Onsen between June and mid-October, consider taking the bus, which goes via the beautifully scenic mountaintop **Orofure Pass** (¥1530).

The Dōnan and Chūō bus terminals stand opposite each other at the southern end of the resort's main shopping street, which runs uphill towards Jigokudani. Just up from the bus terminals is a **tourist information office** (daily 9am–6pm; ☎0143/84-3311) – no English is spoken here, but you can pick up a decent English map and leaflet on the area.

For budget **accommodation**, head for the *Kanefuku Youth Hostel* (☎0143/84-2565, ⓦwww.youthhostel.or.jp/English/menu2.htm; dorm beds ¥2750per person), a run-down and decidedly musty building ten minutes' walk down the hill from the bus station, past the hospital. One of the nicest midrange hotels is the modern ryokan *Hanaya* (☎0143/84-2521, ⓦwww4.ocn.ne.jp/~k-hanaya; ❼), opposite the hospital, five minutes' walk down the hill from the bus station. Run by English-speaking managers, the ryokan has comfortable Western- and Japanese-style rooms, as well as an ornamental garden, and a lovely rotemburo. Prices are slightly higher if you go for the *kaiseki-ryōri* (Japanese haute cuisine) meals, which are mouthwatering. For something really swanky, try the *Dai-ichi Takimoto-kan* (☎0143/84-2111, ⓦwww.takimotokan.co.jp/english/index.html; ❼ including two meals), or the over-the-top *Mahoroba* (☎0143/84-2211, Ⓕ84-2218; ❼ for a Western-style twin) – the latter has the largest collection of residents-only baths in town.

As far as **eating** goes, there are plenty of ramen stalls and tourist restaurants along the main street – all good for a cheap lunch. Also worth trying is the *Takamoto Inn* opposite the *Dai-ichi Takamoto-kan*, which serves Japanese dishes and does a special set lunch for ¥800.

Ainu Villages: Poroto Kotan and Nibutani

Some 30km north of Noboribetsu is **POROTO KOTAN** (daily: April–Oct 8am–5.30pm; Jan–March, Nov & Dec 8.30am–4.30pm; ¥680, ⓦwww.ainu-museum.org.jp/english/english.html), a recreated Ainu village of thatched communal huts and a museum lying beside a small lake, ten minutes' walk east of Shiraoi Station. Although it bears no relation to how the Ainu live today, Poroto Kotan does provide the rare opportunity to see traditionally dressed Ainu men and women perform the ritual dance, Iyomante Rimse. You can also listen to the haunting music of the *mukkur*, a mouth harp made of bamboo and thread that creates a strange, resonating sound. Lectures in Japanese on Ainu culture are given in the large straw huts, which have smoked fish hanging from their rafters. There's also a small museum of Ainu artefacts with good explanations in English, but it's somewhat overshadowed by the pathetic scene of caged bears outside. One of the Ainu's most important ceremonies involved the ritual slaughter and eating of bears. Limited express trains from Sapporo to Shiraoi take just over an hour.

Much better museums can be found in the real Ainu village of **NIBUTANI**, some 50km due east of the port of Tomakomai on Route 237. Eighty percent of the five-hundred-strong population here are of Ainu blood. Just outside the village is the controversial Nibutani dam, which caused uproar in the community when it was built, since it flooded sacred Ainu sites and stopped the salmon runs along the river. A landmark legal verdict in 1997 declared that the dam violated Ainu rights, but also that it would stay.

One of Nibutani's elder statesmen is Kayano Shigeru, an MP from 1994 to 1998; his personal collection of Ainu artefacts is on display in the charming **Kayano Shigeru Ainu Memorial Museum** (April–Nov daily 9am–5pm; Dec & Jan–March open by appointment only on ☎0145/72-3215; ¥400, or ¥700 with the Nibutani Ainu Culture Museum), a five-minute walk up the hill from the main road. Outside there's a collection of traditional Ainu huts (craftsmen creating traditional items can be found at work in one of the huts); inside, look out for the amazing preserved Emperor Fish, a prehistoric-looking giant salmon, and the evocative photographs of Ainu fishermen. In the meeting room you'll find a large number of handsome black- and blue-ink etchings showing Ainu hunting bears and fighting off the Japanese.

The **Nibutani Ainu Culture Museum** (daily 9am–4.30pm; ¥400 or ¥700 with the Kayano Shigeru Ainu Memorial Museum), on the opposite side of the main road through the village, is a strikingly modern concrete and glass facility which also has some original Ainu huts outside. Inside the main building are carefully labelled and displayed exhibits on Ainu daily life and religion, plus videos in Japanese showing dances and explaining the language. Make sure you look through the pull-out display cases, which contain beautifully embroidered traditional costumes. Behind the culture museum lies the **Historical Museum of the Saru Village** (Tues–Sun 9.30am–4.30pm; free), which has a few evocative early photographs of Nibutani but can otherwise be ignored unless you really need to kill some time.

To reach Nibutani by public transport, you'll need to take a local **train** south from Tomakomai to Tomikawa Station, from where buses run to the village – look out for the dam and get off when you see the cluster of Ainu giftshops and a rainbow arch over the side road leading into the main Ainu settlement.

Shikotsu-ko

Despite being the section of the Shikotsu-Tōya National Park closest to Sapporo, tourist development around the beautiful lake of **SHIKOTSU-KO** is remarkably low-key. At 360m, this is Japan's second deepest lake (after Tazawa-ko in Akita-ken) and its blue waters never freeze over.

Buses all stop at laid back **SHIKOTSU KOHAN**, a village nestled in the woods beside the mouth of the Chitose-gawa on the east side of the lake, and mercifully free of the multistorey hotels and tourist tack of Tōya-ko. The **visitor centre** (daily: April–Nov 9am–5.30pm; Jan–March, Nov & Dec 9.30am–4.30pm), just south of the bus terminal, has displays in Japanese on the area's nature and geology, and puts on a good slide show of the lake through the seasons – you can also pick up a free area map here. There are the usual boat rides on the lake, lasting thirty minutes (¥930), as well as a gentle, self-guided **nature walk**, lasting about an hour and twenty minutes, over the bridge across the Chitose-gawa and along the lake shore to the campsite at Morappu, 3km south. You'll get the best view of the lake by **hiking** to the peaks of any of the surrounding mountains and volcanoes. One of the easiest trails starts at the northern end of the village and leads up **Monbetsu-dake**, a 866-metre peak which takes around one hour and twenty minutes to climb. The hike up **Eniwa-dake**, on the north side of the lake above the *Poropinai* campsite, is more challenging and takes at least two and a half hours. After the climb, unwind beside the lake at the foot of the mountain in the lovely rotemburo at **Marukoma Onsen** (see below).

Most people, however, opt for the hike up **Tarumae-zan**, an active volcano (the last eruption was in 1955) south of the lake. The hike begins at the seventh "station", three-quarters of the way up the volcano at the end of a dirt road; the easiest way of reaching the start is to hitch a ride from Shikotsu-ko, although you may be lucky enough to catch one of the irregular buses (check at the bus terminal for times). The walk from the seventh station up to the summit (1024m) shouldn't take more than an hour. At the top you'll be rewarded with great views, though the pungent aroma from the steaming crater discourages much lingering.

Following the northwest trail down from Tarumae-zan towards the lake leads after a couple of hours to the impressive moss-covered gorge of **Koke-no-dōmon**. The sheer rock walls of this narrow passageway look as though they have been wallpapered with soft green velvet and, even if you don't climb the volcano, it's worth hitching, walking or cycling the 5km from Shikotsu-ko Kohan to see this natural wonder.

Practicalities

There are daily buses from Chitose airport (1hr; ¥920 one way) and Sapporo (1hr 30min; ¥1330) to Shikotsu Kohan. **Getting around** the lake is best with your own transport, as there are no local buses. You can rent a bike from the youth hostel in Shikotsu Kohan for ¥1800 a day (or ¥1200 if you're staying at the hostel).

Most of the area's **ryokan and hotels** are within easy walking distance of the bus terminal at Shikotsu Kohan. The best budget place is the large *Shikotsu-ko Youth Hostel* (☎0123/25-2311, ⓦwww.youthhostel.or.jp/English/menu2.htm; ¥2900 per person), which has reasonable bunk-bed and tatami rooms and a friendly atmosphere; it's on the edge of the main car park to the right of the bus terminal as you face the lake. In the winter, the hostel managers organize daily cross-country skiing tours (¥500 an hour). The hostel also serves decent food – a good thing, since there are few cheap options nearby. Of the three **campsites**, *Poropinai*, at the northern end of the lake, has the most attractive location, costs ¥300 per night, and is a good spot for swimming. Further around the lake is the plush ryokan *Marukoma Onsen* (☎0123/25-2341; ❼ including two meals), with wonderful rotemburo (open to non-residents 10am–3pm; ¥1000) and stunning views across Shikotsu-ko to Tarumae-zan. Note that you will need your own transport or take a taxi to get to *Marukoma Onsen*, as access is from a side road off the highway up the hill leading away from the lake.

Central Hokkaidō

On the way to central Hokkaidō or other points north, you're almost certain to find yourself passing through **Asahikawa**, Hokkaidō's second largest city and a major transport hub. Though there's little reason to linger here, Asahikawa is a good place to replenish supplies and change money. **Central Hokkaidō** is a sparsely populated area dominated by the vast (2309 square

Asahikawa	Asahikawa	旭川
Asahikawa Youth Hostel	Asahikawa Yūsu Hosuteru	旭川ユースホステル
Asahikawa Washington Hotel	Fujita Kankō Asahikawa Washinton Hoteru	藤田観光旭川ワシントンホテル
Fitness Hotel 330 Asahikawa	Fittonesu Hoteru 330 Asahikawa	フェトネスホテル３３０旭川
Daisetsu-zan National Park	Daisetsu-zan Kokuritsu-kōen	大雪山国立公園
Asahi-dake	Asahi-dake	旭岳
Asahidake Onsen	Asahi-dake Onsen	旭岳温泉
Kamikawa	Kamikawa	上川
Kuro-dake	Kuro-dake	黒岳
Sōunkyō gorge	Sōunkyō	層雲峡
Tenninkyō Onsen	Tenninkyō Onsen	天人峡温泉
Accommodation		
Ezo Matsu-sō	Ezo Matsu-sō	えぞまつ荘
Lodge Nutapu-Kaushipe	Rojji Nutapu Kaushipe	ロッジヌタプカウシペ
Midori	Minshuku Midori	民宿みどり
Northern Lodge	Hotel Nōzan Rojji	ホテル・ノーザンロッジ
Mount View Hotel	Maunto Byū Hoteru	マウントビューホテル
Daisetsuzan Shirakaba-sō Hotel and Youth Hostel	Daisetsuzan Shirakaba-sō	大雪山白樺荘
Sōunkyō Youth Hostel	Sōunkyō Yūsu Hosuteru	層雲峡ユースホステル
Bibaushi	Bibaushi	美馬牛
Bibaushi Liberty Youth Hostel	Bibaushi Ribatii Yūsu Hosuteru	美馬牛リバティーユースホステル
With You Farm Pension	Fāmu Penshon Uizu Yū	ファームペンションウイズユー
Biei	Biei	美瑛
Minshuku Hōzuki	Minshuku Hōzuki	民宿ほうずき
Furano	Furano	富良野
Alpine Visitors' Centre	Arupain Bijitā Sentā	アルパインビジターセンター
Furano Prince Hotel	Furano Purinsu Hoteru	富良野プリンスホテル
New Furano Hotel	Nyū Furano Hoteru	ニュー富良野ホテル
Pension Phytoncide	Penshon Fitonchiddo	ペンションフィトンチッド

kilometres) and magnificent **Daisetsu-zan**, Japan's largest **national park**, which features Hokkaidō's highest mountain, **Asahi-dake** (2290m), and the spectacular **Sōunkyō gorge**. On the western fringes of the park lie the fertile farmlands that have given Hokkaidō the reputation for being a misplaced slice of Europe in the Orient. The fields around the picturesque village of **Bibaushi** are at their best in summer, when lavender, sunflowers and other blooms create a multicoloured patchwork. Further south is **Furano**, one of Japan's top ski resorts and location of past World Cup skiing competitions.

Asahikawa

Straddling the confluence of the Ishikari, Biei, Chubetsu and Ushibetsu rivers, sprawling **ASAHIKAWA**, 136km northeast of Sapporo, is Hokkaidō's second largest city. Although it has no compelling attractions, you may well find your-self passing through – and even having to stay – as this is an important railway junction, with lines heading from here north to Wakkanai and Abashiri. The city is also the main access point into the Daisetsu-zan National Park (see below), some 40km east, and a free bus runs daily from outside the train station to Asahidake Onsen.

Asahikawa airport (⊕0166/83-3989) lies 18km to the east of the city. **Trains** from Abashiri, Sapporo and Wakkanai arrive at the JR station, at the southern end of Heiwa-dōri, the city's main shopping street. There's a **tourist information booth** (daily: July–Sept 8.30am–7pm; Jan–June & Oct–Dec 10am–5.30pm; ⊕0166/22-6704, ⓔkankou@city.asahikawa.hokkaido.jp) inside the station to the right as you exit the ticket barrier. There should be at least one English-speaking staff member on hand, and they can give you a decent English-language map of the city. There are plenty of department stores and banks close to the JR station – be sure to stock up on supplies and cash before venturing out into Hokkaidō's more remote regions.

Most **hotels** are within easy walking distance of the station. The *Asahikawa Washington* (⊕0166/23-7111, ⓔfront@asahikawa-wh.com; ❺) is a good-value business hotel a couple of minutes' walk north of the station, while the *Fitness Hotel 330 Asahikawa* (⊕0166/26-0330, ⓔasahi330@lime.ocn.ne.jp; ❺), oppo-site the Asahi Building, is even nicer, with a stylish café, a gym and swimming pool (use of the fitness facilities costs an extra ¥500). It's a twenty-minute bus ride out to the *Asahikawa Youth Hostel* (⊕0166/61-2751, ⓦwww.youthhos-tel.or.jp/English/menu2.htm), which has quite tired-looking Western-style dorms (¥3200 per person) and twin rooms (❸), all with ancient, coin-operat-ed TVs. The hostel also serves hearty meals in a café that is also showing its age, and rents out bicycles in summer and ski equipment in winter, which you can use at the small neighbouring ski slope. The hostel can be reached by buses #50, #444 or #550 from stand 11 outside the Chūō Bus Terminal, next to the Malsa department store (last bus 9.30pm).

There are plenty of places to **eat** around the Heiwa-dōri shopping street, including all the main fast-food outlets. One block west is the **Sanroku** enter-tainment district, where you'll find good-value *izakaya* and sushi bars.

Daisetsu-zan National Park

Daisetsu-zan National Park may lack the picturesque lakes of Hokkaidō's other green spaces, but makes up for it with a spectacular range of gorges, hot springs and mountains – including **Asahi-dake**, the island's tallest peak – crisscrossed by hiking trails which could keep you happily occupied for days. Tourism in the park is generally low-key, especially at the wooded and remote **Asahidake Onsen**. **Sōunkyō Onsen**, on the northeast edge of the park, is the only place which attracts tourists in large numbers, though a tasteful redevelopment has made it much nicer than most hot-spring resorts. The highlight here is the famous **gorge**, a twenty-kilometre corridor of jagged cliffs, 150m high in places. In July, the mountain slopes are covered with alpine flowers, while September and October see the landscape painted in vivid autumnal colours; these are the best months for hiking. During the winter, both Asahi-dake and **Kuro-dake** in Sōunkyō are pop-ular skiing spots, enjoying the longest ski season in Japan (usually Oct–June).

Asahidake Onsen

Given that it's only 40km from Asahikawa, and is served by a free bus service, it's surprising that attractive **ASAHIDAKE ONSEN** has remained so uncommercialized. A handful of small hotels and pensions are dotted along the

DAISETSU-ZAN NATIONAL PARK

Kitami

Obihiro

Ōbako

Kobako

Sōunkyō Gorge

Ishikari-gawa

Lake Daisetsu

0   5 km

Kamikawa

Sōunkyō Onsen

Mount View

Northern Lodge
Visitor Centre

Cable Car

Ryusei Falls

Ginga Falls

Sōunkyō Youth Hostel

Chair lift

Ginsendai Hut
(1490 m)

Kuro-dake
(1984 m)

Midori-dake
(2019 m)

Daisetsu Kogen Onsen Hut
(1240 m)

Yanbe Onsen

Tokachidake

Kuro-dake Hut

Hokkai-dake
(2149 m)

Hakuun Hut

Yudoku rōtemburo

Naka-dake rōtemburo

Asahi-dake
(2290 m)

Aizankei Onsen
(1010 m)

Cable Car

Asahidake Onsen

Visitor Centre

Ezo-Matsu-sō

Cross country skiing area

Daisetsuzan Shirakaba-sō Hotel & Youth Hostel

Lodge Nutapu-Kaushipe

Tenninkyō Onsen

N

Kamikawa

Asahikawa

Asahikawa

391

road which snakes up to the cable-car station, from where hikers in the summer and skiers in the winter are whisked up to within striking distance of the summit of Hokkaidō's highest mountain, **Asahi-dake**. The cable car, opened in 2000, has opened up this area somewhat, but the remoteness of the area means that it remains a delightful and little-visited destination for serious hikers and cross-country and downhill skiers. Cross-country skiers in particular will appreciate the kilometres of groomed trails, some of the best in Japan, which wind through beautiful forests of white birch and Hokkaidō spruce.

Just before the cable-car station is the **visitor centre** (daily: June–Oct 9am–5pm; Jan–May, Nov & Dec 10am–4pm), which has some simple nature displays (all in Japanese), information on weather conditions on the mountain and a good hiking map in Japanese for ¥300. The **cable car** (Jan–May 9am–5pm; early to mid-June & Oct 8.45am–5pm; mid-June to Aug 6am–7pm; Sept 6am–5.30pm; Nov–Dec 9am–4pm; closed May 7–19 & Nov 11–30; Jan–June & mid-Oct to Dec ¥1000 one way, ¥1800 return; July to mid-Oct ¥1500 one way, ¥2800 return; ¥3800 for all-day ski passes) takes about fifteen minutes to reach the top station, worth visiting for its ethereal landscape of steaming pools and rocky outcrops even if you're not planning to hike to the summit. Asahi-dake's peak is an arduous, ninety-minute slog over slippery volcanic rock from the cable-car station, but the view from the summit is fantastic.

Apart from the hike across to Sōunkyō (see below), there's a good two-hour walk, mainly downhill and through forests, from the campsite in Asahidake Onsen to **Tenninkyō Onsen**, where a gaggle of concrete tourist hotels stands at the mouth of a dramatic gorge. The soaring cliffs are draped in greenery, and at the end of the gorge are two spectacular **waterfalls**. From the main car park at Tenninkyō Onsen you can catch the bus to Asahikawa or back to Asahidake Onsen. The youth hostel and the visitor centre can advise on other hikes around the park, some of which pass by natural rotemburo.

From June to October there are two **buses** a day from Asahikawa Station to Asahidake Onsen, which stop at Tenninkyō Onsen en route. The ninety-minute journey is free as long as you get off at either onsen, and free also for the return if you pick up a coupon from your hostel or hotel. One of the best **places to stay** is the family-run *Daisetsuzan Shirakaba-sō Hotel and Youth Hostel* (☎0166/97-2246, ☎97-2247; hotel rooms ❺, hostel rooms ❹, dorm beds ¥3360 per person), which offers both hotel and hostel-style lodgings in a lovely wooden building set back from the road, opposite the campsite bus stop, and next to a running stream; the attached log house has a convivial communal lounge. Evening meals include freshly caught river fish and the hostel staff can provide all you need to climb Asahi-dake, including a lunch of *onigiri* (rice balls) and a bell to warn off bears. There's a rotemburo in the woods behind the main building. Just beside the hostel, on the road, is the equally appealing *Lodge Nutapu-Kaushipe* (☎ & ☎0166/97-2150; ❺), an attractive wooden cabin with comfortable, Japanese-style rooms; rates here include two meals. The lodge has a café, a winter-only sauna and a wood-lined indoor bath, as well as a dramatic two-level rotemburo overlooking the cascading river. The biggest hotel in the village, the *Ezo Matsu-sō* (☎0166/97-2321, ☎97-2324; ❼), opposite the visitor centre and designed to look like a Swiss chalet, caters mainly for large tour groups. Apart from the **café** at the *Lodge Nutapu-Kaushipe*, the best places for snacks and drinks are the **canteens** at the cable-car stations.

Sōunkyō Onsen

On the northeastern edge of Daisetsu-zan, some 60km east of Asahikawa, is **SŌUNKYŌ ONSEN**, the park's main resort, which had fallen into disrepair until being saved by town leaders, local business and the environment agency which runs the national park. A **park visitor centre** (8am–6pm Tues–Sun; ☎0165/89-4400) with excellent nature displays sits at the top of the main street, which is lined with stylish hotels, shops and a large bathing complex – the effect is refreshing and natural, and only just a bit too clean. Still, the main attraction here is not urban planning but the astonishing **Sōunkyō gorge**.

The best way to see the gorge, with its jagged rock walls carved out by the Ishikari-gawa, is to rent a **bike** from the shop by the bus station (¥1500) and follow the riverside route for 8km to Ōbako. Just east of the resort, leave the main road and pull into the car park next to the **Ginga and Ryusei waterfalls**. A twenty-minute climb up the opposite hill will lead to a viewpoint from where you'll get a fabulous view of the two cascades of white water tumbling down the cliffs. Continuing along the cycling and walking path, you may notice that the natural formations have been given poetic names, such as "Hime-iwa" (Princess Rock). The narrowest section of the gorge is called **Kobako**, or "Small Box", because of the enclosed feeling imparted by the towering rock pillars shooting up from the riverbanks. The route crosses the new road and enters a tunnel before emerging at the decidedly touristy **Ōbako** (Big Box), where visitors line up to be photographed in front of the river that gushes through the narrow gap in the perpendicular cliffs.

The classic Daisetsu-zan **hike** across the park's central mountain range may be started either from the top of the cable car at Asahidake Onsen or from Sōunkyō Onsen. Two minutes' walk south of the bus terminal you can catch a **cable car** (daily 6am–7pm; ¥900 one way, ¥1650 return), followed by a **chairlift** (¥400 one way, ¥600 return) up to within one hour's hike of the 1984-metre **Kuro-dake** (Black Mountain). From the summit, capped by a small shrine and giving marvellous views of the park, there's a choice of two trails to Asahi-dake – the southern route via Hokkai-dake (2149m) is the more scenic. By the time you reach Asahi-dake's summit, you'll have spent around six hours walking, so returning on foot to Sōunkyō Onsen the same day is only possible if you set out at the crack of dawn. There are overnight huts on the mountain, but the more comfortable option is to continue down to Asahidake Onsen and rest there for the night. If you don't want to backtrack for your luggage, consider having it sent on by *Takkyūbin* (see "Basics", p.61).

Practicalities

The closest **train** station to Sōunkyō Onsen is **Kamikawa**, some 22km north; buses take thirty minutes from here to reach the resort. Some of the **buses** passing through Kamikawa and Sōunkyō originate in Asahikawa and continue on to the central Hokkaidō town of Obihiro, to the south. There's a **tourist information office** (daily 8.30am–5.30pm; ☎0165/85-3350, ⓦwww.sounkyo .net/english/index.html) in the bus-terminal building, where you can pick up a basic English map and pamphlet on the area.

There are many large, expensive **hotels** on the edge of Sōunkyō, of which the *Mount View* (☎01658/5-3011, ⓕ5-3010; ❻), in the valley just outside the main village, is one of the least anonymous. The *Sōunkyō Youth Hostel* (☎01658/5-3418, ⓦwww.youthhostel.or.jp/English/menu2.htm; dorm beds ¥2800 per person) is a ten-minute walk up the path which runs behind the bus terminal, near the *Prince Hotel*. The dorms here have bunk beds, meals are served in a rustic lounge area and there are lots of notes on hiking in the park – but all in Japanese. Within the village itself, the only really inexpensive place is *Midori* (☎01658/5-3315; ❺ including meals), with very basic tatami rooms and a friendly manager. It's at the top of a perilous stairwell to the right of the souvenir shop between the *Northern Lodge* (see below) and the visitor centre; if no one answers at the reception desk, pop down to the souvenir shop, which is run by the same family. If you crave a bit more luxury, all the new hotels in the village are nice, the best probably being *Northern Lodge* (☎01658/5-3231, ⓔmanaboo@h4.dion.ne.jp; ❺), which has a choice of good Western or Japanese meals in their large restaurant, spacious rooms and comfortable public areas. You can also rent basic bikes here for ¥1000 a day.

If you have just come from a backpacking trip or are using the riverside campground, the new public **onsen bath** in the small shopping centre in the middle of town is a great place to soak and get cleaned up. The mall also houses a number of **restaurants**, a bar and some reasonably tasteful craft shops.

Biei and Bibaushi

Outside of Daisetsu-zan National Park, but overlooking its mountains from the east – including the active volcano Tokachi-dake – are the scenic farmlands surrounding the small town of **BIEI** and the tranquil and picturesque village of **BIBAUSHI**. Known for its vast fields of lavender and expanses of sunflowers, the landscape here is faintly evocative of Provençal France, with bales of hay lying around and lone poplar trees etched against the backdrop of snow-capped peaks. The gently undulating countryside is ideal for gentle walks, bike riding and photography – some good examples of which you can check out in the **Post Card Gallery and Café** (daily 9am–6pm), next to *Bibaushi Liberty Youth Hostel*. It's also possible to use Bibaushi as a base for a hike up the 2077-metre active volcano of **Tokachi-dake**, some 20km southwest and within the Daisetsu-zan National Park.

Bibaushi is connected with Asahikawa by frequent **trains** and **buses** and can easily be visited as a day-trip, or en route to and from Sapporo. For **overnight stays**, there's the stylish *Bibaushi Liberty Youth Hostel* (☎0166/95-2141, ⓦwww.biei.com/liberty; dorm beds ¥3200 per person, rooms ❹), next to the train station, with bunk-bed dorms and excellent meals. Staff here can provide a cycling and hiking map of the area, plus mountain bikes for ¥2800 a day, and also organize cross-country skiing and mountain treks. If you have your own transport, consider staying at *With You Farm Pension* (☎0166/95-2748, ⓔwithyou@guitar.ocn.ne.jp; ❺), ten minutes' drive from Bibaushi Station in a lovely location overlooking the mountains and offering both Western-style rooms (❺) and bunk-bed dorms (¥5500 per person); rates include two meals. Two kilometres from Biei Station the charming *Minshuku Hōzuki* (☎ & ⓕ0166/92-1225; ❼ including meals) has an English-speaking owner and Western-style twin rooms.

Furano

The main reason to come to the sleepy farm town of **FURANO**, 120km northeast of Sapporo, is to **ski** at the renowned World Cup resort on the slopes of Mount Kitanomine. Famous for being the location of the old soap opera *Kita no Kuni Kara* (*From the North Country*), which followed the dramas of a Tokyo family adapting to life in Hokkaidō, Furano is also the focus of many a salaryman's dreams about escaping the rat race.

Furano's **ski resort**, overlooking Mount Furano and the smoking volcano Tokachi-dake (both within the southern border of Daisetsu-zan National Park), is run by the *Prince* hotel group. The slopes are challenging but not as varied or as long as those at Niseko (see p.373). Lift passes start at ¥1900 for a night ticket (5–9pm) rising to ¥4500 for a one-day ticket.

Furano is best reached by direct **bus** from Sapporo (around 2hr 30min); ask to be dropped by the road leading up to *ski-jō*, rather than getting off in the centre of town, since you'll only have to backtrack. Check with tourist information in Sapporo (see p.365) about any special bus and lift-pass deals that are on offer. There's a **train** from the capital but it takes longer and costs more; if you're coming from Asahikawa, the train journey is only one hour and fifteen minutes. Buses run from the train station to the ski resort; a taxi will cost less than ¥2000.

A good budget **place to stay** is the former youth hostel, now called the *Alpine Visitors' Centre* (Ⓣ0167/22-1311, Ⓔalpine@furano.ne.jp; dorms ¥3000 per person, rooms ❸), five minutes' walk from the ski lifts, with bunk-bed dorms or twins, and good-value package deals on accommodation and lift passes. The young staff are enthusiastic, and you'll probably find someone who speaks English. They also organize balloon trips all year round, plus adventure sports in summer such as rafting, mountain biking and horseback riding. Only breakfast is served but there are several restaurants nearby. The most aesthetically pleasing place to stay in Furano, if you can get a reservation, is the *Pension Phytoncide* (Ⓣ0167/39-1551, Ⓕ39-1552; ❼). Named after a healing essence produced by green plants, this country inn is a perfect example of Japanese luxury in simplicity. The owners bake their own bread, and serve foods grown on their organic farm. Each of the six Western-style rooms has its own bath/toilet, and one of the rooms is wheelchair-accessible. The two *Prince* hotels are comfortable but pricey – the *Furano Prince* (Ⓣ0167/23-4111, Ⓦwww.princehotels.co.jp/english/index.html; ❼), a giant, tent-shaped lodge rising out of the snow, is closer to the rest of the resort, while the *New Furano* (Ⓣ0167/22-1111, Ⓦwww.princehotels.co.jp/english/index.html; ❼), a more modern, oval-shaped tower block, is tucked away on its own a few kilometres south, and has a heated swimming pool and several restaurants.

There's a decent range of **eating** options on the mountain, though you're likely to eat in your hotel or pension at night, as meals are generally included in room rates. For sheer entertainment value, be sure to try some of the "healthy steak" at the *Cola Company Museum, Restaurant and Bar* (closed first and third Tues of the month), on the right-hand side of the main road leading from Route 38 to the ski lifts. If you follow owner Mitsuhiro Wada's rather bizarre list of rules, and eat some of the "handmade food", he'll show you his amazing collection of Hollywood movie memorabilia.

Wakkanai and Rishiri-Rebun-Sarobetsu National Park

The rather dreary port of **WAKKANAI**, 320km from Sapporo, is the gateway to the far northwestern tip of Hokkaidō and the idyllic **Rishiri-Rebun-Sarobetsu National Park**. The main reason for coming here is to press on to the islands of Rebun-tō and Rishiri-tō, and the quickest way of doing this is to hop on the overnight train from Sapporo, which will deposit you in Wakkanai in good time to board one of the early ferries. If you arrive during the day, however, you'll find a few points of interest to keep you occupied for a few hours.

One impressive spot is by the northern flank of the port, which is protected by the **North Breakwater Dome**, a 427-metre-long arched corridor

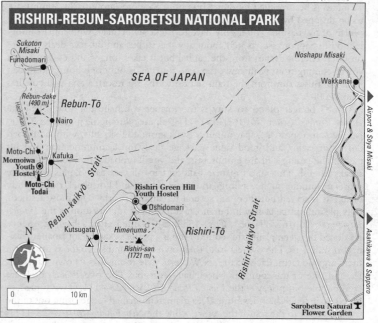

Korsakov (Sakhalin)

RISHIRI-REBUN-SAROBETSU NATIONAL PARK

Sukoton Misaki
Funadomari

Noshapu Misaki

SEA OF JAPAN

Wakkanai

Rebun-dake (490 m)   Rebun-Tō
Hachikura Course
Nairo

Moto-Chi   Kafuka
Momoiwa
Youth
Hostel

Moto-Chi
Todai

Rishiri Green Hill
Youth Hostel
Oshidomari

Kutsugata   Himenuma   Rishiri-Tō

Rishiri-san
(1721 m)

Rebun-kaikyō Strait

Rishiri-kaikyō Strait

N

0   10 km

Sarobetsu Natural
Flower Garden

Airport & Sōya Misaki

Asahikawa & Sapporo

supported by seventy concrete pillars. In July and August, a local **market** is set up here, along with a karaoke stage and barbecue pits at which you can sizzle your own fresh seafood and meat and guzzle beer. With more time to kill, head west of the JR station to the small cable car (¥180 one way, ¥240 return) which will whisk you up to **Wakkanai-kōen**, a grassy park from where, on a clear day, you can see right across to the Russian island of **Sakhalin**, some 60km northwest. Japan occupied Sakhalin in the early twentieth century and there's a monument in the park to nine female telephone operators who committed suicide in the post office on the island at the end of World War II rather than be captured by the Russians. Russo–Japanese relations are now much improved and there's steady trade between Wakkanai and its northern neighbours.

There's not much point carrying on to cape **Sōya Misaki**, 27km east of Wakkanai, other than to say you've been to the northernmost point of Japan. A couple of monuments, "The Bell for World Peace" and the "Tower of Prayer", a memorial to the Korean Airlines plane shot down by Soviet Union just north of the cape, mark the flat and rather dull spot, served by infrequent buses from Wakkanai.

Some 35km south of Wakkanai lies the **Sarobetsu Natural Flower Garden**, best visited between May and September, when its marshlands become a riot of colourful blooms. However, if you're heading over to Rebun, save your energy, as you'll see just as many flowers there, and in a far more dramatic setting. To reach the park, take a local train to Toyotomi Station, a 45-minute journey from Wakkanai, and then catch a bus (¥430) for the last fifteen minutes.

Practicalities

Direct **trains** from Sapporo and Asahikawa pull into Wakkanai Station, just south of the **ferry** terminal. Inside the station a **tourist information counter** (daily 10am–6pm; Ⓔinfo@welcome.wakkanai.hokkaido.jp) provides a Japanese map of the town, an English pamphlet and information on getting to the islands. Wakkanai's **airport** lies 10km east of the port; there are daily flights from here to and from Tokyo, Ōsaka and Sapporo. From the airport, a bus into town will cost around ¥590 for the thirty-minute journey, and a taxi ¥3500.

If you're heading on to Rishiri-tō and Rebun-tō, make sure you're carrying enough Japanese currency, or change some money here, as there are no foreign exchange facilities on either of the islands. The North Pacific Bank, two blocks west of the station walking towards the hillside, has a **foreign exchange** desk on the second floor. From May 7 to October 30 a **ferry service** runs between Wakkanai and the town of **Korsakov** on Sakhalin (¥30,000 one way, ¥45,000 return). The journey takes six hours and thirty minutes, with nine or ten departures a month.

There's no shortage of **accommodation** close to the station and around the port. The most convenient – though not the friendliest – budget option is *Wakkanai Moshiripa* (☎0162/24-0180, Ⓦwww.youthhostel.or.jp/English/menu2.htm; dorm beds ¥3200 per person), a hostel five minutes' walk north from the JR station and east of the ferry terminal; guests must check in before 8pm. More welcoming is *Wakkanai Youth Hostel* (☎0162/23-7162, Ⓦwww.youthhostel.or.jp/English/menu2.htm; dorm beds ¥2900 per person), a ten-minute walk south from JR Minami Wakkanai Station. The *Minshuku Nakayama* (☎0162/22-8868; ❺ including two meals) is a large, old-fashioned place opposite the port, while the *Petit Hotel Joy* (☎0162/22-1007, Ⓔjoy@ph-joy.com; ❺), next to the Pacific North Bank two blocks from the station, has standard Western-style rooms; rates include a simple breakfast. Most luxurious is the *ANA Hotel Wakkanai* (☎0162/23-8111, Ⓦwww.anahotels.com; ❽), directly in front of the ferry terminal. As with many upmarket hotels in Hokkaidō, prices here drop dramatically in the off season.

Plenty of tourist **restaurants** can be found around the JR station, the most famous being *Takechan*, which specializes in fresh fish dishes, including sushi and *tako-shabu* (¥1500), an octopus stew that's worth trying for its novelty value.

Rishiri-tō and Rebun-tō

The stunning and remote islands of **Rebun-tō** and **Rishiri-tō** are quite different: slender Rebun-tō is low-lying, its gentle hills sprinkled with alpine flowers, while Rishiri-tō is a Fuji-like volcano rising 1721m out of the sea. Because of their lovely scenery and mild weather, both islands are exceptionally popular with Japanese tourists in summer, when accommodation should be booked well in advance. At other times of the year, you're likely to have the islands to yourself. It's worth spending a couple of nights on each island.

Rishiri-tō

Hiking up the volcano is the best reason to come to **RISHIRI-TŌ**, a circular island made up of the 1721-metre cone of **Rishiri-san**. The island is sometimes called Rishiri-Fuji because its shape resembles the famous southern volcano, but Westerners might find it looks more like a lone Swiss Alp. Even if the weather is unpromising, it's still worth making the ascent (which takes ten to twelve hours) to break through the clouds on the upper slopes and be rewarded with panoramic views from the summit, which is crowned with a small shrine.

Rishiri-Rebun-Sarobetsu National Park

Wakkanai	*Wakkanai*	稚内
Sarobetsu Natural Flower Garden	*Sarobetsu Gensei Kaen*	サロベツ原生花園
Sōya Misaki	*Sōya Misaki*	宗谷岬
Accommodation		
ANA Hotel Wakkanai	*ANA Hoteru Wakkanai*	ＡＮＡホテル稚内
Minshuku Nakayama	*Minshuku Nakayama*	民宿中山
Petit Hotel Joy	*Puchi Hoteru Joi*	プチホテルジョイ
Wakkanai Moshiripa Youth Hostel	*Wakkanai Moshiripa Yūsu Hosuteru*	稚内モシリパユースホステル
Wakkanai Youth Hostel	*Wakkanai Yūsu Hosuteru*	稚内ユースホステル
Rishiri-tō	*Rishiri-tō*	利尻島
Himenuma pond	*Himenuma*	姫沼
Kutsugata	*Kutsugata*	沓形
Oshidomari	*Oshidomari*	鴛泊
Rishiri-san	*Rishiri-san*	利尻山
Accommodation		
Kitaguni Grand Hotel	*Kitaguni Gurando Hoteru*	北国グランドホテル
Pension Hera-san-no-ie	*Penshon Hera-san-no-ie*	ペンションへらさんの家
Rishiri Green Hill Youth Hostel	*Rishiri Guriinhiru Yūsu Hosuteru*	利尻グリーンヒルユースホステル
Rebun-tō	*Rebun-tō*	礼文島
Funadomari	*Funadomari*	船泊
Kafuka	*Kafuka*	香深
Moto-chi	*Moto-chi*	元地
Sukoton Misaki	*Sukoton Misaki*	スコトン岬
Accommodation		
Kaidō	*Kaidō*	海憧
Momoiwa-sō Youth Hostel	*Momoiwa-sō Yūsu Hosuteru*	桃岩荘ユースホステル
Hotel Rebun	*Hoteru Rebun*	ホテル礼文
Seikan-sō	*Seikan-sō*	星観荘

The most convenient route up the volcano starts some 3km south of the main port of **Oshidomari**, at the *Rishiri Hokuroku* campsite. Information and maps for the climb are available from the island's tourist information centre (see opposite) and occasional climbing groups are organized by staff at the local youth hostel. Around fifteen minutes' climb from the peak of Mount Chokan, the eighth station up the volcano, there's a basic hut where you can take shelter en route. Make sure you take plenty of water with you, as there's none available on the mountain.

If you don't want to climb to the top of Rishiri-san, you can always embark on the less strenuous three-hour hiking trail which starts at the pretty **Himenuma** pond and continues across the slopes of two smaller mountains, Kopon-san and Pon-san, to the Rishiri Hokuroku campsite. To get to Himenuma from the ferry terminal at Oshidomari, follow the coastal road a kilometre or so west until you reach a junction going up into the hills. The walk up to the pond is quite steep – you might be able to hitch a lift – and takes around an hour. At Himenuma, walk left around the lake to find the trail leading to the campsite.

Practicalities

There's an **airport** a few kilometres west of Oshidomari with a daily flight (Apr–Oct) from New Chitose airport (at present there are no commercial flights to the island from Wakkanai), although this may change. There are two to four **ferries** a day from Wakkanai to Oshidomari (1hr 40min; ¥1880 one way for second-class seats). Daily ferry services also run between Kafuka on Rebun-tō and Oshidomari and Kutsugata on Rishiri-tō's west coast (40min; ¥730). If you book ahead, staff at the hostel and most minshuku on the island can meet you at the ferry terminal or the airport. The youth hostel reception group are well-known for their enthusiastic goodbyes to departing guests, when they sing and dance on the docks at Oshidomari.

The **tourist information counter** (mid-April to mid-Oct daily 8am–5.40pm; ☎01638/2-2201, ✉rishiri@seagreen.ocn.ne.jp), inside the ferry terminal at Oshidomari, has a map of the island, plus English notes on the hikes to Rishiri-san and Himenuma pond. **Bicycles** – a good way to get around the island – can be rented from near the ferry terminal and from the youth hostel for around ¥1500 a day. Otherwise, **buses** run in both directions around the island (a circuit which takes 1hr 45min; ¥2100). If you arrive by ferry at Kutsugata on the western side of Rishiri, you'll need to get a bus north to Oshidomari (30min; ¥690).

The best **place to stay** is the *Rishiri Green Hill Youth Hostel* (☎01638/2-2507, ⊛www.youthhostel.or.jp/English/menu2.htm; dorm beds ¥2900 per person). There's accommodation in tatami rooms, good food, organized hiking up the mountain (starting at 4am) and the young staff throw their heart and soul into the nightly communal singalongs and information sessions, during which visitors are given detailed information in Japanese on what to do on the island, with the emphasis on cultural, historical and environmental issues. Note that you may be told when you try to book that you will have to call back closer to your time of intended stay, as the hostel opens and closes according to demand, especially from the middle of September. Near the ferry terminal is *Pension Hera-san-no-ie* (☎ & ☏01638/2-2361; ❺), with nice tatami rooms and a couple of Western-style bedrooms in a modern grey- and red-brick building next to the path leading up the rock which looms over the harbour. Rishiri-tō's most upmarket accommodation, the *Kitaguni Grand Hotel* (☎01638/2-1362, ☏2-2556; ❽–❾), is an unsightly red-brick tower that sticks out like a sore thumb amid the surrounding houses and is overpriced, although rates do include two meals, and drop significantly in the off season. Pitching a tent at the Rishiri Hokuroku **campsite** (☎01638/2-2394; mid-May to mid-Oct), 3km south of the port, will cost you ¥340 – alternatively, you can kip in one of the wooden cabins, which sleep four people (¥2000 per person). The campsite is on the main route up the volcano, so can get busy. For a quieter spot, head for the campsite (☎01638/4-2345; May–Oct) in Kutsugata Misaki-kōen, the park on the promontory south of Kutsugata port.

The best place for **lunch** in Oshidomari is *Aji-no-ichi*, on the main road behind the ferry terminal, where the huge bowls of seafood-topped ramen (¥1000) are delicious. If you're climbing Rishiri-san, you can pick up supplies for a picnic at the grocery stores in town.

Rebun-tō

Shaped like a crab's claw adrift in the Sea of Japan, **REBUN-TŌ** is most famous for its wildflower displays – the island's rolling green slopes are said to bloom with three hundred different types of alpine plants. At the southern tip of the island is its main port, the small and attractive settlement of **Kafuka**,

Rebun-tō hikes

The longest and most popular **hike** on Rebun-tō is the eight-hour **Hachi-jikan**, which runs for 32km along the west coast from Sukoton Misaki, the island's north-ernmost point, to Moto-chi in the south, passing through flower fields and forests. The cliffs at the end of this hike can be slippery and sometimes dangerous; if you don't enjoy struggling, try the easier **Yo-jikan** course, which consists of the first sec-tion of the Hachi-jikan course, thus lasting only four hours and missing the difficult coastal section from Uennai to Moto-chi. The island's youth hostels arrange walking groups for the two hikes and hold briefings the night before. If you want to hike on your own, aim to take the 6.50am bus from Kafuka to Sukoton, arriving at around 7.30am, so you can safely complete the walk during daylight. Stock up on food and drink before you start, as there are no refreshment stops along the way and it's not safe to drink river water on the island.

Another easy and enjoyable hike is the two-hour **Momoiwa** course, a return trip starting just above Kafuka and running to the lighthouse, Moto-chi Todai, at the south-ern tip of the island. The well-marked cliff-top trail takes its name from the Momoiwa (or "Peach-Shaped Rock") on the west coast, which it passes along the way. The views up the coast and over to Rishiri-tō are breathtaking, but be prepared for fero-cious winds and some steep sections. If you don't feel like walking back the way you came, continue down to the road at the lighthouse, and return to Kafuka by bus.

Other hikes include the **Rebun Rindō Hanabatake** course, which runs across the centre of the island (through valleys blooming with flowers), and follows a dirt road. The course can be approached from either Kafuka or Kafukai, 8km to the north, and can also be used as a diversion from the dangerous part of the eight-hour hike. Finally, there's the **Rebun-dake Tozan** course, starting at either Nairo or Kitouse, both on the bus route north from Kafuka. The summit gives fine views of Rishiri-tō and the Hokkaidō mainland.

which climbs uphill from the coast. In the north is the fishing village of **Funadomari**. The whole island is fabulous **hiking** territory (see box above) and attracts hordes of visitors every summer – especially to its scenic western coast.

From May to September five **ferries** a day go from Wakkanai to Kafuka (1hr 55min; ¥2200), and there are at least a couple during the rest of the year. There are also two ferries a day to Oshidomari and Kutsugata on Rishiri-tō (40min; ¥730). Hostels and most minshuku will pick you up from the ferry terminal if you book in advance. As on Rishiri, the youth hostel staff loudly serenade departing guests at the port.

The island's **tourist information counter** (daily 8.00am–5.30pm; ℡01638/6-2655) is in the ferry terminal at Kafuka, and has a good Japanese map of the island, marked with the main hiking routes. Staff here can also help with booking accommodation. **Getting around** the island is by bus, but fares are high and, given the scarcity of services, you'll probably find hitching a bet-ter way of exploring. If time is limited, consider taking one of the three **bus tours** (¥3100–3500), which cover all the scenic highlights and are timed to connect with the ferries. **Bike rental** is available from several shops near the ferry terminal for ¥500 an hour, or ¥2000 a day.

Most of Rebun's **accommodation** is in or around Kafuka. The luxurious *Hotel Rebun* (℡01638/6-1177, ℗6-2007; ❾), in the modern block next to the ferry terminal, is pricey, though rates include two meals. The *Momoiwa-sō Youth Hostel* (℡01638/6-1421, ⓦwww.youthhostel.or.jp/English/menu2.htm; dorm beds ¥2800 per person) occupies a dramatic location on the rocky western coast, south of the small fishing village of Moto-chi and fifteen minutes' drive from Kafuka. It's a good base for the eight-hour Hachi-jikan hiking course, being at the end of the walk (and staff can organize transport to the start). The hostel gets packed at the height of the season and the atmosphere becomes akin to a summer camp, featuring lots of singing and dancing with the high-spirited staff; it was closed in mid-2003 after a massive landslide nearby but may have reopened by the time you read this.

Tranquil **Funadomari**, the small fishing village at the northern end of the island, makes a good base for hikes out to the Sukoton Misaki cape. Accommodation here comprises the comfortable, recently rebuilt minshuku, *Seikan-sō* (☎01638/7-2818; ❺ including two meals), and the larger *Kaidō* (☎01638/7-2717, ☎7-2183; ❺ including two meals), next to the beachside campsite, which has nice tatami rooms and some cheaper dorm accommodation (¥6000 per person; under 40s only).

Eating is best arranged at your hotel or hostel – most can usually provide *bentō* picnic lunches if you're off on a hike. Otherwise, there are grocery shops in both Kafuka and Funadomari where you can pick up supplies. There's a laid-back **café** next to the *Momoiwa-sō Youth Hostel* in Kafuka, which plays jazz and is a relaxing place to chill out.

Eastern Hokkaidō

Without your own transport it's difficult to travel directly down the coastal route from Wakkanai to **eastern Hokkaidō**. There are no through buses along the sparsely populated coast, and by train you'll have to return to Asahikawa before you can transfer to the line out to **Abashiri**. This small port, 350km northeast of Sapporo, is well-known throughout Japan for its old maximum-security prison and is also the starting point in winter for boat tours through the drift ice which floats down from Siberia into the Sea of Okhotsk. Jutting into this inhospitable expanse of water northeast of Abashiri is the amazing **Shiretoko National Park**, one of the country's most remote and primeval areas, featuring abundant wildlife, dramatic cliffs, ancient forests and a volcanically heated waterfall cascading down a mountain into natural bathing pools. Inland, south of the peninsula, the **Akan National Park** pales in comparison to Hokkaidō's other national parks, but is not without its own attractions, including three scenic lakes, home to a winter population of large whooper swans. Heading south, further ecotourist delights abound at **Kushiro Shitsugen National Park** and **Kiritappu Marsh**, while the coast reaches a fittingly dramatic conclusion at the rocky cape of **Erimo Misaki**, which has the distinction of holding the record for the windiest place in Japan, as well as being home to a colony of seals.

Abashiri

The dead of winter is the best time to visit the compact fishing port of **ABASHIRI**, 350km from Sapporo, bordered by a couple of pretty lakes and overlooked by Mount Tento-zan, as this is when snow covers the less appealing modern parts of the town, whooper swans fly in to winter at Lake Tofutsu a few kilometres east of the harbour, and drift ice (called *ryūhyō* in Japanese) floats across the Sea of Okhotsk. By February the sea has frozen over in a remarkable sheet of blue-white ice that stretches as far as the eye can see. The ideal way to witness this astonishing phenomenon is to hop aboard the *Aurora*, an **ice-breaking sightseeing boat**, for a one-hour tour (daily Jan 20 to the

Abashiri · Abashiri · 網走
Abashiri Prison Museum · Hakubutsukan Abashiri Kangoku · 博物館網走監獄
Hokkaidō Museum of Northern Peoples · Hokkaidō Ritsu Hoppōminzoku Hakubutsukan · 北海道北方民族博物館
Okhotsk Ryūhyō Museum · Ohōtsuku Ryūhyō-kan · オホーツク流氷館

Accommodation
Abashiri Central Hotel · Abashiri Sentoraru Hoteru · 網走セントラルホテル
Abashiri Ryūhyō-no-Oka Youth Hostel · Abashiri Ryūhyō-no-Oka Yūsu Hosuteru · 網走流氷の丘ユースホステル
Hotel Shimbashi · Hoteru Shimbashi · ホテルしんばし

Shiretoko National Park · Shiretoko Kokuritsu-kōen · 知床国立公園
Kamuiwakka-no-taki · Kamuiwakka-no-taki · カムイワッカの滝
Rausu · Rausu · 羅臼
Rausu-dake · Rausu-dake · 羅臼岳
Shari · Shari · 斜里
Shiretoko Go-ko · Shiretoko Go-ko · 知床五湖
Shiretoko Shizen Centre · Shiretoko Shizen Sentā · 知床自然センター
Utoro · Utoro · ウトロ

Accommodation
Mine-no-yu · Mine-no-yu · 峰の湯
Minshuku Maruman · Minshuku Maruman · 民宿マルマン
Shiretoko Grand Hotel · Gurando Hoteru · グランドホテル
Shiretoko Iwaobetsu Youth Hostel · Shiretoko Iwaobetsu Yūsu Hosuteru · 知床岩尾別ユースホステル
Shiretoko Yaei-jō · Shiretoko Yaei-jō · 知床野営場
Yūhi-no-Ataru Ie · Yūhi-no-Ataru Ie · 夕陽のあたる家

first Sun in April; ¥3000), which departs at least four times a day, depending on the weather. The boat cracks through the ice sheets, throwing up huge chunks, some over 1m thick. You may well spot seals and eagles lounging on the floating white slabs.

An excellent vantage point from which to take in the ice floes is the summit of Tento-zan, directly behind the train station, where you'll also find several enjoyable museums. For a taste of the extremes of winter in Abashiri, head for the modern and informative **Okhotsk Ryūhyō Museum** (daily: April–Oct 8am–6pm; Jan–March, Nov & Dec 9am–4.30pm; ¥520), where you can touch huge lumps of ice in a room where the temperature is kept at minus 15°C and coats are provided for warmth. A panoramic film of the drift ice is also screened regularly throughout the day. While you're up here, don't miss the **Hokkaidō Museum of Northern Peoples** (Tues–Sun 9.30am–4.30pm; ¥300), a five-minute walk downhill from the Okhotsk Ryūhyō Museum, which has contemporary displays on the native peoples of northern Eurasia and America, prompting comparisons between the different cultures. A colour-coded chart at the start of the exhibition will help you identify which artefacts belong to which races; look out for the Inuit cagoules made of seal intestines.

Most Japanese associate Abashiri with its **maximum-security prison**, featured in a popular series of jail drama films called *Abashiri Bangaichi*. The town's

Akan National Park	*Akan Kokuritsu-kōen*	阿寒国立公園
Ainu Kotan	*Ainu Kotan*	アイヌコタン
Akan Kohan	*Akan Kohan*	阿寒湖畔
Kussharo-ko	*Kussharo-ko*	屈斜路湖
Mashū-ko	*Mashū-ko*	摩周湖
Me-Akan-dake	*Me-Akan-dake*	雌阿寒岳
Ō-Akan-dake	*Ō-Akan-dake*	雄尾阿寒岳
Teshikaga	*Teshikaga*	弟子屈
Accommodation		
Grand Hotel Akan	*Gurando Hoteru Akan*	グランドホテル阿寒
Kiri	*Kiri*	桐
Kussharo-Gen'ya Youth Guesthouse	*Kussharo-Gen'ya Yūsu Gesutohausu*	屈斜路原野ユースゲストハウス
Mashū-ko Youth Hostel	*Mashū-ko Yūsu Hosuteru*	摩周湖ユースホステル
New Akan Hotel Shangrila	*Nyū Akan Hoteru Shangurira*	ニュー阿寒ホテルシャングリラ
Nibushi-no-Sato	*Nibushi-no-Sato*	にぶしのさと
Hotel Park Way	*Hoteru Pāku Uei*	ホテルパークウェイ
Pension Birao	*Penshon Birao*	ペンションビラオ
Kushiro	*Kushiro*	釧路
Kushiro Shitsugen National Park	*Kushiro Shitsugen Kokusai-kōen*	釧路湿原国際公園
Pension Porch	*Penshon Porch*	ペンションPORCH
Erimo Misaki	*Erimo Misaki*	えりも岬
Kaze-no-kan	*Kaze-no-kan*	風の館
Minshuku Semba	*Minshuku Semba*	民宿仙庭
Misakisō	*Misakisō*	岬荘
Obihiro	*Obihiro*	帯広

current prison no longer houses high-grade criminals or political undesirables, and the original nineteenth-century penitentiary has been relocated to the foot of Tento-zan and transformed into the jolly **Abashiri Prison Museum** (daily: April–Oct 8am–6pm; Jan–March, Nov & Dec 9am–5pm; ¥1050). This large, open-air site features waxworks of various detainees (look out for the tattooed *yakuza* in the bathhouse, and Shiratori Yoshie, a famous escapee, crawling across the rafters in the cell block), and is popular with Japanese tour groups. A regular **bus** runs a circular course from Abashiri Station up Tento-zan to the museums on the summit, stopping first at the prison museum on the way up.

Practicalities

Apart from flying, the fastest way to reach Abashiri is on the limited express **train** from Sapporo via Asahikawa (5hr 20min). Cheaper, and only a little slower, are the nine daily **buses** from Sapporo, as well as an overnight bus (¥6210) and train from Sapporo, if you want to save on a night's accommodation. Abashiri can also be reached by the plodding local train from the port of Kushiro (see p.410), 146km south, on the Senmō line. The nearest **airport** is Memanbetsu, 16km south of Abashiri, and 25 minutes from the JR station by bus (¥720), with regular flights to and from New Chitose airport, Hakodate,

Haneda (Tokyo), Ōsaka and Nagoya. The **tourist information office** (Mon–Sat 9am–5pm; ☎0152/44-5849, ⓦhttp://abashiri.jp/tabinavi_en/index.html) is next to the JR station. The friendly assistants can give you a Japanese map of the town, help with accommodation and supply discount tickets for the town's museums.

Of the several **hotels** near the JR station, the *Shimbashi* (☎0152/43-4307, ⓕ45-2091; ❺), directly opposite, has decent tatami rooms. The town's top hotel, the *Abashiri Central* (☎0152/44-5151, ⓕ43-5177; ❻), is well located near the shopping district. The modern *Abashiri Ryūhyō-no-Oka Youth Hostel* (☎0152/43-8558, ⓦwww.youthhostel.or.jp/English/menu2.htm; dorm beds ¥3100 per person) occupies a great location overlooking the Sea of Okhotsk, and rents out bicycles. To reach the hostel, take a bus from the station to Meiji-iriguchi (10min) and then walk uphill towards the right for ten minutes. The last bus leaves the station at 5pm: if you miss it you'll need to catch a taxi or face a forty-minute walk along some unlit, isolated streets.

Abashiri specializes in fresh **seafood** – don't leave town without trying some of its succulent crabs. The best place to head for is *Sushiyasu*, a couple of blocks behind the *Abashiri Central Hotel*, and easily spotted by its outside photograph menu and cheap prices: sushi sets cost from ¥1800. The *Hotel Shimbashi*'s restaurant serves good-value set meals, cheap noodle dishes and sushi, while the stylish *Daihyogen* in the *Abashiri Central Hotel* does beautifully presented set meals of local delicacies from ¥2500 per person – worth the splurge.

△ Hakodate

Shiretoko National Park

Clearly visible from Abashiri is the **Shiretoko peninsula**, a seventy-kilometre-long finger of land thrusting out into the Sea of Okhotsk, 40km to the east. About half the peninsula is covered by the **SHIRETOKO NATIONAL PARK**. *Shiretoko* is an Ainu word meaning "the end of the earth" and this volcanic corner of Hokkaidō, covered with virgin forest, certainly lives up to its name. Giant black rocks scattered along the coast look as though they were newly spewed from a volcano, roads are few, tourist facilities even fewer, and wildlife is abundant – you're almost guaranteed to encounter wild deer, foxes, and even brown bears. In the winter, when freezing temperatures put off all but the hardiest of travellers, drift ice litters the shore, and the magnificent Steller's sea eagle can be observed near Rausu. Most people visit between June and September, the best period for hiking up the mountainous volcanic spine of the peninsula and viewing the five small lakes at Shiretoko Go-ko. This is also a great time to soak in the natural rotemburo, including the hot waterfall of Kamuiwakka-no-taki.

Roads stop halfway up both sides of the peninsula, so the only way you'll get to see the rocky cape, with its unmanned lighthouse and waterfalls plunging over sheer cliffs into the sea, is to take a sightseeing boat from **UTORO**, the area's main onsen resort and fishing port; tours run daily between June and September, departing at midday (3hr 45min; ¥6000). Near Utoro's tiny harbour you'll notice several large rocks, one of which is nicknamed "Godzilla", for reasons which become obvious when you see it.

Apart from being a useful stopover, however, Utoro has few attractions, and you're best off pressing up the coast to the **Shiretoko Shizen Centre** (daily: April 20–Oct 20 8am–5.40pm; Oct 21–April 19 9am–4pm), which has displays on the national park and shows a twenty-minute giant-screen film (¥500) throughout the day, with swooping aerial shots of the mountains and rugged coastline. Behind the centre, a few well-marked nature trails lead through forests and heathland covered with ferns, bamboo grass and wild flowers to cliffs, down which a waterfall cascades.

Some 9km further north, past the *Iwaobetsu Youth Hostel* (see p.406), lies one of the peninsula's top attractions, **Shiretoko Go-ko**, where five jewel-like lakes are linked by wooden walkways and sinuous forest paths. If the weather is fine, some of the lakes reflect the mountains, and a lookout point west of the parking lot provides a sweeping view across the heathland to the sea. In summer, the first couple of lakes can be crowded with tourists, but the further you walk around the 2.4-kilometre circuit, the more serene the landscape becomes. A bus from Utoro runs to the lakes four times a day – hitching is another option. Allow at least an hour to see all five lakes.

Just before the turn-off to the lakes, a dirt road continues up the peninsula. Following this track for about twenty minutes by car, as it rises uphill, will bring you to **Kamuiwakka-no-taki**, a cascading warm-water river and series of waterfalls, creating three levels of natural rotemburo. To reach the bathing pools you'll have to climb up the river. Bring your bathing costume and support the local economy by renting straw sandals at the start of the climb – they make a world of difference on the dangerously slippery rocks. The climb becomes more treacherous the higher you go, but the reward is that the topmost pool is the warmest and has the loveliest waterfall. The water is mildly acidic, so be warned that if you have any cuts it's going to sting, and bring a water bottle to rinse off with afterwards. From June to mid-October, three buses a day continue on from Shiretoko Go-ko to the falls; again, it's easy enough to hitch.

With more time, think about embarking on one of the challenging **hikes** up the volcanic backbone of the peninsula. The peak of **Rausu-dake**, at 1661m the tallest mountain in Shiretoko, can be reached in around four and a half hours from the *Iwaobetsu Youth Hostel*, passing a natural rotemburo on the way. It's a popular hike and the hostel staff can advise on weather conditions. From the top there are spectacular views along the whole peninsula, while to the east you should be able to see Kunashiri-tō, one of the disputed Kuril Islands, or "Northern Territories" as they are known in Japan (see box opposite). It will take you a full day to continue across Rausu-dake to the sleepy east-coast fishing village of Rausu.

Iō-zan, the active volcano that produces hot water for the Kamuiwakka-no-taki waterfalls, is a more difficult climb. The trail begins beside the Shiretoko Ōhashi, the bridge just beyond the entrance to the falls. A hike to the 1562-metre summit and back takes at least eight hours and can be combined with a visit to the hot waterfall. If you are a serious mountaineer you can continue from one peak to the other, connecting the two hikes via a difficult ridge trail, but bring a topographical map, take precautions against bears and plan to stay one or two nights at the campsites along the way. With your own transport, there's a terrific three-hour hike on a trail that leads in to Lake Rausu and back, beginning about a third of the way down to Rausu town from Shiretoko pass on the road that bisects the peninsula. The trail passes through a unique highland environment of swamps and small lakes with gnarled trees and alpine flowers. The trailhead is not well marked from the road, however, so you'll need a good map to find it.

Practicalities

The gateway to the Shiretoko National Park is the rather shabby town of **SHARI**, where there's a JR station on the Senmō line, which links Abashiri with the port of Kushiro, some 100km south. Between May and October, four buses a day (the last at 1.45pm) run up the western side of the peninsula to Shiretoko Go-ko (¥960 one way) from Shari bus station opposite the JR station, all stopping at Utoro on the way. From June to mid-October a daily bus (¥1000 one way) runs from Shari to Rausu, on the east coast, via the Shiretoko Pass in the middle of the peninsula. Rausu is also connected by bus with JR Nemuro-Shibetsu Station on the Nemuro line, which runs out to the Nemuro peninsula, some 40km east of Kushiro.

There's an **information office** in front of Utoro's bus station (daily 8am–7.30pm; ☎01522/4-2639); the assistants can help with accommodation, but don't speak English. Of the four **youth hostels** in the area, the best and most convenient for the park is *Shiretoko Iwaobetsu* (☎01522/4-2311, ⓦwww.youthhostel.or.jp/English/menu2.htm; dorm beds ¥2900 per person), which nestles in a valley beside the Iwaobetsu-gawa. The hostel is large and well managed, with welcoming staff and good food, though it gets busy in summer.

Utoro

If you want to stay in **Utoro**, the *Yuhi-no-Ataru Ie* (☎01522/4-2764, ⓔsiretoko@mb.infoweb.ne.jp; ❼) is expensive in summer but much cheaper off season. It's a fifteen-minute hike up the second road off to the right after the bus station – take the pedestrian pathway and walk straight ahead until you see a building with a painting of a white-tailed eagle on it. The rooms are pretty good, and the rates include two meals, but it's not as handy a base for hikes as *Iwaobetsu*. Next door is the *Shiretoko Yaei-jō*, a well-maintained **campsite**

The disputed Kuril Islands

Despite relatively civil negotiations, which began in earnest in 1997, Japan and Russia have still not put an end to a 55-year territorial dispute over the **Kuril Islands**, some of which can be seen clearly from the Shiretoko peninsula. Technically, Japan is still fighting World War II with the former Soviet Union; a peace accord has never been signed because of Russia's continued occupation of these volcanic islands strung across the Sea of Okhotsk between the Kamchatka Peninsula and north-eastern Hokkaidō.

Known in Japan as the Northern Territories, or *Chishima* (Thousand Islands), and in Russia as the Kurils, only five of the islands are permanently inhabited, with a third of the population of 23,000 being accounted for by Russian soldiers. Japan demands the return of the four southernmost islands of Kunashiri, Shikotan, Etorofu and the Habomai group, the closest of which is less than 20km off Hokkaidō's coast.

The islands themselves are fairly desolate; it is their rich mineral resources and especially the surrounding fishing grounds that make them so desirable. Also, for Russia, the islands – blocking off the Sea of Okhotsk – have an important strategic military position. Although negotiations continue, it is far from clear, given the delicate issues involved, how a settlement will be achieved. A picture history of the negotiations, as well as a great view of Kunashiri, can be seen from the observation deck and café on the steep hill just above Rausu port.

which costs ¥350 per person per night. At the other end of the scale, the opulent *Shiretoko Grand Hotel* (☎01522/4-2021, ✉info@shiretoko.co.jp; ❼–❽) has both Western- and Japanese-style rooms and a rooftop onsen bath and rotemburo with views across the harbour; rates include two meals.

Utoro has a reasonable selection of **restaurants**: try *Ikkyuya*, just north of the bus station, where large bowls of ramen noodles shouldn't cost you more than ¥700. Also worth searching out is *Shiokaze*, a small restaurant where a set lunch of grilled fish, soup, rice and pickles costs ¥800; you'll find it on the hill above the bus station, five minutes' walk east of the campsite.

Rausu

On the opposite side of the peninsula, **RAUSU**, the first place you come to when either descending the trail or coming down the road over the pass, has a free public campsite, across the road from the *Kuma-no-yu* outdoor onsen (which is also free). Proceeding downhill toward the town, you'll come to Rausu's three large onsen hotels, the least shabby of which is the *Mine-no-yu* (☎01538/7-3001; ❼). Further towards town on the left are a few small minshuku including *Minshuku Maruman* (☎01538/7-2479; ❺ including meals), probably the best deal in town.

Akan National Park

Some 50km south of the Shiretoko peninsula is yet another wilderness and lakeland area, the **AKAN NATIONAL PARK**. In any other part of Japan this densely forested park, with its three **lakes** – Mashū-ko, Kussharo-ko and Akan-ko – and the **volcanic peaks** of Me-Akan and Ō-Akan, would rate as a major tourist attraction. In Hokkaidō, though, where breathtaking scenery is a given, Akan National Park is something of an also-ran, not nearly as beautiful as the Shikotsu-Tōya National Park in the south (see p.382), nor as dramatic as the Shiretoko National Park to the north (see p.405). Furthermore, patchy public transport makes this a difficult area to tour unless you have your own wheels or don't mind hitching. Nevertheless, the park is a haven for birdwatchers and walkers and has some pleasant lakeside onsen, while in the resort of **Akan Kohan** you can see traditional Ainu dancing, as well as the rare and fascinating *marimo* weedballs.

Akan Kohan

The compact onsen resort of **AKAN KOHAN**, on the southern shore of Akan-ko, is the most commercialized part of the national park, bursting with ritzy hotels and gift shops – the town's main attraction is as a base for hikes up the nearby peaks of **Me-Akan-dake** (1499m) and **Ō-Akan-dake** (1371m). At the western end of town, a ten-minute walk from the bus station, is the **Ainu Kotan**, a depressingly fake Ainu "village" which is little more than a short road of giftshops selling identical carved wood figures. Two hundred Ainu are said to live here. Visitors can watch a performance of traditional dance and music in the thatched *chise* (house) at the top of the shopping parade, and there's a tiny **museum** (daily 10am–10pm; ¥300) in a hut beside the *chise* with some interesting traditional Ainu costumes.

Just beyond the Ainu Kotan is the **Akan Forest and Lake Culture Centre** (daily 10am–5pm; ¥500), a small exhibition area with an impressive slide show of owls and some excellent examples of woodcarvings – much better than those you'll see in the giftshops. Look out also for a tank of *marimo*, the velvety green weedballs that are native to Akan-ko. Much is made of the *marimo* in Akan Kohan; the lake is one of the few places in the world where this spherical weed, a nationally designated "special natural treasure", is found, and you can buy bottled baby *marimo* in all the giftshops. It can take two hundred years for the weedballs to grow to the size of baseballs.

Dedicated botanists might want to take the boat trip across the lake to the small island of Churui-shima, where the **Marimo Exhibition Centre** (daily 7.30am–5.30pm; ¥400, or ¥1520 including the return boat trip) has an underwater viewing tank. If you're lucky, you'll see the *marimo* balls bobbing up to the surface of the lake as they photosynthesize – thereby producing the gases that make them float – during the day (they sink to the bottom of the lake at night when they aren't synthesizing). Back in Akan Kohan, there's yet more *marimo* on display in the **visitor centre** (daily 9am–5pm) at the eastern end of town, but it's more interesting to head along the pleasant woodland trails which start behind the centre and lead to the **Bokke**, a small area of bubbling mud pools beside the lake.

Many of the hotels in Akan Kohan allow day visitors into their **onsen** baths, usually between 11am and 3pm. This costs around ¥1500 at either the *New Akan Hotel Shangrila* or the *Akan Grand Hotel* which has the most elaborate tubs, including rooftop baths for women, and a landscaped rotemburo with a view across the lake, for men.

Practicalities

There are daily **bus** connections to Akan Kohan from Asahikawa via Sōunkyō (see p.392), and from the port of Kushiro (3hr 5min; ¥2650). Between July and September additional buses run between the lake and Utoro in Shiretoko National Park. The closest **train** station to the lake is in Teshikaga, but it's better to get off at Kawayu further north, where you can board the expensive tourist bus service that runs around the national park's main sights (2hr 30min; ¥3190), including Mashū-ko, before stopping at Akan Kohan.

Help with accommodation bookings plus English maps and leaflets on the area, including good hiking notes on the nearby mountains, are all available from the **sightseeing information office** (daily 9am–6pm; ☎0154/67-2254,

©staff@lake-akan.com), right near the Akan Kohan bus station. There's a decent wooded **campsite** five minutes' walk beyond the Ainu Kotan. Of the several minshuku in the resort, *Kiri* (℡0154/67-2755; ❹), opposite the *Grand Hotel Akan*, has English-speaking owners and is good value, considering two meals are included in the price. At the other end of the scale, both the *Grand Hotel Akan* (℡0154/67-2531, ©reserve@newakanhotel.co.jp; ❽) and the *New Akan Hotel Shangrila* (℡0154/67-2121, ℻67-3339; ❾) have prime lakeside locations, opulent interiors, luxurious onsen baths and top-notch Japanese cuisine, which is included in the rates.

Mashū-ko

Some 25km east of Akan-ko, just outside the park boundaries, is the small and unexciting town of **Teshikaga**, where you'll find the Mashū JR station. The reason for coming here is to see the famed lake of **MASHŪ-KO**, roughly 10km west of the town at the bottom of sheer cliffs that keep all tourists at bay and the waters pristine. There are three lookout points over the 212-metre-deep caldera lake, which on rare occasions sparkles a brilliant blue, though the view is usually obscured by swirling mists and thick cloud, creating a mysterious atmosphere which led the Ainu to christen Mashū-ko "The Devil's Lake". The first lookout point tends to get crowded; a ten-minute walk further around the road will lead you to a quieter viewpoint. If the weather is bad and you want to see the lake in all its glory, the giftshop at the first lookout point shows a free video and slide show about Mashū-ko.

There are infrequent and costly buses from Teshikaga to Mashū-ko – it's much better to hitch here, especially if you're staying at the large and modern *Mashū-ko Youth Hostel* (℡01548/2-3098, ⓦwww.masyuko.jp; dorms ¥3000 per person; rooms ❸), which is halfway to the lake. The hostel runs a number of reasonably priced guided tours of the area, and meals are served next door in the *Great Bear* restaurant (the ¥1050 three-course dinner is especially good value). A good alternative is the homely and friendly *Pension Birao* (℡01548/2-2979, ©birao@d3.dion.ne.jp; ❻ including two meals), which offers neat, Western-style rooms and hearty local cuisine. It's in Teshigaka, about a five-minute taxi ride from the JR station.

Kussharo-ko and around

To the west of Mashū-ko is the Akan National Park's largest lake, picturesque **Kussharo-ko**, which at eighty square kilometres is the biggest **crater lake** in Japan. It's also famous as the home of Kussie, Japan's answer to the Loch Ness Monster. Kussie's mythical status received a boost in 1997 when several people reported seeing a mysterious creature in the lake, though according to most locals it was an oversized trout. Whether it has a monster or not, Kussharo-ko is special because it is fed by onsen water, creating a warm temperature and several natural rotemburo around its edge, such as the piping-hot pools at **Wakoto Hantō**, a mini-promontory on the lake's southern shore. You can hop into another lakeside rotemburo at **Kotan Onsen**, an easy cycle ride from the *Kussharo-Gen'ya Youth Guesthouse* (see p.410). There's also a small **Ainu museum** (daily 9am–4.30pm; ¥300) here in a strikingly modern concrete building, though it's only worth a visit if you've not checked out any of the other collections around Hokkaidō.

A strong whiff of sulphur from the nearby volcano Iō-zan drifts over the area's main village, **KAWAYU ONSEN**, 3km from the lake. Here you'll find several hotels and minshuku, as well as the bus terminal. Be sure to drop into the excellent new **Kawayu Eco-Museum Centre**, where you can pick up an English map and a guide to the many birds you're likely to see in the area (including all five of the Japanese woodpecker species). One of the centre's nature guides speaks English and there are several hiking trails, one of which is wheelchair-accessible. Kawayu's train station is a ten-minute bus journey south of the village; if you arrive late (the last bus to the onsen is 5.30pm) you could **stay** at the *Hotel Park Way* (℡01548/3-2616, ℻3-2817; ❻), which has decent tatami rooms and rotemburo. A great place to stay beside the lake is *Nibushi-no-Sato* (℡01548/3-2294, ⓦwww1.ocn.ne.jp/~kussie; ❻ including two meals), a minshuku run by a friendly English-speaking manager who will come and pick you up at Kawayu Onsen bus terminal if you phone ahead. Bike rental is available (¥1800 per day) and there's an indoor onsen bath with a lake view. This is also a great place to observe the whooper swans (*O-hakucho*) in winter, and lots of other birds and animals all year round.

The park's best **youth hostel** is the *Kussharo-Gen'ya Youth Guesthouse* (℡01548/4-2609, ⓦwww.gogogenya.com/intro/e-intro.htm;¥3500 per person), a distinctive, tent-like wooden building set amid potato fields some thirty minutes' walk from the southern shore of Kussharo-ko. Accommodation is in Western-style rooms and superb Japanese meals are served. Mountain bikes can be rented (¥1000 a day) from here, and the staff organize two-hour canoe tours from the lake up one of the local rivers (¥3500) and cross-country ski tours in the winter.

Kushiro

The main southern gateway to the Akan National Park (see p.407) is the industrial town and port of **KUSHIRO**, which has a domestic airport and is also served by ferries from Tokyo. There's no special reason to linger here except to change money at one of the banks on the main road or to see the excellent natural history exhibits at the **Kushiro City Museum** (9.30am–5pm;¥360), southeast of the train station and across the river. The dramatic exterior is designed to represent the outstretched wings of a tancho crane; inside, you'll see a reconstructed mammoth skeleton, carnivorous marshland plants, detailed life histories of bird, insect, fish and mammal species of the area, displays on prehistoric human life and an excellent collection of Ainu artefacts. There are few signs in English, but staff are happy to try to answer your questions. Another possible time-filler is the colourful **Fisherman's Wharf**, a redeveloped waterside complex of shops and restaurants. The place also goes by the odd nickname of MOO, which apparently stands for "Marine Our Oasis".

If you need a **place to stay**, your best bet is the *Kushiro Royal Inn*, 14-9-2 Kurogane-chō, immediately to your right as you exit the station (℡0154/31-2121, ℻31-2122; ❺ including breakfast); before reserving a room, check out the JR *Hokkaidō* magazine, found on most express services, for special offers of substantially discounted rates.

Kushiro Shitsugen National Park

The Akan bus from Kushiro Station connects Kushiro with Akan-ko, passing through the **Kushiro Shitsugen National Park**. Dedicated birdwatchers will want to spend more time in the Kushiro Marsh and the surrounding area and may want to take one of several tour buses which go from Kushiro Station or the MOO bus terminal through the various observation sites in the park, returning to Kushiro within four to five hours. Information on these is available at the Kushiro Station information centre. If you have your own transport and are headed north to Akan along Route 53, stop in at the **Kushiro Marsh Observatory** (daily 8.30am–6pm,¥360) and the Onnenai Visitor Centre (same hours). Both are within Kushiro Park and have promenade trails and observation points through the marsh, which is a waterfowl reserve on the Ramsar Convention list of Wetlands of International Importance: there should be a staff member in one or both places who can answer a few questions in English.

People come from around the world to see the area's **red-crested cranes**, a majestic bird with a two-metre wingspan. The cranes perform a courtship dance in February which can be seen at several places in the Kushiro and Kiritappu marshlands; the best place to observe it is in the fields near **TSU-RUI** village, outside Kushiro park in a reserve operated by the Wild Bird Association of Japan (*Nihon Yacho no Kai*). Tsurui lies an hour north of Kushiro, on the way to Akan. There's excellent **accommodation** here at the *Hickory Wind* wilderness lodge (T0154/64-2956; ⑥), which has comfortable Western-style accommodation in a new rustic building overlooking the Japanese crane sanctuary, though with just five rooms it quickly gets booked up when the cranes are dancing. The meals are a work of art and the owner speaks English and is a mine of information on nature destinations in eastern Hokkaidō. If you call ahead, he can pick you up at the airport or Tsurui bus station.

Kiritappu Shitsugen and the Shiretoko Peninsula

If you can't get enough of cranes, sea eagles and tufted puffins, and want to try to spot a Kuril seal, a red fox or a sea otter, head east from Kushiro in the direction of the Nemuro peninsula to **Kiritappu Shitsugen** (Wetland) prefectural park, where the town of Hamanaka and the Friends of Kiritappu Marsh have built the **Kiritappu Shitsugen Centre** (9.30am–4pm), with an excellent bookstore, nature museum and restaurant overlooking the marsh. Kiritappu is a two-hour drive from Kushiro on Route 44; the Shitsugen centre lies south of Chanai train station on the MG road. If you plan **to stay** in Kiritappu, continue east on the MG road to Biwase Bay and the friendly *Pension Porch* ecolodge (T0153/62-2772, ⓔporch@cocoa.ocn.ne.jp; ⑥), between Shinkawa and the Biwase Tembodai viewpoint. The English-speaking owner Urita-san can set you up with canoes or take you out to uninhabited **Kenboki Island** to see rare flowers, seabirds, Kuril seals and possibly a whale spout off on the horizon.

From Kiritappu you can continue up the coast with possible stops at the Nemuro and Notsuke peninsulas, before finally coming to the **Shiretoko peninsula** and national park. In this area of Eastern Hokkaidō you can see three of Japan's four greatest ornithological spectacles: Tancho cranes in the Kushiro and Kiritappu regions; whooper swans at Odaito near the Notsuke peninsula; and Steller's sea eagles at Rausu on the Shiretoko peninsula (the fourth are cranes at Arasaki in Kyūshū). The best months for all of these are January, February and March.

Erimo Misaki

One of the most fascinating places along Hokkaidō's eastern coast is the small fishing village of **ERIMO MISAKI**, 160km southwest of Kushiro and a popular stop with tour groups and bikers, who come to take in one of the windiest areas in Japan and gaze at the colony of three hundred Kuril harbour seals living around the rocky cape. This is a dramatic place at any time of the year, but is particularly beautiful in summer, when the grassy hills which ripple down to the cape are dusted with wild flowers. Along the coast on the way to the cape you'll see people fishing for *kombu* seaweed, which is dried out in long strands on the pebbly black-sand beaches.

The pride of this isolated community is reflected in the excellent **Kaze-no-kan** (May–Sept 8am–7pm; Jan–April & Oct–Dec 8.30am–5pm; ¥500), a "wind" **museum** just beyond the giftshops and car park at the cape. The exhibition halls are approached through a curved corridor resonating with swirly, tinkling music. Inside, a wind tunnel gives you the chance to experience what it's like to stand in a 25-metre-per-second gale (in case it's not so windy outside). Other highlights include film and slide shows on the area, with a slide screen that scrolls back to reveal a panoramic view of the cape. There's also a room dedicated to the seals, with telescopes to watch them – if you're lucky they'll be basking on the rocks below. Apart from visiting the museum, simply walking around the cape is extremely pleasant. It's also something of a ritual, if you stay overnight at Erimo Misaki, to visit the cape at dawn and watch the sun rise.

The closest train station to Erimo Misaki is at **Obihiro**, 115km northwest, from where you'll need to take two buses to reach the cape. The Tokachi bus departs from outside Obihiro Station and takes an hour to reach **Hirō**, where you'll need to change to the less frequent (4 daily) JR bus running to the cape and around to **Samani**. From southern Hokkaidō you can take a local train from Tomakomai, which chugs for three hours along the coast to Samani, where you need to pick up the JR bus to the cape.

If you decide to **stay**, your best bet is the *Minshuku Semba* (☎01466/3-1144), ten minutes' walk from the cape, next to the Erimo Gakomae bus stop. Both the bunk-bed dorms (¥4700 per person, including two meals) and slightly pricier private tatami rooms (❺, including two meals) are comfortable, and the dinner (including local salmon and seaweed and a complimentary beer) is well worth booking. Another option is *Misakisō* (☎01466/3-1316, ⓕ3-1317; ❻), a traditional ryokan just below the museum and overlooking the cape, where the rates include two meals. No English is spoken here, but the management is friendly and you're well placed to catch Erimo Misaki's sunrise.

Travel details

Trains

The trains between the major cities listed below are the fastest, direct services. There are also frequent slower services, run by JR and several private companies, covering the same destinations. It's usually possible, especially on long-distance routes, to get there faster by changing between services.

Abashiri to: Asahikawa (6 daily; 3hr 44min); Kushiro (4 daily; 3hr); Sapporo (5 daily; 5hr 19min).

Asahikawa to: Abashiri (5 daily; 3hr 44min); Furano (11 daily; 1hr 8min); Sapporo (40 daily; 1hr 30min); Wakkanai (5 daily; 4hr 3min).

Hakodate to: Aomori (12 daily; 2hr); Morioka (4 daily; 4hr 20min); Ōnuma-kōen (12 daily; 20min);

Sapporo (13 daily; 3hr 30min); Sendai (2 overnight sleeper; 7hr); Tokyo (2 daily; 11hr 10min).

Sapporo to: Abashiri (5 daily; 5hr 19min); Asahikawa (40 daily; 1hr 30min); Hakodate (16 daily; 3hr 30min); Kushiro (8 daily; 3hr 30min); New Chitose airport (30 daily; 37min); Noboribetsu (20 daily; 1hr 13min); Ōsaka (daily; 22hr 15min); Otaru (30 daily; 30min); Tokyo (2 daily; 16hr); Tomakomai (25 daily; 50min).

Wakkanai to: Asahikawa (5 daily; 4hr 3min); Sapporo (3 daily; 6hr).

Buses

Abashiri to: Sapporo (9 daily; 6hr); Shari (5 daily; 1hr).

Asahikawa to: Asahidake Onsen (2 daily; 1hr 30min); Furano (daily; 1hr 30min); Sapporo (every 20–40min; 2hr 30min); Sōunkyō Onsen (8 daily; 1hr 45min); Tenninkyō Onsen (2 daily; 1hr); Wakkanai (daily; 4hr 45min).

Hakodate to: Ōnuma-kōen (5 daily; 1hr); Tōya-ko (daily; 3hr 30min).

New Chitose airport to: Niseko (2 daily; 3hr); Rishiri-tō (April–Oct 1 daily; 65min); Sapporo (at least 20 daily; 1hr 10min); Shikotsu Kohan (3 daily; 45min).

Sapporo to: Abashiri (9 daily; 6hr); Furano (10 daily; 3hr); Kushiro (4 daily; 6hr); Niseko (4 daily; 2hr 30min); Noboribetsu (8 daily; 1hr 40min); Tōya-ko (daily; 3hr); Wakkanai (daily; 6hr 15min).

Ferries

Hakodate to: Aomori (9 daily; 3hr 30min; high-speed 2 daily; 1hr 45min); Ōma (2 daily; 1hr 45min).

Muroran to: Aomori (1 daily; 7hr); Hachinohe (1 daily; 8hr); Naoetsu (3 weekly; 16hr 30min).

Otaru to: Maizuru (1 daily; 31hr); Niigata (1 daily except Mon; 19hr); Tsuruga (1 daily except Sun; 21hr).

Tomakomai to: Akita (4 weekly; 11hr 20min); Oarai (northeast of Tokyo) (1 daily; 30hr); Nagoya

(3–4 weekly; 38hr 45min); Sendai (1 daily; 14hr 45min).

Wakkanai to: Rebun-tō (2–4 daily; 2hr); Rishiri-tō (2–4 daily; 1hr 45min).

Flights

Asahikawa to: Kansai International (2 daily; 2hr); Nagoya (daily; 1hr 50min); Kushiro (2 daily; 45min); Tokyo (7 daily; 1hr 35min).

Hakodate to: Nagoya (1 daily; 1hr 20min); Kansai International (3 daily; 1hr 45min); Sapporo (5 daily; 45min); Sendai (3 weekly; 1hr); Tokyo (7 daily; 1hr 15min).

Kushiro to: Asahikawa (1 daily; 45min); Hakodate (1 daily; 1hr 20min); Kansai International (1 daily; 2hr 30min); Sapporo New Chitose (6 daily; 45min); Tokyo (6 daily; 1hr 45min).

Memanbetsu to: Nagoya (daily; 2hr); Kansai International (daily; 2hr 10min); Sapporo (6 daily; 50min); Tokyo (6 daily; 1hr 40min).

Sapporo (New Chitose) to: Fukuoka (5 daily; 2hr 10min); Kansai International (9 daily; 1hr 50min); Nagoya (12 daily; 1hr 30min); Tokyo (46 daily; 1hr 30min).

Wakkanai to: Rebun-tō (daily; 15min); Rishiri-tō (daily; 15min); Sapporo (daily; 50min); Tokyo (daily; 1hr 45min).

Central Honshū

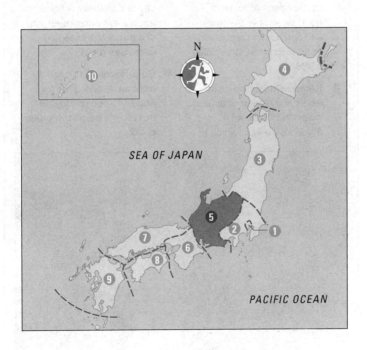

CHAPTER 5

Highlights

* **Zenkō-ji** Search for the key to paradise at Nagano's 1300-year-old temple. **See p.421**

* **Obuse** Attractive rural town boasting traditional architecture and art, plus great food and sake. **See p.427**

* **Matsumoto-jō** Japan's oldest wooden castle, with good views over the town and surrounding mountains from its topmost storey. **See p.436**

* **Kamikochi** Pristine alpine resort at the heart of Japan's magnificent mountains, and a good base from which to tackle the ascent of some of the country's highest peaks. **See p.438**

* **Susaki** Dine in a 300-year-old house on the finest Japanese cuisine at this *ryotei* in Takayama. **See p.450**

* **Kenroku-en** The charming city of Kanazawa is home to the verdant Kenroku-en, one of Japan's top three gardens. **See p.461**

* **Gujō-Hachiman** Dance the night away during the August O-bon holidays in this remote castle town. **See p.482**

△Snow monkeys, yudanaka Onsen

Central Honshū

L ocated roughly midway along the Japanese archipelago, **CENTRAL HONSHŪ**, known as **Chūbu**, offers a wide choice of terrain and travel possibilities. Dominating the region are the magnificent **Japan Alps**, providing spectacular mountain scenery, top onsen and ski resorts, old castle- and temple-towns, and villages caught in a time warp in remote valleys. Just as appealing is the rugged northern coast, **Hokuriku**; shaped by the savage waves of the Sea of Japan, it feels very much set apart from the rest of the country. Expressways and train lines plough a direct route between Tokyo and Kansai through the region's hideously industrialized south coast, yet even here there are places worth stopping to see, including Japan's fourth main city, **Nagoya**.

Even on the shortest trip, make time for the majestic Japan Alps, easily accessible thanks to the Nagano Shinkansen line that zips from Tokyo to **Nagano**, which hosted the 1998 Winter Olympics. Nagano's highlight is its venerable and atmospheric temple, **Zenkō-ji**, while southeast of the city, close to the summer resort of **Karuizawa**, is the stunning lava landscape at **Onioshidashien**. To the northeast is **Obuse**, famous for its sake, old buildings and gallery of works by Hokusai. Of the region's many skiing and onsen possibilities, perhaps the best is the charming village of **Nozawa Onsen**, northeast of Nagano, where you'll find excellent slopes and free hot-spring baths. Northwest of the city, the **Togakushi** area offers ancient shrines surrounded by spiritual forests, and a wacky Ninja warrior museum.

The focus of the southern half of Nagano-ken prefecture is the charming castle town of **Matsumoto**, easily reached from Shinjuku Station in Tokyo. The town is also the jumping-off point for the remote and pristine alpine resort of **Kamikōchi**, popular with mountaineers and hikers in summer, and for a handful of immaculately preserved post towns which line the old Nakasendō route from Kyoto to Tokyo. Between the best of these – **Tsumago** and **Magome** – is a lovely one-day hiking route.

Across the Alps, the small and convivial city of **Takayama** is the centre of the Hida area. Hida is famous for its skilled carpenters, whose craftsmanship is evident in many of the city's houses and temples, as well as in the unusual A-frame thatched houses of the nearby **Shirakawa–gō** and **Gokayama** valleys, where three villages – **Ogimachi**, **Suganuma** and **Ainokura** – have been designated World Heritage Sites. North of here is the elegant, historic city of **Kanazawa**, home of Kenroku-en, one of Japan's top three gardens, as well as a magnificently restored castle and enclaves of old temples and houses. To escape the crowds, head for the tranquil fishing villages dotted around the rugged coastline of the **Noto Hantō** peninsula, northeast of Kanazawa, or the thriving Zen Buddhist community of **Eihei-ji**, a rambling temple in the forested foothills of Fukui-ken's mountains, to the south.

The ugly, urbanized southern coast is generally best passed through as quickly as possible, though **Nagoya** is an excellent base for touring the more scenic parts of the region. From here, it's an easy day-trip to the attractive castle town of **Inuyama**, where you can see summertime displays of the ancient skill of *ukai*, or cormorant fishing. Inuyama is also close to the impressive **Meiji Mura**,

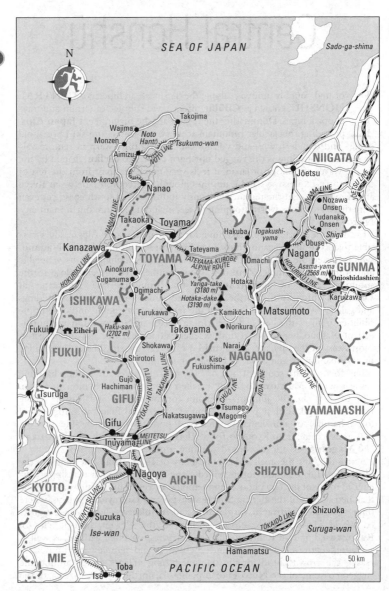

> ## Chūbu cuisine
>
> Wherever you go in Chūbu, there are regional foods to be sampled. The dish you'll come across most frequently is soba, noodles made from buckwheat flour (in Nagano-ken you'll often hear the dish referred to as *shinshu soba*). Nagano is also renowned for its fresh fruit and chestnuts – head to Obuse to sample its many chestnut sweets, not to mention premium sakes. The Hida region of neighbouring Gifu-ken, meanwhile, specializes in beef, mountain vegetables (*sansai*) and miso (fermented bean paste). Ayu river fish are often served in the inland regions, while on the Sea of Japan coast you should make the most of the wonderful fresh seafood. Kanazawa has a particularly refined style of cooking, known as *kaga ryōri*, where each dish is exquisitely displayed, while in Nagoya the local favourite is chicken with flat *kishimen* noodles.

a vast outdoor museum of architecture dating from the beginning of the twentieth century. Further inland, the charming town of **Gujō-Hachiman** is rightly famed for its summer-long O-bon dance festival.

Nagoya is home to Chūbu's main airport, but it's more likely that you'll approach the area by train, either from Tokyo or Kyoto. A couple of train lines cut across from the southern to the northern coasts, but many of the places in the mountains are only served by buses, which can be infrequent and expensive. It's well worth considering renting a car to tour this area, although note that some of the most scenic routes – such as the Skyline drive across the Alps from Gifu-ken to Nagano-ken – are toll roads and are closed in winter because of deep snow. The mountain resort of Kamikōchi and the Tateyama-Kurobe Alpine route are similarly off limits between November and April.

Nagano and around

NAGANO, capital of the province of Nagano-ken, is a modern, compact city some 200km northwest of Tokyo. Surrounded by fruit orchards and mountains, Nagano came to world attention when it hosted the 1998 Winter Olympics, but it's been a focal point for the Japanese for far longer. Every year, around eight million pilgrims come here to pay homage at the temple of **Zenkō-ji**, home of the legendary first image of Buddha, which arrived in Japan in the sixth century. The temple aside, there's not really that much to see in the city itself, although it's worth making full use of the shops and facilities before venturing into the Alps.

If you're travelling to the mountains from Tokyo, it's well worth considering a stop at **Karuizawa**, 90km from Nagano, where the lava flows from the nearby volcano Asama-yama have created a permanent record of a devastating eighteenth-century eruption. Northwest of Nagano lies the scenic mountain area of **Togakushi**, a haven for hikers and skiers and home to the atmospheric shrine of Togakushi Okusha, as well as the Togakushi Minzoku-kan, a folklore museum with an entertaining section on the Ninja warriors who used to train in this area. To the northeast, the country town of **Obuse** features some attractive old buildings and temples, alongside its highlight, the Hokusai-kan museum, displaying several masterpieces by the great *ukiyo-e* artist, Hokusai.

In winter, Nagano turns into one of Japan's top **skiing** destinations, with resorts in nearby Hakuba and Shiga Kōgen. This is also the best time to wallow in the **hot springs** in villages such as **Nozawa Onsen** and **Yudanaka Onsen**,

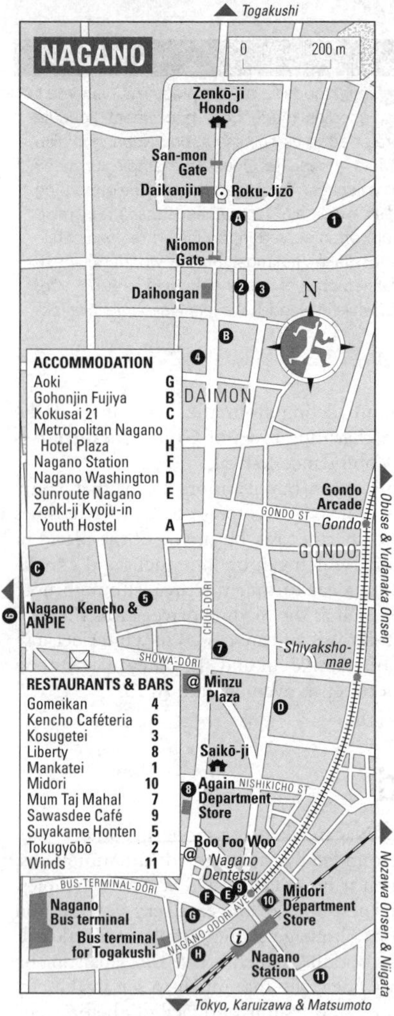
Togakushi
NAGANO
0 200 m
Zenkō-ji Hondo
San-mon Gate
Daikanjin
Roku-Jizō
Niomon Gate
Daihongan
N
DAIMON
ACCOMMODATION
Aoki G
Gohonjin Fujiya B
Kokusai 21 C
Metropolitan Nagano Hotel Plaza H
Nagano Station F
Nagano Washington D
Sunroute Nagano E
Zenkl-ji Kyoju-in Youth Hostel A
Gondo Arcade
GONDO ST
Gondo
GONDO
Obuse & Yudanaka Onsen
Nagano Kencho & ANPIE
CHŪŌ-DŌRI
Shiyakshomae
SHŌWA-DŌRI
RESTAURANTS & BARS
Gomeikan 4
Kencho Caféteria 6
Kosugetei 3
Liberty 8
Mankatei 1
Midori 10
Mum Taj Mahal 7
Sawasdee Café 9
Suyakame Honten 5
Tokugyōbō 2
Winds 11
Minzu Plaza
Saikō-ji
Again Department Store
NISHIKICHO ST
Boo Foo Woo
Nagano Dentetsu
BUS-TERMINAL-DŌRI
Nagano Bus terminal
Bus terminal for Togakushi
NAGANO-ODORI AVE
Midori Department Store
Nagano Station
Nozawa Onsen & Niigata
Tokyo, Karuizawa & Matsumoto

near where *Nihonzaru* (Japanese long-tailed monkeys) also bathe in their own outdoor pool.

Arrival, information and getting around

Nagano's sleek JR station is the terminus for **trains** on the Nagano Shinkansen line from Tokyo, and also the hub for local and express services around the prefecture and up to the Sea of Japan. Most long-distance **buses** pull in at the Nagano Bus Terminal on Basu Tāminaru-dōri, west of the JR station.

The excellent **tourist information centre** (daily 9am–6pm; ⓣ026/226-5626) is inside the station's main concourse. The helpful assistants speak English, can arrange accommodation and hand out a wide range of English maps and pamphlets for the city and prefecture. Information is also available from the International Exchange Lounge **ANPIE** (Mon–Fri 8.30am–5pm; ⓣ026/235-7186), on the second floor of the prefectural office around 1km west of the station. This facility also has a small library, free Internet access and is a good place to meet English-speaking locals. The city website is ⓦwww.city.nagano.nagano.jp.

Getting around is best done on foot – walking the 2km up to Zenkō-ji (see opposite) is an especially good way of taking in the city. Alternatively, you can hop on a bus from the west side of the JR station (¥100) or take the local Nagano Dentetsu, a private railway with its terminus beneath the Midori department store – this is also the line for trains to Obuse (see p.427).

Accommodation

The Olympics naturally caused a boom in **accommodation** and it's likely that, outside the busy summer and winter seasons and weekends, you'll be able to strike bargains at some places. The most atmospheric place to stay is near Zenkō-ji, where you can choose from several pricey ryokan and a good youth hostel. Should you want to stay in temple lodgings (*shukubō* - open only to genuine Zen Buddhist students), call Zenkō-ji's administrative office on ⓣ026/234-3591.

Nagano

Nagano	*Nagano*	長野
Zenkō-ji	*Zenkō-ji*	善光寺

Accommodation

Hotel Aoki	*Hoteru Aoki*	ホテルアオキ
Gohonjin Fujiya	*Gohonjin Fujiya*	御本陣藤屋
Hotel Kokusai 21	*Hoteru Kokusai 21*	ホテル国際２１
Hotel Metropolitan Nagano	*Hoteru Metoroporitan Nagano*	ホテルメトロポリタン長野
Nagano Station Hotel	*Nagano Sutēshon Hoteru*	長野ステーションホテル
Nagano Washington Hotel Plaza	*Nagano Washinton Hoteru Puraza*	長野ワシントンホテルプラザ
Hotel Sunroute Nagano	*Hoteru Sanrūto Nagano*	ホテルサンルート長野
Zenkō-ji Kyōju-in Youth Hostel	*Zenkō-ji Kyōju-in Yūsu Hosuteru*	善光寺教授院ユースホステル

Restaurants

Gomeikan	*Gomeikan*	五明館
Kosugetei	*Kosugetei*	小菅亭
Mankatei	*Mankatei*	萬佳亭
Suyakame Honten	*Suyakame Honten*	すや亀本店
Tokugyōbō	*Tokugyōbō*	とくぎょうぼう

Hotel Aoki Suehiro-chō ☎026/226-1271, ℻226-3445. About the cheapest business hotel in town, with no-frills rooms and a Hawaiian-themed café in the lobby. ❺

Gohonjin Fujiya 80 Daimon ☎026/232-1241, ⓦwww.avis.ne.jp/~fuziya. The stone front and 1920s reception at this venerable hotel on the main approach to Zenkō-ji suggest the setting for an Agatha Christie mystery, but behind it's all Meiji-era elegance, with the most expensive tatami rooms facing onto manicured gardens. Meals are worth the indulgence. ❻

Hotel Kokusai 21 576 Agatamachi ☎026/234-1111, ⓦwww.kokusai21.co.jp. Nagano's top hotel, opposite the prefectural office on the west side of town, is spacious and well appointed, but rather dull. It has a good selection of restaurants and reasonably priced singles. ❻

Hotel Metropolitan Nagano 1346 Minami-Ishido-chō ☎026/291-7000, ⓦwww.metron.co.jp. Good-value luxury hotel beside the west exit of the JR station, with high-standard Western-style rooms and a stylish lobby and restaurants. ❻

Nagano Station Hotel 1359 Suehiro-chō

☎026/226-1295, ℻226-1056. Appealingly old-fashioned, good-value business hotel with both Western and Japanese rooms, nicely decorated. ❺

Nagano Washington Hotel Plaza 1177-3 Kami-Chitose-chō ☎026/228-5111, ⓦwww.wgh.co.jp. Reasonable-value mid-range hotel. The rooms are plainly furnished and on the small side, but have TV with satellite channels. ❺

Hotel Sunroute Nagano 1-28-3 Minami-Chitose-chō ☎026/228-2222, ⓦwww.sunroute-nagano.com. Service is polite and standards high at this slightly old-fashioned mid-range hotel opposite the JR station west exit. The rooms have tiled en-suite bathrooms, rather than the usual moulded plastic affairs. ❺

Zenkō-ji Kyōju-in Youth Hostel 479 Motoyoshi-machi ☎026/232-2768, ℻232-2767. Ideal if you're planning an early-morning visit to Zenkō-ji, which is just one minute's walk away. The friendly management is very protective of the atmospheric old temple building, and you'll have to leave your belongings in lockers in the entrance hall before being shown into the large tatami dorms – if it's not busy you'll have a whole room to yourself. ¥3500 per person.

Zenkō-ji

Believed to house the first image of Buddha to come to Japan, **Zenkō-ji**, Nagano's 1300-year-old temple, has long been a popular place of pilgrimage.

It has traditionally welcomed believers of all Buddhist sects, has never barred women and is run alternately by an abbot of the Tendai sect and abbess of the Jōdo sect. Visitors can join the hundreds of daily petitioners searching for the "key to paradise" which lies beneath Zenkō-ji's main temple building (see below); find it and you'll have earned eternal salvation.

The traditional way to approach the temple is on foot. Head north along Chūō-dōri, west of the JR station, and you'll first pass **Saikō-ji**, a small temple tucked away in a quiet courtyard. Also known as Karukaya-san, after the Buddhist saint who founded it in 1199, the main temple building contains two wooden statues of Jizō, the guardian of children, one carved by Karukaya, and the other by his son Ishidō.

About three-quarters of the way up, the road begins to narrow around the area known as **Daimon**, where you'll find many giftshops, pilgrim stalls and ryokan. To the left is the **Daihongan**, the nunnery and residence of the high priestess of Zenkō-ji, who is also usually a member of the imperial family. In the courtyard, look out for the fountain with a statue of Mizuko Jizō, the patron saint of aborted and stillborn babies – little dolls and toys are left as offerings around the base.

Passing through the impressive 13.6-metre-tall Niō-mon (gate) and a short precinct lined with more souvenir stalls and lodgings, you'll see the **Roku-Jizō** on the right, a row of six large metal statues symbolizing the guardians of the six worlds through which Buddhists believed the soul must pass: hell, starvation, beasts, carnage, human beings and heavenly beings. On the left is **Daikanjin**, the home of the high priest; the entrance is reached by crossing an attractive arched bridge and there is a pretty garden inside.

At the top of the precinct stands the **San-mon**, the huge, double-storey wooden gateway into the temple's central courtyard, the gathering place not only for pilgrims but also pigeons, who have their own elaborate metal coop on the left-hand side. On the same side is the **Kyōzō**, or sutra repository, an elegant wooden building that is only open occasionally. In the centre of the courtyard stands a large metal cauldron decorated with a lion whose mouth exhales the perfumed smoke of incense sticks. As a charm for health and good fortune, pilgrims waft the smoke around their bodies before moving on to the vast, imposing main hall, the Hondō, dating from 1707.

Underneath the Hondō in the Okaidan is the **Ikkō Sanzon Amida Nyorai** (see box below), housed in the dark tunnel where pilgrims grope around for

The Ikkō Sanzon Amida Nyorai

Zenkō-ji's most sacred object is the **Ikkō Sanzon Amida Nyorai**, a triad of Amida Buddha images sharing one halo. This golden statue is said to have been made by Buddha himself in the sixth century BC and is believed to have arrived in Japan some 1200 years later as a gift from Korea to the emperor. For a while, the image was kept in a specially built temple near Ōsaka, where it became the focus of a clan feud. The temple was eventually destroyed and the statue dumped in a nearby canal, from where it was later rescued by **Honda Yoshimitsu**, a poor man who was passing by and apparently heard Buddha call. Honda brought the image back to his home in Nagano (then called Shinano). When news of its recovery reached Empress Kōgyoku, she ordered a temple to be built in its honour and called it Zenkō-ji after the Chinese reading of Honda's name. The empress also ordered that the image should never be publicly viewed again, so a copy was made and it is this that is displayed once every six years in the grand **Gokaichō festival**, held from early April to late May. The next festival is in 2009.

the "key to paradise". Once you've entered the outer sanctuary of the hall, look straight ahead for the worn-out statue of Binzuru, a physician and fallen follower of Buddha; pilgrims rub the statue in the hope of curing their ailments. Just beyond is the awesome worshipper's hall, a vast space with golden ornaments dangling from the high ceiling, where pilgrims used to bed down on futons for the night. Now people traditionally come for the **morning service**, which starts around 5.30am; it's worth making the effort to attend this to witness Zenkō-ji at its most mystical, with the priests wailing, drums pounding and hundreds of pilgrims joined in fervent prayer. Afterwards, the **Ojuzu Chōdai** ceremony takes place in the courtyard in front of the Hondō. Pilgrims kneel and wait for the high priest or priestess to rustle by in their colourful robes, shaded by a giant red paper umbrella, and bless them by tapping prayer beads on their heads.

If you're at all uncomfortable in the dark, don't enter the **Okaidan**, a pitch-black passage that runs beneath the Hondō's innermost sanctum, resting place of the revered original image of Buddha. However, if you fancy a feel of the "key of paradise," buy a ticket (¥300) from one of the machines to the right of Binzuru's statue, and follow the chattering crowds plunging into the darkness. Once you're in, keep your right hand on the wall and chances are you'll find the key (it actually feels more like a door knob) towards the end of the passage.

Eating and drinking

You'll find most places to **eat** clustered on or around Chūō-dōri; in the evenings, try the lively Gondō arcade leading east from Chūō-dōri to Gondō Station. To sample *shōjin ryōri*, the expensive vegetarian cuisine prepared for the monks, head for the area around Zenkō-ji. Soba is available at most places around town. The many small **bars** around Gondō tend to be pricey; if you're looking for a cool spot for a drink in summer, try the beer garden on top of the Nagano Dentetsu Building, at the eastern end of the Gondō arcade.

Restaurants and bars

Gomeikan 515 Daimon-chō ☎026/232-1221. Traditional tourist restaurant in an old white building halfway up Chūō-dōri, across from the *Gohonjin Fujiya Hotel*. The lunch special is ¥1400, the *bentō* box of prepared titbits ¥2500, while full meals clock in at ¥5000. Closed Wed.

Kencho Cafeteria Tenth floor, Prefectural Government Building. This office canteen has cheap food and good views across the city. Check out the plastic food menu first, pay and take your chit to the kitchen counter to collect your meal. Mon–Fri 8.30am–8pm.

Kosugetei Two blocks southeast of the Niomon gate ☎026/232-2439. Cute soba restaurant, decorated with lots of lucky cat statues and old ad posters. The noodles are made on the premises and their tempura zaru-soba set for ¥980 is a good deal. Daily 11am–3pm, April–Nov also 5pm–8pm.

Liberty 1434-1 Kita-ishido-chō (down an alley beside the Again department store). Also known as the *American Bar*, this friendly Western-style pub has light snacks and reasonable cocktails. Open

evenings only; closed Tues.

Mankatei Jōyama-kōen ☎026/232-2326. Enjoy the fine dishes, waitresses in kimono and the twinkling cityscape views at this classy restaurant east of Zenkō-ji in a park overlooking the downtown area. A bentō lunch is ¥2800, a *kaiseki-ryōri* dinner ¥3800.

Midori This department store, connected to the north end of the JR station, has a wide selection of restaurants on the fifth floor. *Keyaki* serves a good-value set meal of local specialities, including soba noodles, tofu and *konyaku* (root vegetable jelly) dipped in mustard and miso. Daily 11am–9pm.

Mum Taj Mahal 2F, 1271 Toigosho ☎026/234-1343. Colourful Indian restaurant about halfway up Chūō-dōri. The tasty lunch sets come in at under ¥1000, and there's an English menu.

Sawasdee Café B1, C-One, 826 Minami-Chitose-chō ☎026/267-6669. In the basement of the trendy C-One shopping plaza, this dark, intimate bar-restaurant serves Thai, Indonesian and Vietnamese dishes, all for under ¥1000.

Suyakame Honten 625 Nishi-go-chō ℡026/35-4022. Restaurant and shop specializing in miso – they even serve miso ice cream. Try the rice balls topped with three different types of miso sauce. Mon–Sat 10.30am–5pm.

Tokugyōbō Motoyoshi, one block southeast of the Niomon gate ℡0262/32-0264. This old pilgrim's inn is a good place to sample *shōjin ryōri*. Prices start from ¥5000 per person and reservations are recommended.

Winds Third floor, Sutera Building, opposite the east exit of Nagano Station. Lively bar serving a good range of snacks.

Listings

Airlines ANA, Suehiro-chō 1361 ℡026/225-0311; JAS, Minami-Ishidō-chō 1282-11 ℡026/225-5888.

Banks and exchange Nagano's main bank, offering full foreign exchange facilities, is Hachijū Ni ("82") Ginkō; there are several branches around the city.

Bookshops Books Heiandō (daily 10am–7.30pm), opposite the west exit of the station, has a small selection of English books and magazines.

Car rental Eki Rent-a-Car (℡026/227-8500), beside the Zenkō-ji exit of the JR station.

Emergencies The main Prefectural Police Office is at 692-2 Habashita (℡026/233-0110). In an absolute emergency, contact the Foreign Advisory Service on ℡026/232-3413. For other emergency numbers, see "Basics" on p.81.

Hospital Nagano's main hospital is Nagano Sekijūji Byōin, 5-22-1 Wakasato ℡026/226-4131.

Internet ANPIE (see p.420) has a free Internet terminal; there are also several terminals on the third floor of Minzu Plaza on Chūō-dōri in the International Exchange Plaza (daily 10am–7pm, except first and third Wed of month). Alternatively, try Boo Foo Woo, a 24-hour Internet and manga café, a few minutes' walk from the station on Chūō-dōri.

Post office The Central Post Office is close to the Prefectural Office (Kencho) at 1085-4 Minami-Agata.

Taxis Try Utsunomiya Taxi ℡026/232-8181; Nagano Kankō Taxi ℡026/226-1234; or Nagano Taxi ℡026/227-2222.

Travel agency The main JTB office is at 1-12-7 Minami-Chitose ℡026/228-0489.

Karuizawa and Onioshidashien

On the eastern edge of landlocked Nagano-ken, and lying on the slopes of Asama-yama (at 2568m Japan's highest triple-cratered active volcano), is the ever-fashionable summer resort of **KARUIZAWA**. It's a pleasant enough town, with a low-key old district, **Kyū-Karuizawa**, where Crown Prince Akihito (now the emperor) met his future wife, Michiko, on the tennis courts in the 1950s. Things can get very hectic in summer, when a mass of clothes shops and giftshops open their doors to the temporary residents of the thousands of hillside villas, but there are still traces of the natural tranquillity that made Karuizawa so appealing to nineteenth-century visitors.

Karuizawa's sights are widely scattered, so the best plan of attack is to pick up the good English map and guidebook of the area from the **tourist information office** (daily 9am–5.30pm; ℡0267/42-2491) at the station. The most enjoyable way of exploring is by **bicycle**; you can rent one from the many outlets near the tourist office (¥500 an hour). Otherwise, hop on a bus from in front of Karuizawa Station for Kyū-Karuizawa and the *Old Mikasa Hotel* (see below).

Heading north from the station, past the row of shops, brings you to a pedestrianized street dubbed "Little Ginza", but more resembling Tokyo's teen-scene Takeshita-dōri (see p.149). At the end of this street, you'll emerge into a forest; look out for the quaint wooden **Nippon Seikōkai** (Anglican) **Chapel**, with a bust of Archdeacon Shaw, who helped popularize the area as a retreat, standing in front. Services are held in the church every Sunday; you can see photographs of the man and his family in the priest's old house behind the church. If you have time, it's a nice two-kilometre cycle ride or hike up to the secluded *Old Mikasa Hotel*, an elegant wooden building dating from 1905, which now houses a small and missable museum. Follow the main road, Mikasa-dōri, due north from the chapel.

The fastest route to Karuizawa is by **train** on the Shinkansen between Tokyo and Nagano. Other services only go as far as Yokokawa Station, from where you have to travel up to Karuizawa by bus from the valley below. There's a lot of expensive, mediocre accommodation in Karuizawa and better deals can be had elsewhere. If you're stuck for somewhere cheap, there's the *Kokumin Shukusha Karuizawa Kōgen-sō* (☎0267/48-2111; ❸, including two meals), a publicly subsidized and rather basic holiday lodge fifteen minutes southwest of Karuizawa Station by taxi. The four *Prince* hotels (☎0267/42-1111, Ⓦwww.princehotels.co.jp; ❻–❼) occupy a sprawling compound just to the south of the station and offer tennis, golf, ice skating, and even their own small ski area; opt for the comfortable cottages in the east complex. The *Mampei Hotel* (☎0267/42-1234, Ⓕ42-7766; ❼–❽), established in 1894, has a quirky rambling elegance, and its food and service are first-rate – John Lennon spent several summers here. While good deals on accommodation are hard to find in Karuizawa, reasonable restaurants are plentiful, especially in Kyū-Karuizawa, where soba shops abound, and many fashionable Tokyo restaurants have branches: try the *Ajanta Indian Restaurant*, a good place for vegetarians, at Kyū-Karuizawa near the fire station, or *Kastanie*, also Kyū-Karuizawa, a cute Western-style restaurant run by an Australian and her Japanese husband.

Karuizawa, Tokagushi and Obuse

Karuizawa	*Karuizawa*	軽井沢
Kokumin Shukusha Karuizawa Kōgen-sō	*Kokumin Shukusha Karuizawa Kōgen-sō*	国民宿舎軽井沢
Kyū-Karuizawa	*Kyū-Karuizawa*	旧軽井沢
Mampei Hotel	*Mampei Hoteru*	万平ホテル
Onioshidashien	*Onioshidashien*	鬼押出し園
Togakushi	*Togakushi*	戸隠
Chūsha	*Chūsha*	中社
Togakushi Kōgen Yokokura Youth Hostel	*Togakushi Kōgen Yokokura Yūsu Hosuteru*	戸隠高原横倉ユースホステル
Togakushi Minzoku-kan	*Togakushi Minzoku-kan*	戸隠民族館
Togakushi Okusha	*Togakushi Okusha*	戸隠奥社
Obuse	*Obuse*	小布施
Ganshōin	*Ganshōin*	岩松院
Hokusai-kan	*Hokusai-kan*	北斎館
Obuse Museum	*Obuse Myūjiamu*	おぶせミュージアム
Takai Kōzan Memorial Hall	*Takai Kōzan Kinenkan*	高井鴻山記念館
Accommodation		
Guest House Obuse	*Gesuto Hausu Obuse*	ゲストハウス小布施
Obuse no Kaze	*Obuse no Kaze*	おぶせの風
Restaurants		
Chikufudō	*Chikufudō*	竹風堂
Kurabu	*Kurabu*	蔵部
Obusedō	*Obusedō*	小布施堂
San Pū Rou	*San Pū Rou*	傘風楼
Senseki-tei	*Senseki-tei*	泉石亭

Onioshidashien

Karuizawa's dominant feature is the volcano **Asama-yama**, which last erupted in 1973 and continues to steam ominously. No hiking is allowed within 4km of the crater, and the best place to get a glimpse of the volcano is on its north side from the **Onioshidashien** area (daily: May–Sept 7am–6pm; Jan–April & Oct–Dec 8am–5pm; ¥400; ☎0279/86-4141), 21km from Karuizawa. Onioshidashien was the scene of a cataclysmic eruption on August 5, 1783, when ashes from the blowout were said to have darkened the sky as far as Europe, and a seven-kilometre-wide lava flow swept away the nearby village of Kanbara. When the lava cooled it solidified into an extraordinary landscape of black boulders and bizarre rock shapes which now sprout alpine plants. To get an idea of the scale of the place, head up to the observation floor in the giftshop and restaurant complex at the entrance. You can then explore the twisting paths that have been laid across the weird landscape. Most of the crowds head for the central temple, **Kannon-dō**, standing on a raised red platform amid the black rocks, but you can easily escape them by continuing past to the quieter area behind.

Regular **buses** run to Onioshidashien (¥1080) from outside Karuizawa Station, in around fifty minutes. There are also direct buses from Karuizawa Station (45min; ¥1150).

Togakushi

One of the best day-trips from Nagano is to the refreshing alpine area of **Togakushi**, 20km northwest of the city, bounded on one side by the jagged ridge of Togakushi-yama and on the other by Mount Iizuna. As well as great scenery, there's a decent museum and a shrine to check out, and if you come in winter there's also good skiing. The best way to approach the area is via the scenic **bus** route. Buses (¥1160) leave from outside the Heiandō Books building across from Nagano train station, and run along the vertiginous Bird-line Driveway, giving panoramic views of the city as they wind up the mountain around a series of hairpin bends. Stay on the bus through the village of Chūsha (see opposite), about one hour from Nagano, and get off a couple of stops later when you reach the entrance to the Togakushi Okusha, the innermost of the three main sanctuaries of the Togakushi shrine.

Before heading off up to the shrine, it's worth crossing the road to the **Togakushi Minzoku-kan** (daily 9am–5pm; ¥500; ☎026/254-2395), a museum complex of traditional farm buildings, some of which have exhibits on the **Ninja warriors**, who were once trained in Togakushi (see box opposite). Within the complex, the Togakure-ryū Ninpō Shiryōkan displays some amazing black-and-white photographs of the stealthy, black-garbed fighters in action, examples of their lethal weapons and even a model Ninja dangling from the rafters. The most fun is to be had next door in the Ninja House, a maze of hidden doors and staircases that is fiendishly difficult to find your way out of.

The **Togakushi Okusha shrine** stands on the lower slopes of the jagged mountain, Togakushi-yama, which, according to ancient Shinto belief, was created when the god Ame-no-Tajikarao tossed away the rock door of the cave where the Sun Goddess Amaterasu had been hiding (see p.839). The shrine is reached via a two-kilometre-long corridor of soaring cedar trees, and the adventurous can continue on along the route up the sharp ridge to the mountain summit; take food and water plus warm waterproof clothing as it's a strenuous route, and you must write your name in the climbers' book at the start of the trail. Having looked round the inner shrine – a rustic collection of small wooden and stone buildings nestling under the rocks – the best option is to

Ninja: the shadow warriors

Long before their ancient martial art was nabbed by a bunch of cartoon turtles, the **Ninja** were Japan's most feared warriors, employed by lords as assassins and spies. They practised **Ninjutsu**, "the art of stealth", which emphasized non-confrontational methods of combat. Dressed in black, Ninja moved like shadow warriors and used a variety of weapons, including *shuriken* (projectile metal stars) and *kusarikama* (a missile with a razor-sharp sickle on one end of a chain), examples of which are displayed in the Togakushi museum (see opposite).

According to legend, Ninjutsu was developed in the twelfth century, when the warrior Togakure Daisuke retreated to the mountain forests of Iga, near Nara, and met Kain Dōshi, a monk on the run from political upheaval in China. Togakure studied Dōshi's fighting ways and it was his descendants who developed them into the **Togakure-ryū school** of Ninjutsu. By the fifteenth century, there were some fifty family-based Ninjutsu schools across Japan, each jealously guarding their techniques.

Although the need for Ninja declined while Japan was under the peaceful rule of the Shogunate, the Tokugawa had their own force of Ninjutsu-trained warriors for protection. One Ninja, Sawamura Yasusuke, even sneaked into the "black ship" of Commodore Perry in 1853 to spy on the foreign barbarians. Today, the Togakure-ryu school of Ninjutsu, emphasizing defence rather than offence, is taught by the 34th master, Hatsumi Masaaki, in Noda, Chiba-ken, just north of Tokyo.

head back downhill along the pleasant and shaded woodland trails through the Togakushi Ōmine Recreational Forest to the attractive village of **CHŪSHA**, a good base for skiing in winter (you can check out details of the Tokagushi ski area at Ⓦ www.valley.ne.jp/~skimenou). Here you'll find the outer sanctuary of the shrine, the **Hōkōsha**, decorated with intricate wooden carvings, along with shops selling all manner of baskets and goods made of woven bamboo strips: the best one (where you can also see a basket weaver at work) is downhill, opposite the Spar grocery store.

Chūsha has a couple of pleasant **accommodation** options, including the excellent-value *Togakushi Kōgen Yokokura Youth Hostel* (Ⓣ 026/254-2030, Ⓕ 254-2540; ¥3000 per person), which offers tatami dorms in a partly thatched, 150-year-old pilgrim's lodge, five minutes' walk south of the shrine and near the ski resort. It's run by a hospitable woman who speaks a little English, and there's also a quaint log-cabin café. If you come in winter for the excellent cross-country or downhill skiing, try *Hutte Yachi Bozu* (Ⓣ 0262/54-2237; Ⓢ), in the woods near the Togakushi ski area base; it has basic tatami rooms, a comfortable living and dining area, English-speaking owners and several friendly golden retrievers.

Back down on the main road, *Uzuraya*, in the thatched farmhouse opposite the Hōkōsha shrine, is Chūsha's top **restaurant** for freshly made soba; at weekends you'll have to stand in line for anything up to forty minutes for lunch. The excellent Italian cuisine and home-made desserts at *Yamabōshi* (Ⓣ 026/254-2624; 10.30am–8.30pm except Wed), on the way to the shrine, are also well worth the journey up here.

Obuse

Some 20km northeast of Nagano, the small town of **OBUSE** is at the vanguard of a quiet revolution in Japanese tourism thanks to the efforts of its committed population and the local sake brewery Masuichi-Ichimura (Ⓦ www.masuichi .com). In the last few years, the already attractive streets around the venerable

Ichimura estate and brewery in the centre of town have been transformed, with old buildings spruced up and turned into excellent restaurants and bars. The brewery is in the process of building a new guesthouse using traditional construction methods but furnished in a contemporary style; they're also restoring the **Hekiiken**, the thatched studio in which the artist **Hokusai** (see p.968) worked. The sidewalks have been relaid with chestnut wood blocks (chestnut farming being a major industry of the area) and some eighty private gardens have been opened to the public, while the whole area brims over with orchards and vineyards. All of this makes it a great place to stay – and makes you think how much better many Japanese towns might be if they followed Obuse's example.

Obuse's main attraction is the **Hokusai-kan** (daily 9am–5pm; ¥500), a small but good museum displaying rare paintings and other works by the master of *ukiyo-e* woodblock prints, **Katsushika Hokusai** – most famous for his image of the Great Wave with Mount Fuji in the background. In 1842, the 83-year-old Hokusai was invited to live and work in Obuse by Takai Kōzan, the town's leading salt merchant and art lover. A special studio was built for the artist, and it was here that he completed four paintings for the ceilings of two large festival floats and a giant phoenix mural for the ceiling of the Ganshōin temple. The beautiful floats, decorated with dragons, seascapes and intricate carvings, are displayed in the museum along with some forty other works, including painted scrolls, delicate watercolours and woodblock prints. You can also watch a slide show on Hokusai's life, with English subtitles. The red-roofed **Ganshōin** (daily: April–Oct 9am–5pm; Jan–March, Nov & Dec 9.30am–4.30pm; ¥200), housing the beguiling phoenix mural (the Great Ho-o), is a pleasant walk or bicycle ride 1km east, towards the hills.

Opposite the Hokusai-kan is the **Takai Kōzan Memorial Hall** (daily 9.30am–4.30pm; ¥200), the atmospheric former home of Hokusai's patron, who was also an accomplished artist and calligrapher. His drawings of ghosts and goblins are meant to be ironic comments on the turbulent early Meiji-era years and are quite intriguing, as is the giant mammoth sketch. In one of the rooms you can see long banners inscribed with *kanji* characters as well as the 2.5-metre-long brush used to paint them.

Also worth checking out is the delightful **Obuse Museum** (daily 9am–5pm; ¥400; ☎026/247-6111), which includes the Nakajima Chinami Gallery, an exhibition of this highly regarded artist's colourful works. Also on display are a couple more of the town's traditional festival floats, along with regularly changing art exhibitions.

Practicalities

Obuse is twenty minutes by **train** (¥650) from Nagano on the Nagano-Dentetsu line. Pick up an English **map** of the town at Nagano's tourist information centre (see p.420) before setting off, or at the Obuse Guide Centre and café (daily 9am–6pm), about five minutes' walk southeast of the station. The best way of **getting around** is to rent a bicycle from the station (around ¥340 per hour) or youth hostel (¥100 per hour). Alternatively, take the shuttle bus that makes a circuit of the town's sights – an all-day ticket costs ¥300. If you come by car on the Jōshin'etsu motorway, pull into the elaborate Obuse **Highway Oasis** service area, worth a look in its own right, and take advantage of the free parking and shuttle bus access to the town.

As for **accommodation**, a great budget choice is the new youth hostel *Obuse no Kaze* (☎026/247-4489, ⊛http://homepage2.nifty.com/obusenokaze; ❷); it's run by a very friendly family and is close by the Hokusai-kan, with a choice of Western-style dorms or tatami rooms. Another pleasant place that has

Western-style rooms is the *Guest House Obuse* (☎026/247-5050, ℉247-5700; ⑤), next to the Obuse Guide Centre. Check the Masuichi website (ⓦwww.masuichi.com) for details of their new guesthouse, which should be opening sometime in 2005.

Linger in Obuse to take advantage of its fine **restaurants**, several of which are attached to the Masuichi brewery. The showcase restaurant at the brewery is *Obusedō* (☎026/247-2027; open lunch only), which offers a *kaiseki ryōri*-style menu (¥2500) of local delicacies which changes on a monthly basis. More casual is *San Pū Rou* (☎026/247-5433), opposite the Hokusai-kan, which has outdoor tables and a bar upstairs. Across the courtyard from *San Pū Rou* is *Kurabu* (☎026/247-5300), the brewery's most animated and convivial space, with an open kitchen where you can watch the chefs at work preparing a good range of local meat and fish dishes to complement their sakes; this is a good place to visit in the evening, when dinner will set you back aroud ¥3000. Opposite the brewery on Obuse's main shopping street, *Chikufudō* (☎026/247-2569; daily 10am–7pm) does good-value set meals in its second-floor restaurant. *Senseki-tei* (☎026/247-5166; 11am–7.30pm; closed Tues), also on the town's main shopping street, has a wider range of dishes and overlooks an exquisite ornamental garden – set menus here range from ¥500 to ¥2000. You can only buy Masuichi's four excellent **sakes** (including one made by the traditional method in huge wooden vats) at the brewery itself (or on the Internet). Finally, don't leave without sampling some of the **chestnut confectionery** for which the town is famous.

Ski resorts and onsen villages around Nagano

Nagano-ken's spectacular mountains are home to several of Japan's best ski resorts and onsen villages. In the northeastern corner of the prefecture is the delightful **Nozawa Onsen**, self-proclaimed home of Japanese skiing and renowned hot-spring village, with thirteen free bathhouses to dip into. West of Nagano is **Hakuba**, a valley with seven different ski resorts to choose from, the most popular being **Happō-one**. **Shiga Kōgen**, 20km north of Nagano, is Japan's biggest skiing area, with 22 interconnected resorts sharing the same lift ticket. It lies within the Jōshinetsu Kōgen National Park, where you'll also find the village of **Yudanaka Onsen**, famous for its "snow monkeys", who splash about in their very own rotemburo.

Nozawa Onsen

The most authentically Japanese skiing and hot-spring village around here is **NOZAWA ONSEN**, nestled at the base of Kenashi-yama (1650m), 50km northeast of Nagano. The ski resort, proudly owned by the five thousand villagers, has a lively yet traditional atmosphere, aided in no small part by the thirteen free bathhouses dotted along the narrow, twisting streets. Most impressive is the **Ōyu bathhouse**, housed in a temple-like wooden building in the centre of the village; each side has two pools, one of which is so hot that it's almost impossible to get into.

Nozawa claims to be the birthplace of Japanese skiing since it was here, in 1930, that Hannes Schneider – an Austrian who popularized the two-pole technique – gave skiing demonstrations to an awestruck audience. One of the resort's runs is named after Schneider, and photos of the man in action, impeccably dressed in suit and tie, can be seen in the **Japan Museum of Skiing** (Fri–Sun 10am–4pm; ¥300), housed in a white, church-like building at the bottom of the Hikage slope.

Nagano ski and onsen resorts

Nozawa Onsen	*Nozawa Onsen*	野沢温泉
Beruku Marukaneya	*Beruku Marukaneya*	べるくまるかねや
Hotel Garni Haus St Anton	*Chiisana Hoteru San Anton no Ie*	小さなホテルサナントンの家
Museum of Skiing	*Sukii Hakubutsukan*	スキー博物館
Pension Schnee	*Penshon Shuné*	ペンションシュネ
Hakuba	*Hakuba*	白馬
Hakuba Alps Backpackers	*Hakuba Aruppusu Bakkupakāzu*	白馬アルップスバックパカーズ
Hakuba Valley Hotel	*Hakuba Bari Hoteru*	白馬バリホテル
Happō-one	*Happō-one*	八方尾根
Shiga Kōgen	*Shiga Kōgen*	志賀高原
Okushiga	*Okushiga*	奥志賀
Okushiga Kōgen Hotel	*Okushiga Kōgen Hoteru*	奥志賀高原ホテル
Shiga Kōgen Prince Hotel	*Shiga Kōgen Purinsu Hoteru*	志賀高原プリンスホテル
Shiga Kōgen Roman Museum	*Shiga Kōgen Roman Hakabutsukan*	志賀高原ロマン博物館
Yudanaka Onsen	*Yudanaka Onsen*	湯田中温泉
Jigokudani Wild Monkey Park	*Jigokudani Yaen-kōen*	地獄谷野猿公園
Kameya Ryokan	*Kameya Ryokan*	亀や旅館
Kanbayashi Hotel	*Kanbayashi Hoteru*	上林ホテル
Kōrakukan	*Kōrakukan*	後楽館

The resort, which hosted the biathlon events at the 1998 Olympics on its excellent cross-country course, has lots of English signs and varied terrain, from long, easy runs for beginners – especially the one on the far right as you face the mountain – to some of Japan's most challenging expert runs. Grand Prix and Jumping are two huge tsunamis of snow and ice that will put any expert through their paces. A one-day lift pass costs ¥4300 and the season runs from mid-December to early May. Try to time your visit to coincide with the spectacular **Dōso-jin fire festival**, held every January 15, when a burning portable shrine is paraded through the village, followed by a fire battle culminating in a monstrous bonfire.

JR **trains** run to Togari–Nozawa-Onsen on the Iiyama line, around one hour by local train from Nagano; Nozawa Onsen is a twenty-minute bus (¥300) or taxi ride from the station. It's also possible to catch direct buses from Nagano (1hr 15min; ¥1300); for timetables, check with the Nagano information office or with the tourism section of the Nozawa village office (Mon–Fri 8.30am–5pm; ☏0269/85-3111; ✉nozawa@avis.ne.jp), where there's an English-speaker. Nozawa Onsen's **tourist information centre** (daily 8.30am–5.30pm; ☏0269/85-3155), opposite the Ōyu bathhouse, has English brochures and maps.

Accommodation rates in Nozawa Onsen usually cover both breakfast and dinner. A pretty place to stay is the Western-style *Pension Schnee* (☏0269/85-2012; ❻), on the mountainside next to the ski museum – it's surrounded by snow in winter and flowers in summer, is run by a friendly couple who were once Olympic competitors, and has a great restaurant. For around the same price, you could also try *Beruku Marukaneya* (☏0269/85-2203; ❻), at the opposite end of the village, whose English-speaking owner offers tatami rooms and home-style cooking. In the heart of the village, near the restaurants and bars, is the cute *Hotel Garni Haus St Anton* (T0269/85-3422; ●), a little piece of Switzerland transplanted to Japan.

There are plenty of **restaurants and cafés** around the ski slopes; try *Atarashiya*, near the *Nozawa Grand Hotel* downhill from Konpara shrine. Also don't miss sampling *onsen manjū*, deliciously plump dumplings with different fillings, best bought from the street vendors out of wooden steam-boxes. To cool down after your onsen, slip into *Stay*, a convivial bar in the centre of town.

Hakuba

There are more than a dozen ski areas around **Hakuba**, in the dramatic northern Japanese Alps 60km northwest of Nagano, where many of the top skiing events of the 1998 Olympics were held. The largest and most popular resort is **HAPPŌ-ONE**, site of the Olympic downhill course, which has a wide range of runs covered by an extensive network of lifts (a one-day lift pass costs ¥4300). Ski Japan Holidays (T0261/72-6663, W www.japanspecialists.com) can arrange all manner of trips here; they're particularly useful if you want to stay at more upmarket places.

The Hakuba valley isn't just a winter destination. There are two very pretty lakes here – Aoki and Kizaki – and the valley makes a fine base for hiking, climbing, canoeing, boating and mountain biking in summer. You can arrange all these activities through the reliable, *gaijin*-run Evergreen Outdoor Centre (W www.evergreen-outdoors.com), who offer everything from rafting and paragliding tours to backcountry ski expeditions and avalanche-awareness courses in the winter. If you want to hike, an English leaflet is available at the information centre in Nagano Station (see p.420) covering some of the area's most popular hiking courses. You may also find advice and leaflets in English at the **tourist information centre** (daily 8.30am–5pm; T0261/72-2279), to the left of Hakuba Station.

To get to Hakuba from Nagano, hop on a **bus** (around 1hr; ¥1400); if you're heading in this direction during winter also enquire about the free bus service which is sometimes run by the Hakuba 47 ski area (W www.hakuba47.co.jp). By **train** the area is best reached from Matsumoto (see p.433) along the JR Ōito line; by express it's about an hour's journey, and there are also direct trains to Shinjuku in Tokyo.

A good place **to stay** at Happō-One is the friendly *Hakuba Valley Hotel* (T0261/72-2448, F72-2137; ●), a Japanese-style inn, run by the English-speaking Hata-san and popular with expats. Rates include two meals and there's a bar and pool table for après-ski socializing. To reach the hotel you need to take the chairlift up the slope from the Happō-One car park, or call ahead and get Hata-san to pick you up in his snow cat. Another great base in both winter and summer is the relaxed *Hakuba Alps Backpackers* (T0261/75 4038, W www.hakubabackpackers.com; dorms ¥3000 per person), in Kamishiro, two stops down the train line from Hakuba. The Kiwi–Japanese couple who run the place are very friendly and the location, close by Goryu Toomi ski field, and price can't be beaten.

Among the places **to eat**, don't miss out on the rustic, log cabin-style *Gravity Worx* (T0261/72-5434), a minute's walk right of Hakuba Station. It's run by welcoming English-speaking staff and serves excellent home-made pizzas, pasta, salads and desserts.

Shiga Kōgen and Yudanaka Onsen

The common complaint about Japanese ski resorts being too small certainly doesn't apply to mammoth **SHIGA KŌGEN** (W www.shigakogen.gr.jp), a collection of 21 resorts strung out along the Shiga plateau within the Jōshinetsu Kōgen National Park, 20km northeast of Nagano. Between mid-December and late April, there's usually good snow here, and the huge variety of terrain makes the one-day ¥4900 lift pass, covering all 21 resorts, great value. You'll find it impossible to ski the whole area in a day, so the best plan of action is to head for the northern end of the mountain range to the resorts at **Okushiga** and **Yakebitai-yama**, where the slalom events of the 1998 Olympics were held.

The closest **train station** to Shiga is Yudanaka (see below) – the ski resorts are a thirty-minute bus ride away from here. During the season, there are direct buses operated by Nagano Dentetsu from the east exit of Nagano Station (¥1800). The best **place to stay** in Okushiga is the comfortable, Western-style *Okushiga Kōgen Hotel* (☎0269/34-2034, ☏34-2827; ❺–❽). In Yakebitai, the *Shiga Kōgen Prince Hotel* (☎0269/34-3111, ☏34-3123; ❻–❽) offers bland but reliably high-standard accommodation. For more advice on lodgings, try the **Shiga Tourism Association** (9am–5pm; ☎0269/34-2404), where some English is spoken.

On the western fringes of the national park is a string of onsen villages, kicking off with **YUDANAKA ONSEN**, which is also the access point for the well-groomed and quiet ski resorts of **Gorin Kōgen** and **Kita-Shiga Kōgen Heights** (tourist information on ☎0269/33-6375), whose five ski areas are fast becoming a snowboarding mecca. The area is most famous, though, for the monkeys who bathe in the rotemburo at the **Monkey Park** (Jigokudani Yaen-kōen; daily 8am–5pm; ¥500), a short walk from the spa village of Kambayashi Onsen. Some two hundred Japanese long-tailed monkeys (*Nihon-zaru*) live in this area; the legend goes that they started to take dips in the hot pools during the 1960s, when a local ryokan owner took pity on them and left food out in winter. A special rotemburo was eventually built for the apes, dubbed "snow monkeys" by *Life* magazine. You can watch them wallowing and fooling around by the pool via webcam at ❾http://shinshu.online.co.jp. Winter is a good time to visit but it's also the main mating season, so there's likely to be some simian hanky-panky going on around the rotemburo.

Yudanaka is the terminus for the Nagano Dentetsu train line from Nagano (40min by express train, 1hr by local train). From the station, it's a fifteen-minute bus journey (¥210) to Kanbayashi Onsen. By the bus stop you can't fail to notice the **Shiga Kōgen Roman Museum** (☎0269/33-8855; ¥500; daily 9am–5pm, closed Thurs Nov–March) in a striking building designed by Kurokawa Kisho. The permanent collection contains some pretty pieces of Roman glass, plus Central Asian kilims and Japanese woodblock prints and paintings – all worth a look if you're hanging around for a bus back to town. To reach the monkey pool, walk uphill from the bus stop until you find a sign for a trail leading through the woods for around 2km. Just beneath the monkey park is *Kōrakukan* (☎0269/33-4376, ☏33-3244; ❻), a rambling wooden ryokan offering homely Japanese-style accommodation; rates include two meals.

There are plenty more ryokan and minshuku in Yudanaka Onsen, although the more attractive base is nearby **Shibu Onsen**, a twenty-minute walk uphill from the station, where there are nine public baths dotted among the narrow streets lined with traditional-style inns. One of the friendliest and cheapest places here is *Kameya Ryokan* (☎0259/33-3585, ☏33-3587; ❻), with decent tatami rooms (without bathrooms). If money's no object, try the elegant *Kanbayashi Hotel* (☎0269/33-3551, ❾www.avis.ne.jp/~senjukak; ❾), set amid the trees in Kanbayashi Onsen, with lovely artworks in its lobby and a view of a Japanese-style garden.

Matsumoto and around

Some 50km southwest of Nagano across the Hijiri Kōgen mountains is the friendly and attractive city of **MATSUMOTO**, the prefecture's second largest, and the gateway to the Japan Alps. The city is famous for its splendid castle, **Matsumoto-jō**, and is also home to **Nakamachi**, an area of traditional white-walled houses, many now renovated into ryokan and shops. To the west is the **Japan Ukiyo-e Museum**, where beautiful traditional prints are displayed inside a surprisingly ugly modern building.

Matsumoto also has a reputation as a centre for classical music. It was the home of **Dr Suzuki Shin'ichi** (who died nine months short of his 100th birthday in 1998), an internationally famous music teacher who encouraged children to learn to play instruments by using their natural gift for mimicry. His "Suzuki Method" is taught in the town's Suzuki Shin'ichi Talent Education Hall, around 1km east of Matsumoto Station. Every September Matsumoto also hosts the ten-day **Saitō Kinen**, a classical music festival in memory of another local talent, Saitō Hideo, celebrated conductor and mentor to many famous musicians, including conductor Seiji Ozawa.

Arrival, information and city transport

Matsumoto is connected to Nagano by **train**, an hour's journey across the mountains on the scenic Shinonoi line. From Nagoya, the limited express train takes two hours. The fastest direct train from Tokyo is the Azusa limited express service from Shinjuku (2hr 30min). All long-distance **buses** stop in front of the train station. Matsumoto's small **airport** (☎0263/57-8818) is 8km southwest of the town centre; buses (¥540) meet all flights and take 25 minutes to reach the city centre.

Japan's friendliest **tourist information office** (daily 9.30am–6pm; ☎0263/32-2814) can be found outside Matsumoto Station. This small bureau is staffed by clued-up English-speakers who can make accommodation book-ings and provide information on areas around Matsumoto, including the Japan Alps and Kamikōchi; you can also pick up a town map and lots of other leaflets. The city's website is ⓦwww.city.matsumoto.nagano.jp. There's free **Internet** access at M Wing on Isemachi-dōri, a five-minute walk north of the station.

Matsumoto's main sights are within easy walking distance of the train station. Alternatively, borrow one of the **free bikes** from various locations around the city – ask the tourist office for details. Convenient Town Sneaker **minibuses** run along two circular routes from the JR station. One ride costs ¥100, or you can buy a ¥300 day pass on the bus; the tourist information office has a map of the routes. Regular **buses** go from the Matsuden Bus Terminal, under the ESPA department store opposite Matsumoto Station, north towards the onsen resort of Asama, where you'll find the local youth hostel, and on to the Matsumoto Folkcraft Museum.

Accommodation

The nicest area to stay is Nakamichi-dōri, where there are several good-value ryokan. The drab youth hostel is several kilometres from the city centre and has the usual curfew; if you want to enjoy a night on the town, check into one of the cheaper business hotels near the station.

Ace Inn Matsumoto 1-1-3 Fukashi ☎0263/35-1188, ⓔace.alpico.co.jp. Handily located modern business hotel with single rooms only. For ¥6700 you also get breakfast, free Internet access and slightly bigger beds than usual.

Asama Onsen Youth Hostel 1-7-15 Asama

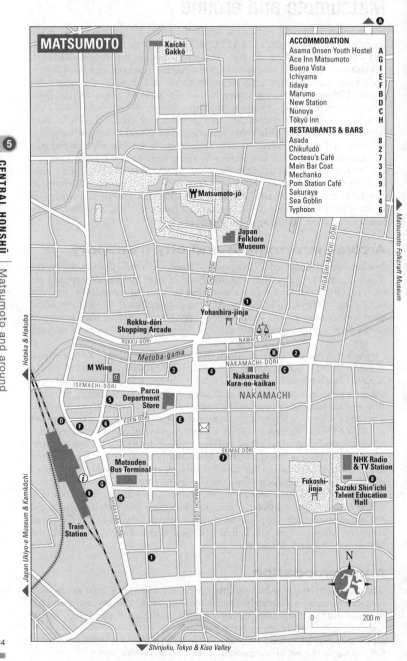

MATSUMOTO

Kaichi Gakkō

Matsumoto-jō

Japan Folklore Museum

Yohashira-jinja

Rokku-dōri Shopping Arcade

ROKKU-DŌRI

Metoba-gama

M Wing

ISEMACHI-DŌRI

Parco Department Store

KŌEN-DŌRI

NAWATE-DŌRI

NAKAMACHI-DŌRI

Nakamachi Kura-no-kaikan

NAKAMACHI

EKIMAE-DŌRI

Matsuden Bus Terminal

SHIBAKABA-DŌRI

HOMMACHI-DŌRI

HIGASHI-MACHI-DŌRI

NHK Radio & TV Station

Fukoshi-jinja

Suzuki Shin'ichi Talent Education Hall

Train Station

ACCOMMODATION
Asama Onsen Youth Hostel	A
Ace Inn Matsumoto	G
Buena Vista	I
Ichiyama	E
Iidaya	F
Marumo	B
New Station	D
Nunoya	C
Tōkyū Inn	H

RESTAURANTS & BARS
Asada	8
Chikufudō	2
Cocteau's Café	7
Main Bar Coat	3
Mechanko	5
Pom Station Café	9
Sakuraya	1
Sea Goblin	4
Typhoon	6

Hotaka & Hakuba

Japan Ukiyo-e Museum & Kamikōchi

Matsumoto Folkcraft Museum

0   200 m

N

▼ *Shinjuku, Tokyo & Kiso Valley*

Matsumoto and around

Matsumoto	*Matsumoto*	松本
Japan Ukiyo-e Museum	*Nihon Ukiyo-e Hakubutsukan*	日本浮世絵美術館
Matsumoto Folkcraft Museum	*Matsumoto Mingeikan*	松本民芸館
Matsumoto-jō	*Matsumoto-jō*	松本城
Nakamachi	*Nakamachi*	中町
Accommodation		
Ace Inn Matsumoto	*Esu In Matsumoto*	エースイン松本
Asama Onsen Youth Hostel	*Asama Onsen Yūsu Hosuteru*	浅間温泉ユースホステル
Hotel Buena Vista	*Hoteru Buena Bisuta*	ホテルブエナビスタ
Hotel Iidaya	*Hoteru Iidaya*	ホテル飯田屋
Ichiyama	*Ichiyama*	いちやま
Marumo	*Marumo*	まるも
Matsumoto Tōkyū Inn	*Matsumoto Tōkyū In*	松本東急イン
Hotel New Station	*Hoteru Nyū Sutēshon*	ホテルニューステーション
Nunoya	*Nunoya*	ぬのや
Restaurants		
Asada	*Asada*	あさだ
Chikufudō	*Chikufudō*	竹風堂
Cocteau's Café	*Kokutōzu Kafe*	コクトーズカフェ
Mechanko	*Mechanko*	めちゃんこ
Sakuraya	*Sakuraya*	桜家
Hotaka	*Hotaka*	穂高
Dai-ō Wasabi Farm	*Dai-ō Wasabi Nōjō*	大王わさび農場
Rokuzan Art Museum	*Rokuzan Bijutsukan*	碌山美術館
Kamikōchi	*Kamikōchi*	上高地
Gosenjaku Lodge	*Gosenjaku Rojji*	五千尺ロッヂ
Kamikōchi Imperial Hotel	*Kamikōchi Teikoku Hoteru*	上高地帝国ホテル
Nishi-itoya Sansō	*Nishi-itoya Sansō*	西糸屋山荘
Yariga-take	*Yariga-take*	槍ヶ岳
Norikura Kōgen	*Norikura Kōgen*	乗鞍高原
Kyūka Mura	*Kyūka Mura*	休暇村
BELL Suzurangoya	*BELL Suzurangoya*	BELL鈴蘭小屋
Norikura Kōgen Youth Hostel	*Norikura Kōgen Yūsu Hosuteru*	乗鞍高原ユースホステル
Pension Chimney	*Penshon Chimunii*	ペンションチムニー
Hirayu Onsen	*Hirayu Onsen*	平湯温泉

Onsen ☎0263/46-1335. Friendly management makes up for the unappealing building and metal bunk beds, though no meals are served. It's twenty minutes by bus from the JR station (take either bus #6 or #7 from the bus terminal at the ESPA department store). Dorms beds ¥3200 per person. **Hotel Buena Vista** 1-2-1 Honjo ☎0263/37-0111, ⓦwww.buena-vista.co.jp. Matsumoto's most opulent Western-style accommodation, with an excellent range of restaurants and bars, and extremely good-value singles. **❼**

Hotel Iidaya 1-2-3 Chūō ☎0263/32-0027, ⓕ36-9223. Standard business hotel, though one of the cheapest in Matsumoto. **❺**

Ichiyama 2-1-17 Chūō ☎0263/32-0122, ℱ32-3968. Good mid-range choice, offering both Western- and Japanese-style rooms with a modern touch. Western-style breakfast included. ❻

Marumo 3-3-10 Chūō ☎0263/32-0115. Set in a white house and Meiji-era wooden building on the banks of the Metoba River, there's an appealing mix of old and modern Japan in this small ryokan, with tatami rooms, a wooden bath, a small enclosed bamboo garden and a nice café (see opposite). ❺

Matsumoto Tōkyū Inn 1-3-21 Fukashi ☎0263/36-0109, ℱ36-0883. Reliable mid-range chain hotel with good-sized rooms, though lacking in atmosphere. ❻

Hotel New Station 1-1-11 Chūō ☎0263/35-3850, ℱ35-3851. Good-value mid-range hotel, with quiet modern rooms, some with a Swiss-chalet feel to them. The attached *Ajian Koyo* is a smart place for a drink and traditional local dishes including horsemeat. ❺

Nunoya 3-5-7 Nakamachi ☎ & ℱ0263/32-0545. Delightful ryokan in a charming wooden building on Nakamachi-dōri, with attractive tatami rooms (but no en-suite bathrooms). Meals costs around ¥3000 per person. ❺

The City

Matsumoto's castle is its big attraction, but you'll find some nice surprises as you make your way to it. Check out the old houses along **Nakamachi-dōri**, which runs parallel to the southern bank of the Metoba River. Among the white-walled inns, antique shops and restaurants, look out for the **Nakamachi Kura-no-Kaikan** (daily 9am–4.30pm; free), a beautifully restored sake brewery with a soaring black-beam interior and traditional cross-hatching plasterwork outside. Cross over the river by any of several bridges and return to Daimyō-chō-dōri along the colourful market street **Nawate-dōri**. The castle grounds are just a couple of hundred metres north of here.

Matsumoto's castle, **Matsumoto-jō**, remains hidden from view until the very last moment, making a sudden dramatic appearance as you enter the outer grounds and approach the moat. The castle (daily 8.30am–5pm; ¥520, or ¥420 with a free discount coupon from the tourist information office), also known as Karasu-jō (Crow Castle) because of its brooding black facade, was started by the Ogasawara clan in 1504, but it was another lord, Ishikawa, who remodelled the fortress in 1593 and built the five-tier **donjon** that is now the oldest keep in Japan. You must take your shoes off before clambering up the dark, steep wooden stairs to the *donjon*'s sixth storey (it has the traditional hidden floor of most Japanese castles), from which you can look out over the town and surrounding mountains. The entrance fee to the castle also includes access to the quirky **Japan Folklore Museum** (daily 8.30am–5pm), which is just before the moat. Inside, the displays include a good model of how Matsumoto looked in feudal times. Around 500m north of the castle is the attractive **Kaichi Gakkō** (Mon–Sat 8.30am–4.30pm; ¥310), the oldest Western-style school building in Japan, dating from 1876. It's just a dusty Victorian school inside, but the handsome, pale-blue facade, decorated with temple-style plasterwork, is worth a look.

Matsumoto's other main sights are out of the city centre. The hideously modern glass-and-concrete **Japan Ukiyo-e Museum** (Tues–Sun 10am–5pm; ¥900), some 3km west of the station, has woodblock prints by all the great masters including Utagawa Hiroshige and Katsushika Hokusai. Only a fraction of the museum's splendid collection of 10,000 prints is ever on display; an English leaflet will help guide you around what is. The simplest way to reach the museum is to hop in a taxi, which will cost around ¥2000 from the town centre.

If you've an interest in Japanese folk crafts, also worth a look is the **Matsumoto Folkcraft Museum** (☎0263/33-1569; Tues–Sun 9am–5pm; ¥210), a fifteen-minute bus ride (¥330) out of the city towards Utsukushigahara Onsen. Set beside a rice paddy and a vineyard, the museum, in a traditional-style building, contains some exquisite objects, including giant pottery urns, lacquerware inlaid with mother of pearl, and wooden chests. Get off the bus at Shimoganai Mingeikanguchi, from where the museum is a minute's walk away.

Eating and drinking

Matsumoto is well served with **places to eat**, particularly around the train station. The local speciality is *Shinshū* (the old name for Nagano) soba, best eaten cold in summer (ask for *zaru-soba*). A more expensive – and delicious – delicacy is *sasamushi*, eel steamed inside rice wrapped in bamboo leaves. The adventurous will want to try horsemeat served in a variety of ways, including raw like sashimi.

Among the city's **bars**, a popular option is the *Gum Tree*, behind the *Hotel Buena Vista*, run by an Australian and serving cans of Fosters and Castlemaine, plus Mexican snacks. Also try the convivial *Sea Goblin* on Nakamachi-dōri, a grunge chic bar with Löwenbräu on tap and electronic darts. There's a ¥300 cover charge, but you do get a bowl of chips and salsa for that. For something more stylish, *Main Bar Coat*, in the Miwa Building at 2-3-5 Chūō (daily 6pm–3am), is known for its cocktails (from ¥800, plus ¥300 cover charge).

Asada Fukashi. In a traditional white-walled building behind the NHK radio and TV station, this restaurant has a good reputation for soba. Tues–Sun 11am–4pm.

Chikufudō 3-4-20 Nakamachi. Local rice dishes and sweets made with chestnuts are served at this chain restaurant in one of the old whitewashed houses on Nakamachi-dōri. Set meals start at ¥900.

Cocteau's Café Ekimae-dōri. Quietly trendy café and bar just past the crossing with Honmachi-dōri. The set lunch is good value at ¥750, while dinner costs ¥2800, and there's excellent French coffee.

Marumo 3-3-10 Chūō. Attached to the ryokan of the same name, this charming café is fitted out in the area's distinctive dark cherry wood furniture. Come for breakfast and be lulled by gentle classical music.

Mechanko 1-7-2 Chūō. Large sushi bar and *izakaya* a couple of minutes' walk north of the station. For once, the food looks better than the photographs in the menu. The all-you-can-eat-and-drink set menus for ¥2300 are great value. Daily 5pm–5am.

Pom! Station Café Relaxed café whose Nepalese chef cooks up Indian dishes. They also have a range of bottled beers from around the world and one free Internet terminal.

Sakuraya 4-9-1 Ōtemachi ☏0263/33-2660. Elegant and traditional restaurant, with waitresses in kimono, on the corner one block east of Daimyō-dōri. Eel dishes (*sasamushi*) are the speciality; a set meal costs ¥2100. Closed Mon.

Typhoon 1-5-17 Chūō ☏0263/33-0905. Casual, cosy restaurant serving spicy Asian foods; all dishes under ¥1000. Closed Mon.

Around Matsumoto

North of Matsumoto, the picturesque rural village of **Hotaka** is known for its *wasabi* (horseradish) farms and is also a starting point for hikes up into the nearby Japan Alps; you can continue from here to reach the beautiful mountain area of Hakuba (see p.431). Serious mountaineers head straight from Matsumoto west to the serene lake and mountain resort of **Kamikōchi**, popularized by British missionary Walter Weston at the beginning of the twentieth century. The mountains get so much snow that Kamikōchi is only open from late April to the end of October, when it can be very busy. A less crowded alternative is the nearby onsen and ski resort of **Norikura Kōgen**. The fabulous **Skyline Road** runs through this area, across to Takayama in neighbouring Gifu-ken (see p.445); drive along it and you'll see why Nagano-ken is known as the "roof of Japan".

Hotaka

Thirty minutes by local train north of Matsumoto lies the quiet country town of **HOTAKA**, a base for hiking in the Alps to the west and well known for its production of *wasabi*, the fiery green horseradish that, made into a paste, accompanies sushi and sashimi. The best way to explore this tranquil area is to pick up a map from the **tourist information office** (daily: May–Oct 9am–5pm; Jan–April, Nov & Dec 10am–3pm; ☎0263/82-9363), to the right of the station exit; you can rent a bicycle from one of many outlets around here (¥300 an hour, ¥1500 a day) and head east out of town through the paddy fields. Keep an eye open along the country roads for the charming *dōsojin*, small stones on which guardian deity couples have been carved.

Some 2km east of Hotaka is the enjoyably touristy **Dai-ō Wasabi Farm** (9am–5pm; free). This is one of the largest *wasabi* farms in Japan and the vast fields of *wasabi* growing in wide, waterlogged gravel trenches make an impressive sight. Within the landscaped grounds you can sample *wasabi* in all manner of foods, including ice cream, which is surprisingly tasty.

Back in Hotaka, a ten-minute walk north of the station along a red-stone paved footpath will bring you to the serene **Rokuzan Art Museum** (Tues–Sun 9am–5pm; ¥500), comprising an ivy-covered, church-like building and a couple of modern galleries. The museum houses the sculptures of **Ogiwara Rokuzan**, known in Japan as the "Rodin of the Orient". The twentieth-century artist, whose career was cut short with his death at 32, was clearly influenced by the French master, but he also turned his hand to painting and sketches, some of which are also on display.

Kamikōchi

Tucked away in the Azusa valley at an altitude of 1500m is the beautiful mountaineering and hiking resort of **KAMIKŌCHI** (Ⓦwww.kamikochi.or.jp). Hardly more than a bus station and a handful of hotels scattered along the Azusa-gawa, Kamikōchi has some stunning alpine scenery, which can only be viewed between late April and the end of October before heavy snow blocks off the narrow roads and the resort shuts down for winter. As a result, during season the place buzzes with tourists and the prices at its few hotels and restaurants are as steep as the surrounding mountains.

Kamikōchi's history as a tourist destination dates back to the late nineteenth century, when British missionary **Walter Weston** (see box, opposite) helped popularize the area as a base for climbing the craggy peaks known as the Northern Alps. The highest mountain here is the 3190-metre **Hotaka-dake**, followed by **Yari-ga-take** (3180m). Both are extremely popular climbs; one trail up Yari-ga-take has been dubbed the Ginza Jūsō ("Ginza Traverse") after Tokyo's busy shopping area, because it gets so crowded. However, the congestion on the mountain is nothing compared to that found at its base, where, at the height of the season, thousands of day-trippers tramp through the well-marked trails along the Azusa valley. The best way to appreciate Kamikōchi is to stay overnight so you can experience the valley minus the crowds in the evening and early morning. Alternatively, come here in June, when frequent showers put off fair-weather walkers.

Hiking around Kamikōchi

With an early start, the scenic spots of the Azusa valley can all be covered in a day's hike. Pick up the English *Kamikōchi Pocket Guide* from the information office at the bus stop for a good map of all the main trails. On the way to the bus stop you'll pass the entrance to the valley, with its fantastic view across the **Taishō-ike**, a glass-like pond reflecting the snowcapped peaks: this is the best place to head first. The hour-long amble starts along the pebbly riverbank and splits after the Tashiro bridge, one leg continuing beside the Azusa-gawa, the other following a nature-observation trail along wooden walkways, over chocolatey marshes. The Taishō-ike was formed when the Azusa-gawa was naturally dammed up after the eruption of the nearby volcano Yake-dake in 1915, and dead tree trunks still poke out of the water. Rowing boats can be rented from the hotel here for ¥800 for thirty minutes.

Returning the way you came, cross over the Tashiro bridge to the opposite bank of the river, where the path leads past some of Kamikōchi's hotels and the rock-embedded relief statue of Walter Weston. In the centre of the village the river is spanned by the much-photographed wooden suspension bridge **Kappa-bashi**. Cross this and continue north for a couple of minutes to the **visitor centre** (daily 9am–5pm), where there are nature displays and evocative black-and-white photographs of Kamikōchi in times past.

The return trip north from the visitors' centre to the picturesque pond, **Myōjin-ike**, with its excellent lunch spot (see p.440), tiny shrine and mallard ducks, will take you around two hours at a leisurely pace. The crowds begin to thin on this trail and really drop away on the "six-hour course" up the valley to the Tokusawa campsite and the Shinmura suspension bridge, named after a famous climber, Shinmura Shōichi.

Climbing around Kamikōchi

Beyond Tokusawa the serious hiking begins. The steep hike up the "Matterhorn of Japan" (so called because of its craggy appearance) to the mountain huts at Ichinomata on the lower slopes of **Yari-ga-take** takes around five hours, and can be done in a long day from Kamikōchi. There are huts on the mountain for overnight stays; a futon and two meals cost around ¥8000 per person, but things can get very crowded during the season.

Reaching the summit of Yari-ga-take may well give you a taste for mountaineering. The popular route to follow is due south across the alpine ridge to **Hotaka-dake** (also known as Oku-Hotaka-dake), the third highest peak in Japan, a three-day loop that will bring you back to Kamikōchi. The route is well covered in *Hiking in Japan* by Paul Hunt (see "Books", p.1018).

Walter Weston

Born in Derbyshire, England, in 1861, the missionary **Walter Weston** was 29 years old when he first set foot in the mountains of Nagano-ken. The phrase "Japan Alps" was actually coined by another Englishman, William Gowland, whose *Japan Guide* was published in 1888, but it was Weston's *Climbing and Exploring in the Japan Alps*, which appeared eight years later, that really put the peaks on the mountaineers' maps. Previously these mountains, considered sacred, were only climbed by Shinto and Buddhist priests, but in fast-modernizing Japan alpinism caught on as a sport and Weston became its acknowledged guru. Weston favoured Kamikōchi as a base from which to climb what he called "the grandest mountains in Japan", and he frequently visited the tiny village from his home in Kōbe. Although he is honoured in Kamikōchi with a monument, and a festival in his name on the first weekend in June at the start of the climbing season, Weston is said to have wept at the prospect of mass tourism ruining his beloved mountains. His ghost can take comfort from the fact that the area's beauty survives largely intact, despite Kamikōchi's popularity.

An adventurous option for approaching Kamikōchi across the mountains from the west is to take the **cable car** (one way ¥1500, return ¥2800, ¥300 extra for large backpacks) up from Shin-Hotaka Onsen in **Gifu-ken**. This onsen resort, best reached by bus from Takayama (see p.445), has the longest cable-car ride in the whole of Asia, which takes you halfway to the 2908-metre summit of Nishi-Hotaka-dake; from here, Kamikōchi is a three-hour hike southeast.

Make sure you pack warm, waterproof clothing, as the weather can change rapidly in the mountains, and even at the height of summer temperatures on the peaks can be freezing, especially early in the morning.

Practicalities

Private vehicles are banned from the valley. If you're **driving**, park your car at the Sawando car park (¥500 a day) in the village of Nakanoyu, 8km outside Kamikōchi. From here buses (¥1000) and taxis (¥4000) make regular runs to and from Kamikōchi, passing through narrow rock tunnels. To get here from Matsumoto, take a thirty-minute **train** journey on the Matsumoto Dentetsu line to Shin-Shimashima Station (¥680), then transfer to a bus (¥2000), which takes 75 minutes to reach Kamikōchi. There is also a direct bus twice a day in summer from Matsumoto bus terminal, opposite the station (¥4400 return). From Takayama, hop on the bus to Hirayu Onsen (¥1530), where you'll have to transfer to the Kamikōchi bus (¥1550), which travels along the scenic Norikura Skyline Road. There's also a daily bus service between Norikura Kōgen (see opposite) and Kamikōchi. Once you've arrived, make sure you reserve your seat on a bus out of Kamikōchi – the sheer number of visitors leaves many people at the mercy of the taxi drivers.

There's an **information centre** (9.30am–5pm; ☏0263/95-2433) at the bus terminal where you can pick up a good English map showing the main hiking trails. The assistants don't speak much English, so if you need more information or want to arrange accommodation, do this at the Matsumoto tourist office (see p.433) before setting out. The staff at the **national park visitor centre** (8am–5pm; ☏0263/95-2606), just past Kappa-bashi, should be able to give some description in English of the many rare animals, plants and songbirds in the valley.

The most convenient **campsite** is at Konashidaira (¥400 per person per night), just beyond Kappa-bashi and the visitor centre. Otherwise, the best budget option is in the large dorm at *Nishi-itoya Sansō* (☏0263/95-2206, ℉95-2208; ¥8000 per person), which has both bunk beds and shared tatami areas. The rates here include two meals – a good deal for Kamikōchi. *Nishi-itoya Sansō* also run a pleasant ryokan where rates (❼ including meals) are slightly higher than those for the smallest rooms at the upmarket *Gosenjaku Lodge* (☏0263/95-2221; ❼) next door. If you really want to push the boat out, book into the luxurious, Western-style *Kamikōchi Imperial Hotel* (☏0263/95-2001, ℉95-2006; ❽), a true classic, with the delightful spookiness of a grand old hotel in a wilderness setting. Putting up at the excellent youth hostel in *Norikura Kōgen* (see opposite) and travelling into Kamikōchi for the day is also a viable option.

Eating options are a bit limited: most hotels serve up standard soba and curry rice at inflated prices. If you're visiting for the day or are planning a hike into the mountains, bring food with you. For lunch, *Kamonjigoya* beside Myōjin-ike (see p.439) is worth stopping at for the *iwana* (river trout) lunch at ¥1500. The fish are roasted on sticks beside an *irori* (charcoal fire), making this an ideal refuge if the weather turns nasty.

Norikura Kōgen Onsen

NORIKURA KŌGEN, an alpine village some 30km southwest of Matsumoto, isn't nearly as crowded as Kamikōchi and has some splendid mountain scenery, easy hiking trails and onsen baths. In winter, ski lifts shoot up the lower slopes of **Norikura-dake**, while in summer the hike to the peak of the same mountain can be accomplished in ninety minutes from the car park, where the Echo Line road leaves Nagano-ken and becomes the **Skyline Road** in Gifu-ken. This is the highest road in Japan, providing spectacular mountain-top views (the upper section is closed Nov–June). The car park is an hour's drive from Norikura Kōgen; there's no public transport on this route.

The village is really no more than several widely spread-out hotels and lodges. The closest thing to a centre is probably the modern onsen complex, **Yukemuri-kan** (daily except Tues 10.30am–9pm; ¥700), which has both indoor wooden baths and rotemburo with mountain views. The nearby **Norikura Kōgen Visitor Centre** (daily except Wed 9am–5pm; free) has unremarkable geology and nature displays in Japanese only; it's better to head on west towards the ski lifts. Continuing on foot up the mountain for around an hour, you'll reach the start of a short trail to **Sanbon-daki**, where three waterfalls converge in one pool.

An alternative route from the ski lifts is to hike south for twenty minutes to another beautiful waterfall, **Zengorō-no-taki**, reached along a clearly marked nature trail, with signs in English – a rainbow often forms in the spray across this impressive fall during the morning. Twenty minutes' hike south of Zengorō, a small reflecting pond, **Ushidome**, provides a perfect view of the mountains. Continuing downhill from the pond, you can choose to walk towards another small lake, **Asami-ko**, or to the main picnic area, **Ichinose**, a picturesque spot at the confluence of two streams. A cycle and walking track leads directly north from Ichinose back to Yukemuri-kan, where the best plan of action is to soak in the rotemburo.

Practicalities

Norikura Kōgen can be reached by infrequent **buses** from both Shin-Shimashima train station on the Matsumoto Dentetsu line (see opposite), and Takayama (see p.445), with a change of buses at Tatamidaira and Hirayu Onsen. From June to October there's also a daily bus between Norikura Kōgen and Kamikōchi. Some of these buses only run once a day, so it's best to check with local tourist offices on the current timetables in advance of your journey.

There's a **tourist information office** (daily 9.30am–4.30pm; ☎0263/93-2952) opposite the Yukemuri-kan onsen complex; the staff don't speak much English, but can provide a hiking map (in Japanese) of the area. Bicycles are handy for getting around and can be rented at the giftshop across from the visitor centre for ¥500 a day. The village's website is ⓦ www.norikura.gr.jp.

As far as **accommodation** goes, the *Norikura Kōgen Youth Hostel* (☎0263/93-2748, ℉93-2162; ¥3500 per person), ten minutes' walk north from the bus stop, and next to the ski lifts, is ideally placed for quick access to the slopes. The young, friendly staff can arrange ski rental (¥3000) and point out the most interesting hikes during the summer. Opposite the ski lifts is *Pension Chimney* (☎0263/93-2902; ❻), an appealing European-style chalet with a steeply sloping roof and cosy rooms. Rates here include two meals; there's a heating charge in the winter. A similar deal is available at the large and friendly *BELL Suzurangoya* (☎0263/93-2001, ℉93-2003; ❻), near the tourist information office. The old rooms are the cheapest, but they're in good condition and in the same building. The "vacation village", *Kyūka Mura* (☎0263/93-2304, ℱ93-2392; ❻), near Ushidome pond, has fine tatami rooms and offers rates which include two meals – and an extra heating charge in the winter. You can get good, inexpensive Japanese **food** at *Kyūka Mura* café; you pay first and are given a tag with a number, then your meal is brought to you.

The Kiso valley

For a taste of how Japan looked before the concrete buildings and neon signs, head for the densely forested river valley of **Kiso**, southwest of Matsumoto, between the Central and Northern Alps. Shogun Tokugawa Ieyasu chose this valley as part of the route for the 550-kilometre Nakasendō, one of the five main highways linking his capital Edo (present-day Tokyo) with the rest of Japan. Eleven post towns (*juku*) lined the Kisoji (Kiso road) section of the Nakasendō, and three of them – **Narai**, **Tsumago** and **Magome** – have been preserved as virtual museums of the feudal past. This is also good **hiking** terrain; Tsugamo and Magome are linked by an easy two-hour hiking trail which follows the original route of the Nakasendō over the hills and through the forests.

Narai

The 34th post town on the Nakasendō, attractive **NARAI**, 30km southwest of Matsumoto, was the most prosperous of the eleven *juku* along the Kisoji. The village's distinctive wooden buildings, with window shutters and *renji-gōshi* lattice-work, have been beautifully preserved – Narai's only drawback is the cars that pass through the main street, making it hard to forget which century you're in.

The main road of restored houses and shops stretches for around 1km south from the train station at the north end of the village. Look out for the shop selling *kashira ningyō*, colourfully painted, traditional dolls and toys made of

The Kiso valley		
Narai	*Narai*	奈良井
Iseya	*Iseya*	伊勢屋
Nakamura House	*Nakamura-tei*	中村邸
Magome	*Magome*	馬籠
Magomejaya	*Magomejaya*	馬籠茶屋
Tajimaya	*Tajimaya*	但馬屋
Tōson Kinenkan	*Tōson Kinenkan*	藤村記念館
Tsumago	*Tsumago*	妻籠
Daikichi	*Daikichi*	大吉
Matsushiro-ya	*Matsushiro-ya*	松代屋
Okuya Kyōdokan	*Okuya Kyōdokan*	奥谷郷土館
Nagiso	*Nagiso*	南木曽
Kiso-Fukushima	*Kiso-Fukushima*	木曽福島
Kiso-Ryojōan Youth Hostel	*Kiso-Ryojōan Yūsu Hosuteru*	木曽旅情庵ユースホステル
Nakatsugawa	*Nakatsugawa*	中津川

wood. About halfway down the road stands **Nakamura House** (daily 9am–4.30pm; ¥200), dating from the 1830s and once the home of a merchant who made his fortune in combs, one of the area's specialities. Side streets lead off to pretty temples and shrines in the foothills and, on the other side, to the rocky banks of the Narai-gawa crossed by the **Kiso-no-Ōhashi**, an arched wooden bridge.

Narai is a 45-minute **train** journey from Matsumoto along the Chūō line. A lovely place **to stay** is *Iseya* (☎0264/34-3051; **❻**), a minshuku in a traditional house along the main street, with an ornamental garden – rates include two meals. Dotted along the main street are several cafés with soaring wooden-beamed ceilings and *irori* – central charcoal fires, serving soba noodles and other local dishes.

Magome

The most southerly of the Kisoji's eleven *juku* is steeply raked **MAGOME**, 55km south of Narai. Standing 800m up in the hills above the Kiso valley, Magome means "horse basket", because this was where travellers on the Nakasendō were forced to leave their nags before tackling the mountainous stretch of road ahead. Plaster and wooden buildings line either side of the stone-flagged path – many of the wooden roofs are still held down by stone. Despite appearances, most of the town's buildings date from the twentieth century, the village having suffered a history of fires, the most recent being in 1915, when 42 houses burnt to the ground. Magome is famous for its native son, **Shimazaki Tōson** (1872–1943), whose historical novel *Yoake Mae* (Before the Dawn) put the town on Japan's literary map. In the middle of the village, the **Tōson Kinenkan** (daily 8.30am–4.45pm; ¥500) celebrates the author's life and makes a pretty place to stroll around. The reverentially displayed fragments of Tōson's life are labelled in Japanese only.

To start the **hike** to Tsumago (see box on p.444), continue up the hill, past the **kōsatsu**, the old town noticeboard on which the shogunate posted rules and regulations. The most notorious rule condemned to death anyone found illegally logging trees in the forests. The steepest part of the three-hour hike is over once you've reached the Magome-tōge (pass), where there's an old tea-house beside the road and a stone monument engraved with a lyrical verse by the haiku master Masaoka Shiki (see p.767). From here, the route enters the forest and later passes two **waterfalls**, O-dake and Me-dake.

The closest **train station** to Magome is in the town of Nakatsugawa, just across the border in Aichi-ken, a 55-minute journey northeast of Nagoya (see p.471) by limited express. **Buses** to Nakatsugawa also run from Nagoya. The bus journey up to Magome from outside Nakatsugawa Station (¥540) takes thirty minutes.

Magome's **tourist information office** (daily 8.30am–5pm; ☎0264/59-2336), opposite the Tōson Kinenkan, has an English map of the area; staff speak Japanese only and can help with accommodation bookings at the village's numerous minshuku. Two good **places to stay** are *Magomejaya* (☎0264/59-2038; **❺**), which has a giant waterwheel outside, and *Tajimaya* (☎0264/59-2048; **❻**), further up the hill towards the information office – both places include two meals in their rates.

Tsumago

Just thirty years ago the now-thriving village of **TSUMAGO**, 80km south of Matsumoto, was virtually a ghost town, with most of its traditional Edo-era houses on the point of collapse. The concerted efforts of the locals helped restore the wooden houses that now line the long main street, earning the village protected status and helping to spark the idea of cultural preservation across Japan. Telegraph poles and TV aerials have been banished from sight, so that the scene that greets you on the pedestrian-only street is probably very similar to that encountered by lords and their samurai passing through the village hundreds of years ago.

The highlight in Tsumago is the folk museum, **Okuya Kyōdokan** (daily 9am–4.45pm; ¥600), inside a rambling mansion that was once one of the village's designated post inns where the *daimyō*'s retinue rested. Inside is a fine range of exhibits on the history of the Nakasendō and the village, including photographs showing just how dilapidated Tsumago once was. For an extra ¥100 you can also enter the Kyū-honjin on the opposite side of the street – this was where the *daimyō* used to stay. The front porch, when it's not thronged with day-trippers, is a fine place to sit and soak up Tsumago's quiet atmosphere. For a bird's-eye view of the village, head uphill to the former site of **Tsumago castle**, destroyed sometime in the late sixteenth century. To get to the hill, follow the path just outside the village on the hiking route to Nagiso (see box below).

The closest **train station** to Tsumago is at Nagiso, from where the village is an hour's walk south or a ten-minute bus ride. There's a **tourist information office** in the centre of Tsumago (daily 8.30am–5pm; ☎0264/57-3123), where you can get help with accommodation and arrange to have your bag forwarded if you're planning to hike to Magome. Two good **places to stay** are the friendly *Daikichi* (☎0264/57-2595; ❺), at the northern end of the village, a minshuku where the rates include two meals of local specialities; and the more upmarket, 140-year-old ryokan, *Matsushiro-ya* (☎0264/57-3022; ❼), in the centre of Tsumago, with large tatami rooms and a shared bathroom.

Although the area's only **youth hostel**, *Kiso-Ryojōan* (☎0264/23-7716; ¥3000 per person), is nowhere near either Tsumago or Magome, it's a gem worth making a detour for. Twenty-five minutes by bus from Kiso-Fukushima Station on the Chūō line between Narai and Nagiso, the hostel is in a large, traditional building in the peaceful mountain village of **Ōhara**. Excellent food, including *nabe* stews and *sukiyaki* (a succulent beef dish), is served by the very friendly staff, and frequent bus connections to Kiso-Fukushima mean you can use the hostel as a base from which to explore the valley's post towns.

Hiking the Kisoji

The traditional way of hiking the Kisoji is to go from Magome to Tsumago to experience the supposedly tough initial climb up into the mountains – though it's actually not that difficult. Although the 7.7-kilometre route is frequently signposted in English, it's a good idea to pick up a map from one of the tourist information offices before you start.

If you don't fancy lugging your bags, there's a **baggage-forwarding service** in operation between March and November, charging ¥500 per piece, to and from the tourist information offices in both Tsumago and Magome. This service is offered daily from late July to the end of August, and on weekends and national holidays only at other times. Get your bag to the offices before 11.30am and they will be delivered at the other end by 5pm.

If you choose to walk in the opposite direction to Magome, start at Nagiso Station on the Chūō line, from where Tsumago is less than an hour's walk south through picturesque fields and small villages. You'll need a whole day to explore both post towns and to complete the hike, and you'll enjoy the experience all the more if you stay in either Tsumago or Magome overnight.

There's no shortage of lunchtime **restaurants and cafés** in Tsumago. Most places serve *sansai* soba (buckwheat noodles topped with mountain vegetables) and *gohei-mochi* (balls of pounded rice on a skewer coated with a sweet nut sauce). A good place to sample these local specialities is *Enoki Zaka*, a bustling café a few doors north of the Okuya Kyōdokan museum (closed Tues).

Takayama and around

Some 110km northeast of Nagoya, on the Gifu-ken side of the Central Alps range in an area known as Hida, lies the lovely town of **TAKAYAMA**. Once an enclave of skilled carpenters employed by emperors to build palaces and temples in Kyoto and Nara, Takayama is now a sprawling modern town, although most of its old merchant houses, small museums, tranquil temples and shrines are clustered into a compact area. Add the area's specialized crafts and cuisine, not to mention warm-hearted locals, and you'll realize why it pulls in the crowds. The best time to visit is out of season or during the week, when it's quiet enough to appreciate the town's timeless atmosphere.

Takayama is famous throughout Japan for two of its festivals – the **Sannō Matsuri** (April 14–15) and the **Hachiman Matsuri** (Oct 9–10). During these events, eleven huge elaborate floats, adorned with mechanical dolls (*karakuri*), are paraded around town, a spectacle that attracts hundreds of thousands of visitors.

You can also view these fabulous floats (*yatai*) at nearby **Furukawa**, a small town which, with its old houses, museums and temples, is like a mini-Takayama,

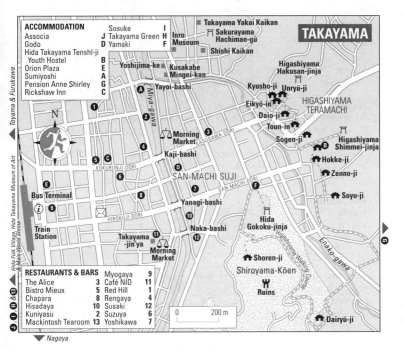

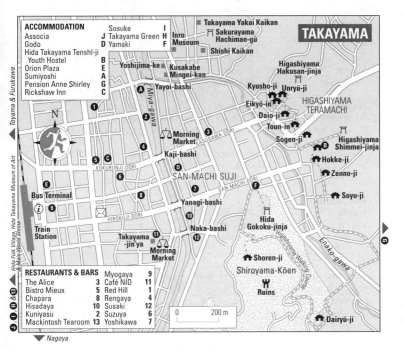

ACCOMMODATION
Associa	J
Godo	D
Hida Takayama Tenshl-ji Youth Hostel	B
Orion Plaza	E
Sumiyoshi	A
Pension Anne Shirley	G
Rickshaw Inn	C
Sosuke	I
Takayama Green	H
Yamaki	F

TAKAYAMA

Takayama Yakai Kaikan
Sakurayama Hachiman-gū
Inro Museum
Shishi Kaikan
Yoshijima-ke
Kusakabe
Mingei-kan
Yayoi-bashi
Higashiyama Hakusan-jinja
Kyusho-ji
Unryū-ji
Eikyo-in
HIGASHIYAMA TERAMACHI
Daio-ji
Morning Market
KASUGAWA-DORI
Kaji-bashi
KOKUBUNJI-DORI
Toun-in
Sogen-ji
Higashiyama Shimmei-jinja
Hokke-ji
SAN-MACHI SUJI
SAN-MACHI-DORI
Zenno-ji
Bus Terminal
Yanagi-bashi
Soyu-ji
HIROKOJI-DORI
Train Station
Naka-bashi
Hida Gokoku-jinja
Takayama -jin'ya
Morning Market
Higashiyama Walking Course
Enako-gawa
Shoren-ji
Shiroyama-Kōen
Ruins
Dairyū-ji

Miya-gawa

N

RESTAURANTS & BARS
The Alice	3	Myogaya	9
Bistro Mieux	5	Café NID	11
Chapara	8	Red Hill	1
Hisadaya	10	Rengaya	4
Kuniyasu	2	Susaki	12
Mackintosh Tearoom	13	Suzuya	6
		Yoshikawa	7

0   200 m

Toyama & Furukawa

Hida Folk Village, Hida Takayama Museum of Art & Main World Shrine

Nagoya

Takayama	*Takayama*	高山
Hida Folk Village	*Hida Minzoku-mura*	飛騨民俗村
Hida Takayama Museum of Art	*Hida Takayama Bijutsukan*	飛騨高山美術館
Higashiyama Teramachi	*Higashiyama Teramachi*	東山寺町
Inrō Museum	*Inrō Bijutsukan*	印籠美術館
Kusakabe Mingei-kan	*Kusakabe Mingei-kan*	日下部民芸館
San-machi Suji	*San-machi Suji*	三町筋
Shishi Kaikan	*Shishi Kaikan*	獅子会館
Takayama-jin'ya	*Takayama-jin'ya*	高山陣屋
Takayama Yatai Kaikan	*Takayama Yatai Kaikan*	高山屋台会館

Accommodation		
Hotel Associa	*Hoteru Asoshia*	ホテルアソシア
Gōdo	*Gōdo*	河渡
Hida Takayama Tenshō-ji Youth Hostel	*Hida Takayama Tenshō-ji Yūsu Hosuteru*	飛騨高山天照寺ユースホステル
Orion Plaza Hotel	*Orion Puraza Hoteru*	オリオンプラザホテル
Pension Anne Shirley	*Penshon An Shārī*	ペンションアンシャーリー
Rickshaw Inn	*Rikisha In*	力車イン
Sōsuke	*Sōsuke*	惣助
Sumiyoshi	*Sumiyoshi*	旅館寿美吉
Takayama Green Hotel	*Takayama Guriin Hoteru*	高山グリーンホテル
Yamaki	*Yamaki*	やまき

Restaurants		
The Alice	*Arisu*	アリス
Hisadaya	*Hisadaya*	久田屋
Kuniyasu	*Kuniyasu*	くにやす
Myōgaya	*Myōgaya*	みょうがや
Rengaya	*Rengaya*	れんがや
Susaki	*Susaki*	州さき
Suzuya	*Suzuya*	寿々や
Yoshikawa	*Yoshikawa*	よしかわ

Furukawa	*Furukawa*	古川
Furukawa Festival Hall	*Furukawa Matsuri Kaikan*	古川まつり会館
Hida Craftsman Culture Hall	*Hida-no-Sanshōkan*	飛騨の山樵館
Shirakabe-dozō	*Shirakabe-dozō*	白壁土蔵
Hida Furukawa Youth Hostel	*Hida Furukawa Yūsu Hosuteru*	飛騨古川ユースホステル

Restaurants		
Maeda	*Maeda*	まえだ
Matsuya	*Matsuya*	まつや
Shinanoya	*Shinanoya*	信濃家

minus the crowds. Less accessible by public transport, but very popular with the tour-bus brigade, are the picturesque villages in the **Shirakawa-gō** and **Gokayama valleys**, northwest of Takayama, where three villages of *gasshō-zukuri* A-frame thatched houses have been designated a UNESCO World Heritage Site.

Arrival, information and accommodation

Takayama is connected by **train** to both Toyama (see p.456) in the north and Nagoya (see p.471) in the south. The bus terminus for services from Hirayu Onsen, where you'll need to transfer if you've taken the bus from Kamikōchi (see p.438), is next to Takayama Station, ten minutes' walk west of the San-machi Suji district, where many of the town's main sights can be found.

Staff at the Hida **tourist information office** (daily: April–Oct 8.30am–6.30pm; Nov–March, 8.30am–5pm; ℡0577/32-5328), immediately in front of the JR station, are among the most clued-up you'll come across in this area – and there's always an English-speaker in the office. The *Rickshaw Inn* (see below) also acts as a tourist office – you can drop in to ask questions, pick up their restaurant map or just read an English newspaper. Takayama is best explored on foot or by **bicycle**. Bikes can be rented from the car park to the right of the station (¥300 per hour, ¥1300 per day) and, less expensively, from the youth hostel (see below) for ¥600 per day. Kankakokan, 40-4 Kamininomachi (daily 10am–5pm), has a couple of **Internet** terminals (¥100 per 30min). The city's website is ⓦwww.hidatakayama.or.jp.

Accommodation

If you're planning on staying in Takayama during either of the festivals, book well ahead. The best places are the town's ryokan and minshuku – a bit pricier than the business hotels near the train station, but a lot more atmospheric, and usually offering rates that include breakfast and dinner.

Hotel Associa 1134 Echigo-chō ℡0577/36-0001, ⓦwww.associa.com/tky. Elegant luxury hotel, a 5km drive southwest of Takayama Station, in the hills overlooking the town. Has several smart restaurants and bars and is next to Kur Alp, a modern onsen complex (¥1300) with baths, saunas, a pool and a water slide. A free shuttle bus runs to and from the station. ❼–❽

Gōdo Kamisanno-machi ℡0577/33-0870. In the heart of San-machi Suji, you pass through a low, paper-covered door to enter this quirkily decorated ryokan. No English is spoken, so you might need to get some help making a booking from the information centre. Rates include breakfast; dinner isn't available. ❻

Hida Takayama Tenshō-ji Youth Hostel 83 Tenshō-ji-machi ℡0577/32-6345, ℻35-2986. If you don't mind the usual rules, this hostel, attached to one of the nicer temples in Teramachi, is a good (and tranquil) place to stay. Dorm beds are ¥3000 per person; for ¥1000 extra you can have a room to yourself, including a TV. Take a bus from the station to the Betsuin-mae stop and walk east for another couple of minutes. Bikes can be rented for ¥600 a day.

Orion Plaza Hotel 6-15 Hana-satochiya ℡0577/34-5677, ℻34-5676. This down-at-heel business hotel beside the station offers cramped, no-frills rooms from ¥3300 with a common bathroom – the cheapest accommodation deal in Takayama. ❹

Pension Anne Shirley 87 1297-1 Yamaguchi-chō ℡0577/32-6606, ℯshirley@lilac.ocn.ne.jp. Delightful Western-style pension on the edge of town, run by an English-speaking couple. There are also some tatami rooms, and evening meals (¥3000) include local delicacies such as *iwana* (river trout). ❺

Rickshaw Inn 54 Suehiro-chō ℡0577/32-2890, ⓦwww.rickshawinn.com. Excellent-value inn in the heart of town, with friendly English-speaking owners. The mainly tatami rooms are all furnished to a high standard and you can relax in the comfy lounge with a daily English newspaper and magazines, and cook in a small kitchen. Good-value single rooms. ❺

Sōsuke 1-64 Okamoto-machi ℡0577/32-0818. Good-value traditional minshuku, about ten minutes' walk west of the station, opposite the *Takayama Green Hotel*. Meals available (from ¥3000 per person per day). ❹

Sumiyoshi 21-4 Honmachi ℡0577/32-0228, ⓦwww.sumiyoshi-ryokan.co. Delightful, *gaijin*-friendly ryokan with a great riverside location. The staff are very friendly and the place is chock full of interesting antiques and knick-knacks. ❺–❻

Takayama Green Hotel 2-180 Nishinoishiki-chō ℡0577/33-5500, ⓦwww.takayama-gh.com. The highlight of this vast upmarket hotel, 1km west of the station, is its spacious onsen baths, which include landscaped rotemburo. There's also a good range of restaurants, including one overlooking a

The Town

The best place to start your explorations in Takayama is at the **Hida Folk Village** (daily 8.30am–5pm; ¥700, ⑩www.hidanosato.org), twenty minutes' walk west of Takayama Station, in a lovely location overlooking the mountains. This outdoor museum of over twenty traditional buildings gathered from the Hida area is a fascinating place to wander around, especially if you're not planning on visiting the *gasshō-zukuri* thatched houses of the Shirakawa-gō and Gokayama districts (see p.452).

The main entrance is roughly 600m uphill, past the first car park and old houses and opposite a row of giftshops. The ticket office has a good English map of the museum and a rather lyrical English-language taped commentary which you can listen to while wandering the grounds. The route winds in a clockwise direction around a central pond, and you're free to explore inside the houses, many of which have displays of farm implements and folk crafts relating to their former owners. At the end of the route, next to the ticket gate, are four old houses where you might catch real artists working at traditional crafts such as lacquering and woodcarving. The old houses at the bottom of the hill comprise the **Hida Folk Museum**, but are little different from those in the main village. If you don't fancy walking or cycling to the museum, take a bus (¥220 each way) from the terminal beside Takayama Station; they run to the village every thirty minutes during the day. Alternatively, the Hida-no-Sato Setto-ken discount return ticket (¥900) includes entrance to the village.

Roughly 1km west of Hida Folk Village is the enormous **Main World Shrine**, headquarters of the Sūkyō Mahikari religious sect. You'll be able to see its golden roof, topped with a huge red snooker ball, quite clearly from the village. It's worth getting closer to check out the shrine's stupendous architecture – including an unbelievably accurate copy of Mexico City's Quetzalcoatl Fountain and two vaguely Islamic-looking towers. The interior, operatically kitsch, is built like a stage set for a cast of thousands. On leaving, you'll probably welcome the offer of a sip of sake to jolt you back to reality.

On the road up to the Hida Folk Village, look out for the elegant and modern **Hida Takayama Museum of Art** (daily 9am–5pm; ¥1300). Although admission is expensive, it's worth forking out to see the wonderful glass collection and Art Nouveau interiors. Near the entrance is a beautiful glass fountain by René Lalique, which once stood in the Paris Lido; further on, the collection includes lustrous objects d'art by Gallè, Tiffany glass lamps and rooms designed by Charles Rennie Mackintosh and the Vienna Secessionists. The museum also has a pleasant café (see p.450).

San-machi Suji

Before you cross the Miya-gawa to the area of old merchants' houses, make your way to the town's feudal-era government complex, **Takayama-jin'ya** (daily 8.45am–4.30pm, April–Oct until 5pm; ¥420), at the end of Hachikenmachi-dōri, five minutes' walk southeast of the station. This small-scale palace, originally built in 1615 and the only building of its kind left in Japan, was the seat of power for the Hida area's governor, appointed by the shogun. Most of the buildings seen today, including a torture chamber and a rice storehouse, date from reconstruction in 1816, and the best way to explore them is to go on one of the free guided tours in English which take around 45 minutes.

Every day country women come into town from the surrounding mountains to sell vegetables, fruit and flowers at one of Takayama's two **morning markets** (*asa ichi*) in front of the *jin'ya*. The more attractive market is strung out along the east bank of the Miya-gawa, between the Kaji-bashi and Yayoi-bashi bridges, and takes place from 7am (6am in summer) until around noon. You can buy local handicrafts here and grab a cheap coffee or local beer.

Cross the Naka-bashi from Takayama-jin'ya and you'll find the **San-machi Suji** area of dark wooden merchant houses dating from the mid-nineteenth century. The quarter's three narrow streets are most evocative at dusk, when the crowds have thinned. During the day, you'll have to negotiate your way through rickshaws and tourists pottering in and out of craft shops, cafés and sake breweries, marked out by the giant balls of cedar leaves hanging in front of their entrances.

You can easily overdose on San-machi Suji's plethora of small and frequently uninteresting museums, many of which are a waste of time and money. The best plan is to head to the north end of the district to the handsome **Kusakabe Mingei-kan** (daily 8.30am–5pm; ¥500), the home of the Kusakabe family, dating from 1879, and an outstanding example of Takayama's renowned carpentry skills. In the shaded courtyard between the main home and the storehouses, now stocked with folkcrafts, you'll be offered a refreshing cup of tea and a rice cracker. The **Yoshijima-ke** (daily 9am–5pm; ¥500) next door is very similar; you'd be better off walking east for a minute to the delightful **Inrō Museum** (April–Nov daily 9am–5pm; ¥500). *Inro* are the antique ornamental boxes of tiered compartments held together on a cord with a *netsuke* (toggle fastener). The highly detailed decoration on the boxes and the *netsuke* is a valued Japanese art, and this museum has some exquisite examples among its collection of three hundred pieces.

Festival floats, temples and shrines

From the Inro Museum turn right and walk east to the precincts of the Sakurayama Hachiman-gū shrine, where you'll find the **Takayama Yatai Kaikan** (daily 8.30am–5.30pm; ¥820), a large exhibition hall for four of the multi-tiered and elaborately decorated *yatai* (floats) used in the town's spring and autumn parades. At least once a year all eleven floats and the golden *mikoshi* (portable shrine) are displayed inside the huge glass case that you wind your way around at different levels so you can see all of the *yatai* decoration, including the *karakuri* (mechanical dolls operated by up to eight puppeteers). Many of the floats date from the seventeenth century; they are usually stored in the tall storehouses (*yatai-gura*) that you'll notice around Takayama. The entrance charge also includes the **Sakurayama-Nikkō-kan**, a hall displaying a dazzling one-tenth scale replica of 28 buildings from Nikkō's Tōshōgu shrine, where a computer controls the lighting to reproduce sunrise and sunset.

If you have time, check out the enjoyable demonstration of automated *karakuri* puppets in the **Shishi Kaikan** (daily 8.30am–5.30pm; ¥600), on the south side of the shrine. A video of a *shishi* (mythical lion) dance, common to festivals in the Takayama area, is screened at regular intervals during the day, and you can also see displays of many lion masks and musical instruments used in these dances.

Following the narrow Enako-gawa southeast, towards the hills from the Sakurayama Hachiman-gū, will bring you to the tranquil area of **Higashiyama Teramachi**, where thirteen temples and five shrines are dotted among the soaring pine trees. None of the holy places is particularly significant, but they are linked by a pleasant walk that goes over the river to

Shiroyama-kōen, a wooded park standing on the remains of Lord Kanamori's castle, destroyed over three hundred years ago; you can still trace the donjon's foundations on the top of the hill, but the view across Takayama is now largely obscured by trees. The route is signposted and you can pick up a map from the tourist information office. The youth hostel (see p.447) is in Tenshō-ji, one of the temples in the middle of the route, around which are clustered the most interesting of the other temples and shrines.

Eating and drinking

The best thing to sample at Takayama's numerous **restaurants** is the area's speciality, *sansai ryōri*, dishes which use local mountain vegetables, ferns and wild plants. Try *sansai soba*, buckwheat noodles topped with the greens, or *hōba miso*, vegetables mixed with miso paste and roasted on a magnolia leaf. *Hoba* beef is also excellent. A delicious snack you'll see sold around town is *mitarashi-dango* – pounded rice balls dipped in soy sauce and roasted on skewers. Many of the San-machi Suji tourist restaurants are only open at lunch, when they can get very busy.

The Asahimachi area between the station and the Miya-gawa is the best place to track down convivial **bars**; a good one to try is *Red Hill*, at the northern end of the district. You'll get a warm welcome on arrival at this small place, which serves a good range of bottled beer from around the world and tasty ethnic food.

Don't leave town without sampling some of the local **sake**; the breweries in San-machi Suji hold free tastings of new sake in January and February. The town has also embraced the *ji-biiru* (regional beer) boom, and several places around the shopping street Kokubunji-dōri now stock the Hida Takayama, Konkon and Kori Kori no Koku labels.

Restaurants and bars

The Alice Yashugawa-dōri. Recently made-over café with aproned waitresses serving faithfully executed *yōshoku*, Japanese takes on Western dishes such as steak and omelettes. The lunchtime set menus (around ¥1000) are good value.

Bistro Mieux 1-55-3 Sowa-chō ☎0577/36-0149. Stylish, modern French bistro where you can eat Hida beef served carpaccio style, among other dishes. Their more casual bar opposite does good set lunch and dinner deals. Closed Thurs.

Cafè NID Cute contemporary café-bar beside the Takayama-jin'ya, serving a range of Asian dishes you can eat while flicking through their style mags. There's a photo menu and a good set lunch for ¥1000. Closed Tues.

Hisadaya 11-3 Kamisanno-machi ☎0577/32-0216. Excellent set lunches of *sansai ryōri* (¥1300 per person) served in the tatami rooms of one of the San-machi Suji's old merchants' houses. Daily 11am–3pm.

Kuniyasu Honmachi dōri. Pleasant riverside vegetarian café with outdoor tables and a good-value buffet (you pay according to the weight of the food). The carrot leaf tempura is delicious. Daily 10am–8pm; Tues till 6pm.

The Mackintosh Tearoom Attached to the Hida Takayama Museum of Art (see p.448) and modelled on the famous tearooms in Glasgow, designed by Charles Rennie Mackintosh. Pasta and pizza cost around ¥1000 and the specially blended tea is a pricey ¥500 a cup, but the view across the mountains is lovely, and you can eat outside. Daily except Tues 9am–5.30pm.

Myogaya There's excellent vegetarian food at this relaxed natural-food restaurant and shop. The brown rice and organic veggie set menu is good value at ¥1000, and the cook will avoid using salt and fat if you ask her. Daily except Tues 8am–5pm, Sat until 7pm.

Rengaya Modern *izakaya* on the west side of the Kaji-bashi, serving some of the local micro-brews on tap. A good place to go with a crowd of people and share a range of nibbly dishes.

Susaki ☎0577/32-0023, ⓦ www.ryoutei-susaki.com. A meal at this *ryōtei* run by the same family since 1794 and serving *honzen* cuisine, similar to *kaiseki* in style and presentation, will be a guaranteed highlight of your visit to Japan. The meal is perfectly balanced in taste and presentation, the service friendly, the setting serene and

atmospheric. Worth every penny of the ¥11,000 or
so per person. It's just across the Nakabashi
Bridge on the edge of San-machi Suji.
Suzuya 24 Hanakawa. Just off Kokubunji-dōri,
this beamed family restaurant is a great place to
sample *sansai ryōri*, and especially the nutty
miso paste cooked on a leaf over a charcoal brazier. There's an English menu with pictures and

friendly waitresses to assist you, and you can
either sit at tables or on tatami. Best for lunch or
an early dinner, since last orders are at 8pm.
Closed Tues.
Yoshikawa 83 Kamisanno-machi. This small, cute
craftsy café with a photo menu is a good place to
sample traditional Japanese sweets, with green
tea or coffee. Daily 9am–6pm.

Furukawa

With its old storehouses by a canal, charming temples and good museums,
FURUKAWA is like a compact version of Takayama, and all the more delightful for that. In addition, this little riverside town, 15km north of Takayama, is
generally free of crowds and giftshops; the only time it's busy is during the
Furukawa Matsuri (April 19 & 20), which celebrates the coming of spring
with a grand parade of wonderfully decorated floats. The highlight is the midnight procession, **Okoshi Daiko**, where hundreds of men, clad only in baggy
white underpants and belly bands, compete to place small drums, tied to long
logs, on top of a portable stage bearing the huge main drum, which is all the
while being solemnly thumped. The men also balance atop tall poles and spin
around on their stomachs.

It shouldn't take you more than three hours to cover the town's main sights,
which are all within easy walking distance of Furukawa Station. West of the station is the **Shirakabe-dozō** district, where a row of white earthen storehouses has been preserved beside a narrow, gently flowing canal, packed with carp.
Follow the canal for five minutes to your left until you reach the main road
leading to the river. Beside the bridge you'll see **Honkō-ji**, an attractive temple decorated with the intricate carving and carpentry for which the town is
famous.

From the temple walk back towards the centre of town along Ichino-machi-
dōri, where you'll find the two-hundred-year-old candle shop **Mishimaya**;
there are regular demonstrations by a candlemaker in the front of the shop.
Further along, look up for the cedar leaf balls hanging outside the **sake breweries**. On the corner of the street, in front of the town's central square, you'll
see a shop where paper lanterns are made.

It's worth buying the ¥1000 ticket to visit all the museums in the square.
The **Hida Craftsman Culture Hall** (daily 9am–5pm; ☎0577/73-3511)
has displays highlighting local carpenters' art and skills, showing how buildings are made from jointed wooden beams without the use of nails. In the
Furukawa Festival Hall (daily 9am–4.30pm) you get up close to two of
the nine *yatai* used in the *matsuri* parade and watch a three-dimensional film
of the festival, see a computer-controlled performance by one of the puppets on the floats and check out local craftsmen at work. Look out, too, for
the convincing crushed beer cans and bowls of peanuts carved from wood
in the display cabinets. The drums used in the festival are in an open hall on
the square; on the second Sunday in October all the *yatai* are displayed in
the square, too.

If you've time to spare, the **Hida Forestry Museum** (9am–5pm; ¥300;
☎0577/73-3321), a couple of minutes' walk east of the station, has displays
of more local crafts and industries, including sculptures woven from straw,
plus a slide show of local beauty spots. The best time to visit is at the weekends, when there are demonstrations of rice-straw sculpture and traditional
weaving.

Practicalities

Furukawa is an easy day-trip from Takayama, with frequent **trains** and **buses** taking at most thirty minutes to reach the town; the local train is the cheapest option, at ¥230. The station name is Hida-Furukawa; the **Kita–Hida tourist information booth** (daily 9am–5.30pm; ☎0577/73-3180) is just outside. You can pick up a town map here and the staff are helpful, but don't speak English; it's best to make detailed enquiries at Takayama first. The town's website is ⓦwww.town.furukawa.gifu.jp.

About the only reason for **staying overnight** is if you're planning on hiking up into the surrounding mountains. The best base to do this from is the modern *Hida Furukawa Youth Hostel* (☎0577/75-2979; ¥3500 per person). The hostel is housed in a homely wooden cabin set amid rice fields a fifteen-minute bus ride from Hida-Furukawa Station; there's good food, and bike rental can be arranged. You need to take a bus to Shinrin-kōen from the stand opposite the JR station – check with the tourist information booth as to the times.

The main **eating** options are clustered within a minute's walk of the station. The best deal is at *Shinanoya* (☎0577/73-2447), a cosy bar with counter seats serving a ¥800 buffet lunch where the freshly cooked dishes just keep coming. Next door is *Matsuya* (☎0577/73-2929; closed Thurs), serving set meals of *sansai ryōri* dishes from ¥2000. If you want to try out the tender local beef, *Maeda* (daily except Thurs 11.30am–2pm; ☎0577/73-2852) on the right-hand corner of the junction with the road from the station, has set meals starting at ¥2500.

Shirakawa-gō and Gokayama

The quaint World Heritage Site villages of the **Shirakawa-gō** and **Gokayama** areas, northwest of Takayama, were among the many fabled bolt holes of the Taira clan after their defeat at the battle of Dannoura (see "History", p.935), though they're no longer quite as remote as they once were, especially with the gradual completion of the new motorway from Takayama to Toyama. Until the mid-twentieth century these villages, with their distinctive, thatched A-frame houses, were almost entirely cut off from fast-modernizing Japan. The damming of the Shō-kawa in the 1960s, together with the drift of population away from the countryside, threatened the survival of this rare form of architecture called *gasshō-zukuri* (see box on p.454). In 1971, local residents began a preservation

Shirakawa-gō and Gokayama

Shirakawa-gō	*Shirakawa-gō*	白川郷
Ogimachi	*Ogimachi*	荻町
Doburoku Matsuri Exhibition Hall	*Doburoku Matsuri-no-Yakata*	どぶろく祭りの館
Gasshō-zukuri Folklore Park	*Gasshō-zukuri Minka-en*	合掌造り民家園
Museum of Daily Life	*Seikatsu Shiryōkan*	生活資料館
Myōzen-ji Temple Museum	*Myōzen-ji Hakubutsukan*	明善寺博物館
Accommodation		
Furusato	Furusato	ふるさと
Yosobe-e	Yosobe-e	よそべえ
Gokayama	*Gokayama*	五箇山
Suganuma	*Suganuma*	菅沼
Ainokura	*Ainokura*	相倉
Murakami-ke	*Murakami-ke*	村上家

movement, which has been so successful that the three tiny communities of **Ogimachi** in Gifu-ken, and **Suganuma** and **Ainokura** in neighbouring Toyama-ken, are in danger of being swamped by the million visitors who now tramp through each year in search of the lost Japan of the popular imagination.

The glut of tourists is unlikely to abate at these villages, designated a World Heritage Site by UNESCO in 1995, but it's still worth braving the crowds to see the remarkable thatched buildings, in idyllic valleys surrounded by forests and mountains. The most popular village is the largest, Ogimachi, which has several small museums and the Gasshō-zukuri Folklore Park, a showcase for 25 unusual buildings. If you want to experience a more authentic atmosphere, head for the smaller villages of Suganuma and Ainokura, and stay overnight in a minshuku in a *gasshō-zukuri* house.

Ogimachi

In the shadow of the sacred mountain Hakusan, **OGIMACHI** village, some 30km northwest of Takayama, is where you'll find the largest collection of **gasshō-zukuri** houses (see box on p.454) within the Shirakawa-gō area of the Shō-kawa valley. Many of the thatched houses were moved here when threatened by the damming of the Shō-kawa, and this makes for rather a contrived scene, not helped by the major road that cuts through its centre, bringing a daily overdose of tourists. It's not all about hype, however; the village is populated by families living in most of the homes, farming rice and other crops in the surrounding rice fields.

A good way to start your explorations is by hiking up to the lookout spot (*tenbōdai*) about ten minutes' walk north of the main Gasshō-Shūraku bus stop, from where you can get a good view of the village's layout and a great photo of the thatched houses. The **Wada-ke** (daily 9am–5pm; ¥300), with a lily pond in front, is the first of several "museum" houses you'll pass on your way back to the village centre. Inside, lacquerware and other household items used by the Wada family, who lived here for over two hundred years, are displayed. Five minutes' walk further south stands the five-storey **Myōzen-ji Temple Museum** (daily 9am–5pm; ¥300). This huge building was once the living quarters for the priests and monks at the attached temple; on its upper floors you can see where over a tonne of silk cocoons were cultivated each year. Gaps in the floorboards allowed the smoke from the *irori* fire to permeate the whole building, preserving the wood and thatch. The thatched temple is connected by a narrow passageway to the main house and outside you'll also notice a thatched bell tower.

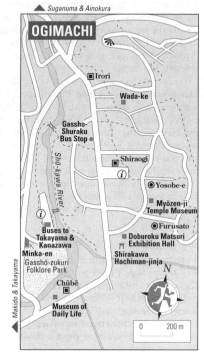

▲ Suganuma & Ainokura

OGIMACHI

- Irori
- Wada-ke
- Gassho-Shuraku Bus Stop
- Shō-kawa River
- Shiraogi
- Yosobe-e
- Myōzen-ji Temple Museum
- Furusato
- Buses to Takayama & Kanazawa
- Minka-en
- Gasshō-zukuri Folklore Park
- Doburoku Matsuri Exhibition Hall
- Shirakawa Hachiman-jinja
- Chūbē
- Museum of Daily Life
- Makido & Takayama

N

0   200 m

Praying-hands houses

Gasshō-zukuri means "praying hands", because the sixty-degree slope of the thatched roofs is said to recall two hands joined in prayer. Although the locals were once fervent Buddhists, it's likely that the roofs were built like this for more practical reasons, since the sharp angle protects the buildings from the effects of the heavy snowfall in this area. The size of the houses is the result of a shortage of land and resources in this remote and mountainous area: generations of the same family had to live together, and the upper storeys of the home were used for industries such as making gunpowder and cultivating silkworms. The thatched roofs – often with a surface area of around six hundred square metres – are made of *susuki* grass, native to the northern part of the Hida region (wooden shingles were used in the south), and have to be replaced every thirty to forty years.

Since it can cost ¥20 million to rethatch an entire roof, many of the houses fell into disrepair until the government stepped in with grants in 1976, enabling the locals to keep up their house-building traditions. The local preservation society decides which buildings are most in need of repair each year and helps organize the *yui*, a two-hundred-strong team who cooperate to rethatch one side of a roof in two days flat. Despite these initiatives, however, there are now fewer than two hundred examples of *gasshō-zukuri* houses left in the Hida region.

Continuing south of the temple will bring you to the village's main shrine, **Shirakawa Hachiman-jinja**, next to which stands the **Doburoku Matsuri Exhibition Hall** (May–Nov daily 9am–4pm; ¥300), devoted to the annual festival (Oct 14–19), which involves the making of *doburoku*, a rough milky sake. The exhibition itself is small, but you can watch a good video in Japanese about life in the village and try a drop of the thick and potent alcohol on the way out. At the far southern end of Ogimachi you'll find the ramshackle **Museum of Daily Life** (daily 9am–4.30pm; ¥300), where you can weave your way through all kinds of intriguing junk, including bearskins and beautifully carved wooden headrests.

Reached by a footbridge across on the west side of the Shō-kawa is the **Gasshō-zukuri Folklore Park** (April, May, July & Sept–Nov daily except Thurs 8.40am–5pm; Aug daily 8am–5.30pm; Jan–March, June & Dec daily except Thurs 9am–4pm; ¥500), an open-air museum of some 25 buildings gathered together from around the region. This is a lifeless place to wander around compared to the real village on the opposite riverbank, but it is quiet and you can see demonstrations of handicrafts, such as weaving and carving, in some of the buildings, as well as rest and have a free cup of tea in the Nakano Chōjirō family house near the entrance. Just outside the park is the **Minka-en**, the village hall where you can don an apron and learn how to make soba noodles. The two-hour sessions cost ¥1800 and must be booked in advance on ☎05769/6-1231.

Practicalities

There are six daily direct **buses** from Takayama to Ogimachi (1hr 45min; ¥2400 one way, ¥4300 return), with two of these services continuing on to Kanazawa. Heading north from Ogimachi to Takaoka (see p.456) there are four daily buses (¥2350). This is a good area to **rent a car**; try Eki Rent-a-Car at Takayama Station (☎0577/33-3522).

The **tourist information office** (daily 9am–5pm; ☎05769/6-1013), next to the car park south of the Gasshō-Shuraku bus stop, is staffed by helpful assistants. They don't speak English, but can provide you with a good English booklet about the village and help arrange accommodation. There's a second information office in car park beside the Gasshō-zukuri Folklore Park, where the buses stop.

The only way of seeing Ogimachi minus the crowds is to **stay** overnight. There are several nice minshuku in the thatched-roof homes to choose from, all of which include breakfast and dinner in their rates. *Yosobe-e* (☎05769/6-1172; ❻) is a small place, one minute's walk northeast of the Gasshō-Shuraku tourist office, recently restored and with an *irori* fireplace. *Furusato* (☎05769/6-1033; ❺), just south of Myōzen-ji, is larger, has a stuffed bear in the hall and other more endearing touches throughout its tatami rooms.

For **eating**, try *Irori* on the main road at the north end of the village, opposite the petrol station, where you can sit around a raised hearth whilst enjoying the good-value set lunches (¥1000), which include fish, noodles or tofu. Overlooking the river next to the Museum of Daily Life is the large *Chūbē* restaurant, where you can feast on the mountain vegetable cuisine, *sansai ryōri*, from ¥1300 per person. *Shiraogi*, opposite the Gasshō-Shuraku tourist office, is a bit more expensive but has an English menu and offers a set menu of local delicacies (ask for the *shiraogi-setto*), including trout and miso bean paste, for ¥2600.

Suganuma, Ainokura and around

Route 156 along the Shō-kawa valley tunnels through the mountains, running for the most part alongside the frequently dammed river as it meanders north. Some 10km from Ogimachi, the road passes the quaint hamlet of **SUGANU-MA**: just fourteen houses, including some *gasshō-zukuri*, beside a sharp bend in the river. This is the smallest village of the three in the World Heritage Site, but it still has two museums, the **Gokayama Minzoku-kan** and the **Enshō-no-Yakata** (daily May–Nov 9am–4pm; ¥210 per museum, or ¥300 combined entrance). The former has more artefacts from daily life, while the latter concentrates on the production of gunpowder, made here because the remote location allowed the ruling Kaga clan to keep it secret.

Some 4km from Suganuma, it's worth stopping off briefly in the modern village of Kaminashi to inspect the **Murakami-ke** (daily except Wed 8.30am–5pm; ¥300), one of the oldest houses in the valley, dating from 1578. The owner gives guided tours around the tatami rooms, pointing out the sunken pit beside the entrance where gunpowder was once made, and finishing with spirited singing of folk tunes accompanied by a performance of the *bin-zasara*, a rattle made of wooden strips.

The last of the three World Heritage Site villages, and possibly the loveliest, is **AINOKURA**, 4km further north of Kaminashi. To reach the village you'll need to hike uphill for around thirty minutes from the modern village of Shimonashi; you could also try hitching a lift, which isn't difficult since Ainokura attracts so many visitors. This is its main problem. Despite the idyllic hillside location and lack of motorized transport in the village itself, Ainokura can feel like hell on earth as you battle past yet another group of camera-toting day-trippers. Catch it on a quiet day, or after the crowds have gone home, however, and you'll think quite the opposite.

Look out for the English map on a sign in the car park at the entrance to the village – it shows various trails up into the surrounding hills. The giftshop in the white building in the centre of the village doubles as the minshuku information centre; if you want to stay overnight in one of the thatched houses, this is the place to head first, although there's no English spoken. There's also the **Ainokura Minzoku-kan** (daily 8.30am–5pm; ¥200), a tiny museum of daily life, including examples of the area's handmade paper and toys.

The infrequent **buses** that run between Ogimachi and Takaoka (see below) also pass by Ainokura and Suganuma. The JR Jōhana line runs from Takaoka to Jōhana, where you can pick up a bus to the Gokayama area.

Takaoka, Toyama and around

Head northeast from the Gokayama valley and you'll reach the modern coastal cities of Takaoka and, further west, the prefectural capital of Toyama. Neither city is worth stopping over in and you'd do well to press on south along the Sea of Japan coast to Kanazawa and the more scenic Noto Hantō peninsula (see p.467).

The only thing **TAKAOKA** is famous for is its Daibutsu, a large statue of the Buddha, cast in 1933, about ten minutes' walk north of the station. The statue is only worth seeing if you have time to kill while waiting for a train – this might be the case if you're using the JR Jōhana line, which starts in Takaoka and goes part of the way towards Gokayama (see p.452). You can pick up a map of the town from the **tourist information booth** (daily 10am–6pm; ☎0766/23-6645), beside the ticket gate at the station; they can make accommodation bookings if you're stuck for somewhere to stay.

Some 17km further west, straddling the mouth of the Jinzū-gawa, is the workaday prefectural capital **TOYAMA**, a good starting point for excursions along the Alpine Route (see opposite) to Nagano-ken. The city's castle, 1km south of the station, is a replica of the original and now houses the **Museum of Local History** (Tues–Sun 9am–4.30pm; ¥210), which is currently under renovation and due to reopen in 2005. If you have time to spare, the best place to head is the **Toyama Municipal Folkcraft Village** (Tues–Sun 9am–4.30pm; ¥630), where eight museums highlighting local arts, crafts and industries are gathered together at the foot of the Kureha hills. Beside the museums you'll also find the atmospheric **Chōkei-ji** temple, with its Gohyaku Rakan terraces, containing over five hundred miniature stone statues of the Buddha's disciples. To reach the village, take a bus from stop #14 in front of the Hokuriku Bank Building opposite Toyama Station to Minzoku Minga Mura, and then walk for five minutes.

Takaoka, Toyama and around

Takaoka	Takaoka	高岡
Toyama	Toyama	富山
Toyama Municipal Folkcraft Village	Toyama Minzoku Minga Mura	富山民族民芸村
Toyoko Inn	Toyoko In	東横イン
Tateyama-Kurobe Alpine Route	Tateyama-Kurobe Arupen Rūto	立山黒部アルペンルート
Murodō	Murodō	室堂
Shinano-Ōmachi	Shinano-Ōmachi	信濃大町
Hotel Tateyama	Hoteru Tateyama	ホテル立山
Tateyama Murodō Sansō	Tateyama Murodō Sansō	立山室堂山荘

The **tourist information booth** (daily 8.30am–8pm; ☏076/432-9751, Ⓦ www.tic-toyamal.or.jp), beside the central exit at Toyama Station, has a good selection of leaflets on local attractions and English-speaking staff who will help book accommodation. You should also be able to get here a copy of *What's Happening*, a monthly English newsletter (with parts in Chinese, Portuguese and Russian), put out by the Toyama International Centre (☏076/444-2500). Toyama's banks, main post office and shops are all within easy walking distance of the station.

If you need **accommodation**, there are plenty of business hotels around Toyama Station; a good option is the *Toyoko Inn* (☏076/405-1045, Ⓦ www.toyoko-inn.com; ❹), including a light breakfast and free Internet access.

Tateyama-Kurobe Alpine Route

If you're in no hurry and don't mind shelling out ¥10,320 – or the constant changes of transport – a dramatic way to travel from the Sea of Japan coast across the Alps to Nagano-ken or vice versa is to follow the **Tateyama–Kurobe Alpine Route**. The ninety-kilometre route, using buses, trains, funicular and cable cars, is only open from about April 20 to November 20, depending on the snow, and is at its busiest between August and October, when on certain sections you may have to wait a while for a seat or spot on the cable car (numbered tickets will be issued for order of boarding). Delays apart, it takes about six hours to traverse the roof of Japan, but it's advisable to start early so you have some time to wander around.

Starting from Toyama, take the Toyama Chihō Tetsudō line to the village of **Tateyama** at the base of Mount Tateyama (45min; ¥1170), one of the three most sacred mountains in Japan after Mount Fuji and Mount Hakusan. Change here onto the Tateyama Cable Railway for the seven-minute journey (¥700) up to the small resort of **Bijo-daira** (Beautiful Lady Plateau). One of the best parts of the journey follows, taking the Tateyama Kōgen bus (55min; ¥1660) up the twisting Alpine road, which early in the season is still piled high on either side with snow, to the terminal at **Murodō**. Only five minutes north of the bus terminal is the **Mikuriga-ike**, an Alpine lake in a fifteen-metre-deep volcanic crater and, twenty minutes' walk further on, **Jigokudani** (Hell Valley), an area of boiling hot springs. There are also several longer hikes you can do around Murodō – through some beautiful and dramatic Alpine scenery – which is the best place to end your journey along the Alpine Route if you're concerned about the cost, and prefer to return to Toyama. There are also several places to stay in Murodō: try *Tateyama Murodō Sansō* (☏076/465-5763; ❺), which is also a good place to head for lunch if you want to avoid the crowds at the pricey *Hotel Tateyama* (☏076/465-3333, Ⓕ465-3336; ❽) at the head of the Tateyama tunnel.

The next section of the journey – a ten-minute bus ride along a tunnel cut through Mount Tateyama to **Daikanbō** – is the most expensive (¥2100). The view from Daikanbō across the mountains is spectacular, and you'll be able to admire it some more as you take the Tateyama Ropeway cable car (¥1260) down to the Kurobe Cable Railway (¥840) for a five-minute journey to the edge of the Kurobe-ko lake formed by the enormous **Kurobe dam** (Ⓦ www.kurobe-dam.com). The ¥51.3 billion dam, blocking one of Japan's deepest gorges, is a highlight of the trip, and there are also boat trips across the lake (30min; ¥930) and some excellent hiking. An easy thirty-minute walk along the lake to the south gets you to a **campsite** on a peninsula, and if you have gear and the Tateyama topographical map – available in any major bookstore – you could continue for days along some of Japan's most spectacular hiking trails.

From the cable railway you'll have to walk 800m across the dam to catch the trolley bus (¥1260) for a sixteen-minute journey through tunnels under Harinoki-dake to the village of **Ogisawa**, across in Nagano-ken. Here you'll transfer to a bus (40min; ¥1330) down to the station at **Shinano-Ōmachi**, where you can catch trains to Matsumoto (p.433) or Hakuba (p.431). You can buy a ticket for the whole trip at either end (¥10,320).

Kanazawa and around

Like several other historic cities on the Sea of Japan coast, **KANAZAWA** has become something of a backwater. Only 150 years ago, this was the fourth largest city in Japan, but despite its diminished importance, the crowds still flock here to visit lovely **Kenroku-en**, one of Japan's top three gardens. In addition, part of the city's **castle** has recently been rebuilt and is well worth visiting, while there are also a number of museums, areas of samurai houses and geisha teahouses, and the fascinating "Ninja" temple, **Myōryū-ji**. As if this wasn't sufficient to persuade you to visit, Kanazawa also makes a conscious effort to welcome *gaijin*, demonstrated by the city's many international centres.

The history of Kanazawa ("Golden Marsh") stretches back over seven hundred years to when the region was known as **Kaga**, a name which is still applied to the city's exquisite crafts, such as silk-dyeing and lacquerware, and its delicately prepared cuisine. The city's heyday was a golden century from 1488, when the ruling Togashi family were overthrown by a collective of farmers and Buddhist monks, and Kanazawa became Japan's only independent Buddhist state. Autonomy ended in 1583, when the *daimyō* Maeda Toshiie was installed as ruler by the warlord Oda Nobunaga, but Kanazawa continued to thrive as the nation's richest province, churning out five million bushels of rice a year.

Around Kanazawa, the rural **Noto Hantō** peninsula north of the city is a great place to kick back and enjoy the slower pace of life. It's also possible on a long day-trip from the city to visit **Eihei-ji**, one of Japan's most atmospheric temples, surrounded by forests and still an active monastery. You can also stay in the temple overnight and experience part of the monks' daily routine.

Arrival, information and getting around

The fastest way of reaching Kanazawa by **train** from Tokyo is to take a Shinkansen to Nagaoka and change to an express train heading west, via Toyama – a total journey time of just under four hours. Slightly cheaper is the daily direct limited express train from Ueno Station in Tokyo, which reaches the city in six hours. Coming from the Kansai area, the Thunderbird express from Ōsaka, via Kyoto, does the journey in two hours and thirty minutes, and there's also a direct express service from Kyoto and Nagoya.

Long-distance **buses** pull up at the bus terminal on the east side of the train station. Komatsu **airport** is 30km southwest of the city and connected to Kanazawa Station by bus (55min; ¥1100). The bus stops first in the Katamachi shopping and entertainment district, close to some hotels.

Providing help for foreign visitors is one of Kanazawa's strengths. In the station is an excellent **tourist information office** (daily 9am–7pm; ☎076/232-6200),

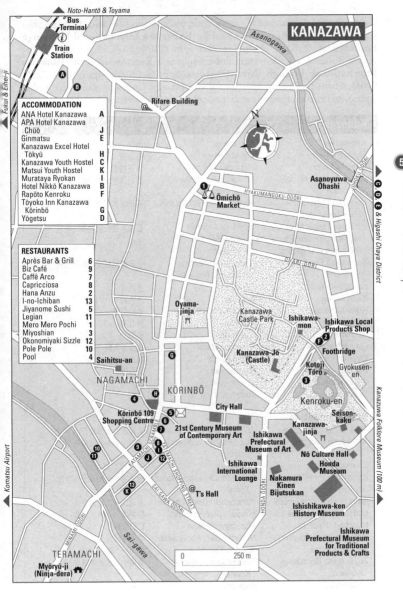

KANAZAWA

Noto-Hantō & Toyama

Bus Terminal

Train Station

Asanogawa

Fukui & Eihei-ji

Rifare Building

ACCOMMODATION

ANA Hotel Kanazawa	A
APA Hotel Kanazawa Chūō	J E
Ginmatsu	
Kanazawa Excel Hotel Tōkyū	H C
Kanazawa Youth Hostel	K
Matsui Youth Hostel	I
Murataya Ryokan	B
Hotel Nikkō Kanazawa	F
Rapōto Kenroku	
Tōyoko Inn Kanazawa Kōrinbō	G D
Yōgetsu	

RESTAURANTS

Après Bar & Grill	6
Biz Café	9
Caffé Arco	7
Capricciosa	8
Hana Anzu	2
I-no-Ichiban	13
Jiyanome Sushi	5
Legian	11
Mero Mero Pochi	1
Miyoshian	3
Okonomiyaki Sizzle	12
Pole Pole	10
Pool	4

Ōmichō Market

HYAKUMANGOKU-ŌDŌRI

Asanoyuwa Ohashi

OHARI-ŌDŌRI

Oyama-jinja

Kanazawa Castle Park

Ishikawa-mon

Ishikawa Local Products Shop

Kanazawa-Jō (Castle)

Footbridge

Saihitsu-an

NAGAMACHI

KŌRINBŌ

Kotoji Tōrō

Gyokusen-en

Kenroku-en

Seison-kaku

Komatsu Airport

Kōrinbō 109 Shopping Centre

City Hall

21st Century Museum of Contemporary Art

Ishikawa Prefectural Museum of Art

Kanazawa-jinja

Nō Culture Hall

Honda Museum

Ishikawa International Lounge

Nakamura Kinen Bijutsukan

T's Hall

Ishishikawa-ken History Museum

Ishikawa Prefectural Museum for Traditional Products & Crafts

KATAMACHI SCRAMBLE

TATEMACHI SHOPPING STREET

SAI-GAWA ŌDŌRI

MINAMI ŌDŌRI

HONDA ŌDŌRI

Sai-gawa

TERAMACHI

Myōryū-ji (Ninja-dera)

0   250 m

CENTRAL HONSHŪ | Kanazawa and around

& Higashi Chaya District

Kanazawa Folklore Museum (100 m)

well stocked with maps and leaflets and with English-speaking staff (daily 10am–6pm) who can book accommodation. You may also be able to arrange for a guide to show you around town for free. Another good place to pop in is the **Ishikawa Foundation for International Exchange** (Mon–Fri 9am–6pm, Sat 9am–5pm; ☎076/262-5931), on the third and fourth floors of the **Rifare Building**, five minutes' walk southeast of the station. This has a library with foreign newspapers and magazines and two widescreen TVs, one showing CNN, the other BBC World, and it's also a good place to meet up with Japanese who want to practise their English. The similar **Kanazawa International Exchange Foundation**, or KIEF (Mon–Fri 9am–6pm; ☎076/220-2522), is also in the Rifare Building, on the second floor, while near Kenroku-en is the **Ishikawa International Lounge** (Mon–Fri 10am–5pm, Sat 10am–4pm; ☎076/221-9901), which runs many free cultural and Japanese-language courses, as well as courses in origami, the tea ceremony, calligraphy and *ikebana*.

Kanazawa

Kanazawa	*Kanazawa*	金沢
Gyokusen-en	*Gyokusen-en*	玉泉園
Higashi Chaya	*Higashi Chaya-gai*	東茶屋街
Ishikawa-ken History Museum	*Ishikawa-ken Rekishi Hakubutsukan*	石川県歴史博物館
Ishikawa Prefectural Museum of Art	*Ishikawa-ken Bijutsukan*	石川県美術館
Ishikawa Prefectural Museum for Traditional Products and Crafts	*Ishikawa-kenritsu Dentō-Sangyō Kōgeikan*	石川県立伝統産業工芸館
Kanazawa Folklore Museum	*Kanazawa Minzoku Bunkazai Tenjikan*	金沢市民俗文化財展示館
Kanazawa Castle	*Kanzawa-jō*	金沢城
Kenroku-en	*Kenroku-en*	兼六園
Komatsu airport	*Komatsu Kūkō*	小松空港
Myōryū-ji	*Myōryū-ji*	妙立寺
Nagamachi	*Nagamachi*	長町
Ōmichō Market	*Ōmichō Ichiba*	近江町市場
Oyama-jinja	*Oyama-jinja*	尾山神社
Saihitsu-an	*Saihitsu-an*	彩筆庵
Seison-kaku	*Seison-kaku*	成巽閣
Teramachi	*Teramachi*	寺町

Accommodation		
ANA Hotel Kanazawa	*ANA Hoteru Kanazawa*	ＡＮＡホテル金沢
APA Hotel Kanazawa Chūō	*Apa Hoteru Kanazawa Chūō*	アパホテル金沢中央
Ginmatsu	*Ginmatsu*	銀松
Kanazawa Excel Hotel Tōkyū	*Kanazawa Ekuseru Hoteru Tōkyū*	金沢エクセルホテル東急
Kanazawa Youth Hostel	*Kanazawa Yūsu Hosuteru*	金沢ユースホステル
Matsui Youth Hostel	*Matsui Yūsu Hosuteru*	松井ユースホステル
Murataya Ryokan	*Murataya Ryokan*	村田屋旅館
Hotel Nikkō Kanazawa	*Hoteru Nikkō Kanazawa*	ホテル日光金沢
Rapōto Kenroku	*Rapōto Kenroku*	ラポート兼六
Tōyoko Inn Kanazawa Kōrinbō	*Tōyoko In Kanazawa Kōrinbō*	東横イン金沢香林坊
Yōgetsu	*Yōgetsu*	陽月

Restaurants		
Capricciosa	*Kapurichōza*	カプリチョーザ
Hana Anzu	*Hana Anzu*	花あんず
Janome Sushi	*Janome Sushi*	蛇の目寿司
Legian	*Rejian*	レジアン
Miyoshian	*Miyoshian*	祢Σ汐籔\

Getting around is easy enough; although Kanazawa is a sprawling city, its main sights are clustered within walking distance of Kōrinbō and Katamachi, the neighbouring downtown areas, ten minutes by bus from the terminal outside the east exit of Kanazawa Station. Kenroku-en is five minutes' walk east of Kōrinbō, and the Nagamachi district of samurai houses lies immediately to the west. **Buses** leave frequently from stops #6, #7 and #8 for both Kōrinbō and Katamachi (¥210).

Accommodation

There are plenty of **hotels** – luxury and mid-range – near the train station, but the most convenient place to be based is in the central **Kōrinbō** district, within easy walking distance of Kenroku-en and other sights. On the east side of the city, **Higashi Chaya** is also a pleasant and atmospheric area to stay – get directions to the minshuku here from the tourist information office at the station.

ANA Hotel Kanazawa 16-3 Shōwa-machi ☎076/224-6111, ⊛www.anahotels-kanazawa.co.jp. Luxury hotel, next to Kanazawa Station, with a grand atrium lobby and comfortable rooms. Its Japanese restaurant overlooks a miniature version of Kenroku-en. **❼**

APA Hotel Kanazawa Chūō 1-5-24 Katamachi ☎076/235-2111, ⊛www.apahotel.com. There are several branches of this rather elegant business hotel in Kanazawa but this is the most central. It also has a hot spring and sauna on the top floor, including outdoor baths, and a Seattle style café in the lobby. Singles start at ¥7000. **❺**

Ginmatsu 1-17-18 Higashi Chaya ☎076/252-3577, ⊜ginmatsu@nifty.com. Pleasant and outstandingly good-value minshuku in the lovely Higashi Chaya district, with a friendly welcome and the cheapest tatami rooms in town. **❹**

Kanazawa Excel Hotel Tōkyū 2-1-1 Kōrinbō ☎076/231-2411, ⊛www.tokyuhotels.co.jp. Upmarket hotel with spacious rooms and old-fashioned decor in an ideal downtown location a short walk from Kenroku-en. **❻**

Kanazawa Youth Hostel 37 Suehiro-machi ☎076/252-3414, ⊕252-8590. Up in the wooded hills on the east side of the city, the larger and more modern of Kanazawa's two hostels has some very nice tatami rooms, does good-value meals, has a kitchen where you can cook for yourself, and rents out bikes. However, the steep, twenty-minute hike up the hill is a disadvantage. Dorm beds ¥2900 per person.

Matsui Youth Hostel 1-9-3 Katamachi ☎076/221-0275. Small, friendly hostel in the heart of Katamachi, with tatami dorms and private rooms for just a little extra. No meals, but free tea and coffee. The 10pm curfew puts a dampener on a night out in the surrounding bars. Dorm beds ¥3100 per person.

Murataya Ryokan 1-5-2 Katamachi ☎076/263-0455, ⊜murataya@spacelan.ne.jp. This small ryokan in the heart of Katamachi has some stylish touches and is run by friendly people used to dealing with foreign guests. The tatami rooms are on the small side, but are well maintained, and you can get a Western-style breakfast for ¥450. **❹**

Hotel Nikkō Kanazawa 2-15-1 Honmachi ☎076/234-1111, ⊛www.hnkanazawa.co.jp. Upmarket, high-rise hotel opposite Kanazawa Station, with a sophisticated modern European design feel to its sleek lobby, restaurants and rooms. **❼**

Rapōto Kenroku 2-5 Kenroku-machi ☎076/231-2000, ⊛www.hokuriku.ne.jp/rapo. A minute's walk from the northern gate of Kenroku-en, this small, pleasant hotel offers good-value Western and tatami rooms, with breakfast included. **❺**

Tōyoko Inn Kanazawa Kōrinbō 1-2-35 Kōrinbō ☎076/265-1045, ⊛www.toyoko-inn.com. Part of the good-value budget business hotel chain. It's a popular place, so it pays to book ahead. **❹**

Yōgetsu 22 Higashi Chaya ☎076/252-0497. Cosy minshuku in a wooden-beamed house dating from the nineteenth century, once the home of a geisha, with small tatami rooms. **❹**

Kenroku-en

Thousands of visitors flock to Kanazawa's star attraction, **Kenroku-en** (daily: March to mid-Oct 7am–6pm; mid-Oct to Feb 8am–4.30pm; ¥300, free third Sun of month), five minutes' walk north of Kōrinbō. Early morning or late afternoon are the best times for catching the garden at its most tranquil, although unless you're exceptionally early you're bound to have your thoughts interrupted at least once by a megaphone-toting guide and party of tourists.

Of the official top three gardens in Japan (Kairaku-en in Mito and Kōraku-en in Okayama are the other two), Kenroku-en – developed over two centuries from the 1670s – is generally regarded as the best. Originally the outer grounds of Kanazawa castle, and thus the private garden of the ruling Maeda clan, Kenroku-en was opened to the public in 1871. Its name, which means "combined six garden", refers to the six horticultural graces that the garden embraces: spaciousness, seclusion, artificiality, antiquity, water and panoramic views. Crowds notwithstanding, it's a lovely place to stroll around, all the more remarkable because an ingenious pumping system keeps the hillside pools full of water and the fountains working.

The main gate to Kenroku-en is on the slope leading up to its western edge and there's another a little further north beside the Renchimon, the original gate to the garden, next to the row of giftshops. From either entrance you'll first see the 300-year-old Hisago-ike (Gourd Pond), so called because it's supposed to have the shape of the vegetable. Into the pond drops the Midori-taki (Green Waterfall), an unusual feature for a Japanese garden and built in 1774, at the same time as the nearby Yūgaotei, a teahouse where you can still take tea for ¥500.

Walking in a clockwise direction up the hill you'll pass Japan's first fountain, constructed in 1861 and operated by the natural pressure of water flowing down from the mountains outside Kanazawa. At the top of the hill is the **Kasumi-ga-ike** (Misty Lake), the largest of Kenroku-en's four ponds and the heart of the garden. The pedestrian jam here is in front of the two-legged **Kotoji Tōrō**, the most famous of Kenroku-en's eighteen stone lanterns, and an obligatory photo opportunity for all tourist groups.

Looking in the opposite direction from the pond, take in the sweeping prospect across towards Kanazawa's old geisha district Higashi Chaya and, weather permitting, the Sea of Japan coast. Throughout the park are many marvellous pine trees, pruned carefully throughout the centuries to achieve a certain shape; look out for the "married pines" at the southern end of the Kasumi-ga-ike, whose trunks are lovingly entwined.

One minute's walk east of the pond is the entrance to the delightful **Seison-kaku** (daily except Wed 8.30am–4.30pm; ¥500), an elegant, two-storey shingle-roofed mansion built in 1863 by the *daimyō* Maeda Nariyasu as a retirement home for his mother. A good English leaflet lists the main architectural and decorative features to look out for, including paintings of fish, shellfish and turtles on the wainscots of the *shōji* sliding screens in the formal guest rooms downstairs. The view from the Tsukushi-no-rōka (Horsetail Corridor) across the mansion's own raked-gravel garden is particularly enchanting, while upstairs the decorative style is more adventurous, using a range of striking colours and materials including, unusually for a Japanese house, glass windows, imported from the Netherlands. These were installed so that the occupants could look out in winter at the falling snow.

Kanazawa-jō and around

Return to the northernmost exit to the gardens to reach the footbridge leading to the **Ishikawa-mon**, the impressive eighteenth-century gateway to the city's castle, **Kanazawa-jō** (daily 9am–4.30pm; ¥300 entry to the castle buildings; ☎076/234-3800). There's been a fortification on the Kodatsuno plateau since 1546, but the castle in its present form dates back mainly to the early seventeenth century. In 2001, part of the inner enclosure was rebuilt using tradi-

△ Matsumoto-jō, Matsumoto

tional methods and plans from the Edo period. These included the three-storey, diamond-shaped Hishi Yagura and Hashizume-mon Tsuzuki Yagura watchtowers, the Gojukken Nagaya corridor linking them, some of the earthern walls, and the Hashizume Bridge and gate leading to the enclosure. The results are stunning, and can best be appreciated inside the buildings, where you can see the intricate joinery and have a look at the one-tenth-scale skeletal model carpenters used to master the complexities of the task.

Parts of the original unrestored castle can be seen within the grounds, as well as an attractive modern garden with traditional elements – an interesting contrast to Kenroku-en. If you head for the Imori-zaka entrance at the southwest corner of the grounds, you'll emerge near the back of the intriguing **Oyama-jinja**, a large shrine dedicated to the first Maeda lord, Toshiie. The shrine is fronted by the **Shinmon**, a square-arched gate with multi-coloured stained glass in its upper tower, designed in 1875 with the help of Dutch engineers and once used as a lighthouse to guide ships towards the coast.

Alternatively, returning to Ishikawa-mon and Kenroku-en's north exit, head along the garden's eastern flank, to the small traditional garden, **Gyokusen-en** (daily April–Nov 9am–4pm; ¥500). Built on two levels on a steep slope, this quiet garden has many lovely features, including mossy stone paths leading past two ponds and a mini waterfall. For ¥500 extra you can enjoy green tea and a sweet in the main villa's tearoom.

Museums southwest of Kenroku-en

There are several museums immediately to the southwest of Kenroku-en, one of the best being the informative **Ishikawa Prefectural Museum for Traditional Products and Crafts** (daily except Thurs 9.30am–4.30pm; ¥300; ☎076/262-2020), in a concrete building beside the Seison-kaku, next to the garden's east exit. The museum displays prime contemporary examples of Kanazawa's rich artistic heritage, including lacquerware, dyed silk, pottery, musical instruments and fireworks. None of the articles is for sale but all have a price tag, so if you take a fancy to one of the gold leaf and lacquer Buddhist family altars, for example, you'll know that it costs ¥4.5 million. A short walk southeast of here, in a lovingly preserved late nineteenth-century wooden school building, the **Kanazawa Folklore Museum** (9.30am–5pm daily; free; ☎076/222-5740) is also worth a look for its eclectic collection of everyday items.

Heading downhill from the gardens you'll pass the **Nō Culture Hall**, where Nō plays are often performed – check with one of the tourist offices (see p.458) for programme details. Beyond here, the **Ishikawa-ken History Museum** (daily 9am–5pm; ¥250; ☎076/262-3236), housed in the striking red-brick army barracks buildings dating from 1910, has displays including a detailed miniature reconstruction of a samurai parade, a grainy black-and-white film of Kanazawa from the early twentieth century, and a reconstruction of a silk-spinning factory.

If you're pressed for time, pass by the small **Honda Museum** (daily except Thurs 9am–5pm; ¥500; ☎076/261-0500), with its family collection of robes, armour and knick-knacks, and the **Nakamura Kinen Bijutsukan** (Mon & Wed–Sun 9am–4.30pm; ¥300; ☎076/221-0751), specializing in tea ceremony *objets d'art*, in favour of the larger **Ishikawa Prefectural Museum of Art** (Tues–Sun 9.30am–5pm; ¥350; ☎076/231-7580), where beautiful examples of calligraphy, kimono, pottery, lacquerware and other relics of the Maeda clan are displayed along with a more eclectic collection of contemporary local art. There are usually special exhibitions held here, which cost extra.

At the time of writing the promising **21st Century Museum of Contemporary Art** (www.art.city.kanazawa.ishikawa.jp), next to the Kanazawa City Hall, was under construction, with a planned opening for 2005.

Nagamachi, Teramachi and Higashi Chaya

Kanazawa escaped bombing during World War II and so was able to preserve some of its traditional inner-city areas. Directly behind Kōrinbō, the **Nagamachi** quarter has a few twisting cobbled streets of samurai houses, protected by thick yellow and grey earthen walls, topped with ceramic tiles. It's an evocative area to wander around, although the modern graffiti scratched into the walls is somewhat distracting. Inside one of the old wooden houses is the *kaga-yūzen* (silk-dyeing) workshop **Saihitsu-an** (daily except Thurs 9–11.45am & 1–4.30pm; ¥500), where a short lecture and demonstration in Japanese is given on this painstaking, highly detailed process of dyeing silk for kimono, after which you can wander around the house and see some of the artists at work behind a glass screen.

A ten-minute walk south of Nagamachi flows the Sai-gawa, on the other side of which is **Teramachi** (Temple Town), an area of narrow streets and several temples. Religious buildings were often grouped together at the entrance to a city in an attempt to deter enemies, a defensive role that is clearly apparent at the unique **Myōryū-ji**, also known as Ninja-dera (daily: March–Oct 9am–4.30pm; Jan, Feb, Nov & Dec 9am–4pm; ¥800), five minutes' walk south of the river. The temple, completed in 1643 and belonging to the Nichiren sect of Buddhism, is associated with the Ninja assassins (see p.427) because of its many secret passages, trick doors and concealed chambers, including a lookout tower that once commanded a sweeping view of the surrounding mountains and coast. To see around the temple you must reserve a place on one of several daily tours (call ☎076/241-0888), conducted in Japanese but pretty self-explanatory.

Also well worth visiting is the **Higashi Chaya** district, a fifteen-minute walk northeast from Kenroku-en across the Asanagawa river. This carefully preserved area of wooden latticed houses on narrow streets was Kanazawa's geisha quarter from 1820, and the winding streets and old-world atmosphere make for an interesting stroll. There are also a couple of teahouses here: the **Ochaya Shima** (9am–6pm daily; ¥400) is the most traditional, while opposite is the **Kaikarō** (9am–6pm, closed Tues; ¥700), which has been refurbished in a more modern style, including an unusual Zen rock garden made entirely of broken chunks of glass and a tearoom with gilded tatami mats. At both you can take tea (without geisha, unfortunately) for a small extra fee. Buses run here directly from Kanazawa Station (get off at the Asanagawa Ōhashi bridge) via the fascinating **Ōmichō Ichiba**, a teeming market brimming with fresh produce and seafood.

Eating, drinking and entertainment

Kanazawa has a great range of **restaurants**. The local cuisine, *kaga ryōri* (see p.419), can be expensive and is best sampled for lunch or at the major hotels, where special set menus are often available. Also worth trying is seafood and sushi; the best place to head is the daily Ōmichō Ichiba market, around which you'll find many small sushi bars and *shokudō* (cafeterias) serving rice-bowl dishes (*donburi*).

The neon-lit drag running south towards the Sai-gawa from Kōrinbō is known locally as the Katamachi Scramble. The warren of streets around here is chock-full of **bars**. Katamachi also has several **cinemas**; pick up a copy of the free English-language newsletter *Uh-huh* from one of the International Exchange offices (see p.460) for performance times. This also has details of Nō plays (enthusiastically nurtured by Kanazawa's arty citizens) and classical music performances.

Restaurants

Biz Café Katamachi ☎076/233 1008. Stylish Southeast Asian café-bar with free Internet access upstairs.

Caffé Arco 1-3-21 Katamachi ☎076/223-7333. The more casual of the two European brasserie-style restaurants in the Prego complex off the main Katamachi scramble. Nice for an alfresco lunch with serve-yourself drinks.

Capricciosa 1-4-18 Tatemachi ☎076/260-8855. Italian chain restaurant serving huge portions of pasta. Close by the Katamachi Scramble, opposite the *Doutor* café.

Hana Anzu ☎076/222-5188. On the 2nd floor of the Ishikawa Local Products shop, a couple of minutes' walk downhill from the north entrance to Kenroku-en. This is an ideal place to sample *kaga-ryōri* with lunch sets starting at ¥1500. The delicious duck stew *jibu* is ¥2500. Daily 11am–6pm.

Janome Sushi Kōrinbō ☎076/231-0093. Set in an attractive building by a gurgling stream, this upmarket sushi restaurant has reasonably priced set menus and also does some *kaga-ryōri* dishes.

Legian ☎076/262-6510. Casual Indonesian café on the east side of Katamachi overlooking the Sai-gawa. Does a good-value lunch (daily noon–3pm) and there's sometimes a cart outside from where you can buy satay sticks.

Miyoshian 1-11 Kenroku-machi ☎076/221-0127. Atmospheric 100-year-old restaurant in Kenroku-en – find it just past the row of shops at the north entrance. Specializes in *kaga ryōri*; try the *bentō* boxed lunches (from ¥1500) or come for a cup of *macha* tea and sweets, overlooking the ornamental pond. You'll need to reserve for the elaborate dinners (¥6000).

Okonomiyaki Sizzle Tatemachi. Fun DIY Japanese pancake restaurant. A photo menu helps you choose which set of ingredients to fry up on the hotplate at your table. Reckon on ¥1000 per person.

Bars and clubs

Après Bar & Grill 3-9 Katamachi ☎076/221-0090. Ground central for the *gaijin* community in Kanazawa and it's easy to see why. The price of a drink gets you free pool, Internet access and even karaoke. The Thai chef does a mean curry and the bar manager's called Elvis. What more could you want? They also have a popular beach bar out at Uchinada, on the coast a few kilometres north of the city, which is popular in summer (July & Aug). Closed Mon.

I-no-Ichiban 1-9-20 Katamachi ☎076/261-0001. The entrance to this hip, modern *izakaya*, on the ground floor of the Sekano Building, is hidden behind a mini bamboo grove. Sit at the bar beside the open kitchen so you can watch the chefs at work.

Mero Mero Pochi Ōmichō Ichiba ☎076/234-5556, ⓦ www.meropochi.com. Non-commerical live house in the Ōmichō Ichiba markets that stages an interesting range of events from art exhibitions to DJ sets. Closed Mon.

Pole Pole 2-31-30 Katamachi ☎076/260-1138. Directly behind the Indonesian restaurant *Legian*, on the road running parallel to the Sai-gawa. Cramped and loud reggae bar serving forty different cocktails and a range of beers, as well as abundant supplies of monkey nuts, the shells of which litter the floor.

Pool 3F Gogui Bldg, 2 Katamachi ☎076/264-4236. This is one of the coolest of the various bars in this building, a short walk behind the 109 building, with a laid-back vibe and a good range of drinks.

Listings

Airlines For ticket reservations, call ANA (☎076/231-3111) or JAL (☎0120-25-5971).
Airport information ☎076/121-9803.
Banks and exchange There are several banks along the main road leading southeast from Kanazawa Station, as well as around Kōrinbō.
Bike rental Bicycles can be rented from outside the west exit of Kanazawa Station (daily

9am–5pm; 2hr for ¥300, or ¥1000 a day).
Bookshops The best selection of English-language books and magazines can be found in the Rifare Building underneath the Ishikawa Foundation for International Exchange, five minutes' walk southeast of Kanazawa Station.
Car rental Toyota Rent-a-lease Ishikawa (☎076/261-4100) and Nippon Rent-a-car

(☏076/263-0919) are both close by Kanazawa Station.

Hospital The main hospital is Kanazawa University Hospital, 13-1 Takaramachi (☏076/262-8151), around 1km southeast of Kenroku-en.

Internet access There's free access at the library on the third floor of the Rifare building, at *Biz Café* and the *Après Bar and Grill*, and at *T's Hall* on Tatemachi street (10.30am–7.30pm; closed Wed). Alternatively, there's 24-hour access at Freaks Cyber Café on the Katamachi Scramble; the first 30 minutes cost ¥280, then it's ¥100 per 30min.

Police The Prefectural Police Office is at 2-1-1 Hirosaka (☏076/262-1161).

Post office The Central Post Office is a long way from any of Kanazawa's main tourist spots. The most convenient branch is the one at Kōrinbō.

Shopping Kanazawa's wealth of local crafts makes it a fantastic place to go shopping for souvenirs and lovely *objets d'art*. Ōhi and Kutani pottery can be bought at many shops around the city (check out the ones along the street leading up to Kenroku-en past City Hall). The Ishikawa Local Products Shop (☏076/222-7788) has a good selection of everything from food products to *washi* paper; it's near the north entrance to Kenroku-en. Also check out the traditional shops of the Hagashi Kuruwa district, in particular the gold-leaf company *Sakuda* (1-3-27 Higashi Chaya ☏076/251-6777) – if you've a few million yen to spare this is the place to get anything from beautiful screens to gold-leaf golf balls.

Taxis Try Ishikawa Kōtsū (☏076/231-4131) or Daiwa Taxi (☏076/221-5166).

Noto Hantō

Jutting out like a gnarled finger into the Sea of Japan is the **Noto Hantō**. One story is that the name "Noto" is derived from an Ainu word, *nopo*, meaning "set apart", but regardless of whether this is true the peninsula's quieter way of life, tied to agriculture and fishery, is certainly worlds away from modern Japan. The

Noto Hantō and Eihei-ji		
Noto Hantō	*Noto Hantō*	能登半島
Hakui	*Hakui*	羽咋
Cosmo Isle Hakui	*Kosumo Airu Hakui*	コスモアイル羽咋
Kami Tokikuni-ke	*Kami-Tokikuni-ke*	上時国家
Keta-taisha	*Keta-taisha*	気多大社
Monzen	*Monzen*	門前
Myōjō-ji	*Myōjō-ji*	妙成寺
Shimo Tokikuni-ke	*Shimo Tokikuni-ke*	下時国家
Sōji-ji	*Sōji-ji*	総持寺
Tsukumo-wan	*Tsukumo-wan*	九十九湾
Wajima	*Wajima*	輪島
Inachu Gallery	*Inachu Bijutsukan*	イナチュウ美術館
Kiriko Kaikan	*Kiriko Kaikan*	キリコ会館
Wajima Kōbō Nagaya	*Wajima Kōbō Nagaya*	輪島工房長屋
Accommodation		
Fukasan	*Fukasan*	ふかさん
Noto Isaribi Youth Hostel	*Noto Isaribi Yūsu Hosuteru*	能登漁火ユースホステル
Shimbashi Ryokan	*Shimbashi Ryokan*	新橋旅館
Wajima Station Hotel	*Wajima Sutēshon Hoteru*	輪島ステーションホテル
Fukui	*Fukui*	福井
Eihei-ji	*Eihei-ji*	永平寺
Eihei-ji Monzen Yamaguchi-sō	*Eihei-ji Monzen Yamaguchi-sō*	永平寺門前山口荘

rugged and windswept west coast has the bulk of what constitutes the Noto Hantō's low-key attractions, while the calmer, indented east coast harbours several sleepy fishing ports, where the silence is broken only by the lapping of waves and the phut-phut of boat engines.

The Noto Hantō is best explored by car or bicycle. Going up the **west coast** of the peninsula from Kanazawa, drive past the wide, sandy Chiri-hama beach, cluttered with day-trippers and their litter, and head briefly inland to the alleged UFO-hotspot of **HAKUI**. Here, in a suitably saucerish hall near the station, you'll find **Cosmo Isle Hakui** (daily except Tues 9am–5pm; ¥800; ⊕0767/22-9888), a fascinating museum devoted to space exploration which houses a great deal of authentic paraphernalia, most impressively the Vostok craft that launched Yuri Gagarin into space in 1961 – it looks like a giant cannonball.

Nearby, set in a wooded grove near the sea, is **Keta-taisha**, Noto's most important shrine. The complex dates from the 1650s, although the shrine is believed to have been founded in the eighth century. It's attractive, but the atmosphere is spoilt by the modern-day commercialization of the place, catering to young lovers who come to seek the blessing of the spirits. A few kilometres further up the coast, **Myōjō-ji** is a seventeenth-century temple with an impressive five-storey pagoda (¥300). Even better is the **Noto-kongō**, a sixteen-kilometre stretch of coast where the pounding Sea of Japan has created fascinating rock formations and cliffs.

Around the midpoint of the west coast is the small town of **MONZEN**, whose most famous attraction is the temple **Sōji-ji** (daily 8am–5pm; ¥300; ⊕0768/42-0005), a training centre for Zen monks. Most of the temple is a twentieth-century reconstruction of much older buildings, but you can take part in the meditation sessions if you get to the temple early enough.

The peninsula's main tourist centre is **WAJIMA**, an appealing fishing port 16km further up the coast, with a colourful morning market (daily 8am–11.30pm, except for the 10th and 25th of each month), where around two hundred vendors set up stalls along the town's main street selling fish, vegetables and other local products. The main street is also home to an incongruous Italian palazzo, inside which is the **Inachū Gallery** (daily 8am–5pm; ¥800). This bizarre museum exhibits reproductions of famous art pieces, such as the *Venus de Milo*, next to original European and Japanese antiques, including a huge pair of jet-black ornamental jars that once belonged to Tokugawa Iemitsu, the third Tokugawa shogun.

Wajima is renowned for its lacquerware and you'll find many shops around town selling it; one of the best is the **Wajima Lacquerware Centre**, beside the Shin-bashi bridge across the Kawarada-gawa on the west side of town. The centre has a display hall (daily 8.30am–5pm; ¥200), where you can see craftsmen at work and see many good examples of their art, some dating from the sixteenth century. Also check out the new **Wajima Kōbō Nagaya** (⊕0768/23-0011) complex of traditional-style wooden buildings where you can engrave lacquerware yourself if you make an advance booking. If lacquerware isn't your thing, head across to the **Kiriko-kaikan** exhibition hall (daily 8am–5pm; ¥600) to see the giant colourful paper lanterns paraded around town in Wajima's lively summer and autumn festivals. The museum also shows videos of the festivals.

The Sosogi coastline between Wajima and the cape Rokkō-zaki is wonderfully scenic, and a great place for hiking past strange rock formations. Near the village of Sosogi you'll pass the **Senmaida**, where over a thousand rice paddies cling to the sea-facing slopes in diminishing terraces. Heading inland towards Iwakura-yama, a steep 357-metre mountain, are two traditional thatched-roof houses that once belonged to the wealthy Tokikuni family, supposed descendants of the vanquished Taira clan (see "Contexts", p.935). The family split in two in the sixteenth century, one part staying in the **Kami Tokikuni-ke** (daily: April–Nov 8.30am–6pm; Jan–March & Dec 8.30am–5pm; ¥420), the other building the smaller **Shimo Tokikuni-ke** (daily: April–Nov 8.30am–5pm; Jan–March & Dec 8.30am–4pm; ¥250), with its attractive attached garden.

On the Noto Hantō's gentler **east coast**, the nicest place to head for is crinkly **Tsukumo-wan**, meaning "99 Indentation Bay". You can get a closer look at the bay's inlets, islands and shoals of fish by hopping on the glass-bottomed boats (daily 8am–5pm; ¥800) that depart from the dock a minute's walk from Tsukumo-wan-Ogi Station on the Noto line. Heading down the coast around Nanao-wan look out for the *Boramachi-yagura*, pyramid-shaped wooden platforms on top of which fishermen once perched waiting for the fish to swim into their nets.

Practicalities

The new **Noto Airport** (T0768/26-2000, Whttp://noto-airport.net), 25 minutes south of Wajima, has two flights a day to and from Tokyo's Haneda Airport (p.97). Otherwise the main access point for the Noto Hantō is Kanazawa, from where you can catch direct **trains** across the lower half of the peninsula to the uninteresting east-coast town of **Nanao** (which can also be reached from Toyama, with a change of trains at Tsubata). More convenient are the **buses** which cruise up the peninsula's central highway from Kanazawa to Wajima, with some going on to Sosogi. There are also direct bus services between Kanazawa and Suzu near the tip of the east coast.

For **getting around** the peninsula, there's again a choice of train or bus. Nanao is where JR is replaced by the **Noto railway**, although some JR trains continue one further stop to the modern resort of Wakura Onsen. The Noto railway is the best option for sightseeing on the east coast, especially since its carriages have large windows to take in the pleasant views. The line runs as far as Takojima on the southern side of the peninsula's tip. Local **buses** connect most places of interest around the peninsula, but they're infrequent and you might want to try hitching instead. The quiet and mainly flat coastal roads make the Noto Hantō an ideal place in which to cycle or rent a car. If you're pushed for time, there are also several daily **tour buses** from Kanazawa which take in all the sights, with an unrelenting Japanese commentary, for around ¥5000.

The best source of **tourist information** is the desk in Kanazawa Station (see p.458). There's also a tourist information booth (daily 8am–7pm; T0768/22-1503) in Wajima Bus Station, where the assistants speak some English and can provide you with maps of the town and the peninsula and book accommodation. There are lockers at the station and you can rent **bicycles** from the nearby Okina Rent-a-cycle (¥800 for 8hr).

Wajima has the widest choice of **accommodation** and is a good base for day-trips around the peninsula. Try *Fukasan* (T0768/22-9933; ❺), a spotless minshuku beside the coast, or *Shinbashi Ryokan* (T0768/22-0236, F22-5626; ❹), with its arty *washi* paper decoration in the lobby (although the management aren't so friendly). If you want Western-style comforts try the acceptable *Wajima Station* business hotel (T0768/22-0177, F22-6751; ❺), beside the station.

There are plenty of minshuku and ryokan in other villages around the coast, as well as campsites and youth hostels; the nicest hostel is *Noto Isaribi Youth Hostel* (T & F0768/74-0150; ❷), facing onto Tsukumo-wan in the sleepy village of **OGI**, twenty minutes' walk from Tsukumo-wan-Ogi station. It has good-quality tatami dorm rooms (❷) and is run by a friendly man who rustles up local seafood feasts. If you're lucky, he might give you a lift in his fishing boat across the bay to the station.

For **eating** in Wajima, try *Meigetsu* (☎0768/22-4477; closed Thurs), a good seafood restaurant; *Etranger*, a Western bistro in an orange building near the station; or *Tokushin*, an izekaya popular in the evenings.

Fukui and Eihei-ji

Some 75km south of Kanazawa is **FUKUI**, the modern capital of Fukui-ken, rebuilt after World War II and a severe earthquake in 1948 left the old city in a heap of rubble. There's little reason to linger here when **Eihei-ji** – the serene "temple of eternal peace" and headquarters of the Sōtō sect of Zen Buddhism – awaits on a mountainside surrounded by forests, 19km to the northeast.

The main approach to Eihei-ji is lined with the usual tacky souvenir shops, but at the top of the hill the temple complex of over seventy buildings blends seamlessly with the trees. Eihei-ji is one of the few ancient temples in Japan where a community is visibly functioning, breathing life into what would otherwise be an attractive but sterile place. Touring around the seven main buildings of the complex, all connected by covered wooden walkways, you'll pass many shaven-headed monks busily going about their daily chores and religious duties.

Eihei-ji is closed on several dates throughout the year for special services, so it's wise to check first with Fukui City Sightseeing Information (see below) or with the temple (☎0776/63-3102) before setting off. The best way to experience the temple is as a *sanrōsha*, or religious trainee, and to **stay the night**. Enquiries should be made at least two weeks (preferably a month) in advance to see if the dates you would like to stay are available – if they are, you'll be sent an application form. Overnight visits begin around 3pm, with a bath to cleanse your body in preparation for the instruction. At 5pm a meal of simple vegetarian food is served, after which you'll take part in your first *zazen* **meditation** session, lasting around thirty minutes. Next comes a video about life in the temple and then bedtime at 9pm. This might seem rather early, but you'll be up at 3.10am for a second *zazen* session before the morning service at 5am, followed by a tour of the temple complex. At 8.30am, after a breakfast of rice gruel and pickles, you're free to leave.

One night at Eihei-ji costs ¥8000, while for ¥1000 extra you can take part in the three-night/four-day programme, which follows more closely the rigorous daily routine of the monks. If this all sounds too much, there's a nearby **youth hostel**, *Eihei-ji Monzen Yamaguchi-sō* (☎0776/63-3123; ❶), where the food is slightly more luxurious, even if the accommodation, in large tatami rooms, is quite basic.

Practicalities

Fukui can be reached by **train** from Kanazawa on the JR Hokuriku line, or from Maibara, on the Tōkaidō Shinkansen line, from where direct express trains take just over an hour to reach Fukui. There are direct buses (¥1030) from Komatsu airport to Fukui bus terminal, a couple of blocks from the JR station. Buses also run to Fukui from the port of Tsuruga, which is connected by ferry to Otaru in Hokkaidō.

You can get information on the city and the prefecture from **Fukui City Sightseeing Information** (daily 9am–6pm; ☎0776/21-6492), next to Fukui Station's central exit ticket barrier. No English is spoken, but the assistants can supply an English city and prefecture maps and leaflets and help arrange accommodation. You can change money at the Hokuriku Bank opposite the central exit of the JR station and there are plenty of fast-food restaurants in the area should you need a quick bite to eat.

Trains to Eihei-ji (¥710) start from the Keifuku Denki Tetsudō Station, accessible from the east exit to the JR Fukui Station or via an underground tunnel that runs from outside the central exit. The journey takes 35 minutes and you'll have to change trains at Higashi-Furuichi. The temple is five minutes' walk uphill from the Eihei-ji Station.

Nagoya and around

NAGOYA, the capital of Aichi-ken, is Japan's fourth largest city and a major transport hub on central Honshū's industrial southern coast. Completely

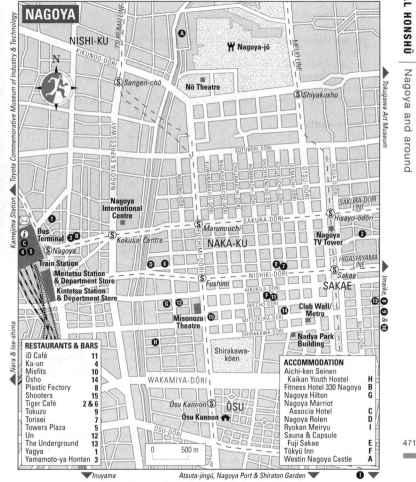

NAGOYA

NISHI-KU

Nagoya-jō

Sengen-chō

Nō Theatre

Shiyakusho

Nagoya International Centre

Bus Terminal

Nagoya Train Station

Meitetsu Station & Department Store

Kintetsu Station & Department Store

Kokusai Centre

Marunouchi

NAKA-KU

Nagoya TV Tower

Hisayo-ōdōri

Fushimi

NISHIKI-DŌRI

Sakae

SAKAE

HIGASHIYAMA LINE

Misonoza Theatre

Club Wall / Metro

Nadya Park Building

Shirakawa-kōen

WAKAMIYA-DŌRI

Ōsu Kannon

ŌSU

Ōsu Kannon

ŌSU-DŌRI

0   500 m

RESTAURANTS & BARS	
iD Café	11
Ka-un	4
Misfits	10
Ōsho	14
Plastic Factory	8
Shooters	15
Tiger Café	2 & 6
Tokuzo	9
Torisei	7
Towers Plaza	5
Un	12
The Underground	13
Yagya	1
Yamamoto-ya Honten	3

ACCOMMODATION	
Aichi-ken Seinen Kaikan Youth Hostel	H
Fitness Hotel 330 Nagoya	B
Nagoya Hilton	G
Nagoya Marriot Associa Hotel	C
Nagoya Rolen	D
Ryokan Meiryu	I
Sauna & Capsule Fuji Sakae	E
Tōkyū Inn	F
Westin Nagoya Castle	A

Kamejima Station   Toyota Commemorative Museum of Industry & Technology

Tokugawa Art Museum

Imaike

Nara & Ise-shima

Inuyama   Atsuta-jingū, Nagoya Port & Shiraton Garden

471

Nagoya	*Nagoya*	名古屋
Atsuta-jingū	*Atsuta-jingū*	熱田神宮
Nagoya-jō	*Nagoya-jō*	名古屋城
Ōsu Kannon	*Ōsu Kannon*	大須観音
Sakae	*Sakae*	栄
Shirotori Garden	*Shirotori-teien*	白鳥庭園
Tokugawa Art Museum	*Tokugawa Bijutsukan*	徳川美術館
Toyota Commemorative Museum of Industry and Technology	*Sangyō Gijutsu Kinenkan*	産業技術記念館

Accommodation		
Aichi-ken Seinen Kaikan Youth Hostel	*Aichi-ken Seinen Kaikan Yūsu Hosuteru*	愛知県青年会館ユースホステル
Fitness Hotel 330 Nagoya	*Fittonesu Hoteru 330 Nagoya*	フィットネスホテル３３０名古屋
Ryokan Meiryu	*Ryokan Meiryū*	旅館名龍
Nagoya Hilton	*Nagoya Hiruton*	名古屋ヒルトン
Nagoya Marriot Associa Hotel	*Nagoya Marioto Asoshia Hoteru*	名古屋マリオットアソシアホテル
Nagoya Rolen Hotel	*Nagoya Rōren Hoteru*	名古屋ローレンホテル
Sauna & Capsule Fuji	*Sauna to Kapuseru Fuji*	サウナ＆カプセル富士
Tōkyū Inn	*Tōkyū In*	東急イン
Westin Nagoya Castle	*Uesutin Nagoya Kyasseru*	ウェスティン名古屋キャッセル

Restaurants		
Ōshō	*Ōshō*	王将
Yagya	*Yagya*	やぎゃ
Yamamoto-ya Honten	*Yamamoto-ya Honten*	山本屋本店

Inuyama	*Inuyama*	犬山
Inuyama Artefacts Museum	*Inuyama-shi Bunka Shiryōkan*	犬山市文化史料館
Inuyama International Youth Hostel	*Inuyama Kokusai Yūsu Hosuteru*	犬山国際ユースホステル
Inuyama-jō	*Inuyama-jō*	犬山城
Meiji Mura	*Meiji Mura*	明治村
Ōgata-jinja	*Ōgata-jinja*	大縣神社
Tagata-jinja	*Tagata-jinja*	田県神社
Uraku-en	*Uraku-en*	有楽苑

rebuilt after a wartime drubbing, it's an overwhelmingly modern city of high-rise buildings, wide boulevards, multi-lane highways and flyovers, where business takes precedence over tourism. This is, after all, the home of **Toyota**, the industrial powerhouse whose healthy balance sheet (US$11 billion in sales per month, and counting) has kept the local economy buoyant throughout the nation's ongoing depression.

Nagoya does have a few decent tourist attractions, the most interesting of which is the grand **Tokugawa Art Museum**, housing belongings of the powerful family that once ruled Japan, and the **Toyota Commemorative Museum of Industry and Technology**, an appropriate tribute to Nagoya's industrial heritage. The city's most hyped attractions – the castle **Nagoya-jō** and the sacred shrine **Atsuta-jingū** – aren't outstanding examples of their kind, but are worth checking out if you have the time.

Nagoya's real attraction is as a base from which to tour the region. To the west, the Kiso-gawa forms the border between Aichi-ken and Gifu-ken, and the ancient night spectacle of *ukai*, cormorant fishing (see box, p.479), is still practised in the small castle town of **Inuyama**. This is also where you'll find the classical Jo-an teahouse in a beautiful traditional garden, and is close by the vast outdoor architectural museum, **Meiji Mura**. Across the river in Gifu-ken, the capital **Gifu** serves up a similar combination of castle, parks and *ukai*, and is well known for its production of paper lanterns and umbrellas. Further into the mountains, along the Nagara River, **Gujō Hachiman** is a refreshing city of clean rivers and traditional houses, with a summer dance festival that is one of the best in Japan. Note that the Shima Hantō covered in the Kansai chapter (p.596) can also easily be visited from Nagoya.

Arrival, information, orientation and city transport

The lines of three **train** companies converge on Nagoya, and their stations are all close to each other on the west side of the city. The **main station** belongs to JR and is where you'll alight from Tōkaidō Shinkansen services from Tokyo, Ōsaka or Kyoto. Direct JR services also run to Nagoya from Takayama (see p.445) to the north and Ise and Toba (see p.596 and p.602), south in Mie-ken. Immediately south of the JR station, beneath the Meitetsu department store, is the **Meitetsu line terminus** for trains to and from Inuyama and Gifu, while next door is the Kintetsu department store, with its **Kintetsu line** for services to Nara and the Shima Hantō region (see p.596). Most long-distance **buses** pull in at the terminal at the north end of the JR station.

Some 10km south of the train stations is the Nagoya-kō port area, where **ferries** arrive from Hokkaidō and Okinawa. The quickest way to reach the city from the port is to hop on the Meijo line of Nagoya's subway system (see p.474). **Nagoya airport**, 12km north of the city, serves scores of local and international destinations and can get busy during peak holiday periods. Buses run from the airport both to the JR station and the neighbouring Meitetsu Bus Centre on the third floor of the Melsa Building. It's anticipated that the new **Chūbu International Airport**, currently being built on a man-made island at Tokoame on Isewan Bay some 30km south of Nagoya, will take over all services when it opens in 2005, and will be connected to the city by a high-speed rail line.

The first stop for information should be the **Nagoya Station Tourist Information Centre** (daily 9am–7pm; ☎052/541-4301), on the central concourse of the JR station. The English-speaking assistants can provide you with maps and guides to the city and help with accommodation bookings. Another useful place to drop by is the International Centre (Tues–Sat 9am–8.30pm, Sun 9am–5pm; ☎052/581-0100), on the third floor of the **Nagoya International Centre Building**, some seven minutes' walk east of the JR station, along Sakura-dōri. The many services on offer here include an excellent library, English-language television, a bulletin board, Internet access (¥250 for 30min) and the opportunity to meet English-speaking locals and arrange home visits and stays. Local English language publications to look out for include the monthly *Japanzine* (see p.64); the excellent quarterly *Nagoya Info Guide* with full, up-to-date listings; and the less useful but occasionally interesting *Avenues*. The Nagoya Convention & Visitors' Bureau's website ⓦ www.ncvb.or.jp is also a useful source of information.

Tokai Welcome Card

The **Tokai Welcome Card** is a discount scheme for overseas tourists covering some 270 hotels, restaurants and transportation and sightseeing facilities; it's valid in Nagoya City, all of Aichi-ken and neighbouring Gifu-ken, Mie-ken and Shizuoka-ken. Cards can be ordered free from ⓦ www.j-heartland.com or you can pick up information leaflets from tourist information centres in the region. For more details on Welcome Cards, see "Basics", p.31.

Orientation and city transport

In front of Nagoya's three train stations, a giant sculpted air vent marks the beginning of **Sakura–dōri**, the main highway cutting directly east towards the Nagoya TV Tower in the heart of the city. Immediately south of here is the main shopping and entertainment district of **Sakae**, where you'll find most hotels, department stores and restaurants. Around 1km north lie the **castle grounds**, while a similar distance south is the temple **Ōsu Kannon**. Some 3km south of the Ōsu Kannon you'll find the main shrine **Atsuta-jingū**. Keep heading south and you'll hit the **Nagoya-kō** port area.

The easiest way to get around is on the **subway**, which has four main colour-coded lines: Higashiyama (yellow), Meijō (purple), Sakura–dōri (red), and Tsurumai (blue). Both the Sakura–dōri and Higashiyama lines connect with the train stations. The extensive **bus** system can also be handy, but it's not as *gaijin*-friendly as the subways, which have everything labelled in English. Single journeys by subway or bus around the city centre cost ¥200; if you plan to travel a lot, consider buying one of the **day tickets** (¥740 for subways only, ¥600 for buses only, ¥850 for subways and buses). If you're going to be doing a lot of sightseeing it might be worth purchasing the **ikomai kippu** (¥1300), a one-day pass which includes free or discounted entrance to practically all Nagoya's major sights; it's available from transport ticket offices.

Accommodation

The cheapest hotel **accommodation** is around the train stations, but the nicest area to stay in is Sakae, 3.5km east of the stations. Apart from the central *Aichi-ken Seinen Kaikan Youth Hostel*, there's also the cheaper *Nagoya Youth Hostel* (☏ 052/781-9845, ☏ 781-7023; ❶), out on a limb at Higashiyama-kōen, some 5km southeast of the city centre – no good if you want to enjoy Nagoya at night.

Aichi-ken Seinen Kaikan Youth Hostel 1-18-8 Sakae, Naka-ku ☏ 052/221-6001, ☏ 204-3508. Great location and very good value, since it's more like a hotel, with big rooms and a huge top-floor communal bath. The downside is the 11pm curfew. Dorm beds ¥2850 per person.

Fitness Hotel 330 Nagoya 3-25-6 Meieki, Nakamura-ku ☏ 052/562-0330, ⓦ www.misawa-resort.co.jp. Pleasantly decorated business hotel, a couple of blocks east of the JR Nagoya Station. ❺

Nagoya Hilton 1-3-3 Sakae, Naka-ku ☏ 052/212-1111, ☏ 212-1225. Classy luxury hotel, with fine rooms and an excellent range of facilities, including a good selection of restaurants with buffet deals. The location is good, and it's worth checking on the special package deals throughout the year. ❽

Nagoya Marriot Associa Hotel 1-1-4 Meieki, Nakamura-ku ☏ 052/584-1113, ⓦ www.associa.com/nma. Not to be confused with the less flashy *Hotel Associa Nagoya Terminal* in the same mammoth station and twin towers complex, these luxurious lodgings start from the 20th floor and go up to the 49th. Rooms are very comfortable, with a chintzy old European look, and there's an excellent range of restaurants and a fitness club with pool. ❼–❽

Nagoya Rolen Hotel 1-8-40 Sakae, Naka-ku ☏ 052/211-4581, ☏ 211-4588. Functional, no-frills business hotel in a good location. The rooms are plain, but clean; the cheapest share communal bathrooms. ❹

Ryokan Meiryū 2-4-21 Kamimaezu, Naka-ku ℡052/331-8686, ⓕ321-6119. This friendly ryokan has tatami rooms with air conditioning and TV; bathrooms are communal and there's a little café for breakfast and dinner. Take exit three at Kamimaezu subway station and walk a couple of minutes east towards the YMCA. ④

Sauna & Capsule Fuji Sakae 3-22-31 Sakae ℡052/962-5711. Nagoya's largest and cheapest capsule hotel (men only) is a snazzy affair, with its own restaurant, sauna and huge bath. If you just want to use the sauna and bath it's ¥1000 for an hour. ¥3800 per person.

Tōkyū Inn 3-1-8 Sakae, Naka-ku ℡052/251-0109, ⓦwww.tokyuhotels.co.jp. This mid-range chain hotel is in an excellent location, has comfortable rooms and a *Starbucks* outlet in the lobby for breakfast and snacks. ⑥

The Westin Nagoya Castle 3-19 Hinokuchi-chō, Nishi-ku ℡052/521-2121, ⓦwww.castle.co.jp. Kept on its toes by the opening of the Marriot, the *Westin Nagoya Castle* has gone all contemporary oriental in its interior design and looks much the better for it. There's a swimming pool and a free shuttle bus from the JR station. ⑦

Central Nagoya

Some 2km northeast of the train stations lies Nagoya's castle, **Nagoya-jō**. The castle was originally built by Tokugawa Ieyasu in 1612 but largely destroyed during World War II – all that survived were three turrets, three gates and sequestered screen paintings from the destroyed Honmaru palace. A handsome concrete replica of the original (daily 9am–4.30pm; ¥500; ℡052/231-1700) was completed in 1959, and the central donjon was topped by huge gold-plated *shachi*, the mythical dolphins which have become a symbol of the city. Money is currently being raised to rebuild the *goten*, the prefectural lord's residence within the grounds; it will house Edo-era painted screens.

More interesting is the **Tokugawa Art Museum** (Tues–Sun 10am–5pm; ¥1200; ℡052/935-6262), 2km further east, along Dekimachi-dōri, which houses a vast array of heirlooms from the Owari branch of the Tokugawa family, who once ruled Nagoya. The collection, displayed in large modern galleries with English explanations, includes items inherited by the first Tokugawa shogun, Ieyasu, reconstructions of the formal chambers of the *daimyō*'s residence and a Nō stage, around which are ranged beautiful traditional costumes. The museum's star attraction is a twelfth-century painted scroll of *The Tale of Genji* (see "Contexts", p.1019). The original is too precious to be exhibited continually, so most of the time you'll only be able to see reproduced panels and video programmes about the scroll.

A handful of other central Nagoya sights are worth checking out. The **Toyota Commemorative Museum of Industry and Technology** (Tues–Sun 9.30am–5pm; ¥500; ℡052/551-6111), in an old red-brick Toyota factory, is nowhere near as dull as it sounds. The museum is made up of two main pavilions, one housing cars, the other textile machinery (though now famous worldwide for its cars, Toyota began life as a textile producer). In the first pavilion, rows of early twentieth-century looms make an incredible racket; in contrast, a computer-controlled air-jet loom at the end of the display purrs like a kitten. In the automobile pavilion, it's the car-making robots, some of which look like giant, menacing aliens, that grab the attention. The museum is around 1km north of JR Nagoya Station and only two minutes' walk east of Sakō Station on the Meitetsu Nagoya line.

In the heart of **Sakae**, the stimulating **Design Museum** (daily except Tues 11am–8pm; ¥300; ℡052/265-2106), on the fourth floor of the Nadya Park Design Centre Building, charts the commercial design of modern products, such as telephones and radios, and has hi-tech displays and computer simulations. Rather more traditional is the **Ōsu Kannon**, a vermilion-painted temple bustling with a steady stream of petitioners, 1km south of Sakae and beside the Ōsu Kannon stop on the Tsurumai subway line. Immediately to the east, check out the bargain-hunters' district of **Ōsu**, where old-style arcades are lined with shops selling discount electronic goods, cheap clothes and used kimono. An antique market is held here on the 18th and 24th of each month.

Panorama House (daily 10am–10pm; ¥700), on the 51st floor of the twin towers which rise 245m above the JR station, provides views as far as the Japan Alps or Ise Bay, if the weather is cooperating. If not, save your cash, since the view from the restaurant floors of the *Nagoya Marriott Associa*'s hostelries is pretty good too.

Atsuta-jingū and around

Some 5km south of central Nagoya, amid extensive wooded grounds, lies the venerable shrine of **Atsuta-jingū**, home of the *kusanagi-no-tsurugi*, or "grass-cutting sword". This, along with the sacred jewels in Tokyo's Imperial Palace and the sacred mirror at Ise-jingū (see p.597), forms part of the imperial regalia and remains hidden – if it exists at all – deep within the shrine, which had to be rebuilt after the war.

Within the shrine grounds there's a small **museum** (daily 9am–4.30pm; closed last Wed & Thurs of the month; ¥300; ☏052/671-4151), where you can see many other swords offered to the Shinto gods at Atsuta-jingū, including a ferocious two-metre-long blade in the entrance hall. Also within the grounds, look out for the giant camphor tree, said to have been planted by the Buddhist saint Kōbō Daishi (see p.954) 1300 years ago. It takes around twenty minutes by subway from Nagoya Station to reach Jingū-Nishi station on the Meijō line, the closest stop to Atsuta-jingū.

While you're out at the shrine, it's worth strolling west from the subway station towards the Hori-kawa, on the other side of which is the charming **Shirotori Garden** (Tues–Sun 9am–4.30pm; closed third Wed of month; ¥200). This classical stroll-garden, arranged around ponds and streams, has an elegant traditional teahouse which is supposed to resemble a swan landing on the water.

Eating, drinking and nightlife

For **eating**, Sakae is the main district to head for, the grid of streets around 3-chōme being packed with lively **restaurants**, as well as numerous bars. The town's signature dish is *kishimen*, flat, floury noodles served in a variety of ways; one of the tastiest comes in a kind of salad called *goma-su*. You should also try the local *cochin* chicken, famed for its succulent taste. The main **drinking** area is around Sakae Ō-chōme on the far eastern side of the central park. Here you'll find many multistorey buildings, decked out in neon, where numerous *nomiya*, clubs, and more dubious establishments are piled on top of each other. East of the centre are Imaike and Ikeshita, up-and-coming districts that sport some relaxed bars and Nagoya's most happening clubs.

Traditional performing arts are well supported in Nagoya, with a splendid Nō **theatre** opposite the castle and the grand Kabuki theatre, Misono-za, in the downtown area of Fushimi; for details of shows, contact the International Centre or check out the listings in the free city **magazines** (see p.473). You could also try your hand at a game of *pachinko* (see p.1006) while here – this is where Japan's top pastime was invented.

Restaurants and cafés

Ka-un 18th floor, *Nagoya Marriot Associa Hotel* ☏052/584-1111. Elegant restaurant offering top-class Japanese cuisine; try their *Hyotan bentō* box at lunch, which comes in a gourd-shaped lacquer-ware container. You'll have to book to get a table with a view across the Zen-pebble garden. Dinner sets start at ¥4000.

Ōshō Cheap and cheerful Chinese café, one block south of the Maruzen bookshop on one of Sakae's main shopping streets. Has an English menu and pictures of the excellent-value set meals, which rarely cost over ¥1000.

Tiger Café 1-8-26 Nishiki, Naka-ku. Fairly authentic 1930s-style French café-bistro, open from 7am for breakfasts of croissant and espresso until 11pm for after-dinner *digestifs*. There's another branch at 1-9-22 Higashi Sakura, Higashi-ku.

Torisei 3-19-24 Sakae, Naka-ku ☎052/951-7337. Excellent yakitori restaurant offering tasty takes on the old standby of bits of chicken on a stick. Closed Sun.

Towers Plaza 11–13th floors of the towers above the JR Nagoya Station. There's a wide selection of restaurants here to please all tastes. *The Queens Street* deli serves good bagel sandwich sets with string fries and has window seats with a view. Also worth checking out is the chic *Library Café Quatre*, which has Internet terminals, plenty of trendy

English-style mags and books to leaf through, and an interesting menu of small Japanese dishes.

Un 1-4-33 Sakae, Naka-ku ☎052/218-1577. Branch of the upmarket nationwide chain offering inventive nouvelle Japanese cuisine in a sleek contemporary setting. Lunch costs around ¥1500, dinner ¥3000.

Yagya 3-13-21 Meieki ☎052/586-5544. Ultramodern Southeast Asian and Japanese restaurant with a vaguely Balinese feel to its interior – the food is a good deal if you come with a crowd and share dishes. Look for the huge Aztec ruin-style facade, a two-minute walk northeast of JR Nagoya Station. There's another branch in Sakae. Daily 5pm–midnight.

Yamamoto-ya Honten B1, Horiuchi Building, Meieki. Chief outlet of noodle café chain, on Sakura-dōri, a few minutes' walk from the JR station. The specialities are *miso nikomi* (thick udon noodles in a bean paste) and locally reared *tori kochin* (chicken). Around ¥1500 per head. Daily 11am–7.30pm.

Bars and clubs

iD Café (The sign outside says *iD Bar*) 3-1-15 Sakae ☎052/251-0382. Psychedelic flowers decorate this funky multi-level bar and club. The ¥1000 entrance gets you two tokens that can be used for food or drinks. Closed Mon.

Metro ⓦhttp://home.att.ne.jp/sky/metroclub. Nagoya's only *gaijin*-friendly gay and lesbian club event has been going for over a decade now – it's currently held every second Saturday of the month at *Club Wall* (☎052/251-5609) in Sakae; check the website for details.

Misfits 4-10-16 Imaike, Chikusa-ku ☎052/733-7525. Convivial bar justly popular with both the foreign community and young Japanese, and the food's not bad, particularly the big salads. On the third floor of a building around the corner from exit 4 of Imaike station.

Plastic Factory 32-13 Kanda-chō, Chikusa-ku ☎052/723-9971, ⓦwww.mangafrog.com. Nagoya's most happening club space hosts an eclectic range of events in – guess what? – an old

plastic factory, three blocks north of Imaike station. Expect anything from Bhangra (1st Sat of the month) to live rock shows.

Shooters 2F Pola Nagoya Bldg, 2-9-26 Naka-ku ☎052/202-7077. If you're looking to pick up, this is the place to do it – or so we're told. Even if you're not, this sports bar and grill is a good place to just hang out and enjoy the boisterous atmosphere. Hosts live bands every Sunday night from 8pm.

Tokuzo 2F Blue Star Bldg, 1-6-8 Imaike, Chikusa-ku ☎052/733-3709. The coolest of Nagoya's current crop of cool bars, and another good reason to head out to Imaike of an evening. Live music most nights.

The Underground 4-3-15 Sakae ☎052/242-1388. On third and fourth floors of a corner building – look for the London Underground symbol. Long-running club known for its *Lush* and *Cypher* dance nights. Dark and crowded at weekends. Entrance is ¥1500 on Fri & Sat, including two drinks.

Listings

Airlines ANA, Sumitomo Shōji Building, 1-1-6 Higashi-Sakura (international ☎0120-029333, domestic ☎0120-029222); JAL, Sakae Sun City Building, 4-1-8 Sakae (international ☎0120-255931, domestic ☎0120-255971).

Airport information Domestic ☎052/28-5633; international ☎0568/29-0765.

Banks and exchange Several major bank

branches can be found around the stations, along Sakura-dōri and Nishiki-dōri in Sakae. These include Citibank, whose ATMs accept some foreign-issued cards.

Bookshops The best places for English-language books are Maruzen, 3-2-7 Sakae (daily except Wed 9.50am–8pm) and Kinokuniya, within the Loft department store in the Nadya Park Building in

Sakae (daily except Tues 11am–8pm).

Car rental Eki Rent-a-Car ☎052/581-0882; Nissan Rent-a-Car ☎052/451-2300.

Consulates Australia, 8F, Ikkō-Fushimi Building, 1-20-10 Nishiki, Naka-ku ☎052/211-0603; Canada, 6F, Nakatō Marunouchi Building, 3-17-6 Marunouchi ☎052/972-0450; USA, 6F, Nishiki SIS Building, 3-10-33 Nishiki, Naka-ku ☎052/203-4011.

Emergencies The Prefectural Police Office is at 2-1-1 Sannomaru (☎052/951-1611). In an absolute emergency, contact the International Centre (☎052/581-0100). For other emergency numbers, see "Basics" p.81.

Hospital The main hospital is the National Hospital of Nagoya, 4-1-1 Sannomaru, Naku-ku

(☎052/951-1111), but it's best to first call the International Centre (☎052/581-0100) and they'll tell you the most appropriate place to go.

Internet access The Nagoya International Centre (see p.473) has Internet terminals. Each of the four Kinko's – at Chiyogaoka, Ikeshita, Sakae and Meikei Minami – offers Internet access, and you can also access the Web at the *Library Café Quatre* (see p.477).

Post office There's a handy post office (Mon–Fri 9am–7pm, Sat 9am–5pm, Sun 9am–12.30pm) at 1-1-1 Meieki, one minute's walk north of the JR station.

Travel agency There's a useful branch of JTB in the *Hilton* hotel (☎052/221-8768).

Inuyama

Easily visited as a day-trip from Nagoya is the castle town of **INUYAMA**, 25km north of the city, beside the Kiso-gawa. The town feels like an affluent suburb of Nagoya, but on summer evenings, displays of *ukai* (cormorant fishing; see box opposite), to which the castle's floodlit exterior provides a dramatic backdrop, will transport you back centuries.

The castle is slightly closer to Inuyama-Yūen Station, but if you approach it from the west side of Inuyama Station – which takes around ten minutes on foot – you'll pass through an area of old wooden houses culminating in the small **Inuyama Artefacts Museum** (daily 9am–5pm; ¥100; ☎0568/62-4802). Here you can see two of the thirteen towering, ornately decorated floats (*yatai*) which are paraded around Inuyama during the town's major festival on the first weekend of April, and a video of the *matsuri*. If you visit the museum on Friday or Saturday, you can also see a craftsman demonstrating the art of making *karakuri*, the mechanical wooden puppets that perform on the *yatai*.

The museum is just in front of **Haritsuna-jinja**, the plain shrine at which the colourful festival takes place. One minute's walk up the hill behind the shrine will bring you to the entrance of the only privately owned castle in Japan, **Inuyama-jō** (daily 9am–5pm; ¥400; joint ticket with Uraku-en ¥1100). This toy-like fortress was built in 1537, making it the oldest in Japan (although parts have been extensively renovated), and it has belonged to the Naruse family since 1618. Inside, the donjon is nothing special, but there's a pretty view of the river and surrounding country from the top, where you can appreciate the defensive role that this white castle played.

East of Inuyama-jō, within the grounds of the luxury *Meitetsu Inuyama Hotel* beside the river, is the beautiful garden of **Uraku-en** (daily 9am–4pm, March–Nov until 5pm; ¥1000). The mossy lawns and stone pathways act as a fancy frame for the subdued **Jo-an**, a traditional teahouse. Originally built in Kyoto by Oda Uraku, the younger brother of the warlord Oda Nobunaga, the yellow-walled teahouse has floor space for just over three tatami mats, though it can only be viewed from the outside. If you want tea (¥500), you'll have to go to one of the garden's larger modern teahouses.

Practicalities

Inuyama is roughly thirty minutes from both Nagoya and Gifu on the Meitetsu railway and is best visited as a day-trip from either city. There's a **tourist information booth** (daily 9am–5pm; ☎0568/61-6000) beside the central exit of Inuyama Station; staff speak a little English and can provide you with English

Ukai

Inuyama on the Kiso-gawa, and Gifu on the Nagara-gawa 20km west (see p.480), are two of the main locations for **ukai**, or night-time **fishing with cormorants**, a skill developed back in the seventh century. The slender-necked birds are used to catch *ayu*, a sweet freshwater fish, in season between May and September. The fishermen, dressed in traditional straw skirts and pointed hats, handle up to twelve cormorants on long leashes, attached at the birds' throats with a ring to prevent them from swallowing the fish. The birds dive into the water, hunting the *ayu*, which are attracted to the light of the fire blazing in the metal braziers hanging from the bows of the narrow fishing boats. The birds are specially bred and trained for the job and get well fed afterwards.

The fast-moving show usually only lasts around twenty minutes, but an *ukai* jaunt is not just about fishing. Around two hours before the start of the fishing, the audience boards long, canopied boats, decorated with paper lanterns, which sail upriver and then moor to allow a pre-show picnic. Unless you pay extra you'll have to bring your own food and drink, but sometimes a boat will drift by selling beer, snacks and fireworks – another essential *ukai* component. Although you can watch the show for free from the riverbank, you won't experience the thrill of racing alongside the fishing boats, the birds splashing furiously in the reflected light of the pine wood burning in the brazier hanging from the boats' prows.

The *ukai* season in Inuyama runs from June 1 to September 30, with boats sailing from the dock beside the Inuyama-bashi bridge, five minutes' walk north of Inuyama Yūen Station. In June, July and August the boats depart at 6pm and the fishing show begins at 7.50pm, while in September the start time is 5.30pm, with the *ukai* kicking off at 7.20pm. In June and September the cost is ¥2500, rising to ¥2800 during the peak months of July and August, when it's best to reserve a place at your hotel or the booking office (☎0568/61-0057). *Ukai* is not performed on nights of the full moon or during and after heavy rain, when the rivers become too muddy.

maps and leaflets, and even free bicycles (except Wed). If you need more detailed assistance, head for the Inuyama International Sightseeing Centre "FRUEDE" (daily 9am–7pm, closed second and fourth Mon of month), five minutes' walk east of the station.

Accommodation includes the *Inuyama International Youth Hostel* (☎0568/61-1111, ⓕ61-2770; ❸), which has no dorms and is really a modern hotel with a good restaurant and free laundry service. With such good facilities, you'll need to book well in advance. To reach the hostel, walk for fifteen minutes from Inuyama-Yūen Station following the Kiso-gawa upstream until you reach the first major turning off to the right, where there's a park and a sign pointing up a steep flight of steps to the hostel. Alternatively, take the monorail from Inuyama-Yūen Station to the Monkey Park (¥150) and walk north for ten minutes past the park, across the main road, and up the hill on your left.

Meiji Mura and around

Some 7km southeast of Inuyama lie the extensive grounds of **Meiji Mura** (daily 9.30am–4pm, March–Oct until 9.30am–5pm; ¥1600; ⓦ www.meijimura.com; ☎0568/67-0314), one of the best of several open-air architectural museums dotted around Japan. This huge park contains 67 structures, including lamps that once stood on a bridge to the Imperial Palace in Tokyo, churches, banks, a Kabuki theatre, a lighthouse and a telephone exchange from Sapporo. The common factor is that all date from around the Meiji era

(1868–1912), when Western influences were flooding into Japan, resulting in some unique hybrid architecture. This stylistic synthesis can be seen in one of the park's highlights, the front of Frank Lloyd Wright's original **Imperial Hotel**, at the north end of the park, a survivor of the Great Kantō Earthquake, which hit Tokyo the day after the hotel opened in 1923.

The sheer size of Meiji Mura means that tour groups are easily swallowed up and you may be tempted to hop on the electric bus (¥600) that beetles from one end of the park to the other, or the old Kyoto tram (¥300) and steam locomotive (¥500), though these only go part of the way. Give yourself half a day and you can cover most of the park on foot. There are several places to snack or eat **lunch** within the park. Coffee and cake inside the *Imperial Hotel* is a rather pricey ¥800; hold out instead for lunch at the reasonable modern restaurant, opposite the elegant reception hall of the Marquis Saigō Tsugumichi (younger brother of Kagoshima's famous general Saigō Takamori), at the southern end of the park.

Buses leave at regular intervals from the east side of Inuyama Station for the twenty-minute journey to Meiji Mura (¥820 return), or you can go directly from Nagoya's Meitetsu bus station (¥1190 return), which takes one hour.

If you're in the mood for a **country walk**, head 3km west towards Gakuden Station on the Meitetsu Komaki line between Inuyama and Nagoya, until you reach the **Ōgata-jinja**, one of a pair of fertility shrines dedicated to the Shinto deities Izanagi and Izanami. Ōgata-jinja is the female's shrine and as such is packed with cleft rocks and the like resembling female genitalia, while **Tagata-jinja**, further southwest, the male shrine, is where you'll find all shapes and sizes of carved penises. Both shrines have festivals, one week apart in early March, which involve the parading of a giant vagina and penis around town and lots of sake drinking. Ōgata-jinja stands around 1.5km east of Gakuden Station, and Tagata-jinja is beside Tagata-jinja-mae Station, one stop further south on the Meitetsu Komaki line.

Gifu

On the other side of the Kiso-gawa from Inuyama is Gifu-ken, whose capital, **GIFU**, lies 20km further west. The city pretty much repeats the Inuyama formula of *ukai* on a meandering river overlooked by a hilltop castle, but is otherwise a bigger and more modern place, rebuilt after the double whammy of an earthquake in 1891 and blanket bombings during World War II. The city is also renowned for its **paper umbrellas** and **lanterns** and it's possible to visit a couple of workshops.

Ukai displays (see box, p.479) run each year from May 11 to October 15 on the waters of the Nagara-gawa, around 2km north of the town's two train stations. You'll have to bring your own picnic for the boat, the cormorant fishing lasts only thirty minutes and, at ¥3300, it's more expensive than in Inuyama, which may persuade you to view the whole thing for free from the riverside. If the water is low, you'll be able to walk out across the rocky river bed for a better view of the proceedings. If you do want to go out on a boat, book first at the boat office (☎0582/62-0104; English spoken) beside the Nagara-bashi, reached on bus #11 (¥200) from either of the train stations.

The small white castle of **Gifu-jō** (daily 9am–5pm; ¥200), perched atop Kinka-zan, is the city's main daytime attraction; it's also sometimes open in the evenings during July and August (check with the tourist office). Set in verdant **Gifu-kōen**, the park around the densely forested hillock looming over the Nagara-gawa, the castle itself is an unremarkable recreation, but it's worth taking the cable car up (daily 9am–5pm; ¥600 one way, ¥1050 return) for the

Gifu	*Gifu*	岐阜
Hotel 330 Grande	*Hoteru 330 Gurande*	ホテル３３０グランデ
Gifu-jō	*Gifu-jō*	岐阜城
Gifu Youth Hostel	*Gifu Yūsu Hosuteru*	岐阜ユースホステル
Gurume-kan	*Gurume-kan*	グルメ館
Kawaraya	*Kawaraya*	かわらや
Ryokan Banshōkan	*Ryokan Banshōkan*	旅館萬松館
Gujō Hachiman	*Gujō Hachiman*	郡上八幡
Gujō-Hachiman-jō	*Gujō-Hachiman-jō*	郡上八幡城
Gujō-Tōsenji Youth Hostel	*Gujō-Tōsenji Yūsu Hosuteru*	郡上洞泉寺ユースホステル
Hachiman Cycling Terminal	*Hachiman Saikuringu Tāminaru*	八幡サイクリングターミナル
Hakurankan	*Hakurankan*	博覧館
Hanamura	*Hanamura*	花むら
Izumisaka	*Izumisaka*	泉坂
Nakashimaya	*Nakashimaya*	中嶋屋
Soba-no-Hiraji	*Soba-no-Hiraji*	そばの駅
Sōgisui	*Sōgisui*	宗ぎ水

panoramic view of the river winding its way past the humpbacked outcrops on Gifu's surrounding plains. The park is reached on the #11 bus which goes out to the Nagara-bashi. While you're out here, pop into **Shōhō-ji**, a temple opposite the park, housing an imposing 13.7-metre-tall sculpture of Buddha made of lacquered bamboo.

Around 1km south of Gifu-kōen, at 1-18 Koguma-chō, is **Ozeki Shōten** (Mon–Sat 9am–5pm), a company which produces traditional **paper lanterns** as well as the contemporary *Akari* light sculptures. The workshops here are closed to the public, but the shop (Mon–Sat 9am–5pm) has a display outlining the way in which the lanterns are made. To see craftsmen at work, head for the paper umbrella company, **Sakaida Honten**, 27 Kanō-Naka Hiroe (Mon–Sat 7am–noon & 2–5pm). The assistants will happily show you a range of the colourful umbrellas, which start at ¥3000 and rise to ¥100,000 for the giant red parasols often seen outside the most traditional of ryokan. The shop is less than ten minutes on foot south of the JR station, but tricky to locate; get the assistants at Gifu tourist information to draw you a map.

Practicalities

Gifu has two **train stations** – JR and Meitetsu – five minutes from one another at the south end of the city's commercial district. The main **tourist information office** (daily 9am–7pm; ☎0582/62-4415) is inside JR Gifu Station, beside the ticket barrier at the Nagara-guchi exit. The helpful assistants speak a little English and can provide English maps and pamphlets on the city and the prefecture and point you towards accommodation.

There's a good range of both Western- and Japanese-style **hotels** and ryokan in the city. As usual, there are several business hotels clustered close by the train stations. One of the better ones is the comfortable *Hotel 330 Grande* (☎058/267-0330, ℱ264-1330; ➎). The *Gifu Youth Hostel* (☎058/263-6631; ➊) is a cheap and clean place run by a chatty manager who speaks a little English, though it's located on top of hilly Kashimori-kōen on the east side of town –

you'll save a lot of sweat by taking a taxi there from the station (around ¥2000) rather than lugging your bags 2km up the hill. Many tourist ryokan line the Nagara-gawa, where the *ukai* displays take place, but if you can afford it head for *Ryokan Banshōkan* (☎058/262-0039; **❼**), a traditional wooden building with raked gravel gardens beside the entrance to Gifu-kōen.

As far as **eating** goes, there are many dining options around the main road heading north from the station, along which trams run; these include the *Gurume-kan*, a corner building with different restaurants on each level. Closer to Gifu-kōen in Honmachi is the venerable, expensive *ayu* (sweetfish) restaurant *Kawaraya* (☎058/262-0039; daily except Tues 11am–2pm & 5–9pm) or the funky, Asian-influenced *Natural Café & Gallery* (☎058/269-5788), set in an old storehouse with a wooden balcony tacked on.

Gujō Hachiman

> It is a town of low, dark, wood-and-plaster buildings, paved lanes, and running water. The windows of the buildings are narrow and slatted. The lanes, too, are narrow, steeply walled, and end in dimly lanterned eating places or in small stone bridges that arch over splashing streams. It was like an Edo-era stage set.
>
> **Alan Booth *Looking for the Lost*, 1995**

Long-distance walker Booth's romantic description of **GUJŌ HACHIMAN** still applies: its old-world atmosphere and mountain-bound location – with two pristine rivers, the Yoshida and Nagara, running through the centre – lend it great appeal. Tucked in a valley on an old trade route which once led to the Sea of Japan, the town lies around 55km north of Gifu. It's worth visiting at any time of year, but the best time is during the **Gujō Odori** (see box below), one of Japan's top three dance festivals.

Gujō is a lovely place just to wander around and make casual discoveries. The tourist office (see opposite) sells the *Jokamachi midokoro tsukotegata*, a ¥1500 ticket giving you access to nine different places of interest including the castle and

---

Gujō Odori

Thousands of communities in Japan put on Bon Odori festivals, but nowhere is the dance so firmly rooted in the life of the community as at Gujō Hachiman, where the **Gujō Odori** has been going since the 1590s. Practically every night from mid-July to early September, from about 8pm to 11pm in a different part of town (the tourist information centre can tell you exactly when and where) the locals don their *yukata* and dance in the streets. At the height of the season, during the O-bon holiday in mid-August, dancing goes on all night and thousands of dancers and observers crowd the town to take part. Over this time the town's hotels are all usually fully booked, but don't worry if you can't find a bed since there's always somewhere in town that will allow revellers a place to rest during the night-long festivities – again check with the tourist office.

The rules of Gujō Odori are simple. Dress in something cool and light: the locals favour a cotton *yukata* and sandals, but you can wear anything comfortable, such as shorts and a T-shirt. People dance in circles around a tall wood-and-bamboo structure from which a singer, drummers, flute player and a chorus call the tune. There are ten kinds of dances and the singer will call their name out before each one commences. Learn the hand movements first – they are pantomime motions usually illustrating farming or other traditional tasks. Next, pick up the steps – typically some combination of step, step, step, kick. Watch the movements of the dancers in the inner circle, as these are the people who learned these steps as children.

a couple of museums. The best of these is the **Hakurankan** (daily 9.30am–5pm; ¥500), on the northern side of the Yoshida river, a ten-minute stroll from the tourist office. This excellent museum has four sections detailing the town's history, arts and crafts, connection with water, and folk dance. A good fifteen-minute climb from the Hakurankan past several attractive temples is **Gujō-Hachiman-jō** (daily 9am–5pm, Nov–Feb until 4.30pm, June–Aug 8am–6pm; ¥300). This photogenic replica of the old castle was rebuilt in 1934 on the stone foundations of the less elaborate original structure. From its ramparts you'll see that the town resembles the shape of a fish, the elegant concrete span of the motorway accenting the tail.

In the summer you might be tempted to take a swim in the sparkling river; if the waters are high enough, a diving contest is held in July from the bridge by the tourist office. Anglers with long poles and tall straw hats can be seen along both of the town's rivers trying their luck for the *ayu* (sweetfish) and trout for which the region is famous. It's also worth seeking out the town's **Fountain of Youth** (Sōgisui): a natural spring that flows into two rectangular pools, located down the stone pathway leading to the pretty red bridge. It's about a kilometre northwest of the tourist office.

Practicalities

The simplest and fastest way to get to Gujō Hachiman from Gifu is by **bus**. Take either the Kōsoku Gifu Line or Shiro Tori line bus (1hr 10min; ¥1480 one way). By **train**, take the JR line to Mino Ōta then transfer to the private Nagaragawa line (1hr 20min; ¥1200). Coming from Hida Takayama or Shirayama, an infrequent bus service passes through Makido before getting to Gujō Hachiman. The **tourist information office** (daily 9am–5pm; ☎0575/67-1819) is set in a handsome Western-style building in the town centre, about 1km north of the train station. You can pick up maps and a simple guide to the area in English here. The town's website is ⓦwww.gujohachiman.com.

The best inexpensive **accommodation** in town is the *Gujō-Tōsenji Youth Hostel* (☎0575/67-0290, ⓕ67-0291; ❷), in the grounds of Tosenji temple. If this is full, there's the *Hachiman Cycling Terminal* (☎ & ⓕ0575/62-2139; ❷), about 5km northeast of town on Route 472. Part of a network of minshuku providing basic accommodation for cyclists, it is a bit spare and the food isn't great, but they can hire out bicycles and can show you the back way to town along the river – a quiet and scenic ride. *Nakashimaya* (☎0575/65-2191; ❻) is a pleasant ryokan right on Shinmachi, the main shopping street where the all-night O-bon dancing takes place.

For somewhere to **eat**, head around the corner from *Nakashimaya* to the convivial *Hanamura* (☎ 0575/67-0056; daily except Thurs 5–10.30pm); the set dinner of local dishes (*omikase*) is a great deal at ¥2500. Alternatively, try *Izumisaka* (☎0575/67-0474), serving *okinomiyaki* and *yakisoba*, and *Soba-no-Hiraji* (☎0575/65-2004), for soba; both are on the north side of the Yoshida river close by the Fountain of Youth.

Travel details

Trains

The trains between the major cities listed below are the fastest direct services. There are also frequent slower services, run by JR and several private com-panies, covering the same destinations. It's usually possible, especially on long-distance routes, to get there faster by changing between services.

Kanazawa to: Echigo-Yuzawa (10 daily; 2hr 30min); Fukui (every 15min; 50min); Kyoto (every

30min; 2hr 20min); Niigata (5 daily; 3hr 40min); Ōsaka (every 30min; 2hr 45min); Tokyo (Ueno Station; one daily; 6hr 5min); Toyama (every 45min; 40min).

Matsumoto to: Hakuba (12 daily; 55min); Hotaka (every 30min; 15min); Nagano (every 30min; 45min); Nagoya (hourly; 2hr); Ōsaka (1 daily; 4hr); Tokyo (Shinjuku Station; hourly; 2hr 30min).

Nagano to: Matsumoto (hourly; 50min); Nagoya (hourly; 2hr 50min); Niigata (2 daily; 3hr); Ōsaka (1 daily; 4hr 50min); Tokyo (every 30min; 1hr 30min).

Nagoya to: Fukui (8 daily; 2hr 5min); Fukuoka (Hakata Station; every 30min; 3hr 25min); Gifu (every 30min; 30min); Hiroshima (at least every 30min; 2hr 20min); Inuyama (every 30min; 35min); Kanazawa (8 daily; 2hr 55min); Kii-Katsuura (4 daily; 3hr 20min); Kyoto (every 10min; 45min); Matsumoto (hourly; 2hr); Nagano (hourly; 2hr 50min); Okayama (every 30min; 2hr); Ōsaka (every 10min; 1hr); Takayama (9 daily; 2hr 35min); Toba (8 daily; 1hr 30min); Tokyo (every 10min; 1hr 50min); Toyama (11 daily; 3hr 40min).

Takayama to: Kyoto (one daily; 4hr 20min); Nagoya (10 daily; 2hr 10min); Ōsaka (one daily; 5hr); Toyama (4 daily; 1hr 20min).

Toyama to: Kanazawa (hourly; 40min); Nagoya (4 daily; 3hr 40min); Niigata (5 daily; 3hr); Ōsaka (hourly; 3hr 15min); Takayama (4 daily; 1hr 30min); Tateyama (hourly; 1hr); Tokyo (Ueno Station; 1 daily; 5hr 40min).

Buses

The buses listed below are mainly long-distance services – often travelling overnight – between the major cities; local services are given where there is no alternative means of transport. For shorter journeys, however, trains are almost invariably quicker and often no more expensive.

Kanazawa to: Fukuoka (1 daily; 12hr 45min); Kyoto (5 daily; 3hr 50min); Matsumoto (2 daily; 4hr 50min); Nagoya (10 daily; 3hr); Niigata (2 daily; 4hr 40min); Sendai (1 daily; 8hr 30min); Takayama (2 daily; 3hr); Tokyo (6 daily; 7hr 30min); Wajima (4 daily; 2hr).

Matsumoto to: Nagano (hourly; 1hr 20min);

Ōsaka (1 daily; 6hr 50min); Tokyo (Shinjuku Station; hourly; 3hr 10min).

Nagano to: Matsumoto (hourly; 1hr 20min); Nozawa Onsen (5 daily; 1hr 15min); Togakushi (5 daily; 1hr 30min); Tokyo (hourly; 3hr 40min).

Nagoya to: Kanazawa (8 daily; 3hr); Kyoto (every 30min; 2hr 15min); Magome (1 daily; 2hr); Ogimachi (1 daily; 4hr); Ōsaka (6 daily; 3hr); Tokyo (hourly; 6hr).

Takayama to: Matsumoto (2 daily; 2hr 30min); Kanazawa (2 daily; 3hr).

Ferries

Nagoya to: Naha (1 daily; 21hr); Sendai (3–4 weekly; 21hr); Tomakomai (1 daily; 38hr 45min).

Tsuruga to: Otaru (daily except Sun; 21hr).

Flights

Komatsu to: Fukuoka (2 daily; 1hr 15min); Hiroshima (3 daily; 1hr 20min); Izumo (6 weekly; 1hr 5min); Kagoshima (5 weekly; 1hr 40min); Naha (1 daily; 2hr 15min); Okayama (2 daily; 55min); Sapporo (1 daily; 1hr 35min); Sendai (1 daily; 1hr 5min); Tokyo (8 daily; 1hr).

Matsumoto to: Fukuoka (1 daily; 1hr 30min); Ōsaka (daily; 1hr); Sapporo (1 daily; 1hr 30min).

Nagoya to: Akita (2 daily; 1hr 10min); Aomori (2 daily; 1hr 20min); Asahikawa (1 daily; 1hr 40min); Fukuoka (hourly; 1hr 15min); Hakodate (2 daily; 1hr 25min); Kagoshima (5 daily; 1hr 20min); Kōchi (2 daily; 55min); Kumamoto (2 daily; 1hr 15min); Matsuyama (2 daily; 1hr); Memanbetsu (1 daily; 1hr 50min); Miyazaki (5 daily; 1hr 15imin); Nagasaki (4 daily; 1hr 20min); Narita (1 daily; 1hr); Niigata (2 daily; 55min); Ōita (3 daily; 1hr 10min); Okinawa (6 daily; 2hr 10min); Sapporo (1 daily; 1hr 35min); Sendai (6 daily; 1hr 5min); Takamatsu (2 daily; 1hr 5min); Tokushima (1 daily; 1hr); Toyama (2 daily; 55min).

Toyama to: Fukuoka (1 daily; 1hr 20min); Hakodate (1 daily; 1hr 50min); Kansai International (1 daily; 1hr 15min); Nagoya (2 daily; 55min); Sapporo (1 daily; 1hr 20min); Tokyo (6 daily; 1hr 5min).

6

Kansai

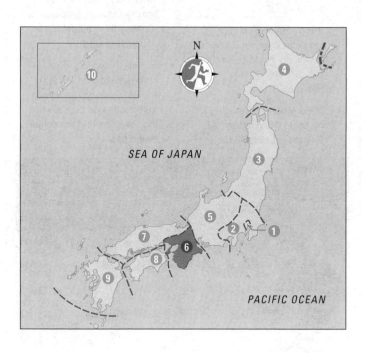

N

SEA OF JAPAN

PACIFIC OCEAN

CHAPTER 6

Highlights

* **Ōsaka Aquarium** The country's best aquarium, housed in an unusual, butterfly-shaped building. See p.504

* **Kinkaku-ji** Kyoto's Golden Pavilion and the city's most beautiful temple, built as a retirement home for a fourteenth-century shogun. See p.545

* **Imobō Hirano-ya** Enjoy a long and luxurious dinner of traditional Kyoto cuisine in this 300-year-old restaurant. See p.552

* **Miho Museum** Stunning art museum designed by I.M. Pei and set deep in the mountains of Shiga Prefecture. See p.567

* **Tōdai-ji** In the ancient capital city of Nara, this enormous temple was founded nearly 1300 years ago and is still the world's largest wooden building. See p.580

* **Kōya-san** Spend a night in temple lodgings atop one of the most holy mountains in Japan. See p.590

* **Himeji-jo** Japan's most impressive castle, dating from the seventeenth century and dominated by a towering six-storey central donjon. See p.615

△ Zen garden, Ryōan-ji, Kyoto

6

Kansai

n a country so devoid of flat land, the great rice-growing plains of **KANSAI**, the district around Ōsaka and Kyoto, are imbued with an almost mystical significance. This was where the first proto-nation took root, in the historic region known as Yamato, and where a distinct Japanese civilization evolved from the strong cultural influences of China and Korea. Kansai people are tremendously proud of their pivotal role in Japanese history and tend to look down on Tokyo, which they regard as an uncivilized upstart. Today, its superb legacy of temples, palaces, shrines, gardens, sculpture and crafts makes Kansai one of Japan's top tourist destinations.

The opening in the early 1990s of the spectacular **Kansai International Airport** – on a man-made island – created a new gateway into Japan, but the downturn in the economy, extremely high landing fees and concerns that the airport is sinking have meant it has not been the success originally envisaged. Nonetheless, it has given a significant tourism impetus to **Ōsaka**, the country's second largest metropolis. A much-maligned city, Ōsaka is not short of impressive attractions and easily makes up for its superficial shortcomings with an excess of commercial spirit – the source of its long-established wealth – and an unqualified love of eating, drinking and general bonhomie. Even on the briefest stay in Kansai it's worth visiting the city's fabulous **aquarium**, the handsomely restored castle **Ōsaka-jō** and the laudable **Liberty Ōsaka**, an uncompromising civil rights museum. You could also take a trip out to **Takarazuka**, home of an eponymous, show-stopping all-female musical drama troupe and the imaginative **Tezuka Osamu Manga Museum**, celebrating a Japanese master of comic-book art.

Until Emperor Meiji decamped for the bright lights of Tokyo in 1868, **Kyoto** was Japan's imperial capital, and to this day the city still represents the last word in cultural refinement – its elaborate cuisine, traditional theatre and even everyday crafts reflect this incomparable lineage. You could spend a lifetime exploring the city's bewildering array of ancient Buddhist **temples** and gorgeously decorated **imperial palaces** wrapped round with exquisite **gardens**, though to avoid cultural overload it's best to take Kyoto in small chunks, and to spend one day in the surrounding districts. **Hiei-zan**, in particular, offers not only majestic temples but also an escape from the city streets, while in **Uji**'s Byōdō-in you'll find one of the country's supreme architectural masterpieces.

Before Kyoto even existed, the monks of **Nara** were busily erecting their great Buddhist monuments under the patronage of an earlier group of princes and nobles. This relaxed, appealing town holds the distinction of being Japan's first permanent capital, founded in the early eighth century. A surprising number of buildings survive, notably the great **Tōdai-ji** with its colossal bronze

Buddha, but Nara's real glory lies in its wealth of statues. Nowhere is this more evident than at the nearby temple complex of **Hōryū-ji**, a treasure trove of early Japanese art.

South of Nara, the monasteries of **Kōya-san** provide a glimpse into contemporary religious practice in Japan. This mountain-top retreat – the headquarters of the Shingon Buddhist sect – has been an active centre of pilgrimage since the ninth century. The monks welcome people of all faiths to stay in their quiet old temples and join in the morning prayer service. Afterwards you can walk through the ancient **Okunoin** cemetery to visit the grave of Shingon's founder, Kōbō Daishi, wreathed in incense smoke under towering cryptomeria trees.

With so many major Buddhist foundations in the Kansai area, it's sometimes hard to remember that Shinto is Japan's native religion. But the balance is redressed over on the far east side of the district at **Ise-jingū**, one of the country's most important Shinto monuments. The Grand Shrine of Ise, as it's known, is dedicated to Amaterasu, the Sun Goddess, from whom all Japan's emperors are descended. **Ise** itself is the gateway to an attractive neck of land called **Shima Hantō**. Though the area has no dramatic sights, the lovely island-speckled bay of **Ago-wan** makes a rewarding destination for boat rides through its unspoiled scenery.

The port of **Kōbe**, now recovered from 1995's devastating earthquake, is less than thirty minutes west of Ōsaka in a dramatic location on the edge of Ōsaka Bay. Kōbe's sights are less of a draw than its relaxed cosmopolitan atmosphere, best experienced in a stroll around its shops and harbourside developments. Close by is the ancient hot-spring resort, **Arima Onsen**, which has managed to retain a little old-world rusticity alongside the modern hotel developments.

Wherever you choose to stay in Kansai, don't miss the opportunity to visit **Himeji**, on the area's western edge, to explore **Himeji-jō**, Japan's most impressive castle. Himeji also has a couple of intriguing museums in buildings designed by top contemporary architects and the lovely **Himeji Kōko-en**, nine connected gardens laid out according to traditional principles.

Kansai cuisine

Kansai folk, and Ōsakans in particular, are rightly proud of their region's long-held reputation of having the best, and most reasonably priced, food in the country. Each of the region's major cities has a number of specialities, with the most down-to-earth being found, somewhat predictably, in Ōsaka. One of the most accessible dishes is **okonomiyaki**, a savoury pancake made from wheat flour, cabbage, eggs and water, to which a variety of fillings is added, from pork to squid, topped off with a special sauce, mayonnaise and powdered seaweed known as *aonori*. Equally synonymous with Ōsaka is **takoyaki** (literally octopus balls), golfball-sized wheat-flour dumplings cooked on a griddle, each one containing a small chunk of octopus, and topped off with a tasty sauce similar to that used on *okonomiyaki*. Those bought hot off a street stall should be treated with caution, as the fillings tend to be red-hot and can burn the inside of your mouth.

Kōbe is home to the world-renowned **Kōbe beef**, originally introduced by Westerners in the late nineteenth century who wanted some real red meat to tuck into, rather than the fish and rice dishes popular with the natives. Kōbe beef is very tender, very succulent and very expensive, and is still something of a status symbol for older Japanese wanting to show both their sophisticated Western ways and their wealth. At the other end of the scale is **sobameishi**, sometimes referred to as "Kōbe soul food", a dish made of chopped up soba noodles mixed with fried rice (*meishi*) and sometimes with bits of pork and other fillings thrown in. It's fairly cheap and filling, but is uncommon outside Kōbe.

Kyoto, with its long imperial tradition, is home to **kyō-ryōri** cuisine, a refined style of cooking that harks back to the city's aristocratic days. The best way to experience this cuisine is *kaiseki*: a multi-course banquet featuring a large variety of vegetables and tōfu-based dishes. These feasts can easily cost upwards of ¥10,000, however, and *kaiseki* restaurants often provide smaller-sized lunchboxes which offer a more affordable way to sample *kyō-ryōri* for those on a budget or in a rush. Kyoto's myriad temples are the main factor behind the city's other noted cuisine, **shōjin-ryōri** (Buddhist vegetarian cooking featuring various mountain vegetable, soya bean and tofu-based dishes). At the cheaper end of the market, Kyoto is noted for its **nishin soba**, a big bowl of soba noodles with a part-dried piece of herring on top.

The most convenient way of **getting around** the Kansai district is by train. The area is crisscrossed by a skein of competing JR and private rail lines, while the Tōkaidō Shinkansen provides a high-speed service between Ōsaka, Kyoto, Kōbe and Himeji. If you plan to travel intensively round the region, you might want to investigate JR-West's Kansai Area Pass. Valid for between one and four consecutive days (¥2000–¥6000), the pass allows unlimited travel on all local services operated by JR West, apart from the Shinkansen. It also offers discounts on admission to various cultural and tourist sights, including art museums and amusement parks along JR lines. For those travelling on to Fukuoka, the San'yō Area Pass covers JR services from Kansai Airport via Ōsaka, Kōbe and Himeji. Another option is to take advantage of the loose alignment which the region's private railway lines, subway networks and bus companies have made under the "Surutto Kansai" umbrella. Buying stored-value tickets – known as *Surutto Kansai kādo*, and available in ¥1000, ¥2000, ¥3000 and ¥5000 denominations – enables travellers to ride on almost any bus, subway or private railway in the whole of the region. Even if you have a JR Rail Pass these cards are handy, as they save the hassle of buying tickets each time you jump on a bus or ride the subway.

Ōsaka and around

The urban equivalent of the Elephant Man, **ŌSAKA**, Japan's third largest city after Tokyo and Yokohama, yearns to be loved despite its ugliness. It may well lack the pockets of beauty and refinement found in nearby Kyoto, but beyond the unrelenting concrete cityscape, Ōsaka is a vibrant metropolis, inhabited by famously easy-going citizens with a taste for the good things in life.

The handsomely renovated castle, **Ōsaka-jō**, dominates Ōsaka's heart just as it did centuries ago, while the venerable **Shitennō-ji** and **Sumiyoshi Taisha** hark back to the city's past importance as a religious centre. In contrast, bizarre modern buildings, such as the spaceship-like **Ōsaka Dome** sports stadium and the fantastic **aquarium** at the Tempozan Harbour Village, sparkle amidst the urban sprawl like shiny gems, while the large-scale theme park, **Universal Studios Japan**, is another of the city's modern attractions.

But what is really special about Ōsaka is its people, who speak one of Japan's more earthy dialects, **Ōsaka-ben**, and are as friendly as Kyoto folk can be frosty. Ōsakans may greet each other saying "Mō kari-makka?" ("Are you making any money?"), but they also know how to enjoy themselves once work has stopped. Whereas Tokyo has shut down its once thriving Harajuku band scene, Ōsakans still thrash out rock tunes by the castle every Sunday. Downtown Shinsaibashi is an eternal fancy-dress parade of matronly shoppers and boozy *bons viveurs*, where bequiffed lads cast their nets for mini-skirted girls on the Ebisu-bashi (fishing bridge). In a city which cultivated high **arts**, such as Bunraku puppetry, the locals also have a gift for lowlife comedy; Takeshi "Beat" Kitano, the internationally famous film director, started his career as a comedian in Ōsaka, while "Knock" Yokoyama, another retired funny man, was elected prefectural governor in the late 1990s, before resigning over a sexual harassment case in late 1999. Ōsaka is also one of Japan's great **food** cities, but Ōsakans are not precious about their cuisine, a typical local dish being *takoyaki*, battered octopus balls, usually sold as a street snack.

Ōsaka also feels a more welcoming place for foreigners. It has Japan's largest community of Koreans and a growing *gaijin* population. There's also a willingness to face up to uncomfortable social issues, exemplified by the city's admirable civil rights museum, **Liberty Ōsaka**, which among other things focuses on Japan's untouchables, the Burakumin.

If you want to escape Ōsaka's urban landscape for a day, take a trip out to **Takarazuka**, home of the eponymous musical drama troupe. As well as taking in one of the all-female troupe's glitzy shows, you can check out the imaginative artwork at the **Tezuka Osamu Manga Museum**, a showcase for local artist Tezuka, widely regarded as the god of *manga* (comic books).

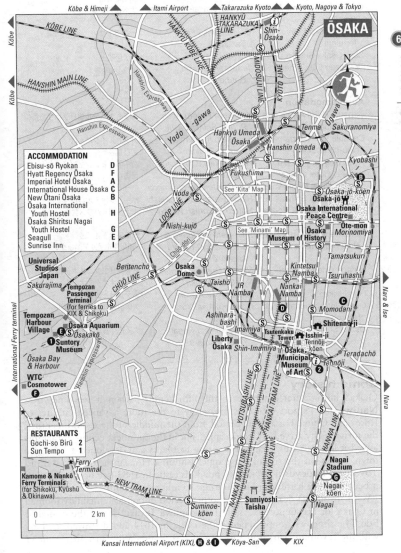

ŌSAKA

6

KANSAI | Ōsaka and around

ACCOMMODATION
Ebisu-sō Ryokan	D
Hyatt Regency Ōsaka	F
Imperial Hotel Ōsaka	A
International House Ōsaka	C
New Ōtani Ōsaka	B
Ōsaka International	
Youth Hostel	H
Ōsaka Shiritsu Nagai	
Youth Hostel	G
Seagull	E
Sunrise Inn	I

RESTAURANTS
Gochi-so Birū	2
Sun Tempo	1

0   2 km

Ōsaka	Ōsaka	大阪
Arrival		
Hankyū Umeda Station	*Hankyū Umeda-eki*	阪急梅田駅
Hanshin Umeda Station	*Hanshin Umeda-eki*	阪神梅田駅
JR Namba Station	*JR Namba-eki*	ＪＲ難波駅
JR Ōsaka Station	*JR Ōsaka-eki*	ＪＲ大阪駅
Kansai International Airport	*Kansai Kokusai-Kūkō*	関西国際空港
Nankai Namba Station	*Nankai Namba-eki*	南海難海駅
Ōsaka International Airport (Itami)	*Ōsaka Kokusai-Kūkō Itami*	大阪国際空港（伊丹）
Ōsaka Nankō Ferry Terminal	*Ōsaka Nankō Ferii Tāminaru*	大阪南港フェリーターミナル
Shin-Ōsaka Station	*Shin-Ōsaka-eki*	新大阪駅
Tenpozan East Wharf	*Tenpozan Higashi Ganbeki*	天保山東岸壁

Accommodation		
Capsule Hotel Asahiplaza Shinsaibashi	*Kapuseru Hoteru Asahi Puraza Shinsaibashi*	カプセルホテル朝日プラザ心斎橋
Capsule Inn Namba	*Kapuseru In Namba*	カプセルインなんば
Ebisu-sō Ryokan	*Ebisu-sō Ryokan*	えびす荘旅館
Hyatt Regency Ōsaka	*Haiatto Rejenshii Ōsaka*	ハイアットレジェンシー大阪
Imperial Hotel Ōsaka	*Teikoku Hoteru Ōsaka*	帝国ホテル大阪
Hearton Hotel Nishi-Umeda	*Hāton Hoteru Nishi-Umeda*	ハートンホテル西梅田
Hearton Hotel Shinsaibashi	*Hāton Hoteru Shinsaibashi*	ハートンホテル心斎橋
Hotel International House Ōsaka	*Hoteru Kokuritsu Hausu Ōsaka*	ホテル国立ハウス大阪
Hotel New Hankyu & Hotel New Hankyu Annex	*Shin-Hankyū Hoteru & Shin-Hankyū Hoteru Anekkusu*	新阪急ホテル ＆ 新阪急ホテルアネックス
Namba Oriental Hotel	*Namba Orientaru Hoteru*	難波オリエンタルホテル
New Ōtani Ōsaka	*Nyū Ōtani Ōsaka*	ニューオオタニ大阪
Hotel Nikkō Ōsaka	*Hoteru Nikkō Ōsaka*	ホテル日光大阪
Ōsaka International Youth Hostel	*Ōsaka Kokusai Yūsu Hosuteru*	大阪国際ユースホステル
Ōsaka Shiritsu Nagai Youth Hostel	*Ōsaka Shiritsu Nagai Yūsu Hosuteru*	大阪市立長居ユースホステル

Some history

Ōsaka's history stretches back to the fifth century, when it was known as **Naniwa** and its port served as a gateway to the more advanced cultures of Korea and China. For a short period, from the middle of the seventh century, the thriving city served as Japan's capital, but in the turbulent centuries that followed it lost its status, changed its name to Ōsaka and developed as a temple town. It was on the site of the temple Ishiyama Hongan-ji that the warlord **Toyotomi Hideyoshi** decided to build his castle in 1583 (see box, p.501) and it became a key bastion in his campaign to unite the country.

With Toyotomi's death in 1598, another period of political instability loomed in Ōsaka for his supporters, as rival **Tokugawa Ieyasu** shifted the capital to Edo. The shogun's troops besieged the castle in 1614 and destroyed it, along with the Toyotomi clan's hopes for power, a year later. With Japan firmly under

Ritz Carlton Ōsaka	*Za Rittsu Kāruton Ōsaka*	ザリッツカールトン大阪
Hotel Seagull	*Hoteru Shiigaru*	ホテルシーガル
Sunrise Inn	*Sanraizu In*	サンライズイン

The City

Dōtombori	*Dōtombori*	道頓堀
Liberty Ōsaka	*Ribati Ōsaka*	リバティ大阪
Museum of Oriental Ceramics	*Tōyo Tōji Bijutsukan*	東洋陶磁美術館
Namba	*Namba*	難波
National Bunraku Theatre	*Kokuritsu Bunraku Gekijō*	国立文楽劇場
Ōsaka-jō	*Ōsaka-jō*	大阪城
Ōsaka Aquarium	*Kaiyūkan*	海遊館
Ōsaka Museum of History	*Ōsaka Rekishi Hakubutsukan*	大阪歴史博物館
Ōsaka Nō Hall	*Ōsaka Nōgaku-kaikan*	大阪能楽会館
Ōsaka Shōchiku-za	*Ōsaka Shōchiku-za*	大阪松竹座
Shinsaibashi	*Shinsaibashi*	心斎橋
Shin-Sekai	*Shin-Sekai*	新世界
Shitennō-ji	*Shitennō-ji*	四天王寺
Sumiyoshi Taisha	*Sumiyoshi Taisha*	住吉大社
Tempozan Harbour Village	*Tempozan Hābā Birejji*	天保山ハーバービレッジ
Tennōji-kōen	*Tennōji-kōen*	
Umeda	*Umeda*	梅田

Restaurants

Burdigala	*Burudigara*	ブルディガラ
Fun Fun Plaza	*Fan Fan Puraza*	ファンファンプラザ
Gataro	*Gataro*	がたろ
Gochi-sō Biru	*Gochi-sō Biru*	ごちそうビル
Herbis Plaza	*Hābisu Puraza*	ハービスプラザ
Kani Dōraku	*Kani Dōraku*	かに道楽
Kisoji	*Kisoji*	木曽路
Kuidaore	*Kuidaore*	くいだおれ
Madonna	*Madonna*	マドンナ
Nawasushi	*Nawasushi*	縄寿司
Ninniku-ya	*Ninniku-ya*	にんにく屋

their control, the Tokugawa shoguns were happy to allow the castle to be rebuilt and for Ōsaka to continue developing as an economic and commercial centre, which it did with spectacular success. The wealth of what became known as the "kitchen of Japan" led to patronage of the arts, such as Kabuki and Bunraku, and an appreciation of fine food, still retained today.

In the twentieth century, Ōsaka has dragged itself up from the rubble of World War II bombings to become one of the wealthiest cities in the world, and the economic engine of a region that has a gross domestic product greater than that of Canada. Although its hopes of hosting the 2008 Olympic Games were misplaced (Nagano having held the 1996 Winter Olympics), the development programme that was pushed through resulted in many new facilities, including the Universal Studios theme park on Ōsaka Bay. Critics, however, say that the city is now so mired in debt as to be on the verge of bankruptcy.

Arrival

Served by two airports, numerous ferries and buses, not to mention a slew of railway companies, you can arrive in Ōsaka from almost any point in Japan and, via Kansai International Airport, from many places overseas, too. There's also a weekly ferry service between Ōsaka and Shanghai in China.

By plane

All international and many domestic flights now arrive at **Kansai International airport (KIX)**, on a man-made island in Ōsaka Bay, some 35km south of the city centre. International arrivals are processed on the first floor of the sleek modern building, topped with a wave-like roof, where you'll also find the small **Kansai Tourist Information Centre** (daily 9am–9pm; ☏0724/56-6025), a separate desk where you can make hotel reservations, and several **bureaux de change** booths. Domestic arrivals are on the second floor.

The fastest way into the city is by train. Services depart from the station connected to the second floor of the passenger terminal building. The regular **Nankai Express**, or *kaisoku* (¥890), takes just over forty minutes to reach Nankai Namba Station, although it's hard to resist the chic **Rapi:t** (pronounced "Rapid"), designed like a train from a sci-fi comic, which costs ¥1390 and does the journey in around thirty minutes. From Nankai Namba Station you can take a subway or taxi to other parts of the city.

JR also runs trains directly to several stations in and around Ōsaka from KIX, and if you have a rail pass voucher you can exchange it at Kansai Airport Station. For pass holders, the services to JR Namba Station (1hr; ¥1010) are a good alternative to the Nankai Express. The **Haruka** limited express is a convenient, but pricey, option, stopping at Tennōji Station (30min; ¥2270; handy for the **Nagai Youth Hostel**; Shin-Ōsaka Station (45min; ¥2980), where you can catch the Shinkansen; and then on to Kyoto (1hr 15min; ¥3490). If you're in no hurry, the regular JR express trains to Tennōji Station (45min; ¥1010) and Ōsaka Station (70min; ¥1160), in the Umeda area of the city, are worth considering. The first Haruka leaves Shin-Ōsaka at 6.17am, while the last one departs at 8.46pm, though regular JR expresses run twice an hour from Ōsaka Station until 10.33pm. From the airport, the first Haruka leaves at 6.29am, the last at 10.18pm. The last through-train from the airport to JR Ōsaka leaves fifteen minutes later – if you miss that you'll need to change at Tennōji Station.

To avoid the hassle of dragging your luggage on and off trains, there are also **limousine buses** and taxis for various locations around Ōsaka, including several hotels, departing from international arrivals. All central city locations take forty minutes to one hour to reach, depending on the traffic, and cost ¥1300. There's also a direct bus to Itami airport (see below; 1hr 20min; ¥1700), and services to Kyoto, Kōbe and Nara. **Taxis** to central Ōsaka are expensive (¥10,000), and no faster than the buses.

Itami airport is 10km north of the city centre; it's also known as Ōsaka International Airport even though it no longer handles overseas flights. From the airport there are regular buses into the city (25–50min depending on destination; ¥340–680) and also to Shin-Ōsaka Station (25min; ¥480), where you can connect to the Shinkansen. There are also direct limousine buses to KIX (1hr 20min; ¥1700) and on to Kyoto and Kōbe. A taxi to Umeda in central Ōsaka costs around ¥5000. There's also a **monorail** (tickets from ¥190), which links the airport with parts of north Ōsaka, connecting at various points to the city subway system and both the Hankyu and Keihan private railways.

By train

Shinkansen, taking around three hours from Tokyo or Fukuoka in Kyūshū (the two termini of the line), pull into **Shin-Ōsaka Station**, north of the city centre. You can transfer here to other JR services around the area or to the city's subway lines.

JR services, along the Tōkaidō line connecting Nagoya, Kyoto and Kōbe with Ōsaka, arrive at the central **Ōsaka Station**, in Umeda, where you'll also find the termini for the Hankyū and Hanshin lines, both of which provide cheaper connections with Kyoto and Kōbe than JR if you're not using a rail pass. Services from Nara (see p.574) on the Kintetsu line arrive at **Kintetsu Namba Station**, in the heart of the Minami district. Those from Ise (see p.596) arrive at Uehonmachi, also on the Kintetsu network.

By bus

Ōsaka has various long-distance **bus stations**. These are located beside the JR Ōsaka Station in Umeda; at the Namba Kaisoku Bus Terminal and Ōsaka City Air Terminal in Namba; at Kintetsu Uehonmachi, south of the castle; and at Abenobashi near Tennōji, 1km further south of the castle. All are beside or near subway and train stations for connections around the city.

By boat

Ōsaka is still a major port of call for many of the **ferries** plying routes around Japan, and sailing into Ōsaka Bay is a memorable way of approaching the city. The port is west of the city centre and has good transport links via the subway and train network. Most ferries use the Ōsaka Nankō Terminal, close to Ferry Terminal Station on the New Tram monorail, which connects to the city's subway network. The nearest station to the less busy Tempozan East Wharf is Ōsaka-kō on the Chūō subway line, a ten-minute walk away.

Moving on from Ōsaka

The international departure lounge at Kansai International Airport is on the fourth floor. The ¥2650 departure tax is now included in the price of most tickets, but some cheap discount tickets might not include it, in which case you'll have to pay it upon check-in. Domestic departures are on the second floor. It's worth noting that Kyoto, Nankai Namba and JR Namba stations all have CAT (city air terminal) facilities, as does the jetfoil terminal on Kōbe's Port Island, where you can go through check-in procedures for Japanese and some other airlines.

If you plan to depart Ōsaka by **bus**, check first with one of the tourist information centres (see p.496) on timetables and which station to go to.

Among other places, there are **ferry** services from Ōsaka to Beppu, Miyazaki and Shin-Moji on Kyūshū (see p.788), and to Kōchi, Matsuyama and several other destinations on Shikoku (see p.711). In addition, there's a slow boat to Shanghai, China, which leaves once a week from Ōsaka Nankō International Ferry Terminal, close by Cosmosquare Station, where the Techno Port line meets the New Tram line. Check current timetables and fares with the tourist information office.

Orientation and information

Like all big Japanese cities, Ōsaka is divided into wards (*ku*), but you'll often hear locals talking of Kita (north) and Minami (south), the split being along Chūō-dōri. **Kita** covers the areas of **Umeda**, where all the main railway companies have stations, and **Shin-Ōsaka**, north of the Yodo-gawa River and location of the Shinkansen station. On the east side of this area is **Ōsaka-jō**, the castle. The shopping and entertainment districts of Shinsaibashi, Dōtombori and Namba are all part of **Minami**.

Slightly further south is **Tennōji**, where you'll find Tennōji-kōen and the temple Shitennō-ji and, further south again, the ancient shrine Sumiyoshi Taisha. West of these districts lies the patchwork of landfill islands edging Ōsaka Bay; the Ōsaka Aquarium is at **Tempozan Harbour Village**, while the Kansai area's tallest building, the WTC Cosmotower, is further south at **Nankō**.

Information

The Ōsaka Tourist Association beats both Tokyo and Kyoto hands down. There are **tourist information** offices all over the city, as well as at KIX, so that no matter where you arrive you're sure to be within walking distance of one. All are open daily from 8am to 8pm, have English-speaking staff and can help you book accommodation. Make sure you also pick up a free copy of the **Ōsaka City Map**, which includes a handy subway and local train map, too.

There's an office in Shin-Ōsaka Station (☎06/6305-3311), handy if you've arrived by Shinkansen, while the main office is in Umeda's JR Ōsaka Station (☎06/6345-2189), tucked away beside the Midōsuji East Gate opposite the Hankyū department store. You should apply at either of these if you're interested in participating in the home-visit programme (see "Listings", p.509). You'll also find tourist information counters beneath the OCAT train terminal at JR Namba Station (☎06/6643-2125) and in Tennōji Station (☎06/6774-3077). If you're going to be in Ōsaka for a while, it's well worth visiting the **International House Ōsaka**, 8-2-6 Uehonmachi (☎06/6772-5931), which has a well-stocked library and cultural exchange facilities.

At all the information counters and in most top hotels you'll find the free quarterly booklet *Meet Ōsaka*, which carries basic **listings** of events. A better outline of what's happening appears in the monthly *Kansai Time Out* (ⓦwww.kto.co.jp), one of Japan's best English-language magazines, which carries detailed information and listings for the whole Kansai area as well as interesting features. *The Japan Times and Daily Yomiuri* newspapers also carry special weekly sections on what's on in the Ōsaka area, while the free weekly *Kansai Flea Market* and the free monthly *Kansai Scene* contain information about bars, accommodation and suchlike, and can be found in places where foreigners tend to congregate.

The Kansai Window site at ⓦwww.kansai.gr.jp offers background information on the region. JNTO's Ōsaka site is at ⓦwww.jnto.go.jp/eng/RTG/RI/kansai/osaka/osaka/osaka.html.

City transport

Ōsaka's extensive **subway and train system** operates exactly like Tokyo's – it even has an overground circular line, called the JR Loop line, with trains running both clockwise and anticlockwise, just like the Yamanote line in Tokyo. The Loop line is handy, especially if you're using a rail pass, but most of the time you'll find the subway more convenient and quicker for getting around the city. You can transfer between the seven subway lines and the New Tram line on the same ticket, but if you switch to any of the railway lines at a connecting station you'll need to buy either another ticket or a special transfer ticket when you start your journey. Most journeys across central Ōsaka cost ¥230. See the colour insert at the back of the book for a **map** of the Ōsaka subway.

Because Ōsaka's attractions are widely scattered, investing in a **one-day pass** (¥850) is worth considering if you're up for a hectic round of the sights. The pass, like a thin telephone card, is valid on all the subways and will be date-stamped when you pass it through the gate machines the first time. On the twentieth of each month (or twenty-first if the twentieth falls on a Sunday) you can buy the "No-My-Car-Day" pass (a consciousness-raising scheme to encourage people to use public transport instead of their cars), which is the same as the one-day pass, but only costs ¥600. If you're spending a few days in Ōsaka, you could also buy a pre-paid subway card which costs ¥3000 but provides ¥3300 worth of travel – these can be bought at subway-ticket vending machines as well as station kiosks.

There are plenty of **buses**, but you'll find the subways and trains with their English signs and maps much easier to use. If you do need to go short distances quickly, flag down a **taxi**; a city-centre journey shouldn't cost more than ¥2000.

Accommodation

Being a commercial city, Ōsaka's **accommodation** ranges from scores of business hotels near the main train stations to some of the swankiest luxury hotels you'll come across in Japan. However, due to a glut of top-class hotels, and the lingering effect of the recession, many special offers and discounts are available – it pays to ask. If you're in search of more traditional ryokan, you'll be better off staying in Kyoto (see p.512). The most convenient locations in Ōsaka are **Umeda** and the shopping and nightlife districts of **Shinsaibashi** and **Namba**. However, local transport is so efficient that it's no great problem to be based elsewhere, such as around Ōsaka Bay or even south of the city closer to Kansai International airport.

Kita

The following are marked on the map on p.498.

Hearton Hotel Nishi-Umeda 3-3-55 Umeda ☎06/6342-1111, ⓦ www.hearton.co.jp/english. Popular new business hotel just behind the main post office next to JR Ōsaka Station. Rooms are smart, clean and functional, and come with cable TV. Ōsaka/Umeda stations. ❹

Imperial Hotel Ōsaka 1-8-50 Temmabashi ☎06/6881-1111, ⓦ www.imperialhotel.co.jp. This gorgeous hotel, overlooking the Ō-kawa river, is just as luxurious as its famous Tokyo parent, from which it borrows many Frank Lloyd Wright touches. Perfumed air, a golf driving range and a select range of elegant restaurants are all part of the experience. Sakuranomiya Station. ❼

Hotel New Hankyu & Hotel New Hankyu Annex 1-1-35 Shibata ☎06/6372-5101, ⓦ http://hotel.newhankyu.co.jp/osaka-e. Enormous mid-range hotel catering to Japanese tourists. Rooms are rather small, though there are a number of Japanese-style rooms if you want to experience a traditional night's rest. The location is excellent, with good transport connections close by. Ōsaka/Umeda stations. ❻

New Ōtani Ōsaka 1-4-1 Shiromi ☎06/6941-1111, ⓦ www.osaka.newotani.co.jp/e/. One of the city's top hotels. Many of the comfortable rooms overlook the castle and rivers, and there's a wide range of restaurants and other facilities, and excellent service. Ōsaka-jō-kōen Station. ❼

Ritz Carlton Ōsaka 2-5-25 Umeda ☎06/6343-7000, ⓦ www.ritzcarlton.com. Luxury hotel with the intimate feel of a European country house, sprinkled liberally with antiques and Japanese objets d'art. Rooms have fantastic views across the city, there's a great range of restaurants and the pool and gym are free to guests. It's worth asking if they're running any special deals. Ōsaka/Umeda stations. ❽

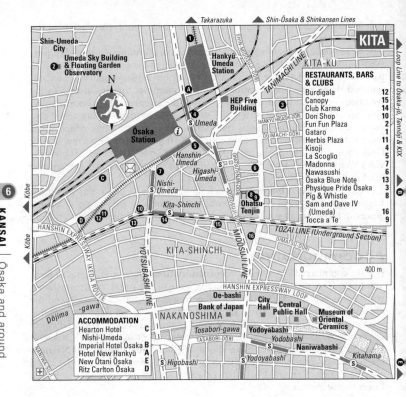

Takarazuka Shin-Ōsaka & Shinkansen Lines

Loop Line to Ōsaka-jō, Tennōji & KIX

Shin-Umeda City
Umeda Sky Building & Floating Garden Observatory
Hankyū Umeda Station
KITA-KU
HEP Five Building
Ōsaka Station
Umeda
Hanshin Umeda
Higashi-Umeda
Nishi-Umeda
Kita-Shinchi
Ohatsu Tenjin
HANSHIN EXPRESSWAY IKEDA ROUTE
Kōbe
KANSAI | Ōsaka and around

RESTAURANTS, BARS & CLUBS

Burdigala	12
Canopy	15
Club Karma	14
Don Shop	10
Fun Fun Plaza	2
Gataro	1
Herbis Plaza	11
Kisoji	4
La Scoglio	5
Madonna	7
Nawasushi	6
Ōsaka Blue Note	13
Physique Pride Ōsaka	8
Pig & Whistle	3
Sam and Dave IV (Umeda)	16
Tocca a Te	9

TOZAI LINE (Underground Section)
KITA-SHINCHI
0 400 m

Oe-bashi
Bank of Japan
City Hall
Central Public Hall
Museum of Oriental Ceramics
NAKANOSHIMA
-gawa
Dōjima
Tosabori-gawa
Yodoyabashi
Yodoyabashi
Naniwabashi
Kitahama
Higobashi
Yodoyabashi

ACCOMMODATION

Hearton Hotel Nishi-Umeda	C
Imperial Hotel Ōsaka	B
Hotel New Hankyū	A
New Ōtani Ōsaka	E
Ritz Carlton Ōsaka	D

Minami

The following are marked on the map on p.499.

Capsule Hotel Asahiplaza Shinsaibashi 2-12-22 Nishi-Shinsaibashi ☎06/6213-1991, ⓦwww.asahiplaza.co.jp/capcel/english.html. Reasonably smart, men-only capsule hotel, with a large bath, sauna and restaurant. Shinsaibashi Station. ¥2600 per person.

Capsule Inn Namba 1-7-16 Namba ☎06/6633-2666. Basic hotel close by all the Namba stations with capsules for both men and women (¥2990), single rooms and small doubles (❸). Namba Station.

Ebisu-sō Ryokan 1-7-33 Nipponbashi-nishi ☎06/6643-4861, ⓦwww.jpinn.com/inn/12-1.html. One of the city's few ryokan. The tatami rooms are a little shabby, but the welcome is friendly and the location, close to Namba, is handy for the city's nightlife. Ebisuchō Station. ❹

Hearton Hotel Shinsaibashi 1-5-24 Nishi-Shinsaibashi ☎06/6251-3711, ⓦwww.hearton.co.jp/english. Another branch of

this Kansai business hotel chain, located in the heart of the Amerika-Mura nightlife district, with clean and functional rooms. There's a third branch a few minutes' walk away in case this one is full. Shinsaibashi Station. ❹

Namba Oriental Hotel 2-8-17 Sennichi-mae ☎06/6647-8111, ⓦwww.nambaoriental-daole.co.jp/hotel. Good-value mid-range hotel in a fine location. Some of the spacious rooms have small balconies overlooking a courtyard with an Italianate fountain. Namba and Nipponbashi stations. ❻

Hotel Nikkō Ōsaka 1-3-3 Nishi-Shinsaibashi ☎06/6244-1281, ⓦwww.hno.co.jp/english/index_e.html. Top-class hotel close to Ōsaka's best nightlife, with spacious and comfortable rooms, attentive service and a good range of restaurants, including a coffee shop which does a huge buffet breakfast. Shinsaibashi Station. ❼

Other areas

The following are marked on the map on p.491.

Hyatt Regency Ōsaka 1-13-11 Nankō-Kita ☎06/6612-1234, ⓕ6614-7800, ⓦwww.hyattregencyosaka.com. Good luxury choice near the Ōsaka World Trade Centre, offering well-appointed rooms with a minimalist design, elegant public areas and restaurants, and indoor and outdoor pools. Nakafutō Station. **⓻**

Hotel International House Ōsaka 8-2-6 Uehonmachi ☎06/6773-8181, ⓕ6773-0777. Used mainly by those attending meetings at the International House, with large and very good-value rooms (mostly singles for ¥7000) and a restaurant and café. Midnight curfew. Uehonmachi Station. **⓹**

Ōsaka International Youth Hostel 4-1-56 Hagoromo, Takaishi-shi ☎0722/65-8539, ⓦhttp://homepage3.nifty.com/osakayh/osakaint.html. This modern, clean youth hostel has both tatami dorm rooms (¥3150 per person) and Western-style en-suite twins (**⓸**). It's midway between KIX and the city centre, ten minutes' walk from Hagoromo Station on the Nankai main line. Hagoromo Station.

Ōsaka Shiritsu Nagai Youth Hostel 1-1 Nagai-kōen ☎06/6699-5631, ⓕ6699-5644. Excellent modern hostel next to Nagai sports stadium with six-bed dorms (¥2500 per person), spacious private doubles (**⓷**) and family rooms. Staff are friendly and speak some English and meals are reasonable (there's also a kitchen for self-catering). The main drawback is the 11pm curfew. Tsurugaoka/Nagai stations.

RESTAURANTS, BARS & CLUBS

Africa	10	Kani Doraku	14
Bears	18	Ken's Chanto Dining	4
Capricciosa	5	Kuidaore	15
The Cellar	8	Murphy's	6
Garb	2	Namaste	3
Green Earth	1	Ninniku-ya	11
Il Gemello	13	Pig & Whistle	9
Joule	7	Rockets	17
Kanadian	16	Underlounge	12

ACCOMMODATION

Capsule Hotel Asahiplaza Shinsaibashi **C**
Capsule Inn Namba **E**
Ebisu-sō Ryokan **F**
Hearton Hotel Shinsaibashi **B**
Namba Oriental **D**
Nikkō Ōsaka **A**

Hotel Seagull 1-5-15 Kaigan-dōri ℡06/6573-0011, ℻6575-5031. Stylish contemporary hotel, part of the Tempozan Harbour Village development. Rooms are decorated in cool blues and there's a bright lobby restaurant. Ōsaka-kō Station. ❼

Sunrise Inn 925 Naka-Kaizuka-shi ℡0724/32-3711, ⓦwww.kanku-city.or.jp/sunrise/. Not far from KIX, this Western-style hotel, a Japanese Inn Group member, is good value and has single rooms from ¥6600. The attached restaurant, Kashin, serves excellent traditional cuisine at reasonable prices. Kaizuka Station. ❺

The City

Ōsaka's best sights are scattered far and wide, but there are some areas worth exploring on foot. A fine place to start is the castle **Ōsaka-jō** and its immediate environs. **Umeda**, north of the centre, also has a few attractions, such as the rarefied **Museum of Oriental Ceramics** and the soaring skyscrapers near the clutch of train stations. The areas south of the Ogawa, including Shinsaibashi, Dōtombori, Amerika-mura and Namba, are almost exclusively shopping, eating and entertainment districts which fully come to life at night (see p.506).

Another good area for strolling around is **Tennōji**, south of the centre, where you'll find **Shitennō-ji**, the city's most important temple, and an evocative old downtown area around **Tennōji-kōen**. Further south is **Sumiyoshi Taisha**, Ōsaka's venerable shrine, an oasis of greenery amid the urban sprawl.

Heading west towards the port area, don't miss out on the enlightening **Liberty Ōsaka**, a museum highlighting aspects of Japanese contemporary history which are usually swept under the carpet. At Tempozan Harbour Village, the ultra-cool **Ōsaka Aquarium** has the best collection of aquatic life on display in Japan, while nearby is the new **Universal Studios Japan**, a giant theme park with eighteen spectacular rides.

Ōsaka-jō and around

Critics often throw scorn on **Ōsaka-jō**, saying the only reason the castle is the single most-visited attraction in Japan – outdoing the country's best fortress Himeji-jō (see p.615) and even Mount Fuji – is because it's the only thing to see in the city. In fact, Ōsaka has plenty to see, but the castle is the main focus, especially since a ¥7 billion facelift, completed in 1997, restored the east outer moat, spruced up the donjon's glittering exterior and modernized the eight floors of displays inside.

There are several entrances to the park (free) surrounding the castle, but the most impressive is through the **Ōte-mon** gate, dating from 1629, on the west side, two minutes' walk east of the Tanimachi 4-chōme subway station. The stone towers on this side of the castle all date from the Tokugawa era and you can visit the pretty **Nishinomaru garden** (Tues–Sun 9am–4.30pm; ¥200) between the west outer and inner moats, where cherry trees bloom in spring. As you head up towards the donjon through the southern Sakura-mon gate, keep an eye out for the 130-tonne **Tako-ishi** (Octopus Stone): with a surface area of sixty square metres, this is the largest rock used in the original construction of the castle walls.

It's long been a point of amusement that Ōsaka-jō's main tower, or **donjon** (daily 9am–5pm; ¥600; ℡06/6941-3044, ⓦwww.museum.or.jp/osakajo/html/info-E.html), has its own elevator inside, and since the recent renovation it also has one outside too, so that the elderly and those in wheelchairs can avoid the steps to the entrance. Head up to the eighth floor for a panoramic view of the city and castle grounds; the plantation of fruit trees you can see between the moats on the castle's eastern flank is a riot of blossom in March. There are also some 3-D displays of famous old Ōsaka views inside the tower. Working your way down the floors you'll be guided through the life of Toyotomi Hideyoshi (see box opposite) and the castle's colourful history. The displays include the highly detailed folding screen painting of the *Summer War of Ōsaka* and a full-scale recreation of Toyotomi's famous golden tearoom. On the first floor it's worth dropping by the mini-theatre to see the free history videos screened with English subtitles.

From the donjon, there's a choice of directions through the park. Returning through the Sakura-mon and turning left past the dry moat through the Tamatsukuri-mon will bring you to the sobering **Ōsaka International Peace Centre** (Tues–Sun 9.30am–5pm; ¥250; ℡06/6947-7208) in the southern corner of the park. As at similar museums in Hiroshima and Nagasaki, the worthy but heavy-going displays attempt to square the destruction of Ōsaka with Japan's provocative actions before and during World War II. A jollier alternative is the route north from the main tower across the Gokuraku-bashi bridge and past the circular concert hall towards the exit for the Ōsaka-jō-kōen Station. On Sunday, between noon and 6pm, **amateur rock bands** crank out their music in front of the station to hordes of fans, mainly teenage girls waggling their arms in unison.

To the southwest of the castle is the stunning new **Ōsaka Museum of History** (Mon & Wed–Sun 9.30am–5pm, Fri until 8pm; ¥600; ℡06/6946-5728, Ⓦwww.mus-his.city.osaka.jp/english), a twelve-storey concrete and glass structure in the shape of a giant ship's funnel – the "edge" pointing towards the castle is made of glass and offers good views. One of the city's premier attractions, the museum is built on the site of the Asuka period Naniwa-Nagara-Toyozaki Palace, remains of which have been preserved in the museum's basement. After entering the museum, a lift whizzes you up to the tenth floor, from where you make your way down through four storeys of excellent displays featuring replicas, antiques, manuscripts and intricate, finely detailed scale models of street scenes and other long-vanished buildings and structures which once played important roles in the city's cultural and social life. There's lots of English-language information on the displays, though not, sadly, for the wide range of video presentations. The ground floor is home to a decent café-restaurant.

The indomitable fortress

Despite being largely a concrete reconstruction, **Ōsaka-jō** can be counted a great survivor, a tangible link with the city's illustrious past as Japan's one-time seat of power. The castle's roots go back to the early sixteenth century, when an influential Buddhist sect built its fortified temple headquarters **Ishiyama Hongan-ji** beside the confluence of the Ōgawa and Neya-gawa rivers. For a decade the monks held out against warlord Oda Nobunaga (see "Contexts", p.937), before handing their fortress over to the first of Japan's three great unifiers, in 1580. Nobunaga's successor, **Toyotomi Hideyoshi**, decided to build the grandest castle in Japan on the temple site. For three years from 1583, tens of thousands of men laboured on the enormous castle, and craftsmen were drafted in from around Japan to give the eight-storey central donjon the finest gold-leaf decoration.

Toyotomi died in 1598, and his son and heir Hideyori was immediately under threat from rival **Tokugawa Ieyasu**. In 1614, the would-be shogun laid siege to the castle, even though his favourite granddaughter Senhime, wife of Hideyori, was inside. A year later he breached the castle and reduced it to ruins. Hideyori and his mother committed suicide rather than surrender, but Senhime survived and went on to become mistress of Himeji-jō (see p.615). When Ieyasu allowed the castle to be rebuilt in the 1620s, he made sure it was not on the same scale as his own residence in Edo. In 1665, the donjon was again burnt to the ground after being struck by lightning. It was not rebuilt until the 1840s and then only lasted another thirty years before the Tokugawa troops set fire to the castle during the civil war that briefly raged before the Meiji Restoration of 1868. Ōsaka's citizens, however, had grown fond of their castle, so the donjon was rebuilt once more in 1931 – this time from concrete – and it has remained standing despite the heavy bombing of the city during World War II.

Adjoining the museum are the mammoth Ōsaka headquaters of the national broadcaster, **NHK** (Tues–Sun 10am–5.30pm, closed fourth Tues of the month; free; ☏06/6941-0431), worth popping into if only to see the next-generation plasma screens and digital TV broadcasts on the ground floor, and to take a peek inside the TV studios on the ninth floor (there's also a good view of the south of the city from a viewing point on the same floor as the studios). TV programmes are produced here, so you might be lucky and see some local stars filming soap operas and the like.

Umeda and around

Around 1km west of the castle, sandwiched between the Dojima and Tosabori rivers, lies a thin island, Nakanoshima, the eastern tip of which is home to a small park. Here, in a squat brick building, you'll find the **Museum of Oriental Ceramics** (Tues–Sun 9.30am–4.30pm; ¥500; ☏06/6223-0055, ⓦwww.moco.or.jp/en/guide/index.html), housing an exemplary collection of mainly ancient Chinese and Korean pottery in a hushed, reverential atmosphere, a world away from the bustling city outside.

Just west of the museum stands the handsome **Central Public Hall**, a Neoclassical beauty dating from 1918 which looks best when floodlit at night. Heading north across the Oe-bashi bridge, and along the broad Midōsuji-dōri, brings you to the heart of the **Umeda** area, the meeting point of the JR, Hankyū and Hanshin railway lines. Tucked into a side street just before the stations is the **Ohatsu–Tenjin**, an atmospheric shrine where local shopkeepers pray for good business and which has a flea market on the first Friday of each month.

Even if you don't plan to take a train, the Baroque entrance hall of the **Hankyū Umeda Station** is worth a look, as is the nearby **HEP Five** eleven-storey shopping and dining extravaganza, complete with a ferris wheel (daily 11am–11pm; ¥700) on its roof, which offers excellent vistas of the city. The ferris wheel is definitely worth a spin, but try to avoid weekends as it's a popular spot for young couples on dates and consequently the queues can be horrendous. Immediately west of the station, a tunnel leads under the railway sidings to the twin towers of the **Umeda Sky Building**, one of the city's more striking skyscrapers, where you can take a glass elevator up to the **Floating Garden Observatory** (daily 10am–10pm; ¥700; ☏06/6440-3855), 170m above the ground. Although there are some other attractions in the tower, this is a rather expensive way to get a bird's-eye view of Ōsaka, and if you've been up the castle already it's not worth doing. The open courtyard at the base of the Umeda Sky Building is the venue for the city's annual **International Beer Summit** (ⓦwww.ibws-npo.org/index-e.html), held in October every year (usually the second weekend) – check the website or Kansai Time Out for details. The festival regularly attracts more than forty thousand ale-swillers during its three days, with traditional musical performances, entertainments and tasty foods from all over the world, plus around 150 types of beer. The basement of the adjacent **Garden Six** building is styled as a late nineteenth-century street called "Fun Fun Plaza" and offers a somewhat surreal shopping and dining experience (see p.505).

Around Tennōji and Sumiyoshi Taisha

Some 2km southeast of Namba lies **Shitennō-ji**, the first state Buddhist temple in Japan. The temple has retained its classical layout but contains none of the buildings originally erected in 593; the oldest feature of this windswept, concrete complex, with turtle ponds and a five-storey pagoda at its centre, is the late thirteenth-century *torii* at the main entrance gate. The **treasure house** (Tues–Sun: April–Sept 8.30am–4.30pm; Jan–March & Oct–Dec 8.30am–4pm;

¥200; ☎06/6771-0066), in the modern white building behind the central courtyard, contains gorgeous orange costumes and enormous mandalas, carved with fantastic birds and dragons, which are used for the ceremonial *bugaku* dances held at the temple on April 22, August 8 and October 22. The main entrance to the temple is five minutes' walk south of Shitennō-ji-mae subway station and fifteen minutes north of the Tennōji overground station.

Festival days apart, spacious Shitennō-ji swallows up visitors with ease, but the more compact precincts of nearby **Isshin-ji**, five minutes' walk west, are always bustling with crowds of petitioners. This atmospheric temple is adorned with striking modern sculptures of the Gods of Thunder and Wind (Raijin and Fūjin) and bare-breasted dancing girls on the steel gate doors.

Leave the temple through its adjacent graveyard and walk south to reach the **Ōsaka Municipal Museum of Art** (☎06/6771-4874; Tues–Sun 9.30am–4.30pm; ¥300), which contains fine examples of ancient and modern Oriental art in its permanent collection and usually has special exhibitions. Behind the gallery is **Keitakuen**, a pretty traditional Japanese garden arranged around a central pond. The garden, left to the city by Baron Sumitomo, whose family owned the mammoth trading company of the same name, is now part of **Tennōji-kōen** (Tues–Sun 9.30am–5pm; ¥150; ☎06/6771-8401), which also includes the modern Great Conservatory, a giant glasshouse brimming with plants and flowers from around the world.

On the western side of the zoo, soak up the low-rent atmosphere of **Shin-Sekai** (New World), a raffish district of narrow shopping arcades, cheap bars and restaurants and *pachinko* parlours. At its centre stands the appealingly retro **Tsūtenkaku Tower** (daily 10am–6.30/7.30pm; ¥600; ☎06/6641-9555). This city landmark was rebuilt in the 1950s after having been destroyed in World War II, though at just 103m it's long been surpassed by Umeda's skyscrapers to the north and the 256-metre WTC Cosmotower by Ōsaka Bay. A few minutes' walk to the south of the tower is the **Festival Gate** amusement park (daily 10am–9pm; entrance free, rides from ¥200), with a number of rides, restaurants and shops, and the intriguing, but pricey, **Spa World** (daily 10am–9pm; ¥2400 for 3hr, ¥2700 for the day; ☎06/6631-0001), which offers a bizarre array of baths and saunas, from *faux*-Roman to herbal Chinese.

From Ebisuchō Station, immediately north of Shin-Sekai, it's a fifteen-minute subway or tram ride south to **Sumiyoshi Taisha**, Ōsaka's grandest shrine, home of the Shinto gods of the sea. Built in 211, after the grateful Empress Jingō (so the legend goes) returned from a voyage to Korea, its buildings, with logs jutting out at angles from the thatched roofs, exemplify *sumiyoshi zukuri*, one of Japan's oldest styles of shrine architecture. Unlike similar complexes at Ise (see p.596) and Izumo Taisha (see p.696), Sumiyoshi Taisha is painted bright red, a sharp contrast with its wooded surrounding. The approach to the complex takes you over the elegant humpbacked Sori-hashi bridge, donated to the shrine by Yodogimi, Toyotomi Hideyoshi's lover.

Some 2km west of Tennōji, a wasteland of factories and flyovers provides the unlikely location for the city's most stimulating museum, **Liberty Ōsaka** (Tues–Sun 10am–5pm; ¥250; ☎06/6561-5891). Its longer name is the Ōsaka Human Rights Museum and it contains remarkable exhibits which tackle Japan's most taboo subjects. There's an excellent English-language leaflet and a portable tape recording to guide you around the displays which include the untouchable caste, the Burakumin, Japan's ethnic minorities and the disabled, the sexist treatment of women, and the effects of pollution, most tragically seen in the exhibition about Minamata disease (see p.831). The museum is an eight-minute walk south of Ashiharabashi Station on the JR Loop line.

Ōsaka Bay

To reach the **Ōsaka Bay** area, take the JR Loop line to Bentenchō Station; on the way you'll pass the UFO-like **Ōsaka Dome**, home of the Kintetsu Buffaloes pro-baseball team. From Bentenchō Station take the Chūō line subway to Ōsaka-kō Station (the Chūō line subway will bring you all the way from other parts of the city), and walk north towards the huge ferris wheel beside Tempozan Harbour Village. Inside an exotic butterfly-shaped building, decorated with a giant fish-tank mosaic, is the fabulous **Ōsaka Aquarium** (daily 10am–7pm; ¥2000; ☎06/6576-5501, ⓦwww.kaiyukan.com/eng/index.htm). The aquarium is constructed so that you wind your way down around fourteen elongated tanks, each representing a different aquatic environment, from Antarctica to the Aleutian Islands. The beauty of the design means you can, for example, watch seals basking on the rocks at the top of the tank and see them swimming, torpedo-like, through the lower depths later. The huge central tank represents the Pacific Ocean and is home to a couple of whale sharks and several manta rays, among many other fish. The giant spider crabs, looking like alien invaders from *War of the Worlds*, provide a fitting climax to far and away Japan's best aquarium.

While at Tempozan, check out what's showing at the **Suntory Museum** (Tues–Sun 10.30am–7pm; ¥1000; ☎06/6577-0001), housed in a striking inverted glass-and-concrete cone, designed by star local architect Andō Tadao. The museum specializes in twentieth-century graphic art and has a collection of over ten thousand posters. There's also an IMAX movie theatre (Tues–Sun 11am–7pm; ¥1000) showing films on a twenty-metre-high screen.

Universal Studios Japan

Covering some 140 acres on Ōsaka's western waterfront, **Universal Studios Japan** (daily 10am–8pm; ¥5500; ☎06/4790-7000, ⓦwww.usj.co.jp/e_top.html) is one of the nation's leading theme parks, with eighteen **rides** and shows including "Jaws", "ET Adventure" and the star attraction, "Jurassic Park – The Ride", which features a near-vertical, 25-metre plunge. All use state-of-the-art special effects and motion simulation, but if you've been to similar theme parks in the US then there's nothing much new here. Crowds tend to thin out come evening time. Among the park's plethora of **eating** options are a French-style café, an Irish pub from Brooklyn, a *Godfather*-style pizzeria and, somewhat bizarrely, a Japanese restaurant based on one in SoHo, New York.

The theme park is served by the new Universal City Station on the JR Sakurajima line, connecting to the JR Loop line at Nishikujo Station. Direct **express trains** run to Universal City Station from JR Ōsaka Station (every 10min; 14min).

Eating

Ōsaka has a reputation as a foodies' paradise, but it can be a daunting task finding the best places to eat in a city crammed with so many restaurants. The trick is to stick to particular areas and to hunt around until something takes your fancy. Both **Umeda** and **Dōtombori** offer rich pickings, while **Tsuruhashi**, on the JR Loop line to the east, is the main place to head for Korean food. *Kansai Time Out* reviews the latest additions to the restaurant scene and it's always a good idea to ask the locals what their favourite places are.

Of the several dishes that Ōsaka specializes in you shouldn't leave town without going to an **okonomiyaki restaurant**, preferably one where you can fry the thick pancakes yourself. Ōsaka's own style of **sushi** is *oshizushi*, layers of vinegared rice, seaweed and fish cut into bite-size chunks, and the city also has a favourite way of cooking chunky udon noodles, simmering them in a veggie, seafood or meat broth.

Restaurants and cafés

The best choice of **restaurants and cafés** is around the Kita areas of Umeda and Sonezaki, and the Minami areas of Shinsaibashi, Dōtombori and Namba. Strolling around the narrow streets dotted with stand-up noodle and *takoyaki* bars and restaurants dolled up with flickering neon signs and crazy displays – especially along Dōtombori-dōri – is an appetizing experience in itself. The major **hotels** and **department stores** are also worth checking out, especially at lunchtime, when many restaurants offer special deals.

Restaurants have been graded according to the **price codes** described on p.165.

Kita
The following are marked on the map on p.498.

Burdigala B1 Herbis Plaza (see below), 2-5-25 Umeda ☏06/6343-7108. Smart-casual wine bar-cum-restaurant with one of the best wine lists in the city plus excellent and surprisingly affordable Franco-Italian cuisine. The only problem is the abominable – and slow – service. Booking advisable. Ōsaka/Umeda stations. Moderate.

Fun Fun Plaza B1 Umeda Sky Building. Concealed beneath one of Ōsaka's high-tech towers, this evocative recreation of a 1920s shopping street has some fifteen restaurants to choose from, all serving traditional dishes including noodles, tempura and *okonomiyaki*. Ōsaka/Nishi-Umeda stations. Moderate to expensive.

Gataro Kappa Yokochōnai, Shibata 1-7-2 ☏06/6373-1484. Intimate, classy *izakaya* hidden away in the warren of restaurants under the Hankyu railway terminus. Sit at the counter to get a view of the food being prepared – you might see the grilled fish being given a finishing touch with a blowtorch. No English menu, but an extensive *jizake* (regional sake) selection and friendly staff more than compensate. Ōsaka/Umeda stations. Moderate to expensive.

Herbis Plaza 2-5-25 Umeda. Excellent range of restaurants serving all kinds of cuisine in imaginative settings on the B2 level of this shopping development west of Ōsaka Station. Try Takara-no-Kura, a hip *izakaya* serving *mukokuseki* (fusion) dishes. Ōsaka or Nishi-Umeda stations. Moderate to expensive.

Kisoji This cubbyhole *izakaya*, on the second floor of the warren of small cafés and restaurants behind Hankyū Umeda Station, serves a good-value ¥500 buffet lunch that has local office workers lining up outside. Ōsaka/Umeda stations. Inexpensive.

La Scoglio 10F Hanshin Department Store, 1-13-13 Umeda ☏06/6341-1235. Hugely popular Italian restaurant that's always packed at weekends thanks to its pizzas – some of the tastiest and best value (¥1000) in town. Pasta dishes are so-so. Ōsaka and Umeda stations. Moderate.

Madonna B2 Hilton Plaza, 1-8-16 Umeda ☏06/6347-7371. Small *okonomiyaki* restaurant where you cook at your own table or sit at the kitchen counter and watch the chefs. Also serves *yakisoba* (fried noodles). Most dishes under ¥1500. Ōsaka or Nishi-Umeda stations. Moderate.

Nawasushi 2-14-1 Sonezaki ☏06/6312-9891. Of the many sushi restaurants east of the Hanshin department store, this one stands out for serving three rather than two pieces of sushi per dish (around ¥400). Higashi-Umeda Station. Moderate.

Minami
The following are marked on the map on p.499.

Africa Karaoke Yubo Building B1F, 2-8-5 Nishi-Shinsaibashi ☏06/6213-4622. Trendy underground restaurant with a kitsch African theme and an excellent menu of French–Italian cuisine. Surprisingly for such a hip joint, the prices won't break the bank, and there's unlimited free bread, freshly baked on the premises. Make sure to have a drink afterwards at the secret bar, hidden at the back of the restaurant – if you can get a seat. Daily from 6pm. Namba Station. Expensive.

Capricciosa 3F Atrium, 1-5-30 Shinsaibashi-suji ☏06/6243-6020. Well-established chain Italian restaurant which has prospered by serving up huge helpings of pasta in a casual atmosphere. Daily 11am–11pm. Namba or Shinsaibashi stations. Moderate.

Garb BBB Building, 1-3F, Baguromachi 4-4-7 ☏06/6258-3341. Hugely popular *mukokuseki* café-restaurant in the city's cool Minami-Semba district amongst the fashion boutiques, art galleries and office blocks. The menu is a fusion of east, west and all points in between, with baked tuna sitting alongside duck pizza and cutting-edge pasta dishes, though the food is more filling and the bill is less wallet-emptying than you might expect. Shinsaibashi Station. Moderate to expensive.

Green Earth 1F Kyuho Bldg., 4-2-2 Kitakyuhoji-chō ☏06/6251-1245. This narrow café is one of the city's few true vegetarian establishments, and offers some of its best-value meals. Jumbo sandwiches (¥400) either come on their own or form the centrepiece of set meals (¥700), which include soup, salad and a drink. Good hummus, too. Tues–Sun 11.30am–5pm. Shinsaibashi Station. Inexpensive.

Il Gemello 2F Daiki Building, 2-4-8 Nishi-Shinsaibashi ☏06/6211-9542. Traditional and friendly Italian restaurant with Rome-trained chefs. English is spoken and meals cost around ¥2000 per person. Mon–Fri 5.30pm–midnight, Sat & Sun 11.30am–2.30pm & 5.30–midnight. Namba Station. Expensive.

Kanadian B1 Miyoshi Manshuon, 2-1-64 Teramachi ☏06/6764-6483. Long-running Asian food restaurant with a funky, bohemian atmosphere and organic curries, samosas and chai. There's sometimes live music on Saturdays (extra charge). Closed Thurs. Tani-machi 9-chōme Station. Inexpensive.

Kani Doraku 1-6-2 Dōtombori ☏06/6344-5091. There are now outlets of this seafood restaurant – easily spotted by the giant red crab above the door – all over Japan, but this is one of the originals, serving fresh crab in a vast range of dishes. Namba Station. Daily 11am–11pm. Expensive.

Ken's Chanto Dining 1-7-28 Higashi-Shinsaibashi ☏06/6282-3838. One of the city's most excitingly designed restaurants. In the second-floor sushi bar, mirror-lined walls combine with the black decor and low-slung tables and chairs to give a feeling of floating in space, while the third-floor dining room is decadent in a jet-set style. The food is a joy too, from tender slices of raw beef *tataki* to Tokyo-style conger eel. The best option may be to go for Ken's Special: five dishes where you're at the mercy of the restaurant's master chef. Afterwards, there's a good range of cigars to enjoy in the first-floor bar. Daily from 5pm. Shinsaibashi Station. Expensive.

Kuidaore 1-8-25 Dōtombori ☏06/6211-5300. One of Ōsaka's oldest restaurant department stores, easily identified by the giant drumming clown outside. Set meals, covering a wide range of cuisines, start at around ¥1000 and there are good plastic food displays. Head to the fourth floor for *nabe* and *shabu-shabu* stews. Namba Station. Moderate to expensive.

Namaste No. 2 Rose Building, 3-7-28 Minami-Semba ☏06/6241-6515. To the east of the Shinsaibashi shopping arcade, on the cross-street before the Maruzen bookshop. Not the cheapest Indian restaurant in Ōsaka, but a good one, serving lots of veg dishes and with set lunches from ¥750. Mon–Sat 11.30am–3pm & 5.30–11pm. Shinsaibashi Station. Moderate.

Ninniku-ya 6F Daimondo Building, 2-3-12 Shinsaibashi-suji ☏06/6212-5770, plus two further branches in Umeda. There's a South Sea Islands feel at this garlic-with-everything restaurant. The portions are large so it pays to go with friends and share a few dishes, and there's an English menu. Namba Station. Moderate.

Other areas

Gochi-sō Biru Restaurant building with eleven floors next to the Kintetsu department store opposite Tennōji Station, offering a good range of reasonably priced cuisines. Head to the basement for excellent-value set Japanese meals. The *Hokuo* bakery on the ground floor is a good place to pick up a breakfast snack. Tennōji Station. Moderate to expensive.

Sun Tempo 1-5-10 Kaigan-dōri ☏06/6577-0001. Rustic Italian restaurant behind the Suntory Museum, with views across Ōsaka Bay, imaginative pizzas and pasta and a decent salad bar. Ōsakakō Station. Moderate.

WTC Cosmotower 1-14-16 Nankō-Kita. Ōsaka's tallest building has several good-value restaurants including *Isamu Sushi*, on the 47th floor, and the *World Buffet Restaurant* on the 48th. Cosmosquare Station. Moderate to expensive.

Nightlife and entertainment

The epicentre of Ōsaka's frenetic nightlife is **Ebisu-bashi**, a dazzling area to wander around, if only to check out the wild youth fashions on view. If you've seen the movie *Black Rain*, you'll recognize the jet-black glass-and-steel microbrewery pub *Kirin Plaza Ōsaka* beside the bridge, but there are plenty of other bars around the area. Don't miss out on strolling through **Amerika-mura**, immediately west, a street crowded with trendy shops and bars. In contrast, the **Hozen-ji Yokochō** area, around the paper-lantern-festooned temple Hozen-ji, is old-time Ōsaka, a narrow alley of tiny watering holes.

The city's **gay scene** is much smaller than that in Tokyo, and historically it's tended to be in Kita rather than Minami. There's a slightly tacky, but relatively accurate, online listing at ⓦhttp://plaza8.mbn.or.jp/~climb/index-e.html – otherwise, Physique Pride Ōsaka (see below) is the place to go. Check the listings magazine *Kansai Time Out* for the latest info on clubs, bars and one-off dance events.

Bars and clubs

Bears B1 Shin-Nihon Namba Bldg, 3-14-5 Namba-naka ☎06/6649-5564; ⓦhome.att.ne.jp/orange/bears. The heart of the city's underground music scene, with a diverse range of experimental and avant-garde acts playing every night. Gigs start and end early (6.30–10pm) so as not to irritate the *yakuza* upstairs. Entrance from ¥1500. There's no bar, so take your own booze. Namba Station.

Canopy IM Excellence Building, 1-11-20 Sonezaki-Shinchi ☎06/6341-0339. A healthy mix of *gaijin* and Japanese rub shoulders in the least-likely-looking – and slightly sleazy – "American delicatessen" in Ōsaka (it appears to be modelled after a beach hut in Thailand). Cool down on the outdoor terrace and enjoy the 5–8.30pm happy hour, when beers are ¥400. Higashi-Umeda or Kita-Shinchi Stations.

The Cellar B1 Dai-3 Hirata Building, 2-17-13 Nishi-Shinsaibashi ☎06/6212-6437. Comfortable neighbourhood bar with reasonably priced drinks and a daily happy hour (6–9pm), plus live music on Wednesday, Friday and Saturday, and a popular jam session on Sunday afternoons. Shinsaibashi Station.

Club Karma Kasai Building, 1-5-18 Sonezaki-Shinchi ☎06/6344-6181. Stark yet roomy bar and club which hosts a range of hip dance events and happenings, with the added bonus of a good food menu and a happy hour until 9pm. The all-night techno and house events are usually held on Friday and Saturday, when there's a cover charge of ¥2500 (more if big-name foreign DJs are in town). *Karma* is the most gay-friendly of the mainstream clubs and stages occasional gay or lesbian events. Nishi-Umeda or Kita-Shinchi Stations.

Don Shop B1 Shimazu Bldg, 2-4-11 Umeda ☎06/6341-2605. If the *Ōsaka Blue Note* over the road is too expensive, catch live jazz (nearly always free; very rarely a ¥1500 cover charge) any night of the week at this legendary all-night jazz club with its bohemian, 1960s atmosphere. Big-name performers sometimes hop over the road from the *Blue Note* for impromptu late-night jam sessions. Good food and reasonable drinks. Ōsaka Station.

Joule 2-3F Brutus Building, 2-11-30 Nishi-Shinsaibashi ☎06/6214-1223. The very popular

younger cousin of *Underlounge* (see p.508), with an equally mainstream music policy but a more laidback atmosphere and a third-floor lounge for relaxing in when the dance floor gets too full. Shinsaibashi Station.

Murphy's 6F Lead Plaza Building, Higashi-Shinsaibashi ☎06/6282-0677. It's seen better days, but the city's original Irish bar still has a traditionally boozy atmosphere to go with the draught Guinness and Kilkenny. Also serves food and has the odd live music show. There are several other bars in the same building in case this one is too rowdy. Nagahoribashi Station.

Ōsaka Blue Note B1 ax Bldg, 2-3-21 Sonezaki-Shinchi ☎06/6342-7722. Top-flight jazz, soul and R&B performers regularly play at this small-scale supper club, but it's pricey, with tickets often in excess of ¥7000. Still, the sound system is excellent and the food's reasonable. Ōsaka Station.

Physique Pride Ōsaka Sanyo Kaikan, 8-23 Doyama-chō ☎06/6361-2430, ⓦwww.physiqueprideosaka.com. Well-established Ōsaka gay bar that's foreigner friendly and has English-speaking staff. No cover charge.

Pig & Whistle B1 Ohatsutenjin Building, 2-5 Sonezaki ☎06/6361-3198 (Higashi-Umeda subway station) and 2F Across Building, 2-6-14 Shinsaibashi-suji ☎06/6213-6911 (Shinsaibashi subway station). Both branches of this British-style pub have Guinness on tap, fish-and-chip suppers, and darts – the place to head if you're feeling nostalgic about the old boozer back home.

Rockets 6025 Namba-pia, 2-8-13 Nambanaka ☎06/6649-3919. Bare concrete and plastic sheeting typify this alternative club, nestling under the railway tracks running south from Namba Station. DJs spin everything from drum 'n' bass to reggae and punk, depending on the night of the week. It's best to ring up since it's not open every night. Entrance ¥2500 including one drink. Namba Station.

Sam and Dave IV (Umeda) 4-15-19 Nishi-Tenma ☎06/6365-1688, ⓦwww.samanddave.jp. Ridiculously popular bar that is always heaving with foreigners and Japanese alike all night every night, and there's a good sound system in case you feel like a bop on the dance floor. Cover charge (around ¥1000) some nights. Two more branches in Minami are just as packed.

Tocca a Te 2-2-15 Sonezaki ☎06/6365-5808. Arty bar-club with film screenings, dance events, salsa nights and a good vibe. Mostly Japanese crowd, but foreigners made to feel welcome. Entry to bar is usually free, or up to ¥2000 if there's a club night or other special event. Occasional gay/lesbian events. Higashi-Umeda Station.

Underlounge B1 634 Building, 2-7-11 Nishi-Shinsaibashi ☎06/6214-3322. Very smart, mainstream club with swish decor and tip-top sound system. Mostly house and techno events at the weekends, with heavyweight national and international DJs on the decks. Midweek events include hip-hop and soul parties. Entrance ¥2500 including one drink. Closed Mon. Shinsaibashi Station.

Traditional performing arts

Ōsaka is where **Bunraku** puppetry flourished during the seventeenth century and performances are still held in Namba at the **National Bunraku Theatre** (☎06/6212-2531, ⓦwww.ntj.jac.go.jp/english/index.html; performances in Jan, April, Jun–Aug and Nov at 11am and 4pm). Tickets (price depends on performance) sell out quickly, but you can try at the theatre box office, a three-minute walk from exit 7 of Nipponbashi Station.

The place to catch **Kabuki** plays is the handsomely restored **Ōsaka Shōchiku-za** (☎06/6214-2211), five minutes' walk north of Namba Station, beside the Dōtombori canal. Tickets start at ¥4200. If you're interested in sampling the more difficult **Nō** plays, the **Ōsaka Nō Hall** (☎06/6373-1726), near Nakazakichō Station on the Tanimachi line, or a short walk east of Hankyū Umeda Station, often holds free performances on weekends and national holidays, usually beginning around 9.30am. Full details of all traditional arts performances appear in the free quarterly booklet *Meet Ōsaka*, available at all the tourist offices, and in *Kansai Time Out*. The performing arts section of the Kansai Window website (ⓦwww.kansai.gr.jp/culture/geinou/index_e.html) has detailed information on the history of the local performing arts scene.

Listings

Airlines ANA domestic ☎0120-02-9222; international ☎0120-02-9333; JAL domestic ☎0120-25-5971, international ☎0120-25-5931; Japan Asia Airways ☎06/6223-2258; Aeroflot ☎06/6271-8471; Air China ☎06/6946-1702; Air France ☎06/6641-1271; Air India ☎06/6246-1781; Air New Zealand ☎03/3287-6311; Alitalia ☎06/6341-3951; Asiana Airlines ☎06/6229-3939; British Airways ☎0120-122881; Cathay Pacific ☎03/6245-6731; China Eastern Airlines

☎06/6448-5161; Continental Micronesia ☎03/3508-6411; Finnair ☎06/6347-0888; Garuda Indonesia Airways ☎06/6635-3222; Iberia ☎06/6347-7201; KLM ☎06/6345-6691; Korean Air ☎0088-21-2001; Lufthansa ☎0120-051-844; Malaysian Airlines ☎06/6635-3070; Northwest Airlines ☎06/6228-0747; Philippine Airlines ☎06/6444-2541; Qantas Airways ☎06/6262-1691; Singapore Airlines ☎06/6345-8801; Swissair ☎06/6345-7811; Thai Airways International ☎06/6202-5161; United Airlines ☎0120-114466; Vietnam Airlines ☎06/6533-2689.

Airport information Kansai International ☎0724/55-2500; Itami ☎06/6856-6781.

Banks and exchange There are plenty of banks around Umeda, Shinsaibashi and Namba. Major department stores also have foreign exchange desks, as does the Central Post Office, beside JR Ōsaka Station.

Bookshops Kinokuniya, behind the main entrance to Hankyū Umeda Station, is open daily 10am–9pm, except the third Wednesday of the month. Athens, in the Shinsaibashi shopping arcade, has a particularly good selection of art books, while the four-storey branch of Tower Records in Amerika-Mura has a wide range of foreign and domestic music and lifestyle magazines at competitive prices.

Car rental Several major car rental firms can be found at both Shin-Ōsaka and Ōsaka stations (both open daily 8am–8pm) including Eki Rent-a-Car (Shin-Ōsaka ☎06/6303-0181, Ōsaka ☎06/6341-3388). Alternatively, try Nippon Rent-a-Car (Ōsaka Reservation Center ☎06/6344-0919) and PanaLife (☎06/6949-1822).

Consulates Australia, 29F, Twin 21 MID Tower, 2-1-61 Shiromi, Chūō-ku ☎06/6941-9271; Canada, 12F Daisan Shoho Building, 2-2-3 Nishi-Shinsaibashi, Chūō-ku ☎06/6212-4910; China, 3-9-2 Utsubohommachi, Nishi-ku ☎06/6445-9481; Germany, 35F Umeda Sky Building Tower East, 1-1-81 Oyodonaka, Kita-ku ☎06/6440-5070; Netherlands, 6F Twin 21 MID Tower, 2-1-61 Shiromi, Chūō-ku ☎06/6944-7272; Russia, 1-2-2 Nishimidorigaoka, Toyonaka-shi ☎06/6848-3451; South Korea, 2-3-4 Nishi-Shinsaibashi, Chūō-ku ☎06/6213-1401; UK, 19F Seiko Ōsaka Building, 3-5-1 Bakuromachi, Chūō-ku ☎06/6120-5600; USA, 2-11-5 Nishitemma, Kita-ku ☎06/6315-5900.

Emergencies The main police station is at 3-1-16 Otemae, Chūō-ku (Mon–Fri 9.15am–5.30pm; ☎06/6943-1234). In an absolute emergency, contact the Foreign Advisory Service on ☎06/773-6533. For other emergency numbers, see "Basics" on p.81.

Home visits Ōsaka runs a programme which allows you to meet local people in their homes for a few hours so you can learn a bit more about Japanese life. If you want to participate you need to take your passport to either of the tourist information desks at Ōsaka or Shin-Ōsaka stations (see p.496) and allow a couple of days for visiting arrangements to be made.

Hospitals and medical advice Yodogawa Christian Hospital, 2-9-26 Awaji, Higashi-Yodogawa-ku (☎06/6322-2250), or the more central Sumitomo Hospital, 5-2-2 Nakanoshima, Kita-ku (☎06/6443-1261). Otherwise contact one of the tourist information counters (see p.496).

Immigration Ōsaka's immigration bureau is a three-minute walk from exit 3 of Temmabashi Station on the Keihan line at 2-1-17 Tanimachi, Chūō-ku (☎06/6941-0771).

Internet access There are four branches of Kinko's around the city offering Internet access (¥200/10min). The Umeda branch is five minutes from the Sakurabashi Exit of JR Ōsaka, opposite the Herbis Plaza. Other branches can be found in Minami-Morimachi, Shinsaibashi and on Sakaisuji-Honmachi. Also try *Bean's B:t Café*, 6-2-29 Uehonmachi, Tennōji-ku (daily 8.30am–9pm), which offers special rates for foreigners. The closest subway station is Tanimachi 9-chōme, and it's also close to Uehonmachi on the Kintetsu line.

Lost property The lost and found department for Ōsaka's buses and subways is at 1-17 Motomachi (☎06/6633-9151).

Post office The Central Post Office is immediately west of JR Ōsaka Station.

Shopping Den-Den Town, the electronic goods area of Ōsaka, five minutes' walk east of Namba, has over 300 discount outlets, those with tax-free signs selling export models. The shops here are closed on Wednesday. Nearby, beside Nipponbashi Station, is the Kuromon-Ichiba, a large food market (Mon–Sat 10am–5pm) that's worth a browse. North of Namba, Amerika-mura and Europe-mura are the main areas to shop for trendy clothes and knick-knacks, while Umeda has several classy department stores and shopping plazas, good for souvenir hunting. Nearby are two giant electronics department stores, Sofmap, next to the Central Post Office, and Yodobashi Camera, opposite the New Hankyu Hotel.

Sports Ōsaka's fifteen-day sumo tournament is held mid-March at Ōsaka Furitsu Taiikukan, a ten-minute walk from exit 5 of Namba Station. Seats for the bouts, which begin at 10am and run through to 6pm, sell out quickly, and you'll need to arrive early to snag one of the standing-room tickets (¥1500), which go on sale each day at 9am.

The Kintetsu Buffaloes play at the huge Ōsaka Dome during the professional baseball season, but the highlight of the city's sporting summer is the All-Japan High School Baseball Championship, held at Kōshien Stadium, a five-minute walk from Kōshien Station on the Hanshin line. For ticket availability, check first with tourist information. **Taxis** Ōsaka Taxi Companies Association T06/6768-1221.

Travel agencies For international tickets, try one of the following English-speaking discount agents: Academy Travel T06/6303-3538; A'cross Travellers Bureau T06/6345-0150; GS Travel T06/6281-1230; Legend Travel T06/6281-8600; No 1 Travel T06/6363-4489; STA T06/6262-7066; Travel Kingdom T06/6309-2199. For domestic journeys, try Academy Travel, or JTB Plaza Higashi-Umeda, at 2-11-5 Sonezaki, Kita-ku T06/6361-7831.

Takarazuka

When the Hankyū railway tycoon Kobayashi Ichizū laid a line out to the tiny spa town of **TAKARAZUKA**, 20km northwest of Ōsaka, in 1911, he had an entertainment vision that extended way beyond soothing onsen dips. By 1924 he'd built the first Takurazuka Grand Theatre, home to the all-female musical drama troupe **Takarazuka** (see box opposite). Some 2.5 million people – mainly women – flock to the town each year to see the reviews and musicals at the plush **Takarazuka Grand Theatre**, ten minutes' walk southeast of the train stations, through the Sonio shopping centre and along an avenue of cherry trees. Shows start at 11am, 1pm and 3pm, with no performances on Wednesday, and tickets cost from ¥3500. Reservations should be made up to a month before performances (daily 10am–5pm except for four-day closures between performance runs; T0797/86-7777; no English spoken, but tourist offices can often make calls on your behalf; W http://kageki.hankyu.co.jp/english/index.html). Shows are also staged regularly in Tokyo; see p.182.

A much more entertaining place for both children and adults is the **Tezuka Osamu Manga Museum** (daily except Wed 9.30am–5pm; ¥500; W http://en.tezuka.co.jp), just beyond the Grand Theatre, which celebrates the comic-book genius Tezuka Osamu, creator of Astro Boy and Kimba the White Lion, an inspiration for Disney's *The Lion King*. Considered Japan's "god of *manga*", Tezuka (1928–89), who was raised in Takarazuka, was the pioneer of story-book comics – the mainstay of today's mammoth *manga* industry. He didn't just create cuddly cartoon characters, but also tackled difficult adult material, such as anti-Semitism in his epic masterpiece *Adorufu ni Tsugu* (Tell Adolf). This colourful museum charts his career, displays art from his books, comics and animated films, screens cartoons and gives you the chance to become an animator in the basement workshop.

Takarazuka

Takarazuka	*Takarazuka*	宝塚
Daihonzan Nakayama-dera	*Daihonzan Nakayama-dera*	大本山中山寺
Kiyoshikōjin Seichō-ji	*Kiyoshikōjin Seichō-ji*	清荒神清澄寺
Takarazuka Grand Theatre	*Takarazuka Gurando Gekijō*	宝塚グランド劇場
Tezuka Osamu Manga Museum	*Tezuka Osamu Kinenkan*	手塚治虫記念館

Accommodation and eating		
Petit House	*Puchi Hausu*	プチハウス
Takarazuka Washington Hotel	*Takarazuka Washinton Hoteru*	宝塚ワシントンホテル
Takarazuka Iroha	*Takarazuka Iroha*	宝塚いろは
Hotel Wakamizu	*Hoteru Wakamizu*	ホテル若水

The wonderful world of Takarazuka

There's a long tradition of men performing female roles in Japanese theatre, acting out a male fantasy of how women are supposed to behave. It's not so strange, then, that actresses playing idealized men have struck such a chord with contemporary female audiences. Along with the glitter, this has been the successful formula of the 700-strong, all-female **Takarazuka Review Company**, founded in 1914.

The company's founder, Kobayashi Ichizū, was mightily impressed by performances of Western operas he'd seen in Tokyo. He sensed that Japanese audiences were ripe for lively Western musical dramas, but he also wanted to preserve something of Japan's traditional theatre, too. So, as well as performing dance reviews and musicals, Takarazuka also act out classical Japanese plays and have developed shows from Western novels, including *Gone with the Wind* and *War and Peace*.

Thousands of young girls apply annually to join the troupe at the age of 16, and devote themselves to a punishing routine of classes that will enable them to embody the "modesty, fairness and grace" (the company's motto) expected of a Takarazuka member. They must also forsake boyfriends, but in return are guaranteed the slavish adoration of an almost exclusively female audience. The male impersonators or *otoko-yaku* attract the most attention from the fans, who buy so many cut flowers for their idols that the town's shops and restaurants receive free daily deliveries of unwanted bouquets.

6

KANSAI | Ōsaka and around

There are a couple of atmospheric **temples** in the hills around Takarazuka that merit a look as part of a day-trip to the spa town. The liveliest, especially on the festival days held on the 27th and 28th of each month, is **Kiyoshikōjin Seichō-ji**, a rambling complex dedicated to a fire deity, high above Hankyū Kiyoshikōjin Station, one stop from Takarazuka. The long slope leading up to the temple from the station is lined with stalls selling souvenirs and traditional sweets, and each autumn the woods surrounding Kōjin-san, as it's nicknamed, burst into a range of rustic colours. The ideal time to visit the nearby **Daihonzan Nakayama-dera** temple, three minutes' walk from Hankyū Nakayama Station, is the end of February when a thousand *ume* (plum) trees blossom with pink and white buds. Although there's been a temple on this spot for 1400 years, the present buildings date from 1610, and people come here to worship and pray for healthy births at the eleven-faced Goddess of Mercy, Jūichimen Kannon Bosatsu, a statue believed to have been carved from a nutmeg tree in the tenth century.

Practicalities

The fastest **train** on the Hankyū Takarazuka line from Ōsaka's Umeda Station takes less than thirty minutes to reach Takarazuka Station (¥270). There are also direct trains on the JR Fukuchiyama line, taking a few minutes more from JR Ōsaka Station to JR Takarazuka Station, next to the Hankyū terminus and department store. The town's **tourist information office** (daily 9am–5.15pm; ☎0797/81-5344) is on the ground floor of the Hankyū department store and is always staffed by English-speakers. You can pick up a map of the town here, but everything is so close that you don't really need one.

Given that performances take place during the day, there's no need to stay over in Takarazuka, especially since **accommodation** is generally expensive and can be difficult to book depending on the popularity of the shows. However, the town is much quieter than Ōsaka and several of the hotels along the Muko-gawa have their own onsen. One of the nicest is *Hotel Wakamizu* (☎0797/86-0151, ℱ86-2846; ❾ including two meals), a top-class establishment with tatami and Western rooms and beautifully designed onsen baths, directly across the river from Hankyū Takarazuka Station. The *Takarazuka Washington Hotel* (⊕0797/87-1771, ⓕ86-2287; ⑤), beside the station, is part of the national business hotel chain. Just about the cheapest accommodation is the women-only dorm at *Petit House* (⊕0797/84-8753;¥4500 per person), a small hotel opposite the *manga* museum, where you can mull over Takarazuka performances with die-hard fans.

There are several **places to eat** in the Sorio 1 shopping mall that you'll pass through on the way to the Takarazuka Grand Theatre, including a *Mister Donuts*. The theatre complex also has a range of restaurants, but they tend to serve rather delicate portions. The best bet is *Takarazuka Iroha* (⊕0797/87-3019), an excellent *okonomiyaki* restaurant a couple of minutes' walk up the hill northeast of the JR station, which is open at lunchtimes and in the evenings and offers an extensive menu of not just *okonomiyaki* but also *yakisoba* and *sobameshi* (a mix of soba noodles and rice, fried). If you really want to make a day of it, go for the lunch and bath package at *Hotel Wakamizu*, starting at ¥3500 per person.

Kyoto

The capital of Japan for more than a thousand years, **KYOTO** is endowed with an almost overwhelming legacy of ancient Buddhist temples, majestic palaces and gardens of every size and description, not to mention some of the country's most important works of art, its richest culture and its most refined cuisine. For many people the very name Kyoto conjures up the classic image of Japan: streets of traditional wooden houses, the click-clack of *geta* on the paving stones, geisha in a flourish of brightly coloured silks, and the inevitable weeping cherry. While you can still find all these things, and much more, first impressions of Kyoto are invariably disappointing. For the most part it's a sprawling, overcrowded city with a population of 1.5 million and a thriving industrial sector. The die-straight streets certainly simplify navigation, but they also give the city an oppressive uniformity which you won't find among the tortuous lanes of Tokyo. And, perhaps not surprisingly, Kyoto is a notoriously exclusive place, where it's difficult for outsiders to peek through the centuries-thick layer of cultural refinement into the city's secretive soul.

However, there's plenty for the short-term visitor to enjoy in Kyoto. In fact, the array of top-class sights is quite mind-boggling: more than 1600 Buddhist temples, hundreds of Shinto shrines, two hundred classified gardens, a clutch of imperial villas and several first-rate museums. With so much choice, the biggest problem is where to start, but it's perfectly possible to get a good feel for Kyoto even in a couple of days. Top priority should go to the eastern, Higashiyama district, where you can walk north from the famous **Kiyomizu-dera** to **Ginkaku-ji**, the Silver Pavilion, taking in a whole raft of interesting temples, gardens and museums on the way. Or you could head for the northwestern hills to contemplate the superb Zen gardens of **Daitoku-ji** and **Ryōan-ji**, and then gorge on the wildly extravagant Golden Pavilion, **Kinkaku-ji**. With more time, you can visit some of the central sights, of which the highlight is **Nijō-jō**, a lavishly decorated seventeenth-century palace, while nearby **Nijō-jin'ya** is an intriguing place riddled with secret passages and hidey-holes. Try also to visit one of the imperial villas, such as **Shūgaku-in Rikyū** or **Katsura**

Rikyū, or the sensuous moss gardens of **Saihō-ji**, all located in the outer districts. And it's well worth making time to wander off the beaten track into Kyoto's old merchant quarters. The best of these, surprisingly, are to be found in the central district **north of Shijō-dōri** and across the river in **Gion**. Here you'll find the traditional **crafts shops** and beautiful old **ryokan** for which the city is justly famous.

Kyoto's **festivals** tend to be more stately than rumbustious. The most famous feature grand costume parades, esoteric ritual and elegant geisha dances, and take place in spring and autumn. These two seasons are undoubtedly the **best time to visit** Kyoto, though also the busiest; after a chill winter, the cherry trees put on their finery in early April, while the hot, oppressive summer months (June–Aug) are followed in October by a delightful period of clear, dry weather when the maples erupt into fiery reds.

Some history

Kyoto became the **imperial capital** in the late eighth century when Emperor Kammu relocated the court from Nara (see p.574). His first choice was Nagaoka, southwest of today's Kyoto, but a few inauspicious events led the emperor to move again in 794 AD. This time he settled on what was to be known as **Heian-kyō**, "Capital of Peace and Tranquillity", which he modelled on the Chinese Tang-dynasty capital Chang'an (today's Xi'an). The new city was built on a rectangular grid of streets, symmetrical about a north–south axis, with the Imperial Palace to the north and the main entrance in the south. By the late ninth century the city was already overflowing onto the eastern hills and soon had an estimated population of 500,000. For the aristocrats at least, it was a life of exquisite refinement, characterized by boating parties and poetry-writing competitions, while Japanese arts were evolving their own identity independent of earlier Chinese influences.

From then on the city had a rather roller-coaster ride. In the late twelfth century a fire practically destroyed the whole place, but two centuries later the **Ashikaga shoguns** were busily building some of the city's finest monuments, among them the Golden and Silver Pavilions (Kinkaku-ji and Ginkaku-ji). Many of the great Zen temples were established at this time and the arts reached new levels of sophistication. Once again, however, almost everything was lost during the **Ōnin Wars** (1467–78), which were waged largely within the city over an Ashikaga succession dispute.

Kyoto's knight in shining armour, however, was **Toyotomi Hideyoshi**, who came to power in 1582 and sponsored a vast rebuilding programme. The **Momoyama period**, as it's now known, was a golden era of artistic and architectural ostentation, epitomized by Kyoto's famous **Kanō school of artists**, who decorated the temples and palaces with sumptuous gilded screens. Even when **Tokugawa Ieyasu** moved the seat of government to Edo (now Tokyo) in 1603, Kyoto remained the imperial capital and stood its ground as the nation's foremost cultural centre. While the new military regime went in for extravagant displays of power, such as the **Nijō-jō** palace built for Ieyasu but rarely used, the emperor and his cohorts cocked a snook at such lack of taste by developing a talent for superb understatement in their architecture, gardens, arts and even everyday utensils; the rustic simplicity of the tea ceremony also evolved during this period. Undoubtedly, this sudden delight in simplicity was born partly from necessity, but it nevertheless spawned many of the crafts for which Kyoto is now famous.

In 1788 another huge conflagration swept through the city, but worse was to come; in 1868 the new **Emperor Meiji** moved the court to Tokyo. Kyoto

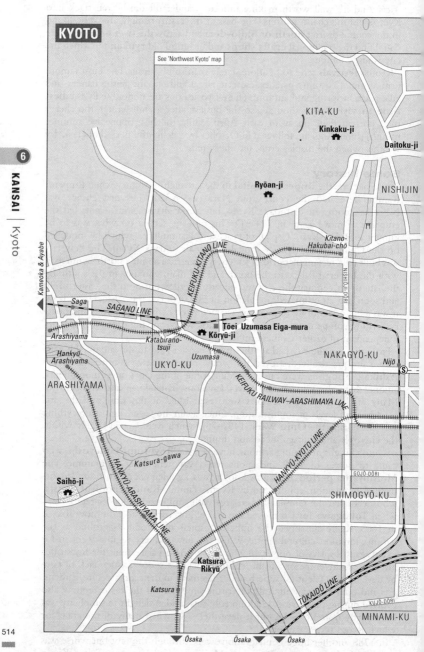

KYOTO

See 'Northwest Kyoto' map

KITA-KU

Kinkaku-ji

Daitoku-ji

NISHIJIN

Ryōan-ji

Kitano-
Hakubai-chō

KEIFUKU-KITANO LINE

NISHIŌJI-DŌRI

Kameoka & Ayabe

Saga

SAGANO LINE

Arashiyama

Tōei Uzumasa Eiga-mura

Kōryū-ji

Katabirano-
tsuji

Uzumasa

NAKAGYŌ-KU

Nijō

Hankyū-
Arashiyama

UKYŌ-KU

KEIFUKU RAILWAY–ARASHIMAYA LINE

S

ARASHIYAMA

HANKYŪ-KYOTO LINE

HANKYŪ-ARASHIYAMA LINE

Katsura-gawa

GOJŌ-DŌRI

Saihō-ji

SHIMOGYŌ-KU

Katsura
Rikyū

Katsura

TOKAIDŌ LINE

KUJŌ-DŌRI

MINAMI-KU

▼ Ōsaka   Ōsaka ▼   ▼ Ōsaka

Kokusai Kaikan ▲ Kurama ▲▲ Ōhara

KARASUMA LINE

Shūgaku-in
Rikyū

Kitayama

Ⓢ

Ⓢ

Shūgaku-in
■ Speakeasy

Takano-gawa

Kita-ōji Ⓢ

Ryokan
◉ Rakuchō

KITAŌJI-DŌRI

EIZAN LINE

SHIRAKAWA-DŌRI

A Womb
■

N

Ⓢ

SAKYŌ-KU

Didi's
■

Japan
Baptist
✚

KAMIGYŌ-KU

Mototanaka

IMADEGAWA-DŌRI

Imadegawa

Demachiyanagi

See 'Central Kyoto' map

See 'East Kyoto' map

Ginkaku-ji

Imperial
Household
Agency

HORIKAWA-DŌRI

Kamo-gawa

HIGASHIŌJI-DŌRI

Imperial
Palace

Daimonji-yama ▲

Hiei-zan ▶

Marutamachi Ⓢ

Keihan-Marutamachi

■ Nijō-jō

Karasuma-
Ōike

Heian-jingū

OIKE-DŌRI

Ⓢ

Ⓢ

ⓘ

Nanzen-ji

Higashiyama

KARASUMA-DŌRI

KAWARAMACHI-DŌRI

Ⓢ

Ⓢ Ⓢ

Ⓢ

Shijō Ⓢ

Kawaramachi

✕

Sanjō-
Keihan

SHIJŌ-DŌRI

Shijō-
Ōmiya

GION

See 'Around Kyoto Station' map

HIGASHIYAMA-KU

TŌZAI LINE Ⓢ

KEIHAN LINE

Kyoto
National
Museum

Kiyomizu-
dera

!

Yamashina & Daigō ▶

Sakamoto & Tsuruga ▶

ⓘ

⊠

Ⓢ

Kyoto
Station

KINTETSU-
KYOTO LINE

Nagoya &
Tokyo ▶

Tō-ji

0   1 km

▼ Nara   ▼ Takeda   ▼ Uji & Nara

went into shock and the economy foundered – but not for long. In the 1890s a canal was built from Biwa-ko to the city, and Kyoto, like the rest of Japan, embarked on a process of industrialization. For all the negative effects of these changes, the city narrowly escaped a far worse fate. At the end of **World War II** Kyoto featured high on the list of potential targets for the atom bomb, but was famously spared by American Defense Secretary, Henry Stimson, who recognized the city's supreme architectural and historical importance.

Kyoto was not immune to the modernization which swept the country after the end of World War II, and though it was largely unaffected by the war, many of the city's old buildings were replaced by new concrete structures. Though some people deplore the destruction of old Kyoto, the truth is that many of the city's residents no longer wanted to live in "charming" (read: cold and rickety) old wooden houses, preferring the comforts of modern urban living. For the most part, historically important buildings have been preserved, while some of the city's major new constructions, particularly the fabulous train station, completed in 1997, are as aesthetically pleasing as the best of the city's ancient temples.

Orientation

Kyoto is contained within a wide valley surrounded by hills on three sides and drained by the Katsura-gawa to the west and the smaller Kamo-gawa to the east. Thanks to its grid-iron street system, this is one of Japan's easier cities to find your way around. The **central district** of banks, shops and the main tourist facilities lies between the Imperial Palace in the north and **Kyoto Station** to the south. Nijō-jō and Horikawa-dōri define the district's western extent, while the Kamo-gawa provides a natural boundary to the east. Within this core, the **downtown** area is concentrated around Shijō-dōri and north along Kawaramachi-dōri to Oike-dōri. Shijō-dōri leads east over the Kamo-gawa into **Gion**, the city's major entertainment district, and to the eastern hills, **Higashiyama**, which shelter many of Kyoto's most famous temples. Much of this central area is best tackled on foot, but the city's other sights are widely scattered. To the northwest, **Kinkaku-ji** and **Ryōan-ji** provide the focus for a second group of temples, while the southwestern suburbs hide the superb gardens of **Saihō-ji** and the **Katsura Rikyū**.

Moving on from Kyoto

If you're heading from Kyoto direct **to Kansai International airport**, it's a good idea to reserve your transport in advance. Limousine buses depart from outside the Avanti department store on the south side of Kyoto Station (hourly 5am–9pm; 1hr 45min; ¥2300; ☎075/682-4400); tickets are available from the ground floor of the nearby *Keihan Hotel*. Reservations are essential on JR's Haruka Limited Express trains, for which you can buy tickets either at an ordinary JR ticket office or in **Kyoto City Air Terminal** (9.30am–5.30pm), in the first basement of Kyoto Station. Ticket holders on international flights with JAL and JAA can also check in here (6am–5pm), as long as you're travelling by Haruka train; you need to check in three hours before your flight departs.

Long-distance **buses** depart from terminals either side of Kyoto Station. JR Highway buses and other services to Tokyo, Nagoya and Kanazawa depart from a stand on the north side of the station, while Keihan Bus uses a terminal on the south side, outside the *Keihan Hotel*. Keihan services cover Nagasaki, Kumamoto, Fukuoka, Tokyo and Kanazawa.

In general, Kyoto **addresses** follow the same pattern as for the rest of Japan (see p.27). There are, however, a few added subtleties which are worth mastering. Unusually, most of the city's main roads are named and the location of a place is generally described by reference to the nearest major junction. Since the land slopes gently south, the most usual indicator is whether a place lies north of (*agaru*, literally "above") or south of (*sagaru*, "below") a particular east–west road. For example, Kawaramachi Sanjō simply means the place is near the intersection of Kawaramachi-dōri and Sanjō-dōri; Kawaramachi Sanjō-agaru tells you it's north of Sanjō-dōri; Kawaramachi Sanjō-sagaru, that it's to the south. At a higher level of sophistication, the address might also indicate whether a place lies east (*higashi*) or west (*nishi*) of the north–south road. Finally, ten east–west avenues are numbered consecutively from Ichijō-dōri (First Street), on a level with today's Imperial Palace, to Jūjō-dōri (Tenth Street) down below the station, which helps pinpoint roughly how far south you are.

Arrival

Most visitors arrive at Kyoto's splendid **JR train station**. The city is linked by Shinkansen to Tokyo and Nagoya to the east and Ōsaka, Hiroshima and Fukuoka to the west. If you're coming direct from **Kansai International airport** (see p.494) the quickest and easiest option is a JR Haruka Limited Express train, which whisks you direct to Kyoto in just over an hour (¥3490); JR rail passes are valid on this service. For those not travelling with a JR rail pass, a cheaper option is to take an express from the airport as far as Ōsaka Station, changing there to an express train on the JR Kyoto line. This method takes a little under two hours and costs about ¥1600. Alternatively, comfortable **airport limousine** buses do the journey in under two hours, traffic permitting, terminating on the south (Hachijō-guchi) side of Kyoto Station (1–2 hourly 5am–9pm; ¥2300). Discounted return tickets (¥3800) are also available, but are only valid for 14 days. Limousine buses also run direct from Ōsaka's **Itami airport** to Kyoto Station (every 30min 6am–7.30pm; 55min; ¥1280), from where local buses and a two-line subway system fan out to all destinations around the city.

 Long-distance buses from Tokyo and other cities terminate outside Kyoto Station. Keihan buses arrive at the southern terminal in front of Avanti department store, while other companies use a stand at the front (north side) of the station.

Information

Conveniently, the station area also contains Kyoto's main information services. Your best bet is the new **Kyoto Tourist Information Centre** (TIC), on the ninth floor of the station building. This has maps, sightseeing brochures, tour information and English-speaking staff who can assist with enquires in person or by phone (daily 10am–6pm except the 2nd & 4th Tues of month; 075/344-3300). If it's shut, try the **Kyoto City Tourist Information Centre** (daily 8.30am–7pm; 075/343-6655) on the station's second floor, near the entrance to Isetan department store. There's usually an English-speaker on hand who can help with accommodation, maps and city-wide information. Failing that, head for the **JR Railway information office** (daily 5.30am–11pm) on the ground floor, which also has English-speaking staff and can make hotel reservations (¥525 commission) for the same night only.

 Closer to the city centre, near Nanzen-ji, **Kyoto International Community House** (Tues–Sun 9am–9pm; ☎075/752-3010, ⓦhttp://www .kcif.or.jp/en/index.html) is aimed primarily at foreign students or longer-

Applications to visit restricted sights

To visit some of Kyoto's most famous palaces and gardens it's necessary to apply in advance. In most cases this is a simple procedure and well worth the effort. Tours of the **Imperial Palace**, **Sentō Gosho**, **Katsura Rikyū** and **Shūgaku-in Rikyū** are all handled by the **Imperial Household Agency** (Mon–Fri 8.45am–noon & 1–4pm; ☏075/211-1215, ⓦwww.kunaicho.go.jp/eindex.html). Their office is located on the west side of the Imperial Park, near Imadegawa subway station. It's best to book your tour two days in advance, though you can often visit the Imperial Palace itself on the same day. All tours are free and conducted in Japanese, with the exception of the Imperial Palace, where there may be an English guide. Note that anyone under 20 years old (still a minor in Japanese law) has to be accompanied by an adult when visiting the Sentō Gosho, Katsura Rikyū or Shūgaku-in Rikyū. Finally, take your passport with you to the office and also for the tour itself, in case it's requested.

Other sights which require reservations are **Nijō-jin'ya**, the interior of **Nishi-Hongan-ji** and **Saihō-ji**. See the individual accounts for details.

term residents, but will happily assist tourists where possible. They have a message board, a library, foreign-language papers and magazines, and CNN or BBC World news playing in the first-floor lobby. Finally, the popular **Tour Club Hostel** (see "Accommodation" on p.523), close to Kyoto Station, offers a fair amount of English-language information whether you're staying there or not.

For most purposes the combined Kyoto–Nara **maps**, available free from the TIC, are perfectly adequate. If you feel in need of something more detailed, look out for the *Kyoto Information Map* (¥300), a book of large-scale maps in English and Japanese, which you should find in major bookstores (see p.559).

The monthly freesheet, *Kyoto Visitor's Guide*, is the best source of information regarding **what's on** in Kyoto. It includes details of festivals and cultural events, as well as area spotlights and selective listings of restaurants, bars and shops; you can usually pick it up in the TIC, major hotels and other tourist haunts. The monthly *Kansai Time Out* magazine (¥300) has good coverage of the Kyoto arts scene, from cinema, theatre and live music to museums and galleries. Keep an eye out in bars, shops and the information centres for the free, weekly *Kansai Flea Market*, which contains classified adverts for accommodation, employment, courses and so on.

The **Kansai Window** site at ⓦwww.kansai.gr.jp offers background information on the region. JNTO's Kyoto site is at ⓦwww.jnto.go.jp/eng/RTG/RI/kansai/kyoto/kyoto/kyoto.html.

City transport and tours

Kyoto's two **subway** lines offer the quickest way to scoot around the city. The **Karasuma line** runs from southerly Takeda, via Kyoto Station and Kita-ōji, to Kokusai Kaikan in the north, while the **Tōzai line** starts at Nijō in the west and cuts east through Sanjō-Keihan and Higashiyama to Daigo in the southeast suburbs; the two lines intersect at Karasuma-Oike Station. Trains run from 5.30am to 11.30pm and fares range from ¥200 to ¥320. Tickets are available from station vending machines. As well as single tickets, you can also buy stored-fare cards (*Torafika Kyō Kādo*) for ¥3000, which you can use both to buy subway tickets and on City Bus services. There are also region-wide stored-value tickets known as *Surutto Kansai kādo*.

Several private railways also operate within the city. Trains on **Hankyū railway**'s Kyoto line for Ōsaka (Umeda) run beneath the city centre from

Kawaramachi Station west along Shijō-dōri; a branch line heads northwest from Katsura Station in west Kyoto to Arashiyama (see p.569). Arashiyama is also served by the **Keifuku Railway** from Shijō-Ōmiya Station, with another branch line (the Kitano Line) looping north. In northeast Kyoto, Demachiyanagi is the terminus for the **Eizan line**, which covers Shūgaku-in Rikyū and Yase-yūen, one of the routes up Hiei-zan (see p.562). **Keihan mainline services** start from a separate station in Demachiyanagi and then head south via Sanjō-Keihan to Ōsaka (Yodayabashi). Finally, trains on the **Kintetsu-Kyoto line** depart from the south side of Kyoto Station, from where they link into the main Kintetsu network, with services to Nara, Kōya-san and Ise.

Kyoto's excellent **bus system** is relatively easy to use. The buses are colour-coded, the majority show their route numbers on the front and the most important stops are announced in English, either on the electronic display or over the loudspeakers. Within the city there's a flat fare of ¥220, which you pay on exit. In most cases you enter via the back door, where you may need to take a numbered ticket if the bus is going into the suburbs, though the flat fare still applies within the central zone. The only problem is that most services stop running around 11pm, or earlier on less popular routes.

Before leaping on board, get hold of the English-language route map from the information offices (see p.517) or the bus terminals. This shows the central zone boundary and routes operated by both **Kyoto City Bus** (light green with a darker stripe) and the far less comprehensive **Kyoto Bus** (cream with a red stripe). You'll need to use Kyoto Bus services for Ōhara and Arashiyama, but otherwise you can stick to City Bus for the central districts. The **main bus terminal** is outside Kyoto Station's Karasuma exit. Nearly all City Bus stands are coded: "A" before the stand number indicates buses headed for east Kyoto, and "B" for the western districts. Of several loop lines around the city, the most useful is #206, with stops near the National Museum, Gion, Heian-jingū, Daitoku-ji and Nijō-jō; buses running clockwise leave from stand B-4, anticlockwise from A-2. The other major terminals are at **Sanjō-Keihan** and **Kita-ōji** in the north. Some loop line buses terminate at Kita-ōji, so check with the driver if you're going that way; the stands at Kita-ōji are colour-coded red for eastbound buses and blue for westbound. A recent development is the introduction of a ¥100 bus service at the weekend and on national holidays. This one-direction-only, circular bus route runs in a loop from Kyoto City Hall to Karasuma Oike to Shijō Karasuma to Shijō Kawaramachi and back to Kyoto City Hall every ten minutes between 10am and 4.50pm. Buses are easy to spot as they have "¥100" written on the side in big letters.

The bus companies offer a range of **discount tickets**. The simplest, *kaisūken*, are booklets of ¥220 tickets available at a small reduction at the bus terminals or from the driver in denominations of ¥1000, ¥3000 and ¥5000, valid on all buses. Next up are the one-day passes (*shi-basu ichi-nichi jyōshaken*; ¥500), which allow unlimited travel on City Bus services within the central zone; if you want to visit anywhere further out, you just pay for the bit outside the zone. These passes are available at information centres, hotels and bus terminals, but not on the bus itself. To validate the pass, put it through the machine beside the driver when you get off the first bus – after that, just show it as you exit. Finally, there are combined subway and bus passes, either one-day (*shi-basu chikatetsu ichi-nichi jyōshaken*; ¥1200) or two-day (*shi-basu chikatetsu futsuka jyōshaken*; ¥2000), covering unlimited travel on the subways, City Bus and Kyoto Bus within a wider area marked on the bus maps in white. They're sold at hotels, the TIC, bus terminals, subway information windows or travel agents. You can buy them in advance, though you have to specify a date.

Though traffic in central Kyoto often gridlocks during rush hour, **taxis** (see "Listings", p.562) can be useful for hopping short distances. The minimum fare is ¥580 for 2km. Renting a **bike** is a viable option for exploring central Kyoto, though not much use along the eastern hills, where you're better off walking. See "Listings", p.561 for outlets.

City tours

Kyoto is best appreciated at a leisurely pace, but if you're really short of time JTB's Sunrise Tours (☎075/341-1413, ⓦwww.jtb.co.jp/sunrisetour/kyoto) offers English-speaking guides on their **city tours**; prices start at ¥5300 for a half-day tour of selected sights. Tours start from the lobby of the New Miyako Hotel south of Kyoto station, with pick-up services available from some of the city's other major hotels. Alternatively, Keihan Bus and City Bus run a more varied programme at slightly cheaper prices, but all in Japanese. Tickets for all these tours are available through travel agents or at the bus terminals. If you fancy a more personal tour, **Johnny Hillwalker** (otherwise known as Hirōka Hajime), an English-speaking veteran tour guide with more than forty years' experience, takes small groups on a slow amble through southern Kyoto from Higashi-Hongan-ji to Kiyomizu-dera (March–Nov Mon, Wed & Fri, except national holidays; ¥2000 per person; ☎075/622-6803). Alternatively, long-term resident **Peter Macintosh** offers a glimpse into the hidden world of the geisha (tours from ¥3000 per person; ring to arrange one on ☎090/5169-1654; ⓦwww.kyotosightsandnights.com).

Accommodation

Kyoto's **accommodation** options range from basic guesthouses, youth hostels and temple lodgings (*shukubō*) to luxurious international hotels and top-class ryokan. One night in a full-blown Kyoto **ryokan**, enjoying the world's most meticulous service, is an experience not to be missed, though some are hideously expensive and may refuse to accept foreigners – or indeed anyone without a prior recommendation, but we've listed one or two of the more accessible traditional ones below. Needless to say, it's essential to make **reservations** at these places as far in advance as possible, but all accommodation in Kyoto gets pretty busy during the autumn and spring peaks, at holiday weekends and around the major festivals (see p.556). Note that during these times room rates may rise considerably.

Central Kyoto is obviously a popular choice, with its easy access to the main shopping and nightlife districts as well as good transport links to sights around the city. That said, with a few notable exceptions most downtown hotels are either big, luxury places or offer poor value for money. Because city transport is so good, however, you can stay in the cheaper outer districts and still enjoy everything the city has to offer. Many places in **eastern Kyoto** are within walking distance of Gion and the city centre, while also being in quieter, more attractive surroundings. It's also worth considering one or two nights in **northern** Kyoto to explore the region around Kinkaku-ji and west to Arashiyama. Even the **station area** has a lot going for it, especially the group of inexpensive ryokan to the northeast.

Central Kyoto

The following are marked on the map on p.526.

Hotel Gimmond Takakura Oike, Nakagyō-ku ☎075/221-4111, ⓦwww.gimmond.co.jp/kyoto/kplan-e.htm. Elegant mid-range hotel with pleasant en-suite rooms and a smart in-house restaurant. ❺

Hiiragiya Fuyachō Anekoji-agaru, Nakagyō-ku

Kyoto: accommodation

Central Kyoto

Hotel Gimmond	*Hoteru Gimmondo*	ホテルギンモンド
Hiiragiya	*Hiiragiya*	柊家
Hiiragiya Bekkan	*Hiiragiya Bekkan*	柊家別館
Kinmata	*Kinmata*	近又
Kyoto Brighton Hotel	*Kyōto Buraiton Hoteru*	京都ブライトンホテル
Kyoto Garden Hotel	*Kyōto Gāden Hoteru*	京都ガーデンホテル
Kyoto Hotel Okura	*Kyōto Hoteru Ōkura*	京都ホテルオークラ
Hotel Oaks	*Hoteru Ōkusu*	ホテルオークス
Palace-Side Hotel	*Paresu Saido Hoteru*	パレスサイドホテル
Ryokan Hinomoto	*Ryokan Hinomoto*	旅館ひのもと
Sanjō Karasuma Hotel	*Sanjō Karasuma Hoteru*	三条烏丸ホテル
Sun Hotel	*San Hoteru*	サンホテル
Yoshikawa Ryokan	*Yoshikawa Ryokan*	吉川旅館

Around the station

Bekkan Heainbō	*Bekkan Heainbō*	別館平安坊
Budget Inn	*Bajetto In*	バジェットイン
Heianbō	*Heianbō*	平安坊
Hotel Granvia Kyoto	*Hoteru Guranvia Kyōto*	ホテルグランヴィア京都
J-Hoppers	*Jei Hoppāzu*	ジェイホッパーズ
K's House Kyoto	*Keizu Hausu Kyōto*	ケイズハウス京都
Kyoto 2 Tower Hotel	*Kyōto Dai-Ni Tawā Hoteru*	京都弟2タワーホテル
Matsuba-ya Ryokan	*Matsuba-ya Ryokan*	松葉家旅館
New Hankyū Hotel	*Shin-Hankyū Hoteru*	新阪急ホテル
Pension Station Kyoto	*Penshon Sutēshon Kyōto*	ペンションステーション京都
Riverside Takase	*Ribāsaido Takase*	リバーサイド高瀬
Ryokan Hiraiwa	*Ryokan Hiraiwa*	旅館平岩
Ryokan Yuhara	*Ryokan Yuhara*	旅館ゆはら
Tōjian	*Tōjian*	とうじ庵
Tour Club	*Tsuā kurasu*	ツアークラブ

East Kyoto

Higashiyama Youth Hostel	*Higashiyama Yūsu Hosuteru*	東山ユースホステル
Kiyomizu Sansō	*Kiyomizu Sansō*	清水山荘
Ryokan Seiki	*Ryokan Seiki*	旅館晴輝
Shinnyo-sansō	*Shinnyo-sansō*	真如山荘
Three Sisters' Inn	*Ryokan Surii Shisutāsu*	旅館スリーシスターズ
Travellers' Inn	*Toraberāzu In*	トラベラーズイン
Westin Miyako Hotel	*Miyako Hoteru*	ウェスティン都ホテル京都

North Kyoto

Aoi-sō Inn	*Aoi-sō In*	あおい荘イン
Kitayama Youth Hostel	*Kitayama Yūsu Hosuteru*	北山ユースホステル
Kyoto Takaragaike Prince Hotel	*Kyoto Takaragaike Purinsu Hoteru*	京都宝ヶ池プリンスホテル
Myōken-ji	*Myōken-ji*	妙顕寺
Myōren-ji	*Myōren-ji*	妙蓮寺
Ryokan Rakuchō	*Ryokan Rakuchō*	旅館洛頂
Tani House	*Tani Hausu*	谷ハウス
Utano Youth Hostel	*Utano Yūsu Hosuteru*	宇多野ユースホステル

☎075/221-1136, ⓦwww.hiiragiya.co.jp. One of Kyoto's most famous traditional ryokan, which has hardly changed since samurai stayed here in the mid-nineteenth century – guests have included Elizabeth Taylor, Charlie Chaplin and Mishima Yukio. You need to book well in advance, but it's worth it for this quintessential Kyoto experience. ❾

Hiiragiya Bekkan Gokomachi Nijō-sagaru, Nakagyō-ku ☎075/231-0151, ⓕ231-0153. The annexe of *Hiiragiya* (see above) offers slightly less grand accommodation. Though you can stay without meals, their *kaiseki* cuisine is superb. ❼

Kinmata 407 Gokomachi Shijō-agaru, Nakagyō-ku ☎075/221-1039, ⓦwww.kinmata.com. Leave the hustle and bustle of Shijō-dōri behind in this beautiful old inn, established in 1801. It offers the full ryokan experience, with *kaiseki ryōri* served in your room, a cedar-wood bath, meticulous service and a tiny classical garden – though the modern breakfast room is a tad incongruous. Prices are a little less than the competition and, while you really should try one evening meal, they do offer breakfast-only rates. English spoken. ❾

Kyoto Brighton Hotel Nakadachiuri, Shinmachi-dōri, Kamigyō-ku ☎075/441-4411, ⓦwww.brightonhotels.co.jp. Excellent-value top-class hotel a stone's throw from the Imperial Palace. Rooms are stylish and elegant, and even standard rooms have a lounge area that gives the impression of being in a suite. Imadegawa subway station. ❽

Kyoto Garden Hotel Muromachi-dōri, Oike Minami-iru, Nakagyō-ku ☎075/255-2000, ⓦwww.kyoto-gardenhotel.co.jp. Superior but good-value (especially off-peak when prices drop sharply) mid-range hotel in a convenient location very close to Karasuma-Oike subway station. There's free Internet access in the hotel lobby. ❹

Kyoto Hotel Okura Kawaramachi-Oike, Nakagyō-ku ☎075/211-5111, ⓦwww.kyotohotel.co.jp. This centrally located hotel offers an elegant mix of European and Japanese style. Rooms are of a good size and offer great views of the city, while

facilities include a fitness centre and swimming pool. Shiyakusho-mae subway station. ❽

Hotel Oaks Nishinotōin Shijō, Shimogyō-ku ☎075/371-0941, ⓦwww.h-oaks.co.jp/kyoto-shijo/english/index.html. This comfortable, mid-range business hotel (part of a Kansai-wide chain) offers excellent value for its location. All rooms come with small bathroom, phone, TV and minibar as standard and there are both Western- and Japanese-style dining facilities. ❺

Palace-Side Hotel Shimodachiuri Karasuma, Kamigyō-ku ☎075/431-8171, ⓦwww.palaceside-hotel.co.jp. Large, slightly bland hotel overlooking the Imperial Palace, with good views from the more expensive, higher rooms. Substantial discounts if you stay six days or more. Three minutes north of Marutamachi subway station. ❺

Ryokan Hinomoto 375 Kotake-chō, Kawaramachi Matsubara-agaru, Shimogyō-ku ☎075/351-4563, ⓕ351-3932. This friendly ryokan is one of the few inexpensive places to stay in central Kyoto. The recently refurbished rooms are nicely done in Japanese style, though none has private bathrooms. City Bus #17 and #205 stop at the nearby Kawaramachi Matsubara junction. ❹

Sanjō Karasuma Hotel 80 Mikura-chō, Sanjō Karasuma Nishi-iru, Nakagyō-ku ☎075/256-3331, ⓕ256-2351. This large, modern hotel offers well-priced, comfortable rooms, all with satellite TV, extra-wide beds and en-suite bathrooms. There's also a communal bath with garden views, a bar, restaurant and tea lounge. ❺

Sun Hotel Kawaramachi Sanjō-sagaru, Nakagyō-ku ☎075/241-3351, ⓕ241-0616. Nothing special, but the best of several lower-end hotels bang in the centre of town. Inevitably boxy but more than adequate. In-house Italian restaurant and coin-laundry facilities. English spoken. ❺

Yoshikawa Ryokan Tominokoji Oike-sagaru, Nakagyō-ku ☎075/221-5544, ⓕ221-6805. Intimate, traditional inn that's also renowned for its *tempura kaiseki* cuisine. Cypress-wood bath, immaculate garden and all the understated luxury you could want. ❽ including two meals.

Around the station

The following are marked on the map on p.531.

Budget Inn 295 Aburanokoji-chō, Aburanokoji, Shichijō-sagaru, Shimogyō-ku ☎075/344-1510, ⓦwww.budgetinn.jp. The closest hostel to JR Kyoto, this brand new establishment is run by the same friendly folk who operate *Tour Club* (see opposite) and offers a similar range of services. Dorm rooms ¥2500 per person, rooms ❹

Hotel Granvia Kyoto 657 Higashi-Shiokoji-chō, Karasuma Shiokoji-sagaru, Shimogyō-ku

☎075/344-8888, ⓦwww.granvia-kyoto.co.jp/e/index.html. Sleek new hotel incorporated into the Kyoto Station building, with rooms on the upper floors. Facilities include a range of restaurants and bars, indoor swimming pool, boutiques and business suites. Excellent value in this price range. ❻

Heianbō 725 Heian-chō, JR Kyoto-eki-mae, Shimogyō-ku ☎075/351-0650. This little wooden inn is a real surprise among all the high-rises. Rooms (some with bathrooms) are nicely refurbished in Japanese style. The recently opened annexe, *Bekkan Heainbō*, is just a few minutes' walk northwest and has cheaper rooms (❹). Enquiries should be directed to the main inn. ❺

J-Hoppers 51-2, Nakagoryō-chō, Higashikujō ☏075/681-2282, ⓦwww.j-hoppers.com. New backpackers' hostel with dorm beds (¥2500 per person) and private rooms (❸), plus bike rental, Internet access, laundry facilities and satellite TV.

K's House Kyoto 418 Nayachō, Shichijō-agaru, Shimogyō-ku ☏075/342-2444, ⓦwww.kshouse.jp. Brand new guesthouse with smart furnishings, four- to six-bed dorms (¥2500 per person) and private doubles, plus bicycle rental and Internet access. English spoken. ❷

Kyoto 2 Tower Hotel Higashinotōin Shichijō-sagaru, Shimogyō-ku ☏075/361-3261, ⓕ351-6281. Immediately outside the station, this is the nicest of the three Kyoto Tower hotels, with fairly cheerful rooms and English-speaking staff. ❺

Matsuba-ya Ryokan Kamijuzumachi Higashinotōin nishi-iru, Shimogyō-ku ☏075/351-3727, ⓦwww.matsubayainn.com/index.htm. Homely ryokan established in 1884 and located in an atmospheric Meiji-era building. All rooms (none en suite) are Japanese-style; the more expensive ones overlook a tiny garden. ❹

New Hankyū Hotel JR Kyoto-eki-mae, Shiokoji-dōri, Shimogyō-ku ☏075/343-5300, ⓦhttp://hotel.newhankyu.co.jp/kyoto-e/index.html. An efficient, upmarket hotel that's a cut above the neighbouring Kyoto Tower hotels. ❼

Pension Station Kyoto Shinmachi Shichijō-sagaru, Shimogyō-ku ☏075/882-6200, ⓕ862-0820. Located in an interesting old neighbourhood west of Higashi-Hongan-ji, this cheerful and relaxed place has a choice of Western and Japanese rooms – those without bath are better value. ❹

Riverside Takase Kiyamachi Kaminokuchi-agaru,

Shimogyō-ku ☏075/351-7925, ⓦhttp://web.kyoto-inet.or.jp/people/kyoka/takase.html. Though basic, these tatami rooms are among the cheapest available in the city centre, but as there are only five rooms it tends to fill up quickly. On the Takase Canal near *Ryokan Hiraiwa*. ❹

Ryokan Hiraiwa 314 Hayao-chō, Ninomiyachō Kaminokuchi-agaru, Shimogyō-ku ☏075/351-6748, ⓦwww2.odn.ne.jp/hiraiwa. Efficient, popular place in an attractive area of backstreets east of the Takase Canal. The tatami rooms are slightly spartan, and none are en suite, but they're all clean and tidy. It's a short walk from the Kawaramachi-shōmen stop on City Bus #17 or #205. ❹

Ryokan Yuhara Kiyamachi Shōmen-agaru, Shimogyō-ku ☏ & ⓕ075/371-9583. Slightly more elegant ryokan on the Takase Canal, with comfortable tatami rooms and English-speaking owners. ❹

Tōjian Hitotsume Nishi-iru Kitagawa, Hachi-jō-sagaru, Minami Ōmiya-dōri ☏075/691-7017, ⓕ691-0304. Friendly guesthouse, popular with backpackers, with air-conditioned dorms (¥2000 per person) and single rooms (¥2300), plus free laundry, use of a kitchen and bike rental (¥500) – and there's no curfew. Bathing facilities aren't wonderful (only one shower), but the guesthouse subsidizes most of the entry fee to the local bathhouse.

Tour Club 362 Momiji-chō Kitakoji-agaru, Higashi-Nakasuji-dōri, Shimogyō-ku ☏075/353-6968, ⓕ353-6978, ⓦwww.kyotojp.com. The best backpacker hostel in town: conveniently located, tastefully decorated and with very friendly, English-speaking owners.Dorms and en-suite twins are available, and facilities include a Japanese-style communal living room, Internet access, coin laundry, plenty of showers, money-changing facilities, kimono try-outs and very reasonable bicycle rentals. Rates get cheaper the longer you stay. Dorm beds ¥2415 per person, rooms ❸

East Kyoto

The following are marked on the map on p.534.

Higashiyama Youth Hostel 112 Sanjō-dōri Shirakawa-bashi, Higashiyama-ku ☏075/761-8135, ⓦwww.biwa.ne.jp/~kyoto-yh/inde-f-higasi-e.html. Kyoto's smartest hostel is conveniently located just east of Higashiyama subway station. However, it's run like a boarding school and there's a 10.30pm curfew. The food's not bad, but you definitely want to eat out at night in Kyoto. ❷

Kiyomizu Sansō 3-341 Kyomizu, Higashiyama-ku ☏075/561-6109. There are only four rooms in this hundred-year-old family inn, hidden down an alley

off the Sannen-zaka pedestrian street. Meals are optional, but excellent value. Reservations essential. ❹

Ryokan Seiki 188-1 Kadowaki-chō, Yamatoōji Gojō-agaru higashi-iru, Higashiyama-ku ☏075/551-4911, ⓕ551-9251. Modern ryokan within walking distance of Gion. Rooms are small but adequate, though none is en suite. Take City Bus #206 heading anticlockwise to the Gojō-zaka stop, then walk back down Gojō-dōri till you find their sign on the right. ❹

Shinnyo-sansō 82 Shinnyo-chō, Jōdo-ji, Sakyō-ku ☎075/751-8073, ℻771-1304. Modern *shukubō* in the grounds of Shinnyo-dō temple, in a quiet corner of northeast Kyoto, offering tatami rooms with separate bath and toilet. You can order mini-*kaiseki* dinners (¥3150) or other meals as required. The nearest bus stop, Shinnyodō-mae, is about 300m east on Shirakawa-dōri. There's an 11pm curfew. ❸

Three Sisters' Inn Kurodani-mae, Okazaki, Sakyō-ku ☎075/761-6336, ℻761-6338. The Yamada sisters run this homely ryokan, opened in 1957, and a nearby annexe set in a small garden. All rooms (some en-suite) are beautifully appointed, and they're located in an interesting residential area behind Heian-jingū. Meals are optional. English spoken. ❺

Travellers' Inn 91 Enshoji-chō, Okazaki, Sakyō-ku ☎075/771-0225, ℻771-0226. Tidy, no-frills Japanese- and Western-style rooms at an excellent price for the location, within walking distance of Heian-jingū and the surrounding sights. Rooms have baths, but there's a huge communal bath, too. From the station, take City Bus #5. ❺

Westin Miyako Hotel Sanjō Keage, Higashiyama-ku ☎075/771-7111, ⓦwww.westinmiyako-kyoto.com. Huge, efficient, top-class hotel complete with landscaped gardens, bird sanctuary and range of restaurants. There's a choice of elegant Japanese-style rooms, some in the garden annexe, or Western-style accommodation, where higher rates get you balconies with views over Kyoto. Free shuttle buses operate between the hotel, Sanjō-dōri and Kyoto Station. ❼

North Kyoto

The following are marked on the map on p.542.

Aoi-sō Inn Karasuma Shimei, Kita-ku ☎075/431-0788. Popular *gaijin* guesthouse, offering functional private rooms with shared toilets and showers. Weekly and monthly rates also available. Two minutes' walk west from Kuramaguchi subway station. ❷

Kitayama Youth Hostel Takagamine, Kita-ku ☎075/492-5345. This small, older hostel on the northwest fringes of Kyoto makes a good base for Kinkaku-ji and surrounding sights. You'll get a warm welcome and lots of local information from the jovial English-speaking manager and, though there's a 9.30pm curfew, it's all pretty relaxed. Take the subway to Kita-Ōji station, then take a City Bus (Kita #1) from the Kita-Ōji Bus Terminal to the Takagamine Genkō-an-mae stop (15min), then walk west until you find the signed right-hand turn. Dorm beds ¥2800 per person.

Kyoto Takaragaike Prince Hotel Takaragaike, Sakyō-ku ☎075/712-1111, ⓦwww.princehotels.co.jp/kyoto. Located in leafy north Kyoto close to the International Conference Center (which will be familiar to anyone who has seen the 1975 Robert Mitchum classic, *The Yakuza*), this is one of the city's few top-class Western-style hotels – and certainly the only one shaped like a doughnut. Rooms are large and service is good, as you'd expect at the price. The hotel's surroundings are pleasantly green and relaxing, though the location is a tad inconvenient. Kokusai Kaikan subway station. ❻

Myōken-ji Teranouchi Shinmachi nishi-iru, Kamigyō-ku ☎075/414-0808. Lovely, traditional *shukubō* with a delightful garden at the back of the temple complex, but you need to be able to speak some Japanese. At busy times you'll be asked to share the tatami rooms. It's slightly west of Horikawa Teranouchi bus stop, northwest of the Imperial Palace. From the station, take City Bus #9. 10pm curfew. ❹

Myōren-ji Teranouchi Ōmiya higashi-iru, Kamigyō-ku ☎075/451-3527. Welcoming, relaxed *shukubō* with refurbished tatami rooms behind a thirteenth-century temple with a celebrated rock garden. There's no bath – you'll be given tickets to the local public bath – and no meals, but guests can attend the 6.30am service in the temple. It's just east of the Horikawa Teranouchi bus stop, in the opposite direction to *Myōken-ji* (see above); look for an unusual bell tower in the front courtyard. English spoken. 11pm curfew. ❸

Ryokan Rakuchō 67 Higashi-Hangi-chō, Shimogamo, Sakyō-ku ☎075/721-2174, ⓦwww.rakucho-ryokan.com. Friendly, well-kept inn with tatami rooms and shared washing facilities. Internet access. It's about 500m east from Kita-Ōji subway and bus station and also on the #206 City Bus loop line (50m north of Furitsu-daigaku-mae stop); turn north off Kitaōji-dōri in front of the sub-post office. English spoken. ❹

Tani House 8 Daitokuji-chō Murasakino, Kita-ku ☎075/492-5489, ℻493-6419. Reservations are essential at this welcoming, cluttered house among quiet lanes to the east of Daitoku-ji. There's a choice of shared tatami-mat dorms, or basic private rooms, plus use of a shared kitchen and cheap bikes for rent (¥500 per day). They also run an annexe in central Kyoto, though it's often filled with long-term guests. To find it, walk west from the Kenkun-jinja-mae stop (City Bus #206) and turn north beside the walls of Daitoku-ji. English spoken. ❷

Utano Youth Hostel 29 Nakayama-chō, Uzumasa, Ukyō-ku ☎075/462-2288, ⓦhttp://web.kyoto-inet.or.jp/org/utano-yh. A big, bustling hostel with a good atmosphere and helpful, English-speaking staff, set in its own grounds on Kyoto's western outskirts. The buffet breakfast is excellent value, and you can work it off by bik-ing (¥800 per day) to nearby Ryōan-ji and Kinkaku-ji, or west to Arashiyama. Vegetarian meals available with prior notice. There's a 10.30pm curfew. Three City Bus lines (#10, #26 and #59) stop near the hostel, just within the ¥700-bus pass zone. Dorm beds ¥2500 per person, twins ❸

The City

For decades Kyoto-lovers have been lamenting the loss of old wooden neighbourhoods to concrete modernity, the diminishing number of traditional craftsmen and the demise of their ancient city's unique culture. While the onslaught has been relentless – witness the giant JR station complex and the more insidious redevelopment of countless private plots – Kyoto's "**world of shadows**" still exists, lurking behind the secretive screens of traditional inns or exclusive restaurants, and within the lantern-lit facades of Gion and Pontochō. The spirit of old Kyoto is not all so elusive, however, and the key to enjoying this massive city is to leave the tourist haunts behind occasionally and delve into the quiet backstreets, among age-old craftshops and distinctive *machiya* houses (see box, p.537), or to seek out the peaceful garden of some forgotten temple.

The account below starts in central Kyoto and then heads south to the station before crossing east over the Kamo-gawa to work anticlockwise around the outer districts. Much of the city centre and the eastern hills can be covered on foot, but you'll need to hop on a few trains and buses to explore the more scattered sights to the north and west.

Central Kyoto

Before the emperor moved to Tokyo in 1868, Kyoto's **Imperial Palace** symbolized the nation's physical and spiritual centre. Today's palace is by no means a high priority among Kyoto's wealth of sights, but it's a good idea to come here early in your stay to make arrangements for visiting the city's more rewarding imperial villas and gardens (see box, p.518). If you're not pushed for time, then the **Sentō Gosho** garden, also in the Imperial Park, is worth seeing, but otherwise it's better to concentrate on **Nijō-jō**'s magnificent screen paintings and the intriguing **Nijō-jin'ya**.

The Imperial Park and Palace

Dun-coloured earth walls enclose the **Imperial Park**, inside which wide expanses of gravel and clipped lawns have replaced most of the former palaces and subsidiary buildings. In the park's northwest corner, the **Imperial Household Agency** office handles applications to visit the former royal palaces (see box, p.518); the nearest subway station is Imadegawa, or take a bus to Karasuma Imadegawa. As long as you arrive twenty minutes before, it's usually possible to sign up for the next tour of the nearby **Imperial Palace** (Mon–Fri & third Sat each month – and every Sat in April, May, Oct & Nov – at 10am & 2pm; free). The tour lasts around one hour and is often in English, though it's still worth investing in the English-language guidebook (¥200) for its interior views. Though it originally stood about 2km further west, the palace was relocated to the present site in the late twelfth century. Nearly all the buildings, however, date from the mid-nineteenth century and the overwhelming impression is of sterile spaces of pure white gravel set off against regal halls built in austere Heian style (794–1185). The most important build-

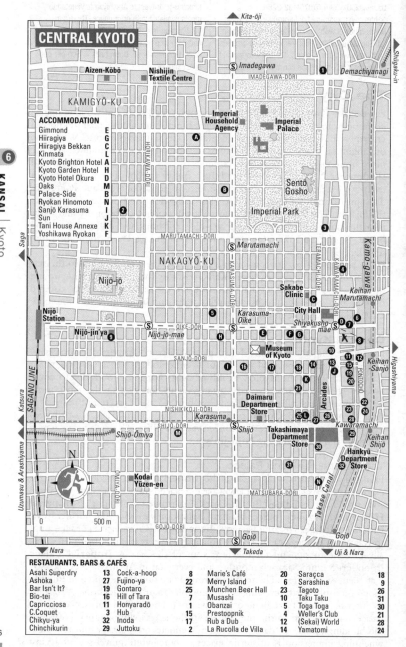

CENTRAL KYOTO

Kita-ōji

Shigaku-in

Imadegawa

Demachiyanagi

IMADEGAWA-DORI

Aizen-Kōbō

Nishijin Textile Centre

KAMIGYŌ-KU

ACCOMMODATION

Gimmond	E
Hiiragiya	G
Hiiragiya Bekkan	C
Kinmata	L
Kyoto Brighton Hotel	A
Kyoto Garden Hotel	H
Kyoto Hotel Okura	D
Oaks	M
Palace-Side	B
Ryokan Hinomoto	N
Sanjō Karasuma	I
Sun	J
Tani House Annexe	K
Yoshikawa Ryokan	F

Imperial Household Agency

Imperial Palace

Sentō Gosho

Imperial Park

MARUTAMACHI-DORI

Marutamachi

NAKAGYŌ-KU

Nijō-jō

Nijō Station

Nijō-jin ya

Nijō-jō-mae

OIKE-DORI

SANJŌ-DORI

Sakabe Clinic

City Hall

Karasuma-Oike

Shiyakusho-mae

Museum of Kyoto

Keihan Marutamachi

Kamo-gawa

Keihan-Sanjō

Higashiyama

NISHIKIKOJI-DORI

Daimaru Department Store

Arcades

Karasuma

SHIJŌ-DORI

Shijō

Shijō-Ōmiya

Takashimaya Department Store

Kawaramachi

Keihan Shijō

Kodai Yūzen-en

Hankyū Department Store

MATSUBARA-DORI

Takase Canal

0   500 m

N

GOJŌ-DORI

Gojō

Gojō

Nara

Takeda

Uji & Nara

Saga

Katsura

Uzumasu & Arashiyama

SAGANO LINE

KANSAI | Kyoto

6

526

RESTAURANTS, BARS & CAFÉS

Asahi Superdry	13	Cock-a-hoop	8
Ashoka	27	Fujino-ya	22
Bar Isn't It?	19	Gontaro	25
Bio-tei	16	Hill of Tara	7
Capricciosa	11	Honyaradō	1
C.Coquet	3	Hub	15
Chikyu-ya	32	Inoda	17
Chinchikurin	29	Juttoku	2

Marie's Café	
Merry Island	6
Munchen Beer Hall	23
Musashi	10
Obanzai	4
Prestoopnik	
Rub a Dub	12
La Rucolla de Villa	14

Saraçca	18
Sarashina	9
Tagoto	26
Taku Taku	31
Toga Toga	30
(Sekai) World	28
Yamatomi	24
Weller's Club	21

ing is the ceremonial **Shishin-den**, flanked by two cherry and citrus trees, where the Meiji, Taishō and Shōwa emperors were all enthroned. Further on, you can peer inside the Seiryō-den, which was once the emperor's private residence, while beyond there's a tantalizing glimpse of a pond-filled stroll-garden (see p.528) designed by the landscape gardener Kobori Enshū (1579–1647).

Kyoto: the city

Central Kyoto and around the station

Higashi-Hongan-ji	*Higashi-Hongan-ji*	東本願寺
Imperial Palace	*Kyōto Gosho*	京都御所
Kyoto Station	*Kyōto-eki*	京都駅
Museum of Kyoto	*Kyōto Bunka Hakubutsukan*	京都文化博物館
Nijō-jin'ya	*Nijō-jin'ya*	二条陣屋
Nijō-jō	*Nijō-jō*	二条城
Nishi-Hongan-ji	*Nishi-Hongan-ji*	西本願寺
Pontochō	*Pontochō*	先斗町
Tō-ji	*Tō-ji*	東寺

East Kyoto

Chion-in	*Chion-in*	知恩院
Eikan-dō	*Eikan-dō*	永観堂
Fureaikan	*Fureaikan*	ふれあい館
Ginkaku-ji	*Ginkaku-ji*	銀閣寺
Gion	*Gion*	祇園
Gion Kōbu Kaburenjō	*Gion Kōbu Kaburenjō*	祇園甲部歌舞練場
Heian-jingū	*Heian-jingū*	平安神宮
Kawai Kanjirō's House	*Kawai Kanjirō Kinenkan*	河井寛次郎記念館
Kiyomizu-dera	*Kiyomizu-dera*	清水寺
Kōdai-ji	*Kōdai-ji*	高台寺
Konchi-in	*Konchi-in*	金地院
Kyoto National Museum	*Kyōto Kokuritsu Hakubutsukan*	京都国立博物館
Murin-an	*Murin-an*	無隣庵
Nanzen-ji	*Nanzen-ji*	南禅寺
Nomura Art Museum	*Nomura Bijutsukan*	野村美術館
Sanjūsangen-dō	*Sanjūsangen-dō*	三十三間堂
Shimbashi	*Shimbashi*	新橋
Shōren-in	*Shōren-in*	青連院
Shūgaku-in Rikyū	*Shūgaku-in Rikyū*	修学院離宮
Yasaka-jinja	*Yasaka-jinja*	八坂神社
Yasui Konpira-gū	*Yasui Konpira-gū*	安井金比羅宮

West Kyoto

Daisen-in	*Daisen-in*	大仙院
Daitoku-ji	*Daitoku-ji*	大徳寺
Katsura Rikyū	*Katsura Rikyū*	桂離宮
Kinkaku-ji	*Kinkaku-ji*	金閣寺
Kita-ōji Station	*Kita-ōji-eki*	北大路駅
Kōryū-ji	*Kōryū-ji*	広隆寺
Ryōan-ji	*Ryōan-ji*	龍安寺
Ryōgen-in	*Ryōgen-in*	龍源院
Saihō-ji	*Saihō-ji*	西芳寺
Tōei Uzumasa Eiga-mura	*Tōei Uzumasa Eiga-mura*	東映太秦映画村

You can enjoy Enshū's work to the full in the **Sentō Gosho**, which occupies the southeast quadrant of the Imperial Park. Again, you have to join a guided tour (Mon–Fri & third Sat each month, and every Sat in April, May, Oct & Nov; free), and this time it's all in Japanese. Originally built as a retirement home for former emperors, the palace last burnt down in 1854 and now only the peaceful garden remains. Apart from several graceful pavilions, its main features are a zigzag bridge – stunning when its wisteria trellis is in full bloom – and a cobbled "seashore", which lends the garden an extra grandeur.

Nijō-jō and Nijō-jin'ya

One kilometre southwest of the Imperial Park, the swaggering opulence of **Nijō-jō** (daily 8.45am–5pm, closed Tues in Jan, July, Aug & Dec; ¥600; ☎075/841-0096) provides a complete contrast to imperial understatement. Built as the Kyoto residence of Shogun Tokugawa Ieyasu (1603–16), the castle's double moats, massive walls and watchtowers demonstrate the supreme confidence of his new, Tokyo-based military government. Inside, the finest artists of the day filled the palace with sumptuous gilded screens and carvings, the epitome of Momoyama style (see "Contexts", p.967), leaving the increasingly impoverished emperor in no doubt as to where power really lay. The castle took 23 years to complete, paid for by local *daimyō*, but Nijō-jō was never used in defence and rarely visited by a shogun after the mid-1600s. More than two hundred years later, however, it was here that the young Emperor Meiji had the satisfaction of receiving the resignation of the last Tokugawa shogun in 1867.

The entrance to Nijō-jō lies via the main East Gate on Horikawa-dōri, near the Nijō-jō-mae subway station and bus stop. Inside, follow the crowds through Kara-mon gate and under the magnificent sweeping roofs of the **Ninomaru Palace**. Its five buildings face onto a lake-garden created by Kobori Enshū and run in a staggered line connected by covered corridors. Each room is lavishly decorated with **screen paintings** by the brilliant Kanō school of artists, notably Kanō Tanyū and Naonobu, while some of the intricately carved transoms are attributed to Hidari Jingoro. In keeping with the rigid stratification of feudal society, each room's function was reflected in the degree of decoration and in the motifs themselves. *Daimyō* seeking an audience with the shogun cooled their heels among scenes of imposing leopards and tigers – animals the artists had never seen – before being ushered into the Second Grand Chamber (in the third building). Here they would prostrate themselves before the shogun on his raised dais, surrounded by bold, shimmering screens of pines and peacocks beneath an equally ornate ceiling. The fourth building, reserved for the trusted Inner Lords, eschews such grandeur for more delicate herons and cherry blossoms, while the fifth is positively subdued. This last was the shogun's living quarters, which only his female attendants were allowed to enter; it's decorated with monochrome screens of craggy Chinese landscapes and sleeping sparrows.

Ieyasu built Nijō-jō in the grounds of the original Heian-era Imperial Palace. Today only a tiny fragment of the earlier palace remains – a pond-garden, **Shinsen-en** – trapped between two roads immediately south of the castle walls. Through the garden, continue walking south down Ōmiya-dōri to find the mysterious **Nijō-jin'ya** behind a fence on the right-hand side. Since this is a private house, **tours** (daily except Wed at 10am, 11am, 2pm & 3pm; 1hr; ¥1000; ☎075/841-0972) are by appointment only and must be booked by phone, in Japanese, a day before; they also ask that non-Japanese-speakers bring an interpreter. All this effort is rewarded with a glimpse into a treacherous world – the seemingly ordinary house is riddled with trap doors, false walls and ceilings, squeaking "nightingale" floors, escape hatches, disguised staircases and confusing dead ends to trap intruders. It was built in the early seventeenth century as an inn for feudal lords who came to pay homage to the emperor. As these were days of intrigue and high skulduggery, the owner spent thirty years incorporating this splendid array of security devices. It's the stuff of countless samurai epics, but Ian Fleming, researching locations for *You Only Live Twice* (see "Books", p.1021), found it excessive: "I wouldn't dare write this for Bond," he said. "There must be some show of plausibility."

Downtown Kyoto

Kyoto's **downtown** district is contained within the grid of streets bounded by Oike-dōri and Shijō-dōri to the north and south, Karasuma-dōri to the west and the Kamo-gawa in the east. While there are few specific sights, the backstreets still hide a number of traditional wooden buildings, including some of Kyoto's finest ryokan (see "Accommodation", p.520). You'll also come across fine old craft shops (see p.557) among the boutiques and department stores, while the colourful arcades of **Teramachi-dōri** and neighbouring **Shinkyōgoku** are worth a browse. The alleys east of Shinkyōgoku are home to a scattering of forgotten temples which were banished to this area in the late sixteenth century. Beyond here, towards the Kamo-gawa, lies the former geisha district of **Pontochō** – best at night, when lantern-light fills the district's narrow lanes, but also attractive by day, particularly along the willow-lined Takase Canal. In July and August Pontochō restaurants open terraces over the cooling Kamo-gawa – their mellow lamps are a memorable feature of Kyoto's sweltering summer nights.

A little further west, **Nishikikoji** street market provides a feast for the eyes and nose. Since the early seventeenth century this narrow covered alley has been one of Kyoto's main fish and vegetable markets, supplemented nowadays by the city's famous *tsukemono* – great vats of brightly coloured pickled vegetables. Where the stalls end, turn north on Takakura-dōri to find the downtown district's only conventional sight, the **Museum of Kyoto** (Tues–Sun 10am–6/7.30pm; ¥500; ☎075/222-0888), in a trendy area of galleries and cafés. The museum incorporates a Meiji-era bank building and a replica Edo-period shopping street with craft shops and some reasonable restaurants. Upstairs, the main display halls deal with local history, culture and modern crafts. Despite the charming historical dioramas, the exhibitions are rather disappointing – ask for one of the museum's volunteer guides if you want to fathom what's going on. However, the small section on Kyoto's film industry is enlivened by screenings of classic movies (in Japanese) at 1.30pm and 5pm on weekdays.

Around the station

Historically, the principal entrance to Kyoto lay through its great southern gate, so it's only fitting that this district, south of the city centre, should be home to the monumental **Kyoto Station**. Uncompromisingly modern, the shiny new station and its associated developments have already begun to revitalize the area, which also contains a few of the city's more venerable temples. In their day, when their massive wooden halls were filled with shimmering gold, **Nishi–Hongan-ji** and **Higashi–Hongan-ji** were probably equally awe-inspiring as the modern train station. Across the tracks, **Tō-ji** boasts Japan's tallest wooden pagoda and some of the city's oldest surviving buildings.

Nishi-Hongan-ji

One of Japan's most popular and wealthy Buddhist sects is the Jōdo Shinshū (True Pure Land), founded by the Kyoto-born priest Shonin Shinran (1173–1262). His simple creed, which at the time was regarded as heresy, asserts that merely chanting the *nembutsu*, "Praise to Amida Buddha", can lead to salvation. Not surprisingly, the sect grew rapidly, despite opposition from the established hierarchy, until eventually Toyotomi Hideyoshi granted them a plot of land in southern Kyoto in 1591. By 1602, however, Shogun Tokugawa Ieyasu was sufficiently alarmed at the sect's power to sponsor a splinter group just a few hundred metres to the east – even today the two groups continue to differ over doctrinal affairs.

The more interesting of the two temples is the original **Nishi-Hongan-ji** (daily: March, April, Sept & Oct 5.30am–5.30pm; May & Aug 5.30am–6pm; Nov–Feb 6am–5pm; free; ☎075/371-5181; ⓦhttp://www2.hongwanji.or.jp/english/), which faces onto Horikawa-dōri about ten minutes' walk north of Kyoto Station. The gravel courtyard contains two huge halls, the oldest of which is the **Founder's Hall** (1636) on the left, dedicated to Shinran, while the **Amida Hall** dates from 1760. Both are decked with gold, including some screens by Kanō artists in the Amida Hall. Unfortunately, you won't be able to see much of the Founder's Hall, as a ten-year reconstruction programme (which started in 1998) means that it has been enclosed in what looks like an enormous aircraft hangar as the battered tiles are restored and, in many cases, replaced. The temple's real highlights, however, are the even more ornate **Shoin** and **Kuro-shoin Chambers**. Entrance is by guided tour (daily at 10.45am & 2.45pm; free; ☎075/371-5181) – ask in the green-roofed building, left of the Founder's Hall. To be on the safe side, however, it's best to reserve two weeks before by writing to the Nishi-Hongan-ji Reception Office, Hanayachō-sagaru, Horikawa-dōri, Shimogyō-ku, Kyoto 600-8358, giving your name, address, phone number, number of people and dates you'll be in Kyoto; remember to enclose a stamped-addressed envelope, or an international reply coupon if sending from abroad.

The tour starts with an introductory talk – you'll be lent an English-language pamphlet – after which you can explore at your own pace. The chambers date from the mid-seventeenth century and were relocated here from various palaces around the city by order of Tokugawa Ieyasu. Kanō-school artists covered the walls and screens with what are regarded as some of the finest Momoyama-period paintings, showing classical landscapes, birds and flowers, all lavishly sprinkled with gold. The temple's dry garden is noted for its exotic cycad palms and is similarly elaborate, in stark contrast to the two austere **Nō stages**. Dated 1581, the northern stage is held to be the oldest in Japan.

Higashi-Hongan-ji

Shōmen-dōri leads east from Nishi-Hongan-ji, past shops selling Buddhist accessories, to the back wall of **Higashi-Hongan-ji** (daily: March–Oct 5.50am–5.30pm; Nov–Feb 6.20am–4.30pm; free; ☎075/371-9181). Though similar in style to its rival, Higashi-Hongan-ji had to be completely rebuilt after a fire in 1864. Only the two main halls are open to the public. The more northerly **Founder's Hall** is among Japan's largest wooden buildings – when the new halls were built, ordinary ropes proved too weak to lift the massive roof beams, so female devotees from around the country sent in enough hair to plait 53 ropes; an example of these black coils is preserved in the open corridor connecting the halls. Two blocks further east, the temple's shady **Kikoku-tei** garden (daily 9am–4pm; free) provides a welcome respite from the surrounding city blocks.

AROUND KYOTO STATION

ACCOMMODATION

Bekkan Heianbō	F
Budget Inn	G
Granvia Kyoto	M
Heianbō	J
J-Hoppers	O
K's House Kyoto	I
Kyoto 2 Tower	L
Matsuba-ya Ryokan	D
New Hankyū	K
Pension Station Kyoto	H
Riverside Takase	A
Ryokan Hiraiwa	B
Ryokan Yuhara	C
Tōjian	N
Tour Club	E

RESTAURANTS, CAFÉS & BARS

Izusen	1
Suishin	2

0 ————— 500 m

Kyoto Station and Kyoto Tower

There was much local controversy in the 1990s about the new **Kyoto Station**, designed by Tokyo architect Hara Hiroshi, which dominates the southern aspect of this low-rise city, but now that it has been completed many people have come to appreciate its steel-grey bulk. The hugely ugly 131-metre-high **Kyoto Tower**, built in the 1960s, is far more objectionable, though it does prove a useful landmark when walking around the city. Save your money on the tower's observatory (daily 9am–9pm; ¥770) and head for the station's twelfth-floor Sky Garden instead: the views may be less dramatic, but it's free and the building's extraordinary central atrium, with its grand stairways and suspended walkway, is well worth exploring. Apart from the station itself, there's a department store, restaurants and underground shopping malls, plus a hotel, theatre and an unusually good Joypolis amusement hall (daily 10am–11pm; from ¥1500 for three attractions). Already the station is providing a new focus to southern Kyoto and it's likely that this area will see more development.

Tō-ji

There's little reason to venture into the bleak districts south of Kyoto Station, with the noteworthy exception of **Tō-ji** (daily: mid-March to mid-Sept 8.30am–5.30pm; mid-Sept to mid-March 8.30am–4.30pm; ☎075/691-3325). This historic temple, founded by Emperor Kammu in 794, contains some of Japan's finest Esoteric Buddhist sculpture. If possible, it's best to visit during the monthly flea market (the 21st of each month), when Tō-ji throngs with pilgrims, hustlers and bargain hunters.

The main entrance to eighth-century Heian-kyō lay through the great south gate, Rashō-mon, which stood at the junction of Kujō-dōri and Senbon-dōri. After the problems in Nara (see p.574), Emperor Kammu permitted only two Buddhist temples within the city walls: Tō-ji and Sai-ji, the East and West temples, stood either side of Rashō-mon and were charged with the young capital's spiritual wellbeing. While Sai-ji eventually faded in the thirteenth century, Tō-ji prospered under **Kōbō Daishi**, the founder of Shingon Buddhism (see p.954), who was granted the stewardship in 823. Over the centuries, the temple gathered a treasure trove of calligraphy, paintings and Buddhist statuary, the oldest of which were supposedly brought from China by the Daishi himself.

The back gate of Tō-ji lies about ten minutes' walk southwest of Kyoto Station. Its most distinctive feature is a **five-storey pagoda** – Japan's tallest – which was erected in 826 and last rebuilt in the mid-seventeenth century. It now stands in an enclosure alongside Tō-ji's greatest treasures, the Kō-dō and more southerly Kon-dō (¥500, or ¥800 including the Hōmotsu-kan). These solid, confident buildings both date from the early seventeenth century, but it's the images inside that are the focus.

The red-lacquered **Kō-dō** (Lecture Hall) is the temple's most important building. Inside the cool, slightly musty hall, 21 gilded polychrome statues are arranged in a mandala representing the eternal realm. Five Buddhas hold centre stage, flanked by two splendid groups of statues, all of which date from the early Heian period. To the right (east), five Bodhisattvas sit on their lotus thrones and to the left stand the Godai Myō-ō (Five Fearful Kings), whose ferocious demeanour is meant to scare off evil. The mandala's corners are protected by the no less fierce Shi-Tennō (Four Heavenly Kings), with between them the glorious Taishaku-Ten, astride a lumpy white elephant, and the four-headed, four-armed Bon-Ten, perched precariously on a quartet of geese.

By contrast, the plain wooden **Kon-dō** (Main Hall) contains just three images within its dark, high-roofed sanctuary. Here, Yakushi Nyorai, the Buddha of physical and spiritual healing, is accompanied by his two assistants, Nikkō and Gakkō, all carved around four centuries ago. Take a close look at the twelve sacred generals gathered around Yakushi's throne – one of these small but lusty characters shades his eyes to search out evil, while another eagerly tests the edge of his sword.

Kōbō Daishi is said to have lived in the **Miei-dō**, the Founder's Hall, located in the temple's northwest corner. The present building, erected in 1380, houses a thirteenth-century statue of the saint which can be seen on the 21st of each month. On this day, which marks the entry of the Daishi into Nirvana, hundreds of pilgrims queue up to pay their respects. Beyond the Miei-dō, the modern **Hōmotsu-kan** contains Tō-ji's remaining treasures, including priceless mandala, portraits of Kōbō Daishi and a six-metre-tall Senjū Kannon (thousand-armed Buddhist Goddess of Mercy) carved in 877. The museum opens twice a year (March 20–May 25 & Sept 20–Nov 25 daily 9am–4.30pm; ¥500), with a different exhibition on each occasion.

East Kyoto

If you only have one day in Kyoto, it's best to concentrate on the wealth of temples and museums lining the eastern hills. Not only does this district include many of Kyoto's more rewarding sights, but it's also fairly compact and contains areas of attractive lanes and traditional houses set against the wooded slopes behind. Beginning in the south, the massed statues of **Sanjūsangen-dō** are a tremendous sight, but if you're pushed for time head straight for **Kiyomizu-dera**, with its distinctive wooden terrace, and then follow cobbled **Sannen-zaka** north. **Gion**, the famous entertainment district traditionally associated with geisha and teahouses, retains a surprising number of wooden facades and photogenic corners, though its seductive charms are best savoured after dark. Further north, **Heian-jingū** rings the changes as both a major shrine and a relatively recent addition to the cityscape, while the nearby **Fureaikan** provides a comprehensive introduction to Kyoto's myriad traditional crafts. It's worth seeking out the quiet gardens of **Murin-an** and **Konchi-in**, before taking the philosopher's path north to **Ginkaku-ji** – the Silver Pavilion may be unexpectedly low-key, but it makes a startling combination with the garden's mass of sculpted white sand. Garden lovers should also arrange to visit **Shūgaku-in Rikyū** on the northeast edge of Kyoto, for its inspired use of borrowed scenery on a grand scale – you'll need an extra half-day for this.

Sanjūsangen-dō to Kiyomizu-dera

Don't be put off by the turnstile entrance to **Sanjūsangen-dō** (daily: April to mid-Nov 8am–5pm; mid-Nov to March 9am–4pm; ¥600; ☎075/561-4137), on the southeastern edge of Kyoto – the ranks of 1001 gilded statues inside the hall are a truly memorable sight. At first the impassive, haloed figures appear as identical images of Kannon, the Buddhist Goddess of Mercy, portrayed with eleven heads and a thousand arms. But they all have subtle differences in their faces, clothes, jewellery or the symbols held in their tiny, outstretched hands. Rather than a thousand arms, the statues have been given only forty apiece (excluding the two hands in prayer), but each of these can save 25 worlds. In addition, every figure represents 33 incarnations, giving a total of 33,033 Kannon to help save mankind. It's perhaps not surprising to learn that they were commissioned by the devout former emperor Go-Shirakawa in 1164, during the bloody Genpei Wars (see p.935).

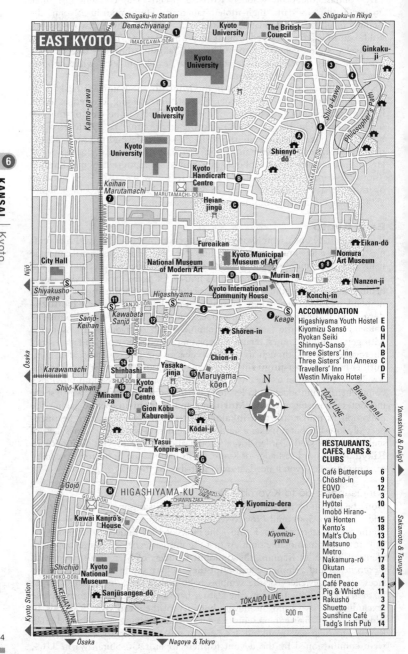

EAST KYOTO

▲ Shūgaku-in Station   ▲ Shūgaku-in Rikyū

Demachiyanagi ❶

IMADEGAWA-DŌRI

Kyoto University

The British Council

Kyoto University

Ginkaku-ji

❷ ❸
❹

Kyoto University

❺

Shira-kawa

❻

Philosopher's Path

Kyoto University

Kamo-gawa

KAWARAMACHI-DŌRI

Shinnyo-dō Ⓐ

Kyoto Handicraft Centre Ⓑ

Keihan Marutamachi ❼

MARUTAMACHI-DŌRI

Heian-jingū

Fureaikan

Nomura Art Museum

City Hall

Nijō

Shiyakusho-mae Ⓢ

National Museum of Modern Art

Kyoto Municipal Museum of Art

Ⓓ ⑩ Murin-an

Eikan-dō ⛩

❾ 8

Kyoto International Community House

Konchi-in

Nanzen-ji

ACCOMMODATION

Higashiyama Youth Hostel	E
Kiyomizu Sansō	G
Ryokan Seiki	H
Shinnyō-Sansō	A
Three Sisters' Inn	B
Three Sisters' Inn Annexe	C
Travellers' Inn	D
Westin Miyako Hotel	F

SHIRAKAWA-DŌRI

Higashiyama Ⓢ

SANJŌ-DŌRI

⑪ Ⓢ Ⓔ

Keage Ⓢ

Sanjō Keihan

Kawabata Sanjō

⑫

KAWABATA-DŌRI

HIGASHIŌJI-DŌRI

Shōren-in ⛩

Chion-in ⛩

TOZAILINE

Biwa Canal

Yamashina & Daigō

Osaka

Karawamachi

⑬

PONTOCHŌ

⑭ Shinbashi

Yasaka-jinja ⑮ Maruyama-kōen

Shijō-Keihan

SHIJŌ-DŌRI

⑯ ⑱ Kyoto Craft Centre

Minami -za

Gion Kōbu Kaburenjō

⑲

Kōdai-ji ⛩

Sakamoto & Tsuruga

N

RESTAURANTS, CAFÉS, BARS & CLUBS

Gojō

YAMATOŌJI-DŌRI

Yasui Konpira-gū ⛩

Ⓖ

HIGASHIYAMA-KU

KIYOMIZU-ZAKA

Gojō

GOJŌ-DŌRI

Ⓗ

CHAWAN-ZAKA

Kawai Kanjirō's House

⛩

Kiyomizu-dera ⛩

Kiyomizu-yama ▲

Café Buttercups	6
Chōshō-in	9
EQVO	12
Furōen	3
Hyōtei	10
Imobō Hirano-ya Honten	15
Kento's	18
Malt's Club	13
Matsuno	16
Metro	7
Nakamura-rō	17
Okutan	8
Omen	4
Café Peace	1
Pig & Whistle	11
Rakushō	2
Shuetto	5
Sunshine Café	5
Tadg's Irish Pub	14

Shichijō

Kyoto National Museum

Sanjūsangen-dō ⛩

KEIHAN LINE

Kyoto Station

SHICHIKŌ-DŌRI

TŌKAIDŌ LINE

0   500 m

▼ Ōsaka   ▼ Nagoya & Tokyo

The statues were carved by some seventy craftsmen under the direction of the renowned sculptor, **Tankei** (c.1173–1256). He completed the central, seated Kannon at the age of 82 and is also attributed with several of the superb images along the front row. Of these, 28 are disciples of Kannon, while Fūjin and Raijin, the muscular gods of Wind and Thunder, bring up the two ends. Unfortunately, many of the original statues were lost in a fire in 1249, but 156 Kannon and the head of the main image were saved, and by 1266 a replica hall had been completed with the Kannon back up to full strength. In the early seventeenth century, the west veranda of the 118-metre-long hall became a popular place for samurai to practise their **archery**. This developed into a competition, **Tōshiya**, in which archers had to fire arrows from a squatting position along the length of the building without hitting a pillar. Nowadays, the event is commemorated with an archery display outside the hall on January 15.

Sanjūsangen-dō lies south of Shichijō-dōri (on bus routes #206 and #208), immediately across from the Kyoto National Museum (Tues–Sun 9am–4.30pm, Fri until 7.30pm; ¥420, plus extra for special exhibitions; ☎075/541-1151, ⊛www.kyohaku.go.jp/indexe.htm). The museum's permanent collection, covering Kyoto culture from prehistory up to 1868, is held in its new wing, while the original hall, built in 1895, is reserved for special exhibitions. Many of the items on display are national treasures and the museum is a manageable size, if rather old-fashioned in style.

Heading north along Higashiōji-dōri, anyone interested in Japanese folk crafts should make a brief detour to **Kawai Kanjirō's House** (Tues–Sun 10am–5pm; closed Aug 11–20 & Dec 24–Jan 7; ¥900; ☎075/561-3585), the tastefully rustic home of the innovative potter Kawai Kanjirō (1890–1966), who helped revive *mingei* (folk crafts) in the 1930s. The house is as he left it, beautifully furnished with ceramics and sculptures from his long career, including the kilns where many of these pieces were made. To find the house, turn west off the main road shortly before the Gojō-dōri flyover.

Just north of the flyover a right fork brings you to Chawan-zaka, a road lined with shops selling local pottery. This is also a quieter, back entrance to **Kiyomizu-dera** (daily 6am–6pm; ¥300; ☎075/551-1234). If you'd rather use the traditional approach, continue to Kiyomizu-zaka, where you'll find a colourful, crowded parade of souvenir shops and craft galleries. The closest bus stops are Kiyomizu-michi or Gojō-zaka on Higashi-ōji-dōri (served by buses #202, #207 and #206).

Kiyomizu-dera, with its trademark wooden platform overhanging the valley, is one of Kyoto's defining sights. There's been a temple here since 778, when a visionary priest came across its fount of clear water (*kiyo-mizu*). Nearly all the buildings you see today, however, date from 1633. Passing the newly painted three-storey pagoda, the monumental **Hon-dō** (Main Hall) is strangely peaceful inside, though there's little to see – its principal image, an eleven-headed Kannon, only goes on show every 33 years. Instead, most people head straight for the terrace in front, originally a stage for sacred dances, for the famous view over the wooded gorge and Kyoto beyond.

On the hill behind the Hon-dō a jumble of shrine buildings competes for the attention of students and young couples. **Jishū-jinja** is dedicated to several Shinto gods, of whom the most popular is Okuninushi-no-mikoto, an ancient deity in charge of love and good marriages; his messenger is a rabbit. To test your current love life, try walking in a straight line between the two "blind stones", set 18m apart, with your eyes closed and intoning your partner's name. If you arrive at the other stone intact, without erring, all is well. If not, well, it's time for a new relationship. Finally, head down beside the wooden terrace to the **Otowa waterfall**, a sip of which is reputed to cure any illness, and then follow the short path up the opposite hillside from where you get the best views of Kiyomizu-dera.

North to Gion

Leaving Kiyomizu-dera via Kiyomizu-zaka, head north down a set of stone steps along an inviting, cobbled lane. Known as **Sannen-zaka** (Three-Year Slope) and **Ninen-zaka** (Two-Year Slope), these lanes preserve some of the last vestiges of the old Kyoto townscape (see box, opposite). A few paving stones were laid in the ninth century, while the two-storey wooden townhouses date from the late 1800s. Many still cater to passing pilgrims and souvenir hunters in time-honoured fashion, peddling Kiyomizu pottery, bambooware, pickles and refreshments. Just at the bottom of the steps, look out for Hyōtan-ya, which has been selling gourd flasks (*hyōtan*) for two hundred years. Be careful walking along these two lanes, though: according to popular belief, a fall here brings two or three years' bad luck.

At the north end of Ninen-zaka, make a dogleg round to the left to find the entrance to the peaceful gardens of **Kōdai-ji** (daily 9am–5pm; ¥600; ☎075/561-9966). This temple was granted to Kita-no-Mandokoro, the wife of Toyotomi Hideyoshi, when she became a nun after his death in 1598. Kōdai-ji owes its finery, however, to the generosity of Hideyoshi's successor, Tokugawa Ieyasu, who donated buildings from his own castles and financed paintings by Kanō artists, before he wiped out the Toyotomi dynasty at Ōsaka in 1615 (see box, p.501). Nowadays, the temple buildings blend beautifully into their attractive, hillside garden, its two ponds graced by a moon-viewing pavilion and the aptly named "Reclining Dragon Corridor". Between the two, the ceilings of the pretty Kaisan-dō are made from recycled panels from Ieyasu's ship and from the carriage of Kita-no-Mandokoro. But the temple's most important building lies at the top of the scaly-backed corridor – you have to walk round by path – where statues of Hideyoshi and his widow are enshrined. The exquisite gold-inlay lacquerwork is among the finest of its kind in Japan.

Continuing north, a phoenix-tipped tower is a bizarre 1920s replica of a float from the Gion Matsuri (see opposite). A right turn in front of it brings you to an attractive public park called **Maruyama-kōen**, beyond which lie a pair of markedly different temples. The first, **Chion-in**, is a big, busy complex, where everything is built on a monumental scale. Chion-in was founded in 1175 by the priest Hōnen, and is the headquarters of his popular Jōdo (Pure Land) sect of Buddhism. On entering via the huge San-mon gate, look up to the right, and you'll see the colossal Daishō-rō bell, the biggest in Japan, hanging in its belfry; at New Year it takes seventeen priests to ring the 67-tonne monster. Behind the cavernous main hall – all dark wood and sumptuous gold – red arrows lead to the entrance to the Ōhōjō and Kohōjō halls and a garden representing Amida's paradise (daily: March–Nov 9am–4pm; Dec–Feb 9am–4.30pm; ¥400; ☎075/531-2111). The halls' main features are their rooms filled with Momoyama-period screens, but, since you can only peer in, they've placed replicas of the screens in a room behind the ticket desk – the most famous features a cat with uncannily lifelike eyes.

Next door, **Shōren-in** (daily 9am–5pm; ¥500) is a quiet little place surrounded by gardens and ancient camphor trees. The temple started life in the ninth century as lodgings for Tendai-sect priests from Enryaku-ji (see p.563) and later served as a residence for members of the imperial family. After seeing the collection of painted screens, there's not a lot to do here apart from enjoy the paths winding through the hillside garden.

Back in Maruyama-kōen, take any path downhill to come in at the back of **Yasaka-jinja**. The main entrance to this bustling shrine faces west onto Higashiōji-dōri where, instead of the usual *torii*, there's a brightly coloured Buddhist-style gate – a legacy of the days before 1868 when Buddhism and Shinto often cohabited. Yasaka-jinja lies on the eastern edge of **Gion** and each July hosts one of Kyoto's biggest spectacles, the **Gion Matsuri**. This festival dates back to the ninth century, since when the ritual purification to ward off plague in the humid summer months has developed into a grand procession of richly decorated floats.

From Yasaka-jinja, Shijō-dōri runs west through the heart of Gion and across the Kamo-gawa into Kyoto's main downtown district. One of the most distinctive buildings along here, on the corner overlooking the river, is the **Minami-za**. This famous Kabuki theatre was established in the early seventeenth century, though last rebuilt in 1929; each December it's the venue for a major Kabuki festival featuring Japan's most celebrated actors. Kabuki has been an integral part of Gion life since the late sixteenth century when a female troupe started performing religious dances on the river banks. Eventually this evolved into an equally popular, all-male theatre, and, patronized by an increasingly wealthy merchant class, Kabuki joined geisha and the teahouses in Kyoto's vibrant **pleasure quarters**. Of these, Gion was perhaps the most famous, and you can still get a flavour of this "floating world" if you walk south along Hanamikoji-dōri, where many of the lovely wooden buildings still function as exclusive teahouses with geisha holding court. It's best after dark when red lanterns hang outside each secretive doorway, allowing the occasional glimpse down a stone-flagged entranceway; early evening is also a good time to spot geisha, or trainee *maiko*, arriving for an appointment.

During April's Miyako Odori local geisha give performances of traditional dance at the **Gion Kōbu Kaburenjō**, a theatre near the south end of Hanamikoji-dōri. This is also the venue for a touristy display of traditional arts known as **Gion Corner** (March–Nov daily 7.40pm & 8.40pm; ¥2800; ℡075/752-0225). Though it's far better to spend a little extra for the real thing, this is an opportunity to see brief extracts of court dance, Bunraku puppet theatre and the slapstick *kyōgen*. (See p.556 for further details of events in Kyoto.)

Bedrooms of eels

Kyoto's **traditional townhouses**, *machiya*, were built to a unique architectural style known colloquially as "bedrooms of eels" (*unagi no nedoko*). They consist of a succession of rooms along a single corridor stretching back up to 100m – the reason being that taxes were levied according to street frontage. *Machiya* were usually built by **merchants**, with a shop space at the front, then living quarters and with a warehouse at the rear. They generally have one courtyard garden to allow in light and air.

Machiya were also built almost entirely of wood, which means that few today are more than a century old. While some of the best are now protected by law, *machiya* are still being destroyed at an alarming rate. But walk along **Sannen-zaka** (see opposite) or through **Shinbashi** (see p.538), two of the city's historical preservation areas, and you'll find some almost complete rows of these beautiful old houses, each dark facade showing subtle variations on the same overall design. Note the distinctive gutter-guards made of curved bamboo, and the narrow-slatted ground-floor windows, which keep out both the summer heat and prying eyes.

On the southern fringes of Gion, "love hotels" have replaced the brothels of earlier times. This area is also home to a little-visited shrine, **Yasui Konpira-gū** (Tues–Sun 10am–4pm; ¥500; ℡075/561-5127); to get there, turn left at the end of Hanamikoji-dōri and then second right. Founded in 1659, the shrine itself is relatively new, but over the years it's amassed an interesting collection of *ema*, the wooden boards on which people write their prayers. Ask the priest if you can also see the Glass Gallery, which features some lovely Art Deco pieces and a huge creation by American Dale Chihuly, layered like a seashell and set under a glass floor.

Gion north of Shijō-dōri consists mainly of high-rise blocks packed with clubs, bars and restaurants. But walk up Kiritoshi, one block west of Hanamikoji-dōri, and you eventually emerge into another area of teahouses. **Shimbashi**, as the district is known, only comprises two short streets, but the row of slatted facades reflected in the willow-lined Shirakawa Canal makes a delightful scene, day or night.

Heian-jingū and around

In the late nineteenth century, after Emperor Meiji had moved his imperial court to Tokyo, Kyoto authorities felt the need to reaffirm their city's illustrious past. The result is **Heian-jingū** (March–Nov 8.30am–5pm/5:30pm; Dec–Feb 8.30am–4.30pm; free; ℡075/761-0221, ⓦwww.heianjingu.or.jp/index_e.html), an impressive though rather garish shrine which was modelled on a scaled-down version of the original, eighth-century emperor's Hall of State. Completed in 1895 to commemorate the 1100th anniversary of the founding of the city, it is dedicated to emperors Kammu and Komei (1846–67), Kyoto's first and last imperial residents. The present buildings are a 1979 reconstruction, but this is still one of Kyoto's most famous landmarks. The shrine lies about ten minutes' walk north of Higashiyama subway station, or you can take one of the many bus routes along Higashiōji-dōri.

The shrine's bright-orange and white halls have an unmistakably Chinese air. Two wings embrace a huge, gravelled courtyard, at the north end of which sits the main worship hall flanked by a couple of pretty two-storeyed towers representing the protective "Blue Dragon" and "White Tiger". More interesting are the gardens behind (same hours; ¥600), which were also designed in Heian style. They're divided into four sections, starting in the southwest corner and ending beside a large pond in the east. The south garden features a collection of plants mentioned in Heian literature, while the middle (third) garden is famous for a row of stepping stones made from the columns of two sixteenth-century bridges. Lastly, the more spacious east garden boasts the shrine's most attractive buildings – the graceful Taihei-kaku pavilion and its covered bridge.

Heian-jingū faces south towards a large vermilion *torii* across a park dotted with museums and other municipal buildings. The most rewarding of these is the **Fureaikan**, or Kyoto Museum of Traditional Crafts (Tues–Sun 10am–6pm; free; ℡075/762-2670), in the basement of the modern Miyako Messe building. Well designed and informative, the museum provides an excellent introduction to the whole range of Kyoto crafts, from roof tiles and metalwork to textiles, confectionery and ornamental hairpins. Allow plenty of time to take it all in.

Close to Fureaikan, the **National Museum of Modern Art** (Tues–Sun 9.30am–5pm; Fri April–Oct until 8pm; ¥420, extra for special exhibitions; ℡075/761-4111, ⓦwww.momak.go.jp/menu_e.html) and the brick-built **Kyoto Municipal Museum of Art** (Tues–Sun 9am–5pm; varying prices; ℡075/771-4107) stand on opposite sides of the big *torii*. The modern art museum focuses on local twentieth-century artists, while the Municipal

Museum hosts temporary exhibitions from its vast collection of post-1868 fine arts.

At the same time as Heian-jingū was being built, Marshal Yamagata Aritomo, a leading member of the Meiji government, was creating a delightful haven for himself beside the Biwa Canal. From the *torii*, walk east along the canal to find his villa, **Murin-an** (daily 9am–4.30pm; ¥350; ☎075/771-3909), where the road bends to the right. Even today, as you look east from the garden to the Higashiyama hills beyond, it's hard to believe you're in the middle of a busy city. Designed by Yamagata himself, the unusually naturalistic garden incorporates a meandering stream, pond and lawns in a surprisingly small space. There are also three buildings: take a look upstairs in the two-storeyed brick house, where parquet floors and wood panelling blend beautifully with Kanō-school painted screens.

Continuing east, cross over the canal again in front of **Kyoto International Community House**, an excellent resource centre for Kyoto's foreign residents (see p.517), and head uphill towards **Nanzen-ji** (daily 8.30am–4.30/5pm; ¥400; ☎075/771-0365). This large, active temple belongs to the Rinzai sect of Zen Buddhism and is one of the most important in Kyoto. Before entering the main compound, however, it's worth exploring its quiet sub-temple, **Konchi-in**, on the right in front of the first gate. An arched gate leads straight into one of Kyoto's most beautiful dry gardens – one of the rare works by the ubiquitous Kobori Enshū with documents to prove it. Its centrepiece is a large rectangle of raked gravel with two groups of rocks set against a bank of clipped shrubs. The right-hand, vertical rock group represents a crane, in balance with the horizontal "tortoise" topped by a twisted pine, on the left; both these animals symbolize longevity.

After Konchi-in, the looming bulk of **San-mon**, the main gate to Nanzen-ji, seems excessively monumental. It was erected in 1628 to commemorate the soldiers killed during the siege of Ōsaka Castle (see p.501). However, Nanzen-ji's prize possessions are in the **Hōjō** (March–Nov 8.40am–5pm Dec–Feb 8.40am–4.30pm; ¥400), up to the right behind the San-mon. These include the "Leaping Tiger" garden, also attributed to Enshū, though working in a much more confined space, and a series of screens painted by Kanō Tanyū depicting tigers in a bamboo grove. Nanzen-ji is also famous for its **shōjin-ryōri**, Buddhist vegetarian cuisine, which can be sampled in a number of sub-temples (see "Eating", p.548).

North to Ginkaku-ji

The final sight along this stretch of Kyoto's eastern hills is the famous Ginkaku-ji. Though you can get there by bus (see p.540), by far the best approach is to walk along the canalside of **Philosopher's Path**, which starts just north of Nanzen-ji (see above). The name of the two-kilometre-long path refers to a respected philosopher, Nishida Kitarō (1870–1945), who took his daily constitutional along the wooded hillside. To reach the path from Nanzen-ji, follow the road curving northeast past the small, extremely esoteric **Nomura Art Museum** (Tues–Sun mid-March to mid-June & Sept–Dec 10am–4pm; ¥700; ☎075/751-0374), which holds rotating exhibitions of tea-ceremony utensils and related paraphernalia. A little further on, you might want to pop into **Eikan-dō** (Jan–Oct & Dec daily 9am–4/5pm; Nov daily 8.30am–5pm & 5.30–9.30pm; ¥600, Nov daytime ¥1000; ☎075/761-0007, ⓦ www.eikando.or.jp/English/index_eng.htm), also known as Zenrin-ji for its unusual Amida statue. Eikan-dō was founded in the ninth century by a disciple of Kōbō Daishi (see p.954), but later became the headquarters of a sub-sect of Jōdoshū (Pure

Land Buddhism). In 1082 the then head priest, Eikan, was circling the altar and chanting the *nembutsu*, "Praise to Amida Buddha", when the Amida statue stepped down and started walking in front of him. When Eikan stopped in his tracks, Amida turned to encourage him. Soon after, the priest commissioned the statue you see today of Amida looking over his left shoulder. Eikan-dō is also a popular location for **maple leaf viewing** during November (hence the higher admission price during this month). Viewing the floodlit leaves in the evening is quite magical, if you don't mind sharing the experience with big crowds of other people. Avoid weekends if at all possible.

On exiting Eikan-dō, the first right turn leads to the philosopher's path. Every so often stone bridges link the tempting residential lanes on either side, while the occasional souvenir shop or bijou teahouse provides an additional distraction. **Hōnen-in** (daily 7am–4pm; free; ☎075/771-2420) makes for a pleasant stop before the crowds of Ginkaku-ji. Restored in 1680 by the (then) head priest of Chion-in, it is a tranquil place with a pleasing carp pond and small garden, which attracts few visitors. The head priest is quite progressive, and occasional events and exhibitions are held here. Without too many halts, however, you should emerge beside the Ginkaku-ji bridge about thirty minutes later. If you're coming by bus, on the other hand, routes #5, #203 and #204 stop nearby at Ginkaku-ji-michi.

The Temple of the Silver Pavilion, **Ginkaku-ji** (daily: mid-March to Nov 8.30am–5pm; Jan to mid-March & Dec 9am–4.30pm; ¥500; ☎075/771-5725), is one of Kyoto's most celebrated sights. Though modelled on its ostentatious forebear, the golden Kinkaku (see p.545), this simple building sits quietly in the wings. Here, it's the garden that takes centre stage, dominated by a truncated cone of white sand whose severity offsets the soft greens of the surrounding stroll-garden. Ginkaku originally formed part of a much larger villa built in the fifteenth century for Shogun **Ashikaga Yoshimasa** (1436–90), the grandson of Kinkaku's Ashikaga Yoshimitsu. Interrupted by the Ōnin Wars (1467–77) and plagued by lack of funds, the work continued for thirty years, until Yoshimasa's death in 1490. During those years, however, it became the focal point of Japanese cultural life. Yoshimasa may have been a weak and incompetent ruler, but under his patronage the arts reached new heights of aesthetic refinement. In this mountainside retreat, significantly turned away from the city, he indulged his love of the tea ceremony, poetry and moon-viewing parties while Kyoto burned. After 1490, the villa became a Rinzai Zen temple (Jishō-ji) and eventually fires razed all except two buildings, one of which was the famous pavilion.

It's worth savouring the approach to Ginkaku-ji. Despite the crowds, there's a wonderful sense of anticipation as you're funnelled between tall, thick hedges down an apparently dead-end lane. Turning the corner, a high wall now blocks the view except for one teasing glimpse through a small, low window. Inside, you're directed first to the **dry garden**, comprising a raised, rippled "Sea of Silver Sand" – designed to reflect moonlight – and a large "moon-facing" cone. The jury's out on whether these enhance the garden or intrude, but it's almost certain that they weren't in the original design, and were probably added in the early seventeenth century. Behind the cone to the west, the small, dark two-storeyed building with the phoenix topknot is **Ginkaku-ji**. Some scholars argue that Yoshimasa never intended to cover it with silver, while others say he ran out of money; whatever, it must be a glorious, ethereal sight under the reflected light of a full moon.

The villa's other extant building, the **Tōgū-dō**, lies east of the main hall. Though not generally open to the public, it contains a small tatami room with a central sunken hearth and decorative *tokonoma* (alcove) which is considered to be the forerunner of the tea-ceremony house. The more classical pond-garden in front of the Tōgū-dō is attributed to the gifted Sōami (died 1525) and is full of literary allusions.

Shūgaku-in Rikyū

In the far northeast of Kyoto, the foothills of Hiei-zan (see p.562) provide a superb setting for one of Japan's finest examples of garden design using borrowed scenery. Entry to **Shūgaku-in Rikyū**, an imperial villa, is by appointment only (see box, p.518) and requires you to join a guided tour (Mon–Fri & occasionally Sat 5 tours daily; free). To get there, hop on City Bus #5 to the Shūgaku-in Rikyū-michi stop on Shirakawa-dōri, from where the villa is a signed ten-minute walk to the east. Alternatively, take a train on the private Eizan line from Demachiyanagi Station (in northeast Kyoto) to Shūgaku-in Station (10min), located a couple of minutes west of Shirakawa-dōri.

Emperor Go-mizuno'o (1611–29) built Shūgaku-in Rikyū in the late 1650s as a pleasure garden rather than a residence. Just 15 years old when he ascended to the throne, the artistic and highly cultured Go-mizuno'o fiercely resented the new shogunate's constant meddling in imperial affairs – not least being forced to marry the shogun's daughter. After Go-mizuno'o abdicated, however, the shogun encouraged him to establish an imperial villa. He eventually settled on the site of a ruined temple, Shūgaku-in, and set about designing a series of gardens, which survived more than a century of neglect before the government rescued them in the 1820s. Though some of the original pavilions have been lost, Go-mizuno'o's overall design remains – a delightfully naturalistic garden that blends seamlessly into the wooded hills.

In fact, Shūgaku-in Rikyū is made up of three separate gardens, each in their own enclosure among the terraced rice-fields. Of these, the top lake-garden is the star attraction, though the middle villa's **Kyaku-den** guesthouse is also of interest. Look out for a complicated, fragile set of shelves – the "shelves of mist" – hanging in one alcove, and some painted wooden panels. One set shows festival floats from the Gion Matsuri (see p.537), while another is embellished with three scaly carp – it's said that the nets were added later to keep the fish from slipping out at night to the nearby pond.

From here you start climbing towards the upper villa, passing between tall, clipped hedges before suddenly emerging at the garden's highest point. An airy pavilion, **Rin-un-Tei**, occupies the little promontory, with views over the lake, the forested, rolling hills in the middle distance and the mountains beyond. Walking down through the garden, the grand vistas continue with every twist and turn of the path, passing the intricate Chitose bridge, intimate tea-ceremony pavilions and rustic boathouses which decorate the garden.

West Kyoto

Compared to east Kyoto, sights in the city's **western districts** are more dispersed and therefore require a little more effort to get to. Nevertheless, it's well worth devoting one day to this area, particularly the northwest fringes, where the city meets the encircling hills. Here you'll find the outrageously extravagant **Kinkaku-ji**, the Golden Pavilion, rubbing shoulders with **Ryōan-ji's** supreme example of an austere, enigmatic Zen garden. If puzzling over Zen riddles is your thing, then don't miss the dry gardens of **Daitoku-ji**, where **Daisen-in** attracts all the attention, though several other sub-temples allow quieter contemplation.

Moving south, **Kōryū-ji** houses one of Japan's most perfect images, a serene statue of the Future Buddha, carved fourteen centuries ago. Nearby

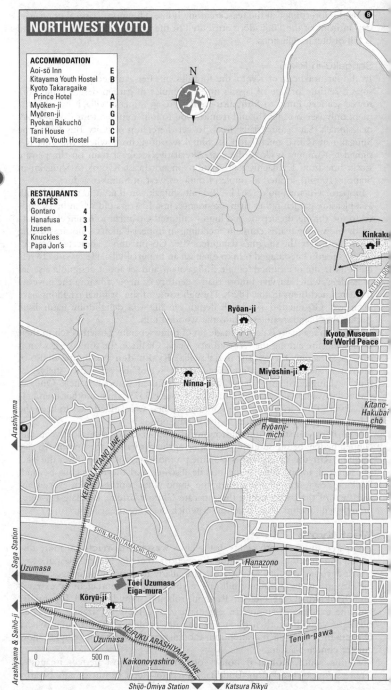

ACCOMMODATION

Aoi-sō Inn	E
Kitayama Youth Hostel	B
Kyoto Takaragaike Prince Hotel	A
Myōken-ji	F
Myōren-ji	G
Ryokan Rakuchō	D
Tani House	C
Utano Youth Hostel	H

RESTAURANTS & CAFÉS

Gontaro	4
Hanafusa	3
Izusen	1
Knuckles	2
Papa Jon's	5

N

Kinkaku-ji

Ryōan-ji

Kyoto Museum for World Peace

Ninna-ji

Miyōshin-ji

Kitano-Hakubai chō

Ryōanji-michi

KEIFUKU KITANO LINE

SHIN-MARUTAMACHI-DORI

Arashiyama

Saga Station

Uzumasa

Hanazono

Tōei Uzumasa Eiga-mura

Kōryū-ji

KEIFUKU ARASHIYAMA LINE

Uzumasa

Tenjin-gawa

Arashiyama & Saihō-ji

Kaikonoyashiro

Shijō-Ōmiya Station   ▼   ▼ Katsura Rikyū

KITSUJI-DORI

6

KANSAI | Kyoto

542

0   500 m

KITA-KU

KITAYAMA-DŌRI

Botanical
Gardens

Kokusai Kaikan-mae Station

Kamo-gawa

Imamiya
Jinja

Daisen-
in

Kita-ōji Ⓢ

Daitoku-
ji Ⓒ

Ryōgen-
in ❶

KITAŌJI-DŌRI

❷

SHIMEI-DŌRI

❸

Kenkun
Shrine

Ⓔ

Kuramaguchi

KURAMAGUCHI-DŌRI
Ⓢ

⌂ Hirano
Jinja

TERANOUCHI-DŌRI

Ⓖ ⌂ Ⓕ

⌂ Kitano
Tenman-gū

NISHIJIN

KAMITACHIURI-DŌRI

❺

Nishijin
Textile
Centre

Doshisa
University

IMADEGAWA-DŌRI

Imadegawa Ⓢ

KAMIGYŌ-KU

OMIYA-DŌRI

HORIKAWA-DŌRI

KARASUMA-DŌRI

Imperial
Palace

SENBON-DŌRI

MARUTAMACHI-DŌRI

SAGANO LINE

Marutamachi Ⓢ

NAKAGYŌ-KU

Nijō-jō

Nijō Ⓢ

TŌZAI LINE

Nijō-jō-mae Ⓢ

ŌIKE-DŌRI

Karasuma-Ōike Ⓢ

Sanjō-Keihan & Daigō

▼ Kyoto Station

▼ Kyoto Station

Tōei Uzumasa Eiga-mura, on the other hand, celebrates the celluloid world. This "movie village", styled "Japan's Hollywood", turns working film sets and studios into a theme park, complete with battling samurai, winsome geisha and sci-fi monsters. The city's southwestern suburbs contain two outstanding gardens: **Katsura Rikyū**, one of Japan's first stroll-gardens, belongs to the languid world of moon-viewing parties and tea ceremonies, while the dappled mosses of **Saihō-ji** herald from an older tradition of Buddhist paradise gardens.

Daitoku-ji

Lying halfway between the Kamo-gawa and the Kitayama hills, **Daitoku-ji** is one of Kyoto's largest Zen foundations, with over twenty sub-temples in its large, walled compound. Of these only four are open to the public, but within them you'll find a representative sampler of the dry gardens (*kare-sansui*) for which Japanese Zen Buddhism is renowned. The temple lies roughly 1500m west of Kita-ōji subway station (on the Karasuma line), or can be reached by City Bus #101, #205 and #206 – get off at Daitoku-ji-mae.

Entering from the south, head past the huge San-mon gate to **Daisen-in** (daily 9am–5pm, Dec–Feb until 4.30pm; ¥400; ☎075/491-8346) in the north of the compound. This sub-temple contains two gardens, of which the most famous lies to the right as you enter the main hall. In fact, you'd be forgiven for overlooking it – the miniaturized, allegorical landscape is squeezed into a narrow strip, then cut in two by a corridor with a bell-shaped window. Replicating a Chinese landscape painting, the garden uses only carefully selected rocks, pebbles and a few scaled-down plants to conjure up jagged mountains, from which a stream tumbles down to the plain, then broadens into a gently flowing river. Just in front of the bell-window, a boat-shaped rock "floats" seawards – enhancing the garden's allusion to the passage of life.

Follow the "river" south and it opens into the second, larger garden. Here an expanse of raked, white gravel represents the "Sea of Nothingness", into which two cones of purity are sinking; the idea is that a soul must be pure, or empty, to face its destiny. A statue of Kogaku Shukō, the temple's founder, sits in the room behind. He's also credited with the river-and-mountain garden, which dates from the early sixteenth century, possibly in collaboration with the great Sōami, while it's likely that the south garden was added later.

It pays to visit Daisen-in early in the day before the crowds arrive. However, Daitoku-ji's other sub-temples remain surprisingly quiet. Of these, probably the most interesting is **Ryōgen-in** (daily 9am–4.30pm; ¥350; ☎075/491-7635), lying just south of the San-mon gate. The temple was also founded in the early sixteenth century and claims Japan's smallest Zen rock garden. As you enter, the first garden is another narrow rectangle of gravel containing three rocks. This represents "A-un", the essential dichotomy and harmony of the universe – heaven and earth, male and female, inhale and exhale – which lies at the heart of Zen. Once you've got that sorted out, move on to the minuscule Tōtekiko garden, on your right. The meaning's a bit less obtuse here: waves of sand round a rock symbolize a Zen saying that the harder a stone is thrown, the bigger the ripples. The hall's south side looks out on a bigger garden, Isshidan, where vertical rocks represent the mythical Mount Horai, which lies at the centre of the Buddhist universe, flanked by its Crane and Turtle islands (symbols of longevity). Finally, Ryōgin-tei, the north garden, is not only the oldest in Daitoku-ji but is also attributed to Sōami. Again its subject is the essential truth at the core of the universe, rising from a sea of moss.

Kinkaku-ji and Ryōan-ji

West of Daitoku-ji, the wooded hills of Kitayama are home to **Kinkaku-ji** (daily 9am–5pm; ¥400; ℡075/461-0013), the famous Temple of the Golden Pavilion. The pavilion originally formed part of a larger retirement villa built by the former Shogun Ashikaga Yoshimitsu (1358–1408) on the site of an earlier aristocratic residence; on his death it was converted into a Zen temple. A noted scholar of Chinese culture, Yoshimitsu incorporated various Chinese motifs into both the pavilion and the surrounding garden, whose focus is a lake studded with rocks and pine-covered islets.

Even the crowds can't diminish the impact of seeing the temple for the first time – a hint of gold glimpsed though the trees, and then the whole, gleaming apparition floating above the aptly named Kyōko-chi (Mirror Pond). If you're lucky enough to see it against the autumn leaves, or on a sunny winter's day after a dusting of snow, the effect is doubly striking. Note the different architectural styles of the pavilion's three floors and the phoenix standing on the shingle roof. It's an appropriate symbol: having survived all these years, Kinkaku was torched in 1950 by an unhappy monk. The replica was finished in just five years, and in 1987 the building was regilded at vast expense.

Kinkaku-ji lies on several bus routes, of which the most convenient are #12 and #59. To get to the next stop, Ryōan-ji, either hop back on a #59 bus or walk southwest along Kitsuji-dōri for about twenty minutes.

If you're not planning on visiting Hiroshima, or if you simply fancy a short break from the temples, the **Kyoto Museum for World Peace** (Tues–Sun 9.30am–4.30pm; ¥300; ℡075/465-8151, Ⓦwww.ritsumei.ac.jp/mng/er/wp-museum/e/eng.html), located halfway between Kinkaku-ji and Ryōan-ji on the campus of Ritsumeikan University, makes for an interesting diversion. Consisting of one large exhibition room, the displays include a look at Japan's twentieth-century military history, an outline of the plan to drop an atomic bomb on the city and a replica of a wartime house. The two large reliefs on the wall depicting the mythical phoenix – intended to symbolize the living energy of all creatures on earth – were painted by noted manga artist Tezuka Osamu (see Takarazuka, p.510).

While Kinkaku-ji is all about displays of wealth and power, the dry garden of **Ryōan-ji** (daily: March–Nov 8am–5pm; Dec–Feb 8.30am–4.30pm; ¥400; ℡075/463-2216) hides infinite truths within its riddle of rocks and sand. It was probably laid out in the late fifteenth century (some say it's the work of Sōami), but went largely undiscovered until the 1930s. Now it's probably Japan's most famous garden, which means you're unlikely to be able to appreciate the Zen experience thanks to intrusive tape-recorded explanations and almost constant crowds, though very early morning tends to be better.

The garden consists of a long, walled rectangle of off-white gravel in which fifteen stones of various sizes are arranged in five groups, some rising up from the raked sand and others almost completely lost. In fact, the stones are placed so that wherever you stand one of them is always hidden from view. The only colour is provided by electric-green patches of moss around some stones, making this the simplest and most abstract of all Japan's Zen gardens. It's thought that the layout is a *kōan*, or riddle, set by Zen masters to test their students, and there's endless debate about its "meaning". Popular theories range from tigers crossing a river to islands floating in a sea of infinity. Fortunately, it's possible to enjoy the garden's perfect harmony and in-built tension without worrying too much about the meaning. Walk round the veranda of the main hall and you'll find a stone water basin inscribed with a helpful thought from the Zen tradition: "I learn only to be contented".

Leaving the main hall, it's worth strolling round Ryōan-ji's refreshingly quiet lake-garden. This dates back to the twelfth century, when a noble of the Fujiwara clan built his villa here, before the estate was donated to the Rinzai Buddhist sect in the fifteenth century.

Kōryū-ji and Tōei Uzumasa Eiga-mura

Uzumasa district, due south of Ryōan-ji, is home to both the art treasures of Kōryū-ji and the Tōei film studios. The easiest way to get here is to take a train on the private Keifuku Arashiyama line from Shijō-Ōmiya Station in central Kyoto to Uzumasa Station. If you're coming straight from Ryōan-ji, it's probably quickest to backtrack into Kyoto and pick up the train or a bus; City Bus #11 and Kyoto Bus #71, #72 and #73 all stop outside Kōryū-ji.

Kōryū-ji (daily 9am–4.30/5pm; ¥600; ☏075/861-1461) is said to have been founded in the early seventh century by Nara's Prince Shōtoku (see p.575), but some scholars believe that the real founder was actually a friend of the prince's by the name of Hata no Kawakatsu, who had a lineage that stretched back to Korea, and possibly all the way to Turkestan. The first Hata family members are said to have ended up in Japan in search of religious freedom in about 400 AD, several generations before the time of Hata no Kawakatsu. Whatever the truth behind these stories, Uzumasa shares the same Chinese characters (though a different reading) as the Da Qin monastery in the Chinese city of Xi'an, and records indicate that Kōryū-ji used to be known as Uzumasa-dera. All of which fuels speculation that there was a strong Christian link between China and Japan before the Buddhist one.

The Kōdō (Lecture Hall) – the first inside the gate – dates from 1165 and is one of the oldest buildings in Kyoto. The three Buddhas inside are imposing enough, but Kōryū-ji's main attractions are the statues kept in the modern Reihōden (Treasure House) at the back of the compound. The "newest" of these images is a thirteenth-century statue of Prince Shōtoku aged 16 years, his sweet face framed by bun-shaped pigtails. The oldest is the exquisite **Miroku Bosatsu**, the Future Buddha rendered as a Bodhisattva pondering how to save mankind. It is believed to have been gilded originally and was probably a gift to Shōtoku from the Korean court in the early seventh century; its soft, delicate features are certainly unlike contemporary Japanese images. The small, slim figure sits, elbow on knee, leaning forward slightly and head tilted in a pose of utter concentration.

Having come out this way, you might want to visit the nearby **Tōei Uzumasa Eiga-mura** (daily: April–Nov 9am–5pm; Dec–March 9.30am–4pm, closed Dec 21–Jan 1; ¥2200, plus extra charges for some attractions; ☏075/864-7716), where Tōei, one of Japan's major film companies, opens its sets to the public. The entertainment complex here, **Padios**, is more like a theme park, with its roller-coaster rides, games arcades and huge souvenir malls, but the **studios** behind hold more general appeal. One of the indoor studios is usually in action, nowadays mostly making TV dramas, while the outdoor sets – an Edo-period street, thatched farms, Meiji-era Western-style buildings and so on – are enlivened by roaming geisha, battling samurai and a superbly cheesy "special effects" zone. On the way out, don't miss the Movie Museum, where film buffs can take a nostalgic romp through the archives.

Katsura Rikyū

Few people trek out to the southwest corner of Kyoto, but the journey is rewarded with two magnificent gardens, though in both cases admission is by appointment only. The more accessible garden belongs to **Katsura Rikyū**

(Mon–Fri and occasionally Sat 4 tours daily; free), a former imperial palace; applications to visit should be made through the Imperial Household Agency (see p.518). Located on the west bank of the Katsura-gawa, it's fifteen minutes' walk from Katsura Station, on the private Hankyū line from central Kyoto. Alternatively, City Bus #33 will drop you at Katsura Rikyū-mae, the first stop after crossing the river, from where it's a five-minute walk north to the gate. Note that this bus stop lies just outside the bus-pass zones, so if you want to save a few yen get off before the river and walk over.

Katsura palace was built in the early seventeenth century as a residence for the imperial Prince Toshihito, and then expanded by his son, Toshitada, in the 1650s. Toshihito was a highly cultured man, who filled his villa and garden with references to *The Tale of Genji* and other literary classics, while also creating what is considered Japan's first **stroll-garden**. As the name suggests, these gardens were to be enjoyed on foot – rather than from a boat or from a fixed viewpoint – and were designed to look "natural". In fact they were planned in minute detail so that scenes unfold in a particular order as the viewer progresses round the garden. Focused on a large, indented lake, the Katsura garden is famed for its variety of footpaths and stone pavings, and for its stone lanterns, all of which helped create the desired mood. Several tea pavilions occupy prime spots around the lake, the most attractive of which is **Shokin-tei**, but perhaps the most interesting aspect about the Katsura garden is the designer's sheer ingenuity. Unlike Shūgaku-in Rikyū (see p.541), there's no help here from the site itself and very little opportunity to use borrowed scenery to expand the view. Instead, Toshihito managed to wrestle a splendidly harmonious, seemingly spacious garden out of an unexciting bit of floodplain.

Unfortunately, the **palace** buildings themselves are not open to the public, though even from outside they're beautiful structures. The low-slung, wood and shingle pavilions were all built in the seventeenth century in an innovative architectural style. Two sections are raised up on platforms to allow cooling air to circulate in summer, while individual rooms are variously oriented to avoid the fierce summer sun, catch the winter rays or face the full autumn moon.

Saihō-ji

Three kilometres northwest of Katsura Rikyū in a narrow, tree-filled valley you'll find the voluptuous moss gardens of **Saihō-ji** (daily; ¥3000; ☎075/391-3631), also known as Koku-dera (the "Moss Temple"). Not surprisingly, many people are put off by the exorbitant entry fee (termed a "donation"), but if you've got time to spare after the major sights this temple is well worth visiting, not least because it's one of the few you really can enjoy in peace.

To visit Saihō-ji you have to make an **application**. Japanese speakers can try phoning a few days before to see if there's space – or ask someone to phone on your behalf. But the more assured method is to write to Saihō-ji, 56 Kamigatani, Matsuo, Nishikyō-ku, Kyoto-shi, Kyoto-fu, giving your name, address, age, occupation and proposed date of visit. It's best to allow one or two weeks' notice – longer if sending from abroad – and remember to enclose a stamped-addressed postcard or international reply coupon. Within Japan you can buy special reply-paid "double postcards" (*ofuku hakagi*) at post offices for this type of application.

Saihō-ji lies at the terminus of the #73 Kyoto Bus route, which takes a circuitous route from Kyoto Station via Arashiyama (see p.569). Unless you're visiting Arashiyama at the same time, it's quicker to take a City Bus (#28 and #29) to Matsuo Taisha-mae, just west of the river, and change to the #73. At the end of the line, walk up the road for a minute or so to find the temple gate on your right. All visitors are required to attend a short Zen service during which you'll chant a sutra, trace the sutra's characters in *sumi-e* ink and finally write your name, address and "wish" before placing the paper in front of the altar. After that you're free to explore the garden at your leisure.

Like Kōryū-ji (see p.546), the temple apparently started life in the seventh century as another of Prince Shōtoku's villas. Soon after, Jōdo Buddhists adopted the site for one of their "paradise gardens", after which the gifted Zen monk, **Musō Kokushi**, was invited to take over the temple in 1338 and restore the gardens. The present layout dates mostly from his time, though the lakeside pavilion – the inspiration for Kinkaku-ji (see p.545) – and nearly all Saihō-ji's other buildings burnt down in the Ōnin Wars (1467–77). In fact, given the temple's history of fire, flooding and periods of neglect, it seems unlikely that today's garden bears much resemblance to Musō's original. Saihō-ji was in complete ruins by the eighteenth century and some sources even attribute the famous mosses to accident, arguing that they spread naturally as the garden reverted to damp, shady woodland.

Whatever their origin, the swathes of soft, dappled moss – some 120 varieties in all – are a magical sight, especially after the rains of May and June, when the greens take on an extra intensity. The garden is divided into two levels with the serene, strangely melancholic lake area followed by an upper slope where a powerful, rocky cascade tumbles down the hillside. This "dry waterfall" is held to be one of the first examples of *kare-sansui*, dry gardening; though it's a world away from Zen's enigmatic rocks and gravel, the design was also conceived as an aid to meditation.

Eating

With such an august history, it's not surprising that Kyoto is home to Japan's most refined cuisine, **Kyō-ryōri** (Kyoto cooking), which is known for its subtle flavours and use of only the freshest ingredients. The ultimate Kyoto dining experience is **kaiseki**, originally designed to accompany the tea ceremony, and a feast for both the eyes and taste buds. Everything about the meal is an expression of cultured refinement, from the artful arrangement of seasonal delicacies, each on its carefully chosen lacquer or earthenware dish, to the picture-perfect garden outside the window. Of course such meals aren't cheap (generally ¥10,000 per head), but at lunchtime many *kaiseki* restaurants offer a usually excellent-value mini-*kaiseki* or *bentō* – a boxed sampler of their specialities.

Kyoto's other gastronomic highlight is **fucha-ryōri**, a Zen version of the exquisite Buddhist vegetarian cuisine, *shōjin-ryōri*, and still mostly found in restaurants near the great Zen temples of Daitoku-ji and Nanzen-ji. *Fucha-ryōri* includes a good deal of *yuba* (dried soya-bean curd) and *fu* (wheat gluten), dressed up in the most appetizing ways, while restaurants around Nanzen-ji also specialize in *yudōfu*, which is tofu simmered in a kelp-flavoured stock. Though generally cheaper than *kaiseki*, the best of these restaurants are also found in lovely old houses overlooking a classic garden.

It's well worth treating yourself to one traditional Kyoto restaurant, but after that there are plenty of more modest establishments to choose from. Some of these have been serving their simple home-cooking for a century or more and are as much a part of Kyoto life as the high-class places. There's also a fair sprinkling of Indian, Italian and other international cuisines nowadays, as well as a growing number of vegetarian and health-food restaurants. **Reservations** are nearly always essential at top-end *kaiseki* restaurants in the evening; elsewhere it's not a bad idea to book ahead at weekends and during peak holiday times.

Central Kyoto

Bio-tei	Bio-tei	びお亭
Capricciosa	Kapurichōza	カプリチョーザ
Chikyū-ya	Chikyū-ya	地球屋
Chinchikurin	Chinchikurin	珍竹林
Fujino-ya	Fujino-ya	藤の家
Gontaro	Gontaro	権太呂
Honyaradō	Honyaradō	ほんやら洞
Musashi	Musashi	むさし
Obanzai	Obanzai	おばんざい
Saracça	Sarasa	サラサ
Sarashina	Sarashina	更科
Tagoto	Tagoto	田ごと
Yamatomi	Yamatomi	山とみ

Around the station

Izusen	Izusen	泉仙
Suishin	Suishin	すいしん

East Kyoto

Chōshō-in	Chōshō-in	聴松院
Furōen	Furōen	ふろうえん
Hōnen-in	Hōnen-in	法然院
Hyōtei	Hyōtei	瓢亭
Imobō Hirano-ya Honten	Imobō Hirano-ya Honten	いもぼう平野屋本店
Matsuno	Matsuno	松乃
Nakamura-rō	Nakamura-rō	中村楼
Okutan	Okutan	奥丹
Omen	Omen	おめん
Rakushō	Rakushō	洛匠
Shuetto	Shuetto	しゅえっと

Northwest Kyoto

Gontaro	Gontaro	権太呂
Izusen	Izusen	泉仙

Central Kyoto

The best place to look for somewhere to eat in Kyoto is the central shopping district around **Shijō-dōri and Kawaramachi-dōri**, including the back-streets north of Shijō. Among the plethora of fast-food chains there are a number of decent foreign restaurants and also several old Kyoto establishments hiding down alleys and among the more expensive names of **Pontochō**. Below, we've also recommended one or two places on the fringes of this central district where they're handy for nearby sights.

The following are marked on the map on p.526.

Ashoka 3F, Kikusui Building, Teramachi Shijō-agaru ☏075/241-1318. Once you've tried a few of the Japanese restaurants below, give your taste buds a workout at Kyoto's most popular Indian restaurant. It's a smart place, but their lunchtime sets offer reasonable value (Mon–Fri ¥900–2000,

Sat–Sun ¥1200–2000). Moderate.
A Womb 35-2 Ichijōji Hinokuchi-chō ☏075/721-1357. Ultra-modern café-bar a street back from Shirakawa-dōri whose Zen-simple architecture is softened with smooth jazz and colourful stools. The food offers an equally contemporary twist on

the traditional – try one of their unusual sushi platters. Moderate.

Bio-tei 2F, Higashinotōin Sanjō ℡ 075/255-0086. Laidback health-food restaurant with an appetizing range of vegetarian daily specials, plus some meat dishes. Count on spending around ¥1000 at lunchtime or ¥2000 in the evening for a good feast. Tues–Sat 11.30am–2pm & 5–8.30pm; closed Thurs evening, Sat lunch and all day Mon and Sun. Inexpensive to moderate.

Capricciosa 2F, Vox Building, 44 Daikoku-chō, Kawaramachi Sanjō ℡ 075/221-7496. Ever-popular member of the cheerful Tokyo chain, selling huge portions of pizza and pasta. Moderate.

C. Coquet Teramachi Marutamachi-agaru ℡ 075/212-0882. Stylish new café next to the Imperial Palace offering tasty lunch sets (¥800) and free Internet access. Full breakfasts are also available for the same price as lunch. Wash your food down with a Guinness for extra satisfaction. Closed Thurs. Moderate.

Chikyu-ya Kawaramachi Shijō-sagaru ℡ 075/344-6159. There's a faintly hippy air to this bustling, student *izakaya*, with its shared wooden tables and rug-covered ceiling. Prices are cheap and the food's not bad, with standard *izakaya* small dishes ranging from tofu to tuna salad, some listed on their English menu. Daily 5pm–midnight. Inexpensive to moderate.

Chinchikurin Kiyamachi Shijō-sagaru ℡ 075/351-9205. Inexpensive country-style restaurant specializing in *kamameshi*, kettle-steamed rice with a whole range of toppings. In winter, *nabe* stews or *zōsui* rice gruel make a good choice. Located behind the Hankyū department store on the street parallel to Kawaramachi-dōri. Closed Wed. Moderate.

Fujino-ya Pontochō Shijō-agaru ℡ 075/221-2446. One of the more affordable Pontochō restaurants with a river view. The simple menu (in English) offers either tempura or *kushi-katsu* (deep-fried pork skewers), with standard sets from around ¥2800. In the summer you can eat on the riverside terrace, but the price of dinner increases to ¥3800. Daily except Wed 5–10pm. Moderate to expensive.

Gontaro Fuyachō Shijō-agaru ℡ 075/221-5810. Home-made noodles are the order of the day at this welcoming little restaurant just north of busy Shijō-dōri. Despite the elegant entrance, prices are reasonable, starting at under ¥1000 for standard dishes and rising to around ¥4000 for the house speciality, *Gontaro nabe*. Daily except Wed. Inexpensive to moderate.

Honyarado Teramachi Imadegawa nishi-iru ℡ 075/222-1574. Cluttered but relaxed "ethnic" café-restaurant just northeast of the Imperial Palace. Great for a long coffee break – especially upstairs, where you can read a book or magazine for a while – or a satisfying meal. The food's wholesome – don't miss their home-made bread – and excellent value, with set meals around ¥600–700 for lunch or dinner. English menu. Inexpensive.

La Rucolla de Villa #2/1928 Building, Gokomachi-kado, Sanjō-dōri ℡ 075/257-6521. Part of the Kyoto Complex alongside a café and gallery, this trendy restaurant has bright-red screens and a bank of TV monitors on one wall. The well-priced menu offers Euro-Japanese concoctions like stuffed rolled eel and miso-flavoured beef tongue salad. English menu. Moderate to expensive.

Merry Island Kiyamachi-dōri ℡ 075/213-0214. Very good Asian-flavoured and themed café-restaurant serving a range of ever-changing *mukokuseki* dishes which are a definite cut above the norm, especially the soups and fish platters. Also has outside seating, an English menu, attentive staff and great music. Moderate.

Musashi Kawaramachi Sanjō-agaru ℡ 075/222-0634. The original branch of the excellent, region-wide *kaitenzushi* (conveyor-belt sushi) chain. Located right on the junction, it also does a brisk trade in takeaway bentō with nearby office workers. Unless you're ravenous, lunch – or dinner – shouldn't set you back more than ¥1000, and the cheapest dishes are just ¥120. Inexpensive.

Obanzai Koromonotana Oike-agaru ℡ 075/223-6623. It's well worth searching out this nicely designed and very popular cafeteria-style restaurant east of Nijō-jō for their excellent-value vegetarian buffets (¥840–1050 for lunch, ¥2100 in the evening). Closed Wed evenings. Inexpensive to moderate.

Saracça Wood Inn, Tominokoji Sanjō-sagaru ℡ 075/432-5075. This friendly haven in the midst of central Kyoto is difficult to define – a restaurant, café, bar and record shop all in one. There's a definite arty touch to its high ceilings, wooden tables and scattered fabrics, while the menu is similarly eclectic – tofu with tuna and spicy miso, sandwiches, preservative-free wine and home-made cheesecake. English menu. Closed Wed. Moderate.

Sarashina Ōmiya Aneyakoji-agaru ℡ 075/841-5933. If you're feeling peckish out near Nijō-jō, join the locals for a hearty bowl of soba or udon. Prices are very reasonable and there's an English menu. Mon–Sat 10.30am–7.30pm. Moderate.

Tagoto Shijō Teramachi higashi-iru ℡ 075/221-6286. This welcoming little restaurant is a good place to sample *kyō-ryōri* without breaking the bank. Try their beautiful *kōetsu-mizusashi-bentō*

(¥3000) or, at lunchtime only, choose between a smaller bentō (¥1500) or a mini-*kaiseki* (¥3000). Reservations are required for an evening *kaiseki* meal (from ¥4500). It's just off Shijō-dōri up a tiny alley next to the Takano jewellery shop near the Central Hotel. Expensive to very expensive.
Yamatomi Pontochō Shijō-agaru ☎075/221-

3268. Another unpretentious, Pontochō restaurant a few doors down from *Fujino-ya*. There's plenty of good, wholesome fare on offer (English menu available), such as sashimi, *oden* and *okonomiyaki*. Count on about ¥4000 for dinner including drinks. In summer you can eat on their riverside terrace. Expensive.

Around the station

The area immediately around **Kyoto Station** isn't particularly well endowed with restaurants, but since the enormous station complex has well over a hundred places to eat at, this needn't be a problem. Apart from the places recommended below, your best bet is the eleventh-floor "Eat Paradise" in the station's Isetan department store, The Cube's eleventh-floor restaurant mall (adjoining Eat Paradise) or the Porta underground shopping mall, where a branch of the faux-Italian nationwide chain *Capricciosa* serves up hearty portions.

The following are marked on the map on p.531.

Izusen 2F, Bright Building, Karasuma Shichijō-sagaru ☎075/343-4211. Not the most brilliant surroundings, but the Zen vegetarian cuisine is beautifully presented, with sets starting from ¥1800; there's an English menu and also a window display to choose from. Daily 11am–8pm.

Moderate to expensive.
Suishin SK Building, Kyoto-eki-mae ☎075/365-0271. The ground floor of this big restaurant houses a clean, modern sushi bar (it's better value at lunchtime), while in the evening head for the huge, popular *izakaya* in the basement. Moderate.

East Kyoto

If you want to treat yourself to traditional Kyoto cuisine, then head for the city's **eastern districts**. We've recommended one or two of the more affordable restaurants below, which still offer a glimpse into the world of kimono-clad waitresses, elegant tatami rooms, carp ponds and tinkling bamboo water spouts. Northeast Kyoto, on the other hand, is home to a number of lively student cafeterias, which make a welcome break on the temple trail.

The following are marked on the map on p.534, except for *Didi's* and *Speakeasy*, which appear on p.514.

Café Buttercups 103 Shimobanba, Jōdo-ji ☎075/751-9537. Arty *gaijin* hangout serving a well-priced menu of scrumptious daily specials including avocado and cream cheese sandwiches, fried rice and tacos, all accompanied by fruit-shakes and free coffee refills; there are also newspapers to browse and Internet access (¥250/30min). English spoken. Closed Tues. Inexpensive.
Café Peace 3F Domus Hyakumanben, 28-20 Tanaka-monzencho ☎075/707-6856. Popular vegetarian restaurant located close to Kyoto University and opposite Chion-ji. Has all sorts of organic produce on the menu, including juices and wine, and is one of the few places in town where you can get a satisfying veggie burger. Closed Sun. Inexpensive.
Chōshō-in Fukuchi-chō, Nanzen-ji ☎075/761-2186. A sub-temple of Nanzen-ji which offers Zen *yudōfu* cuisine in its attractive gardens, with the option of an outside terrace in fine weather. If you

don't want the full "Matsu" meal (around ¥3000), there are individual dishes such as *fu no dengaku*, three wheat-gluten cakes with different toppings. English menu. Daily except Tues 11am–4pm. Moderate to expensive.
Didi's Higashiōji Imadegawa-agaru ☎075/791-8226. Follow your nose to this cheerful ethnic restaurant, using all-natural ingredients to create delicious curries, wholewheat pancakes and blueberry muffins. It's a great place for breakfast, and the weekday veggie lunch sets are a snip at ¥750. No smoking. Closed Wed. Inexpensive.
EQVO Higashiyama-Sanjō ☎075/525-7039. Located halfway down the Furukawa-chō shopping arcade, this smart new Italian restaurant and wine bar offers soft lighting and a stylish interior. Lunch sets run from ¥850 to ¥2500; dinner can be considerably more. The (Japanese-only) menu changes weekly, and there's little English spoken, but the staff are friendly. Closed first Wed of each month. Moderate to expensive.

Furōen Ishibashi-chō, Jōdo-ji ☏075/771-1276. Earthen walls, bamboo fixtures, rustic tables and Elvis make odd bedfellows, but this little place is less touristy than most around Ginkaku-ji. The food's equally eclectic, and prices aren't bad, with a choice of *teishoku* at under ¥1500, or, if you feel like splashing out, a decent steak for ¥2600. Closed all day Tues and Wed lunchtime. Moderate.

Hyōtei Nanzen-ji ☏075/771-4116. Hidden behind Murin-an garden, this thatch-roofed garden-restaurant started serving *kaiseki* cuisine more than a hundred years ago. Their specials are *asagayu*, a summer breakfast, and *uzuragayu* (rice gruel with quail eggs) in winter. Prices are lower in the new annexe, but even here expect to pay ¥4000 for the cheapest meal. Reservations essential; English spoken. Daily until 7.30pm; closed 2nd & 4th Tues of the month. Very expensive.

Imobō Hirano-ya Honten Maruyama-kōen-uchi ☏075/561-1603. Delightful, 300-year-old restaurant located inside the north entrance to Maruyama park. Their specialities are *imobō* incorporating an unusual type of potato (*ebi-imo*), and finding ingenious ways to make preserved fish taste superb. Try an *imobō teishoku* for about ¥2500, but expect to pay upwards of ¥7000 for a wonderful *kaiseki* experience. Daily 10.30am–8pm. Expensive to very expensive.

Matsuno Shijō-dōri ☏075/701-1577. If you like eel (*unagi*), which is traditionally eaten in the hot summer months to revive one's stamina, this is the place for you. The Matsuno family have been broiling eels for a century and devising all sorts of delicious ways to present them. Sets start at around ¥2000. English menu. Daily except Thurs 11.30am–9pm. Moderate to expensive.

Nakamura-rō 509 Gion-machi minami-gawa

☏075/561-0016. This wonderful old restaurant has been serving exquisite Kyoto cuisine for the last four hundred years. It's surprisingly relaxed and informal, with tatami rooms overlooking a lush garden, but even a lunchtime bentō will set you back ¥3600, or ¥5250 for a mini-*kaiseki* meal – worth every yen, of course. Full *kaiseki* dinners start at ¥13,000 and go up to ¥30,000. Daily 11.30am–10pm (enter before 7pm); closed twice a month – days vary. Very expensive.

Okutan 86-30 Fukuchi-chō, Nanzen-ji ☏075/771-8709. If *Chōshō-in* (see p.551) is full, try this small restaurant half hidden in a bamboo grove on the east side of the same garden. Daily except Thurs 10.30am–5pm. Expensive.

Omen Shishigadani-dōri ☏075/771-8994. This informal noodle restaurant makes a useful pit stop at the north end of the Philosopher's Path, with lunchtime sets (around ¥2000) and daily specials; if you're simply after a quick fix, a bowl of udon costs just ¥900. English menu. Closed Thurs. Moderate to expensive.

Speakeasy Shūgakuin Station ☏075/781-2110. Casual American-style bar-diner with all-day breakfasts (9am–6pm), toasted sandwiches and coffee refills. CNN and foreign newspapers ensure its popularity with local foreign residents. English menu and vegetarian options. Daily 9am–2am. Moderate.

Sunshine Café 4 Ushinomiya-chō, Yoshida ☏075/761-9944. A veritable jungle of pot plants fills this popular organic café housed in the Italian Institute near Kyoto University, serving tasty, innovative meals in generous portions. There's a daily lunch for ¥800, a longer evening menu (around ¥800 for a main dish), plus sandwiches, salads, herb teas and organic beer. Inexpensive.

Northwest Kyoto

This **northwestern district** covers a huge area with no particular centre to aim for. Instead, the restaurants below are chosen for their proximity to Daitoku-ji and Kinkaku-ji.

The following are marked on the map on p.542.

Gontaro Kinkake-no-michi ☏075/463-1039. Useful branch of the Shijō soba shop just a few minutes' walk west of Kinkaku-ji. Nothing fancy, but you'll still find the same welcome and well-priced noodle dishes. Inexpensive to moderate.

Izusen Daitoku-ji ☏075/491-6665. One of the nicest places to sample vegetarian *shōjin-ryōri* at an affordable price, though it's still around ¥3000 for the simplest meal. It's located in the garden of Daiji-in, a sub-temple of Daitoku-ji, with tables outside in fine weather. Reservations are recom-

mended in spring and autumn. They also have a cheaper branch near the station (see p.551). Daily except Thurs 11am–5pm. Expensive.

Knuckles 1-9 Murasakino Nishinochō ☏090/5463-0533. A "New York deli" just west of Daitoku-ji's Zen gardens. As you'd expect, there are bagels and rye-bread sandwiches, plus a few Mexican dishes and good lasagne. The lunch deal (11am–2.30pm) includes soup and tea or coffee for ¥850. English menu available. Closed Mon. Inexpensive.

Drinking and nightlife

Kyoto isn't all about high culture. After you've finished tramping the streets, there are plenty of **coffee houses** and cosy **bars** where you can kick back and quench your thirst. And, if the aching feet can stand it, Kyoto's late-night scene offers a fair range of **clubs**, **discos** and **live music** venues. It may not compete with the likes of Ōsaka and Tokyo, but you should be able to find somewhere to party till the wee hours. The prime entertainment districts are **Pontochō** and **Gion**, both of which are stuffed to the gunwales with bars, clubs and much else besides. But be warned: even fairly innocuous-looking establishments can be astronomically expensive, so check first to make sure you know exactly what you're letting yourself in for. And don't be surprised if you get a frosty reception, or are even turned away. It may be because you're a foreigner or because you need a formal introduction – which is invariably the case with the exclusive geisha houses.

Coffee shops and teahouses

Caffeine addicts need never go short in Japan, and Kyoto is no exception. If all you want is a quick break, then look out for the *Doutor* and *Pronto* chains – they're cheap, reasonably smart and the coffee's decent. For something more classy you might want to try the places listed below, while *Rakushō* offers traditional green tea in delightful surroundings.

Central and east Kyoto

Inoda Sakaimachi Sanjō-sagaru ☏075/221-0507. It's hard to ignore the delicious aroma of roasting coffee outside this traditional coffee shop, established over one hundred years ago. They have a range of coffees (from ¥450), plus sandwiches, cakes and other snacks, served in a 1920s Western-style tearoom overlooking a small garden. There are six other branches around Kyoto (including one in the Daimaru department store) – not as atmospheric as the original, but the coffee tastes as good. Daily 7am–8pm.

Rakushō Washiyo-chō Kōdai-ji-mae ☏075/561-6892. On the hike through eastern Kyoto, stop off at this charming old teashop for a cup of green tea and *warabi mochi* (green-tea rice cake). They also serve coffee, ice cream, cakes and other light snacks – and don't miss their tiny pond filled with enormous carp. Open 9am–5pm; closed one day each week.

Shuetto Shirakawa-dōri ☏075/762-1311. Small, organic "juice salon" at the north end of Shirakawa, 10min from Ginkaku-ji, which serves light lunches like fried rice and sandwiches (from ¥600) in addition to a wide range of wonderful fruit and vegetable juices, as well as organic coffee and tea. Takeaway service available. English menu. Daily except Tues 10am–8pm.

Northwest Kyoto

Hanafusa Kitaōji Tōnangawa, Nishiōji ☏075/462-5292. Kyoto's oldest siphon coffee shop (established in 1955) serves up thirty-odd varieties at this branch not far from Kinkaku-ji. Coffees start at ¥480, and there are a number of tasty, if slightly expensive, sandwiches on the menu. Daily 7am–2am.

Papa Jon's Kamidachiuri Karasuma higashi-iru ☏075/415-2655. Located north of Doshisha University, this airy little coffee shop serves luscious home-made cheesecake, as well as herbal teas and all kinds of coffee – from espresso, latte and frothy cappuccino to liqueur coffees with attitude. No smoking.

Bars, clubs and live music

From dingy dives to swanky hostess **bars**, Kyoto is well endowed with places to while away the evening. The epicentre of this activity is Gion and Pontochō, the two traditional pleasure quarters either side of the Kamo-gawa in downtown Kyoto. Even if you're not keen on propping up bars, make sure you take an evening stroll up Pontochō-dōri and along Gion's Hanamikoji-dōri. In summer, look out for rooftop **beer gardens** on top of the big hotels – the *Miyako Hotel* is a popular venue.

The contemporary music scene is also alive and well in Kyoto. Whether you're into jazz, rock, folk or drum 'n' bass, or simply want a good bop, the city has enough **clubs**, discos and **live music** venues to satisfy most tastes. To find out who or what's on, pick up a copy of the *Kyoto Visitors' Guide* or *Kansai Time Out* (¥300).

Central Kyoto and Pontochō

Asahi Superdry Kawaramachi Sanjō-sagaru ☏075/221-1882. This big, casual Japanese take on a German-style beer restaurant on the main Kawaramachi-dōri drag is a fine place to start the evening.

Bar Isn't It? B1, 67-3 Daikoku-chō, Kawaramachi Sanjō-sagaru ☏075/221-5399. Loud, lively pub-cum-disco with a predominantly *gaijin* crowd. Drinks and snacks are all ¥500. There's a DJ on Friday and Saturday, and live music most Sundays (¥1000 entry, including one drink).

Cock-a-hoop 7F, Empire Building, Kiyamachi Sanjō-agaru ☏075/221-4939. Relaxed, inexpensive bar with river views and salsa on the turntable (daily except Wed 6pm–2am). In the same building, there's the cool *Teddy's Bar*, and *Live Spot Rag*, which hosts local and international bands, mainly playing jazz, most nights (from ¥1600).

Hill of Tara Kawaramachi higashi-iru ☏075/213-3330. Excellent and very popular Irish pub right next to the *Kyōto Hotel Okura*. There's Kilkenny and Guinness on tap, voluminous portions of hearty – and high-quality – Irish fare, and a great atmosphere, especially on the regular live music nights. Happy hour 5–8pm.

Hub 71,Daikoku-cho, Kawaramachi Sanjō-sagaru ☏075/212-9027. Kyoto branch of the faux-British pub chain which boasts a massive range of cocktails and an impressive range of world beers – as well as lager by the yard. Reasonable pub grub and a convenient location make it an excellent pit stop if you've been traipsing around town all day. Happy hour 5–7pm.

Juttoku 815 Higashiya-chō, Ōmiya Marutamachi-agaru ☏075/841-1691. A bit out of the way, north of Nijō-jō, this wonderful old *kura* hosts mostly rock and blues bands. Cover charge ¥800–3000.

Marie's Café Kiyamachi Rokkaku-sagaru ☏075/253-1625. This large, attractive café-bar, popular with university students and a similarly young crowd, opens onto the west bank of the Takase Canal. Drinks are mostly ¥500 and there's a wide range of reasonable, tasty food. There's an adjoining karaoke bar (fifty percent off for café customers) if you've had too much to drink and feel like a warble.

Munchen Beer Hall Shijō Kawaramachi-agaru higashi-iru ☏075/221-3917. No-nonsense German-style beer restaurant in an interesting area of back alleys between Kawaramachi and Pontochō. Daily noon–10/11pm.

Prestoopnik B1, Kawaramachi Tokyū Bldg ☏075/213-2208. Stylish bar-cum-late-night diner with glass bar, TV sets at the tables and an English menu and international cuisine including Thai, Mexican and Indian dishes alongside a large selection of spirits.

Rub a Dub B1, Kiyamachi Sanjō-sagaru ☏075/256-3122. Sup a piña colada in this compact reggae beach bar decked out with fairy lights, palm trees and plastic fruit. Occasional DJ nights. It's at the north end of canalside Kiyamachi-dōri – look for a small signboard on the pavement.

Taku Taku Tominokoji Bukkoji-sagaru ☏075/351-1321. This *kura* (traditional storehouse) makes a great live venue. The music's pretty varied but tends towards rock and blues, with someone on stage most nights (7–9pm), including the occasional international artist. It's in the blocks southwest of Takashimaya department store. Cover charge from ¥1600 (depending on performer), including one drink.

Toga Toga B1, Teramachi Shijō-sagaru ☏075/361-6900. Another small live music club just south of Shijō-dōri, with performers most nights (from ¥1500).

The Weller's Club 5F Rapport Building, 146 Aburaya-chō, Fuyachō Nishi-iru, Takoyakushi-dōi ☏075/253-0753. A shrine to all things mod, with an emphasis on Paul Weller in his various incarnations. Occasional Northern Soul nights and regular scooter parties. Daily 8pm–3am.

Sekai (also known as *World*) B1-B2 Imagium Building, Shijō Kawaramachi-agaru Higashi-iru ☏075/223-2965. Attracts relatively mainstream top-notch, big-name reggae, house, hip-hop and techno DJs from Japan and abroad. Weekday nights are quieter, but the place rocks come the weekend. Average entry is ¥2000–2500 (including one drink). Open most nights from 9pm.

Gion

Kento's 2F, Hitosujime nishi-iru, Hanamikoji Shijō-sagaru ☏075/551-2777. The golden 1950s are still rocking at *Kento's* – all greased quiffs, polka dots and naff suits. Entry is ¥3500, but this includes the music cover charge, a portion or two of food and free drinks all night. It's just south of

Shijō-dōri behind an old Gion facade. Daily
6.30pm–2am, Sun till midnight.
Malt's Club Nexus Building, Hanamikoji Shinbashi
nishi-iru ☎075/551-5678. Extraordinary "concept" bar. The food's a bit expensive but the drinks
aren't so bad and it's worth it for the decor –
choose between jazz lounge, casual Japanese or

Mongolian yurt.
Tadg's Irish Pub & Restaurant 2F Ōto Bldg,
Keihan Shijō Station, Exit 8 ☎075/525-0680.
Popular expat hangout with plenty of dark wood
and a warm and friendly atmosphere. There's
good-quality food, thanks to master chef Tadg, and
a decent range of beers.

East Kyoto

Metro exit 2, Keihan Marutamachi Station
☎075/752-4765. Commendably catholic selection
of music on offer at Kansai's most progressive
club, in the guts of the train station, from local guitar bands to big-name foreign techno DJs, via
drag-queen dramas and hardcore dub reggae parties. It's small, loud and very popular. Check the
club section of *Kansai Time Out* for details.

Entrance ¥500–2000 (more for foreign DJs or
bands), including one drink. Daily from around
9pm.
Pig & Whistle 2F, 115 Ōhashi-chō, Sanjō-ōhashi
higashi-iru ☎075/761-6022. If you're craving a
game of darts or feel homesick for an Axminster
carpet, then hurry along to this well-established
British pub just east of Sanjō-Keihan Station.

Dance, theatre and cinema

Kyoto is famous for its performances of traditional **geisha dances** – geisha and
maiko (trainee geisha) from each of the city's former pleasure quarters have
been putting on these *odori* since the late nineteenth century, though the music
and choreography are much older. By turns demure and coquettish, they glide
round the stage in the most gorgeous kimono, straight out of an Edo-period
woodblock print of Japan's seductive "floating world". If you're in Kyoto at the
time, it's well worth going along. Performances take place several times a day,
so it's usually possible to get hold of tickets; you can buy them from the theatre box offices, ticket agencies, travel agents (see p.562) and major hotels.

The year kicks off with the **Miyako Odori** (April 1–30) performed by
geisha from the Gion teahouses. These dances, on a seasonal theme, take place
in the local theatre, Gion Kōbu Kaburenjō (see p.537; ☎075/541-3391; tickets from ¥1900). The ladies of Pontochō stage their **Kamo-gawa Odori** twice
a year (May 1–24 & Oct 15–Nov 7) in Pontochō Kaburenjō, at the north end
of Pontochō-dōri (☎075/221-2025; tickets from ¥2000) – Jean Cocteau and
Charlie Chaplin were both fans. In fact, autumn brings a whole flurry of activity: the **Onshukai** dances are held during the first week in October at the
Gion Kaikan theatre, near Yasaka-jinja (☎075/561-0224; from ¥4000), followed by **Kotobukikai** (around Oct 8–12) in northwest Kyoto's Kitano Kami-
shichiken Kaburenjō (☎075/461-0148; ¥6000); finally, the **Gion Odori** wraps
things up in early November (Nov 1–10; from ¥3300), again in the Gion
Kaikan. If your visit doesn't coincide with any of these, you can see a rather
disappointing sampler of traditional arts from March to November at **Gion
Corner** (see p.537; ☎075/561-1119). As well as a dance by *maiko*, there are
short extracts from court dances, a puppet play (Bunraku) and *kyōgen* theatre,
and demonstrations of the tea ceremony and flower arranging (*ikebana*).

Colourful and dramatic, **Kabuki** theatre is said to have originated in Kyoto.
Unfortunately, performances these days are fairly sporadic, but in December
there's a major Kabuki-fest at Gion's eye-catching Minami-za theatre (see
p.537; ☎075/561-1155). During this *kaomise*, or "face-showing" (Dec 1–25),
big-name actors give snippets from their most successful roles. **Nō** theatre is a
far more stately affair – and often incomprehensible even to Japanese, though
it can also be incredibly powerful. Kyoto's main venue is the Kanze Kaikan
(☎075/771-6114), south of Heian-jingū, with performances of Nō or *kyōgen*

Thanks to its central role in Japanese history, Kyoto is home to a number of important **festivals**, of which the major celebrations are listed below. The **cherry-blossom** season hits Kyoto in early April – famous viewing spots include the Imperial Park, Heian-jingū and Arashiyama – while early November brings dramatic **autumn colours**. Many **temples** hold special **openings** in October and November to air their inner rooms during the fine, dry weather. This is a marvellous opportunity to see paintings, statues and other treasures not normally on public display; details are available in the free *Kyoto Visitors' Guide*. Note that Kyoto gets pretty busy during major festivals and national holidays, especially Golden Week (April 29–May 5).

Feb 2–4 Setsubun. The annual bean-throwing festival is celebrated at shrines throughout the city. "Ogres" scatter beans and pray for good harvests at Yasaka-jinja, while Heian-jingū hosts performances of traditional *kyōgen* theatre (see p.970) on Feb 3.

April 1–30 Miyako Odori. Performances of traditional geisha dances in Gion (see p.537).

May 15 Aoi Matsuri. The Hollyhock Festival dates back to the days when this plant was believed to ward off earthquakes and thunder. Now it's an occasion for a gorgeous parade of people dressed in Heian-period costume (794–1185). They accompany the imperial messenger and an ox cart decked in hollyhock leaves from the Imperial Palace to the Shimo-gamo and Kami-gamo shrines, in north Kyoto.

May 1–24 Kamo-gawa Odori. Performances of traditional dances by geisha in Pontochō (see p.529).

June 1–2 Takigi Nō. Nō plays performed by torchlight at Heian-jingū.

July 17 Gion Matsuri. One of Kyoto's great festivals, the Gion Matsuri, also dates back to Heian times, when ceremonies were held to drive away epidemics of the plague – a curse of the hot, humid summer months. The festivities focus on Yasaka-jinja and culminate on July 17 (though there are related events throughout the whole of the month), with a grand parade of tall, pointy *yama-boko* floats, richly decorated with local Nishijin silk.

Aug 16 Daimonji Gozan Okuribi. Five huge bonfires etch *kanji* characters on the hills around Kyoto; the most famous is the character for *dai* (big) on Daimonji-yama, northeast of the city. The practice originated from lighting fires after Obon (see p.67), to guide the ancestral spirits back "home".

Oct 22 Jidai Matsuri. A comparative newcomer, this "Festival of the Ages" was introduced in 1895 to mark the city's 1100th anniversary. More than two thousand people, wearing costumes representing all the intervening historical periods, parade from the Imperial Palace to Heian-jingū.

Oct 22 Kurama-no-Himatsuri. After the Jidai parade, hop on a train north to see Kurama's more boisterous Fire Festival. In 940, Yuki-jinja, the local shrine, was moved here from central Kyoto, a journey which was accomplished by torchlight over three nights. To commemorate the event, the villagers light bonfires outside their houses and local lads carry giant, flaming torches (weighing up to 50kg) up to the shrine. Events climax around 9pm, after which there's heavy-duty drinking, drumming and chanting till dawn. It's primitive, exciting and extremely crowded. To get to Kurama, take the Eizan line from Kyoto's Demachiyanagi Station (30min); it's best to arrive early and leave around 10pm unless you want to see it through.

Dec 1–25 Kabuki Kaomise. Grand Kabuki festival (see p.555).

Dec 31 Okera Mairi. The best place to see in the New Year is at Gion's Yasaka-jinja. Apart from the normal festivities (see p.65), locals come here to light a flame from the sacred fire with which to rekindle their hearths back home. As well as general good luck, this supposedly prevents illness in the coming year.

most weekends (tickets from ¥2500; occasional free performances). Both the Kongo Nō-gakudō (☎075/221-3049; around ¥6000), near west Kyoto's Karasuma Shijō junction, and Kawamura Nō Kaikan (☎075/451-4513; from ¥4000), put on plays every month or so. The latter is a lovely old theatre run by the Kawamura family – a long line of famous Nō actors – located on Karasuma-dōri near Doshisha University.

A recent addition to the local arts scene is the refurbished **Kyoto Art Center** (☎075/213-1000, ⓦwww.kac.or.jp/english/index.html) which hosts a range of exhibitions and art performances as well as lectures, field trips and a well-regarded series of "Traditional Theatre Training" workshops (held every July) for those who want to find out more about Nō and other Japanese performing arts.

Alternatively, you can catch the latest Hollywood **movies** at the local cinema. These are mostly grouped along Kawaramachi-dōri north of Shijō and in the backstreets immediately to the west. For art-house movies, try Asahi Kaikan, on Kawaramachi-dōri south of the *Royal Hotel*, which often screens them in their original language, and Minami Kaikan, near the junction of Ōmiya and Kujō, southeast of Kyoto Station. The Japan Foundation, 8F Yasuda Kasai Building, Karasuma Nishikinokoji-agaru (☎075/211-1312), hosts free showings of Japanese classics for foreigners only; films are subtitled in English and are usually on Wednesday at 2pm. Finally, the British Council occasionally puts on home-grown English-language films (see "Listings", p.561).

Details of these and other events in Kyoto are available at the Tourist Information Centre (see p.517), and also in the two monthly publications, the *Kyoto Visitor's Guide* and *Kansai Time Out*.

Crafts and shopping

Over the centuries the finest craftsmen in Japan were drawn to Kyoto's Imperial Court as the city's workshops spawned an array of exquisite crafts. Gold-dusted **lacquerware**, shimmering **brocades** and folding paper **fans** were all favourites of the royal household. In the sixteenth century the popularity of the formal tea ceremony, with its appreciation of rustic understatement, created a fashion for rough-cast **pottery** and simple **bamboo utensils**. The nouveau-riche merchants, on the other hand, favoured a more flamboyant style, epitomized by the gorgeous **silks** and ornate **hair ornaments** worn in the pleasure quarters. Even everyday items, such as **boxwood combs**, brooms and buckets, show a certain pizzazz in Kyoto.

You can still find **shops** in Kyoto producing crafts in the traditional way, using skills passed down the generations. These offer superb, if often pricey, souvenirs of the city. And there's no shortage of conventional shops, department stores and even one or two flea markets where you can pick up less august mementos. To learn more about local crafts, take a look round the Fureaikan museum (see p.538) or join one of the **craft classes** listed below and have a go yourself.

Textiles

Kyoto has long been famous for its high-quality **weaving**. The centre of the city's textile industry is the **Nishijin** district, located northwest of the Imperial Palace. Even today you'll still hear the clatter of looms in dozens of family-run workshops as you walk through the area. Some of these families have been here since the early 1500s when their ancestors, returning to Kyoto after the ravages of the Ōnin Wars (1467–77), settled in an abandoned military camp called

Nishi-jin. They revived the production of *aya*, a unique style of elaborately patterned weave, which eventually became synonymous with Nishijin. During the Edo period (1603–1868) these sumptuous **silk brocades** were much in demand – it's estimated that the area boasted more than five thousand looms at its peak – but business collapsed after the Meiji Restoration as Western fashions took over. To counteract the decline, several Nishijin craftsmen travelled to France to study modern techniques, and came back with the revolutionary Jacquard mechanical loom. Nowadays, the vast majority of Nishijin fabrics are produced on computerized looms, but the more complex designs are still woven on the Jacquard or the even more labour-intensive hand loom.

You can see samples of these gorgeous fabrics and demonstrations of traditional Nishijin weaving at the **Nishijin Textile Centre** (daily 9am–5pm; free), just south of the Horikawa Imadegawa junction. Take a close look at the incredibly painstaking *tsuzurebata* technique, aptly known as fingernail weaving – it can take a whole day to complete 1cm. The centre also puts on occasional kimono shows (¥600; tickets available at the ground-floor information desk) showcasing the season's fashions.

In Nishijin weaving, silk threads are dyed before being woven into their intricate patterns. Originally, only the aristocracy could afford these fabrics, and when merchants began to patronize the same tailors in the late seventeenth century the shogun promptly forbade such extravagance. However, an enterprising Kyoto craftsman, Yūzensai Miyazaki, soon came up with a method for hand-dyeing fabrics to create the same elaborate effect. **Yūzen dyeing** is still an incredibly complex process, involving successive applications of glutinous-rice paste and dye to produce detailed, multicoloured designs. Afterwards, the pattern is often augmented with powdered gold or silver leaf, or embroidered with gold threads. Some of these wonderful fabrics are on display in the **Kodai Yūzen-en** gallery (daily 9am–5pm; ¥500), located on Takatsuji-dōri, southwest of the Hirokawa Shijō junction Ask to see their introductory video in English first and then, if you're inspired, you can try hand-dyeing yourself on a handkerchief or table centrepiece (from ¥1050).

When luxury fabrics went out of fashion in the Meiji era, many weavers turned to other areas of textile production. One of these was the Utsuki family, who saw the potential in making good-quality indigo-dyed cloth which was traditionally worn by farmers. Hand-woven clothes, *noren* curtains, bags and so forth are still produced in the lovely old **Aizen-kōbō** workshop (Mon–Fri 9am–5.30pm, Sat & Sun 9am–4pm; free, but prior reservation essential at the weekends; ☏075/441-0355), two blocks west of the Nishijin Textile Centre, on Nakasuji-dōri. The English-speaking owner will explain the laborious techniques involved in hand-dyeing the cloth with natural indigo and then sun-drying it to give a glorious, rich shade of blue.

Craft classes and cultural activities

In addition to Yūzen dyeing (see above), you can try several other crafts at various venues around the city. The Kyoto Handicraft Centre (see "Shopping", p.560) offers **demonstration classes** for beginners in woodblock printing, *cloisonné* (enamel-work) and doll-making (¥1500 for 1hr; book at the ground-floor information desk 1–4pm). Classes in *ikebana*, origami and calligraphy, among other things, are available through Kyoto International Community House (see p.517). At Tō-ji temple, south of Kyoto Station (see p.532), you can also try painting on lacquerware (daily 9.30am–3pm; ¥1000–1500).

Kyoto's most famous **tea-ceremony** school, Urasenke, is open to visitors one afternoon a week (⊛www.urasenke.or.jp; ¥1000). After an English-language introduction to the ceremony's form and history, you'll take part in the ritual itself. Phone the centre on ☎075/451-8516 for the latest schedule and to make a reservation. Alternatively, the *Miyako Hotel* offers the tea ceremony every day (10am–7pm; ¥1150); reservations required.

Recently it's become popular to dress up as a *maiko* (trainee geisha) and, if you can afford it, wander round the streets of Kyoto for an hour or two – much to the horror of the genuine *maiko*. Some hotels and guesthouses now offer the opportunity to their guests, or you can don a kimono, wig and make-up at the Nishijin Textile Centre (see opposite) for around ¥10,000 and have your photo taken.

Shopping

Kyoto's main shopping district is focused around the junction of **Shijō-dōri** and **Kawaramachi-dōri**, and spreads north of Shijō along the Teramachi and Shinkyōgoku arcades. Here you'll find the big-name **department stores**, notably Takashimaya, Hankyū and Daimaru, as well as all manner of souvenir shops, smart boutiques and even a few traditional craft shops, especially on Sanjō-dōri just west of the river. The **station area** has improved enormously with the opening of the huge Isetan department store and a revamped underground shopping mall, Porta, under the northern bus terminal.

East Kyoto is best known for its wealth of shops around Kiyomizu-dera selling the local pottery, while nearby Sannen-zaka hosts a lovely parade of traditional craft shops. Further north, Gion's Shinmonzen-dōri specializes in antiques – prices are predictably high, but it's a good area to browse. Listed below are some of the more interesting shops to aim for, but anyone in Kyoto for more than a few days should invest in a copy of Diane Durston's labour of love, *Old Kyoto* (see "Books", p.1017).

Books and music

Kyoto's largest range of foreign-language **books** is to be found on the eighth floor of the Maruzen store on Kawaramachi-dōri north of the Shijō junction. Alternatively, you'll find a more limited selection of foreign-language titles in the Kinokuniya bookstore; it's in the Zest underground mall beneath the Kawaramachi Oike crossroads.

For the city's biggest choice of **records and CDs**, try the Virgin Megastore, on Kawaramachi-dōri just up from Maruzen, or Tower Records, in the backstreets to the west. Joe's Garage, at 82-3 Nishimachi, Kitashirakawa (daily 11am–11pm), is also worth seeking out if you're into nostalgia; this tiny outlet specializes in records, posters and pop memorabilia of the 1960s and 1970s – with a soft spot for Frank Zappa. It's on Imadegawa, the road leading east to Ginkaku-ji, about halfway between Higashiōji and Shirakawa-dōri. Alternatively, for reasonably priced funk, soul and hip-hop, try A-Sign Records (daily 1–9pm) on the ground floor of the Empire Building on Kiyamachi-dōri – the same building as Cock-a-hoop (see "Bars, clubs and live music", p.553). There's good vinyl in the Wood Inn building too (see Saracça in "Eating" p.550). Otonokinoko (literally, "sound mushrooms") is a bizarre little shop on Ninenzaka-dōri, as you approach Kiyomizu-dera. The owner, professional sound recordist Fujiwara Kazumichi, has been collecting sounds from around the world since 1968 and now has a collection of over fifty CDs, DVDs and videos for sale (¥600–3900) featuring a most unusual range of subjects, from beans frying in a pan to elephants breaking wind. Listening stations enable you to tune in before deciding whether you want to splurge on one of these idosyncratic aural delights.

Crafts and souvenirs

Asahi Tōan 1-287-1 Kiyomizu. The best and most famous of several pottery shops on the road up to Kiyomizu-dera. They sell a wide variety of locally produced *Kiyomizu-yaki*.

Jūsan-ya Shijō Teramachi higashi-iru. This little shop on Shijō-dōri is crammed with beautiful combs and hair ornaments in plain boxwood or covered in lacquer. All the items are handcrafted using traditional techniques.

Kungyoku-dō Horikawa-dōri, Nishi-Hongan-ji-mae. Though you wouldn't guess it from its modern, grey-stone frontage, this shop has been selling incense since 1594 – their original customers were Buddhist temples and court nobles indulging in incense parties (players had to guess the ingredients from the perfume). The shop lies opposite the west gate of Nishi-Hongan-ji. Closed 1st and 3rd Sun of the month.

Kyoto Craft Centre Shijō-dōri. This large modern shop showcases the best of Kyoto's contemporary designers working with traditional crafts and is great for unusual, stylish souvenirs. It's located in Gion, towards the east end of Shijō-dōri. Closed Wed.

Kyoto Handicraft Centre Marutamachi-dōri. Five floors packed with souvenirs from all over Japan at a range of prices. The smaller Amita Plaza, next door, is also worth a look for its selection of foodstuffs. Both shops offer tax-free prices for goods over ¥10,000 (see p.72 for more on this). Find them near the northwest corner of Heian-jingū.

Kyoto Tōjiki Kaikan Gojō-zaka. West of Kiyomizu-dera, this place stocks a good selection of *Kiyomizu-yaki* and other local ceramics. It's also worth popping into the next-door gallery to see what's on display.

Naitō Sanjō-ōhashi. You might not be in the market for a broom, but this old shop just west of the Sanjō bridge is a treasure trove of beautifully made hemp brushes of every size and description (from ¥700). The traditional shop selling rice crackers and confectionery next door is also a delight.

Tachichiki Shijō Tominokoji. An elegant shop on Shijō-dōri, with fine ceramics and china on three floors and modern crafts in the basement. Closed occasionally on Wed.

Tanakaya Shijō Yanaginobanba. Dolls of all shapes and sizes fill this shop on Shijō-dōri. There's also a gallery upstairs with changing exhibitions of antique dolls. Closed Wed.

Tsujikura Kawaramachi Shijō-agaru. Traditional paper and modern plastic umbrellas spill out of this shop (established in 1690) onto the pavement of Kawaramachi-dōri. They also stock jaunty paper lanterns in a variety of styles. Closed Wed.

Yamato Mingei-ten Kawaramachi Takoyakushi-agaru. The best place in Kyoto to buy folk crafts. The main shop has two floors stuffed full of tempting items from all over Japan, while the annexe round the corner displays furniture and more modern designs. Find them on Kawaramachi-dōri, near Maruzen bookstore. Closed Tues.

Food and markets

Kyoto is as famous for its beautiful **foodstuffs** as it is for crafts, all made with the same attention to detail and love of refinement. You can see this in even the most modest restaurant, but also in the **confectionery** shops, whose window displays look more like art galleries. In the centre of Kyoto, take a look in Masune (closed Thurs), on the southeast corner of the Sanjō Kawaramachi junction, or Kagiya Yoshifusa (closed Mon), on Gion's Shijō-dōri, for a sample of the best. This latter shop has a tearoom upstairs where you can enjoy one of their dainty sweetmeats (*wagashi*) over a cup of green tea.

The other local delicacy is **pickled vegetables** (*tsukemono*). You'll be eating them at every meal, but if you want to buy some pickles – they're often sold vacuum-packed – head for **Murakami-jū** (closed occasionally on Wed). This traditional shop, southeast of Hankyū department store, is famous throughout Japan for the quality of its old-style pickles. Otherwise, take a walk down **Nishiki-koji** market street (see p.529), where pickles predominate among a whole range of foodstuffs.

If you're in Kyoto on the 21st or 25th of the month, don't miss the two big **flea markets** held respectively at Tō-ji temple (see p.532) and Kitano Tenmangū, a shrine in northwest Kyoto with its entrance on Imadegawa-dōri. Both kick off at 7am and it's worth getting there early if you're looking for bargains. There's a fantastic carnival atmosphere at these markets, where stalls sell everything from pots and socks to lacquerware and long johns. A similar monthly market at Chion-ji on the 15th of every month (16th if wet) is a little less frantic. Chion-ji sits on the corner of Imadegawa-dōri and Higashiōji-dōri, close to Kyoto University. Tō-ji has another market – for antiques – on the first Sunday of every month.

A mammoth **antiques** fair is held three times a year in the Pulse Plaza in the south of the city, near Takeda Station (on both the private Kintetsu line and the subway). Exact dates vary – check *Kansai Time Out* magazine. Entrance is free and there's something for every pocket. Even if you're not buying, the chance to see every conceivable kind of Japanese antique under one roof makes the fair well worth a visit.

Listings

Airlines JAL, JR Kyoto Station (international ☎0120-25-5931; domestic 0120-25-5971); Korean Airlines, Toho Seimei Blg, Aidano-chō higashi-iru, Nakagyō-ku (☎0088-212001).

Airport information Itami ☎06/6856-6781; Kansai International ☎0724/55-2500.

Banks and exchange Note that most banks in Kyoto don't open their exchange desks until 10.30/11am. Kyoto's main banking district is around the Karasuma Shijō junction, extending east towards the river and north to Oike-dōri, where Sumitomo Mitsui Banking Corporation, UFJ and Tokyo Mitsubishi banks all have foreign-exchange facilities. Down near the station, the Central Post Office (see p.562) also handles foreign exchange (Mon–Fri 9.30am–6pm). In addition to the post office ATMs (see "Basics", p.32), ATM machines in the All Card Plaza (in the Teramachi arcade, just north of Shijō-dōri) and the underground Zest Mall (under the Kawaramachi Oike junction, near Kyoto City Hall) accept a range of credit cards, including some cards registered on foreign accounts. Otherwise, you can get cash advances over the counter without a PIN number at the following: for Visa go to Sumitomo Mitsui Banking Corporation's main branch on Karasuma just south of Sanjō-dōri, or a handy sub-branch in Hankyū department store; for MasterCard, head for Nanto Bank, on the Karasuma Oike junction; and UFJ Bank, at Shijō Karasuma, for American Express.

Bike rental Renta-cycle Yasumoto (☎075/751-0595; daily 9am–5pm), on the riverbank just north of Sanjō-Keihan Station, charges ¥1000 per day or ¥200 an hour; you'll need to leave a deposit of ¥10,000 or ID of some sort. Ordinary town bikes at Taki Renta Bike (daily 8am–8pm; ☎075/341-7586), near *Hiraiwa Ryokan*, cost ¥1000 for 24hr (¥1300 for three-speed machines). If you're staying at *Tōjian*, *Utano Youth Hostel* or *Tani House* (see p.524), you could rent their more reasonable

bikes (¥500–800 per day). The popular backpacker hostel *Tour Club* has large, Westerner-friendly bikes which can be rented for ¥800 a day, or ¥630 if you're staying there.

British Council The Council's library, at Karasuma Chuo Building 8F, 659 Tearaimizu-chō (Mon–Fri 10am–8pm, Sat 10am–5pm; ☎075/229 7151), stocks English-language newspapers and magazines. They also have occasional screenings of British films (¥500) and a varied lecture programme.

Car rental Nippon Rent-a-Car (☎075/671-0919), Nissan Rent-a-Car (☎075/351-4123) and Eki Rent-a-Car (☎075/371-3020) all have offices near Kyoto Station.

Emergencies The main police station is at 85-3 Yabunouchi-cho, Shimodachiuri-dori, Kamaza Higashi-iru, Kamigyo-ku (☎075/451-9111). In an absolute emergency, contact the Foreign Advisory Service on ☎075/752-3010. For other emergency numbers, see "Basics" on p.81.

Hospitals and clinics The main Kyoto hospital with English-speaking doctors is the Japan Baptist Hospital, 47 Yamanomoto-chō, Kitashirakawa, Sakyō-ku (☎075/781-5191). Otherwise, Sakabe Clinic, 435 Yamamoto-chō, Gokomachi Nijō-sagaru (closed Thurs & Sat afternoons and all day Sun; ☎075/231-1624), is run by the English-speaking Dr Sakabe. They have a general clinic (6.30–8.30pm), or take appointments between 9am and 12.30pm. Consultations cost around ¥4000 for the first visit and ¥2000 thereafter. For more information about medical facilities with English-speaking staff in Kyoto or throughout the region, call the AMDA International Medical Information Centre (☎06/6636-2333).

Immigration To renew your tourist or student visa, apply to the Immigration Bureau, 4F, 34-12 Higashi Marutamachi, Kawabata Higashi-iru, near Keihan Marutamachi Station (☎075/752-5997).

Internet access A number of places offer Internet

access, but it's probably best to check with the Tourist Information Centre first, as they have an up-to-date list of places and rates. Try *Café Buttercups* (see "Eating", p.551; ¥250 for 30min) or for free at the Kyoto Prefectural Tourist Office on the ninth floor of Isetan department store in Kyoto Station. Alternatively, downtown, log on at the popular organic bakery *God Mountain* on the west side of Shinkyōgoku, 50m north of Shijō (daily 8am–9pm; ¥150 for 15min) or at C. Coquet (see "Eating", p.550), where it's free as long as you buy something.

Language courses Kyoto Japanese Language School, Ichijō-dōri Muromachi-nishi, Kamigyō-ku ☎075/414-0449, ⓦ www.kjls.or.jp; Kyoto Kokusai Gaikokugo Centre, 21 Kamihate-chō, Kitashirakawa, Sakyō-ku ☎075/722-5066, ⓔ kicl@kca.kyoto-art.ac.jp; Kyoto YMCA Japanese Language School, Sanjō Yanaginobanba ☎075/255-3287, ⓔ education@kyotoymca.or.jp; and Kyoto International Academy, Sanjō Hanamikoji ☎075/752-2837, ⓦ www.kia-ac.jp. The Kyoto International Community House, 2-1 Torii-chō Awataguchi, Sakyō-ku (☎075/752-3010), also runs basic courses in survival Japanese (¥3000 per term), while Berlitz, 9F, Ishizumi Building, Shijō Tominokoji nishi-iru, Shimogyō-ku (☎075/255-

2311), is recommended for its intensive courses.

Post office The Central Post Office, 843-12 Higashi Shiokoji-chō, Shimogyō-ku, Kyoto-shi, is located in front of Kyoto Station. They accept poste restante mail and there's a 24hr window for stamps and express mail.

Taxis If you phone in advance, MK Taxi (☎075/721-2237) can provide English-speaking drivers. Otherwise, Kyōren (☎075/661-2121) offers decent rates.

Ticket agencies Tickets to theatre, films, concerts and sports events are available at Pia, in the basement of the Kawaramchi Vivre department store just off the west side of Kawaramachi halfway between Sanjō and Shijō. There are also similar agencies in the Daimaru and Hankyū department stores.

Travel agents For international tickets, A'cross Travellers Bureau, 2F Royal Plaza Building, Rokkaku-sagaru Higashinotōin (☎075/255-3559), and No 1 Travel, 3F Shinkyōgoku Shijō-agaru (☎075/251-6970), have English-speaking staff. Alternatively, try T.I.S. (☎075/352-5341), in the first basement of Kyoto Station. The main domestic agents are Japan Travel Bureau (JTB; ☎075/361-7241) and Kinki Nippon Tourist (☎075/681-7211), with branches all over the city.

Around Kyoto

There's so much to see in Kyoto itself that most people don't explore the surrounding area, although it's worth making one trip out into the countryside. First priority should probably go to **Hiei-zan**, the mountain overlooking northeast Kyoto, where age-old cedars shelter the venerable temples of **Enryaku-ji**. Below Hiei-zan, **Ōhara** contains a scattering of beguiling temples in an attractive valley, while over on the west side of Kyoto the more urbanized **Arashiyama** is also famous for its gardens and temples. Arashiyama has less highbrow attractions as well: take a toy-town train through the Hozu-gawa gorge and then ride the rapids back down. It's back on the temple trail south of Kyoto, where **Uji** is home to the magnificent **Byōdō-in**, whose graceful Phoenix Hall is a masterpiece of Japanese architecture. Finally, if you have had your fill of temples and historical sights, a visit to the stunning **Miho Museum**, nestled in the Shigaraki mountains, should be at the top of your to-do list.

Hiei-zan

Protecting Kyoto's northeastern flank (traditionally considered the source of evil spirits threatening the capital), the sacred mountain of **Hiei-zan** is the home of Tendai Buddhism, whose headquarters are housed in an atmospheric collection of buildings, **Enryaku-ji**. There's not much else up on the mountain, so it's a good area to go at a leisurely pace, following ancient paths among the cedar forests to the temple's less-frequented halls. Though there are several ways of getting to Enryaku-ji (see "Practicalities", p.566), the easiest route is by bus from Kyoto, wriggling up the mountain side and then following a ridge road north. On a clear day you'll be rewarded with huge views west over **Biwa-ko**, Japan's largest lake and the second oldest freshwater lake in the world after Lake Baikal in Siberia.

Enryaku-ji

The top of Hiei-zan consists of a narrow ridge, at the south end of which stand the central halls of **Enryaku-ji** (daily 8.30/9am–4/4.30pm; ¥550; ☎077/578-0047). From this core area, known as the **Tō-tō** (Eastern Pagoda), the ridge

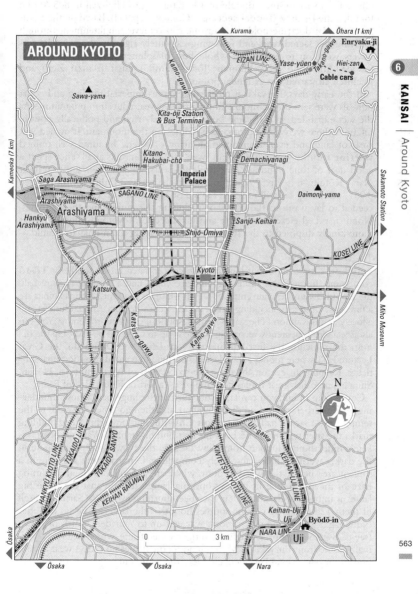

AROUND KYOTO

Kurama

Ōhara (1 km)

Enryaku-ji

EIZAN LINE

Yase-yūen

Hiei-zan

Takano-gawa

Cable cars

Kamo-gawa

Sawa-yama

Kita-ōji Station & Bus Terminal

Kitano-Hakubai-chō

Demachiyanagi

Kameoka (7 km)

Saga Arashiyama

SAGANO LINE

Imperial Palace

Daimonji-yama

Arashiyama

Arashiyama

Hankyū Arashiyama

Sanjō-Keihan

KOSEI LINE

Shijō-Ōmiya

Kyoto

Katsura

Katsura-gawa

Kamo-gawa

Sakamoto Station

Miho Museum

N

TOKAIDŌ LINE

HANKYŪ KYOTO LINE

TOKAIDŌ SANYŌ

Uji-gawa

KEIHAN-UJI LINE

KINTETSU KYOTO LINE

KEIHAN RAILWAY

Keihan-Uji

Uji

Byōdō-in

Ōsaka

0   3 km

NARA LINE

Uji

Ōsaka

Ōsaka

Nara

slopes gently northwest down to the **Sai-tō** (Western Pagoda). A third compound, Yokawa, lies further north again, but this was a later addition and contains little of immediate interest. Most buses from Kyoto terminate at the Tō-tō car park beside a souvenir shop; walk behind it to find the temple's main entrance.

Enryaku-ji was founded in 788 AD by a young Buddhist monk called Saichō (767–822), later sanctified as **Dengyō Daishi**. Saichō built himself a small hut on the mountain and a temple to house an image of Yakushi Nyorai (the Buddha of Healing), which he carved from a fallen tree. He then went to China for a year to study Buddhism. On returning to Hiei-zan in 805 AD he founded the Japanese **Tendai sect** (see "Contexts", p.953). Based on the Lotus Sutra, Tendai doctrine holds that anyone can achieve enlightenment through studying the sacred texts and following extremely rigorous practices. Its followers went on to establish a whole host of splinter groups: Hōnen (who founded the Jōdo sect), Shinran (Jōdo Shinshū), Eisai (Rinzai Zen) and Nichiren all started out as Tendai priests.

In the early days, Enryaku-ji received generous imperial funding and court officials were sent up the mountain for a twelve-year education programme. As the sect expanded, so it became both enormously rich and politically powerful, until there were three thousand buildings on the mountain. It owned vast areas of land and even maintained an army of several hundred well-trained **warrior monks** – many of whom were not really monks at all. They spent a good deal of time fighting other Buddhist sects, notably their great rivals at Nara's Kōfuku-ji (see p.579), but in the end the warlord **Oda Nobunaga** (see p.937) put a stop to it all in 1571. He led 30,000 troops up Hiei-zan and proceeded to lay waste to the complex, including the monks and their families. Nobunaga died eleven years later and his successor, Toyotomi Hideyoshi, was more kindly disposed to the Tendai sect, encouraging the monks to rebuild.

Tō-tō

Enryaku-ji's most important buildings are concentrated in the southerly **Tō-tō** compound. Immediately inside the entrance you'll find a modern treasure hall, the **Kokuhō-den** (separate entrance fee of ¥450). Its most interesting exhibits are a fine array of statues, including a delicate, thirteenth-century Amida Buddha and a lovely Senjū Kannon (Thousand-Armed Kannon) of the ninth century. You can also see a scroll apparently recording Saichō's trip to China in 804 AD. Up the hill from the museum, the first building on your left is the **Daikō-dō**, the Great Lecture Hall, where monks attend lectures on the sutras and discuss doctrinal subtleties. Keeping an eye on them are life-size statues of Nichiren, Eisai, Hōnen, Shinran and other great names from the past – a sort of Tendai Hall of Fame.

Continuing uphill, you can take your turn at the huge bell, whose thundering peal reverberates around the mountain, and then go down the steps to the temple's most sacred hall, the **Konpon Chū-dō**. This powerful, faded building marks the spot where Saichō built his first hut; his statue of Yakushi Nyorai is kept inside, though hidden from view. Despite the crowds, the atmosphere in the dark, cavernous hall is absolutely compelling. Unusually, the altars are in a sunken area below the worship floor, where they seem to float in a swirling haze of incense smoke lit by low-burning lamps. It's said that the three big lanterns in front of the main altar have been burning ever since Saichō himself lit them 1200 years ago. Some sources hold that the lanterns did go out after Nobunaga's attack, and that a monk was sent up to Yamadera, north of Tokyo (see p.284), to bring back a light from their sacred flame, which had itself originally come from Enryaku-ji. Monks tending the flames nowadays wear a mask in case they sneeze and accidentally blow the flame out.

Arashiyama	*Arashiyama*	嵐山
Daikaku-ji	*Daikaku-ji*	大覚寺
Giō-ji	*Giō-ji*	祇王寺
Ōkōchi Sansō	*Ōkōchi Sansō*	大河内山荘
Seiryō-ji	*Seiryō-ji*	清涼寺
Tenryū-ji	*Tenryū-ji*	天竜寺
Accommodation and eating		
Nishiki	*Nishiki*	錦
Sagano	*Sagano*	嵯峨野
Minshuku Tsujimura	*Minshuku Tsujimura*	民宿辻村
Tenryū-ji Shigetsu	*Tenryū-ji Shigetsu*	天龍寺篩月
Tsurezure	*Tsurezure*	つれずれ
Hiei-zan	*Hiei-zan*	比叡山
Eizan Cable	*Eizan Kēburu*	叡山ケーブル
Enryaku-ji	*Enryaku-ji*	延暦寺
Jōdo-in	*Jōdo-in*	浄土院
Konpon Chū-dō	*Konpon Chū-dō*	根本中堂
Ninai-dō	*Ninai-dō*	にない堂
Sai-tō	*Sai-tō*	西塔
Sakamoto Cable	*Sakamoto Kēburu*	坂本ケーブル
Shaka-dō	*Shaka-dō*	釈迦堂
Tō-tō	*Tō-tō*	東塔
Yase-Hiei-zan-guchi Station	*Yase-Hiei-zan-guchi*	八瀬比叡山口駅
Miho Museum	*Miho Miyūjiamu*	ミホ ミュージアム
Ōhara	*Ōhara*	大原
Hōsen-in	*Hōsen-in*	宝泉院
Jakkō-in	*Jakkō-in*	寂光院
Sanzen-in	*Sanzen-in*	三千院
Seryō	*Seryō*	芹生
Shōrin-in	*Shōrin-in*	勝林院
Uji	*Uji*	宇治
Byōdō-in	*Byōdō-in*	平等院
Magozaemon	*Magozaemon*	孫座ェ門

From Konpon Chū-dō, walk ahead to the paved road and then follow it generally west, passing the bell again on your right. The next little hillock sports the pretty **Kaidan-in**, the Ordination Hall, and beyond it stands the recently reconstructed **Amida-dō** and its two-storey pagoda. Behind this bright-red hall, a path leads off through the woods to the Sai-tō compound.

Sai-tō

It takes around thirty minutes to walk from the Amida-dō to the centre of the **Sai-tō** compound, with a few stops en route. First of these is the **Jōdo-in**, which you'll come to after about ten minutes at the bottom of a lantern-lined staircase. Inside the temple's courtyard and round to the right of the main hall, **Saichō's mausoleum**, a red-lacquered, sun-burnt building, stands in a carefully tended gravel enclosure.

Marathon monks

Followers of the Buddhist **Tendai sect** believe that the route to enlightenment lies through chanting, esoteric ritual and extreme physical endurance. The most rigorous of these practices is the "thousand-day ascetic mountain pilgrimage", in which **marathon monks**, as they're popularly known, are required to walk 40,000km through the mountains and streets of Kyoto in a thousand days – the equivalent of nearly a thousand marathons. The thousand days are split into hundred-day periods over seven years; during each period the monk has to go out every day in all weathers, regardless of his physical condition. He must adhere to a strict vegetarian diet and, at one point during the seven years, go on a week-long fast with no food, water or sleep, just for good measure.

Not surprisingly, many monks don't make it – in the old days they were expected to commit ritual suicide if they had to give up. Those that do finish (nowadays, about one person every five years) are rewarded with enlightenment and become "living Buddhas". Apparently, the advice of modern marathon monks is much sought after by national baseball coaches and others involved in endurance training.

Continuing northwest, the path eventually leads to two identical square halls standing on a raised area. These are commonly known as **Ninai-dō**, which roughly translates as "shoulder-carrying hall". The name refers to the legendary strength of a certain Benkei, who's said to have hoisted the two buildings onto his shoulders like a yoke. Their official names are Jōgyō-dō, the Hall of Perpetual Practice on the left, and the Hokke-dō, or Lotus Hall. They're used for different types of meditation practice: in the former monks walk round the altar for days reciting the Buddha's name, in the latter they alternate between walking and sitting meditation while studying the Lotus Sutra.

Walk between the pair of buildings and down more steps to reach the **Shaka-dō**, another imposing hall, which marks the centre of the Sai-tō area. Though smaller and not so atmospheric as Konpon Chū-dō, this building is much older. It was originally erected in the thirteenth century on the shores of Biwa-ko, but was moved here in 1595 to replace the earlier hall destroyed by Nobunaga's armies. It enshrines an image of Shaka Nyorai (Sakyamuni, the Historical Buddha), which is also attributed to Saichō, but again you can't see it. Otherwise, the Shaka-dō is similar to the Tō-tō, with its sunken centre and three lanterns. It's a lovely, quiet place to rest before you start heading back.

Practicalities

The quickest and simplest way of getting to Enryaku-ji is to take a **direct bus** (1hr; ¥800) from either Kyoto Station or Sanjō-Keihan Station in east Kyoto. The timetable varies according to the season, so check in Kyoto for the latest schedule and note that in winter the road is sometimes closed by snow. Enryaku-ji lies about 800m above sea level and can get pretty chilly in winter. Even in summer you'll find it noticeably cooler than Kyoto.

The alternative is to take one of two **cable cars** up the mountain. The most convenient of these is the eastern **Sakamoto Cable** (every 30min; 11min; ¥840, or ¥1570 return), which has the added benefit of views over Biwa-ko. To reach the cable car, take a JR Kosei line train from Kyoto Station to Hiei-zan Sakamoto Station (every 15min; 20min; ¥320), then a bus (¥210). From the top station it's a 700-metre-walk north to the central Tō-tō area along a quiet road. The main disadvantage of the western **Eizan Cable** (every 30min; 20min; ¥840 one way, or ¥1640 return) is that it dumps you about 1.5km from the Tō-tō at the Sanchō Station, from where you can catch a shuttle bus (see opposite), or walk along a footpath from behind the ski lift. However, it's slightly cheaper, especially if you've got a bus pass covering Kyoto's outer districts (see p.513). Eizan Cable leaves from near Yase-Hiei-zan-guchi Station on the private Eizan line; to get there, either take a Kyoto Bus headed for Ōhara, or a train from Kyoto's Demachiyanagi Station (every 12min; 14min; ¥260).

Once you've arrived on the mountain, the best way to get around is on foot. If you're in a hurry, **shuttle buses** run during most of the year from Sanchō via the central Tō-tō car park to Sai-tō and Yokawa (March 20 to Dec 1; every 30min). The whole journey only takes about twenty minutes and costs ¥740. If you plan to use this bus a lot, buy a one-day pass (*hiei-zannai ichi-nichi jyōshaken*; ¥900) from the bus driver or at the Tō-tō bus terminal. The pass allows unlimited travel and also entitles you to a ¥100 discount on the entrance to Enryaku-ji.

Miho Museum

Taking six years to build at a cost of $215 million, the I.M. Pei-designed **Miho Museum** (Tues–Fri & Sun 10am–5pm, Sat 10am–7pm; ¥1000; ☎0748/82-3411, ⓦwww.miho.or.jp/english) is one of the architectural high points of the Kansai region, although it's only open for a few months every year – exact dates vary; check the website for details. Located in a rural, mountainous part of Shiga Prefecture, best-known for its Shigaraki pottery, the museum provides an unlikely setting for an incredible collection of artworks belonging to Koyama Mihoko and her daughter Hiroko. Koyama is the head of one of Japan's so-called "new religions", Shinki Shumeikai, founded in 1970, which has an estimated 300,000 followers worldwide, hundreds of whom can be found living and working here at the museum. The central tenet of Shinki Shumeikai's philosophy is that spiritual fulfilment lies in art and nature, hence the setting.

From the entrance and cafeteria (serving excellent, if pricey, organic vegetarian cuisine), access to the museum proper is on an electric shuttle bus through a tunnel which opens on to a beautiful valley spanned by a 120-metre-high bridge; alternatively, you can walk – it takes about 15 minutes on foot. Opposite is a series of tetrahedrons, all that can be seen of the museum, most of which is actually built inside the mountainside due to planning restrictions. Inside, a continually shifting pattern of light and shadow is created by the innovative use of skylights, pyramid-shaped wall lights and ever-so-slightly uneven corridors which look out – through windows fitted with aluminium screens – on to bamboo gardens and tranquil green landscapes.

The museum has two wings. The **north wing** houses Japanese art, including priceless porcelain, scrolls, screens and Buddhist relics; the **south wing** has antiquities from the rest of the world, amongst them jewellery, frescoes, textiles and statues produced by a range of civilizations from ancient Egyptian to classical Chinese. Amongst the numerous treasures are a 3000-year-old silver-and-gold cult figure of a falcon-headed deity from Egypt's 19th Dynasty, a limestone Assyrian relief unearthed in Nimrud, and the splendid Sanguszko Carpet from Iran. Each artwork is labelled in English and Japanese, and there are explanatory leaflets in some of the galleries, but the overall effect is one of art which is meant to be experienced for its intrinsic beauty rather than its historical or cultural import.

The easiest way to visit the Miho Museum is by joining the **organized half-day tour** run by JTB's Sunrise Tours (☎075/341-1413, ⓦwww.jtb.co.jp/sunrisetour/ kyoto; ¥13,000 per person). It's far cheaper, but a little more complicated, to do it yourself. From JR Kyoto Station take a local train on the JR Biwako Line (for Nagahama or Maibara) two stops to JR **Ishiyama Station** (every 10–15min; 13min; ¥230). Infrequent buses (50min; ¥800), run by the Teisan Bus Company, leave for the museum from outside Ishiyama Station's south exit. On weekdays, buses leave at ten minutes past the hour between 9.10am and 12.10pm. If you miss the 12.10pm bus, you'll have to take an (expensive) taxi. On Saturdays, Sundays and national holidays, the weekday timetable is supplemented by buses at 9.50am, 1.55pm, 2.55pm and 3.55pm.

Ōhara

Though only a short bus ride from Kyoto, the collection of temples that makes up **ŌHARA** is almost in a different world. All are sub-temples of Enryaku-ji (see p.563), but the atmosphere here is quite different: instead of stately cedar forests, these little temples are surrounded by maples and flower-filled gardens, fed by tumbling streams. The sights used to be divided into two sections: the easterly **Sanzen-in** and the melancholy **Jakkō-in** across the rice fields, but the latter's main hall was gutted in an arson attack in 2000, leaving Sanzen-in as Ōhara's main attraction.

The temples

From the Ōhara bus terminal, cross over the main road and follow the lane leading east, uphill beside a small river and between stalls selling "beefsteak-leaf" tea (*shiso-cha*), mountain vegetables and other local produce. At the top of the steps, roughly ten minutes from the bus terminal, a fortress-like wall on the left contains Ōhara's most important temple, **Sanzen-in** (daily 8.30am–4/4.30pm; ¥550; ☎075/744-2531). The temple is said to have been founded by Saichō, the founder of Tendai Buddhism, but its main point of interest is the twelfth-century **Hon-dō**, a small but splendid building standing on its own in a mossy garden. Inside is an astonishingly well-preserved tenth-century Amida Buddha flanked by smaller statues of Kannon (on the right as you face them) and Seishi, which were added later.

The hillside behind Sanzen-in is covered with hydrangeas, at their best in June, but at other times of year walk back past the entrance and north along the lane a short distance to **Jakkō-in** (daily 9am–5pm; ¥600, including green tea; ☎075/744-2545, ⓦ www.jakkoin.or.jp/index-e.html). This monastery's prime attraction is a quiet garden, landscaped in the late Edo period and fringed by a row of tufted pines, but the May 2000 arson attack has robbed the temple of much of its charm. The temple's main hall is currently being rebuilt, but it will be 2005 at the earliest before it is completed.

Continuing north, the lane takes a sharp left in front of **Shōrin-in** (daily 9am–5pm; ¥200; ☎075/744-2409) where, if you're lucky, you might hear monks chanting, though it's generally deserted. The large hall, reconstructed in the 1770s and containing another image of Amida, is used for studying *shōmyō*, Buddhist incantations practised by followers of Tendai. *Shōmyō* were first introduced from China in the eighth century and have had a profound influence on music in Japan; some temples have CDs for sale if you're interested in hearing more.

The last temple in this section, **Hōsen-in** (daily 9am–5pm; ¥600, including green tea; ☎075/744-2409) lies at the end of the lane, on the left. Like Jakkō-in, the highlight here is the garden, this one much more enclosed and almost swamped by a magnificent aged pine and a lovely maple. The attendants will give you a brief history of the temple while you sip tea.

Practicalities

To reach Ōhara from central Kyoto, take a cream-and-red **Kyoto Bus** either from Kyoto Station (#17 and #18), Sanjō-Keihan Station (#16 and #17) or Kita-ōji Station (#15). The journey takes between thirty and fifty minutes and costs a maximum of ¥580, or you can use the Kyoto-wide subway and bus pass (see p.518). The route takes you past Yase-yūen, the starting point of the Eizan cable car up Hiei-zan (see p.562), making it possible to visit both places in one rather hectic day.

There are numerous small **restaurants** in Ōhara, but one of the nicest places to eat is *Seryō* (daily 11am–5pm), at the top of the steps up to Sanzen-in, on the left. They serve a beautifully presented *bentō* of seasonal vegetables (¥2500) as well as more expensive meals; in good weather you can eat outside on a riverside terrace. If you want to enjoy Ōhara once the crowds have gone, they also run a fine **ryokan** with a choice of tatami or Western-style rooms and both open-air and indoor baths (℡075/744-2301, ⓦwww.seryo.co.jp/english .htm; ❼, including two meals).

Arashiyama

Western Kyoto ends in the pleasant, leafy suburb of **ARASHIYAMA**. Set beside the Hozu-gawa, Arashiyama was originally a place for imperial relaxation, but the palaces were later converted into Buddhist temples and monasteries. The most famous of these is **Tenryū-ji**, noted for its garden, while the smaller, quieter temples have a more intimate appeal. In contrast with Tenryū-ji's somewhat introspective garden, that of **Ōkōchi Sansō** – the home of a 1920s movie actor – is by turns secretive and dramatic, with winding paths and sudden views over Kyoto. For a break from temples and gardens, take the little Torokko train tootling up the Hozu valley to **Kameoka**, from where boats ferry you back down the fairly gentle **Hozu rapids**.

A good way to explore the area is to rent a bike and spend a day pottering around the lanes and through magnificent bamboo forests. Alternatively, if you're pushed for time, you can combine Arashiyama with the sights of western Kyoto (see p.541). Note that central Arashiyama can get unbearably crowded, particularly on spring and autumn weekends. Just head north along the hillside, however, and you'll soon begin to leave the crowds behind.

Temples and gardens

Arashiyama is centred on the long **Togetsu-kyō** bridge, which spans the Hozu-gawa (known as the Katsura-gawa east of the bridge). This is a famous spot for viewing spring cherry blossoms or maples in autumn, and is also the scene of night-time **cormorant fishing** expeditions (see box, p.478); boats depart for an hour-long fishing trip (July & Aug 7pm & 8pm, Sept 1–15 7.30pm; ¥1700) from the river's north bank just upstream from the bridge.

The town's most interesting sights, as well as the majority of its shops, restaurants and transport facilities, lie north of the Hozu-gawa. First of these is the Zen temple of **Tenryū-ji** (daily 8.30am–5/5.30pm; ¥600, or ¥500 for the garden only; ℡075/881-1235), which started life as the country retreat of Emperor Kameyama (1260–74), grandfather of the more famous **Emperor Go-Daigo** (1318–39). Go-daigo overthrew the Kamakura shogunate (see p.936) and wrested power back to Kyoto in 1333 with the help of a defector from the enemy camp, **Ashikaga Takauji**. The ambitious Takauji soon grew exasperated at Go-Daigo's incompetence and staged a counter-coup. He placed a puppet emperor on the throne and had himself declared shogun, thus also gaining the Arashiyama palace, while Go-Daigo fled south to set up a rival court in Yoshino, south of Nara. After Go-Daigo died in 1339, however, a series of bad omens convinced Takauji to convert the palace into a temple to appease Go-Daigo's restless soul.

The temple buildings are nearly all twentieth-century reproductions, but the **garden** behind dates back to the thirteenth century. It's best viewed from inside the temple, from where you get the full impact of the pond and its artfully placed rock groupings against the tree-covered hillside. The present layout of the garden is the work of **Musō Kokushi**, the fourteenth-century Zen monk also responsible for Saihō-ji (see p.547), who incorporated Zen and Chinese motifs into the existing garden. There's still an argument, however, over who created the garden's most admired feature, the dry, Dragon Gate waterfall on the far side of the pond. Apparently inspired by Chinese Sung-dynasty landscape paintings, the waterfall's height and bold vertical composition are extremely unusual in Japanese garden design. The temple is also home to **Shishiku-no-niwa** ("The Garden of the Lion's Roar"), a noted Zen garden of the dry, landscape type, with some particularly striking fence-work. Dating back to the Muromachi period (1338-1573), the garden opened to the public for the first time in 130 years in 2003, albeit for limited periods in spring and autumn. It's especially attractive in the autumn, when the maple trees are turning red.

When you've had your fill, follow the paths through the garden to its back (north) entrance, where you'll emerge into some of the bamboo groves for which Arashiyama is renowned. Heading northwest along the hillside, look out on the left for the entrance to **Ōkōchi Sansō** (daily 9am–5pm; ¥1000, including green tea; ☎075/872-2233), just before you reach the train tracks. This was once the home of Ōkōchi Denjirō, a silent-movie idol of the 1920s, who chose a spectacular location for his traditional Japanese villa. The route takes you winding all over the hillside, past tea-ceremony pavilions, a moss garden, a dry garden and convenient stone benches, up to a ridge with views over Kyoto on one side and the Hozu gorge on the other. Finally, you drop down to a small museum devoted to the actor.

From here continue north past Torokko Arashiyama Station, where you can join the train for Kameoka (see opposite), and keep following the attractive lanes along the hillside. After passing two minor temples, Jōjakkō-ji and Nison-in, a left turn leads up to **Giō-ji** (daily 9am–5pm; ¥300; ☎075/861-3574), a pretty little Buddhist nunnery, with a mossy, maple-shaded garden and more bamboo groves. The nunnery is named after one of its former inhabitants, Princess Giō, a concubine of the notoriously ruthless Taira Kiyomori (1118–81), who was head of the Taira clan and effective ruler of Japan for a number of years. On falling from favour, Giō came to Arashiyama to retire, bringing along her mother, sister and a friend. Their statues are on display in a small pavilion – from the left, Giō's mother, Giō, her sister and her friend – alongside a Buddha image and Kiyomori half hidden from view.

While the lanes carry on along the hills, the last two sights in Arashiyama – both of moderate interest – are off to the west. It's only worth popping into **Seiryō-ji** (daily 9am–4pm; ¥400; ☎075/861-0343), 1km from Giō-ji, on the eighth day of the month, when the statue of Shaka Nyorai (the Historical Buddha) is on show. The image was carved in China in 985 AD and is a copy of a much older, Indian statue, which in turn was said to have been modelled on the Buddha while he was alive. The rest of the time you'll have to be content with his internal organs – when the statue was opened in 1953, they found several little silk bags in the shape of a heart, kidneys and liver, which are now on display in the temple museum. One kilometre northeast from here, the more impressive **Daikaku-ji** (daily 9am–4.30pm; ¥500; ☎075/871-0071) was founded in 876, when Emperor Saga ordered that his country villa be converted to a Shingon-sect temple. The main Shin-den hall was moved here from Kyoto's Imperial Palace in the late sixteenth century and still contains some fine screens painted by renowned artists of the Kanō school. Behind this building, the Shoshin-den is also noted for its panels of a hawk and an endearing group of rabbits. Afterwards you can wander along the banks of Ōsawa-ike, Emperor Saga's boating lake.

Along the Hozu-gawa

Northwest of Arashiyama the **Hozu-gawa** flows through a fairly narrow, twisting gorge just over 15km long. It's a popular, though fairly expensive, half-day excursion to take the old-fashioned Torokko train upriver to **Kameoka** and come back down by boat. You can board the train at Torokko Arashiyama Station, just north of Ōkōchi Sansō (see opposite), or at the Torokko Saga terminus one stop further east. Wherever you get on it's the same price (¥600 one way) for the 25-minute journey, which takes you through tunnels and criss-crosses the river. It's a good idea to reserve seats in advance during the main holiday periods, especially when the cherries and autumn colours are at their peak, though at other times you should be able to buy tickets on the day. Reservations can be made through JTB and other major travel agents, at JR's Green Windows, or by phone direct to Torokko (☎075/861-7444). Trains leave hourly between 9.25am and 5.25pm (daily except Wed March–Dec).

At the Torokko Kameoka terminus buses wait to take you to the landing stage (15min; ¥280), from where chunky wooden **punts** set off down the Hozu-gawa (4 daily; ¥3900). The **rapids** aren't the most fearsome in the world, but it's a fun trip and the gorge is that much more impressive from water level. Back in Arashiyama, the boats land on the river's north bank just short of the Togetsu bridge. Regular **sightseeing boats** depart from this same landing stage for a very overpriced thirty-minute jaunt to the mouth of the gorge (¥1100 per person), or you can rent your own three-person rowing boat for ¥1400 per hour.

Practicalities

Three train lines and several bus routes connect Arashiyama with central Kyoto. Unless you've got a bus or JR rail pass, the quickest and most pleasant way to get here is to take a **train** on the private Keifuku Electric Railway from Kyoto's Shijō-Ōmiya Station (every 10min; 20min; ¥200). This brings you into the main Arashiyama Station in the centre of town – make sure to pick up a free bilingual map of the town available at the station. Keifuku offers a one-day pass (¥650) covering unlimited travel on this Arashiyama line and also the Keifuku Kitano line, which connects with Kitano-Hakubai-chō Station in northwest Kyoto. Alternatively, the JR Sagano line runs from Kyoto Station to Saga-Arashiyama Station (every 20min; 15min; ¥230), which is handy for the Torokko trains, but it's roughly fifteen minutes' walk to central Arashiyama from here; make sure you get on a local JR train and not the express, which shoots straight through. Finally, there's the less convenient Hankyū Electric Railway; from central Kyoto you have to change at Katsura Station, and you end up in the Hankyū Arashiyama Station on the south side of the river.

Buses are slightly more expensive and take longer, especially when the traffic's bad. However, Arashiyama is on the main Kyoto bus network and falls within the limits for the combined bus and subway pass (see p.518). City Bus routes #11, #28 and #93, and Kyoto Bus routes #61, #71, #72 and #73, all pass through central Arashiyama. If you plan to do more than just the central sights, it's worth considering **bike rental**. There are rental outlets at each of the train stations (¥800–1000 per day).

If you want **to stay** out here, the nicest option is *Minshuku Tsujimura* (☎075/861-3207, ℱ862-0820; ❺). It's a small, tidy place, with tatami rooms and shared washing facilities, located several minutes west of JR Saga Station. To get there, walk along the north side of the tracks, cross a small river and follow the road for a further 100m – there's a sign outside in Japanese, on the left side of the road.

Restaurants

Arashiyama is famous for its Buddhist vegetarian cuisine, *shōjin-ryōri*, and particularly for *yudōfu* (simmered tofu), which is closely associated with the Zen tradition. Of several **restaurants** serving *shōjin-ryōri*, Tenryū-ji's *Shigetsu* (daily 11am–2pm; ☎075/882-9725) offers the best surroundings, though you're a bit on public display. There's a choice of three meals (from ¥3500) and reservations are recommended; note that if you're eating in the restaurant the temple's ¥600 entry fee will be waived. A good alternative is *Sagano* (☎075/871-6946; daily 11am–7pm), a cheerful little place buried in a bamboo grove south of Tenryū-ji. Their *yudōfu* set meal, with lots of sauces and non-meat side dishes, costs ¥3800. But the town's most famous restaurant is undoubtedly *Nishiki* (daily except Tues 11am–7.30pm; ☎075/871-8888), located on the low island in the middle of the Hozu-gawa. They specialize in Kyoto cuisine, whose subtle flavours and exquisite presentation follow a seasonal theme; seven- to thirteen-course meals start at ¥3800. Though not too busy on weekdays, it's a good idea to reserve at weekends. Arashiyama also has plenty of cheaper places to eat, mostly clustered around the main station. If you're following the temple route, look out for *Tsurezure* (daily except Thurs 11am–4.30pm), a small Japanese restaurant on a corner 200m before Giō-ji. This has excellent and reasonably priced noodle and rice dishes, including the house speciality, *tsurezure gohan* – a set meal of rice, pickles, *goma miso* and miso soup for just ¥600.

Uji

The town of **UJI**, thirty minutes' train ride south of Kyoto, has a long and illustrious past and boasts one of Japan's most fabulous buildings, the **Byōdō-in** – for a preview, look at the reverse side of a ¥10 coin. Somehow this eleventh-century hall, with its glorious statue of Amida Buddha, survived war, fire and years of neglect and preserves a stunning display of Heian-period art at its most majestic. Unfortunately, there's not a lot else to do in Uji, except sample their famous green tea; since the fourteenth century this area's tea leaves have been rated among the best in the country. Most people visit Uji on a half-day excursion from Kyoto, but it's only a little bit further from Nara (see p.574).

Byōdō-in

Arriving at JR Uji station, cross over the main road and turn left along the next, parallel, road for a quieter route down to the Uji-gawa. Just before the bridge – a modern successor to the seventh-century original – turn right on to a narrow shopping street and follow the river southeast through a fragrant haze of roasting tea. Then, where the lane forks left up onto the embankment, continue straight ahead and you'll find the entrance to the **Byōdō-in** (daily: March–Nov 8.30am–5pm; Jan, Feb & Dec 9am–4.30pm; ¥600; ☎0774/21-2861), roughly ten minutes' walk from the station.

After the imperial capital moved to Kyoto in 794 AD, Uji became a popular location for aristocratic country retreats. One such villa was taken over in the late tenth century by the emperor's chief adviser, **Fujiwara Michinaga**, when the Fujiwara clan was at its peak (see "History", p.935). His son, Yorimichi, continued developing the gardens and pavilions until they were the envy of the court. Those pavilions have long gone, but you can still catch a flavour of this golden age through the great literary masterpiece, *The Tale of Genji* (see "Books", p.1019), written in the early eleventh century. The book's final chapters are set in Uji, which the authoress, Murasaki Shikibu, would have known intimately – a distant relative of Fujiwara Michinaga, she served as lady-in-waiting to his daughter, Empress Akiko. In 1052, some years after *The Genji* was completed, Yorimichi decided to convert the villa into a temple dedicated to Amida, the Buddha of the Western Paradise. By the following year the great Amida Hall, popularly known as the **Phoenix Hall** (*Hōō-dō*), was completed. Miraculously, it's the only building from the original temple to have survived (though it's currently closed for refurbishment until August 2005).

The best place to view the Phoenix Hall is from the far side of the pond in which it sits on a small island. The hall itself is surprisingly small, but the architect has added two completely ornamental wings which extend in a broad U, like a pair of open arms. The whole ensemble is in perfect balance, while the little turrets, upward-sweeping roofs and airy, open spaces create a graceful, gossamer-light structure which appears to float on the reflecting water. A third corridor extends west behind the main hall, giving the building its distinctive, birdlike ground plan from which its name is said to derive. However, the phoenix is also an ancient Chinese image of rebirth, which is what this building, and its now much-diminished garden, represents. According to Buddhist teachings, Amida promised to save all souls who faithfully beseech his name and to lead them to the Pure Land, the Western Paradise. The splendour of the hall and the images inside are all reminders of that promise of ultimate salvation.

The gilded statue of **Amida** dominates the hall. It was created by a sculptor-priest called Jōchō, using a new method of slotting together carved blocks of wood, and is in remarkably fine condition. Interestingly, at this time Chinese influence in Japan was waning and artists were establishing a fresh, purely Japanese stylistic form. Already, the statue's gentle expression and softer, more human body set it apart from earlier Buddhist images. Again the impression is one of Amida floating on his lotus throne – a clever, stylistic trick in which a narrow pedestal supports four layers of gilded petals in strict alignment rather than the normal staggered arrangement. A golden, flaming halo, decorated with twelve barely visible Bodhisattvas, swoops up behind the statue to a richly decorated canopy inlaid with mother-of-pearl.

At one time the hall must have been a riot of colour, but now only a few traces of the **wall paintings** remain, most of which are reproductions. If you look very carefully, you can just make out faded images of Amida and a host of heavenly beings descending on billowing clouds to receive the faithful. Meanwhile the white, upper walls are decorated with a unique collection of 52 carved Bodhisattvas, which were also painted at one time. Each delicate, wooden figure rides a wisp of clouds, and they're all busy either dancing, playing an instrument, praying or carrying religious symbols.

The original wall paintings, as well as the temple bell and two phoenixes, are now preserved in a modern **treasure hall** (*Hōmotsu-kan*; ¥500) on a hill behind the Phoenix Hall. Unfortunately, the treasures only go on view in spring and

KANSAI | Around Kyoto

autumn, but if you get the chance it's worth seeing them close up. These are now the oldest examples of the emerging *Yamato-e* style of painting (see p.967) still in existence.

On the opposite, north side of the temple compound, the twelfth-century **Kannon-dō** houses a gently smiling statue of the eleven-headed Kannon, while behind it you'll find a fenced-off triangle of grass. This "**fan-shaped lawn**" is revered as the place where Minamoto Yorimasa, a valiant warrior of the Genpei Wars (see p.935), committed ritual suicide in 1180, at the age of 76. After a bitter struggle, his small army was completely overrun when the rival Taira army swept across the river. Yorimasa retreated inside the temple gates and, while his son held off the attackers, penned a quick poem on his war fan before disembowelling himself. His words: "How sad that the old fossil tree should die without a single blooming."

Practicalities

Uji lies on the JR Nara line between Kyoto and Nara, with **trains** roughly every fifteen minutes from Kyoto (15–30min) and every twenty minutes from Nara (30–50min). There's a **tourist information office** (daily 9am–5pm; ☎0774/23-3334) further along the riverbank from the Byōdō-in, next door to a traditional **teahouse**, the *Taiho-an*, where you can try Uji's famous green tea (Jan 10 to Dec 20 daily 10am–4pm; ¥500). On summer evenings the river here is used for demonstrations of **cormorant fishing** (see p.478); it's best experienced from one of the fishing boats (mid-June to early Sept 7–8.30pm; ¥1800).

In fine weather it's a nice idea to buy a bentō and eat it on the little island in the Uji-gawa. You'll find plenty of snack shops and **restaurants** as you walk down from the station, but *Magozaemon*, opposite the entrance to the Byōdō-in, has especially good and inexpensive handmade noodle dishes – try their green-tea udon, either hot or cold.

Nara and around

Before Kyoto became the capital of Japan in 794 AD, this honour was held by **NARA**, a town some 35km further south in an area which is regarded as the birthplace of Japanese civilization. During this period, particularly the seventh and eighth centuries, Buddhism became firmly established within Japan under the patronage of court nobles, who sponsored magnificent temples and works of art, many of which have survived to this day. Fortunately, history subsequently left Nara largely to its own devices and it's now a relaxed, attractive place set against a backdrop of wooded hills. Its greatest draw is undoubtedly the monumental bronze Buddha of **Tōdai-ji**, while **Kōfuku-ji** and several of the smaller temples boast outstanding collections of Buddhist statuary. However, even these are outclassed by the images housed in **Hōryū-ji**, a temple to the southwest of Nara, which also claims the world's oldest wooden building. The nearby temples of **Yakushi-ji** and **Tōshōdai-ji** contain yet more early masterpieces of Japanese art and architecture.

Nara has the added attraction of packing all these sights into a fairly compact space. The central area is easily explored on foot, and can just about be covered in a long day, with the more distant temples fitting into a second day's outing. Many people visit Nara on a day-trip from Kyoto, but it more than deserves an overnight stop, not least to enjoy it once the crowds have gone. If at all possible, try to avoid Nara on Sundays and holidays.

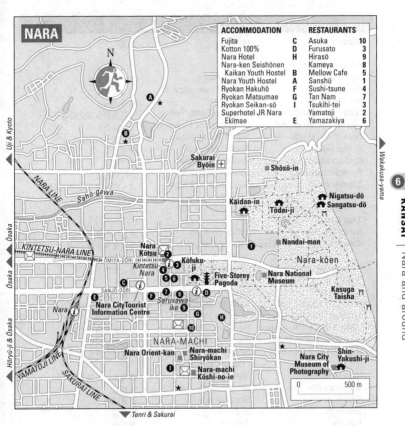

NARA

ACCOMMODATION		RESTAURANTS	
Fujita	C	Asuka	10
Kotton 100%	D	Furusato	3
Nara Hotel	H	Hirasō	9
Nara-ken Seishōnen		Kameya	8
Kaikan Youth Hostel	B	Mellow Cafe	5
Nara Youth Hostel	A	Sanshū	1
Ryokan Hakuhō	F	Sushi-tsune	4
Ryokan Matsumae	G	Tan Nam	7
Ryokan Seikan-sō	I	Tsukihi-tei	3
Superhotel JR Nara		Yamatoji	2
Ekīmae	E	Yamazakiya	6

Some history

During the fifth and sixth centuries a sophisticated culture evolved in the plains east of Ōsaka, an area known as **Yamato**. Close contact between Japan, Korea and China saw the introduction of Chinese script, technology and the Buddhist religion, as well as Chinese ideas on law and administration. Under these influences, the regent **Prince Shōtoku** (574–622) established a strictly hierarchical system of government. However, he's probably best remembered as a devout Buddhist who founded numerous temples, amongst them the great **Hōryū-ji**. Though Shōtoku's successors continued the process of centralization, they were hampered by the practice of relocating the court after each emperor died. In 710 AD, therefore, it was decided to establish a permanent capital modelled on China's imperial city, Chang'an (today's Xi'an). The name chosen for this new city was **Heijō**, "Citadel of Peace", today known as **Nara**.

In fact Heijō lasted little more than seventy years, but it was a glorious period, which saw Japanese culture beginning to take shape. A frenzy of building and artistic creativity culminated in the unveiling of the great bronze Buddha in **Tōdai-ji** temple by **Emperor Shōmu** in 752 AD. But beneath the surface things were starting to unravel. As the temples became increasingly powerful, so the monks began to dabble in politics, until one Dōkyō seduced a former empress and tried to seize the throne in 769. In an attempt to escape such

Nara	Nara	奈良

Accommodation

Hotel Fujita	Hoteru Fujita	ホテルフジタ
Kotton 100%	Kotton Hyaku-pāsento	古っ都ん１００％
Nara Hotel	Nara Hoteru	奈良ホテル
Nara-ken Seishōnen Kaikan Youth Hostel	Nara-ken Seishōnen Kaikan Yūsu Hosuteru	奈良県青少年会館ユースホステル
Nara Youth Hostel	Nara Yūsu Hosuteru	奈良ユースホステル
Ryokan Hakuhō	Ryokan Hakuhō	旅館白鳳
Ryokan Matsumae	Ryokan Matsumae	旅館松前
Ryokan Seikan-sō	Ryokan Seikan-sō	旅館靜観荘
Superhotel JR Nara Ekimae	Sūpahoterū JR Nara Ekimae	スーパーホテルJR奈良駅前

The City

Ashibi-no-Sato	Ashibi-no-Sato	あしびの郷
Kikuoka Kampō Yakkyoku	Kikuoka Kampō Yakkyoku	菊岡漢方薬局
Kasuga Taisha	Kasuga Taisha	春日大社
Kōfuku-ji	Kōfuku-ji	興福寺
Nara-kōen	Nara-kōen	奈良公園
Nara City Museum of Photography	Nara-shi Shashin Bijutsukan	奈良市写真美術館
Nara-machi Kōshi-no-ie	Nara-machi Kōshi-no-ie	ならまち格子の家
Nara-machi Shiryōkan	Nara-machi Shiryōkan	奈良町資料館
Nara National Museum	Nara Kokuritsu Hakubutsukan	奈良国立博物館
Nara Orient-kan	Nara Oriento-kan	奈良オリエント館
Sangatsu-dō	Sangatsu-dō	三月堂
Shin-Yakushi-ji	Shin-Yakushi-ji	新薬師寺
Shōsō-in	Shōsō-in	正倉院
Tōdai-ji	Tōdai-ji	東大寺

Restaurants

Asuka	Asuka	飛鳥
Furusato	Furusato	ふる里
Hirasō	Hirasō	平宗
Kameya	Kameya	かめ屋
Sanshū	Sanshū	三秀
Sushi-tsune	Sushi-tsune	寿し常
Tsukihi-tei	Tsukihi-tei	月日亭
Yamatoji	Yamatoji	大和路
Yamazakiya	Yamazakiya	山崎屋

shenanigans, Emperor Kammu decided to move the court out of Nara in 784, and eventually founded Kyoto.

Arrival, information and city transport

Nara has two competing **train stations**: the JR Nara Station (currently being redeveloped), on the west side of the town centre, and the private Kintetsu-Nara Station right in the thick of things. Arriving **from Kyoto**, the quickest option is a Limited Express train on the private Kintetsu–Kyoto line (every 30min; 33min; ¥1110); the ordinary express takes a little longer and you have to change at Yamato-Saidaiji (1–2 hourly; 45min; ¥610). JR also has a choice of express trains (8 daily; 45min; ¥740) and regular trains (every 30min; 1hr 20min; ¥740) from Kyoto. Travelling **from Ōsaka**, trains on the private Kintetsu–Nara line (from Ōsaka's Kintetsu-Namba Station) arrive at the Kintetsu–Nara Station (every 15min; 30–40min; ¥540–1040). Alternatively, take a JR line train from Ōsaka Station (every 20min; 40min; ¥780) or from JR Namba Station (every 20min; 30–40min; ¥740) to JR Nara Station. If you're coming here **from Kansai International airport**, you can go into central Ōsaka to pick up a train, or hop on a limousine bus (hourly; 1hr 35min; ¥1800), which stops at both Nara's train stations.

Nara is also well provided with **information offices**. The most useful of these is the Nara City Tourist Information Centre (daily 9am–9pm; ℡0742/22-3900, ℻22-5595), located on Sanjō-dōri. They have English-speaking staff, plentiful **maps** and information, and can also help arrange volunteer "Goodwill Guides" (see p.28). There's also an office in the JR Station (daily 9am–5pm; ℡ & ℻0742/22-9821) – the English-speaking staff here can make hotel bookings – and another in the Kintetsu Station (daily 9am–5pm; ℡ & ℻0742/24-4858). Finally, you'll find a small booth on the hill above the Sarusawa pond, near the five-storey pagoda (daily 9am–5pm; ℡ & ℻0742/26-1991), on the eastern edge of central Nara. The Nara City office carries some information about **what's on**, as does the region-wide magazine, *Kansai Time Out* (see p.496). JNTO's Nara website is at ⓦwww.jnto.go.jp/eng/RTG/RI/kansai/nara/nara/nara.html.

City transport

The centre of Nara is small enough to be covered on foot, though you'll need to use local **buses** for some of the more far-flung sights. The main termini are outside the JR and Kintetsu-Nara train stations. Nearly all the timetables and route maps are in Japanese, but the one-sheet "Nara Sightseeing Map", available at the tourist offices, has a summary of the most useful routes. The standard fare is ¥180 within the city centre, which you usually pay as you get on, though buses going out of central Nara employ a ticket system – take a numbered ticket as you board and pay the appropriate fare on exit. If you're heading for the sights around Nara, there is a range of **bus passes**, of which the most helpful is the *Nara Nishinokyō Ikaruga Furii-ken* (¥1600). This covers unlimited travel for one day in central Nara and the western districts, including Hōryū-ji, Yakushi-ji and Tōshōdai-ji. A cheaper version, which excludes Hōryū-ji, is available for ¥810. A third kind of one-day pass, the *Gurutto Basu Furii Jōshaken* (¥800), allows you to jump on a special sightseeing bus (daily late March to early June & Oct–Nov; Sat & Sun only early to late March and mid-June to Sept) that covers Nara's main sights, including Yakushi-ji and Tōshōdai-ji. The advantage of this is that it takes you directly to the main sights and you don't have to wrestle with the city's public bus service; the disadvantage is that the bus only makes its rounds once an hour. The first bus leaves from in front of JR Nara Station at 8:57am. You can buy all these passes in the Nara Kōtsū bus office (daily 8.30am–6pm), across Ōmiya-dōri from the Kintetsu train station.

Nara Kōtsū (℡0742/22-5263) runs a number of **bus tours** where you'll be given a cassette recorder with taped information in English. Again, the tours covering the surrounding sights are most useful: a full day-trip round the Nishinokyō and Ikaruga areas, for example, costs ¥6660. JTB's Sunrise Tours (℡075/341-1413) also offers half-day excursions to Nara from Kyoto and

Ōsaka. They're accompanied by an English-speaking guide, but only cover Tōdai-ji and Kasuga Taisha.

Another option for central Nara is **bike rental**. You'll find Eki Rent-a-Cycle (daily 9am–5pm; ¥1000 per day) outside the JR Station, and Sunflower Rent-a-Cycle (daily 9am–5pm; ¥1000–1200 per day, or ¥2000 for two days) southeast of the Kintetsu Station.

Accommodation

Nara has some unusual **accommodation** options, ranging from a former geisha house to the grand old *Nara Hotel*, whose guests have included Albert Einstein and Deng Xiaoping. There's plenty of choice in the city centre, but you'll need to book ahead at weekends and during the spring and autumn peaks. Note that the smarter places tend to put their rates up at these times.

Hotel Fujita 47-1 Sanjō-chō ℡0742/23-8111, Ⓦwww.fujita-kanko.co.jp/english/city/hfnara/index.html. A reasonably smart, surprisingly affordable business hotel right on Sanjō-dōri. The rooms are nothing exciting, but they're all comfortable and en suite. **⑥**

Kotton 100% 1122-21 Bodai-chō, Takabatake ℡0742/22-7117. The rooms are small and rather worn, but the central location on the edge of Nara-kōen, just east of Sarusawa-ike, is a plus. **⑤**

Nara Hotel Nara Deer Park ℡0742/26-3300, Ⓦwww.hotels.westjr.co.jp/nara. Nara's top hotel occupies a stylish, Meiji-era building, set in its own gardens within Nara-kōen. Ask for a room in the old wing for the full works – high ceilings, fireplaces, period furniture and original baths. **⑦**

Nara-ken Seishōnen Kaikan Youth Hostel 72-7 Ikenoue Handa, Hiraki-chō ℡0742/22-5540, Ⓔnaseikan@galaxy.ocn.ne.jp. You're assured of a friendly welcome at the Nara Prefecture hostel, located in a residential area just behind the main *Nara Youth Hostel* (see below). They also offer very reasonable bike rental (¥300 per day). There are several buses from the stations (#12, #13, #131, #140) which will drop you at the Ikuei Gakuen-mae stop, a five-minute walk from the hostel. Dorm beds ¥2650 per person, rooms **②**

Nara Youth Hostel 1716 Horen-chō ℡0742/22-1334, Ⓦhttp://www5.ocn.ne.jp/~narayout/english/neweng.html. Large, modern hostel with dor-

mitory rooms and good facilities, though a little soulless. Check-in is from 3pm and there's a 10pm curfew. The hostel's in northwest Nara, a ten-minute bus ride (bus #108, #109, #111, #115, #130) from either the JR or Kintetsu stations; get off at the Shieikujō stop in front of the hostel. Dorm beds ¥3150 per person.

Ryokan Hakuhō 4-1 Kamisanjō-chō ℡0742/26-7891, Ⓕ26-7893. This friendly little guesthouse on Sanjō-dōri offers a choice of tatami rooms with or without bath. Slightly aged, but reasonable value for the location. **⑤**

Ryokan Matsumae 28-1 Higashi-Terabayashi-chō ℡0742/22-3686, Ⓕ26-3927. Welcoming ryokan in an interesting area south of Sarusawa-ike. The spruce, Japanese-style rooms come with or without private bathrooms. **④**

Ryokan Seikan-sō 29 Higashi-Kitsuji-chō ℡ & Ⓕ0742/22-2670. Though it's a little out of the centre and the rooms are a bit frayed, this old ryokan has a lovely atmosphere and a colourful past – half of it was once a geisha house. It's in the Nara-machi area, about ten minutes' walk south of Sanjō-dōri. **④**

Superhotel JR Nara Ekimae 500-1 Sanjō-dōri ℡0742/20-9000, Ⓕ20-9008. The city's newest hotel, right in front of the JR Nara Station and part of the hugely popular Superhotel chain. Rooms are functional and clean, if a bit small, but offer excellent value, especially the singles. **⑤**

The City

More a large town than a city, Nara is an enjoyable place to explore. There are plentiful English-language signs, the grid street system makes for easy navigation, and the main sights are all gathered on the city's eastern edge in the green expanse of **Nara-kōen**. The route outlined below starts with the most important temples, **Kōfuku-ji** and **Tōdai-ji**, before ambling south along the eastern hills. Here you'll find a sprinkling of second-tier sights, including Nara's holiest shrine, **Kasuga Taisha**, and splendid displays of Buddhist statuary in two historic temples, **Sangatsu-dō** and **Shin-Yakushi-ji**. With an extra hour or two to spare, it's worth wandering the streets of southerly **Nara-machi**, a tra-ditional merchants' quarter where some attractive old shophouses have been converted into museums and craft shops.

Nara-kōen

The most pleasant route into **Nara-kōen** is along Sanjō-dōri, which cuts across the central district and brings you out near Sarasuwa-ike with the **Five-Storey Pagoda** rising from the trees to your left. The pagoda belongs to **Kōfuku-ji**, which in the eighth century was one of Nara's great temples. It was founded in 669 AD by a member of the Fujiwara clan, and moved to its present location when Nara became the new capital in 710. For a while it prospered, but when the Fujiwara star began to fade in the twelfth century, Kōfuku-ji lost its power-ful patrons and now only a handful of buildings remain from that period.

The prime draw here is the fine collection of **Buddhist statues** contained in the Tōkon-dō (daily 9am–5pm; ¥300; ☎0742-22-7755) and the Kokuhōkan (same hours; ¥500). The **Tōkon-dō**, a fifteenth-century hall to the north of the Five-Storey Pagoda, is dominated by a large image of Yakushi Nyorai, the Buddha of Healing. He's flanked by three Bodhisattvas, the Four Heavenly Kings and the Twelve Heavenly Generals, all beady-eyed guardians of the faith, some of which date from the eighth century. Perhaps the most interesting statue, though, is the seated figure of Yuima Koji to the left of Yakushi Nyorai; depicting an ordinary mortal rather than a celestial being, it's a touchingly realistic portrait.

Festivals and annual events

Several of Nara's **festivals** have been celebrated for well over a thousand years. Many of these are dignified court dances, though some of the fire rituals are more lively affairs. In spring and autumn the New Public Hall (☎0742/27-2630) in Nara-kōen stages a series of **Nō dramas**, while the biggest cultural event of the year is undoubt-edly the autumn exhibition of **Shōsō-in treasures** at the National Museum (see p.580).

Jan 15 Yama-yaki (Grass-burning festival). On a winter evening at 6pm, priests from Kōfuku-ji set fire to the grass on Wakakusa-yama – watched by a few hundred firemen. The festival commemorates the settlement of a boundary dispute between Nara's warrior monks.

March 1–14 O-Taimatsu and O-Mizutori (Torch lighting and water drawing). A 1200-year-old ceremony which commemorates a priest's dream about Kannon draw-ing water from a holy well. The climax is on the night of March 13. At around 6.30pm priests on the second-floor veranda light huge torches and scatter sparks over the assembled crowds to protect them from evil spirits. At 2am the priests collect water from the well, after which they whirl more lighted flares round in a frenzied dance.

May 11–12 Takigi Nō. Outdoor performances of Nō dramas by firelight at Kōfuku-ji.

September Uneme Matsuri. Every September, on the night of the harvest moon, the Uneme Matsuri takes place at the Sausawa-ike Pond. The festival is a dedica-tion to Uneme, a court lady who drowned herself in the pond after losing the favour of the emperor. At around 7pm two dragon-bowed boats bearing costumed partic-ipants and *gagaku* musicians commemorate the lady's death in multicoloured splen-dour. The festival lasts until 9.30pm.

Early to mid-Oct Shika-no-Tsunokiri (Antler cutting). You might want to give Sundays a miss during October. This is the season when the deer in Nara-kōen are wrestled to the ground and have their antlers sawn off by Shinto priests. It all takes place in the Roku-en deer pen, near Kasuga Taisha. Check locally for exact dates.

Dec 17 On-matsuri. At around midday a grand costume parade sets off from the prefectural offices to Kasuga Wakamiya-jinja, stopping on the way for various cere-monies. It ends with outdoor performances of Nō and various courtly dances.

The modern **Kokuhōkan** is a veritable treasure trove of early Buddhist statues. The most famous image is the standing figure of **Ashura**, one of Buddha's eight protectors, instantly recognizable from his three red-tinted heads and six spindly arms. Look out, too, for his companion Karura (Garuda) with his beaked head. Though they're not all on display at the same time, these eight protectors are considered to be the finest dry-lacquer images of the Nara period. Surprisingly, the large, **bronze Buddha head**, with its fine, crisp features, comes from an even earlier period. Apart from a crumpled left ear, the head is in remarkably good condition considering that the original, complete statue was stolen by Kōfuku-ji's warrior priests from another temple sometime during the Heian period (794–1185). Then, after a fire destroyed its body, the head was buried beneath the replacement Buddha, only to be rediscovered in 1937 during renovation work.

From Kōfuku-ji you can stroll generally northeast through the park, towards Tōdai-ji. The large, grassy area is kept trim by more than a thousand semi-wild **deer**. They were originally regarded as divine messengers of one of Kasuga-jinja's Shinto gods, and anyone who killed a deer was liable to be dispatched shortly after. During World War II the numbers dwindled to just seventy beasts, but now they're back with a vengeance – which makes picnicking impossible and presents something of a hazard to young children.

In the midst of the park you'll come across a grey, Western-style building, erected in 1894, which houses the main exhibits of the **Nara National Museum** (Tues–Sun 9am–4.30pm; ¥420, ¥830 for special exhibitions; ℡0742/22-7771, ⓦwww.narahaku.go.jp/index_e.html). As you'd imagine, the museum's strong point is its superb collection of statues, of which only a small part is on display at any one time. They're arranged chronologically, so you can trace the development of the various styles, and there's plenty of English-language information available, though the presentation is pretty unexciting. Each autumn (late Oct to early Nov) the museum is closed for two weeks while an exhibition of the **Shōsō-in treasures** takes place in the newer annexe next door. This priceless collection was donated to Tōdai-ji in 756 by Empress Kōmyō, on the death of her husband Emperor Shōmu, and then added to in 950. It contains unique examples of Buddhist art and ritual objects, musical instruments, household utensils, glassware and games, not only from eighth-century Japan but also from China, Korea, India and Persia. The exhibition takes a different theme each year, so what you see is very much the luck of the draw.

Tōdai-ji

For many people Nara is synonymous with **Tōdai-ji**. This great temple was founded in 745 by **Emperor Shōmu**, ostensibly to ward off the terrible epidemics that regularly swept the nation, but also as a means of cementing imperial power. In doing so he nearly bankrupted his young nation, but the political message came across loud and clear and soon an extensive network of sub-temples spread throughout the provinces, where they played an important role in local administration. It took more than fifteen years to complete Tōdai-ji, which isn't surprising when you learn that the main hall is still the world's largest wooden building. Even so, the present structure (last rebuilt in 1709) is only two-thirds the size of the original. Avoid visiting Tōdai-ji at weekends, especially during the spring and autumn, the two peak times for visiting Nara, when the temple is overrun with thousands of tourists.

The main entrance to Tōdai-ji lies through the suitably impressive **Nandai-mon**, or Great Southern Gate. Rebuilt in the thirteenth century, it shelters two wonderfully expressive guardian gods (*Niō*), each over 7m tall. Beyond, you begin to see the horned, sweeping roof of the **Daibutsu-den**, the Great Buddha Hall (daily: March–Oct 7.30am–5/5.30pm; Jan, Feb, Nov & Dec 8am–4.30pm; ¥500; ☎0742/47-5511), which houses Japan's largest bronze statue. A fifteen-metre-tall, blackened figure on a lotus throne, the great Buddha (*Daibutsu*) seems to strain at the very walls of the building. It depicts Rushana (later known as Dainichi Nyorai), the Cosmic Buddha who presides over all levels of the Buddhist universe, and was a phenomenal achievement for the time. Not surprisingly, several attempts at casting the Buddha failed, but in 752 the (then) retired Emperor Shōmu, his wife Empress Kōmyō and the reigning Empress Kōgen gathered to dedicate the gilded statue by symbolically "opening" its eyes. To achieve this, an Indian priest stood on a special platform and "painted" the eyes with a huge brush, from which coloured strings trailed down to the assembled dignitaries, enabling them to participate in the ceremony. Not only were there hundreds of local monks, but also ambassadors from China, India and further afield, bearing an amazing array of gifts, many of which have been preserved in the Shōsō-in treasury – as has the original paintbrush.

The Buddha has had a rough time of it since then. As early as the ninth century an earthquake toppled his head, then it and his right hand melted in a fire in 1180 and again in 1567. As a result only tiny fragments of the original statue remain intact, the rest being made up of patchwork parts put together over the centuries – not that you're likely to notice, however. Nonetheless, the remodelled giant is definitely large, and it's hard not to be impressed by the technological triumph involved in recreating it. As you walk round the hall, don't be surprised to see people trying to squeeze through a hole in one of the rear supporting pillars – success apparently reserves you a corner of paradise.

Walk west from the Daibutsu-den compound and you'll find the more modest **Kaidan-in** (daily 7.30/8am–4.30/5pm; ¥400), which was established in 754 as Japan's first, and foremost, ordination hall. It was founded by a Chinese high priest, Ganjin, who Emperor Shōmu hoped would instil some discipline into the rapidly expanding Buddhist priesthood. He had to be patient, however; poor Ganjin's ship eventually arrived on the sixth attempt, by which time the priest was 67 years old and completely blind. His ordination hall was rebuilt in the Edo period, but the statues inside include eighth-century representations of the Four Heavenly Kings (*Shi-Tennō*). These small, beautifully crafted clay figures, each standing on a different demonic beast, protect a diminutive Buddha inside a wooden pagoda.

If you've got time to spare, circle round behind the Daibutsu-den to take a peak at the **Shōsō-in** (Mon–Fri 10am–3pm; free). Though it looks like a modern log cabin on stilts, this storehouse was erected in the eighth century to hold the massed treasures of Tōdai-ji. Whatever the secret, it preserved them in immaculate condition – as witnessed at the National Museum's annual exhibition (see opposite). Nowadays, however, they're kept in a specially designed concrete repository. The nearby **Daibutsu Pond** is a tranquil spot even on busy weekends – a good place to relax and watch the local amateur painters who gather here with their brushes and canvases.

Along the eastern hills

Two of Tōdai-ji's sub-temples were built on the slopes of Wakakusa-yama, which forms Nara's eastern boundary. Northerly **Nigatsu-dō** (daily 8am–5pm; free) offers good views over the city from its wooden terrace. Next door, **Sangatsu-dō** (daily 8am–4.30/5pm; ¥400) is Nara's oldest building, completed in 729, and contains another rare collection of eighth-century, dry-lacquer statues. The main image is a dimly lit, gilded figure of Kannon, bearing a silver Amida in its crown, while all around stand gods, guardians, Bodhisattvas and other protectors of the faith.

From Sangatsu-dō it's a pleasant stroll south along the Wakakusa hillside, past a handy string of restaurants and up the lantern-lined approach to **Kasuga Taisha** (Kasuga Grand Shrine). This was founded in 768 as the tutelary shrine of the Fujiwara family and, for a while, held an important place in Shinto worship; indeed, the emperor still sends a messenger to participate in shrine rituals. As with many shrines, however, there's not a great deal to see unless you happen to coincide with a special service or festival (see p.579). The four sanctuaries, gleaming after their 59th reconstruction, are just visible in the inner compound, while the thousand beautifully crafted bronze **lanterns** hanging round the outer eaves are easier to admire. Donated over the years by supplicants, they bear intricate designs of deer, wisteria blooms, leaves or geometric patterns. The best time to see them is in early February (Feb 3) and mid-August (Aug 14–15), when these and the nearly two thousand stone lanterns are lit at dusk.

Continuing south through the woods from Kasuga Taisha, cross over the main road into an attractive residential area. Five minutes further on you'll come to the venerable **Shin-Yakushi-ji** (daily 9am–5pm; ¥500; ☎0742/22-3736). This quiet temple stands in a courtyard full of bush clover, much as it has done for the last 1250 years. It was founded by Empress Kōmyō to pray for Emperor Shōmu's recovery from an eye infection; apparently she had some success since he lived for another decade. Though the hall may not look terribly imposing, it's the original, and inside you'll find more Buddhist statues of a similar age. The central image is a plump-faced, slightly cross-eyed Yakushi Nyorai (the Buddha of Healing), carved from one block of cypress wood. He's surrounded by clay statues of the Twelve Heavenly Generals, of which only one has had to be replaced. It's worth the walk just to see their wonderful expressions and innovative hairdos.

Another good reason for visiting this area is the **Nara City Museum of Photography** (Tues–Sun 9.30am–5pm; ¥500; ☎0742/22-9811), which lies a few metres west of Shin-Yakushi-ji in a sleek, modern and almost completely underground building. Its core collection consists of some 80,000 photos by the late Irie Taikichi, who spent most of his life capturing Nara and its temples on film. In addition, there's a fascinating group of two thousand photos of Nara during the Taishō period (1912–25) taken by Kudo Risaburo. The exhibitions change every three months, but the collection can always be viewed on video in the museum's Hi-Vision gallery.

Nara-machi

The southern district of central Nara is known as **Nara-machi**. There are no great temples here, but instead an attractive area of traditional shops and lattice-front houses off the main tourist path. The best approach is to start by the southwest corner of willow-fringed Sarusawa-ike, a good spot for views of the Five-Storey Pagoda, and then head south. At the end of the road is an enticing little shop, **Kikuoka Kampō Yakkyoku**, selling all sorts of traditional Chinese medicines and, next door, **Nara-machi Monogatari-kan** (daily 10am–5pm; free; ☎0742/26-3476), which shows changing exhibitions of local crafts. Turn right (west) in front of these two and you'll find **Nara-machi Shiryōkan** (Tues–Sun 10am–4pm; free; ☎0742/22-5509), on the next corner. Marked by strings of red-cloth monkeys hanging outside, this small museum occupies the former warehouse of a mosquito-net manufacturer and houses a wonderful jumble of household utensils, shop signboards, Buddhist statues, pots and so forth from the local area.

Turn left (south) beside the Shiryōkan for the **Nara Orient-kan** (Tues–Sun 10am–5pm), an interesting old merchant's house consisting of two traditional storehouses (*kura*) linked by a long corridor. It's now home to a sub-studio of Nara FM radio station, as well as doubling as a café during the day and a relaxed, intimate setting for all sorts of live music in the evening. Follow this road round to the left and turn south again, past a sub-post office. Just before the next corner the lovingly restored latticed facade of **Nara-machi Kōshi-no-ie** (Tues–Sun 9am–5pm; free) announces one of the area's best-preserved traditional townhouses. Inside, you can see the line of tatami rooms off a high-ceilinged corridor, inner courtyard garden and beautiful wooden furniture favoured by successful Edo-period merchants.

You're now near the southern limits of Nara-machi. To return to central Nara, take the next road parallel to the west, which will eventually lead to the arcades and Sanjō-dōri. On the way, look out for **Ashibi-no-sato**, an old-style shop selling pickles and tea, where you can also have light meals, and **Esaki** on the corner – unmissable thanks to its jaunty lanterns and shopful of traditional umbrellas.

Eating

You're spoiled for choice when it comes to eating in Nara. The central Higashimuki arcade is the best place to look, or along Sanjō-dōri, where you'll find a range of hamburger joints, coffee shops and a clutch of decent **restaurants** serving classy local cuisine. Like Kyoto, Nara has its own brand of *kaiseki*, the elaborate meals that originally accompanied the tea ceremony, but **local specialities** also include some rather less appetizing dishes. *Cha-ga-yu* evolved from the poor people's breakfast into a fairly expensive delicacy, but there's no escaping the fact that it's basically a thin rice gruel, boiled up with soya beans, sweet potatoes and green tea leaves. It's best as part of a *teishoku*, when the accompaniments add a bit of flavour. *Tororo* is pretty similar: thickened grated yam mixed with soy sauce, seaweed and barley, then poured over a bowl of rice – full of protein and rather sticky. Less of an acquired taste is sushi wrapped in persimmon leaves and *Nara-zuke*, vegetables pickled in sake.

Asuka 1 Shonami-chō ☎0742/26-4308. A sleek tempura restaurant in the attractive Nara-machi district. At lunchtime you can feast on their beautifully presented bentō (¥1500), or menus from around ¥2000. Closed Mon.

Furusato 10 Higashimuki-dōri ☎0742/22-2828. This unpretentious restaurant serving a range of hearty Japanese fare is hidden behind a traditional sweet shop near the north end of the arcade. There's an English menu, or see what catches your eye in their window display. Tues–Sun 11.30am–8.30pm.

Hirasō 30-1 Imanikadō-chō ☎0742/22-0866. Hirasō specializes in persimmon-wrapped sushi, though you'll also find all sorts of other tasty delicacies on the menu. Sushi sets start at ¥820, with more varied meals from around ¥2400, including *cha-ga-yu*. Closed Mon.

Kameya 6 Hashimoto-chō ☎0742/22-2434. Popular, nicely decorated *okonomiyaki* joint. Prices start at ¥600 and there's an English menu available. Closed Tues.

Mellow Café Axe Unit, 1–8 Konishi-chō ☎0742/27-9099. Large, open-plan café-restaurant with a counter bar and cake shop to boot, located in a faux-Spanish-style shopping arcade 50m south of the Vivre department store, on the opposite side of the road. Lunch specials start at ¥700, while the daily "Mellow Lunch" offers unlimited amounts of freshly baked bread. Daily 11am–10.30pm.

Sushi-tsune Konishi-dōri ☎0742/22-2310. Tastefully decorated sushi bar in a traditional building opposite Vivre department store. They do a good-value lunchtime *teishoku* for around ¥1000, as well as *chirashi* (a box of rice topped with sashimi and vegetables), or individual pieces (from ¥350). Closed Tues.

Sanshū Isui-en ☎0742/25-0781. *Tororo* isn't everyone's cup of tea, but this is an attractive place to find out, located in an old wooden house overlooking the secluded, Meiji-era Isui-en garden. There are just two meals on the menu: plain *mugi tororo* (¥1200) or *unagi tororo* laced with eels

(¥2500). Daily except Tues 11.30am–1.30pm.

Tan Nam 1F, Hattori Building, 15-2 Tsunofuri-chō ☎0742/22-9498. Cheerful Vietnamese restaurant down a small alley off Sanjō-dōri – the big sign makes it hard to miss. Food is authentic and portions filling. There's no English on the menu, but colour photos make ordering a breeze.

Tsukihi-tei 2F, Higashimuki-dōri ☎0742/23-5470. One of the best places to sample Nara *kaiseki* at an affordable price. A full *kaiseki* course starts at ¥6300, with mini-*kaiseki* from ¥3500; reservations are required for your own tatami dining room. They also do cheaper *teishoku*.

Yamatoji 4F & 5F, 6 Nakasuji-chō ☎0742/24-4529. Located above the Nara Kōtsū bus office, these two restaurants offer reasonable-value meals. The fourth floor is an *izakaya*-style place where you can get *cha-ga-yu* for breakfast (¥860) and cheap *teishoku*. Upstairs is smarter, with tempura, shabu-shabu and *so on* (sets from ¥1500).

Yamazakiya Higashimuki-dōri ☎0742/27-3715. Pleasantly relaxed restaurant behind a large pickle shop at the south end of the arcade. They offer *kaiseki* cuisine from ¥4000 for a sampler, and *cha-ga-yu* (¥2200 for a *teishoku*), or try the excellent-value Nara bentō (¥1500). Closed Mon.

Listings

Banks and exchange You'll find several banks with foreign-exchange desks, including Kinki Ōsaka Bank, Mizuho Bank and Nara Bank, on Sanjō-dōri.

Buses Long-distance buses for Tokyo (Shinjuku) and Yokohama stop outside both the Kintetsu and JR Nara train stations.

Car rental Eki Rent-a-Car (☎0742/26-3929) is next door to JR Nara Station, while Toyota Rent-a-Car (☎0742/22-0100) and Nippon Rent-a-Car (☎0742/24-5701) have branches near the Kintetsu Station.

Hospital Nara's main hospital is the Sakurai Byōin, 2 Imako-chō (☎0742/26-0277), with a 24hr emergency department. It's located on the main road, Tegai-dōri, northwest of Tōdai-ji.

Internet access Nara City Tourist Information Centre has a full list of places offering Internet access. The snazziest place in town is the new NTT West Nara@Square (daily 10am–7pm) on Sanjō-dōri. Computers are state-of-the-art, the staff are friendly, the fibre-optic broadband connection is superfast and, best of all, it's free.

Post offices Nara's Central Post Office is on Ōmiya-dōri, a fair walk west of centre. It has 24hr mail services, but for other purposes the sub-post offices in the centre of town (see map on p.575) are more convenient.

Shopping Among a range of local crafts, Nara is particularly renowned for its high-quality *sumi-e* ink, calligraphy brushes (*fude*), tea whisks (*chasen*) and bleached hemp cloth (*sarashi*). You'll find all these on sale along the main shopping streets, or try the Nara Prefectural Commerce, Industry and Tourist Hall, on Ōmiya-dōri to the east of Kintetsu-Nara Station, which stocks the full range of Nara crafts.

Taxis The main taxi companies are Kintetsu Taxi ☎0742/22-5501, Hattori Taxi ☎0742/22-5521 and Kai-Nara ☎0742/22-3383.

Around Nara

Even before Nara was founded, the surrounding plains were sprinkled with burial mounds, palaces and temples. A few of these still survive, of which the most remarkable is **Hōryū-ji**, about 10km southwest of Nara in Ikaruga district. In 1993 this temple complex was recognized by UNESCO as a World Heritage Site for its unique collection of Buddhist architecture and statues (some of which are now housed in Tokyo's National Museum; see p.134). The temple was founded when Buddhism was gaining a foothold in Japan, and its statues and buildings are a fascinating record of the transition from monumental Chinese to a more intimate Japanese artistic style. A supreme example of this is the delicate Miroku Bosatsu statue housed in the **Chūgū-ji** nunnery, next to Hōryū-ji. Closer to Nara, the two temples of Nishinokyō district, **Shin-Yakushi-ji** and **Tōshōdai-ji**, continue the story of the transition from Chinese to Japanese art and architecture.

The route described below starts at Hōryū-ji and then works back towards Nara. All these temples are served by the same **buses** (routes #52 and #97)

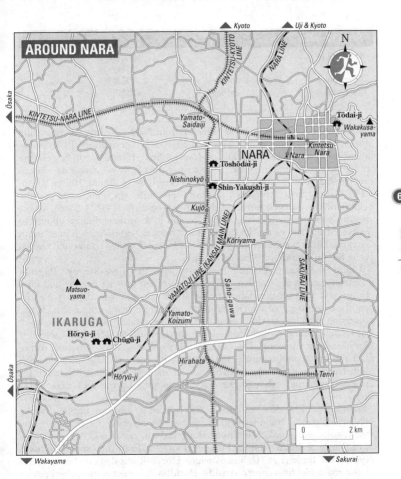

from Nara's JR and Kintetsu stations. If you're just doing the journeys outlined here, it's cheaper to buy single tickets. For anything more complicated, however, it's worth investigating the discount bus passes offered by Nara Kōtsū (see p.577). Note that it's a good idea to take a **torch** when visiting Hōryū-ji, as the statues can be difficult to see on grey days.

Hōryū-ji and Chūgū-ji

As you walk round the historic temple of **Hōryū-ji** (daily: April–Oct 8am–5pm; Jan–March, Nov & Dec 8am–4pm; ¥1000; ☎0745-75-2555, ⓦwww.horyuji.or.jp/horyuji_e.htm), completed in 607 AD, it's worth bearing in mind that Buddhism had only really got going in Japan some fifty years earlier. The confident scale of Hōryū-ji and its superb array of Buddhist statues amply illustrate how quickly this imported faith took hold. One of its strongest proponents was Prince Shōtoku (574-622), the then regent, who founded Hōryū-ji in accordance with the dying wish of his father, Emperor Yōmei. Though the complex burnt down in 670, it was soon rebuilt, making this Japan's oldest-surviving Buddhist temple.

Chūgū-ji	*Chūgū-ji*	中宮寺
Hōryū-ji	*Hōryū-ji*	法隆寺
Tōshōdai-ji	*Tōshōdai-ji*	唐招堤寺
Yakushi-ji	*Yakushi-ji*	薬師寺

The simplest way of getting to Hōryū-ji from Nara is by **bus** (every 30min; 50min; ¥760); get off at the Hōryū-ji-mae stop. Alternatively, JR's Ōsaka-bound trains stop at Hōryū-ji Station (every 10min; 15min; ¥210), from where it's a good twenty-minute walk to the temple on a fairly busy road, or you can catch a #72 bus (weekdays 2–3 hourly, weekends every 10min; 10min; ¥170).

The main approach to Hōryū-ji is from the south, which takes you past the helpful **information centre** (daily 8.30am–6pm; ☎0745/74-6800), where you can pick up English-language maps and look at their displays about the temple. At the end of the wide, tree-lined avenue, Nandai-mon (Great South Gate) marks the outer enclosure. Inside lies a second, walled compound known as the **Sai-in Garan**, or Western Precinct.

Within the Sai-in Garan's cloister-gallery, the **Five-Storey Pagoda** inevitably catches the eye first. This is Japan's oldest five-tier pagoda, and for a change you can see the statues inside. In this case they're all early eighth-century clay images, of which the most appealing is that in the north alcove, portraying Buddha entering nirvana watched by a nicely realistic little crowd. But it's actually the right-hand building, the **Kon-dō** (Golden Hall), which is Hōryū-ji's star attraction. This is the world's oldest wooden structure, dating from the late seventh century, and although it's not very large, the building's multi-layered roofs, sweeping eaves and elaborate, second-floor balustrade are extremely striking – though the dragons propping up the roof were added later.

Entering the Kon-dō's east door, you're greeted by a bronze image of Shaka Nyorai (Historical Buddha) flanked by two Bodhisattvas still bearing a few touches of original gold leaf; this **Shaka triad** was cast in 623 AD in memory of Prince Shōtoku, who died the previous year. To its right stands **Yakushi Nyorai**, the Buddha of Healing to which Hōryū-ji was dedicated in 607, and to the left a twelfth-century **Amida Buddha** commemorating the Prince's mother. Four Heavenly Kings (*Shi-Tennō*), carved of camphor wood in the late seventh century, protect the corners of the platform. Though they're perched symbolically on chunky demons, these images are stolid and rather half-hearted compared to the far more aggressive figures introduced in the eighth century – for example, the *Shi-Tennō* of Nara's Kaidan-in (see p.581). On the walls behind, it's possible to make out murals depicting the Buddhist paradise, similar to those of the Byōdō-in near Kyoto (see p.572); sadly, the original frescoes were damaged by a fire in 1949 and these are now replicas.

Exiting the Sai-in compound, walk east past two long, narrow halls, once monks' quarters, and a small shrine dedicated to Prince Shōtoku's horse. Once past these, the **Daihōzō-den** (Gallery of Temple Treasures), which houses Hōryū-ji's priceless temple treasures, comes into view. This museum consists of two halls. The first features statues of Prince Shōtoku aged 2 and 7, as well as a portrait of him as a young man, and the bronze **Yume-chigae Kannon**. A delicate creature with a soft, secretive smile, this "Dream-Changing" Kannon is credited with turning bad dreams into good. One of the museum's two unique Buddhist altars is also housed in the first hall. Known as the **Tamamushi Altar** after the *tamamushi* beetle, whose iridescent wings once decorated the bronze filigree-work round its base, it's thought to have been the property of Empress Suiko. Paintings on the sides depict scenes from Buddha's life, of which the most famous shows him neatly folding his shirt, hanging it on a tree and then throwing himself off a cliff to feed a starving tigress and her cubs. Connecting the two museum halls is the newly constructed **Kudara Kannon Dōi** which houses the wooden **Kudara Kannon** statue, thought to be seventh-century. Nothing is known about where this unusually tall, willowy figure came from or who carved it, but it's long been recognized as one of Japan's finest Buddhist works of art.

The second of the Daihōzō-den buildings contains a number of percussion instruments and masks used in *gigaku* and *bugaku* performances, in addition to a number of swords and silk scroll paintings, some of which date back to the fourteenth century. But its most important treasure is the second of the two unique Buddhist altars, the **Lady Tachibana Altar**, which once belonged to Prince Shōtoku's consort. It's larger and less beautifully ornamented than the Tanamushi Altar, but contains bronze statues of Amida – wearing a lovable grimace – and two attendant Bodhisattvas balanced on long-stemmed lotus blossoms.

From the treasure house a lane leads east between old clay walls to the **Tō-in Garan** (same ticket). This eastern precinct was added in 739, when the monk Gyōshin Sōzu dedicated a temple to Shōtoku on the site of the prince's former palace. Its centrepiece is the octagonal **Yume-dono** (Hall of Dreams), with its magnificent statue, the **Kuze Kannon**. Until recently this gilded wooden figure, said to be the same height as Prince Shōtoku (or even modelled on him in the early seventh century), was a *hibutsu*, a hidden image, which no one had seen for centuries. Somewhat surprisingly, it was an American art historian, Ernest Fenellosa, who was given permission to unwrap the bundle of white cloth in the 1880s. He revealed a dazzling statue in an almost perfect state of repair, carrying a sacred jewel and wearing an elaborate crown, with the famous enigmatic smile playing around its youthful lips. Unfortunately, the Kannon is still kept hidden for most of the year, except for brief spells in spring and autumn (April 11–May 15 & Oct 22–Nov 22). Also inside the Yume-dono, you'll find a Nara-period dry-lacquer statue of Gyōshin Sōzu, holding a rod, on the east side, and on the west, a clay statue of a thin, worried-looking monk. This is Dōsen Risshi, who supervised repairs to the hall during the Heian era (794–1185).

Chūgū-ji

A gate in the northeast corner of the Tō-in Garan leads directly into **Chūgū-ji** (daily 9am–4/4.30pm; ¥400; ☎0745/75-2106). This intimate, surprisingly quiet nunnery was originally the residence of Prince Shōtoku's mother, which he converted into a temple on her death in 621. The main reason for coming here, however, sits inside a modern hall facing south over a pond. If you've already visited Kyoto's Kōryū-ji (see p.546), you'll recognize the central image of a pensive, boy-like **Miroku Bosatsu** (Future Buddha) absorbed in his task of trying to save mankind from suffering. In this case the statue is of camphor wood, burnished black with age, and is believed to have been carved by an immigrant Korean craftsman in the early seventh century. The pose is the same – his right arm rests on his knee, one leg is crossed and one hand is raised to the chin in a classic gesture of deep concentration – but here the figure dressed in cascading robes has an even softer, more natural quality and its gently smiling face a mystical realism.

△ Bamboo forest, Kyoto

Beside the altar, a few fragments of silk embroidery are replicated remnants of a pair of tapestries known as the **Tenjukoku Mandala**. The mandala was commissioned by Lady Tachibana in 623 to commemorate Prince Shōtoku's death by depicting him in Buddha's Paradise. A thirteenth-century nun rescued what she could and patched the pieces together into the square that survives today. It's still possible to make out some celestial figures as well as symbolic tortoises and phoenixes.

Chūgū-ji marks the eastern extent of the Hōryū-ji complex. From here it's about an eight-minute walk south down to the main road and the Chūgū-ji-mae bus stop. Buses heading south will take you back to JR Hōryū-ji Station, while those going north pass Yakushi-ji en route to Nara; in either case, you'll want a #52 or #97 bus.

Yakushi-ji and Tōshōdai-ji

Six kilometres northwest of Hōryū-ji, the Nishinokyō area is home to two great temples which are again famed for their age and wealth of statuary. The older of the pair is southerly **Yakushi-ji** (daily 8.30am–5pm; ¥800; ☎0742-33-6001). Emperor Tenmu first ordered its construction sometime around 680 AD when his wife was seriously ill. Although she recovered, Tenmu died eight years later, leaving the empress to dedicate Yakushi-ji in 697. Over the centuries, fires have destroyed all but one of the original buildings, though the statues themselves have fared better.

Arriving by **bus** from Hōryū-ji (35min; ¥560) or Nara (20min; ¥240) – buses #52, #97 – get off at the Yakushi-ji Higashi-guchi stop, from where it's roughly ten minutes' walk to the temple's north gate. Alternatively, Kintetsu-line **trains** run from Nara to Nishinokyō Station with a change at Saidai-ji; the north gate is a three-minute walk east of the station.

Since Yakushi-ji faces south, you are, in effect, entering by the back door. The first building, in the compound's northeast corner, is a modern **treasure hall**. It's open three times a year (Jan 1–15, late March to early April & Oct 8–Nov 10; ¥500), and during two of those periods (Jan & Oct–Nov) a rare, Nara-period painting of Kissho-ten, the Buddhist goddess of peace, happiness and beauty, is the prime attraction. She is portrayed as a voluptuous figure with cherry-red, butterfly lips, and dressed in an intricately patterned fabric whose colours are still remarkably clear.

Continuing south through the outer compound you come to a long, low wooden hall on your left, the **Tōin-dō**. This hall, rebuilt around 1285, houses a bronze image of **Shō-Kannon**, an incarnation of the goddess of mercy, which dates from the early Nara period. The graceful, erect statue framed against a golden aureole shows distinctly Indian influences in its diaphanous robes, double necklace and strands of hair falling over its shoulders.

The only building of note in Yakushi-ji's inner compound is the three-storeyed **East Pagoda**, which Ernest Fenellosa famously described as "frozen music". Apart from its obvious beauty, he was referring to the rhythmical progression of smaller double roofs that punctuate the pagoda's upward flow. It's the sole surviving remnant of the original temple and stands out like a sore thumb against the spanking-red lacquer of the new West Pagoda, the Daikō-do (Great Lecture Hall) and the Kon-dō (Golden Hall), all of which have been rebuilt in the last 25 years. But inside the Kon-dō the temple's original seventh-century bronze **Yakushi triad** sits unperturbed. Past fires have removed most of the gold and given the statues a rich black sheen, but otherwise they are in remarkably fine condition. A rather pudgy, seated Yakushi Nyorai, Buddha of Healing, is flanked by two only slightly less ample Bodhisattvas of the sun and moon. Their poses are symmetrical, resting gracefully on one leg, though there are subtle differences in their ornate jewellery, headdresses and the drape of their garments; Nikkō, the sun, stands on the right (east), with Gakkō the moon to the left. As you leave by the back of the hall, take a look at Yakushi's **pedestal**, which is decorated with so-far-unexplained figures with Polynesian features, and a grapevine motif of Middle Eastern origin.

Tōshōdai-ji

Retracing your steps, head north from Yakushi-ji's north gate for five minutes and you'll find the front entrance to **Tōshōdai-ji** (daily 8.30am–4.30/5pm; free; ☎0742/33-7900). The weathered, wooden halls in their shady compound here are superb examples of late eighth-century architecture, though the main attraction, the **Kon-dō** (Golden Hall), is being rebuilt and will be closed until 2009. The temple was founded in 759 by the eminent Chinese monk Ganjin – he of Nara's Kaidan-in (see p.581) – when he was granted permission to move from the city to somewhere more peaceful.

The first thing you'll see upon entering the south gate is the enormous aluminium and concrete structure inside which the Kon-dō is being entirely rebuilt. A video presentation (in Japanese only) explains the process and visitors are allowed to peek into the area where the work is progressing. There is also a small, ad hoc exhibition of photographs showing the statues which are the temple's main treasures. Craftsmen who accompanied Ganjin from the mainland are also responsible for the three dry-lacquer statues that usually fill the hall. Pole position goes to a seated Rushana Buddha, a slightly later cousin of Tōdai-ji's Daibutsu (see p.581), surrounded by a halo of a thousand mini-Buddhas. Yakushi Nyorai stands on one side and a phenomenally busy Senju Kannon, this time with the full complement of a thousand arms, on the other. The Four Heavenly Kings who are supposed to protect this trio do their best to look menacing, but they're way outclassed on the height stakes.

The **Kō-dō** (Lecture Hall) behind also dates from the late eighth century, though this low-slung hall with its gabled roof is more Japanese in styling. In spring and autumn Tōshōdai-ji's treasures go on display in the concrete **Shin-Hōzō** (daily 8.30am–4.30/5pm; ¥100) on the compound's east side. Again, these are mostly statues, of which the most celebrated is a headless Buddha known as the "Venus of the Orient". Just once a year – on June 6, the anniversary of Ganjin's death – the doors of the **Miei-dō** are opened to reveal a lacquered image which was carved just before he died in 763 at the grand age of 76. He's buried next door, in the far northeast corner of the compound, in a simple grave within a clay-walled enclosure.

When you've finished, walk back to the main gate and then east for about five minutes to the main road where you can pick up a bus back to Nara – the same #52 or #97 (20min; ¥240). Alternatively, head back to Yakushi-ji and catch a Kintetsu line train, changing at Saidaiji.

Kōya-san

Ever since the Buddhist monk Kōbō Daishi founded a temple here in the early ninth century, **KŌYA-SAN**, some 50km south of Ōsaka, has been one of Japan's holiest mountains. On top is an elongated, cedar-filled valley perched 800m above sea level, where more than one hundred monasteries cluster round the head temple of the Shingon sect, **Kongōbu-ji**. This isolated community is protected by two concentric mountain chains of eight peaks each, which are said to resemble an eight-petalled lotus blossom.

Whatever your religious persuasion, there's a highly charged, slightly surreal atmosphere about this group of temples suspended among the clouds. The journey alone, a dramatic ride by train and cable car, more than repays the effort, but Kōya-san is also a good place to step out of Japan's hectic city life for a day or two. One of its great delights is to stay in a *shukubō*, or **temple lodgings**, and attend a dawn prayer service. Afterwards, head for the **Garan**, the mountain's spiritual centre, or wander among the thousands of ancient tombs and memorials which populate the **Okunoin cemetery**, where Kōbō Daishi's mausoleum is honoured with a blaze of ten thousand oil-fuelled brass lanterns.

Of course, Kōya-san is not undiscovered. Some six thousand people live in the valley and each year thousands of pilgrims visit the monasteries. Even here, loudspeakers, ugly concrete buildings and commercialization intrude, and one or two women travelling alone have complained of some mildly unmonkish behaviour. Be aware also that, while the mountain can be pleasantly cool in summer, winter temperatures often fall below freezing.

The biggest **festival** in Kōya-san takes place on the 21st day of the third lunar month (usually mid-April), when all the monks gather for a service at the Mie-dō. Everyone's out in force again for Kōbō Daishi's birthday (June 15), while during Obon several thousand lanterns light the route through Okunoin cemetery as part of Japan's festival for the dead (Aug 13).

Some history

The first monastery on Kōya-san was founded in the early ninth century by the monk Kūkai (774–835), known after his death as **Kōbō Daishi**. As a young monk Kūkai travelled to China to study Esoteric Buddhism for two years. On his return in 806 he established a temple in Hakata (now Fukuoka) before moving to Takao-san near Kyoto, where his ardent prayers for the peace and pros-

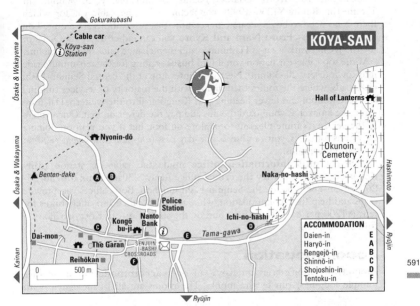

perity of the nation won him powerful supporters. Kūkai was soon granted permission to found the **Shingon** sect which, in a break from contemporary belief, held that enlightenment could be achieved in one lifetime (see p.954 for more on Shingon Buddhism). But city life was too disruptive for serious meditation, so Kūkai set off round Japan to find a suitable mountain retreat.

According to legend, when Kūkai left China he prayed for guidance on where to establish his monastery. At the same time he flung his three-pronged *vajra* (the ritual implement of Shingon monks) clear across the ocean. Later, as he drew near **Kōya-san**, he met a giant, red-faced hunter, who gave him a two-headed dog. The dog led Kūkai to the top of the mountain where, of course, he found his *vajra* hanging in a pine tree. In any event, the historical records show that Kūkai first came to Kōya-san in 816 and returned in 819 to consecrate the first temple. For a while after 823 he presided over Kyoto's Tō-ji temple (see p.532), but eventually returned to Kōya-san, where he died in 835. Even without his religious work it seems that Kūkai was a remarkable man; he's credited with inventing the *hiragana* syllabary and founding Japan's first public school, as well as being a gifted scholar, calligrapher and spiritual healer.

After his death, Kūkai's disciple **Shinzen** continued developing the monasteries, then collectively known as **Kongōbu-ji**, until at its height there were more than 1500 monasteries and several thousand monks on the mountaintop. The sect then had its ups and downs, of which the most serious was during the anti-Buddhist movement following the 1868 Meiji Restoration. In recent years, however, the temples have been extensively repaired and Kōya-san is once again a major centre of pilgrimage.

Arrival and information

Access to Kōya-san's mountain-top hideaway is via a cable car which departs every thirty minutes from **Gokurakubashi Station**, arriving at Kōya-san station five minutes later. Direct express and super-express trains on the private Nankai line run **from Ōsaka**'s Namba Station (every 20–30min; 1hr 15min–1hr 40min; ¥1230–1990), connecting with the cable car for which there is no need to buy a separate ticket; note that reservations are required on the super-express. **From Nara and Kyoto** you can either travel via Ōsaka or use the JR network as far as Hashimoto and then change onto the Nankai line.

At the top cable-car station you'll find **buses** waiting for the ten-minute ride into town (every 20–30min). Nearly all buses stop at the central Senjuin-bashi crossroads, where the routes then divide, with the majority of services running east to Okunoin and fewer heading past Kongōbu-ji to the western, Dai-mon gate; take a ticket as you board the bus and pay the driver on exit. Once you're in the centre it's more pleasant to explore on foot, but if you plan on doing a lot of bus journeys, you can buy a one-day pass (*ichi-nichi furii kippu*; ¥800) at the station terminus.

There's a small **information office** inside the cable-car station (daily 8.30am–5/5.30pm), or try the central office (daily 8.30am–5pm; ☎0736/56-2616, ℻56-2889) beside the Senjuin-bashi junction. Both offices can provide maps and help fix accommodation, while the main office also offers **bikes** for rent (¥1200 per day). **Taxis** wait outside the station, or call Kōya-san Taxi on ☎0736/56-2628.

Accommodation

Around fifty monasteries on Kōya-san offer **accommodation** in *shukubō* (temple lodgings) run by the monks. The rooms are all Japanese-style with communal washing facilities, and in some cases look out over beautiful gardens or are decorated with painted screens or antique hanging scrolls. These are primarily places of worship, so don't expect hotel-style service, and you'll be asked to keep to fairly strict meal and bath times. However, guests are usually welcome to attend the early-morning prayers (around 6am or 6.30am) and all the *shukubō* offer excellent **vegetarian meals** (*shōjin-ryōri*).

While the local information offices (see opposite) can help book *shukubō*, it's a good idea to make reservations in advance. Either approach the temples recommended below direct, or contact the Kōya-san Tourist Association at 600 Kōya-san, Kōya-chō, Itō-gun, Wakayama-ken (℡0736/56-2616, ℻56-2889). Prices generally start at around ¥9000 per person per night, including two meals.

Daien-in ℡0736/56-2009, ℻56-2971. Small, highly recommended *shukubō* near the centre of Kōya-san. No English spoken, but it's a friendly place. ⑥

Haryō-in ℡0736/56-2702, ℻56-2936. One of the cheapest places to stay on the mountain. They even offer rooms without meals, though it would be a shame to miss out. The temple's located about ten minutes' walk from the centre of town on the road to the cable-car station, or take a bus to the Isshin-guchi stop. ⑤

Rengejō-in ℡0736/56-2233, ℻56-4743. Foreigners are assured a warm welcome at this lovely old temple, founded in 1190, opposite *Haryō-in*. They'll even conduct the prayer ceremony in English if there's enough demand, and again rooms are available without meals. ⑥

Shinnō-in ℡0736/56-2227, ℻56-3936. One of Kūkai's leading disciples founded this attractive temple in a secluded spot just behind the Garan. No English spoken. ⑥

Shōjōshin-in ℡0736/56-2006, ℻56-4770. One of the larger temples, located on the edge of town near Okunoin's west entrance, *Shōjōshin-in* started life as a grass hut erected by Kūkai himself. It boasts a lovely garden, a warm atmosphere and there's usually someone who speaks English. ⑥

Tentoku-in ℡0736/56-2714, ℻56-4725. On a lane south of Kongōbu-ji, *Tentoku-in* is best known for its sixteenth-century garden. More expensive rooms come with glorious garden views. ⑥

The Town

The road into Kōya-san from the cable-car station winds through cool, dark cryptomeria forests for about 2km before passing a small temple called **Nyonin-dō**. This "Women's Hall" marks one of the original seven entrances to the sacred precincts, beyond which women weren't allowed to proceed; the practice continued until 1906 despite an imperial edict issued in 1872. In the meantime, female pilgrims worshipped in special temples built beside each gate, of which Nyonin-dō is the last. Beyond the hall, you begin to see the first

Kōya-san		
Kōya-san	*Kōya-san*	高野山
Danjō Garan	*Danjō Garan*	壇上伽藍
Gokurakubashi Station	*Gokurakubashi-eki*	極楽橋駅
Hashimoto	*Hashimoto*	橋本
Kongōbu-ji	*Kongōbu-ji*	金剛峯寺
Okunoin	*Okunoin*	奥/院
Reihōkan	*Reihōkan*	霊宝館
Accommodation		
Daien-in	*Daien-in*	大円院
Haryō-in	*Haryō-in*	巴陵院
Rengejō-in	*Rengejō-in*	蓮華定院
Shinnō-in	*Shinnō-in*	親王院
Shōjōshin-in	*Shōjōshin-in*	清浄心院
Tentoku-in	*Tentoku-in*	天徳院

monasteries and, 1km further on, reach the main **Senjuin-bashi crossroads**. This junction lies at the secular centre of Kōya-san. Nearby you'll find the information office, post office, police station and restaurants alongside shops peddling souvenirs and pilgrims' accessories. The main sights are located either side of this crossroads: head west for Kōya-san's principal temple, **Kongōbu-ji**, and its religious centre, the **Garan**, or east for the mossy graves of **Okunoin cemetery**.

Kongōbu-ji and the Garan

Though it originally applied to the whole mountain community, the name **Kongōbu-ji**, Temple of the Diamond Mountain (daily: April–Oct 8am–5pm; Jan–March, Nov & Dec 8.30am–4.30pm; ¥350; ℡0736/56-2011), now refers specifically to the sect's chief monastery and administrative offices, located three minutes' walk west of the central crossroads. In fact, this temple was a late addition to the complex, being founded in 1592 by the then ruler Toyotomi Hideyoshi in honour of his mother. It only later became Shingon's headquarters.

Rebuilt in 1861 in the original style, the graceful building is famous largely for its late sixteenth-century **screen paintings** by Kyoto's Kanō school of artists. The best of these are the cranes and pine trees by Kanō Tanyū decorating the Great Hall, and Kanō Tansai's *Willows in Four Seasons* two rooms further along. This Willow Room is also the spot where Hideyoshi's nephew **Toyotomi Hidetsugu** killed himself in 1595. Hidetsugu was the adopted heir of the childless Hideyoshi, but things got complicated when Hideyoshi fathered a lusty son, Hideyori, in 1593. To forestall any arguments over the succession, Hideyoshi ordered his now inconvenient nephew to commit suicide and then had Hidetsugu's wife and family murdered just to be on the safe side.

Beside the temple's front entrance, the **Rokuji-no-kane** (Six O'Clock Bell), cast in 1547, sits on a castle-like foundation; a monk comes out to ring it every even hour (6am–10pm). Opposite the bell a gravelled path leads into the **Garan**, Kōya-san's sacred precinct. This large sandy compound, filled with cryptomeria trees, lanterns and wooden halls wreathed in incense, is where Kōbō Daishi founded his original monastery. Only one of those early buildings still stands and many are much newer, such as the **eastern stupa**, which marks the entrance to the Garan from this side. It's followed by three older halls, of which the most interesting is the middle **Daie-dō**, housing an impressive statue of Amida Buddha attended by two Bodhisattvas. The Daie-dō was rebuilt in 1638, while the hall in front of it, the **Fudō-dō**, is the oldest building in the Garan, dating from 1198.

The Garan's most important building, however, is the monumental **Konpon Daitō** (¥100), the Fundamental Great Stupa, covered in strident, orange lacquer – it was last rebuilt in the 1930s. Inside, Dainichi Nyorai and four other blue-coiffed Buddhas symbolize the ideal universe. They're surrounded by a gaudy forest of pillars painted with Bodhisattvas, while the eight patriarchs who helped propagate Shingon decorate the walls. South of the stupa, the more restrained **Kon-dō** (¥100), also rebuilt in the 1930s, marks the spot where Kūkai gave his first lectures. He reputedly lived where the **Mie-dō** now stands, just to the west. There's nothing much to see inside, but this attractive building, dating from 1843, is regarded as one of the mountain's most holy places. Note the two sacred pines in front which are said to be offspring of the tree in which Kūkai's *vajra* landed.

Continuing west past the little **Juntei-dō** and **Kujakū-dō** – peer in to see a mini-Kannon and a statue of the peacock divinity Kujakū – you finally reach the nicely weathered **western stupa**. Circling round to the south, the pretty hexagonal building was once a scripture repository, and the long, low wooden hall is where priests still hold monthly debates and monks sweat over their exams. Behind the exam hall, there's a reminder that Kōya-san was a sacred mountain long before Kūkai arrived; the ornate, vermilion Shinto shrine **Miyō-jinja** is dedicated to Kōya-san's guardian deities – Kūkai's red-faced hunter and his mother.

The main road in front of the Garan eventually leads to the **Dai-mon**, or Great Gate, which was Kōya-san's main entrance until the cable car was built in the 1930s. The huge, rust-red gate sits on the mountain's western edge but the views are blocked by trees and it's not really worth the five-minute walk. Instead, follow the main road back towards town to see the temples' greatest treasures in the **Reihōkan** (daily 8.30am–4.30pm; ¥600). Though the old buildings don't really do the exhibits justice, and there's very little in English, this collection includes a number of priceless works of art. The displays are changed five times a year, but look out for a triptych of Amida welcoming souls to the Western Paradise, painted in 965, and a Heian-era silk painting of Buddha entering nirvana. Among the statues there's the original Kujakū Myō-ō, the peacock deity, and an apoplectic Fudō Myō-ō. In Shingon Buddhism this god is regarded as an incarnation of Dainichi Nyorai and he's usually accompanied by eight youthful servants – those in the museum are attributed to the gifted twelfth-century sculptor, Unkei. The rest of the collection is made up of mandala, scrolls and documents, including some by Kūkai, and also a number of ritual implements (*vajra*) he's said to have brought back from China.

Okunoin

About 1km east of Kōya-san's central crossroads, the buildings give way once more to stately cedar trees. Turn left here over a broad, white bridge, **Ichi-no-hashi**, to follow the path into a mysterious, mossy forest. This is **Okunoin**, Kōya-san's vast **cemetery**. Stretching away to either side, the forest floor is scattered with more than 200,000 stone stupas of all shapes and sizes, some jumbled and decaying like fallen logs, others scraped clear of lichen so that you can make out vague inscriptions. Here and there you'll also find Jizō statues, their red bibs bright against the muted greens, and the occasional war memorial. The most obvious is a white-winged structure beside Ichi-no-hashi, commemorating students who died in the Pacific War, but along the path keep an eye open for campaign maps of Papua New Guinea and Borneo. A great number of historical characters are also buried here, among them the great general Oda Nobunaga, and the monks Dōgen, Shinran, Nichiren and Hōnen, all founders of Buddhist sects.

It's best to walk through Okunoin in the early morning or around dusk, when lamps light up the path; at these times the only other people you're likely to meet are the occasional, white-garbed pilgrims with their tinkling bells. It takes roughly twenty minutes to reach the cemetery's spiritual centre beyond the little **Tama-gawa** river. Before entering the sacred precinct, people offer paper or bamboo strips bearing names of deceased relatives to one of the seven bronze statues – five Jizō, Fudō and Miroku, the Future Buddha – and then douse the statue with water as a service to the dead. Above the bridge, a line of wooden stakes in the river represents memorials to those who died by drowning and to miscarried foetuses.

Across the bridge you begin the approach to the **mausoleum of Kōbō Daishi**. First comes the **Hall of Lanterns**, where ten thousand oil lamps donated by the faithful are kept constantly alight. Two of them are said to have been burning since the eleventh century, one donated by the former Emperor

Shirakawa and another by an anonymous poor woman. After this blaze of light and colour, the **tomb** itself is mercifully restrained. Indeed, it's only just visible within a gated enclosure behind the hall, sheltered by lofty cryptomeria trees.

According to Shingon tradition, the Great Master, Daishi, did not die in 835 but rather entered "eternal meditation". He's now waiting the coming of Miroku, the Future Buddha, when he will help lead the faithful to salvation – which is one reason why so many Japanese wish to have their ashes buried on Kōya-san. Next to the Daishi's tomb you'll see the octagonal ossuary where ashes are collected. Many of these are destined for the **modern cemetery**, which lies south of the Tama-gawa bridge on a short cut back to the main road. It's the custom now for big companies to maintain plots on Kōya-san for past employees – the space rocket is probably the most famous memorial, but look out, too, for familiar names such as Yakult and UCC's coffee cup. And note also the "letter boxes" on some monuments for company employees to leave their *meishi* (business cards), just to say they called or perhaps to petition a former colleague for a bit of spiritual assistance.

You emerge on to the main road beside a clutch of restaurants and a bus park. If you don't want to walk back, take any bus heading west from the Okunoin-mae stop across the road.

Shima Hantō

East of Ōsaka and Nara, on the far side of the Kii Peninsula, a small knuckle of land sticks out into the ocean. Known as the **Shima Hantō**, this peninsula has been designated a national park, partly for its natural beauty but also because it contains Japan's spiritual heartland, **Ise-jingū**. Since the fourth century the Grand Shrine of Ise, on the edge of **Ise** town, has been venerated as the terrestrial home of the Sun Goddess Amaterasu, from whom it was once believed all Japanese emperors are descended. Unfortunately, there's not a great deal to see, but if you're passing through Ise it's worth making a brief excursion, joining the reverent throng of Japanese tourists who try to make a pilgrimage here once in their lifetimes. Beyond Ise it's **pearl** country. The world-famous Mikimoto company started up in **Toba** when an enterprising restaurant owner discovered the art of cultivating pearls. Now there's a whole island dedicated to his memory, including a surprisingly interesting museum. Most of today's pearls are raised further east in **Ago-wan**, where hundreds of rafts are tethered in a beautiful, island-speckled bay.

Ise

The town of **ISE** wears its sanctity lightly. Although many visitors find the town a disappointingly ordinary place, at **Ise-jingū**, Japan's most sacred Shinto shrine, even non-Japanese visitors can appreciate its deeper spiritual significance. Apart from their historical importance, there is an unquestionable sense of awe and mystery about these simple buildings buried in the cedar forest and an understanding as to why 6.5 million Japanese make the journey here every year. After you've seen the two sanctuaries, however, there's really nothing else to detain you in Ise.

Ise-jingū is naturally a top choice for the first shrine visit of the New Year (*hatsu-mōde*) on January 1. This is followed by more than 1500 annual **ceremonies** in honour of Ise's gods. The most important of these revolve around the agricultural cycle, culminating in offerings of sacred rice (Oct 15–17). In

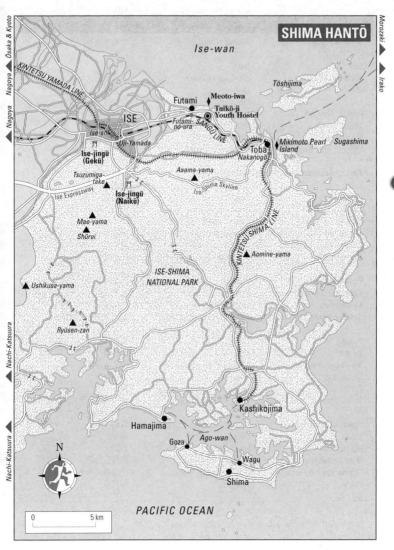

spring (April 5–6) and during the autumn equinox (around Sept 22), ancient Shinto dances and a moon-viewing party take place at the inner shrine.

The Town

Central Ise is bounded to the north by the JR and Kintetsu line train tracks and by the Seta-gawa river to the east. The southwestern quarter, however, is taken up by a large expanse of woodland (which accounts for a full third of the city's area), in the midst of which lies the first of **Ise-jingū**'s two sanctuaries, the **Gekū**, or Outer Shrine. This is within easy walking distance of both train stations, but to reach the **Naikū** (Inner Shrine), some 6km to the southeast,

Shima Hantō	*Shima Hantō*	志摩半島
Ise	*Ise*	伊勢
Akafuku Honten	*Akafuku Honten*	赤福本店
Gekū	*Gekū*	外宮
Ise-jingū	*Ise-jingū*	伊勢神宮
Ise-shi Station	*Ise-shi eki*	伊勢市駅
Naikū	*Naikū*	内宮
Oharai-machi	*Oharai-machi*	おはらい町
Uji-Yamada Station	*Uji-Yamada eki*	宇治山田駅
Accommodation and restaurants		
Daiki	*Daiki*	大喜
Hoshide-kan	*Hoshide-kan*	星出館
Ise City Hotel	*Ise Shitii Hoteru*	伊勢シティーホテル
Kawasaki-kan	*Kawasaki-kan*	河崎館
Okadaiya	*Okadaiya*	岡田屋
Okuno	*Okuno*	おく乃
Yamada-kan	*Yamada-kan*	山田館
Futami	*Futami*	二見
Futami-no-ura Station	*Futami-no-ura eki*	二見浦駅
Meoto-iwa	*Meoto-iwa*	夫婦岩
Taikō-ji Youth Hostel	*Taikō-ji Yūsu Hosuteru*	太江寺ユースホステル
Toba	*Toba*	鳥羽
Awami	*Awami*	阿波海
Mikimoto Pearl Island	*Mikimoto Shinju-shima*	御木本真珠島
Sazanami	*Sazanami*	さざなみ
Tenbinya	*Tenbinya*	天びん屋
Toba International Hotel	*Toba Kokusai Hoteru*	鳥羽国際ホテル
Kashikojima	*Kashikojima*	賢島
Goza	*Goza*	御座
Hamajima	*Hamajima*	浜島
Ryokan Ishiyama-sō	*Ryokan Ishiyama-sō*	旅館石山荘
Shima Kankō Hotel	*Shima Kankō Hoteru*	志摩観光ホテル
Wagu	*Wagu*	和具

you'll need to take a bus (see "Practicalities", p.600). The two shrines follow roughly the same layout, so if you're pushed for time, head straight for the more interesting Naikū.

What is now the Inner Shrine was established sometime in the fourth century to house a **mirror** representing the Sun Goddess, **Amaterasu**. According to legend, this was the very mirror that Amaterasu gave her grandson Ninigi-no-Mikoto when she sent him to rule Japan (see "Contexts", p.949). At first it had been stored in the imperial palace, along with the sacred sword and beads (these are now held respectively in Nagoya's Atsuta-jingū and Tokyo's Imperial Palace), but the goddess gave instructions to move her mirror to somewhere more remote. Eventually they settled on a wooded spot beside Ise's Isuzu-gawa, which has been the mirror's home ever since and the country's most sacred centre. The Outer Shrine was added in the fifth century to honour the god of food and industry. Not that the shrines look old: according to custom they are rebuilt every twenty years in order to re-purify the ground. Each is an exact replica of its predecessor, following a unique style of architecture that has been passed down the centuries and is free of any Chinese or Korean influences. Only plain *hinoki* (Japanese cypress) and grass thatch are used, plus a few gold embellishments, but the most distinctive features are the two crosspieces (*chigi*) standing up at each end of the roof and the chunky, horizontal bars (*katsuogi*) lined up between them. When the buildings are dismantled, the old timbers are passed on to other shrines around the country to be recycled.

Gekū

The entrance to the **Gekū** (sunrise to sunset; free) lies over a small humped bridge and along a gravel path leading into the woods. After passing under two unpainted *torii*, you reach a sacred dance platform and, nearby, the shrine office – ask for a copy of their excellent English-language leaflet. Just beyond, a high wooden fence contains the shrine itself, a thickly thatched, gleaming structure in a sea of white gravel. It's dedicated to the goddess **Toyouke-no-Ōmikami**, who was sent by Amaterasu to look after the all-important rice harvests. Another of her duties is to provide Amaterasu with sacred food, so twice a day priests make offerings to Toyouke in a small hall at the back of the compound. Presumably she then passes this on to the Sun Goddess.

As you leave, take a look at the empty plot next door. This is reserved for the new shrine, which will be built in 2013, when the Naikū will also be reconstructed. It takes about a year to complete the buildings and refurbish them with hundreds of sacred objects, all of which are handmade according to age-old techniques. The dedication of the new shrine takes place at night, when the secret treasures symbolizing the goddess are carried from one building to the other. This solemn ceremony is believed to renew the blessings brought by the gods on the Japanese people.

Having paid their respects to Toyouke by bowing deeply twice, clapping and bowing deeply a third time, most people hurry off to visit the Naikū. Buses heading east leave from a stand on the main road opposite the Gekū's main entrance; hop on either a #55 or #51 for the Naikū stop (every 10min; 15min; ¥410).

Naikū

The **Naikū** (sunrise to sunset; free), Ise-jingū's inner shrine, is a much grander affair. The shrine is dedicated to Amaterasu Ōmikami, the ancestress of the imperial family, and stands on the edge of a large expanse of sacred woodland across a beautiful arched bridge, **Uji-bashi**, which spans the Isuzu-gawa. On the far side, turn right and walk through a small, formal garden to reach the purification fountain just in front of the first sacred *torii*. A little further on, the path goes down to the river. Traditionally, pilgrims would purify themselves here as well, but most people nowadays just go to see the fat, multicoloured carp that laze in the shallows.

The path turns away from the river towards a collection of buildings which include the shrine office – where they also stock the English-language leaflets – and a purple-curtained music hall. Here worshippers dedicate performances of sacred dance or Nō theatre to the gods for services rendered or in the hope of securing divine intervention. Next come various halls where sacred foods are stored and prepared; to ensure their purity, rice, sake, salt, fruit and vegetables are all produced on plots of shrine land. Finally, the path loops round to approach the **inner sanctum** from the south. As in the Gekū, the main building is contained within four increasingly sacred enclosures, though in this case the inner sanctum is further away and it's even more difficult to see the details. Nevertheless, the architecture's pure, strong lines hold the same mystical power. Only members of the imperial family and head priests can enter the inner sanctuary where Amaterasu's **sacred mirror** is enshrined. It's wrapped in layers of cloth and, according to the records, no one's laid eyes on it for a thousand years.

Rather than retracing your steps, follow the paths round to the west of the main sanctuary. This route takes you past an attractive rice storehouse and treasury, to the auxiliary shrine of Aramatsurinomiya, where you can get a better look at the architecture.

If you've got time to spare after exploring the Naikū, turn right immediately over the Uji-bashi and take a stroll down the shopping street known as **Oharai-machi**. This pedestrian-only area replicates a Meiji-era merchants' quarter; it's all rather touristy, but the buildings are well done and there are some decent places to eat (see opposite). If you just want a snack, head for *Akafuku Honten* restaurant, about halfway along on the right beside a little bridge – look for the lovely red wood-burning steamers in front. They serve the local speciality, *akafuku mochi*, steamed rice cakes covered with red-bean paste (¥230 for three pieces including tea); in summer, try them cold with ice. To return to central Ise from the Naikū area take a bus (#51 or #55 again) from stop 1 (every 30min; 15–20min; ¥410).

Practicalities

There are regular **trains** to Ise from Nagoya, Kyoto and Ōsaka. In all cases the private Kintetsu network offers the quickest and most convenient service, particularly if you're travelling from Kyoto or Ōsaka. Note that there are two stations in central Ise. The more easterly, **Uji-Yamada Station**, is Kintetsu's main station. However, some Kintetsu trains also stop at **Ise-shi Station**, which is shared with JR. **From Nagoya** the fastest option is an express on the Kintetsu-Ise line to Uji-Yamada Station (hourly; 1hr 20min; ¥2690). If you've got a JR Rail Pass, you can use JR's limited express trains direct from Nagoya to Ise-shi (hourly; 1hr 35min), but note that you have to pay a small supplement (¥440) for travelling on a section of Kintetsu track. Kintetsu also runs direct trains **from Ōsaka's** Uehonmachi Station (every 15min; 1hr 45min; ¥3030) and **from Kyoto** (hourly; 2hr; ¥3520). For those planning on spending a few days in the area, a ¥3800 three-day Kintetsu line rail pass spanning the whole of the extensive Kintetsu network is available, but this doesn't include the surcharge for using the fastest, special express trains.

Each train station has its own **bus** terminal, with regular departures for the two shrines; buses #51 and #55 run via the Gekū to Naikū, after which the #51 route circles back round to the stations.

Ise's main **tourist information office** (daily 8.30am–5pm; ☎0596/28-3705) is located opposite the entrance to the Gekū. You can pick up maps and brochures at the ground-floor window, but if you need English-language help try the office upstairs (Mon–Fri only). Alternatively, there's a useful office with English-speaking staff in the Uji-Yamada Station (daily 9am–5.30pm; ☎0596/23-9655), where staff can also help arrange accommodation throughout the Shima Hantō area. Ise's main **shopping area** lies south of Ise-shi Station. For **foreign exchange**, try the Daisan Bank opposite the JR Station, or walk down the pleasant, lantern-lined street leading from the station to the Gekū, where'll you'll find UFJ Bank. **Car rental** is available through Kinki Nippon Rent-a-Car (☎0596/28-0295), at Uji-Yamada Station, and Eki Rent-a–Car (☎0596/25-5019), at Ise-shi Station. **Bike rental** is available at Ise-shi Station (¥1030 per day).

Accommodation

Surprisingly, Ise doesn't have a great choice of **accommodation**. One of the most interesting places is *Yamada-kan* (☎0596/28-2532, ℻28-4440; ❼ including two meals), a traditional ryokan in a distinctive seventy-year-old building on the lantern-lined road in front of Ise-shi Station. Accommodation is in Japanese-style rooms with shared bathroom facilities. On the main road north of Uji-Yamada Station, the *Ise City Hotel* (☎0596/28-2111, ℻28-1058; ❺) is a reasonable business hotel with English-speaking staff and comfortable en-suite rooms; they also have a slightly more expensive annexe. Continue up this road to find *Hoshide-kan* (☎0596/28-2377, ℻27-2830; ❻), on the right before the next main junction. This delightful, higgledy-piggledy old ryokan offers tatami rooms, all with shared bathrooms, and serves excellent vegetarian meals in the restaurant next door. Behind the *Hoshide-kan* there's a small, interesting area of old streets, known as Kawasaki, along the Seta-gawa river.

Restaurants

Ise's **speciality foods** include lobster (*Ise-ebi*) and the rather less exciting *Ise udon*, which consists of thick, handmade noodles served in a thin soy sauce – in summer they'll ask if you want it cold. By far the nicest **restaurant** in town is the *Daiki* (☎0596/28-0281), despite its rather unpromising location on the north side of the Uji-Yamada Station forecourt. The restaurant made its name catering to the emperor, but it's a nicely relaxed place and eating here doesn't have to blow the budget. Set meals start at under ¥2000, though if you want to splurge they also do *Ise-ebi* at ¥6000. In the Naikū area, *Okadaiya* (daily except Fri 10.30am–5pm) and *Okuno* (daily 10am–5pm) both serve *Ise udon* (¥400) and well-priced set meals – find them on the main street of Oharai-machi before the Akafuku shop. Finally, if you're wandering the Kawasaki area, look out for the jazz coffee house *Kawasaki-kan* (daily 8am–7pm) in a nicely restored traditional warehouse. They serve a variety of freshly roasted coffees, as well as cakes and light snacks.

Toba and Ago-wan

East of Ise the ragged Shima Peninsula juts out into the Pacific Ocean. Most of this mountainous area belongs to the Ise-Shima National Park, whose largest settlement is the port of **Toba**, home to the famous **Mikimoto Pearl Island**. After learning everything you ever wanted to know about cultured pearls, you can head on south to **Kashikojima** on the shores of **Ago-wan**, a huge, sheltered bay scattered with wooded islands between which float banks of oyster rafts – magical at sunset.

Travelling from Ise, there's a choice of routes into the area. If the weather's clear the best option is via the **Ise-Shima Skyline**, which runs between Ise and Toba over the summit of Asama-yama. From the top you get excellent views over Ise-wan and, on an exceptional day, all the way to Mount Fuji. **Buses** depart twice a day (12.05pm & 2.20pm; 40min; ¥1120) from outside Ise's Naikū shrine (see p.599), while a new bus service, Canbus, covers the area between Ise and Toba, taking in all the major sights. Canbus departs from Uji-Yamada Station (Mon–Fri hourly, Sat & Sun every 30min). One-day (¥1000) and two-day (¥1600) passes are available – both passes come with a book of coupons offering further discounts to attractions in the area.

Alternatively, both Kintetsu (¥290) and JR (¥230) **trains** continue east of Ise. Of these, the JR services are less frequent and don't go beyond Toba. However, their lines are routed closer to the coast where they pass through **FUTAMI**, which is famous for its "wedded rocks", **Meoto-iwa**. Joined by a hefty, sacred rope, this pair of "male" and "female" rocks lies just offshore about fifteen minutes' walk northeast of Futami-no-ura Station. They're revered as representations of Izanagi and Izanami, the two gods who created Japan (see p.949), and it's the done thing to see the sun rise between them – the best season is from May to August, when the sun's in the right place. Perhaps more interesting, however, is Futami's excellent **youth hostel**, located ten minutes' walk inland from the rocks; ask at the train station for a map. As the name suggests, the *Taikō-ji Youth Hostel*, 1659E, Futami-chō (☎0596/43-2283; ❷), is located in a temple. It's on a quiet knoll among trees, nothing luxurious but a lovely relaxed place to recharge the batteries.

Toba

Although it's on an attractive bay, the town of **TOBA** is not somewhere to linger. The seafront is a strip of car parks, ferry terminals and shopping arcades, behind which run the main road and train tracks. Really the only point in stopping here, unless you need accommodation or are catching a ferry, is to pay homage to the birthplace of cultured pearls.

In 1893 **Mikimoto Kokichi** (1858–1954), the son of a Toba noodle-maker, produced the world's first cultivated pearl using tools developed by a dentist friend. Just six years later he opened his first shop in Tokyo's fashionable Ginza shopping district, from where the Mikimoto empire spread worldwide. His life's work is commemorated – and minutely detailed – on **Mikimoto Pearl Island** (daily: April–Oct 8.30am–5/5.30pm; Jan–March, Nov & Dec 9am–4.30pm; ¥1500; ☎0599/25-2028, ⓦwww.mikimoto-pearl-museum.co.jp), lying just offshore five minutes' walk south of Toba's train and bus stations. Even if you're not a pearl fan, the museum is extremely well put together, with masses of information in English describing the whole process from seeding the oyster to grading and stringing the pearls. There's also a section devoted to Mikimoto's extraordinary pearl artworks, including a spinning globe, a model of the Yume-dono pavilion (see p.587) with a revolving top, and a modest little crown containing 872 pearls and 188 diamonds. The unsung heroines of all this are the **women divers** (*ama*) who stoically come out every hour or so in all weathers to demonstrate their skills. Though *ama* are no longer employed in the pearl industry, some two thousand local women still earn their living this way, collecting abalone, sea urchins and seaweed from the rocky coast. On average they'll spend three to four hours a day in the water, going down to a depth of 10–15m, and some are still diving at the age of 60. The argument for using women is that they can apparently hold their breath longer than men and are blessed with an extra layer of insulating fat.

Practicalities

Toba's JR and Kintetsu **stations** and the bus terminal are all located next door to each other in the centre of town. There's an **information booth** (daily 9am–5pm; ☎0599/25-2844) beside the taxi stand at the bottom of the Kintetsu Station steps. The staff don't speak English, but can help with accommodation.

If you're leaving the Shima Hantō area, one of the nicest ways to travel is by **ferry** across the bay to a couple of ports south of Nagoya. Ise-wan Ferry (☎0599/25-2880) operates regular services to both Irako (50min; ¥1050) and

Morozaki (1hr 10min; ¥1150), from where buses connect with the rail network. The boats leave from Ise-wan Ferry Terminal, two minutes' walk south along the seafront from Mikimoto Pearl Island; if you're travelling by Kintetsu line train, get off at Nakanogō Station.

Toba is not well endowed with **accommodation** options, so you'd be better off staying in Ise (see p.596) or travelling on to Kashikojima (see below). If you're stuck, one of the most reasonable places to stay is *Awami*, 300-7 Kohama (T0599/25-2423, F25-2701; ❸). This small, friendly ryokan is actually located in the Kohama district, an attractive fishing port ten minutes' walk north of Toba Station; follow the train tracks but keep going straight ahead when they veer left. The rooms are simple but clean, meals are available and the owners speak a little English. Otherwise, the choice is a resort hotel, such as the *Toba International Hotel*, 1-23-1 Toba (T0599/25-3121, Wwww.j-hotel.or.jp/member/MIE/TOBA_HOTEL_ INTERNATIONAL/welcome-e.html; ❼), in a fine position on the headland overlooking Toba Bay. It takes about fifteen minutes on foot from the station.

Eating in Toba is less of a problem. Seafood restaurants abound, with oyster as the predictable speciality. Though it looks a bit grim, the Pearl Building, opposite Toba Station, offers a pretty good choice on its *Ichibangai* restaurant floor. Here *Tenbinya* is recommended for its well-priced seafood *teishoku*, but you'll also find noodle shops and Western-style restaurants. If you're after something smarter, try *Tenbinya*'s main shop (closed Mon) in the streets just inland from Mikimoto Pearl Island, where you can eat well for under ¥2000. Nearby, *Sazanami* is another popular seafood restaurant with slightly higher prices.

Ago-wan

The Shima Hantō ends in a chaos of islands known as **Ago-wan**. This large, sheltered bay is a classic ria coastline, formed by the sea rising along river valleys to create myriad islands and deep inlets. For centuries, divers have been collecting natural pearls from its warm, shallow waters, but things really took off when Mikimoto started producing his cultured pearls in Ago-wan early in the twentieth century. Nowadays, hundreds of rafts moored between the islands trace strangely attractive patterns on the water, while, in the nets beneath, thousands of oysters busily work their magic.

The main reason to visit Ago-wan is to take a **boat trip** round the bay. Boats depart from the tiny port of **KASHIKOJIMA** at the end of the Kintetsu train line (40min; ¥460). The station lies just one minute north of the harbour, where you'll find a choice of sightseeing boats and ferries. For ¥1500 you can cruise in a very mock-Spanish galleon (every 30min, according to demand; 50min), and there are also small boats (*yūransen*) which take you further in among the islands (50–60min; ¥1400). But perhaps the best option is one of the passenger **ferries** (*teikisen*). There are two ferry routes: across to **Goza**, on the long arm forming the bay's southern edge, and back via **Hamajima** to the west of Kashikojima (6 daily; 1hr 15min; ¥1800 for the round-trip); or via Monsaki island in the middle of the bay to **Wagu**, a village east of Goza (hourly; 25min; ¥600 one way). You can get tickets and information about the ferries and Spanish cruise boats from an office beside the harbour – on the right as you walk down from the station – or buy *yūransen* tickets from a small booth opposite.

For local maps and general **information**, try the Kashikojima Ryokan Annaijo (daily except Mon & Thurs 9am–4.30pm; T0599/43-3061) at the bottom of the escalator leading from the station to the pier. They can help with all types of **accommodation**, while the unofficial help desk in the train station handles

Kintetsu hotels. Kintetsu mainly owns big, resort establishments, such as their flagship *Shima Kankō Hotel* (T0599/43-1211, F43-3538; ⑥), in a magnificent position overlooking the bay; there's a free shuttle bus for the two-minute ride from the station. At the other end of the scale, the wonderfully atmospheric *Ryokan Ishiyama-sō* (T0599/52-1527, F52-1240; ④, including Western breakfast) is a great place to spend the night. The rooms are nothing fancy but the main thing here is its location on an island, Yokoyama-jima, two minutes by boat from Kashikojima pier – the English-speaking owner will collect you. After dining on a feast of fresh seafood, you can watch the sun go down over Ago-wan.

Kōbe and around

A historic port and distinct city in its own right, **KŌBE**, the capital of Hyōgo-ken, now seems more like the fashionable western suburb of sprawling Ōsaka, 33km east around Ōsaka Bay. You don't visit Kōbe for the sights, which are of limited interest, but more for its human scale, dramatic location on a sliver of land between the sea and Rokkō-san, its cosmopolitan atmosphere and great range of food.

Although Kōbe has almost totally recovered from the 1995 **earthquake**, it has far from forgotten this horrific event – the gracelessly named **Disaster Reduction and Human Renovation Institution** documents the quake and its aftermath. The **Kōbe City Museum**, covering the port's earlier illustrious history, is also worth a look, as is the space-age **Fashion Museum** on the man-made Rokkō Island, east of the city harbour.

Heading into the hills, you can relax at **Arima Onsen**, one of Japan's oldest spa resorts. West of the city is the **Akashi Kaikyō Ōhashi**, the longest suspension bridge in the world (see p.612), linking Kansai directly with Shikoku via Awaji-shima. Continue some 55km further west along the coast and you'll arrive at **Himeji**, home of Japan's best original castle Himeji-jō, a UNESCO World Heritage Site since 1993.

Some history

Kōbe's history is dominated by two important events; the opening of Japan's ports to foreign trade in 1868 and the Great Hanshin Earthquake of 1995. Although it had been a port as long ago as the eighth century, Kōbe's fortunes really took off when **foreign traders** set up shop in the city in the latter part of the nineteenth century, bringing their new ways and styles of living with them. Japan got its first taste of beef and soccer in 1871 in Kōbe, the first cinema film was shown here in 1896, and the first golf course was laid down close to the city in 1903, designed by Arthur Gloom, a Brit.

This trendsetting nature and booming trade made Kōbe a very popular place and, despite suffering heavy bombing during World War II, by the 1960s the city was bursting out of its narrow stretch of land between the mountains and the sea. A solution was found by levelling the hills and dumping the rubble in the sea to create Port Island and Rokkō Island in the bay. All this came to a sudden halt, though, at 5.46am, January 17, 1995, when a devastating **earthquake** struck the city and surrounding area. As dawn broke, Kōbe resembled a war zone, with buildings and highways toppled, whole neighbourhoods in flames, some 5500 people dead and tens of thousands homeless. Although the authorities were criticized for not responding promptly to the disaster, Kōbe has tried its best to get back to business and the city bears little physical sign of its tragedy today.

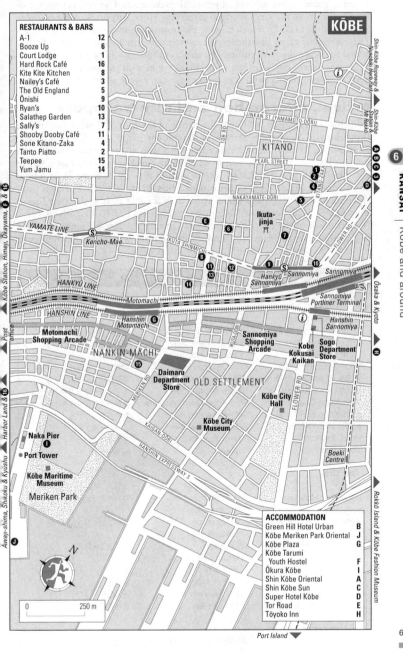

KŌBE

RESTAURANTS & BARS	
A-1	12
Booze Up	6
Court Lodge	1
Hard Rock Café	16
Kite Kite Kitchen	8
Nailey's Café	3
The Old England	5
Ōnishi	9
Ryan's	10
Salathep Garden	13
Sally's	7
Shooby Dooby Café	11
Sone Kitano-Zaka	4
Tanto Piatto	2
Teepee	15
Yum Jamu	14

Shin-Kōbe Ropeway & Nunobiki Herb Park

Shin-Kōbe & Mt Rokkō

A B C 3

D

Kōbe Station, Himeji, Okayama, F & 16

Ōsaka & Kyoto

Post Office

Harbor Land & 16

Awaji-shima, Shikoku & Kyushu

Rokkō Island & Kōbe Fashion Museum

IJINKAN ST (YAMAMOTO-DŌRI)

KITANO

TOR RD

PEARL STREET

KITANO-ZAKA

NAKAYAMATE-DŌRI

FLOWER RD

YAMATE LINE

Kencho-Mae

Ikuta-jinja

IKUTA SHINMICHI

HANKYŪ LINE

Hankyū Sannomiya

Sannomiya

Motomachi

Sannomiya Portliner Terminal

HANSHIN LINE

Hanshin Motomachi

Hanshin Sannomiya

Motomachi Shopping Arcade

NANKIN-MACHI

Sannomiya Shopping Arcade

Kōbe Kokusai Kaikan

Sogo Department Store

KUTA-DŌRI

MEIKEN RD

Daimaru Department Store

OLD SETTLEMENT

Kōbe City Hall

KAIGAN-DŌRI

Kōbe City Museum

FLOWER RD

Naka Pier

HANSHIN EXPRESSWAY 3

Port Tower

Kōbe Maritime Museum

Boeki Centre

Meriken Park

N

0   250 m

ACCOMMODATION	
Green Hill Hotel Urban	B
Kōbe Meriken Park Oriental	J
Kōbe Plaza	G
Kōbe Tarumi Youth Hostel	F
Ōkura Kōbe	I
Shin Kōbe Oriental	A
Shin Kōbe Sun	C
Super Hotel Kōbe	D
Tor Road	E
Tōyoko Inn	H

Port Island

Nonetheless, a lingering recession still affects the city, and economic activity is stalled at about eighty percent of pre-earthquake levels. The primary source of angst for many of the city's residents is the new Kōbe Airport (due for completion sometime in 2005) which is being built on a man-made island off the coast. The authorities claim that the airport, which will only handle domestic flights, is vital to secure the city's future. The airport's thousands of opponents, however, say it is a gross misuse of municipal funds – and with two perfectly good airports already in service within an hour of the city centre, they're probably right.

Arrival, information and city transport

Shinkansen **trains** stop at Shin-Kōbe station at the foot of Rokkō-san, around 1km north of Sannomiya Station in downtown Kōbe. As well as JR trains, those on the Hankyū and Hanshin lines also stop at Sannomiya Station, and are the cheaper way of connecting with Ōsaka and Kyoto to the east if you're not using a JR pass. The fastest way of getting directly to Kōbe from Kansai International airport is by **limousine bus** (1hr; ¥1800). **Ferries** from Shikoku, Kyūshū and Awaji-shima arrive at Naka Pier next to the Port Tower, ten minutes' walk south of Motomachi Station, and at Rokkō Island Ferry Terminal, east of the city. From here you can take the Rokkō Liner monorail to JR Sumiyoshi or Hanshin Uozaki Stations, from where it's ten minutes to either JR Sannomiya or Hanshin Sannomiya stations.

Kōbe		
Kōbe	*Kōbe*	神戸
Accommodation		
Green Hill Hotel Urban	*Guriin Hiru Hoteru Āban*	グリーンヒルホテルアーバン
Kōbe Meriken Park Oriental Hotel	*Kōbe Merikenpāku Orientaru Hoteru*	神戸メリケンパークオリエンタルホテル
Kōbe Plaza Hotel	*Kōbe Puraza Hoteru*	神戸プラザホテル
Kōbe Tarumi Youth Hostel	*Kōbe Tarumi Yūsu Hosuteru*	神戸垂水ユースホステル
Hotel Ōkura Kōbe	*Hoteru Ōkura Kōbe*	ホテルオークラ神戸
Shin-Kōbe Oriental Hotel	*Shin-Kōbe Orientaru Hoteru*	新神戸オリエンタルホテル
Shin-Kōbe Sun Hotel	*Shin-Kōbe San Hoteru*	新神戸サンホテル
Super Hotel Kōbe	*Sūpā Hoteru Kōbe*	スーパーホテル
Hotel Tor Road	*Hoteru Toa Rōdo*	ホテルトアロード
Tōyoko Inn	*Tōyoko In*	東横イン
The City		
Kitano	*Kitano*	北野
Kōbe City Museum	*Kōbe Shiritsu Hakubutsukan*	神戸市立博物館
Kōbe Fashion Museum	*Kōbe Fasshon Hakubutsukan*	神戸ファッション博物館
Kōbe Maritime Museum	*Kōbe Kaiyō Hakubutsukan*	神戸海洋博物館
Motomachi	*Motomachi*	元町
Nankin-machi	*Nankin-machi*	南京町
Sannomiya Station	*Sannomiya-eki*	三ノ宮駅
Shin-Kōbe Station	*Shin-Kōbe-eki*	新神戸駅
Restaurants		
Ōnishi	*Ōnishi*	大西

The main **tourist information** office (daily 9am–7pm; ☎078/322-0220), south of Sannomiya Station on Flower Road, is well stocked with English maps and leaflets and is always staffed by English-speakers. There's also an information counter inside Shin-Kōbe Station and one at the top of Kitana-zaka, the main slope leading up to the Kitano area. For more general information on what's happening around Kōbe, pick up a copy of *Kansai Time Out* (see p.496), which has full listings of local events. JNTO's Kōbe site is at ⓦ www.jnto.go.jp/eng/RTG/RI /kansai/hyogo/hyogo.html

Being less than 3km wide, Kōbe is a great city for **walking** around. About the only reason for using the subway is to go from Shin-Kōbe to Sannomiya Station (¥200). If you feel like taking things easy, hop on the **city loop** tourist bus (¥250 per ride, or ¥650 for a day pass, offering substantial discounts to many of the city's major sights), which runs a regular circuit around Kōbe's main sights.

Accommodation

There's plenty of top-end and mid-range **accommodation** in Kōbe, though few budget options. If you're really stuck for somewhere cheap, try the love-hotel district between Shin-Kōbe and Sannomiya stations.

Green Hill Hotel Urban 2-5-16 Kanno, Chūō-ku ☎078/222-1221, ℗242-1194. The cheapest of this mini-chain of hotels (the *Green Hill Hotel* and *Green Hill Hotel Annex* are up the hill, closer to Shin-Kōbe Station) is a reasonable deal since the rates include breakfast. ❺

Kōbe Meriken Park Oriental Hotel 5-6 Hatoba-chō ☎078/325-8111, ℮rooms@meriken-oh.co.jp. Very reasonably priced upmarket hotel, whose distinctive humpback shape juts out into Kōbe Harbour. Rooms have balconies and lovely views and there's a good range of in-house restaurants. Single rooms are just over ¥10,000. Room rates almost double at weekends and at peak holiday times, however. ❼

Kōbe Plaza Hotel 1-13-12 Motomachi-dōri ☎078/332-1141, ℗331-2630. Good-value mid-range hotel in a convenient location opposite Motomachi Station, near Chinatown, although the decor's slightly old-fashioned. Room rates include breakfast. ❻

Kōbe Tarumi Youth Hostel 5-58 Kaigan-dōri, Tarumi-ku ☎078/707-2133. This hostel, eight train stops west of Sannomiya Station, is worth considering because there's no curfew, the trains are frequent and there are kitchen facilities, as well as single rooms for ¥5000 (but no doubles). To reach the hostel from Tarumi Station, walk west along the main road running parallel to the shore for around ten minutes. The main road makes it a noisy choice, however. Dorm beds ¥2940.

Hotel Ōkura Kōbe 2-1 Hatoba-chō ☎078/333-0111, ⓦwww.kobe.hotelokura.co.jp/english/

overview.htm. Elegant luxury hotel, with smartly designed rooms, beside the Port Tower. Facilities include indoor and outdoor swimming pools and several restaurants and bars. It's worth stopping by to check out the beautiful paintings by Hirayama Ikuo in the main lobby. ❼

Shin-Kōbe Oriental Hotel 1-7-14 Kitano-chō ☎078/291-1121, ⓦwww.orientalhotel.co.jp/e/index.htm. This upmarket hotel occupies a soaring skyscraper next to Shin-Kōbe Station, with fantastic views from its (smallish) rooms and a good range of restaurants both in the hotel and the connected shopping plaza. ❼

Shin-Kōbe Sun Hotel 2-1-9 Nunobiki-chō ☎078/272-1080, ℗272-1088. Reasonably priced if undistinguished business hotel towards the Shin-Kōbe end of the Flower Road. ❺

Super Hotel Kōbe 2-1-11 Kanō-chō ☎078/261-9000, ℗261-9090. Smart new business hotel on Flower Road halfway between Sannomiya and Shin-Kōbe stations. ❸

Hotel Tor Road 3-1-19 Nakayamate-dōri ☎078/391-6691, ℗391-6570. Mid-range hotel with spacious rooms and a little more character than similar establishments, plus a better than average café-restaurant. Breakfast included. ❻

Tōyoko Inn 2-2-2 Miyuki-dōri ☎078/271-1045, ⓦwww.toyoko-inn.com/eng. A brand new member of a nationwide chain of business hotels – it's a little east of the city centre, but very good value for money. Breakfast included. ❹

The City

Kōbe's sights are split into three main areas. South of the band of rail lines passing through Sannomiya Station is the city's commercial centre covering the old settlement area and, to the west, **Nankin-machi**, Kōbe's Chinatown. Immediately south of here are the **harbour** developments of Meriken Park, Kōbe Harbor Land, Port Island and Rokkō Island. North of Sannomiya Station lies Shin-Kōbe Station and **Kitano** where the *ijinkan* (foreigners' houses), dating from the turn of the twentieth century (most were reconstructed after the 1995 quake), are clustered on the slopes of Maya-san. For the best view of the whole city and the Inland Sea take the cable car up Rokkō-san, where you might also be lucky enough to see one of the many wild boars which roam the city's mountainous northern districts.

South of Sannomiya Station

Around a century ago, the area south of Sannomiya Station was Kōbe's principal foreign settlement, although there's little evidence of it today. To get a better idea of what it once looked like, head for the **Kōbe City Museum** (Tues–Sun 10am–4.30pm; ¥200; ☎078-391-0035), ten minutes' walk south of either Sannomiya or Motomachi stations, which contains a finely detailed scale model of early twentieth-century Kōbe and many woodblock prints from the same era. The highlight of the museum, however, is its collection of *Namban* (southern barbarian) art. These paintings, prints and screens – some of extraordinary detail and beauty – by Japanese artists of the late sixteenth and seventeenth century, show how they were influenced by the art of the first Europeans, or "southern barbarians", to come to Japan. Most of the pieces are so precious that they're only displayed for short periods each year.

Immediately west of the museum is **Nankin-machi**, Kōbe's Chinatown, the entrance to which is marked by the ornate Choan-mon gate opposite the Daimaru department store. The area is packed with Chinese restaurants and is a colourful spot to browse for Asian trinkets, CDs and old vinyl records.

Kōbe Harbour and Kitano

Kōbe's **harbour** lies directly south of Nankin-machi. Here you'll find the city's most striking architectural feature – the filigree roof of **Kōbe Maritime Museum** (Tues–Sun 10am–4.30pm; ¥600, or ¥900 including entrance to the Port Tower; ☎078/322-5670), a swooping white framework symbolizing waves and sails, contrasting with the tapered red casing of the adjacent Port Tower, best viewed at dusk from the wharf of the Harbor Land development. The museum itself contains detailed models of a wide range of ships, intriguing audiovisual displays and has good English explanations, although it lacks the impact of its exterior. If you want a bird's-eye view of the city, go up to the top of Kōbe City Hall, back on Flower Road, rather than pay ¥600 to enter the Port Tower.

The surrounding **Meriken Park** is a pleasant place to chill out and take in harbour views, as is the newer **Harbor Land** development, directly across the bay, where spruced-up brick wharf buildings have been joined by modern shopping malls, a cinema complex and a huge Ferris wheel.

Of primary interest to the hordes of Japanese visitors to Kōbe, but less so to others, are the *ijinkan*, or Western-style brick and clapboard houses of **Kitano**, 1km north of Sannomiya Station. The area's steep, narrow streets, lined with fashionable cafés, restaurants and shops, are pleasant to explore and throw up odd surprises, such as a mosque and a Jain temple. However, virtually all the *ijinkan* had to be reconstructed after the 1995 earthquake and most are just not that interesting inside for Westerners.

From the top of Kitano, it's a short walk across to the **Shin-Kōbe Ropeway** (March 20–July 19 & Sept–Nov Mon–Fri 9.30am–5.30pm, Sat 9.30am–9pm,

Sun 9.30am–8pm; July 20–Aug daily 9.30am–9pm; Dec–March 19 daily 9.30am–5pm; ¥550 one way, ¥1000 return; closed 2nd & 4th Mon each month). This cable car provides sweeping views of the bay on the way up to the restful **Nunobiki Herb Park** (opens 30min later and closes 30min earlier than the cable car; ¥200), a flower garden with a field of lavender and glass houses stocked with more exotic blooms. Hiking up the hill along the course, starting behind Shin-Kōbe Station, takes around thirty minutes.

The rest of the city

East of the city centre, **Rokkō Island** is something of a *gaijin* ghetto of multinational offices and expat apartments. The main tourist attraction here is the **Kōbe Fashion Museum** (Mon–Sat 10am–6pm; ¥500; ☎078-858-0050). Housed inside what looks like a docked *Starship Enterprise*, this museum is a must for clothes junkies, with regular special exhibitions and an extensive library of fashion mags and books. The only disappointment is that it's surprisingly light on Japanese fashion. Rokkō Island is popular with many Japanese who like to marvel at the island's "international atmosphere". Only ten percent of the island's inhabitants are foreign, but that's still enough to make the place decidely different from anywhere else in the whole of Kansai. To reach the museum, take the Rokkō line monorail from JR Sumiyoshi or Hanshin Uozaki stations to Island Centre Station, from where it's a couple of minutes' walk from the southeast exit.

Located about ten minutes' walk from Hanshin Iwaya or JR Nada stations' south exits (both stations are one station east of Sannomiya on their respective lines) is the **Disaster Reduction and Human Renovation Institution** and the associated **Great Hanshin-Awaji Earthquake Museum** (Tues–Sun 9.30am–4.30pm, Fri & Sat until 6pm; ¥800 for both, ¥500 for one; ☎078/262-5050). Hi-tech multimedia facilities, interactive exhibits and film screenings devoted to the 1995 disaster are just some of the attractions on offer at the multistorey complex and help to make this one of Kōbe's must-see destinations. If you're able to spare the time, a visit to the nearby Andō Tadao-designed **Hyogo Prefectural Museum of Art** (Tues–Sun 10am–6pm; ¥500, more for special exhibitions; ☎078/262-0901, ⓦwww.artm.pref.hyogo.jp) is highly recommended. Exhibitions tend to focus on artists from the prefecture, but as this includes the postwar Gutai – a controversial group of loosely aligned 1950s artists who went very much against the local grain with their "happenings" and visceral visual art – the quality is extremely high. There's a coffee shop-cum-bar here with a terrace overlooking the waterfront that makes for a good place to recuperate with a reasonably priced glass of wine.

Eating, drinking and nightlife

Kōbe is a gourmet's paradise, its long history of international exchange blessing it with a diverse range of excellent **restaurants**. The most cosmopolitan dining area is between **Sannomiya Station** and **Kitano-zaka**, where you can eat everything from Sri Lankan curries to the local delicacy, Kōbe beef – expensive slices of meat heavily marbled with fat. Another exciting place to head of an evening is the **Harbor Land** development, where you can take your pick from a multitude of cafés and restaurants in the bayside Mosaic Mall. Fans of Chinese cuisine shouldn't miss out on **Nankin-machi** (Chinatown), where long queues form outside the most popular restaurants; if you can't wait, there are plenty of street stalls selling takeaway dumplings, noodles and other dishes.

While Kōbe doesn't have as strong a club scene as neighbouring Ōsaka, it does have a good range of **bars**, most clustered around Sannomiya and Motomachi – all within easy walking distance of each other. There are also several **cinemas** around Sannomiya, and a four-screen multiplex at the Mosaic mall.

Restaurants and cafés

A-1 2-2-9 Shimoyamate-dōri ☎078/331-8676. Renowned Kōbe beef restaurant where the steaks are served *teppan-yaki*-style on a hot grill. This place is particularly hospitable to foreigners. Daily 5–10pm. Expensive to very expensive.

Court Lodge 1-23-16 Kitano-chō ☎078/222-5504. Next door to *Tanto Piatto*, this excellent Sri Lankan restaurant serves rich coconut-milk-flavoured curries, best eaten with *godamba* bread. The set lunches are the best deal, at around ¥1000. Moderate to expensive.

Hard Rock Café 1-3-3 Higashi-Kawasaki-chō ☎078/366-5369. Located in the HarborCircus complex in Harbor Land, Japan's latest *Hard Rock* is exactly as you'd expect – large burgers and lots of rock memorabilia, though the Mt Fuji burger does add a little local flavour to the menu. Expensive.

Kite Kite Kitchen 4-7-17 Shimoyamate-dōri ☎078/334-7568. Café specializing in *gyoza*, a kind of small Chinese dumpling filled with meat, cabbage and other tasty treats. Lunch sets, including soup and rice, go for as little as ¥600. Inexpensive to moderate.

Nailey's Café 2-8-12 Kanō-chō ☎078/231-2008. Trendy bar-café with a simple but tasty menu – the ¥1000 lunches include soup, salad and coffee in addition to the main course, and the open front is a nice place to sit at during the summer. Internet access also available. Inexpensive.

Ōnishi 3F Yūberu Building, 1-4-16 Nakayamate-dōri ☎078/332-4029. Photos and autographs of famous baseball players (Japanese and foreign), sumo wrestlers and other personalities decorate the walls of this long-established *teppan-yaki* restaurant which serves excellent Kōbe beef at prices considerably less than at more stuffy estab-

lishments. Popular with both foreign and Japanese business types unwinding in a convivial atmosphere, Ōnishi also serves *okonomiyaki* if beef doesn't take your fancy. Good for late-night dining, too. Daily except Mon 5pm–3am, Sun until 9.30pm. Expensive to very expensive.

Salathep Garden 8F Grand Plaza Tor, 2-11-5 Kitanagasa-dōri ☎078/322-7033. Authentic Thai cuisine at affordable prices, with course dinners starting at ¥1800. Some English spoken, though the full-colour picture menu makes ordering a breeze, and the staff are happy to make accommodations for vegetarians. Moderate.

Shooby Dooby Café 2-5-5 Shimoyamate-dōri ☎078/321-3550. This hip diner attracts Kōbe's stylish youth, with colourful leather banquette seats and a counter bar where you can get Western snacks like sandwiches and pizza. The ¥1000 set lunch includes a beer and salad. Moderate.

Tanto Piatto 1-23-16 Kitano-chō ☎078/242-1589. Tasty pasta and other Italian dishes in a stylish, contemporary restaurant with an open kitchen. Lunch specials are a great deal. Closed Mon. Moderate to expensive.

Teepee 3F KCS Building, 1-2-26 Sakae-machi ☎078/327-7177. Hidden away in a backstreet of Chinatown, this wonderful, semi-outdoor restaurant does a great line in pizzas straight from a wood-fired oven. The clientele is young and friendly and it's a great place to relax, especially if the weather's good. Closed Tues. Moderate.

Yum Jamu 3F Hirose Building, 3-2-17 Kitanagasa-dōri ☎078-322-0135. Eclectic Oriental restaurant and good veggie choice, using organic and additive-free produce. Has an English menu. Around ¥1000 per person. Moderate.

Bars and clubs

Booze Up 2-15-3 Nakayamate-dōri ☎078/322-2873. Laid-back bar, tucked away in the backstreets north of Ikuta Shinmichi, with a great collection of classic soul and hip-hop LPs.

The Old England 1-13-7 Nakayamate-dōri ☎078/392-7033. Quiet, authentic British-themed bar-restaurant with a range of draught beers and an enormous selection of malt whiskies. Haggis and steak and kidney pie (¥800 each) are among

the menu's delights. Daily from 5pm until late.

Ryan's 7F Condo Building, opposite Sannomiya Station ☎078-391-6902. Lively bar, popular as much for its convenient location opposite Kōbe's main station as for its draught Kilkenny. Occasional live music and big-screen sports. Daily from 5pm until late.

Sally's 1-5-8 Nakayamate-dōri ☎078/333-5534. Popular bar-club catering to mainstream tastes –

it's usually packed with a young, foreign crowd and can get very rowdy at weekends. There's a small pool hall off to one side. Daily 7pm until late. **Sone Kitano-zaka** ☎078-221-2055. This famous jazz club is the best in the Kansai area and attracts many top international artists as well as local talent. The first live set starts around 7pm; ¥700 cover charge. Decent food, too. Daily from 5pm.

Listings

Airlines JAL ☎078/331-2811; JAS ☎078/391-7611.

Banks and exchange UFJ Bank and Sumitomo-Mitsubishi Bank are a 5min walk south of Sannomiya Station, just off Flower Road.

Bookshops The excellent secondhand bookstore Wantage Books, 1-13 Ikuta-chō (Mon–Fri 10am–5.30pm), is just south of Shin-Kōbe Station, below the offices of the monthly magazine *Kansai Time Out* – you can get copies of the magazine in the bookshop. For new books, head to Kinokuniya (daily 11am–8pm), in the Loft department store next to the Kōbe Kokusai Kaikan.

Car rental Nippon Rent-a-Car (☎078/231-0067), Kobe Rent-a-Car (☎078/241-5151) and Eki Rent-a-Car (☎078/241-2995) all have branches near Sannomiya Station.

Emergencies The main police station is at 5-4-1 Shinoyamate-dōri, chūō-ku (☎078/341-7441). In an absolute emergency, contact the Foreign Advisory Service on ☎078/291-8441. For other emergency numbers, see "Basics" on p.81.

Hospital and medical advice Kōbe Adventist Hospital, 8-4-1 Arinodai, Kita-ku (☎078/981-0161), has many English-speaking staff, but is a 30min drive north of the city. Kōbe Kaisei Hospital, 3-11-15 Shinohara Kitamachi, Nada-ku (☎078/871-5201), has an International Division with many English-speaking staff, but, like the Adventist Hospital, is a little awkward to reach, being a fifteen-minute walk uphill from Hankyu Rokkō Station. Kōbe University Hospital, 7-5-2 Kusunoki-chō (☎078/341-7451), is ten minutes' walk north of Kōbe Station. You could also try CHIC (Community House and Information Centre) for medical advice in English (☎078/857-6540; Mon–Fri 9.30am–4.30pm).

Internet access Kinko's, 1F Kobe Isuzu Recruit Building, 4-2-2 Kumoi-dōri, five minutes' walk east of JR Sannomiya Station on Route 2; it's the large main road running in front of the Sogo department store on the south side of the station (open 24hr; ¥100 for 10min).

Post office Kōbe Central Post Office is a two-minute walk northeast of Kōbe Station. There's also a convenient branch in the Kōbe Kokusai Kaikan Building, next to Sogo Department Store directly south of Sannomiya Station.

Shopping Kōbe has several large department stores, including Daimaru, south of Motomachi Station, and Kōbe Hankyū, part of the Harbor Land development beside Kōbe Station. The shopping arcades shadowing the train tracks between Motomachi and Sannomiya stations are a favourite cruising ground of Kōbe's youth, while the arcades around Nankin-machi have several cut-price electrical outlets.

Taxis Try Kōbe Mainichi Kōtsū (☎078/691-0055), which has English-speaking staff on request, or Kōbe Sogō Taxi (☎078/431-0081).

Travel agency World Express (☎078/222-5050), a reputable discount ticket agency, is on the north side of Sannomiya Station; the main JTB office is inside the station (☎078/231-4118).

Arima Onsen

It may be one of Japan's oldest hot-spring resorts, but **ARIMA ONSEN**, on the northern slopes of Rokkō-san, northeast of the city, has become blighted by ugly overpriced tourist hotels and giftshops galore. Fortunately, there's still an area of small wooden ryokan, twisting narrow streets and several rustic temples and shrines dotted up the hillside. If you've not been to an onsen resort, Arima is worth dropping by to see what one is like, and it's also possible to hike to the top of the mountain in around an hour.

The small **public bath** (daily 8am–10pm; closed first and third Tues of the month; ¥520) is five minutes' walk uphill from the train station, close by the bus station and **tourist information office** (daily 9am–7pm; ☎078/904-0708). It's nothing special and is usually full of pensioners who come to take the sludgy brown waters for their health. Slightly more attractive, but more expensive, are the baths at **Kanpo no Yado Arima** (daily 10.30am–3.30pm; ¥1000), a hotel ten minutes' walk further up the hill past a cluster of shrines.

Arima Onsen, Awaji-shima and Himeji

Arima Onsen	*Arima Onsen*	有馬温泉
Goshobō	*Goshobō*	御所坊
Kami-ō-bō	*Kami-ō-bō*	上大坊
Kampo no Yado Arima	*Kampo no Yado Arima*	かんぽの宿有馬
Awaji-shima	*Awaji-shima*	淡路島
Akashi Straits Suspension Bridge	*Akashi Kaikyō Ōhashi*	明石海峡大橋
Awaji Youth Hostel	*Awaji Yūsu Hosuteru*	淡路ユースホステル
Iwaya	*Iwaya*	岩屋
Maiko	*Maiko*	舞子
Hotel Perla	*Hoteru Perūra*	ホテルペルーラ
Qkamura Minami Awaji	*Kyūkamura Minami Awaji*	休暇村　南淡路
Sun Yat Sen Memorial Museum	*Sun Yat Sen Kinenkan*	孫中山記念館
Himeji	*Himeji*	姫路
Himeji-jō	*Himeji-jō*	姫路城
Himeji Kōko-en	*Himeji Kōko-en*	姫路好古園
Hyōgo Prefectural Museum of History	*Hyōgo-kenritsu Rekishi Hakubutsukan*	兵庫県立歴史博物館
Hyōgo Prefectural Museum of Literature	*Hyōgo-ken Bungaku Hakubutsukan*	兵庫県文学博物館
Accommodation and restaurants		
Fukutei	*Fukutei*	福亭
Hotel Himeji Plaza	*Hoteru Himeji Puraza*	ホテル姫路プラザ
Himeji Washington Hotel	*Himeji Washinton Hoteru*	姫路ワシントンホテル
Seinen-no-le	*Seinen-no-le*	青年の家

To reach the resort by **train** from Kōbe, take the subway from Sannomiya to Tanigami, transfer to the Kōbe Dentetsu line to Arima Guchi, where you may have to change again to reach the terminus at Arima Onsen. The journey takes around 45 minutes and costs ¥900. There are also direct **buses** from Sannomiya and Shin-Kōbe stations to Arima; they take around forty minutes and cost ¥680. If you're coming from Ōsaka, take a local JR train to Sanda (JR Fukuchiyama line), where you can change to the Kōbe Dentetsu line. The journey costs ¥1290 and takes about 80 minutes. Alternatively, comfortable air-conditioned coaches from the Hankyū Bus Station underneath Hankyū Umeda station cost ¥1330 one way and take just over an hour.

The tourist office has a hand-drawn English map of the town and can help arrange **accommodation** should you wish to stay over. One of the more traditional small ryokan is *Kami-ō-bō* (☎078/904-0531, ⓕ904-0515; ❺), just up the main street from the public bath, where the rates include two meals. For lunch, *Goshobo*, opposite the tourist office in the rustic lodge, has set menus of local dishes from around ¥2000 per person.

Awaji-shima and around

The **Akashi Straits Suspension Bridge**, at 3.91km the longest suspension bridge in the world, links mainland Hyogo-ken to **AWAJI-SHIMA**, the largest island in the Inland Sea (see p.621) after Shikoku. The bridge has naturally become a tourist draw in its own right and has a commanding presence, in a concrete-and-steel way, with fishermen and artists gathering on the promenades around its imposing base.

If you want all the facts and figures on this marvel of civil engineering, there's the **Bridge Exhibition Centre** (daily 9.30am–6pm; ¥200), within easy walking distance of **Maiko** Station. A hundred metres or so further east is, for Japan, a rather pleasant beach, with a sheltered swimming area. If this isn't diversion enough there's a viewing platform that looks like a giant revolving doughnut on a stick. This is a rather better bet for a view than paying to enter the pylon of the bridge itself (¥500) and wander out 150m along the undercarriage of the structure. Nestling beside all this, rather incongruously, is the **Sun Yat Sen Memorial Museum** (Tues–Sat 10am–6pm; ¥400; ☎078/783-7172), housed in an early twentieth-century mansion relocated here when the bridge was built. The museum is lovingly tended by members of Kōbe's ethnic Chinese community, but it's unlikely to be of much interest to most visitors.

Best known for its largely unspoilt **beaches** – not to mention its particularly tasty onions, which are prized throughout the Kansai region – Awaji-shima provides an escape for Kansai residents from the urban sprawl of Honshū and is especially appealing in spring and summer, when flowers and fruit crops scent the air and colour the landscape. It was at the epicentre of the Great Hanshin Earthquake of 1995 and took the brunt of the tremor's force. Luckily, the island is not nearly as populated as Kōbe, so although the damage was extensive, the loss of life was not. The most notable casualty was the bridge, which grew longer by 1m as Awaji-shima moved away from Honshū.

With the bridge and fast boat connections to Kansai International Airport, Awaji-shima is quickly shedding its sleepy demeanour and get-away-from-it-all atmosphere – if this is what you're after, you'd be better off visiting one of the smaller islands of the Inland Sea, such as Shōdo-shima (see p.723). The biggest changes have taken place at **Iwaya**, the landing point for the Akashi Kaikyō Ōhashi. A mountain-side landscaped park lies behind the small fishing village – a better attraction than Iwaya's current claim to fame: a splodge of rock next to the ferry port called **Esima-jima**. Believed to be Japan's first island created by the ancient gods, it's so small that it's hardly worth visiting.

Of Awaji-shima's **beaches**, Ōhama, on the east of the island, is a long sandy stretch that attracts crowds during summer. Goshiki, on the west, is pebbly but more tranquil, better for swimming and renowned for its golden sunsets.

Practicalities

Maiko is the most convenient station to the bridge; outside you can catch buses to the island and onwards to Tokushima on Shikoku. Direct **buses** from several places in central Ōsaka and Kōbe run to Awaji-shima across the Akashi Kaikyō Ōhashi, with many continuing on to Tokushima. From Tokushima, several buses a day leave from outside the bus terminal and go directly to Awaji-shima, stopping in Naruto on the way. **Ferries** run roughly every twenty minutes during the day from Akashi, on the main JR line from Kōbe, to Iwaya, and cost ¥320 one way. Buses running the length of the island (a trip of around 2hr) depart from outside the ferry terminal.

There's a fairly good range of **accommodation** around the island, particularly in the tourist resorts such as **Ōhama**. The youth hostel (☎0799/52-0460; ❷; closed Sept–Feb), 4.5km from Fukura on the southern coast, is isolated, basic and very institutional, but does have a splendid view across to the bridge joining the island to Shikoku. Meals are available but, if you want

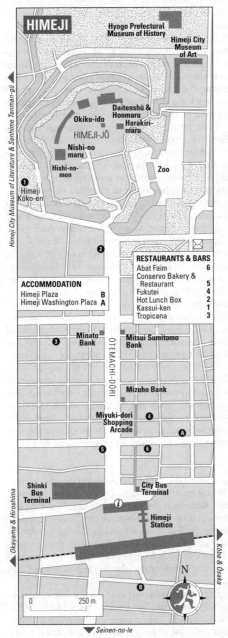

HIMEJI

Hyogo Prefectural Museum of History

Himeji City Museum of Art

Daitenshū & Honmaru

Okiku-ido

HIMEJI-JŌ

Harakiri-maru

Nishi-no maru

Hishi-no-mon

Zoo

1 Himeji Kōko-en

2

RESTAURANTS & BARS

Abat Faim	6
Conservo Bakery & Restaurant	5
Fukutei	4
Hot Lunch Box	2
Kassui-ken	1
Tropicana	3

ACCOMMODATION

Himeji Plaza	B
Himeji Washington Plaza	A

3 Minato Bank

ŌTEMACHI-DŌRI

Mitsui Sumitomo Bank

Mizuho Bank

Miyuki-dori Shopping Arcade **4**

A

5 **6**

Shinki Bus Terminal

City Bus Terminal

i

Himeji Station

B

0 250 m

N

Himeji City Museum of Literature & Senhime Tenman-gū

Okayama & Hiroshima

Kōbe & Ōsaka

▼ _Seinen-no-Ie_

6

KANSAI | Kōbe and around

something tasty, pack your own food. A pricier but good-value year-round option is *Qkamura Minami-Awaji* (☎0799/52-0291, ℱ52-3651; **6**), a national vacation village on the opposite side of Fukura Bay from the youth hostel. Accommodation is in tatami rooms, and various set meal options are available. Back on the mainland, the smart *Hotel Perla* (☎078/708-6780; **6**) stands beside the bridge at Maiko; all the rooms are spacious, have sea views and are pleasantly furnished.

Himeji

Of Japan's twelve surviving feudal-era fortresses, by far the most impressive is the one in the city of **HIMEJI**, 55km west of Kōbe. The fortress made the memorable backdrop to the Bond adventure *You Only Live Twice*, as well as countless feudal-era dramas and the recent Tom Cruise film, *The Last Samurai*, part of which was filmed in the city. The splendid gabled donjons of **Himeji-jō** – also known as Shirasagi-jō, or "white egret castle", since the complex is supposed to resemble the shape of the bird in flight – miraculously survived the World War II bombings that laid waste to much of the city, and in 1993 it was added to UNESCO's World Heritage list. Himeji is best visited as a day-trip; after you've explored the castle, it's also worth taking in the beautiful **Himeji Kōko-en**, nine linked traditional-style gardens, and a couple of intriguing **museums** around the fortress walls.

Himeji-jō

Around 1km directly north of Himeji Station lies the main gateway to **Himeji-jō** (daily 9am–4pm, June–Aug until 5pm; ¥600; ☎0792/85-1146, ⓦwww.himeji-castle.gr.jp). The present complex of moats, thick defensive walls, keeps and connecting corridors dates from the early seventeenth century, although there has been a fortress in the town since around 1346. By the time Tokugawa Ieyasu's son-in-law, Ikeda Terumasa, took control of the area in 1600, the country was at peace and so when he set about rebuilding Himeji-jō, adding the central five-storey donjon and three smaller donjons, the aim was to create something visually impressive. Even so, the castle incorporates many cunning defensive features, only really appreciated if you go on one of the **free guided tours** in English, which take around ninety minutes; guides are usually waiting at the main castle gate, but it's best to ask when buying your ticket.

If you don't have a guide, finding your way around the castle is no problem, since the route is clearly marked and there are English explanations on plaques at many points of interest. To the west of the main gateway, the Hishi-no-mon, are the open grounds of the **Nishi-no-maru** (western citadel), where the *daimyō* and his family lived, the central donjon only being used in times of war. All that remains of the original palace are the outer corridor and "cosmetic tower" where Princess Sen adjusted her kimono and powdered her nose during the mid-seventeenth century. It was Sen's dowry that enabled the castle to be built in its present form.

A zigzag path through more gates and past turrets and walls from which defending soldiers could fire arrows, shoot muskets and drop stones and boiling liquids, leads up to the **Honmaru** (inner citadel), dominated by the magnificent central donjon, **Daitenshū**. There are six levels within the dark and chilly keep, supported by a framework of huge wooden pillars, one of which is made from a 780-year-old cypress tree; touch it and it's said you'll have long life. On the top level, where the lord and his family would commit suicide if the castle was captured (which it never was), you can now look out across the city and as far as the Inland Sea on clear days.

Beside the **Harakiri-maru**, a small courtyard on the east side of the Daitenshū where samurai are believed to have committed ritual suicide (*seppuku*), is an alternative route to the donjon from the moat grounds. Before leaving, pass by **Okiku-ido**, a well south of the donjon. According to the castle's most famous ghost story, *Banshu Sara-Yashiki*, the body of a servant girl called Okiku – who had been falsely accused of stealing a valuable dish – was dumped here after she was tortured to death. Her ghost, it is said, can be heard wailing from inside the well.

The rest of the town

Himeji's other sights are conveniently located around Himeji-jō's moats. On the west side of the castle is the splendid **Himeji Kōko-en** (daily: Jan–May & Sept–Dec 9am–4.30pm; June–Aug 9am–5.30pm; ¥300, or ¥720 combined ticket with the castle), nine connected Edo-era style gardens built in 1992 on the former site of the Nishi Oyashiki, the *daimyō*'s west residence for his samurai. The gardens are separated by mud walls topped with roof-tiles, like those which would have stood around each samurai villa, and include mini-forests, carp-filled pools, rockeries and an elegant teahouse where you can experience the tea ceremony (¥500).

Ignore the depressing zoo on the east side of Himeji-jō and follow the moat grounds north past the red-brick building that once housed an armoury and is now the **Himeji City Museum of Art** (daily: Jan–May & Sept–Dec

9am–4.30pm; June–Aug 9am–5.30pm; ¥200; ☎0792/22-2288), opened in 1983 and displaying a range of Japanese paintings, ceramics and swords along-side changing exhibitions of Western art. Ahead, in a striking building designed by the founding father of modern Japanese architecture, Tange Kenzō, is the informative **Hyōgo Prefectural Museum of History** (Tues–Sun 10am–4.30pm; ¥200; ☎0792/88-9011), which includes detailed scale models of the twelve donjons across Japan that survive in their original form, plus Tokyo's Edo Castle, the largest of the keeps, which was largely destroyed by fire in 1657 and finally destroyed during World War II. There's also the opportuni-ty to try on a twelve-layered court kimono and samurai armour (11am, 2pm & 3.30pm).

Tange's contemporary rival, Andō Tadao, has made his mark on Himeji at the city's **Museum of Literature** (Tues–Sun 10am–4.30pm; ¥200; ☎0792/93-8228), some 600m directly west of the History Museum across the moat and just beyond the entrance to Princess Sen's shrine, **Senhime Tenman-gū**. The exhibits inside the museum are all in Japanese and their authors are mostly unknown in the West, but the imaginative displays and an excellent English-language leaflet make the entrance fee worth considering. If nothing else, come here to admire Andō's ultra-modern design – a disjointed arrangement of squares, circles and walkways made from rough concrete – which also respects traditional principles, such as the *shakkei* (borrowed scenery) of the castle behind the museum and the use of water.

Practicalities

Himeji is a stop on the **Shinkansen** line between Ōsaka and Okayama, and is also served by slower but cheaper *shinkaisoku* **trains**, which take forty minutes from Kōbe or an hour from Ōsaka to the east. Long-distance **buses**, from Tokyo, Ōsaka and Kōbe, also stop beside the train station, which is around 1km south of the castle at the end of Ōtemae-dōri, the main shopping street.

Himeji's major sights are within easy walking distance of the station. Stash your bags in one of the station's coin lockers, and pick up a map of the town from the **Himeji Tourist Information Centre** (daily 9am–5pm; ☎0792/85-3792), staffed by English speakers between 10am and 3pm. If you decide to stop over, the assistants can also make **accommodation** bookings, although there's little reason for staying overnight in Himeji beyond walking around the floodlit castle. The centre offers a free **bicycle rental** service to tourists; bikes can be rented between 9am and 4pm and must be returned by 6pm. Another convenient service is the retro-styled city "**loop bus**" (Sat & Sun 9am–5pm, every 15–30min), which starts from outside Himeji Station and stops at all the major tourist attractions. Rides are ¥100, though a one-day pass (¥300) may be better value as it offers a twenty percent discount on entry to a number of the city's major sights, including the castle and some of the museums.

Only consider the run-down prefectural youth hostel *Seinen-no-Ie* (☎0792/93-2716) if you're running low on cash – it has very cheap dorms (¥700 per person) and cooking facilities, but is very basic and has a 9pm cur-few. To reach the hostel, take bus #37 to the Chūō-kōen-guchi bus stop and walk 600m west across the river and past a Japanese garden. Immediately south of Himeji Station is the *Hotel Himeji Plaza* (☎0792/81-9000, ℉84-3549; ❺), one of the cheaper mid-range business hotels, with a sauna and communal bath. The singles are slightly more expensive, but the rooms more modern, at the *Himeji Washington Plaza* (☎0792/25-0111, ℉25-0133; ❺), part of the national chain of business hotels, three blocks east of the north side of the station.

The Miyuki-dōri covered shopping arcade, to the north from the station, is a good place to stop off for a **snack** or to pick up a bentō to enjoy within the castle grounds. The *Conservo* bakery and restaurant on Ōtemae-dōri does reasonably priced sandwiches, salads and cakes, while closer to the castle the *Hot Lunch Box* serves heated takeaway bentō. For something classier, try the *Kassuiken* **teahouse** within Himeji Kōko-en; the lunch of *anago* (grilled conger eel) is a local speciality and worth the expense, if only for the beautiful views of castle and gardens. A block behind the *Himeji Hotel Plaza* is the traditional Japanese **restaurant** *Fukutei* (℡0792/23-0981), which does good-value set lunches from ¥1400, including sashimi and tempura, while almost opposite the hotel is a branch of the excellent Italian restaurant, *Abat Faim* (℡0792/82-0844). Pasta lunch specials here are under ¥1000 and it's open until 9pm if you fancy dinner after seeing the castle. If you're staying the night, the city's most swinging joint is the Latin bar *Tropicana* (℡0792/22-5837), which stays open until late and hosts various club events and parties at weekends.

Travel details

Trains

The trains between the major cities listed below are the fastest direct services. There are also frequent slower services, run by JR and several private companies, covering the same destinations. It's usually possible, especially on long-distance routes, to get there faster by changing between services.

Himeji to: Fukuoka (Hakata Station; every 30min; 2hr 15min); Hiroshima (hourly; 1hr); Kōbe (every 30min; 20min); Kyoto (every 30min; 1hr); Nagoya (30 daily; 1hr 50min); Okayama (every 30min; 22min); Ōsaka (every 30min; 30min); Tokyo (hourly; 3hr 40min).

Ise to: Futaminoura (1–3 hourly; 6min); Kashikojima (1–3 hourly; 50min–1hr); Kyoto (hourly; 2hr); Nagoya (every 20–30min; 1hr 20min–1hr 35min); Nara (every 15–20min; 2–3hr); Ōsaka (every 15min; 1hr 45min); Toba (every 20–30min; 15–20min).

Kashikojima to: Ise (1–3 hourly; 50min–1hr); Kyoto (hourly; 2hr 45min); Nagoya (1–2 hourly; 2hr 15min); Ōsaka (1–2 hourly; 2hr 20min).

Kōbe (Shin-Kōbe) to: Fukuoka (Hakata Station; 20 daily; 2hr 8min); Himeji (every 30min; 20min); Hiroshima (every 30min; 1hr 7min); Kyoto (every 30min; 30min); Nagoya (every 30min; 1hr 8min); Okayama (every 30min; 35min); Ōsaka (every 15min; 15min); Tokyo (every 30min; 2hr 50min).

Kōya-san (Gokurakabashi) to: Hashimoto (every 20–30min; 45min); Nara (every 15–20min; 3hr); Ōsaka (every 20–30min; 1hr 15min–1hr 40min).

Kyoto to: Fukuoka (Hakata Station; 1–2 hourly; 2hr 50min); Himeji (1–3 hourly; 50min); Hiroshima

(1–2 hourly; 1hr 40min); Ise (hourly; 2hr); Kanazawa (1–2 hourly; 2hr); Kansai International (every 30min; 1hr 15min); Kashikojima (hourly; 2hr 45min); Kobe (1–3 hourly; 30min); Nagoya (every 15min; 40min); Nara (every 15–20min; 40min); Ōsaka (every 15min; 17min); Toba (hourly; 2hr 20min); Tokyo (every 15min; 2hr 10min); Toyama (hourly; 2hr 40min); Uji (every 15–20min; 20min).

Nara to: Ise (every 15–20min; 2–3hr); Kōya-san (every 15–20min; 3hr); Kyoto (every 15–20min; 40min); Ōsaka (every 15min; 30min).

Ōsaka (Hankyū Umeda) to: Takarazuka (every 30min; 30min).

Ōsaka (Kintetsu-Namba) to: Nara (every 15min; 30min).

Ōsaka (Namba) to: Kansai International airport (every 30min; 35min); Kōya-san (every 20–30min; 1hr 15min).

Ōsaka (Ōsaka Station) to: Akita (1 daily; 12hr); Aomori (1 daily; 15hr); Kanazawa (24 daily; 2hr 30min); Matsumoto (1 daily; 4hr); Nagano (1 daily; 4hr 50min); Takarazuka (every 30min; 30min); Toyama (14 daily; 3hr 5min).

Ōsaka (Shin-Ōsaka) to: Fukuoka (Hakata Station; every 30min; 2hr 17min); Himeji (every 20min; 35min); Hiroshima (every 15min; 1hr 15min); Kansai International (every 30min; 45min); Kōbe (every 15min; 15min); Kyoto (every 15min; 17min); Nagoya (every 15min; 1hr 7min); Okayama (every 15min; 1hr 5min); Tokyo (every 15min; 2hr 30min).

Ōsaka (Uehonmachi) to: Ise (every 15min; 1hr 45min); Kashikojima (1–2 hourly; 2hr 20min); Toba (every 20–30min; 2hr).

Toba to: Kashikojima (every 30min; 30–40min); Kyoto (hourly; 2hr 20min); Nagoya (every

20–30min; 1hr 45min); Ōsaka (every 20–30min; 2hr).

Buses

The buses listed below are mainly long-distance services – often travelling overnight – between the major cities, and local services where there is no alternative means of transport. With the ongoing recession, long-distance bus travel has become more popular with cost-conscious passengers. Star Express (℡06/6692-8857, ⓦwww.nightbus.info) is one company offering return tickets between the Kansai region and Tokyo for just ¥4800 one way or ¥9500 return, and other routes connecting major cities are also available. For shorter journeys, however, trains are almost invariably quicker and often no more expensive.

Himeji to: Tokyo (Shibuya; 1 daily; 9hr).

Ise to: Toba (3 daily; 40min).

Kyoto to: Fukuoka (1 daily; 9hr 35min); Kanazawa (5 daily; 4hr); Kansai International (hourly; 1hr 45min); Kumamoto (1 daily; 11hr); Nagasaki (1 daily; 11hr); Nagoya (13 daily; 2hr 30min); Ōsaka (Itami; every 30min; 55min); Tokyo (3 daily; 8hr); Tottori (3 daily; 4hr); Yokohama (1 daily; 7hr 30min).

Kōbe to: Fukuoka (1 daily; 10hr); Kagoshima (1 daily; 12 hr); Kumamoto (1 daily; 9hr); Tokyo (1 daily; 8hr); Tottori (7 daily; 3hr 10min); Uwajima (1 daily; 7hr 30min); Yokohama (1 daily; 9hr); Yonago (5 daily; 4hr).

Nara to: Fukuoka (1 daily; 10hr); Tokyo (1 daily; 8hr); Yokohama (1 daily; 9hr).

Ōsaka to: Beppu (1 daily; 9hr); Fukuoka (1 daily; 9hr); Niigata (1 daily; 9hr); Hagi (1 daily; 12hr); Kagoshima (1 daily; 12hr); Kansai International (every 15min; 40min); Kumamoto (1 daily; 9hr); Miyazaki (1 daily; 12hr); Nagano (1 daily; 8hr); Nagasaki (1 daily; 10hr); Ōsaka (Itami; every 20–30min; 50min); Tokyo (3 daily; 8hr 50min); Tottori (19 daily; 4hr); Yonago (18 daily; 5hr).

Ferries

Kōbe to: Imabari (1 daily; 7hr 10min); Matsuyama (2 daily; 8hr); Ōita (2 daily; 12hr); Shinmoji (1 daily; 12hr); Takamatsu (5 daily; 3hr 30min).

Ōsaka to: Ashizuri (1 daily; 9hr 20min); Beppu (1 daily; 11hr 30min); Kannoura (1 daily; 5hr); Kōchi (1 daily; 9hr 10min); Matsuyama (1 daily; 9hr 20min); Miyazaki (1 daily; 12hr 50min); Shibushi (1 daily; 14hr 40min); Shinmoji (2 daily; 12hr).

Toba to: Irako (frequent; 50min); Morozaki (4 daily; 1hr 10min).

Flights

Ōsaka (Itami) to: Akita (1 daily; 1hr 20min); Aomori (2 daily; 1hr 30min); Fukuoka (7 daily; 1hr); Kagoshima (11 daily; 1hr 10min); Kumamoto (8 daily; 1hr 5min); Miyazaki (6 daily; 1hr 5min); Nagasaki (6 daily; 1hr 10min); Niigata (6 daily; 1hr); Ōita (6 daily; 1hr); Okinawa (Naha; 5 daily; 2hr 20min); Sapporo (Chitose; 9 daily; 2hr); Sendai (12 daily; 1hr 10min); Tokyo (Narita; 3 daily; 1hr 15min); Tokyo (Haneda; 27 daily; 1hr); Yamagata (4 daily; 1hr 20min).

Ōsaka (Kansai International) to: Akita (1 daily; 1hr 30min); Fukuoka (6 daily; 1hr); Ishigaki (2 daily; 2hr 50min); Kagoshima (2 daily; 1hr 10min); Kōchi (2 daily; 40min); Kumamoto (1 daily; 1hr 5min); Matsuyama (2 daily; 50min); Miyako (2 daily; 2hr); Miyazaki (2 daily; 1hr); Nagasaki (1 daily; 1hr 10min); Niigata (1 daily; 1hr 10min); Ōita (1 daily; 1hr); Okinawa (Naha; 6 daily; 2hr); Sapporo (6 daily; 2hr); Tokyo (Haneda; 14 daily; 1hr).

Western Honshū

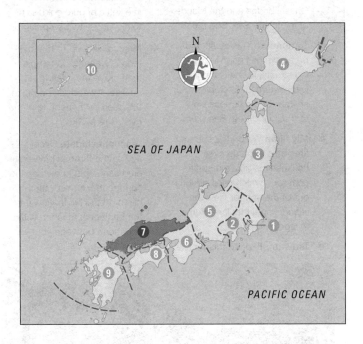

* **Okayama International Villas** Stay in one of the prefecture's international villas – locations include a traditional farmhouse at Hattōji, the old copper-mining village of Fukiya, and the island of Shiraishi-jima. **See p.628**

* **Washūzan** Climb to the summit of Washūzan and watch the sun set over the Seto Ōhashi bridge and the islands of the Inland Sea. **See p.638**

* **Tomonoura** This quaint old port town has narrow, twisting streets, liberally sprinkled with picturesque temples and shrines, and a famous view of the Inland Sea. **See p.642**

* **Miyajima** Watch the summer fireworks explode over Itsukushima-jinja's magnificent *torii*, which rises directly out of the sea, or view the island's spectacular autumn foliage **See p.660**

* **Tsuwano** Explore this picturesque old castle town by bicycle, then climb up to the Taikodani Inari-jinja through a tunnel of over a thousand red *torii*. **See p.685**

* **Adachi Museum of Art** The Adachi Museum of Japanese art is famed for its exquisite gardens, and you can finish your visit with a bowl of green tea made with water heated in a kettle of pure gold, said to aid longevity. **See p.696**

* **Misasa** Hike up to the mysterious Nageire-dō temple, then brave the gaze of passers-by and take a dip in the open-air hot spring in the river. **See p.700**

* **Amanohashidate** Cycle across the famous pine-covered sand spit, known as the "Bridge to Heaven", then climb up the hill to view it in the traditional manner: with your head between your legs. **See p.703**

△ Kintai-kyō, Iwakuni

7

Western Honshū

A lso known as *Chūgoku*, meaning "middle country", **Western Honshū** used to be at the centre of the Japanese nation, lying between the country's earliest settlements in Kyūshū and the imperial city of Kyoto. The region is split geographically into two distinct areas. The southern **San'yō coast** is blighted by heavy industry but borders the enchanting Inland Sea, while the rugged and sparsely populated northern **San'in** coast boasts some delightful small towns and a generally pristine landscape. The southern coast is easy to travel around, with Shinkansen lines, good local railway services and highways, while the northern coast takes more planning to tour by public transport, but easily repays the effort.

The Inland Sea

"They rise gracefully from this protected, stormless sea, as if they had just emerged, their beaches, piers, harbors all intact . . . Wherever one turns there is a wide and restful view, one island behind the other, each soft shape melting into the next until the last dim outline is lost in the distance."

Donald Richie, *The Inland Sea*, 1971.

It's difficult to improve on American author Donald Richie's sublime description of the **Inland Sea** (Seto Naikai) and, despite his fears that it would all be ruined in Japan's rush to the 21st century, this priceless panorama has changed remarkably little. Boxed in by the islands of Honshū, Kyūshū and Shikoku, and dotted with more than three thousand other islands, the sea is one of Japan's scenic gems, often likened to the Aegean in its beauty.

Several islands are now connected by bridges and fast ferries to the mainland, reducing their isolation and much of their charm, but on many others you'll be struck by the more leisurely pace of life and the relative lack of modern-day blight. The most popular islands to head for are Awaji-shima (p.612), Ikuchi-jima (p.647) and Ōmi-shima (p.650), Miyajima (p.660) and Shōdo-shima (p.647), although a host of others are served by ferries and have accommodation and tourist facilities.

If you don't have time to linger, consider taking one boat trip across the sea or heading to a vantage point such as Washū-zan (p.638) or Yashima (p.722) to look out over the islands. JNTO publishes a fact sheet, detailing several sightseeing cruises, though these are expensive for what they offer; you're better off putting together your own itinerary using individual ferry services. If you take a ferry between Kyūshū and Kōbe, Ōsaka or Tokyo, you'll pass through the Inland Sea anyway, although check whether it will be daylight.

WESTERN HONSHŪ

Though Chūgoku is rich in history, with burial mounds on both coasts dating from the first century, it's a more contemporary event that brings most visitors to the region. Lying midway along the San'yō coast, **Hiroshima**, site of the first atom bomb attack and the region's largest city, is the one place you'll want to stop off en route to or from Kyūshū. At the eastern end of the San'yō coast, **Okayama** has one of Japan's best gardens, **Kōrakuen**, and makes a good base for visiting the beautifully preserved Edo-era town of **Kurashiki**. Heading west along the coast, one of the treasures of Hiroshima-ken is the timeless fishing village of **Tomonoura** with its gorgeous views across the Inland Sea. The raffishly appealing port of **Onomichi**, just to the north, is also the jumping-off point for the laid-back island of **Ikuchi-jima**, home to Japan's wackiest temple complex and a lovely art museum.

The one island of the Inland Sea you won't want to miss is verdant **Miyajima**, just west of Hiroshima and site of the ancient shrine **Itsukushima-jinja** with its red *torii* rising straight up from the sea. On the southern coast of neighbouring Yamaguchi-ken, pause to admire the elegant Kintai-kyō bridge at **Iwakuni** and the spectacular view across the narrow Kanmon Straits to Kyūshū from Hino-yama in the port of **Shimonoseki**, at the tip of Honshū. Inland, the highlights of the prefecture's small capital, **Yamaguchi**, are an impressive pagoda and classic Zen rock and moss garden.

East along the frequently deserted San'in coast, the old castle town of **Hagi** boasts a lovely cluster of old samurai houses and atmospheric temples. Perhaps even more beautiful is **Tsuwano**, another small castle town nestling in a tranquil valley inland, further east in Shimane-ken. This prefecture is the heartland of Japan's eight million Shinto deities, who gather each year in October at the ancient shrine Izumo Taisha, near the appealing capital of **Matsue**. Marking the approximate midpoint of the San'in coast, Matsue has the region's only original castle tower, as well as some old samurai houses and interesting museums. In neighbouring Tottori-ken you'll find **Mount Daisen**, the highest peak in the Chūgoku region, with great hiking in the summer and skiing in winter. The sand spit of **Amanohashidate** marks the end of the San'in coast and provides some of Japan's most scenic views.

If you only have a few days, you should also aim to take in the old towns of Kurashiki and Matsue, as well as the island of Miyajima. In a couple of weeks, you could make a circuit of both coasts taking in most of the region's highlights. A regular JR Rail Pass is the most convenient way of getting around the region, but if you plan to stick only to the San'yō coast consider the cheaper **JR West San'yō Area Pass**, covering all Shinkansen and local rail routes between Ōsaka and Fukuoka. For quicker access to the region there are several **airports**, including two near Hiroshima, plus others at Okayama, Ube (close to Shimonoseki), Yonago (near Matsue) and Tottori. If time isn't an issue, then don't miss out on a leisurely **ferry** ride across the Inland Sea (see box p.621). **Renting a car** is a good idea, especially if you're planning to tour the quieter San'in coast, as you can make good use of the fast **Chūgoku Expressway**, which threads its way through the region's central mountainous spine, from where you can branch off to sights on either coast.

If you're going to be travelling in Hiroshima-ken and Yamaguchi-ken in Western Honshū, and Ehime-ken in Shikoku, make sure you get a **Seto Inland Sea Welcome Card**. This free card, which lasts a year, provides discounts of up to twenty percent at over 300 hotels, restaurants and tourist facilities in these three prefectures bordering the western end of the Inland Sea. To qualify for the card you need to be an overseas visitor who has been in Japan for less than a year, or a foreign student. The cards are available from the TICs in Tokyo, Narita and Kansai International airports, as well as at the TICs and international centres in the three prefectures. You'll need to take along your passport or alien registration card, plus student ID if you're a full-time student. The card comes with a useful booklet in English outlining all the participating organizations and businesses.

Western Honshū cuisine

As in other areas of Japan, Chūgoku has its own distinct styles of cuisine. Along the San'yō coast, seafood, unsurprisingly, is the thing to eat. Oysters are especially popular around Hiroshima: you'll find them served in various mouthwatering dishes during the season, which runs from November to spring. The notorious *fugu* (blowfish) is Shimonoseki's top dish, where it's known as *fuku*, homonymous with the character for fortune and wealth, in order to attract good luck and happiness. Both Iwakuni and Kurashiki make their own varieties of sushi: Iwakuni's is a block of rice topped with cooked fish and vegetables, while Kurashiki's is the delicious *mamakari sushi*, small fingers of rice topped with a sardine-like raw fish. In Miyajima *anago*, or conger eel, is the local favourite, delicious served as *sashimi*, tempura, or cooked and sliced on top of rice, while Tomonoura is famous for its *tai* (sea bream). On the San'in coast, Hagi's speciality is spring whitebait (*shirauo*), Matsue is renowned for its *kyōdo ryōri*, seven dishes made with fish and seafood from Lake Shinji-ko (see box p.695), while if you're visiting Shimane or Tottori in the autumn or winter, a dinner of *matsuba* crab is a must.

Hiroshima has its own special way of preparing *okonomiyaki*, with the various components of shredded cabbage, bean sprouts, meat or seafood and noodles layered between two thin batter pancakes rather than mixed altogether in the more common Ōsaka style. And if you like noodles, be sure to try the ramen in Onomichi, served in a delicious beef or pork broth, or the Izumo soba buckwheat noodles, found in almost every restaurant in the vicinity of the Izumo Shrine. The Chūgoku area also produces fine fruits and sweets: Okayama, with its high number of sunshine hours, produces superb peaches, and Tottori is the number one producer of *nashi* – a type of large, round, juicy pear with crisp flesh – and watermelon. Matsue is well known as a tea ceremony town, and many famous confectionery shops produce all manner of sweets to be served with green tea. Hiroshima and Miyajima's most famous souvenir is *momiji-manjū*, a delicious maple-leaf shaped cake filled with sweet-bean paste.

It's worth taking a look at the plates you're eating off, too: both Hagi, at the far western end of the San'in coast, and Imbe, east of Okayama, are famous for their distinctive pottery – *Hagi-yaki* and *Bizen-yaki* respectively.

Okayama and around

The main reason for stopping off in the capital of Okayama-ken, **OKAYAMA**, 730km west of Tokyo, is to stretch your legs in its famous garden, **Kōrakuen**, considered one of Japan's top three. The spacious gardens are overlooked by the castle, **Okayama-jō**, around which the city developed in the Edo period, but aside from the intriguing **Okayama Orient Museum** there's little else of note in this modern town.

Okayama is also the transport hub for trips out to surrounding attractions. The top draw is **Kurashiki**, just fifteen minutes west of the city, with its well-preserved enclave of picturesque old merchant houses and canals. From Kurashiki you can head inland to **Takahashi** to discover Japan's highest castle, **Bitchū Matsuyama**, looking down from its mountain-top over a town of old temples. For a spectacular view of both the Inland Sea and the Seto Ōhashi bridge, aim

Okayama and around

Okayama	Okayama	岡山
Hayashibara Museum of Art	Hayashibara Bijutsukan	林原美術館
Kōrakuen	Kōraku-en	後楽園
Okayama-jō	Okayama-jō	岡山城
Okayama Orient Museum	Okayama-shiritsu Oriento Bijutsukan	岡山市立オリエント美術館
Okayama Prefectural Museum of Art	Okayama-kenritsu Bijutsukan	岡山県立美術館
Okayama Prefectural Museum	Okayama-kenritsu Hakubutsukan	岡山県立博物館

Accommodation
Dai-ichi Inn Okayama	Dai-ichi In Okayama	第一イン岡山
Excel Okayama	Ekuseru Okayama	エクセル岡山
Hotel Granvia	Hoteru Guranvia	ホテルグランヴィア
Hollywood	Hariuddo	ハリウッド
Matsunoki Ryokan	Matsunoki Ryokan	まつのき旅館
Okayama-ken Seinen-kaikan Youth Hostel	Okayama-ken Seinen-kaikan Yūsu Hosuteru	岡山県青年会館ユースホステル
Okayama New Station Hotel	Okayama Nyū Sutēshon Hoteru	岡山ニューステーションホテル
Saiwai-sō	Saiwai-sō	幸荘

International villas
Fukiya	Fukiya	吹屋
Hattōji	Hattōji	八塔時
Koshihata	Koshihata	越畑
Shiraishi-jima	Shiraishi-jima	白石島
Takebe	Takebe	建部
Ushimado	Ushimado	牛窓

Restaurants
Bukkake-tei	Bukkake-tei	ぶっかけ亭
Marinporisu	Marinporisu	マリンポリス
Musashi	Musashi	武蔵

for the mountain of **Washū-zan** on the southern tip of the prefecture, while fragments of the area's ancient history can be seen along the **Kibi bicycle route**, west of the city, which runs past fifth-century burial mounds and rustic temples and shrines. For an even more off-the-beaten-track experience, stay at one of the prefecture's **International Villas** (see box p.628), self-catering accommodation in scenic locations specially reserved for foreign visitors.

Arrival and information

Shinkansen and regular **trains** stop at Okayama Station, just over 1km west of Kōrakuen. This is where you'll need to change from the Shinkansen to the JR Seto Ōhashi line if you're heading across to Shikoku. Long-distance **buses** arrive either at the Ekimae bus station on the east side of Okayama Station or the Tenmaya Bus Centre, in the heart of the city's shopping district. Okayama **airport** is around 20km northwest of the train station; buses run from the airport into the city every hour or so (¥680; 40min). Ferries arrive at Shin-Okayama Port, 10km south of the city; buses run from the port into the Tenmaya Bus Centre every hour or so (30min).

Kōrakuen and the city's other main sights are clustered around the Asahi-gawa, fifteen minutes' walk down Momotarō-dōri (see p.628), the main road heading directly east from Okayama Station, which **trams** run along. If you don't fancy walking or taking the tram, a bicycle is a good way to get around; the cheapest daily **bike rental** is from the youth hostel (see below).

Of the city's three sources of **tourist information**, the most convenient is the counter inside Okayama Station (daily 9am–6pm; ☎086/222-2912, ☏224-2572), where you'll find English-speakers and plenty of information and maps. The Okayama Prefecture International Exchange Centre, 2-2-1 Hokan-chō (Tues–Sun 9am–5pm; ☎086/256-2000, ⓦwww.opief.or.jp), five minutes' walk from the eastern exit of the station, has a good library and information centre, plus free Internet access. Finally, I-Plaza, the city's international centre along the Nishi-gawa Greenway Canal, 500m southeast of the station, is the place to head if you want to arrange a visit to a Japanese home.

Accommodation

There are plenty of inexpensive business **hotels** around Okayama Station, with the marginally cheaper ones and the youth hostel being on the west side. If you want to stay in a ryokan or minshuku, head for nearby Kurashiki (see p.631).

Dai-ichi Inn Okayama 16-17 Ekimoto-chō ☎086/253-5311, ⓦwww.daiichihotels.com/hotel/okayama. Conveniently located and friendly place, with good-sized Western-style rooms. ❹–❺
Excel Okayama 5-1 Ishiseki-chō ☎086/224-0505, ☏224-2625. Good-value mid-range hotel, smartly decorated and conveniently located near Kōrakuen and Okayama's shopping arcades. ❹
Hotel Granvia 1-5 Ekimoto-chō ☎086/234-7000, ☏234-7099. The city's top Western-style hotel, next to the station, with tastefully furnished, spacious bedrooms and elegant public areas, plus several restaurants, bars and shops. ❻
Hollywood 1-2-6 Ekimoto-chō ☎086/226-2188. This men-only capsule hotel and sauna, above a pachinko parlour in the shopping arcade opposite Okayama Station, may have a tacky name, but it's

spacious and clean inside. Capsules are available 5pm–10am for ¥3500. There's another branch at 10-4 Chūō-chō if this is full.
Matsunoki 19-1 Ekimoto-chō ☎086/253-4111, ☏253-4110. A five-minute walk from the west side of the station, this hotel has both Western-style and tatami rooms, the cheaper ones with shared bath. A Japanese-style breakfast (¥700) is served in a communal dining hall. ❹
Okayama-ken Seinen-kaikan Youth Hostel 1-7-6 Tsukura-chō ☎086/252-0651. In a residential area, ten minutes by bus #5 or #15 from the JR station, this hostel has comfortable rooms, friendly management and a relaxed atmosphere. Accommodation is in shared tatami rooms, meals are available and you can rent bikes for ¥300 a day. Cross the footbridge from the bus stop and

OKAYAMA

Kōbe & Ōsaka ▲

Kōrakuen

Okayama Prefectural Museum

Shin-Tsurumi-bashi

Tsurumi-bashi

Tsukimi-bashi

Asahi-gawa

Okayama Prefectural Museum of Art

Okayama Orient Museum

Okayama Symphony Hall

Shiroshita

Hayashibara Museum of Art

Okayama-jō

SHIROSHITA-SUJI

Tenmaya Department Store

OMOTECHO-SHOTENGAI

KENCHO-DŌRI

MOMOTARŌ-DŌRI

Central Post Office

Tenmaya Bus Centre

YANAGAWA-DŌRI

Nishi-gawa Greenway Canal

Okayama Prefecture International Exchange Centre

Train Station

KIBI LINE

Eki-mae Bus Station

I-Plaza

SHIYAKUSHO-SUJI

N

0   250 m

Hiroshima ▼▼   Shikoku & Kurashiki   ◀ A ▼

ACCOMMODATION
Dai-Ichi Inn Okayama	E
Excel Okayama	G
Granvia	H
Hollywood	F
Matsunoki	C
Okayama-ken Seinen-kaikan Youth Hostel	A
Okayama New Station	D
Saiwai-sō	B

RESTAURANTS & BARS
Aussie Bar	1
Bukkake-tei	9
Hunter	7
Il Gondola	5
Marinporisu	2
Musashi	4
Neverland Café	6
Niki Niki	3
Vecchio Mercato	8

Okayama-ken set up the first of its **International Villas** in Fukiya in 1988 in order to provide foreign visitors with affordable, authentic accommodation. The villas range from restored farmhouses to specially commissioned modern buildings, and all are in interesting locations. The six properties can be booked up to three months in advance with the Okayama International Villa Group, Okayama International Centre, 2-2-1 Hokan-chō, Okayama ☏086/256-2535, ⊛www.harenet.ne.jp/villa (Tues–Sun 9am–5pm). All villas cost ¥3000 per person per night for non-members, ¥2500 for members, and ¥500 extra for single occupancy; a two-year membership costs ¥500. You may have to share your villa with other visitors. All the properties have fully equipped kitchens and basic cooking ingredients (though in practice the cookers are fiddly to use and supplies are often missing). Each villa has booklets of information in English about where to get food locally and what to do in the area. There should also be a caretaker around to let you in and answer any questions. Few of the villas are easy to reach by public transport, so having your own car is very useful.

Two of the nicest villas are at **Fukiya** (see p.638) and **Hattōji** (see p.640). One of the smallest, sleeping a maximum of eight people, is at **Koshihata** in a nineteenth-century, thatched farmhouse in the remote Chūgoku mountains, in the north of Okayama-ken. It's a bit run-down, but is in a beautiful location. It can feel quite damp though, so be sure to buy coal and matches in Tsuyama for the *irori* fire whatever time of year you visit. The nearest train station is Tsuyama (on the Tsuyama line from Okayama, Kishin line from Himeji and Imbi line from Tottori), from where two buses a day make the seventy-minute journey to the villa. **Shiraishi-jima**, a modern villa with one tatami and four Western-style rooms, is extremely popular because of its idyllic location on a small island in the Inland Sea. The villa has sea views and a sun deck, as well as access to the island's hiking trails, small temples and rocky coastline. To reach Shiraishi-jima, take a ferry from Kasaoka, 45 minutes west of Okayama by train. Despite its modern design, **Takebe** International Villa is showing its age, with damaged furniture and an interior that is overly minimalist. Its pluses are an adjacent onsen overlooking the gushing Asahi-gawa and an easily accessible location, one hour north of Okayama by direct train or bus to Fukuwatari Station. Sadly, the spacious, modern villa at **Ushimado**, spectacularly perched on a hill overlooking the Inland Sea, is also fraying at the edges. However, it still makes a good base for exploring the seaside town, the neighbouring olive groves or the small island of Maejima, a five-minute boat ride from Ushimado harbour. The nearest JR station is Oku, from where you can take a 25-minute bus ride to Ushimado.

follow the YH sign down the first road on your right. Dorm beds ¥2940 per person.
Okayama New Station Hotel 18-9 Ekimoto-chō ☏086/253-6655, ℱ254-2583. Simple Western-style rooms at this business hotel on the west side

of the station. ❹
Saiwai-sō 24-8 Ekimoto-chō ☏086/254-0020, ℱ254-9438. Small, good-value business hotel with tatami and Western rooms – the cheaper ones share a bathroom. ❹

The City

Although you can hop on a tram and travel the length of **Momotarō-dōri** to Shiroshita (¥140), the closest stop to Kōrakuen, the walk from the station is easy enough and takes you across the tree-lined **Nishi-gawa Greenway Canal**, a pleasant spot for a stroll. At the main crossroad, Shiroshita-suji, turn north and you'll soon arrive at the atmospheric **Okayama Orient Museum** (Tues–Sun 9am–5pm; ¥300), an unusual and well-presented collection of Near Eastern antiquities, ranging from Mesopotamian pottery and Syrian mosaics to Roman sculptures. A block further north, you'll see an angular modern building which is home to the **Okayama Prefectural Museum of Art** (Tues–Sun

You can save a little money if you buy **combined tickets** to Kōrakuen and other attractions in Okayama. The gardens and the Okayama Prefectural Museum ticket is ¥440; the gardens and castle ticket costs ¥520; and the gardens, castle and Hayashibara Art Museum ticket is the best value, at ¥670.

9am–5pm; ¥300), a collection of more recent and local art. As well as dreamy ink paintings by the fifteenth-century artist and priest Sesshū Tōyō, there are examples of the local pottery style, Bizen-yaki (see p.639), and regularly changing special exhibitions, for which you'll have to pay an additional fee.

Just north of the museum, turn east and head across the Tsurumi-bashi (bridge) to the northern end of the comma-shaped island on which you'll find Okayama's star attraction, **Kōrakuen** (daily: April–Sept 7.30am–6pm; Jan–March & Oct–Dec 8am–5pm; ¥350). Founded in 1686 by Lord Ikeda Tsunamasa, this landscaped garden is notable for its wide, lush lawns, highly unusual in Japanese garden design. Other than this, all the traditional elements, including teahouses, artificial lakes, islands and hills, and borrowed scenery (in this case, the black keep of Okayama-jō), are present. The strange bleating sound you'll hear on entering the garden comes from a flock of caged red-crested cranes. Fortunately, Kōrakuen is large enough to soak up the crowds that deluge other famous gardens, such as Kenroku-en in Kanazawa and Ritsurin-kōen in Takamatsu, both of which are more interesting.

Outside the main gate to Kōrakuen is the lacklustre **Okayama Prefectural Museum** (Tues–Sun: April–Sept 9am–6pm; Jan–March & Oct–Dec 9.30am–5pm; ¥200), where the historical exhibits are presented with little ceremony and no English captions. Better to head for the smartly renovated castle, **Okayama-jō** (daily 9am–5pm; ¥300), reached by walking round the island and crossing the Tsukimi-bashi (Moon-viewing Bridge). Its nickname, U-jō (Crow Castle), refers to the black-wooden cladding of the donjon, from the top of which you get an excellent view of the surrounding area. Founded in 1573 by Lord Ukita Hideie, the adopted son of the great warlord Toyotomi Hideyoshi, the castle fell foul of both the Meiji restoration and World War II bombings, with the only original bit of the building now being the Tsukimi Yagura (Moon-Viewing Turret), at the western corner of the compound. You can pick up a good English-language leaflet from the ticket desk at the entrance to the donjon, and inside there's the chance to dress up in kimono as a samurai lord or lady for no extra charge.

A final stop on the way back to the station is the small **Hayashibara Museum of Art**, 2-7-15 Marunouchi (daily 9am–5pm; ¥300), which displays selections from the Oriental art collection of local businessman Hayashibara Ichiro. There are some beautiful items in the collection, including delicate ink scroll paintings and exquisite Nō theatre robes from the sixteenth century, but they're not always on display, so take a moment to leaf through the catalogue while sipping a free cup of green tea in the lounge.

Eating, drinking and entertainment

Okayama has the widest range of **eating** and **drinking** options between Kōbe and Hiroshima. The main districts to head for are immediately east of Okayama Station, where you'll find all the usual fast-food outlets and many other restaurants, and along Omotechō-shōtengai, the covered shopping street closer to the river. Local dishes include *sōmen*, handmade noodles dried in the sun and often

Kibi Plain bicycle route

A trip along the fifteen-kilometre-long **Kibi Plain bicycle route**, accessed either from Okayama or Kurashiki (see p.631), is an enjoyable way to see an area of countryside studded with ancient burial grounds, shrines and temples. Running from Bizen-Ichinomiya Station in the east to Sōja Station in the west, the route takes about four hours to cycle, or a full day to walk. Bikes can be rented at either station (¥200 per hour, or ¥1000 for the day) and dropped off at the other end.

In the fourth century this area was known as Kibi-no-kuni and was the centre of early Japanese civilization. Lords were buried in giant keyhole-shaped mounds known as *kofun*, one of which can be visited along the cycle route. Starting from **Bizen-Ichinomiya Station**, three stops from Okayama on the JR Kibi line, cross the tracks and follow the cycle path to Kibitsuhiko-jinja, an ordinary shrine beside a pond notable only for its huge stone lantern, one of the largest in Japan. Around 300m further southwest is the much more impressive **Kibitsu-jinja**, dating from 1425 and dedicated to Kibitsu-no-mikoto, the valiant prince who served as the inspiration for the legend of **Momotarō**, Japan's famous fairytale of a child who pops out of the centre of a giant peach after being rescued from a river by a childless farmer's wife. This shrine nestles at the foot of Mount Naka and has a magnificently roofed outer sanctum, with twin gables.

Several kilometres further west is the **Tsukuriyama-kofun**, a burial mound constructed in the fifth century in the characteristic shape of a keyhole (only really appreciated from the air). Measuring 350m in length and 30m at its highest point, this wooded mound in the midst of rice fields is the fourth largest *kofun* in Japan. Around 1km east of here is a cluster of sights, including the foundation stones of Bitchū Kokubunniji, an eighth-century convent, another burial mound and the five-storeyed pagoda of **Bitchū Kokubun-ji**, a temple dating from the seventeenth century.

It's another couple of kilometres to the train station at **Sōja**, from where you can either return to Okayama or to Kurashiki. Before leaving, check out **Iyama Hōfuku-ji**, a pretty Zen Buddhist temple, 1km north of Sōja Station along a footpath that follows the railway line. The celebrated artist and landscape gardener Sesshū Tōyō (1420–1506) trained here as a priest.

Kibi Plain Bicycle Route	*Kibi-ji Saikuringu Rūto*	吉備路サイクリングルート
Bitchū Kokubun-ji	*Bitchū Kokubun-ji*	備中国分寺
Bizen-Ichinomiya Station	*Bizen Ichinomiya-eki*	備前一宮駅
Kibitsu-jinja	*Kibitsu-jinja*	吉備津神社
Sōja	*Sōja*	総社
Tsukuriyama-kofun	*Tsukuriyama-kofun*	造山古墳

served cold in summer, and *Okayama barazushi* (festival sushi), a mound of vinegared rice covered with seafood and regional vegetables.

There's not a huge variety of **nightlife**, but several jolly *izakaya* cater to a mainly younger crowd. The mauve cylindrical building at the start of the Omotechō-shōtengai is the **Okayama Symphony Hall**; check with tourist information as to what concerts are on. Towards the southern end of the arcade are several cinemas showing mainstream films, while more arty movies get an airing at Cinema Claire near the Okayama Prefectural Museum of Art; for schedules pick up a copy of *Okayama Insider*, a free monthly English newsletter available from the tourist information centres.

Restaurants

Applause At the *Hotel Granvia*, 1-5 Ekimoto-chō. The main lounge bar on the nineteenth floor of this upmarket hotel often does good-value buffet lunches. The cityscape view, especially at night, is unbeatable, and there are several other restaurants in the hotel, including *Prix d'Or* for French food and *Bisai* for *teppanyaki* (beef and seafood cooked at your table).

Bukkake-tei 2-6-59 Omotechō-shōtengai. Located inside a shopping arcade, this restaurant specializes in udon noodles, served in cheap set menus (around ¥800 per head) with tempura on rice. Look upwards to the second floor for the grand piano playing by itself. Daily except Tues 11am–7.30pm.

Il Gondola Omotechō-shōtengai. This friendly café near the Momotarō-dōri end of the arcade does pizzas, pastas, risottos, salads and paninis, plus cakes, coffees and ice cream. Closed Tues.

Marinporisu Ekimae-shōtengai. Brightly lit revolving sushi restaurant in the arcade immediately opposite the east exit of Okayama Station. Take your pick from fingers of vinegared rice and fish, plates of melon, jelly and potato chips.

Musashi Momotarō-dōri. Near where the main road crosses the Nishi-gawa Greenway Canal, this traditional restaurant is the best place to try Okayama cuisine. The set lunches from ¥1200 are the best value, while dinner starts at ¥3000 per head. Closed Sun.

Niki Niki 1-2-4 Marunouchi. Stylish *mukokuseki* ("no nationality") restaurant with a Mediterranean feel, opposite Okayama civic hall on the way to Kōrakuen. Lunch specials start at ¥700. Closed Mon.

Vecchio Mercato 6-8 Nishiki-chō. This compact bistro a couple of minutes' walk east of the station offers Italian dishes starting at ¥500. Evenings only; closed first Mon of month.

Bars and izakaya

Aussie Bar Popular bar by the Nishi-gawa Greenway Canal, north of Momotarō-dōri. Look for the 000X sign outside.

Hunter 2F, YA Building, 3-22 Nishikimachi. Spacious American-style bar with free pool tables if you buy a drink (around ¥800). The food is also worth checking out, with hamburgers and sand-wiches for under ¥1000.

Neverland Café Honmachi. The low tables make you feel like one of Peter Pan's Lost Boys at this cheerfully designed *izakaya*. Half-price drinks before 7pm and a varied and reasonably priced food menu, including fish'n'chips in newspaper.

Listings

Airlines ANA ☎0120-029222; JAC and JAS ☎0120-511283; JTA ☎0120-255971; KAL ☎086/221-3311.

Banks and exchange There are several banks along Momotarō-dōri, and you can also change money at the Central Post Office (see below).

Bookshops Located beneath the Symphony Hall, Maruzen (daily 10am–8pm; closed second Tues of month) has the best selection of English books and magazines. Alternatively, try Kinokuniya, a block west of Tenmaya Bus Station (daily 10am–7.30pm).

Car rental Nippon Rent-a-Car ☎086/235-0919; Toyota Rent-a-Car ☎086/254-0100.

Hospital Okayama University Medical Research Hospital, 2-5-1 Shikata-chō ☎086/223-7151.

Internet access You can get thirty minutes' free

Internet access at the Okayama Prefecture International Exchange Centre, 2-2-1 Hokan-chō (Tues–Sun 9am–5pm; ☎086/256-2914); *Lit Café*, down the arcade opposite the station, offers two hours' Internet access for ¥300, plus the price of a drink.

Police Okayama Prefectural Police HQ, 2-4-6 Uchisange ☎086/234-0110.

Post office Central Post Office, 2-1-1 Nakasange (Mon–Fri 9am–7pm, Sat 9am–5pm, Sun 9am–12.30pm).

Shopping The Okayama Tourist Product Centre (daily 10am–8pm) on the ground floor of the Symphony Hall, is a good one-stop emporium for local arts and crafts, including Bizen-yaki pottery, masks and weaving.

Kurashiki

At first sight, **KURASHIKI**, 26km west of Okayama, looks like just another bland identikit Japanese town with a recreation of Copenhagen's Tivoli Park tacked onto one side. But ten minutes' walk south of the station, the modern buildings and shops are replaced by a delightful enclave of black-and-white walled merchants' homes (*machiya*) and storehouses (*kura*) dating from the town's Edo-era heyday, when it was an important centre for trade in rice and rush reeds. The compact **Bikan** historical area, cut through by a narrow, willow-fringed canal, in which swans drift and carp swim, is endowed with museums and galleries, the best of which is the excellent

Ōhara Museum of Art, containing four separate halls for Western art, contemporary Japanese art and local crafts. Kurashiki is hugely popular with tourists and can get very busy during the day; to really appreciate the town's charm it's best to stay overnight and take an early-morning or evening stroll through the Bikan district, or visit on Monday, when most of the museums and galleries are shut.

Arrival and information

Local **trains** arrive at Kurashiki Station, fifteen minutes west of Okayama on the San'yō line. Shinkansen don't stop at Kurashiki, so you'll need to change to a local train at Okayama. Regular buses from Okayama and Kojima (see p.638) stop in front of Kurashiki Station. The **tourist information office** (daily: April–Nov 9am–6pm; Jan–March & Dec 9am–5pm; ☎086/426-8681), inside Kurashiki Station, has maps of the town's sights and the English-speaking staff can make accommodation bookings. There's also another helpful tourist information office in the Bikan district (daily 9am–5pm; ☎086/422-0542), beside the canal, with a rest area where you can grab a drink from a bank of vending machines.

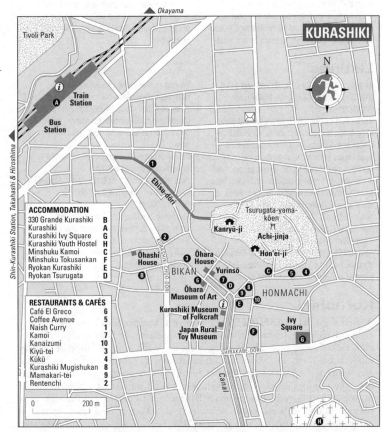

KURASHIKI

Okayama

Tivoli Park

Train Station

Bus Station

Ebisu-dōri

Tsurugata-yama-kōen

Kanryū-ji

Achi-jinja

Hon'ei-ji

ACCOMMODATION

330 Grande Kurashiki	B
Kurashiki	A
Kurashiki Ivy Square	G
Kurashiki Youth Hostel	H
Minshuku Kamoi	C
Minshuku Tokusankan	F
Ryokan Kurashiki	E
Ryokan Tsurugata	D

RESTAURANTS & CAFÉS

Café El Greco	6
Coffee Avenue	5
Naish Curry	1
Kamoi	7
Kanaizumi	10
Kiyū-tei	3
Kūkū	4
Kurashiki Mugishukan	8
Mamakari-tei	9
Rentenchi	2

KURASHIKI CHUO-DORI

Ōhashi House

Ōhara House

BIKAN

Yurinsō

Ōhara Museum of Art

Kurashiki Museum of Folkcraft

Japan Rural Toy Museum

HONMACHI

Ivy Square

SHIRAKABE-DŌRI

Canal

0   200 m

Kurashiki	Kurashiki	倉敷
Bikan	Bikan	美観
Japan Rural Toy Museum	Nihon Kyōdo Gangukan	日本郷土玩具館
Kurashiki Museum of Folkcraft	Kurashiki Mingeikan	倉敷民芸館
Kurashiki Tivoli Park	Kurashiki Chibori-kōen	倉敷チボリ公園
Ōhara Museum of Art	Ōhara Bijutsukan	大原美術館
Ōhashi House	Ōhashi-tei	大橋邸
Tsurugata-yama Park	Tsurugata-yama kōen	鶴形山公園

Accommodation

Hotel 330 Grande Kurashiki	Hoteru 330 Gurande Kurashiki	ホテル３３０グランデ倉敷
Hotel Kurashiki	Hoteru Kurashiki	ホテル倉敷
Kurashiki Ivy Square Hotel	Kurashiki Aibii Sukuea Hoteru	倉敷アイビースクエアホテル
Kurashiki Youth Hostel	Kurashiki Yūsu Hosuteru	倉敷ユースホステル
Minshuku Kamoi	Minshuku Kamoi	民宿カモ井
Minshuku Tokusankan	Minshuku Tokusankan	民宿特産館
Ryokan Kurashiki	Ryokan Kurashiki	旅館くらしき
Ryokan Tsurugata	Ryokan Tsurugata	旅館鶴形

Restaurants and bars

Café El Greco	Kafe Eru Gureko	カフェエルグレコ
Kamoi	Kamoi	カモ井
Kanaizumi	Kanaizumi	かな泉
Kiyū-tei	Kiyū-tei	亀遊亭
Kūkū	Kūkū	空空
Kurashiki Mugishukan	Kurashiki Mugishukan	倉敷麦酒館
Mamakari-tei	Mamakari-tei	ままかり亭
Naish Curry	Nasshu Karii	ナッシュカリー
Rentenchi	Rentenchi	煉天地

Accommodation

Kurashiki is an excellent place to stay if you want to experience a traditional ryokan or minshuku, the best being in the Bikan district. The town is also well served with upmarket Western-style hotels. In contrast, the cheaper business hotels tend to be shabby and overpriced and are best avoided in favour of those in Okayama. Rates at most hotels rise by a couple of thousand yen at weekends and during holidays.

Hotel 330 Grande Kurashiki 2-2-26 Chūō ☎086/421-0330, ℻421-0335. Stylish modern hotel, with tastefully decorated rooms that are surprisingly well priced for what they offer. Also has a restaurant next to the lobby. ❺

Hotel Kurashiki 1-1-1 Achi ☎086/426-6111, ℻426-6163. Although it's above Kurashiki Station, this reasonably priced upmarket hotel, owned by JR, has a hushed atmosphere, as well as a couple of restaurants and attractive rooms, some with views over the neighbouring Tivoli Park. ❺

Kurashiki Ivy Square Hotel 7-2 Honmachi ☎086/422-0011, ℻424-0515. Part of a renovated factory complex at the southern corner of the Bikan district, this is a good mid-range hotel with pleasantly decorated rooms, a couple of restaurants, a bar and shops. Rates are cheaper for rooms without en-suite baths. ❺

Kurashiki Youth Hostel 1537-1 Mukoyama ☎086/422-7355, ℻422-7364. Homely hostel set atop a hill overlooking the Bikan district at the southern end of Kurashiki. Has dorms with bunk beds, excellent food, a kitchen for self-caterers and a comfortable lounge area with bilingual TV.

Dorm beds ¥2800 per person.

Minshuku Kamoi 1-24 Honmachi ☎086/422-4898, ℱ427-7615. On the slope leading up to Tsurugata-yama park, this modern minshuku, built in traditional style, has some rooms overlooking the Bikan district, antiques in the entrance hall and a pretty garden. Rates are good value considering meals are included. **⑤**

Minshuku Tokusankan 6-12 Honmachi ☎086/425-3056, ℱ425-3053. Reasonably priced minshuku with simply furnished tatami rooms – it's tucked away one street east of the southern end of the Bikan canal above a giftshop of the same name. Rates include two meals. **⑤**

Ryokan Kurashiki 4-1 Honmachi ☎086/422-0730, ℱ422-0990. Classic ryokan housed in three converted rice and sugar storehouses in the midst of the Bikan district. Each individual suite of rooms is filled with antiques, and women in blue kimono minister to your needs. Expensive, but the genuine article. **⑨**

Ryokan Tsurugata 1-3-15 Chūō ☎086/424-1635, ℱ424/1650. Slightly cheaper than *Ryokan Kurashiki*, set in a 250-year-old canal-side merchant's house with atmospheric tatami rooms overlooking a traditional rock garden. Guests are served top-class *kaiseki ryōri* meals, which are also available to non-residents. **⑦**

The Town

It's around a one-kilometre walk from Kurashiki Station along Kurashiki Chūō–dōri to the Bikan district of seventeenth-century granaries and merchant houses, but, before heading there, peel off west after the fourth set of traffic lights to check out **Ōhashi House** (Tues–Sun 9am–5pm; ¥500). A rich merchant family, the Ōhashi prospered through salt production and land holdings. When they built their home in 1796 it was designed like those of the high-ranking samurai class, indicating how wealth was beginning to break down previously rigid social barriers. After passing through a gatehouse and small courtyard, you're free to wander through the spacious, unfurnished tatami rooms.

Returning to the main road, the start of the **Bikan** district is marked by the inevitable cluster of shops and dawdling tourists. Either side of the willow-lined canal are beautifully preserved houses and warehouses, including the **Ōhara House**, with its typical wooden lattice windows, and the adjacent **Yūrinsō**, the Ōhara family guesthouse with its distinctive green roof tiles. Opposite, across a stone bridge decorated with carved dragons, is the **Ōhara Museum of Art** (see opposite), the best of Kurashiki's many galleries and museums. The next most engaging is the **Kurashiki Museum of Folkcraft** (Tues–Sun: March–Nov 9am–5pm; Jan, Feb & Dec 9am–4.15pm; ¥700), in a handsomely restored granary around the canal bend, next to a stylish Meiji-era wooden building, which houses the tourist information centre. The museum displays a wide range of crafts, including Bizen-yaki pottery, baskets and traditional clothes, and has a small shop attached, selling souvenirs a cut above those found in most of Kurashiki's other giftshops.

A few doors down from the folkcraft museum, another excellent giftshop attached to the **Japan Rural Toy Museum** (daily 9am–5pm; ¥500) sells colourful, new versions of the traditional playthings on display in the museum. Among this vast collection of dolls, spinning tops, animals and suchlike – most faded and tatty with age and use – the best displays are of huge kites and masks in the hall across the garden at the back of the shop.

Rather than spending more yen at Kurashiki's other lacklustre museums, retrace your steps north over the canal and amble past the seventeenth-century merchant houses in the district of **Honmachi**, where you'll find some artsy craft shops, or stroll up the hillside to **Tsurugata-yama Park**, which includes the grounds of the simple **Achi-jinja** shrine and **Hon'ei-ji** and **Kanryū-ji** temples. If you have time, you could also potter around **Ivy Square**, east of the canal, where the ivy-covered late nineteenth-century Kurashiki Spinning Mill has been redeveloped into a shopping, museum and hotel complex. There's another good craft shop here, as well as an atelier where you can try your hand at pottery (¥1800).

Grafted onto the town as if from another planet is **Kurashiki Tivoli Park** (Mon–Fri 10am–8pm, Sat & Sun 9am–10pm; ¥2000), a mini-Danish theme park in storybook colours, immediately north of Kurashiki Station. Modelled on the famous Copenhagen funfair, the park (with its street entertainers, giant Ferris wheel, Hanseatic palaces and shopping plazas, landscaped gardens and artificial lakes) is amusingly kitsch, and has some reasonably priced restaurants and cafés. However, the rides are all tame and cost extra on top of the already expensive entrance fee. Hang around, though, to watch the Hans Christian Andersen-inspired automatons spring to life on the hour from inside the musical clock between the station and the park.

Ōhara Museum of Art

Apart from the Bikan district's historical townscape, Kurashiki's top draw is the impressive **Ōhara Museum of Art** (Tues–Sun 9am–5pm; ¥1000), easily spotted by its creamy Neoclassical facade. This is the entrance to the original gallery established by local textile tycoon Ōhara Magosaburō to house his collection of Western art in 1930, including works by Cézanne, El Greco, Matisse, Monet, Picasso and Rodin, which were hand-picked by his friend, the painter Kojima Torajirō, in Europe in the 1920s. The first gallery to exhibit Western art in Japan, it was a roaring success and has been continually expanded ever since, with Magosaburō's heirs adding Western and Japanese contemporary art to the collection, as well as ancient Chinese artworks and an excellent range of top-class Japanese folkcrafts.

The entrance to the **Main Gallery** is flanked by bronze sculptures of St John the Baptist and the Burghers of Calais by Rodin – both were nearly melted down to make armaments during World War II. Starting with Ōhara's nine-teenth-century purchases, the paintings are displayed in roughly chronological order, with works by Kandinsky, Pollock, Rothko and Andy Warhol included in the twentieth-century and contemporary art sections. Despite the impressive range of artists displayed, however, there are few truly memorable works in this collection.

In contrast, the **Craft Art Gallery**, housed in an attractive quadrangle of converted wooden-beamed storehouses, leaves a much stronger impression. The ceramics rooms display beautiful and unusual works by four potters who were prime movers in the resurgence of interest in Japanese folk arts (*mingei*) earlier this century: Hamada Shōji (1894–1978), Kawai Kanjirō (1890–1966), Kenkichi Tomimoto (1886–1963) and Bernard Leach (1887–1979), the British potter who worked with Hamada both in Japan, at Mashiko (see p.206), and in England at St Ives. A room filled with the strikingly colourful and sometimes abstract woodblock prints of Munakata Shikō (1903–75) follows, with the last section devoted to Serizawa Keisuke, a textile dyer and painter whose exqui-site work features on kimono, curtains and fans, and who designed both the craft galleries and the adjoining **Asiatic Art Gallery**. This smaller collection, on two levels, provides another change of pace with its cool displays of ancient East Asian art, including seventh-century Tang Dynasty ceramics and sculp-tures, and serene Buddhas.

The ground floor of the **Annexe**, in a separate building behind the main gallery, displays unmemorable pastiches of modern Western-style art by Japanese artists, while downstairs you'll find bizarre contemporary works, made from Day-Glo perspex and the like.

Eating, drinking and entertainment

There's a bewildering choice of **restaurants** in Kurashiki, with the Bikan district being the place to head to for excellent-value set-lunch deals. In the evenings many places are closed, so you might have to head towards the station area, which is also where you should go if you want fast food. The town's signature dish is *mamakari sushi*, a vinegared sardine-like fish on top of sushi rice.

Bars and evening entertainment aren't Kurashiki's strong point; the liveliest spot at night is Tivoli Park (see p.635), which is certainly more charming once the fairy lights spark into action.

Restaurants and cafés

Café El Greco Classic Bikan café in an ivy-clad building facing the canal next to the Ōhara Museum of Art. It's a favourite pit stop with visitors, even though it has a limited menu of drinks and cake. Seating is at shared tables and a coffee will set you back ¥400. Tues–Sun 10am–5pm.

Kamoi 1-3-17 Chūō. Good-value *sushi-ya* in an old granary facing the canal. Choose from the plastic food display in the restaurant window. Tues–Sun 10am–6pm.

Kanaizumi Honmachi. Koto music tinkles in the background at this traditional restaurant, specializing in freshly made noodles and serving excellent-value set meals throughout the day, all illustrated in a photo menu. A good place to sample *mamakari sushi* at only ¥750 for a set meal. Daily 11.30am–8pm.

Kiyū-tei Chūō. Rustic steak restaurant at the head of the canal running through the Bikan district. The lunches start at ¥800 for curry rice. The fixed three-course lunch or dinner menu for ¥2500 is also worth considering. Daily 11.30am–3pm & 5–8.30pm.

Kūkū Honmachi. This quaint restaurant, located away from the bustle of the tourist track, serves up great Indian and Thai curries (from ¥700) and great chai and lassis. Tues–Sun noon–8pm.

Kurashiki Mugishukan 10-19 Honmachi. Microbrewery with attached restaurant and bar in an old storehouse. Try the combination taster of two types of Kurashiki Beer – Kölsch and Alt – with a snack for ¥500 before deciding which one to go for. Snacks are available and a ¥950 set lunch is served daily (11.30am–2.30pm). Daily except Wed 11am–6pm.

Mamakari-tei 3-12 Honmachi. Fine place to try the local speciality *mamakari sushi*, just up some steps off the street. A set lunch including the sushi, along with baked fish, tofu and soup, is ¥2500.

Naish Curry Nishinaka-shinda 78-2. Just off the Ebisu-dōri arcade, this great little curry restaurant and bar gets pretty lively at night. Delicious sets from ¥800 – they'll ask you how spicy you want your curry and how much rice. Mon–Fri 6pm–3am, Sat & Sun 11.30am–3am.

Rentenchi Kurashiki Chūō-dōri. Intimate, dimly lit Italian restaurant with pasta and pizza meals for around ¥1500 per person.

Terrace de Ryokan Kurashiki 4-1 Honmachi. Elegant café at the back of the *Ryokan Kurashiki*, opening out onto a beautiful traditional garden which is particularly enchanting at dusk. Indulge in tea and biscuits for ¥840. Daily 9am–8pm.

Bars

Coffee Avenue Honmachi. Cool coffee shop in the middle of a street of old merchant houses. At 7pm it transforms into *Your Jazz Life* bar, with live jazz (Wed–Sat; cover charge ¥500).

Ivy Square 7-2 Honmachi. In July and August you can chill out at the beer garden in the inner courtyard of this red-brick, ivy-clad complex. July & Aug daily 6–9.30pm.

Takahashi

Some 40km northwest of Okayama, in the foothills of the mountain range which divides Western Honshū, is **TAKAHASHI**, a small and charming time-warped castle town. Few visitors venture here despite the fine old buildings and temples in the **Ishibiya-chō Furusato Mura** ("Hometown Village") area, a name evoking images of a long-lost Japan. Except for the steep hike up to the castle – Japan's highest – all of Takahashi's sights are within easy walking distance of Bitchū Takahashi Station and can be covered in half a day. Finding your way around is simple, since there are plenty of direction signs in English.

The row of temples, ranged attractively at staggered levels along the hillside and heading north towards Furusato Mura, lies mainly on the eastern side of the train tracks. The single most impressive is **Raikyū-ji** (daily 9am–5pm; ¥300), ten minutes' walk from the train station, with its serenely beautiful raked-gravel garden. The exact date of the temple's construction is lost in the mists of time, though it is known that in 1604 Kobori Enshū, governor of the province and expert gardener, lived in the temple. The Zen garden he designed is maintained today exactly as he left it, with its islands of stones, plants and trimmed azalea hedges carefully placed to resemble a crane and a tortoise in the "well-wishing garden" style, and featuring the distant borrowed scenery of Mount Atago.

Rest by Raikyū-ji's garden before tackling the strenuous hour-long hike up to the castle, **Bitchū Matsuyama-jō**, following a shaded track through the hillside forest; even if you take a taxi from the station (¥1200), it's still a steep fifteen-minute walk from the car park. Takahashi's fortunes prospered from the mid-thirteenth century, when warlord Akiba Saburoshigenobu built the original fortress on top of the nearby Mount Gagyū. Don't bother paying to go into the **donjon** (daily 9am–4.30pm; ¥300), restored this century, since there are few relics inside and not much of a view from its narrow windows. The vistas on the walk back downhill make the effort of hiking up worthwhile.

On returning to the town, if you have time, explore the **Ishibiya-chō Furusato Mura** area of old houses and buildings, sandwiched between the rail tracks and the Takahashi-gawa and cut through by a stream crossed by stone

7

WESTERN HONSHŪ | Okayama and around

Takahashi, Kojima and Imbe

Takahashi	*Takahashi*	高梁
Bitchū Matsuyama-jō	*Bitchū Matsuyama-jō*	備中松山城
Bitchū Takahashi Station	*Bitchū-Takahashi-eki*	備中高梁駅
Local History Museum	*Kyōdo Shiryōkan*	郷土資料館
Raikyū-ji	*Raikyū-ji*	頼久寺
Samurai House Museum	*Buke-yashiki-kan*	武家屋敷館
Accommodation		
Fukiya	*Fukiya*	吹屋
Takahashi Cycling Terminal	*Takahashi-shi Saikuringu Tāminaru*	高梁サイクリングターミナル
Takahashi Kokusai Hotel	*Takahashi Kokusai Hoteru*	高梁国際ホテル
Takahashi Youth Hostel	*Takahashi Yūsu Hosuteru*	高梁ユースホステル
Kojima	*Kojima*	児島
Bridge Museum	*Seto Ōhashi Kinenkan*	瀬戸大橋記念館
Mukashi Shimotsui Kaisendonya	*Mukashi Shimotsui Kaisendonya*	むかし下津井回船問屋
Seto Ōhashi	*Seto Ōhashi*	瀬戸大橋
Washū-zan	*Washū-zan*	鷲羽山
Washū-zan Youth Hostel	*Washū-zan Yūsu Hosuteru*	鷲羽山ユースホステル
Imbe	*Imbe*	伊部
Hattōji	*Hattōji*	八塔寺
Shizutani School	*Shizutani Gakkō*	閑谷学校

637

bridges topped with miniature shrines. Of the several buildings here which have been turned into museums, the most interesting are the **Buké-yashiki-kan samurai house** (daily 9am–5pm; ¥300) and the wooden, Meiji-era Takahashi Elementary School, now the **Local History Museum** (daily 9am–5pm; ¥300), housing a jumble of items running from *mikoshi* (portable shrines) to a morse code machine. At the back of the ground floor are some evocative black-and-white photos of the town, while on the second floor you should look out for the dancing doll models made from old cigarette packets – a nod to Japan Tobacco, which has a factory in Takahashi.

Practicalities

Takahashi's train station, **Bitchū–Takahashi**, is on the JR Hakubi line, just under an hour from Okayama or 45 minutes from Kurashiki. You can pick up a Japanese map of the town from the **information office** (Mon–Fri 8am–6pm, Sat 8.30am–5pm; ☎0866/21-0461) at the bus terminal, next to the station. The staff here only speak Japanese, but are welcoming and can point you towards **accommodation**, if you decide to stay overnight.

The *Takahashi Youth Hostel* (☎0866/22-3149; dorms ¥2800 per person), a small place run by a chatty old lady, is next to the Kofuku-ji temple on the way to Raikyū-ji, and overlooks the temple's gardens. Budget accommodation is also available some way out of town at the *Takahashi-shi Cycling Terminal* (☎0866/22-0135, ℱ22-0935; ❸ including meals), which has both Japanese and Western-style rooms. Bicycles can be rented here (¥500 for 4hr). The *Cycling Terminal* is a twenty-minute bus journey from the bus terminal; get off at Wonderland Iri-guchi and walk for twenty minutes. For upmarket accommodation, try the *Takahashi Kokusai Hotel* (☎0866/21-0080, ℱ21-0075; ❺), two minutes' walk north of the station. Alternatively, you could explore Takahashi from the International Villa (see box, p.628) in the charming hamlet of **FUKIYA**, an old copper-mining centre with streets of nineteenth-century merchants' houses made of wood, plaster and tiles. The villa is a modern building mixing Western and Japanese styles, about an hour by bus (3 daily) from Bitchū–Takahashi.

Eating options in Takahashi are centred around the station, where there are several restaurants with plastic food displays. *Jūjū-tei* (closed Thurs), near the *Takahashi Kokusai Hotel*, is an inexpensive *okonomiyaki* restaurant, while across the road is *Sushi Hana-kan* (daily until 7pm), a take-out sushi shop, ideal for a picnic lunch at the castle.

Kojima and Seto Ōhashi

Twenty-five kilometres south of Okayama, **KOJIMA**, with its sprawling shopping centres and newly laid roads, has boomed since the opening in 1988 of the nearby 12.3-kilometre-long **Seto Ōhashi**, a series of six bridges and four viaducts hopping from island to island across the Inland Sea to Shikoku. One of the most memorable ways to view this engineering wonder is to take an hour-long boat tour (daily: March–Nov 9am–4pm; Jan, Feb & Dec 10am–2pm; ¥1550) from the sightseeing pier immediately to the east of Kojima Station. The boats depart on the hour, except at noon.

If you'd prefer to view the Seto Ōhashi and islands from dry land, head 4km south of Kojima to **Washū-zan**, a 134-metre-high hill jutting out into the Inland Sea. Regular buses run to the lookout point, from outside both Kojima and Kurashiki (see p.631) stations. Stay on the bus past the fishing hamlet of **Shimotsui** and Washū-zan Highland, a tacky amusement park, and get off at the car park by the official lookout spot. From here you can climb to Washū-zan's summit and take in what has to be one of Japan's most glorious panoramas. If you have time, stop off in Shimotsui and check out the interesting **Mukashi Shimotsui Kaisendonya** (daily except Tues 9am–5pm; free), a museum of fisherfolk life, and wander around the old streets, taking in the castle ruins, the covered wells from which passing boats stocked up on fresh water, and the Gion-jinja shrine.

Back in Kojima, the **Bridge Museum** (Tues–Sun 9am–5pm; free), a ten-minute walk west of the train station, is a wacky attraction, well worth a look if you have the time. You can actually walk over the arched museum building, inspired by a *taiko-bashi* (drum bridge), and enjoy the small park over the road containing eleven amusing mini-bridges, a chessboard-like square decorated with bizarre silver statues (supposedly symbolizing the seasons) and a model of Stephenson's *Rocket*. Inside the museum, which displays scale models of bridges from around the world, the eye is drawn immediately to the roof, painted with a lively mural of Edo-era travelling performers, craftsmen, merchants and priests. The rather less unusual **Nozaki House** (Tues–Sun 9am–4.30pm; ¥500), the handsomely kept mansion of salt tycoon Nozaki Buzaemon, lies five minutes' walk northwest of the Bridge Museum. The house dates from the 1830s and includes three picturesque storehouses, identical to those found in Kurashiki.

The **tourist office** (daily 9am–6pm; ☎086/472-1289) in Kojima Station has a friendly, English-speaking assistant who can provide you with an English map and booklet on the area. The best **place to stay** in the area is at the *Washū-zan Youth Hostel* (☎ & ℱ086/479-9280; ❶), which has bunk-bed dorms (¥2100 per person) and good food, as well as impressive views of the Seto Ōhashi and the Inland Sea from its location at the tip of a promontory. It takes twenty minutes to reach the hostel on one of the frequent buses (last bus at 4.20pm) leaving for Washū-zan from platform 2 outside Kojima Station.

Imbe and around

Only dedicated lovers of ceramics will want to linger in drab **IMBE**, 30km east of Okayama and home of Bizen-yaki, Japan's oldest method of making pottery, developed here over a thousand years ago. The ceramics' distinctive earthy colour and texture are achieved without the use of glazes by firing in wood-fuelled kilns, whose brick chimneys you'll see dotted around Imbe Station. Beside the station is a **tourist information** counter (daily except Tues 9am–6pm; ☎0869/64-1100), where you can pick up an English leaflet about Bizen-yaki and get directions to the local pottery museums, the best being the **Bizen Pottery Traditional and Contemporary Art Museum** (Tues–Sun 9.30am–4.30pm; ¥500), in the grey concrete block immediately north of the station. This museum displays both old and new examples of the ceramics, providing an overview of the pottery's style and development.

There are plenty of kilns with attached shops which you can mooch around in Imbe, and at some these are studios where you can sculpt your own blob of clay, for around ¥3000. This is then fired and shipped to your home (for overseas deliveries you'll need to pay extra). The most convenient place to try your hand at making pottery is the **Bizen-yaki Traditional Pottery Centre** (☎0869/64-1001), on the third floor of Imbe Station, where workshops are held each weekend and on holidays.

If you have a car, it's worth exploring the area around Imbe and in particular heading northeast to visit the **Shizutani School** (daily 9am–4.30pm; ¥300), 3km south of the Yoshinaga Station on the JR San'yō line. Secluded in a leafy vale, this elegant walled compound of buildings was established by feudal lord Ikeda Mitsumasa in 1666 as a school open to all, regardless of social position. The gateways and large lecture hall are roofed with warm brown and grey Bizen-yaki tiles, contrasting sharply with the green lawns and gently rounded stone walls.

Returning to Yoshinaga Station, you can catch occasional buses north to the picturesque village of **HATTŌJI**, setting for the anti-war movie *Black Rain* by Imamura Shohei, and home to the oldest and perhaps loveliest of Okayama's International Villas (see box, p.628). The restored thatched-roof village farmhouse, on the slopes of Mount Hattōji, has an open hearth and a *goemonburo* – a traditional stone and metal bath – and all the rooms have tatami and *fusuma* (sliding screens).

Fukuyama and around

Some 65km west from Okayama along the industrialized San'yō coast is the old castle town of **Fukuyama**, now the key industrial city of Hiroshima-ken's Bingo district. The main reason to visit Fukuyama, apart from a few quirky museums, is as a jumping-off point for the characterful seaside towns of **Tomonoura** and **Onomichi**, from where you can also explore the islands of the Inland Sea.

The Town

One of Japan's less interesting castles, **Fukuyama-jō** (Tues–Sun 9am–4.30pm; ¥200), immediately north of the train station, can be safely ignored in favour of the more memorable **Hiroshima Prefectural Museum of History**, just west of the station (Tues–Sun 9.30am–4.30pm; ¥290). Designed around the excavation of the ruins of **Kusado Sengen**, a medieval town buried in the nearby riverbed of the Ashida-gawa, the museum has some imaginatively displayed artefacts and haunting background music, as well as a reconstructed village street from Kusado Sengen, lit to recreate twilight in May. Next door is the **Fukuyama Museum of Art** (Tues–Sun 9.30am–5pm; ¥300), with a permanent collection of mainly Japanese art, focusing on contemporary works by local artists. The most striking pieces of sculpture are in the surrounding gardens. The gallery also hosts visiting exhibitions, for which there's an extra charge.

Fifteen minutes' walk north of Fukuyama Station is the odd **Fukuyama Automobile and Clock Museum** (daily 9am–6pm; ¥900, or ¥700 with a discount coupon from the tourist information desk), combining vintage vehicles, including a motorbike taxi, with clocks and music machines. To liven things up there are also waxwork models of celebrities such as Elvis Presley and James Dean. If you don't fancy walking there, take a bus to Kitayoshizu-Jūtaku from platform 3 outside the east exit of Fukuyama Station.

Keeping up the quirky museum theme are the **Japan Footwear Museum** and the **Japan Folk Toy and Doll Museum** (daily 9am–5pm; ¥1000 joint ticket), five minutes' walk east of Matsunaga Station, two stops west of Fukuyama. It's only natural that the town of Matsunaga, which has produced *geta* (traditional wooden sandals) for over a century, hosts Japan's only museum dedicated to shoes. It's a large and surprisingly intriguing collection – from straw sandals to a pair of lunar boots used on one of the Apollo missions – that would make Imelda Marcos drool with envy. The toy museum next door is less unique, but just as extensive, with over fifty thousand colourful exhibits. Most of the toys are linked to festivals and religious beliefs and there's also a fascinating display of Kachina dolls made by the Hopi people in Arizona.

Fukuyama	*Fukuyama*	福山
Fukuyama Automobile and Clock Museum	*Fukuyama Jidōsha Tokei Hakubutsukan*	福山自動車時計博物館
Fukuyama Museum of Art	*Fukuyama Bijutsukan*	福山美術館
Hiroshima Prefectural Museum of History	*Hiroshima-kenritsu Rekishi Hakubutsukan*	広島県立歴史博物館
Japan Folk Toy and Doll Museum	*Nihon Kyōdo Gangu Hakubutsukan*	日本郷土玩具博物館
Japan Footwear Museum	*Nihon Hakimono Hakubutsukan*	日本はきもの博物館

Accommodation		
Fukuyama Oriental Hotel	*Fukuyama Orientaru Hoteru*	福山オリエンタルホテル
Marunouchi Hotel	*Marunouchi Hoteru*	まるのうちホテル
New Castle Hotel	*Nyū Kyassuru Hoteru*	ニューキャッスルホテル

Tomonoura	*Tomonoura*	鞆の浦
Fukuzen-ji	*Fukuzen-ji*	福善寺
Hōsen-ji	*Hōsen-ji*	法宣寺
Iō-ji	*Iō-ji*	医王寺
Nunakuma-jinja	*Nunakuma-jinja*	沼名前神社
Sensui-an	*Sensui-an*	仙粋庵
Sensui-jima	*Sensui-jima*	仙酔島
Tomonoura Museum of History	*Tomonoura Rekishi Minzoku Shiryōkan*	鞆の浦歴史民俗資料館
Uonosato	*Uonosato*	うをの里

Accommodation		
Keishōkan	*Keishōkan*	景勝館
Kokuminshukusha Sensui-jima	*Kokuminshukusha Sensui-jima*	国民宿舎仙酔島
Hotel Ōfūtei	*Hoteru Ōfūtei*	ホテル鴎風亭
Tomo Seaside Hotel	*Tomo Shiisaido Hoteru*	鞆シーサイドホテル

Onomichi	*Onomichi*	尾道
Fukuzen-ji	*Fukuzen-ji*	福善寺
Jōdo-ji	*Jōdo-ji*	浄土寺
Saikoku-ji	*Saikoku-ji*	西国寺
Senkō-ji	*Senkō-ji*	千光寺
Senkō-ji-kōen	*Senkō-ji-kōen*	千光寺公園

Accommodation		
Alpha-1	*Arufa-1*	アルファ1
Dai-Ichi Hotel	*Dai-Ichi Hoteru*	第一ホテル
View Hotel Seizan	*Byū Hoteru Seizan*	ビュウホテルセイザン

Practicalities

Fukuyama Station is on both the Shinkansen and JR San'yō **train** lines. The bus terminus, from where services run to Tomonoura (see p.642), is beside the station's south exit. Inside the station, beside the north exit, is the **tourist information desk** (daily 8.30am–5.15pm; ☎0849/22-2869), where the helpful assistants speak English and can provide you with English maps and leaflets on Fukuyama and

Tomonoura. If for some reason you need to **stay** overnight, the best selection of hotels can be found north of the station. The *Marunouchi Hotel* (℡0849/23-2277, ℻23-6557; ❹) has the cheapest rates, while the *Fukuyama Oriental Hotel* (℡0849/27-0888, ℻27-0991; ❺) offers smart, spacious en-suite rooms with TVs and fridges. Top of the range is the characterless *New Castle Hotel* (℡0849/22-2121, ℻23-6813; ❻), one minute south of the station.

There are plenty of **restaurants** along the south side of the JR station, including the usual fast-food outlets. The *Delhy Curry Shop* behind the Tenmaya department store on the Motomachi arcade, five minutes' walk south of Fukuyama Station, has tasty curries and good-value lunch sets. If you're after a few beers in the evening try the *izakaya Eki-no-Shita*, which is open until midnight.

Tomonoura

There are few more pleasant ways to spend half a day or more in Japan than exploring the enchanting fishing port of **TOMONOURA**, at the tip of the Numakuma Peninsula, 14km south of Fukuyama. The town has one of the most beautiful locations on the Inland Sea, and its narrow, twisting streets and surrounding hills, liberally sprinkled with picturesque temples and shrines, are easi-

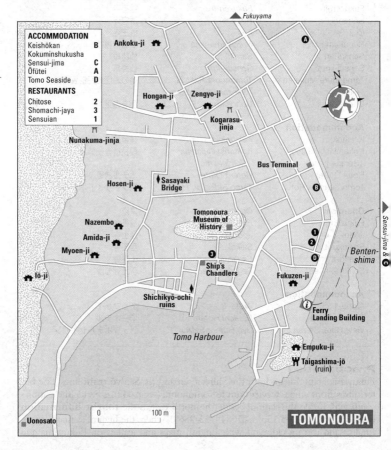

ly explored on foot or by bicycle. Boats unload their catch daily beside the horse-shoe-shaped **harbour**, which has hardly changed since the town's Edo-era heyday, when trading vessels waited here for the tides to change direction or rested en route to mainland Asia. Now, you're just as likely to see locals dreaming the day away on the sea walls, rod in hand, waiting for the fish to bite, or selling catches of prawns, squirming crabs, and other seafood on the streets.

The best way to get your bearings is by climbing up to the ruins of the castle **Taigashima-jō** on the headland immediately above the ferry landing and pausing to take in the view from the Empuku-ji temple, where you'll also find a small monument to the celebrated haiku poet Bashō. To the west, you can see the gentle sweep of the harbour and the temple-studded slopes of Taishiden hill, while to the east is tiny **Benten-jima**, an outsized rock crowned with a temple to the Buddhist deity, and the larger island **Sensui-jima**, the best place to stay the night (see p.644).

Heading west into the town from the bus terminal, you'll soon hit the steps leading up to the **Tomonoura Museum of History** (Tues–Sun: 9am–5pm; ¥150), which has a few mildly diverting exhibits including a miniature model of the sea bream-netting show held every day in May, when the local fishermen use age-old methods to herd the fish into their nets. Even if you don't go into the museum, the view from its hilltop location in the middle of the town, across a patchwork of grey and blue tiled roofs dropping away to the harbour, is one of Tomonoura's most pleasant.

Returning to the foot of the hill, follow the narrow road west past the ship's chandler's shop and then turn left into the street lined with wood and plaster warehouses dating from the eighteenth and nineteenth centuries, some of which have been converted into gift and coffee shops. At the end of the street is the confusingly named **Shichikyō-ochi Ruins** (daily except Tues 10am–5pm; ¥400), a perfectly intact old sake brewery that briefly sheltered a band of anti-shogun rebels in the turbulent times prior to the Meiji Restoration. The water-washed steps of the harbour, topped off by a handsome stone lantern, are directly ahead.

Much of the locally caught fish ends up being processed at **Uonosato** (Tues–Sun 9am–5pm; free), a surprisingly engaging snack-food factory in a commanding hillside position on the far western side of the harbour. There's more of a craft shop than a factory atmosphere inside and you can try your hand at making your prawn paste *sembei* (crackers) and other snacks after watching demonstrations by the friendly, blue-clothed workers (¥850). Outside the workshops, seafood dries in the sunlight on large wooden racks and there are craft shops on the surrounding terraces, all of which provide marvellous views across the harbour.

Returning towards the town, keep an eye open for the sign pointing up a narrow pedestrian alley up Taishiden hill to the pretty temple **Iō-ji**. If you're cycling it's best to leave your bike on the main road before hiking up to the temple, one of many founded by the revered Buddhist priest Kōbō Daishi (see p.954). You can hike down the hill eastwards past several more temples, including **Hōsen-ji**, where only a truncated stump remains of the previously 14.3-metre-wide Tengai pine tree. As the street turns the corner, just beyond Hōsen-ji, glance down to see the mini-stone bridge **Sasayaki**, where a couple of ill-fated lovers are said to have once whispered sweet nothings before drowning.

Continuing north for a couple of minutes, you'll arrive at the hillside approach to **Nunakuma-jinja**, a large shrine which, although ancient, has been recently rebuilt in concrete. More impressive is the traditional wooden Nō stage within the shrine grounds that used to be taken around battlefields so the warlord Toyotomi Hideyoshi could be entertained. A couple of minutes' walk further north is **Ankoku-ji** (daily 9am–5pm; ¥100), founded around 1270, and containing two wooden statues of Buddha, designated as national treasures, though neither they nor the temple's tatty sand and rock garden are worth going out of your way for.

Either wind your way back to the ferry landing along the narrow streets or follow the seafront to the south, then hike up the hill immediately to the north to take in one more view from the Taichoro reception hall of **Fukuzen-ji** temple (daily 9am–5pm). It costs ¥200 to enter the airy tatami space with paper screens that open to reveal a striking panorama of the Inland Sea, a view which has changed little since 1711, when a visiting Korean envoy hailed it "the most beautiful scenery in Japan".

Practicalities

Buses leave platform 11 at Fukuyama bus terminus roughly every fifteen minutes, and take around thirty minutes to reach Tomonoura. They stop at the ferry landing building, inside which is an **information desk** (daily 9am–5.45pm), where you can pick up an English map of the town. **Bikes** can be rented from the adjoining car park (¥100 for 2hr, plus ¥500 deposit).

Accommodation in Tomonoura is limited to expensive ryokan-type hotels in charmless modern buildings. Both the *Keishōkan* (℡084/982-2121, ℻982-2510; ❽) and the *Tomo Seaside Hotel* (℡084/983-5111, ℻983-5333; ❼) have traditional tatami rooms with sea views, meals included, but are geared towards the tastes of old-fashioned tour parties. The most upmarket choice is the *Hotel Ōfūtei* (℡084/982-2480; ❽), whose highlight is its collection of huge rooftop baths; thankfully the strikingly ugly building is safely out of view at the north end of the town. However, a much better option is to take the ferry that regularly shuttles across to **Sensui-jima** (5min; ¥240 return) and stay in the smartly refurbished *Kokuminshukusha Sensui-jima* (℡084/970-5050, ℻970-5035; ❻), which has superior-quality tatami rooms and a relaxing set of public baths, including an outdoor rooftop pool. Breakfast and dinner are ¥2800 per person extra and, admirably for a Japanese hotel, there are no TVs in the rooms; instead, you'll find pens and paper and a note encouraging guests to write a letter or even a poem. At a small visitors' centre beside the hotel, you can pick up a map showing four trails around the island, including one across its hilly centre and another passing secluded beaches.

Being a fishing port, Tomonoura has a decent range of seafood **restaurants**, the best being *Chitose* (closed Tues), a friendly joint just behind the car park on the town's eastern waterfront. A delicious set meal of many dishes, including Tomo's trademark catch of *tai* (sea bream), costs ¥1680. In the same row of shops, pop into the charming *Sensuian*, a café serving *macha* tea and *dango* rice balls in winter and shaved ice desserts in the summer. Also worth checking out is *Shomachi-jaya* (Tues–Sun 9am–7.30pm), which serves tempura set meals for ¥1400, in an atmospheric wooden building near the chandler's shop on the east side of the harbour.

Onomichi

Twenty kilometres west of Fukuyama lies the appealingly raffish port of **ONOMICHI**, overlooked by the houses and temples that tumble down the steep face of the wooded hill, Senkōji-san. Many Japanese come here to linger along the town's vertiginous byways, imagining scenes from their favourite movies by local director Ōbayashi Nobuhiko. Onomichi is also a gateway to

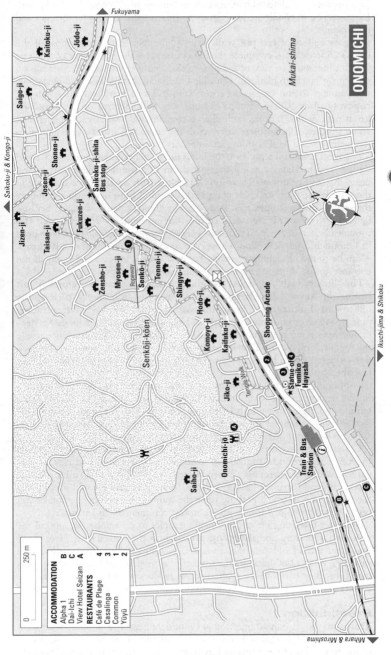

Fukuyama

▲ *Saikoku-ji & Kongo-ji*

Kaitoku-ji

Jōdo-ji

Saigo-ji

Shonen-ji

Josen-ji

Jizen-ji

Taisan-ji

Fukuzen-ji

Saikoku-ji-shita
Bus stop

Zensho-ji

Myosen-ji

Senkō-ji

Tennei-ji

Shingyo-ji

Hodo-ji

Ropeway

Senkōji-kōen

Konoyo-ji

Kaitoku-ji

Jiko-ji

Temple Walk

Onomichi-jō

Saiho-ji

Mukai-shima

ONOMICHI

Shopping Arcade

Statue of
Fumiko
Hayashi

Ikuchi-jima & Shikoku ▶

Train & Bus
Station

▲ *Mihara & Miroshima*

0   250 m

ACCOMMODATION
Alpha 1   B
Dai-Ichi   C
View Hotel Seizan   A

RESTAURANTS
Café de Plage   4
Casalinga   3
Common   1
Yūyū   2

some of the islands of the Inland Sea, including Ikuchi-jima and Ōmi-shima (see opposite), and to Shikoku via ferry or by road along the Nishi-Seto Expressway, a sixty-kilometre highway to Imabari that crosses ten bridges and nine islands.

There's a pleasant **temple walk** from Onomichi Station past most of the town's 25 temples; to complete the full course takes the better part of a day, by which time you'll be sick of temples, so skip those at the start by hopping on the regular bus from platform 1 outside Onomichi Station and heading east for five minutes to the Nagaeguchi stop (¥140). From here, you can catch the **ropeway** (daily 9am–5.15pm; ¥280 one way, ¥440 return) up to **Senkō-ji-kōen** park, which blooms with cherry blossom and azaleas each spring. The views from its hilltop observatory across the town and narrow sea channel to the nearest island Mukai-shima are impressive.

The most colourful temple on the hill is the scarlet-painted **Senkō-ji**, packed with *jizō* statues and doing a lively trade in devotional trinkets, particularly heart-shaped placards which visitors scribble a wish on and leave dangling in the temple for good luck. Heading back downhill from here, you can follow the section of the temple walk known as the "literary path", so called because famous writers' words are inscribed on stone monuments along the way. The most celebrated of the local writers is Hayashi Fumiko, a female poet who lived in Onomichi from 1917 and whose bronze statue – something of a landmark – can be found crouching pensively beside a wicker suitcase and brolly at the entrance to the shopping arcade a minute east of the station.

The "literary path" continues past the pagoda at the temple **Tennei-ji**, just behind the ropeway base station, from where you can head east back up the hill towards **Fukuzen-ji**. This temple, dating from 1573, has a vast spreading pine tree in its grounds, said to be shaped like an eagle, and its main gate is decorated with some beautiful wood carvings of cranes and dragons. Once inside the temple, look out for **Tile-ko-michi** (Little Tile Street), a narrow alley back down the hill which has been plastered over the last 25 years with ceramic slabs inscribed by visitors.

Continuing east along the flagstoned streets, head north up the hill when you hit the next main crossroads, and you'll arrive at **Saikoku-ji**, one of the largest temple complexes in western Japan and easily spotted by the giant straw sandals which hang either side of the imposing entrance gate; pray here and it's said you'll find the strength to continue your journey.

The last temple worth visiting is **Jōdo-ji** at the eastern end of the route. Pigeons flock around its squat two-storey pagoda, and there's an elegant Zen garden, with a tea-ceremony room transported from Kyoto's Fushimi castle, hidden behind the main hall of worship. To see the garden you'll have to pay the attendant ¥500; he'll perk up once the money's handed over and take you on a personally guided tour with a nonstop commentary in Japanese.

Don't get too hung up in Onomichi's temples to miss pottering around the evocative waterfront and **shopping arcade** near the train station. Here you'll find remnants of old Asia rare in squeaky-clean modern Japan, including a shrinking crescent of shacks by the sea that have miraculously survived the combined forces of earthquakes, typhoons and redevelopment. In and around the arcades are several antique and junk emporiums that are also worth a browse.

Practicalities

Trains on the JR San'yō line stop at Onomichi Station, a minute's walk from the waterfront. The closest Shinkansen station, Shin-Onomichi, is 3km north of the town; from here a regular bus takes fifteen minutes to reach Onomichi

Station (¥180). **Buses** leave from outside Onomichi Station for Ikuchi-jima (see below) and Hiroshima Airport (see p.654), thirty minutes west. Ferries to Setoda on Ikuchi-jima leave from the jetty immediately in front of Onomichi Station. Tourist **information** is available to the right of Onomichi Station inside the Teatro Shell-rune building (daily 9am–6pm; ☎0848/20-0005, ℗20-1361). The assistants don't speak English, but you can pick up an English map here that marks out the walking route around the temples.

The cheapest **accommodation** options are business hotels, of which there are several immediately west of the station, including the *Alpha-1* (☎0848/25-5600; ❺) and the *Dai-Ichi Hotel*, just round the corner (☎0848/23-4567, ℗23-2112; ❺) – rooms at the latter have sea views. *View Hotel Seizan* (☎0848/23-3313, ℗22-3780; ❹–❺) is a friendly place up by the castle with great views out over the Inland Sea and discounted off-peak rates.

Onomichi fancies itself as something of a gourmet destination and the tourist office produces a map in Japanese detailing an impressive range of **eating** options. Being a port, fresh seafood is the thing to go for, especially at the sushi restaurants clustered along the harbour front east of the station. There are plenty of Western-style restaurants, too, such as *Casalinga* (daily except Thurs 11.30am–3pm & 5.30–8.30pm), a funky Italian joint between the shopping arcade and the water-front, with red-checked tablecloths and graffiti on the walls; lunch here costs around ¥1000, and dinner not much more. Just round the corner, on the water-front, you can get a cheap lunch of salad and a drink at the trendy *Cafe de Plage*, which also opens in the evenings at weekends. In the arcade itself, you'll find *Yūyū* (daily 10am–7pm), a café-bar and giftshop with a 1920s feel, while, at the base of the ropeway, *Common* (daily 10am–5pm) specializes in freshly made Belgian waffles (¥400–670 with a drink). There are plenty of bars and late-night eateries in the entertainment district south of the bus stop Saikoku-ji-shita, in the narrow streets between the railway line and the waterfront.

Ikuchi-jima and Ōmi-shima

Among the Geiyo archipelago of islands clogging the Inland Sea between Onomichi and the northwest coast of Shikoku, **IKUCHI-JIMA** and **ŌMI-SHIMA** are both worth a visit. Of the two, Ikuchi-jima is the place to stay and has the best attractions, including **Kōsan-ji**, a dazzling Disneyland-esque temple complex, and the exquisite **Hirayama Ikuo Museum of Art**.

Whilst part of the fun of visiting these islands is the **ferry** ride there, you can also get to Ikuchi-jima by bus from Onomichi, since the islands are connected to the mainland by a series of bridges that carry the Nishi-Seto Expressway. Ikuchi-jima is best explored, like its neighbour, by bicycle.

Ikuchi-jima

Sun-kissed **IKUCHI-JIMA** is covered with citrus groves and attracts plenty of tourists each summer to its palm-fringed beaches, in particular the sweeping man-made Sunset Beach on the west coast. The potato-shaped island can comfortably be toured by bicycle in a day, as can the islet Kōne-shima, which is linked by bridge to Ikuchi-jima's main settlement, the quaint **Setoda** on the island's northwest coast. Around the island, you should look out for the fourteen bizarre contemporary outdoor sculptures, including a giant saxophone and a stack of yellow buckets, which form part of Ikuchi-jima's "Biennale" modern art project.

Ikuchi-jima	*Ikuchi-jima*	生口島
Hirayama Ikuo Museum of Art	*Hirayama Ikuo Bijutsukan*	平山郁夫美術館
Chōseikaku	*Chōseikaku*	潮聲閣
Kōsan-ji	*Kōsan-ji*	耕三寺
Setoda	*Setoda*	瀬戸田
Accommodation		
Ikuchi-jima Shimanami Youth Hostel	*Ikuchi-jima Shimanami Yūsu Hosuteru*	生口島しまなみユースホステル
Sazanami	*Sazanami*	さざなみ
Setoda Youth House	*Setoda Yūsu Hausu*	瀬戸田ユースハウス
Suminoe	*Suminoe*	住之江
Ōmi-shima	*Ōmi-shima*	大三島
Inokuchi	*Inokuchi*	井口
Miyaura	*Miyaura*	宮浦
Ōyamazumi-jinja	*Ōyamazumi-jinja*	大山祇神社

Kōsan-ji

A giftshop-lined street leads directly from Setoda's ferry landing to the unmistakeably gaudy entrance to Ikuchi-jima's wackiest attraction – the technicolour temple complex of **Kōsan-ji** (daily 9am–5pm; ¥1000). Kōsan-ji was the creation of steel-tube manufacturer Kanemoto Kozo, who made much of his fortune from the arms trade. A devoted son, Kanemoto used some of his funds to build his mother a holiday retreat in their home town of Setoda. When she died, the bereft Kanemoto decided to build a temple in her honour, so bought a priesthood from Nishi-Hongan-ji temple in Kyoto and took over the name of a minor-league temple, Kōsan-ji, in Niigata. He resigned from his company, grew his hair, changed his name to Kōsanji Kozo, and began drawing up plans for the new Kōsan-ji – a collection of copies of the most splendid examples of Japanese temple buildings – which now includes about ten halls, three towers, four gates, an underground cave and an enormous statue of Kannon, the Goddess of Mercy. Although many of the recreations are smaller than the originals, Kanemoto cut no corners when it came to detail, even adding his own embellishments, most famously to the already over-the-top replica of the Yōmei-mon from Nikkō's Tōshō-gū. Behind Kanemoto's seemingly barmy project lay sound business sense. Despite its costly upkeep, Kōsan-ji has attracted millions of paying visitors since its opening in 1936, and continues to do so. And since it's recognized as an official temple, Kōsan-ji's considerable income is tax-free.

The Sanmon entrance gate is modelled on one from the imperial palace in Kyoto. Inside, the central focus is on a faithful reproduction of the Yōmei-mon (Sunshine Gate) from Tōshō-gū in Nikkō – it was this gate, completed in the mid-1950s, that earned Kōsan-ji its nickname Nishi-Nikkō, the "Nikkō of the west". To the right of the main temple building is the entrance to the **Sembutsudō** (Cave of a Thousand Buddhas) and the Valley of Hell. An underground passage leads past miniature tableaux showing the horrors of damnation, followed by the raptures of a heavenly host of Buddhas. You then wind your way up to emerge beneath the beatific gaze of a fifteen-metre-tall statue of the Buddhist Goddess of Mercy, Kannon. From here you can walk up to the

Hill of Hope, a collection of bizarre modern marble sculptures with names like "Cat of the Sky", "Flame of the Future" and "Stage of the Noble Turtle".

Kōsan-ji's five-storeyed pagoda, modelled on the one at Murō-ji in Nara, is the last resting place of Kanemoto's beloved mother, whose holiday home, **Chōseikaku**, is right by the exit (daily 9am–5pm; ¥700). The home is a fascinating combination of Western and traditional styles, with two of the rooms having beautiful painted panels on their ceilings and a Buddha-like model of Mrs Kanemoto resting in one of the alcoves. Opposite the mother's retreat is Kōsan-ji's **art gallery**, a plain building housing sober displays of mainly religious paintings and statues.

Hirayama Ikuo Museum of Art and around

Topping Kōsan-ji's treasures takes some doing, but the **Hirayama Ikuo Museum of Art**, next door to the temple's art gallery (daily 9am–5pm; ¥700), eclipses it with a superior calibre of art. Hirayama Ikuo, one of Japan's greatest living artists, was born in Setoda in 1930 and was a junior-high-school student in Hiroshima when the bomb dropped – his famous painting "Holocaust at Hiroshima" can be seen in the Hiroshima Museum of Art. Despite travelling the world and becoming famous for his series of paintings on the Silk Road, he continually returns to the Inland Sea for inspiration. Hirayama uses a traditional Japanese painting technique for his giant canvases, working very quickly with

△ Amanohashidate sandbar

fast-drying paint – the resultant swift brush strokes give the finished paintings a distinctively dreamy quality. Because the special paint (*iwaenogu*) needed for this method is much less flexible and dries faster than oil paint, each picture has its own series of preparatory sketches. These full-sized blueprints for the final painting are known as *oshitazu*, and this museum contains many such sketches of Hirayama's most celebrated works, as well as original paintings and watercolours.

After the Hirayama museum, you can take in the view that inspired one of the artist's most beautiful paintings by hiking up to the summit of the hill behind Setoda. A small park here overlooks the attractive three-storey pagoda of **Kōjō-ji**, breaking out of the pine trees below, with the coloured tiled roofs of the village and the islands of the Inland Sea beyond. If you have some time to kill while waiting for a ferry or bus, you could drop by the **Folk Museum** (Mon & Wed–Sun 10am–4.30pm; free) in the old building beside the ferry terminal, where you'll find a mildly diverting collection of antique boats and everyday household objects.

Practicalities

There are **ferries** to Ikuchi-jima from either Onomichi (40min; ¥760 one way) or Sunami, slightly further along the coast, which is on the San'yō rail line and offers the cheapest ferry fare (¥340 one way). The **bus** from Onomichi (1hr; ¥1250) leaves from platform 7 in front of Onomichi Station and terminates at the southern end of Setoda; you might have to change buses at the terminus on Ino-shima along the way. For a map of Ikuchi-jima and a well-illustrated brochure on the island's attractions, partly in English, drop by the **tourist information booth** (daily 9am–5pm; ℡08452/7-0051, ℻6-4001), across from the Hirayama Ikuo Museum of Art. **Bikes** can be rented from here (¥500 per day, plus ¥1000 deposit).

The slightly run-down *Ikuchi-jima Shimanami Youth Hostel* (℡08452/7-3137; ❶), beside Sunset Beach a couple of kilometres south of Setoda, provides cheap **accommodation**, bike rental and meals, and they'll pick you up from the ferry port. Alternatively, there's the distinctive *Setoda Youth House* (℡08452/7-0224; ❷), easily spotted on the hill five minutes' walk south of the ferry terminal by the rainbow painted on one side. Inside, the hostel is just as colourful, decorated with many dolls, including the Seven Dwarfs skulking under the stairs. The tatami rooms have fans and TVs and meals are available. Setoda also has several ryokan: *Sazanami* (℡ & ℻08452/7-3373; ❺), a couple of blocks from the waterfront along the main approach to the Kōsan-ji, is one of the cheapest, while the nicest is *Suminoe* (℡08452/7-2155, ℻7-2156; ❼), a very traditional establishment next to the ferry terminal, with an elegant courtyard garden and spacious tatami rooms. Rates at both include two meals.

Most of Setoda's **eating** options are along the Shiomachi-shōtengai shopping street leading up to the temple. Opposite Kōsan-ji, *Mansaku* and *Chidori* are two smart fish restaurants serving pricey set lunches of local cuisine. For something cheaper, head back towards the ferry terminal for sushi at the down-to-earth *Keima*, or try *Restaurant Fuji* or *Jurobian*, friendly places serving a mish-mash of dishes. If you're cycling around the island, either pack a picnic from Setoda's shops or stop off at Mien, a small *okonomiyaki* joint (closed Thurs) on the coastal road near the Kōmyōbo temple.

Ōmi-shima

While Ikuchi-jima's top attraction is a temple, the big draw of neighbouring **Ōmi-shima** is one of the oldest shrines in the country, **Ōyamazumi-jinja**, dating back to the end of the Kamakura era (1192–1333). Dedicated to

Ōyamazumi, the elder brother of the Shinto deity Amaterasu, the shrine is around a fifteen-minute walk from the small, undistinguished port of **Miyaura**, on the west side of the island. Between the twelfth and sixteenth centuries it used to be a place of worship for pirates, who used the island as a base before being brought to heel by the warlord Toyotomi Hideyoshi.

To the right of the main shrine grounds you'll find three modern buildings comprising Ōyamazumi-jinja's **museum** (daily 8.30am–5pm; ¥1000, including entrance to the Kaiji Museum). The Shiyōden hall and connected Kokuhō-kan are reputed to contain the largest collection of armour in Japan, but unless you're a samurai freak you'll find the dry displays very dull. More intriguing is the **Kaiji Museum**, next door (same hours and entrance fee as above), which houses the Hayama-maru, the boat built for Emperor Hirohito so he could undertake marine biology research. Beside the boat are some meticulously catalogued displays of fish, birds and rocks, some of the sea life looking like pickled aliens.

After visiting the shrine, there's not a huge amount to do on Ōmi-shima other than explore the coast by bike (the best way of getting around the island) – which will take half a day – or linger on some of its less than fine beaches. The interior is hilly, but there is a decent five-kilometre cycle track mainly downhill from **Inokuchi**, the ferry port closest to Ikuchi-jima, across the island to Miyaura.

There are **ferries** from Miyaura to Imabari on Shikoku, and from Mihara (also a Shinkansen stop) on Honshū to Inokuchi. There's also a **bus** to Onomichi from Ōmi-shima bus station (¥1500 one way); the bus station is located just below the Tatara Ōhashi (the bridge linking Ōmi-shima with Ikuchi-jima), from where a local bus will take you to Miyaura.

Hiroshima and around

Western Honshū's largest city needs little introduction. Since August 6, 1945, **HIROSHIMA** has become a byword for the devastating effects of the atom bomb, and for this reason alone millions visit the city every year to pay their respects at the Peace Park and museum. But more than either of these formal monuments, the reconstructed city – bigger, brighter and more vibrant than ever – is eloquent testimony to the power of life over destruction. Where once there was nothing but ashes for as far as the eye could see, there now stands a modern city that still retains an old-world feel with its trundling trams and sunny disposition.

Poised on the coast at the western end of the Inland Sea, Hiroshima is also the jumping-off point for several islands, most notably verdant **Miyajima**, home of the beautiful shrine **Itsukushima-jinja**. The view out to the red *torii* gate standing in the shallows in front of the shrine is rightly one of Japan's most celebrated, and although the island is often swamped by day-trippers it's a delightful place to spend the night.

Some history

During the twelfth century, the delta of the Ōta-gawa on which Hiroshima now stands was known as **Gokamura** (Five Villages). The delta was ruled by Taira no Kiyomori, a scion of the Taira clan who was for a while the power behind the emperor in Kyoto and who commissioned the Ikutsushima-jinja shrine on Miyajima. All this ended when the Taira were vanquished by the

Hiroshima	*Hiroshima*	広島
A-bomb Dome	*Gembaku Dōmu*	原爆ドーム
Hiroshima-jō	*Hiroshima-jō*	広島城
Peace Memorial Museum	*Heiwa Kinen-shiryōkan*	平和記念資料館
Peace Memorial Park	*Heiwa Kinen-kōen*	平和記念公園
Hiroshima City Museum of Contemporary Art	*Hiroshima-shi Gendai Bijutsukan*	広島市現代美術館
Hiroshima Prefectural Museum of Art	*Hiroshima kenritsu Bijutsukan*	広島県立美術館
Shukkei-en	*Shukkei-en*	縮景園

Accommodation

ANA Hotel	*Zennikkū Hoteru*	全日空ホテル
Aster Plaza International Youth House	*Asutēru Puraza Kokusai Yūsu Hausu*	アステールプラザ国際ユースハウス
Dormy Inn Hiroshima	*Dōmī In Hiroshima*	ドーミーイン広島
Hiroshima Kokusai Hotel	*Hiroshima Kokusai Hoteru*	広島国際ホテル
Hiroshima Youth Hostel	*Hiroshima Yūsu Hosuteru*	広島ユースホステル
Mikawa Ryokan	*Mikawa Ryokan*	三河旅館
Rihga Royal Hotel	*Riiga Roiyaru Hoteru*	リーガロイヤルホテル
Hotel Sunroute	*Hoteru Sanrūto*	ホテルサンルート
World Friendship Centre	*Sekai Yūkō Sentā*	世界友好センター

Restaurants and bars

Geishū	*Geishū*	芸州
Kissui	*Kissui*	吉水
Naka-chan	*Naka-chan*	中ちゃん
Namuche Bazaar	*Namuche Bazāru*	ナムチェバザール
Okonomi-mura	*Okonomi-mura*	お好み村
Pacela	*Pasēra*	パセーラ
Suishin	*Suishin*	酔心
Tokugawa	*Tokugawa*	徳川

Minamoto clan (or Genji) at the Battle of Dannoura in 1185. However, Gokamura continued to grow and became crucial during warlord **Mōri Motonari**'s campaign to take control of Chūgoku during the latter half of the fifteenth century. When Motonari's grandson Terumoto built his castle, the city was renamed **Hiroshima** (Wide Island), and by the Meiji era the city had become an important base for the imperial army, a role that placed it firmly on the path to its terrible destiny.

As a garrison town, Hiroshima was an obvious target during World War II, but until August 6, 1945 it had been spared Allied bombing. It's speculated that this was an intentional strategy by the US military so that the effects of the atom bomb when exploded could be fully understood. Even so, when the B29 bomber *Enola Gay* set off on its mission, Hiroshima was one of three possible targets (the others being Nagasaki and Kokura) whose fate was sealed by reconnaissance planes above the city reporting clear skies.

When "Little Boy", as the bomb was nicknamed, exploded 580m above the city at 8.15am it unleashed the equivalent of the destructive power of 15,000 tonnes of TNT. Beneath, some 350,000 people looked up and saw the sun fall

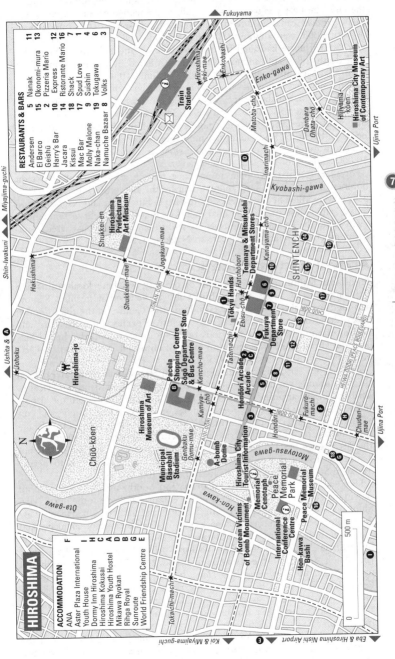

HIROSHIMA

ACCOMMODATION

ANA F
Aster Plaza International I
Youth House
Dormy Inn Hiroshima H
Hiroshima Kokusai C
Hiroshima Youth Hostel A
Mikawa Ryokan D
Rihga Royal B
Sunroute G
World Friendship Centre E

RESTAURANTS & BARS

Andersen 11
El Barco 13
Geishū 2
Harry's Bar 10
Jacara 14
Kissui 18
Mac Bar 17
Molly Malone 9
Naka-chan 4
Namuche Bazaar 8

Nanak 5
Okonomi-mura 15
Pizzeria Mario 2
Express 12
Ristorante Mario 16
Shack 7
Spud Love 1
Suishin 4
Tokugawa 6
Volks 3

▲ *Fukuyama*

Train Station

Hiroshima-eki-mae

Enkobashi

Enko-gawa

Hiroshima Prefectural Art Museum

Shukkei-en

Hakushima

Matoba-chō

Dambara Ohata-chō

Hijiyama-kōen

■ **Hiroshima City Museum of Contemporary Art**

Kyobashi-gawa

Inarimachi

▼ *Ujina Port*

7

WESTERN HONSHŪ | Hiroshima and around

Shukkeien-mae

Jogakuin-mae

Tenmaya & Mitsukoshi Department Stores

Kanayama-chō

SHIN'TENCHI

CHŪO-DŌRI

Tōkyū Hands

Hatchōbori

Ebisu-chō

Fukuya Department Store

Tatemachi

Hondōri Arcade

Kamiya-chō

Kencho-mae

Pacela Shopping Centre Sōgō Department Store & Bus Centre

Hiroshima-jō

★ Johoku

Chūō-kōen

Ōta-gawa

N

Hiroshima Museum of Art

Municipal Baseball Stadium

Genbaku Dōmu-mae

A-bomb Dome

Hiroshima City Tourist Information

Peace Park

Memorial Cenotaph

Korean Victims of Bomb Monument

International Conference Centre

Peace Memorial Museum

Hon-kawa

Motoyasu-gawa

HEIWA-ŌDŌRI PEACE BOULEVARD

Hondōri

Fukuro-machi

Chuden-mae

Chūden-mae

500 m

0

▲ *Ushita & ▲*

▲ *Shin-Iwakuni* ▲ *Miyajima-guchi*

▲ *Koi & Miyajima-guchi*

▲ *Eba & Hiroshima Nishi Airport*

▼ *Tokaichi-machi*

▼ *Ujina Port*

Hon-kawa Bashi

653

to earth. In less than a second a kilometre-wide radioactive fireball consumed the city. The heat was so intense that all that remained of some victims were their shadows seared onto the rubble. Immediately some 70,000 buildings and 80,000 people were destroyed. But this was only the start. By the end of the year, 60,000 more had died from burns, wounds and radiation sickness. The final death toll is still unknown, the figure offered by the Hiroshima Peace Memorial Museum being "140,000 (plus or minus 10,000)".

Many survivors despaired of anything growing again for decades in the city's poisoned earth, but their hopes were raised on seeing fresh buds and blossom on the trees less than a year after the blast. The reborn Hiroshima, with its population of more than a million, is now a self-proclaimed "city of international peace and culture", and one of the most memorable and moving days to visit the city is August 6, when a **memorial service** is held in the Peace Park and 10,000 lanterns for the souls of the dead are set adrift on the Ōta-gawa delta.

For all Hiroshima's symbolic importance, though, it's important to put the number of those killed into context. During the Battle of Okinawa, 265,000 people were killed in a few weeks, more than in Hiroshima and Nagasaki combined, while close to 200,000 died in Tokyo in a single night of bombing in 1945 – and the Japanese themselves are said to have brutally massacred a similar number of soldiers and civilians in Nanking, China.

Arrival and information

Hiroshima Station, on the east side of the city, is where local **trains** and Shinkansen arrive. Long-distance **buses** also arrive beside Hiroshima Station, although some also terminate at Hiroshima Bus Centre on the third floor of Sogō department store in the city centre. **Ferries** from Imabari and Matsuyama in Shikoku, and various other locations around the Inland Sea, arrive at Hiroshima Port, some 4km south of Hiroshima Station and connected to the city by regular trams (¥150).

Two airports serve the city, the closest being **Hiroshima Nishi airport**, on the bay around 4km from the city centre. Hiroshima Nishi handles services to smaller regional airports, such as Niigata and Miyazaki; buses from the airport to the city centre leave every forty minutes or so, take thirty minutes and cost ¥240; a taxi will set you back around ¥3000. Flights from Tokyo Haneda airport and several other cities arrive at **Hiroshima airport**, some 40km east of the city; regular buses run from here to Hiroshima Station and the central bus centre in around fifty minutes (¥1300), or you can take a bus to nearby Shiraichi Station and transfer to a local train to the city.

There are three small **tourist information** booths in Hiroshima Station; one in the concourse at the south (*minami*) entrance and one at the north (*kita*) Shinkansen entrance (both daily 9am–5.30pm), and one in the basement (daily 9am–7pm). They can provide maps, leaflets in a wide range of languages and assist with hotel bookings. Hiroshima's main tourist information centre is the **Hiroshima City Tourist Association** (daily: April–Sept 9.30am–6pm; Jan–March & Oct–Dec 8.30am–5pm; ☎082/247-6738, ⊛www.hiroshima-navi.or.jp) in the *Hiroshima Rest House* beside the Motoyasu bridge to the Peace Park. The Association has the best range of tourist literature, including information on other areas of Hiroshima-ken, and a small souvenir shop.

If you want to arrange a **home visit**, you'll need to apply in person at the International Exchange Lounge of the International Conference Centre (daily: May–Nov 9am–7pm; Jan–April & Dec 10am–6pm; ☎082/247-9715), at the southwest end of the Peace Park, at least a week in advance. The centre also provides information on local events and has an excellent library and reading area with lots of magazines and newspapers, plus three computers where you can get thirty minutes' free Internet access.

City transport

The city is well served by public transport, with nine **tramlines**, an extensive network of **city buses** and the zippy Astram **monorail** line which transforms into a subway in the city centre, terminating beneath the Hondōri arcade. In practice, however, traffic can make catching a bus or a tram a frustratingly slow business; to get around the central sights quickly, you're often better off **walking**.

Within the city centre the minimum tram and city bus fares are ¥150. From the station, trams #1 and #5 head south to Hiroshima Port past Hijiyama-kōen, while #2 and #6 head west to the Peace Park and beyond. Tram #9 shuttles back and forth from Hatchobōri past the Shukkei-en garden. If you need to transfer from one tram to another to get to your destination, ask for a *norikae-kippu* from the driver; drop this in the fare box when you leave the second tram. If you need to transfer again, a second *norikae-kippu* costs ¥50.

With fares so cheap, neither of the one-day tram tickets is worth buying. A better option is the **pre-paid travel card**, which can be used on the buses, trams and monorail/subway – the ¥1000 card gets you ¥1100-worth of travel. These cards can only be bought at the tram terminus at Hiroshima Station, the bus centre and the main JTB office on Rijo-dōri.

Accommodation

Hiroshima has plenty of inexpensive **accommodation**, and the only time of year you might have a problem finding somewhere to stay is August 6 when the annual peace ceremony is held. Although there are many business hotels in the charmless area around Hiroshima Station, it's better to stay closer to the Peace Park, west of which are more business hotels, minshuku and, if all else fails, love hotels. Hiroshima's main **youth hostel** is a couple of kilometres to the north of the city centre, though if you're planning on visiting nearby Miyajima (p.660) you might find it more convenient to stay at the *Miyajima-guchi Youth Hostel* and travel into Hiroshima for the day. This island also has some luxury ryokan.

ANA Hotel 7-20 Nakamachi, Naka-ku ☎082/241-1111, ⓦ www.anahotels.com/eng/hotels/hij. Reasonably priced luxury hotel with spacious rooms only a couple of minutes' walk from the Peace Park. The comfy lobby overlooks an ornamental garden and there's a swimming pool as well as several restaurants and a few single rooms. ❼

Aster Plaza International Youth House 4-17 Kakomachi, Naka-ku ☎082/247-8700, ⓕ246-5808. Accommodation at this municipal culture centre a block south of the Peace Park is meant for students, but is also available at the same rates to foreign tourists. The large, comfortable Western and tatami rooms have en-suite bathrooms and good views. There's a midnight curfew. ❹

Dormy Inn Hiroshima 3-28 Komachi, Naka-ku ☎082/240-1177, ⓕ240-1755. Friendly new hotel in a central location, with its own onsen and sauna and free washing machines. ❺

Hiroshima Kokusai Hotel 3-13 Tatemachi, Naka-ku ☎082/248-2323, ⓦ www.kokusai.gr.jp/room/index-english.html. Good-value mid-range hotel, one minute's walk from the Hondōri shopping arcade. Some of the rooms are a bit flowery in design, but it also has a few economy singles, plus a 14th-floor revolving restaurant and a good Japanese restaurant, *Geishū*. ❺

Hiroshima Youth Hostel 1-13-6 Ushita-shin-machi, Higashi-ku ☎082/221-5343, ⓕ221-5377. This large institutional hostel, with bunk-bed dorms, is Hiroshima's cheapest option. There are extra charges, though, for bedsheets (¥140), heating in winter and air conditioning in summer (¥170), and for use of the outdoor swimming pool. The main drawbacks are its distance from the sights and the 10pm curfew. If you arrive by train, the information counter in Hiroshima Station can give details of where to catch the bus to the hostel;

if you arrive at the Bus Centre, take any bus from platform 11 and get off at Ushita-shinmachi-itchōme (¥210). From here, the hostel is an eight-minute uphill walk. Dorm beds ¥2562 per person.
Mikawa Ryokan 9-6 Kyobashi-chō, Minami-ku ☎082/261-2719. Small minshuku five minutes' walk from Hiroshima Station towards the city centre. The rooms (all tatami, and sharing a common bathroom) are gloomy, but cheap. ❸
Rihga Royal Hotel 6-78 Motomachi, Naka-ku ☎082/502-1121, ⓦwww.rihga.com/hiroshi. Hiroshima's grandest hotel soars 33 floors and is supposedly designed in the image of its neighbour, the reconstructed castle. Inside there are spacious rooms, eight restaurants, a pool and fitness centre and a stunning painting of Itsukushima-jinja by Hirayama Ikuo (see p.649) in the plush lobby. ❼

Hotel Sunroute 3-3-1 Ōtemachi, Naka-ku ☎082/249-3600, ⓦwww.sunroute-hiroshima.com/panfe.htm. One of the more upmarket branches of this nationwide chain of business hotels, with a couple of good restaurants (the Italian *Viale* and the Japanese *Kissui*), a non-smoking floor and rooms specially equipped for disabled guests. It's a five-minute walk east of the Peace Park, on Heiwa-ōdōri. ❻
World Friendship Centre (WFC) 8-10 Higashi-Kannonmachi, Nishi-ku ☎082/503-3191, ⒻFAX503-3179. This small and homely non-smoking B&B has tatami rooms and is run by a friendly American couple who can also arrange meetings with A-bomb survivors and guided tours around the Peace Memorial Park for non-guests. ❷

The Peace Memorial Park and Museum

The most appropriate place to start exploring Hiroshima is beside the twisted shell of the Industrial Promotion Hall, built in 1914 and now better known as the **A-bomb Dome**. Almost at the hypocentre of the blast, the hall was one of the few structures in the surrounding 3km that remained standing. It's been maintained ever since in its distressed state as a historical witness of Hiroshima's suffering and packs a powerful punch as you emerge from the modern-day hustle and bustle of the Hondōri arcade.

On the opposite bank of the Motoyasu-gawa is the verdant **Peace Memorial Park**, dotted with dozens of statues and monuments to the A-bomb victims. One of the most touching is the **Children's Peace Monument**, a statue of a young girl standing atop an elongated dome and holding aloft a giant origami crane – the symbol of health and longevity. The monument's base is eternally festooned in multicoloured garlands of origami cranes, folded by schoolchildren from all over Japan and many other countries, a tradition that started with radiation victim Sasaki Sadako who fell ill with leukaemia in 1955. The 12-year-old Sasaki started to fold cranes on her sick bed in the hope that if she reached 1000 she'd be cured; she died before reaching her goal, but her classmates continued after her death and went on to build this monument.

The main monument – a smooth concrete and granite arch aligned with the A-bomb Dome and the Peace Memorial Museum – is the **Memorial Cenotaph**, designed by architect Kenzō Tange in the style of protective objects found in ancient Japanese burial mounds. Underneath the arch lies a stone coffin holding the names of all the direct and indirect A-bomb victims, and beside it burns the **Flame of Peace**, which will be put out once the last nuclear weapon on earth has been destroyed. It is before this monument that a memorial service is held every August 6, when white doves are released.

One final monument to take note of before proceeding to the museum is the **Monument in Memory of the Korean Victims of the Bomb**, on the eastern bank of the Hon-kawa, inside the Peace Park, just north of the Hon-kawa-bashi. Some two thousand forced labourers from Korea, a Japanese colony at the time of the war, died anonymously in the A-bomb blast, but it took decades before this monolith, mounted on the back of a turtle, was erected in their memory.

The Hibakusha

I saw, or rather felt, an enormous bluish white flash of light, as when a photographer lights a dish of magnesium. Off to my right, the sky split open over the city of Hiroshima.

Ogura Toyofumi, *Letters from the End of the World* (Kodansha).

There are more than 300,000 **hibakusha** (A-bomb survivors) in Japan who, like Ogura, lived through the A-bomb, and some 95,000 still live in Hiroshima today. Ogura's poignant account – a series of letters penned to his dead wife in the immediate aftermath of the war – stands alongside many others, including the videotaped testimonies of survivors that can be viewed at the Peace Museum.

Through the museum it's also possible to meet with a *hibakusha*. To do this you need to make a request in writing to the Heiwa Bunka Centre (℡082/541-5544, ℻542-7941), stating the dates you'd prefer and whether you'll need an interpreter. The World Friendship Centre (see "Accommodation", opposite) also arranges meetings and occasionally hosts discussions with experts and visiting scholars.

The **Peace Memorial Museum** (daily: April–July & Aug 16 to Nov 9am–6pm; Aug 1–15 8.30am–7pm; Jan–March & Dec 9am–5pm; ¥50) deserves to be seen by every visitor to Hiroshima. Expanded into two sections for the fiftieth anniversary of the bombing, it presents a balanced picture of why the atrocity took place, as well as its harrowing effects. The newer displays in the **east building** revolve around two models of the city before and after the explosion, and explain the lead-up to the bombing, including Japan's militarism. A watch in one case is forever frozen at 8.15am. To one side of the ground floor is a video theatre where you can see two short documentary films in English; in one a doctor's voice breaks as he recalls his realization that vast numbers of childhood leukaemia cases were caused by radiation.

On the third floor, after displays on the nuclear age post-Hiroshima, a connecting corridor leads to the old museum in the **west building**. There are counters here where you can rent a taped commentary (¥300) in one of sixteen different languages – worth doing, although the appalling injuries shown in photographs and recreated by models need no translation. This is strong stuff, which shirks none of the horror of the bomb's aftermath. At the end, you'll walk along a corridor overlooking the Peace Park and the resurrected city, providing a chance for contemplation on the bomb that wiped it all out over half a century ago.

North of the Peace Park

At the northern end of the Peace Park, east of the T-shaped bridge – Aioi-bashi – that was the A-bombers' target, is the **Municipal Baseball Stadium**, home ground of the Toyo Carp, Hiroshima's professional team. Locals are avid supporters of the team and it's well worth trying to catch a game. Tickets start from ¥1500 and can be bought on the gate; for information and advance bookings, call ℡082/223-2141.

Five minutes' walk northeast of the stadium lies the pricey **Hiroshima Museum of Art** (daily 9am–5pm; ¥1000), which specializes in late nineteenth- and twentieth-century French art, including minor works by Monet, Renoir, Matisse, Van Gogh and Picasso. The airy museum with an elegant central dome also has a less enthralling section of modern Western-style Japanese paintings. If you have limited time, skip this and head for some of Hiroshima's better art museums.

If you've seen other castles in Japan, there's little reason either to proceed to **Hiroshima-jō** (daily: April–Sept 9am–5.30pm; Jan–March & Oct–Dec 9am–4.30pm;¥320), whose main entrance is directly behind the museum, next to three reconstructed turrets containing temporary exhibitions and fronting the Ninomaru compound beside the castle moat. The original castle was built in 1589 by Mōri Terumoto, one of Toyotomi's Hideyoshi council of "five great elders", but just eleven years later he was forced to retreat to Hagi (see p.678) following defeat in the battle of Sekigahara. Eventually the shogun passed control of Hiroshima to the Asano clan who held sway until the Meiji restoration. Inside the smartly rebuilt five-floor donjon are various historical displays, the most entertaining of which is the combined model and video show with a guard giving a comical English commentary.

Shukkei-en and the Hiroshima Prefectural Museum of Art

Ten minutes' walk east of Hiroshima-jō (or catch tram #9 from the Hatchōbori stop, getting off at Shukkei-en-mae) is a much better post-bomb reconstruction, **Shukkei-en** (daily: April–Sept 9am–6pm; Jan–March & Oct–Dec 9am–5pm; ¥250), a beautiful stroll-garden with a central pond and several teahouses. Built originally by Asano Nagaakira after he had been made *daimyō* of Hiroshima in 1619, the garden aims to present in miniature the Xihu lake from Hangzhou, China, and its name aptly means "shrunk scenery garden".

Adjacent to the garden is **Hiroshima Prefectural Museum of Art** (Tues–Fri & Sun 9am–5pm, Sat 9am–7pm;¥500), an impressive modern facility worth visiting to see two paintings alone: the fiery, awe-inspiring *Holocaust at Hiroshima* by Hirayama Ikuo (see p.649), who was in the city when the bomb dropped, and the floppy watches of Salvador Dalí's surreal masterpiece *Dreams of Venus*. Check out what's showing in the temporary exhibition area, too, for which you'll pay an extra fee. A combined ticket for the museum and garden costs ¥600; you'll need to buy this in the museum and enter the garden from there.

Hiroshima City Museum of Contemporary Art

Around 1km south of Hiroshima Station, on the crest of Hiji-yama, is the challenging **Hiroshima City Museum of Contemporary Art** (Tues–Sun 10am–5pm;¥320) with its ultra-modern collection of art inspired in part by the atomic bombing. Whether or not the often weird, sometimes wonderful, sculptures and paintings in this museum are to your taste, it's a collection that the city has clearly lavished money on. The surrounding leafy park, **Hijiyama-kōen**, is dotted with more modern sculptures, including some by Henry Moore, and provides splendid views across the city. To reach the museum, take trams #1, #3 or #5 to Hijiyama-shita and hike up the hill. On Saturday, Sunday and holidays, there's a free shuttle bus from the bus centre to the museum.

Eating

Hiroshima's excellent selection of **restaurants** is the best you'll find in this part of Japan. There are also the usual **fast-food** chains, including a branch of the American sandwich bar *Subway*, just south of the east end of the Hondōri arcade, the epicentre of Hiroshima's entertainment district. The Pacela shopping complex connecting the *Rihga Royal Hotel* and Sogo department store also has four floors of restaurants and a food court in the basement with many fast-food operations and cafés, such as *Mister Donut* and *Café du Monde*.

Hiroshima's specialities are fresh seafood from the Inland Sea, in particular **oysters**, which are cultivated on thousands of rafts in Hiroshima Bay, and **okonomiyaki**. The local tradition is to make these delicious batter pancakes with the diner's choice of separate layers of cabbage, bean sprouts, meat, fish and noodles, unlike in Ōsaka, where all the ingredients are mixed up – don't leave Hiroshima without sampling one. Where the reviews below list a telephone number, it's a good idea to book.

Andersen 7-1 Hondōri. With its ground-floor deli, top-notch bakery and café, and second-floor restaurants, this is a true gourmet's paradise.

Geishū 2F, *Hiroshima Kokusai Hotel*, 3-13 Tate-machi. Pricey but beautifully presented local seafood dishes. *Le Train Blue*, the revolving restaurant on the top floor of the same hotel, is worth dropping by for a romantic evening cocktail.

Kissui 15F, *Hotel Sunroute*, 3-3-1 Ōte-machi ℡082/249-3600. Elegant *shabu shabu* (beef) restaurant overlooking the Peace Park, where the waitresses wear pale-green kimono. Dinner (last orders at 8.30pm) is very pricey, but the ¥1800 lunch is much more affordable.

Namuche Bazaar 2F, K Building, 2-22 Fukuro-machi ℡082/246-1355. Oriental trinkets decorate this compact *mukokuseki* (no nationality) restaurant, which serves dishes like Spanish omelette alongside Thai salads and Japanese-style beef stew. There's an English menu and they cater for vegetarians. Daily 5pm–midnight.

Nanak 2-2 Fukuro-machi. Popular Indian chain restaurant with curries to suit all tastes and a decent lunch special for ¥880.

Okonomi-mura 5-13 Shin-tenchi. Behind the Parco department store in the heart of the lively entertainment district, this building has 28 small *okonomiyaki* stalls crammed into three floors. You're unlikely to go wrong at any of them, but *Hasshō* on the first floor and *Itsukushima*, the first stall you see on emerging from the elevator on the fourth floor, are reputed to be two of the best in town. Daily 11am–9pm.

Pizzeria Mario Express 7-9 Fukuro-machi. Lively pizzeria with outside tables overlooking a small park. A nice spot to chill out over a coffee and dessert if you don't fancy a full meal.

Ristorante Mario 4-11 Nakaji-machi ℡082/248-4956. Authentic and deservedly popular Italian restaurant in the ivy-clad mock-Tuscan villa beside the Peace Bridge. As usual, the set lunches for ¥1200 and ¥1800 offer the best deal, but it's not too expensive for dinner.

Spud Love 13-1 Hatchōbori. Good-value filled baked potatoes, snacks and barbecue food, plus cheap beer. It's tucked away in the backstreets behind Tōkyū Hands – look for the Union Jack painted on the outside wall.

Suishin 6-7 Tatemachi ℡082/247-2331. Long-established fish restaurant that serves dishes in the local style, in particular *kamameshi* (rice casseroles). Closed Wed.

Tokugawa 2F, Tohgeki Building, Ebisu-chō. Cook up your own *okonomiyaki* for around ¥1000 at this restaurant, whose entrance is halfway down the covered arcade running behind Tenmaya department store. Has an English menu and a bright, family-orientated atmosphere. Daily 11am–3am.

Volks Hondōri. At the west end of the main shopping arcade, this inexpensive chain steak restaurant is also a good choice for vegetarians because of its all-you-can-eat salad bar.

Drinking

Come sundown, the thousands of **bars** crammed into the Nagarekawa and Shin-tenchi areas of the city, at the east end of the Hondōri arcade, fling open their doors. In summer, several beer gardens sprout on city rooftops, including one at the *ANA Hotel*.

El Barco & Barco Tropical 3F, Sanwa Building 2, Yagembori 7-9. This is the place to come if you want some Latin vibes and salsa dance. ¥1000 cover gets you one drink, and they do food too.

Harry's Bar B1, Apple 2 Building, 3-15 Ebisu-chō. Not quite up to its Venice namesake, but does have a more spacious and stylish ambience than many other bars. Cocktails cost around ¥1000,

snacks are available and there's sometimes live music.

Jacara 5F, Shatore No.3 Building, 13-13 Ginzan-chō, Naka-ku. The best of Hiroshima's late-night dance bars, *Jacara* has a friendly vibe and the DJs play a wide range of sounds. The entry charge of ¥1000 includes one drink.

Mac Bar 2F, Hiroshima Rakutenchi Building,

Nagarekawa 6-18. Laidback bar with a vast CD collection and beers from ¥500.

Molly Malone 4F, Teigeki Building, Chūō-dōri. This very popular Irish bar is a good place for meeting the local foreigners, and the Irish chef rustles up generous-sized portions of tasty Irish fare – try the Jamieson chicken.

Naka-chan This very traditional drinking shack at the south end of Yagembori, near the police box (*kōban*), has bags of atmosphere, especially late at night, with pavement tables where you can sip beers and tuck into dishes like grilled fish. You'll find things more easy-going if you take a Japanese-speaker.

Shack 6F Takarazuka Building, 2-10 Shintenchi. Popular place for beers, burgers and Tex Mex food, and there's a pool table and a couple of dart boards if you're pining for a bit of pub-style entertainment.

Listings

Airlines ANA, 2-1 Ōtemachi (domestic ☎243-2231, international ☎082/246-0211); JAL, 1-1-17 Kamiya-chō (☎0120-255971); JAS, Kamiya-chō (☎0120-511283).

Banks and exchange There are several banks clustered around the Hondōri arcade as it crosses Rijo-dōri, including Hiroshima Bank, Sumitomo Bank and Tokyo Mitsubishi Bank. You can make cash withdrawals with cards including Visa and Mastercard at the Tokyo Mitsubishi Bank (Mon–Fri 9am–3pm). Foreign-exchange facilities are also available at the central post office (see below) and Higashi post office next to Hiroshima Station.

Bookshops There's a small selection of English-language books and magazines at Kinokuniya, on the 6th floor of Sogō department store, and at Maruzen in the Hondōri arcade, opposite *Andersen*. The Book Nook, 201 Nakano Building, 1-5-17 Kamiya-chō, Naka-ku, near the *Hiroshima Kokusai Hotel*, has an excellent selection of secondhand books in English.

Car rental Eki Rent-a-Car is at Hiroshima Station (☎082/263-5933). Alternatively, there are local branches of Avis (☎0120-390784) and Budget (☎082/262-4455).

Cinema Salon Cinema (☎082/241-1781), near the city hall, has by far the most adventurous programme of European and American art-house films and revivals.

Emergencies The main police station is at 9-48 Moto-machi (☎082/224-0110). In an absolute emergency, contact the Foreign Advisory Service on ☎082/247-8007. For other emergency numbers, see "Basics" on p.81.

Hospital Hiroshima Municipal Hospital, 7-33 Moto-machi ☎082/221-2291.

Internet access You can get thirty minutes' free Internet access on one of the three public computers at the International Exchange Lounge in the Peace Park (daily 10am–6pm). There's 24hr Internet access at the *I Love You* Internet Café on the 6th floor of the Futaba bookshop outside the south exit of Hiroshima station (¥390 per hr, plus ¥100 membership, and drinks are free).

Post office The main central post office is on Rijo-dōri near the Shiyakusho-mae tram stop (Mon–Fri 9am–7pm, Sat 9am–5pm & Sun 9am–12.30pm). Other convenient branches are the Higashi post office beside the south exit of Hiroshima Station (also open Sat until noon) and the Miru Paruku post office next to Sogō department store.

Sports The Big Wave sports centre, with a swimming pool in summer and two ice rinks during the winter, sits beside the Ushita stop on the Astram line. There's also a pool and other fitness facilities at the Hiroshima Prefectural Sports Centre behind the Municipal Baseball Stadium.

Travel agents The main JTB office is at Kamiya-chō Biru, 2-2-2 Kamiya-chō ☎082/542-5005.

Miyajima

The most famous attraction on **MIYAJIMA**, officially known as Itsukushima, is the venerable shrine of **Itsukushima-jinja**, whose vermilion gate rising grandly out of the sea is considered one of Japan's most beautiful views. In the right light, when the tide is high and the many day-trippers have left, you may be tempted to agree.

The shrine and temples clustered around Miyajima's only village at the northern tip of this long, mountainous island can comfortably be seen in a half-day trip from Hiroshima. If you have more time, there are plenty of other attractions, including beaches to laze on, and hikes over **Mount Misen**, whose summit provides panoramic views across the Inland Sea. Consider splashing out on a night's accommodation at one of the island's classy ryokan so that you

Miyajima	Miyajima	宮島
Daishō-in	Daishō-in	大聖院
Itsukushima-jinja	Itsukushima-jinja	厳島神社
Misen	Misen-san	弥山
Momiji-dani	Momiji-dani	紅葉谷
Senjōkaku	Senjōkaku	千畳閣
Miyajima History and Folklore Museum	Miyajima Rekishi Minzoku Shiryōkan	宮島歴史民俗資料館

Accommodation

Jukei-sō	Jukei-sō	錦水館
Hotel Kamefuku	Hoteru Kamefuku	ホテルかめ福
Guest House Kikugawa	Gesuto Hausu Kikugawa	ゲストハウス菊川
Kinsuikan	Kinsuikan	錦ヒ3館
Kokuminshukusha Miyajima Morinoyado	Kokuminshukusha Miyajima Morinoyado	国民宿舎みやじま杜の宿
Minatokan	Minatokan	みなと館
Miyajima-guchi Youth Hostel	Miyajima-guchi Yūsu Hosuteru	宮島口ユースホステル

Restaurants

Fujitaya	Fujitaya	ふじたや
Komitei	Komitei	こみ亭
Watanabe	Watanabe	わたなべ

can enjoy the after-hours atmosphere with only tame deer and a few other guests for company. Autumn is a particularly beautiful time to visit, when the myriad maple trees turn a glorious red and gold, perfectly complementing the vermilion Itsukushima-jinja shrine.

Getting there and information

From Hiroshima you can get to Miyajima either directly by ferry or by a combination of tram and ferry or train and ferry. High-speed **ferries** (¥1460) from Hiroshima's port – connected by tram #5 to Hiroshima Station and tram #3 to the city centre – take twenty minutes. Alternatively, tram #2 will take you to the ferry terminal at Miyajima-guchi, a 55-minute journey. A one-way trip costs ¥270, and the ten-minute ferry fare is ¥170. If you plan to return to Hiroshima the same day and travel a bit around the city, you'll save money buying a ¥840 one-day ticket. The **train** plus ferry route is only worth considering if you have a rail pass or special excursion ticket that will cover the cost of both the thirty-minute journey from Hiroshima to Miyajima-guchi Station and the crossing on the JR-run ferry.

There's a **tourist information** booth (daily 9am–7pm; ☎0829/44-2011, ⓕ44-0066) inside the island's ferry terminal, where you can pick up a basic map and book accommodation. The assistants speak a little English. Also in the terminal, you can **rent bikes** from the JR ticket counter from ¥320 for two hours (or ¥630 for an electric bike), though the only reason you'd want to do this is to pedal to the northern beaches, since all the main sights are within easy walking distance of the ferry.

Accommodation

The only budget accommodation options around Miyajima are the **Tsutsumigaura Recreation Park and Campsite**, at the northern end of the island (☏0829/44-2903; ¥300 per person per night), which also has fairly plush cabins with air conditioning, kitchen and bathroom (from ¥15,210 for a four-person cabin); and the **youth hostel** on the mainland at Miyajima-guchi. The best deal on the island is the *Kokuminshukusha*, but if you can afford it you should splash out on one of the island's more upmarket **ryokan** or the excellent Western-style pension. Also try and visit midweek, since at weekends and during peak holiday seasons rates at many of the hotels rise.

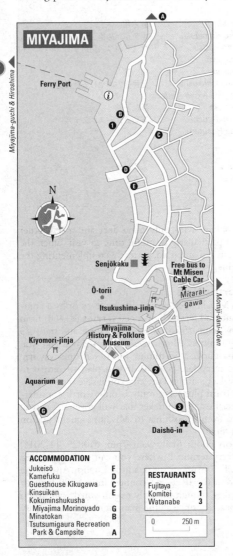

Jukeisō ☏0829/44-0300, ℻44-0388. This ryokan has an excellent hillside location south of Itsukushima-jinja and overlooking the shrine. There's a choice of Western and tatami rooms and of Japanese and French restaurants. It's possible to stay here without taking meals, which start at ¥8000 per person. ⑧

Hotel Kamefuku ☏0829/44-2111, ℻44-2554. Large, modern waterfront hotel, with spacious Japanese and Western-style rooms. Rooms have nice touches, including fresh flowers, and there are luxurious public baths and several restaurants. ⑦

Guest House Kikugawa ☏0829/44-0039, ℻44-2773. Set back in the village a couple of minutes from the ferry, this delightful Western-style pension (formerly *Pension Miyajima*) is clean and comfortable. The owner Kikugawa-san speaks a little English and is an excellent chef. ⑤, or ⑥ with meals.

Kinsuikan ☏0829/44-2131, ℻44-2137. Luxurious ryokan on the waterfront one minute's walk from the ferry. Some of the tatami rooms also have sunken *irori* charcoal fires, ideal for chilly winter nights. ⑧

Kokuminshukusha Miyajima Morinoyado ☏0829/44-0430, ℻44-2248. Book ahead for Miyajima's only accommodation bargain, at the quiet southern end of the island, beyond the aquarium. Rooms are available without meals from around ¥4800 per person, a choice of meal plans start at ¥2000 for dinner, and there's a good public bath which non-residents can use for ¥300. ⑥

Minatokan ☏0829/44-0362. Small minshuku, one minute's walk south of the ferry terminal, with slightly cramped tatami rooms and shared bathrooms. No meals. ⑤

Itsukushima-jinja and around

Ancient records tell that a sea deity has been worshipped on Miyajima since the sixth century, but it wasn't until 1168 that **Itsukushima-jinja** (daily March to mid-Oct 6.30am–6pm; Jan, Feb & mid-Oct to Dec 6.30am–5pm; ¥300) took on its present splendid form courtesy of the warlord Taira-no-Kiyomori. When the sea is lapping beneath its low-slung halls and red-colonnaded, lantern-fringed corridors, you can see why it's called the "floating shrine". More than likely, though, the tide will be out and the muddy seabed revealed. Still, the classical beauty of the architectural ensemble, modelled after the *shinden*-style villas of the Heian period, endures, although the shrine is at its most enchanting come dusk, when the lights of the surrounding stone lanterns flicker on.

From the ferry landing the shrine is around a ten-minute walk south either along the seafront, where the island's many tame deer amble, or through the parallel shopping arcade crammed with giftshops and cafés. There's only one way to walk through the shrine, from its most northern entrance to its southern exit beside the Nishi-matsubara sand spit. Most of the attached halls are closed, but in the centre, 200m ahead of the projecting stage for Nō plays, you'll see the famed sixteen-metre-tall **Ō-torii**, dating from 1875. This is the seventeenth incarnation since the original gate was erected by Taira-no-Kiyomori, its position in the sea indicating that the entire island is a Shinto holy place.

The shrine is the obvious place to head, which is why it's often better to hang back from the crowds and explore some of the other surrounding attractions first. From the ferry landing, head up the hill to the south towards the red-painted five-storey pagoda that you'll see poking through the trees. Beside this is the "hall of a thousand tatami", **Senjōkaku** (daily 9am–4pm; ¥100), part of Hokoku-jinja, a shrine started by Toyotomi Hideyoshi but left unfinished when the warlord died. Votive plaques decorate the inside of the large, airy hall, which was originally a library for Buddhist sutras.

Miyajima festivals

As well as the regular festivals, such as New Year, there are special **festivals** held most months on Miyajima at both the Itsukushima-jinja shrine and the main temple Daishō-in. From time to time, *bugaku* (traditional court dancing) is also performed on the shrine's Nō stage; check with the main tourist information offices in Hiroshima (see p.654) for details.

February (second Sat of the month): **Kaki Matsuri**. Free oysters, an island speciality, are served to sightseers.

April 15 & November 15: **Spring and Autumn festivals** at Daishō-in, including fire-walking displays by the resident monks.

April 16–18: **Jin-Nō**. Sacred Nō plays, first performed for the *daimyō* Mōri Motonari in 1568, are re-enacted on the shrine's stage as part of the spring peach-blossom festival.

June 16: **Kangensai**. Itsukushima-jinja's main annual festival includes an atmospheric night-boat parade, accompanied by traditional music.

August 14: **Hanabi Matsuri**. The largest fireworks display in western Japan explodes in front of Itsukushima-jinja.

December 31: **Chinkasai**. Huge pine torches, blazing in front of Itsukushima-jinja, are fought over by groups of young men.

Better still is the island's main temple **Daishō-in**, on the hillside around ten minutes' walk south of Itsukushima-jinja. This attractive temple complex, with ornate wooden pavilions, arched bridges across lily-pad-dotted ponds and stone lanterns, belongs to the Shingon sect of Buddhism associated with the revered Kōbō Daishi, who blessed the island with a visit in the ninth century. Look out for the "universally illuminating cave" towards the back of the complex, hung with hundreds of lanterns and packed with mini-Buddhas laden down with lucky talismans.

Misen-san and around

If you're feeling energetic, the 530-metre **Misen-san**, Miyajima's sacred mountain, can be climbed in a couple of hours. Otherwise a two-stage **ropeway** (daily: March–Nov 8am–5pm; Jan, Feb & Oct–Dec 9am–4.20pm; ¥1000 one way, ¥1700 return) provides a thrilling and somewhat scary 1.7-kilometre cable-car ride up to within easy walking distance of the summit. The ropeway base-station is beside **Momiji-dani-kōen** (Maple Valley Park), a leafy hillside park around a twenty-minute hike from the ferry terminal; a free minibus runs up to the station from opposite the *Iwasō Ryokan*.

Around the Shishiwa station on top of the mountain, you'll see a colony of wild **monkeys** as well as more deer. Cute as they may look, it's important to keep your distance from the monkeys, who can occasionally turn vicious. There's an excellent lookout spot across the Inland Sea near the station, but the actual summit is a good twenty minutes further on. The path initially drops down but then starts to climb past various small temples built in honour of Kōbō Daishi. Opposite the Misen Hondō, the main hall of worship on the mountain, is the **Kiezu-no-Reikadō**, in which a sacred fire said to be originally lit by the Daishi has burnt for over 1200 years. Legend has it that, if you drink tea made from the boiling water in the suitably blackened iron pot which hangs over the fire, all your ills will be cured.

Five more minutes' climb will take you past giant mysterious boulders to the rest-house at the summit; if you haven't packed refreshments you can buy them here, but at accordingly high prices. The main route down passes more small temples and provides stunning views over Itsukushima-jinja, especially as you near Daishō-in.

If you have enough time, the beachside walks along a pine-tree-lined sand spit south of the shrine are pleasant, and there's a rather dated **aquarium** (daily 8.30am–5.30pm; ¥1050) nearby, which has sea-lion and sea-otter feeding shows. Opposite the aquarium is the marginally diverting **Miyajima History and Folklore Museum** (Tues–Sun 8.30am–5pm; ¥300), with a mishmash of exhibits, including traditional boats, farm equipment and furniture, in an attractive nineteenth-century merchant's home.

Several kilometres north of the ferry landing is the **Tsutsumigaura Recreation Park**, with a long stretch of sandy beach and shallow waters ideal for paddling in. Further north still are beautiful empty beaches with crystal-clear water and fantastic views.

Eating and drinking

Because most people dine at their hotels, other than at lunch **eating** options on the island are limited. Besides oysters, another local speciality is **anago**, a long eel-like fish, cooked and served sliced on top of rice (*anagoburi*). The most famous place to sample this dish is the refined *Fujitaya*, a small, busy restaurant a couple of minutes' walk uphill from the shrine, towards Daishō-in. A large serving of *anagoburi*, accompanied by soup and pickles, costs ¥2300. Less expensive is the *Watanabe* restaurant, beside the main gate to Daishō-in, which has an *anago* set lunch for ¥1600, as well as many other dishes.

The arcade of tourist shops leading to the shrine has several restaurants, all with plastic food displays. *Komitei*, closer to the ferry terminal, serves *okonomiyaki*, as well as having an English menu and a pretty ornamental garden at the back. You can have your *okonomiyaki* Hiroshima-style (layered and cooked for you) or Kansai-style (cook it yourself).

Iwakuni

Heading south along the San'yō coast from Miyajima, you'll soon cross the border into western Honshū's last prefecture, Yamaguchi-ken. The first place to pause briefly is the pleasant old castle town of **IWAKUNI**, some 40km west of Hiroshima and home to an American military base. Two kilometres west of the present town centre is one of the country's top three bridges, **Kintai-kyō**, an elegant five-arched structure, spanning the rocky Nishiki-gawa like a tossed pebble skipping across the water. It was *daimyō* Kikkawa Hiroyoshi who ordered the construction of the bridge in 1673 to solve the problem of crossing the Nishiki-gawa every time it flooded. The first bridge was quickly washed away during the rainy season of 1674, but the second attempt – a 210-metre-long structure built without a single nail and bound together with clamps and wires – survived until Typhoon Kijiya swept it away in 1950. What you see today – and can walk across for ¥220 – is the 1953 reconstruction, no less impressive for that. For once, the hordes of tourists add something to the bridge's attraction, as they parade across the steep arches like figures in a *ukiyo-e* print.

Out of regular office hours, you're supposed to drop the bridge toll in the box beside the ticket office, or you can avoid it altogether by crossing the river on the nearby modern concrete span, the Kinjō-kyō, a good vantage point for a photo. It's also worth checking out the bridge at night, when it's glamorously floodlit. The ticket office also sells a **combination ticket** (¥840) for the bridge, the return cable-car ride up Shiro-yama and entry to the castle, which, if you do all three, gives you a small saving.

Adjoining the bridge on the west bank of the Nishiki-gawa is a landscaped park, **Kikkō-kōen**, once the estate of the ruling Kikkawa clan. With its grass lawns and cooling fountains, the park preserves some of the layout and

Iwakuni

Iwakuni	Iwakuni	岩国
Chōko-kan	Chōko-kan	徴古館
Iwakuni Kokusai Kankō Hotel	Iwakuni Kokusai Kankō Hoteru	岩国国際観光ホテル
Iwakuni Historical Art Museum	Iwakuni Rekishi Bijutsukan	岩国歴史美術館
Iwakuni Youth Hostel	Iwakuni Yūsu Hosuteru	岩国ユースホステル
Kikkawa Historical Museum	Kikkawa Shiryōkan	吉川史料館
Kikkō-kōen	Kikkō-kōen	吉香公園
Kintai-kyō	Kintai-kyō	錦帯橋
Shiratame Ryokan	Shiratame Ryokan	白為旅館

buildings of the former estate, despite also having some modern features. Immediately ahead from the bridge, on the right, is the **Nagaya-mon**, the wooden gate to the home of the Kagawa family, samurai to the Kikkawa *daimyō*. There are several other samurai houses you can wander around and, at the far west side of the park, the Kikkawa family **graveyard**, a compact series of white-walled enclosures with moss-covered gravestones. There's a mildly interesting collection of old maps and plans from feudal times, photos and prints featuring the bridge through the centuries, as well as craftwork from Iwakuni's past, on display at the **Chōko-kan** (Tues–Sun 9am–5pm; free), at the north end of the park. Just round the corner from there is the **Kikkawa Historical Museum** (daily except Wed 9am–5pm; ¥500), which has various artefacts from the Kikkawa family collection, including swords, jewellery and hanging scrolls, although the explanations are all in Japanese. The information office sometimes hands out tickets giving a ¥100 discount to the Kikkawa Historical Museum and the Iwakuni Historical Art Museum.

Just outside the park, opposite the cable-car station, is a small **white-snake research centre** (daily 9am–5pm; entry free, ¥100 donation for an English pamphlet), worth a visit for those interested in the area's zoological oddity. The albino-like snakes are unique to Iwakuni and are thought to have evolved here because of the slightly warmer temperatures in winter. A guide will show you the observation tanks where four of the snakes live. Right next to the cable-car station, the **Iwakuni Historical Art Museum** (daily except Thurs 9am–5pm; ¥500) displays the unexceptional art collection of local resident Nishimura Shigenori.

The **cable car** (¥320 one way, ¥540 return), rather confusingly marked "tram" on the town maps, saves a forty-minute hike up Shiro-yama – if you fancy the workout, the route begins beside the youth hostel in the southwest corner of Kikkō-kōen. An impressive view of the meandering river, town and Inland Sea from the summit makes the effort worthwhile. Unless you're interested in displays of armour, swords and a miniature wooden model of the Kintai-kyō, however, the **castle** (daily 9am–5pm; ¥260) isn't worth entering. Set back from the 1960 reconstruction is the original base of the fortress built by Kikkawa Hiroie in 1608, and torn down by the *daimyō* just seven years later in obeyance of the Tokugawa government's edict that each province should only have one castle (Hagi's took precedence). If you have time, follow the nature trail along the mountain ridge for just over 1km to the lonely **Gokanjin** shrine, keeping an eye out for the many giant spiders in their webs along the way.

If you are in Iwakuni overnight between June 1 and August 31, don't miss the **cormorant fishing** (*ukai*), which takes place on the Nishiki-gawa beside the bridge between 6.30pm and 9pm. This colourful and exciting method of fishing with birds (see box on p.479) can be watched from boats for ¥3500, or for free from the pebbly riverbank.

Practicalities

The Kintai-kyō is roughly midway between Iwakuni's Shinkansen and local train stations. **Shinkansen** stop at Shin-Iwakuni Station, ten minutes by bus west of the bridge, while trains on the JR San'yō line stop at Iwakuni Station, a fifteen-minute bus journey east of the centre. Buses from both stations are operated by the Shiden bus company; the fare to Iwakuni is ¥240, to Shin-Iwakuni, ¥280.

There are **tourist information** booths in Iwakuni Station (Tues–Sun 9am–5pm; ☎ & ℱ 0827/21-6050) and in Shin-Iwakuni Station (daily except Wed 10.30am–4pm); both provide maps and pamphlets, and the assistants might speak some English. Another information booth, by the bridge, has the same leaflets, but is only open daily during the peak holiday seasons, and at weekends during the rest of the year (8.30am–5pm; ☎ 0827/41-2037).

All Iwakuni's sights can be comfortably seen in a couple of hours. If you decide **to stay** the night, the cheapest option is *Iwakuni Youth Hostel* (☎ 0827/43-1092, ℱ 43-0123; dorm beds ¥2835), in the southwest corner of the park, ten minutes' walk from the bus stop by the bridge, which has shared Japanese-style rooms with TVs – its peaceful location and considerate managers make this a good place to stay. The best ryokan is the pretty *Shiratame Ryokan* (☎ 0827/41-0074, ℱ 41-1174; ❽), which has rooms overlooking the bridge; even if you can't afford to stay, try to go for lunch. The *Iwakuni Kokusai Kankō Hotel* (☎ 0827/43-1111, ℱ 41-2483; ❼) has branches on both sides of the river, with the east-bank main hotel being decorated in kitsch 1970s style.

There are several **eating** options on the east side of the bridge; try the local fish dishes, such as *Iwakuni-zushi*, a block of vinegared rice topped with bits of cooked fish and vegetables, at *Yoshida*, which lies just beyond some interesting antique shops leading up to the Kintai-kyō. In the summer months be sure to try the *ayu*, sweet fish, caught by cormorants, available at many of the restaurants near the bridge. Otherwise, pack a picnic and enjoy it in the park.

Yamaguchi and around

Yamaguchi-ken is perhaps Chūgoku's most appealing prefecture, but the coastal route further west from Iwakuni is blighted by heavy industry. Better to head inland to the hills, where an old-world atmosphere hangs over the sleepy prefectural capital, **YAMAGUCHI**, cut through by the narrow scenic river, Ichinosaka-gawa. It's a modern city, but one can see why it's also known as the "Kyoto of western Japan". The local highlights are the beguiling temple garden of **Jōei-ji**, designed by the fifteenth-century artist and priest Sesshū; the handsome five-storey pagoda at **Rurikō-ji**; and the recently reconstructed **St Francis Xavier Memorial Cathedral**, an ultra-contemporary church commemorating the first Christian missionary to Japan.

Many of the temples spread around Yamaguchi, not to mention its artistic sensibilities, date from the late fifteenth century, when war raged around Kyoto, and the city became an alternative capital for fleeing noblemen and their retinues. The tolerant ruling family of **Ōuchi Hiroyo**, who settled in the area in 1360, allowed the missionary Francis Xavier to stay in Yamaguchi in 1549. By the Edo period, the **Mōri** clan had gained power over the whole of western Japan and several of the Mōri lords are buried in Kōzan-kōen, including Mōri Takachika, who was a key figure in the overthrow of the Tokugawa government in 1867.

The closest of the surrounding attractions is the hot-spring resort **Yuda Onsen**, just one train-stop to the west of Yamaguchi, and practically a suburb of the city. Some 20km northwest are the intriguing caverns and rocky plateau of **Akiyoshi-dai** quasi-national park. The **SL Yamaguchi-gō**, a highly popular steam train service, also passes through the city on its way to the delightful castle town of Tsuwano (see p.685).

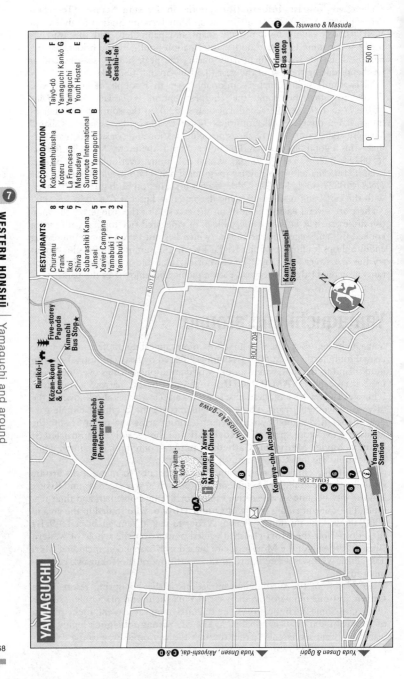

YAMAGUCHI

RESTAURANTS

Churamu	8
Frank	4
Ikoi	6
Shiva	7
Subarashiki Kana	5
Jinsei	
Xavier Campana	1
Yamabuki 1	3
Yamabuki 2	2

ACCOMMODATION

Kokuminshukusha	
Koteru	F
La Francesca	
Matsudaya	
Sunroute International	
Hotel Yamaguchi	
Taiyō-dō	F
Yamaguchi Kankō	G
Yamaguchi	A
Youth Hostel	E
	D
	B

Rurikō-ji

Five-storey Pagoda

Kōzan-kōen & Cemetery

Kimachi Bus Stop ★

Yamaguchi-kenchō (Prefectural office)

Kame-yama-kōen

St Francis Xavier Memorial Church

Ichinosaka-gawa

ROUTE 9

ROUTE 204

Koneya-chō Arcade

EKIMAE-DŌRI

Kamiyamaguchi Station

Yamaguchi Station

Orimoto Bus stop

Jōei-ji & Sesshū-tei

▲ ⓔ ▲ Tsuwano & Masuda

Yuda Onsen & Ogōri

Yuda Onsen, Akiyoshi-dai, ⓒ & ⓓ

0   500 m

Yamaguchi and around

Yamaguchi	*Yamaguchi*	山口
Jōei-ji	*Jōei-ji*	常榮寺
Kōzan-kōen	*Kōzan-kōen*	香山公園
Rurikō-ji	*Rurikō-ji*	瑠璃光寺
Sesshū-tei	*Sesshū-tei*	雪舟庭
St Francis Xavier Memorial Church	*Sabieru Kinen Seido*	サビエル記念聖堂

Accommodation

Kokuminshukusha Koteru	*Kokuminshukusha Koteru*	国民宿舎小てる
La Francesca	*Ra Furanchesuka*	ラフランチェスカ
Matsudaya Hotel	*Matsudaya Hoteru*	松田屋ホテル
Sunroute International Hotel Yamaguchi	*Sanrūto Kokusai Hoteru Yamaguchi*	サンルート国際ホテル山口
Taiyō-dō	*Taiyō-dō*	太陽堂
Yamaguchi Kankō Hotel	*Yamaguchi Kankō Hoteru*	山口観光ホテル
Yamaguchi Youth Hostel	*Yamaguchi Yūsu Hosuteru*	山口ユースホステル

Restaurants

Churamu	*Churamu*	チュラム
Frank	*Furanku*	フランク
Ikoi	*Ikoi*	いこい
Shiva	*Shiba*	シバ
Subarashiki Kana Jinsei	*Subarashiki Kana Jinsei*	素晴しきかな人生
Yamabuki	*Yamabuki*	山吹

Around Yamaguchi

Akiyoshi-dai	*Akiyoshi-dai*	秋吉台
Ogōri	*Ogōri*	小郡
Yuda Onsen	*Yuda Onsen*	湯田温泉

Arrival and information

To reach Yamaguchi by **train**, take the branch JR Yamaguchi line, which runs between **Ogōri** on the southern coast (also a Shinkansen stop) and the north coast town of Masuda in Shimane-ken. From Ogōri, the journey takes twenty minutes. The line is famous because it's one of the very few left in Japan on which a **steam train** service, the SL Yamaguchi-gō, operates most weekends and holidays between mid-March and November. A gleaming 1937 locomotive, pulling restored antique carriages, takes two hours to run from Ogōri to the castle town of Tsuwano, where it waits for just under three hours before making the return journey. Seat bookings are essential for this highly popular service. For the current schedule, check with JR and tourist information offices. Regular **bus** services run to the city from Hagi (p.678) and Tsuwano, and there are also connecting buses for flights into **Yamaguchi Ube Airport**, some 40km south near the coastal city of Ube. All buses stop in front of Yamaguchi Station.

The **tourist information centre** (daily 9am–6pm; ☎083/933-0090, ⓔkanko@city.yamaguchi.yamaguchi.jp) is on the second floor of Yamaguchi

Station. English-language maps and leaflets are available, and one of the assistants speaks English. There's also an information counter at Ogōri Station beside the exit from the Shinkansen tracks, where you can get English-language leaflets on most attractions in Yamaguchi-ken.

Yamaguchi might be the smallest of Japan's prefectural capitals, but its main sights are too widely spread out to walk between them. There are plenty of local buses, but the easiest way to get around is to rent a **bicycle** outside the station (¥320 for 2hr, ¥840 for the day; they will look after your baggage for free). The city's commercial heart is where Ekimae-dōri, the main street heading northwest towards the hills from the station, crosses the shopping arcade of Komeya-chō. The central **post office** is on the west side of the arcade, and there are **banks** and a JTB **travel agent** to the east. All the main sights are north of here.

Accommodation

An **overnight stay** in Yamaguchi will allow you to enjoy the city's relaxed atmosphere or take a hot-spring bath in nearby Yuda Onsen. The cheapest option, the *Yamaguchi Youth Hostel*, is several kilometres east of the city, although easily reached by JR buses from Yamaguchi Station or city buses from Miyano Station, two stops along the line from Yamaguchi.

Kokuminshukusha Koteru 4-3-15 Yuda Onsen ☎083/922-3240, ℻ 928-6177. Good-value Japanese-style accommodation in Yuda Onsen, around ten minutes' walk northwest of the station. Two meals cost ¥2000 extra per person. ⑤

La Francesca 7-1 Kame-yama ☎083/934-1888, ℻ 934-1777. This romantic Tuscan-style villa hotel, nestling at the base of the hilltop Xavier Church, has Western-style suites with twin beds, as well as a lovely garden and a top-class Italian restaurant. ⑧

Matsudaya Hotel 3-6-7 Yuda Onsen ☎083/922-0125, ℻ 925-6111. A historic three-hundred-year-old ryokan, cocooned by high walls, on the main road running through the onsen resort. Has a modern high-rise extension, but the elegant tatami rooms, delicious meals and a lovely traditional garden make it worth the expense. ⑨

Sunroute International Hotel Yamaguchi 1-1 Nakagawara-chō ☎083/923-3610, ⓦ www.sunroute.jp/AreaHotelSelectJSE.jsp. Standard business hotel, part of a nationwide chain, in a convenient location fifteen minutes' walk from the station. ⑤

Taiyō-dō Komeya-chō ☎083/922-0897, ℻ 922-1152. Surprisingly large ryokan, with a small central garden, and tatami rooms with shared bathrooms. It's good value when you consider that rates include two meals. The entrance is on the east side of Komeya-chō arcade. ⑤

Yamaguchi Kankō Hotel ☎083/922-0356, ℻ 925-5668. Convenient budget hotel with plastic herons and a bamboo garden by the entrance. Inside, the atmosphere is no less cheesy, but the tatami rooms are clean. ④

Yamaguchi Youth Hostel 801 Miyano-kami ☎083/928-0057. Set in a peacefully rural location a few kilometres east of the city in an ivy-clad building with tatami dorms, good food, English-speaking owners and a quirky art collection. The nearest train station is Miyano-eki, two stops east of Yamaguchi – if you call the owners they will come and collect you from there. Dorm beds ¥2730 per person.

The City

The twin towers of the modern **St Francis Xavier Memorial Church** (Mon–Sat 9am–5.30pm; ¥100) are easily spotted atop Kame-yama-kōen on the northwest side of the city. The church was named after the pioneering Spanish missionary Francis Xavier who, having already had success in Goa and Malacca, landed in Japan on August 15, 1549, and in the following year was granted leave to preach in Yamaguchi. When he left, the city had a community of more than five hundred Christians, many of whom later died for their beliefs under the less tolerant Tokugawa government. In 1991, the original church, built in 1952 to commemorate the four-hundredth anniversary of Xavier's visit, burnt down. It has recently been completely replaced by a striking contemporary structure incorporating a pyramid-like main building, and twin square towers topped by metallic sculptures, one hung with nine bells.

A more traditionally Japanese place of worship is the charming temple and park of **Rurikō-ji** and **Kōzan-kōen**, in the foothills around 1km north of Kame-yama-kōen. The temple dates from the high point of the Ōuchi clan's reign and epitomizes the Kyoto style of the Muromachi era (1333–1573). Its highlight is a beautifully preserved **five-storey pagoda** (designated one of the top three pagodas in the country), made from Japanese cypress and picturesquely sited beside an ornamental pond. Beside the temple is a small exhibition hall (daily 9am–5pm; ¥300) containing a diverting collection of model pagodas, photographs of the other 53 pagodas scattered around Japan, and strange masks.

Next to Rurikō-ji, the park of Kōzan-kōen, with its peaceful and atmospheric graveyard, is the last resting place of the *daimyō* Mōri Takachika and his offspring. Takachika was one of the prime movers in planning the overthrow of the Tokugawa government at the end of the Edo era, and there are a couple of old wooden houses preserved in the park where he secretly met with fellow plotters. The closest bus stop to Rurikō-ji is Kimachi.

Some 2km east of the park, along the major road Route 9, is the enchanting **Sesshū-tei** garden at the **Jōei-ji** temple (daily 8am–5pm; ¥300). The priest and master-painter Sesshū, born in Okayama-ken in 1420, settled in Yamaguchi at the end of the fifteenth century. After travelling to China to study the arts, he was asked by the *daimyō* Ōuchi Masahiro to create a traditional garden for the grounds of his mother's summer house. Sesshū's Zen-inspired rock and moss design remains intact behind the temple and, if you're fortunate enough to avoid the arrival of a tour group, you'll be able to sit in quiet contemplation of the garden's simple beauty, looking for the volcano-shaped rock that symbolizes Mount Fuji. The surrounding forest and the lily-pad pond add brilliant splashes of colour, particularly in autumn, when the maple trees flame red and gold. Orimoto, the closest bus stop to Jōei-ji, is around ten minutes' walk south of the temple.

On the way back to the city centre, follow the meandering path of the **Ichinosaka-gawa**, a pretty stream crossed by pedestrian bridges. The cherry trees along the riverbanks turn candy-floss pink each spring, while in early summer fireflies buzz around the azaleas and reeds.

One train station before Yamaguchi or a short bus ride south of the city centre is **Yuda Onsen**, easily spotted by the cluster of large (and not particularly attractive) hotels. A cute legend about a white fox curing an injured leg in the natural springwater explains both how the onsen and the town's mascot, immortalized by an eight-metre-high cartoon-like fox statue beside the station, developed. **Onsen no Mori** (daily 10am–midnight; ¥1000), a modern spa complex about ten minutes' walk north from Yuda Onsen Station, has several different Jacuzzi baths, a sauna and a rotemburo; you're given towels to use when you enter.

Eating

There's a limited range of **restaurants** in Yamaguchi, with most options clustered along Ekimae-dōri and the Komeya-chō arcade, with a few cafés along the riverside beyond the arcade. Many shops also sell the local speciality *uirō*, a glutinous sweet made from pounded rice, a supposed favourite of the ruling Ōuchi clan six hundred years ago.

Churamu Cosy café specializing in cheap pasta and curry dishes. The wooden interior and local art add some character to the place. Open daily until 8.30pm.

Frank 2F, Ekimae-dōri. Reasonably priced eatery serving staple Japanese café fare including curry rice and pilaf. Closed Tues.

Ikoi Ekimae-dōri. Restaurant serving a decent range of Japanese staple dishes, including fish. The plastic food display outside will help you choose from the menu.

La Francesca 7-1 Kame-yama. Top-class Italian restaurant attached to the hotel of the same name which does excellent-value pasta lunches (¥1200 or ¥2200) and more expensive dinners. Sometimes closed Sat & Sun lunchtime.

Shiva Ekimae-dōri. Small Indian restaurant opposite Yamaguchi Station serving a good set lunch of authentic Indian curry and nan bread for ¥800, and more expensive à la carte evening meals.

Subarashiki Kana Jinsei Ekimae-dōri. Lively little *izakaya* if you're looking for some evening entertainment.

Xavier Campana 5-2 Kame-yama. Mouthwatering bakery and restaurant serving a wide range of breads, cakes, salads and a mixture of European cuisines, including German-style dishes, fondu and pasta.

Yamabuki There are two outlets of this inexpensive and authentic noodle operation in town, both identifiable by their traditional wooden exteriors. Bowls of tempura, udon and soba cost as little as ¥470. Daily 11.30am–5.30pm.

Akiyoshi-dai

Midway between Yamaguchi and the northern coast city of Hagi, in the heart of the prefecture are the vast caverns and rock-strewn tablelands of **AKIYOSHI-DAI**. This rather bleak landscape has been designated a quasi-national park, though it isn't worth going out of your way for. The park's main attraction is **Akiyoshi-dō** (daily 8.30am–4.30pm; ¥1200), the largest limestone cave in Japan, stretching around 10km underground, although only about a tenth of it is open to the public. The main entrance is a five-minute walk from Akiyoshi-dō bus station along a pedestrianized street of giftshops, a sure sign that the cave gets its full complement of tour groups. Look out for the cheeky He-no-Kappa statues, a bug-eyed water sprite clutching his penis.

A raised walkway through a copse of lofty, moss-covered pine trees provides an atmospheric introduction to the gaping cavern mouth. However, inside, the booming loudspeakers of competing tour-group leaders, combined with unimaginative lighting, detracts from the huge cave's potential impact. It took more than 300,000 years of steady erosion and dripping to create some of the rock walls and formations, which have since been given names like the "Big Mushroom" and the "Straw-Wrapped Persimmon".

From the bowels of the earth an elevator whisks you up to the alternative cave entrance **Yano-ana**, a short walk from the Akiyoshi-dai, Japan's largest karst plateau. A lookout point commands an impressive view of rolling hills spread out in all directions, and there is a range of hikes you can follow across the 130 square kilometres of the plateau. If you return to the cave in the elevator, you'll be charged ¥100, but you can just as easily either walk down the hill or catch a bus back to the station.

Practicalities

Buses run to Akiyoshi-dō from Hagi, Ogōri, Shimonoseki and Yamaguchi. The fastest connection is from Ogōri Station, a Shinkansen stop (1hr 10min). If you have a JR Rail Pass, it's best to take the JR bus service from Yamaguchi. **Tourist information** is available from the counter inside the bus centre (daily 8.30am–5pm; ☎0837/62-1620), where you can pick up an English-language pamphlet on the area.

The only reason **to stay** overnight is if you arrive late in the day and want to see the cave early the next morning before the tour buses arrive. The

Akiyoshi-dai Youth Hostel (☎0837/62-0341, ⑤62-1546; dorm beds ¥2730 per person), on the hill leading up to the plateau, is a twenty-minute steep hike from the bus centre. If you have heavy luggage, you can take a taxi there for ¥570. It's an institutional place, geared to large groups, but the food is fine. In a more scenic location overlooking the plateau is the down-at-heel *Kokuminshukusha Wakatakesan-sō* (☎0837/62-0126, ⑤62-0127; ❺, including meals). Rates include two meals (or you can have a room only for ¥4200 per person). **Eating** options are thin on the ground, and practically nonexistent at night. The pedestrian arcade, which houses a number of Japanese eateries, is your best bet.

Shimonoseki and around

Most travellers pass through the port of **SHIMONOSEKI** at the southern tip of Honshū, 65km west of Yamaguchi, as quickly as possible en route to Kyūshū, or to Pusan in South Korea on the daily ferry. However, this unpretentious city is not without its attractions. The narrow **Kanmon Channel**, which separates Honshū from Kyūshū, is best viewed from Hino-yama, the mountain park that rises above the port. The channel was the scene of the battle of Dannoura, the decisive clash between the Taira and Minamoto clans in 1185, and the colourful shrine **Akama-jingū** is dedicated to the defeated Taira. If you have enough time, you should consider a short trip to the neighbouring town of **Chōfu**, with its authentic enclave of samurai houses and streets, sleepy temples and lovely garden.

Shimonoseki		
Shimonoseki	*Shimonoseki*	下関
Akama-jingū	*Akama-jingū*	赤間神宮
Hino yama	*Hino yama*	火の山
Kaikyō-yume	*Kaikyō-yume*	海峡ゆめ
Karato	*Karato*	唐戸
Chōfu	*Chōfu*	長府
Chōfu-teien	*Chōfu-teien*	長府庭園
Kōzan-ji	*Kōzan-ji*	功山寺
Accommodation		
Kaikyō View Shimonoseki	*Kaikyō Byū Shimonoseki*	海峡ビュー下関
Shimonoseki Grand Hotel	*Shimonoseki Gurando Hoteru*	下関グランドホテル
Shimonoseki Hino-yama Youth Hostel	*Shimonoseki Hino-yama Yūsu Hosuteru*	下関火の山ユースホステル
Shumpanrō	*Shumpanrō*	春帆楼
Via Inn Shimonoseki	*Via In Shimonoseki*	ヴィアイン下関
Eating		
Chayashō	*Chayashō*	茶屋祥
Furue Shōji	*Furue Shōji*	古江小路
Kappō Nakao	*Kappō Nakao*	割烹なかお
Yaburekabure	*Yaburekabure*	やぶれかぶれ
Yasumori	*Yasumori*	やすもり

Arrival, information and city transport

If you're travelling by **Shinkansen**, you'll need to change **trains** at Shin-Shimonoseki Station, and go two stops on the San'yō line to Shimonoseki Station. Long-distance **buses** arrive at the bus station in front of Shimonoseki Station. The fastest way of connecting with Kyūshū is by train or road across Kanmon suspension bridge; traditionalists can still make the short ferry hop (¥270) from Karato Pier, around 1.5km east of Shimonoseki Station, to Moji on Kyūshū's northwest tip. If you arrive by ferry from South Korea, you'll come in at the Shimonoseki Port International Terminal, five minutes' walk from Shimonoseki Station.

Maps and local sightseeing literature in English are available from the **tourist information** booth in Shin-Shimonoseki Station (daily 9am–7pm; ☎ & ☏ 0832/56-3422) by the Shinkansen exit. The main tourist office, whose assistants speak English and can help arrange accommodation, is on the concourse of Shimonoseki Station (daily 9am–7pm; ☎ & ☏ 0832/32-8383).

Shimonoseki's main sights are several kilometres east along the waterfront from the station so it's best to use the local **buses** to get around, though if you're staying at the youth hostel you can hire a bike (¥300 per day, or ¥350 for a mountain bike). The buses departing from platforms 1 and 2 outside Shimonoseki Station are the most convenient, passing Akama-jingū and Hino-yama on their way to Chōfu.

Accommodation

It doesn't take long to see the port's sights, but if you do want to stay overnight there's the usual cluster of business **hotels** around Shimonoseki Station and the international ferry terminal. More spectacular views can be had from the youth hostel and the *kokuminshukusha* on the slopes of Hino-yama, around 2km east of the station, near the Kanmon Bridge.

Kaikyō View Shimonoseki 3-58 Mimosusogawa-chō ☎ 0832/29-0117. This low-rise concrete block has a fantastic view across the Kanmon Channel and spacious tatami rooms. ⑤

Shimonoseki Grand Hotel 31-2 Nabe-chō ☎ 0832/31-5000, ☏ 35-0039. Comfortable, upmarket hotel beside Karato Pier with Western-style rooms and a couple of restaurants and bars. ⑥

Shimonoseki Hino-yama Youth Hostel 3-47 Mimosusogawa-chō ☎ & ☏ 0832/22-3753. Fine hostel with good views across to the Kanmon Bridge. The dorms have bunk beds (¥2900 per person) and the friendly English-speaking manager is a reasonable cook. From Shimonoseki Station, take the bus from platform 1 to the Hino-yama ropeway, from where the hostel is a two-minute

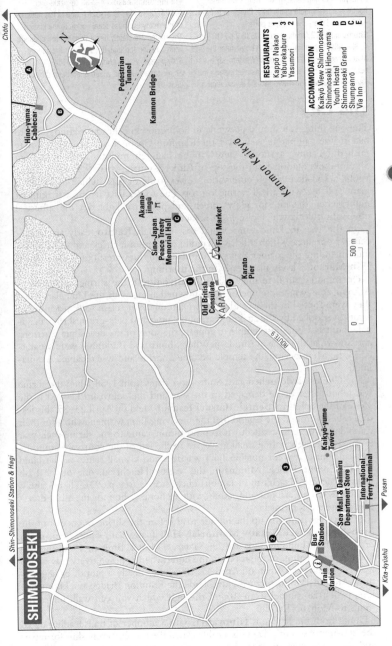

SHIMONOSEKI

◀ Shin-Shimonoseki Station & Hagi

◀ Chōfu

Hino-yama Cablecar

Pedestrian Tunnel

Kannon Bridge

Kannon Kaikyō

Akama-jingū

Sino-Japan Peace Treaty Memorial Hall

⛩ Fish Market

Old British Consulate

KARATO

Karato Pier

ROUTE 9

Kaikyō-yume Tower

Sea Mall & Daimaru Department Store

International Ferry Terminal

Bus Station

Train Station

▶ Pusan

▶ Kita-kyūshū

N

0   500 m

RESTAURANTS

Kappō Nakao	1
Yaburekabure	3
Yasumori	2

ACCOMMODATION

Kaikyō View Shimonoseki	A
Shimonoseki Hino-yama Youth Hostel	B
Shimonoseki Grand	C
Shunpanrō	D
Via Inn	E

walk downhill. More buses stop at the base of Hino-yama at Mimosuso-gawa, from where the hostel is a ten-minute uphill hike. Check-in is from 4.30pm and there's a 9.30pm curfew.
Shumpanrō 4-2 Amida-dera ☏0832/23-7181, ℗32-7980. Expensive, top-notch hotel, near the Akama-jingū, with large suites of Western-style bedrooms and tatami sitting rooms overlooking the Kanmon Channel. The meals include lavish *fugu*

dishes. ❾
Via Inn Shimonoseki 4-2-33 Takezaki-chō ☏0832/22-6111, ℗24-3261. One of the newest of the many business hotels close to the station. The rooms are plainly decorated, but the beds are wide and comfortable. If it's full, try the nearby *Shimonoseki Station Hotel* or *Hotel 38 Shimonoseki*, both of which offer much the same deal. ❺

The City

The one thing you should do while in Shimonoseki is head up Hino-yama to take in the panoramic view over the Kanmon Channel (see below). If you're pushed for time, a similar view can be had ten minutes' walk east from Shimonoseki Station from the top of **Kaikyō-yume** (daily 9.30am–9.30pm; ¥600), a 153-metre-high observation tower made of glass, which looks like a giant golf tee with a ball resting on top. The tower is at its most striking at night, when the interior glows green and points of light dot the spherical observation deck, which also has a restaurant.

On the way to Hino-yama you'll pass through **Karato**, early twentieth-century port area, which still has a handful of handsome brick and stone buildings, including the former British Consulate. On the waterfront is the **Karato Fish Market**, a lively place early in the morning.

Ten minutes' stroll further east is **Akama-jingū**, the shrine dedicated to Antoku, an 8-year-old emperor who drowned along with the Taira clan when they were routed in the naval battle of Dannoura. The clash took place in the straits overlooked by the striking vermilion, gold and pale-green shrine, originally built as a Buddhist temple to appease the souls of the dead Taira warriors, and known at the time as Amida-ji. When Shinto and Buddhism were separated in the Meiji period, the temple became a shrine and was renamed Akama-jingū.

The Chinese-style arched gate, Suite-mon, dates from 1958 when the shrine was rebuilt after being damaged in the war, and the courtyard beyond is the scene of the colourful **Sentei Matsuri festival**. Held on April 23–25, this festival is based around the legend that the surviving Taira women, who after their clan's defeat were forced to turn to prostitution, came to the shrine each year to purify themselves. In a small graveyard to the left of the courtyard are fourteen ancient graves for notable Taira warriors and a small statue of the blind and deaf priest, Hōichi Miminashi, the "earless Hōichi" in one of the Irish writer Lafcadio Hearn's most famous ghost stories (see p.693). There's also a small museum of armour and scrolls, with an honesty box for the ¥100 donation requested for entry.

If you've got time, nip up the hillside road before the shrine to check out the **Sino-Japan Peace Treaty Memorial Hall** (daily 9am–5pm; free), in an ornate, gabled building next to the *Shumpanrō* hotel. Built in 1936, the hall includes a recreation of the room in the hotel where a peace treaty was signed between China and Japan on April 17, 1895, after nearly a month of negotiations. Around 1km further east, just beside the Kanmon Bridge, is a kilometre-long pedestrian tunnel (6am–10pm) through which you can walk under the straits to Moji, on Kyūshū.

Uphill from the bridge is **Hinoyama**, with a number of trails leading up to the 268-metre summit. There is a cable car to the top, currently shut for repair and due to reopen in April 2005; the view from the roof of the cable-car station takes in the whole of the Kanmon Straits and the islands to the west of Shimonoseki – particularly memorable towards sunset. Over a thousand ships a day sail through this narrow waterway, making it one of Asia's busiest maritime crossroads.

Chōfu

Heading east along Route 9 from Hino-yama for around 3km, ignore the lack-lustre aquarium and amusement park in favour of the elegant garden **Chōfu-teien** (daily 9am–5pm; ¥200), which makes a civilized introduction to **CHŌFU**, an old castle town of the Mōri family. The garden dates from the Taishō era and has several teahouses dotted around an ornamental pond and babbling river.

After the garden, branch off from the main road at the next turning and head inland towards a compact enclave of old **samurai houses**, shielded by wooden gates and crumbling earthen walls, topped with glazed tiles, with the roads bordered by narrow water channels. Further up the hill in a leafy glade approached by a broad flight of stone steps is **Kōzan-ji**, the Mōri family temple dating from the fourteenth century. Next to the temple, you'll see the small **Chōfu Museum** (Tues–Sun 9am–5pm; ¥200), displaying some beautiful scrolls decorated with calligraphy and some intriguing old maps, as well as a statue of General Nogi Maresuke, a key military figure in both the Sino-Japanese War of 1894–95 and the Russo-Japanese War of 1904–05.

One of the joys of Chōfu is a relative lack of tourist development, making it easy to feel you have slipped back several centuries while wandering round the samurai district. The one shop you should search out is **Chayashō**, a marvellous antique emporium selling kimono, pottery and other colourful knick-knacks, with a special display area in the *kura* (storehouse) at the back; it also serves coffee and tea in an atmospheric lounge (see below). Look for the large red-paper umbrella by the entrance to the century-old house, downhill from Kōzan-ji.

Buses to Chōfu (25min; ¥350) run from platforms 1 and 2 at Shimonoseki Station, every forty minutes or so. For the samurai district, get off at **Jōka-machi** bus stop and head uphill; for Chōfu-teien get off at Bijutsukan-mae bus stop.

Eating

Shimonoseki is packed with **restaurants** specializing in *fugu* (see box on p.678), but the daily ferry connection with Pusan means that Korean cuisine is almost as popular. There are several restaurants around the Green Mall near the station that specialize in Korean barbecue dishes, called *yakiniku*, while for *fugu* head for the parade running parallel to Route 9. Another good area for fish restaurants is Karato.

The area around the station has plenty of **fast-food** options too, with branches of *KFC*, *Lotteria* and *Mister Donut* in the Sea Mall. The seventh floor of Daimaru department store, connected to the mall, also has a variety of restaurants, all with inexpensive set menus and plastic food displays.

Restaurants and cafés

Chayashō Chōfu. Delightful café in an antique shop in Chōfu (see above), where ladies in kimono serve tea and coffee with cakes for ¥500. The delicious chocolate cake comes on indigo china plates and is decorated with a gold maple leaf. ⑥

Furue Shōji Chōfu ☎0832/45-5233. Elegant *kaiseki ryōri* restaurant in an old samurai house. The light but visually splendid lunch for ¥2500 is worth trying (11.30am–2.30pm). Dinner is at least twice the price.

Fugu

Shimonoseki revels in its role as Japan's centre for **fugu**, the potentially deadly blowfish or globefish which provides inspiration for many local sculptures and souvenirs of spiky, balloon-shaped fish. It is known in Shimonoseki as *fuku*, homonymous with the character for fortune and wealth, in order to attract good luck and happiness. About half the entire national catch (3000 tonnes a year) passes through Haedomari, the main market for *fugu*, at the tip of the island of Hiko-shima, some 3km west of Shimonoseki Station.

Chomping on the translucent slivers of the fish, which are practically tasteless, you may wonder what all the fuss is about. Only the *fugu*'s ovaries, liver and a few other internal organs contain dangerous amounts of tetrodotoxin, a poison more lethal than cyanide, and *fugu* chefs spend up to seven years in training before they can obtain a government licence to prepare the fish. Even so, a small number of people do die, the most famous fatality being Kabuki actor Bandō Mitsugorō – a national treasure – who dropped dead after a globefish banquet in Kyoto in January 1975.

Kappō Nakao Karato. ☎0832/31-4129. Excellent fish restaurant set back from the road where a team of motherly waitresses serves hearty set lunches for around ¥1200. The *fugu* course is ¥5000 at dinner. Closed Sun except during *fugu* season (Nov–March).

Yaburekabure ☎0832/34-3711. Look out for the large plastic *fugu* hanging outside the door of this restaurant on the shopping parade east of the sta-

tion. The speciality is a meal including seven different *fugu* dishes for ¥5000.

Yasumori 2-1-13 Takeza ki-chō. One of Shimonoseki's best *yakiniku* restaurants: you order plates of raw meat and vegetables to sizzle on a table-top cooker. Also try *pivinpa*, a traditional mix of rice and vegetables in a stone bowl. Around ¥2000 per person. Closed Thurs.

Hagi and around

Heading east from Shimonoseki along the **San'in** coast, the landscape becomes much more rugged and sparsely populated. Here the savage Sea of Japan has eroded the rocks into jagged shapes, and if you take the train you'll see some marvellously bleak shorelines. The next town of any consequence is **HAGI**, some 70km northeast of Shimonoseki, which dates back to 1604 when warlord Mōri Terumoto built his castle at the tip of an island between the Hashimoto and Matsumoto rivers. Hagi's castle is long ruined, but the atmospheric graveyards of the Mōri *daimyō* and the layouts of the samurai and merchants' quarters – **Horiuchi** and **Jōkamachi** – and the temple district of Teramachi remain, with several significant buildings intact. These attractive plaster-walled streets are the town's main attraction, together with its renowned pottery, **Hagi-yaki**, considered Japan's next-best style of ceramics after Kyoto's Raku-yaki – you can hardly move around Hagi without coming across a shop selling the pastel-glazed wares. The town is also famous for the role that some of its citizens played in the Meiji Restoration, such as Yoshida Shōin (see box on p.683), enshrined at **Shōin-jinja**, who was executed by the Tokugawa Shogunate for his radical beliefs.

Sharing the relaxed, friendly atmosphere of other Yamaguchi-ken towns, Hagi is certainly worth visiting. If you rent a bike (see p.681), you can easily take in the most important sights in a day and still have time to crash out on **Kikugahama**, a fine stretch of beach beside the castle ruins.

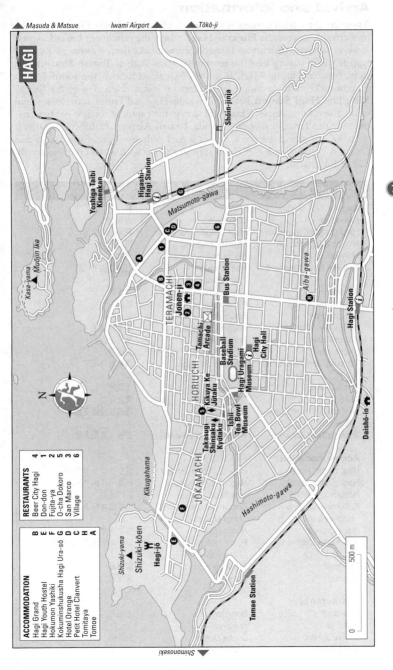

HAGI

Shōin-jinja

Yoshiga Taibi
Kinenkan

Higashi-
Hagi Station

Muōjin Ike

Kasa-yama

Matsumoto-gawa

Aiba-gawa

Ⓐ

Ⓑ

TERAMACHI

Jonen-ji

Ⓒ Ⓓ

❶

❷

❸

❹

Bus Station

Tamachi
Arcade

Baseball
Stadium

HORIUCHI

Kikuya Ke
Jūtaku

Hagi Uragami
Museum

Hagi
City Hall

Ⓗ

Hagi Station

Ⓖ

❻

JŌKAMACHI

Takasugi
Shinsaku
Kyūtaku

❺

Ishii
Tea Bowl
Museum

Kikugahama

Ⓕ

Hashimoto-gawa

Daishō-in

N

500 m

Shizuki-yama

Shizuki-kōen

Hagi-jō ♨

Ⓔ

0

Tamae Station

ACCOMMODATION	
Hagi Grand	B
Hagi Youth Hostel	E
Hokumon Yashiki	F
Kokuminshukusha Hagi Ura-sō	G
Hotel Orange	D
Petit Hotel Clanvert	C
Tomitaya	H
Tomoe	A

RESTAURANTS	
Beer City Hagi	4
Don-don	1
Fujita-ya	2
O-cha Dokoro	5
San Marco	3
Village	6

7

WESTERN HONSHŪ | Hagi and around

Arrival and information

There are three train stations around Hagi. The main train station, close to the modern side of town, is **Higashi-Hagi**, where the infrequent limited express (*tokkyū*) services, which pass through Shimonoseki from Kokura in Kyūshū, stop. If you're staying near the remains of Hagi-jō, then **Tamae Station**, two stops west of Higashi-Hagi, is more convenient, though the journey from Shimonoseki entails a couple of changes on either the San'in or the San'yō Mine line. **Hagi Station**, between Higashi-Hagi and Tamae, is the least useful of the three. Long-distance **buses** all stop in the centre of town at the bus centre, near the Tamachi shopping arcade. **Iwami Airport** (☎0856/24-0010) is an hour east along the coast, and is served only by flights from Tokyo and Ōsaka. A connecting bus (¥1560) runs to the town's bus station, a short walk east of Jōkamachi.

Hagi and around

Hagi	Hagi	萩
Daishō-in	Daishō-in	大照院
Hagi Uragami Museum	Hagi Uragami Kinenkan	萩浦上記念館
Higashi-Hagi Station	Higashi-Hagi-eki	東萩駅
Horiuchi	Horiuchi	堀内
Ishii Tea Bowl Museum	Ishii Chawan Bijutsukan	石井茶碗美術館
Jōkamachi	Jōkamachi	城下町
Kasa-yama	Kasa-yama	笠山
Kikugahama	Kikugahama	菊ヶ浜
Kikuya-ke Jūtaku	Kikuya-ke Jūtaku	菊屋家住宅
Shizuki-kōen	Shizuki-kōen	指月公園
Shōin-jinja	Shōin-jinja	松陰神社
Takasugi Shinsaku Kyūtaku	Takasugi Shinsaku Kyūtaku	高杉晋作旧宅
Tamae Station	Tamae-eki	玉江駅
Tōkō-ji	Tōkō-ji	東光寺
Yoshida Shōin History Museum	Yoshida Shōin Rekishi-kan	吉田松陰歴史館
Yoshiga Taibi Kinenkan	Yoshiga Taibi Kinenkan	吉賀大眉記念館

Accommodation

Hagi Grand Hotel	Hagi Gurando Hoteru	萩グランドホテル
Hagi Youth Hostel	Hagi Yūsu Hosuteru	萩ユースホステル
Hokumon Yashiki	Hokumon Yashiki	北門屋敷
Kokuminshukusha Hagi Ura-sō	Kokuminshukusha Hagi Ura-sō	国民宿舎萩浦荘
Hotel Orange	Hoteru Orenji	ホテルオレンジ
Petit Hotel Clanvert	Puchi Hoteru Kuranbēru	プチホテルクランベール
Tomitaya	Tomitaya	富田屋
Tomoe	Tomoe	常茂恵

Restaurants

Don-don	Don-don	どんどん
Fujita-ya	Fujita-ya	ふじた屋
O-cha Dokoro	O-cha Dokoro	お茶処
San Marco	San Maruko	サンマルコ

There are **tourist information** booths at Higashi Hagi (daily 9am–5.30pm; ⓣ & ⓕ0838/25-3145) and Hagi stations (daily 9am–5.30pm; ⓣ0838/25-1750, ⓕ25-2073), both to the left as you leave the station buildings. Both provide bilingual maps and pamphlets, although you'll have to pay for the useful, pocket-sized *Hagi Sightseeing Guide* (¥200). However, neither is staffed by English-speakers, so if you have more detailed enquiries, contact the tourism section (desk 14) at **Hagi City Office** (Mon–Fri 8.30am–5.15pm; ⓣ0838/25-3131), where there's a helpful English-speaking assistant.

Hagi's sights are spread over a wide area. From Higashi-Hagi Station, the samurai district of Jōkamachi and the remains of Hagi-jō in Shizuki-kōen are a good thirty minutes' walk west, while other major temples and shrines are similar distances to the east and south. The best way of getting around, therefore, is by **bicycle** and there are plenty of bike rental shops at Higashi-Hagi Station, with rates starting from ¥150 per hour. The cheapest day rentals are available from the outfit directly opposite the station entrance, beside the river, and the youth hostel – both charge ¥500 per day.

Accommodation

Hagi has a good range of **accommodation** spread evenly between Higashi-Hagi Station and Shizuki-kōen. The two main ryokan – *Hokumon Yashiki* and *Tomoe* – are top-notch places to indulge in traditional Japanese hospitality and cuisine at hefty prices. At the opposite end of the scale, there is a *kokumin-shukusha* and a fairly decent youth hostel.

Hagi Grand Hotel 25 Furuhagi-chō ⓣ0838/25-1211, ⓕ25-4422. Large Western-style hotel close to the modern heart of town, with dated decor but spacious and well-furnished rooms. ⑥

Hagi Youth Hostel 109-22 Horiuchi ⓣ0838/22-0733. Beside Shizuki-kōen, this hostel has bunk-bed dorms (¥2940 per person) around a central open courtyard. It's not a modern place, but the manager is very helpful and can advise on the area's attractions. Bike rental is also available. From Tamae Station, walk fifteen minutes north across the Hashimoto-gawa. ❶

Hokumon Yashiki 210 Horiuchi ⓣ0838/22-7521, ⓕ25-8144. Set in a picturesque area close to the castle ruins, Hagi's most luxurious ryokan combines traditional Japanese rooms, gardens and cuisine with a Western-style lobby backed by an English garden. ⑨

Kokuminshukusha Hagi Ura-sō Higashi Hagi Kaisaku ⓣ0838/22-2511, ⓕ26-0143. Located five minutes' walk south of Higashi-Hagi Station, facing the Matsumoto-gawa, this place is nothing fancy, but the manager is friendly, the Japanese-

style rooms are clean and rates include two meals. ⑤

Hotel Orange 370-48 Hijiwara ⓣ0838/25-5880, ⓕ25-7690. This business hotel doesn't look much from outside, but the rooms are all well turned out, with air conditioning, TV and compact en-suite bathrooms. ❹

Petit Hotel Clanvert 370-9 Hijiwara ⓣ0838/25-8711. Good-value modern hotel with comfy Western-style rooms, all with twin beds, a kids' play area and a smart café. Breakfast and dinner cost ¥3600 extra. ⑤

Tomitaya Hashimoto-chō ⓣ0838/22-0025, ⓕ25-8232. Friendly new *ryokan*. Rates include two beautifully presented meals, and each room has an alcove featuring a suitably seasonal hanging scroll. ⑥

Tomoe Hijiwara ⓣ0838/22-0150, ⓕ22-0152. The warm orange walls of this swanky modern ryokan offset the Zen minimalism of the rest of the decor. Rooms overlook the surrounding raked-gravel gardens, rather than the less-than-scenic stretch of the Matsumoto-gawa. ⑨

The Town

Much of Hagi's charm is as a place for meandering strolls and bike rides. The tourist map suggests several cycling routes varying from two to six hours, but if you set off early the main sights can be seen in a day. There are frequent direction signs in English around the town, and at each of the sights you'll usually find an English explanation, too.

If time is limited, head first to the scenic **Jōkamachi** district. If you're starting from Higashi-Hagi Station, you'd be wise first to check out the temples and shrines in the hills to the south or the coastal routes, leaving Jōkamachi as the final stop, to be enjoyed once most of the day-trippers have gone home.

Jōkamachi and around

From Higashi-Hagi Station, the most direct route to the **Jōkamachi** district is along the main road heading west across the river, which will take you through Hagi's central shopping area and the **Teramachi** district (so-called because it contains some twenty temples, or *tera*). Bordering Jōkamachi is the surprisingly clean and picturesque **Kikugahama** beach, officially open for swimming only from mid-July to mid-August, after which you'll have to watch out for jellyfish.

At the end of the beach, across a narrow channel, rises Shizuki-san, a 143-metre hill surrounded by **Shizuki-kōen** (daily: March 8.30am–6pm; April–Oct 8am–6.30pm; Jan, Feb, Nov & Dec 8.30am–4.30pm; ¥210). The park is home to an atmospheric shrine, the rustic *Hananoe* teahouse (tea costs ¥500) and the moat and sloping stone walls of **Hagi-jō**, all that remains of the castle destroyed in 1874 when Mōri Takachika shifted court to Yamaguchi (see p.667). It takes twenty minutes to hike to the top of Shizuki-san, or you can relax beside the quiet cove with modern sculptures on the west side of the park.

Immediately south of the park are several large pottery factories with showrooms and a long wood and plaster tenement building where soldiers of the Mōri clan once lived. Entry to soldiers' residence is covered by the same ticket as for Shizuki-kōen, and as you walk the path outside the building you can look into the various rooms and imagine life two centuries ago. From here, return east through the **Horiuchi** quarter, where high-ranking samurai once lived. In summer you'll notice *natsu mikan* (summer orange) trees heavily laden with fruit behind the high stone and mud walls; these were planted in 1876 as a way for the redundant samurai to earn some money.

The neighbouring quarter, **Horiuchi**, contains the old homes of lower-ranking samurai and rich merchants, and is the most picturesque part of Hagi, with narrow lanes lined by whitewashed buildings decorated with distinctive black-and-white lattice plasterwork. Several of the houses are open to the public, the most interesting being the **Kikuya-ke Jūtaku** (daily 9am–5pm; ¥500), built in 1604 for a wealthy merchant family. The house has a particularly lovely garden, which you can see from the main tatami guest room, as well as displays of many household items. Just south of the Kikuya residence is the **Takasugi Shinsaku Kyūtaku** (daily 8am–5pm; ¥100), home of Takasugi Shinsaku, a leading figure in the fight to restore the emperor to power. Like his mentor, Yoshida Shōin (see box opposite), Takasugi died tragically young at 29, a year before the Meiji Restoration in 1868.

If you have time to kill or are particularly interested in the tea ceremony, drop by the tiny (but pricey) **Ishii Tea Bowl Museum** (Mon & Wed–Sun 9am to noon & 1–4.45pm; ¥1000), at the southern end of Jōkamachi, which contains the bizarre collections of Ishii Kigensai, a merchant who died in 1982. In addition to a few prime examples of Hagi-yaki tea bowls, the museum's second floor contains a jumble of knick-knacks including toys, lamps and old cameras. A little further south is the **Hagi Uragami Museum** (Tues–Sun 9am–5pm;

¥190), which houses a collection of *ukiyo-e* prints and oriental ceramics. Exhibits change regularly, and there are also special exhibitions relating to *ukiyo-e* and ceramics (separate entrance charge).

South of Higashi-Hagi Station

One kilometre southeast of Higashi-Hagi Station, on the mountain side of the Mastumoto-gawa, is **Shōin-jinja**, Hagi's largest shrine, dedicated to the nineteenth-century scholar and revolutionary figure Yoshida Shōin (see box on below). Within the shrine grounds is **Shōka Sonjuku**, the small academy where Yoshida lived and taught during the final years of his life, the **Yoshida Shōin History Museum** (daily 9am–5pm; ¥650) illustrating various scenes from Yoshida's life, and the **Museum of Shōin's Writings** (daily 9am–5pm; ¥110), with more artefacts of Yoshida's life, all in Japanese.

Following the riverside cycle path uphill from the shrine leads to one of the family temples of the Mōri clan, **Tōkō-ji** (daily 8.30am–5pm; ¥300), where there's an atmospheric graveyard packed with neat rows of more than five hundred moss-covered stone lanterns. The temple, founded in 1691, has a Chinese flavour to its many handsome buildings and gates. Look out for the giant wooden carp gong hanging in the courtyard as you walk behind the main hall towards the graveyard. Here you'll find the tombs of five Mōri lords, all odd-numbered generations, save the first lord buried with the even-numbered generations in nearby Daishō-in (see p.684), guarded by an army of lanterns. On August 15, during the Obon festival, the lanterns are lit to send off the souls of the dead.

Cycling up the hill behind the temple will bring you to **Tanjōchi**, the birthplace of Yoshida Shōin, marked by a bronze statue of the samurai revolutionary and one of his followers. Take in the view of the town before heading back downhill, past the small thatched home of **Itō Hirobumi**, another Yoshida disciple who later became prime minister and drafted the Meiji constitution. Cross over to the west bank of the Matsumoto-gawa and follow the river south to the start of the **Aiba-gawa**, a narrow canal teeming with carp.

Yoshida Shōin

Born into a Hagi **samurai** family in 1830, the charismatic **Yoshida Shōin** believed that the only way self-isolated, military-ruled Japan could face up to the industrialized world – knocking at the country's door in the insistent form of Commodore Perry (see p.939) – was to ditch the Tokugawa government, reinstate the emperor and rapidly emulate the ways of the West. To this end, he tried to leave Japan in 1854 on one of Perry's ships, together with a fellow samurai, but was handed over to the authorities who imprisoned him in Edo (Tokyo) before banishing him back to Hagi.

Once at home, Yoshida didn't let up in his revolutionary campaign to "revere the emperor, expel the barbarians". From 1857 he was kept under house arrest in the Shōka Sonjuku (now within the shrine grounds of Shōin-jinja), where he taught many young disciples, including the future Meiji-era prime minister Itō Hirobumi. Eventually Yoshida became too big a thorn in the shogunate's side and he was executed in 1860, aged 29, for plotting to assassinate an official.

Five years later, samurai and peasants joined forces in Hagi to bring down the local Togukawa government. This, together with similar revolts in western Japan (see p.940), led to Yoshida's aim being achieved in 1867– the restoration of the emperor to power.

The final sight to check out on a tour of this side of Hagi is the **Daishō-in** temple (daily 8am–5pm; ¥200), around ten minutes' bike ride from the Aiba-gawa, west of Hagi Station on the south bank of the Hashimoto-gawa. The temple was built after the death of Mōri Hidenari, the first lord of the Hagi branch of the Mōri clan. A rickety gate leads to another lantern-filled grave-yard, where you'll find the tombs of all the even-numbered Mōri lords, as well as Hidenari's and those of eight samurai who committed *seppuku* (ritual sui-cide) on his death. The serenity of the spot can be ruined, though, by the squealing of pigs from the farm next door.

North to Kasa-yama

Along the coastal route Highway 191, directly north of Higashi-Hagi Station, is **Yoshiga Taibi Kinenkan** (daily 9am–5pm; ¥500), one of Hagi's most respected pottery kilns, with an attached museum displaying an outstanding collection of Hagi-yaki. If you call in advance (☎0838/26-5180) you can make your own pottery for ¥2000, which will be fired and sent to you for an extra fee after a couple of months. Unlike some other kilns, this one will post pot-tery abroad.

A fifteen-minute bike ride further north along the indented coast will take you past several fishing villages, where drying squid hang on lines like wet underwear, out along a narrow peninsula to the **Myōjin-ike**, a saltwater pond teeming with fish, at the foot of a mini-volcano, **Kasa-yama**. Set back from the pond, beside a small shrine, is an interesting natural phenomenon: the **Kazeana**, a shaded glade cooled by cold air rushing from cracks in the lava. Naturally, you'll find a café in this amenable spot, which is a good place to cool down after hiking the 112m up Kasa-yama. At the summit there are panoram-ic views along the coast and you can inspect the thirty-metre crater, one of the smallest in the world.

Eating and drinking

You'll find many of Hagi's **restaurants** around the central Tamachi shopping arcade and the main cross street, Route 262. There's not a huge choice, but you won't go wrong if you opt for a cheap noodle bar or fish restaurant. The local speciality is whitebait, and in spring you'll see fishermen on the Matsumoto-gawa sifting the water for the fish with giant nets hung from their narrow boats.

At night the town reveals its true colours as a fishing village, where everyone goes to bed early. This isn't a town to party in, but if you're in search of a **drink**, try *Beer City Hagi* or the jazz café-bar *Village* – you might be lucky enough to catch a live performance.

Restaurants and cafés

Beer City Hagi 19-4 Tōdachō. Surprisingly stylish and modern *izakaya* serving a good range of beers, cheap set lunches and the usual selection of nibbly dishes in the evening.

Don-don 177 Hijiwara 3-ku. Bustling, inexpensive noodle joint near the Hagi-bashi across the Matsumoto-gawa. A bowl of udon noodles plus *taki-kome gohan* (vegetable rice) and pickles costs ¥700. Order at the counter, and point at the plastic dishes in the window if you can't read the menu.

Fujita-ya Very small but popular noodle shop on a street north of the Tamachi arcade and one block west of the temple Jonen-ji. Specializes in *sairo soba*, handmade buckwheat noodles served in five-tiered cypress-wood boxes.

O-cha Dokoro Jōkamachi. A pleasant place to rest and sample various types of Japanese tea (¥500). Sit either on tatami or at a low table, admire the mini-garden, and try the pounded rice and bean-paste cake, served by waitresses in kimono.

San Marco On the second floor of the building next to *Beer City Hagi* (see above). This bright

Italian restaurant has a photo-menu and does passable pizza as well as pasta, pilaf rice and gratin dishes. A meal will cost around ¥1300.
Village 291-1 Hijiwara. Laid-back café-bar on the second floor of a white building on the way to the Matsumoto-bashi. Serves cheap meals of spaghetti or pilaf as well as yummy yoghurt drinks. Top jazz artists play here when they're in town. Closed Tues.

Tsuwano

Some 80km east of Hagi, in the neighbouring prefecture of Shimane-ken, is the older and even more picturesque castle town of **TSUWANO**. Nestling in the shadow of the 908-metre-high extinct volcano, **Aono-yama**, around which mists swirl moodily each autumn, this is yet another small town that touts itself as a "Little Kyoto", and for once there really is an air of courtly affluence along the tourist-jammed streets of **Tonomachi**, the well-pre-served central area of samurai houses, with their distinctive cross-hatched black-and-white plaster walls.

Arrival and information

By **train**, Tsuwano is reached on the cross-country JR Yamaguchi line. From Ogōri, where the Shinkansen stops, the fastest journey is just over an hour, while from Masuda (near Iwami Airport; see p.680), on the San'in coast, express trains take thirty minutes, only ten minutes faster than the local service. Tsuwano is also the ter-minus for the **SL Yamaguchi-gō** steam train service (see p.669); the fare from Ogōri to Tsuwano is ¥1620, and reserva-tions are essential. There are also daily direct **bus** services to Tsuwano from Hagi (1hr 40min) and Yamaguchi (1hr). All buses stop in front of Tsuwano Station, at the northern end of town, seven minutes' walk from Tonomachi, the heart of the old samurai district.

▲ *Masuda*

TSUWANO

Train Station

Otometōge Maria Seidō

Via Dolorosa

Kakuōzan Yōmei-ji

TONOMACHI

Katsushika Hokusai Museum of Art

Catholic Church

Yōrōkan

Yasaka-jinja

Taikodani Inari-jinja

Musée de Morijuku

Chairlift

Tsuwano-jō (Ruin)

Tsuwano-kawa

ACCOMMODATION

Hoshi Ryokan	A
Meigetsu	C
Mimuraya	B
Tsuwano Lodge	E
Tsuwano Youth Hostel	F
Wakasaginoyado	D

RESTAURANTS

Furusato	2
Iwami-ji	1
Saranoki Shōintei	4
Yūki	3

Mori Ōgai Kyūtaku & Mori Ōgai Memorial Museum

Washibari-Hachimangū

0   250 m

▼ *Yamaguchi & Ogōri*

Tsuwano	*Tsuwano*	津和野
Kakuōzan Yōmei-ji	*Kakuōzan Yōmei-ji*	覚皇山永明寺
Katsushika Hokusai Museum of Art	*Katsushika Hokusai Bijutsukan*	葛飾北斎美術館
Musée de Morijuku	*Morijuku Bijutsukan*	杜塾美術館
Otometōge Maria Seidō	*Otometōge Maria Seidō*	乙女峠マリア聖堂
Taikodani Inari-jinja	*Taikodani Inari-jinja*	太皷谷稲成神社
Tonomachi	*Tonomachi*	殿町

Accommodation		
Hoshi Ryokan	*Hoshi Ryokan*	星旅館
Meigetsu	*Meigetsu*	明月
Mimuraya	*Mimuraya*	みむらや
Tsuwano Lodge	*Tsuwano Rojji*	津和野ロッジ
Tsuwano Youth Hostel	*Tsuwano Yūsu Hosuteru*	津和野ユースホステル
Wakasaginoyado	*Wakasaginoyado*	若さぎの宿

Eating		
Furusato	*Furusato*	ふる里
Iwami-ji	*Iwami-ji*	石見路
Saranoki Shōintei	*Saranoki Shōintei*	沙羅の木松韻亭
Yūki	*Yūki*	遊亀

To the right of the station is the **tourist information centre** (daily 9am–5pm; ☎0856/72-1771, ✉tsuwanok@iwami.or.jp), where the friendly assistants speak some English. It's worth picking up the excellent English guidebook to the town (¥200), updated every April by the local tourism association.

Tsuwano's sights are somewhat spread out, so if you intend to explore beyond Tonomachi rent a **bicycle** from one of the many operations around the station, all charging ¥500 for two hours, ¥800 for the day. Alternatively, infrequent **buses** run to the southern end of town, from where you can walk back towards the station seeing most of the sights in a couple of hours.

Accommodation

There's little more than a day's leisurely sightseeing and walks around Tsuwano, but an **overnight stay** is recommended if you want to sample a traditional ryokan or minshuku, of which the town has several. Rates mostly start at a reasonable ¥6000 per person including two meals, and the tourist office by Tsuwano Station can help you find a place if the ones below are full.

Hoshi Ryokan Ekimae ☎0856/72-0136. This is the most convenient ryokan for the station. All the rooms are tatami and the very reasonable rates include two meals. ⑤

Meigetsu Uochō ☎0856/72-0685, ℱ72-0637. Tsuwano's most charming ryokan, with paper umbrellas by the front door, polished wood fittings, spacious tatami rooms and a small traditional garden. Rates include two meals, which feature seasonal mountain vegetables and carp. ⑦

Mimuraya Shinchō ☎0856/72-1171, ℱ72-3053.

Small minshuku above a fishmonger's, so you know the fish served in the meals will be fresh. All tatami rooms, and rates include two meals. ⑤

Tsuwano Lodge Washibara ☎0856/72-1683, ℱ72-2880. Friendly hotel set on the west bank of the Tsuwano-kawa. Also has a small rotemburo. ⑥

Tsuwano Youth Hostel Washibara ☎0856/72-0373. Run-down hostel 3km south of the station. A possibility if you're on a really tight budget, though it's not so much of a bargain once you factor in the breakfast and dinner you'll be missing at Tsuwano's minshuku and ryokan. Infrequent buses bound for Nagano run from the station to within three minutes' walk of the hostel. Dorm beds ¥3045 per person.

Wakasaginoyado Mori ⊤ & ⓕ 0856/72-1146. Homely minshuku with an English-speaking owner and good tatami rooms with TV and air conditioning. Rates include two meals. ❻

The Town

The first place to head for in Tsuwano is the old streets of **Tonomachi**, southeast of the station. At the north end of the main pedestrian thoroughfare, Tonomachi-dōri, pause at the small **Katsushika Hokusai Museum of Art** (daily 9.30am–5pm; ¥500) to view its refined collection of woodblock prints, illustrations and paintings by the famous nineteenth-century artist Hokusai Katsushika.

Tonomachi's streets are bordered by narrow canals, home to carp, which outnumber the town's nine thousand residents by more than ten to one; they were originally bred as emergency food supplies in the event of famine. The town's prosperity born of peace and enlightened rule by local *daimyō* is evident from the handsome buildings. Look out for sake breweries and shops selling traditional sweets, including *genji-maki*, a soft sponge filled with sweet red-bean paste.

Easily spotted behind the white, tile-capped walls is the grey spire of the **Catholic Church**, built in 1931, which combines stained-glass windows and an organ with tatami flooring. Further along, near the banks of the Tsuwano-kawa, is the **Yōrōkan**, the former school for young samurai, now containing an uninspiring folk-art museum (daily 8.30am–5pm; ¥200).

Make a short detour across the Tsuwano-kawa, around which the fireflies buzz each June, to the fancifully named **Musée de Morijuku** (daily 9am–5pm; ¥500), a restored farmhouse fronted by raked-gravel gardens which has been converted into a smart modern gallery showing works by local contemporary artists, plus a small collection of etchings by Goya. Upstairs, get the attendant to show you the pinhole camera in the *shōji* screen, capturing an image of the garden outside.

Back across the river, just west of the train tracks, is the **Yasaka-jinja** shrine, where each July 20–27 the ancient *Sagi-Mai* (Heron Dance) is performed by men dressed as the white birds, complete with flapping wings and long-necked hats. Nearby, a path, covered by a tunnel of over a thousand red *torii*, leads uphill towards the **Taikodani Inari-jinja**, one of the five largest Inari shrines in Japan. The bright-red and gold shrine bustles with tourists who say prayers to the local Shinto deities outside the splendid main hall.

The views of Tsuwano from the shrine's hillside location are good, but not as dramatic as those from the top of the hill where the ruins of the town's castle, **Tsuwano-jō**, stand. The castle was built in 1295 by Lord Yoshimi Yoriyuki as protection against potential Mongol invaders. The Yoshimi clan followed their allies, the Mōri, to Hagi after they both fought on the losing side in the Battle of Sekigahara in 1600. Sakazaki Naomori was installed in Tsuwano by the Tokugawa clan but, even though he later proved his loyalty by rescuing the Princess Senhime from the siege of Ōsaka castle, he was refused her hand in marriage. The castle was dismantled at the start of the Meiji era, but you can still walk around the remnants of the walls. If you fancy an energetic hike, follow the pathway leading up to the old castle grounds (around a 30min walk), or take the **chair lift** (daily 10am–4pm; ¥450 return).

Going downhill from the bottom of the chair lift, you'll find yourself at the southern end of Tsuwano. If you cross over the river and head south along the main road, you'll pass several more inconsequential museums, before reaching

WESTERN HONSHŪ | Tsuwano

the **Mori Ōgai Kyūtaku**, on the right, the preserved wood and mustard-plaster home of a famed Meiji-era novelist. Personal effects of the writer, and his death mask, are displayed next door in the modern **Mori Ōgai Memorial Museum** (daily 9am–5pm; ¥500). Crossing back over the river again and following it southwest, you'll reach the **Washibari Hachimangū** shrine, well worth braving the crowds to see its annual Yabusame Horseback Archery Competition, held on the second Sunday in April.

Otometōge Maria Seidō to Kakuōzan Yōmei-ji

If you have an hour or so to spare, there's a very pleasant woodland hike in the hills immediately west of Tsuwano Station. Head south and cross the train tracks at the first opportunity, then double back and continue to the car park, from where a footpath leads up to the cosy chapel of **Otometōge Maria Seidō**, nestling in a leafy glade. In 1865, the Tokugawa shogunate transported some 150 Christians from Nagasaki to Tsuwano; 36 were eventually put to death for their beliefs before the new Meiji government bowed to international pressure, lifting the ban on the religion in 1874. This chapel was built in 1951 to commemorate the martyrs, and the quaint wooden building is the scene of the **Otometōge festival** on May 3.

From the chapel a series of wooden signs counts down the stations of the Cross along the **Via Dolorosa footpath**, winding up the hillside. The path emerges from the forest onto a wider dirt track leading downhill to the charming temple of **Kakuōzan Yōmei-ji** (daily 8.30am–5pm; ¥300). Stone steps lead up to the elegant collection of wooden, thatched buildings, used by generations of Tsuwano lords since 1420. Inside, look out for the lovely screen paintings decorating some of the tatami rooms, and take a moment to sit and admire the verdant traditional garden. From the temple it's around a fifteen-minute walk back to Tsuwano Station.

Eating

Being a tourist town, Tsuwano isn't short of **restaurants**, with several *shokudō* and noodle shops close to the station and around the scenic Tonomachi area of town. Finding an evening meal can be more tricky, since most visitors who stop over eat in their ryokan or minshuku. *Uzume-meshi*, the traditional local dish of rice in a broth with shredded green mountain vegetables, pieces of tofu and mushrooms, is worth trying, as is the carp.

Furusato Gion-chō. This small restaurant, in a traditional plaster house, specializes in *uzume-meshi*, served as part of a set meal (¥1200) with slices of white root-vegetable jelly coated in lemon sauce and pickles. Daily 11am–3pm.

Iwami-ji Eki-dōri. One of the better restaurants close to the station, this small place does good set meals including tempura and sashimi for around ¥1500. Also a good option for dinner. Closed Thurs.

Saranoki Shōintei Yamane-chō. From the large tatami room you can gaze out on a lovely traditional garden while eating either a set meal (¥2000 or ¥3000) of *kaiseki ryōri* haute cuisine. There's an attached *omiyage* shop. Daily until 6pm.

Yūki Honmachi. At the northern end of Tonomachi, this famous and busy restaurant has lots of traditional touches, including a stream running through the dining room filled with carp, some of which end up on the plate as sashimi or in the miso soup. The best deal is the ¥2000 *Tsuwano teishoku*, a set meal of local dishes. Daily except Thurs until 7pm.

Matsue and beyond

Straddling the strip of land between the lagoons of Nakaumi and Shinji-ko is **MATSUE**, the appealing prefectural capital of Shimane-ken, 180km east of Tsuwano, and one of the highlights of the San'in coast. Although the city's main sights – one of Japan's few original castles, **Matsue-jō**, an area of samurai residences, the museum and one-time home of nineteenth-century expat writer **Lafcadio Hearn** (see box, p.693) – are so closely grouped together that they can all easily be seen in half a day, it's worth lingering in Matsue. The lakes, rivers and castle moat lend this modern city a soothing, faintly Venetian atmosphere, and it's still possible to catch glimpses of the old Japan that so enchant-

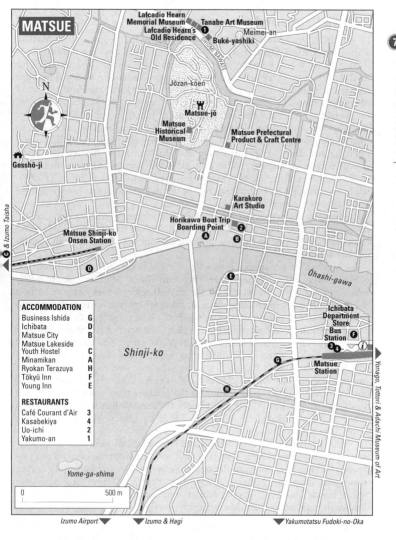

MATSUE

Lafcadio Hearn Memorial Museum
Lafcadio Hearn's Old Residence
Tanabe Art Museum
Meimei-an
Buké-yashiki

SHIOMI NAWATE

N

Jōzan-kōen

Matsue-jō

Matsue Historical Museum

Matsue Prefectural Product & Craft Centre

Gesshō-ji

← & Izumo Taisha

Karakoro Art Studio

Horikawa Boat Trip Boarding Point

Matsue Shinji-ko Onsen Station

Ōhashi-gawa

Ichibata Department Store
Bus Station

ACCOMMODATION

Business Ishida	G
Ichibata	D
Matsue City	B
Matsue Lakeside Youth Hostel	C
Minamikan	A
Ryokan Terazuya	H
Tōkyū Inn	F
Young Inn	E

RESTAURANTS

Café Courant d'Air	3
Kasabekiya	4
Uo-ichi	2
Yakumo-an	1

Shinji-ko

Matsue Station

Yome-ga-shima

0 ———— 500 m

Yonago, Tottori & Adachi Museum of Art

689

Izumo Airport   Izumo & Hagi   Yakumotatsu Fudoki-no-Oka

ed Hearn a century ago, such as fishermen casting their nets in **Shinji-ko**, or prodding the lake bed with poles, searching out shellfish.

There's also plenty to see in the area around Matsue, including the stunning landscapes at the **Adachi Museum of Art**, the shrines and burial tumuli at **Fudoki-no-Oka**, and **Izumo Taisha**, one of Japan's most important shrines, holiday home of the Shinto pantheon of deities, and the reason that Matsue was dubbed "chief city of the province of the gods", by Hearn. Some 130km east of Matsue, there's stunning scenery at **Mount Daisen**, at the cluster of hot-spring resorts around **Kurayoshi**, and along the coastal sand dunes by the prefectural capital of **Tottori**. Further east again, the onsen town of **Kinosaki** makes a pleasant stopover en route to **Amanohashidate**.

Arrival and information

JR **trains** arrive at **Matsue Station**, south of the Ōhashi-gawa, while **Matsue Shinji-ko Onsen Station** (complete with public hot-spring footbath outside), just north of where the river flows into Lake Shinji, is the terminus for Ichibata trains from the grand shrine of Izumo Taisha (see p.696). The most convenient Shinkansen stop is Okayama, from where local trains run to Matsue (the fastest takes 2hr 20min). There are also sleeper train services from Tokyo via **Yonago**, the main San'in coast railway junction, some 25km east of Matsue. Most long-distance **buses** arrive beside Matsue Station; the rest go to Matsue Shinji-ko Onsen Station. There are overnight services to Tokyo and Fukuoka and daily services to Ōsaka and Hiroshima. For **flights**, the closest airport is **Izumo Airport**, 35km west, although **Yonago Airport** to the east is also an option. There are direct buses from Izumo to Matsue Station (¥1000), while from Yonago it's best to take one of the frequent buses to Yonago Station and then catch a train to Matsue.

The **tourist information** office (daily 9am–6pm; ☎0852/21-4034, ℱ27-2598), just outside the north exit of Matsue Station, has plenty of leaflets and maps and is staffed by an English-speaking assistant who can help with accommodation bookings.

The best way to get around is to walk or cycle. Bikes can be rented from the Nippon Rent-a-Car office over the road from Matsue Station (daily 9am–6pm; ¥500 for 2hr, ¥1100 for the day). Regular **buses** connect Matsue Shinji-ko Onsen with Matsue Station, from where you can catch buses to other parts of the city and surrounding area. From outside both stations you can also pick up the **Lakeside bus** service, a motorized red trolley bus that makes a leisurely circuit of Matsue's sights (¥200 a trip). The day-pass for ¥500 is hardly worth it, since it's far quicker to walk parts of the route. However, if you're planning to visit Izumo Taisha the same day, you might save money if you buy the one-day L&R ticket (¥1000), which covers the Lakeside bus and one leg of the round trip to Izumo on the Ichibata train – you'll have to pay for the return journey (¥790). In addition, a Matsue Walker bus service (¥100) connects Matsue Station and Matsue Shinji-ko Onsen Station on a loop around the main sights.

If you visit Matsue between March and November, an ideal way to appreciate the city's watery charms is to take an hour-long **boat** trip around the castle moat and canals. There are departures between 9am and 5pm (July & Aug 9am–6pm) from the Horikawa Boat Trip Boarding Point, near Karakoro Square beside Matsue's shopping district, south of the castle. The fare is ¥1200, though the open-top boats don't run if it's raining.

Matsue and around

Matsue	*Matsue*	松江
Buké-Yashiki	*Buké-Yashiki*	武家屋敷
Lafcadio Hearn Memorial Museum	*Koizumi Yakumo Kinenkan*	小泉八雲記念館
Lafcadio Hearn's Old Residence	*Koizumi Yakumo Kyūkyo*	小泉八雲旧居
Matsue Historical Museum	*Matsue Kyōdokan*	松江郷土館
Matsue-jō	*Matsue-jō*	松江城
Matsue Shinji-ko Onsen Station	*Matsue Shinji-ko Onsen-eki*	松江しんじこ温泉駅
Meimei-an	*Meimei-an*	明々庵
Tanabe Art Museum	*Tanabe Bijutsukan*	田部美術館
Tiffany Museum	*Tiffanii Bijutsukan*	ティファニー美術館
Accommodation		
Business Ishida	*Bijinesu Ishida*	ビジネス石田
Hotel Ichibata	*Hoteru Ichibata*	ホテル一畑
Matsue City Hotel	*Matsue Shitii Hoteru*	松江シティーホテル
Matsue Lakeside Youth Hostel	*Matsue Reikusaido Yūsu Hosuteru*	松江レイクサイドユースホステル
Minamikan	*Minamikan*	皆美館
Ryokan Terazuya	*Ryokan Terazuya*	旅館寺津屋
Tōkyū Inn	*Tōkyū In*	東急イン
Young Inn	*Yangu In*	ヤングイン
Eating		
Uo-ichi	*Uo-ichi*	魚一
Yakumo-an	*Yakumo-an*	八雲庵
Around Matsue		
Yakumotatsu Fudoki-no-Oka	*Yakumotatsu Fudoki-no-Oka*	八雲立つ風土記の丘
Izumo Kambe-no-sato	*Izumo Kambe-no-sato*	出雲かんべの里
Kamosu-jinja	*Kamosu-jinja*	神魂神社
Adachi Museum of Art	*Adachi Bijutsukan*	足立美術館
Izumo Taisha	*Izumo Taisha*	出雲大社
Arakiya	*Arakiya*	荒木屋
Ebisuya Youth Hostel	*Ebisuya Yūsu Hosuteru*	ゑびすやユースホステル
Hi-no-Izukan	*Hi-no-Izukan*	日の出館
Hino-misaki	*Hino-misaki*	日御碕
Takenoya	*Takenoya*	竹の屋

Accommodation

Accommodation options in Matsue are split across two main areas. There's the usual cluster of business hotels around Matsue Station, while on the lake south of Matsue Shinji-ko Onsen Station are the upmarket, expensive hotels catering to the hot-spring crowd.

Business Ishida 205-11 Tera-machi ☏0852/21-5931. Plain hotel offering Japanese-style rooms with shared bathrooms. It doesn't look much, but it's clean and they're used to *gaijin*. ④

Hotel Ichibata 30 Chidori-chō ☏0825/22-0188, ℻22-0230. Upmarket lakeside hotel in Matsue

Onsen with cheaper Western-style rooms (⑥) and much more expensive tatami rooms (⑨) – the cheap rooms don't have lake views, but you can always admire the scenery from the top-floor onsen.

Matsue City Hotel Suetsugu-Honmachi ☎0852/25-4100, ⑤25-5100. Convenient and comfortable business hotel, with a quirky display of eighteenth-century antique clocks on one floor. Most rooms are singles, starting from ¥5250. ⑤

Matsue Lakeside Youth Hostel 1546 Kososhi-chō ☎ & ⑤0852/36-8620. Spacious hillside hostel, inconveniently located a few kilometres west of Matsue, but with fine bunk-bed dorms, friendly staff, good meals and a great view across Shinji-ko. Take the Ichibata line one stop from Matsue Shinji-ko Onsen Station to Tiffany Bijutsukan-mae station, then follow the signs for around ten minutes to the hostel. If you arrive late at night, they will collect you from Matsue Station. Dorm ¥2940 per person, plus a couple of private rooms (⑦).

Minamikan 14 Suetsugu-Honmachi ☎0852/21-5131, ⑤26-0351. Matsue's top ryokan is in a modern complex, but has a distinctly traditional feel, from the courteous service to the neatly clipped pines in the gravel garden. Huge suites of tatami rooms and the best local cuisine push up the prices. ⑧

Ryokan Terazuya 60-3 Tenjin-machi ☎0852/21-3480, ⑤21-3422. Set in a quiet location above a sushi restaurant, this excellent-value ryokan is run by a friendly English-speaking couple and has well-kept Japanese-style rooms with air-conditioning and TV. For two meals, add ¥3000 per person. ④

Tōkyū Inn 590 Asahi-machi ☎0852/27-0109, ⑩www.tokyuhotels.co.jp/en/TI/TI_MATUE/index.shtml. Very conveniently located opposite Matsue Station, this national chain hotel has clean, though dated, Western-style rooms. ⑥

Young Inn 5 Uo-machi ☎ & ⑤0852/25-4500. There's a 1970s retro feel to this business hotel and bar. The rooms are cheap because they're cramped and share shower rooms (no baths), but they're clean, and the hotel is conveniently sited just south of the main sights. ②

Matsue-jō and around

The brooding, five-storey donjon of **Matsue-jō** (daily: April–Sept 8.30am–6.30pm; Jan–March & Oct–Dec 8.30am–5pm; ¥550), standing on top of the hill, Oshiro-yama, is still the focal point of the city, as it was when the *daimyō* Horio Yoshiharu first built his castle in 1611. Compared to Himeji-jō's donjon (see p.615), this one looks as if it's been squashed, but it is, in fact, the largest of the twelve remaining original castle towers scattered around Japan – its sinister aspect is enhanced by the black-painted wood decorating the walls. The castle was extensively renovated in the 1950s and the surrounding grounds, defined by the inner moat, have been turned into a pleasant park, **Jōzan-kōen**. English-speaking guides are available at weekends, and on weekdays if you book at the tourist information office (☎0852/21-4034, ⑤27-2598).

If you're taking a bus from Matsue Station to the castle, get off at Kencho-mae and you'll see the castle grounds dead ahead. You'll have to change into slippers before entering the donjon, but if you have large feet it will be safer to climb the slippy wooden stairs to the fifth-floor Tengu (Long-Nosed Goblin) room in your socks. This is where the lords would have commanded their armies if there had been any battles (which there weren't), and the room now has displays of armour, weapons and other artefacts, including the original *shachi* (mythical dolphins) that topped the roof. The views across the city towards the lake and sea are still splendid.

Tickets for Matsue's sights

If you plan to visit Matsue-jō, the Lafcadio Hearn Museum and the Buké-yashiki samurai residence it's best to buy the **Universal Pass** (¥800) at the first of the sights you visit. This ticket, which is valid for three days, will save you money on the separate entrance fees, and get you discounts at other attractions around the city.

Lafcadio Hearn

"There is some charm unutterable in the morning air, cool with the coolness of Japanese spring and wind-waves from the snowy cone of Fuji..."

Lafcadio Hearn, *My First Day in the Orient*

From the moment he set foot in the country, the journalist **Lafcadio Hearn** was clearly enchanted by Japan. Of all expat writers, Hearn is by far the most respected by the Japanese, and has been adopted as a mascot of Matsue, where he lived on and off between August 1890 and November 1891. Books such as *Glimpses of Unfamiliar Japan* and *Kwaidan* are considered classics, but if Hearn had chosen to chronicle his own remarkable life he'd have surely had a bestseller on his hands.

The son of a passionate but doomed liaison between an Anglo-Irish army surgeon and a Greek girl, and named after the Greek island of Lefkada on which he was born on June 27, 1850, Hearn was destined to be an outsider. Growing up in Dublin, a contemporary of Bram Stoker and Oscar Wilde, it was also on the cards that he would become a writer. A schoolyard accident in 1866 left Hearn permanently blind in his left eye, something he remained ashamed of for the rest of his life, as shown by the many photographs where the writer carefully presents his right profile.

In 1869, the young and penniless Hearn decided to chance his fortune in the United States, eventually becoming a reporter for the *Cincinnati Inquirer*, where he built a reputation as a brilliant but difficult writer. However, in 1875 Hearn was sacked and had to leave the city because he broke a social taboo, not to mention the law, by marrying a black girl. The marriage didn't last, but Hearn ended up in more tolerant New Orleans, where he threw himself into writing about Creole culture.

After a couple of years living on the West Indian island of Martinique and penning his first novel, *Chita*, Hearn was commissioned by *Harper's Monthly* to write about Japan. He arrived in Yokohama at 6am on April 4, 1890, and by the end of the day had decided to stay, get a teaching job and write a book. The teaching post brought Hearn to Matsue, where he met and married Koizumi Setsu, the daughter of an impoverished samurai family.

Hearn would happily have stayed in Matsue, but the freezing winter weather made him ill and he was forced to move south to Kumamoto, in Kyūshū, closer to Setsu's relatives. The couple had four children and in 1896 he adopted the name Koizumi Yakumo (Eight Clouds) and Japanese nationality. By the beginning of the new century, Hearn's novels and articles had become a great success, he had started teaching at the prestigious Waseda University in Tokyo, and was invited to give a series of lectures at London University and in the United States. However, he was never to return to the West, since on September 30, 1904, at the age of 54, Hearn suffered a series of heart attacks and died. His grave at Zoshigaya cemetery near Ikebukuro in Tokyo is marked by a stone that proclaims him a "man of faith, similar to the undefiled flower blooming like eight rising clouds who dwells in the mansion of right enlightenment".

Hearn's books stand as paeans to the beauty and mystery of old Japan, something he believed worth recording because it seemed to be fast disappearing in the nonstop modernization of the early Meiji years.

Within Jōzan Kōen you'll also find the **Matsue Historical Museum** (daily 8.30am–5pm; free), in an elegant whitewashed wooden building, whose combination of pillars, verandas and ornate gabled roof are typical of the hybrid style of the Meiji era. The two-storey mansion was built in 1903 to accommodate the emperor on the off chance that he might visit the city, which he never did. It now contains an interesting collection of colourful local arts and crafts, including plenty of tea-ceremony utensils.

Leave the park by the bridge in the northwest corner, follow the moat as it turns east and you'll come to **Shiomi Nawate**, a parade of samurai residences, some converted into museums, that remain protected by high walls capped with grey tiles. On the corner is the **Lafcadio Hearn Memorial Museum** (daily: April–Sept 8.30am–6.30pm; Jan–March & Oct–Dec 8.30am–5pm; ¥300), which provides an excellent introduction to the life and works of the revered writer (see box on p.693) and is curated by Hearn's great-grandson, Bon Koizumi. There are lots of English explanations and you can also see Hearn's favourite writing desk and chair, specially designed so that he could better use his one good eye. Next door is **Lafcadio Hearn's Old Residence** (daily 9am–5pm; ¥250), the small, old samurai house where the writer lived from May to November 1891 and in which he began work on two of his most famous books, *Glimpses of Unfamiliar Japan* and the ghost story collection *Kwaidan*. Sit in the calm of the tatami rooms, read the English leaflet containing extracts from Hearn's essay, "In a Japanese Garden", which is about the house, and see how little has changed.

The next high wall shields the contemporary building of the **Tanabe Art Museum** (Tues–Sun 9am–5pm; ¥500), established by the late prefectural governor Tanabe Chōemon XXIII, who was also a respected artist with a particular interest in the aesthetics of the tea ceremony. The museum contains the Tanabe family's refined collection, centred around pottery tea bowls and tea utensils. There's a pleasant, airy café where you can take tea (¥350) overlooking the museum's garden.

Further along Shiomi Nawate is the largest samurai house remaining in Matsue, the **Buké-yashiki** (daily: April–Sept 8.30am–6.30pm; Jan–March & Oct–Dec 8.30am–5pm; ¥300), built in 1730 as the home of the Shiomi family, high-ranking retainers to the ruling Matsudaira clan. The attractive complex of buildings has been well preserved and you can wander round the exterior looking into tatami and wood rooms, which give some sense of what eighteenth-century samurai life was like.

The dusty grounds of the Buké-yashiki are a contrast to the precise Zen beauty of the raked gravel and artfully positioned stones around the **Meimei-an teahouse** (grounds daily 9am–5pm; ¥300), a short walk up the hill directly behind Shiomi Nawate. Originally designed by the *daimyō* Matsudaira Fumai to exact tea-ceremony principles, the tiny cottage has creamy beige plaster walls which hardly look capable of holding up the heavily thatched roof. In 1966, Meimei-an was restored and moved to this spot beside an existing samurai mansion with a good prospect of the castle – to celebrate its 150th anniversary. You can't enter the teahouse itself, but it's still worth taking time to admire it from the veranda of the adjoining mansion. About 800m south of Meimei-an, by the Kyobashi Bridge is the **Karakoro Art Studio** (daily 9.30am–6.30pm; free), housed in a stately former bank. The complex contains a small gallery exhibiting locally produced glass art, kimono and fabric and a number of craft shops selling jewellery, clothing and stained glass. There's also a classy restaurant with affordable lunchtime specials and a café serving up cappuccino and mouthwatering Italian ice cream that can be enjoyed in the breezy courtyard.

If art nouveau is your thing, you might fancy a trip out to the **Tiffany Museum** (Tues–Sun 10am–6pm; ¥200), one stop west of Matsue Shinji-ko Onsen Station en route to Izumo Taisha. The museum boasts a collection of exquisite pieces by Louis Tiffany, including paintings, jewellery, furniture and stained glass, and is set in a beautiful English-style garden on the shores of Lake Shinji. Follow the signs from Tiffany Bijutsukan-mae station.

The best place to head at the end of the day, especially if the weather is good, is the eastern shore of **Shinji-ko**. This is where a mass of photographers gather, lenses poised, to capture the golden sunset behind Yōme-ga-shima, a tiny pine-studded island in the lake.

Epicureans flock to Matsue for its **Kyōdo ryōri**, seven types of dishes using fish and seafood from Shinji-ko, best sampled in winter, when all the fish are available and tasting their freshest. The seven dishes are *amasagi*, smelt either cooked as tempura or marinated in teriyaki sauce; *koi*, carp baked in a rich, sweet sauce; *moroge-ebi*, steamed prawns; *shijimi*, small shellfish usually served in miso soup; *shirauo*, whitebait eaten raw as sashimi or cooked as tempura; *suzuki*, bass wrapped in paper and steam-baked over hot coals; and *unagi*, grilled freshwater eel. To sample the full seven courses, make an advance reservation with one of the top ryokan, such as *Minamikan* (☎0852/21-5131), and have at least ¥10,000 in your wallet.

Eating and drinking

Matsue doesn't have a wide range of **restaurants**, but those it does have are of a high quality and reasonably priced; a good place to head for is the Suetsugu Honmachi area beside the canal just south of the castle. If you're on a budget, pack a picnic to enjoy in the castle grounds or at Meimei-an. For **fast-food** fans there's a *Mister Donut* by Matsue Station, and a *McDonald's* on the main road, Kunibiki-dōri, to the east of the town centre. You'll find a few cheap **drinking** options: *Filament*, about five minutes' walk from Matsue Station, is generally recommended as a *gaijin*-friendly bar, but is pretty expensive. If your Japanese is up to it, take pot luck in the Isemiya district near Matsue Station or Tohonchō between the canal and the Ōhashi-gawa, two areas teeming with small bars and *izakaya*.

Café Courant d'Air 494-13 Asahi-machi. Sophisticated café, with subdued lighting, classical music and classy decor, specializing in thick slices of creamy sponge cake and fancy coffees.

Kasabekiya Matsue Station. Reasonably priced Italian restaurant just outside the station, with good food and friendly service. Daily until 8pm.

Uo-ichi Katahara-chō. On the corner by the Kyobashi bridge over the canal, this is a good place to try some of the *Kyōdo ryōri* fish dishes.

The set course costs ¥3500, but there are cheaper meals, starting at around ¥1000, which include sashimi and tempura. Friendly service either at the counter or at tables on tatami. Closed Tues.

Yakumo-an Shiomi Nawate. Popular, picturesque restaurant in a former samurai residence, with a central garden, teahouse and carp-filled pond, specializing in soba and udon noodles, including *warigo soba* (see p.698). Most dishes under ¥1000. Daily until 4.30pm.

Yakumotatsu Fudoki-no-Oka

The area around Matsue, once known as Izumo, is one of the longest settled in Japan, with a written history dating back to the seventh century *Izumo-no-Kuni Fudoki* (*The Topography of Izumo*). Keyhole-shaped burial tumuli (*kofun*) from this period can be seen in the rice field-dotted countryside at **Yakumotatsu Fudoki-no-Oka**, a museum and park thirty minutes by bus south of Matsue Station. The dry **museum** (Tues–Sun 9am–5pm; ¥200) is mainly of interest to archeology and history buffs, with a small display of finds from excavations of nearby burial tumuli, including impressive pottery horses, and some first- and second-century bronze daggers and bells. There's also a recreated thatched hut, half-buried in the ground, while you can get an overview of some of the tumuli from the roof. The park has several pleasant forest and nature walks, plus the **Izumo Kambe-no-sato**, a couple of buildings promoting local culture where you can watch woodworkers, basket-makers, weavers, potters and a specialist in *temari*, the art of making colourful thread-decorated balls. With advance reservation (☎0852/28-0040) you can even take craft lessons here.

Before leaving, check out the nearby fourteenth-century shrine, **Kamosu-jinja**, dedicated to the Shinto mother deity Izanami. The impressive raised wooden structure, in a glade of soaring pines reached via stone steps lined by cherry trees, is one of the few remaining examples of *Taisha-zukuri* or "Grand shrine style" left in Japan.

Adachi Museum of Art

While in Matsue, don't miss taking a trip to the stunning **Adachi Museum of Art** (April–Sept 9am–5.30pm; Jan–March & Oct–Dec 9am–5pm; ¥2200, half-price to foreign visitors), some 20km east of the city near the village of Yasugi, en route to Yonago. The large collection of Japanese artworks, dating from 1870 to the present day, includes masterpieces by Yokoyama Taikan and Uemura Shoen, though these take second place to the exquisite surrounding gardens, covering 43,000 square metres.

The founder of the museum, Adachi Zenkō, was an enthusiastic gardener and his passion for the artform shows through in the beautiful landscapes which envelop the galleries and steal your attention at every turn. The museum is designed so that, as you move around, the views of the Dry Landscape Garden, the White Gravel and Pine Garden, the Moss Garden and the Pond Garden appear like living picture scrolls when viewed through the museum's carefully placed windows. A couple of the gardens have traditional teahouses where you can take tea and sweets (from ¥850). *Juryū-an* is a copy of a teahouse in the former Imperial Palace, Katsura Rikyū, in Kyoto, and looks over a peaceful moss-covered garden; in the smaller *Juraku-an* visitors are served a bowl of green tea made with water boiled in a kettle of pure gold, said to aid long life. The two coffee shops in the museum are less atmospheric but cheaper, and the views just as fine.

Give yourself plenty of time here because, once you've dragged yourself away from the gardens, the art itself isn't bad, either. The museum has the largest collection of paintings by **Yokoyama Taikan**, whose delicate ink drawings and deep colour screens set the standard for modern Japanese art. The curators can't resist pandering to the Japanese love of the cute by including a section of kitsch art from children's books, but recover credibility in the tasteful ceramics hall, which includes works by Kawai Kanjirō, a brilliant local potter who participated actively in the *mingei* (folk art) movement begun by Yanagi Sōetsu, and Kitaōji Rosanjin, a cook and potter, whose pieces were designed to complement and enhance the food served on them.

Direct buses from Matsue's and Yonago's JR stations take around fifty minutes to reach the museum (get off at Saginoyu Onsen), or you can take a train to Yasugi, which is only twenty minutes away from the museum by free shuttle bus (8 daily); the tourist information offices in Matsue or at Yonago Station can provide a timetable.

Izumo Taisha and around

The grand, graceful shrine of Izumo Oyashiro, second only in importance to that at Ise, is better known as **IZUMO TAISHA**, after the town it's situated in, 33km west of Matsue. Although most of the current buildings date from the nineteenth century, the original shrine was built, if you believe the legend, by Amaterasu, the Sun Goddess, and is still visited each October by all eight million Shinto deities for their annual get-together – in this region the tenth month is traditionally known as the "month with gods", while in all other parts of Japan it's known as the "month without gods". Since the shrine is dedicated to Okuninushi-no-mikoto, the God of Happy Marriage, many couples visit in the hope that they will live happily ever after. It's also a popular stop for tour groups, but the shrine precincts are large enough to absorb the crowds and most pass through pretty quickly anyway.

A giant concrete *torii* stands at the southern end of Shinmon-dōri, the main approach to the shrine, along which you'll also find Izumo Taisha Station, the terminus for the Ichibata train from Matsue Shinji-ko Onsen. More in keeping with the shrine's natural grace is the wooden *torii* that marks the entrance to the forested grounds at the foot of Yakumo-yama. To the left, you'll pass an old steam locomotive, quietly rusting away, while closer to the central compound, to the right of the Seki-no-Baba, an avenue of gnarled pine trees leaning at odd angles, is a large, modern statue of the deity Okuninushi.

Straight ahead, beyond the bronze *torii*, is the shrine's central compound, the **Oracle Hall**, in front of which hangs a giant *shimenawa*, the traditional twist of straw rope. Inside the hall, Shinto ceremonies take place all day, with accompanying drumming and flute-playing. To the right is a modern building containing the **treasure hall** (daily 8am–4.30pm; ¥150), on the second floor of which you'll find a small collection of swords, statues, armour, painted screens and a map of the shrine, dating from 1248, painted on silk and in remarkably good condition. There's also an illustration of the shrine as it was supposed to have been in the Middle Ages, when it was 48m tall and the highest wooden structure in Japan, topping Nara's Tōdai-ji, home of the great statue of Buddha.

The current inner shrine, or **Honden**, last rebuilt in 1744 and directly behind the Oracle Hall, is still the country's tallest, at 24m in height, with projecting rafters that shoot out from the roof. Unless you've paid to take part in a Shinto ceremony, you'll have to stand outside the **Eight-Legged East Gate** entrance, decorated with beautiful unpainted wooden carvings, and peer through to the inner courtyard. Even pilgrims are not allowed anywhere near the central Holy of Holies hall, buried deep within the Honden and the province only of the head priest.

The branches of the trees surrounding the shrine, on which visitors tie *omiku-ji* (fortune-telling) papers for good luck, are so heavily laden they look as if they have been coated with snow. In the woods behind the Honden is the **Shōkōkan** (daily 8am–4.30pm; ¥50), the former treasure house, now displaying many jolly statues of Daikoku (one of the guises of Okuninushi), and his *bon viveur* son Ebisu, who usually has a fish tucked under his arm.

Leaving the shrine by the west exit (the closest to the Bus Centre and main car park), you'll see a large modern hall, where more daily ceremonies take place and which is also used for the sacred kagura dances performed on festival days. In front of the hall hangs another *shimenawa* into which people fling coins, hoping they will stick and bring them luck.

Izumo Taisha festivals

Apart from the usual Shinto festival days (see "Basics", p.66), the important festivals at Izumo Taisha are:

May 14–16: **Imperial Grand Festival**. The welcome mat is rolled out for an envoy from the imperial family.

End of October or beginning of November: **Kamiari-sai**. Celebration for the annual gathering of the Shinto gods.

Apart from the shrine, there are only a couple of other sights worth seeing in Izumo Taisha. Near the cement Ōtorii is the **Kichō-kan** (daily 9am–5pm; free), a modern hall with colourful exhibits on the town's festival, including costumes, banners and video films. Also look out for **Iwaidakoten**, where traditional Izumo kites have been made for over seventy years (the large ones cost ¥40,000); it's on the same street as the soba shop *Arakiya* (see below), close to Shinmon-dōri.

If you have time, head 10km northwest to the scenic cape of **Hino-misaki**, where you'll find a quieter shrine complex, **Hinomisaki-jinja**, built in 1644 under the shogun Tokugawa Ieyasu, and boasting a 44-metre-tall white stone lighthouse dating from 1903. Climb the steep spiral staircase to the top of the lighthouse (daily 9am–4.30pm; ¥150) for a splendid view out to the nearby islands (though note that you can't go up in bad weather). Around the cape are several bathing beaches, too. Hino-misaki is a twenty-minute bus ride (¥530) from Izumo Taisha Bus Centre.

Practicalities

From Matsue, the easiest way to reach Izumo Taisha is by **train** on the Ichibata line from Matsue Shinji-ko Onsen Station. You'll have to change at Kawato for the final leg to Izumo Taisha. The journey takes an hour and costs ¥790. If you're travelling round both Matsue and Izumo Taisha in the same day you can save a little money by buying the ¥1000 L&R Free Kippu (see p.690). JR trains stop at Izumo-shi Station, from where you'll have to transfer to the Ichibata line, changing again at Kawato. The Izumo Taisha-mae terminus is five minutes' walk south of the shrine. There's also a direct Ichibata bus from Izumo-shi Station, which is slower and more expensive than the train; both the train and bus leave from the Ichibata department store beside the JR station. Buses stop at the Izumo Taisha bus centre, a minute's walk west of the shrine, where you can also catch buses to Hino-misaki.

The **tourist information** office (daily 9am–5.30pm; ℡ & ℻0853/53-2298) is on Shinmon-dōri between the station and the shrine grounds. No English is spoken, but a few English leaflets are available. It's only worth renting a bicycle at the station (¥500 for 3hr, ¥800 for the day) if you plan to cycle out to Hino-misaki, which takes around thirty minutes.

With Matsue so close, there's no pressing reason to stay overnight in Izumo Taisha, and especially not at the *Ebisuya Youth Hostel* (℡0853/53-2157), which has plain bunk-bed dorms (¥3050 per person) and a sterile, unwelcoming atmosphere. A ryokan is a better option, especially since you'll be served dinner, almost impossible to come by otherwise, as all the tourist restaurants shut around 5pm. The *Hi-no-Izukan* (℡0853/53-3311, ℻53-2014; ❼) and the slightly more expensive but better-kept *Takenoya* (℡0853/53-3131, ℻53-3134; ❼) are both attractive, friendly places on the main Shinmon-dōri approach to the shrine.

There are lots of bland tourist **restaurants** around the bus centre near the shrine. For something more interesting, try the local speciality, **warigo soba**, cold buckwheat noodles seasoned with seaweed flakes, served in three-layer dishes, over which you pour *dashi* stock. The best place to try it is at *Arakiya*, a hospitable outfit about five minutes' walk south of the main throng of tourist canteens. You'll pay ¥780 for *warigo soba*, or you can try one layer of noodles for just ¥250. Both are served with a cup of hot soba-water soup, which you can flavour with *dashi*.

Mount Daisen to Tottori

The main rail and road routes east of Matsue continue along the coast, crossing into the neighbouring prefecture of Tottori-ken and through the uninteresting industrial city of **Yonago**; trains from Okayama on the JR Hakubi line terminate here. Yonago is the gateway to **Mount Daisen**, at 1711m the highest mountain in western Japan and home to beautiful beech forests and ancient temples. Buses (9 daily) depart from bus stop 4 outside Yonago station for the village of **DAISEN-JI** (50min; ¥800), the main hub for accommodation on Mount Daisen, with access to the ski slopes in winter and hiking paths in summer. Daisen has the largest **ski slopes** in western Japan and sees heavy snowfall from November to April; it's also known for the **Daisen Ice and Snow Festival**, which takes place over three days at the end of January, with fireworks lighting up the night sky and an amazing display of ice sculptures. As the snow melts in the spring the hiking paths open up, alpine flowers come into bloom, and walkers can enjoy panoramic views of the surrounding countryside and out over the Sea of Japan. Later in the year the trees form a stunning tapestry of red and gold, making it a popular place to come and view the autumn leaves.

A couple of minutes' walk east from the bus stop, the **tourist information booth** has plenty of maps of the area and staff can help book accommodation. The *Goen'yama Camp Ground* (☎0859/52-2165; closed Oct–April), five minutes' walk further east, has tents for hire. En route to the camp ground you'll pass the conveniently located *Daisen Youth Hostel* (☎0859/52-2501; dorm beds ¥2888 per person), which is very close to the ski slopes and has skis for rent.

Tottori and around		
Mount Daisen	*Daisen*	大山
Daisen-ji	*Daisen-ji*	大山寺
Daisen Youth Hostel	*Daisen Yūsu Hosuteru*	大山ユースホステル
Goen'yama Camp Ground	*Goen'yama Kyampu-jō*	豪円山キャンプ場
Yonago	*Yonago*	米子
Kurayoshi	*Kurayoshi*	倉吉
Akagawara	*Akagawara*	赤瓦
Misasa	*Misasa*	三朝
Jizō-dō	*Jizō-dō*	地蔵堂
Kiya-ryokan	*Kiya-ryokan*	木屋旅館
Misasa Museum of Art	*Misasa Bijutsukan*	みささ美術館
Mount Mitoku	*Mitoku-san*	三徳山
Monju-dō	*Monju-dō*	文殊堂
Nageire-dō	*Nageire-dō*	投入堂
Sambutsu-ji	*Sambutsu-ji*	山仏寺
Tōgō-chō	*Tōgō-chō*	東郷町
Suimeisō	*Suimeisō*	国民宿舎水明荘
Tottori	*Tottori*	鳥取
Dunes	*Sakyū*	砂丘
Uradome Coast	*Uradome-kaigan*	浦富海岸
Accommodation		
Hotel New Ōtani Tottori	*Hoteru Nyū Ōtani Tottori*	ホテルニューオータニ鳥取
Sakyū Centre Hotel	*Sakyū Sentā Hoteru*	砂丘センターホテル
Tottori Green Hotel Morris	*Tottori Guriin Hoteru Mōrisu*	鳥取グリーンホテルモーリス
Washington Hotel	*Washinton Hoteru*	ワシントンホテル

Kurayoshi and around

An hour further east along the coast by train brings you to **KURAYOSHI**, a small town in central Tottori-ken and the jumping-off point for the hot-spring resort of **Misasa** and the temple hike up to **Nageire-dō** on Mount Mitoku. The **tourist information booth** (daily 10am–6pm), to the left outside the station by the bus stands, has maps, English information on the surrounding area and free bikes with which to explore the town. If you have an hour or two to spare, head for the picturesque **Akagawara** area, a fifteen-minute cycle ride from the station, where a number of recently refurbished Edo- and Meiji-era black-and-white storehouses stand next to the shallow Tama-gawa. These are now home to various souvenir and craft shops selling local goods including beautiful *Kurayoshi-gasuri* items made from the locally woven, indigo-dyed cloth. *Café Mela* (closed Thurs), on the second floor of the Sadar Chowk crafts shop opposite the storehouses, serves up authentic Indian curry, lassi and chai, while a little way along the river either side of the storehouses you'll find a couple of peaceful little temples.

The hot-spring resort **MISASA** is situated in the mountains twenty minutes by bus (¥420) south of Kurayoshi. Its hot springs boast a high level of radium, famed for its curative powers: cancer rates around Misasa are noticeably lower than elsewhere in Japan, and people come from all over the country to take the waters. There's a free rotemburo in the river if you're passing through and feeling brave – there are bamboo screens by the pools, but as onlookers from the nearby bridge have a bird's-eye view of proceedings, this is one communal bathing experience that's not for the shrinking violet. Misasa is a picturesque place to spend the night, and you'll come across *yukata*-clad visitors wandering through the streets from inn to rotemburo or bar and back again. If you want **to stay**, *Kiya Ryokan* (☎0858/43-0521, ℱ43-0523; ❼ including meals) is a friendly place with fine food and a choice of baths located on the narrow street east of the river, dotted with craft shops and tea rooms. On the other side of the river you'll find the **Misasa Museum of Art** (daily except Tues 9am–5pm; ¥500), home to a collection of wonderful contemporary wood-block prints by local artist Hasegawa, plus a fine collection of Buddhist and Hindu statuary and ornaments from India and Pakistan.

While in the area it's well worth taking the bus from Misasa (15min; ¥370) 8km up the road to **Mount Mitoku** to visit the famous **Nageire-dō** temple, part of the Sambutsu-ji temple. The main Sambutsu-ji temple complex is just over the road from the bus stop. From here it's an hour's climb up a rugged path (there are chains in places to help you scramble over the massive boulders) past a belfry and a number of smaller temple buildings including Monju-dō and Jizō-dō, both spectacularly perched on a precipice and with marvellous views. At the very top is Nageire-dō, a wooden structure nestling under an overhanging rock and balanced precariously on stilts which grip the cliff face below. It's an incredible feat of engineering, and no one knows quite how it was built. Legend has it that it was thrown into place by an ascetic priest named Ennogyoja; certainly Sambutsu-ji has been a centre for Buddhism since the eighth century, and Nageire-dō is thought to date back to the eleventh or twelfth century. On your way down, be sure to try the local speciality of **san-sai-ryōri**, mountain vegetables and tofu, at one of the restaurants at the foot of the main temple complex, near the bus stop. Make sure you check bus times for the return trip, however, or you could end up with a long wait for the next bus back to Misasa.

Heading east from Kurayoshi, a five-minute train ride (or 20min by bus) brings you to **TŌGŌ-CHŌ**, another hot-spring resort on the shores of Lake

Tōgō, its sparkling blue water edged by reeds and wild rice. Fishermen here still use traditional four-handled nets to catch shrimp, which you can see strung out from a rice-thatched hut perched on stilts in the lake and connected to the land by a rickety-looking bridge. *Suimeisō* (⊕0858/32-0411, ⑤32-0130; ❻ including meals), on the lake a couple of minutes' walk from the station, was the first *kokuminshukusha* in Japan. It was rebuilt in 1993 and now boasts modern facilities, including a rooftop rotemburo overlooking the lake. They also have free bikes, and you could spend a pleasant day cycling around the lake (12km) or visiting the area's shrines and waterfalls.

Tottori and around

At the easternmost end of the prefecture, an hour's train ride from Kurayoshi, lies the provincial capital of **TOTTORI**, famous in Japan for the sixteen-kilometre-long **sand dunes** at nearby Hamasaka. Although they've been designated a national monument, there's nothing especially unique about the dunes and they're not worth going out of your way to see. However, it is an atmospheric place, where tourists get swallowed up by the enormity of the sand hills, and there are also camels imported for would-be Lawrence of Arabias to pose on.

The dunes are a twenty-minute **bus** journey north of Tottori Station. Buses leave from platform 3 at the bus centre next to the station and pass through the city centre on the way to either Sakyū Kaikan, beside the dunes, or the Sakyū Centre, overlooking them from a hill. The centre is nothing more than a souvenir and food stop for the tour buses that pile in daily. There's a **chair lift** (daily 8am–5pm; ¥200), which runs between the centre and the edge of the dunes, but you can just as easily walk between the two.

More scenic is the **Uradome coastline**, which covers the 15km between the edge of the sand dunes and the eastern edge of the prefecture, and which, together with the dunes, forms part of the **San'in Coast National Park**. The shore is fringed with strangely shaped rocks and islands jutting out of the water, some topped with pine trees, and many sculpted with wave-carved tunnels, caves and openings. The views from the cliff-top paths along much of the pine-covered coastline looking out over the blue-green Sea of Japan are stunning, and if you follow one of the steep paths down through the trees to the shore, you'll find numerous sandy bays and bathing beaches. If you have a car you can drive along the coast from the sand dunes on Route 178, stopping at any of the many parking places along the way to enjoy the beautiful views from the cliff top, or follow one of the many paths down to the secluded beaches below. If using public transport, take a bus bound for Iwai-onsen from platform 3 outside Tottori Station and get off at **Uradome-kaigan-iriguchi** (40min; ¥520), from where you can explore the cliff-top paths and beaches at your leisure, before catching a bus back to the city.

Practicalities

Tottori Station, on the San'in line, is the terminal of the JR Tsuyama line from Okayama. The **bus terminal** next to the station is where long-distance buses from Tokyo, Himeji, Hiroshima, Kyoto and Ōsaka stop. Tottori **airport** (⊕0857/28-1150), 10km northwest of the city, has daily flights to Tokyo and Ōsaka. A bus to the city from the airport takes twenty minutes and costs ¥450.

The **tourist information** booth (daily 9.30am–6.30pm; ⊕0857/22-3318) is inside Tottori Station, to the right of the north exit. The assistants don't speak English, but there are English leaflets and maps of the city and prefecture. If you need a hotel, there are several options close to the station's north side. *Tottori Green Hotel Morris* (⊕0857/22-2331, ⑤26-5574; ❹) is a good-value business hotel behind the Daimaru department store across from the station; it has neat rooms and serves Western-style breakfast for ¥550. Nearby is the ever-reliable *Washington Hotel* (☎0857/27-8111, ℱ27-8125; ❺), while the upmarket *Hotel New Ōtani Tottori* (☎0857/23-1111, ℱ23-0979; ❼) sits next to Daimaru. If you want to stay out by the dunes, the *Sakyū Centre Hotel* (☎0857/22-2111, ℱ24-8811; ❻) is old-fashioned, but has good-value Japanese-style rooms overlooking the coast, with two meals included in the rates and, in summer, an outdoor pool.

Although there is a handful of **restaurants** at the dunes, you'll be better served by the choice near Tottori Station. Several restaurants can be found in the shopping arcades that run under the train tracks, all with plastic food displays. Directly across from the station is *Mister Donut*, while on the fourth floor of the Daimaru department store you'll find *Marguerite* (11am–6.30pm), a Japanese restaurant with a good range of set meals and special daily dishes.

Kinosaki

Roughly halfway between Tottori and Amanohashidate, in the northern part of Hyōgo Prefecture, is the atmospheric onsen town of **KINOSAKI**, a mecca for hot-spring aficionados, who flock in droves – especially in the winter months – to soak in the therapeutic waters and sample crab from the nearby Sea of Japan. There isn't much to see, although you might spot people sauntering down the ryokan-lined street in *geta* and *yukata*, and there are a couple of mildly interesting temples and a willow-fringed canal reminiscent of Kurashiki. If you're after an indulgent onsen experience, however, Kinosaki makes a worthwhile overnight stop. Because of its compact size, the town is easily explored on foot.

There are a total of six hot-spring **bathhouses** and one **rotemburo** open to the public (most daily 7am–11pm; ¥500–800). Guests at any of Kinosaki's plush ryokan can get complimentary passes to visit any of the *soto-yu* (outside bathhouses). When you've had your fill of onsen you might want to check out **Gokuraku-ji** (daily 8am–6pm; free) and nearby **Onsen-ji** (daily except Thurs 9am–4.30pm; ¥300), both located just west of the Goshono-yu bathhouse on the west bank of the Ōtani River. Gokuraku-ji is home to a miniature rock garden, while Onsen-ji, located halfway up a mountain, has a small collection of Buddhist antiquities and boasts a scenic view of the town below. Although there's a **ropeway** (daily except second and fourth Thurs of month 9.10am–5.10pm; ¥280 one way to the temple, ¥450 one way to the mountain peak lookout), Onsen-ji is best reached by following the row of ancient stone steps, flanked by towering cedar trees and a carpet of moss, that starts not far from the base of the ropeway. The walk takes about fifteen minutes, and when you've come back down you can soak your feet in the public footbath near the base of the ropeway; there's another public footbath just outside the station.

Practicalities

Kinosaki is located on the JR San'in line, making it accessible by **train** from Tottori to the west on a very scenic train ride along the coast, or Kōbe, Kyoto and Ōsaka to the south. If you're approaching from Amanohashidate, take the Kita-Kinki Tango Tetsudō to Toyooka and then change to the San'in line. **Buses** from Kōbe and Ōsaka to Kinosaki Station run twice a day and take roughly three and a half hours.

A small **tourist information booth** (daily 9am–5pm; ☎0796/32-3663, ℮info@kinosaki-spa.gr.jp) in the Kinosaki-chō Bungeikan dispenses good

Kinosaki	Kinosaki	城崎
Bungeikan	*Bungeikan*	文芸館
Gokuraku-ji	*Gokuraku-ji*	極楽寺
Onsen-ji	*Onsen-ji*	温泉時

Accommodation		
Akaishiya	*Akaishiya*	赤石屋
Mikuniya	*Mikuniya*	三国屋
Morizuya	*Morizuya*	森津屋

Amanohashidate	*Amanohashidate*	天橋立
Chion-ji	*Chion-ji*	智恩寺
Fuchū	*Fuchū*	府中
Hashidate Jaya	*Hashidate Jaya*	はしだて茶屋
Ine	*Ine*	伊根
Monju	*Monju*	文珠
Nariai-ji	*Nariai-ji*	成相寺
Tango-hantō	*Tango-hantō*	丹後半島
Toyooka	*Toyooka*	豊岡

Accommodation		
Amanohashidate Youth Hostel	*Amanohashidate Yūsu Hosuteru*	天橋立ユースホステル
Gemmyōan	*Gemmyōan*	玄妙庵
Maruyasu	*Maruyasu*	まるやす
Monjusō Shōrotei	*Monjusō Shōrotei*	文珠荘松露亭
Young Inn	*Yangu In*	ヤングイン

English pamphlets and maps written in Japanese. The staff are helpful, but don't speak English. To find the booth, turn right after exiting the station and follow the main street until you reach the fishmonger; turn left and you'll find the Bungeikan about 150m down the street on your left.

Across from Kinosaki Station, the **ryokan association** (☎0796/32-4141, ⓕ 32-4560) handles bookings and has information about places to stay, though again, they don't speak English. **Accommodation** in Kinosaki doesn't come cheap, but a stay in one of the many first-class ryokan is well worth the money. *Morizuya* (☎0796/32-2106, ⓕ32-3789; ❼, meals included) is next to the Ichino-yu bathhouse and has exquisite rooms and a cave-like bath with inviting blue water. *Mikuniya* (☎0796/32-2414, ⓕ32-2679; ❼, including meals), conveniently located on the main street not far from the station, has immaculate, spacious rooms and an English-speaking owner, while *Akaishiya* (☎0796/32-3333, ⓕ32-3335; ❽, including meals), just up the street from *Morizuya*, offers clean and comfortable rooms, some with views of the canal below. Though it's customary to eat at the ryokan where you're staying, there are a number of undistinguished **restaurants** clustered around the station.

Amanohashidate and around

At the far eastern end of the San'in coast, some 90km from Tottori, the stubby peninsula of Tango-hantō leans protectively over Wakasa Bay, shielding the sand

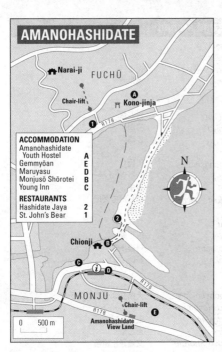

AMANOHASHIDATE

♠ Narai-ji   FUCHŪ

Chair-lift

Ⓐ
⛩ Kono-jinja
R178
❶

ACCOMMODATION
Amanohashidate
  Youth Hostel   A
Gemmyōan   E
Maruyasu   D
Monjusō Shōrotei   B
Young Inn   C

RESTAURANTS
Hashidate Jaya   2
St. John's Bear   1

N

Chionji 卍 Ⓑ

Ⓒ ⓘ Ⓓ
R178
MONJU
 ⚓ Chair-lift
R178   Ⓔ
Amanohashidate
View Land

0   500 m

spit of **Amanohashidate**, the "Bridge to Heaven". As one of the trio of top scenic views in Japan (the other two being Matsushima and Miyajima), Amanohashidate has a lot to live up to. The "bridge" is actually a 3.6-kilometre ribbon of white sand and pine trees slinking its way between the touristy villages of **Monju** to **Fuchū** across the bay, and the recommended way to view it is from one of the hills above the bay with your head stuck between your legs, so that the sandspit seems to float in midair.

Once you're standing upright, you'll find that Amanohashidate and the surrounding attractions of the Tango-hantō are to northern Kyoto prefecture what Hakone is to Tokyo – a pleasureland of scenic delights, old temples and shrines and, rare for Japan, good beaches. Expensive and limited public transport keeps the crowds down, particularly out of season, and you'll need your own transport to get the most out of the area.

On Mount Nariai above Fuchū, the splendidly atmospheric **Nariai-ji** is one of the 33 temples on the Saigoku Kannon pilgrimage route, while closer to the summit there is a fantastic view of the bay and coast as far away as the Noto-hantō, some 500km northeast. East along the Tango-hantō lies the picturesque fishing hamlet of **Ine**, while across the bay in Monju is another attractive wooden temple, **Chion-ji**, standing on the brink of the sandbar – a lovely area for a quiet stroll or cycle ride, or simply lazing on the beach.

Arrival, information and local transport

Trains to Amanohashidate Station in Monju run along the scenic Kita-kinki Tango Tetsudō line. If you're approaching the Tango-hantō from the west, you'll need to change from the JR line at **Toyooka**. The standard fare from here for the seventy-minute journey to Amanohashidate is ¥1160, but for ¥930 extra you can save yourself thirty minutes by taking the more comfortable limited express trains, whose carriages have large picture windows and TV screens showing the view from the front of the train. There are a few direct JR trains from Kyoto and Ōsaka, which take around two hours and thirty minutes, but you'll have to pay for the Kita-kinki Tango Tetsudō portion of the journey if you're using a JR pass. **Buses** from both Kyoto and Ōsaka take around two hours and forty minutes.

The assistants at the **tourist information desk** (daily 10am–6pm; ☎0772/22-8030, ✉monju@tango.or.jp) inside Amanohashidate Station are helpful but don't speak much English, although they can provide a couple of

English-language pamphlets on the area and help with accommodation bookings.

Buses across the bay to Fuchū (20min; ¥510), where you'll find the youth hostel, and around the Tango-hantō, leave from outside the station until 7pm. Alternatively, you can take the more regular and faster **ferry** (12min; ¥520; last ferry 5.30pm) from the jetty beside Chion-ji, five minutes' walk from the station, to the Fuchū-side jetty at Ichinomiya. If you fancy some exercise, **bicycles** can be rented from various shops close to the station and jetty (¥500 for 2hr), or you could stroll the 4km across the sandbar.

Accommodation

Monju is the main tourist hub of Amanohashidate and has the widest range of **accommodation**, including several inexpensive minshuku near the station and a couple of top-class ryokan. Both the youth hostels are across the bay in Fuchū.

Amanohashidate Youth Hostel Fuchū ☎0772 /27-0121, ℱ27-0939. This secluded hostel has bunk-bed dorms, a comfy lounge, a helpful English-speaking manager and cheap bike rental (¥500 per day). It's a ten-minute hike uphill to the right from the ferry and bus stop at Ichinomiya, behind the shrine, Kono-jinja. Dorm beds ¥3098 per person.

Gemmyōan ☎0772/22-2171, ℱ25-1641. On the hillside above Monju, with good views of the sandbar, this ryokan has the feel of an English cottage with dark wooden beams and white plaster walls. The rooms are traditional tatami and there's an outdoor pool in the summer. ❾

Maruyasu Eki-dōri, Monju ☎0772/22-2310, ℱ22-8200. Cosy but colourless minshuku offering tatami rooms with shared bath. Rates include two meals. ❺

Monjusō Shōrotei ☎0772/22-2151, ℱ22-2153. Exquisite ryokan behind Chion-ji temple, surrounded by private gardens at the tip of a mini-peninsula overlooking the sandbar. Rates can climb as high as ¥60,000 per person, depending on the room and your choice of meals. ❾

Young Inn Eki-dōri ☎0772/22-0650, ℱ22-7735. No-frills Western-style hotel, beside the lake. Cheaper rooms share a bathroom. ❹

Amanohashidate and Monju

Five minutes' walk north of Amanohashidate Station, at the end of a shopping street leading towards the sand spit, is the attractive temple, **Chion-ji**, dedicated to the Buddhist saint Chie-no-Monju. Beside the main hall (Monjudo), which houses a revered image of the saint, stands the Tahoto, a squat wooden pagoda dating from 1500. In the temple precincts, near the ferry jetty, you'll also see the Chie-no-wa Torō, a granite ring monument symbolizing wisdom, which has been adopted as an emblem of the town.

To reach the pine-forested sand bar, **Amanohashidate**, cross the red bridge, Kaisenkyō, which swings around to allow boats through the narrow channel to the open sea. The sandy, crescent-shaped beaches on the east side of the spit are at their busiest from July to August. The pine-shaded lane is a lovely spot for a quiet stroll or you can hop in one of the pedicabs (¥3000 for 30min).

The best place from which to view the sand spit in its entirety is from Kasamatsu-kōen above Fuchū (see below), but if you're pushed for time there's also a lookout point in the hills behind **Monju**. A five-minute walk over the rail tracks and up the hill behind Amanohashidate Station brings you to the **chair lift** (daily 8.30am–5pm; ¥850 return), which takes six minutes to reach the touristy Amanohashidate View Land, a mini-amusement park where loudspeakers pump out a 1950s musical soundtrack.

Fuchū and around

The walking trail across Amanohashidate and the ferry brings you close to the precincts of **Kono-jinja**, the oldest shrine in the area, guarded by a pair of stone dogs dating from the Kamakura era. A short walk up the hill to the left, past a row of souvenir stalls, is the station for both the funicular railway and chair lift (daily 8am–5.30pm; ¥1340 return, including bus to and from Nariai-ji) up the lower slopes of Mount Nariai to Kasamatsu-kōen, the principal look-out point over Amanohashidate, where tourists gather for official group photos. Signs demonstrate how best to stand, with your head between your legs, so the sand spit seems to float in midair like a bridge.

From the park you can either catch a bus or walk for twenty minutes further up the mountain to the gate to **Nariai-ji** (daily 8am–5pm; ¥500), a charmingly rustic temple surrounded by lofty pines, founded in 704 and dedicated to Kannon, the Buddhist goddess of mercy. This is one of the 33 temples on the Saigoku Kannon pilgrim route, and so attracts a steady stream of visitors, many of whom clutch elaborate hanging scrolls which are specially inscribed at each temple. Legend has it that if you pray at the temple and make a vow to Kannon, your prayer will be granted.

As you climb the stone steps leading up to the main temple building you'll pass a 33-metre-tall pagoda, recently rebuilt for the first time since it burnt down five hundred years ago, and a small wooden bell tower. An interesting legend is attached to the bell, which has never been rung since it was first cast in 1609. A mother who claimed to be too poor to contribute money to the temple accidentally dropped her baby into the vat of molten copper being cast as the bell. When the bell was first struck, it is said that the people could hear the baby calling out for its mother, so it was decided never to ring the bell again.

If you have time, it really is worth making the effort to continue on to the **Nihon Ichi Tembōdai**, a panoramic lookout spot around 1km further up the mountain from Nariai-ji. The sublime view across Amanohashidate and Wakasa Bay, as far away as the Noto-hanō and the sacred mountain Hakusan on the Hokuriku coast, is straight out of a woodblock print.

If you have time, back down in Fuchū you can catch a bus 16km up the coast to the charming fishing hamlet of **INE**, sheltering in a hook-like inlet towards the eastern end of the Tango-hantō. The best way to see the traditional wooden houses built over the water, with space beneath for the boats to be stored, is to take a yellow sightseeing boat from Ine harbour (closed Feb; daily 9am–4.30pm; ¥660) on a thirty-minute tour of the inlet. If you have your own transport, you'll find it easier to proceed around the rest of the rugged peninsula, with its dramatic cliffside roads, sweeping coastal views and quiet beaches.

Eating and drinking

You'll find more **restaurants** and **cafés** in Monju than Fuchū, although there are few stand-out options. One of the nicest places is *Hashidate Jaya* (daily except Thurs 9am–5pm), nestling amid the pines at the Monju end of the sand spit, which serves good-value meals and snacks, including *asari-don*, small shellfish and spring onions on a bowl of rice. The *Young Inn* (see p.705) has an attached French restaurant with views of the bay and does a four-course lunch deal for ¥1500. Over in Fuchū, try *St John's Bear* (daily 8am–8pm) at the water's edge down from the chair-lift station, a Western-style café-bar which also serves pizza.

Travel details

Trains

The trains between the major cities listed below are the fastest, direct services. There are also frequent slower services, run by JR and several private companies, covering the same destinations. It is usually possible, especially on long-distance routes, to get there faster by changing between services.

Amanohashidate to: Kinosaki (8 daily; 1hr 15min); Kyoto (7 daily; 2hr 30min); Ōsaka (8 daily; 2hr 30min); Toyooka (8 daily; 1hr 20min).

Hagi to: Matsue (3 daily; 3hr 45min); Shimonoseki (3 daily; 2hr).

Hiroshima to: Fukuoka (Hakata Station) (every 15min; 1hr 10min); Kyoto (every 15 min; 1hr 50min); Matsue, via Okayama (1 hourly; 4hr); Okayama (every 15min; 40min); Shin-Ōsaka (every 15min; 1hr 30min); Tokyo (at least 25 daily; 4hr 50min).

Matsue to: Izumo Taisha (10 daily; 1hr); Kokura (daily; 5hr 35min); Okayama (14 daily; 2hr 20min); Tokyo (daily; 13hr); Tsuwano (3 daily; 2hr 30min).

Okayama to: Hiroshima (every 15min; 40min); Matsue (hourly; 2hr 20min); Shin-Ōsaka (every 30min; 55min); Takamatsu (3 hourly, 1hr); Tokyo (every 20min; 3hr 53min).

Tottori to: Ōsaka (15 daily, 2hr 20min).

Yamaguchi to: Tsuwano (17 daily; 50min–1hr 20min); Ogōri (every 20min; 20min).

Buses

The buses listed below are mainly long-distance services, often travelling overnight – between the major cities – and local services where there is no alternative means of transport. For shorter journeys, however, trains are almost invariably quicker and often no more expensive.

Amanohashidate to: Kyoto (daily; 2hr 40min); Ōsaka (daily; 2hr 40min).

Hagi to: Ōsaka (daily; 9hr); Tokyo (daily; 14hr).

Hiroshima to: Hagi (2 daily; 2hr 30min); Izumo (8 daily; 3hr 30min); Kyoto (daily; 8hr); Matsue (12 daily; 3hr 30min); Ōsaka (daily; 7hr 30min); Tokyo (daily; 12hr).

Kurashiki to: Ōsaka (2 daily; 5hr); Tokyo (daily; 11hr).

Ogōri to: Akiyoshi-dai (12 daily; 40min); Hagi (6 daily; 1hr 26min).

Okayama to: Chiba (1 daily; 10hr 55min); Fukuoka (1 daily; 9hr); Kōbe (2 daily; 2hr 50min); Kōchi (8 daily; 2hr 30min); Matsue (4 daily; 3hr 10min); Matsuyama (6 daily; 2hr 40min); Ōsaka (2 daily; 4hr); Tokyo (2 daily; 10hr 20min); Yonago (6 daily; 2hr 10min).

Onomichi to: Imabari (Shikoku) (10 daily; 1hr 30min); Matsuyama (Shikoku) (2 daily; 2hr 50min); Omishima (10 daily; 55min).

Tottori to: Hiroshima (5 daily; 4hr 50min); Kyoto (3 daily; 4hr); Ōsaka (19 daily; 3hr 35min); Tokyo (daily; 10hr 30min).

Yamaguchi to: Akiyoshi-dai (19 daily; 55min); Hagi (11 daily; 1hr 15min).

Ferries

Hiroshima to: Beppu (1 daily; 3hr 10min); Matsuyama (12 daily; ferry 2hr 40min, hydrofoil 1hr 10min); Miyajima (every 20min; 10min).

Okayama to: Shōdo-shima (1 hourly; 1hr 10min).

Onomichi to: Ikuchi-jima (9 daily; 30min).

Shimonoseki to: Pusan (daily; 13hr 30min).

Flights

Hiroshima to: Okinawa (10 weekly; 1hr 50min); Sapporo (2 daily; 2hr); Sendai (2 daily; 1hr 35min); Tokyo Haneda (18 daily; 1hr 15min); Tokyo Narita (daily; 1hr 40min).

Hiroshima Nishi to: Kagoshima (5 daily; 1hr); Miyazaki (2 daily; 45min); Niigata (daily; 1hr 25min).

Iwami (Hagi) to: Ōsaka (daily; 1hr); Tokyo (2 daily; 1hr 40min).

Izumo to: Fukuoka (3 daily; 1hr 15min); Nagoya (daily; 1hr 10min); Ōsaka (6 daily; 1hr); Tokyo (5 daily; 1hr 20min).

Okayama to: Kagoshima (3 daily; 1hr 15min); Komatsu (2 daily; 1hr 5min); Okinawa (2hr); Sapporo (daily; 2hr); Sendai (daily; 1hr 30min); Tokyo (4 daily; 1hr 15min).

Tottori to: Ōsaka Nishi (daily; 50min); Tokyo Haneda (3 daily; 1hr 10min).

Yamaguchi Ube to: Tokyo Haneda (8 daily; 1hr 30min).

Yonago to: Fukuoka (daily; 1hr 10min); Nagoya (daily; 1hr 5min); Tokyo Haneda (5 daily; 1hr 15min); Seoul (3 weekly; 1hr 30min).

8

Shikoku

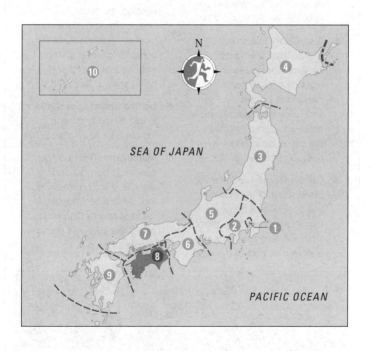

N

SEA OF JAPAN

PACIFIC OCEAN

CHAPTER 8

Highlights

* **Ritsurin-kōen** Japan's largest garden, whose creation took three feudal lords over a century to complete. See p.719

* **Kompira-san** One of Shinto's major places of pilgrimage – and the climb up all 1346 steps to the innermost shrine is rewarded by splendid views. See p.731

* **Awa Odori** Tokushima's annual festival attracts over a million spectators and eighty thousand participants, dressed in colourful *yukata* and half-moon-shaped straw hats, who parade through the city to an insistent two-beat rhythm. See p.736

* **Ōboke Gorge** Hidden away in the heart of the island, this spectacular gorge is especially dramatic in winter, while in summer you can admire it as part of a pleas-ant boat trip along the river. See p.743

* **Shimanto-gawa** Japan's most beautiful river, twisting through verdant countryside past pine-clad slopes and terraced rice fields. See p.755

* **Bullfights** More akin to bull sumo than to Spanish bullfighting, the contests of bovine strength at the rural town of Uwajima make for compelling viewing, and without a drop of blood being spilled. See p.762

* **Uchiko** Charming and little-visited historical town in remote Ehime-ken. See p.764

* **Matsuyama** This compact castle city boasts good nightlife, a strong literary history, a famous hot-spring resort at nearby Dōgo and one of the country's strangest temples. See p.767

△ Bullfight, Uwajima

8

Shikoku

I t has beautiful scenery, a laid-back atmosphere, friendly people and several notable sights, yet **SHIKOKU**, Japan's fourth main island, is usually at the bottom of most visitors' itineraries – if it appears at all. This is a shame, since this tranquil island, nestling in the crook between Honshū and Kyūshū, offers elements of traditional Japan that are often hard to find elsewhere. An ancient Buddhist pilgrimage, original castles and distinctive arts and crafts are

Shikoku cuisine

Though the least populous of Japan's four main islands, Shikoku has plenty of tasty treats – but make sure you eat early in the evening, especially in the countryside, as most restaurants usually shut by 9pm. The white wheat **noodles** known as *sanuki-udon* are found in Kagawa-ken and best enjoyed in Takamatsu. Sanuki is the old name for the area which now includes Kagawa-ken, and the noodles have a history which allegedly dates back to the ninth century, when they were introduced from China. *Kake-udon* is simply *udon* in a hot broth topped off with minced spring onion and ginger, to which can be added pieces of tempura and the like.

Bukkake-udon is much simpler and in some cases plain soy sauce is used instead of soup stock so the taste and texture of the raw noodles can be enjoyed to the full. *Kama-age-udon* is hot *udon* straight from the pot dipped in soup stock just before being eaten. If the *udon* isn't served up in the water it's been boiled in, but in regular hot water, it's called *yudame-udon*. In *Zaru-udon*, the boiled noodles are rinsed and served on a wickerwork platter, then dipped in a sauce just before being eaten. *Shippoku-udon* is more of a stew, with taros (starchy root vegetables), carrots, *daikon*, *shiitake*, spring onions and other ingredients thrown together in the soup stock and cooked, then heaped on the boiled noodles. One final variation is *uchiko-mi-udon*, similar to *shippoku-udon*, although here the noodles are cooked together with the ingredients in the soup.

If you don't like noodles, get down to Kōchi-ken for some **katsuo-no-tataki** (lightly roasted bonito served with grated radish). After being lightly cooked, the inside of the fish – which is still raw – is sliced open and served as sashimi. If done properly, compliment the chef with a cry of *makkoto umaizeyo*, which means "Very tasty!" in the local dialect. Bonito is common in the waters off the prefecture and *katsuobushi* (dried bonito; also known locally as *tosabushi*) is famous throughout the country. Tokushima is famed for the citrus fruit known as **sudachi**, a cross between a lemon and a lime. *Sudachi* juice is used to add flavour to many local dishes, while recent creations such as *sudachi* juice, *sudachi shōchū* and *sudachi* vinegar have widened the fruit's appeal. Ehime-ken is home to the filling potato-based stew known as **imo-taki**, traditionally cooked in a large iron pot into which sweet potatoes, pieces of dried *tōfu*, *shiitake*, *konnyaku* (a jelly-like food made from the starch of a tuber known as devil's tongue) and chicken are thrown and slowly boiled.

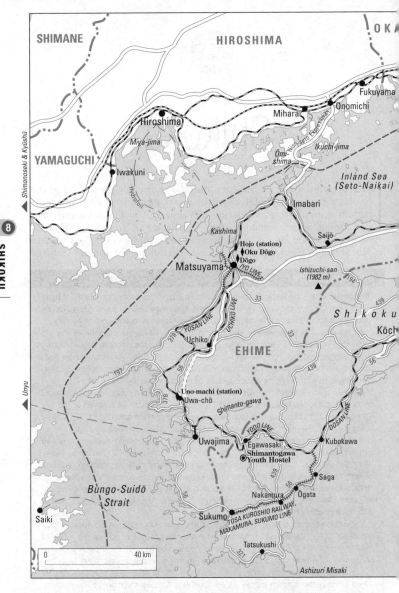

some of Shikoku's attractions – but equally appealing is the island's rural pace of life and little-visited villages. You'll need a week or so to get around all Shikoku's four prefectures. If you only have a day, though, head straight for either of the island's justly famous draws: **Matsuyama's** splendid castle and the hot springs at nearby **Dōgo**, or the landscape gardens of **Ritsurin-kōen** in Takamatsu.

According to legend, Shikoku was the second island (after Awaji-shima) born to Izanagi and Izanami, the gods who are considered to be Japan's parents. Its

Ōsaka

Maiko Kōbe

Okayama HYŌGO Akashi
Akashi Kaikyō
Ōhashi
Iwaya

Tonoshō Shōdo-shima
Nao-shima
Seto-Ōhashi
SETO-ŌHASHI LINE Awaji-shima
Goshiki

Megi-jima
Takamatsu Yashima Sumoto
Ōhama
Marugame KOTOKU LINE Wakayama
KOTODEN LINE
Zentsū-ji 11 Ōnaruto-bashi Fukura
Kotohira KAGAWA Ōtani Naruto Whirlpools
438 NARUTO Naruto
Yoshino-gawa LINE
TOKUSHIMA LINE 192 Tokushima
Awa Ikeda 438
Ōboke TOKUSHIMA
Kazura-bashi 438 193
439 Minokoshi
Oku Iya
Kaeura-bashi Tsurugi-san
32 (1893 m) MUGI LINE
195 55
Hiwasa
KŌCHI 193
Shishikui Kaifu
Gomen TOSA KUROSHIO RAILWAY ASA KAIGAN LINE
55 GOMEN-NAHARI LINE 493 Kannoura
Katsurahama Aki
Nahari N

Hotsumisaki-ji
(Temple & Youth Hostel)
Tosa-wan Muroto Misaki

PACIFIC OCEAN

Ōsaka ▶
Kansai International Airport ▶
Hydrofoil
Tokyo ▶

ancient name was Iyo-no-futana and it was divided into four main areas: Awa (now Tokushima-ken), Iyo (Ehime-ken), Sanuki (Kagawa-ken) and Tosa (Kōchi-ken). These epithets are still used today when referring to the different prefectures' cuisines and traditional arts. Apart from being the scene of a decisive battle between the Taira and Minamoto clans in the twelfth century (see "History", p.935), Shikoku has had a relatively peaceful history, due in part to its isolation from the rest of Japan. This isolation finally ended with the opening of the **Seto Ōhashi** in 1989, a series of six bridges which leapfrog the islands of the Inland Sea, carrying both trains and cars. It has now been joined by the **Akashi Kaikyō Ōhashi** – the longest single-span suspension bridge in the world – connecting Shikoku to Honshū via Awaji-shima, the island to the west of Tokushima, and the **Nishi Seto Expressway**, running along ten bridges spanning nine islands between Onomichi in Hiroshima-ken and Imabari on the island's northern coast.

Most of Shikoku's population of just over four million lives in one of the island's four prefectural capitals: Takamatsu, Tokushima, Kōchi and Matsuyama. The island is split by a vast mountain range that runs from Tsurugi-san in the east, to Ishizuchi-san, Shikoku's tallest peak, in the west. The northern coast, facing the Inland Sea, is heavily developed, in contrast to the predominantly rural south, where the unimpeded *kuroshio* (black current) of the Pacific Ocean has carved a rugged coastline of sheer cliffs and outsized boulders. The climate throughout the island is generally mild, although the coasts can be lashed by typhoons and the mountains see snow in the winter.

The Shikoku pilgrimage

Wherever you are in Shikoku, you'll seldom be far from Japan's longest and most famous pilgrimage, established by disciples of the Buddhist saint **Kōbō Daishi**, founder of Shingon Buddhism. It takes over two months to walk the 1400km between the 88 temples on the prescribed route, and plenty of pilgrims, known as *henro-san*, still complete the journey on foot, though far more travel the route by car or on bus tours. It's even possible to do the tour by helicopter. The number of temples represents the 88 evils that, according to Shingon Buddhism, bedevil human life.

Henro-san are easy to spot, since they usually dress in traditional short white cotton coats, coloured shoulder bands and broad-rimmed straw hats, and generally clutch rosaries, brass bells and long wooden staffs – for support on the steep ascents to most of the temples. The characters on their robes and staffs translate as "Daishi and I go together". Most pilgrims are well past retirement age, as few young Japanese have the inclination or the vacation time needed for such a pilgrimage.

Kōbō Daishi (known during his lifetime as Kūkai) was born in 774, 30km from Takamatsu. This pious man walked all over the island as an itinerant priest and spent two years in China studying esoteric Buddhism, before apparently gaining enlightenment at Muroto Misaki in Kōchi-ken and founding the **Shingon** (True Word) sect of Buddhism. Shingon was influenced by Central Asian tantric Buddhist traditions and this is reflected in the Shikoku temples, with their often exotic decor and atmosphere. Kūkai died on April 22, 835, the exact day he predicted he would. For his achievements, he was posthumously awarded the title **Daishi** (Great Saint) by the imperial court. Soon after his death, his disciples began a tour around the temples of Shikoku associated with the Daishi, thus establishing the pilgrimage as it is known today.

The present-day headquarters of the Shingon sect is **Kōya-san**, in Wakayama-ken (see p.590), and this is the traditional start of the once-in-a-lifetime pilgrimage. The first temple visited on Shikoku is **Ryōzen-ji**, near Naruto in Tokushima-ken. Pilgrims then follow a circular route that winds its way clockwise around the island, stopping at all the temples on the way to the 88th temple, **Ōkubo-ji**, in Kagawa-ken. Around half the temples allow pilgrims to stay for around ¥4000 per person including meals. You'll see many pilgrims dropping coins by the thousands of Buddhas along the way, and they fork out again at the temples, where an official stamp costs around ¥300.

Several books in English describe the 88-temple hike, including Oliver Statler's classic *Japanese Pilgrimage*. For slightly more up-to-date details, check out ⓦ www.mandala.ne.jp/echoes/index.html, created by Don Weiss, the author of *Echoes of Incense* and a resident of Tokushima.

You're most likely to begin your journey around the island in **Kagawa-ken** on the northern coast, after crossing the Seto Ōhashi. Stop in Takamatsu to visit the delightful gardens of **Ritsurin-kōen**, the **Yashima** plateau, immediately east of the city, site of a historic clan battle, and, in the west of the prefecture, the shrine at **Kotohira**. If you have a bit more time, take a trip out to one of the nearby Inland Sea islands, such as **Shōdoshima** or **Naoshima**. Eastern Shikoku and the central, secluded **Iya valley** are part of **Tokushima-ken**, famous for its capital city Tokushima's annual **Awa Odori** dance festival, the whirlpools at **Naruto** and the turtles who come to lay their eggs at **Hiwasa** each summer. Shikoku's southern coast, fanning out between the capes at Ashizuri and Muroto, is covered by **Kōchi-ken**, where fighting sumo dogs and long-tailed roosters are the local attractions, along with an original castle in the capital, Kōchi. Flowing through the west of the prefecture is the **Shimantogawa**, one of Japan's most beautiful rivers. **Matsuyama**, the capital of the eastern prefecture of **Ehime-ken**, is justly famous for its castle – one of the best in Japan – and the onsen at Dōgo, where emperors and commoners have come to bathe for centuries. Just outside Matsuyama, the small towns of **Uwa-chō** and **Uchiko**, relatively untouched by industrialization, give glimpses of a Japan long since past.

Despite being off the beaten track, Shikoku has good tourist facilities. In the prefectural capitals you'll find a decent range of hotels, restaurants and bars, not to mention international centres and tourist information offices, while the island's famous 88-temple **pilgrimage** (see box, opposite) means that even in the countryside you're unlikely to be stuck for accommodation. **Getting around** by public transport is easy enough, though a rented car will obviously give you more flexibility and really comes into its own if you want to get to the villages of the Iya Valley or explore Western Kōchi-ken and the Shimantogawa area. JR Shikoku runs regular express trains, though local train services are not as frequent as on the mainland. Nonetheless, the island's compact size means you can easily cross it in a day.

Of the island's several **discount schemes**, JR's Young Weekend Card gives 16- to 29-year-olds forty percent off all rail travel on the island from after 5pm on Friday until midnight on Sunday and public holidays. The card costs ¥500 and is available from all JR stations – worth looking into if you don't qualify for a JR rail pass. Also useful are the Seto Inland Sea Welcome Card for Ehime-ken and the similar Kagawa Welcome Card. These free cards last a year and provide discounts of up to twenty percent on a good range of hotels, restaurants and tourist attractions; they're available from all the major tourist information offices and come with handy information booklets in English, Korean and Chinese.

Takamatsu and around

On the northern coast of Shikoku, breezily cosmopolitan **TAKAMATSU**, the capital city of **Kagawa-ken**, is likely to be your first stop on Shikoku. Even before the Seto Ōhashi connected Shikoku's rail network with that on Honshū, the city's port was a major gateway into the island. Warlord Chikamasa Ikoma built his castle here in 1588, but the city and surrounding area's history goes back a long way before that. The priest and mystic Kōbō Daishi (see box, opposite) was born in the prefecture, the banished Emperor Sutoku was murdered here in 1164 and, 21 years later, the Taira and Minamoto clans clashed at nearby **Yashima**. In air raids during World War II, Chikamasa's castle was virtually destroyed, along with most of the city.

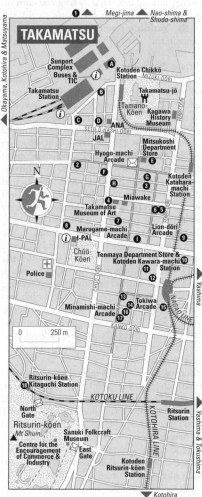

TAKAMATSU

Megi-jima ▲ Nao-shima &
Shodo-shima

Okayama, Kotohira & Matsuyama

Sunport
Complex
Buses &
TIC ⓘ A
Kotoden Chikkō
Station
MIZUKI-DŌRI

Takamatsu
Station B
Takamatsu-jō
Tamano-
Kōen
Kagawa
History
Museum

ⓘ C D ANA
SETO-Ō-HASHI-DŌRI
JAL

Mitsukoshi
Department
Store
Hyogo-machi
Arcade E
② F
H G G
Kotoden
Katahara-
machi
Station
Miyawake
④ Takamatsu
Museum of Art
⑦ ⑥ ⑤
N
Lion-dōri
Arcade
⑧ Marugame-machi
Arcade
ⓘ I-PAL
⑨
Chūō-
Kōen
Tenmaya Department Store &
Kotoden Kawara-machi
Station ⑩
Police ⑪
⑫
⑬ Tokiwa
Arcade
Minamishi-machi
Arcade ⑭ ⑮
⑯
⑰
0 250 m
KANKO-DŌRI

Yashima

NAGAO LINE

Ritsurin-kōen
⑱ Kitaguchi Station

KOTOKU LINE

North
Gate
Ritsurin-kōen
Mt Shuin
Centre for the
Encouragement
of Commerce &
Industry
Sanuki Folkcraft
Museum
East
Gate
Ritsurin
Station

KOTOHIRA LINE

Yashima & Tokushima

Kotoden
Ritsurin-kōen
Station

▼ Kotohira

ACCOMMODATION

ANA Hotel Clement Takamatsu	A	Rihga Hotel Zest Takamatsu	H
Business Hotel Wakaba	E	Takamatsu Terminal Hotel	D
Ebisutei	C	Takamtsu Tōkyū Inn	F
Kawaroku	G	Takamatsu Washington Hotel	I
		Urban Hotel Takamatsu	B

RESTAURANTS, CAFÉS & BARS

Delta Market	9	Kawariyasu	9	Sea Dragon	7
Enia	10	Kikugetsu-tei	18	Sicily Island	17
Imagine	5	Macou's Bagel		Spice Kingdom	13
Jammingway's Café		Café	8	Tenkatsu	2
Kanaizumi	4	Mikayla	1	Tokiwa Saryō	14
Kaname-zushi	6	Nice Time Muzik	16	Tuk Tuk	12
		Queensberry Café	15	Uo Ichiba	3

Today, Takamatsu is a sprawling but fairly attractive modern city of 350,000 inhabitants, peppered with covered shopping arcades and designer stores. As 21st-century as all this is, the city's star attraction remains **Ritsurin-kōen**, one of Japan's most classical, spacious and beautifully designed gardens. The gardens are easily accessible on a day-trip from Honshū, but it's well worth staying overnight so you can also take in **Shikoku Mura**, the open-air museum of traditional houses at Yashima, or **Kotohira-gū** (see p.731), the ancient shrine less than one hour by train west of the city. And, if you're on your way to Kotohira, consider visiting nearby **Zentsū-ji**, the atmospheric temple at the birthplace of Kōbō Daishi. Takamatsu is also a gateway to two of the most appealing islands in the Inland Sea: **Shōdoshima**, a mini-Shikoku with its own temple circuit and scenic attractions; and **Naoshima**, home of the imaginative Benesse Island cultural village and contemporary art museum, designed by Ando Tadao.

Arrival, information and city transport

The JR **train** station is at the northern, seaside end of the central thoroughfare, Chūō-dōri, and ten minutes' walk from the heart of the city. Several direct trains arrive daily from Kōchi, Matsuyama, Okayama and Tokushima, and there's an overnight service to Tokyo. Long-distance and most local **buses** pull in nearby, at the north end of Chūō-dōri. **High-speed boats** from Kōbe (5 daily; ¥6390 one way, ¥9990

SHIKOKU | Takamatsu and around

8

return) dock some way from the city centre at Tokushima-East; a free shuttle bus transports passengers to JR Takamatsu Station. Boats from Ōsaka (2 daily; ¥5800 one way, ¥10500 return) and **ferries** from Shōdoshima and Naoshima dock at the new Sunport ferry terminal, five minutes' walk east of the train station. Takamatsu **airport** (☎087/835-8110) lies 16km south of the town centre, 35 minutes away by bus (¥740) or taxi (¥4000).

The **tourist information office** (daily 9am–5pm; ☎087/851-2009), on the west side of the plaza outside the train station, usually has someone who can speak English and provides useful free maps and booklets on the area. Alternatively, pay a visit to the Kagawa International Exchange Centre, better known as **I-PAL**, at 1-11-63 Banchō (Tues–Sun 9am–6pm; ☎087/837-5901). This excellent facility has a library of foreign-language books, magazines and newspapers from around the world, free Internet access (for 30min), and a TV lounge where you can catch up on CNN news. It's also a good place to meet Japanese who speak English and foreigners who live in town, and you can pick up the free information sheets *Kagawa Journal* and *Takamatsu Information Board* (TIA), which carry details of what's on in town. From the JR station, I-PAL is a twenty-minute walk down Chūō-dōri to the crossing with Central Park – turn right and I-PAL is just on the left.

Takamatsu and around

Takamatsu	Takamatsu	高松
Kagawa History Museum	Kagawa-ken Rekishi Hakubutsukan	香川県歴史博物館
Kawaramachi	Kawaramachi	瓦町
Kotoden	Kotoden	琴電電鉄
Ritsurin-kōen	Ritsurin-kōen	栗林公園
Takamatsu Museum of Art	Takamatsu-shi Bijutsukan	高松市美術館
Tamamo-kōen	Tamamo-kōen	玉藻公園

Accommodation

ANA Clement Takamatsu	Zennikkū Hoteru Kuremento Takamatsu	全日空ホテルクレメント高松
Business Hotel Wakaba	Bijinesu Hoteru Wakaba	ビジネスホテルWAKABA
Ebisutei	Ebisutei	えびす亭
Kawaroku	Kawaroku	川六
Rihga Hotel Zest Takamatsu	Riiga Hoteru Zesuto Takamatsu	リーガホテルゼスト高松
Takamatsu Terminal Hotel	Takamatsu Tāminaru Hoteru	高松ターミナルホテル
Takamatsu Tōkyū Inn	Takamatsu Tōkyū In	高松東急イン
Takamatsu Washington Hotel	Takamatsu Washinton Hoteru	高松ワシントンホテル
Urban Hotel Takamatsu	Āban Hoteru Takamatsu	アーバンホテル高松

Eating

Kanaizumi	Kanaizumi	かな泉
Kaname-zushi	Kaname-Zushi	要寿司
Kawariyasu	Kawariyasu	吾割安
Kikugetsu-tei	Kikugetsu-tei	菊月亭
Spice Kingdom	Supaisu Ōkoku	スパイス王国
Tenkatsu	Tenkatsu	天勝
Tokiwa Saryō	Tokiwa Saryō	ときわ茶寮
Uo Ichiba	Uo Ichiba	魚市場

City transport

Laid out on a grid plan, Takamatsu is an easy city to walk or cycle around. Bicycles can be rented at the JR station for just ¥100 (see "Listings", p.721). Otherwise, you'll find trains and buses perfectly user-friendly, and good for getting to sights outside the city. As well as local JR train services, Takamatsu has the **Kotoden** network, which uses old-fashioned trains and is useful for getting to Yashima or Kotohira. Kawaramachi Station, where the Kotoden's three main lines intersect, is beside the Tenmaya department store at the end of the Tokiwa arcade, while Takamatsu Chikkō Station is next to Tamano-kōen, a few minutes' walk from JR Takamatsu Station. If you're heading from Takamatsu Chikkō Station to Yashima, you'll need to change at Kawaramachi. Buses for Ritsurin-kōen and Yashima run from the stops outside Chikkō Station at the top of Chūō-dōri.

Accommodation

The nearest youth hostel to Takamatsu, at Yashima (see p.722), is very basic, but if you want to stay in the centre of Takamatsu there are also a few small **hotels** with Japanese-style rooms for around ¥4000 per person, near the station. If these are full, go for one of the many business hotels clustered in the same area – the better ones are listed below and have single rooms from around ¥6000. More upmarket options can be found around Chūō-dōri.

ANA Clement Takamatsu 1-1 Hamanochō ☎087/811-1111, ⓦwww.anaclement.com. The city's newest and swankiest hotel, boasting great sea views. There are six bars and restaurants and all the other trimmings you would associate with this sort of hotel. ⑥–⑦

Business Hotel Wakaba 2-20 Uchi-machi ☎087/823-7177, ⒻTT 823-7182. Modern business hotel, with small but smart rooms – a cut above others in this price range. ⑤

Ebisutei 13-13 Nishinomaru-chō ☎ & Ⓕ 087/821-4112. This small, family-run ryokan near the station is central Takamatsu's best budget choice, with good tatami rooms with TV, and a spotless shared bathroom. ④

Kawaroku Hyaken-machi ☎087/821-5666, Ⓕ 821-7301. Excellent tatami rooms and decent Western-style ones too. The original was bombed during World War II, but an attempt has been made to add some traditional ambience, with raked gravel gardens on the lobby roof, which is overlooked by some of the guest rooms. ⑤

Rihga Hotel Zest Takamatsu 9-1 Furujin-machi ☎087/822-3555, ⓦwww.rihga.com. Pleasant, upmarket hotel with comfortable, good-value rooms and several restaurants, conveniently located for shopping and nightlife. ⑥–⑥

Takamatsu Terminal Hotel 10-17 Nishinomaru-chō ☎087/822-3731, ⓦwww.webterminal.co.jp. There are both Western- and Japanese-style rooms at this standard business hotel. Some rooms have a sofa that can be turned into a bed if you want to share a room between three and bring the cost down. ⑤

Takamatsu Tōkyū Inn 9-9 Hyogo-machi ☎087/821-0109, Ⓕ821-0291. Nothing fancy, but the rooms at this chain hotel are reasonably priced and have a good range of facilities. ⑤

Takamatsu Washington Hotel 1-2-3 Kawaramachi ☎087/822-7111, Ⓕ822-7110. Upmarket business hotel, with high-standard rooms and lots of restaurants. Non-smoking rooms are also available. ⑤

Urban Hotel Takamatsu 2-23 Nishnomaru-chō ☎087/821-1011, Ⓕ821-1012. Basic business hotel close to the train station, with Western- and Japanese-style rooms. They're well furnished, with small en-suite bathrooms and coin-operated TVs. ④

The City

Takamatsu's one must-see sight, **Ritsurin-kōen**, is 2km south down Chūō-dōri from the JR station, but there are several sights worth a stop on the way. Just beside the Kotoden Chikkō Station, opposite the JR station, is **Tamamo-kōen** (daily 9am–5pm; ¥200), a park which contains what's left of the city's castle, **Takamatsu-jō**. Four hundred years ago this was one of the three major Japanese fortresses protected by sea, with three rings of moats surrounding the central keep. All that remains today are a couple of turrets and parts of the moat, and the grounds are only a ninth of their original size. Still, it's a pleasant enough park, with winding pathways and a fantastic display of blossom on the cherry trees in spring. If you climb the raised mound of the keep, you'll get a great view out across the Inland Sea. At the east end of the park, also have a look around the very traditional **Hiunkaku**, a sprawling wooden mansion, surrounded by stunted pines. Rebuilt in 1917, it's now used as public rooms. This area is set for change, however, thanks to the enormous **Sunport** development, in a prime position facing the Inland Sea. At the moment the development, which is still under construction, includes a luxury hotel (the *ANA Hotel Clement*), the JR train station, a convention centre and the ferry wharves – it's eventually intended to house a shopping centre, a seaside promenade plus beach and a new Kotoden train station.

Immediately east of the park is the new **Kagawa History Museum** (Tues–Sun 9.30am–5pm; ¥400), built on part of the old castle grounds. Head to the fourth floor to see the main exhibition, which has lots of high-tech displays, including a mobile phone device you can use to get an English (or Korean or Chinese) explanation of what you're seeing. To make the device work, press the green dial button, wait for the dial tone to finish and for the Japanese announcement, and then punch in the code marked up at the display you're in front of. It's all quite fun, with some impressive relics and life-size replicas of local landmarks, such as the seven-metre-tall copper lantern from Marogame. On the third floor is a special section relating to Kōbō Daishi (see box, p.714), with some amazing giant mandala paintings and ancient statues. Next to the ground-floor library is a hands-on section, where you can dress up in old Japanese costumes and have your photo taken.

South of the park, heading down Chūō-dōri, are the main commercial and entertainment districts, threaded through with covered shopping arcades (*shotengai*) – one stretches for 2.7km and is said to be the longest in Japan. Just off Chūō-dōri on Bijutsukan-dōri is the modern **Takamatsu Museum of Art** (Tues–Sun 9am–6pm; ¥200). The small permanent collection includes Sanuki lacquerware and Western and Japanese contemporary art. There's also a library of art books and videos – some in English – and the spacious entrance hall is also used for dance and music performances. A fifteen-minute walk further down Chūō-dōri is the main entrance to the gardens of Ritsurin-kōen.

Ritsurin-kōen

At the foot of Mount Shuin lies **Ritsurin-kōen** (daily; opening hours vary but at least 7am–5pm; ¥400), at 750,000 square metres the largest garden in Japan. Three feudal lords had a hand in constructing these splendid gardens over a period of one hundred years, starting in the early seventeenth century. In the following century Ritsurin became the private gardens of the powerful Matsudaira family and was opened to the public in 1875. The gardens were designed to present magnificent vistas throughout the seasons, from an arched red bridge amid a snowy landscape in winter, to ponds full of purple and white irises in early summer.

You're most likely to enter the park from the East Gate, a twenty-minute walk from the port. Alternatively, you can take the bus from platform 2 outside the JR station. JR trains stop at least once an hour at Ritsurin-kōen Kita-guchi, one minute's walk from the North Gate – a quieter entrance to the park. At the East Gate there's an **information booth** where you can pick up a free English map of the gardens and buy tickets, at a modest discount, combining entrance with tea in the Kikugetsu-tei Pavilion (see p.720). Ignore the shabby zoo to the left of the

East Gate, and head instead for the **Sanuki Folkcraft Museum** (daily 8.45am–4.30pm, Wed until 4pm; free), worth checking out for its good examples of local basketwork, ceramics and furniture and especially its huge, brightly painted banners and kites. By contrast, the rather pompously named **Centre for the Encouragement of Commerce and Industry** – housed in an impressive two-storey traditional building – is little more than a glorified giftshop.

From the East Gate you can either follow a route through the Nantei (South Garden) to the left or Hokutei (North Garden) to the right, though your priority will probably be to head in the opposite direction to the many tour groups that descend daily on the park. The more stylized **Nantei** garden has paths around three lakes, dotted with islands sprouting carefully pruned pine trees. The highlight here is the delightful *Kikugetsu-tei*, or "Scooping the Moon" **teahouse**, overlooking the South Lake. Dating from around 1640 and named after a Tang-dynasty Chinese poem, the teahouse exudes tranquillity, with its empty tatami rooms with screens pulled back to reveal perfect garden views. The Nantei also has the less elaborate, more secluded *Higurashi-tei* teahouse set in a shady grove.

Hokutei has a more natural appearance, and is based around two ponds – Fuyosho-ike, dotted with lotus flowers, and Gunochi-ike, where feudal lords once hunted ducks and which now blooms with irises in June. Keep an eye out for the Tsuru Kame no Matsu, just to the left of the main park building, a black pine tree shaped like a crane spreading its wings and considered to be the most beautiful of the 29,190 trees in the gardens. Behind this is a line of pines called the "Byōbu-matsu", after the folding-screen painting (*byōbu*) they are supposed to resemble.

Eating, drinking and nightlife

Takamatsu has a wide range of **restaurants** and **cafés**, many conveniently concentrated around the central arcade district, just off Chūō-dōri. Like Shikoku's other seaside cities, this is a great place to sample fish and **seafood** – in some restaurants, served live and still wriggling on your plate. The other local speciality is **sanuki udon**, thick white noodles usually served with a separate flask of stock and condiments. For snacks and fast food, there's a *Willie Winkie* bakery at the station (as there is at all major JR stations in Shikoku), which serves up freshly baked pastries, cakes and sandwiches, and a branch of *Mister Donuts* next to the Tenmaya department store. Coffee fiends can find *Doutor*, *Starbucks* and *Seattle's Best Coffee* outlets in the Marugame-machi arcade.

Among the city's several **bars**, a favourite with expat teachers and young Japanese is *Sea Dragon*, just off the Marugame-machi arcade. It's a spacious, convivial place with a surfboard hanging from the ceiling and potted palms. Apart from being an Internet café (see opposite), the *Queensberry Café*, near the Tenmaya department store, is also a rather cool bar serving beer and cocktails. Nearby are *Tuk Tuk*, a funky *izakaya* which perpetually pounds to a reggae beat and has Australian wines, and *Nice Time Muzik* in Tokiwa-chō, a laid-back bar-cum-record shop also serving food to a soundtrack of reggae classics.

Takamatsu has few **clubs**. Those worth checking out include *Jammingway's Café* (☎087/837-3669) and *Imagine* (☎087/811-2056), both of which host live music events and club nights at the weekends, usually charging ¥1500, including one drink. The *Sicily Island* bar, a block south of the Tokiwa arcade, has live music on Thursday and Sunday nights and is a good spot to find out what's happening on the local club scene. Though mainly an Italian restaurant-cum-bar, *Mikayla* (☎087/811-5357), part of the new Sunport development, sometimes hosts all-night events featuring big-name DJs and bands. There are also several **cinemas** around the Tokiwa arcade that show English-language films.

Restaurants and cafés

Delta Market 6-5 Fukudamachi ☎087/823-0375. On a busy street of bars and restaurants, this funky *izakaya* has an English menu, a long bar and jazz vibes, and is a good bet for intriguing dishes like prawn-and-pear salad, a coffee or a drink at night.

Kanaizumi 9-3 Konyamachi ☎087/822-0123. Main branch of the noted *sanuki udon* chain: go upstairs for a spot of luxury and service (¥1000 and up) or serve yourself downstairs if you're on a budget (¥500). If you're not sure what to do, don't worry, just imitate one of the other diners – the place is always busy. Open 7am–5.30pm (downstairs), 11am–8.30pm (upstairs). Closed Mon (upstairs only).

Kaname-zushi Lion arcade. On a corner halfway down the Lion Arcade, this smart sushi shop does good-value evening set meals of sushi, tempura, sashimi and fried fish for ¥1500.

Kawariyasu 6-3 Fukudamachi ☎087/851-5030. This atmospheric *izakaya*, decorated with nostalgic posters, record covers and other memorabilia, specializes in ramen but also does a fine range of other dishes. Also a good place to try *sudachi-shu*, a very tasty, and not-too-potent, liquor made from the regional citrus fruit *sudachi* – try it on the rocks. The same company runs the nearby *Enia* (☎087/821-1822), a lively *mukokuseki* (no nationality) *izakaya* with a rustic design. Open daily 6pm–3am.

Kikugetsu-tei Ritsurin-kōen. The best way fully to appreciate Ritsurin-kōen's beautiful "Scooping the Moon" teahouse is to sip *sencha* (green tea) for ¥510 or *macha* (powdered green tea) for ¥710. You can buy a ticket at either of the garden's gates, which will get you into the grounds and entitle you to a cup of tea at a small discount.

Macou's Bagel Café Ban-chō 1-9-11 ☎087/822-3558. Good cappuccino and a range of bagels, freshly made on the premises and served up with an imaginative range of fillings, either to eat in or take away. Ideal for breakfast, lunch or a late cuppa. Daily 8am–9pm.

Spice Kingdom Corner of Minamishin-machi and Tokiwa arcades ☎087/835-1722. This second-floor Indian chain restaurant, decorated in dusky-pink curtains, does the full range of Indian dishes and has a picture menu. The set lunches are good value at ¥850 and curries are available in different grades of spiciness.

Tenkatsu Nishizumi Hiroba, Hyogo-machi ☎087/821-5380. Reputable fish restaurant in the square at the far west end of the Hyogo-machi arcade. The interior is dominated by a central sunken tank around which you can sit either at the jet-black counter bar or in tatami booths. Kimono-clad waitresses will bring you your pick of the fish served raw or cooked in *nabe* stews. Has good-value set meals in the evening for ¥1500.

Tokiwa Saryō 1-8-2 Tokiwa-chō ☎087/861-5577. This old ryokan has been transformed into a restaurant and *izakaya* and is well worth searching out if only to see the magnificent interior decoration of the main banquet room. Set courses start at as little as ¥1000 for lunch, and the contemporary *izakaya* section at the front is rather stylish.

Uo Ichiba Hyaken-machi ☎087/826-2056. Colourfully decorated, lively restaurant on several floors, just off the Marugame-machi arcade, with a circular wooden tank of fish ready for the picking. Lunchtime set menus start as low as ¥900, but dinner is considerably more expensive.

Listings

Airlines Both ANA (☎087/825-0111) and JAL (☎0120-25-5971) have offices at the north end of Chūō-dōri, five minutes from the JR station. JAS is at 1-1-5 Banchō (☎0878/26-1111).

Banks and exchange The main branch of Hyakujyushi Bank is at 5-1 Kameichō; Kagawa Bank is at 6-1 Kameichō; and Sumitomo Mistui Bank is at 10 Hyōgo-machi. There's a cash machine that accepts foreign cards at the main post office (see below); it's accessible Mon–Fri 7am–11pm, Sat & Sun 9am–7pm.

Bike rental From the rent-a-cycle offices beneath JR Takamatsu Station. At ¥100 for 24 hours this is an absolute steal and the best way to see the city. Ask at the tourist information office for precise details, as you have to register first.

Bookshops Miawake, 4-8 Marugame-chō (daily 9am–10pm), has a good selection of English-language books and magazines on the fifth floor.

Car rental Eki Rent-a-Car Shikoku, 1-10 Hamanchō ☎087/821-1341; Toyota Rent-a-Lease Kagawa, 2-2-5 Kotobuki-chō ☎087/851-0100.

Hospitals and clinics Kagawa Kenritsu Chūō Byōin (Prefectural Central Hospital) is at 5-4-16 Banchō (☎087/835-2222).

Internet access Apart from the free terminals at I-PAL (see p.635), *Queensberry Café*, beside the Sogō department store, charges ¥100 for 30mins' access (daily 11am–midnight). The *ANA Hotel Clement* also has a business salon with Internet access.

Laundry Flower Coin Laundry, 1-11-15

Hananomiya-chō (daily 8am–10pm).

Police The main police station is at 4-1-10 Banchō (☎087/833-2111). Emergency numbers are listed in "Basics" on p.81.

Post office The main post office (Mon–Fri 9am–7pm, Sat 9am–5pm, Sun 9am–12.30pm) is at the north end of the Marugame arcade, opposite the Mitsukoshi department store.

Shopping Sanuki lacquerware and papier-mâché dolls are the main local crafts. Apart from the gift-shops in Ritsurin-kōen and the Kagawa History Museum, shops in the arcades and the Mitsukoshi and Tenmaya department stores are good places for souvenirs. Also worth checking out is Mingei

Fukuda (Tues–Sun 10am–5.30pm), Hyakean-machi, opposite the *Kawaroku Hotel*, a fine empo-rium packed with folk crafts, pottery and paper goods. Music fans should head to *More Music* (daily 11am–8pm), just around the corner from the police box opposite the Indian restaurant *Spice Kitchen*, for a wide selection of cheap vinyl and CDs, both secondhand and new.

Taxis Try Okawa Taxi ☎087/851-3358 or Tosan ☎087/821-0777.

Travel agencies The main JTB office (☎087/851-4981) is on Chūō-dōri close to Chūō-kōen. The assistants speak some English.

Yashima

Twenty minutes by train to the east of Takamatsu lies **YASHIMA**, a 293-metre-high plateau formed from volcanic lava, and best reached by cable car. The name literally means "rooftop island" (which thousands of years ago it was) and it was here that, in 1185, the Taira and Minamoto clans famously bat-tled to determine who ruled Japan (see "History", p.935). A small detachment of Minamoto forces surprised the Taira by attacking from the land side of the peninsula – the Taira had expected the attack to come from the sea. Within a month the Taira were defeated at the Battle of Dannoura and forced to flee to the mountainous hinterland of Shikoku.

JR trains run at least every hour to Yashima Station (15min; ¥210), from where it's a ten-minute walk north to the base of the plateau. More conven-ient is the Kotoden line (every 20min; 20min; ¥310 from Takamatsu Chikkō Station), as Kotoden Yashima Station is only a five-minute walk from the cable-car station and the outdoor Shikoku Mura museum. A bus also runs from out-side the JR station directly to the top of the plateau three times a day (35min; ¥740).

Yashima's rather antiquated **cable car** takes five minutes (daily 8am–5.40pm; departures every 20min; ¥700 one way, ¥1300 return) to reach the park on the top of the plateau. You can also hike up a steep, winding path starting to the west of the cable-car station. Once at the top, apart from the stunning views (weather permitting) of the Inland Sea, you might be a little disappointed. On the southern ridge of the plateau are some rather dingy tourist hotels, souvenir shops, and the tacky Yashima Sanjo Aquarium, where dolphins and sea lions are kept in appallingly small pools. More appealing is **Yashima-ji** temple, supposedly constructed in 754 and number 84 on the Shikoku pilgrimage. Look out for the saucy granite carvings of raccoons next to the temple. Yashima-ji's **Treasure House** (daily 9am–5pm; ¥500) is worth popping into for its collection of screens, pottery and a mixed bag of relics from the battle between the Taira and Minamoto. There's also a traditional garden behind the Treasure House, with the distinctly unbloody "Pond of Blood", believed to be the spot where the Minamoto soldiers cleansed their swords.

By far the best reason for visiting Yashima is **Shikoku Mura** (daily: April–Oct 8.30am–5pm; Jan–March, Nov & Dec 8.30am–4.30pm; ¥800), which lies at the base of the plateau, five minutes' walk to the east of the cable-car station. Twenty-one traditional houses and buildings were relocated here from across the island, and a cleverly landscaped park links the buildings. The park starts with a replica of the Iya Valley's Kazura-bashi, a bridge made of vines and bamboo which crosses a pond to a traditional thatched-roof Kabuki theatre from Shōdoshima. Plays are occasionally performed here – check with the tourist information office in Takamatsu (see p.717). Look out also for the circular Sato Shime Goya (Sugarcane Press Hut) with a conical roof – a unique feature in Japanese architecture. There's also a guardhouse of the Marugame clan, and a fisherman's hut, complete with a couple of boats. Each of the houses has an excellent English explanation of its history.

In late 2002, the Ando Tadao-designed **Shikoku Mura Bijutsukan** (same hours as Shikoku Mura; ¥500) opened inside the park. Snugly fitting a hillside, this museum consists of a single long gallery featuring original paintings by the likes of Marc Chagall and Pablo Picasso, a selection of Claude Monet's letters, Natsume Soseki's hand-painted picture postcards and a particularly large Kofun-era horse. Equally impressive is the landscaped water garden, comprising a number of descending staircases and waterfalls surrounded by beds of roses. The garden has been designed so that the sound of the water changes in intensity as you walk up and down the staircases, from a gentle trickle to a raging torrent.

A visit to the **Isamu Noguchi Garden Museum** (by appointment only Tues, Thurs & Sat 11am, 1pm & 3pm; ¥2100; ☎087/870-1500, ⓦ www.isamunoguchi.or.jp) completes the day-trip to Yashima, though to visit you'll need to make an appointment at least two weeks in advance. A Japanese-American sculptor of exceptional talent, Noguchi eventually came to terms with his mixed upbringing, and at the time of his death (in 1988, at the age of 84) had studios both in New York and in the town of Mure, where the museum (actually his house, showroom and studio as they were when he died) is located. The museum aims to replicate Noguchi's working environment, and numerous statues are displayed in the garden and two large storehouses known as *kura*, one of which houses his enormous signature work, the circular *Energy Void*. To get to the museum, hop on the Kotoden train at Kotoden Yashima Station heading towards Shido and alight at **Yakuri Station** (every 20min; 5min; ¥180), from where it's a twenty-minute walk northeast.

Practicalities

Being so close to Takamatsu, there's little reason to search for **accommodation** at Yashima. If you're desperate, head for the *Takamatsu Yashima Sansō Youth Hostel*, 77-4 Yashima Naka-machi (☎087/841-2318), next to the entrance to Shikoku Mura – a run-down place, with grubby futons in small tatami dorm rooms (¥2000 per person). You can't get food here, but fortunately there are several good **restaurants** nearby. *Ikkaku*, a minute's walk east of Kotoden Yashima Station, is a contemporary beer hall specializing in spicy chicken, served with leaves of raw cabbage, at around ¥1000 a head. Wash it down with a beer brewed on the premises. *Waraya* is a justly famous *sanuki udon* restaurant at the foot of the plateau next to Shikoku Mura. The main building has a thatched roof and a water wheel and gets so busy that there's an overflow section in a temporary wooden building in the car park. You sit at shared tables and slurp the noodles (¥380) from large wooden bowls.

Shōdo-shima

The third largest island in the Inland Sea, **Shōdoshima** is also one of the most interesting to visit, with splendid natural scenery and some worthwhile sights. The mountainous, forested island styles itself as a Mediterranean retreat, and has whitewashed windmills and mock-Grecian ruins strategically placed in its terraced olive groves. But native culture also gets a look in, since Shōdoshima

– which translates as "island of small beans" – promotes its own version of Shikoku's 88-temple pilgrimage and its connection with the classic Japanese book and movie *Nijūshi-no-Hitomi* (*24 Eyes*), the anti-war tale of a teacher and her twelve young charges set on Shōdoshima between the 1920s and 1950s, written by local author Tsuboi Sakae.

Midweek, Shōdoshima makes a delightfully peaceful escape, and you may find yourself tempted to linger. During the summer, however, and at weekends for most of the rest of the year, the island absolutely teems with tourists. Though the main sights can be covered in a day, it's a bit of a rush if you don't have your own transport, in which case it's better to allow yourself a full two days – taking advantage of the two-day bus ticket (see below) – and spending a night on the island. If you're short of time, it's best to start exploring at the main port of **Tonoshō** and then head up into the mountains on the bus bound for the 612-metre-high spot of Kanka-kei. Along the way, the bus stops for thirty minutes at **Choshi-kei monkey park** (daily 10am–4.30pm; ¥370), where apes from Africa, Southeast Asia and South America are kept in cages

Shōdoshima and Yashima

Shōdoshima	*Shōdoshima*	小豆島
Choshi-kei	*Choshi-kei*	銚子渓
Kanka-kei	*Kanka-kei*	寒霞渓
Kusakabe	*Kusakabe*	草壁
Olive-kōen	*Oriibu-kōen*	オリーブ公園
Sakate	*Sakate*	坂手
Tanoura	*Tanoura*	田の浦
Tonoshō	*Tonoshō*	土庄
24 Eyes film set	*Nijūshi-no-Hitomi Eigamura*	二十四の瞳映画村
Accommodation		
Benesse House	*Benesse Hausu Honkan*	ベネッセハウス本館
Chūhichi	*Chūhichi*	忠七
International Campground	*Kokusai Kyampu-jo*	国際キャンプ所
Maruse	*Maruse*	マルセ
Shōdoshima Olive Youth Hostel	*Shōdoshima Oriibu Yūsu Hosuteru*	小豆島オーリフユースホステル
Uchinomi-chō Cycling Terminal	*Saikuringu Tāminaru Uchinomi-chō*	サイクリングターミナル 内海町
Yashima	*Yashima*	屋島
Isamu Noguchi Garden Museum	*Isamu Noguchi Teien Bijutsukan*	イサムノグチ庭園美術館
Kotoden Yashima	*Kotoden Yashima*	琴電屋島
Shikoku Mura	*Shikoku Mura*	四国村
Takamatsu Yashima Sansō Youth Hostel	*Takamatsu Yashima Sansō Yūsu Hosuteru*	高松屋島山荘ユースホステル
Yakuri	*Yakuri*	八栗
Restaurants		
Ikkaku	*Ikkaku*	一鶴
Waraya	*Waraya*	鬼ヶ島
Marugame	*Marugame*	丸亀
Zentsū-ji	*Zentsū-ji*	善通時s

while the local wild monkeys roam free. It's rather unsettling to be surrounded by so many monkeys, especially as the apes often fight viciously among themselves over the food. The bus makes a five-minute stop at a lookout point before arriving at the park at **Kanka-kei**, which has breathtaking vistas across the Inland Sea.

Another way of getting here is by **cable car** (daily 8am–5pm; ¥700 one way, ¥1250 return) from Kountei, a fifteen-minute bus ride from Kusakabe port on the south of the island. From the cable car you can look down into the three-million-year-old granite gorge, where the rocks sprout trees that explode in a palate of brown, gold and red every October. It's a fairly easy forty-minute hike up the gorge from Kountei, while to continue up to the summit of Hoshigajō, the island's highest point at 817m, will take another hour. The youth hostel (see p.726) can provide a basic hiking map in Japanese, though it's not necessary if you're just going from Kountei to Kanka-kei. Note that if you decide to hike or take the cable car up to Kanka-kei with the intention of catching the bus to Tonoshō, the last bus doesn't stop at the monkey park.

The best way to appreciate the indented **coast** of Shōdoshima is to rent a bicycle or motor scooter; the seventy-kilometre circuit of the island will take you a day to cover. Along the main Highway 436 heading east from Tonoshō lies **Olive-kōen** (daily 9am–5pm; free), a pleasant but touristy park of olive groves and fake Grecian ruins where, among other things, you can buy green-olive chocolate. Just as touristy, but far more interesting, is the **24 Eyes film set** (daily 9am–5pm; ¥630), located at the tip of a crooked isthmus sticking out into Uchinomi Bay on the south of the island. The film set was left over from the 1980s remake of *24 Eyes*, and you can wander around a recreated village, do some souvenir shopping and watch the movie. There is also a museum dedicated to the prolific author Tsuboi Sakae, best known for the novel the film was based on. Just before Eigamura is the rustic fishing village of **Tanoura**, where the original schoolhouse that served as an inspiration for the book is also open to visitors (daily 9am–5pm; ¥200).

The east and north coasts of the island are less attractive, scattered as they are with stone quarries. At Omi and Iwagatani, however, you can see **Zannen Ishi**, "rocks which are sorry to be left behind". These huge chiselled blocks were originally ordered by Toyotomi Hideyoshi (the warlord who unified Japan) in the sixteenth century as construction materials for Ōsaka castle. Every block is stamped with the seal of the general in charge of its shipment.

Practicalities

The best way to get to Shōdoshima is from Takamatsu via one of the many **ferries** (1hr; ¥510 one way, ¥970 return, valid for one week) and **high-speed boats** (35min; ¥1020 one way) that depart daily for several ports on the island. If you're coming from Honshū, there are also ferries from Himeji, Hinase, Kōbe, Ōsaka, Okayama and Uno. The main port of Tonoshō, on the west coast, is served by the most services. If you intend to stay at the youth hostel, take a ferry from Takamatsu to Kusabe and, if you're heading for the *Uchinomi-chō Cycling Terminal*, take the boat to Sakate. There's a **tourist information desk** (daily 8.30am–5.15pm; ☎0879/62-6256) inside Tonoshō's ferry terminal; the assistant speaks a little English and can provide you with an English map and bus timetables. If you're coming from Takamatsu, you can pick up information on the island from the tourist information centre there (see p.717).

Buses for main points around the island depart from next to the Tonoshō Port building, two minutes' walk from the ferry terminal. At the bus company office you can buy a one-day ticket for ¥1980, or a two-day ticket for ¥2550

– a good deal if you intend to make your way around the island's main sights by bus, since individual fares are expensive. Buses are not that frequent on some routes, so careful planning is advised. The best deal for **motor scooters** is from Ryōbi Rent-a-bike (¥2990 per day including fuel; ☎0879/62-6578), near Tonoshō ferry terminal; **bicycles** are available at either the youth hostel or the *Cycling Terminal* at Sakate (¥500 for 4hr; mountain bike ¥1000 for 4hr).

Tonoshō has plenty of business and tourist **hotels** charging around ¥8000 per person, including two meals (a safe bet, as restaurants are thin on the ground). A slightly cheaper option is the *Maruse* (☎0879/62-2385; ➍), a small, clean minshuku next to the Tonoshō post office. This place is often full, however, in which case ask for a room at their new "annexe", the Western-style *New Port*. Alternatively, try *Chūhichi* (☎0879/62-3679; ➍), a ramshackle minshuku ten minutes' walk from the ferry terminal that, though a bit primitive in some respects, has decent tatami bedrooms. It's run by a very welcoming elderly Japanese woman who, though she doesn't speak English, is always happy to receive foreign guests – and her home cooking is a knockout. The real flavour of Shōdoshima, however, is perhaps best appreciated at the smaller seaside villages along the southern coast. The friendly *Shōdoshima Olive Youth Hostel* (☎0879/82-6161, ☎82-6060; ➍), a ten-minute walk west of Kusabe port, has high-standard dorms (¥3100 per person) and private tatami rooms, and serves good meals. A fine alternative is the *Uchinomi-chō Cycling Terminal* (☎ & ☎0879/82-1099; ➊), beside Sakate port, which has the cheapest dorm rooms on the island and is run by Yokoyama-san, president of Shōdoshima's International Friendship Club (☎ & ☎0879/82-0469) and author of an informative, free English booklet on the island. For **lunch**, try *Santarō*, next to Kusabe port, where you can enjoy a sea breeze while tucking into delicious freshly made udon noodles.

Naoshima and Megijima

If you have more time, there are a few other islands easily reached from Takamatsu that merit a look. The main one to aim for is **NAO-SHIMA**, home to the unique **Benesse Island Naoshima Cultural Village**, with accommodation in an encampment of Mongolian *pao* (circular tents), an Ando Tadao-designed contemporary art museum and hotel (*Benesse House*), and the associated **Art House Project**, a fascinating collaboration between the local community and innovative artists.

Although it's much closer to the port of Uno in Okayama-ken, the island group (Naoshima is the largest of the 27 in the group) is administratively part of Shikoku's Kagawa-ken and can just as easily be reached from Takamatsu. The cultural village, occupying the attractive southern end of Naoshima (you can safely ignore the industrialized northern part of the island), is part of a project that was begun in 1987 by the publishing company Fukutake Shoten to display its collection of contemporary art. Now called the Benesse Corporation, hence the name Benesse Island, the publisher pulled off a major coup in hiring award-winning architect Ando, who designed the striking **Naoshima Contemporary Art Museum** (daily 8am–5pm; ¥1000 for those not staying at the campsite or hotel), occupying a commanding position on a hill overlooking the rugged coast and Inland Sea. The spacious galleries include some stunning art that justifies a journey here in its own right. Works by Jasper Johns, Jean Michel Basquiat, Andy Warhol, Issey Miyake and David Hockney grab the eye, but particularly notable are the sculptural paintings of Frank Stella and the beguiling *100 Live and Die* installation by Bruce Nauman, which dominates a cylindrical space near the entrance. New works are added all the time, including the winners of the annual Benesse Prize. Just west of *Benesse House* hotel is the new **Chichu Museum**, also designed by Ando Tadao and scheduled to open during 2004. The museum is intended to house five paintings by Monet plus site-specific installations by James Turrell and Walter de Maria.

Art House Project

Naoshima's art isn't restricted to its museum but also spills over into hotel rooms (see p.728) and other parts of the island. The most ambitious of the public works are displayed in the old village of **Honmura**, located midway down Naoshima's east coast, some 3km from the museum. This is the base for the **Art House Project**, a plan to restore two- or three-hundred-year-old houses in the village and turn them into works of art.

So far four "works" have been completed. On approaching the village from the main road, the first one you'll come across is **Minamidera** (Tues–Sun 10am-1pm & 2pm-4pm), a collaboration between Ando Tadao and American artist James Turrell. Ando designed the stark new building that stands on the site of a long-since-demolished temple, and incorporates the charred wooden walls that are typical of the village. Inside everything is pitch-black; it takes about ten minutes for your eyes slowly to adjust to Turrell's artwork – an enigmatic blue void in the midst of the otherwise empty space.

The art in **Kodoya** (Tues–Sun 10am-1pm & 2–4pm), a restored house further into the village, is more immediately accessible, although you'll have to look carefully to spot one of the three pieces by Miyajima Tatsuo here. As you enter the courtyard, pause by the bamboo lattice fence and you'll see it's been created in the shape of digital display numbers, a trademark of the artist. Inside, the traditional house has become the forum for the dynamic light-and-water installation *Sea of Time '98*. **Kinza** (Tues & Fri–Sun 10am–1pm & 2–4pm), a short walk to the west from here, occupies an old fisherman's house. Visitors are only allowed to enter the darkened interior one at a time for precisely fifteen minutes. As one's eyes become accustomed to the lack of light, the collections of small objects made of wood, glass and stone slowly reveal themselves. On the small hill to the east stands **Gō Jinja** (open 24hr), renovated in late 2002. This shrine has been a place of worship since the Edo Period and the modern renovation includes a stone chamber and a glass staircase, unifying the ground below with the world above. Entrance to Gō Jinja is free; a one-day ticket to the other three structures is ¥500. Guided tours (¥1000; Tues & Fri–Sun at 9.45am and 12.45pm) are available with advance reservation, leaving from Benesse House. Email ℮naoshima@mail.benesse.co.jp for details. More information can be found at ⓦwww.naoshima-is.co.jp.

Back near the museum and campsite, several pieces of outsized **sculpture** dot the shoreline, including Cai Gui Quang's witty and practical *Cultural Melting Bath*, an open-air Jacuzzi in a glade surrounded by 36 jagged limestone rocks imported from China. Bookings to use the bath (free if you're staying in the hotel or campsite, otherwise ¥500) can be made between 4pm and 10pm.

Practicalities

There are regular ferries to Miyanoura on Naoshima from Takamatsu (1hr; ¥510 one way) and Uno (20min; ¥280). Minibuses or cars will meet you, if you've called ahead either to book accommodation or arrange a visit to the museum. If you elect not to stay overnight and want to take your time exploring the island, the simplest way of **getting around** is to bring your own transport over on the ferry – a bicycle would be ideal. There is an infrequent bus service; you can get details and a basic map of the island from the tourist information office in

Takamatsu (see p.717). Alternatively, an excellent, pocket-sized bilingual guidebook to the island is available at various locations, price ¥800.

Although Naoshima can easily be visited in a day, an **overnight stay** is recommended to soak up the true magic of the place. Don't pass up the chance to bunk down at the *International Campground* (☏087/892-2030, Ⓦwww.naoshima-is.co.jp/eindex.htm; ④), which resembles Genghis Khan's barracks as designed by Walt Disney. The genuine Mongolian *poas*, with beautiful carved and painted doors and support poles, are furnished with comfortable beds and furniture that would do a four-star hotel very nicely. Rabbits bounce around the campsite in the morning, and the beach immediately on the doorstep is clean and inviting. There's a shower block with a giant communal bath and a restaurant where you can pre-order breakfast (¥900), lunch (from ¥850) and dinner, typically a DIY barbecue for ¥3000. The camp is very busy with school groups from July through August, but at other times you might end up having the place pretty much to yourself. If it's full, there's a separate campsite, with similar facilities, on the adjacent beach.

Up the hill and attached to the museum (or in the separate annexe) is the very stylish **Benesse House** (☏087/892-2030, Ⓦwww.naoshima-is.co.jp/eindex.htm; ⑥–⑨); each room is decorated with the work of an individual artist and all have serene views of the Inland Sea. The ones in the annexe are the most luxurious, and some have even had their walls painted by artists. To preview each of the rooms (and find out which piece of art you could be sleeping with), click on to the website. There's a café in the museum and a restaurant serving *kaiseki ryōri* from ¥3500 for lunch and ¥6000 for dinner.

Megijima

Less of a priority, but just 4km from Takamatsu, is compact **MEGI-JIMA**, also popularly known as Onigashima, or Devil's Island. The name relates to one of Japan's best-known fairy stories – that of Momotaro, the boy born inside a peach who grew up to slay the people-eating demon of this island. Halfway up the central peak is a long **cave** (daily 8.30am–5pm; ¥500), where the devil is supposed to have lived – to drive the point home, the place is decorated with jolly plaster demons. It's fun for kids, but otherwise save your cash and take in the view from the platform above the cave. The attractive fishing village at the foot of the hill, where the ferry docks, has distinctive high stone walls, called *ote*, to provide protection from the elements. Boats run six times a day from the Prefectural Pier at the end of Chūō-dōri in Takamatsu to Megijima (¥330), and take twenty minutes.

Ferries continue from Megijima for another twenty minutes to the even smaller island of **Ogi-jima** (¥450 from Takamatsu, ¥210 from Megijima). Here you can hike from the hillside village across scenic slopes to a European-style lighthouse built in the Meiji era.

West of Takamatsu: Marugame and Zentsū-ji

Heading west from Takamatsu, you'll first pass the lush green slopes of **Goshiikidai**, five forested peaks each believed to have a subtly different colour (which they do seem to, at sunset). Enjoy this burst of unspoiled countryside while you can; the rest of the coastline is heavily developed, a consequence of the proximity of the Seto Ōhashi.

Some 30km from Takamatsu, the port of **MARUGAME** has a few points of minor interest. **Marugame-jō** castle, 1km south of the station, dates from 1597, and is one of only twelve left in Japan with an original wooden donjon, while **Nakatsu Banshō-en** (daily 9.30am–5pm;¥1000) is a pretty seaside garden dating from 1688, with art and pottery museums attached to the grounds. From the port you can reach the **Shiwaku Islands**, once the hideout of pirates who terrorized ships on the Inland Sea.

At Tadotsu the train line splits into the Yosan line, which continues around the coast to Matsuyama, and the Dosan line, which runs south to Kotohira and Kōchi. Taking the inland route and alighting one train stop before Kotohira will get you to atmospheric **Zentsū-ji**, the 75th temple on the pilgrim circuit, and featuring a picturesque five-storey pagoda, a treasure hall containing statues and portraits of Kōbō Daishi (daily 9am–5pm;¥500), and wooded grounds. Kōbō Daishi was born here, so the temple is one of the three most sacred places associated with the Buddhist saint – the others are Kōya-san in Wakayama-ken, and Tō-ji in Kyoto. A map outside the JR station will direct you up the main road to the temple, a twenty-minute walk away. A visit here is well worth combining with Kotohira as a day-trip from Takamatsu.

Kotohira

Some 30km southwest of Takamatsu, **KOTOHIRA** should be high on your list of places to see in Shikoku, thanks to its ancient shrine, Kotohira-gū, popularly known as **Kompira-san**. After the Grand Shrines of Ise and Izumo Taisha, Kotohira is one of the major places of pilgrimage of the Shinto religion, attracting around four million visitors a year. The town itself is pleasantly located, straddling the Kanakura-gawa at the foot of the mountain Zozu-san, so called because it is said to resemble an elephant's head (*zozu*). Kotohira can easily be visited on a day-trip from Takamatsu, one hour away by train, or en route to Kōchi or the mountainous interior.

Arrival and information

JR Kotohira Station is a ten-minute walk northeast of the town centre. To the left as you exit the station is a cloakroom for left luggage (daily 6.30am–9pm;

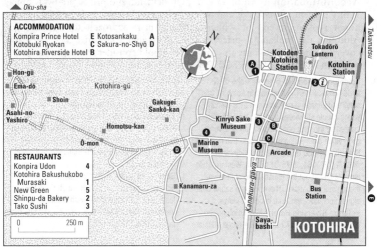

▲ *Oku-sha*

ACCOMMODATION

Kompira Prince Hotel	E	Kotosankaku	A
Kotobuki Ryokan	C	Sakura-no-Shyō	D
Kotohira Riverside Hotel	B		

RESTAURANTS

Konpira Udon	4
Kotohira Bakushukobo Murasaki	1
New Green	5
Shinpu-da Bakery	2
Tako Sushi	3

Hon-gū
Ema-dō
Shoin
Kotohira-gū
Asahi-no-Yashiro
Homotsu-kan
Ō-mon
Gakugei Sankō-kan
Kinryō Sake Museum
Marine Museum
Arcade
Kanamaru-za
Kanekura-gawa
Saya-bashi
Kotoden Kotohira Station
Tokadōrō Lantern
Kotohira Station
Bus Station
Takamatsu
Awal keda & Kōchi ▼

KOTOHIRA

0   250 m

Kotohira	Kotohira	琴平
Kanamaru-za	Kanamaru-za	金丸座
Kinryō Sake Museum	Kinryō-no-Sato	金陵の郷
Kotohira-gū	Kotohira-gū	琴平宮
Saya-bashi	Saya-bashi	鞘橋

Accommodation

Kotobuki Ryokan	Kotobuki Ryokan	ことぶき旅館
Kompira Prince Hotel	Kompira Purinsu Hoteru	金比羅プリンスホテル
Kotohira Riverside Hotel	Kotohira Ribāsaido Hoteru	琴平リバーサイドホテル
Kotosankaku	Kotosankaku	琴参閣
Sakura-no-Shiyō	Sakura-no-Shiyō	桜の抄

Restaurants

Kompira Udon	Kompira Udon	こんぴらうどん
Kotohira Bakushukobo Murasaki	Kotohira Bakushukobo Murasaki	ことひら麦酒工房村さ来
New Green	Nyū Guriin	ニューグリーン
Shumpu-dō	Shumpu-dō	春風堂
Tako Sushi	Tako Sushi	たこ寿司

¥200 per bag). If you've travelled by Kotoden train from Takamatsu, you'll arrive at the smaller station closer to the town centre on the banks of the Kanekura–gawa. The **tourist information** office, or *kankō kaikan* (daily 9.30am–8pm) is on the main street between the two stations; very little English is spoken here, but you can pick up a map, check on accommodation options and rent a bicycle (¥100 per hour or ¥500 per day). **Buses** from Takamatsu terminate at the bus station at the eastern end of the covered shopping arcade leading to the main approach to the shrine.

Accommodation

Accommodation in Kotohira is in high demand, and prices rise by as much as fifty percent at weekends and public holidays. The town is famed for its top-notch ryokan, several of which line the main approach to Kotohira-gū. Although the ryokan are pricey, it's worth remembering that their rates also cover two meals. Those on a tight budget should consider staying at the youth hostel in Awa Ikeda (see p.742), 20km to the south.

Kotobuki Ryokan 245-5 Kotohira-chō ⓣ & ⓕ0877/73-3872. The best deal in Kotohira, this small and charming ryokan is run by a friendly young couple and oozes tradition. It's conveniently located by the river and shopping arcade. Very good value considering rates include two meals. ⑤
Kompira Prince Hotel 709 Enai, Kotohira-chō ⓣ0877/73-3051, ⓕ75-3143. This Western-style place is just about the cheapest hotel in town, though still no bargain. There's a nice sauna on the eighth floor, however, with excellent views. ④
Kotohira Riverside Hotel 246-1 Kotohira-chō, ⓣ0877/75-1880, ⓕ75-2890. Mid-range business

hotel with fairly spacious modern rooms, on the west bank of the Kanekura-gawa a few minutes' walk south of the JR station. ⑤
Kotosankaku 685-11 Kotohira-chō ⓣ0877/75-1000, ⓕ75-0600. Enormous complex, located just west of the JR station, with top-notch facilities including a rooftop pool, luxurious spa baths and restaurants. ⑧
Sakura-no-Shiyō ⓣ0877/75-3218, ⓦwww.hananoyu.co.jp. At the foot of the steps leading up to Kompira-san, with comfortable Japanese and Western-style rooms and some nice public baths. ⑧

The Town

Kotohira's main attraction is **Kotohira-gū**, usually known as **Kompira-san**, which comes from the nickname for Omono-nushi-no-Mikoto, the spiritual guardian of seafarers. This is appropriate enough, since Kompira was originally Kumbhira, the Hindu crocodile god of the River Ganges, and was imported as a deity from India well before the ninth century, when Kōbō Daishi chose the shrine as the spot for one of his Buddhist temples. For one thousand years Kompira-san served as both a Buddhist and Shinto holy place and was so popular among the Japanese that those who could not afford to make the pilgrimage themselves either dispatched their pet dogs, with pouches of coins as a gift to the gods, or tossed barrels of rice and money into the sea, in the hope that they would be picked up by sailors, who would take the offering to Kompira-san on their behalf.

When the Meiji Restoration began, Shinto took precedence, and the Buddhas were ousted from the shrine, along with Kompira, who was seen as too closely associated with the rival religion. While there are no representations of Kompira at the shrine today, an open-air gallery decorated with pictures and models of ships serves as a reminder of the shrine's original purpose, and the Chinese flavour of some of the buildings hints at the former Buddhist connection.

A big deal is made of climbing the 785 steps to reach the main shrine buildings, and you'll see many people huffing and puffing on the lower slopes beside the tourist shops. Some elderly tourists choose to part with ¥5000 to be carried up in cramped palanquins, but the climb is far from strenuous and shouldn't take you more than thirty minutes.

The shrine grounds begin at the Ō-mon, a stone gateway just inside which you'll pass the Gonin Byakushō – five red-painted stalls shaded by large white umbrellas. The souvenir sellers here stand in for the five farmers who were once allowed to hawk their wares in the shrine precincts. Further along to the right of the main walkway, lined with stone lanterns, are the Hōmotsu-kan (Treasure House) and the Gakugei Sankō-kan (both daily 8.30am–5.30pm; ¥500), two small museums which can be passed over in favour of the **Shoin** (see below).

Just before climbing up to the next stage of the shrine, you'll notice a giant gold ship's propeller, a gift from a local shipbuilders, as well as the shrine stables where the sacred white horses (*shinme*) are kept. From here, steps lead on upwards to the main shrine. Soon after leaving the stables and continuing your ascent, you'll see the **Shoin** (daily 9am–4pm; ¥500) on your right, a study and reception hall built in 1659. Press the buzzer on the right-hand post to alert the staff inside that you're entering, and then remove your shoes. You can walk around the verandas and peer through the grills at the delicate screen paintings by the celebrated artist Okyo Maruyama (1733–95).

At the top of the steps is the grand **Asahi-no-Yashiro** (Sunshine Shrine), dedicated to the Sun Goddess Amaterasu, decorated with intricate woodcarvings of flora and fauna and topped with a green copper roof. Two flights of steep steps lead from here to the thatched-roof **Hon-gū**, the main shrine, built in 1879 and the centre of Kompira-san's daily activities. Priests and their acolytes in traditional robes rustle by along a raised wooden corridor linking the shrine buildings. Visitors bow deeply, clap their hands, toss their coins and sigh with relief on reaching here, but the hardy, and truly faithful, trudge on up a further 583 steps to the **Oku-sha** following a path to the left of the main shrine. It's actually an easier ascent than the one up to the main shrine, but very few people bother to make the effort. This inner shrine, located almost at the top of Zozu-san, sports two rather cartoonish stone carvings of the long-nosed demon Tengu on the side of a cliff.

Returning to the main shrine area, head for the wooden platforms for magnificent views of the surrounding countryside – on a clear day you can see as far as the Inland Sea. To the left of the main shrine is the open-air **Ema-dō** gallery, which displays votive plaques, paintings and models of ships. These are from sailors who hope to be granted good favour on the seas. The commendations extend to one from Japan's first cosmonaut, a TV journalist who was a paying passenger on a Russian Soyuz launch in 1990.

The Takadōrō Lantern to Saya-bashi

Kotohira's other sights include the **Takadōrō Lantern**, the 27.6-metre-tall wooden tower next to the Kotoden station, which was built in 1865 and served as a warning beacon in times of trouble. Also worth a look is the **Kinryō Sake Museum** (daily 9am–5pm; ¥310), located at the start of the shrine approach. There has been a sake brewery on this spot since 1616, and the buildings arranged around a large courtyard have been kept pretty much as they have always been. Inside, the exhibition runs step by step through the sake-making process, using life-size displays. Ask for the leaflet with an English explanation. You can also sample three types of sake at ¥100 per shot.

Closer to the shrine steps, a road to the left leads past the lacklustre Marine Museum (daily 9am–5pm; ¥400) up the hill to the **Kanamaru-za** (Mon & Wed–Sun 9am–4pm; ¥300). This performance hall, built in 1835, is said to be the oldest-surviving Kabuki theatre in Japan and was fully restored when it was moved to this location from the centre of Kotohira in 1975. Plays are only performed here in April, but the theatre itself merits a visit, especially for its wooden-beamed and lantern-lit auditorium.

Just before the turning up the hill to the Kanamaru-za, a twisting path leads down to the river, and if you head south along the banks you'll soon come to the **Saya-bashi**, an attractive arched wooden bridge with a copper-covered roof. The bridge is only used during the grand Otaisai festival, in which sacred *mikoshi* are paraded through the town, held every October.

After climbing up to Kompira-san and exploring the rest of Kotohira, you might want to rest your aching bones at the luxurious *Yu-no-sato* **baths**, part of the *Kotosankaku* hotel complex and open to the public from 10.30am to 3.30pm (¥1200).

Eating and drinking

The best advice for **lunch** in Kotohira is to pack a picnic and enjoy it with the view from Kompira-san. You can stock up on supplies at *Shumpu-dō* bakery, en route from the JR station to the shrine, which serves rolls, sandwiches and cakes. The ryokan-lined approach to the shrine also has several tourist restaurants, many with stout ladies outside shouting the praises of the food inside. Try *Kompira Udon*, where the speciality is *shōyu udon*, thick noodles topped with dried fish flakes and bits of tempura batter for ¥500 a bowl. Closer to the shopping arcade, on the corner beside the bridge, is the *New Green*, a quirkily decorated café which serves Japanese and Western food, including good-value set menus (¥700). For a more traditional setting, try *Tako Sushi*, easily spotted on the main shopping street by the large red octopus (*tako*) above the door. Apart from sushi (a set plate costs ¥800), the restaurant also does the usual noodle dishes. Also worth a look is the *Kotohira Bakushukobo Murasaki*, a modern *izakaya* that serves the local *ji-biru* Konpira Beer – the liveliest place in town in the evenings.

Tokushima and around

Built on the delta of the Yoshino-gawa – Shikoku's longest river – and bisected by the Shinmachi-gawa, **TOKUSHIMA**, the capital of Tokushima-ken, is known across Japan for its summer dance festival, the **Awa Odori**, which is attended every year by over one million people. The city has other attractions besides the festival: the **Awa Odori Kaikan** and **ropeway** up Mount Bizan; the high-tech **ASTY** crafts and exhibition centre; and the historic **Awa Jūrōbē Yashiki**, where puppet performances are held. The opening of the Akashi Kaikyō Ōhashi – providing a new road route from Honshū to Shikoku, via Awaji-shima – has brought more visitors and development to Tokushima, but it remains a laid-back, friendly place.

Tokushima also makes a good jumping-off point from which to explore the rest of the prefecture. North of the city are the whirlpools of **Naruto** and several **craft villages**. Heading south, there's the pretty coastal village of **Hiwasa**, where turtles lay their eggs on the beach each summer, seaside communities like **Shishikui** where surfing rules and, across the border in Kōchi-ken, the jagged cape at **Muroto**. Inland to the west are mountains, which cover eighty percent of the prefecture, including **Mount Tsurugi**, the second highest in Shikoku, and the spectacular **Iya Valley**, including the gorge at **Ōboke** and several bridges made of vines and bamboo, such as the **Kazura-bashi**.

Tokushima (meaning "Virtuous Island") was named by Hachisuka Iemasa, a supporter of the warlord Toyotomi Hideyoshi. Hachisuka built his castle here in

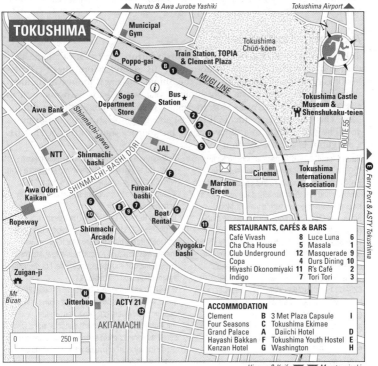

1586, and his clan ruled the area until the fall of the Tokugawa Shogunate in 1867. The following year the prefecture of Tokushima-ken was established.

Arrival and information

Trains from Takamatsu via the Kotoku line, and from Kōchi via the Dosan and Tokushima lines, pull in at Tokushima Station, next to the Clement Plaza shopping centre, at the head of Shinmachibashi-dōri, the main thoroughfare. Tokushima's **airport** (T088/623-5111) lies 8km north of the city centre; a bus from here to the terminal, in front of Clement Plaza, takes 25 minutes and costs ¥430. There's a **ferry** from Wakayama (¥2420) to Okinosu port, 3km east of the centre, and fifteen minutes by bus from Clement Plaza. From Kansai International airport there's now a direct bus via Awaji-shima (¥4000), though the ferry from the airport is considerably cheaper (¥1730). Buses also arrive from Maiko, on the Honshū side of the Akashi Kaikyō Ōhashi. **Buses** arrive and depart from the terminal outside Clement Plaza; there's an information office to help you find the right platform. The city's sights are all within easy walking distance of here.

For **information** on the city and prefecture, the best place to head is the Tokushima Prefecture International Exchange Association (TOPIA), on the sixth floor of Clement Plaza (daily 10am–6pm; T088/656-3303, W www.tk2.nmt.ne.jp/~topia). Staff here are helpful and speak English, and there's a small library of English books and magazines, as well as information on other parts of Japan and Internet access (¥50 per 10min). The Tokushima International Association (Mon–Fri 9am–6pm; T088/622-6066), one block beyond the city hall to the east of the JR station, offers similar services, as well as Japanese classes.

Accommodation

Tokushima has a decent range of **accommodation**, most of it of a high standard and conveniently located around the JR station. More cheap business hotels can be found across the river, the Shinmachi-gawa, about five minutes' walk from the station. The only time of year you'll have to **book** well in advance is during the Awa Odori in August. If you're having problems finding somewhere to stay, pop into TOPIA (see above), who can make enquiries for you. The youth hostel is a thirty-minute bus journey south of the city, but has a delightful beachside location.

Hotel Clement 1-16 Terashima Honchō Nishi T088/656-3111, W www.hotelclement.co.jp. Right beside the JR station, this splendid hotel has spacious and tastefully furnished rooms. There's an eighteenth-floor bar with a view of Mount Bizan, and Chinese, French and Japanese restaurants on the premises. ❺

Four Seasons 1-54 Terashima Honchō Nishi T088/622-2203, F656-6083. Small business hotel with an attached café. More stylish than average. ❹

Grand Palace 1-60 Terashima Honchō Nishi T088/626-1111, F626-4565. Upmarket hotel going for the sleek black look in a big way. The lobby is all gleaming surfaces and odd angles and the rooms are large, with decent-sized en-suite bathrooms. ❺

Hayashi Bekkan 2 Naka Torimachi T088/622-9191, F626-3346. Tucked away in the side streets near the station, this Japanese-style place

has spacious tatami rooms and friendly management. Thirty percent discount if you stay more than one night. Rates include two meals but fall to ¥7000 per person if you opt for accommodation only without food. ❼

Kenzan Hotel 2-11 Minami Uchimachi T088/654-3331, F655-1651. Good-value hotel, a stone's throw from the Shinmachi-gawa, with mainly Western-style rooms, plus a few Japanese ones. It helps if you speak Japanese, but the management are approachable. ❹

3 Met Plaza Capsule 1-8 Ōmichi T088/622-1177, F622-7822. Men-only 24hr sauna and capsule hotel (overnight stays 4pm–10am) next to the Akitamachi entertainment district – not as seedy as some capsule hotels, and also has bigger-than-standard capsules for ¥4500 (ordinary ones are ¥3500).

Tokushima	Tokushima	徳島
Awa Jūrōbe Yashiki	Awa Jūrōbe Yashiki	阿波十朗部べ衛屋敷
Awa Odori Kaikan	Awa Odori Kaikan	阿波おどり会館
ASTY Tokushima	Asuti Tokushima	アスティ徳島
Tokushima Chūō-kōen	Tokushima Chūō-kōen	徳島中央公園
Zuigan-ji	Zuigan-ji	瑞巌寺

Accommodation

Hotel Clement	Hoteru Kuremento	ホテルクレメント
Four Seasons	Fō Shiizunzo	フォーシーズンズ
Grand Palace	Gurando Paresu	グランドパレス
Hayashi Bekkan	Hayashi Bekkan	はやし別館
Kenzan Hotel	Kenzan Hoteru	剣山ホテル
3 Met Plaza Capsule	3 Meto Puraza Kyapuseru	３メトプラザキャプセル
Tokushima Ekimae Daiichi Hotel	Tokushima Ekimae Daiichi Hoteru	徳島駅前第一ホテル
Tokushima Youth Hostel	Tokushima Yūsu Hosuteru	徳島ユースホステル
Washington Hotel	Washinton Hoteru	ワシントンホテル

Eating

Café Vivash	Kafe Bibashu	カフェビバシュ
Clement Plaza	Kuremento Puraza	クレメントプラザ
Hiyashi Okonomiyaki	Hiyashi Okonomiyaki	ひやしお好み焼
Tori Tori	Tori Tori	とりとり

Craft villages and Naruto

Aizomi-chō Historical Museum	Ai-no-Yakata	藍の館
Hall of Awa Japanese Handmade Paper	Awa Washi Dentō Sangyō Kaikan	阿波和紙伝統産業会館
Naruto	Naruto	鳴門
Ōtani	Ōtani	大谷
Shōzui	Shōzui	勝瑞
Uzu-no-Michi	Uzu-no-Michi	うずの道

Tokushima Ekimae Daiichi Hotel 2-21 Ichibanchō ☏088/655-5005, ⓦwww.tokushima-daiichihotel.co.jp. Tiny, clean rooms at one of the city's cheapest business hotels. Payment is fully automated, but there are plenty of obliging clerks on hand to help you check in. Rates are ¥1000 lower on Fri, Sat and Sun, and they only charge ¥2000 extra if a room is used by two people rather than one. ❹

Tokushima Youth Hostel 7-1 Hama, Ohara-machi ☏088/663-1505, ⓕ663-2407. Next to a crescent-shaped stretch of beach fringed by pine trees, this hostel has a peaceful location and friendly English-speaking management. Meals are available, and bikes can be rented for ¥800 a day. Take the bus bound for Omiko, the last one leaving from outside Tokushima Station around 6pm, then catch the bus to Omiko-guchi and walk the remaining 3km to the beach. ❶

Washington Hotel 1-61-1 Ōmichi ☏088/653-7111, ⓕ654-3111. Another of the city's identikit upmarket business hotels. The rooms are nothing special, but the lobby coffee shop is a light, popular spot, and gives free coffee refills. ❻

The City

Five minutes' walk to the east of the JR station is the attractive **Tokushima Chūō-kōen**, a park on the site of the fortress of *daimyō* Hachisuka Iemasa, built in 1586. His clan lived in the castle for the next 280 years and created the town that is now Tokushima. The building was destroyed in 1896 and all that remains of the castle today are a few stone walls, part of the moat and the **Shenshuku-teien**, a beautiful formal garden (¥50). Beside the garden is the small **Tokushima Castle Museum** (Tues–Sun 9.30am–5pm; ¥300; ☎088/656-2525), with informative, modern displays explaining the history of the Hachisuka clan and a large model which gives a good idea of what the castle and its surrounding compound once looked like. Train buffs might like to have a snoop around the immaculately preserved **steam locomotive** in the park directly behind the train station. Japan may now be the land of the bullet train, but this old puffer was in service locally until as recently as 1970.

Walking directly south out of the JR station along the main road brings you to the **Shinmachi-gawa**. There are several bridges and prettily designed promenades along the river, with places to sit and some clever pieces of modern sculpture – look out for the street mosaics of Awa Odori dancers reflected in the metallic bollards on the bridge Shinmachi-bashi. Boats can be rented from ¥500 for thirty minutes at a booth beside the Ryogoku-bashi, and there are also free sightseeing boat trips several times a day.

Five minutes' walk south of the river, at the base of the 280-metre-high **Mount Bizan**, is the wedge-shaped **Awa Odori Kaikan** building (daily 9am–5pm, closed second and fourth Wed of the month; ☎088/611-1611). As well as an excellent giftshop on the ground floor and the **ropeway** (daily: April–Sept 9am–6.30pm, March–Aug Sat & Sun until 9pm; Jan–March & Oct–Dec 9am–5.30pm; one way ¥600, return ¥1000), on the fifth floor, the building is also home to the **Awa Odori Hall** (¥500), where there are at least three live performances daily of the city's famous dance (in which you can take part) as well as the missable Awa Odori Museum (¥300). If you plan to do the lot, go for the discount ¥1500 ticket that covers all the attractions.

The dancing fools

Every year in mid-August many Japanese return to their family homes for **O-bon** (Festival of the Dead), which is as much a celebration as a remembrance of the deceased. Towns all over the country hold *bon* dances, but none can compare to Tokushima's **Awa Odori** – the "Great Dance of Awa" – a four-day festival which runs every year from August 12 to 15. Over a million spectators come to watch the eighty thousand participants, dressed in colourful *yukata* (summer kimono) and half-moon-shaped straw hats, who parade through the city, waving their hands and shuffling their feet to an insistent two-beat rhythm, played on *taiko* drums, flutes and *shamisen* (traditional stringed instruments). With plenty of street parties and sideshows, this is as close as Japan gets to Rio's Mardi Gras.

The history of the Awa Odori goes back to 1587, when the first *daimyō* of Tokushima, Hachisuka Iemasa, is said to have initiated the celebration on the completion of his castle. The people enjoyed themselves so much that the party was held again the following year, and so on for the centuries that followed. The festival only became known as the Awa Odori after World War II, and it now also attracts participants from abroad. Some feel the festival has become too big and organized – there are now viewing stands for which you must purchase tickets, for example. But there's still plenty of fun to be had – mostly from mingling with the dancers, who famously chant, "The dancing fool and the watching fool are equally foolish. So why not dance?"

If you plan to attend the festival, book your accommodation well in advance or arrange to stay in one of the nearby towns and travel in for the dances, which start at 6pm and finish at 10.30pm (street parties continue well into the night). If you fancy taking part as a dancer, contact the Tokushima International Association (see p.734), which organizes a dance group on one of the festival nights.

On a clear day, it's worth ascending Mount Bizan for the panoramic view, and it's not too difficult a hike if you want to save on the ropeway fee; a route starts from the temple to the left of the *kaikan* at the end of Shinmachibashi-dōri. An excellent, full-colour bilingual hiking map detailing ten different hiking courses is available at the tourist information centre. At the summit there's a park with a stupa, called **Tokushima Pagoda**, to the memory of the Japanese soldiers who served in Burma during the war, and the marginally interesting **Moraesu-kan** (daily 9.30am–5pm, closed second and fourth Wed of the month; ¥200; ☎088/623-5342), a tiny museum dedicated to Wenceslão de Morães, a Portuguese naval officer and former consul-general in Kōbe who lived in Tokushima for 16 years until his death in 1929 and who wrote many books on Japan.

Walk east around the base of Bizan and you'll come to the delightful Buddhist temple, **Zuigan-ji**. The street approaching the temple has an ornamental stream running down one side and you can see a picturesque red pagoda poking out of the mountainside woods. Built in the Momoyama-style, Zuigan-ji dates from 1614 and has an elegant traditional garden with carp-filled pools, a waterfall and rock paths across mossy lawns leading up to the pagoda.

If you want to see all that Tokushima-ken offers without the bother of actually travelling, **ASTY Tokushima** is a state-of-the-art conference and exhibition hall, some 2km southeast of the JR station (the name stands for Attractive Space in Tokushima Yamashiro), which presents the prefecture's highlights in one place. Head for the second floor of the complex, where you'll find the **Experience Tokushima Area** (daily 9am–5pm, closed third Tues of the month; ¥910; ☎088/624-5111), an impressive exhibition with high-tech devices, including simulated bus, bike and windsurf rides. The highlight is a 360-degree cinema in which you are surrounded by the story of three childhood friends who are reunited as adults at the Awa Odori, travelling from some of the prefecture's most scenic locations in the process. Outside the cinema, assistants will help you practise the festival dance routines and play the instruments. In the *ningyō jōruri* section puppets are displayed; shows are performed daily by robots and at the weekends by human puppeteers. Also worth checking out is the "arts village" (*Kōgei-mura*) – a large shopping area where you can watch, and participate in, the making of local crafts, including *washi* paper, indigo-dyeing and lacquerwork. There are regular buses from the bus terminal to ASTY, which take ten minutes. The centre has several restaurants.

If you're interested in Bunraku puppetry, known locally as *ningyō jōruri*, head for the historic premises of the Jūrobei family, **Awa Jūrōbē Yashiki** (daily 8.30am–5pm; ¥400), 4km to the north of Tokushima Station. This former samurai residence, with an enclosed garden and display room of beautifully made antique puppets, was once the home of the tragic figure Jūrōbē, immortalized in *Keisei Awa no Naruto*, the epic eighteenth-century play by Chikamatsu. You can see part of the play performed here, usually the classic scene where Jūrōbē's wife Oyumi turns away their daughter Otsuru as a stranger. Live performances are held in the wooden outdoor theatre on Saturdays and Sundays at 3pm, and between April and November at 10.30am on Sunday (call ☎088/665-2202 first to check). A video of the play is also shown inside a large tatami hall. To reach the building, take a fifteen-minute bus journey from platform 7 at the bus terminal.

Eating, drinking and nightlife

Tokushima has a good choice of **restaurants**; an easy option is to make your way to the fifth floor of Clement Plaza, where several places serve Japanese, Chinese and Western food. The major hotels do inexpensive buffet lunches – *Café Clements*, on the ground floor of *Hotel Clement*, is a good bet. A local speciality is *taki-no-yakimochi*, a sweet patty of pounded rice and red beans toasted on a griddle – try it at *Awa Odori Kaikan* or in Clement Plaza. There are also delicious home-made *gelati* at the *Luce Luna* ice-cream bar on Higashi Shinmachi.

For a **drink**, one of the favourites is *R's Café* (see below); *Copa*, a narrow café/bar close to the train station on Terashimahonchō, is no longer quite so popular, but serves a cheap lunch set for ¥650 and has a selection of English magazines. Rooftop beer gardens open during the summer at several hotels, including the *Marston Green* on Ryōgoku Honmachi, while **Akitamachi**, Tokushima's lively entertainment area, bulges with bars and restaurants. For dancing try *Club Underground* in the basement of the ASTY Ijinkan Building, just down from the ASTY21 Building, which hosts drum 'n' bass and other club events at the weekends. Live music fans should head to the small club *Jitterbug* (☏088/669-3286), a stone's throw from the *Washington Hotel*. All manner of local bands play here, most nights of the week; admission is usually ¥1500.

Restaurants and cafés

Café Vivash 1-18 Higashi Semba. Cool café-bar with friendly staff which does a mean set lunch of bagel sandwich, salad and chips with drink for ¥750. Also serves cocktails and a good range of coffees. Open till midnight.

Cha Cha House 2-19 Yaoyamachi ☏088/622-2907. Cute corner café that still has the expat community raving about the quality of its coffees and set-meal menus, all very reasonably priced. The ¥1200 dinner is an absolute bargain.

Hiyashi Okonomiyaki 1-30 Minami Uchimachi. Fine *okonomiyaki* joint, where you can cook your own meal from ¥600. One of the owners speaks a little English.

Indigo 2-8 Higashi Semba ☏088/655-4110. This stylish restaurant has a terrace overlooking the river and specializes in lobster with dinner costing around ¥2000. Lunch is a better deal at ¥800.

Masala 5F Clement Plaza, above JR Tokushima ☏088/654-7122. Not the best Indian in the world, but reasonable grub at reasonable prices ensures a steady flow of customers.

Masquerade 2-41 Higashi Semba ☏088/622-3365. Smoky and a bit grungy, this *gaijin*-friendly compact second-floor restaurant does a mean *pilau* and plays hip-hop music.

Ours Dining 1-28-2 Minami Shinmachi ☏088/652-5560. High-end café run by a husband-and-wife couple who serve tasty Western dishes using ingredients solely sourced from organic farms across the nation. Lunch 11.30am–2.50pm; dinner by reservation only. Closed Tues.

R's Café Second floor, 3-30 Ichiban-chō ☏088/623-4787. R speaks English and has an English menu, which includes pasta, pizza, sandwiches and a wide range of cocktails. Open 11am–3am.

Tori Tori 2-16 Ichiban-chō. Serried ranks of *sake* bottle-keeps and fading Awa Odori posters set the tone at this convivial *izakaya*, next to the *Lawsons* convenience store. *Yakitori* is the speciality – if you're adventurous, go for the pizza-flavoured chicken, pig's stomach or *wani* (alligator). There's an English menu.

Listings

Airlines ANA, 2-11 Yaoya-chō (☏088/625-8800); JAL is on the 4F of the Tokushima Aoba Building, diagonally opposite Sogō department store (☏0120-25-5971).

Banks and exchange The main branch of Awa Bank, beside the Kasuga-bashi, offers the full range of foreign exchange services. Mizuho Bank is just off from Shinmachi-dōri, while UFJ Bank is opposite Sogō department store.

Bookshops There's a very limited selection of English-language books at the Koyama bookstore, a block east of the JR station.

Car rental Eki Rent-a-Car (☏088/622-1014) is in front of Tokushima Station, while Kōkō Rent-a-Car (☏088/699-6671) is at the airport; both offer similar rates.

Hospitals and clinics Tokushima Prefectural Central Hospital (Kenritsu Chūō Byōin), 1-10-3 Kuramoto-chō ☏088/631-7151.

Internet access Available at TOPIA (see p.734; ¥50 for 10min) and free at *R's Café* (see above), if R isn't using the computer.

Laundry A short walk from the station is the Aozara coin laundry, at 3-3 Nakajo-sanjima, open

daily from 8am–10pm.
Police The main police station is close to
Kachidoki-bashi ☎088/622-3101. Emergency
numbers are listed in "Basics" on p.81.
Post office The central post office is just south of
the JR station at 1-2 Yaoya-chō (Mon–Fri
9am–7pm, Sat 9am–5pm & Sun 9am–12.30pm).
Shopping Clement Plaza, beside the JR station,
and Sogō department store are good places to
hunt out souvenirs and food supplies. Both Awa
Odori Kaikan and ASTY Tokushima have fine

ranges of local products. The main shopping
arcade is the covered Higashi Shinmachi, just off
Shinmachi-dōri. Harada Koto Sangenten specializes in *shamisen* and koto musical instruments,
just next door to the Isaku ryokan. The kind owners will likely pull a *shamisen* out and give you a
demonstration.
Taxis Try Anzen Taxi ☎088/631-4988 or Chūō
Taxi ☎088/622-8898.
Travel agents The main JTB office is at 1-29
Ryogoku Honmachi ☎088/623-3181.

Around Tokushima: craft villages and Naruto

Tokushima is a good base for visiting local **craft factories** specializing in indigo-dyeing, paper-making and pottery. **ŌTANI**, around 10km north of the city
on the JR Naruto line, is the home of Ōtani-yaki, the name given to the distinctive local pottery, which has a heavy, earthen texture and is traditionally
crafted into enormous standing vessels. There are several workshops where you
can try your hand at creating your own cups or plates, but you need to make
an appointment first – try Yano Toen (☎088/689-0006) and Harumoto Togyo
Kaikan (☎088/689-0048). Making a simple pottery cup will cost you around
¥3000.

You can learn about natural indigo-dyeing at the **Aizomi-chō Historical
Museum** (daily 9am–5pm; ¥300; ☎088/692-6317), 10km east of Tokushima
near the Yoshino-gawa. In Tokushima this craft dates back at least four hundred
years and until the late eighteenth century was the source of much of the area's
wealth. As well as visiting the museum, where there are informative mini-dioramas showing the whole colouring process and examples of blue patterned
cloth, you can wander around the old buildings that make up the complex and
have a go at dyeing yourself. The museum is about twenty minutes by bus from
Tokushima Station (get off at Higashi Nakatomi) or five minutes' walk west
from JR Shōzui Station, which is three stops north of Tokushima (at least 1
hourly; 12 min; ¥210).

Some 30km west of Tokushima is the **Hall of Awa Japanese Handmade
Paper** (Tues–Sun 9am–5pm; ¥300; ⓦwww.awagami.com/index.html), which
holds exhibitions, sells a wide range of multicoloured papers and has a huge
working space where you might catch a glimpse of master paper-maker
Fujimori Minoru at work. You can also make your own *washi* postcards, and
there are also annual, week-long workshops costing ¥100,000 (including
accommodation and meals). To get there, take the JR Tokushima line and get
off at Awa Yamakawa Station, from where the hall is a fifteen-minute walk
south.

NARUTO, around 13km north of Tokushima, marks the start of the 88-
temple pilgrimage (see p.714), but the town is more famous for the
whirlpools which form as the tides change and water is forced through the
narrow straits between Shikoku and Awaji-shima. This is one of Tokushima's
most heavily hyped attractions, but it's not an event you can bank on catching.
The whirlpools are at their most dramatic on days of the full and new moon,
but to avoid a wasted journey check first on the tidal schedule with tourist
information in Tokushima (see p.734). To see the whirlpools up close you can
either hop on one of the tourist cruise **boats** (¥1500–2000 for around 30min),

8

SHIKOKU | Tokushima and around

or traverse the **Uzu-no-Michi** (daily April–Sept 9.30am–5.30pm; Jan–March & Oct–Dec 9.30am–4.30pm; ¥500), a walkway under Naruto-Ōhashi bridge, which puts you 45m directly above the maelstrom. The cheaper alternative is a bird's-eye view from Naruto-kōen, the park on Oge island, just to the north of Naruto town.

Although there are several trains daily from Tokushima to Naruto, the bridge is a fair way from the station, so it's more convenient to hop on the regular direct bus from Clement Plaza, which takes around an hour and costs ¥600.

South to Hiwasa

Heading south by rail or road from Tokushima you'll be following the rugged coastline, passing by a string of small fishing villages – the best one to stop at is picturesque **HIWASA**, 55km from the city, for its intriguing temple, quaint harbour and beach. **Yakuō-ji**, the 23rd temple on the Shikoku pilgrimage, is on the hillside as you pull into the train station; the temple's base is surrounded by hotels and giftshops catering to the hordes of pilgrims who regularly pass through. Climbing the steps to the main temple you'll probably notice lots of ¥1 coins on the ground: some pilgrims place a coin on each step as they head up for luck. At the top of the steps is the main temple area, whose buildings date from 815 and where there's a striking statue of a goddess carrying a basket of fish and flanked by lotus blooms. Off to the right is a more recently built single-storey pagoda. There's a good view of Hiwasa's harbour from the platform, but the highlight here is to descend into the pagoda's darkened basement, where for ¥100 you can fumble your way around a pitch-black circular corridor to a central gallery containing Brueghel-like painted depictions of all the tortures of hell. In a second gallery is long scroll showing the steady decay of a beautiful, but dead, young woman.

About 1km south of the harbour, the reconstructed castle **Hiwasa-jō** (daily 9am–5pm; ¥200; ☎08847/7-1370) is only worth visiting for its impressive view of the town. The better option is to head directly to Ōhama beach, north of the harbour, where **turtles** lay their eggs between May and August. During this time, the beach is roped off and spectators must watch the action from a distance. For a closer look at the turtles, make your way to the **Sea Turtle Museum** (daily 8.30am–5pm; ¥600; ☎08847/7-1110), beside the beach. The displays are mainly in Japanese, but are very visual, with step-by-step photos of turtles laying eggs; you can also see some turtles here swimming in indoor and outdoor pools.

Hiwasa is 55 minutes from Tokushima by limited express **train**, or one hour and 45 minutes by the more frequent local trains, and makes a good day-trip or a stop en route to or from Muroto Misaki (see opposite). You can leave your bags (¥200 a bag) at the small **tourist information office**, on your right as you leave the station, where you can also pick up a map of the town and rent a bicycle for the day for just ¥100 – a good idea, as the sights are a bit spread out. Close to the museum is a national lodge, *Umigamesō* (☎08847/7-1166; ❺, including two meals). If this is full (it sometimes has parties of school children staying there), try the *White Lighthouse* (☎08847/7-1170; ❼), where the rates also include two meals in a restaurant with a good view of the beach. For lunch, there are a couple of big *udon* restaurants on the main road near Yakuō-ji, but if you've had your fill of noodles, head back to the station and stop at *Hisayama Shokudō*, a clean, friendly establishment serving staple fare like curry rice. This place is packed at lunchtime, so it helps to get there just before noon. It's on the left as you walk out of the station.

Aki	Aki	安芸
Hisayama Shokudō	Hisayama Shokudō	ひさやま食堂
Hiwasa	Hiwasa	日和佐
Hotsumisaki-ji	Hotsumisaki-ji	最御崎寺
Hotsumisaki-ji Youth Hostel	Hotsumisaki-ji Yūsu Hosuteru	最御崎寺ユースホステル
Kannoura	Kannoura	甲浦
Kokuminshukusha Mitoko-sō	Kokuminshukusha Mitoko-sō	国民宿舎みとこ荘
Muroto Misaki	Muroto Misaki	室戸岬
Nahari	Nahari	奈半利
Sea Turtle Museum	Umigame Hakubutsukan Karetta	うみがめ博物館カレッタ
Shishikui	Shishikui	宍喰
Umigamesō	Umigamesō	うみがめ荘
White Beach Hotel	Houito Biichi Hoteru	ホワイトビーチホテル
Yakuō-ji	Yakuō-ji	薬王寺

8

SHIKOKU | Tokushima and around

On to Shishikui, Kannoura and Muroto Misaki

Some 26km south of Hiwasa is **Kaifu**, a popular surfing spot, where the JR train line ends and is replaced with the private Asa Kaigan railway. You'll nearly always have to change trains here (simply cross over to the opposite platform). Even if you don't, you'll have to pay ¥270 extra to travel the remaining two stops – the first is **SHISHIKUI**, Tokushima's top surf beach, where there's a good range of accommodation including the reasonable *Kokuminshukusha Mitoko-sō* (☎0884/76-3150, Ⓕ76-3609; ❺, including two meals).

The end of the line is **KANNOURA**, a sleepy village with a pleasant stretch of gravelly sand framed with rocky outcrops. It has a surprisingly stylish **place to stay**, the *White Beach Hotel* (☎0887/29-3344, Ⓕ29-3032; ❼), where there's also a decent **restaurant**, *El Mare*, serving good-value set lunches. You can rent a bicycle at the station office (daily 10am–3pm) for just ¥200, though you'll need to leave a ¥1000 deposit. If you want to continue south from Kannoura, you'll have to take the bus – several continue around the cape to Kōchi, while there are more frequent services to Nahari and Aki, from either of which you can catch a train towards Kōchi.

You can reach the cape, **MUROTO MISAKI**, an important stop on the pilgrimage route, by bus from either Kannoura (1hr; ¥1490) or Kōchi (2hr 30min; ¥2770). The route from Kannoura takes you past rocky, black-sand beaches and **Meotoiwa** – two huge rock outcrops between which a ceremonial rope has been strung, creating a natural shrine. Virtually at the cape, you can't fail to notice the towering white **statue of Kōbō Daishi**, commemorating the spot where the priest gained enlightenment when he had a vision of the Buddhist deity Kokūzō in a nearby cavern. Pilgrims pay their respects here before heading up to a glade of lush vegetation high above the sharp cliffs and boulders at the cape where **Hotsumisaki-ji** stands. This appealingly shabby Buddhist temple, known locally as Higashi-dera (East Temple), is the 24th on the pilgrimage circuit.

The cape is now famous for its "deep-sea-water" products, made from mineral water pumped from under the ocean. Besides this there's little more to

Muroto than a few weather-beaten shops and small hotels, and a series of pathways along the shore and up the mountainside to the temple. If you decide to **stay**, the best option is *Hotsumisaki-ji Youth Hostel* (☎0887/23-0024, ℱ22-0055; dorm beds ¥3200 per person), just behind the temple. This new concrete block has spacious and elegant tatami rooms with separate bathrooms and toilet; its main custom is from coach loads of OAPs on pilgrimage. Order your meals when you book, or bring your own food, because there's nothing else up here. And be prepared for a long steep climb up the mountainside. Pop into the **information centre** (daily 8.30am–5pm; ☎0887/22-0574), close to the bus stop, if you get stuck for somewhere to stay.

If you're continuing around the coast to Kōchi, you'll probably need to change buses at Aki. Alternatively, and more comfortably, take the bus as far as either Nahari or Aki and then get a train on the brand new Gomen-Nahari line on the privately run **Tosa Kuroshio Railway**. Most trains run from Nahari all the way to Kōchi, though the Gomen to Kōchi stretch is on JR lines. From Nahari it costs ¥1040 to get to Gomen and takes about an hour. With careful planning, and an early start from Tokushima, it's possible to visit the cape and make it all the way to Kōchi in a day, but you should allow two days if you want to spend a decent amount of time in Hiwasa.

Inland to the Ōboke Gorge

Highway 192 shadows the JR Tokushima line for around 70km inland from Tokushima to the railway junction at **AWA IKEDA**, also easily reached from Kotohira. If you want to explore the mountainous heart of Shikoku, this is where you'll need to change trains. There's little of interest in the town itself, aside from a fine **youth hostel** (☎ & ℱ0883/72-5277; ¥2850 per person in large tatami rooms), which is part of a temple with a spectacular location on the side of the mountain overlooking the town and the Yoshino-gawa river. The priest Kondo-san will pick you up at the station if you call. Accommodation is in high-standard tatami rooms, there's a cosy lounge with TV, and Kondo-san's wife cooks excellent meals. There's a pleasant restaurant, *Chamise*, at the station which serves the local speciality, Iya soba, as well as staple fare like udon and curry rice for about ¥500. Alternatively, buy some

Inland to Ōboke Gorge		
Awa Ikeda	*Awa Ikeda*	阿波池田
Iya Onsen	*Iya Onsen*	祖谷温泉
Kazura-bashi	*Kazura-bashi*	かずら橋
Lapis Ōboke Stone Museum	*Rapisu Ōboke Ishi-no-Hakubutsukan*	ラピス大ぼけ石の博物館
Minokoshi	*Minokoshi*	見ノ越
Mount Tsurugi	*Tsurugi-san*	剣山
Nishi Iya	*Nishi Iya*	西祖谷
Ōboke	*Ōboke*	大歩危
Oku Iya Kazura-bashi	*Oku Iya Kazura-bashi*	奥祖谷かずら橋
Toyonaga Station	*Toyonaga-eki*	豊永駅
Accommodation		
Hikyō-no-yu	*Hikyō-no-yu*	秘境の湯
Hotel Iya Onsen	*Hoteru Iya Onsen*	ホテル祖谷温泉
Jōfuku-ji Youth Hostel	*Jōfuku-ji Yūsu Hosuteru*	定福時ユースホステル
Hotel Kazura-bashi	*Hoteru Kazura-bashi*	ホテルかずら橋

provisions from the shops on the main street directly in front of the station and have a picnic in **Heso Kōen** (Belly-button Park, so called because of the town's claim to be Shikoku's belly button), immediately on your right as you walk out of the station.

From Awa Ikeda the road and railway enter the spectacular **Ōboke Gorge**, one of the highlights of Shikoku. The vertiginous mountains here and in the adjacent Iya Valley can be thickly coated in snow during the winter, while, less than one hour south, the palms of Kōchi sway in the sunshine. This remoteness from the rest of the island made the gorge an ideal bolt hole for the Taira clan after their defeat at Yashima in 1185. Here the warriors traded their swords for farm implements and built distinctive thatched-roof cottages on the mountainsides. Few of these remain in their original form, their thatched roofs now covered in rusty tin and their wooden walls in plastic sheeting, but one that does – and that it's often possible to stay at – is **Chiiori**, in the village of Tsurui, some 20km east from JR Ōboke, the nearest train station. This delightfully rustic building belongs to Alex Kerr and is described in his book, *Lost Japan*. Kerr and like-minded colleagues have set up the Friends of Chiiori (Ⓦ www.chiiori.org) and host regular volunteer weekends and workshops on traditional crafts at the cottage. Rates are reduced if you're involved in a volunteer weekend, but you can stay at other times, vacancies permitting. Full details can be found on the website.

To get to Chiiori and many of the area's other attractions, you'll need your own transport – either a car or bicycle (but take note: pedalling up and down these valleys is tough work). With your own wheels you'll have the choice of taking the quieter old Route 32 through the Iya Valley – this is the road that starts across the blue bridge at Iya-guchi, and continues past the *Iya Kei Camp Village* and **Iya Onsen**, where you can take a short funicular train ride down to the hot spring right beside the river (¥1500 if you're not staying at the attached hotel). The road eventually ends up at **Nishi Iya**, home of the **Kazura-bashi**, one of several bridges in the area whose style dates from Taira times when they were made out of *shirakuchi* (mountain vines) and bamboo, so they could easily be cut down to block an enemy. The Taira would have a tougher time chopping down the Kazura-bashi today, since it's strengthened with carefully concealed steel cables. The 45-metre-long bridge is rebuilt every three years and, though it is not that high, the swaying motion as you cross induces enough of a thrill to justify the rather expensive admission price of ¥500. Otherwise, you can get a perfectly good view for free from the secure footing of the adjacent concrete bridge.

Even more picturesque are the **Oku Iya Kazura-bashi**, a pair of vine bridges, also known as the "Fufu-bashi" (Husband and Wife Bridges), some 15km further into the Iya Valley from Nishi Iya and en route to **Mount Tsurugi** – at 1955m, Shikoku's second highest mountain. A four-hour round-trip climb starts at **Minokoshi**, from where there's a ropeway part of the way up the mountain, if you want to save time and effort.

To learn more about the area's geology, pop into the **Lapis Ōboke Stone Museum** (daily 9am–5pm; ¥500; ☎0883/84-1489), in the modern building with the distinctive rippling roof across the river from Ōboke Station. The exhibition begins with a clever piece of technology that transposes a video of a Japanese Indiana Jones character onto a model of the gorge and features all manner of stones, including a meteorite from Mars and many glittering gems. To get to the museum, after alighting at Ōboke Station, cross the bridge over the river and turn right, following the fairly busy main road for a kilometre or so. It's about a 20-minute walk, and the scenery makes up for the roar of the trucks as they hurtle past.

If the weather is good you can take a thirty-minute **boat trip** (¥1000) down the spectacular river gorge. Boats leave from the *Manaka* restaurant (☎0883/84-1211), a five-minute walk past the museum. More exciting **rafting trips** are offered by Mont-bell Outdoor Challenge (☎06/6538-0208, ⓦwww.montbell.com/english/contact/index.html), an Ōsaka-based adventure tour operator; a half-day trip costs ¥10,000 and there are one-, two- and three-day options, too.

Practicalities

Regular **express trains** from Okayama and Kōchi stop at Awa Ikeda (most also stop at Ōboke). Several daily local **trains** ply the route through the Iya Valley between Awa Ikeda and Ōboke, but they are infrequent. If you don't have a car there are very infrequent buses into the valley from Awa Ikeda and Ōboke – the information office beside Awa Ikeda Station has details (they're also posted at Ōboke Station). You can also check with the Shikoku Transit Information Bureau (☎0883/72-1231) about the "Bonnet Bus" tours, running from March to the end of November, and taking in most of the area's sights for ¥5200.

If you're staying at the *Jōfuku-ji Youth Hostel* (see below), you can rent a bicycle for ¥1000 per day, but be prepared to pedal up some seriously steep roads. Following the road up from Ōboke you'll eventually reach a tunnel which takes you into the west side of the Iya Valley. On the route down to the bridge you'll pass the **Hikyō-no-Yu**, an onsen and hotel complex, where you can take a bath for ¥1500.

Jōfuku-ji **youth hostel** (☎0887/74-0301, ⓕ74-0302; ❷) is a twenty-minute uphill walk from Toyanaga Station and makes a good base for exploring the area. Set in the grounds of a beautiful hillside temple, the hostel is surrounded by little stone statues (*jizō*), considered guardians of children and travellers. Tsurui-san, the beaming Buddhist priest who runs the hostel, has devised a series of cycling and walking routes in the mountains and valleys. You can also join the priest in **zazen meditation** at the temple daily at 7am. Accommodation is either in bunk beds or huge tatami rooms. Note that between December and April the hostel is only open Friday to Sunday and there's no food, so bring your own supplies.

In Nishi Iya, 500km along the river from the Kazura-bashi, you'll find a good **campsite** (℡0883/87-2848), which charges ¥200 per person for a pitch, and has tents for rent and wooden cabins (sleeping four) for ¥5200 per night. For something more luxurious, try the *Hotel Kazura-bashi* (℡0883/87-2171, ℻87-2175; ➒), a fine ryokan on the main road about twenty minutes' walk before the bridge. A highlight here is the open-air baths on the hillside above the hotel, open to non-guests for ¥1000. *Hotel Iya Onsen* (℡0883/75-2311; ➐) also comes highly recommended for its luxurious rooms with beautiful riverside views and fine food. Buses to both of these hotels run from Awa Ikeda Station. The *Hotel Kazura-bashi* is also served by a bus from Ōboke Station.

Several tourist **restaurants** around the Kazura-bashi serve *yakisakana* – fish roasted on sticks over hot coals; set meals start at around ¥1000. The management at *Woody Rest*, near Iya-guchi Station, speak English; it's a rustic place serving good, inexpensive food. For a splurge, the best place is the *Kazura-bashi Hotel*. In Ōboke, the *Manaka* is the place to eat, serving set Japanese meals starting at ¥1200. There's also a coffee shop, *Alex*, in the museum, or you can get basic provisions at a shop near the station if your budget is tight.

Kōchi and around

Sun-kissed **KŌCHI** lies dead in the centre of the arch-shaped southern prefecture of Shikoku. Texts from 712 refer to the area as "Takeyoriwake", meaning "brave and manly country" – a reputation enforced by the city being the birthplace of some of Japan's most impressive historical figures. Tosa was the next name of the area and is still used by people today, particularly when referring to the local cuisine. It wasn't until 1603, when ruling *daimyō* Yamaguchi Katsutoyo named his castle Kōchiyama (now Kōchi-jō), that the city adopted its present name.

The **castle** is still the highlight of any visit to Kōchi. To see anything else of interest requires a short journey out of the city centre. The most immediately rewarding trip is to **Godai-san-kōen**, a mountain-top park overlooking the city, and the nearby **Chikurin-ji**, the 31st temple on the pilgrimage circuit. South of the city lies Katsurahama, with its celebrated beach and Tosa fighting dogs, though in fact the most interesting attraction here is the **Sakamoto Ryōma Memorial Museum**, dedicated to a local hero of the Meiji Restoration.

Kōchi-ken is predominantly rural, and the people here are refreshingly down-to-earth, something you'll discover if you time your visit to coincide with a three-hundred-year-old institution, the weekly **Sunday market** on Kōchi's Otesuji-dōri, when farmers from all over the prefecture bring their produce to town. Even so, the capital is no hick town. On the contrary, Kōchi has a distinctly cosmopolitan feel, with its wide, palm-lined avenues, network of rivers and shopping arcades, and gently trundling trams. It's also well worth attending the **Yosokoi Matsuri**, Kōchi's O-bon festival – with 14,000 plus dancers, it might not be as big as Tokushima's Awa Odori, which it immediately precedes from August 9–12, but it's just as colourful.

▲ Ry;ga-dl, Awa Ikeda & Takamatsu

▲ Kōchi Prefectural Museum of Art & Godai-san-kien

DENCHA-DŌRI

Yokoyama Ryuiichi Memorial Manga Museum

250 m

0

Bicycle Rental Shop

Kōchi-eki (tram terminus)

Kōchi Station

N

Hasuike-machi

HARIMAYA-BASHI-DŌRI

Daimaru Department Store

Tōden Seibu

Bus Station

Bus Station

Police Station

Bowl Jumbo Centre

Harimaya-bashi (Remains)

Harimaya-bashi

Chūō-kōen

Enokuchi-gawa

Yanagi-machi

Kagami-gawa

Horizume

OTESUJI-DŌRI

Obiya-machi Arcade

OBIASAN-DŌRI

Sunday Market

Ohashi-dōri

Kōchijō-mae

NTT

Fuji Bookstore

Kōchi International Association

Itagaki Taisuke Statue

Ōte-mon

DENCHA-DŌRI

Kōchi-jō

Dōrin

KENCHO-MAE DŌRI

Kyu-Yamanouchi-ke Shimoyashiki Nagaya

Kencho-mae

Grando-dōri

Masugata

Iriake Station

▲ Nakamura & Uwajima

Ferries & Katsurahama Beach ▶

Umenotsuji

KŌCHI

ACCOMMODATION	
Big 1	A
Joseikan	I
Hotel No.1 Kōchi	F
Kōchi Green Kaikan	H
Los Inn Kōchi	B
Manhattan Hotel	E
New Hankyū Kōchi	G
Petit Hotel Kōchi	C
Sansuien	J
Tosa Bekkan	D

RESTAURANTS, CAFÉS & BARS	
A Bar	3
Baffone	6
BB Café Hall	7
Beans Deli	16
Café de Blue	6
Faust	18
Get	13
Habana	5
Hakobe	8
Hirome Ichiba	14
Irish Pub Amontillado	12
Jungri-la	20
Love Jamaica	11
Mamma Italia	2
Masala	9
Mephistopheles	19
Nakamachi's	4
Ninnikuya	17
Tosahan	10
Viva	15
Yatai Stalls	1

Kōchi and around

Kōchi	*Kōchi*	高知
Chikurin-ji	*Chikurin-ji*	竹林寺
Godai-san-kōen	*Godai-san-kōen*	五台山公園
Harimaya-bashi	*Harimaya-bashi*	はりまや橋
Katsurahama	*Katsurahama*	桂浜
Kōchi-jō	*Kōchi-jō*	高知城
Kōchi Prefectural Museum of Art	*Kōchi Kenritsu Bijutsukan*	高知県立美術館
Kōchi Prefectural Sakamoto Ryōma Memorial Museum	*Kōchi Kenritsu Sakamoto Ryōma Kinenkan*	高知県立坂本龍馬記念館
Makino Botanical Garden	*Makino Shokubutsu-en*	牧野植物園
Sakamoto Ryōma Memorial Museum	*Sakamoto Ryōma Kinenkan*	坂本竜馬記念館
Yokoyama Ryuichi Memorial Manga Museum	*Yokoyama Ryuichi Kinen Mangakan*	横山隆一記念まんが館

Accommodation

Big 1	*Biggu 1*	ビッグ1
Jōseikan	*Jōseikan*	城西館
Katsurahama Kokuminshukusha	*Katsurahama Kokuminshukusha*	桂浜国民宿舎
Kōchi Green Kaikan	*Kōchi Guriin Kaikan*	高知グリーン会館
Los Inn Kōchi	*Rosu In Kōchi*	ロスイン高知
Manhattan Hotel	*Manhattan Hoteru*	マンハッタンホテル
New Hankyū Hotel Kōchi	*Shin-Hankyū Hoteru Kōchi*	新阪急ホテル高知
Hotel No.1 Kōchi	*Hoteru No.1 Kōchi*	ホテルNo.1 高知
Petit Hotel Kochi	*Puchi Hoteru Kōchi*	プチホテル高知
Sansuien	*Sansuien*	三翠園
Tosa Bekkan	*Tosa Bekkan*	とさ別館

Restaurants

Baffone	*Baffone*	バフォネ
Hakobe	*Hakobe*	はこべ
Jungri-la	*Jangurira*	ジャングリラ
Tosahan	*Tosahan*	土佐藩

Western Kōchi-ken

Ashizuri Misaki	*Ashizuri Misaki*	足摺岬
Ashizuri Youth Hostel	*Ashizuri Yūsu Hosuteru*	あしずりユースホステル
Hotel Ashizurien	*Hoteru Ashizurien*	ホテル足摺園
John Mung House	*Jon Mung Hausu*	ジョン万ハウス
Hotel Kaijōkan	*Hoteru Kaijōkan*	ホテル海上館
Kongōfuku-ji	*Kongōfuku-ji*	金剛福寺
Hotel Matsu-ya	*Hoteru Matsuya*	ホテルマツヤ
Ōgata	*Ōgata*	大方
Shimanto-gawa	*Shimanto-gawa*	四万十川
Shimantogawa Youth Hostel	*Shimantogawa Yūsu Hosuteru*	四万十川ユースホステル
Sukumo	*Sukumo*	宿毛
Sukumo Youth Hostel	*Sukumo Yūsu Hosuteru*	宿毛ユースホステル
Tatsukushi	*Tatsukushi*	竜串

Arrival, information and city transport

All **trains** and most **buses** arrive at Kōchi Station, at the head of Harimaya-bashi-dōri, north of the city centre. Most buses coming from Muroto Misaki to the east arrive at the bus station next to the Seibu department store (now closed) at Harimaya-bashi, a few continue to the JR station, 800m north. Kōchi's **airport** (☎088/882-6171; officially the Kōchi Ryoma Airport) is a forty-minute drive east of the city; a bus (¥700) runs from the airport to opposite Kōchi Station, while a taxi into the city will cost around ¥4000. **Ferries** from Tokyo (via Katsura in Wakayama-ken) and Ōsaka arrive at the port, a fifteen-minute tram ride south of the city centre.

Kōchi's excellent **tourist information centre** (daily 9am–8pm; ☎088/882-1634) is on the left outside Kōchi Station. There is always someone who can speak English on hand and they can provide useful maps and booklets both for the city and prefecture. There are also plans to offer a bicycle rental service from the summer of 2004. Another useful resource is the **Kōchi International Association (KIA)**, close to the castle on the second floor of the Marunouchi Biru, 4-1-37 Honmachi (Mon–Fri 8.30am–5pm; ☎088/875-0022, ⓦwww.pref.kochi.jp/english/index.htm), which also has a small library of English books and magazines as well as free Internet access.

While central Kōchi is easily negotiated on foot, the distances between the major sights makes catching a **tram** or **bus** a sensible option. The tram terminus is just to the left as you exit Kōchi Station. The system consists of two lines, one running north to south from the station to the port, crossing the east–west tracks at Harimaya-bashi. To travel within the city area costs a flat ¥180, paid to the driver on leaving the tram; you'll need to ask for a transfer ticket (*norikaiken*) when you switch lines at Harimaya-bashi. A one-day ticket covering the central city area costs ¥500; an ¥800 ticket gives you access to everywhere on both lines. Buses for Godai-san and Katsurahama leave from both Kōchi Station and the bus station at Harimaya-bashi. If you're travelling on to Matsuyama, the most direct route is via JR express bus from Kōchi Station.

Accommodation

There's no shortage of **accommodation** in Kōchi, with a cluster of identikit business hotels close to the train station. More convenient for the shopping and entertainment districts are the hotels between Dencha-dōri and the city's principal river, Kagami-gawa. If you want to stay by the beach, head for the good *kokuminshukusha* (national lodging house) at Katsurahama.

Big 1 3-9-45 Kitahonmachi ☎088/883-9603. Large, men-only sauna and capsule hotel, with a swimming pool and relaxation area where you can watch widescreen movies (some in English). Capsules (¥3700 per night) are available from 4pm.

Hotel No.1 Kōchi 16-8 Nijōdai-chō ☎088/873-3333, ⓕ088/875-9999. Reasonable business hotel with nearby annexe (*bekkan*) close to the city's nightlife. Both buildings have an open-air rooftop bath (men-only in the main hotel, women-only in the annexe) offering a view of the castle – very atmospheric when it's lit up at night. The annexe offers preferential service to women, and boasts a women-only floor. Cheap singles. ❹

Jōseikan 2-5-34 Kamimachi ☎088/875-0111, ⓕ824-0557. Elegant and expensive, this ryokan has spacious tatami rooms and offers service fit for an emperor – which is why he stays here when he visits town. ❽ including two meals.

Katsurahama Kokuminshukusha Katsurahama ☎088/841-2201, ⓦwww.kochi-f.co.jp/katsurahamasou. Located 13km south of central Kōchi, this modern hotel has spectacular views across the beach from its cliff-top location and very good-value, high-standard rooms. ❻ including two meals.

Kōchi Green Kaikan 5-6-11 Honmachi ☎088/825-2701, ⓕ825-2703. Good-value mid-range hotel, close to the castle and with friendly management. Rooms are a decent size and have all the usual amenities. ❹

SHIKOKU | Kōchi and around

Los Inn Kōchi 2-4-8 Kitahonmachi ☎088/884-1110, ☎884-1095. Close to the station, this place has kitsch decor (a mixture of reproduction antiques, heavy leather sofas and 1970s-style chandeliers), an English-speaking manager and reasonably comfortable Western- and Japanese-style rooms. ⑤

Manhattan Hotel 5-16 Nijudai-chō ☎088/821-2111, ⊚www.manhattan.co.jp. This centrally located hotel is more stylish and better value than similar accommodation in this price range, and has a choice of three restaurants. ⑤

New Hankyū Kōchi 4-2-50 Honmachi ☎088/873-1111, ⊚hotel.newhankyu.co.jp/kochi-e/index.html. Kōchi's top Western-style hotel, with well-appointed rooms, a good selection of restaurants (the Chinese is recommended), a fitness centre and a swimming pool. Internet reservations offer substantial discounts over rack rates. ⑤

Petit Hotel Kochi 1-8-13 Kita-Honmachi ☎088/826-8156, ☎826-8157. One of the city's newest business hotels, and with very competitive rates. Rooms are a little small, but are clean and equipped with all mod cons, including broadband Internet connections. Couples should pay the extra ¥1000 for a full double room rather than an economy one – the extra space is worth it. ④

Sansuien 1-3-35 Honmachi ☎088/822-0131, ☎822-0145. Although it's housed in a large, ugly building, this ryokan has a refined interior, while the attached traditional gardens and buildings beside the Kagami-gawa add some atmosphere. Regular rates include two meals; a "business plan" without meals almost halves the cost. ⑧

Tosa Bekkan 1-11-34 Sakurai-chō ☎088/883-5685. Very friendly and relaxed Japanese-style hotel. The fine tatami rooms have TV, air con and toilet, though bathrooms are communal. Meals are available, and there's a coin laundry outside. ④

The City

Kōchi's best-known fable concerns a romantic monk who courted a lady beside the **Harimaya-bashi**. A small recreation of this red-railed bridge can be found ten minutes' walk south from the station – either side of which are pleasant landscaped promenades for the stream below. Also look out for the telephone box (on the left as you emerge from Kōchi Station) crowned with a small statue of the monk and his kimono-dressed paramour. Once you've checked out the bridge, pop into the nearby **Yokoyama Ryuichi Memorial Manga Museum** before proceeding on to the city's main attraction, Kōchi **castle**, best followed up with a visit to the **Kōchi Prefectural Museum of Art** to the east. Kōchi's other main sights – **Godai-san-kōen**, the temple **Chikurin-ji** and the beach at **Katsurahama** – are all short journeys from the city centre by bus.

Kōchi-jō and three museums

West of Harimaya-bashi, at the end of the Obiya-machi shopping arcade, is the hilltop castle of **Kōchi-jō** (daily 9am–4.30pm; ¥350 to enter the donjon; ☎088/824-5701). Construction was begun in 1601 by the feudal lord Yamaguchi Katsutoyo and finished in 1611, when the outer walls went up, but what you see today dates mainly from 1748, when reconstruction of the donjon turrets and gates was completed, following a major fire 21 years earlier.

The main approach is through the Ōte-mon, an impressive gateway flanked by high stone walls at the end of Otesuji-dōri. On the walk up to the donjon you'll pass a statue of Itagaki Taisuke, the founder of the People's Rights Movement, which promoted democracy in Japan during the early years of the Meiji era. For his efforts, Itagaki suffered an assassination attempt, during which he cried out "Itagaki may die, but liberty never!" The politician survived the knife attack, living to the ripe old age of 82, and his defiant phrase was adopted across Japan as the patriotic *cri de coeur* for democracy.

In the anti-feudal fervour that heralded the start of the Meiji era, almost all the castle's buildings were demolished, leaving the steeply sloping walls surrounding empty courtyards. The exception was the three-storey donjon, within the inner citadel (*honmaru*), reached through the Tsume-mon gate. To the left

△ Pilgrims on the 88-temple route

of the entrance there's an exhibition of old samurai armour and a scroll from 1852 showing the English alphabet, written by John Mung (see p.756). In the main building look out for a beautifully painted palanquin, before you ascend to take in the superb view from the uppermost storey. To the right is the corridor leading to the *daimyō's* main chambers. By the time the donjon was rebuilt, the threat of war had evaporated, so these rooms did not need to be heavily fortified; hence the sliding screens and wooden balconies.

From the castle, it's only a five-minute walk south along Kenchomae-dōri to Kōchi's other main building of historic interest: the **Kyu-Yamanouchi-ke Shimoyashiki Nagaya**, on the banks of the Kagami-gawa, and next to the *Sansuien Ryokan*. Once the barracks of foot soldiers during the late Tokugawa period, the narrow two-storey wooden building is now a National Treasure and houses a small museum (daily 7am–5pm; free) with some mildly interesting models of boats and displays showing the original use of the rooms.

In stark contrast is the stylish modern building housing the **Kōchi Prefectural Museum of Art** (Tues–Sun 9am–5pm; ¥350; ☏088/866-8000, ⓦwww2.net-kochi.gr.jp/~kenbunka/museum/english_page/welcome.htm). Set in landscaped grounds some 3km east of the city centre, the museum houses an impressive collection of modern Japanese and Western art, including a gallery of lithographs and paintings by Marc Chagall and a theatre with a specially designed stage for Nō plays. Films and other performances are occasionally held here, too, and there's a decent restaurant, *Pizzicato*. The museum is a fifteen-minute tram journey east of Harimaya-bashi (ask to get off at Kenritsu Bijutsukan-dōri).

Closer to the town centre, a five-minute walk east of Harimaya-bashi tram stop, the new Kōchi Municipal Culture Plaza is home to the **Yokoyama Ryuichi Memorial Manga Museum** (Tues–Sun 9am–7pm; ¥400; ☏088/883-5029, ⓦwww.bunkaplaza.or.jp/mangakan). Though Tezuka Osamu is credited with revolutionizing the world of manga after World War II, it was Yokoyama (died 2001) who paved the way for Tezuka's success by founding the *Shinmanga ha Shudan* manga group in Tokyo in 1932 – it was the members of this group who brought a new freshness and vitality to the previously staid world of Japanese cartoons. The museum is full of examples of Yokoyama's work, most obviously his signature creation, the "Eternal Boy" Fuku-chan, a comic strip which clocked up a record 5534 serializations before bowing out in 1971. There's also an exact replica of one of his ateliers, as well as a mock-up of the bar he used to have in his house.

Gōdai-san-kōen and Chikurin-ji

Perched on the wooded mountain-top overlooking Kōchi's harbour, 2km south of the city centre, is the attractive park of **Godai-san-kōen**. Buses run from Kōchi Station to Yama no Moto (around 20min), from where it's a thirty-minute walk up the hill. Check at the tourist information office, however, as there may be buses direct to the park in summer.

Alongside Godai-san-kōen lie the equally pleasant grounds of the **Chikurin-ji** temple. This was founded in 724, making it one of the oldest temples in the prefecture, and its atmospheric main building, decorated with intricate carvings of animals, dates from the Muromachi period. The pagoda, built in the 1970s, is said to contain a bone of the Buddha from Bodh Gaya in India, but there's no way of verifying this since the tower is closed to the public. The **Treasure House** (daily 9am–5pm; ¥400), to the right of the temple's main entrance gate, is worth a visit for its tranquil traditional gardens, overlooked by an Edo-era villa, and small collection of Tantric statues and Buddhas.

Opposite the temple lies the large **Makino Botanical Garden** (daily 9am–5pm; ¥500; ☎088/882-2601), which has lovely views out to the coast and is dedicated to celebrated local botanist Dr Makino Tomitaro, who died aged 95 in 1957. Apart from the large greenhouse and a fossil gallery, easily spotted since it has a giant model of a tyrannosaurus rex outside, there's the rather more tasteful **Makino Museum of Plants and People**, crafted from wood and opened in 1999. While you're out here, the garden's restaurant, *Arbre*, is worth trying – you don't need to pay entrance to the garden to eat here.

Katsurahama

Katsurahama, some 13km south from the centre of Kōchi, is famous for two things: its beach and the Tosa fighting dogs, who compete in mock sumo tournaments. Neither attraction is what it's cracked up to be. The crescent-shaped beach, though capped off at one end with a picturesque cliff-top shrine, is rather pebbly and swimming isn't allowed, while the dogs in the **Tosa Tōken Centre** (daily 9am–4pm; ☎088/842-3315) are such lethargic, over-fed lumps that it's hard to believe they walk for 10km every day, let alone take part in sometimes bloodily vicious fights (¥1500). Animal lovers should give these bouts a wide berth, as well as the small museum, which includes several *Onagadōri* roosters cooped up in cramped boxes designed to display their long tail feathers, and a Tosa dog lounging in a small cage. The rest of the centre is a giant giftshop selling tacky souvenirs, including cuddly toy sumo dogs.

Far more interesting is the **Kōchi Prefectural Sakamoto Ryōma Memorial Museum** (daily 9am–5pm; ¥400; ☎088/841-0001), the architecturally stunning building on the headland above the beach. Dedicated to local hero Sakamoto (see box below), the building uses bold colours and a radical freestanding design for the main exhibition halls. Inside there are state-of-the-art displays using computers, as well as the blood-spotted screen from the room in which Sakamoto was assassinated in Kyoto. If the weather is good, you can walk out on to the top of the building for spectacular views of the Pacific. Next to the beach is a large statue of Sakamoto and a small **aquarium** (daily 8.30am–5pm; ¥1000), which has dolphin and sea-lion shows.

To get to Katsurahama from Kōchi by public transport, you'll need to take a **bus** (¥560) from Harimaya-bashi (every 30min; 35min). Buses also leave from beside Kōchi Station, but they're very infrequent.

Sakamoto Ryōma

You'd have to be blind to miss the scowling features of **Sakamoto Ryōma** on posters and other memorabilia around Kōchi. The city is immensely proud of this romantic figure who died young but whose political ideas helped lay the groundwork for the Meiji Restoration of 1868. Born in 1835 to a half-samurai, half-farmer family, Sakamoto directly challenged the rigid class structure of the Shogunate years by leaving Kōchi to start a trading company in Nagasaki (samurai never normally dirtied their hands in business). In his travels around Japan, he gathered support for his pro-imperial views, eventually forcing the shogun, Tokugawa Yoshinobu, to agree to give supreme power back to the emperor. But, one month later, on November 15, 1867, Sakamoto was assassinated in Kyoto. Although he was just 33 at the time, his writings included an enlightened plan for a new political system for Japan, aspects of which were later embraced by the Meiji government.

Eating, drinking and entertainment

Around Obiya-machi arcade is the best area for **eating and drinking** in Kōchi, although on Wednesday you'll find several places closed. There are also many cheap *yatai* (street stalls) around town, serving *oden*, ramen, *gyōza* and beer – a good location on a balmy night is beside the Enokuchi-gawa near the Bowl Jumbo centre. The top floor of the Seibu department store, next to the Harimaya-bashi, has a range of restaurants with picture menus and plastic-food window displays. If you are looking for a cheap pick-me-up, *Mister Donuts* is your best bet: it does bottomless cups of coffee at two outlets on Dencha-dōri.

For a relatively small city, Kōchi has an awful lot of *pachinko* parlours and amusement arcades. If these forms of entertainment don't thrill, head for one of the several **cinemas** along the Obiya-machi arcade or Dechan-dōri, which sometimes show English-language films, or try your hand at ten-pin bowling at Bowl Jumbo beside the Enokuchi-gawa. There's sometimes **live music** at *Mephistopheles* and *BB Café Hall*. Also check with tourist information (see p.748) to see whether there are any **cultural performances** happening out at the Museum of Art.

Restaurants and cafés

Baffone 1-2-10 Obiya-machi ☎088/822-3884. At the Harimaya-bashi end of Kōchi's famous drinking street, you can watch the drunken revellers pass by from this continental-style café's outdoor tables. The daily menu is a mixture of French and Italian styles. Around ¥2500 per head. Occasional live music.

Beans Deli 1-5-18 Harimaya-machi ☎088/882-8182. Good for a light lunch or snack, this modern café facing onto a pleasant promenade boasts "the best homemade sandwiches and coffee in town". Closed Wed.

Habana Harimaya-bashi-dōri ☎088/885-6891. Spacious self-service café with an outdoor terrace facing Harimaya-bashi-dōri, serving the usual range of coffees, sandwiches and cakes, as well as beer.

Hakobe 1-2-5 Obiya-machi Arcade ☎088/822-4423. The place for *okonomiyaki* and *yakisoba*. You cook up the dish yourself at the hotplate on your table. Difficult to spend over ¥1000. Closed Wed.

Hirome Ichiba At the end of the Obiya-machi Arcade. Lively market of stalls selling a range of Japanese food and cheap beer; you're almost always guaranteed to find one of the local expat community here. Also has a good Chinese food stall.

Jungri-la Densha-dōri ☎088/873-9966. Above the corner *pachinko* parlour, this pub-restaurant has palms and vines which sprout up and around the large dining space, built around a fake waterfall. The standard *izakaya* food is a lot less adventurous, but they do serve alligator and have Guinness on tap.

Mamma Italia Nijudai-chō ☎088/873-3131. Opposite the *Manhattan Hotel*, this stylish Italian is run by an English-speaking chef who learned his craft in Rome. The speciality is pizza baked in a wood-fired oven. Around ¥2500 a head. Closed Wed.

Masala Obiya-machi Arcade ☎088/885-0065. New Indian restaurant, already a favourite of local expats, serving lunches from ¥800. Look for the big yellow sign in the arcade, opposite Daimaru.

Mephistopheles Opposite the west end of Obisan-dōri. Dark, comfy and convivial, this café serves a wide range of coffees and set-meal menus from as little as ¥650. Also has occasional live music, including jazz. Daily 7am–9.30pm.

Ninnikuya Obisan-dōri ☎088/826-0200. Pretty good branch of the nationwide garlic restaurant *Ninnikuya* franchise – try the fried whole garlic bulb. Otherwise, you can't go wrong with their pizza and pasta dishes.

Tosahan Obiya-machi Arcade. The place to go to savour *Tosa ryōri*, the local speciality fish cuisine. The decor is all dark-wood beams and red lanterns and the set lunches at around ¥1000 are good value. For dinner expect to pay at least ¥4000 per head.

Bars and clubs

As the largest city on Shikoku's southern coast, Kōchi attracts many people looking for a night on the town, so it's not short of a **bar** or ten and has a lively atmosphere, especially on weekends. The city's famous drinking street is

Yanagi-machi, which runs parallel to the Obiya-machi Arcade. During the summer Kōchi's many *yatai* and rooftop beer gardens are the ideal places to relax with a cold brew on a sultry night. For **dancing**, try *Get* near the Harimaya-bashi Shotengai, which plays all the faves from the 1980s and has a ¥1200 cover charge, or *Love Jamaica*, just off Obiya-machi Arcade.

A's Bar Look for the white corrugated-iron building on a street behind Otesuji-dōri – the door is decorated with a giant black A on an orange background. This is a spacious, laid-back place with comfy sofas and soul, blues and jazz on the sound system. All drinks ¥600. Mon–Sat from 8pm. Closed Sun.

BB Café Hall A basement nightspot just off the Obiya-machi Arcade, which attracts a trendy young crowd and triples up as a café, bar and live music venue. The cover charge for the live music ranges from ¥500 to ¥2500, depending on who is playing.

Café de Blue 5F, 1-2-10 Obiya-machi ☎088/823-2660. In the same building as *Baffone*, this is a stylish bar-club that comes into its own at the weekends, especially if there's an all-night techno event, as there usually is on a Saturday. Wed–Sun 10pm until late.

Irish Pub Amontillado Obiya-machi. Just behind the Daimaru department store, it's a mystery why this Irish bar has a Spanish name, but the Guinness and Kilkenny on tap (¥900 a pint) are worth coming for, as are the fish 'n' chips, Irish stew and darts. Sometimes has live music.

Kōchi Yosakoi Brewery Kagami-gawa-zoi. This new *ji-biru* brew-pub has a riverside location and is a stylish place, serving *izakaya*-type nibbles to go with its three regular beers – Pilsner, lager and ale – as well as other drinks.

Nakamachi's Funky hangout for the foreign community on the second floor of a building just off Harimaya-bashi-dōri, on the east side of Otesuji-dōri – look for the wooden sliding door. Spacious interior with scatter cushions around low tables on one side and a long bar on the other. Also serves food. Open daily 8pm–3am.

Viva Obisan-dōri, just west of Chūō-kōen. New basement restaurant-cum-bar that turns into a club after 11pm on Fridays and Saturdays.

Listings

Airlines ANA, 1-5-1 Harimaya-chō ☎088/882-0747; JAL, 1-5-33 Harimaya-chō ☎0120-25-5971; JAS, Dentetsu Taminaru Biru, 1-5-15 Harimaya-chō ☎088/883-9611.

Banks and exchange Shikoku Bank is on the corner at Harimaya-bashi; there's a branch of Kōchi bank further west, along Dencha-dōri. Credit cards can be used in the cash machine at the post office on Dencha-dōri.

Bike rental Bikes can be rented from Kagiyama Rental Cycle, 4-11 Aioi-chō (☎088/882-1585), for ¥600 for 2hr or ¥1200 for a day.

Bookshops Fuji Bookstore, on the corner of Kōchijōmae-dōri (Mon–Sat 9am–9pm, Sun 10am–7pm), has a few English paperbacks on the second floor.

Car rental Try Eki Rent-a-Car ☎088/882-3022; Toyota Rent-a-Car ☎088/823-0100; Nissan ☎0888/83-4485; or Budget ☎0120–23-0543.

Hospitals and clinics The Red Cross Hospital (☎088/822-1202) is behind Kōchi Station.

Internet access There's free access at the Kōchi International Association (see p.748). Otherwise, try Hotto Station (☎088/820-6741; ¥100 for 15min), at 5F Bell Epoch Building on Otesuji-dōri.

Laundry There are coin-operated machines outside the *Tosa Bekkan* (see p.749).

Police The main police station is opposite Kōchi Station. Emergency numbers are listed in "Basics" on p.81.

Post office The main post office is just to the west of Kōchi Station (Mon–Fri 9am–7pm, Sat 9am–5pm, Sun 9am–12.30pm).

Shopping The main department stores are Daimaru on the Obiya-machi Arcade and Seibu on the corner of Harimaya-bashi, which includes an outlet of Muji. On Harimaya-bashi Shotengai, Hana Usagi sells beautiful secondhand and antique kimono and *obi*. For Kōchi's handmade *washi* paper, try Pepie at 2-8-11 Harimaya-machi.

Sports There's an outdoor swimming pool at the Sogō Taikokan (City Gym) next to the baseball stadium across the Yanagihara-bashi south of the Kagami-gawa.

Taxis Call Kenko Hire ☎088/882-6166 or Mikuni Hire ☎088/882-3660.

Travel agencies The main branch of JTB is at Harimaya-bashi, but you're not guaranteed to be served by English-speaking staff.

Whale-watching tours

It's said that the whaling industry in Kōchi dates from 1591, when the local *daimyō* Chokosabe Motochika gifted the warlord Toyotomi Hideyoshi in Ōsaka a whale and in return received 800 bags of rice. Japan and whales have, in recent times, become a controversial combination, but along Kōchi-ken's coast few are complaining as whale-watching tours replace the old way of making a living. Tours typically last three hours and cost around ¥5000 per person in small boats holding eight to ten people. The best time to see whales is May and June, though the season runs from spring through to autumn. Nothing's guaranteed, but with a good skipper expect to see the large Bryde's whales and medium-sized false killer whales as well as schools of white-sided and Risso's dolphins. For details, contact the Ōgata Town Leisure Fishing Boats Owners Association (℡0880/43-1058) or Saga Town Fishermen's Association (℡0880/55-3131).

Western Kōchi-ken

The western side of Kōchi-ken has some of Shikoku's best scenery, either inland beside the **Shimanto-gawa** or along the rugged coast, washed by the savage current of the Pacific Ocean. There are several fishing villages, of which Ōgata is perhaps the best known, from where you can take **whale-watching tours** (see box above). The rocky cape at **Ashizuri Misaki**, 180km southwest of Kōchi, with its twisting scenic roads, temple and lush foliage, is well worth the journey. Continue around the coast to reach **Tatsukushi**, where outlandish rock formations stretch out towards coral reefs, and **Sukumo**, a recommended spot for scuba diving and jumping-off point for the undeveloped islands of Okino-shima and Uguru-shima.

Shimanto-gawa

Often claimed to be the last free-flowing river in Japan, the **Shimanto-gawa** actually has one small dam along its 196-kilometre length. This doesn't detract from the wide river's beauty, twisting through verdant countryside past pine-clad slopes and terraced rice fields, splashed with scarlet *higanbena* flowers in September. This is the place to head for tranquil boating, canoeing and fishing – local fishermen still use a traditional method to catch *ayu* fish, waving flaming torches to coax them into waiting nets. Again, having your own transport helps since bus and train services are scarce, and on Sunday there are no buses at all.

As a base, you can't go far wrong with the charming *Shimantogawa Youth Hostel* (℡0880/54-1352, www.netwave.or.jp/~shimanto; ❷), run by a friendly couple and about as far off the beaten track as you could wish for in Shikoku. It sleeps just fifteen people, has good food and a regular programme of canoeing trips down the river (from ¥5500, full tuition and equipment included). The nearest train station is Ekawasaki on JR's plodding Yodo line, which runs from Kubokawa on the bay side of Kōchi-ken, to Uwajima along a very scenic route. From March to November it's possible to ride in open-air carriages (*torroko ressha*) for part of the route on most weekends and holidays and almost all of August. From Ekawasaki you'll need to catch a bus (3 daily) to Kuchiyanai, from where the hostel is 4.5km across the river; if you call the hostel manager he will arrange to meet you. It's also possible to catch a bus to Kuchiyanai from Nakamura, on the Tosa Kuroshio train line to Sukumo.

Ashizuri Misaki

The tourist trail has beaten a steady path to the small, scenic village of **ASHIZURI MISAKI**, standing on the most southerly point of Shikoku, but don't let this put you off checking it out. Pilgrims have long been coming here to pay their respects at **Kongōfuku-ji**, the 38th temple on the sacred circuit. This picturesque temple, dedicated to the Buddhist deity Kannon, who symbolizes infinite compassion, has a two-storey pagoda and nestles amid a palm grove in the centre of the village. Ashizuri's white-painted lighthouse stands atop the eighty-metre-high cliffs, while at shore level there's a natural rock arch, crowned by a small shrine. All these sights are within easy walking distance of each other, along cliff-top pathways that each February burst forth with crimson camellia blossoms.

On the way to the lighthouse you'll pass the statue of Nakahama Manjirō, better known as **John Mung** (see box, below), the local lad who travelled the world and pioneered relations between Japan and the USA in the early years of the Meiji Restoration. Opposite Kongōfuku-ji is the small **John Mung House** museum (Mon & Wed–Sun 10am–6pm; ¥300; ☏08808/8-0939), which includes some of Mung's personal possessions and miniature tableaux describing his life and the whaling industry he was once part of.

Reaching the cape by public transport can be costly (around ¥4000) and time-consuming. There are direct **buses** from Kōchi to Ashizuri Misaki (around 4hr 40min). **Trains** only go as far as Nakamura, where you'll have to catch one of the local buses (9 daily; ¥1930) from directly outside the station. The bus journey takes ninety minutes and becomes progressively more spectacular the closer to the cape you get, the driver whipping the bus around the narrow, cliff-hugging road. In your own car, you can opt for the less hair-raising but equally scenic Skyline road down the middle of the peninsula to the cape. The bus stop is next to Kongōfuku-ji.

John Mung

In the normal course of life, Nakahama Manjirō, born in 1827 into a poor family living in Tosa Shimizu, near Ashizuri Misaki, would have lived and died a fisherman. His lucky break came when he was marooned on Tori-jima, an uninhabited volcanic island some 580km south of Tokyo, along with five shipmates. After nearly five months, they were saved by a landing party from a passing US whaling ship, who had come to the island in search of fresh water.

The ship's captain, John Whitfield, took a shine to the 14-year-old Nakahama and renamed him **John Mung**. When the ship docked at Honolulu, Mung decided to remain with the Americans and served with Whitfield's crew for four years, before returning with the captain to his home in Bedford, Massachusetts. The bright lad mastered English, mathematics, surveying and navigation, and undertook journeys to Africa, Australia and around Southeast Asia. After making some money in the California Gold Rush of 1849, Mung returned to Japan in 1851. He was sought out by the feudal lord of Tosa, who realized it was only a matter of time before Japan would open up to the West and so was eager to have the likes of Mung on his side.

Two years later, Mung was summoned to Tokyo to assist with the drawing up of international trade treaties. In 1860 he returned to the US as part of a national delegation and in 1869 paid visits to London and other places in Europe. Before his death in 1898 he taught at the Kaisei School for Western Learning in Tokyo (later to become part of the prestigious Tokyo University), sharing the knowledge he had accumulated during a period when Japan was still living in self-imposed isolation from the rest of the world.

Buses run regularly from Ashizuri Misaki to the nearby town of Tosa Shimizu (¥820), where you'll usually have to change at the Shimizu Bus Centre to continue north up the coast. There are two **youth hostels** at Ashizuri Misaki: *Kongōfuku-ji* (℡08808/8-0038, ℻8-0688; ●), next to the temple, is the slightly more attractive (¥3200 per person plus ¥1600 for two optional meals), though it's often busy with groups of pilgrims; and *Ashizuri* (℡08808/8-0324; ●), a very friendly and relaxed place next to the small shrine, which offers accommodation in tatami rooms (¥2900 per person plus ¥1600 for two optional meals). Both hostels serve breakfast and evening meals. There are several ryokan in town, including the *Hotel Kaijōkan* (℡08808/8-0503, ℻8-0211; ●) and the *Hotel Ashizurien* (℡08808/8-0206, ℻8-0033; ●), which includes dinner in its rate.

Tatsukushi and Sukumo

Heading north for 24km around the coast from Ashizuri Misaki brings you to the small town of **TATSUKUSHI**, which gets its name (meaning "dragon's skewers") from the remarkable rock pillars that protrude, like dinosaur bones, from the sea. The various formations have been given names like "dragon's skeleton" and "big bamboo tree" to jolly things up, but there's really no need: the honeycombed rocks, split by swirling indentations where the sea water has sluiced in, are fascinating enough in their own right.

The Minokoshi coastline around Tatsukushi was designated a national under-water park in 1970, the first of its kind in Japan. It's possible to take glass-bottomed boats (¥850) from the jetty near the bus station to view the coral reefs and then explore the weird rock formation along the coast, created over tens of thousands of years. Don't expect much from the reefs – they're hardly up to tropical standards, but the oddly shaped cliffs on what is dubbed the "hidden coast" make it worth the trip.

Tatsukushi is just twenty minutes' bus ride (¥560) from the Shimzu Bus Centre in Tosa Shimizu. You can leave your bags at the bus station (¥100) while exploring the area. Next to the bus station in the Chinese-style red-and-green building is the **Coral Museum** (daily 8am–5.30pm; ¥300), which has a large collection of *sango*, the pink coral found in the area. Mini-dioramas show how the coral used to be raised to the surface, and there are some showpiece models made from the stuff, including a detailed castle and a life-size tiger. The café next to the shop on the ground floor is also about the best bet for something to **eat**. Five minutes' walk around the coast, past a sandy beach and an unremarkable aquarium, is the **Ashizuri Sea-Floor Museum** (April–Aug 8.30am–5pm; Jan–March & Sept–Dec 9am–5pm; ¥900). You walk out to the red, white and blue cross-shaped pod, stranded in the ocean, along a gantry from the rocks, and then descend a spiral staircase to the sea bed to watch the fish swirling around the observation room's windows. Emperor Hirohito, a keen marine biologist, visited many times, but unless you're mad on fish you could give it a miss.

Buses continue up the coast for 50km to **SUKUMO** (¥1470), a small and quiet fishing port where it's possible to take a trip out to the nearby islands, **Okino-shima** and **Uguru-shima**, though there's little to do in Sukumo itself. On these islands you can camp, follow hiking trails, fish and go scuba-diving. Ferries also make a three-hour crossing from Sukumo to Saeki in Kyushu. If you want to bypass the cape, the Tosa Kuroshio train line links Sukumo with Kubokawa on the JR line and there are also through-trains from Kōchi. Direct buses also run from here to Uwajima several times a day (¥1750), departing from outside Sukumo station – considerably quicker than making the long detour via Kubokawa by rail.

A very pleasant **place to stay**, although it is far from convenient to reach by public transport, is the *Sukumo Youth Hostel* (℡0880/64-0233, ℱ64-0162; ❶). Run by an enthusiastic young couple, the hostel is 9km out of town, next to a river where fireflies appear in June. There is a school bus which runs from Sukumo to Matsudagawa, a fifteen-minute walk from the hostel. If you miss this, you can call the wardens, who speak a little English and may be able to pick you up. If you don't fancy hiking out to the youth hostel, the recently refurbished hotel *Matsu-ya* (℡0880/63-1185, ℱ63-1991; ❹) offers large rooms and all mod cons at reasonable rates. It's a ten-minute walk from Sukumo station. Turn left out of the south exit, then right at the pachinko parlour, walk straight for about five minutes (passing a convenience store on your right) until you come to a petrol station on the corner of an intersection. Turn right here and continue straight on for five minutes. The hotel is on the right and has a half-decent restaurant that's open until 9pm.

Uwajima and around

From Sukumo, Route 56 continues through countryside before emerging on the coast. The cliff-side road, passing though small fishing communities, provides spectacular views of the deep-blue sea, carpeted with nets held up by a criss-cross network of buoys. The next major stop is the port of **UWAJI-MA**, 60km north of Sukumo, famous for its sumo-style bullfights (see box, p.762), when the otherwise quiet and compact town comes alive. The main sights – which include a castle and a fertility shrine – can be seen easily in half a day, though an overnight stop will allow you more time to explore the town's real selling point: its tranquil backstreets lined with old wooden houses and temples.

You can easily walk between Uwajima's main sights, but they are a little scattered, so renting a bike (available from the youth hostel or the information centre at ¥100 per hour) is a good idea. The castle is a fifteen-minute walk south of the JR station, while the Taga-jinja sex shrine, across the Suka-gawa river, is a ten-minute walk to the north. The municipal bullfighting ring is a twenty-minute walk up the hill to the east. Route 56 cuts through the centre of Uwajima, running past the castle and the JR station and parallel to the main covered shopping arcade, Uwajima Gintengai.

Arrival and information

Uwajima Station is the **train** terminus for both the JR Yodo line running from Kubokawa and the JR Yosan line from Matsuyama. Buses to and from Sukumo stop in front of the station as well as at the main bus centre at the foot of the castle hill on Route 56. Uwajima is also connected by a daily ferry to Beppu in Kyūshū; the port is around twenty minutes' walk west of the city centre.

Just south of the exit from the JR station, on the wide, palm-lined avenue, is an **information centre** (Mon–Sat 8.30am–5pm, Sun 9am–5pm; ℡0895/22-3934), where you can pick up a good English-language map and booklet of the town. The assistants speak English and there's free Internet access (for checking mail only). You can change money at Iyo Bank just off the Gintengai, and there's a cash machine at the main post office near the Kōri Gate to the castle.

Uwajima and around

Uwajima	*Uwajima*	宇和島
Uwa-chō	*Uwa-chō*	宇和町
Taga-jinja	*Taga-jinja*	多賀神社
Tensha-en	*Tensha-en*	天赦園
Togyū-jō bullring	*Togyū-jō*	闘牛場
Uwajima-jō	*Uwajima-jō*	宇和島城
Warei-jinja	*Warei-jinja*	和霊神社

Accommodation

Business Hotel Shirakabe	*Bijinesu Hoteru Shirakabe*	ビジネスホテル白壁
Hotel Clement	*Hoteru Kuremento*	ホテルクレメント
Dai-ichi Hotel	*Dai-ichi Hoteru*	第一ホテル
Kokusai Hotel	*Kokusai Hoteru*	国際ホテル
Park Hotel	*Pāku Hoteru*	パークホテル
Tsukigase	*Tsugikase*	月ヶ瀬
Uwajima Oriental Hotel	*Uwajima Orientaru Hoteru*	宇和島オリエンタルホテル
Uwajima Youth Hostel	*Uwajima Yūsu Hosuteru*	宇和島ユースホステル

Restaurants

Gaiya	*Gaiya*	がいや
Gansui	*Gansui*	丸水
Hozumi-tei	*Hozumi-tei*	ほづみ亭
Kadoya	*Kadoya*	かどや
Suzu	*Suzu*	鈴
Tomiya	*Tomiya*	とみや

Uchiko	*Uchiko*	内子
Historic Folkways Materials, Business and Livelihood Museum	*Akinai-to-Kurashi Hakubutsukan*	商いと暮らし博物館
Hon-Haga Residence	*Hon-Haga-tei*	本芳我邸
Kami Haga Residence	*Kami-Haga-tei*	上芳我邸
Ōmura Residence	*Ōmura-ke*	大村家
Uchiko-za	*Uchiko-za*	内子座
Yōkaichi	*Yōkaichi*	八日市

Uwa-chō	*Uwa-chō*	宇和町
Kaimei School	*Kaimei Gakkō*	開明学校
Museum of Ehime History and Culture	*Ehime-ken Rekishi Bunka Hakubutsukan*	愛媛県歴史文化博物館
Uwa Folkcraft Museum	*Uwa-chō Mingu-kan*	宇和町民具間
Uwa Memorial Museum of Great Predecessors	*Uwa-chō Sentetsu Kinenkan*	宇和町先哲記念館
Uwa Rice Museum	*Uwa-chō Kome Hakubutsukan*	宇和町米博物館

Accommodation and restaurants

Farm Inn Raum Kokuriko	*Fāmu In Raumu Kokuriko*	ファームインRAUM古久里来
Ishidatami-no-Yado	*Ishidatami-no-Yado*	石畳の宿
Kabachū	*Kabachū*	かば忠
Karari	*Karari*	からり
Komachi	*Komachi*	こまち
Matsunoya	*Matsunoya*	松乃屋
Ōse-no-Yakata	*Ōse-no-Yakata*	大瀬の館

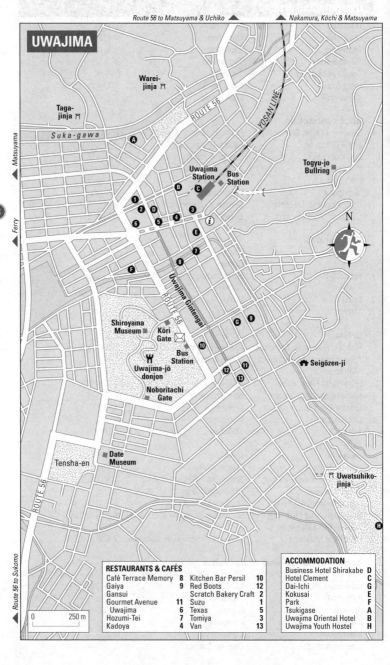

UWAJIMA

Route 56 to Matsuyama & Uchiko ▲ ▲ Nakamura, Kōchi & Matsuyama

Warei-jinja ⛩

Taga-jinja ⛩

ROUTE 56

YOSAN LINE

Suka-gawa

Ⓐ

Uwajima Station

Bus Station

Togyu-jo Bullring

Matsuyama ◀

Ferry ◀

Ⓑ
Ⓒ

N

① Suzu
②
Ⓓ
⑤ ④
Ⓔ
⑥
③
ⓘ
⑦
⑧

Ⓕ

Uwajima Gintengai

ROUTE 56

Shiroyama Museum

Kōri Gate ✉

Bus Station

Uwajima-jō donjon

Noboritachi Gate

Ⓖ ⑨

⑩

⑫ ⑪
⑬

♨ Seigōzen-ji

Date Museum

Tensha-en

ROUTE 56

⛩ Uwatsuhiko-jinja

Ⓗ

Route 56 to Sukomo ◀

0   250 m

RESTAURANTS & CAFÉS

Café Terrace Memory	8	Kitchen Bar Persil	10
Gaiya	9	Red Boots	12
Gansui		Scratch Bakery Craft	2
Gourmet Avenue		Suzu	1
Uwajima	11	Texas	5
Hozumi-Tei	7	Tomiya	3
Kadoya	4	Van	13

ACCOMMODATION

Business Hotel Shirakabe	D
Hotel Clement	C
Dai-Ichi	G
Kokusai	E
Park	F
Tsukigase	A
Uwajima Oriental Hotel	B
Uwajima Youth Hostel	H

Accommodation

There are several **hotels** near Uwajima Station and you'll find even more towards the port area, though this is not so convenient a base for sightseeing. The youth hostel is at the top of a steep hill, twenty minutes' walk south of the JR station. If you're carrying heavy luggage, it's best to take a taxi up (for around ¥900).

Business Hotel Shirakabe 2-22 Tsurusanchō ☏0895/22-3585, ⓌWWW3.netwave.or.jp/~sirakabe/infomation.htm. Nothing fancy, with some rather musty single rooms (for ¥4200), but the doubles are fine and the accommodating management speak a little English. ❹

Hotel Clement 10-1 Nishiki-machi ☏0895/23-6111, Ⓦwww.shikoku.ne.jp/clement-uwajima. Smart mid-range hotel, directly above the JR station, with a few Japanese-style rooms and a rooftop beer garden in summer. ❹

Dai-ichi Hotel 1-3-9 Chūō-chō ☏0895/25-0001, Ⓕ25-0002. Decent-enough business hotel, with a café attached, and relatively good-value single rooms, but pales a bit when compared to the *Clement* or *Oriental* in the same price range. ❹

Kokusai Hotel 4-1 Nishiki-machi ☏0895/25-0111, Ⓕ25-0715. Traditional Japanese-style holiday hotel with large, well-appointed tatami rooms. ❼ including two meals.

Park Hotel 1-5-5 Sakamachi Minato ☏0895/22-5589, Ⓕ22-2261. The best of several smaller, unspectacular hotels close to the port, with clean and functional rooms. ❹

Tsukigase 1-5-6 Miyukimachi ☏0895/22-4788, Ⓕ22-4787. The town's top ryokan, this attractive, if somewhat formal place is very handy for the Taga-jinja just across the river and also has a fine attached restaurant (see p.763). ❼ including two meals.

Uwajima Oriental Hotel 607-2 Tsurushima-chō ☏0895/23-3838, Ⓦwww.oriental-web.co.jp/uwajima. Smart, stylish business hotel a few minutes' walk from the station. There are cheap singles, plus a nice restaurant serving local seafood delicacies. ❹

Uwajima Youth Hostel Atago-kōen ☏0895/22-7177, Ⓦwww2.odn.ne.jp/~cfm91130/eigo.htm. The building's a tad institutional, but the views on the way up the hill and the friendly reception once you arrive make the hike worth the effort. Run by a young couple who speak English and are good cooks; also has a pool table and bikes for rent (¥800 per day). Dorm beds ¥3360 per person. ❷

The City

Uwajima's most notorious attraction, the fertility shrine **Taga-jinja**, is set back from the Suka-gawa river, a short walk north of the JR station. The shrine has an attached **sex museum** (daily 8am–5pm; ¥800) and is set in a small compound packed with various statues, some of which assume the shape of penises if looked at from a certain angle – there's no mistaking the shape of the carved log beside the main shrine building, though. To the right you'll see a smaller shrine, clogged with dolls, strings of paper cranes, women's clothes and other articles – all fertility offerings. The museum is spread over three floors of a modern building. Inside, it's wall-to-wall erotica, with display cases packed with all manner of sexual objects, literature and art. The ground floor is home to a collection of Japanese fertility symbols and figurines dating back centuries, while the first floor holds similar objects from around the world, including displays devoted to Tibet, India, Europe and elsewhere; some exhibits are claimed to be the best part of two thousand years old. The top floor hosts an impressive and unique collection of five hundred hand-carved wooden statues depicting all sorts of sexual shenanigans – no two are alike. Also on this floor is a large selection of Japanese erotic books and prints (*shunga*) dating back to the Edo and Meiji periods.

Taga-jinja is to the left as you cross the bridge over the Suka-gawa, while the larger shrine to the right is **Warei-jinja**, the focal point of the spectacular Warei Taisai, one of Shikoku's major festivals. Held from the evening of July 22 to July 24, the festival involves huge models of devil bulls (*ushi-oni*) being paraded in the streets, along with ornate portable shrines, the aim being to dispel evil. The bulls, like giant pantomime horses, eventually do battle in the river, while at the shrine there's much banging of *taiko*, bonfire burning and a fireworks finale.

Walking back into the town, keep an eye out for the rather forlorn-looking **Uwajima-jō** (daily 9am–4pm; ¥200), at the top of the hillside park that rises west of Route 56. The compact, three-storey donjon may be original and certainly gives a fine view of the surrounding city and port, but there's little reason to pay the entrance charge, unless you want to look at the photos of other Japanese castles displayed inside. There are two routes up to the donjon, either from the north through the gate of the Kōri samurai family (transferred to the castle ground in 1952), tucked back from the main road behind the post office, or from the Noboritachi-mon gate on the south side of the castle hill. On the way up, it's worth popping into the **Shiroyama Museum** (daily 9.30am–4pm; free) to see its eclectic collection of local antiques and artefacts, ranging from giant masks of a long-nosed goblin and a smiling woman to an early radio set.

A short walk south of the castle park, the small formal garden of **Tensha-en** (daily: April–July 8.30am–5pm; Jan–March & Aug–Dec 8.30am–4.30pm; ¥300) is a popular place to hang out. The garden dates from 1866 and is laid out in circular style with a feature made of a wisteria trellis. You can safely skip the nearby **Date Museum** (Tues–Sun 9am–4.30pm; ¥500) and its dusty collection of heirlooms from the local ruling family and instead explore the narrow residential streets immediately southeast of the centre. Here shrines, temples and graveyards are huddled on the slopes leading up to the *Uwajima Youth Hostel*. Climb this hill, even if you're not staying at the hostel, for sweeping views of the town.

Bullfighting Japanese-style

Although it's said that the novelty wears thin fast, the best time to visit Uwajima is for one of its **bullfights**, or *tōgyū*, the bovine equivalent of sumo wrestling. Some accounts date the sport back four hundred years, while others pinpoint the origins in the nineteenth century, when a Dutch captain made a gift of bulls to the town, after local fishermen came to his ship's aid during a typhoon. The bulls, weighing in at up to a tonne and treated like pampered pets by their owners, lock horns and struggle either to push each other to the floor or out of the tournament ring. Fights are held at the **Tōgyū-jō**, a white-walled arena in the hills above the city, between noon and 3pm. Get there an hour early to soak up the atmosphere and watch the bulls being paraded around the ring. The bouts are very good-natured and the enthusiastic crowd is welcoming and friendly. Some food and beer is available, but it's advisable to pack a picnic as supplies never seem to suffice. There are bouts on January 2, July 24, August 14 and the second Sunday in November, and sometimes also in April and May; call ☎0895/25-3511 to check. Tickets cost ¥3000 and can be bought on the day at the arena. A free shuttle bus from the station to the bullring runs from 10am to noon on fight days. Ask at the tourist information office for details. More information (in English) can be found at ⓦ www.tougyu.com.

Uwajima is not the only place in Japan that hosts such contests – bullfights are popular in **Okinawa**, too, particularly on the main island Okinawa-Hontō, where the sport is called *Ushiorase*. Here it's claimed the contests began in the seventeenth century as a form of distraction for farmers and their bulls during the slack farming seasons.

Eating and drinking

Not surprisingly for a port, Uwajima offers ample opportunity to eat **fresh fish** – two popular dishes are *tai-meshi* (marinated sea bream on top of rice) and *satsuma-jiru* (minced fish and miso paste on rice). There are several good **restaurants** close by the JR station, but none of the usual fast-food outlets; your best bet for a quick snack is either the *Willie Winkie* bakery at the station or the *Scratch Bakery Craft* on the way to the Taga–jinja.

For a **drink**, you could try *Gaiya*, east of the Gintengai, a modern *izakaya*, painted bright yellow outside and serving a good range of seafood, vegetable and meat dishes. Just beyond the southern end of the arcade, *Van* (closed Thurs), with its collection of Meissen pottery, is the sophisticated option, serves good food and is also open for lunch. The nearby *Red Boots* (closed Mon) has more of a Wild West vibe and very *genki* management. You may well run into someone from the expat community and plenty of lively Japanese at *Texas Bar* on the main road three blocks west of the station; it's run by Seiji, a hefty judo black belt.

Restaurants and cafés

Café Terrace Memory Ebisumachi ☎0895/22-8004. Bright place on the second floor of a building just outside the arcade, serving mainly Japanese takes on Western dishes, such as spaghetti and pilaf, with lunch costing around ¥800.

Gansui Honmachi Otē ☎0895/22-3636. Upmarket *izakaya* east of the Gintengai, with a picture menu and daily set dishes from as little as ¥1300. Daily except Tues 11am–9pm.

Gourmet Avenue Uwajima Tsurushimachi. This brand-new eating complex offers plenty of variety, with a *yakiniku* restaurant, a ramen joint and a branch of the family restaurant chain *Donto*. Open until 11.30pm.

Hozumi-tei 2-3-8 Shinmachi ☎0895/25-6590. Appealingly rustic fish restaurant with both tables and tatami seating areas overlooking a stream.

Kadoya Tsurushimachi ☎0895/22-1453.

Reasonably priced seafood dishes and other set menus for around ¥1000, and a useful picture menu.

Kitchen Bar Persil 1-10-5 Chūō-chō ☎0895/23-7558. Cool bar-restaurant with glass tables, funky red seats and Western-style dishes like pizza, garlic toast and pasta. Open until late.

Suzu Miyukimachi 2-chōme ☎0895-25-1738. Excellent coffee in a dark, smoky old-style coffee shop packed with jazz and blues LPs. The master speaks a little English.

Tomiya Tsurushimachi ☎0895/22-1697. Also near the station, but slightly cheaper and more basic than *Kadoya*.

Tsukigase 1-5-6 Miyukimachi. Set around a fish-pond and specializing in *fugu* (in winter) and *tempura*. Pricey at night, though has lunch sets for ¥1400.

Uwa-chō

Less than 20km north of Uwajima, the small country town of **UWA-CHŌ** (ⓦ www.islands.ne.jp/uwa/e_index.html) is a very pleasant half-day trip, and also makes a convenient stop on the way to Matsuyama. The highlight is the excellent **Museum of Ehime History and Culture** (Tues–Sun 9am–5pm; ¥500; ☎0894/62-6222). At first glance this ultra-modern building sticks out from the hillside like an ugly grey growth, but move closer and the natural stone walls and gently rounded roofs look more appealing and provide ample space for the spectacular displays inside. These include full-sized replicas of buildings, including a Yayoi-era (330 BC–300 AD) hut, a street of Meiji-era shops and a small wooden temple. In the centre of the museum is a folklore exhibit, which includes examples of the fabulous portable shrines, costumes and other decorations used in local festivals, such as Uwajima's Warei Taisai. TV screens also show videos of the festivals.

The **train** station for Uwa-chō is Uno-machi, less than twenty minutes from Uwajima by the hourly limited express. The museum can be reached by an infrequent bus (¥150) from the stop about five minutes' walk south of the JR station, along Route 56. To walk up the hill to the museum takes around twenty minutes. On the way, you'll pass the other reason for visiting this town, a street of well-preserved, white-walled houses known as **Naka-chō**, which is also the name given to this part of town. Along here is **Kaimei School** (Tues–Sun 9am–5pm; ¥200), a lovely and well-preserved example of a Meiji period school and one of the oldest extant in western Japan; there's also a temple and a church house you can look into. Opposite the old schoolhouse is the **Uwa Folkcraft Museum** (Tues–Sun 9am–5pm; free), an immaculate new folkcraft museum that contains a wide range of interesting items which were in daily use in the town over the years, from bamboo swords and deer costumes used in local festivals to record players and dioramas depicting life during the Edo Period. There's also a full-scale mock-up of a Taishō-period living room, and an intact fuel tank dropped by a US fighter bomber during World War II.

You can pick up a simple map-cum-guide to the town's sites in English here, as well as a special ¥400 ticket offering entry to the school, the nearby **Memorial Museum of Great Predecessors** (Tues–Sun 9am–5pm; ¥200) and the **Rice Museum** (Tues–Sun 9am–5pm; ¥200) on the other side of town. If you're in a hurry, the latter two can be safely skipped as there's little in the way of English explanations, though the rice museum is housed in a lovely 109-metre-long wooden school building. To reach this street, walk straight ahead from the station through the arch and turn right at the pedestrianized shopping street. Take the first left and then follow the road as it forks right.

Lunch options in Uwa are limited. There's a takeaway sushi joint and a coffee shop offering light meals in the small branch of the Takashimaya department store on the main road a minute's walk from the station, but your best bet is the *Ristorante Station*, which serves pizza and Yebisu beer. As its name might imply, it's bang opposite the station. If you're on a budget, the next-door coffee shop *Jun* offers Japanese-style curry rice for just ¥530.

Uchiko

Some 45km northeast of Uwajima is the small town of **UCHIKO**, once an important centre for the Japanese **wax** industry, and also the birthplace of Oe Kenzaburo, Japan's second winner of the Nobel Prize for literature. The wax (*moku-rō*) is made from the crushed berries of the sumach tree and used for candles, polishes, in cosmetics, crayons, food, and even computer disks. The wealth generated by wax production has left Uchiko with many fine houses preserved in the Yōkaichi district of the town, and there are several shops where craftsmen can still be seen making candles by hand. A picturesque six-hundred-metre stretch of nineteenth-century merchants' houses is promoted as an "Antique Road"; if you plan to enter all the buildings and museums – an interesting enough way to pass half a day – a small saving can be made by purchasing the ¥700 combination ticket.

The best place to start your tour of Uchiko – which is easily explored on foot – is at the **Historic Folkways Materials, Business and Livelihood Museum** (daily 9am–4.30pm; ¥200; ☎0893/44-5220). The museum is set in a charmingly converted merchant's house, with mechanical dummies that help show the daily life of a shopkeeper during the Taishō era (1912–26). The mannequins, which are electronically activated to start speaking when you enter a room, are quite fun (especially the moaning pharmacist in the upstairs storeroom), and the museum gives a good idea of what it was like to live in such a house.

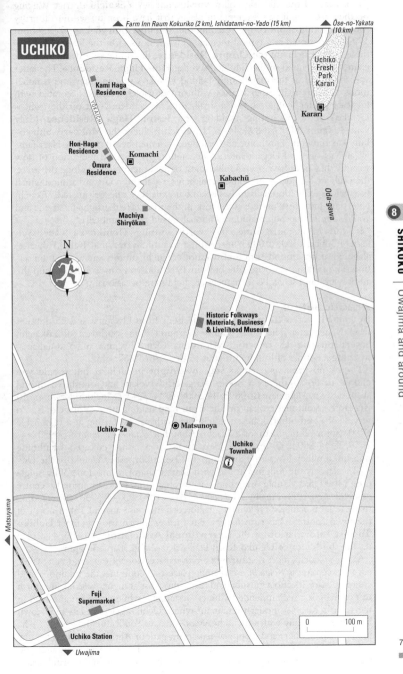

UCHIKO

Kami Haga Residence

Uchiko Fresh Park Karari

YOKAICHI

Karari

Hon-Haga Residence

Komachi

Ōmura Residence

Kabachū

Oda-gawa

Machiya Shiryōkan

N

Historic Folkways Materials, Business & Livelihood Museum

Uchiko-Za

Matsunoya

Uchiko Townhall

ⓘ

◀ Matsuyama

Fuji Supermarket

Uchiko Station

▼ Uwajima

0　　　100 m

Northeast of the Historic Folkways Museum lies **Yōkaichi** district. Walking up the street you'll pass a couple of places that have been turned into touristy souvenir and teashops before reaching the **Machiya Shiryō-kan**, dating from 1793, and restored as a typical merchant's town house. On the left as you continue up Yōkaichi are the **Ōmura Residence**, the home of a dyehouse merchant from the end of the Edo era, and the **Hon-Haga Residence**. The latter was the home of the main family behind Uchiko's wax industry and is rather more elaborate than other houses, with ornate gables, a facade decorated with intricate plaster sculptures, and a small, attractive garden. Next on the right is Uchiko's most interesting building, the **Kami Haga Residence** (daily 9am–4.30pm; ¥400; ☎0893/44-2771), which includes the **Muko-rō Shiryō-kan** wax museum. This home also belonged to a member of the Hon-Haga family and its size and elegant interior decoration give a good indication of how wealthy they must have been. Unlike most of the other buildings along the street, the walls are a golden sand colour, and there's a spacious courtyard around which the various exhibition halls and a decent but expensive café are situated. Yōkaichi peters out just north of here at the fork in the road; take the right-hand side and you'll soon find a shop making traditional waxed paper umbrellas.

If you have more time, it's worth visiting **Uchiko-za** (Tues–Sun 9am–4.30pm; ¥300; ☎0893/44-2840), a beautifully restored Kabuki theatre, although it lies around 1km southwest of Yōkaichi, on the way to the train station. The theatre was originally built in 1916 and you can wander around the auditorium and stage. Performances are held here occasionally.

Practicalities

By limited express **train** Uchiko is one hour from Uwajima and 25 minutes from Matsuyama. The train station is around 2km southwest of Yōkaichi. Several **buses** a day run from Matsuyama, Ōzu, Uwajima and Yawatahama, stopping a couple of hundred metres to the east of Yōkaichi.

There's no pressing need to **stay overnight** in Uchiko, but should you choose to do so, there are some characterful ryokan and minshuku in and around town. *Matsunoya* (☎0893/44-5000, ℱ44-2244; ❼ including two meals) is a large, traditional ryokan on the main road leading up to Yōkaichi. It also serves soba and other dishes at lunchtime, with prices starting at a reasonable ¥700. Some 2km north of Yōkachi, *Farm Inn Raum Kokuriko* (☎0983/44-2079, ℱ44-2094; ❻ including two meals) is a rather cultured farmhouse minshuku which hosts art exhibitions. In Ōse, 10km east of Uchiko, is the *Ōse-no-Yakata*, a rustic lodging house with shared tatami rooms for ¥3000 single use, ¥4000 for double use; book it through the Ōse community centre (☎0893/47-0102). Finally, *Ishidatami-no-Yado* (☎0893/44-5730; ❺ including two meals) is a lovely ryokan in a restored farmhouse around 15km north of the town centre; a bus runs nearby. For further information, contact **Uchiko Tourist Information** or the **International Association** (☎0893/44-2111) on the third floor of Uchiko Town Hall (Mon–Fri 8.30am–5.15pm).

Along Yōkaichi, most **restaurants** are overpriced tourist traps and best avoided; an exception is *Komachi*, a charming place that combines the traditional and contemporary. It's also a giftshop and turns into a bar at night. *Kabachū*, just north of Yōkaichi, is a recommended Chinese restaurant, while down on an island in the river is *Karari*, a modern restaurant where Uchiko celebrates its twin-town links with Germany with a menu heavy on sausages. You'll also find a lively fresh-produce market here and a popular ice-cream parlour. Another option is to pack some provisions at the large Fuji supermarket, which you'll pass soon after you leave the train station and head into town, and have a picnic in the island's park.

Matsuyama and around

If you have time to visit only one place on Shikoku, make it **MATSUYAMA**. Although it's the island's largest city, with a population of over 450,000, Matsuyama feels more like a convivial town and makes the most of its literary pedigree as Japan's centre for haiku poetry (see box below). Most points of interest are centred around the impressive castle, **Matsuyama-jō**, and the popular hot-spring suburb of **Dōgo**, 2km east of the centre. The city is also a good base from which to launch your assault on Shikoku's highest mountain, **Ishizuchi-san**.

Local warlords from the Kono clan built a fortress in Dōgo in the fourteenth century, while Matsuyama was created in 1602 by *daimyō* Katō Yoshiakira when he built his castle on Katsuyama Hill. In 1635, the Matsudaira clan took charge of the castle and ruled the area until the Meiji Restoration in 1868. Matsuyama was made the capital of Ehime-ken in 1889 and has since expanded across its corner of Shikoku's northwest coast to swallow up several neighbouring towns and suburbs, including Dōgo. The city centre was pretty much destroyed during World War II and is now largely modern, though the handy tram network harks back to a less frantic era. You can see the city's highlights in a day, but it's better to give yourself an extra couple of days to savour the relaxed mood induced by Dōgo's onsen.

Arrival, information and city transport

Trains and **buses** pull in at the JR Matsuyama Station, just west of the city centre – from here it's roughly a ten-minute walk to the castle. Matsuyama's **airport** lies 6km west of the centre; bus #52 from here takes about twenty minutes to reach the JR station (¥300) and continues on to Dōgo; there's also a more comfortable, though less frequent, limousine bus for the same price. A

Masaoka Shiki

At many tourist spots in Matsuyama you'll find wooden postboxes bearing the Japanese for "Haiku post". **Haiku** is a traditional poetic form just three lines long containing respectively five, seven and five syllables, and the subject of the poem is usually connected with the seasons. Anyone can drop their poems into the boxes and souvenirs are sent to those who submit praiseworthy efforts. The postboxes were established in 1967 to commemorate the centenary of the birth of Matsuyama's most famous haiku poet, **Masaoka Shiki**.

Befitting his profession, Masaoka was a rather tragic figure, who died at 35 from tuberculosis. He took his pen name Shiki from that of a bird, which according to legend coughs blood as it sings. His life story, which included a spell reporting on the Sino-Japanese War, can be traced at the Shiki Kinen Museum in Dōgo (see p.775) and there are two houses connected with the poet preserved as tourist attractions in the city, including the villa he shared for a short time with Matsuyama's other adopted literary son, Sōseki Natsume (see p.1019). Masaoka is particularly remembered in Japan for encouraging reforms to the rather hidebound haiku artform – he thought it should be more reflective of real life. He famously criticized the master of the genre, Bashō, and advocated that poets be allowed to use whatever words they wanted for haiku, on any subject matter. One of his most famous poems is: *"Kaki kueba kane-ga narunari Hōryū-ji"* ("I was eating a persimmon. Then, the bell of Hōryū-ji temple echoed far and wide"), which is both realistic and immediate, two qualities that Masaoka argued poets should be striving for.

MATSUYAMA

RESTAURANTS

Cappuccio	10
Club Bibros	11
Doutor	17
Fishbone	7
Freshness Burger	15
Goshiki	12
Indie's Kashi Mashi	9
Jett Rockbar	6
Kani Dōraku	2
Kawasemi	5
Le Mas de Provence	8
Murasaki	3
Paradiso	4
Rarekii	13
Rue de Bac	16
Sara Sol	14
Underground Café	1

ACCOMMODATION

Business Hotel Taihei	B
Capsule Hotel New Grand	J
Chateautel Matsuyama	I
Heiwa	A
International	C
Hotel JAL City	F
Matsuyama ANA Hotel	E
Matsuyama New Grand	H
Matsuyama Tōkyū Inn	D
Washington	G

Dōgo

Minami-machi

Kenmin Bunka Kaikan (Prefectural Cultural Centre)
EPIC

Sekijuji Byōin-mae

Heiwa-dōri-chōme

Kami-ichiman

Keisatsusho-mae

Katsuyama-chō

Teppō-chō

Shinonome Jinja

Ropeway & Chairlift Entrance

Ichiban-chō

Matsuyama-jō

Bansui-so (Annex of the Prefectural Art Museum)

Okaidō

Cinema Sunshine

Katsuyama

Ninomaru Shiseki Teien

Kenchō-mae

Kents & Ex

Cine Riente

Cinema Lunatic

Honmachi 4-chōme

Honmachi 3-chōme

Shiyakusho-mae

NTT

JAL

Gintengai Arcade

Imabari

Komachi

Nishi-Horibata

Minami-Horibata

Kinokuniya

München

Shiki-dō

Shoshu-ji

Ferry

Miyata-chō

COMS

Matsuyama International Centre & Internet

Shieki-mae

ANA

Shieki & Sōgo Department Store (Matsuyama City Station trains & buses)

Otemachi

JR Ekimae

Matsuyama Community Centre

Train Station

N

0   250 m

Imabari, Okayama & Takamatsu

Uchiko & Uwajima

Uwajima

Tobe (13 km)

Ishite-gawa

Takamatsu

taxi from the airport will set you back around ¥2000. **Ferries** from several ports in Western Honshū and Kyūshū dock at Takahama and Matsuyama Kankō ports – both around 10km north of Matsuyama. The terminus of the Iyo Tetsudō train line is within walking distance of both ports, from where it's a 25-minute journey (¥400) into Shi-eki Station, just south of the castle. The fastest connection with Honshū is the **hydrofoil** from Hiroshima (1hr; ¥5800).

Matsuyama has several **information** points. You can pick up English maps and leaflets at the small tourist booth (daily 8.30am–5.15pm) just to the left as you exit the JR station. For more detailed help head for **EPIC – Ehime Prefectural International Centre** (Mon–Sat 8.30am–5pm; ☎089/917-5678), just west of the Kenmin Bunka Kaikan a couple of minutes' walk from the Minami-machi tram stop, where you can also browse through the small library of English-language books. EPIC offers many free services to residents and visitors alike: classes on Japanese traditional arts, Internet access and bicycle rental (for up to two weeks). Make sure you pick up the free Seto Inland Sea Welcome Card from either EPIC or the tourist booth, which will give you discounts at many places around town. Finally, the **Matsuyama International Centre** (Tues–Sat 9am–5.30pm; ☎089/943-2025), on the ground floor of COMS, 6-4-10 Sanbanchō, can arrange free volunteer guides to show you around the city and also publishes the free monthly *What's Going On?* booklet, available here, at EPIC and on the fourth floor of the Kinokuniya bookstore.

Getting around

Matsuyama's city centre is easily covered on foot, but to travel between here and Dōgo you'll almost certainly use the **tram** network. There are four tram routes: one loop line and three other routes all running through the city centre at Ichiban-chō, past the castle and ending at the delightfully old-fashioned Dōgo terminal. **Fares** are a flat ¥150 and must be paid to the driver on leaving the tram. A **one-day ticket**, offering unlimited travel on the trams and the Loop Bus, is a bargain at ¥300, and can be bought from the ticket offices at Ōtemachi (a five-minute walk east from the JR station), Shi-eki and the Dōgo terminus, or on the trams themselves. Alternatively, you can buy pre-paid **travel cards** for ¥1000 (worth ¥1100) from vending machines on the trams. These should be inserted into the machine beside the driver as you exit. Travel cards can also be used on city **buses** – most useful for reaching further-flung areas of the city, such as the airport and Oku Dōgo. Apart from the castle hill, Matsuyama is reasonably flat, making this a good city to **cycle** in, although you'll need to keep an eye out for trams on the main roads.

Accommodation

The most pleasant **place to stay** in Matsuyama is Dōgo, which lies 2km east of the centre and has one of the best youth hostels in Japan, as well as a good selection of hotels and ryokan. If you want to be based more centrally, you'll find plenty of cheap business hotels around the JR station – expect to pay no more than ¥4000 for a single room or ¥7000 for a double or twin. If you can afford a little more, head for the hotels around the castle and Ōkaidō shopping arcade. These are generally a lot nicer and more convenient for sightseeing.

Matsuyama	Mastuyama	松山
Bansui-sō	Bansui-sō	萬翠荘
Matsuyama-jō	Matsuyama-jō	松山城
Ninomaru Shiseki Teien	Ninomaru Shiseki Teien	二之丸史跡庭園
Ōtemachi Station	Ōtemachi-eki	大手町駅
Shi-eki Station	Shi-eki	市駅
Shiki-dō	Shiki-dō	子規堂
Shinonome-jinja	Shinonome-jinja	東雲神社
Raikō-ji	Raikō-ji	来迎時
Russian cemetery	Roshia-jin no bochi	ロシア人の墓地

Accommodation		
Business Hotel Taihei	Bijinesu Hoteru Taihei	ビジネスホテル泰平
Capsule Hotel New Grand	Kapuseru Hoteru Nyū Gurando	カプセルホテルニューグランド
Chateautel Matsuyama	Shatōteru Matsuyama	シャトーテル松山
Hotel Heiwa	Hoteru Heiwa	ホテル平和
International Hotel	Kokusai Hoteru	国際ホテル
Hotel JAL City	Hoteru JAL Shiti	ホテルJALシティ
Matsuyama ANA Hotel	Matsuyama Zennikkū Hoteru	松山全日空ホテル
Matsuyama New Grand Hotel	Matsuyama Nyū Gurando Hoteru	松山ニューグランドホテル
Matsuyama Tōkyū Inn	Matsuyama Tōkyū In	松山東急イン
Washington Hotel	Washinton Hoteru	ワシントンホテル

Eating		
Goshiki	Goshiki	五色
Kani Dōraku	Kani Dōraku	かに道楽
Kawasemi	Kawasemi	川瀬見
Murasaki	Murasaki	村さ来
Paradiso	Paradiso	パラディソ
Rarekii	Rarekii	ラルキー

Dōgo	Dōgo	道後
Dōgo Onsen Honkan	Dōgo Onsen Honkan	道後温泉本館

Matsuyama

Business Hotel Taihei 3-1-15 Heiwa-dōri
☏089/943-3560, ℻ 932-2525. The best busi-
ness-type accommodation on the north side of
the castle. The rooms are of a good standard, with
larger beds and TVs than normal. Also has an outdoor spa bath and cheap single rooms. ④

Capsule Hotel New Grand Minato-machi
☏089/945-7089. Capsule hotel, opposite the Sōgo
department store and the Shi-eki Station, taking
both men and women. It's clean and spacious, if a
little shabby, and capsules cost just ¥2600.

Chateautel Matsuyama 4-9-6 Sanban-chō
☏089/946-2111. Not the most stylish of hotels,
but the rooms at this central mid-range establish-

ment are large, comfortable and light, management is helpful and there's a rooftop beer garden
from May to August. ④

Hotel Heiwa 3-1-34 Heiwa-dōri ☏089/921-3515,
℻ 921-3520. A two-minute walk from the
Shimizu-machi tram stop north of the castle, this
modern business hotel has standard rooms,
friendly management and a café. ④

International Hotel 1-13 Ichiban-chō
☏089/932-5111. Good-value mid-range hotel
near the castle, with comfortably furnished rooms
and some striking interior designs in its public
areas and restaurants. The kitsch top-floor Chinese
restaurant has to be seen to be believed. ④

Hotel JAL City 1-10-10 Ōtemachi ☏089/913-

Isaniwa-jinja	*Isaniwa-jinja*	伊佐爾波神社
Ishite-ji	*Ishite-ji*	石手寺
Oku Dōgo	*Oku Dōgo*	奥道後
Seki Art Gallery	*Seki Bijutsukan*	せき美術館
Shiki Kinen Museum	*Shiki Kinen Hakubutsukan*	子規記念博物館
Tsubaki-no-yu baths	*Tsubaki-no-yu*	椿の湯

Accommodation

Dōgo Business Hotel	*Dōgo Bijinesu Hoteru*	道後ビジネスホテル
Dōgo Kan	*Dōgo Kan*	道後館
Funaya	*Funaya*	ふなや
Matsuyama Youth Hostel	*Matsuyama Yūsu Hosuteru*	松山ユースホステル
Minshuku Miyoshi	*Minshuku Miyoshi*	民宿みよし
Hotel Patio Dōgo	*Hoteru Pateo Dōgo*	ホテルパテオ道後

Eating and drinking

Café do Namo	*Kafe-do-Namo*	カフェドなも
Dōgo Bakushukan	*Dōgo Bakushukan*	道後麦酒館
Nikitatsu-an	*Nikitatsu-an*	にきたつあん

Around Matsuyama

Imabari	*Imabari*	今治
Imabari-jō	*Imabari-jō*	今治城
Hojo	*Hojo*	北条
Hojosuigun Youth Hostel	*Hojosuigun Yūsu Hosuteru*	北条水軍ユースホステル
Kashima	*Kashima*	鹿島
Kurushima Bridge	*Kurushima Kaikyo Ōhashi*	来島海峡第一大橋
Ishizuchi-san	*Ishizuchi-san*	石鎚山
Jōju	*Jōju*	成就
Nishi-no-Kawa	*Nishi-no-Kawa*	西之川
Saijō	*Saijō*	西条市
Shiraishi Ryokan	*Shiraishi Ryokan*	白石旅館
Tsuchigoya	*Tsuchigoya*	土小屋

2580. Rivalling the *Matsuyama ANA Hotel* as the city's best, this has several good restaurants and comfortable rooms – ask for one overlooking the castle grounds. ⑤

Matsuyama ANA Hotel 3-2-1 Ichiban-chō ☎089/933-5511, ℻ 921-6053. The city's top hotel lives up to its reputation, with well-appointed rooms, many with excellent views of the castle. Also has several restaurants and a shopping arcade. Weekday rates are considerably lower than those at weekends. Weekends ⑥, weekdays ④–⑤

Matsuyama New Grand Hotel 3-4-10 Niban-chō ☎089/933-3661, ℻ 933-3960. Not so new, nor that grand, but it does have single rooms from around ¥4000 and cheaper doubles (④) in its older section (ask for the *honkan*) if you're on a budget. The newer doubles (⑤) are pricier but a bit more comfortable. For ¥1500, male guests can take advantage of the large communal baths and sauna.

Matsuyama Tōkyū Inn 3-3-1 Ichiban-chō ☎089/941-0109, ℻ 934-3725. Opposite the Ōkaidō arcade, this relatively upmarket branch of the national hotel chain has stylishly furnished rooms in cool green tones with large beds – some rooms have views of the castle hill, and there's also a decent range of restaurants and a good breakfast buffet for just ¥950. ⑥

Washington Hotel 1-7-1 Niban-chō ☎089/945-8111, ℻ 947-3110. A pleasantly light lobby leads

on to identikit rooms of a reasonably high standard. The location is convenient for those who
wish to throw themselves into the city's nightlife.
6

Dōgo

Dōgo Business Hotel 2-25 Yumo-machi ☎089/
943-2911, ⓕ 943-2913. Friendly, no-frills hotel
with both tatami and Western-style rooms. **4**
Dōgo Kan 7-26 Dōgo Tako-chō ☎089/941-777.A
night at Dōgo's grandest traditional hotel doesn't
come cheap: it's ¥50,000 per night for even the
cheapest doubles – and be prepared to pay double
that for one of the elegant Art Deco-style rooms.
The real attractions are the Japanese restaurant
area and the "Grand Baths", an imaginatively
designed series of indoor and outdoor onsen. **9**
including two meals.
Funaya 1-33 Dōgo Yumo-machi ☎ 089/947-
0278. One of the oldest and most expensive
ryokan in Dōgo, this isn't much to look at from the

outside, but inside it has immaculate tatami
rooms, its own baths, and a beautiful central garden. **9** including two meals.
Matsuyama Youth Hostel 22-3 Himezuka Otsu,
Dōgo ☎089/933-6366, ⓕ 933-6378. Fantastic
hostel, which regularly comes top of the annual
JYH popularity poll. The management goes out of
its way to make your stay enjoyable: there's an
excellent-value restaurant, and free tea and
snacks are served every evening in the comfy
lounge. Also has private double rooms (**2**) with
their own TVs and washbasins. Dorm beds ¥3360
per person.
Minshuku Miyoshi 3-7-23 Ishite ☎089/977-
2581. Large tatami rooms with air conditioning,
washbasins and TVs. No English spoken. **3**
Hotel Patio Dōgo Honkan-mae ☎089/941-4128.
You couldn't get more convenient than this friendly, mid-range hotel, opposite the Honkan. The
attached sushi restaurant is good value, and
there's free Internet access for guests. **6**

The City

The 132-metre-high Katsuyama dominates the centre of Matsuyama and on
its summit stands the city's prime attraction, **Matsuyama-jō** castle (daily
9am–5pm; ¥500; ☎089/921-2540). Warlord Katō Yoshiakira began building his
fortress in 1602, but by the time it was finished, 26 years later, he had moved
to Aizu in Tōhoku. Like many Japanese castles hailed as "original", the
Matsuyama-jō has gone through several editions during its lifetime. The main
five-storey donjon was destroyed by lightning on New Year's Day in 1784 and
rebuilt two storeys shorter in 1820 – the three lesser donjons are all modern-
day reconstructions. Despite this, the castle is one of the more impressive
fortresses in Japan, particularly since its location provides commanding views
of the city and Inland Sea.

You can get up to the castle using the cable car or chairlift (¥160 each way)
on the eastern flank of the hill. It's also possible to walk up. There are several
steep routes – the main one starts just beside the cable car, at the steps up to
Shinonome-jinja, also on the castle hill's east side. This picturesque shrine is
famous for its Takigi festival, held every April, when Nō plays are performed
by the light of fire torches. Other routes run up the west side of the hill, and
can be combined with a visit to the Ninomaru Shiseki Teien (see below).
Whichever route you take, you'll end up at the Tonashi-mon gateway to the
castle, past which you emerge onto a long plateau surrounded by walls and turrets and planted with blossom trees. Inside the main donjon, climb up to the
top floor for the view and, on the way down, pass through the museum with
displays of calligraphy, old maps, samurai armour and some gorgeously painted
screens.

Heading down the western side of the hill leads to the tranquil gardens of the
Ninomaru Shiseki Teien (April–Aug Mon–Sat 9am–4.30pm, Sun
9am–7pm; Jan–March & Sept–Dec daily 9am–4.30pm; ¥100; ☎089/921-
2000). Looking a bit like a giant geometry puzzle, the gardens are built on the
site of the Ninomaru, the outer citadel of the castle. The pools and pathways
at the front of the gardens represent the floor plan of the former structure,
which succumbed to fire in 1872. To the rear, as the grounds climb Katsuyama,

the design becomes more fluid, with rockeries, a waterfall and two tea-ceremony houses, one of which serves tea and *okashi* (a sweet cake) for ¥300.

At the base of the south side of the hill is the striking French-style villa, **Bansui-sō**. Built in 1922 for Count Sadakoto Hisamatsu, the fifteenth lord of Matsuyama-jō, the villa now houses the Annexe of the Prefectural Art Museum (Tues–Sun 10am–6pm; ¥800; ☎089/921-3711). The twentieth-century Japanese art displayed inside is changed every three months, but it's the exterior of the building which is most impressive, particularly the juxtaposition of trees pruned like poodles and the wild palms on the forecourt.

From the exit to Bansui-sō you are well placed to start exploring the main shopping arcade of Ōkaidō, at the entrance of which is a branch of the upmarket Mitsukoshi department store. At the end of the arcade, cross the main road and turn right into the Gintengai arcade, which eventually leads to the Shi-eki Station and Sogō department store. A couple of minutes' walk south of here, across the Iyo Tetsudō rail line, is the **Shiki-dō** (daily 9am–5pm; ¥50; ☎089/945-0400), an evocative recreation of the poet Masaoka Shiki's home sandwiched between his family's local temple, Shoshu-ji, and the cemetery. Inside the tiny one-storey house are some of the poet's personal effects, his writing desk and examples of his calligraphy.

In the north of the city lie a number of temples in the Yamagoe district, whose purpose it was to defend the area immediately to the north of the castle. None of these is today of any major interest, save perhaps for **Raikō-ji**, originally located in Dōgo but reconstructed in its present location in the eighteenth century. The temple itself is currently being rebuilt, though the main point of interest is in the grounds outside. Head around the corner and walk a hundred metres up a steep incline to find the **Russian Cemetery**. Some six thousand Russian prisoners were interred at the POW camp here during the Russo-Japanese War of 1904–5. The prisoners – being something of a novelty and having little chance of escaping back to Russia – were allowed a fair amount of freedom. Ninety-eight prisoners died from natural causes during their imprisonment, and their graves are still kept immaculate, with fresh flowers placed in front of each of the crosses. An impressive commemorative bust of a fierce-looking Russian officer stands watch at the entrance to the cemetery. Raikō-ji is a fifteen-minute walk northeast of the Takasago-chō tram stop.

Dōgo

Like many other onsen resorts, **DŌGO** has its strip shows, porn shops and women on street corners, as well as mundane tourist giftshops lining its arcade. However, Dōgo's bathtime delights more than make up for this. Once you've sampled the **onsen**, there are a couple of interesting museums to explore, along with the appealing **Isaniwa-jinja** shrine and over-the-top temple **Ishite-ji**.

The onsen

If you went first class, for only 8 sen they lent you a bathrobe, an attendant washed you, and a girl served you tea in one of those elegant, shallow cups that they use in the tea ceremony. I always went first class.

Botchan, by Sōseki Natsume, 1906

It may no longer be so cheap, nor do the attendants scrub your back, but a bath at the grand **Dōgo Onsen Honkan** (daily 6.30am–11pm) remains the highlight of any trip to Matsuyama. This is the oldest hot spring in Japan and is mentioned in the 1300-year-old book *Nihon-shoki*, one of the most ancient written histories of Japan. According to legend, a white heron dipped its

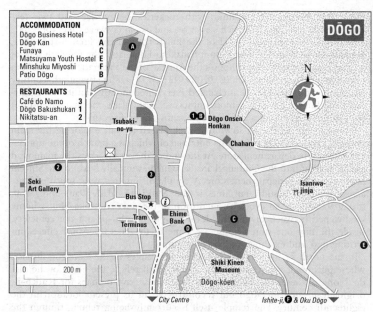

ACCOMMODATION
Dōgo Business Hotel   D
Dōgo Kan   A
Funaya   C
Matsuyama Youth Hostel E
Minshuku Miyoshi   F
Patio Dōgo   B

RESTAURANTS
Café do Namo   3
Dōgo Bakushukan   1
Nikitatsu-an   2

N

Tsubaki-no-yu

Dōgo Onsen Honkan

Chaharu

Seki Art Gallery

Isaniwa-jinja

Bus Stop

Tram Terminus

Ehime Bank

Shiki Kinen Museum

Dōgo-kōen

0   200 m

▼ City Centre   Ishite-ji, **F** & Oku Dōgo ▼

injured leg into the hot water gushing out of the rocks and found that it had healing properties. By the sixth century the onsen's fame reached the ears of Prince Shōtoku, and his royal patronage cemented its reputation, creating the first tourist town in Japan. By the seventeenth century the local *daimyō* Matsudaira Sadayuki had segregated the baths into those for monks and samurai and those for the lower-class merchants and craftsmen. He also introduced women-only baths and created facilities for animals to soak away their ills (the animal baths were only closed in 1966).

The present architectural extravaganza was built in 1894 and the heron, which has become the symbol of the baths, is commemorated in a statue astride the three-storey building's ornate roof. Inside there are two types of bath, plus the Yushinden, a special bath built in 1899 for the imperial family, but now drained of water. At the entrance you'll be confronted by a slightly bewildering range of prices – an English leaflet provides a basic explanation of what's on offer. The cheapest deal is to pay ¥300 to use the rather raucous **Kami-no-yu**, or "Hot Water of the Gods", a section with two identical baths, decorated with mosaics of the heron, on each side of the changing rooms. For ¥620 you still bathe in the Kami-no-yu, but get to relax afterwards in the second-floor public room, where you'll be served green tea and rice crackers, and you also get a towel and a cotton *yukata* robe – head here first to deposit your belongings before going to the bath. Pricier and more serene is the **Tama-no-yu** (Hot Water of the Spirits), a bath at the back of the complex, which costs ¥980 and gets fewer people. There's a view of a small garden from the changing room and you relax afterwards in a separate section on the second floor. Finally, the top price of ¥1240 entitles you to a **private room** on the third floor, where you'll be offered green tea and three-coloured *dango* (sweet rice dough balls on a stick) after your dip. This is the first-class experience recommended by the title character of *Botchan*, which relates the comic misadventures of a maths teacher posted from Tokyo to the countryside. The private room experience is still well worth the extra expense today.

Even if you opt for the no-frills bath, the staff will allow you to explore the rest of the building. On the second floor, look out for a display of tea-ceremony items and old calligraphy scrolls to the side of the large tatami resting room with carved wooden verandas. On the third floor, the corner room has a small exhibition (all in Japanese) of items related to *Botchan* and his creator **Sōseki**, one of Japan's most famous authors, whose portrait adorns the ¥1000 note. You'll need to return to the second floor to gain entrance to the **Yushinden** (daily 6.30am–9pm), for which you have to pay an extra ¥210. The bath has been empty since 1950 (it was only ever used ten times), but the imperial apartments, with their silver- and gilt-coated screens and ornamental gardens, have been preserved. You'll be guided around by one of the no-nonsense female attendants who'll explain, in Japanese, how the rooms were specially constructed to foil any would-be assassins.

A minute's walk along the arcade from the Honkan is the separate modern bathhouse **Tsubaki-no-yu** (daily 6.30am–11pm; ¥300), meaning "Hot Water of Camellia". The granite bath here is much larger than those at the Honkan and uses water from the same hot-spring source. You won't find so many tourists here; rather, elderly locals who take their bathing seriously.

Most of the top-class ryokan in Dōgo also have their own baths, some open to non-residents on weekdays only, including the *Dōgo Kan* (¥1500) and *Chaharu*, whose rooftop indoor and outdoor baths provide splendid views of the city, and where a dip for ¥1600 includes lunch, but must be booked a day in advance – see p.772 for addresses.

The most exotic baths can be found at **Oku Dōgo**, 4km towards the hills northeast of Dōgo, where the **Jungle Onsen** (daily 6am–10.30pm; ¥500) lives up to its name, offering no fewer than eleven different bathing pools in a botanical garden setting; there's even a sake bath, smelling a little too pungently of the rice liquor. Several pretty walks lead through the gardens beside the baths. Lengthy trellises bloom with lilac wisteria in May, and further up the valley is the golden temple of **Kinseiden**, a slightly tacky replica of Kyoto's famous Kinkaku-ji. Buses #52 and #53 (¥320) run out to Oku Dōgo roughly every hour from beside the Dōgo tram terminal.

Other sights

Just before Dōgo's old-fashioned tram terminus you'll pass **Dōgo-kōen**, a pleasantly landscaped park, built on the former site of Yuchiku-jō, the fourteenth-century castle of the Kono clan. The summit of the mound in the centre of the park gives a good view of the surrounding area. In the park's eastern corner is the **Shiki Kinen Museum** (Tues–Sun 9am–5pm; ¥300; ☎089/931-5566), which houses rather dry displays telling the life story – with English translations – of Masaoka Shiki (see box, p.767), and setting his literature in its cultural context. The bulky, ivory-coloured building with a curved copper roof is supposed to suggest a *kura*, the storehouse often attached to old Japanese homes.

Walking directly up the hill from the tram terminus, you'll see a flight of 140 old stone steps and lanterns leading up to the beautiful **Isaniwa-jinja**. It hardly feels appropriate that this captivating shrine, built by Matsudaira Sadanaga in 1667 and decorated with delicately painted carvings of animals, birds, plants and the sea, was once called Yuzuki Hachiman-gū and is still dedicated to Hachiman, the god of war. Returning to the Dōgo shopping arcade, take the first turning on the left along the arcade, and walk down past the beer and sake brewery to the **Seki Art Gallery** (Wed–Sun 10am–5pm; ¥500; ☎089/946-5678), a small museum containing the collection of a local printing tycoon which includes a room of sketches and a statue by Rodin, as well as some good examples of twentieth-century Japanese art.

Ishite-ji

Eight of the 88 temples on Shikoku's sacred circuit are in Matsuyama, but the most famous is the 51st, **Ishite-ji**, which gained its name from a legend involving Kōbō Daishi (see box opposite). Ishite-ji is one of the most memorable temples you're likely to visit, but not for the usual reasons. Unlike Shikoku's other 87 temples, Ishite-ji has used its accumulated wealth to branch out into surreal forms of religious expression. Tucked away behind the main temple buildings are dimly lit tunnels lined with hundreds of Buddhas and other icons. Condensation drips heavily from the tunnel ceiling if it's been raining, adding to the slightly foreboding atmosphere. Further on, in the tunnel which heads upwards, flashing fairy and strobe lights, activated as you approach, and the piped sound of a priest wailing mantras, create the impression that you've stumbled into an esoteric rave.

The main tunnel emerges from behind a rock on the hill above the temple, close to the entrance to a park containing more bizarre statues – and plenty of wild cats – at the centre of which is a squat, golden-domed 3-D mandala. Enter this circular hall and you'll be confronted by a two-hundred-strong congregation of wooden *jizō*, between 1m and 3m high, carved with Buddhist sexual symbols, and arranged in tiered circles. Oddly, while the main temple is usually heaving with pilgrims, very few bother to head up to the park, making it a nice place to relax for a few minutes and take in your unusual surroundings. Climbing up the slope from the mandala will lead to a large graveyard and, on the summit of the adjoining hill, the looming statue of Buddhist saint Kōbō Daishi, founder of Shikoku's pilgrim trail (see p.714).

Next to all this, the temple's classical Kamakura-era architecture, which includes a three-storey pagoda, seems almost mundane. Behind the main gate, Niō-mon, built in 1318, are two giant straw sandals, along with many normal-sized ones, left by pilgrims who hope to have their feet and leg ailments cured. There's also a drab **museum** (¥300) on the east side of the complex, where the temple's treasures are rather poorly presented.

To get to Ishite-ji, you can either walk for fifteen minutes east of the Dōgo tram terminus – stick to the main road, or cross the first small bridge on your left, which leads to a more scenic riverside approach to the temple – or hop on the #8 or #52 bus (¥160) to Oku Dōgo from the tram terminus, which will drop you outside the temple gate.

Eating, drinking and entertainment

Matsuyama is undoubtedly the best place for **eating** in Shikoku, with a wide range of restaurants, cafés and bars. You'll come across a number of local foods – all worth trying – including the sponge roly-poly cake called *taruto*, inspired by a Portuguese confection introduced to Japan 350 years ago through the port of Nagasaki; the three-coloured rice dumplings on sticks called *Botchan dango*, after the character's favourite sweet; and *goshiki sōmen*, thin noodles made in five colours. There are also plenty of fast-food options in the city centre along the shopping arcades, including *KFC*, *Mister Donuts*, a branch of the home-grown *Freshness Burger* chain and a branch of the cheap coffee shop *Doutor* on Gintengai.

Saburō Emon

There's a curious legend to explain how Ishite-ji gained its name, which involves **Saburō Emon**, a rapacious landlord, and **Kōbō Daishi**, whose saintly halo slips somewhat in the telling. Not knowing who the Daishi was, Saburō is said to have repeatedly refused to help the itinerant priest who came begging for food. On the eighth occasion, Saburō beat the priest and cast his begging bowl into the street, shattering it into eight pieces. The next day, Saburō's eldest son became mysteriously ill and died, and within the week his other seven sons had followed suit. Too late, Saburō realized that the monk was Kōbō Daishi and that he had exacted a terrible revenge. Desperate for salvation, he gave away all that he owned and went in search of the Daishi.

Over four years, Saburō circled Shikoku twenty times, but the Daishi always remained one step ahead of him. On the 21st circuit, Saburō, exhausted to the point of death, went in the opposite direction, hoping to meet the priest coming towards him. Daishi finally appeared and granted Saburō his dying wish to be reborn as a powerful man, so that he might do good works. The Daishi took a stone, wrote on it "Saburō Emon is reborn" and pressed it into the dying man's hand. Nine months later, the wife of the Lord of Iyo (present-day Ehime-ken) gave birth to a son whose fist was tightly clenched. When the baby's grip was eventually loosened, out fell the inscribed stone. In commemoration, the local temple was renamed Ishite-ji – "stone hand temple".

Matsuyama is also well served with places to **drink**. The tight grid of streets between Niban-chō and Sanban-chō in the centre heaves with bars and, in the summer, beer gardens sprout on the roofs of the *ANA*, *Chataeutel* and *Sunroute* hotels. Standard beer and nibbles joints include *München*, a German-style beer-hall, serving Sapporo beer. Many of the bars in Dōgo are pricey hostess joints and best avoided.

The **cinemas** on and around the Ōkaidō arcade show mainstream Hollywood and Japanese movies, while you can usually catch independent foreign films at Cinema Lunatic (℡089/933-9230), south of the city centre, close to the Tachibana-bashi across the river Ishite-gawa. Theatre, dance and orchestral performances are held at the Matsuyama City Hall (℡089/921-8222) and the Prefectural Cultural Centre (Kenmin Bunka Kaikan) (℡089/923-5111). Check the monthly *What's Going On?* booklet for details.

Restaurants and cafés

Café do Namo Dōgo. Artsy café, easily spotted halfway along the covered shopping arcade: it's in the stone igloo-like building with the wooden interior. The set lunches for ¥700 are good value.

Cappuccio 2-1-1 Ōkaido ℡089/946-0046. Cheap 'n' cheerful second-floor pizza 'n' pasta joint with an entrance on the Ōkaido arcade itself. Food is better than appearances may suggest, and the weekday lunchtime special is generously available until 3pm.

Castle Grill *ANA Hotel* ℡089/933-5511. This romantic restaurant serves European dishes, and has a lovely view of Katsuyama Hill and the Bansui-sō villa, especially when the buildings are spotlit at night.

Fishbone 2-5-10 Niban-chō ℡089/934-8445.

Cool dining bar a block east of Ōkaido with unusually shaped tables to complement the international fusion food, from Chinese to Italian. Open until 3am.

Goshiki 3-5-4 Sanban-chō ℡089/933-3838. Matsuyama's most famous place to sample *sōmen*, the five-coloured noodles. In front of the restaurant is a shop where you can buy the noodles, packed as souvenir sets from around ¥300. Lunchtime set menus start at ¥1100; noodles on their own are cheaper.

Indie's Kashi Mashi 2-1-1 Niban-chō ℡089/913-0769. Drag yourself away from the rather synthetic collection of cakes in the upstairs café and enjoy the funky *izakaya* downstairs serving pizza, pasta and other nibbles along with beer and cocktails. Open until 4am.

Kawasemi 2-5-18 Niban-chō ☎089/933-9697. Avant-garde *kaiseki* (Japanese haute cuisine) restaurant. The portions are small, but your taste buds will be subtly challenged. Look for the world "club" in English on the mauve sign and go up to the second floor. Best visited for lunch (around ¥1500); dinner is a more expensive affair.

Kani Dōraku 2-6-3 Ichiban-chō ☎089/941-2448. Branch of the nationwide chain specializing in crab, but also serving other seafood dishes. Hard to miss due to the giant crab sign on the side of the building.

Le Mas de Provence 6-23 Minami-Horibata-chō ☎089/998-2811. Saucy postcards on the wall, wooden beams and excellent French country cooking all under the careful eye of masterful French chef Phillip. The set lunches for ¥1000 are a taster of the delights on offer at dinner, which averages ¥4000 without drinks.

Nikitatsu-an Dōgo Shitamachi ☎089/924-6617. Seating is on tatami in a contemporary setting,

and the imaginative modern Japanese cooking complements the local beer. The set meals (lunch starts at ¥1000) include a range of tasty morsels, beautifully presented on a wicker plate, and accompanied by special rice and soup. There's also an outdoor deck for quaffing beer on balmy nights.

Paradiso 1-10-1 Niban-chō ☎089/941-5077. Occupying two corner spots facing each other, this highly rated pizzeria and bar is open 5pm–3am and has some outdoor tables.

Rareki 5-9 Hanazono-machi ☎089/948-0885. Indian-run Indian restaurant serving great curries and huge, freshly baked nan breads. Fill up for around ¥1000.

Rue de Bac 5-5-5 Minato-machi ☎089/932-6505. A favourite Parisian café was the inspiration for this appealing restaurant and wine bar, set up by a freelance photographer. The menu, flitting from Vietnamese spring rolls to pasta, reflects the rest of his travels. On the second floor opposite the Sogō department store.

Bars and clubs

Club Bibros Niban-chō. Small dance club, three blocks east of Ōkaido. The cover charge varies depending on the event (hip-hop to techno) and they sometimes host all-you-can-drink parties.

Dōgo Bakushukan Opposite Dōgo Onsen Honkan ☎089/924-6617. An *izakaya* owned by the same independent brewery that runs Nikutatsu-an (see above). The three beers to try are the Botchan lager, a stout and the slightly sweet Madonna ale – all very refreshing after an onsen dip.

Jett Rockbar 1-8-4 Niban-chō ☎089/933-0001. The place to go if you want to hear some down 'n' dirty rock 'n' roll. The popular basement bar (open until 4am) also stages the occasional rock-style club event.

Murasaki Niban-chō. Look for the large red lantern hanging outside this appealingly ramshackle *izakaya* near the Ōkaidō. There's a picture menu and it's popular with a young, lively Japanese crowd.

Sara Sol Ciel Biru, 2-3-5 Sanban-chō. Top-floor bar that serves Thai food in the early evenings and serves as a popular hangout for the foreign community. Open until 4am.

Underground Café 3-3-6 Ōkaido. Retro-chic café-bar on the way to the castle chairlift, with a very laid-back vibe. The food is reasonable and there's a happy hour 5–7pm, plus occasional club events. Closed second and fourth Wednesday of month. Open until 4am.

Listings

Airlines ANA, 5 Minato-machi ☎089/948-3131; JAL, 4 Chifune-machi ☎0120-25-5971.

Banks and exchange Ehime Ginkō has several branches in downtown Matsuyama. There's also a branch by the Dōgo tram terminus.

Bookshops Kinokuniya, 5-7-1 Chifune-machi, has an extensive range of English books and magazines on the fourth floor (daily 10am–7.30pm).

Car rental Budget Rent-a-Car has a branch at the airport (☎089/974-3733).

Hospital and clinics The central prefectural hospital, Ehime Kenritsu Chūō Byōin (☎089/947-1111), is in Kasuga-machi, south of the Shi-eki Station.

Internet access There's free Internet access at the *Matsuyama Youth Hostel*, if you're staying there. Otherwise the best deal is at COMS, 6-4-20 Sanbanchō; go to the second-floor library and sign up at the desk. It's ¥100 per hour (Tues–Sat 9am–8.30pm, Sun 9am–5pm).

Laundry Okaya Coin Laundry, 43 Minami-Mochida (daily 6am–10.30pm).

Police The main police station is at 2 Minami Horibata (☎089/941-0111). Emergency numbers are listed in "Basics" on p.81.

Post office Matsuyama's main post office is at 3 Sanban-chō (Mon–Fri 9am–7pm, Sat 9am–5pm & Sun 9am–12.30pm). There's also a branch in Dōgo

(Mon–Fri 9am–5pm), to the west of the shopping arcade.

Shopping Local products to look out for include *iyo-gasuri*, an indigo dyed cloth; *hime temari*, colourful thread-covered balls that bring good luck; and *Tobe-yaki*, distinctive blue-patterned pottery. Check out the Ōkaidō and Gintengai arcades for souvenir shops. Also try the Mitsukoshi and Sogō department stores. There's a branch of Muji, the trendy, no-brand goods shop, in the Laforet building next to Mitsukoshi. Hamashō, a large shop specializing in basket-weaving, is close by Ishite-ji, on the way from Dōgo. *Tobe-yaki* pottery is distinguished by its robust feel and simple blue-and-white glaze. The centre of the local pottery industry is Tobe-cho, 13km from Matsuyama. Take a bus here from the Shi-eki station (45min; ¥650) to visit the Tobe-yaki Kankō Centre (☎089/962

2070), where you can watch pottery being made and make or decorate some pieces yourself. Modelling 1kg of clay costs ¥1500, while glazing ready-made plates and cups starts from ¥600.

Sports There's an open-air public swimming pool in the park beside EPIC (closest tram stop is Shiyakusho-mae; open July & Aug only; ¥200). Otherwise, try the pool at the Matsuyama Municipal Community Centre (¥100 per hr; daily 9am–9pm).

Taxis Hinomaru Taxi ☎089/946-1123 and Ehime Kintetsu Taxi ☎089/924-8112 are two of the city's bigger taxi firms.

Travel agents For cheap international flights, try HIS, Yasui Biru 3-2, Hanazono-machi ☎089/931 6121. For domestic travel arrangements, JTB's main office (English spoken) is at 4-12-10 Sanban-chō ☎089/931-2281.

Kashima and Imabari

Around thirty minutes by train north along the coast from Matsuyama is **Hojo** (JR station Iyo-Hojo), a small fishing port that is the jumping-off spot for **KASHIMA**, a tiny island park that's a favourite getaway for locals. The island is so close to the mainland you could swim there, but if that doesn't appeal there's a regular ferry (¥300 return). Once on Kashima, you can climb to the summit of Mount Takanawa (986m), a forested hillock, watching out for the wild deer that give the island its name. There are beaches, but they're nothing much to rave about, although the view from the far side of the island out to the shrine Futami-no-Iyo, strung across three rocks, is picturesque. Kashima's basically a place to relax, especially during the week, when you're likely to have it pretty much to yourself save for a few fishermen.

The other good reason to come here is the *Hojosuigun Youth Hostel* (☎089/992-4150, ✪www.hojosuigun.com; ¥2500 per person), a stone's throw from the ferry landing. A small and appealing place run by the English-speaking Sakate-san, the hostel has both tatami and bunk rooms and you can get fresh fish dinners for ¥1000. There's also free Internet access. If you're looking for somewhere quiet, but within easy reach of Matsuyama, this is ideal.

The next major town, **IMABARI**, perched on Shikoku's northwest coast 45km from Matsuyama, is the access point to the larger and more interesting Inland Sea islands of Ōmi-shima and Ikuchi-jima (see p.647 & 650), via the nearby **Kurushima bridge**, part of the Nishi-Seto Expressway linking Honshū to Shikoku. Imabari itself is nothing special, but it does have a rare example of a castle in an open field: **Imabari-jō**, built in 1604 by local warlord Tōdō Takatora. The present buildings date from 1980, but are surrounded by the original moat. Inside the castle grounds is an attractive shrine with lots of red-painted *torii*, while the keep contains a rather musty museum (daily 9am–4.30pm; ¥300; ☎0898/31-9233), displaying armour and painted screens, plus a natural history section with local rocks, embalmed fish and stuffed birds. The castle is a ten-minute walk from JR Imabari Station.

Maps and booklets on the area are available at the helpful **tourist information** centre (daily 9am–5pm; no English spoken) inside the JR station.

Ishizuchi-san

Some 25km further east along the coast from Imabari is **Saijō** (JR station Iyo-Saijō), the main access point for **ISHIZUCHI-SAN**, Shikoku's tallest mountain and a sacred place of pilgrimage. Legend has it that the 1982-metre mountain was first climbed in 682 by En no Ozuno, a *yamabushi*, or mountain ascetic, while Kōbō Daishi undertook the hike in 797. Ishizuchi's temple, **Ōhō-ji**, in the valley below the mountain, is the sixtieth on the pilgrimage route. Saijō itself is known for the purity of its groundwater, which bubbles up through some two thousand *uchinuki* springs. No wonder the beer giant Asahi has opened a new brewery in the city.

At one time, the mountain was climbed only by male pilgrims – women were strictly forbidden from setting foot on it. This tradition is still upheld for the annual official opening ceremony on July 1, when *yamabushi*, dressed in white robes and blowing on conch shells, hike up to the shrine at the summit. It's possible to scale the mountain from April, once the winter snow has melted, but the climbing season officially runs from July until the end of August and there are more frequent bus connections to the trails during this time, enabling you to get up and down the mountain in a day, as long as you set off early from Matsuyama.

The Ishizuchi Quasi National Park, in which the mountain stands, was established in 1955 and has several hiking trails, plus limited skiing in the winter. The relatively warm climate means there are trees on the slopes of the mountain, almost to the summit. There's a **cable car** (times vary throughout year: at least 9am–4pm; Jan–April Mon–Fri 2–6pm, Sat & Sun 9am–5pm; ¥1000 one way, ¥1900 return) at **Nishi-no-Kawa**, which cuts out some of the foot-slogging, taking you to within three hours' hike of the top. A short walk from the cable car is a **chair lift** (late April to early Nov; ¥300 one way, ¥450 return), which saves a little bit more effort on the way up to **Jōju**, where you'll find the **Ishizuchi-jinja** shrine, plus several places to eat and buy souvenirs. There are good views from here, if you don't wish to go any further.

The 3.5-kilometre route from Jōju to the summit is clearly marked. Along the way are several spots where *kusari*, thick metal chains, have been hammered into the rock to help you climb. If this doesn't appeal there's always a marginally easier walking path. Most people stop at the mountain-top shrine (beside which, during the climbing season, is a refreshments hut), but the official summit is the even higher peak of Tengu-dake, approached along a razor-edge ridge, about ten minutes away. If you don't want to retrace your steps, there's an alternative route down the mountain to **Tsuchigoya**, from where infrequent buses (you might have to change buses at Mimido) run back to Matsuyama.

Plenty of trains from Matsuyama go to Iyo-Saijō, on the Yosan line, from where it's a 55-minute bus ride (¥970) to Nishi-no-Kawa via the scenic Omogo-kei gorge (the first bus is at 7.41am; the next isn't until 10.23am). Alternatively, the Iyo Railway company in Matsuyama offers a return bus ticket, via Tsuchigoya, for ¥4700, available at the Shi-eki station. The one-way fare for the approximately three-hour journey is ¥2680, and if you want to get to the summit and back in a day you'll need to be on the first bus at 8am. The last bus back to Matsuyama from Tsuchigoya is at 4.30pm, but double-check this before setting out.

Standard Japanese **meals**, such as noodles and curry rice, are available at various mountain huts and in the tourist restaurants at Nishi-no-Kawa, Jōju and Tsuchigoya, but generally you'd do better to pack a picnic and enjoy it at the summit. If you do choose to eat on the mountain, Jōju's *Shiraishi Ryokan* (☏ 0897/59-0032; ❹) serves decent food and is also a reasonable place to bunk down in large tatami rooms (¥5000 per person, or from ¥8000, including two meals).

Travel details

Trains

The trains between the major cities listed below are the fastest, direct services. There are also frequent slower services, run by JR and several private companies, covering the same destinations. It is usually possible, especially on long-distance routes, to get there faster by changing between services.

Kōchi to: Awa Ikeda (16 daily; 1hr 5min); Kotohira (16 daily; 1hr 30min); Nakamura (8 daily; 1hr 50min); Okayama (14 daily; 2hr 25min); Takamatsu (5 daily; 2hr 15min).

Matsuyama to: Okayama (14 daily; 2hr 45min); Takamatsu (17 daily; 2hr 30min); Uwajima (15 daily; 1hr 20min).

Takamatsu to: Matsuyama (16 daily; 2hr 30min); Kōchi (6 daily; 2hr 5min); Kotohira (20 daily; 1hr); Okayama (every 30min; 1hr); Tokushima (15 daily; 1hr 15min); Uwajima (1 daily; 4hr).

Tokushima to: Awa Ikeda (6 daily; 1hr 10min); Kaifu (3 daily; 1hr 40min); Naruto (14 daily; 40min); Takamatsu (15 daily; 1hr 15min).

Uwajima to: Kubokawa (6 daily; 2hr); Matsuyama (16 daily; 1hr 20min).

Buses

Kōchi to: Okayama (9 daily; 2hr 30min); Ōsaka (12 daily; 5hr 35min); Tokyo (1 daily; 11hr 40min).

Matsuyama to: Kōchi (11 daily; 2hr 30min); Okayama (6 daily; 2hr 50min); Onomichi (2 daily; 2hr 30min); Ōsaka (4 daily; 7hr); Takamatsu (11 daily; 2hr 35min); Tokyo (1 daily; 12hr); Tokushima (4 daily; 3hr 25min).

Takamatsu to: Kōchi (13 daily; 2hr); Matsuyama (11 daily; 2hr 35min); Tokyo (1 daily; 11hr); Yokohama (1 daily; 10hr 30min).

Tokushima to: Awaji-shima/Tsuna (6 daily; 1hr 30min); Ōsaka (21 daily; 3hr 10min); Takamatsu (8 daily; 2hr); Tokyo (2 daily; 10hr 40min).

Ferries

Ashizuri to: Ōsaka (3 weekly; 16hr 30min).
Kōchi to: Ōsaka (1 daily; 9hr 10min).
Imabari to: Hiroshima (5 daily; 1hr 50min); Kōbe (2 daily; 7hr 10min).
Matsuyama to: Aga (18 daily; 1hr 50min); Beppu (daily; 2hr 25min); Hiroshima (hydrofoil; 16 daily; 1hr 10min; ferry, 10 daily; 2hr 40min); Iwakuni (4 daily; 1hr 20min); Kōbe (3 daily; 9hr); Kokura (daily; 7hr); Oita (daily; 3hr 25min); Yanai (18 daily; 2hr 20min).
Sukumo to: Saeki (6 daily; 2hr 45min).
Takamatsu to: Kōbe (hydrofoil: 2 daily; 2hr 20min; ferry: 5 daily; 3hr 40min); Megijima (6 daily; 20min); Naoshima (5 daily; 1hr); Ōsaka (2 daily; 3hr 5min); Shōdoshima (hydrofoil, 17 daily; 30min; ferry, 33 daily; 1hr); Uno (50 daily; 1hr).
Tokushima to: Kansai International Airport (9 daily; 3hr 15min); Kitakyūshū (daily; 17hr); Tokyo (daily; 17hr 30min); Wakayama (12 daily; hydrofoil 1hr, ferry 2hr).
Uwajima to: Beppu (6 daily; 2hr 30min).

Flights

Kōchi to: Fukuoka (3 daily; 50min); Nagoya (3 daily; 1hr); Naha (daily; 1hr 45min); Miyazaki (2 daily; 45min); Ōsaka (7–10 daily; 40min); Tokyo (9 daily; 1hr 25min).
Matsuyama to: Fukuoka (2 daily; 45min); Kagoshima (2 daily; 1hr); Miyazaki (daily; 55min); Nagoya (3 daily; 1hr 25min); Naha (daily; 1hr 55min); Ōsaka (11 daily; 50min); Sapporo (daily; 2hr); Seoul (2 weekly; 1hr 30min); Tokyo (10 daily; 1hr 30min).
Takamatsu to: Fukuoka (daily; 1hr 10min); Kagoshima (daily; 1hr 15min); Nagoya (2 daily; 1hr); Naha (1 daily; 2hr 5min); Sapporo (daily; 2hr); Sendai (daily; 1hr 20min); Tokyo (10 daily; 1hr 20min).
Tokushima to: Fukuoka (2 daily; 1hr 40min); Nagoya (2 daily; 1hr); Tokyo (7 daily; 1hr 15min).

Kyūshū

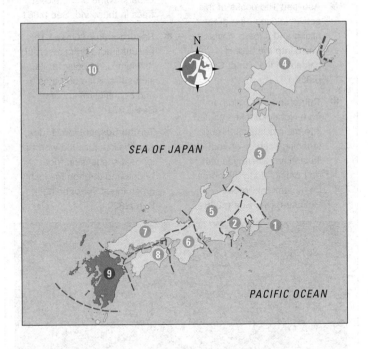

N

SEA OF JAPAN

PACIFIC OCEAN

CHAPTER 9

Highlights

* **Fukuoka** Slurp a bowl of ramen noodles at one of the open-air *yatai* stalls along the Tenjin river. See p.790

* **Dazaifu** Enjoy a gourmet meal based entirely around tofu at the renowned Ume-no-hana restaurant. See p.800

* **Aso-san** The peaks of this active volcano offer great hiking and superb views down into the largest caldera in the world. See p.834

* **Takachiho** The train ride from Nobeoka takes you up into the mountains through stunning scenery en route to Takachiho, where you can go boating along the gorge on the emerald-green Gokase-gawa. See p.838

* **Furusato Onsen** Take a *yukata*-clad soak at this sacred hot spring on Sakurajima, dedicated to a local dragon god. See p.854

* **Yakushima** Go hiking in the rainiest place in Japan, through lush green forests up to the ancient *yaku-sugi* cedars, some of the oldest trees in the world. See p.861

* **Sakura-sakura Onsen** This beautiful hot-spring resort in Kirishima is popular for its skin-softening mud baths and beautiful rotemburo. See p.871

* **Teruha Suspension Bridge, Aya** Walk across the world's longest suspension foot-bridge and through the lush green forest surrounding it. See p.880

△ Sakurajima

9

Kyūshū

apan's third largest island, **KYŪSHŪ**, lies off the south end of Honshū, surrounded by a spray of smaller islands which trail off in a long arc across the East China Sea. It's a relaxed, uncomplicated place, with its own distinctive character and enough variety to make it a feasible holiday destination on its own. Though Kyūshū has no absolutely compelling sights, there's something for everyone here, from dynamic cities to ancient folk dances, grumbling volcanoes and steaming hot-spring baths. It's perfectly possible to scoot round the main cities in a week, but you'll need more like two to do it justice, allowing time for the splendid mountainous interior and a few of the more far-flung islands.

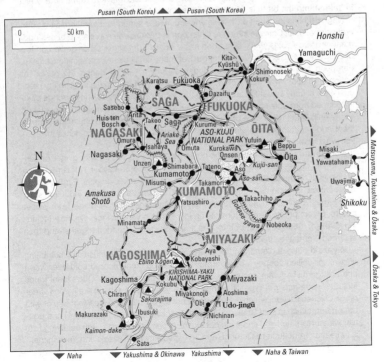

This area has long had close links with the Asian mainland, and Kyūshū's chief city, **Fukuoka**, is again becoming an important regional hub. An energetic city on the island's heavily developed north coast, most people pass Fukuoka by, but it's a shame to miss out on its superb modern architecture and vibrant nightlife. If you've only got a couple of days on Kyūshū, however, **Nagasaki** represents the best all-round destination. Though its prime draw is the A–Bomb museum and related sights, the city also has a picturesque harbour setting, a laid-back, cosmopolitan air and a spattering of temples and historical museums. From here it's a short hop east to **Kumamoto**, famous for its castle and landscaped garden, and the empty, rolling uplands of central Kyūshū beyond. Dominated by the spluttering, smouldering cone of **Aso-san**, this is great hiking country, while hot-spring enthusiasts will also be in their element – from **Kurokawa Onsen's** delightful rotemburo to the bawdy pleasures of Beppu on the east coast. The mountain village of **Takachiho** requires a fair detour, but it's worth it for the thrilling train ride along the Gokase gorge and to see traditional dance performances depicting the antics of Japan's ancient gods.

Kyūshū cuisine

Kyūshū, like the rest of Japan, is full of local specialities. The ubiquitous ramen can be enjoyed in several varieties: **Fukuoka** is famous for its hundreds of *yatai* stalls serving Hakata-ramen, noodles in a thick pork broth, and somehow the experience of eating outdoors at a tarpaulin-covered street stall just adds to the flavour. In **Kumamoto** you'll find *takana*-ramen, where the noodles are served in a garlicky soup with a healthy dollop of pickled *takana*, a vegetable native to Kumamoto, while in **Yakushima** the broth is flavoured with smoked fish.

Nagasaki has long had a Chinese enclave, and is famed for *champon*, sara udon and *shippoku*, all Chinese in origin. *Champon* is thick noodles in a soup of seafood, meat and vegetables, while sara udon has a similar but thicker sauce served on top of crispy noodles. *Shippoku* is a banquet of many small dishes combining Chinese, European and Japanese flavours. Sugar, a rarity in Japan during the period of national isolation, was easily obtained in the port town of Nagasaki, so many dishes have a slightly sweet flavour. It's also the home of Castella, a honey-sponge cake introduced from Spain by Portuguese cooks in the sixteenth century, and popular as a souvenir. **Ōita** is the home of *dango-jiru*, thick flat noodles in a tasty rustic soup of meat and vegetables, and of *seki-saba*, sashimi of mackerel whose necks are broken when caught to preserve the freshest of flavours.

Kumamoto is known for *basashi*, horsemeat sashimi, served with ginger or garlic – low in cholesterol, it's prized for its melt-in-the-mouth flavour. Kumamoto also prides itself on the quality of its rice, and has many fine sakes on offer. Further south, **Kagoshima** is Japan's biggest producer of *shōchū*, a hangover-inducing spirit sometimes made from rice, though Kagoshima's speciality is made from sweet potato. Sweet potato also features as an ingredient in various local sweets – including *karukan*, made of sweet potato, rice flour and sugar, kneaded together and then steamed – and even in ice cream.

Miyazaki offers a plethora of local flavours, one of its most unusual dishes being *hiyajiru*, or chilled soup – a concentrated miso soup stock poured cold over warm rice and garnished with cucumber, seaweed and spring onions. Other local foods include *hyūga natsu*, a type of orange where you eat the pith as well; *jidori*, free-range chicken *yakitori*, which is very chewy but full of taste; and *inoshishi niku* or wild boar meat, which is said to warm the body – *shishi nabe* (wild boar stew) is a popular winter dish, and you can even get *inoshishi* curry rice. Finally, *tobiuo* (flying fish) is in season from June to October, and is a speciality of Miyazaki and Yakushima.

The island's southern districts contain more on the same theme – volcanoes, onsen and magnificent scenery. Highlights include **Sakurajima**, one of the world's most active volcanoes, which looms over the city of **Kagoshima**, while nearby **Chiran** was a World War II air base for kamikaze pilots, who are the subject of a somewhat perturbing museum. After this, the perfect tonic is provided by the lush island of **Yakushima**, roughly 100km south of Kyūshū, designated a World Heritage Site in honour of its towering, thousand-year-old cedar trees.

Kyūshū is connected to Honshū by road and rail. **Trains** on the Tōkaidō Shinkansen terminate in Fukuoka's Hakata Station and are covered by JR West's Sanyō Area Pass. From Hakata, JR Kyūshū trains fan out to all the major cities, and the company offers its own five- and seven-day **rail passes** (¥15,000 and ¥20,000) for travelling round the island. These allow unlimited travel on all local, limited express and express trains, but not the Shinkansen or JR buses, and you have to buy the exchange voucher before arriving in Japan; see p.37 for more on JR passes and discount tickets.

In the central uplands and southern Kyūshū, however, you'll be more reliant on **local buses**, particularly in the south, and a limited number of private train lines. For exploring these more remote areas, car rental is an excellent option – as elsewhere in Japan, there are **car rental** outlets in almost every town and in all the main tourist areas.

Some history

The ancient chronicles state that **Emperor Jimmu**, considered to be Japan's first emperor, set out from southern Kyūshū to found the Japanese nation in 660 BC. Though the records are open to dispute, there's evidence of human habitation on Kyūshū from before the tenth century BC, and by the beginning of the Yayoi period (300 BC–300 AD) the small kingdom of **Na** was trading with China and Korea. Local merchants brought rice-farming and bronze-making techniques back to Japan, while in the twelfth century monks introduced Zen Buddhism to northern Kyūshū. Less welcome visitors arrived in 1274 and 1281 during the **Mongol invasions** under Kublai Khan. The first ended in a narrow escape when the Mongols withdrew, and the shogun ordered a protective wall to be built around Hakata Bay. By 1281 the Japanese were far better prepared, but their real saviour was a typhoon, subsequently dubbed *kami kaze*, or "wind of the gods", which whipped up out of nowhere and scattered the Mongol fleet on the eve of their massed assault.

Three hundred years later, in 1543, the first **Europeans** to reach Japan pitched up on the island of Tanegashima, off southern Kyūshū. Finding an eager market for their guns among the local *daimyō*, the Portuguese sailors returned a few years later, bringing with them **missionaries**, among them the Jesuit priest Francis Xavier. Within fifty years the Catholic Church, now also represented by Spanish Franciscans and Dominicans, was claiming some 600,000 Christian converts. The centre of activity was **Nagasaki**, where Chinese, Dutch and British merchants swelled the throng. In the early 1600s, however, the government grew increasingly wary of the Europeans in general and Christians in particular. By fits and starts successive shoguns stamped down on the religion and restricted the movement of all foreigners, until eventually only two small communities of Dutch and Chinese merchants were left in Nagasaki.

This period of isolation lasted until the mid-1850s, when Nagasaki and Kagoshima in particular found themselves at the forefront of the modernizing revolution which swept Japan after the **Meiji Restoration**. Indeed, it was the armies of the Satsuma and Chōshū clans, both from Kyūshū, which helped restore the emperor to the throne, and many members of the new government hailed from the island. In 1877, however, Kagoshima's **Saigō Takamori** led a revolt against the Meiji government in what became known as the **Satsuma Rebellion**. Saigō's army was routed, but he's still something of a local hero in Kyūshū, where they pride themselves in being different from the rest of Japan – perhaps not surprising, considering Kyūshū is closer to Korea than Tokyo.

North Kyūshū

Kyūshū's five northern prefectures (Fukuoka, Saga, Nagasaki, Kumamoto and Ōita) contain the bulk of the island's population, industry and economic power. Though coal-mining and shipbuilding, the region's traditional money-earners, have been in slow decline for many years, there's been a massive boom in electronics industries – Kyūshū now produces ten percent of the world's semiconductors and has been dubbed "silicon island". Nowhere is this renewed optimism more visible than in **Fukuoka**, with its high-tech research centres reflected in futuristic urban renewal projects, but the upturn is also visible in other cities such as Kita-Kyūshū and Kumamoto.

But north Kyūshū isn't just about industry. Its ragged western shores, from Fukuoka round to **Nagasaki's** misshapen headland and down through the Amakusa Islands, display magnificent stretches of coastal scenery. From here you could strike east via **Unzen-dake**, one of Kyūshū's several active volcanoes, to the castle-town of **Kumamoto**. This is the main jumping-off point for exploring **Aso-san's** vast caldera, which dominates the island's wild, relatively empty central highlands. Most people then continue on to **Beppu**, on Kyūshū's east coast, where bathing is taken to such an extreme that it's earned the accolade of Japan's hot-spring capital. Further south, on the edge of the central highlands, the isolated village of **Takachiho** is accessible from either Aso or Beppu. It's a bit of a trek, but the effort is amply rewarded with a dramatic journey and the opportunity to see lively folk dances recalling the ancient gods and goddesses.

Kita-Kyūshū

A narrow strip of water little more than 1km wide separates Kyūshū from the southern tip of Honshū. Three tunnels and a soaring suspension bridge funnel road and rail traffic south from Shimonoseki into the sprawling, industrial conurbation of **KITA-KYŪSHŪ**. Most people travel straight through to Fukuoka (see p.790), but if you're arriving by ferry or changing trains for Beppu and other east-coast towns, you may need to make an overnight stop here. Kita-Kyūshū was created in 1963 out of five towns, of which Kokura is the largest. Here you'll find the city's main train station, administrative offices, the majority of its hotels and ferries to Matsuyama (Shikoku). Neighbouring **Yahata**, however, offers the area's cheapest accommodation, while over on the east coast **Shin-Moji-kō** now serves as the area's main ferry terminal.

Kita-Kyūshū

Kita-Kyūshū	*Kita-Kyūshū*	北九州
Kokura	*Kokura*	小倉
Chisan Hotel	*Chisan Hoteru*	チサンホテル
Kurofune	*Kurofune*	黒舟
Rihga Royal Hotel	*Riiga Roiyaru Hoteru*	リーガロイヤルホテル
Ryokan Hanosō	*Ryokan Hanosō*	旅館葉尾荘
Yutaka Business Hotel	*Yutaka Bijinesu Hoteru*	ユタカビジネスホテル
Shin-Moji-kō	*Shin-Moji-kō*	新門司港
Yahata	*Yahata*	八幡
Gusto	*Gasuto*	ガスト
Kisaragi	*Kisaragi*	きさらぎ
Kita-Kyūshū Youth Hostel	*Kita-Kyūshū Yūsu Hosuteru*	北九州ユースホステル

Despite its industrial surroundings, central **Kokura** is not an unattractive place. It has a small but lively downtown area south of Kokura JR Station, while the northern, port-side districts are catching up fast. It also boasts the area's only notable sight, the reconstructed castle of **Kokura-jō** (daily: April–Oct 9am–6pm; Jan–March, Nov & Dec till 5pm; ¥350), twenty minutes' walk west of the station. Built in the mid-seventeenth century, the castle was home to the Ogasawara clan for two hundred years until they were forced to abandon it in 1866. It then lay in ruins until 1959 when the keep was rebuilt in the original style, including its distinctive, overhanging fifth floor. While it's now all concrete inside, it's worth venturing in to see a scale model of seventeenth-century Kokura peopled by 1500 paper figures, full of life and energy despite their diminutive size; use the knee-high telescopes to take a closer look.

Practicalities

Kita-Kyūshū's main **train station** is the new Kokura Station, a stop on the Shinkansen between Tokyo and Fukuoka, where you can pick up trains to Beppu and Miyazaki. **Ferries** from Matsuyama (Shikoku) pull in at the Sunatsu pier, a five-minute walk north of Kokura Station. Boats from Kōbe, Ōsaka and Tokushima (also on Shikoku) use Shin-Moji-kō over on the east coast; from the port there's a free shuttle bus to Kokura, or alternatively take a taxi (around ¥2000) to JR Moji Station, then a train (6min; ¥200) to Kokura. There's a **tourist information** booth (daily 9am–6pm; ☏ & ℗093/541-4189) beside the ticket barrier at the station's north exit where you can make hotel reservations and get basic information in English. For anything more complicated, try the **Kita-Kyūshū International Association** desk (Mon–Fri 9am–5.30pm; ☏093/551-0555) on the ground floor of the distinctive modern Conference Centre, next to Sunatsu pier. At weekends, only their **main office** in Yahata is open (Tues–Sun 9am–5.30pm; ☏093/662-0055); it's in a black-glass building about ten minutes' walk south of Yahata Station. Overseas visitors are eligible for the **Kitak-yūshū Welcome Card** which entitles the holder to various discounts at hotels, restaurants, shops and attractions. The card is available at all the tourist offices listed above – you'll need to show your passport – and comes with a booklet outlining the various discounts on offer.

You'll find a clutch of middle- and top-end **hotels** immediately north of Kokura Station, including the *Rihga Royal Hotel* (☏093/531-1121, ℗521-2068; ➐), behind the Laforet department store – its deluxe, top-floor tower rooms are the work of Japanese designer Hanae Mori. In the next block east, the new *Chisan Hotel* (℡093/531-4000, ℱ531-5120; ❺) is a more straightforward business hotel offering well-appointed, comfortable rooms at reasonable rates. The *Yutaka Business Hotel* (℡093/511-0101, ℱ511-0120; ❹) is decidedly functional but represents about the best budget accommodation in central Kokura; it's located two blocks west of the Laforet store, overlooking the station car parks. Otherwise, hop down the line to Yahata, where you'll find the *Ryokan Hanosō* (℡093/671-3617, ℱ661-2160; ❹), three blocks south of the station. *Kita-Kyūshū Youth Hostel* (℡093/681-8142; ❶) lies further south past Kita-Kyūshū International Centre, over the expressway and then up to the Sarakura-yama cable-car station on the hillside – the hostel is the low, white building hidden among trees to the right, 25 minutes' walk from Yahata Station. Alternatively, a taxi will cost about ¥600.

The warren of streets south of Kokura Station is a good area to trawl for **restaurants**. One of the most atmospheric places is *Kurofune* (daily 5–11pm), a giant *izakaya* where you can wash down the local speciality, *karashi mentaiko* (salted cods' roe marinated in salt and red pepper), with a jar or two of beer. To find it, walk south from the station down the main road, Mikage-dōri, till you spot its large, black triangular sign on the corner opposite Quest bookstore. South of Tobata Station (between Kokura and Yahata Stations), you'll find lots of restaurants serving steaming bowls of *champon*, thick noodles laced with deep-fried chicken chunks, or sizzling hot plates of *yakisoba* for ¥700–900. Out on the ring road south of Yahata Station (walk past Kita-Kyūshū International Centre and turn right) are two more reasonable restaurants: *Kisaragi*, on the left next to a golf-driving range, serves well-priced Japanese sets from ¥700, while a bit further along is *Gusto* family restaurant, offering everything from sandwiches to *tonkatsu*. There's 24-hour **Internet** access at Media Café in the Laforet department store just north of the station (¥460 per hour including free drinks).

Fukuoka

A big, semi-industrial city at the southern end of the Shinkansen, **FUKUOKA** was until recently simply a place to negotiate as quickly as possible en route to Kyūshū's more picturesque regions. However, over the last few years it has established itself as western Japan's major cultural centre and an important international gateway. Though not a huge place (just under 1.3 million people), the city combines tremendous vitality with a determination to make the rest of Japan sit up and take notice – already it claims the country's biggest hotel, longest bar, largest cinema complex and most advanced baseball stadium. For the visitor this translates into a thoroughly modern city with all the energy and atmosphere of a Tokyo or Ōsaka, contained within manageable proportions.

Though Fukuoka offers few historical sights, it does have one or two excellent museums plus more than enough outstanding modern architecture to justify at least a day in transit. The highlights are **Canal City** (ⓦwww.canalcity.co.jp), a sparkling new self-contained cinema, hotel and shopping complex built around a semicircular strip of water, and **Hawks Town** (ⓦwww.hawkstown.com), which forms part of a major seafront redevelopment incorporating a shopping mall, over fifty eateries, beach, cinema and amusement arcade (see p.797). The city is also renowned for its festivals and folk crafts, which are presented at **Hakata Machiya Folk Museum**. As with any self-respecting

FUKUOKA

▲ Fukuoka Airport

◄ Kita-Kyūshū & Tōkyō

◄ Kita-Kyūshū

◄ Kaizuka

Okinawa & South Korea ▲

HAKATA-KU

KAGOSHIMA LINE

Nagasaki & Kumamoto ▶

Dazaifu ▶

Hakata Station

ℹ️

E

C

B Gion

Hakata Machiya Furusato-kan

Kushida-jinja

F

Canal City

Naka-gawa

Hakata-wan

Hakata Asian Art Museum

Hakata Futō Ferry Terminals

S

G

H

NAKASU

Nakasu

Kawabata

Akarenga Cultural Centre

Tenjin

ACROS Fukuoka

IMS Building

Nishitetsu Fukuoka

WATANABE-DŌRI

I

J

NISHITETSU-OMUTA LINE

D

2 3

4

5

6

Akasaka

TENJIN NISHI-DŌRI

10

11

Aratsu Ōhashi

SHOWA-DŌRI

MEIJI-DŌRI

Ōhori-kōen

Ōhori-kōen

Fukuoka Castle

Fukuoka-shi Bijutsukan

CHŪŌ-KU

Tōjin-machi

9

KYŪSHŪ | Fukuoka

Fukuoka Dome

Hawks Town

Fukuoka Tower

Fukuoka-shi Hakubutsukan

MOMOCHI

Nishijin

Meinohama ▲

N

RESTAURANTS & BARS

Apetito	6
Capricciosa	9
El Liston	8
Happy Cock	10
The Hard Rock Café	1
International Bar	2
Nanak	4
Off Broadway	3
Sizzler	7
Ume-no-hana	11
Voodoo Lounge	5

ACCOMMODATION

Ark	D
Arty Inn	I
Canal City Washington	G
Grand Hyatt Fukuoka	H
Green	E
Kashima Honkan	B
Marukō Inn	F
Nanak	J
New Ōtani	C
New Simple	A

0 ___ 1 km

791

Japanese city of this size, Fukuoka maintains a lively entertainment district, in this case crammed onto the tiny island of **Nakasu**, though it's safer on the wallet to head for the less glitzy bars and restaurants of **Tenjin**, the city's main downtown area.

Arrival, information and city transport

Central Fukuoka is split in two by the Naka-gawa. To the east of this river, **Hakata** district centres on Fukuoka's main **train station**, confusingly known as Hakata Station – a historical legacy from before the two neighbouring towns of Fukuoka and Hakata were combined. Hakata Station is the terminus of the Tōkaidō Shinkansen and the focal point of Kyūshū's local JR services. West of the Naka-gawa, in **Tenjin**, the city's commercial heart, stands Nishitetsu-Fukuoka Station, where trains from Dazaifu terminate (see p.800). These central districts are linked by subway to **Fukuoka airport**, handily located only two stops down the line from Hakata (5min; ¥220). From the **ferry** terminal you have to take a Nishitetsu city bus for the ten-minute ride to either Tenjin or Hakata Station (¥200). **Long-distance buses** call at the Tenjin Fukuoka Bus Centre (above the Nishitetsu Station), before terminating at the Fukuoka Kōtsu Centre outside Hakata Station.

Fukuoka has a good sprinkling of **information** offices. There are desks at the airport, but the main tourist information centre (daily 8am–8pm; ☎092/431-3003, ℻431-3005) is located in Hakata Station's central concourse; the English-speaking staff can provide city maps, hotel lists and the *Fukuoka City Visitor's Guide*. If you're in Tenjin, or need more serious English-language assistance, Fukuoka International Association (daily 10am–8pm, closed third Tues of the month; ☎092/733-2220) offers a broad range of information, from tourist brochures to English-speaking doctors, plus English-language newspapers and free Internet access; you'll find them in the Rainbow Plaza, on the eighth floor of Tenjin's IMS Building. Finally, the Prefectural Cultural Information Centre (daily 10am–7pm, closed second and fourth Mon of the month; ☎092/725-9100, ℻725–9102) has plenty of information on Fukuoka events and other Kyūshū destinations; it's in east Tenjin on the second floor of the ACROS Fukuoka building.

Overseas visitors are eligible for the **Fukuoka Welcome Card**, which entitles the holder to discounts of up to thirty percent at 140 participating hotels, restaurants and tourist facilities. The card is available at the Fukuoka Airport Information, Fukuoka City Tourist Information, Rainbow Plaza, Cultural Information Centre (ACROS), Hakata Machiya Folk Museum, Canal City Hakata Information, Tenjin Chikagai Information, *Sea Hawk Hotel and Resort* and Nishitetsu Solaria Information; you need to show a passport or alien registration card. All these places also dish out free city **maps**, but it's also worth asking in the subway for the useful English booklet, *Guide to Main Subway Station Vicinities*, which contains five detailed area maps. *Rainbow* is a free monthly **newsletter**, available at Rainbow Plaza, aimed at residents but with some interesting articles and listings of what's happening around town. The monthly *Fukuoka Now* (🌐www.fukuoka-now.com) gives snippets of local news together with club and restaurant reviews; it can be picked up at the information desk at the airport, the tourist information booth at Hakata Station, Rainbow Plaza and various hotels in Fukuoka.

The easiest way of **getting around** Fukuoka is on its fast and efficient **subway** system. There's plenty of English-language information and, though there are only two lines, most places of interest fall within walking distance of a station. The main Kūkō line runs from the airport through central Fukuoka, via Hakata Station and Tenjin, to Meinohama in the west, while the shorter Hakozaki line splits off at Nakasu-kawabata (one stop east of Tenjin) for the northeast suburb of Kaizuka. Trains run from 5.30am to around 11pm, every three to eight minutes depending on the time of day, and the minimum fare is ¥200; buy your tickets at the station vending machines. If you anticipate doing several journeys, it's worth buying a one-day **subway** card (¥600), which also gets you small discounts at several museums and the Fukuoka Tower. For those places not within immediate striking distance of the subway, such as the Hawks Town area, you'll need to use Nishitetsu **city buses**, most of which funnel through the Hakata Station–Tenjin corridor. Take a numbered ticket from the machine as you enter and pay the driver on exit; the screen at the front of the bus shows how much you have to pay – the minimum fare is ¥100. A day-pass (¥600) is available for the central zone, but you probably won't cover enough ground in a day to make it worthwhile.

Accommodation

Fukuoka has several modern, world-class **hotels** which aren't a bad deal compared to what you'd pay for similar accommodation in Tokyo. For those on more modest budgets, there's a good choice of business hotels and some truly bargain-basement rooms, mostly located around Hakata Station. You can make hotel **reservations** in the station at the desk (Mon–Sat noon–2.30pm & 3.30–8pm, Sun 11am–12.30pm & 3.30–7pm) next to the tourist information centre – note that there's a small commission charge – and at the airport.

Ark Hotel 3-7-22 Tenjin ☎092/781-2552, ℱ781-2606. Spruce, marble-lobbied business hotel located in the thick of the Tenjin restaurant and bar district, five minutes' walk from the subway. The rooms are well equipped and reasonably priced for such a central location. ⑤

Arty Inn 5-1-2 Watanabe-dōri ☎092/724-3511, ℱ714-3200. Good-value business hotel. Rooms are simple but well decorated, with unusually large beds and bathrooms. The entrance is down a side road just off the main street. ⑤

Canal City Fukuoka Washington Hotel 1-2-20 Sumiyoshi ☎092/282-8800, ℱ282-0757. This slightly upmarket member of the Washington chain is a good option if you want to stay in Canal City but can't afford the *Hyatt* (see below). Rooms are relatively spacious and come with TV, fridge and phone, and good-size bathrooms. ⑥

Grand Hyatt Fukuoka 1-2-82 Sumiyoshi ☎092/282-1234, ℱ282-2817. Fukuoka's top hotel occupies a large chunk of Canal City, between Hakata Station and the Nakasu nightlife district. The understated entrance opens into an oval-shaped lobby and a plunging atrium looking out over fountains. The big, beautifully designed rooms incorporate Japanese touches, such as *shōji* screens and contemporary artwork, and have huge bathrooms. ⑦

Green Hotel 1 & 2 3-11 Hakataeki-chūōgai ☎092/451-4111, ⓦwww.hakata-green.co.jp/

english/index.html. These adjacent hotels offer some of the cheapest accommodation around Hakata Station. The mostly single rooms are basic boxes, but come with TV and tiny bathroom. They also have a few doubles with very small beds, plus slightly more expensive and larger twins. ④

Kashima Honkan 3-11 Reisen-machi ☎092/291-0746, ℱ271-7995. This homely, eighty-year-old ryokan is located on a pleasant backstreet, just round the corner from Gion subway station. The 23 tatami rooms are traditional and elegant, with antique screens and wall hangings. Rooms are available with or without meals. English spoken. ⑤

Marukō Inn 3-30-25 Hakata-eki-mae ☎092/461-0505, ℱ475-2680. A short walk west of Hakata Station, this good-value, mid-range business hotel offers rooms that are comfortable, cheery and well kept, all with TV, minibar and bathroom. ⑤

Hotel New Ōtani 1-1-2 Watanabe-dōri ☎092/715-2000, ℱ715-5658. Predictably efficient hotel offering all the usual facilities, including restaurants, shopping arcade, non-smoking rooms, CNN and BBC TV. The bedrooms are slowly being revamped in brighter tones, but they're all a good size and well appointed. The only drawback is the location, about fifteen minutes' walk south of Tenjin subway station. ⑦

Hotel New Simple 1-23-11 Hakata-eki-mae

℡092/411-4311, ℻411-4312. Basic but welcoming hotel near Gion subway station, with the cheapest, hardest beds in Fukuoka, mostly in single rooms with communal washing facilities. They also have two dorms with bare, wooden cubicles, though are sometimes reluctant to use them. English spoken. Dorm beds ¥2800 per person; rooms ❸

Sea Hawk 2-2-3 Jigyohama ℡092/844-8111, ⓦ www.hawkstown.com/etc/english/index.html. Japan's biggest hotel, out near Momochi Seaside Park. Most of the 1052 rooms overlook Hakata Bay, with sea-view Jacuzzis at the luxury end. They're stylish but by no means as spacious or luxurious as the *Hyatt's*. The hotel has any number of bars and restaurants, while baseball enthusiasts can walk to the next-door Fukuoka Dome. ❻

The City

Even today the old cultural and economic divide between the original castle town, Fukuoka, and the former merchants' quarter of Hakata can be traced, albeit faintly, in the city's streets. Much of **Hakata** consists of dull office blocks, but the district is also home to the city's oldest **shrine** and its most rumbustious festival. You'll also still find the occasional wooden building, narrow lane or aged wall, while some of the unique Hakata culture is showcased in its well-presented **folk museum**. Not surprisingly, many **craft industries** originated in this

Fukuoka

Fukuoka	Fukuoka	福岡
Fukuoka Asian Art Museum	Fukuoka Ajia Bijitsukan	福岡アジア美術館
Fukuoka-shi Bijutsukan	Fukuoka-shi Bijitsukan	福岡市美術館
Fukuoka-shi Hakubutsukan	Fukuoka-shi Hakubutsukan	福岡市博物館
Fukuoka Tower	Fukuoka Tawā	福岡タワー
Hakata	Hakata	博多
Hakata Machiya Furusato-kan	Hakata Machiya Furusato-kan	博多町家ふるさと館
Hawks Town	Hōkusu Taun	ホークスタウン
Kushida-jinja	Kushida-jinja	櫛田神社
Nakasu	Nakasu	中洲
Ōhori-kōen	Ōhori-kōen	大濠公園
Tenjin	Tenjin	天神

Accommodation

Ark Hotel	Āku Hoteru	アークホテル
Arty Inn	Aruti In	アルティイン
Canal City Fukuoka Washington Hotel	Kyanaru Shiti Fukuoka Washinton Hoteru	キャナルシティ福岡ワシントンホテル
Grand Hyatt Fukuoka	Gurando Haiatto Fukuoka	グランドハイアット福岡
Green Hotel	Guriin Hoteru	グリーンホテル
Kashima Honkan	Kashima Honkan	鹿島本館
Marukō Inn	Marukō In	マルコーイン
Hotel New Ōtani	Hoteru Nyū Ōtani	ホテルニューオオタニ
Hotel New Simple	Hoteru Nyū Shimpuru	ホテルニューシンプル
Sea Hawk	Shii Hōku	シーホーク

Restaurants

Nanak	Nanakku	ナナック
Ume-no-hana	Ume-no-hana	梅の花
Uosue	Uosue	魚末

area, most famously Hakata dolls and *ori* silks, while *geisha* still work the traditional **entertainment district** of Nakasu. Hakata is also home to one of Fukuoka's most famous landmarks, the futuristic **Canal City** complex, a startling contrast to the rest of the district.

West of the Naka-gawa, **Tenjin** has upmarket boutiques, department stores and "fashion buildings", but there's little in the way of sights until you go further west to the ruins of Fukuoka castle in **Ōhori-kōen**. As well as an attractive lake, this park also contains an **art museum** with an important collection of twentieth-century works. North and west again, you reach the high-tech **Fukuoka City Museum** of local history and, beyond, the coastal Momochi area dominated by the **Fukuoka Tower** and the **Hawks Town** development.

Hakata and Tenjin

Kami-Kawabata-dōri, now a covered arcade, was once the city's main shopping street, and its small stores, selling a mix of clothes, daily provisions, crafts and household shrines, now have a pleasantly old-world feel. If you're coming by subway, exit 5 of Hakata's Nakasu-Kawabata station brings you straight out onto the street. At weekends, look out for a towering festival float filling one of the shops, where you can sample Kawabata *zenzai*, a hot, sweet red-bean soup topped with rice cakes, washed down with green tea (Sat & Sun 11am–5pm; ¥400).

At the far end of the arcade, a left turn under a *torii* brings you to the back entrance of Hakata's principal shrine, **Kushida-jinja**, founded in 757 AD. However, since its halls are reconstructed every 25 years, the prime attraction is another of the twelve gaudy, top-heavy floats displayed during Hakata's annual **Gion Yamakasa festival** (July 1–15). The climax of these lively celebrations is a five-kilometre dawn race finishing at Kushida-jinja, in which seven teams manhandle one-ton floats through the streets while spectators dowse them with water. Like Kyoto's Gion festival, this harks back to the Kamakura period (1185–1333) when Buddhist priests sprinkled sacred water to drive away summer epidemics. There's a small **museum** (daily 10am–5pm; ¥300) of shrine treasures in the grounds, not of great interest, though it stocks English-language leaflets about Kushida-jinja and the festival. As you leave by the main, east gate, look out for a couple of hefty stone anchor weights, supposedly left behind by the Mongol fleet (see p.936), lying beneath a thousand-year-old ginkgo tree.

A short walk east of Kushida-jinja you can't miss the traditional whitewashed walls and grey roofs of **Hakata Machiya Furusato-kan** (daily 10am–6pm; ¥200) which records the history of Hakata over the last two hundred years. Made up of three buildings, the museum is well designed, with plenty of scale models, reconstructed interiors and good coverage of Hakata's many festivities, including a twenty-minute video of the Gion Yamakasa festival (regular shows 10am–5pm). The middle block comprises a late-nineteenth-century weaver's workshop, with a soaring roof space, where craftsmen demonstrate traditional Hakata-ori silk weaving on aged looms.

Immediately west of Kushida-jinja, the **Nakasu** entertainment district is built on a sandbank in the middle of the Naka-gawa. At its most atmospheric at night, the district can still provide an interesting wander during daylight. The island is a mere 1500m long by 250m wide, but its size is deceptive – somehow more than 2500 restaurants, bars and foodstalls manage to squeeze themselves on. Its southernmost point lies just off the weird and wonderful, multicoloured blocks of **Canal City**, Fukuoka's vision of the future. Apart from two large hotels, a major theatre, a thirteen-screen cinema with seating for nearly 2600, and an amusement hall, the complex also houses a shopping arcade and multi-media store, plus a host of bars and restaurants. The liveliest part, however, is the interior court, where the pink, purple and blue buildings wrap round the "canal", which erupts occasionally into five-storey-high jets of water.

From Nakasu, a pedestrian bridge leads west across the Naka-gawa to Tenjin. Immediately over the river, the European-style building is the former **Prefectural Hall** (Tues–Sun 9am–5pm; ¥240). Built for a trade fair in 1910, the hall's interior plaster cornices, marble fireplaces and wooden panelling will probably be of greater interest to Japanese visitors. The next block west, how-ever, is dominated by a bizarre building with a name to match. **ACROS Fukuoka**, meaning "Asian Crossroads Over the Sea", was completed in 1995 as a cultural centre. Its terraced south side forms a "step garden" (daily 9am–5.30pm; free), giving it the vague air of an Inca ruin, while inside lurk a symphony hall, an information centre (see p.792) with an interesting prefec-tural crafts exhibition space, shops and restaurants. The **Akarenga Cultural Centre** (Tues–Sun 9am–9pm; free), one block north of **ACROS Fukuoka**, was erected in 1909 for a life insurance company and designed by Tatsuno Kingo, one of Japan's first modern architects, who went in for busy, white-stone detailing, domes and turrets. The interior offices, now given over to exhibition space and a coffee shop, are more sedate and have some attractive touches, par-ticularly the cashiers' windows and iron grille-work. Just across the river near the corner of Hakata Ōhashi and Meiji dōri, the **Fukuoka Asian Art Museum** (daily except Wed 10am–8pm; ¥200) is a recent addition to the Fukuoka cultural scene. Located on the seventh and eighth floor of the trendy Hakata Riverain shopping complex, the museum boasts a modest but interest-ing collection of contemporary art from Asia, as well as temporary exhibitions (additional charge).

Ōhori-kōen and around

In 1601 the Kuroda lords built their castle on a low hill sitting among coastal marshes to the west of the Naka-gawa. Today, just a few old stone walls and ruined watchtowers remain, but the castle grounds have been landscaped to form **Ōhori-kōen**, a large public park. It's most easily accessible from the sub-way; exit 3 of Ōhori-kōen Station brings you up beside a large lake spanned by a pleasing necklace of islets and bridges. The park's foremost attraction is the city's art museum, **Fukuoka-shi Bijutsukan** (Tues–Sun 9.30am–5.30pm; ¥200), situated in its southeast corner about ten minutes' walk from the sub-way. Its three ground-floor galleries contain a hotchpotch of early Japanese and Asian art, including the Kuroda family treasures and several eye-catching stat-ues of Buddhism's twelve guardian generals (Jūni Jinsho), each crowned with his associated zodiacal beast. Upstairs you leap a few centuries to the likes of Warhol, Miró and Lichtenstein in a great retrospective of twentieth-century Western art, displayed alongside contemporary Japanese works.

The district west of here, known as **Momochi**, has only recently been reclaimed from the sea and handed over to ambitious city planners. By far their most striking project is the 234-metre, pencil-thin **Fukuoka Tower** which has become one of the city's most famous icons. The closest subway station is Nishijin, about fifteen minutes' walk to the south, or city bus number #305 from Tenjin stops just outside. Primarily a communications tower, the first section is an empty shell coated with 8000 sheets of mirror glass, while the top third bristles with radio transmitters. In between, at 123m, the architects slipped in an observation deck (daily 9.30am–9pm, April–Sept till 10pm; ¥800) to cap-italize on the spectacular views of Fukuoka and Hakata Bay. On the ground floor there's a moderately interesting **Doll Museum** (daily 9.30am–6pm; free), displaying just some of the thirty thousand dolls amassed by a local collector.

Five minutes' walk south from the tower, the excellent local history museum, **Fukuoka-shi Hakubutsukan** (Tues–Sun 9.30am–5.30pm; ¥200), occupies an imposing, late-1980s structure of mirrored glass and grey stone. The museum's most famous exhibit is the two-centimetre-square **Kin-in gold seal**, ornamented with a dumpy, coiled snake. According to its inscription, the seal was presented by China's Han emperor to the King of Na (see p.787) in 57 AD – it was only rediscovered in 1784 in a grave on an island in Hakata Bay. The main exhibition hall, containing the seal, is divided into seven chronological periods from the kingdom of Na to the 1950s, with a final section devoted to folk culture. An English-language guidebook provides selective details, or you can borrow headphones for a fuller commentary. The museum is well laid-out and enlivened by videos, maps and models, including one of the Yamakasa Festival (see p.799).

Before heading back to central Fukuoka, it's worth walking over to the neighbouring reclamation area, roughly 800m east through an area of high-tech research centres, to visit **Hawks Town** and the *Sea Hawk* hotel (see also p.794), one of Fukuoka's top hotels. It also passes muster as a tourist attraction, partly for its extraordinary boat-shaped floor plan and luxurious interior design, but mainly for the jungle-filled, hot-house atrium on the seaward side. Parrots squawk unhappily from cramped cages, but that apart it works well: a waterfall slides down one wall, model giant stag beetles and crabs hide among the palms, while tropical sunshades, exotic birdcalls and the sound of rustling leaves add extra "authenticity". The humidity is boosted regularly with a fine spray and, so they say, alpha waves transmitted to ensure "stable bio-rhythms and a tranquil spirit" – which makes ¥700 for a coffee at the atrium's *Lugg Nagg Café* an absolute steal.

Opened in 1993, **Fukuoka Dome** easily outclasses Tokyo's older rival: it's not only larger but is the first stadium in Japan to sport a retractable roof. The Dome also boasts the world's longest bar, *The Big Life*, an 188-metre counter overlooking the pitch, though it's marred by a rather tacky row of themed service outlets and game machines (daily 11am–midnight; cover charge ¥500; during matches, ¥1000 after 4pm).

To return to central Fukuoka from the Dome you can walk south for fifteen minutes to Tōjin-machi subway station. Alternatively, for a scenic ride along the seafront expressway and over the Aratsu-Ōhashi suspension bridge, pick up a Nishitetsu bus either from the *Sea Hawk* or the Fukuoka Dome-mae bus stop on the main road; bus #305 goes via Tenjin to Hakata Station.

Eating, drinking and entertainment

Fukuoka's most notorious **speciality food** is *fugu*, the poisonous blowfish eaten only in winter (Nov–March); though you'll find *fugu* throughout Japan, the best is said to come from this region. Cheaper food is on offer at the city's mobile street-kitchens, **yatai**, the plastic sheets cocooning a steamy, pungent world where you squeeze in at the counter for hearty bowls of ramen, or, less traditionally, *oden* and tempura, accompanied by flasks of sake. A typical stall charges roughly ¥500 for ramen, though some are going more upmarket. *Yatai* can be found around the intersection of Tenjin Nishi-dōri and Shōwa-dōri, and along the southwest bank of Nakasu island. Tenjin is also a good bet for more traditional restaurants, particularly the blocks west and north of Tenjin Station. Sun Plaza, under the west side of Hakata Station, has a host of mostly downmarket eating houses, while the station itself is a cheap place to try out *karashi mentaiko*, the spicy fish eggs for which north Kyūshū is famed; you'll find both *mentaiko onigiri* (rice balls) and bentō at the station stalls.

Fukuoka's famous **Nakasu** nightlife district occupies an island in the Naka-gawa, seemingly just staying afloat under the weight of clubs, restaurants, bars and soft-porn cinemas. It's a great area to wander round, but most places are extortionately expensive and only take customers by recommendation, if they accept foreigners at all. A happier hunting ground lies around Tenjin's main crossroads, particularly **Oyafukō-dōri** and streets immediately to the east which are packed with bars and clubs. Roughly translated, Oyafukō-dōri means street of disobedient children, originally referring to a local school but nowa-days more applicable to groups of college kids in various stages of inebriation who gather here at weekends under the blind eye of the *kōban* on the corner.

As for more formal **entertainment**, Fukuoka is large enough to be on the circuit for pop stars, musicals and major theatre productions. The main venues are Canal City's Fukuoka City Theatre, ACROS Symphony Hall, or Fukuoka Dome for the real biggies. To find out what's on, consult the *Rainbow* newslet-ter (see p.792) or ask at any of the information centres; tickets are available through PIA (℡092/708-9999). Movie fans should check the current week's showings at Japan's biggest cinema, AMC Canal City 13, on Canal City's fourth floor; cut-price seats (¥1000) are available on weekdays up to 7pm (ring ℡092/272–2222 for 24hr recorded information). Finally, jazz aficionados should check out the *Blue Note* club, at 2-7-6 Tenjin (℡092/715-6666).

Restaurants

Apetito 29-5 Daimyō. Hugely popular bakery-cum-restaurant on Tenjin's Meiji-dōri, especially for the excellent-value lunchtime deals. Western food ranges from sandwiches and salads to more substantial fish and meat dishes, all for well under ¥2000. But star attraction is the bread bar – help yourself for an extra ¥200.

Capricciosa 2F, 2-6-5 Daimyō ℡092/716-7701. The well-known Tokyo chain of Italian restaurants has hit Kyūshū, offering the same value for money, mammoth portions and queues at peak times.

Food Live *Grand Hyatt Fukuoka*, 1-2-82 Sumiyoshi. This basement-floor food court is your best option for somewhere to eat in Canal City, both for atmosphere and value for money. Choose between the appetizing aromas of five open-plan, stylish eating spaces; a moderate meal should cost around ¥2000 per person.

Hard Rock Cafe Fukuoka 2-2-1 Jigyohama, Chou-ku. Located next to the Fukuoka Dome, the "Rock" offers its formulated dose of Americana along with generous portions of nachos, burgers

and ribs starting at around ¥1000. Closed Sun.

Nanak 2F, 3-2-1 Maizuru. On the corner of Oyafukō-dōri, this branch of the reliable Indian chain offers excellent-value lunchtime sets and reasonable evening menus, but outside these spe-cial deals count on at least ¥2000 per head.

Sizzler 13F, IMS Building, Tenjin. This large, bright steak restaurant does a great salad-bar lunch, kids' menus and a decent evening buffet. As well as big, juicy steaks, they serve hamburgers and other variations on the theme.

Ume-no-hana 4F, Canal City. If you can't get to the Dazaifu outlet of this popular tofu restaurant (see p.803), this is the next best thing. Try the silky-smooth *yudōfu*, cooked in famously pure water from Ureshino onsen. No smoking.

Uosue 2-1-30 Daimyō. Small, traditional restau-rant famous for having the freshest fish in town. Menus change daily and there aren't any displayed prices, but count on at least ¥2500 for a satisfying evening meal. Even on weekdays it pays to get here before 6pm.

Bars

El Liston *Il Palazzo Hotel*, 3-13-1 Haruyoshi. An opulent little bar attached to a designer hotel. Not surprisingly, it's not cheap: there's a ¥500 cover charge and the lowliest beer is ¥600. Daily from 7pm.

Happy Cock 9F, 2-1-51 Daimyō. It's elbowroom only at weekends in this large, laid-back bar oppo-site *Capricciosa* (see above). Drinks are all ¥500 – buy your own beer from vending machines – and they do a range of foods, such as nachos, pizzas and Thai soup, with an all-you-can-eat-and-drink deal in the early evening (6–9pm; ¥2500). Tues–Sat from 6pm.

International Bar 4F, 3 Tenjin. This ordinary little bar is a good place to network with local *gaijin*. No cover charge and inexpensive snacks and curry rice. Look out for the English sign on the main street opposite Matsuya Ladies store, north of the main Tenjin crossroads. *Bolero*, in the basement of the same building, is a similarly relaxed, inexpensive place. Daily from 6.30pm.

Off Broadway 2F, Tenjin Centre Building, 3-2-13 Tenjin. Dark, lively bar playing everything from jazz to hip-hop plus regular reggae and Latin nights.

Though there's no cover charge, you're expected to buy at least one drink, with prices starting at ¥400 for a beer; midweek, beer pitchers are half price until 10pm. They claim to serve the "best hamburgers in Kyūshū", besides large portions of fries, buffalo wings and daily set meals. One street east of Oyafukō-dōri. Daily from 7.30pm.

The Voodoo Lounge 3F, Tenjin Centre Building. Boogie the night away with the hip crowd or chill out while watching sports in this capacious bar one floor above *Off Broadway*. Live bands nightly. The cheapest beer is ¥400 and there's a ¥500 cover charge on Fri & Sat after 9pm. Tues–Sun from 7pm.

Listings

Airlines Air China ☏092/282-5611; ANA ☏0120-029222; Air New Zealand ☏092/724-3211; Asiana Airlines ☏092/441-8800; Cathay Pacific ☏092/441-1806; China Airlines ☏092/471-7788; China Eastern Airlines ☏092/472-8383; Eva Air ☏092/412-3553; Garuda ☏092/475-3400; JAL ☏0120-255971; Korean Air ☏092/441-3311; Northwest Airlines ☏092/262-2771; Philippine Airlines ☏092/415-3232; Qantas ☏092/761-1821; Singapore Airlines ☏092/731-7052; Thai Airways International ☏092/734-6409.

Airport information ☏092/621-6059. Note that Fukuoka airport has three terminals: numbers 1 and 2 for domestic flights and 3 for international.

Banks and exchange There's a whole cluster of banks with foreign exchange desks outside the front, west entrance of Hakata Station, including Sumitomo Mitsui Banking Corporation and Fukuoka Ginkō. In Tenjin, head for Meiji-dōri, near the junction with Watanabe-dōri, where you'll also find Fuji Bank and Sanwa Bank.

Bookshops Kinokuniya, on the sixth floor of the bus centre building outside Hakata JR station, has a good English-language section.

Buses Long-distance buses depart from outside Hakata JR Station, with a stop at Tenjin. There are connections to cities on Kyūshū, as well as express buses to Kyoto, Ōsaka and Tokyo.

Consulates Australia, 7F, Tsuruta-keyaki Building, 1-1-5 Akasaka ☏092/734-5055; Canada, 9F, FT Building, 4-8-28 Watanabe-dōri ☏092/752-6055; China, 1-3-3 Jigyohama ☏092/713-1121; South Korea, 1-3-3 Jigyohama ☏092/771-0461; US, 2-5-26 Ōhori ☏092/751-9331.

Car rental Eki Rent-a-Car (☏092/431-8775), Nissan Rent-a-Car (☏092/471-1623), Nippon Rent-a-Car (☏092/414-7535) and Toyota Rent-a-Car (☏092/441-0100) all have offices in or near Hakata Station.

Emergencies The main police station is at 7-7 Higashikoen, Hakata-ku (☏092/641-4141). In an absolute emergency contact the Foreign Advisory Service on ☏092/733-2220. For other emergency numbers, see "Basics" on p.81.

Ferries The RKK Line (☏092/291-3362) operates weekly ferries from Hakata Futō, northwest of Hakata Station, to Naha on Okinawa (26hr; ¥13,220). There's also a choice of services to Pusan in South Korea, from Hakata Futō's International Terminal. Beetle 2 is a daily hydrofoil service (3hr; ¥13,000; ☏092/281-2315), with a free shuttle bus to the port from Hakata Station, while the Camellia Line (☏092/262-2323) operates conventional ferries on Monday, Wednesday and Friday (13–14hr; from ¥9000).

Festivals Hakata celebrates a whole host of festivals, of which the biggest are the summertime Gion Yamakasa (July 1–15) and the Hakata Dontaku, now held during Golden Week (May 3 & 4). In feudal times, Hakata townspeople were permitted across the river once a year to convey New Year greetings to their lord. Today's festival centres on a parade along Meiji-dōri to the old castle.

Hospitals The largest general hospital with English-speaking staff is National Kyūshū Medical Centre, 1-8-1 Jigyohama (☏092/852-0700), near Hawks Town. In a more central location, there's the Saiseki Fukuoka General Hospital, 1-3-46 Tenjin (☏092/771-8151), south of the ACROS building.

Immigration For visa renewals, contact Fukuoka Regional Immigration Bureau, 1–22 Okihama-chō, Hakata-ku (☏092/281-7431).

Internet access You can surf the Internet for a pricey ¥200 for 10min at any one of the six Kinko's in Fukuoka. The two most convenient branches are found in front of Hakata Station (IF, Daiichi Seimei Building, 1-4-1 Hakata-eki-mae;

☎092/473-2677) and south of Tenjin Station across from Kego Park (1F, Hummingbird, 1-22-17 Ima-Izumi; ☎092/722-4222). Open 24 hours a day. Fukuoka International Association, 8F, IMS building in Tenjin, has free, but slow, Internet access (daily 10am–8pm) if you register. Cybac Internet Café, halfway up the west side of Tenjin Nishi-dorri, has 24 hour access, you pay ¥300 to become a member, then ¥480 an hour, and drinks are free.

Police ☎092/641-4141. Emergency numbers are listed in "Basics" on p.81.

Post offices Fukuoka Central Post Office, just north of Tenjin subway station at 4-3-1 Tenjin, offers a poste restante service. There's also another big branch beside the west exit of Hakata Station.

Shopping Fukuoka's main department stores are Iwataya and Daimaru in Tenjin, and Izutsuya built over Hakata Station. All of these sell a selection of local crafts, the most famous of which are Hakata *ningyō*, hand-painted, unglazed clay dolls fashioned as samurai, Kabuki actors, or demure, kimono-clad women. Hakata *ori* is a rather more

transportable, slightly rough silk fabric traditionally used for *obi* (sashes worn with kimono), but now made into ties, wallets and bags. *Champon* are totally impractical – a long-stemmed, glass toy with a bowl at the end which makes a clicking sound when you blow into it. Apart from the big stores, try Hakata Machiya Furusato-kan (p.795), the Kawabata-dōri arcade (p.795) or Hakata Station's Ming arcade for local souvenirs.

Sumo Japan's last *basho* of the season, the Kyūshū Grand Sumo Tournament, takes place in Fukuoka's Kokusai Centre (☎092/272-1111) during November. Phone the centre for tickets and information.

Taxis For a taxi, call Nishitetsu Taxi on ☎092/521-1331.

Travel agents For domestic travel, JTB (☎092/752-0700) has English-speaking staff; their main office is in the Yamato Seimei Building, on Meiji-dōri west of the ACROS building. International tickets are available at A'cross Travellers Bureau, 2F, Dayton Building, 2-4-5 Tenjin (☎092/761-9309), and H.I.S. No 1 Travel, 3F, ACROS Building, 1-1-1 Tenjin (☎092/761-0957).

South to Nagasaki

The plains south of Fukuoka are pretty much built-up all the way to the ancient temple town of **Dazaifu**, once the seat of government for all southern Japan, but now a pleasant backwater best known for its collection of temples and shrines set against a backdrop of wooded slopes. For centuries, Dazaifu's monks, priests and officials sought solace in the healing waters of nearby **Futsukaichi Onsen**. Both towns are easily accessible by train and can either be combined as a day-trip from Fukuoka or as a stopover en route to Nagasaki. Travelling on from Futsukaichi, the Nagasaki line peels off south on a picturesque run beside the Ariake Sea, while the Sasebo line continues via **Takeo**, another recommended dip for hot-spring enthusiasts, and through the pottery town of **Arita** towards Kyūshū's west coast. Arita's 150 kilns punch out the world-renowned Arita-yaki, but it's not a particularly attractive town, and unless you're a real enthusiast or happen to be here during the annual pottery fair (April 29–May 5) there's little reason to stop. At the coast, the line splits again: the southern branch passing the improbable yet intriguing **Huis ten Bosch**, a replica Dutch town which doubles as a holiday resort, then skirting round the shores of Ōmura Bay before dropping down into Nagasaki.

Dazaifu and around

A mere 15km from Fukuoka, **DAZAIFU** only just squeaks free of the urban sprawl, but manages to retain a definite country air. The town is very much on Kyūshū's tourist map, especially in late February and March, when cherry blossoms signal both the start of spring and the onset of the exam season. Anxious students descend on **Tenman-gū**, Japan's foremost shrine dedicated to the god

South to Nagasaki

Dazaifu	*Dazaifu*	太宰府
Guest House Dazaifu	*Gesuto Hausu Dazaifu*	ゲストハウス太宰府
Kanzeon-ji	*Kanzeon-ji*	観世音寺
Kōmyōzen-ji	*Kōmyōzen-ji*	光明禅寺
Rankan	*Rankan*	蘭館
Tenman-gū	*Tenman-gū*	天満宮
Ume-no-hana	*Ume-no-hana*	梅の花
Futsukaichi Onsen	*Futsukaichi Onsen*	二日市温泉
Daimaru Bessō	*Daimaru Bessō*	大丸別荘
Maizuru-sō	*Maizuru-sō*	舞鶴荘
Takeo	*Takeo*	武雄
Ryokan Kagetsu	*Ryokan Kagetsu*	旅館花月
Sagi-no-yu	*Sagi-no-yu*	鷺乃湯
Takeo Onsen Youth Hostel	*Takeo Onsen Yūsu Hosuteru*	武雄温泉ユースホステル
Arita	*Arita*	有田
Huis ten Bosch	*Hausu ten Bosu*	ハウステンボス
Hotel den Haag	*Hoteru den Hāgu*	ホテルデンハーグ
Hotel Tulip	*Hoteru Chūrippu*	ホテルチューリップ

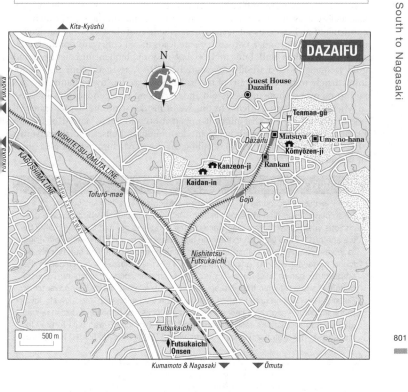

of learning, but the nearby **temples** and other historical relics remain surprisingly peaceful. Everything is within easy walking distance of the station, making it possible to cover the main sights in a day. A popular stop en route to or from Dazaifu is **Futsukaichi Onsen**, around 3km further south, where you can take a dip in its healing waters.

Dazaifu rose to prominence in the late seventh century, when the emperor established a regional seat of government and military headquarters (known as the Dazaifu) here, responsible for defence, trade, and diplomatic ties particularly with China and Korea. For more than five hundred years successive governor generals ruled Kyūshū from Dazaifu, protected by a series of ditches, embankments and hilltop fortresses, until political circumstances changed in the twelfth century and the town gradually fell into decline.

The Town

Dazaifu Station sits on the town's main crossroads, facing north, with the tourist information right outside. From here it's a short walk east along Kazami-dōri to Dazaifu's main sight, **Tenman-gū** (daily 8.30am–5pm; free), a tenth-century shrine dedicated to Tenjin, the guardian deity of scholars (see box below). The shrine information office (daily 8.30am–5pm), on the right as you enter the grounds, rents out radio-headsets (¥300) providing English-language information about Tenman-gū, though the quality of the reception is not brilliant.

The approach to Tenman-gū lies over an allegorical stone bridge, **Taiko-bashi**; its first, steep arch represents the past, the present is flat, while the final, gentler hump indicates difficulties yet to come. While negotiating the bridge, take a close look at the second of the two little shrines on the right, which was constructed in 1458 – its intricate, Chinese-style roof shelters some particularly fine carving. Beyond, a two-storey gate leads into a courtyard dominated by the main **worship hall**, built in 1591 but now resplendent in bright red and gold lacquer under a freshly manicured thatch. A twisted plum tree stands immediately to the right (east) of the hall. Known as the "flying plum tree", it's said to be over a thousand years old and, according to legend, originally grew in Michizane's Kyoto garden. On the eve of his departure he wrote a farewell poem to the tree, but that night it upped roots and "flew" ahead of him to Dazaifu. Behind the worship hall, a modern building houses a small **museum** (Tues–Sun 9am–4.30pm; ¥200) detailing the life of Michizane through a series of tableaux.

To escape the crowds at Tenman-gū just walk south from the shrine entrance for about 100m to the nearby temple of **Kōmyōzen-ji** (daily 8am–5pm; ¥200 donation), founded in the mid-thirteenth century. This small, serene temple is an appealing collection of simple, wooden buildings whose tatami rooms contain Buddha figures or works of art. There's usually no one around, but you're free to walk around – take off your shoes and follow the polished wooden corridors round to the rear, where there's a contemplative garden made up of a gravel sea swirling round moss-covered headlands and jutting rocks, caught against a wooded hillside. The stones in the garden at the front of the temple are arranged in the character for "light", referring to the halo of the Buddha.

Dazaifu's three other major sights lie about twenty minutes' walk west of the station; to avoid the main road, follow signs to the right after the post office. This route brings you in at the back of **Kanzeon-ji** – watch out for the footpath off to the left just before a set of old foundation stones lying in the grass. Founded in 746 AD by Emperor Tenji in honour of his mother, Empress Saimei, at one time Kanzeon-ji was the largest temple in all Kyūshū and even rated a mention in the great, eleventh-century novel, *The Tale of Genji* (see "Books", p.1019). Only some Buddhist statues and the bronze **bell**, the oldest in Japan, remain from the original temple, while the present buildings – unadorned and nicely faded – date from the seventeenth century.

Kanzeon-ji's main hall holds a graceful standing Buddha, but you'll find its most magnificent statues in the modern **treasure house** (daily 9am–5pm; ¥500) next door. The immediate impression is the sheer power of the thirteen huge wooden figures, of which even the newest is at least 750 years old. The oldest is Tobatsu-Bishamonten, standing second in line, which was sculpted from a single block of camphor wood in the eighth century. An informative English brochure provides further details, starting with the Jizō figure facing you as you come up the stairs and working clockwise.

From the Treasure Hall, walk west in front of Kanzeon-ji towards the two-tiered roof of **Kaidan-in**, built in the late eighth century for the ordination of Buddhist priests. This is one of only three such ordination halls in Japan – the other two being in Tochigi and Nara – and again the statuary is of interest, in this case an eleven-headed Kannon from the Heian period, dressed in fading gold.

Practicalities

The easiest way of **getting to Dazaifu** from Fukuoka is on a private Nishitetsu train from Tenjin's Nishitetsu-Fukuoka Station direct to Dazaifu (40min; ¥390). Alternatively, Japan Rail pass holders can save a few yen by travelling via Futsukaichi (see p.804); from JR Futsukaichi Station it's a ten-minute walk north to Nishitetsu-Futsukaichi Station, where you can join a Nishitetsu train for the last five minutes to Dazaifu (¥150) – ask at the JR station for a map to the Nishitetsu station.

The town's **tourist information office** (daily 8.30am–5pm; ☎092/925-1880) is located right outside Dazaifu Station, where you can pick up local maps and brochures in English. Though no one speaks English, they do rent out bikes (¥500 per day), which is worth considering for the western sights.

The only **place to stay** in town is the *Guest House Dazaifu* (☎092/922-8740, ✉ghdazaifu@hte.highway.ne.jp ❹), in a grand position up on a hill ten minutes' walk north of the station. It's a relaxed, welcoming tatami B&B with dorms (¥4500), twin and family rooms. The English-speaking manager is a mine of local information.

There's more choice when it comes to **restaurants**. By far the best is *Ume-no-hana* (daily 11am–3pm & 4–8pm), east of Kōmyōzen-ji, which is worth

KYŪSHŪ | South to Nagasaki

tracking down for its melt-in-the-mouth tofu creations served in tatami rooms overlooking a pretty garden. Prices rise steeply in the evening, but their set lunches and bentō are reasonable at just over ¥2000; try to arrive before noon or be prepared for a wait. Youth hostel members can get a small discount at *Rankan* (daily 8.30am–10pm), on the main road south of the station, which serves good coffee and a basic selection of meals. Otherwise, there are a number of places along Kazami-dōri, including a couple of cheap noodle restaurants behind the tourist office. *Matsuya*, second on the right walking east from the station, is a good place to sample the local delicacy, *Umegae-mochi*, a steamed rice cake stuffed with sweet, red-bean paste.

Futsukaichi Onsen

People have been coming to **FUTSUKAICHI ONSEN** since at least the eighth century to soothe muscle pain, skin complaints and digestive troubles in its healing waters. Despite being the closest hot spring to Fukuoka, the resort is still surprisingly undeveloped. There are three **public baths** (daily 9am–9pm), all grouped together in the centre of Futsukaichi, about ten minutes' walk south of JR Futsukaichi Station. The first, and easiest to spot by its English sign, is Baden House (¥460) – it's also the newest and biggest, with a rotemburo and sauna as well as a whole variety of other pools. Next door, Hakata-yu (¥100) is a tiny old bathhouse favoured by Futsukaichi's senior citizenry, while over the road Gozen-yu (¥200) is the perfect compromise, with three large pools in an attractive, old-style building.

Frequent **trains** run from Fukuoka's JR Hakata Station direct to Futsukaichi Station (20min; ¥270). Coming from Dazaifu, take a train to Nishitetsu-Futsukaichi Station, then walk or take a local bus (6min; ¥100). The local **information office** (daily 9am–6pm; ⊤ & Ⓕ092/922-2421), inside the JR station, provides useful town maps, in Japanese only, as well as Dazaifu maps if you're heading that way. As usual, you can leave bags in the station lockers, and the two main bathhouses will take care of luggage while you soak.

If you fancy combining your bath with gourmet dining, or even an overnight stay, *Daimaru Bessō* (⊤092/924-3939, Ⓕ924-4126; ❾) is an atmospheric old **ryokan** on the south side of town, set round a traditional garden of pine trees and carp ponds. The beautifully appointed tatami rooms come with two meals included, and the excellent **restaurant** also serves good-value set lunches (from ¥1500), and includes the use of their huge hot-spring bath. For more affordable accommodation, try *Maizuru-sō* (⊤092/922-2727, Ⓕ922-6750; ❺), a new business hotel on the road in from the station, with just eleven cheerful rooms and a small, black-stone onsen bath.

Takeo

Roughly one hour from Futsukaichi by train on the JR Sasebo line, **TAKEO** is another **onsen resort** which makes a relaxed stopover on the way to Nagasaki. Squeezed in a narrow valley between low hills, the town is more developed than Futsukaichi, though its public baths draw fewer day-trippers. According to legend, it's also a lot older, dating back to the third century AD when Empress Jingu rested here on her way home from invading Korea. Out walking one day, the tip of her staff slipped between two stones, causing a spring of crystal-clear water to gush forth. Later, in the sixteenth century, Toyotomi Hideyoshi used Takeo as a watering hole for his troops on their way to another Korean invasion (see p.937).

The town centre lies ten minutes' walk northwest of the station, where the onsen buildings are clustered behind a squat, Chinese-style gate, built in 1914 without the use of nails. First on the left through the gate is Moto-yu (daily 6.30am–11pm; ¥300), the most traditional of the **public baths**, where locals lying out on the hot stones swap gossip. If you prefer outdoor bathing, the nearby *Ryokan Kagetsu* (see below) has a beautiful rotemburo (¥700), while *Sagi-no-yu* boasts a smaller rotemburo and sauna (daily 9am–4.30pm; ¥600). The waters are renowned, amongst other things, for their power to heal burns and cure physical exhaustion.

You'll find Takeo **information centre** (Mon–Fri 9am–5.30pm, Sat & Sun 9am–5pm; ℡0954/22-2542, ℻23-7102) upstairs in the JR train station, directly opposite the ticket barriers. Among several **ryokan** gathered round the onsen, the *Kagetsu* (℡0954/22-3108, ℻22-2120; ❺) offers elegant, tatami rooms with or without meals, while *Sagi-no-yu* (℡0954/23-2111, ℻23-9205; ❹) charges lower rates for a simple tatami room including breakfast. *Takeo Onsen Youth Hostel* (℡ 0954/22-2490, ✉takeo@jyh.gr.jp; closed late May/early June; dorm beds ¥2730 per person) provides the cheapest option with its bunk beds; it's a seven-minute bus ride south of town on a pine-covered hilltop. Buses for the hostel – direction Hōyō Centre, also known as Kampo – stop on the road outside the station (¥220); the last bus up leaves just after 5pm. If you arrive later, the English-speaking hostel manager will collect you, but after 7pm the choice is a taxi (¥800) or a steep forty-minute hike.

Huis ten Bosch

Where the train from Takeo turns south beside Ōmura Bay there's a surprise in store as the horizon fills with an unmistakeably European-style building, announcing your arrival at **HUIS TEN BOSCH** (ⓦwww.huistenbosch .co.jp). Opened in 1992 at a cost of ¥250 billion, this resort town is a meticulously engineered replica of a Dutch port caught somewhere between the seventeenth and twenty-first centuries. As such, it might not seem a natural destination for most Western visitors, but the overall concept – part theme park, part serious experiment in urban living – and its top-quality design lift it above the ordinary.

Huis ten Bosch (meaning "house in the forest" in Dutch, and named after the official residence of Queen Beatrix of the Netherlands) owes its existence to the drive and vision of **Kamichika Yoshikuni**, a local entrepreneur who was so impressed with Dutch land reclamation and environmental management that he persuaded his financiers it could work in Japan as a commercial venture. The complex took six years to plan and build on an abandoned block of reclaimed land. Twenty million baked-clay bricks were imported from Holland and Dutch technicians came to advise, but Huis ten Bosch is predominantly a Japanese venture, employing thousands of local people. The development has boosted the economy not only of Nagasaki but all Kyūshū through increased tourism, especially from Southeast Asia.

While Huis ten Bosch may seem quaintly olde worlde, it's equipped with the latest technology developed specially to manage its sophisticated heating systems, wave control, desalination, water recycling and security. All the pipes, cables and wires are hidden underground and, as far as possible, it's designed to be environmentally benign.

The Town

Huis ten Bosch (daily 9am–9pm, Jan & Feb until 8pm; last admission two hours before closing) is divided into an exclusive residential district, Wassenaar, and the public areas where you'll find a bewildering choice of museums and attractions, plus dozens of souvenir shops and numerous restaurants.

Fortunately, there are plenty of signposts in English, while the 105-metre-high Utrecht tower (Domtoren) provides a prominent landmark, and a bird's-eye view from its observatory.

It's just a couple of minutes' walk from Huis ten Bosch Station to the entrance gate where there's a choice of three **tickets**. The One Day Passport (¥4800) gets you entry to most attractions; the Official Hotel Resort Passport (¥5800; only available to foreign tourists staying in the resort) covers admission over two days to most facilities in Huis ten Bosch and Holland Village, an older prototype mostly of interest to children; and the Basic Entry Ticket (¥3200) covers admission only, although you can buy a pass card for most attractions once inside the park (¥1600). Though there's a fair amount to explore for "free" inside, especially in summer when they stage more outdoor events, it's worth visiting at least a couple of the attractions.

The best way to get around Huis ten Bosch is on foot, wandering along the canals and past quaint, brick-faced houses on streets refreshingly free of advertising hoardings, loudspeakers and the electrical spaghetti you find elsewhere in Japan. In the far southwest corner, **Paleis Huis ten Bosch** is a perfect replica of the Dutch royal palace – at least on the outside. It's used for art exhibitions but, unless there's something special on, there's not a lot to see, beyond a vast love-it or hate-it computer-designed mural by Dutch artist Rob Scholte. The palace's formal gardens follow an original eighteenth-century design, never realized at the time, by Frenchman Daniel Marot for The Hague. Among other museums, the **Porcelain Museum** is notable for its impressive reproduction of the Charlottenburg's porcelain room as well as some actual genuine pieces of local Imari-ware.

Most of Huis ten Bosch's **attractions** are a touch on the cutesy side. However, three stand out for their high-quality special effects and outrageous ambition. The **Great Voyage Theatre** shows a short film about the first Dutch ships to reach Japan, during which the whole seating area pitches and rolls – sit in the middle if you get seasick. In **Mysterious Escher** you enter a topsy-turvy world to watch a sickly-sweet but well-executed 3D film based on Escher's famous graphics. Last but not least, **Horizon Adventure** stages a real-life flood with 800 tons of water cascading into the theatre.

Practicalities

The easiest way of getting to the resort is on JR's special **Huis ten Bosch Express** from Fukuoka (1hr 40min) or the Seaside Liner from Nagasaki (1hr 20min). For those in a hurry, high-speed boats zip across Ōmura Bay direct to Huis ten Bosch from Nagasaki airport (9 daily; 45min; ¥1420). You'll find **information** counters at the entrance gate and in the main square, as well as a bank, post office, medical centre and Internet café. Huis ten Bosch can easily be explored in a day. Should you decide to stay, however, the cheapest **accommodation** is the nearby *Hotel Tulip* (☎0956/58-7777, ℱ58-7788; ➎), which runs a shuttle bus to the resort entrance. The four hotels on site are top quality and expensive, but if you want to push the boat out, the *Hotel Den Haag* (☎0956/27-0011, ℮intsales@huistenbosch.co.jp ➒) is the most attractive option. **Eating** inside Huis ten Bosch won't break the bank. There's a huge choice of restaurants and cafés, serving everything from sandwiches and tacos to sushi and fresh seafood. Note that you're not allowed to take your own food into the resort.

Nagasaki

As the passage into the harbour widened we had our first glimpse of Nagasaki town in the haze of the morning, nestled in a most beautiful inlet at the foot of wooded hills.

Although few visitors these days arrive by boat and the woods are diminished, many would agree with British landscape painter Sir Alfred East, who

Nagasaki		
Nagasaki	*Nagasaki*	長崎
Atomic Bomb Museum	*Nagasaki Gembaku-shiryōkan*	長崎原爆資料館
Dejima	*Dejima*	出島
Dutch Slopes	*Oranda-zaka*	オランダ坂
Fukusai-ji	*Fukusai-ji*	福済寺
Glover Garden	*Gurabā-en*	グラバー園
Inasa-yama	*Inasa-yama*	稲左山
Kōshi-byō	*Kōshi-byō*	孔子廟
26 Martyrs' Memorial	*Nihon Nijū-roku seijin junkyōchi*	日本26聖人殉教地記念館
Megane-bashi	*Megane-bashi*	眼鏡橋
Museum of Traditional Performing Arts	*Dentō Geinō-kan*	伝統芸能館
Nyoko-dō	*Nyoko-dō*	如己堂
Peace Park	*Heiwa-kōen*	平和公園
Shianbashi	*Shianbashi*	思案橋
Shōfuku-ji	*Shōfuku-ji*	聖福寺
Sōfuku-ji	*Sōfuku-ji*	崇福寺
Suwa-jinja	*Suwa-jinja*	諏訪神社
Urakami	*Urakami*	浦上
Urakami Cathedral	*Urakami Daiseidō*	浦上大聖堂
Accommodation		
Hotel Belle View Nagasaki	*Hoteru Beru Byū Nagasaki*	ホテルベルビュー長崎
Dai-ichi Hotel	*Dai-ichi Hoteru*	第一ホテル
Fumi	*Fumi*	富美
Holiday Inn	*Horidei In*	ホリデイイン
Miyuki-sō	*Miyuki-sō*	三幸荘
Nagasaki Grand Hotel	*Nagasaki Gurando Hoteru*	長崎グランドホテル
Nagasaki Ebisu Youth Hostel	*Nagasaki Ebisu Yūsu Hosuteru*	長崎ゑびすユースホステル
Hotel New Nagasaki	*Hoteru Nyū Nagasaki*	ホテルニュー長崎
Park Side Hotel	*Pāku Saido Hoteru*	パークサイドホテル
Minshuku Tampopo	*Minshuku Tampopo*	民宿たんぽぽ
Washington Hotel	*Washinton Hoteru*	ワシントンホテル
Restaurants		
Futabaya	*Futabaya*	双葉や
Hamakatsu	*Hamakatsu*	浜勝
Kagetsu	*Kagetsu*	花月
Kōzanrō	*Kōzanrō*	江山楼
Robin Hood no Mori	*Robin Fuddo no Mori*	ロビンフッドの森
Shirokiya	*Shirokiya*	白木屋

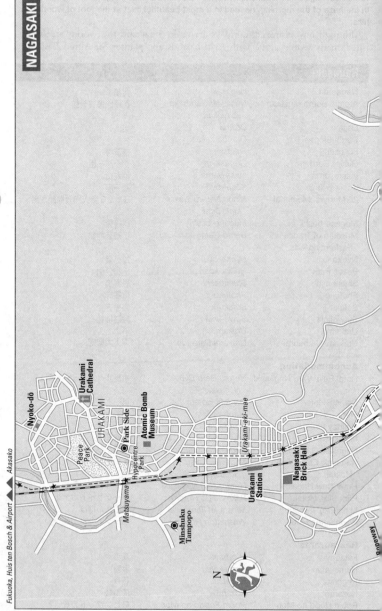

Fukuoka, Huis ten Bosch & Airport   Akasako

Nyoko-dō

Urakami
Cathedral

URAKAMI

Peace
Park

Park Side

Atomic Bomb
Museum

Hypocentre
Park

Matsuyama

Urakami-eki-mae

Minshuku
Tampopo

Urakami
Station

Nagasaki
Brick Hall

N

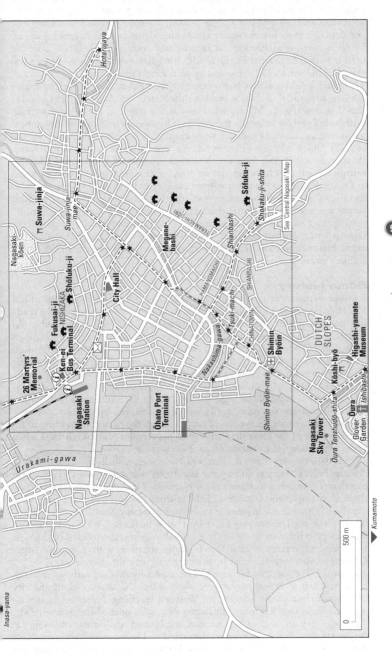

Nagasaki-kōen

⛩ **Suwa-jinja**

Suwa-jinja-mae

Shōfuku-ji

Fukusai-ji

NISHIZAKA

Ken-ei Bus Terminal

26 Martyrs' Memorial

ⓘ

ⓘ

Nagasaki Station

Urakami-gawa

Inasa-yama

City Hall

Ōhato Port Terminal

Sōfuku-ji

Shokaku-ji-shita

Shianbashi

TERAMACHI-DŌRI

Megane-bashi

HAMANOMACHI

Tsuki-machi

SHIANBASHI

Nakashima-gawa

See 'Central Nagasaki' Map

CHINATOWN

✚ **Shimin Byōin**

Shimin Byōin-mae

DUTCH SLOPES

Kōshi-byō

Higashi-yamate Museum

⛩

Ōura Tenshudō-shita

Nagasaki Sky Tower

Glover Garden

Ōura Ishibashi

0   500 m

▶ *Kumamoto*

809

came here in 1889, that **NAGASAKI** is one of Japan's more picturesque cities, gathered in the tucks and crevices of steep hills rising from a long, narrow harbour supposedly shaped like a crane in flight. It's not a particularly ancient city, nor does it possess any absolutely compelling sights. Instead, Nagasaki's appeal lies in its easy-going attitude and an unusually cosmopolitan culture, resulting from over two centuries of contact with foreigners when the rest of Japan was closed to the world, and cemented by its isolation from Tokyo.

Nagasaki would probably have remained just a pleasant, attractive city with a bustling harbour if a chance break in the clouds on August 9, 1945 hadn't seared it into the world's consciousness as the target of the second **atomic bomb** dropped on Japan. It's the A–Bomb hypocentre and nearby museum, as harrowing as that in Hiroshima, that brings most people to Nagasaki, yet the city has much else to offer. Successive communities of Chinese, Dutch, Portuguese and British have left their mark here, building colourful **Chinese temples**, Catholic **churches** and an array of European-style houses gathered in Glover Garden, as well as imported cuisines and festivals. Despite efforts to stamp out another European import, the Catholic faith, Nagasaki remains Japan's centre of **Christianity**, claiming one sixth of the country's believers. It's possible to cover the two main areas – the hypocentre and around Glover Garden – in a day, but Nagasaki deserves at least one extra night's stopover to explore its backstreets, soak up some atmosphere and sample a few of the city's culinary treats.

Some history

Portuguese traders first sailed into Nagasaki, then a small fishing village of just 1500 inhabitants, in 1570. They returned the following year to establish a **trading** post and **Jesuit mission** at the invitation of the local *daimyō*, who was already a Catholic convert. The merchants built up a flourishing business exchanging Chinese silks for copper and silver, while the Jesuit fathers financed their missionary activities by taking a turn on the profits. The Portuguese were soon the most powerful force in Nagasaki, despite competition from Chinese traders and, later, Spanish Franciscan and Dominican fathers. For a brief period, Christianity was all the rage, but in the late sixteenth century Toyotomi Hideyoshi, fearing the missionaries would be followed by military intervention, started to move against the Church. Though the persecutions came in fits and starts, one of the more dramatic events occurred in Nagasaki in 1597 when Hideyoshi ordered the crucifixion of 26 Franciscans.

After 1616 the new shogun, Tokugawa Hidetada, gradually took control of all dealings with foreigners and by the late 1630s only Chinese and Portuguese merchants continued to trade out of Nagasaki. The latter were initially confined to a tiny island enclave called **Dejima**, but in 1639 even they were expelled following a Christian-led rebellion in nearby Shimabara (see p.824). Their place on Dejima was filled by Dutch merchants who had endeared themselves to the shogun by sending a warship against the rebels. For the next two hundred years this tiny Dutch group together with a slightly larger Chinese community provided Japan's only link with the outside world.

Eventually, the restrictions began to ease, especially after the early seventeenth century, when technical books were allowed into Nagasaki, making the city once again Japan's main conduit for **Western learning**. Nevertheless, it wasn't until 1858 that five ports, including Nagasaki, opened for general trade. America, Britain and other nations established diplomatic missions as Nagasaki's foreign community mushroomed and its economy boomed. New inventions flooded in: the printing press, brick-making and modern shipbuilding techniques all made their Japanese debut in Nagasaki.

In the early twentieth century the city's industrial development was spearheaded by the giant **Mitsubishi dockyards**. Nagasaki became an important naval base with huge munitions factories, an obvious target for America's second **atomic bomb** in 1945. Even so, it was only poor visibility at Kokura, near Fukuoka, that forced the bomber, critically short of fuel, south to Nagasaki. The weather was bad there too, but as "Bock's Car" flew down the Urakami-gawa at 11am on August 9 a crack in the cloud revealed a sports stadium just north of the factories and shipyards. A few moments later "Fat Boy" exploded. It's estimated that 73,000 people died in the first seconds, rising to 140,000 by 1950, while 75,000 were injured and nearly forty percent of the city's houses destroyed in the blast and its raging fires. Horrific though these figures are, they would have been higher if the valley walls hadn't contained the blast and a spur of hills shielded southern Nagasaki from the worst. An American naval officer visiting the city a few weeks later described his awe at the "deadness, the absolute essence of death in the sense of finality without resurrection. It's everywhere and nothing has escaped its touch." But the city, at least, did rise again to take its place with Hiroshima as a centre for anti-nuclear protest and an ardent campaign for world peace.

Arrival, information and city transport

Nagasaki is a long, thin city which fills the flatland beside the harbour, spreads its tentacles along tributary valleys, and is slowly creeping up the hillsides, eating away at the green woods. The city's main **downtown** area lies in the south, concentrated round Hamanomachi shopping centre and the compact Shianbashi entertainment district, both on the south bank of the Nakashima-gawa, while administrative and commercial offices occupy land between the river and Nagasaki Station. North of the station, the city slims down to a narrow corridor along the **Urakami valley**, with Inasa-yama rising to the west.

Nagasaki **airport** occupies an artificial island in Ōmura Bay, 40km from town and connected by limousine bus (¥1200 return; 1hr) to Nagasaki Station. The **train station** sits at the south end of the highway running into Nagasaki, roughly 1km north of the city's main downtown area. Most long-distance **buses** either stop outside the station or pull into Ken-ei bus terminal on the opposite side of the road. **Ferries** from Kumamoto dock at the Ōhato Port Terminal, fifteen minutes' walk south of Nagasaki Station.

The best source of **information** is Nagasaki Prefectural Tourist Federation (daily 9am–5.30pm; ⑦095/826-9407, ⑤824-3087), located on the second floor above Ken-ei bus station. The English-speaking staff can help with hotel reservations and there's plentiful information about the local sights and transport to them. When the office is closed, city maps and a few English pamphlets are available at Nagasaki City Tourist Information (daily 8am–7pm; ⑦095/823-3631, ⑤822-1954), inside the station by the ticket barrier, though staff here don't speak English.

City transport

Given its elongated shape, Nagasaki's sights are all fairly spread out. However, it's one of the easier cities for getting around, thanks mainly to its cheap and easy **tram system**. There are four lines, numbered #1 to #5 (#2 is missing), each identified and colour coded on the front. The two north–south lines (#1 and #3) are the most handy, running from either side of the downtown area to meet at the station and then continuing north to the A-Bomb sights. To reach the Glover Garden area, however, you'll need line #5 for Ishibashi; you can transfer onto this line at Tsuki-machi – ask for a transfer ticket

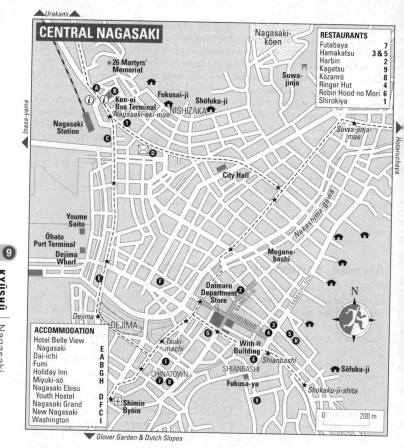

CENTRAL NAGASAKI

RESTAURANTS	
Futabaya	7
Hamakatsu	3 & 5
Harbin	2
Kagetsu	9
Kōzanrō	8
Ringer Hut	4
Robin Hood no Mori	6
Shirokiya	1

Nagasaki-kōen

Urakami

26 Martyrs' Memorial

Suwa-jinja

Ken-ei Bus Terminal

Fukusai-ji

Shōfuku-ji

NISHIZAKA

Nagasaki-eki-mae

Suwa-jinja-mae

Inasa-yama

Hotaruchaya

Nagasaki Station

City Hall

Nakashima-gawa

Youme Saito

Ōhato Port Terminal

Dejima Wharf

Megane-bashi

Daimaru Department Store

KANKO-DORI

HAMANOMACHI

TERAMACHI-DORI

N

Dejima

DEJIMA

With Building

Shianbashi

SHIANBASHI

Sōfuku-ji

Tsuki-machi

CHINATOWN

Fukusa-ya

Shokaku-ji-shita

Shimin Byōin

0   200 m

ACCOMMODATION	
Hotel Belle View Nagasaki	E
Dai-ichi	A
Fumi	B
Holiday Inn	G
Miyuki-sō	H
Nagasaki Ebisu Youth Hostel	D
Nagasaki Grand	F
New Nagasaki	C
Washington	I

Glover Garden & Dutch Slopes

9

KYŪSHŪ | Nagasaki

(*norikae-kippu*). Trams run from approximately 6.30am to 11pm, though check the timetables at each stop for precise times, and there's a flat fare of ¥100 which you feed into the driver's box on exit. Alternatively, you can buy a one-day pass (¥500) at the information centres and hotels, but not on the trams themselves. While you're clanking along, take a look around: some of these trolley-cars are museum pieces – the oldest dates from 1911 – which were snapped up when other Japanese cities were merrily ripping up their tramlines.

City buses are more complicated, but the only time you're likely to need them is getting to the Inasa-yama ropeway (see p.819). In this case you need a Nagasaki Bus (#3 or #4) from a stop on the road outside Nagasaki Station. The normal system operates: take a numbered ticket on entry and pay the driver as you get off according to the fare-display board.

Accommodation

Nagasaki offers a broad range of **accommodation** widely dispersed around the city. Cheaper places cluster round the station, but otherwise the main choice is whether to stay near the station or in the southern, downtown district. There are also a couple of reasonable places near the hypocentre, in the north of the city, if that's your main area of interest.

Around Nagasaki Station

Dai-ichi Hotel 2-1 Daikoku-machi ☎095/820-1111, ⒡823-8745. Friendly and efficient business hotel with some English-speaking staff and a wide range of rooms, up to a six-berth family room. The standard rooms aren't enormous but are comfortable enough, and all en suite. **❹**

Fumi 4-9 Daikoku-machi ☎095/822-4962, ⒡824-5633. After the capsules, this minshuku is the cheapest place near the station, located behind the Ken-ei bus terminal. Its tatami rooms and shared bathrooms have seen better days, but the welcome is warm and there's lots of local information available. Charges are on a room-only basis. **❹**

Nagasaki Ebisu Youth Hostel 6-10 Ebisu-machi ☎ & ⒡095/824-3823. Tiny, friendly and relaxed hostel, with laundry facilities and evening meals. All accommodation is in bunk-bed dorms (¥2940) and there's an 11pm curfew. It's a popular place, so book in advance. Turn right after the post office, then first left, then right and right again. **❶**

Hotel New Nagasaki 14-5 Daikoku-machi ☎095/826-8000, ⒡823-2000. Nagasaki's best hotel, conveniently placed outside the station, with all the trimmings: grand marble lobby, shopping arcade, restaurants, bar and fitness centre (¥2000). The rooms are mostly Western-style, some boasting harbour views – not a lot of character, but generously sized. **❼**

Downtown

Hotel Belle View Nagasaki 1-20, Edo-machi ☎095/826-5030, ⒡826-5051. Reasonably priced business hotel with friendly and efficient service plus a restaurant, bar and in-room Internet access. **❹**

Holiday Inn 6-24 Doza-machi ☎095/828-1234, ⒡828-0178. For mid-range accommodation in central Nagasaki, you can't beat this elegant, well-priced hotel. The lobby sets the tone with its low-level lighting, Japanese screens and antique silk embroideries, mixed with European dark-wood furniture and deep sofas. The standard rooms don't quite go that far, but they're more than adequate in pinky browns with a choice of three different bed sizes. **❻**

Miyuki-sō 6-46 Kajiya-chō ☎095/821-3487, ⒡821-7831. It's worth tracking down this good-value budget hotel, in a five-storey red-brick building with a blue sign, on the far east side of town. Its basic tatami and Western rooms offer pay-TV and phone, while the more expensive have their own bathroom and toilet. The owner speaks a little English. **❹**

Nagasaki Grand Hotel 5-3 Manzai-machi ☎095/823-1234, ⒡822-1793. This big, older hotel offers reasonable rates in a good location midway between the station, downtown and Glover Garden area. The cheaper rooms are pretty standard, all equipped with TV, bathroom and mini-bar. **❺**

Washington Hotel 9-1 Shinchi-machi ☎095/828-1211, ⒡825-8023. A touch more expensive than other hotels in the Washington chain, but with a good selection of rooms. **❺**

North Nagasaki

Park Side Hotel 14-1 Heiwa-machi ☎095/845-3191, ⒡846-5550. This smart and spacious hotel benefits from a peaceful, out-of-town location. All its generous-sized rooms are Western style, while modern art works jolly up the cool, cream walls. **❻**

Minshuku Tampopo 21-7 Hoei-chō ☎095/861-6230, ⒡864-0032. A member of the Japanese Inn Group, this small, tidy minshuku is about ten minutes' walk from the Peace Park. Overnight rates aren't bad for its tatami rooms, all without bath, and well-priced meals are also on offer. It's a ten-minute walk from the Matsuyama tram stop and fifteen from JR Urakami Station; if you phone from Urakami Station, the owners will collect you. **❹**

The City

Nagasaki's principal sights are widely spread, starting in the north with the Peace Park and the gruelling but informative **Atomic Bomb Museum**. From there it's a tram ride down to Nagasaki Station and a gentle stroll along the slopes of Nishizaka from the 26 Martyrs' Memorial round to Nagasaki's most imposing shrine, Suwa-jinja. The focus of interest in the central district is a row of quiet **temples**, notably Sōfuku-ji, founded by the city's Chinese community, while **Chinatown** itself consists of a colourful, compact grid of streets. Slightly further west, the former Dutch enclave of **Dejima** is commemorated with a museum and scale model of the old settlement.

Down in the far south, several European houses have been preserved on the former hilltop concession, now known as **Glover Garden**, overlooking Nagasaki's magnificent harbour and a colourful Confucian shrine. To round it all off, take a twilight ropeway ride up to the top of Inasa-yama before hitting the bars and clubs of Shianbashi. There's more than enough here to fill two days; if you've only got one to spare, it's probably best to skip the sights along Nishizaka and head straight for Sōfuku-ji or Glover Garden.

North Nagasaki: A-Bomb Hypocentre

As you walk around the district of **Urakami** these days it's hard to link these quiet, reasonably prosperous residential suburban streets with the scenes of utter devastation left by the atomic explosion in August 1945. If you've already visited Hiroshima, which was destroyed by uranium bomb three days earlier, Nagasaki's memorials might seem a little less striking. However, the new museum is notable for its balanced approach.

Urakami's main sights can be covered on a circular route from Matsuyama tram stop, roughly ten minutes north of Nagasaki Station. A long flight of steps leads up into the **Peace Park**, which is as popular among anti-nuclear lobbyists trawling for signatures as it is for young kids skateboarding among the donated plaques and memorials, watched over by sculptor Kitamura Seibō's muscular **Peace Statue**. The figure, right hand pointing skyward at the threat of nuclear destruction, left extended to hold back the forces of evil, was unveiled in 1955. As Kazuo Ishiguro remarked in *A Pale View of the Hills* (see "Books", p.1019), from a distance the figure resembles a "policeman conducting traffic", but when some elderly figure pauses on the way past, head bowed, it's not easy to be cynical.

Signs behind the Peace Statue point the way to **Nyoko-dō** (Tues–Sun 9am–5pm; ¥100), the former home of **Dr Nagai Takashi**, who wrote the *Bells of Nagasaki* amongst a dozen other books about the atomic bomb's aftermath. Though his house, now a public library with a few personal mementoes, isn't particularly worth the detour, his life story is remarkable. A radiologist working in Nagasaki, Dr Nagai had already developed leukaemia before he received further exposure from the bomb. He continued to help other survivors until he himself became bedridden, and lived for another four years, cared for by his two young children in a tiny shack, courageously recording his experiences with radiation victims right up to his death, aged 43, in 1951.

From the Peace Park you can see the twin red-brick towers of **Urakami Cathedral** dominating a small rise 400m to the east. The present building is a postwar replica of the original, completed in 1925, which was destroyed when the atomic bomb exploded only 500m away. The blast left scorch marks on the statues now preserved beside the front porch, and tore off huge chunks of masonry, including a section of the tower which still rests on the bank under the north wall. All that remained of the congregation were a few melted rosaries.

Nowadays, a pleasant shopping street leads southwest from the cathedral back towards Matsuyama. Before reaching the main road, turn left into the **Hypocentre Park**, where an austere black pillar marks the exact spot where the bomb exploded 500m above the ground. Overlooking the park to the east, behind an incongruous row of Love Hotels peering over the willows, you'll find the **Atomic Bomb Museum** (daily 8.30am–5.30pm; ¥200). You enter via a symbolic, spiralling descent, then views of pre-war Nagasaki lead abruptly into a darkened room full of twisted iron girders, blackened masonry and videos constantly scrolling through horrific photos of the dead and dying. It's strong stuff, occasionally too much for some, but the most moving exhibits are always those single fragments of an individual life – a charred lunchbox, twisted pair of glasses or the chilling shadow of a man etched on wooden planks.

The purpose of the museum isn't only to shock, and the displays are packed with information, much of it in English, tracing the history of atomic weapons, the effects of the bomb and the heroic efforts of ill-equipped rescue teams who had little idea what they were facing. There's a fascinating video library of interviews with survivors, including some of the foreigners present in Nagasaki at the time; figures vary, but probably more than 12,000 foreigners were killed in the blast, mostly Korean forced-labour working in the Mitsubishi shipyards, as well as Dutch, Australian and British prisoners of war. The museum then broadens out to examine the whole issue of nuclear weapons and ends with a depressing film about the arms race and test-ban treaties.

Along Nishizaka

East of Nagasaki Station, a quiet lane hugs **Nishizaka** hillside, starting in the north at a bizarre, mosaic-clad church dedicated to Japan's first Christian martyrs. In 1597 six foreign missionaries and twenty Japanese converts were the unlucky victims of the shogunate's growing unease at the power of the Church. They were marched from Kyoto and Ōsaka to Nagasaki where they were crucified on February 2 as a warning to others. The group were canonized in 1862 and a century later the **26 Martyrs' Memorial** was erected on the site, together with a small **museum** (daily 9am–5pm; ¥250) telling the history – mostly in Japanese – of the martyrs and of Christianity in Japan. A surprising amount survives, including tissue-thin prayer books hidden in bamboo and statues of the Virgin Mary disguised as the goddess Kannon. One document records the bounties offered to informers: 500 silver pieces per priest, down to 100 for a lowly catechist.

Heading south along Nishizaka, a giant statue of Kannon marks **Fukusai-ji** (daily 7am–5pm; ¥200), founded in 1628 by a Chinese Zen priest. The original temple was destroyed in 1945 and replaced with a tasteless, turtle-shaped building topped by the eighteen-metre-tall, aluminium-alloy goddess and a circle of supplicating infants. Inside, a 25-metre-long Foucault's pendulum represents a perpetual prayer for peace, oscillating over the remains of 16,500 Japanese war-dead buried underneath. Nearby **Shōfuku-ji**, on the other hand, survived the bomb and consists of an attractive collection of aged, wooden buildings surrounded by rustling bamboo stands and shady trees. Another early-seventeenth-century Zen temple, rebuilt in 1715, its main attributes are some detailed carving on the gates and unusual decorative features such as the red balustrade around the worship hall.

From Shōfuku-ji it's a ten-minute walk east along the hillside, along the edge of Nagasaki-kōen, to the side entrance of Nagasaki's major shrine, **Suwa-jinja**, which was founded in 1625 when the shogunate was promoting Shintoism in opposition to the Christian Church. Ask at the office, beside a bronze horse by Kitamura Seibō, for their comprehensive English brochure. Suwa-jinja's main hall, rebuilt in 1869, is fresh and simple, but for most foreigners its greatest attraction is the English-language fortune papers on sale beside the collecting box (¥200). The grounds are scattered with unusual subsidiary shrines, notably two *koma-inu* (guardian lions) known as the "**stop lions**", where people vowing to give up unwanted habits fasten paper strings round the front legs, like plaster casts; you'll find them in a small garden to the left as you face the main hall.

Each autumn, Suwa-jinja hosts the famous **Kunchi Matsuri** (October 7–9). This festival is believed to have originated in 1633 when two courtesans performing a Nō dance attracted huge crowds during celebrations to mark the ninth day of the ninth lunar month. Gradually, European and Chinese elements were incorporated – this was one of the few occasions when Dutch merchants were allowed to leave Dejima – and the jollities now consist of dragon dances and heavy floats, some fashioned as Chinese and Dutch ships, being spun round outside the shrine.

Central Nagasaki: down the Nakashima-gawa

Below Suwa-jinja the **Nakashima-gawa** flows west through central Nagasaki under a succession of stone bridges linked by a pleasant riverside walk. The most noteworthy of these is the double-arched **Megane-bashi**, aptly named "spectacles bridge", which is Japan's oldest stone bridge, dating from 1634. Across Megane-bashi, Teramachi-dōri (Temple-town Street) parallels the river along the valley's eastern slopes.

Turn right here, past a row of traditional shops, and then follow signs pointing left to **Sōfuku-ji** (daily 8am–5pm; ¥300). This is Nagasaki's most important Chinese Zen temple, founded in 1629 by Fujian immigrants and containing rare examples of Ming-period Chinese architecture. The entrance lies under a stocky, vermilion gate followed by a wooden inner gate, **Dai-ippon-mon**, decorated with polychrome, jigsaw-puzzle eaves. Both this gate and the **Buddha hall**, first building on the left inside the temple's stone-flagged courtyard, were actually shipped over from China and then pieced back together in Nagasaki in 1646 and 1696 respectively. Sakyamuni, the historical Buddha, occupies the hall's altar, flanked by eighteen individually expressed, gilded statues of Buddhist saints. A smaller, more faded hall lies at the back of the compound, its interior gloom broken only by the gorgeous robes and spangly headdress of a Chinese goddess, the protectress of sailors, and her two assistants. Finally, don't miss the vast cauldron, against the courtyard's south wall, in which monks supposedly boiled up porridge for five thousand people per day during a famine in 1681.

In the seventeenth century, Nagasaki's Chinese community comprised over fifteen percent of the population. Like the Europeans, they were restricted to a designated area which lay just inland from Dejima, near today's **Chinatown**. Four elaborate gates, recently built by Chinese craftsmen, signpost this colourful grid of six blocks packed with restaurants, while a bare-earth park over on the south side houses an older wooden gate and a Chinese pavilion where old men sit and gossip over the chess pieces.

There's more to see immediately to the northwest, where traces of **Dejima** (daily 9am–7pm; ¥300), the Portuguese and (later) Dutch enclave, can still be found along a curve of the old sea wall. Created in 1636, this tiny artificial island provided Japan's only access to the Western world for over two hundred years. The island was swallowed up in later land reclamations, but a restoration project now aims to restore the area to its former island state by 2010. There's plenty to see, with recreated warehouses and a captain's quarters from the eighteenth and nineteenth centuries; a theatre showing a short film on the history of Dejima, narrated from the viewpoint of a Dutch interpreter in 1865; and several museums. The **Dejima Museum Main Building** has exhibits on daily life on Dejima, including displays of various items from the period such as pottery, firearms, and even a Dutch golf club and ball; the **Museum Annexe** has more historical artefacts, including some unearthed during excavation work. There's an interesting display on the restoration of the Dejima buildings in the **No.1 Warehouse**, while the neighbouring **No.2 Warehouse** shows early examples of Japan absorbing (and improving upon) Western technology, with models of scientific devices such as telescopes and slide projectors created by the Japanese. There's also a scale model of how the whole site will eventually look in a small garden by the river in the east corner of the island.

South Nagasaki

When Japan's period of isolation effectively ended in the mid-1850s, the newcomers were allowed to live in Nagasaki itself, although still only within a prescribed area until 1899. Trading companies and customs offices sprouted along the seafront south of Dejima, while houses soon clothed the steep slopes above. A small river split the area into two districts known as Minami-yamate and Higashi-yamate – the south and east bluffs. Today a fair number of the old buildings still survive, most notably in the southern **Glover Garden** and in pockets along Higashi-yamate's **Dutch slopes**, where you'll also find an exotic little piece of China in Nagasaki's **Confucian shrine**.

Glover Garden

From the Ōura Tenshudō-shita tram stop (Line 5), a parade of souvenir shops leads to Japan's oldest church, **Ōura Catholic Church** (daily: April–Nov 8am–6pm; Jan–March & Dec 8.30am–5pm; ¥250). A pretty little white structure, with nothing much to see inside, it was built by French missionaries in 1864 to serve Nagasaki's growing foreign community. A few months later Father Petitjean was astonished to find outside his door a few brave members of Nagasaki's "hidden Christians" who had secretly kept the faith for more than two centuries.

Madame Butterfly

Puccini's opera, written in the early twentieth century, tells the story of an American lieutenant stationed in Nagasaki who marries a Japanese woman known as **Madame Butterfly**. Whereas she has given up her religion and earned the wrath of her family to enter the marriage, Lt. Pinkerton treats the marriage far less seriously, and is soon posted back to the States. Unknown to Pinkerton, Butterfly has given birth to their son and is waiting faithfully for his return when he arrives back in Nagasaki three years later. Butterfly pretties up her house and prepares to present her child to the proud father. Pinkerton, meanwhile, has remarried in America and brings his new wife to meet the unsuspecting Butterfly. When he offers to adopt the child, poor Butterfly agrees and tells him to come back later, then embraces her son and falls on her father's sword.

The opera was adapted from a play by David Belasco, though some attribute it to a book by Frenchman Pierre Loti who wrote *Madame Chrysanthème* after spending a month in Nagasaki in 1885 with a young Japanese woman called Kane. Whatever its origin, the opera was not well received at its debut and Puccini was forced to rewrite Pinkerton and his American wife in a more sympathetic light. Efforts to trace the real Pinkerton have led to a William B. Franklin, but there are many contenders; it was common practice in the late nineteenth century for Western males stationed in Japan to "marry" a geisha in order to secure their companion's faithfulness and reduce the spread of venereal disease. In return, they provided accommodation plus some remuneration. As soon as the posting ended, however, the agreement was considered null and void on both sides.

The path continues on up to **Glover Garden** (daily: Jan–July 19 & Oct 10 to Nov 8am–6pm; July 20–Oct 9 8am–9.30pm; Dec 8am–8pm; ¥600), which is named after the bluff's most famous resident, Thomas Glover. Despite the crowds and piped music, the garden's seven late-nineteenth-century, European-style buildings are surprisingly interesting, mostly for the life stories of their pioneering inhabitants. The houses are designed in full colonial style with wide verandas and louvred shutters, while their high-ceilinged, spacious rooms contain odds and ends of furniture and evocative family photos. The best approach is to start at the top – there are escalators up the hill – and work down, visiting at least the four houses recommended below.

A modest bungalow, **Walker House** was built in 1877 for the British-born captain of a Japanese passenger ship after he helped provide transport for government troops in the Satsuma Rebellion (see p.850). On retiring from the sea in 1898 he joined Thomas Glover in setting up Japan's first soft drinks company which produced a popular line in "Banzai Lemonade" and "Banzai Cider". **Ringer House** is a more comfortable, stone-built bungalow erected in 1865. Frederick Ringer began life as a tea inspector in Canton, then moved to Nagasaki in 1864 where he ran a tea export business, flour-mill, gas and electricity company, as well as founding an English-language paper, the Nagasaki Press. The **Alt House**, also built in 1865, is more imposing again, with its deep verandas, carriage porch and fountain, while the servants made do in the red-brick kitchen block behind. William Alt, another tea merchant, only lived here for three years before heading on to Ōsaka and then Yokohama.

By far the bluff's most colourful and illustrious resident, however, was the Scotsman **Thomas Glover**, who arrived from Shanghai in 1859, aged just 22, and became involved in various enterprises, including arms dealing. In the mid-1860s, rebels seeking to overthrow the shogun approached Glover for his assistance. Not only did he supply them with weapons, but also he furthered their revolutionary cause by smuggling some of them abroad to study, including Ito Hirobumi, who eventually served as prime minister in the new Meiji government. For this, and his subsequent work in modernizing Japanese industry, Glover was awarded the Second Class Order of the Rising Sun, a rare honour, shortly before his death in Tokyo aged 73.

Thomas built the bungalow now known as **Glover House** in 1863, where he lived with his wife Tsuru, a former geisha, and his son from an earlier liaison, Tomisaburo. After his father's death, Tomisaburo was a valued member of both the Japanese and foreign business communities, but as Japan slid towards war in the mid-1930s his companies were closed and Tomisaburo came under suspicion as a potential spy. Forced to move out of Glover House, with its bird's-eye view of the harbour, and kept under virtual house arrest, he committed suicide two weeks after the atomic bomb flashed above Nagasaki.

The exit from Glover Garden takes you through the rewarding **Museum of Traditional Performing Arts** (same ticket), which displays the beautifully fashioned floats and other paraphernalia used during the Kunchi festivities (see p.816). There's also a short film giving a glimpse of the action, including lithe dragon dances and ships spinning furiously.

The Dutch Slopes

From Ōura Church, take the footpath heading east through a little graveyard and along the valley side until you pick up signs to the **Dutch Slopes**. Though it's only five minutes' walk, few visitors bother to venture into this area where several more Western-style period houses have been preserved on the terraced hillsides reached by roads still paved with their original flagstones. The first group of wooden houses you see on the left consists of two neat rows: the lower three house a **photography museum** (Tues–Sun 9am–5pm; ¥100) displaying early photos of Nagasaki, while the **Higashi-yamate Museum** (same hours; free), in the middle of the upper row, exhibits materials about the district and efforts to rescue the old buildings.

Walking along the Dutch slopes you can't miss the bright yellow roofs of **Kōshi-byō** (daily 8.30am–5pm; ¥525), nestling at the foot of the hill within its stout, red-brick wall. Interestingly, the land beneath this **Confucian shrine**, completed in 1893, belongs to China and is administered by the embassy in Tokyo. Its present pristine state is due to an extensive 1980s rebuild using materials imported from China, right from the glazed roof tiles to the glittering white marble flagstones and statues of Confucius's 72 disciples filling the courtyard. After the restrained tones of Japan's religious architecture, Kōshi-byō's exuberant use of colour comes as a bit of a surprise, as does the gorgeously bedecked statue of Confucius flashing an endearing pair of snow-white buckteeth in the old, incense-stained sanctuary. Behind, the shrine museum is packed with priceless treasures, including hefty silver ingots, gold seals and rich brocades.

Inasa-yama

Nagasaki is not short of good viewpoints, but none can compare with the spectacular night-time panorama from **Inasa-yama**, a 333-metre-high knobble to the west of the city. A **ropeway** (daily: Jan–Feb & Dec 9am–9pm; March–Nov 9am–10pm; closed for maintenance early Dec; ¥700 one way, ¥1200 return) whisks you up there in just five minutes; cars run every twenty minutes and you can pick up discount vouchers at most hotels. To reach the ropeway, take Nagasaki Bus #3 or #4 from outside the train station and get off across the river at Ropeway-mae bus stop, from where the entrance is up the steps in the grounds of a shrine.

Eating, drinking and entertainment

Nagasaki's international heritage extends to its most famous **speciality food**, *shippoku*, which combines European, Chinese and Japanese tastes in lots of small dishes eaten Chinese-style at a round table. It's not a cheap meal, starting at around ¥4000 per head, and for the best *shippoku* you need to reserve the day before, although most of the big hotels also offer a less formal version. Nagasaki's other home-grown dishes include the cheap and cheerful *champon*, in which morsels of seafood, meat and vegetables are served with a dollop of thick noodles in piping-hot soup. Sara udon uses similar ingredients but blends them into a thicker sauce on a pile of crispy strands.

You can sample *champon* and sara udon at some of the **restaurants** listed om p.820, or try the little street immediately across from Nagasaki Station, where yellow flags announce a couple of good-value eating houses. Also check out the extensive food court in the basement of the Youme Saito shopping centre, next to the Ōhato Port Terminal. Just a stone's throw away, the colourful Nagasaki Dejima Wharf houses a number of trendy restaurants with views of the harbour. There's also a good choice of restaurants in the southern districts, specifically around Teramachi-dōri and across the tram tracks into Shianbashi and Chinatown, but these tend to shut quite early, around 8 or 9pm.

Nagasaki's entertainment district, **Shianbashi**, is sandwiched between Hamanomachi shopping district and Chinatown, in the south of the city. Ironically, *shi-an* translates as something like "peaceful contemplation", which is the last thing you'll find in this tangle of lanes, packed with bars, clubs, *pachinko* parlours, *izakaya* and "soaplands", where nothing really gets going until 10pm and ends at dawn. The choice, as ever, is bewildering, and prices can be astronomical, but a safe place to start is the With Nagasaki Building, on the east edge of the district on Kankō-dōri. It's a one-stop night out, starting in the basement with the Mikado *yakitori* or *Plaisir de Vin* winebar, and working upwards through a host of bars and nightclubs.

Restaurants

Futabaya 8-12 Shinchi-machi. Specialist cake shop in Chinatown selling *daifuku*, delicious *mochi* pounded rice cakes filled with all manner of fruits, and even chocolate or cream cheese, at about ¥140 a piece. Very moreish. Daily 9.30am–8.30pm.

Hamakatsu 1-14 Kajiya-chō. Popular restaurant on Teramachi-dōri specializing in *tonkatsu* (pork cutlets). Though it looks smart, with its gold signboard and iron lantern, prices are extremely reasonable and you can eat all you want of the extras – soup, rice and salad.

Hamakatsu 6-50 Kajiya-chō ☎095/826-8321. This smarter *Hamakatsu* offers *shippoku* meals at reasonable prices. You can try a mini-*shippoku* at around ¥3000 or the real thing from ¥4000 up to ¥15,000 per person; note that you must order in advance and they require at least two people per group.

Harbin 2F, 4-13 Yorozuya-machi ☎095/824-6650. On Kankōdōri arcade, this Nagasaki institution has been serving French and Russian cuisine since 1959. It's nicely decked out with dark wooden furniture and an impressive array of vodkas, and there's plenty of choice, from borscht to Azerbaijan-style *pot au feu*, and good lunchtime sets from ¥1000.

Kagetsu 2-1 Maruyama-machi ☎095/822-0191. Set on the corner of an attractive square and surrounded by a traditional garden, this place is even more famous than *Harbin* – although it started life as a brothel – and is the best spot in town for *shippoku*. Prices start at ¥4550 for a lunchtime *ship-*

poku bentō or ¥8000 for the regular set; expect to pay at least double that in the evening. Booking is essential and you need two people or more.

Kōzanrō 12-2 Shinchi-machi. Chinatown is packed with tempting restaurants, but this Fukien establishment is recommended for its reasonably priced *champon* and sara udon, as well as more mainstream Chinese dishes. Daily 11.30am–9.30pm.

Ringer Hut Towards the south end of Teramachi-dōri, this basic, reliable café-style restaurant belongs to another Kyūshū chain. The extensive menu includes *champon* sets from ¥600. Daily until 4am.

Robin Hood no Mori 4F, 5-8 Motoshikkui-machi. Look for their small Robin Hood logo just as you walk south into Shianbashi, and make sure you're hungry enough to appreciate their eat-and-drink-all-you-want deals (from ¥2100). Men pay slightly more than women, there's a two-hour time period and everyone in the group must choose the same type of menu. *Shabu-shabu*, barbecue-beef and seafood are the main options, though there's also a salad bar. It's a bit of a scrum at peak times, when you'll have to queue. Daily from 5pm.

Shirokiya 9-28 Daikoku-machi. Big, bright *izakaya* opposite the station with something for everyone on its picture-menu – sushi, *sukiyaki*, *yakitori*, salads and so on. Service can be slow, but the beers are cheap and you can count on ¥2000 or less per person for a good feast. Daily 5pm–5am.

Listings

Airlines ANA ☎0120-029-222; China Eastern Airlines ☎095/828-1510; JAL ☎0120-255971; JAS ☎0120–511283; Korean Air ☎095/824-3311.

Airport information ☎095/752-5555.

Banks and exchange The 18th Bank, next to the *New Nagasaki Hotel*, is the closest foreign exchange service to the train station. Otherwise, there are branches of major banks around the central Hamanomachi shopping district.

Bookshops Nagasaki's biggest bookshop,

Kinokuniya, is located on the fourth floor of the Youme Saito shopping centre, near the Ōhato Port Terminal. It has a decent selection of English books and magazines. Also try Kobundo, located in Hamanomachi arcade. Foreign titles are up on the second floor. Look out for *Crossroads* (¥600), an excellent journal about Nagasaki history and culture published annually by two American academics.

Car rental Eki Rent-a-Car ☎095/826-0480; Nippon Rent-a-Car ☎095/821-0919; Nissan Rent-

a-Car ☏095/825-1988; Toyota Rent-a-Car
☏095/825-0100.
Ferries Yasuda company (☏095/836-2613) operates daily express and regular ferries from Mogi-
kō south to the Amakusa islands (40min, ¥1750 by
express ferry; 1hr 10min, ¥1220 by regular ferry).
Mogi-kō is a thirty-minute bus ride from Nagasaki
Station.
Festivals New Year is celebrated in Chinatown
with a Lantern Festival, dragon dances and acrobatic displays (Jan 1–3). Dragon-boat races, here
called Peiron, were introduced by the Chinese in
1655 and are still held in Nagasaki harbour every
summer (June–July). The last evening of Obon
(Aug 15) is celebrated with a "spirit-boat" procession, when recently bereaved families lead
lantern-lit floats down to the harbour. But the
biggest bash of the year occurs at the Kunchi
Matsuri held in early October at Suwa-jinja (see
p.816).
Hospitals Shimin Byōin, 6-39 Shinchi-machi
(☏095/822-3251) is an emergency hospital on the
western edge of Chinatown.
Internet access Try Chikyū Shimin Hiroba, on the
second floor of Nagasaki Brick Hall, 2-38, Mori
machi (daily 9am–8pm; ¥100 per hr), south of

Urakami station; they also have international
papers. Alternatively, there's the Cyba Internet
café, just beyond Hamano-machi-dōri (¥300 membership plus ¥480; open 24hr).
Police 6-13 Okeya-machi (☏095/822-0110).
Emergency numbers are listed in "Basics" on p.81.
Post office Nagasaki Central Post Office is 300m
east of the station at 1-1 Ebisu-machi and has a
poste restante service.
Shopping The main department stores, Daimaru
and Hamaya, are in the Hamanomachi shopping
arcades. The most popular local souvenir is
Castella (*kasutera*) sponge cake – the best-known
kasutera bakeries are Fukusa-ya and Bunmei-dō,
both of which have outlets all over the city. If you
want to buy it at source, however, try Fukusa-ya's
original shop in a picturesque building on the edge
of Shianbashi – look for its distinctive bat logo
(daily 8.30am–8pm).
Taxis Lucky Cab ☏095/822-4123.
Travel agencies For domestic travel, the main
JTB office is at 14-9 Dōzamachi (☏095/823-
1261). International tickets can be bought at H.I.S.,
5F, Yamato-seimei Building, 3-4 Manzai-machi
(☏095/820-6839), in the streets west of the City
Hall.

Shimabara Hantō

East of Nagasaki, the **Shimabara Hantō** bulges out into the Ariake Sea, tethered to mainland Kyūshū by a neck of land just 5km wide. The peninsula owes
its existence to the past volcanic fury of **Unzen-dake**, which still grumbles away,
pumping out sulphurous steam, and occasionally spewing lava down its eastern
flanks. Buddhist monks first came to the mountain in the eighth century,
followed more than a millennium later by Europeans from nearby Nagasaki,
attracted by the cool, upland summers and mild winters. Even today, **Unzen**, a
small onsen resort surrounded by pine trees and billowing clouds of steam, draws
holidaymakers to its hot springs, malodorous "hells" and scenic hiking trails. One
of the most popular outings is to the lava dome of **Fugen-dake**, which roared
back into life in 1990 after two centuries of inactivity, and now smoulders
menacingly above the old castle town of **Shimabara** – this was protected from
the worst of the eruption by an older lava block, but still suffered considerable
damage to its southern suburbs, which are slowly being rebuilt. Previously,
Shimabara was famous largely for its association with a Christian-led rebellion in
the seventeenth century when 37,000 peasants and their families were massacred.
Both towns can be covered on a long day's journey between Nagasaki and
Kumamoto, but if time allows Unzen makes a relaxing overnight stop.

Unzen

You can feel the air temperature dropping as the road from Obama leaves sea
level and climbs up towards the **Unzen plateau** (727m). The name means
"fairyland among the clouds", perhaps inspired by the pure mountain air and

colourful flourishes of vegetation – azaleas in spring and autumn leaves – against which the **onsen** and their alter egos, the spitting, scalding **jigoku** ("hells"), compete for attention. Unzen town consists largely of resort hotels and souvenir shops strung out along the main road, but fortunately there's plenty of space around and a variety of **walking trails** lead off into the surrounding national park. The best hikes explore the peaks of Unzen-dake, though the highest paths are still off limits following the 1990 eruption. However, you can take a **rope-way** part way up **Fugen-dake**, affording splendid views of the Ariake Sea and, if you're lucky, across to Aso-san's steaming cauldron.

Without your own transport, the best way of **getting to Unzen** is by bus. Frequent direct services depart from either Nagasaki's Ken-ei bus terminal or outside the station (¥1900); JR pass holders can take the train to Isahaya and pick up the bus there. Isahaya's bus station is right in front of the JR station, to the left of the pedestrian footbridge. From here, both Ken-ei and Shimatetsu buses run up to Unzen. (¥1300).

The Town

UNZEN is pretty much a one-street town. The main road enters from the southwest, does a dog-leg east and then north, before exiting east towards Shimabara. Unzen's commercial centre lies in the north, concentrated round the bus stations, while its geographical centre consists of a steaming, barren area known as **jigoku**. These *jigoku* and an assortment of **onsen baths**, renowned for their silky smooth water, constitute Unzen's foremost attractions. The first commercial onsen bath was opened in 1653, while two hundred years later Europeans arriving from Nagasaki, Hong Kong, Shanghai and east Russia prompted the development of a full-blown resort, complete with mock–Tudor hotels and one of Japan's first golf courses, laid out in 1913.

The nicest of Unzen's **public baths** is the old-style **Kojigoku** (daily 9am–8pm; ¥400), which occupies two octagonal wooden buildings opposite the Seiun-sō hotel, roughly ten minutes' walk south of town. More in the centre of things, **Shin-yu** (daily 10am–11pm; ¥100) is a small but traditional bathhouse

Shimabara Hantō		
Unzen	*Unzen*	雲仙
Fugen-dake	*Fugen-dake*	普賢岳
Fukuda-ya	*Fukuda-ya*	福田屋
Kaseya	*Kaseya*	かせや
Kokuminshukusha	*Kokuminshukusha*	国民宿舎青雲荘
Seiun-sō	*Seiun-sō*	
Unzen Kankō Hotel	*Unzen Kankō Hoteru*	雲仙観光ホテル
Shimabara	*Shimabara*	島原
Business Hotel Toraya	*Bijinesu Hoteru*	ビジネスホテルとらや
Hotel Hakusan	*Hoteru Hakusan*	ホテル白山
Hotel Hanamizuki	*Hoteru Hanamizuki*	ホテル+スパ花みずき
Himematsu-ya	*Himematsu-ya*	姫松屋
New Queen Hotel	*Nyū Kuiin Hoteru*	ニュークイーンホテル
Ōsaka-ya	*Ōsaka-ya*	大阪屋
Shimabara-jō	*Shimabara-jō*	島原城
Shimabara Youth Hostel	*Shimabara Yūsu Hosuteru*	島原ユースホステル
Sushi-katsu	*Sushi-katsu*	すし勝

just south of the *jigoku*. Lastly, there's the more glitzy **Unzen Spa House** (daily 10am–8pm; ¥800), offering sauna, Jacuzzi and all sorts of baths, including a rotemburo, in a half-timbered building on the main road into town.

A Shingon Buddhist priest is credited with "founding" Unzen when he built a temple here in 701 AD; the area developed into a popular retreat where monks could contemplate the 84,000 tortures awaiting wrongdoers in the afterlife as they gazed at Unzen's bubbling mudpools. The volcanic vents are less active nowadays but still emit evil, sulphurous streams and waft steam over a landscape of bilious-coloured clay. Only the hardiest of acid-tolerant plants can survive, and local hoteliers have added to the satanic scene by laying a mess of rusting, hissing pipes to feed water to their onsen baths.

Nevertheless, the *jigoku* provide an interesting hour's diversion, particularly the more active eastern area. The paths are well signposted, with lots of maps and information along the way, and there's also a descriptive English-language brochure, *A Round in Unzen Hell*, available at the Visitors' Centre (see below). The highest and most active *jigoku*, **Daikyōkan Jigoku**, takes its name from the "scream" produced as it emits hydrogen sulphide steam at 120°C. The noise is likened to the cries of souls descending to hell, but could well be the howls of 33 Christian martyrs, commemorated on a nearby monument, who were scalded to death here around 1630 by the Shimabara lords (see box on p.824). Another unhappy end is remembered at **Oito Jigoku** which, according to legend, broke out the day a local adulteress, Oito, was executed for murdering her husband. The tiny, bursting bubbles of **Suzume Jigoku**, on the other hand, supposedly resemble the twittering of sparrows. Over in the western section, the main point of interest is **Mammyō-ji** temple, founded nearly 1300 years ago and now home to an intriguing gilded Shaka Buddha with a startling blue hairdo.

Fugen-dake

While Unzen-dake is the name of the whole volcanic mass, **Fugen-dake** (1488m) refers to a newer cone on its east side that now forms the highest of the Unzen peaks. Fugen-dake erupted suddenly in November 1990 and reached a crescendo in June 1991 when the dome collapsed, sending an avalanche of mud and rocks through Shimabara town. Forty three people were killed and nearly 2000 homes destroyed. Since then, Fugen-dake continues to smoke gently, but the eruption officially ended in May 1995.

A **ropeway** (daily 8.30am–5.30pm; ¥1220 return) takes visitors up to an observation platform to the west of Fugen-dake. Cars run every twenty minutes, though not in bad weather or if the volcano is misbehaving; the last ride down is at 5.30pm. From the top station, you can walk to the nearest summit, Myōken-dake (1333m), in just ten minutes and then continue to Kunimi-dake (1347m). Buses to the ropeway depart from Unzen's Ken-ei bus terminal (20min; ¥740 return; 5–6 daily). The last bus down to Unzen leaves at 4.30pm, after which you'll have to walk, which takes an hour; the path starts to the west of the information centre in the ropeway car park and ends beside the Ikenohara golf course, on the main road 1km east of Unzen town.

Practicalities

Unzen has two **bus terminals**: Ken-ei buses, by far the most frequent, pull in at the north end of town, while Shimatetsu buses stop a little further back down the main road. For general **information** about accommodation and transport, try Unzen Information Centre (daily 9am–5pm; ☎0957/73-3434, ℱ73-2261), located on the main road in from the south. There are no English-speaking staff, but they can give you English guide-maps to the area.

Most **accommodation** in Unzen consists of expensive resort hotels, but there are a couple of reasonable choices, which it's advisable to reserve even out of season. The best option is *Kokuminshukusha Seiun-sō* (☎0957/73-3273, ℻73-2698; ❺), a rambling place offering basic tatami rooms, a big onsen bath and excellent-value meals – or the option of room only – in a nicely wooded position ten minutes' walk south of town (phone to be collected from the bus station). *Kaseya* (☎0957/73-3321, ℻73-3322; ❺), an attractive old ryokan on the main road near the bus stations, has clean bright tatami rooms, a wooden bath and optional meals. Set in gardens at the south end of town, the *Unzen Kankō Hotel* (☎0957/73-3263, ℻73-3419; ❻) is one of the original European-style hotels, built in 1935. The cheaper rooms are all Western style; small but comfortable, and equipped with large, old-fashioned bathtubs. Just south of there, *Fukuda-ya* (☎0957/73-3388, ℻73-3389; ❻–❼) is an atmospheric ryokan in a beautiful old wooden building by the river, with a choice of rotem-buro. For budget travellers, there's a campsite on the road into Unzen from the south (☎0957-73-2642; closed Dec–March).

When it comes to **eating**, you're best off taking meals in your hotel. However, there's a lovely café attached to *Fukuda-ya* called *Mingeijayariki* by the river which serves huge sizzling plates of *yōgan* (lava) soba noodles for two, and delicious sweet potato desserts and ice cream. The *Unzen Kankō Hotel* has a pricey gourmet restaurant which is open to non-residents, and there are a few uninspiring but inexpensive cafés along the main road. If you fancy a few beers, the *Unzen Tabi no Beer Kan*, near the Ken-ei Bus Centre, brews three kinds of beer on the premises and does curry rice, a lunch buffet, and all-you-can-eat German-style *yaki-niku* in the evenings (daily 11am–8pm).

Shimabara

The port town of **SHIMABARA** has had a chequered history. Following the ructions of the **Shimabara Rebellion** (see box below), it was decimated when Unzen-dake erupted in 1792, sending rock and hot ash tumbling into Shimabara Bay. An estimated 15,000 people died in the disaster, mostly from huge tidal waves that swept the Ariake Sea. The volcano then lay dormant until Fugen-dake burst into life again in 1990 (see p.823) and cut a swathe through the town's southern reaches; they're still busily restoring the roads and rice terraces, while photos of the eruption appear all over Shimabara. Though the brooding mountain makes a dramatic backdrop, the only reason to stop here is to visit its castle, **Shimabara-jō**, which hosts an interesting museum about Japan's early Christians and the local rebellion.

The Shimabara Rebellion

In 1637, exorbitant taxes and the oppressive cruelty of two local *daimyō* sparked off a large-scale **peasant revolt** in the Shimabara area, though the underlying motive was anger at **Christian persecutions** taking place at the time. Many of the rebels were Christian, including their leader, a 16-year-old boy known as Amakusa Shirō, who was supposedly able to perform miracles. His motley army of 37,000, including women and children, eventually sought refuge in abandoned Hara castle, roughly 30km south of Shimabara town. For three months they held off far-superior government forces, but even Shirō couldn't save them when Hara was stormed in April 1638 and, so it's said, all 37,000 were massacred. Rightly or wrongly, Portuguese missionaries were implicated in the rebellion and soon after all foreigners were banished from Japan as the country closed its doors.

Completed in 1625, the castle took seven years to build – it was partly the taxes and hard labour demanded for its construction that provoked the Shimabara Rebellion. Entry to the grounds is free, while the reconstructed turrets contain a **museum** (daily: April–Oct 9am–5.30pm; Nov–March 9am–5pm; ¥520), spread over four floors – most interesting are the main keep's local history exhibits, including some relics of clandestine Christian worship. The modern building in the northwest corner shows a short video in English about Fugen-dake's most recent eruption, while fans of Nagasaki's Peace Statue (see p.814) will be interested in the Kitamura Seibō Memorial Museum located in the southeast turret. Kitamura, a local sculptor who died in 1987, specialized in powerful bronzes, the best of them gripped by a restless, pent-up energy. If you have more time, walk ten minutes northeast of the castle to reach the *buké-yashiki*, a pretty little street of samurai houses.

Practicalities

Shimabara straggles along the coast for more than 2km from its southerly **Shin-kō ferry terminal** to the main centre, **Ōte**, just below the castle. **Buses** from Unzen call at the Shin-kō terminal before proceeding into town, where they either terminate at the Shimatetsu bus terminal or stop a little further on in Ōte. **Trains** running south from Isahaya on the private Shimabara line stop at the main Shimabara Station, a couple of minutes' walk east of Ōte, and then continue three more stops to Shin-kō Station (also known as Gai-kō Station) near the ferry port.

Shimabara's **information office** (daily 9am–5pm; ☎ & ℗0957/62-3986) is inside the Shin-kō terminal building. For **onward transport** to Kumamoto, there's a choice of two ferry crossings: either to Kumamoto Shin-kō or Misumi (last sailings 6.35pm & 4.40pm respectively), both of which take one hour and cost ¥590 for foot passengers. There are buses from Kumamoto Shin-kō into the city (35min; ¥470), while from Misumi it's a longer, fifty-minute train ride, though free to JR pass holders.

If you need **accommodation**, one of the nicest central places is *Hanamizuki* (☎0957/62-1000; ❺), a small, bright business hotel five minutes' walk southwest from Shimabara Station. Near the ferry terminal, there's the cheap and basic *Business Hotel Tōraya* (☎0957/63-3332; ❹), offering either Western or tatami rooms, or *Shimabara Youth Hostel* (☎0957/62-4451; dorm beds ¥2750 per person), roughly three minutes' walk west across the train tracks, which has its own onsen bath. For something smarter, try either the *New Queen Hotel* (☎0957/64-5511, ℗63-0051; ❺) or the slightly cheaper *Hotel Hakusan* (☎0957/63-5400, ℗62-3334; ❹), both on the main road north.

Shimabara's **speciality food**, *guzoni*, is a delicious clam broth packed with rice-cakes, fish, pork, lotus root, tofu and egg. You can try it at *Himematsu-ya* (daily 10am–8pm), an attractive **restaurant** opposite the entrance to Shimabara-jō, or there's a choice of well-priced sets and mainstream Japanese dishes. *Sushi-katsu* (daily 10am–8pm) is a fine old sushi bar on Ōte's central square, where you should be able to eat for under ¥2000. For a late-night bite, *Ōsaka-ya* (daily 6pm–3am), south of this square, serves a cracking mixed-cheese *okonomiyaki*.

Kumamoto

Situated halfway down the west coast, within striking distance of Aso to the east and Unzen to the west, **KUMAMOTO** makes a good base for exploring central Kyūshū. The city itself is reasonably attractive and boasts a couple of worthwhile sights, namely the fearsome, fairy-tale **castle** dominating the town centre, and one of Japan's most highly rated gardens, **Suizenji-kōen**, in the western suburbs. Wars and development have meant that little else of particular note survives, though you've got to admire a city which invented the endearingly offbeat "Kobori-style" swimming which "involves the art of swimming in a standing posture attired in armour and helmet".

Kumamoto owes its existence to the Katō clan, who were given the fiefdom in the late sixteenth century in return for supporting Tokugawa Ieyasu during his rise to power. **Katō Kiyomasa**, first of the feudal lords, not only built a magnificent fortress but is also remembered for his public works, such as flood control and land reclamation. However, political intrigue resulted in the Katō being ousted in 1632 in favour of the **Hosokawa** clan, who had previously held Kokura. Thirteen generations of Hosokawa lords ruled Kumamoto for more than two centuries, during which time the city thrived as Kyūshū's major government stronghold, until feudal holdings were abolished in 1871. Six years later, the final drama of the Meiji Restoration was played out here when Saigō Takamori's rebel army was defeated by government troops, but not before destroying much of Kumamoto's previously impregnable castle.

Kumamoto

Kumamoto	*Kumamoto*	熊本
Kumamoto-jō	*Kumamoto-jō*	熊本城
Kumamoto Kōtsū Centre	*Kumamoto Kōtsū Sentā*	熊本交通センター
Kumamoto Shin-kō Port	*Kumamoto Shin-kō*	熊本新港
Kyū-Hosokawa Gyōbutei	*Kyū-Hosokawa Gyōbutei*	旧細川刑部邸
Prefectural Art Museum	*Kumamoto-kenritsu Bijutsukan*	熊本県立美術館
Prefectural Traditional Crafts Centre	*Kumamoto-ken Dentō Kōgei-kan*	熊本県伝統工芸館
Suizenji-kōen	*Suizenji-kōen*	水前寺公園
Accommodation		
Ark Hotel	*Āku Hoteru*	アークホテル
Hotel Ichiban-kan	*Hoteru Ichiban-kan*	ホテル一番館
Kajita	*Kajita*	梶田
Komatsu-sō	*Komatsu-sō*	小松荘
Kumamoto-ken Seinenkaikan	*Kumamoto-ken Seinenkaikan*	熊本県青年会館
Maruko Hotel	*Maruko Hoteru*	丸小ホテル
Mitsui Garden Hotel	*Mitsui Gāden Hoteru*	三井ガーデンホテル
Hotel New Otani	*Hoteru Nyū Ōtani*	ホテルニューオオタニ
Suizenji Youth Hostel	*Suizenji Yūsu Hosuteru*	水前寺ユースホステル
Restaurants		
Aoyagi	*Aoyagi*	青柳
Daimonji	*Daimonji*	大文字
Hanaichimomme	*Hanaichimomme*	花いちもんめ
Ichinosōko	*Ichinosōko*	壱之倉庫
Shankar	*Shankā*	シャンカー
Takamatsu	*Takamatsu*	高松
Yōrōnotaki	*Yōrōnotaki*	養老乃瀧

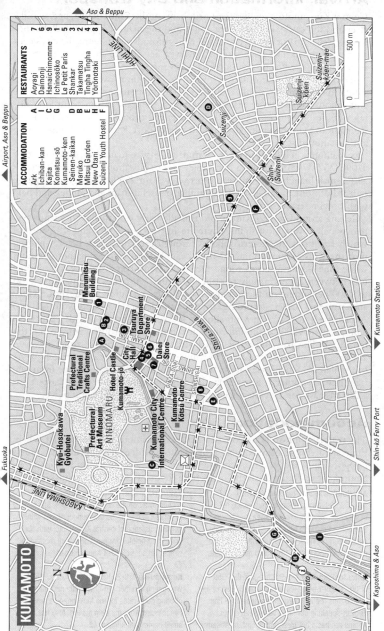

KUMAMOTO

Aso & Beppu

Airport, Aso & Beppu

Fukuoka

HŌHI LINE

Suizenji-kōen

Suizenji-
kōen-mae

Suizenji

Shin-
Suizenji

Marumitsu
Building

Tsuruya
Department
Store

City
Hall

Daiei
Store

Prefectural
Traditional
Crafts Centre

KAMI-TŌRI

SHIMO-TŌRI

GINZA-DŌRI

SHIN-SHIGA

SHIN-SHIGA

Hotel Castle

Kumamoto-jō

NINOMARU

Kumamoto City
International Centre

Kumamoto
Kōtsū Centre

Prefectural
Art Museum

Kyū-Hosokawa
Gyōbutei

KAGOSHIMA LINE

Kumamoto Station

Shin-kō Ferry Port

Kagoshima & Aso

Kumamoto

Kumamoto

0   500 m

N

Arrival, information and city transport

Central Kumamoto occupies the north bank of the **Shira-kawa**, between the river and the castle. This is where you'll find the main shopping mall, Shimo-tōri, as well as major hotels, banks and Kumamoto Kōtsū Centre, the city's central bus terminal. The main station, however, lies 2km to the south, creating a secondary hub, with its own hotels and bus services.

Arriving at Kumamoto **airport**, roughly 15km northwest, limousine buses shuttle into town in roughly one hour (¥670), stopping at Shimo-tōri and the Kumamoto Kōtsū Centre before ending up at the train station. Most long-distance buses terminate at the Kōtsū Centre, though a few continue to Kumamoto Station, while buses from the ferry port, Kumamoto Shin-kō, stop at the station first.

Kumamoto's helpful **tourist information** service (daily 9am–5.30pm; ⊕ & ⑲ 096/352-3743) occupies a desk inside the train station's central exit; there's also a small branch office in the airport (daily 8am–8.30pm). English-language staff at both offices can give you a number of useful maps and guides, and help with hotel reservations.

Getting around central Kumamoto is made fairly easy thanks to a **tram** system which covers most sights. There are just two lines (#2 and #3), both of which run from the eastern suburbs through the city centre before splitting near the Kōtsū Centre. Line #2 then heads off south to Kumamoto Station, while Line #3 loops north round the castle. Trams run every five to ten minutes between approximately 6.30am and 11pm, with fares ranging from ¥130 to ¥200 depending on the distance travelled; take a numbered ticket on entry and pay the driver according to the fare-display board as you get off. Alternatively, if you're moving about a lot, you can buy a one-day pass (*ichinichi jōshaken*; ¥500) at the information centre, in the Kōtsū Centre or on the tram itself. This pass also covers Shiei buses within the central zone; however, as there are four bus companies in Kumamoto and it's not immediately obvious which are Shiei **buses**, it's best to stick to trams. You can change from one tram line to another at Karashima-chō, where the lines split; if you haven't got a day pass, ask for a transfer ticket (*norikae-kippu*) to avoid paying twice.

Accommodation

The majority of **hotels** are concentrated in Kumamoto's central district, where there are a couple of reasonable ryokan plus a wider selection in the business category and above. Most cheaper places are located around Kumamoto Station, while the two youth hostels both lie out west near Suizenji-kōen.

Ark Hotel 5-16 Jōtō-machi ⊕096/351-2222, ⑲326-0909. Nicely designed mid-range hotel beside the castle. The rooms are a reasonable size and decked out with batik-style bed covers and contemporary prints. You pay slightly more for a castle view, though the NHK radio mast intrudes. ⑥

Hotel Ichiban-kan 1-3-9 Nihongi ⊕096/359-6600, ⑲359-6949. Five minutes' walk east of the station, this friendly bargain business hotel has English-speaking staff and very green decor. Rooms are basic but clean and bright, in Western or Japanese style. The cheapest share a bathroom. ❹

Kajita 1-2-7 Shin-machi ⊕ & ⑲096/353-1546. Tucked away on the castle's west side, this homely minshuku is one of the few budget places within walking distance of central Kumamoto, with good prices and helpful owners. The tatami rooms are simple yet smart, with TV but no en-suite facilities. ❹

Komatsu-sō 1-8-23 Kasuga ⊕096/355-2634. Welcoming if rather run-down little minshuku offering good rates for the location, on a lane just five minutes from the train station. Also has a small communal kitchen. ❹

Kumamoto-ken Seinen-kaikan 3-17-15 Suizenji ⊕096/381-6221, ⓔkaikan@ks-kaikan.com. Set in a modern building, with tatami rooms with English TV, plus a restaurant on the ground floor. There's a flexible curfew. Walk straight ahead out of Suizenji Station, take the second left, walk for five minutes then bear left at the next set of traffic lights. ❸

Maruko Hotel 11-10 Kamitōri-chō ℡096/353-1241, ℻353-1217. Modern, well-decorated hotel in an interesting area to the north of the centre. Rooms are mostly Japanese style and all are en suite, and there's also a Japanese bath with views on the sixth floor. English spoken. ❺

Mitsui Garden Hotel 1-20 Koyaima-machi ℡096/352-1131, ℻322-5847. Despite the grand marble lobby, prices at this mid-range business hotel on the south edge of the centre aren't too bad, and the rooms are comfortable and come with bathroom, TV and minibar. ❺

New Ōtani 1-13-1 Kasuga ℡096/326-1111, ℻326-0800. The smartest hotel near Kumamoto Station, with efficient service, a choice of formal restaurants, a coffee shop, sauna and shopping area. Rooms are well equipped and ample, with generous-size beds. ❻

Suizenji Youth Hostel 1-2-20 Hakuzan ℡096/371-9193. Book ahead for this small, spotless hostel out near Suizenji-kōen, with accommodation in shared tatami rooms. It's five minutes' walk west of Shin-Suizenji Station on the JR Hōhi line, and two minutes from the Misotenjin-mae tram stop; from the tram, walk back (west) to the last crossroads, turn left and follow the road round and you'll find the hostel before the next main road. Note that no meals are served, and there are no cooking facilities. Dorm beds ¥3045 per person. ❶

The City

Completed in 1607 after only seven years' work, **Kumamoto-jō** is Japan's third largest castle (after Ōsaka and Nagoya) and one of its most formidable. It was designed by lord **Katō Kiyomasa**, a brilliant military architect who combined superb fortifications with exquisitely graceful flourishes – as Alan Booth observed in *The Roads to Sata* (see "Books", p.1016), the main keep seems like "a fragile bird poised for flight". At its peak, Kumamoto-jō had an outer perimeter of 13km and over 5km of inner wall built in what's called *musha-gaeshi* style, meaning that no invading warrior could scale their smooth, gently concave surfaces. In case of prolonged attack, 120 wells were sunk, while camphor and ginkgo trees provided firewood and edible nuts. These defences were severely tested during the 1877 **Satsuma Rebellion** (see p.850), when Saigō Takamori's army besieged Kumamoto-jō for fifty days. Government reinforcements eventually relieved the garrison and trounced the rebels soon after. Though the castle held, most of its surrounding buildings were burnt to the ground and left in ruins until 1960, when the main keep was magnificently restored around a concrete shell.

The best approach to the castle is from its south side, which brings you up into the grassy expanse of **Ninomaru**. Before entering the inner citadel, you might want to visit the **Prefectural Art Museum** (Tues–Sun 9.30am–4.30pm; ¥260), over to the west, which takes in a broad sweep from ancient ornamented tombs to an impressive collection of contemporary Japanese and Western art. Otherwise, pass through the castle's main, west gate into the **Honmaru** (daily: April–Oct 8.30am–5.30pm; Nov–March 8.30am–4.30pm; ¥500). Inside to the left, **Uto Yagura** was the only turret to survive the 1877 battle, while straight on, a high-sided defile leads to the imposing central keep. It now hosts an excellent historical **museum** about the castle and the Hosokawa lords.

Continuing down the castle's eastern slope, you reach **Akazu-no-mon**. Traditionally this northeastern gate was never opened – the northeast being the direction from which evil was thought to emanate – but castle waste was pushed through a nearby sluice to be collected by local farmers for fertilizer. One enterprising gatekeeper made such a profit selling the refuse that he was later deified by grateful benefactors in his home town.

Opposite the Akazu gate, the **Prefectural Traditional Crafts Centre** (Tues–Sun 9am–4.30pm) hosts free exhibitions promoting local artists and an excellent display of Kumamoto crafts on the second floor (¥200). The most famous traditional craft is *Higo zogan*, a painstaking method of inlaying gold and silver in a metal base. Developed in the seventeenth century for ornamenting sword hilts, it's now used for jewellery, decorative boxes and the like. Look out among the toys for a little red-faced fellow with a black hat, the ghost Obake-no-kinta – try pulling the string.

Below the Prefectural Art Museum you'll find the **Kyū-Hosokawa Gyōbutei** (daily: March–Oct 8.30am–5.30pm; Jan–Feb & Nov–Dec 8.30am–4.30pm; ¥300 or ¥640 including entry to the castle), an immaculately restored and unusually large high-ranking samurai residence in beautiful grounds, one of the few buildings of its kind remaining in Japan.

Suizenji-kōen

It pays to visit **Suizenji-kōen** (daily: March–Nov 7.30am–6pm; Jan–Feb & Dec 8.30am–5pm; ¥400) early, before crowds arrive. In any case, the garden is at its best with an early-morning mist over the crystal-clear, spring-fed lake, its surface broken by jumping minnows or the darting beak of a heron. Plump, multicoloured carp laze under willow-pattern bridges, while staff sweep the gravel paths or snip back an errant pine tuft. Considered to be one of Japan's most beautiful stroll-gardens, Suizenji-kōen was created over eighty years, starting in 1632, by three successive Hosokawa lords. The temple from which the garden took its name is long gone, but the immaculate, undulating landscape, dotted with artfully placed shrubs and trees, has survived. The design supposedly mimics scenes on the road between Tokyo and Kyoto, known as the "53 stations of the Tōkaidō", although the only ones most people will recognize are Fuji and Lake Biwa.

Considering Suizenji's prestige, it's surprising to find the garden cluttered with souvenir stalls, and it's also quite small, taking only thirty minutes to walk round. On the way, you'll pass the Izumi shrine, dedicated to the Hosokawa lords, and a four-hundred-year-old teahouse overlooking the lake. If it's not too early, you can drink a cup of green tea on the benches outside (8.30am–5pm; ¥500) or in the tea ceremony room (¥600), while admiring one of the best views of the garden; the price includes an *izayoi*, a white, moon-shaped cake made using egg white.

Eating, drinking and nightlife

Central Kumamoto splits into two distinct areas either side of the tram tracks. South of the tracks, **Shimo-tōri** arcade and its offshoots, Sannenzaka-dōri, Ginza-dōri and Shinshigai-Sunroad, are the classic entertainment district, packed with neon-lit **bars**, **clubs** and a mix of **restaurants** from fast food to expense-account dining. North of the tracks, on the other hand, there's a younger, less hectic feel among the small boutiques and ethnic cafés around Kami-tōri.

Local **speciality foods** include horse-meat sashimi (*basashi*) eaten with lots of garlic, and *karashi renkon*, which consists of lotus-root slices stuffed with a mustard and bean paste, dipped in batter and deep fried. In addition to the restaurants listed opposite, most big hotels, notably the *Castle* and *New Ōtani*, have well-rated dining-rooms, while Kumamoto Station has a good variety of outlets on its second floor. You'll find the usual chains either at the station or in the central arcades, including *Capricciosa*, *Nanak* and *Ringer Hut*.

Minamata's poisoned sea

In the mid-1950s, fisherfolk living around Minamata, a town in south Kumamoto Prefecture, began suffering from a mysterious disease. The illness attacked the nervous system, causing convulsions, loss of speech and hearing, often severe mental disability and an agonizing death. The first case of what came to be known as **Minamata disease** was officially diagnosed in 1956, but it took another three years to identify the cause as organic mercury poisoning, and it was nearly another decade before Chisso, a local chemical company, stopped pumping their mercury-laden waste into the sea.

The victims, aided by a local teacher, Ishimure Michiko, battled for years against the local authorities, the company and the national government to win recognition of their suffering and adequate compensation. Eventually, a number of families took the company to court in 1969, by which time a nationwide support movement had evolved. Four years later, Chisso was finally judged liable – too late for many, of course.

To date, although the government recently declared the bay mercury-free, nearly 2000 people have died of Minamata disease, while around 13,000 have been certified as afflicted and eligible for compensation. Though the true extent of the tragedy will never be known, some estimates put the total number of people affected as high as 100,000.

Restaurants

Aoyagi 1-2-10 Shimotōri-chō. Large, elegant restaurant behind the Daiei store, with a choice of counter, tatami room or tables. Despite appearances, prices aren't astronomical; lunch sets start at just over ¥1000, though you could spend a lot more. Beautifully presented house specialities include *basashi* (from ¥2000).

Daimonji Tiny *okonomiyaki* place on the second floor above Angelus Bakery at the north end of Shimo-tōri. The food is cheap, cheerful and filling, with a big cook-yourself bowl for around ¥600, and plastic examples to choose from.

Hanaichimomme A good bet if you're staying at the nearby *Suizenji Youth Hostel*. It's a bit run-down but friendly and cheap, serving up huge helpings of curry rice, chicken cutlets, fried noodles, and occasionally *basashi*. The garrulous host speaks a little English and can regale you with songs in any language. Daily 5–11pm.

Ichinosōko 2-8 Kachikōji. A tiny door leads into this spacious, wood-beamed beer restaurant which started life as a silk-weaving workshop. The food is a typical mix of Western and Japanese, both snacks and full meals, and you should be able to eat well for around ¥2000.

Le Petit Paris 3-12 Tetorihon-chō ☎096/359-5252. Pink tablecloths and classical music set the tone at this little French restaurant above a pharmacy behind City Hall. There's a choice of four different menus, with lunchtime prices from around ¥1300. Closed Tues.

Shankar 2F, 7-11 Kamitori-chō. This atmospheric Indian restaurant on Kami-tōri is worth tracking down for its excellent-value set meals (from ¥950), including salad, chai and yoghurt.

Takamatsu 11-10 Kamitori-chō. You can hear the buzz outside this popular basement restaurant which serves an East–West menu (in English) plus daily specials. Portions are on the small side, but the authentic pasta dishes are recommended. Expect to pay around ¥2000 per head. Daily 5–11pm.

Tingha Tingha World Food Café and Lounge 2F, 2-17 Tetorihon-chō. Funky restaurant offering eclectic world cuisine, with good-value happy hour sets between 7pm and 8pm on weekdays (¥1000–1200 with drink). Mon–Thurs 7pm–1am, Fri–Sun 6pm–2am.

Yōrōnotaki Shinshigai-Sunroad. Popular *izakaya* which attracts a young crowd with its cheap beers and lively atmosphere. There's a big choice of well-priced dishes on its picture menu.

Listings

Airlines ANA ☎0120-029222; JAL ☎0120-255971; JAS ☎0120-511283; Korean Air ☎096/323-3311.

Airport information ☎096/232-2810.
Banks and foreign exchange There are foreign-exchange desks in Mizuho Bank, beside the

Tsuruya department store, Higo Bank just across the road, and Daiwa Bank near the Kumamoto-jō-mae tram stop. Higo Bank also has a branch just north of Kumamoto Station.

Bookshops The best is Kinokuniya on the second and third floors on Shimo-tōri, near the corner with Ginza-dōri arcade. English books and magazines are on the third floor.

Car rental Nippon Rent-a-Car (☎096/324-0335), Eki Rent-a-Car (☎096/352-4313), and Mazda Rent-a-Car (☎096/326-5656) all have branches near Kumamoto Station.

Ferries Kyūshū Shōsen (☎096/329-6111) operates hourly ferries from Kumamoto Shin-kō to Shimabara (1hr; ¥590). To get to the port, take a bus from Kumamoto Station (35min; ¥420).

Festivals Kumamoto's main event is the Fujisaki Hachiman-gū autumn festival (Sept 11–15). On the final day there are two processions, morning and afternoon, when some twenty thousand people parade through the streets in historical garb.

Hospital The Kumamoto National Hospital (Kokuritsu Kumamoto Byōin; ☎096/353-6501) is conveniently located immediately south of Ninomaru park.

Internet access The Kumamoto City International Centre, 4–8 Hanabatacho (daily 9am–8pm; closed second and fourth Sunday of the month; ☎096/359-2121; ¥50 for 5min), has Internet access on the second floor, plus English-language newspapers and TV. Alternatively, try Media Café Popeye, on the second floor of Kami-tōri, opposite *Shankar* restaurant (open 24hr; ¥230 for 30min).

Police Kumamoto Prefectural Police Headquarters, 6-18-1 Suizenji ☎096/381-0110.

Travel agents JTB (☎096/322-4111) is a good bet for domestic travel, while HIS (☎096/351-0561) handles international tickets.

Aso and the central highlands

Central Kyūshū is dominated by sparsely populated, grassy highlands, in places rising to substantial peaks, which offer some of the island's most magnificent scenery and best walking country. These mountains are relics of ancient volcanic upheavals and explosions of such incredible force that they collapsed one gigantic volcano to create the **Aso caldera**, the world's largest crater. Today the floor of the caldera is a patchwork of fields like so many tatami mats, and the surrounding uplands a popular summer playground, but the peaks of Aso-san at its centre provide a potent reminder that the volcano is still very much alive. Most people come here to peer inside its steaming crater, eruptions permitting, and then scale some of the neighbouring peaks or walk over the lush green meadows at its base.

All this subterranean activity naturally means a wealth of hot springs to wallow in, mostly within the caldera itself, although there are a few gems hidden deep in the highlands. One is the picturesque village of **Kurokawa Onsen**, squeezed in a narrow gorge on the Senomoto plateau, which makes an indulgent overnight stop on the road to Beppu. The village lies a few kilometres off the **Yamanami Highway**, the main tourist route between Aso and Beppu, providing a spectacular mountain ride through the **Aso-Kujū National Park**. Heading in the opposite direction, another dramatic road climbs over the crater wall and heads southeast to **Takachiho**. Perched above an attractive gorge of angular basalt columns, this is where the mythical Sun Goddess Amaterasu hid, according to legends about the birth of the Japanese nation. A riverside cave and its neighbouring shrine make an easy excursion, but a more compelling reason to stop here is to catch a nightly performance of the story told through traditional folk dances.

The Aso region is one place where having your own **transport** is a definite advantage; it's perfectly feasible to get around by public transport, but everything just takes a lot longer. From Kumamoto the recommended route is the JR Hōhi line across the caldera floor, which is a great journey in its own right, to spend a night or two in Aso Town. It's also possible to visit Aso-san on a day-

Aso	*Aso*	阿蘇
Mount Aso	*Aso-san*	阿蘇山
Aso Volcano Museum	*Aso Kazan Hakubutsukan*	阿蘇火山博物館
Aso Youth Hostel	*Aso Yūsu Hosuteru*	阿蘇ユースホステル
Botchū Campground	*Botchū Kyampu-jō*	坊中キャンプ場
Kokuminshukusha Aso	*Kokuminshukusha Aso*	国民宿舎阿蘇
Minshuku Aso	*Minshuku Aso*	民宿あそ
Minshuku Aso-no-Fumoto	*Minshuku Aso-no-Fumoto*	民宿阿蘇のふもと
Naka-dake	*Naka-dake*	中岳
Yume-no-yu	*Yume-no-yu*	夢の湯
Kurokawa Onsen	*Kurokawa Onsen*	黒川温泉
Aso Senomoto Youth Hostel	*Aso Senomoto Yūsu Hosuteru*	阿蘇瀬の本ユースホステル
Hozantei	*Hozantei*	帆山亭
Okyaku-ya Ryokan	*Okyaku-ya Ryokan*	御客屋旅館
O-yado Kurokawa	*O-yado Kurokawa*	お宿玄河
Senomoto plateau	*Senomoto-kōgen*	瀬の本高原
Shinmei-kan	*Shinmei-kan*	新明館
Yamabiko Ryokan	*Yamabiko Ryokan*	やまびこ旅館
Yamamizuki	*Yamamizuki*	山みずき
Yumotosō	*Yumotosō*	湯本荘
Takachiho	*Takachiho*	高千穂
Amano Iwato-jinja	*Amano Iwato-jinja*	天岩戸神社
Asagi	*Asagi*	あさぎ
Hatsu-e	*Hatsu-e*	初栄
Kamino-ya	*Kamino-ya*	かみの家
Kenchan	*Kenchan*	けんちゃん
Nobeoka	*Nobeoka*	延岡
Takachiho-jinja	*Takachiho-jinja*	高千穂神社
Takachiho gorge	*Takachiho-kyō*	高千穂峡
Takachiho Youth Hostel	*Takachiho Yūsu Hosuteru*	高千穂ユースホステル
Takamori	*Takamori*	高森
Tateno	*Tateno*	立野
Yamato-ya	*Yamato-ya*	大和屋

trip from Kumamoto, or break the journey here for a couple of hours en route to Beppu. If you're heading that way, the Yamanami Highway offers the most scenic option, though the train continues via Bungo-Taketa and Ōita to Beppu and is a good alternative for JR pass holders on a strict budget, providing a fabulous journey through lush green forest deep in the mountains before joining the eastern coast of Kyūshū. You'll have to overnight in Aso, however, if you're combining the crater with Takachiho.

The Aso Caldera

The train from Kumamoto changes direction twice as it zigzags up the formidable wall of the **Aso Caldera**. This ancient crater, 18km from east to west,

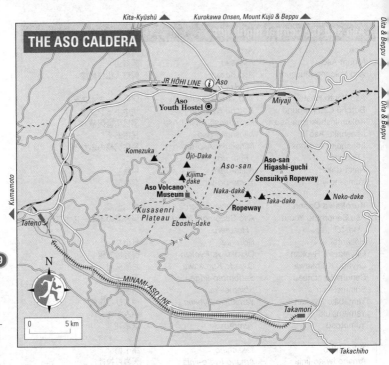

THE ASO CALDERA

JR HŌHI LINE ⓘ Aso

Aso Youth Hostel ◉

Miyaji

Komezuka ▲   Ōjō-Dake ▲   *Aso-san*   **Aso-san Higashi-guchi** // **Sensuikyō Ropeway**

Kijima-dake ▲

Aso Volcano Museum ■   Naka-dake ▲ ▲ Taka-dake   ▲ Neko-dake

Kusasenri Plateau   **Ropeway**

Eboshi-dake ▲

Tateno

N

MINAMI-ASO LINE

Takamori

0   5 km

▼ Takachiho

24km north to south and over 120km in circumference, was formed about 100,000 years ago when a vast volcano collapsed. As the rock cooled, a lake formed, but the eruptions continued, pushing up five smaller cones, today known collectively as **Aso-san**, in the crater's centre. Eventually the lake drained and the area became inhabited; local people attribute their fortune to the god Takeiwatatsu-no-mikoto, grandson of Emperor Jimmu, who kicked a gap in the western wall – the same gap the train uses – to give them rice-land. Now some 70,000 people live within the crater, working the rich volcanic soils, while cattle and horses graze the higher meadows in summer.

Aso Town is a grandiose name for a scattered group of villages located in the northern caldera, including a tourist area around Aso Station where you'll find an information desk (see "Practicalities", opposite), accommodation and buses heading up the mountain or north to Beppu.

Aso-san

The five peaks of **Aso-san** line up across the caldera. At the eastern end of the chain lies the distinctively craggy Neko-dake (1433m), while the next peak west is Taka-dake (1592m), the highest of the five summits, and its volcanic off-shoot Naka-dake (1506m). West of here lie Eboshi-dake (1337m) and Kijima-dake (1321m). Of the five, only **Naka-dake** (1323m) is still active; it's really just a gash on the side of Taka-dake, formed by a volcanic explosion which created a secondary peak. Naka-dake's most recent eruptions occurred in the early 1990s, since when it has calmed down considerably, but it's wise to treat the mountain with respect. Notices are posted in Aso Station when Naka-dake is closed, but if you plan to do any long-distance walks around the crater it's wise to check at the station's information desk. Note that anyone suffering from asthma or other respiratory problems is advised not to approach the crater rim because of strong sulphur emissions.

Seven daily **buses** shuttle visitors from the Sankō terminal outside Aso Station on a dramatic thirty-minute journey up towards the peaks of Aso-san (¥620; last bus up at 3.20pm). There's a five-minute photo break at the pass between Kijima-dake and Eboshi-dake, from where you look down on the perfect cone of **Komezuka**, the "hill of rice" – its dimpled top is said to have been created when Takeiwatatsu-no-mikoto scooped up a handful of rice to feed his starving people. Turning the other way, you get your first glimpse of Naka-dake's gaping mouth across the grassy bowl of **Kusasenri** plateau, speckled with shallow crater lakes.

Before the bus continues along the road to Naka-dake, you might want to get off at the next stop for a quick tour of the informative **Aso Volcano Museum** (daily 9am–5pm; ¥840). Satellite photos reveal Japan's major fault lines in awesome clarity and there are films of recent eruptions around the world, but the museum's most interesting display takes you inside Naka-dake crater courtesy of two cameras inserted in the mountain wall. Afterwards, you can hop on the next passing bus, or walk 3km across the plateau to the base of Naka-dake itself. Alternatively, there's a popular detour up **Kijima-dake** (1321m), an easy thirty-minute climb from behind the museum, and then you can descend via a ski slope to join the road about halfway along.

Buses terminate at the foot of **Naka-dake** in a scruffy area of souvenir shops and restaurants, while a toll road continues to the top for cars. You can walk up in twenty minutes, or there's a **ropeway** (daily 9am–5pm; ¥410) running every eight minutes or so from the bus terminus up to the crater. However you arrive, the crater's evil-coloured rocks and glimpses of a seething grey lake through turbulent, sulphurous clouds of steam, are a sobering sight. Most activity takes place in a hundred-metre-deep cauldron at the northern end, and this area is strictly off limits. Near the ropeway, however, you can approach the unfenced crater lip and then walk south beside barren, dormant craters – mercifully out of earshot of the loudspeakers.

Rather than backtracking, there's a great **hiking trail** round the crater's southern rim to the actual summit of Naka-dake, followed by a possible side trip to Taka-dake and then down to Aso-san Higashi-guchi, the terminus of the Sansuikyō Ropeway. It takes between four and five hours, depending on whether you include Taka-dake, and the path's a little tricky to find at the beginning. After that it's not too difficult as long as you've got good boots, plenty of water and you keep well away from the edge. With any luck, you'll coincide with the cable car down the eastern, Sansuikyō Ropeway (every 25min; ¥750), from where you'll have to hitch a ride or set off on the ninety-minute downhill trot to Miyaji Station, one stop east of Aso Station.

Practicalities

Aso **train station** is the centre of local life. **Buses** congregate at the Sankō terminal, on the left as you exit the station, while inside there's a well-organized **tourist information centre** (daily except Wed 9am–5pm; ☏ & ℻ 0967/34-0751), with English-speaking staff and a wealth of information on local transport and accommodation.

Right outside Aso Station, the yellow *Kokuminshukusha Aso* (☏ 0967/34-0317, ℻ 34-1882; ❸) offers basic tatami **rooms** with or without meals. Ten minutes' walk west, the welcoming *Minshuku Aso-no-Fumoto* (☏ 0967/34-0624; ❸) offers eight nicely decorated tatami rooms in an attractive setting among old farms.

The owners, who speak a little English, will collect you from the station; otherwise, walk west along the main highway, Route 57, for a couple of minutes until you see their blue signboards pointing right. *Minshuku Aso* offers traditional rooms in a beautiful setting (☎0967/34-0194, ℉34-1342; ❺). It's a 500-metre walk south of the station, and is signposted in Japanese. Dormitory beds are available at *Aso Youth Hostel* (☎0967/34-0804; dorm beds ¥2573 per person) which lies twenty minutes' walk uphill from the station on the road to Aso-san; buses heading up the mountain stop outside the hostel (¥130), or a taxi should cost around ¥500. The helpful manager speaks good English and is a real enthusiast for the mountains, with a detailed knowledge of hiking routes and bus timetables. They don't offer meals, however, so you'll have to eat down in the town. Nearby you'll find the *Botchū Campground* (☎0967/34-1262; open June to mid-Sept), from where there are some great hiking trails up to Aso-san.

Most people eat where they're staying, but there are a handful of **restaurants** around the station, of which *East Coffee Plaza* (daily 9am–10pm; closed first and third Thurs of the month) has a good range of well-priced Japanese and Western meals, including substantial breakfast sets. They're on the main highway, two minutes' walk straight ahead from Aso Station. There's a coffee shop with basic dishes in the station (daily 9am–4/5pm). Finally, if you fancy a soak at the end of the day, Yume-no-yu (daily 10am–10pm; ¥400; closed first and third Mon of the month) is a decent **onsen** in the centre of town, with a large rotemburo and sauna. It's on the road between *Kokuminshukusha Aso* and *East Coffee Plaza*.

North on the Yamanami Highway

From Aso the **Yamanami Highway** heads north over the Kujū mountains to Beppu. The road breaches the caldera wall at Ichinomiya, from where the classic profile of Aso-san's five peaks supposedly conjures up a sleeping Buddha with head to the east and Naka-dake's steaming vent at his navel, although it's a little more convincing from Daikambō lookout further west. North of here, **Kurokawa Onsen** offers a choice of rotemburo along a picturesque valley. The highway then climbs again through the Kujū range, which for some reason receives far less attention than Aso-san or Ebino Kōgen, although it contains the Kyūshū mainland's highest peaks (up to 1787m, 148m short of Yakushima's highest) and offers good hiking. The highest peak, Mount Kujū, is no longer active, but even here wisps of steam mark vents high on the north slopes, while more spa towns lie strung along the valley and then break out again at Yufuin before the road makes its final descent into Beppu.

Though the Yamanami Highway is best avoided during peak holiday periods, for the most part it's fairly traffic free. Every day, four sightseeing **buses** ply the route between Kumamoto and Beppu, stopping at Aso, Senomoto, Yufuin and a few other places en route. You can join or leave the bus at any stop, either buying your ticket in advance at the local station or taking a numbered ticket on entry and paying the driver when you get off, as with any normal bus. The cheapest fare between Aso and Beppu costs ¥2950; prices and journey length vary according to whether lunch is included.

Kurokawa Onsen

One of the most popular hot-spring resorts in Japan, the twenty-odd ryokan that make up **KUROKAWA ONSEN** lie higgledy-piggledy at the bottom of a steep-sided, tree-filled valley scoured into the **Senomoto plateau** some 6km west of the Yamanami Highway. The village is completely devoted to hot-

△ Sand bath, Beppu

spring bathing and most of its buildings are at least traditional in design, if not genuinely old, while *yukata*-clad figures wandering the lanes add to its slightly quaint atmosphere. The village is particularly famous for its rotemburo: there are 23 in total, with rocky pools of all shapes and sizes shrouded in dense vegetation. Out of season, when the crowds have gone, it's well worth the effort of getting here, and if you don't mind paying a little extra on accommodation, Kurokawa makes an excellent overnight stop.

Though it helps if you have your own **transport**, it's possible to reach Kurokawa Onsen on one of the four daily buses from the Sankō bus station in Aso Town, taking roughly an hour – check locally for current times. The last bus back to Aso leaves Kurokawa at 4.55pm, so there is time to explore a few of the ryokan baths. If you're heading for Beppu, however, you can take a taxi (approximately ¥1000) back up to the Senomoto Kōgen junction to connect with the last, mid-afternoon Yamanami Highway bus; the bus shelter lies just north of the crossroads, and make sure you arrive at least ten minutes early since these buses occasionally run ahead of schedule.

Arriving in Kurokawa, you'll find the **tourist information** office (daily 9am–6pm; ℡0967/44-0076, ℻44-0819) beside a car park on the north side of the river, next to the bus stop and taxi rank. They have a good English map showing the location of all the **public rotemburo** (daily 8.30am–9pm), with photos and a key indicating whether they're mixed or segregated. All the baths are attached to ryokan and you can either buy tickets at reception (¥500) or get a day pass (¥1200) at the tourist office allowing entry to any three. If you only have time for one and don't mind mixed bathing, try the central **Shinmei-kan** for its cave-bath and choice of open-air pools, or **Yamabiko Ryokan** for its unusually large rotemburo. **Yumotosō** has a gorgeous little rotemburo and women can bathe in old-fashioned iron tubs. If you have your own transport it's worth travelling a few kilometres out of central Kurokawa to try the baths at **Yamamizuki** or **Hozantei**, set in wooded hills away from the crowds.

Yamabiko Ryokan (℡0967/44-0311, ℻44-0313; ❽) is a pleasant **place to stay** if you want to splash out. For something a touch cheaper, both *Okyaku-ya Ryokan* (℡0967/44-0454, ℻44-0551; ❼) and the slightly more rustic *O-yado Kurokawa* (℡0967/44-0651, ℻44-0690; ❼) are atmospheric ryokan right in the centre of things. All these rates include two meals. For those on a budget, the *Aso Senomoto Youth Hostel* (℡0967/44-0157, ✉senomoto@jyh.go.jp; dorm beds ¥2415 per person) lies 5km away, just off the Yamanami Highway. They offer onsen tours to Kurokawa every night for just ¥300, and as the closest youth hostel to Mount Kujū will also take you to and from the base of the mountain if you want to climb it. If travelling by train, they'll pick you up from Miyaji Station.

Takachiho

The small town of **TAKACHIHO** lies on the border between Kumamoto and Miyazaki prefectures, where the Gokase-gawa has sliced a narrow channel through layers of ancient lava. In winter, when night temperatures fall below freezing, local villagers perform time-honoured **Yokagura dances** in the old farmhouses, bringing back to life the gods and goddesses who once inhabited these mountains. The main reason for visiting Takachiho is to see a few excerpts from this dance-cycle, but combine that with **Takachiho gorge**, a pretty spot whose strange rock formations are woven into local myths, plus a dramatic journey from whichever direction you arrive, and Takachiho becomes somewhere to include on any Kyūshū tour.

According to legend, the **Sun Goddess Amaterasu** took umbrage at the offensive behaviour of her brother, the Storm God Susano-ō, after he destroyed her rice fields and desecrated her sacred palace. So she hid in a cave and plunged the world into darkness. The other gods tried to entice her out with prayers and chants, but nothing worked until, finally, a goddess broke into a provocative dance. The general merriment was too much for Amaterasu who peeped out to see the fun, at which point they grabbed her and hauled her back into the world. Locals also claim that Takachiho – not the mountain of Ebino Kōgen (see p.869) – is where Amaterasu's grandson, Ninigi-no-mikoto, descended to earth with his mirror, sword and jewel to become Japan's first emperor.

To **get here** from Aso Town and points west, you need to take a private Minami-Aso line train from Tateno round the caldera's south side as far as Takamori (¥470), from where buses continue to Takachiho (¥1280). Coming from the east coast, or vice versa, the private TR Takachiho line links Takachiho with Nobeoka's JR station (¥1470); its one-car train tracks the Gokase valley, criss-crossing high above the river before pausing over the gorge as it draws in to Takachiho.

The Town

Takachiho sits on the north bank of the Gokase-gawa, with its main street, National Highway 218, running southwest from the town's central crossroads. Both the gorge and Takachiho-jinja, where nightly Yokagura dances are held, are within easy walking distance down this road, on the southwest edge of town, while its other main sight, a mildly interesting riverside cave, lies a short bus ride to the east. It's possible to cover both areas in a day, see a Yokagura performance in the evening and travel on the next morning.

The main road southwest to the gorge first passes **Takachiho-jinja**, roughly 600m from the town's central crossing. It's a simple, wooden building, engulfed in ancient cryptomeria trees and mainly of interest for a carving on its east wall of the guardian deity dispatching a demon. The new, wooden **Kagura-den** next door is where the nightly **Yokagura** (8pm; ¥500) dances are held. Though this is a much-shortened version of the complete cycle, it still gives a good sense of the flavour of the whole. In one hour you see three dances relating the story of Amaterasu and her cave, followed by an explicit rendition of the birth of the Japanese nation in which the two "gods" leave the stage to cavort with members of the audience – to the great delight of all concerned. The performers are drawn from a pool of around 500 local residents, aged from 5 to 80 years, who also dance in the annual **Yokagura festival** (mid-Nov to mid-Feb). In a combination of harvest thanksgiving and spring festival, 24 troupes perform all 33 dances in sequence, lasting through the night and into the next day. The locations vary; check in the tourist office (see p.840) for schedules.

Rather than continuing on the main road for the last kilometre to **Takachiho gorge**, you can take a steep footpath that cuts down from behind the shrine to emerge beneath a soaring road bridge. Cross the old stone bridge to follow another path running 600m along the gorge's most scenic stretch. At its narrowest point, where you recross the river, it's just 3m wide and plunges 100m between cliffs of basalt columns which in one place fan out like a giant cockle shell. If you want to see what it looks like from below you can hire rowing boats at the southern end (¥1500 for 30min; 3 people per boat); though this is a little expensive, the gorge is impressive when viewed from the emerald-green river. Another road heads back into town by the boat station, but it's more pleasant to retrace your tracks along the river. On the way, you might want to stop off at the restaurant-cum-souvenir shop beside the stone bridge for a sup of the local speciality, kappo sake, in which sake is heated in a pipe of fresh green bamboo (¥950).

Suitably revived, the next stop is the central bus terminal to board a bus for an attractive ride east along the Iwata-gawa to **Amano Iwato-jinja**, some 8km from Takachiho (hourly; 15min; ¥370). The shrine buildings are closed to the public, but it's an attractive setting among venerable cedars, and from behind the shrine it's just possible to make out Amaterasu's cave on the river's far bank. Unfortunately, you can't reach it, but, when her fellow gods were deciding their strategy, they fortunately convened in the more accessible **Amano Yasugawara**, on the same side as the shrine. It's about a fifteen-minute walk east, down some steps and beside the river, to find the cave with its diminutive shrine beneath a sacred rope.

Practicalities

From Takachiho **train station**, on the north side of town, it takes roughly ten minutes to walk to the town's central crossroads; the **bus station** lies a couple of hundred metres southeast of the crossroads. The **tourist information** office (daily 8.30am–5pm; ℡0982/72-4680) resides in a small white hut outside the station, where you can pick up maps and, if you're lucky, a brief English-language brochure plus hotel information, though you can't make reservations. **Bus tours** leave four times daily from the bus station, with a choice of a full three-hour tour (¥1660) or a shorter trip missing out Amano Iwato-jinja ¥1150); though all commentary is in Japanese, these are an efficient way of seeing the sights. Local **shops** are full of dried mushrooms, sweet potatoes and other mountain produce alongside *kagura* dolls and locally crafted camphor-wood masks which make an unusual souvenir.

Takachiho has a good choice of **places to stay**. On the main road just below the NTT radio mast, *Yamato-ya* (℡0982/72-2243, ℱ72-6868; ❺) is an affordable ryokan. All the rooms are Japanese-style and, while you don't have to eat in, it's well worth opting for at least the evening meal. If you phone from the station, the English-speaking owner will come to collect you; alternatively, take a taxi (around ¥600) or walk (about fifteen minutes). *Kamino-ya* (℡0982/72-2111, ℱ72-5040; ❻), a couple of minutes' walk south of the central junction, is another friendly ryokan with a nice, rustic atmosphere, where the screens and corridors are decorated with original ink paintings. Again, their meals are good value, though you can opt for room only, and they'll also collect you from the train station. The *Takachiho Youth Hostel* is 3km from the train station but is run by a wonderfully friendly woman who will happily pick you up from the station and take you back out for the Yokagura dances (℡0982/72-3021, ℮takachiho-yh@mx6.tiki.ne.jp; dorm beds ¥2835 per person).

There are plenty of decent **restaurants** in town. On the main crossing, you can't miss the farmhouse-style frontage of *Asagi* (daily 8am–10pm), a souvenir shop which also serves simple snacks, such as udon and soba, and a tasty, hot-ginger drink called *shōga-yu*. In the backstreets just northeast of here, *Hatsu-e* (closed Sun) provides a warm welcome on cold evenings with its table-top braziers for cooking *yakiniku*; sets start at ¥1000. Finally, *Kenchan* (Mon–Sat 5pm–midnight) is a cosy *yakitori* opposite Kamino-ya; a good meal, excluding drinks, will set you back about ¥2000 per person.

Beppu

The best approach to **BEPPU**, on Kyūshū's northeast coast, is on the Yamanami Highway, which drops down into town from the western hills. It's an extraordinary sight: spirals of steam rise from chimneys and billow out of the ground itself in dramatic confirmation that this is one of the world's most geothermally active

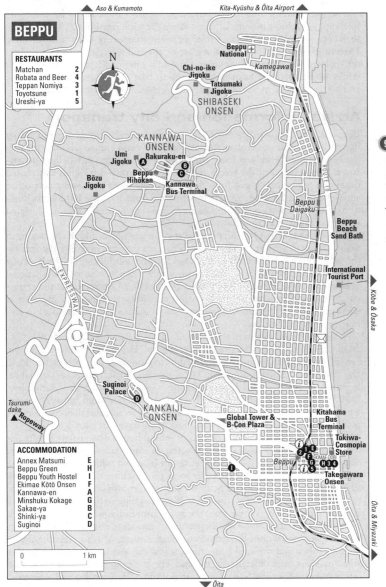

regions. Over 100 million litres a day of near-boiling water gush out of more than 3000 springs, to be harnessed for local swimming pools, heating and medicinal purposes or to fill the dozens of public and private baths that make this one of Japan's most popular **onsen** resorts. Unashamedly dedicated to pleasure, from the refined to the bawdy, this town of only 130,000 people receives over twelve million visitors a year. Most of these are domestic tourists; many foreigners who come here find Beppu all too tacky, but its sheer vulgarity can also be huge fun – the trick is just to jump in and enjoy yourself.

When not soaking in a tub or buried in hot sand, there isn't a lot else to do in Beppu. The most popular attractions are the nine **jigoku**, or "hells", which spew out steaming, sulphurous mud or form simmering lakes in lurid hues. Despite the hype, only two or three are of any real interest, and you'd do better to head for **Tsurumi-dake** and the hills ringing Beppu to the west. If you're leaving Kyūshū from here, be sure to take the daytime ferry for Kōbe and Ōsaka, a glorious voyage right through the island-spattered Inland Sea.

Arrival, information and city transport

Beppu is a medium-size, low-rise city wrapped round an attractive, east-facing bay with mountains to both south and west. The main highway, Route 10, hugs the coast while the railway loops through the city centre, sandwiching **downtown** Beppu between the tracks and the sea. **Ekimae-dōri** splits this central district in two, running east from the station concourse past banks, post office and department stores to end where it meets Route 10 at the **Kitahama** junction. Though Beppu's onsen are scattered far and wide, most *jigoku* are clustered in the northerly Kannawa district.

Beppu is served by **Ōita airport** located on the north side of the bay, from where frequent airport buses run south to Ōita city, stopping at Kitahama on the way (1hr; ¥1450). **Ferries** from Ōsaka, Kōbe and Hiroshima dock a couple of kilometres north of the centre at the grandly named International Tourist Port; take a local Kamenoi bus (#20 or #26) from outside the terminal to either Kitahama or the station. Long-distance **buses** mostly stop at Kitahama, but the Yamanami Highway Bus continues up Ekimae-dōri to terminate at Beppu Station.

The town's main **information desk** (daily 8.30am–5.30pm; ☎0977/24-2838) lies just inside the central east exit of Beppu Station. They supply English-language maps and brochures, information on local bus routes and will also assist with hotel reservations. If you need English-language assistance, Beppu's Foreign Tourist Information Service (Mon–Sat 9am–5pm; ☎0977/23-1119, ⓕ21-6220), run by volunteer staff, should be able to help. Their office is inside the station's north shopping arcade, and they have a computer on which foreign tourists can check their email (free for 10min).

Local buses are the best way of getting around Beppu. Fortunately, they're not too complicated and there's a fair amount of information in English for the major routes. In general, Kamenoi buses, in blue and white livery with route numbers indicated on the front, cover most places within the city limits. Nearly all bus routes start at Beppu Station's east exit and pass along Ekimae-dōri, though a few use the station's west side. If you're going to be doing more than a couple of long journeys – say, from the station out to Kannawa's *jigoku* and back – it's worth investing in a "My Beppu Free" one-day "mini pass" (¥900). This includes all buses within the city centre after 9.30am, which covers the *jigoku*, Suginoi Palace and the sand baths, though you can also use them to go further afield by paying the difference at the end. The passes are available at the station information desk or the Kamenoi bus stations in both Kitahama and Kannawa.

Beppu	Beppu	別府
Beppu Beach Sand Bath	Beppu Kaihin Suna-yu	別府海浜砂湯
Beppu Hihōkan	Beppu Hihōkan	別府秘宝館
Bōzu Jigoku	Bōzu Jigoku	坊主地獄
Chi-no-ike Jigoku	Chi-no-ike Jigoku	血の池地獄
International Tourist Port	Kokusai Kankō-kō	国際観光港
Kankaiji	Kankaiji	観海寺
Kannawa	Kannawa	鉄輪
Kitahama	Kitahama	北浜
Rakuraku-en	Rakuraku-en	楽々園
Takegawara Onsen	Takegawara Onsen	竹瓦温泉
Tsurumi-dake	Tsurumi-dake	鶴見岳
Umi Jigoku	Umi Jigoku	海地獄

Accommodation

Hotel Annex Matsumi	Hoteru Anekkusu Matsumi	ホテルアネックス松美
Beppu Green Hotel	Beppu Guriin Hoteru	別府グリーンホテル
Beppu Youth Hostel	Beppu Yūsu Hosuteru	別府ユースホステル
Ekimae Kōtō Onsen	Ekimae Kōtō Onsen	駅前高等温泉
Kannawa-en	Kannawa-en	神和苑
Minshuku Kokage	Minshuku Kokage	民宿こかげ
Sakae-ya	Sakae-ya	サカエ家
Shinki-ya	Shinki-ya	しんき屋
Suginoi Hotel	Suginoi Hoteru	杉乃井ホテル

Restaurants

Matchan	Matchan	松ちゃん
Teppan Nomiya	Teppan Nomiya	鉄板呑み家
Toyotsune	Toyotsune	とよ常
Ureshi-ya	Ureshi-ya	うれしや

Accommodation

The most convenient place to look for accommodation is **around Beppu Station**, where you'll find a clutch of business hotels and a couple of good-value ryokan. Though less central, the **Kannawa** area offers some interesting alternatives buried among its old streets, while Beppu's top hotel lies in Kankaiji district on the town's western outskirts.

Around the station

Hotel Annex Matsumi 6-28 Ekimae-honchō ☏0977/25-5822, ℻25-3699. This smart business hotel is surprisingly reasonable for a central location. The rooms are mostly Western-style and not huge, but all nicely decorated in beige or peach, with good views from the upper floors. ❹

Beppu Green Hotel 1-3-11 Kitahama ☏0977/24-0020, ℻24-5770. Well-priced bargain business hotel halfway along Ekimae-dōri with a few small semi-doubles (❹) and much larger en-suite twins (❺) with phone and TV.

Beppu Youth Hostel 2 Kankaiji ☏0977/23-4116, ℮beppuyh@ma4.justnet.ne.jp. Large, modern hostel with English-speaking staff, hot-spring bath and dormitory accommodation in bunk-bed tatami rooms. It's a fifteen-minute walk from the station, or take Kamenoi bus #16 or #17 from the station's east exit as far as the Yakyūba-mae bus stop, then walk back the way you came for two minutes and you'll see the building. ❷

Ekimae Kōtō Onsen Ekimae-dōri ☏0977/21-0541. This old, half-timbered onsen building with loads of character doubles as a cheap, clean lodging house offering dormitory beds (men only) and four spartan tatami rooms. Customers can use the on-site onsen for free. Dorm beds ¥1500 per person.

Minshuku Kokage 8-9 Ekimae-chō ☎ 0977/23-1753, ℱ 23-3895. Another popular place in a great location two minutes' walk east of the station. Go down Ekimae-dōri, turn right after Ekimae Kōtō Onsen, then right again down a little alley and it's on your left. Though slightly more upmarket than the *Kagetsu*, it's still excellent value, with a choice of tatami or Western rooms, with or without bath, plus an onsen downstairs. ❹

Kannawa and Kankaiji

Kannawa-en Kannawa ☎ 0977/66-2111. This beautiful old ryokan boasts nineteen lovely tatami rooms, some in individual buildings, set in a classic, hillside garden. Rates include breakfast and an evening meal. ❾

Sakae-ya Kannawa ☎ 0977/66-6234, ℱ 66-6235. Another attractive, wooden building hidden in the eastern, less touristy part of Kannawa. They offer twelve rooms at either minshuku rates (singles are ¥3500) or in the more upmarket ryokan, with an option on meals. ❸–❻

Shinki-ya Kannawa ☎ & ℱ 0977/66-0962. Near the Sakae-ya, this simple, homely minshuku has well-priced tatami rooms and a shared onsen bath; meals can be provided or there's also a small kitchen area. It's three minutes downhill from the Kamenoi bus terminal, past the "Young Centre" theatre and then right up an alley behind a coin laundry. ❸

Suginoi Hotel 1 Kankaiji ☎ 0977/24-1141, ℮ info@suginoi-hotel.com. Beppu's top hotel is a one-stop holiday resort, complete with vast bathing complexes and baseball simulator, as well as shopping malls, restaurants and nearly six hundred rooms. The rooms are bland but comfortable, and the best have stunning views over Beppu bay. ❼–❾

The Town

There are eight distinct hot-spring "towns" dotted about Beppu, each characterized by the varying proportions of iron, sulphur and other minerals in the water. Most activity, however, is concentrated in **Kannawa**. Not only is this northern district home to seven of the nine *jigoku* ("hells"), but it's also a spa in its own right with a beautiful garden rotemburo, as well as an outrageously tacky museum of erotica. Dedicated bathers might want to try one of Beppu's **sand baths** or take a dip in one of the many baths on offer at the **Suginoi Palace**. Alternatively, you can ride the ropeway to the top of Tsurumi-dake for superb views over Beppu bay and inland to the Kujū mountains.

Kannawa and the jigoku

Noxious pools of bubbling mud, super-heated lakes, geysers and other geothermal outpourings are generally known in Japan as **jigoku**, after the word for Buddhism's hell. Beppu's *jigoku* are located in three clusters: six in central Kannawa, one on Kannawa's western edge and two in Shibaseki Onsen, 3km further north. Though each *jigoku* has its own "personality" and you could cover them all in two to three hours, only those recommended below are really worth it – any more and you'll tire of the tacky commercialism, loudspeakers and tour groups. You can buy individual tickets (¥400) as you go round, or get a day pass (¥2000) covering all except Bōzu Jigoku. Frequent buses ply between Beppu Station and Kannawa (20min; ¥320–350). If you plan to visit any of the district's **public baths**, it's a good idea to bring a towel, though you can always buy or rent one on the spot.

Starting from Kannawa's Kamenoi bus terminal, signs point west to a line of six *jigoku* in quick succession. At the far end, **Umi Jigoku** is the most attractive, set in a bowl of hills among well-tended gardens. Its main feature is a sea-blue pool – 120m deep and, at 90°C, hot enough to cook eggs – set off by a bright-red humped bridge and *torii* swathed in clouds of roaring steam. From here it's about 750m on up the main road to **Bōzu Jigoku**, which takes its name from the resemblance between mud bubbles and the bald pate of a

Buddhist monk, a *bōzu*. Again it's surrounded by greenery, but the speciality here is mud – boiling, smelly, steaming, hiccuping pools of mud.

The remaining Kannawa *jigoku* are generally best avoided, being either full of gaudy statues or unfortunate elephants, crocodiles and monkeys in their own personal hell. However, if you fancy an onsen, it's definitely worth heading for the ryokan *Kannawa-en* (see "Accommodation" opposite), whose picturesque, milky-white ryokan is open to the public (daily 10am–2.30pm; ¥800). Built on a hillside to the east of Umi Jigoku, the ryokan has a beautiful, classic garden enclosing a small lake and hidden rocky pools reached by winding paths.

On the way back down to Kannawa bus station, directly opposite Oniyama Jigoku, connoisseurs of the bizarre might like to join the giggling young couples at **Beppu Hihōkan** (daily 9am–10pm; ¥1000), a sex museum (although the coy sign in English on the sign outside says "Beppu Utamaru Gallery"). Buxom statuary graces the entrance, while inside there's a collection of erotic *ukiyo-e*, sacred phalluses from Shinto shrines and then a downhill slide into pornographic tableaux, notably a gleeful Snow White and her seven dwarfs, which grind into action at the push of a button. Finally, if you fancy trying another of Kannawa's baths, **Rakuraku-en** (daily 8.30am–midnight; ¥200), in a ryokan behind the bus station, is a bit run-down, but inexpensive. It offers a mixed and a women-only rotemburo, sauna and ordinary indoor pool.

Beppu's last two *jigoku* are in **Shibaseki Onsen**, five minutes' bus ride north of Kannawa (#16 or #2 from Kannawa bus terminal). **Chi-no-ike Jigoku**, "Blood Pond", is the better of the two, a huge bubbling pool whose vermilion fringes result from a high iron-oxide content. Fifty metres down the road, **Tatsumaki Jigoku** consists of an unimpressive geyser which spouts around 5m into the air roughly every half-hour; it used to reach 50m until a stone block was placed over it for safety.

The sand baths

Beppu is one of only two places in Japan where it's possible to take a genuine sand bath, or *suna-yu*. Ibusuki (see p.856) may be more famous and have the better scenery, but Beppu's two sand baths are less touristy and far more relaxed. **Takegawara Onsen** is a grand, old Meiji-era edifice in the backstreets south of Ekimae-dōri. Its ordinary bath (daily 6.30am–10.30pm; ¥100) is nicely traditional, but first of all try the **sand bath** (8am–9.30pm; ¥780). After rinsing in hot water, you lie face up – take a towel to cover your front – on a bed of coarse, black sand while an attendant gently piles a heavy, warm cocoon (around 42°C) up to your neck. Then just relax as the heat soaks in for the recommended ten minutes, followed by another rinse before soaking in the hot tub.

On a fine day, the seaside location of **Beppu Beach Sand Bath** (daily: April–Oct 8.30am–6pm; Jan–March, Nov & Dec 9am–5pm; ¥780) sounds preferable, but it's slightly marred by a busy main road behind and a concrete breakwater dominating the view – the end result, however, is still an overall sense of wellbeing. You'll need a swimsuit, but they provide *yukata* to wear in the "bath". Shoninga-hama lies on Kamenoi bus route #20 or #26 from central Beppu (20min; ¥230), near Beppu Daigaku Station.

Kankaiji and Tsurumi-dake

Kankaiji onsen spews out its hot water high up on a hill overlooking western Beppu, where it feeds the multifarious baths of the *Suginoi Hotel*'s **Suginoi Palace** (daily 9am–10.30pm; ¥2000; free to hotel guests). This is Beppu's foremost bathing extravaganza, with an enormous terraced outdoor bath, Tana-yu, boasting fantastic views over the city and Beppu Bay, plus the Aquabeat resort, a huge indoor pool with a wave machine, rides and slides.

On the way up to Kankaiji, you pass by the futuristic **Global Tower** (daily 9am–7pm, April–Nov until 9pm; ¥300) which serves as both viewing platform and a landmark for **B-Con Plaza**, Beppu's lavish convention centre and concert hall. The hundred-metre-high open observation deck provides giddying views, but if you've got time you'll get a better all-round panorama from the western hills. A **ropeway** (daily 9am–4.30/5pm; ¥1400) carries you to the top of **Tsurumi-dake** (1375m) in five minutes, from where you can see Shikoku on a clear day. Kamenoi buses #31 to #37 depart Beppu Station every half-hour for the forty-minute ride to the ropeway (¥490; ¥180 extra on the mini-pass), passing below *Suginoi Hotel* en route.

Eating and drinking

Beppu's **speciality foods** include *fugu* (blowfish) and *karei* (flounder), both winter dishes, and the piping-hot *dango-jiru*. This cheap, filling soup comes with thick white noodles, assorted vegetables and chunks of either chicken or pork. When it comes to finding a **restaurant**, you're best off in the downtown area. There are dozens of *izakaya* and Japanese restaurants in the streets south of Ekimae-dōri, while the Tokiwa–Cosmopia store on Ekimae-dōri also has a decent choice of outlets on its fourth-floor "Gourmet Plaza" (daily 10am–7.30pm).

Matchan Beppu Station. This rustic little place in the station's north shopping arcade is one of the best places in town to try *dango-jiru*. They also serve hearty meals of *champon*, *donburi* and tempura at reasonable prices. Daily 9am–7pm.

Robata and Beer 1-15-7 Kitahama. Popular *robatayaki* at the east end of Ekimae-dōri with English-speaking staff and an English menu listing a good range of fish, vegetable and tofu dishes, as well as *yakitori* skewers and daily specials. Service is a bit slow and prices aren't the cheapest, but you should be able to eat for under ¥2000, and it's open till late. Daily 5pm–midnight.

Teppan Nomiya 1-3-19 Kitahama. Great little *okonomiyaki* restaurant on the shopping arcade off Ekimae-dōri. Either choose your ingredients and cook it at your table or get the staff to make it for you.

Toyotsune Ekimae-chō. Traditional restaurant opposite Beppu Station specializing in *fugu*, either as sashimi (¥2500 per person) or a full, two-hour-long meal (¥7000). Other, more reasonable fare includes tempura and sashimi sets, and they offer a good range of local *Shōchū*. Closed Thurs.

Ureshi-ya 7-12 Ekimae-chō. Tables fill up early at this small, friendly restaurant where you can choose from a tempting array of ready-prepared dishes, such as vegetable tempura, pumpkin, sashimi and fried fish. They also serve up standard rice and noodle dishes for under ¥800. Tues–Sun 5pm–2am.

Listings

Airport information ☎0975/37-2800.

Banks and exchange You can change money at banks along Ekimae-dōri, including Iyo Bank, Beppu Shinyo Bank and Fukuoka City Bank.

Buses Long-distance buses between Ōita and Nagoya, Nagasaki and Fukuoka stop at the Kitahama junction in passing.

Car rental Eki Rent-a-Car (☎0977/24-4428), Nippon Rent-a-Car (☎0977/22-6181) and Toyota Rent-a-Car (☎0977/22-7171) all have offices in Beppu.

Ferries Kansai Kisen (☎0977/22-1311) operates two ferries daily from Beppu's International Tourist Port to Ōsaka via Kōbe, with one service daily to Matsuyama (Shikoku). Uwajima Onyu Ferry (☎0977/21-2364) services connect Beppu with Misaki and Yawatahama on Shikoku.

Hospital Beppu National Hospital (☎0977/67-1111) is in north Beppu's Kamegawa district, inland from Kamegawa Station.

Police The main police station (☎0977/21-2131) is opposite the post office on Route 10.

Post office Beppu Central Post Office is at 4-23 Motigahama-chō, opposite the International Tourist Port, and offers poste restante. There's also a more convenient sub-office on Ekimae-dōri.

Shopping The Beppu region is famed for its bamboo handicrafts, which you'll find in the station

South Kyūshū

Southern Kyūshū consists of two huge prefectures which offer plenty of stunning scenery – mostly of the volcanic variety – and further stops on the onsen trail. The most interesting area is westerly **Kagoshima**, whose main city sits in the shadow of a grumbling, ash-spewing volcano, **Sakurajima**. Some people come simply to view this troublesome beast, but Kagoshima also has one or two worthwhile museums celebrating its role in the Meiji Restoration, as well as providing a gateway to the Satsuma Peninsula. Here, the small town of **Ibusuki** is devoted to hot-spring bathing, including a seaside sand bath, while nearby **Chiran** houses another of Japan's disturbingly ambiguous war museums. In this case it commemorates the kamikaze suicide bombers who rallied to the imperial cause at the end of World War II. From either Kagoshima or Ibusuki, ferries ply south to **Yakushima**. A paradise for botanists and hikers, this mountainous island is covered in ancient, misty forests which are home to five-thousand-year-old cedar trees. Back on the Kyūshū mainland, there's very different walking country around **Ebino Kōgen**, a high, open plateau ringed by volcanic peaks, before the mountains fade out towards **Miyazaki**. The only large town on southern Kyūshū's southeast coast, Miyazaki is a useful base but has little to detain you. Its artificial, indoor beach, **Seagaia**, is an extraordinary concept, though the real coast probably holds more of immediate interest, notably **Aoshima**'s subtropical gardens and the celebrated cave-shrine of **Udo-jingū**.

Kagoshima

With a population of nearly 500,000, **KAGOSHIMA** curls round the west shore of Kagoshima Bay, a mere 4km from **Sakurajima**, one of the world's most active volcanoes. Sakurajima's smouldering cone constitutes the city's most obvious and compelling attraction, but Kagoshima contains a few sights of its own which justify a day's exploration. Foremost of these are its classical garden, **Sengan-en**, which uses Sakurajima in the ultimate example of borrowed scenery, and several excellent **museums** of local history and culture. The best are devoted to Kagoshima's mid-nineteenth-century heyday, when Saigō Takamori (amongst other local heroes) played a major role in Japan's modernization.

Some history

Originally known as **Satsuma**, the Kagoshima region was ruled by the powerful **Shimazu** clan for nearly seven centuries until the Meiji reforms put an end to such fiefdoms in 1871. The area has a long tradition of overseas contact and it was here that Japan's first Christian missionary, the Portuguese Jesuit **Francis Xavier**, arrived in 1549. Welcomed by the Shimazu lords – who were primarily interested in trade and acquiring new technologies – he spent ten months working in Kagoshima, where he found the poorer classes particularly receptive to Christian teachings. After just a few months Xavier declared "it seems to me that we shall never find among heathens another race to equal the Japanese".

Soon after, Japan was closed to foreigners and remained so for the next two hundred years. As central control crumbled in the mid-nineteenth century, however, the far-sighted **Shimazu Nariakira** began introducing Western technology, such as spinning machines, the printing press and weapons manufacture, and it was Kagoshima that saw Japan's first gas light, steamships, electric lights, photographs and Morse code transmission. Not that all relations were cordial. In 1862 an Englishman was decapitated in Yokohama by a Shimazu retainer for crossing the road in front of the *daimyō*'s procession. When the Shimazu refused to punish the loyal samurai or pay compensation, seven

Kagoshima

Kagoshima	*Kagoshima*	鹿児島
City Art Museum	*Kagoshima Shiritsu Bijutsukan*	鹿児島市立美術館
Central-Kagoshima Station	*Kagoshima Chūō-eki*	西鹿児島駅
City Aquarium	*Kagoshima Suizokukan*	かごしま水族館
Chūō Park	*Chūō-kōen*	中央公園
Furusato Onsen	*Furusato Onsen*	古里温泉
Museum of the Meiji Restoration	*Ishin Furusato-kan*	維新ふるさと館
Kita-Futō	*Kita-Futō*	北埠頭
Reimeikan	*Reimeikan*	黎明館
Saint Xavier's Church	*Zabieru Kyōkai*	ザビエル教会
Sakurajima	*Sakurajima*	桜島
Sengan-en	*Sengan-en*	仙巌園
Terukuni-jinja	*Terukuni-jinja*	照国神社
Tenmonkan	*Tenmonkan*	天文館
Accommodation		
Kagoshima Shiroyama Youth Hostel	*Kagoshima Shiroyama Yūsu Hosuteru*	鹿児島城山ユースホステル
Nakahara Bessō	*Nakahara Bessō*	中原別荘
Nakazano Ryokan	*Nakazano Ryokan*	中薗旅館
Nanshūkan	*Nanshūkan*	南洲館
Sakurajima Youth Hostel	*Sakurajima Yūsu Hosuteru*	桜島ユースホステル
Hotel Taisei Annex	*Hoteru Taisei Anekkusu*	ホテルタイセイアネックス
Tōkyū Inn	*Tōkyū In*	東急イン
Washington Hotel Plaza	*Washinton Hoteru Puraza*	ワシントンホテルプラザ
Young Inn Kagoshima	*Yangu In Kagoshima*	ヤングインかごしま
Restaurants		
Ajimori	*Ajimori*	あぢもり
Densuke	*Densuke*	でんすけ
Edokko-zushi	*Edokko-zushi*	江戸ッ子寿司
Homba Ōsaka no Takoyaki	*Homba Ōsaka no Takoyaki*	本場大阪のたこやき
Satsuma-aji	*Satsuma-aji*	さつま路
Taiheiyō Bīru-kan	*Taiheiyō Bīru-kan*	太平洋ビール館

KAGOSHIMA

ACCOMMODATION

Kagoshima Shiroyama	A
Youth Hostel	D
Nakahara Bessō	G
Nakazono Ryokan	F
Nanshūkan	B
Taisei Annex	C
Tōkyū Inn	E
Washington Hotel Plaza	C
Young Inn Kagoshima	H
Sakurajima	
Youth Hostel	I

RESTAURANTS

Ajimori	8
Café du Tati	1
Capricciosa	3
Curry A-1	4
Densuke	7
Edokko-zushi	6
Homba Osaka no	
Takoyaki	5
Satsuma-aji	2
Taiheiyo Biru-kan	9

Sengan-en (3 km)

Miyazaki & Kumamoto

Shiroyama

Terukuni-jinja

Saint Xavier's

City Art Museum

Reimeikan Museum

Loyal Retainers' Monument

Statue of Saigo Takamori

Chūō Park

City Hall

Kagoshima Kenmin Kōryū Senta

Shiyakusho-mae

Suizokukan-guchi

Sakurajima Sambashi-dōri

Kagoshima Station

 IZURO-DŌRI

Asahi-dōri

Kagoshima Products Showroom

ASAHI-DŌRI

Iwasaki Hotel

Tenmonkan

Yamakataya Store

Takashimaya Plaza

TENMONKAN-DŌRI

Izuro-dōri

Izuro Bus Centre

MINAMI-DŌRI

I'm Building

Diamond Building

Takamibaba

Takami-bashi

Kajiya-chō

Nishida-bashi

Kagoshima Central Station

Kagoshima-chūō-eki-mae

Nanshu-bashi

Museum of the Meiji Restoration

Shiritsu-Byōin-mae

City

Kōtsuki-gawa

NAPPORI-DŌRI

PERTH-DŌRI

Sakurajima Pier

City Aquarium

KITA-FUTŌ

Sakurajima & ①

Minami-Futō

Shin-kō (800 m)

Ibusuki

200 m

0

N

849

British **warships** bombarded Kagoshima Bay in 1863. Fortunately there was little loss of life and the Shimazu were so impressed by this show of force that three years later they dispatched nineteen "**young pioneers**" to study in London – many of these young men went on to assist the new Meiji government in its mission to modernize Japan.

Easily Kagoshima's most famous son, however, is **Saigō Takamori**. Born in 1827, Saigō made his name as one of the leading figures in the **Meiji Restoration**. Though aware of the need for Japan to modernize, he grew increasingly alarmed at the loss of traditional values and eventually left the government to set up a military academy in Kagoshima. He soon became a focus for opposition forces – mainly disaffected samurai but also peasants protesting at punitive taxes. Things came to a head in January 1877 when Saigō led an army of 40,000 against the government stronghold in Kumamoto, in what came to be known as the **Satsuma Rebellion**. After besieging the castle for nearly two months, the rebels were forced to withdraw before the 60,000-strong Imperial Army. They retreated to Kagoshima where they were gradually pinned down on Shiroyama. On September 24, the imperial forces closed in and Saigō, severely wounded, asked one of his comrades to kill him. His courage, idealism and heroic death earned Saigō enormous popular support – so much so that he was officially pardoned by imperial decree in 1891.

Arrival, information and city transport

Kagoshima **airport**, served by flights to Seoul and Shanghai as well as domestic routes, is located some 30km from the city. Limousine buses depart roughly every ten or twenty minutes for the hour's ride into town (¥1200), stopping at central Kagoshima's Tenmonkan crossroads before terminating just west of the river at the newer **Central Kagoshima Station**. Though this is the main station, some trains also call at the old **Kagoshima Station** to the north of the city. The first part of the new Kyūshū **Shinkansen**, opened in March 2004, links Kagoshima with Yatsushiro in Kumamoto prefecture in just 35 minutes. Most **long-distance buses** stop at Tenmonkan before proceeding to Central Kagoshima Station.

Kagoshima's two main **tourist offices** are located outside the train stations. Of these, the Kagoshima Station branch (daily 8.30am–5pm; ☎ & ℉ 099/222-2500) is a lot quieter and more helpful, though the Central Kagoshima office (daily 8.30am–6pm; ☎ 099/253-2500, ℉ 250-8462) can provide city maps and assist with accommodation. Other options in the centre of town include the International Exchange Plaza on the eleventh floor of the I'm Building on Izurō-dōri (Mon–Sat 9am–5.30pm; ☎ 099/225-3279), and the Update Visitors Centre (Mon–Fri 9.30am–5pm; ☎ 099/224-8011) on the ground floor of the same building. Finally, there's the Prefectural Information Office (Mon–Fri 8.30am–5pm; ☎ 099/223-5771) on the third floor above the Kagoshima Products Showroom on Asahi-dōri. All of these offices have English-speaking staff.

Moving around central Kagoshima is simplified by a highly efficient **tram system** which has been in operation since 1912 – some of the original cars are still used. There are only two lines, both of which start outside Kagoshima Station and run down the main street, past the City Hall (Shiyakusho-mae) and Tenmonkan before splitting at Takamibaba, just past the *Washington Hotel*. Trams on Line 2 then continue southwest to Nishi-Kagoshima Station, while Line 1 turns southeast. There's a flat fare of ¥160, which you pay on exit; trams run roughly every eight minutes from 6.30am to 10.30pm.

The local **bus system** is a lot more complicated, with services run by five different companies. The easily recognizable, retro-style **City View** tourist bus (every 30min; ¥180) does a circuit of the main sights from Nishi-Kagoshima Station (stand #4) via the Museum of the Meiji Restoration, Reimeikan and Shiroyama observatory to Sengan-en, before returning through the city centre. Alternatively, you can buy a one-day pass (¥600) which also covers the trams; it's available at the tourist information centres, or from bus and tram drivers.

Local **ferries** to Sakurajima depart from a pier near Kagoshima Station. The new Kita-Futō (North Pier) next door is used by services to Yakushima, Ibusuki and Okinawa; the slower daily ferry service to Yakushima leaves from Minami-Futō (South Pier), just south of Kita-Futō. "A Line" ferries to Okinawa operate out of the quite separate and even more southerly Shin-kō.

Accommodation

Kagoshima is well provided with mid-range business hotels, offering comfortable if unexciting **accommodation**, but has little in the way of good-value budget places apart from two **youth hostels**. *Kagoshima Shiroyama Youth Hostel*, 2-40-8 Soumuta (☎099/223-2648; dorm beds ¥3200 per person) has only twelve beds but is handily located, an eight-minute ride on bus #3 from Kagoshima Central Station; get off at Naka-Sōmuta, from where it's a five-minute walk. The other youth hostel, the *Sakurajima Youth Hostel* (☎099/293-2150; dorm beds ¥2650 per person), is a big, relaxed hostel with an onsen bath. The hostel is on Sakurajima (see p.853) at Hakama-goshi Sakurajima-chō, a signposted ten-minute walk uphill from the ferry terminal.

Nakahara Bessō 15-19 Higashi-Sengoku-chō ☎099/225-2800, ℉226-3688. Nicely decorated onsen hotel in the city centre overlooking Chūō Park. The Japanese-style rooms are better value, and though they do offer room-only rates, the meals are highly recommended. ❻–❼

Nakazono Ryokan 1-18 Yasui-chō ☎099/226-5125, ℮shindon@satsuma.ne.jp. The best budget option in central Kagoshima, this welcoming ryokan offers homely tatami rooms with shared facilities. It's tucked behind a temple opposite Kagoshima City Hall, about five minutes' walk from Kagoshima Station and handy for the Sakurajima pier. ❹

Nanshūkan 19-17 Higashi-Sengoku-chō ☎099/226-8188, ℉226-9383. Well-priced business hotel with fair-sized rooms – all en suite – in a good location near Chūō Park. ❹

Hotel Taisei Annex 4-32 Chūō-chō ☎099/257-1111, ℉257-1113. Reasonable business hotel

near Nishi-Kagoshima Station. The rooms are nothing special, but they're clean, comfortable and all en suite. ❺

Tōkyū Inn 5-1 Chūō-chō ☎099/256-0109, ℉253-3692. Smartish business hotel three minutes' walk from Nishi-Kagoshima Station. The rooms are all Western-style and come with TV, phone and bath as standard. There's also a coffee shop and restaurant. ❻

Washington Hotel Plaza 12-1 Yamanokuchi-chō ☎099/225-6111, ℉224-2303. This well-appointed business hotel is conveniently located on Izuro-dōri, slightly south of the centre. Rooms are a good size, with satellite TV and telephone; ask for one at the back with views of Sakurajima. ❻

Young Inn Kagoshima 16-23 Izumi-chō ☎099/223-1116, ℉225-1509. Small, very basic guesthouse with a few Japanese and Western rooms. It's buried in the backstreets east of the centre, towards the ferry terminals. ❸

The City

Kagoshima's handful of central sights are gathered round the informative **Reimeikan** museum at the foot of Shiroyama. Next, you can either walk or take a tram south to the banks of the Kōtsuki-gawa, where there's a gimmicky but entertaining **Museum of the Meiji Restoration**. A few kilometres north of town, the Sengan-en area is of interest not only for its traditional garden, but also for a museum celebrating the modernizing zeal of the enterprising Shimazu lords. All these sights are served by the City View bus (see above), but you'll need to catch a ferry over to **Sakurajima** itself. A circuit of the volcano includes lava fields and observatories, but it's also worth stopping off at **Furusato** village to soak in a superb, sacred hot spring.

The city centre

The best place to start exploring Kagoshima is in **Chūō Park**, west of the Tenmonkan arcades. A bronze statue of the close-cropped, portly Saigō Takamori (see p.850) stares seaward across the park's north corner. Unlike the more relaxed portrait in Tokyo's Ueno-kōen (see p.132), this shows Saigō as the uncompromising military leader. Behind him, carp-filled moats and some bullet-pocked walls are all that remain of **Tsurumaru-jō** following the 1877 Satsuma Rebellion. The castle site is now occupied by a collection of public buildings, kicking off with the **City Art Museum** (Tues–Sun 9.30am–6pm; ¥200). This spacious modern building houses a good collection of Impressionist and twentieth-century Western art, besides well-rated local artists Kuroda Seiki and Fujishima Takeji.

Walking north, an arched stone bridge leads up to the **Reimeikan** museum (Tues–Sun 9am–5pm, closed 25th of every month; ¥300), which provides an excellent introduction to local history and culture. Dioramas, life-size models and video presentations take you from Stone-age villages to post-1945 recovery on the ground floor, while upstairs is devoted largely to folk culture and festivals. Apart from a delightful mock-up of the Tenmonkan arcade in the 1930s, the most interesting displays cover the southern islands' distinct traditions, showing the strong influence of Okinawan and Melanesian culture.

Follow the castle walls round to the northwest and you'll find the **Loyal Retainers' Monument** dedicated to Kagoshima labourers who died in Gifuken, central Honshū, in 1755. On the shogun's orders the Satsuma clan sent a thousand men to tame the wild Kiso-gawa. It took two attempts and fifteen months to complete the embankments, in appalling conditions which cost the lives of 84 men from disease, accident and suicide. One of these was the chief retainer, Hirata Yukie, who killed himself in order to atone for the project's huge financial and human cost. Beside the otherwise uninteresting monument, a path leads up through impressive stands of mature, subtropical trees to the top of **Shiroyama**. The twenty-minute climb is worth it for superb views over Kagoshima and the smouldering cone of Sakurajima.

Heading back downhill, the right fork brings you down a gentler route to **Terukuni-jinja**. This shrine is dedicated to Shimazu Nariakira (see p.848), whose statue – with its determined face and oversize shoes – stands immediately to the north. Straight ahead from the shrine you're back in Chūō-kōen. Following the road heading down to the Kōtsuki-gawa from the park's south corner, after a couple of minutes you'll reach **Saint Xavier's Church**. The small gothic building was erected in 1949 to commemorate the four-hundredth anniversary of Francis Xavier's landing. Across the road a memorial park occupies the site of a stone church, built in 1891 by a French Jesuit, which was destroyed in 1945 bombing raids.

From here it's about 600m further south to where the stone **Nishida-bashi**, built in 1846, spans the Kōtsuki-gawa. Turn left before the bridge for a pleasant riverside stroll down to the splendid **Museum of the Meiji Restoration** (daily 9am–5pm; ¥300). No expense has been spared to recreate the "golden age" of Kagoshima, when Saigō and other local luminaries were instrumental in returning power to the emperor and then spearheading the Meiji reforms. The highlight is a 25-minute son et lumière in which robots re-enact scenes from the restoration. It's best to sit near the doors, facing the white screen, from where you get the best view of Saigō and his disconcertingly realistic eyes. All the dialogue is in Japanese, so it's a good idea to visit the rest of the museum first, after which you should be able to identify the main characters. The show takes place roughly once an hour in the basement theatre (9.15am–4.30pm).

The final sight in central Kagoshima is the **City Aquarium** (daily 9am–6pm; ¥1500) on a man-made island in the harbour. Thanks to the warm Kuroshio current sweeping across from the East China Sea, the waters around Kagoshima's southern islands are rich in temperate and subtropical aquatic life, a broad range of which is on show in this well-designed installation, from Sakurajima's unique tube worm, to colourful sea anemones, sharks and dolphins in a huge glass-sided tank.

Sengan-en

When their base at Tsurumaru-jō was destroyed during the Satsuma Rebellion, the Shimazu lords set up residence in their lovely garden-villa Iso Tei-en, now known as **Sengan-en**, 3km east of the city centre (daily 8.30am–5.30pm; ¥1000, or ¥1500 including entry to the residence). Though the villa itself is a beautiful building, the main points of interest are the garden, with its views of Sakurajima, unfortunately now interrupted by the main road and train tracks, and the neighbouring history museum. The easiest way to reach Sengan-en is to take the City View Bus or a local Hayashida Bus from Nishi-Kagoshima Station or Tenmonkan (every 30min; 7min; ¥180); check the destination when you get on, as a few buses skip Sengan-en.

The entrance to Sengan-en lies through a raft of souvenir shops and restaurants, selling everything from Satsuma glass to *imo* (sweet potato) ice cream. Inside, it's worth joining a tour of the **villa** (an English leaflet is provided) as much for the fine interior decoration, including ornamental nail heads, painted screens and carved transoms, as for the views of the volcano. Apart from this stunning backdrop, the **garden** is also noted for its collection of stone lanterns – the first gas lanterns in Japan – and an Okinawa-style Bōgaku-rō pavilion, presented by the king of the Ryūkyū Islands. The cliffs behind are etched with an eleven-metre-tall kanji saying "thousand-fathom crag"; it takes about thirty minutes to walk up beside the stream for even more dramatic panoramas of the bay.

Beside Sengan-en, an old, stone, machine factory, known as the **Shōko Shūseikan** (same times and ticket as Sengan-en), serves as a local history museum. Inside, you'll find a moderately interesting array of Shimazu family heirlooms, from early cannonballs and carding machines to tea-ceremony utensils. An annexe hosts changing exhibitions, behind which is a series of workshops where they still make Satsuma glass and ceramics.

Sakurajima

Just 4km from Kagoshima, the volcanic cone of **Sakurajima** grumbles away, pouring a column of dense black ash into the air. This is one of the world's most active volcanoes and major eruptions have been recorded from the early eighth century till as recently as 1947, though the most violent in living memory was that of 1914. After a period of increased activity in the early 1990s, the volcano is now fairly quiet and makes an enjoyable half-day excursion from Kagoshima. A single road (40km) circles Sakurajima at sea level, with stops along the way at lava fields, onsen baths and a couple of observation points, plus the obligatory souvenir shops where you can buy *Sakurajima-yaki*, pottery glazed with volcanic ash, and various local produce.

Ferries from Kagoshima (15min; ¥150) dock at a small pier on Sakurajima's west coast. The service operates 24 hours a day, with hourly sailings between

10.30pm and 5.30am, and every ten minutes during peak hours (7am–8pm); buy a ticket from the machines before boarding. At the other end, a handy **sightseeing bus** departs twice daily (9.30am & 1.30pm; ¥1700) for a circuit of the volcano from beneath Sakurajima ferry terminal. Tickets are available in the terminal.

As you **tour the island** you'll see plenty of crops growing in the volcanic soil, particularly on the more gentle, northern slopes. This is Sakurajima's most attractive side, where the road wriggles through the pine trees, past coves filled with fishing hamlets. As you turn down the east coast, however, Sakurajima's brooding presence becomes more apparent as you start to see the first grey lava fields. Look out on the right, too, for the buried *torii* of Kurokami-jinja. Originally 3m tall, now just the top cross-bars protrude from a bed of ash and pumice left by the 1914 eruption. During this particularly violent explosion enough lava spilled down the southeast slopes to fill a 400-metre-wide channel that previously separated Sakurajima from the mainland.

Just beyond this narrow neck of land, you can explore the still-barren 1914 lava fields at the **Arimura Observatory**. A little further on the settlements start again, at **Furusato Onsen**, but here it's all resort hotels capitalizing on the abundant supplies of hot water. The best of these, the *Furusato Kankō Hotel* (☏099/221-3111, ℱ221-2345; ❼), features a large, cliff-side rotemburo (closed Mon morning & Thurs afternoon; ¥1050) shaded by a sacred camphor tree. Since it doubles as a shrine dedicated to a local dragon god, you'll be given a white *yukata* to wear when bathing. There's a free shuttle bus service from the ferry port to the hotel between 8.45am and 5pm.

The route then takes you up a tortuous road on the volcano's west flank to the **Yunohira Observatory** (373m). This is the closest you can get to the deeply creviced summit, which in fact comprises three cones, from the highest, northerly Kita-dake (1117m) to Minami-dake (1040m), the most active, in the south. Weather permitting, you'll also be treated to sweeping views of Kagoshima.

The final port of call is the **Sakurajima Visitors' Centre** (daily 9am–5pm; ☏099/293-2443), located less than ten minutes' walk south of the ferry terminal, so you can make your own way back if you want to spend more time here than the tour allows. With the aid of an English-language guide tape you can bone up on volcanoes and gauge Sakurajima's present mood from a seismograph. There's also interesting material about how the islanders cope with their restless home, whose fertile soils produce the world's largest radish – up to 40kg in weight and over 1m in diameter – and its smallest mandarin, measuring a mere 3cm across.

Eating, drinking and nightlife

Kagoshima's most popular **speciality food** is *Satsuma-age*, a deep-fried, slightly sweet patty of minced fish and sake, eaten with ginger and soy sauce. The prettiest dish, however, is *kibinago sashimi*, in which slices of a silvery, sardine-like fish are arranged in an eye-catching flower head. *Keihan* chicken mixes shredded meat with carrot, egg, mushroom and spring onions over a bowl of rice in a hot, tasty broth, while *saké-zushi* consists of sushi with a drop of sake. For snacks, there's *Satsuma-imo* ice cream (made with sweet potato) and *Jambo mochi* – rice cakes smothered in sweet sauce on bamboo skewers. Kagoshima is also Japan's biggest producer of *Shōchū*, a potent liquor traditionally brewed from grain but also sweet potato.

The city's prime **restaurant** area is centred around the Tenmonkan and Sennichi arcades, to either side of Izuro-dōri, though you'll also find places around Nishi-Kagoshima Station and in Sengan-en. As for **nightlife**, head east of Izuro-dōri to the Sennichi-gai area, where the Diamond Building alone provides plenty of choice for a good night out. Particularly recommended is *Rush* in the basement – a big, friendly place with good food, funky vibes and live jazz every night (daily 7pm–3am; ¥500 cover charge).

Bars and restaurants

Ajimori 13-21 Sennichi-chō. Nicely informal *tonkatsu* (fried pork cutlet) restaurant east of the arcade, with a good choice of set meals (¥700–2800), plus a more formal *shabu-shabu* (thinly sliced beef cooked in broth at your table) restaurant upstairs.

Café du Tati Shiroyama-chō. Look out for this small, jolly café in an interesting area of back-streets west of Chūō-kōen, offering a limited menu of sandwiches, crêpes and cakes. (Daily noon–9/10pm.) Upstairs, there's a tree growing through the middle of the nicely relaxed *Treetop Terrace* bar.

Capricciosa Higashi-Sengoku-chō. You'll find this outlet of the reliable Italian chain just round the corner from the *Iwasaki Hotel*. Daily 11am–11pm.

Curry A-1 12-22 Higashi-Sengoku-chō. Cheap and cheerful Japanese-style curry house on Izuro-dōri under the *Iwasaki Hotel* with a branch nearer Kagoshima Station. Their lunch menus (¥700) are particularly good value. Daily 11am–8pm.

Densuke 5-16 Yasui-chō. Join the locals at the counter of this welcoming, traditional *izakaya* for sashimi, *yakitori* and copious glasses of *Shōchū*. It's just round the corner from *Nakazono Ryokan*, whose owner will be more than happy to take you. Mon–Sat 5pm–midnight.

Edokko-zushi 2-16 Sennichi-chō. Sparkling sushi bar on a corner of the street west of Izuro-dōri. It's best at lunchtime for its reasonably priced sets (around ¥1000), and they also do sashimi and tempura dishes.

Homba Ōsaka no Takoyaki 12-18 Higashi-Sengoku-chō. A great *okonomiyaki* place next to the Tenmonkan bus stop. Eat at the little counter downstairs, or at tables in the larger area upstairs. The beer and *okonomiyaki* set for ¥800 is good value.

Reimeikan 7-2 Shiroyama-chō. There's a good restaurant on the ground floor of this museum (see p.852) serving excellent lunchtime sets – try the *yaki-niku donburi* set for ¥750. Tues–Sun 11am–3pm.

Satsuma-aji 6-29 Higashi-Sengoku-chō. Though fairly pricey, this elegantly rustic restaurant is one of the nicest places to try Kagoshima's local speciality dishes, such as *Satsuma-age*, *kibinago sashimi* and *sake-zushi*. There's a picture-menu and lunch deals from ¥2000.

Taiheiyō Bīru-kan Izumi-chō. It's a bit out of centre, but this old stone storehouse near the harbour makes a great venue for a microbrewery and beer restaurant specializing in barbecued meat cooked at your table (¥1500 per head). Mon–Sat 5–10pm.

Listings

Airlines ANA ☏0120-029222; Japan Air Commuter ☏0120-511283; JAL ☏0120-255971 (domestic); ☏0120-255931 (international); JAS ☏0120-511283; Korean Air ☏099/227-3311.

Airport information ☏099/558-2740.

Banks and exchange You'll find foreign exchange banks, such as Sumitomo and Fuji, along Izuro-dōri near Yamakataya department store and around the junction with Asahi-dōri. The Central Post Office has international ATMs.

Bookshops Junkudō bookshop has a small English-language section in the basement. Turn north onto Terukuni-dōri from Izuro-dōri and the shop is a couple of blocks up on the left.

Buses Airport buses leave from Nishi-Kagoshima Station, stand #8 (every 10–20min; 1hr; ¥1200), with a stop in front of Tenmonkan's *Iwasaki Hotel*. Most long-distance buses either depart from Nishi-Kagoshima Station or the city-centre Izuro bus ter-

minus, but also stop at Tenmonkan. Buses to Chiran and Ibusuki use the Yamakataya bus centre, under the department store.

Car rental Eki Rent-a-Car (☏099/258-1412), Nippon (☏099/258-3336) and Nissan Rent-a-Car (☏099/250-2123) all have offices near Nishi-Kagoshima Station.

Ferries A Line ferries (☏099/226-4141) sail to Okinawa from Kagoshima Shin-kō, the city's southern harbour, while RKK Line (☏099/226-1652) uses Kita-Futō (North Pier), which is also the departure point for Toppy jetfoils (Kagoshima Shōsen; ☏099/255-7888) to both Yakushima and Ibusuki. The slower Orita Kisen (☏099/226-0731) ferry to Yakushima leaves from the neighbouring Minami-Futō (South Pier).

Hospitals and medical care The most central hospital with English-speaking staff is the Kagoshima City Hospital, 20-17 Kajiya-chō

(☎099/224-2101), near the Shiritsu Byōin-mae tram stop (line #1). Otherwise, contact the International Exchange Plaza (see p.850) for lists of English-speaking doctors.

Internet access You can surf the Internet for ¥500 an hour on the fourth floor of Best Denki Kagoshima, 1-5 Kajiya-chō (daily 10am–8pm; ☎099/223-2291), on Izuro-dōri just west of the Kajiya-chō tram stop. You can also access the Net free for thirty minutes on the ground floor of the Kagoshima-kenmin Kōryū Sentā (Tues–Sun 9am–5pm).

Police Kagoshima-Chūō Police Station, 13-1 Yamashita-chō ☎099/222-0110.

Post office Kagoshima Central Post Office, 1-2 Chūō-chō, next to Nishi-Kagoshima Station, oper-ates a poste restante service (open 24hr). There's also a handy sub-office on Asahi-dōri near Chūō-kōen. Both have ATMs which take international bank cards.

Shopping Local crafts include Satsuma-yaki (cracked-glaze or earthy black ceramics), Ōshima hand-woven silks and various concoctions made from sweet potato. You'll find all these in the Kagoshima Products Showroom, at the east end of Asahi-dōri, in the sprawling Yamakataya store and Nishi-Kagoshima Station's shopping malls. For sweet-potato products check out Satsumaimo-no-yakata, near the west end of Tenmonkan arcade.

Taxis Kagoshima City Taxi Association ☎099/226-5966.

Ibusuki and around

South of Kagoshima, the great claw of the Satsuma Peninsula extends into the East China Sea, to culminate in a perfect, cone-shaped mountain and a clutch of onsen resorts. The most famous of these is **Ibusuki**, whose trademark is a piping-hot, open-air sand bath on Surigahama beach. The town also has a certain subtropical appeal, with average annual temperatures of 19°C, but its

Ibusuki and around

Ibusuki	Ibusuki	指宿
Ibusuki Station	Ibusuki eki	指宿駅
Ibusuki Port	Ibusuki-kō	指宿港
Moto-yu	Moto-yu	元湯
Saraku	Saraku	砂楽

Accommodation and restaurants

Chō Chō	Chō Chō	蝶蝶
Iwasaki Hotel	Iwasaki Hoteru	いわさきホテル
Kōryū	Kōryū	紅龍
Marutomi	Marutomi	丸富
Satsuma-aji	Satsuma-aji	さつま味
Minshuku Takayoshi	Minshuku Takayoshi	民宿たかよし
Tamaya Youth Hostel	Tamaya Yūsu Hosuteru	圭屋ユースホステル
Yunosato Youth Hostel	Yunosato Yūsu Hosuteru	湯の里ユースホステル

Around Ibusuki

Anglo-Satsuma Museum	Satsuma-Eikoku-kan	薩摩英国館
Buké-yashiki	Buké-yashiki	武家屋敷
Chiran	Chiran	知覧
Chōju-an	Chōju-an	長寿庵
Kaimon-dake	Kaimon-dake	開聞岳
Nagasaki-bana	Nagasaki-bana	長崎鼻
Special Attack Peace Hall	Tokkō Heiwa-kaikan	特攻平和会館
Taki-an	Taki-an	高城庵
Tōsen-kyō	Tōsen-kyō	唐船峡

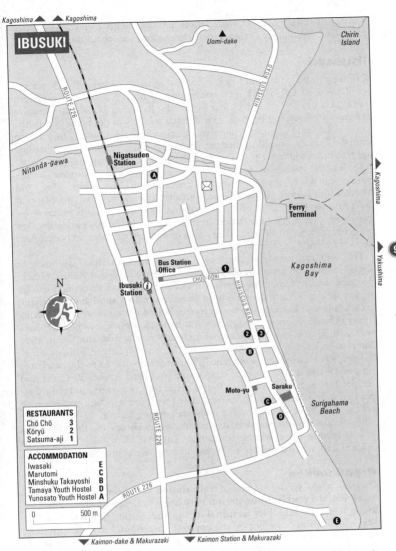

IBUSUKI

Kagoshima ▲ ▲ Kagoshima

Uomi-dake

Chirin Island

HIBISCUS ROAD

ROUTE 226

Nitanda-gawa

Nigatsuden Station

A

Kagoshima

Ferry Terminal

Yakushima

Bus Station Office

CHŪŌ-DŌRI

①

Ibusuki Station *i*

Kagoshima Bay

② **③**

HIBISCUS ROAD

B

N

Moto-yu **Saraku**

C

Surigahama Beach

D

0   500 m

E

▼ Kaimon-dake & Makurazaki   ▼ Kaimon Station & Makurazaki

KYŪSHŪ | Ibusuki and around

9

prime attraction is as a base for the surrounding region. Dominating the landscape, **Kaimon-dake**'s volcanic cone makes a good hike and a perfect backdrop for the flower gardens of nearby **Nagasaki-bana**, the peninsula's most southerly point. Heading north, the road skirts a large crater lake, **Ikeda-ko**, then climbs to join the Ibusuki Skyline – a dramatic ridge road – before dropping down to **Chiran**. The centre of this small town contains a strip of beautifully preserved samurai houses, each with a diminutive traditional garden, but it's perhaps best known as the air base from which kamikaze suicide pilots took off during the closing days of World War II.

The easiest and quickest way **to reach Ibusuki** is by JR train or Toppy jetfoil from Kagoshima – both offer good views across Kagoshima Bay to

Sakurajima and the Sata Peninsula. Jetfoils also operate between Yakushima (see p.861) and Ibusuki; see "Practicalities", below, for more about these ferries.

Ibusuki

Claiming to be Japan's third-largest hot-spring resort by volume of water, the small town of **IBUSUKI** is a strange mix of luxury hotels and expensive restaurants next to seedy bars and nightclubs. Its saving grace is an attractive setting on a sweeping bay and a **sand bath** where you get buried up to the neck in hot sand – a more enjoyable experience than it sounds. Once you've rinsed off the grains and strolled the promenade, however, you're best heading off to Chiran and other places in the neighbourhood (see opposite).

Ibusuki lies spread out along a bay between the Iwasaki promontory to the south and Uomi-dake hill and Chirin island in the north. The main north–south avenue, Hibiscus Road, is shadowed a few hundred metres inland by a road passing in front of the JR station. Chūō-dōri, Ibusuki's prime shopping street, leads from the station to meet the sea at the bay's midpoint. Ten minutes' walk south of here, there's a second clutch of shops and restaurants gathered around the famous sand bath.

This southern stretch of beach is known as **Surigahama**. Like much of Japan's coast it's protected by concrete breakwaters, but a few stretches of black, volcanic sand remain, from which wisps of scalding steam mark the presence of hot springs. It's the done thing in Ibusuki to take a **sand bath** (*suna-yu*), which is best at low tide when everyone is buried on the beach itself, leaving a row of heads under snazzy sunshades; at high tide a raised bed beside the sea wall is used. You can buy tickets and change into a *yukata* in the modern **Saraku** bathhouse immediately behind the beach (daily 8.30am–noon & 1–9pm; ¥900, including *yukata* rental). You then troop down to the beach and lie down – take a small towel to wrap round your head. At over 50°C, the sand temperature is much hotter than Beppu's rival bath (see p.845) and most people find it difficult to last the recommended ten minutes. Once you've rinsed off the sand, however, it's a wonderfully invigorating feeling.

Ibusuki also has several indoor onsen baths which are open to the public. The best of these is the charming, traditional **Moto-yu** (daily 6am–10pm, closed 5th and 25th of each month; ¥200), five minutes' walk from Saraku.

Practicalities

Ibusuki's bright-yellow and orange **train station** lies on the west side of town. You'll find the **tourist information** desk (daily 9am–6pm; ☎0993/22-4114) inside, while the main **bus terminal** occupies the station forecourt, with the Kagoshima Kōtsū bus office on the opposite corner. You can walk to Ibusuki port in ten minutes, from where Toppy **jetfoils** (☎0992/55-7888) sail to Kagoshima (daily; 40min; ¥2100) and Yakushima (daily; 1hr 15min; ¥6000); you need reservations to get on these boats. As Ibusuki is so spread out, it's worth **renting bikes** to get around the central district. The main outlet is Eki Rent-a-Car (¥300 for 2hr, or ¥950 per day) outside the station, while those staying at *Yunosato Youth Hostel* (see below) can take advantage of their more reasonable rates (¥600 per day). For car rental there is Eki Rent-a-Car (☎0993/23-3879), and Toyota (☎0993/22-4009).

Among all the expensive resort **hotels**, Ibusuki does have a number of reasonable places to stay, including no less than three youth hostels. The nicest and newest is the *Yunosato Youth Hostel* (☎0993/22-5680; dorm beds ¥3045 per person), ten minutes' walk north of the station beside a small park. The slightly cheaper *Tamaya Youth Hostel* (☎0993/22-3553; dorm beds ¥2650 per person) is fifteen minutes from the station but more in the thick of things, on Hibiscus Road just south of the sand bath. Going more upmarket, *Minshuku Takayoshi* (T & F 0993/22-5982; ⑤ including meals), offers cheerful tatami rooms and an onsen bath; it's ten minutes southeast of the station and west of Hibiscus Road, just before you reach the sand bath; it's slightly cheaper if you don't have dinner. You'll need to book well in advance for *Marutomi* (T 0993/22-5579, F 22-3993; ⑤ including meals), an attractive old ryokan famous for its seafood dinners – it's also in the backstreets inland from the sand bath. Finally, one of the smartest options around is the *Iwasaki Hotel* (T 0993/22-2131, F 24-3215; ⑦), on the headland south of Ibusuki. Set in lush gardens, this sprawling hotel boasts three onsen baths (including a spectacular, cliff-edge rotemburo), a golf course, swimming pool and numerous restaurants; it's on several bus routes from the station, or a taxi will cost around ¥700.

In general, you're probably best off **eating** in your hotel, since the choice of restaurants in Ibusuki is pretty limited, especially in the winter season. For a bit of atmosphere try *Satsuma-aji* (11.30am–3pm & 5.30–10pm; closed Thurs), near the Hibiscus Road junction on Chūō-dōri, which offers a good choice of local specialities such as *Satsuma-age* and *kibinago* (see p.854) and excellent seafood; you'll get a decent meal for around ¥2500 and there's a helpful English menu. *Kōryū* is a good Chinese on Hibiscus Road – you'll spot a ghostly pair of chopsticks dipping in and out of a huge bowl of noodles outside. Another possibility is the modern *Chō Chō* (Tues–Sun 7pm–5am) on the seafront south of Chūō-dōri. It's primarily a coffee shop and bar, but they'll also rustle up hamburgers, pizza, curry rice and other light meals.

Around Ibusuki

The Ibusuki region is dominated by a beautifully proportioned extinct volcano, **Kaimon-dake**, and a lake whose giant eels have fostered tales of a mythical monster named "Isshy". Subtropical gardens and nurseries also thrive in the mild climate, particularly near the tip of the peninsula, **Nagasaki-bana**. The rest of the area is peppered with missable tourist developments, though **Tōsen-kyō**, a narrow canyon full of outdoor noodle restaurants, makes a fun snack stop. One sight you shouldn't miss, however, is **Chiran**, with its museum commemorating the notorious kamikaze pilots and a street of old samurai houses.

If you're pressed for time and travelling on public transport, the most convenient way of exploring the region is on the **sightseeing bus** which runs from Ibusuki to Kagoshima calling at Nagasaki-bana, Flower Park Kagoshima, Kaimon-dake, Lake Ikeda, and finally the Special Attack Peace Hall and samurai houses in Chiran, before arriving in Kagoshima at 5.30pm. The bus departs at 10.10am from a stand in front of Ibusuki Station; buy your ticket from the Kagoshima Kōtsū office opposite the station (¥3750). If you don't want to go all the way to Kagoshima you can catch a local bus from Chiran to Ibusuki, but note that the last bus leaves Chiran at 3.50pm. You can also reach Chiran by bus direct from Ibusuki (3 daily; 1hr; ¥940) or Kagoshima (3 daily; 1hr 20min; ¥860) – buses depart from the Yamakataya bus centre (see p.855).

The southern sights

The Satsuma Peninsula comes to a halt 13km southwest of Ibusuki at **Nagasaki-bana**. This is a popular tourist spot, but it's still worth walking past the souvenir stalls and out along the rocky promontory to get a classic view of Kaimon-dake and, on clear days, the distant peaks of Yakushima. Next to the bus stop and car park, the oddly named **Parking Garden** (daily 8.20am–5pm,

July–Sept to 6pm; ¥1200) is a moderately interesting subtropical garden where parrots, monkeys and flamingos roam free.

Though a rather pint-size version at 922m, the triangular peak of **Kaimon-dake** is known locally as "Satsuma Fuji". The volcano last erupted some 15,000 years ago and much of it is now a nature park (daily 6am–7pm; ¥350) inhabited by wild Tokara ponies. The classic route up Kaimon-dake is from Kaimon Station, the start of a five-kilometre-long path which spirals round the cone. It takes about two hours and the effort is rewarded with views south to the Satsunan Islands of Yakushima and Tanegashima, and north beyond Sakurajima to Kirishima. Kaimon Station is a stop on the JR line between Ibusuki and Makurazaki (6 daily; 1hr).

From Kaimon-dake the route turns inland towards **Tōsen-kyō**, where three noodle restaurants shelter in the bottom of a narrow tree-filled gorge. They specialize in *sōmen*, thin wheat-noodles, which you fish out from a spinning bowl of ice-cold spring water in the centre of the table. It's gimmicky but quite fun, especially in summer when the gorge makes a welcome refuge from the heat, and pretty cheap – one helping of *sōmen* costs ¥500, and set meals start from ¥1200. In winter they also do hot stews, while at any time of year fresh rainbow trout, raised in the nearby fish farms, makes a tasty side dish. Of the three **restaurants**, southernmost **Chōju-an** (daily 10am–5pm, or 7pm in summer) is recommended for its natural setting beside a waterfall. All the restaurants have plastic-food displays and you pay first at the cashier's window.

The Tōsen-kyō river is fed by a spring from the crater lake, **Ikeda-ko**, lying just over the ridge. Apart from being Kyūshū's largest lake, it's famous for its giant eels, which grow up to 2m long and a hefty 5kg in weight. But there's no real reason to stop here, other than to admire Kaimon-dake rising above the crater's southern rim. Turning north, the **Ibusuki Skyline** climbs over Sansu-yama, flanked by the immaculate tea-fields for which the region is noted, following a ridge of hills north towards Chiran.

Chiran

A small town lying in a broad valley, **CHIRAN** owes its fortune to the Shimazu lords of Kagoshima (see p.847). In the eighteenth century, the Shimazu's chief retainers, the Sata family, were permitted to build a semi-fortified village, and a number of their lovely **samurai houses** survive today. After exploring the samurai quarter, next stop is a former airfield on the outskirts of town where the kamikaze suicide bombers were based. The site has now been turned into a **museum**, documenting the history of the kamikaze and commemorating the hundreds of young pilots who died.

Central Chiran consists of one main road oriented roughly east–west. The **samurai houses**, *buké-yashiki* (daily 9am–5pm; ¥500), are grouped along an attractive lane running parallel to the south of this road, behind ancient stone walls topped by neatly clipped hedges. Arriving by bus, you should get off at the Buké-yashiki-iriguchi stop near the east end of the samurai street; it's the last stop on the sightseeing bus from Ibusuki and on the local Ibusuki–Chiran bus.

Since many of the houses are still occupied, you can't see inside, but the main interest lies in their small but intricate **gardens**, some said to be the work of designers brought from Kyoto. Seven gardens, indicated by signs in English, are open to the public. Though each is different in its composition, they mostly use rock groupings and shrubs to represent a classic scene of mountains, valleys and waterfalls taken from Chinese landscape painting. In the best of them, such as the gardens of Hirayama Katsumi and Hirayama Ryoichi, the design also incorporates the hills behind as "borrowed scenery". Look out, too, for defensive features such as solid, screened entry gates and latrines beside the front gate – apparently, this was so that the occupant could eavesdrop on passers-by.

If you've got time to spare, the **Anglo-Satsuma Museum** (daily 11am–5pm, closed every second Wed; free) has interesting coverage of the "war" between Britain and the Shimazu clan in 1863. Most exhibits are in Japanese, but newspaper reports from London indicate how seriously the incident was taken at the time. The museum is on the main road near the Buké-yashiki bus stops – look for the red double-decker bus. Alternatively, take a pit-stop in *Taki-an* **restaurant** (daily 10am–5pm), in a thatched building in another beautiful garden on the samurai street; their speciality is home-made soba and udon, or try the sweet *jambo-mochi*, pounded rice on bamboo skewers.

Further along the main road (lined with stone lanterns, one for each pilot) on the way to the Peace Hall, you'll find **Hotaru-kan** (daily 9am–5pm, ¥300), another museum commemorating the pilots who died. This was a tiny restaurant frequented by the pilots in Chiran, run by a motherly figure called Torihama Tome, who saw hundreds of these young men pass through on their way to certain death. Many of them left personal possessions and messages for their family with Tome-san, and there are deeply moving pictures, letters and personal effects.

The last stop in Chiran is a five-minute ride southwest from the Buké-yashi-ki-iriguchi bus stop, where the **Special Attack Peace Hall** (daily 9am–5pm; ¥500, or ¥600 including Museum Chiran) marks the site of a military airfield established in 1942. At first it was a training camp, but from mid-1944 Chiran became the base for the "Special Attack Forces" whose mission was to crash their bomb-laden planes into American ships – they're better known in the West as the **kamikaze**, in reference to a "divine wind" which saved Japan from Mongol invasions in the late thirteenth century (see p.936). Hundreds of young men, most of them mere teenagers, rallied to the call, eager to die for the emperor in true samurai style. Their opportunity came during the battle of Okinawa (see p.888), when an estimated 1035 pilots died. Before leaving, they were given a last cigarette, a drink of sake and a blessing, after which they donned their "rising sun" headband and set off on the lonely, one-way mission with enough fuel to last for two hours. It seems that many never reached their target: the toll was 56 American ships sunk, 107 crippled and 300 seriously damaged.

The "peace hall", which was only established in 1975, is essentially a memorial to the pilots' undoubted courage and makes little mention of the wider context or moral argument. That aside, the photos, farewell letters and often childish mascots are tragic mementoes of young lives wasted. Several pilots' letters reveal that, though they knew the war was lost, they were still willing to make the ultimate sacrifice – you'll see many older Japanese people walking round in tears and it's hard not to be moved, despite the chilling overtones.

If you have time you might like to visit the more cheerful **Museum Chiran** (daily except Wed 9am–5pm; ¥300) beside the Peace Hall. Concentrating on local history and culture, the exhibits are beautifully displayed, with the most interesting showing the strong influence of Okinawan culture on Kagoshima's festivals and crafts.

Yakushima

Kagoshima Prefecture includes an arc of islands trailing south over nearly 500km of ocean to Okinawa. Among the most northerly of these, long, low **Tanegashima** has the dubious distinction of being both where the first firearms were introduced to Japan – by shipwrecked Portuguese in 1543 – and the home of Tanegashima Space Centre, Japan's Cape Canaveral. A little further south, some 60km off Kyūshū, a great lump of rock clothed in dripping, subtropical rainforest rises from the ocean. This is **Yakushima**, blessed with an average annual rainfall of at least 4m on the coast and a staggering 8–10m in its mountainous interior. Not surprisingly, the locals are a little touchy about their weather, and it doesn't sound an obvious holiday destination, but all this rain feeds tumbling streams and a lush, primeval forest famous for its magnificent **Yaku-sugi** cedar trees, which are at least a thousand years old and are honoured with individual names (younger trees are known as Ko-sugi, or "small cedars"). The oldest is the **Jōmon-sugi**, estimated to be between five and seven thousand years old, growing high in the mountains. Logging companies worked Yakushima's forests until the early 1970s, but most of the area is now protected within the Kirishima-Yaku National Park, and in 1993 was placed on UNESCO's World Heritage list.

Yakushima's fairly sizeable population is concentrated in **Miyanoura**, either in its main town, Anbō, or in other small settlements scattered round the coast. An increasingly popular tourist destination, the island now boasts a number of swish hotels in addition to more basic accommodation. Most people, however, come to hike and camp among the peaks, where the older cedars are found. For the less adventurous, **Yaku-sugi Land** contains a few more accessible trees and can be reached by public bus. Otherwise, there's a good **local museum**, a seaside **onsen** and several **beaches**, two of which – Isso and Nakama – offer decent snorkelling. There are no dry months here, but the best time to visit is May or during the autumn months of October and November. June sees by far the highest rainfall, followed by a steamy July and August, while winter brings snow to the peaks, though the sea-level temperature stays around 15°C.

The island

The first impressions of the scruffy little port of **MIYANOURA** aren't very favourable. The town is, however, home to the informative **Yakushima Environmental and Cultural Village Centre** (Tues–Sun 9am–5pm; ¥500), in a dramatic new building five minutes' walk up from the ferry terminal. The exhibits are arranged in a spiral, proceeding from the ocean up through village life and the cedar forests to the mountain tops. Allow time to see the Omnimax film (hourly; 25min), projected onto a huge screen, which takes you on a fabulous helicopter ride swooping over the island – not recommended for anyone prone to motion sickness.

From Miyanoura, the main road leads east past the airport to **ANBŌ**, a much more attractive place to stay. From here you can turn inland for a fantastic forty-minute ride up into the mountains. The single-track road, in places almost washed away or blocked by fallen trees, corkscrews up into a lost world wreathed in drifting cloud banks. Every so often there are glimpses of plunging, tree-filled valleys, the lush greens accentuated by cascading, ice-white torrents. Keep an eye open, too, for wild deer (*shika*) and red-faced macaque monkeys (*saru*), which often feed beside the road at dusk. They're noticeably smaller than their relatives on the mainland.

Twelve kilometres later, and 1000m above sea level, a wooden resthouse marks the entrance to **Yaku-sugi Land** (daily 9am–5pm; ¥300). This forest reserve contains four walking trails varying in length from 800m (around 30min) to 3km (around 2hr 30min). The three shortest and most popular walks wind along an attractive river valley which is home to two thousand-year-old cedar trees, their gnarled roots clinging to the rock. The two shorter routes consist mostly

EAST CHINA
SEA

N

Isso
Beach

Isso

Inaka Beach

Nagata Beach

Nagata

Yakushima Cultural
Centre

Miyanoura

Kusugawa

Koseda

Nagamine

Jōmon-
sugi

Miyanoura-
dake

Tachū-
dake

Jamon-
sugi

Anbō-gawa

Anbō

9

Ōko-no-taki

Kigen-
sugi

YAKU-SUGI
LAND

Haruta
Beach

Hirano

Kurio

PACIFIC
OCEAN

Nakama
Beach

Hirauchi

Koshima

Onoaida

0   5 km

Hirauchi
Kaichū Onsen

YAKUSHIMA

Miyanoura-gawa

Kusugawa Hiking Path

Arakawa Hiking Path

Onoaida Hiking Path

of wooden pathways with handrails, so a pair of flat, nonslip shoes will do, but hiking boots are a must on the two longer trails. If you've got the time and energy, the longest course is by far the most interesting, taking you deeper into the forest and past another four Yaku-sugi, of which the oldest is the 2600-year-old **Jamon-sugi**. Alternatively, continue up the paved road from the resthouse for about 6km to the **Kigen-sugi**, a grand old lady of 3000 years.

All these are mere saplings compared to the great **Jōmon-sugi**, whose mossy, tattered trunk looks more like rock face than living tissue. The tree is estimated to be at least 5000 years old, possibly up to 7200 years old. Growing 1300m up and five-hours' hike from the nearest road, the tree was only discovered in 1968, an event which sparked moves to protect the forests and also created the tourist industry which now accounts for over half the island's economy. The Jōmon-sugi stands on the north face of **Miyanoura-dake** (1935m), the highest of Yakushima's seven peaks and the highest mountain in Kyūshū. There are two main routes up to the tree: the Kusugawa Hiking Path from east of Miyanoura, and the eastern, Arakawa, trail starting at the Arakawa Dam. In both cases you can get a fair way up by road if you've got your own transport.

These are just two of the many **hiking** trails snaking through Yakushima's mountains. If you're going to be walking, try to get hold of Shōbunsha's 1:50,000 "Area map" #66 (¥714), and note that you should be well prepared for the arduous terrain. Even in summer you'll need warm clothes and a proper sleeping bag to ward off the chill at higher altitudes. The paths are so steep

Yakushima	*Yakushima*	屋久島
Anbō	*Anbō*	安房
Hirauchi Kaichū onsen	*Hirauchi Kaichū onsen*	平内海中温泉
Jōmon-sugi	*Jōmon-sugi*	縄文杉
Kurio	*Kurio*	栗生
Miyanoura	*Miyanoura*	宮之浦
Mountain hut	*Koya*	小屋
Nagata	*Nagata*	永田
Ōko-no-taki	*Ōko-no-taki*	大川の滝
Onoaida	*Onoaida*	尾之間
Yakushima Environmental and Cultural Village Centre	*Yakushima Kankyō Bunka Mura Sentā*	屋久島環境文化村センター
Yaku-sugi Land	*Yakusugi-rando*	ヤクスギランド

Accommodation		
Backpackers' Support	*Bakkupakkāzu Sapōto*	バックパッカーズサポート
Chinryū-an	*Chinryū-an*	枕流庵
Kamome-sō	*Kamome-sō*	かもめ荘
Minshuku Shiho	*Minshuku Shiho*	民宿志保
Minshuku Takesugi	*Minshuku Takesugi*	民宿岳杉
Minshuku Yaedake	*Minshuku Yaedake*	民宿八重岳
Seaside Hotel Yakushima	*Shiisaido Hoteru Yakushima*	シーサイドホテル屋久島
Shisuikan	*Shisuikan*	紫水館
Sōyōtei	*Sōyōtei*	送陽邸
Yakushima Iwasaki Hotel	*Yakushima Iwasaki Hoteru*	屋久島いわさきホテル
Yakushima Youth Hostel	*Yakushima Yūsu Hosuteru*	屋久島ユースホステル

Restaurants		
Kabochaya	*Kabochaya*	かぼちゃ家
Rengaya	*Rengaya*	れんが屋
Shimamusubi	*Shimamusubi*	島むすび
Wakatake	*Wakatake*	若竹

in places that 1km per hour is good going, and trails often get washed away, so check locally for the latest information. It's also a good idea to leave your itinerary with someone; special forms (*tozan todoke*) are available in the ferry building, airport and at information offices. There are plenty of places to camp and very basic mountain huts along the trails.

One of the hiking paths climbs up from **ONOAIDA** on the south coast, which also has some good accommodation options. Around here you'll see orchards of tropical fruits, such as mango, papaya and lychee, alongside the more traditional orange groves, while bright sprays of bougainvillea and bird-of-paradise flowers decorate the villages. A few kilometres west of Onoaida, **Hirauchi Kaichū onsen** (free) makes the perfect place to kick back with the locals in a hot rockpool overlooking the sea. You just have to get the timing right – the pool is only uncovered for an hour or so either side of low tide.

Practicalities

Miyanoura is the largest centre for supermarkets and other facilities. The main **post office** is located in the town centre, just west of the river, but there's no **money exchange** on Yakushima, so stock up with cash in Kagoshima. Both Anbō and Onoaida have sub-post offices and supermarkets.

Getting to the island

Kagoshima serves as the main **access** point for Yakushima, though you can also reach the island from Ibusuki. There are five **flights** daily from Kagoshima airport (40min; ¥10,620 one way) operated by an associate of JAS (☏0120-511283). Yakushima airport (☏0997/42-1200), lies on the island's northeast coast roughly midway between the two main towns, Miyanoura and Anbō, and is served by local buses and taxis.

By the time you've included transport to and from the airports, however, the Toppy **jetfoil** is almost as speedy. There are four sailings daily from Kagoshima's Kita-Futō terminal (2hr–2hr 30min; ¥7000, or ¥12600 return), one of which comes via Ibusuki. Note that some of these jetfoils also stop at Tanegashima en route and that while most dock at Miyanoura, one or two use Anbō port, so check beforehand. Reservations are required and can be made through a travel agent or with the ferry company (Kagoshima Shōsen; ☏099/255-7888), or you can buy advance tickets at the terminals. Jetfoils stop running in bad weather.

Finally, daily **ferries**, operated by Orita Kisen (☏099/226-0731), depart from Kagoshima's Minami-Futō (4hr; ¥5000 single, ¥8000 return). If you're not in a hurry, these ships are a great way to travel – there's even a sauna and coin-laundry on board – and reservations aren't necessary except for private rooms. You might want to bring your own food, however, since there's not a great choice, and very little seating, just tatami mats or carpets.

For jetfoil information and reservations on Yakushima call the Toppy office in Miyanoura (☏0997/42-0034) or Anbō (☏0997/46-3399). Orita Ferry's local office is on ☏0997/42-0008.

Information

Both Yakushima's main towns have **information offices**. In Miyanoura there's a useful desk in the ferry terminal building (daily 8.30am–5pm; ☏0997/42-1019, ℱ42-1044) where you can pick up bus timetables, hotel lists and maps – look out for the colour "Landsat Map", which gives names in Japanese and English. For English-language assistance walk up the road to the smart new Yakushima Environmental and Cultural Village Centre (Tues–Sun 9am–5pm; ☏0997/42-2900). Though not an official tourist office, the staff will usually help call hotels and so on, if you're stuck. Anbō's tiny tourist information office (daily 8.30am–5pm; ☏0997/46-2333) is located in the centre of town on the main road just north of the river.

There are a number of **dive shops** in Miyanoura that rent gear; enquire at the tourist information centre in the ferry terminal for details. The Yakushima Nature Activity Centre (☏0997/42-0945) on the main drag in Miyanoura runs one-day ecotours of the island with a choice of hiking, kayaking or scuba-diving packages for ¥15,000. An English-speaking guide is available.

Island transport

Yakushima's road system consists of one quiet highway circumnavigating the island, plus a few spurs running up into the mountains. **Buses** depart from the

Miyanoura ferry terminal for Nagata in the west (30min; ¥870), or on the more useful route east via the airport and Anbō to terminate in Kurio or a little further on at Ōko-no-taki (1hr 30min; ¥1820). There's roughly one bus per hour between Miyanoura and Kurio, with the last service in each direction leaving around 5pm. For most of the year (March–Nov) buses also operate twice daily from Miyanoura via Anbō to Yaku-sugi Land (1hr 15min; ¥1330). The timetable varies according to the season so check locally, and note that there's an extra charge for large rucksacks and luggage over 10kg; for example, you'll pay an additional ¥400 from Miyanoura to Yaku-sugi Land.

It's well worth renting your own transport. A day's **car rental** costs ¥6000–10,000 for the smallest car, depending on the season. Local companies are generally cheaper, such as Terada Rent-a-Car (☎0997/42-0460) and Matsubanda Rent-a-Car (☎0997/42-0027), while Nippon Rent-a-Car (☎0997/42-1105) also has offices here. Make sure you keep the tank topped up since there are no petrol stations on west Yakushima between Onoaida and Nagata, while those on the rest of the island close at 6pm; on Sundays, only one station – in Miyanoura – stays open on a rotating basis. **Motorbikes** are available at You Shop (April–Oct; ☎0997/46-2705) on the main road in Anbō. You can rent **mountain bikes** (¥1200 per day, ¥600 for 3 hours) at the Backpackers' Support shop opposite the information center in Anbō, while in Miyanoura you'll find bicycles at the Yakushima Kankō Center, on the main road opposite the ferry terminal. The three main taxi companies on the island are Yakushima Kōtsū Taxi (☎0997/46-2321), Anbō Taxi (0997/46-2311) and Matsubanda Kōtsū Taxi (☎0997/42-0027).

Accommodation

Yakushima has a fair range of **accommodation**, but you still need to plan well ahead during holiday periods. In **Miyanoura**, you can't get more convenient than the *Seaside Hotel Yakushima* (☎0997/42-0175, ℱ22-0502; ❼ including meals), built on the promontory overlooking the ferry port. It's a comfortable place with Western and tatami rooms, plus several restaurants. For something cheaper, try the modern *Minshuku Takesugi* (☎ & ℱ0997/42-0668; ❺ including meals), easily identified by its "Lodging House" sign on the main road overlooking the harbour, or *Minshuku Yaedake* (☎ & ℱ0997/42-2552; ❺), a couple of minutes further east where the road starts to descend to the river.

If you'd rather stay in **Anbō**, book early for the welcoming *Shisuikan* (☎0997/46-2018; ❻ including meals) in a traditional, white building 100m west of the main road, two streets north of the river; the owner speaks English and lays on excellent meals. On the same street the *Kamome-sō* (☎0997/46-2544, ℱ46-3104; ❻) is less attractive but offers a couple of en-suite rooms, while *Minshuku Shiho* (☎09974/6-3288; ❹) is the best option near the port. A white bungalow shaded by palm trees, it's the first building you come to on the road up from the pier, and provides spick-and-span, no-frills tatami rooms with breakfast only. *Backpackers' Support* (☎0997/49-7101, ℱ49-7102; ❶) also offers dorm accommodation and information on hiking and camping. You can rent walking boots, rainwear, snorkelling gear and camping equipment here as well.

Continuing round the island, **Onoaida** is home to the island's plushest hotel, the *Yakushima Iwasaki Hotel* (☎0997/47-3888, ℱ47-3788; ❽), complete with its own *yaku-sugi* in the atrium. Guests are met at the airport or ferry terminal, but the hotel is also on the public bus route, west of central Onoaida. At the other end of the scale, the nearby *Chinryu-an* (☎ & ℱ0997/47-3900; dorm ❸; room ❺ including meals) offers dormitory bunks or private tatami rooms in a cedar-wood chalet buried among trees. The cheerful, English-speaking owner is a fount of local information and also provides hearty meals, though you can use the kitchen for a small fee. To get here, take the bus to the Iwasaki Hoteru-iriguchi stop and walk west for a few minutes, keeping your eyes peeled for a sign on the right. *Yakushima Youth Hostel* (☎0997/47-3751, ⓕ47-2477; dorm beds ¥2940 per person) lies 5km west of Onoaida in **Hirauchi**. The hostel only has six rooms, so make sure you book ahead, and is run along military lines, with a strict policy of lights out at 10pm. It's five minutes' walk east from the Hachimansho gakkō, signed down a quiet lane.

Last but not least, there's the *Sōyōtei* (☎ & ⓕ0997/45-2819; ❼) at **Inaka Beach** in the northwest of the island. This tasteful, antique-decorated ryokan was painstakingly constructed using new materials and hundred-year-old beams; it has some rooms with verandas and stunning views of the finest beach in Yakushima, as well as an outside bath where you can take in the sunset. Meals are provided, but the owner doesn't speak English. The ryokan is located at the western tip of Inaka Beach next to the road leading to Nagata.

Eating and drinking

All the places above offer room rates without meals, but in general you're best off **eating** in your accommodation, especially in the evenings. **Miyanoura** has a few restaurants along the main road, of which *Kabochaya* (Tues–Sun 11am–3pm) makes a good, inexpensive lunch stop. The English-speaking chef rustles up a pretty fair curry rice, but his real speciality is Yakushima ramen made with smoked fish. The restaurant is on the main road, halfway between the two minshuku (see opposite), near the Nisseki petrol station. *Shimamusubi* (Tues–Sun 5am–5pm), run by an affable Argentinian of Japanese extraction, offers bentō box lunches to take on your walking trips; cross the bridge and proceed along the main road towards Anbō for about five minutes until you see the log cabin exterior on your left.

Anbō has a lively little *izakaya* called *Wakatake* (Mon–Sat 11.30am–1.30pm & 6–10pm) beside the river immediately south of the *Kamome-sō* ryokan. Fresh seafood is the order of the day, served as *sashimi* or as part of their *omakase* course-menu (from ¥3000); get here early to be sure of a seat. The pleasantly rustic *Rengaya* (daily 10am–2pm & 6–10pm), on the road down to the harbour, is another popular spot. It offers a varied menu, including *yakiniku* (meat barbecued at your table), *tonkatsu* (pork cutlets) and steaks, with set meals from around ¥1400. Try the sashimi set, which comes complete with deep-fried flying-fish, "wings" set at a jaunty angle.

Kirishima National Park

On the border between Kagoshima and Miyazaki prefectures, **Kirishima National Park** is Japan's oldest and comprises no less than 23 volcanic mountains, ten crater lakes and numerous hot springs. The park's main centre is the plateau-village of **Ebino Kōgen**, a cluster of shops, hotels and campsites, from where it's a short scramble up the park's highest peak, Karakuni-dake (1700m). The park's easternmost peak, Takachiho-no-mine (1574m), however, holds greater significance, since according to legend this is where Ninigi-no-miko-to, grandson of the Sun Goddess Amaterasu (see p.949) and legendary founder of the Japanese imperial line, descended to earth. The traditional approach to Takachiho is from the park's southern gateway, **Kirishima Jingū**, stopping first at a shrine shrouded in cryptomeria trees. The peaks are linked by a skein of

hiking trails – it's worth scaling at least one of them for superb views over a foreground of jagged craters filled with perfectly round, cobalt-blue lakes to Sakurajima puffing angrily on the southern horizon.

The Kirishima range lies at the north end of Kagoshima Bay, with sporadic **transport** links to both Kagoshima and Miyazaki. Coming **from Kagoshima**, the quickest option is bus #8 from Nishi-Kagoshima Station to Ebino Kōgen (1hr 30min; ¥1550). Operated by Hayashida Bus company, these services run three times daily, but only the first bus is direct; the others involve a change at the *Kirishima Iwasaki Hotel* in Hayashida Onsen just below the park. If you're using a JR pass, take a train from Kagoshima to Kirishima Jingū Station, then a bus to Hayashida Onsen to connect with the Ebino Kōgen

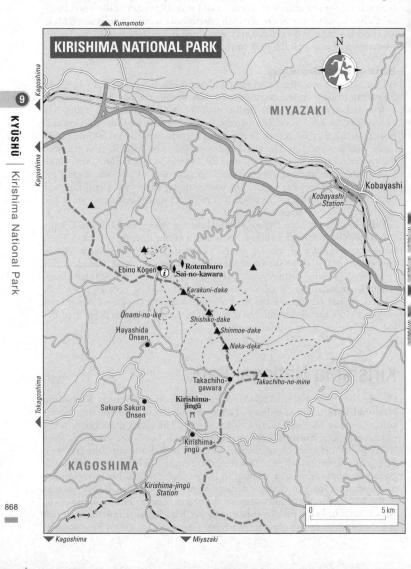

Ebino-kōgen	*Ebino Kōgen*	えびの高原
Ebino-kōgen campsite	*Ebino-kōgen kyampu-mura*	えびの高原キャンプ村
Ebino-kōgen-sō	*Ebino-kōgen-sō*	えびの高原荘
Karakuni-sō	*Karakuni-sō*	からくに荘
Kirishima Iwasaki Hotel	*Kirishima Iwasaki Hoteru*	きりしま岩崎ホテル
Minshuku Kirishima-ji	*Minshuku Kirishima-ji*	民宿きりしま路
Kirishima-jingū	*Kirishima-jingū*	霧島神宮
Kirishima-jingū-mae Youth Hostel	*Kirishima-jingū-mae Yūsu Hosuteru*	霧島神宮前ユースホステル
Kobayashi	*Kobayashi*	小林
Sakura Sakura Onsen	*Sakura Sakura Onsen*	さくらさくら温泉
Takachiho-gawara	*Takachiho-gawara*	高千穂河原
Takachiho-gawara campsite	*Takachiho-gawara kyampu-jō*	高千穂河原キャンプ場

buses. Miyakō Bus runs daily services **from Miyazaki**'s Miyakō City bus terminal to Ebino Kōgen (2hr 15min–3hr; ¥2450 for direct service; ¥2740 via Kobayashi in the north). Again, JR pass holders can save a few yen by taking a train from Miyazaki to Kobayashi Station (3 daily; 1hr 30min) before joining the bus.

Ebino-kōgen

Whichever route you take to **EBINO-KŌGEN** the views are stunning. At 1200m above sea level, temperatures on the plateau rarely exceed 20°C in summer and dip well below freezing when winter gives the peaks a dusting of snow and hoar frost. This is the best time to appreciate the local **onsen** – Kirishima is Japan's highest hot-spring resort – while spring and autumn provide perfect hiking weather.

The centre of Ebino-kōgen consists of a coach park, edged by a few useful buildings: the **Rest Centre** has souvenir shops and fast-food stands downstairs and a restaurant upstairs, the bus centre has an **information desk** (daily 8am–5pm; ℡0984/35-1111), and there's also a small **Visitors' Centre and Eco Museum** (daily 9am–5pm; ℡0984/33-3002). The last two provide local sketch maps, though you'll need something more detailed for the longer **hikes**. If it's a clear day, try tackling **Karakuni-dake** at the very least. The quickest trail starts 1km northeast of the village beside a steaming, sulphurous scar known as Sai-no-kawara, and then climbs steeply along a heavily eroded ridge. It's not a difficult climb, taking under two hours, though you'll want good footwear on the loose stones. From here you can circle south to Ōnami-no-ike, Japan's largest crater lake, and then back to Ebino-kōgen, which will take about another three and a half hours. The classic walk, however, is east along Kirishima's magnificent volcanic peaks from Karakuni-dake to Takachiho-gawara; allow about four hours for the hike and remember to carry plenty of water. The path leads over Shishiko-dake (1428m), the still-active Shinmoe-dake (1421m) and Naka-dake (1345m) with its two grassy hollows and then descends to the hiking base of Takachiho-gawara. Here you've got the choice of the Takachiho-gawara **campsite** (℡0995/57-0969; closed Sept–May) or a seven-kilometre trot down to the comforts of Kirishima Jingū (see p.870), though if you time it right, you may be able to catch the once-daily bus back down – check times locally (see opposite).

There are also more gentle ambles across Ebino plateau. The most popular is a four-kilometre walk starting from behind the Visitors' Centre, through forests of white fir and maple, and past three crater lakes before emerging beside Sai-no-kawara. In May and June, on the other hand, head southeast to where wild azaleas give the hillsides a dusty-pink tinge. As a reward for all this exercise, you can't do better than wallow in an **onsen**. Most local hotels open their baths to the public – the best is Ebino-kōgen-sō's smart **rotemburo** (daily 11am–3pm; ¥500) – but in summer the most atmospheric bathing spot is the public rotemburo (July & Aug; ¥300) on the plateau's northern edge a short distance beyond Sai-no-kawara; the water's a cool 28°C. If you don't fancy a full onsen, you can always ease aching feet in the free hot-spring footbath next to the Rest Centre.

Ebino Kōgen village is just a handful of somewhat pricey **hotels** among the pine forests. The revamped *Ebino-kōgen-sō* (☎0984/33-0161, ℱ33-0114; ❼ including two meals) offers the swishest accommodation, four minutes' walk west of the central junction; their most expensive rooms look out over Karakuni-dake. Alternatively, there's the small but equally sparkling *Karakuni-sō* (☎ & ℱ0984/33-0650; ❺–❼), north of the Visitors' Centre, which has Western and Japanese rooms, including one with a private onsen and mountain views. For cheaper accommodation, the local **campsite**, *Ebino-kōgen kyampu-mura* (☎0984/33-0800), has tents and basic wooden cabins and dorm beds (¥1250). Alternatively, *Kirishima Jingū* (see below) offers a choice of homely minshuku.

If you're not **eating** in your hotel, it's a good idea to bring food with you to the plateau. The shop by the bus centre sells little more than souvenirs, snacks and drinks. The restaurant in the Rest Centre offers either cheap fast food downstairs – *yakitori*, noodles, curry rice and so forth – or a more expansive array of set lunches in the dining room upstairs, with sets for under ¥1000. It stops serving food at 4pm.

Kirishima Jingū

The small town of **KIRISHIMA JINGŪ**, built on the southern slopes of Takachiho-no-mine, makes a possible alternative base to Ebino Kōgen. The top end of town, partly enveloped in cedar forests and focused round a cheerful, red-lacquer bridge, has an appealing, village atmosphere. It also boasts a number of reasonable accommodation options and a couple of mildly interesting sights.

The first of these is a small **craft village** (daily 9am–5/5.30pm; free) immediately south of the lacquered bridge. Though it's a mite touristy, some of the demonstrations are worth a look and there's also a short riverside walk. Heading over the bridge, walk under the bright vermilion *torii* and up a steep flight of steps to the shrine, **Kirishima-jingū**, after which the town is named. A surprisingly imposing complex, it's dedicated to Ninigi-no-mikoto and his fellow gods who first set foot in Kirishima at the dawn of Japan's creation. Although there are fine views of Kagoshima Bay from the shrine, they're better from the summit of **Takachiho-no-mine** (1574m) itself, roughly three hours' walk to the northeast. With your own transport you can halve the walking time by driving 7km up the road to **Takachiho-gawara**. It's then a steady climb on a well-marked path, ending in a short scramble on scree to the crater rim where a replica of Ninigi's sacred sword points skywards. Takachiho last erupted in 1913, and now only faint wisps of steam indicate that it's still active.

As well as a **Visitors' Centre** (daily 8.30am–5pm), Takachiho-gawara also has a good **campsite** just south of the road. Otherwise, if you're looking for

places to stay, try one of the cluster of minshuku at the top end of Kirishima Jingū village. Among these, the friendly *Minshuku Kirishima-ji* (T & F 0995/57-0272; ❻ including meals) beside the bridge is a pleasant place with just four rooms. Take the road east in front of the *Kirishima-ji* for *Kirishima Jingū-mae Youth Hostel* (T & F 0995/57-1188; ¥2625 per person). It's basic, with small tatami rooms which you'll have to share if it's busy, but pretty relaxed, and the food's plentiful and tasty. Both these places have their own hot-spring baths and offer rooms without meals. There are several small **restaurants** (though most close between 5pm and 7pm) and convenience stores on the main square, plus a **post office** and bus stops for services down to Kirishima Jingū Station or on up to Hayashida Onsen, where you'll need to change for Ebino Kōgen.

If you're a big onsen fan you might fancy a visit to *Sakura Sakura Onsen* (T 0995/57-1227, ⓔ info@sakura-sakura.jp; ❻–❼). There are several rotemburo here, but the speciality is *doro*, volcanic mud, which is especially popular with young women for its skin-softening effects – you smear yourself from head to toe in the pungent grey stuff, let it dry, then rinse it off and relax in a selection of different indoor and outdoor pools. The baths are open to non-residents (daily 6am–11pm; ¥500), and there's also a very good-value restaurant with lunch sets from ¥700. The onsen is on the bus route to *Kirishima Iwasaki Hotel* at Hayashida Onsen, 3km west of Kirishima-Jingū shrine. Get off at Yokodake-shimo bus stop then just follow the sign up the path.

Miyazaki and around

Perched on the southeast coast of Kyūshū, the breezy, semi-tropical city of **MIYAZAKI** claims the longest sunshine hours in Japan, while the brightly coloured blooms and phoenix palms, the city's emblems, give the streets a relaxed, summery feel. Actual sights are a little thin on the ground – a historic shrine, municipal park and the world's largest indoor beach – but Miyazaki makes a good base for exploring the **Nichinan coast**. A short train ride south, the island of **Aoshima** is a subtropical garden ringed by platforms of heavily scored rocks, while further along the coast **Udo-jingū**'s main shrine nestles in a sacred cave. From here you can continue down the peninsula to **Cape Toi**, or turn inland to circle round via **Obi**, an attractive castle town with a passable collection of museums and old houses. **Aya**, to the northwest of Miyazaki, is another pleasant town, worth visiting for its reconstructed castle and lively art scene.

Miyazaki's **festivals** are launched on January 15 with a dip in the sea off Aoshima to pray for the coming year. While north Japan is still wrapped in snow, in mid-March the city's flower festival announces the arrival of spring, but the most important event is autumn's Miyazaki-jingū Taisai (last weekend in Oct). This takes the form of a costume parade in honour of Emperor Jimmu, Japan's first emperor, featuring women dressed in gorgeous wedding kimono.

Arrival, information and city transport

Arriving in Miyazaki by **long-distance bus**, you end up at Miyakō City Bus Centre, south of the river, though most services also call at Miyazaki Station or at the city's central crossroads at the junction of Tachibana-dōri and Takachiho-dōri on their way through town. Likewise, **trains** stop at both Miyazaki Station and southerly Minami-Miyazaki Station, just east of Miyakō City. The **airport**

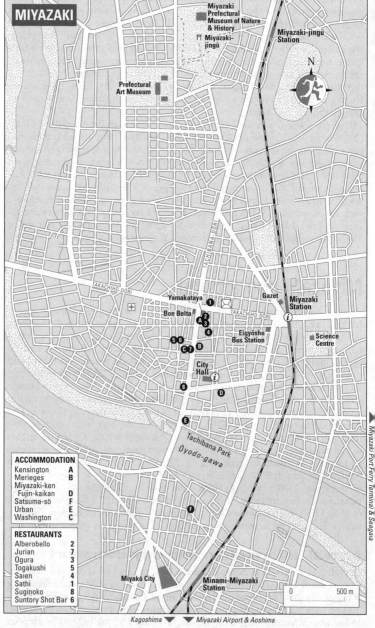

MIYAZAKI

Heiwadai-kōen (400 m) ▲   ▲ Heiwadai-kōen (800 m)   ▲ Nobeoka & Beppu

Miyazaki
Prefectural
Museum of Nature
& History

⛩ Miyazaki-
jingū

Miyazaki-jingū
Station

N

Prefectural
Art Museum

TACHIBANA-DORI

TAKACHIHO-DORI

Yamakataya
Bon Belta

❶

Gazet

Miyazaki
Station
ℹ

TAKACHIHO-DORI

Ⓐ❷
❸
❹

Eigyōsho
Bus Station

Science
Centre

Ⓑ
❺❻
Ⓒ❼

City
Hall
ℹ

❽

Ⓓ

Ⓔ

Tachibana Park
Ōyodo-gawa

Ⓕ

Miyakō City

Minami-Miyazaki
Station

0   500 m

Kagoshima ▼   ▼ Miyazaki Airport & Aoshima

Miyazaki Port Ferry Terminal & Seagaia

ACCOMMODATION
Kensington	A
Merieges	B
Miyazaki-ken Fujin-kaikan	D
Satsuma-sō	E
Urban	C
Washington	C

RESTAURANTS
Alberobello	2
Jurian	7
Ogura	3
Togakushi	5
Saien	4
Sathi	1
Suginoko	8
Suntory Shot Bar	6

also lies 5km south of the city centre. It's connected by both train (1–3 hourly; 10min; ¥340) and limousine bus (every 20min; 25min; ¥400) to Miyazaki Station via Minami-Miyazaki. Finally, **ferries** from Kawasaki, Naha and Ōsaka dock at Miyazaki Port Ferry Terminal, east of the city centre. You'll find buses waiting outside the terminal buildings to bring you to Miyazaki Station or Miyakō City (15–20min; ¥240).

Miyazaki is well provided with English-language information. Both the main **tourist information office** inside Miyazaki Station (daily 9am–7pm; ℡0985/22-6469, ℻22-6505), and the airport desk (daily 7am–8.30pm; ℡0985/51-5114) have English-speaking staff. The Prefectural International Centre, 6F Higashi-Bekkan, 1-6 Miyata-chō (Mon–Fri 8.30am–5.15pm; ℡0985/32-8457), beside the City Hall, is another useful resource, aimed primarily at long-term residents.

The useful *Discovering Miyazaki* leaflet is available from the above tourist offices and contains helpful tips about using **local buses**. Though most services depart from Miyakō City, a few use the Miyazaki Eigyōsho terminus, opposite Miyazaki Station's west entrance, or depart from the station concourse. However, almost all buses call at stops around the city's central crossroads, so the best thing is to head for this junction and ask which stop you need; getting off here, ask for Depāto-mae. Destinations are shown on the front of the bus in *kanji*; take a numbered ticket as you board and pay the driver on exit according to the fare on the display panel.

⑨

KYŪSHŪ | Miyazaki and around

Miyazaki and around

Miyazaki	*Miyazaki*	宮崎
Heiwadai-kōen	*Heiwadai-kōen*	平和台公園
Minami-Miyazaki	*Minami-Miyazaki*	南宮崎
Miyakō City	*Miyakō Shitii*	宮交シティー
Miyazaki-jingū	*Miyazaki-jingū*	宮崎神宮
Miyazaki Prefectural Museum of Nature and History	*Miyazaki-kenritsu Sōgō Hakubutsukan*	宮崎県立総合博物館
Miyazaki Port Ferry Terminal	*Miyazaki-kō Ferii Tāminaru*	宮崎港フェリーターミナル
Prefectural Art Museum	*Miyazaki-kenritsu Bijutsukan*	宮崎県立美術館
Science Centre	*Kagaku Gijutsukan*	科学技術館
Seagaia	*Shiigaia*	シーガイア
Accommodation		
Hotel Kensington	*Hoteru Kenjinton*	ホテルケンジントン
Hotel Merieges	*Hoteru Meriiju*	ホテルメリージュ
Miyazaki-ken Fujin-kaikan	*Miyazaki-ken Fujin-Kaikan*	宮崎県婦人会館
Satsuma-sō	*Satsuma-sō*	さつま荘
Urban Hotel	*Āban Hoteru*	アーバンホテル
Washington Hotel	*Washinton Hoteru*	ワシントンホテル
Restaurants		
Jurian	*Jurian*	寿里庵
Ogura	*Ogura*	おぐら
Saien	*Saien*	菜苑
Sathi	*Sati*	サティ
Suginoko	*Suginoko*	杉の子

Accommodation

If you're looking for **accommodation** in Miyazaki, the best option is to head for Tachibana-dōri, south of the central crossroads, where you'll find a sprinkling of mid-range business hotels. Cheaper places cluster round Miyazaki Station and in Minami-Miyazaki, while the local youth hostel is a bit of a hike from the station, but within walking distance of Tachibana-dōri.

Hotel Kensington 3-4-4 Tachibana-dōri Higashi ☎0985/20-5500, ⓕ32-7700. "Nostalgic days of England" are promised at this smartish business hotel south of Miyazaki's central crossroads. Cheaper rooms lack windows, but they're all equipped with phone, TV and en-suite bath. ➎
Hotel Merieges 3F, 3-1-11 Tachibana-dōri Higashi ☎0985/26-6666, ⓕ26-6111. Sleek, professional business hotel offering comfortable rooms, a business centre and choice of restaurants. ➏
Miyazaki-ken Fujin-kaikan 1-3-10 Asahi ☎0985/24-5785. Miyazaki's youth hostel is about fifteen minutes' walk southwest of the station, across from the Prefectural Office. Accommodation consists of shared tatami rooms in the Prefectural Women's Centre – though men are welcome – and there's a 10pm curfew. There's a cheap café downstairs and bike rental is available (around

¥1000 per day). Dorms beds ¥2600 per person.
Satsuma-sō 3-6-9 Ota ☎0985/51-4488. Set in a residential area ten minutes' walk north of Miyakō City (near the Nakamura 1-chōme bus stop), this is one of the nicest places to stay in Minami-Miyazaki, with friendly staff and bright, clean tatami rooms (but ask for one facing away from the road). Bathrooms are shared and meals are optional. ➌
Urban Hotel 1-5-8 Tachibana-dōri Higashi ☎0985/26-7411, ⓕ26-7532. Just east of the Tachibana bridge, this odd-looking, turreted business hotel hides a few well-priced rooms – simple but spacious, and all are en suite. ➎
Washington Hotel 2F, 3-1-1 Tachibana-dōri Nishi ☎0985/28-9111, ⓕ22-6222. Oldish member of the Washington chain just off the main drag, with boxy but perfectly adequate rooms, and in-house bars and restaurants. ➏

The City

Central Miyazaki's wide boulevards, colourful shopping arcades and boisterous entertainment district make it an appealing stop on a tour round Kyūshū. Though they won't appear on anyone's must-see list, the city's sights are sufficiently interesting to fill a leisurely day. In the northern suburbs, **Heiwadai-kōen** is a hilltop park with a delightful collection of clay *haniwa* figurines – replicas of statues found in ancient burial mounds. The grounds of nearby **Miyazaki-jingū**, the city's foremost shrine, contain a good municipal museum, while the city's sleek new **art museum** lies nearby, and the station area boasts the entertaining **Miyazaki Science Centre**. Much is made of the riverside **Tachibana Park**; by day it's just a narrow strip of green with a few tables and chairs, but comes into its own at dusk, when the palm trees glitter with fairy lights.

The northern districts

Low hills rise to the north of Miyazaki, where the rather Stalinist "Tower of Peace" dominates a large public park, **Heiwadai-kōen**. To reach the park take a #8 bus from Miyakō City or the Depāto-mae stop outside Bon Belta department store (10–20min; ¥230). The 37-metre-high tower was built in 1940 using stones presented from around the world – the name was coined after the war. The only reason to visit the tower, however, is for its odd acoustic effects; stand on the hexagonal stone on the path in front of the tower, clap your hands and listen to the oddly metallic sound bounce back. Further into the park you'll find the **Haniwa Garden**, where dozens of clay statues of houses, animals and people populate a mossy wood. Look out for the charming warriors with elaborate uniforms and the pop-eyed, open-mouthed dancers. These are copies of the haniwa figures discovered in fourth-century burial mounds at nearby Saitobaru; it's believed the statues were used to "protect" aristocratic tombs. You can buy smaller versions in the park shop, though they make rather fragile souvenirs.

Around 1km southeast of Heiwadai-kōen, **Miyazaki Prefectural Museum of Nature and History** (Tues–Sun 9am–5pm; ¥300) gives a good overview of local history, including the haniwa figurines, with much information in English. The same complex includes an archeological centre, where you can watch people patiently glueing together pottery shards, and the **Minka-en** (daily 10am–4.30pm; free), a slightly unkempt collection of four thatched farmhouses from around the area. Don't miss the two traditional stone-and-clay baths at the end of the path; the water was heated by lighting a fire underneath, like giant cauldrons. These museums stand in the extensive woodlands surrounding **Miyazaki-jingū**, a shrine dedicated to Japan's first emperor, Jimmu Tennō. An unusually large shrine at the end of an imposing avenue, the sanctuary itself is typically understated, though if you're lucky you'll catch a festive ceremony, or at least spot some of the colourful, semi-wild chickens scurrying round the raked-gravel compound.

Art lovers should walk five minutes west to an impressive new complex of public buildings, including a concert hall, theatre and library, in the aptly named Culture Park. Here, the monumental **Prefectural Art Museum** (Tues–Sun 10am–6pm; ¥300) hosts temporary exhibitions alongside its permanent collection of twentieth-century painting and Italian sculptures. To get back into central Miyazaki you can catch a bus from the main road east of the Culture Park, or from the southern entrance to Miyazaki-jingū (¥160).

Miyazaki Science Centre and Seagaia

Immediately behind Miyazaki's jolly, blue-and-yellow station, a forty-metre-high satellite launcher pinpoints the city's excellent **Science Centre** (Tues–Sun 9am–4.30pm; ¥520, or ¥730 including planetarium). Using examples from Kyūshū, the museum covers everything from microorganisms, wind power and pulleys to robots and satellite imagery. Most of the displays are interactive and huge fun – ask for a copy of their very thorough English-language brochure. The museum also boasts the world's largest **planetarium** – 27m in diameter – which is well worth the extra expense. The shows (Tues–Sat 3 daily, Sun 5 daily), give you a superb fifty-minute ride through the heavens.

The last sight in Miyazaki city is the **Seagaia** resort, a short bus ride to the northeast. Buses run roughly every twenty minutes from Miyazaki Station or every thirty from Miyakō City (20–40min; ¥470). The complex contains a golf course, zoo, spa, onsen, luxury hotels and a man-made indoor beach, **Ocean Dome**, just a few hundred metres from the coast. Bizarre though it might seem, Ocean Dome (daily 10am–5pm, July & Aug until 8pm; occasionally closed Tues or Wed; ¥2000 ☎0985/21-1177) attracts plenty of holiday-makers to its "paradise island", complete with unsalted water at a constant 28°C, balmy, tropical air at 30°C and a white beach of crushed stones. The whole lot is topped with the world's largest retractable roof – so at least the sunshine's real. At regular intervals a wave machine creates 3.5-metre-high breakers for a none-too-spectacular surfing display, but afterwards you can have a go, if you don't mind forking out ¥1000 for body board rental (2hr). There's also a water slide (¥500).

Eating, drinking and entertainment

Beef, wild boar, *ayu* (sweet fish) and shiitake mushrooms from the mountains, clams, flying fish and citrus fruits – Miyazaki has a good spread of edible delicacies. There's also the local sushi – *retasu-maki* – containing shrimp, lettuce and mayonnaise; chicken Namban, deep-fried, succulent chicken morsels with tartar sauce; and *kama-age* udon, a simple noodle dish with a tasty dipping sauce. The best choice of **restaurants** is in the streets either side of Tachibana-dōri, but the Gazet building, outside Miyazaki Station, also has an interesting selection. The city's energetic **nightlife** district is squeezed into the backstreets west of Tachibana-dōri, behind the Bon Belta department store and south to the *Washington Hotel*.

Alberobello 3-4-26 Tachibana-dōri Higashi. Cheerful pizza parlour down an alley one block south of Yamakataya department store. Choose from a list of imaginative toppings on their English menu, with pizzas from ¥1000 and slightly cheaper pasta dishes. Daily except Tues until 9pm.

Jurian 3-1-3 Tachibana-dōri Nishi. This popular, modern *izakaya* specializes in seafood straight from the tank, and you can eat well for around ¥2000. There's a huge picture menu to choose from, with *yakiniku*, fries, salads and other standard *izakaya* fare. Daily 5pm–midnight.

Ogura Tachibana-dōri Higashi. A café-style restaurant offering good, cheap food (but no atmosphere), tucked down an alley immediately behind the Yamakataya store. They invented chicken namban (¥900) here in 1968, and they also do burgers, fried pork cutlets, curry rice and other comfort food in generous portions. Daily until 8.30pm.

Saien 2F, Tachibana-dōri Higashi. Vegetarian haven on a backstreet east of Tachibana-dōri, with well-priced lunch deals (¥700), fresh juice, brown rice and tofu burgers. Service can be slow. Daily until 8.30pm.

Sathi Haikara-dōri. Popular Indian serving tasty curries and plump naan bread. Sets from ¥1500. Tues–Sun until 9.30pm.

Suginoko 2-1-4 Tachibana-dōri Nishi. One of the city's most famous restaurants, at the south end of Tachibana-dōri, serving tasty country cooking in elegant surroundings. Try their lunchtime Kuroshio *teishoku* (¥1000) or bentō sampler (¥1600). Evening meals start at ¥4000. Closed Sun.

Suntory Shot Bar Chūō-dōri. Funky little bar popular with locals and foreigners alike. In keeping with its name there's a huge array of different alcohols and cocktails, but only a couple of beers to choose from. Daily 6pm–2am.

Togakushi Tachibana-dōri Nishi. Down a backstreet west of Chūō-dōri, this is a great little place for a late-night snack of *kama-age* udon. Look out for the autographs of famous customers on the walls. Daily 5pm–1am.

Listings

Airlines Air Nippon Company ☎0985/23-5101; ANA ☎0120-029222; JAS & Japan Air Commuter ☎0120-511283.

Airport information ☎0985/51-5111.

Banks and exchange Miyazaki Bank, Ōita Bank and Fukuoka Bank all have foreign exchange desks. You'll find them on Tachibana-dōri, with branches of Miyazaki Bank also near Miyazaki Station and in the Miyakō City complex.

Buses Most long-distance buses start from the Miyakō City Bus Centre and call either at Miyazaki Station or the Depāto-mae stops in the city centre. A few services start at the station, but then travel via Miyakō City.

Car rental Eki Rent-a-Car ☎0985/24-7206; Nippon Rent-a-Car ☎0985/25-0919; Toyota Rent-a-Car ☎0985/26-0100.

Emergencies For English-language assistance call the Helping Hands volunteer helpline on ☎090/3320-2158 (daily 8.30am–10pm). Emergency numbers are listed in "Basics" on p.81.

Ferries Marine Express (☎0985/29-8311) has services to Ōsaka (daily; 12hr 30min; from ¥8230) and Kawasaki, between Tokyo and Yokohama (every other day; 20hr 30min; from ¥17,710), departing from Miyazaki-kō Ferry Terminal, a short bus ride east of central Miyazaki (15–20min; ¥290). You can buy tickets at local travel agents (see opposite).

Hospitals and medical care The Prefectural Hospital, 5-30 Kita-takamatsu-chō (☎0985/24-4181), is on Takachiho-dōri, west of the central crossroads. The International Centre (see p.873) has information about English-speaking doctors.

Internet access You can access the Net for a free thirty minutes at Yotten Plaza (daily noon–7pm) on Tachibana-dōri, next to the *Hotel Kensington*. Other possibilities are Manga Wakusei, on the corner of Takachiho-dōri and Kurosako-dōri, west of Tachibana-dōri (open 24hr; ¥480 per hour) and Tip Top, on the northwest corner of Higashifutaba-dōri and Futabakōenkita-dōri behind the cinema just west of the Takachiho-dōri and Tachibana-dōri junction (Mon–Sat 10.30am–7.30pm & Sun 11am–7pm, closed every second and fourth Sun of the month; ¥800 per hour).

Police Miyazaki-Kita Police Station, 2-10-1
Higashi, Tachibana-dōri Miyazaki (☎0985/27-
0110).
Post office Miyazaki Central Post Office, 1-1-34
Takachiho-dōri, is on the main road east of the

Tachibana junction. They accept poste restante
and operate a 24hr service for express mail.
Travel agents For domestic travel arrangements,
try JTB (☎0985/29-2111), or Joy Road
(☎0985/24-2626) in Miyazaki Station.

Around Miyazaki

South of Miyazaki, the hills close in as road and railway follow the coast down to **Aoshima**. This low, oval island lying just offshore is best known for the surrounding platforms of "devil's washboard" rocks, scored into deep grooves as if by a giant's comb. These rock formations stretch over several kilometres south to **Udo-jingū**, an eye-catching shrine halfway up the cliffs. Even here, as in much of Japan, the cliffs are plastered with great swathes of concrete, but as you head down the Nichinan coast to Cape Toi, famed for its wild horses, there are more sandy coves and picturesque islands. Apart from the scenery, the only specific sights along here are the castle ruins and old samurai houses of **Obi**, a small, attractive town lying 6km inland. Both Aoshima and Obi are stops on the JR Nichinan Line from Miyazaki to Shibushi, but the best way to explore the coast is by road. With a careful eye on the timetables, you can travel from Aoshima to Obi by public bus and then pick up a train for the return trip to Miyazaki, or do the trip in reverse. Northwest of Miyazaki is the likeable town of **Aya**, distinguished by its castle, microbrewery and craft scene.

Aoshima

Five kilometres south of Miyazaki, the tiny island of **AOSHIMA**, just 1500m in circumference, is little more than a heap of sand capped by a dense forest of betel palms and other subtropical plants. It's best at low tide when you can explore the rock pools trapped on the surrounding shelf of washboard rocks. After that the only other thing to do is walk round the island – it takes all of fifteen minutes – and drop in at its small shrine, **Aoshima-jinja**. Swathed in tropical creepers, this is dedicated to Yamasachi Hiko, a god of mountain products. Each year he's honoured with a couple of lively **festivals**: on June 17 portable shrines are paraded round the island on boats and then manhandled back to Aoshima, while mid-January sees men rushing semi-naked into the sea to welcome the god back as part of the New Year celebrations.

The island is accessible via a causeway from the neighbouring town, also known as Aoshima, which is a stop on the JR Nichinan line **from Miyazaki**. Trains leave Miyazaki Station (25min; ¥360) every hour or so, stopping also at

Around Miyazaki		
Aoshima	Aoshima	青島
Aya	Aya	綾
Aya-chō Cycling Terminal	Aya-chō Saikuringu Tāminaru	綾町サイクリングターミナル
Cactus Garden	Saboten Hābu-en	サボテンハーブ園
Obi	Obi	飫肥
Obi-jō	Obi-jō	飫肥城
Obi-ten Jaya	Obi-ten Jaya	おび天茶屋
Udo-jingū	Udo-jingū	鵜戸神宮
Ryōyōtei	Ryōyōtei	綾陽亭
Shusen no Mori	Shusen no Mori	酒泉の杜
Teruha Suspension Bridge	Teruha Ōtsuri-bashi	照葉大吊り橋

Minami-Miyazaki (23min; ¥270) – the island is a six-minute walk east from Aoshima Station. The alternative is a bus from Miyazaki Station (45min; ¥670) via the Miyakō City Bus Centre (30min; ¥540); buses run roughly every fifteen minutes and drop you on the main road (Route 220) just behind Aoshima beach. You can pick up sketch maps at the small **tourist information** kiosk (daily 9am–6pm) outside Aoshima Station, and there are touristy **restaurants** on the main road and lining the approach to the causeway.

Udo-jingū

Four kilometres south of Aoshima, the road climbs over the **Horikiri Pass**, along an attractive stretch of coast fringed with heavily ridged rocks, where fishermen and cormorants try their luck. Nine kilometres further south, **Cactus Garden** (daily 9am–5/5.30pm; ¥670) is home to over one million cacti of five hundred different species. They mostly bloom in early summer (April–June), but at any time of year you can sample vitamin-packed cactus ice cream and cactus steaks at the garden's restaurant.

Around 5km further down the road, a cleft in the rock hides one of this area's most famous sights, **Udo-jingū** (free). The main shrine fills the mouth of a large, low cave halfway down the cliff face, its striking, vermilion *torii* and arched bridges vivid against the dark rock. According to legend, Udo-jingū was founded in the first century BC and marks the spot where Emperor Jimmu's father was born. The rounded boulders in front of the cave are said to represent his mother's breasts – expectant women come here to pray for an easy birth and newlyweds for a happy marriage.

The shrine is protected to the rear by a wooded hill, where you'll find various other sanctuaries, but first you have to run the gauntlet of souvenir stalls clustering round the entrance. Arriving by **bus** from Miyazaki's Miyakō City (hourly; 1hr 30min; ¥1440) or Aoshima (hourly; 40min; ¥990), drivers generally let you off at the turning to the shrine, to save a steep climb up from the village. You can then cut through a tunnel from the car parks, but it's nicer to follow the old, mossy steps over the hill-top, to rejoin the crowds by the shrine's distinctly Buddhist entrance gate. When you've finished, walk south along the coast to Udo village (roughly 15min) to catch the bus back to Miyazaki or onwards to Obi; there are three buses from Udo to Obi in the morning, then nothing until 5pm.

Obi

The JR Nichinan line sweeps inland round the Udo headland, passing through **OBI**, an old **castle town** 43km south of Miyazaki. It's a pristine little place with a number of samurai houses and a fine collection of traditional white-washed warehouses, many of them immaculately restored, clustered under the castle walls. Obi's heyday was under the Itō family, who were granted the fiefdom in 1588 and then spent much of their time feuding with the neighbouring Shimazu clan of Kagoshima. Only the walls of their once formidable castle remain, though the main gate and lord's residence have been rebuilt in the original style.

Central Obi lies in a loop of the Sakatani-gawa, with its historic core concentrated north of the main east–west highway. Here you'll find a few streets of **samurai houses** and the castle, **Obi-jō** (daily 9.30am–4.30pm; ¥600, including Yoshōkan and Komura Memorial Hall), on the low hill behind. Walking north up Ōte-mon-dōri, under the great southern gate, you reach a white-walled history museum full of Itō family heirlooms. Beyond is the Matsu-no-maru, an exact replica of the sprawling Edo-period buildings where the lords once lived, including the reception rooms, women's quarters, tea-ceremony room and a lovely "cooling-off" tower, where the lord could catch the summer breezes after his steam bath.

The rest of the castle grounds are now just grass and trees, but on the way out take a quick look at Obi's largest samurai house, the **Yoshōkan** (same ticket and hours), immediately west of Ōte-mon gate. When the Meiji reforms abolished feudal holdings in the late-nineteenth century, the Itō family moved to this more modest villa which had previously belonged to their chief retainer. Though you can't go in, the house is a lovely, airy building surrounded by a spacious garden that's looking a bit worse for wear. On the opposite side of Ōte-mon from the Yoshōkan, the **Komura Memorial Hall** (same ticket and hours) commemorates a famous Meiji-era diplomat who was born in Obi in 1855. He's best remembered for his part in concluding the 1905 peace treaty following the Russo-Japanese War; the museum's most interesting material, much of it in English, revolves around this period.

Practicalities
The quickest way to reach Obi is by **train** on the JR Nichinan line from Miyazaki via Aoshima (1–2 hourly; 1hr 15min; ¥910). Obi Station lies on the east side of town, about fifteen minutes' walk across the river from the castle. Alternatively, **buses** from Aoshima and Udo-jingū (4 daily; 40min; ¥820) terminate a short walk west of Ōte-mon-dōri. Though Obi is small enough to tackle on foot, you can **rent bikes** at the station kiosk (daily 8.30am–5.30pm; ¥300 for 3hr) for scooting into town.

Obi has its own **speciality food**, *Obi-ten*, which consists of minced flying-fish mixed with tofu, miso and sugar, rolled into a leaf shape and deep fried. *Obi-ten Jaya*, a nicely rustic **restaurant** on Ōte-mon-dōri south of the Komura Memorial Hall, serves a good-value *teishoku*, including rice, soup and salad for ¥900.

Aya
About 40km northwest of Miyazaki is the pleasant organic farming town of **AYA**, whose castle was once an important military base for the reigning Itō clan in their war against the Shimazu of Kagoshima. First stop should be the **Aya International Craft Centre** (daily 9am–5.30pm; ¥350 including castle), located in the centre of town a short walk north of the tourist information centre (see p.880). An impressive array of locally produced, handmade bamboo ware, pottery, furniture and *aizomeorimono* (indigo-dyed fabric) is on sale, and you can try your hand at pottery, weaving and cloth-dyeing (from ¥1000). Just beyond the craft centre is the **castle** itself, built in 1345, destroyed in 1615, then rebuilt with rigorous attention to detail in 1985 (historical drawings were used for reference). Though it doesn't hold a candle to some of the more famous castles in Japan, it's still worth a visit, with a superb view of the Aya basin and an attractively rustic exterior – built of stone, tile and local wood – which makes a pleasing picture against the background of coniferous forest. Inside there are displays of local artefacts, including a small collection of samurai swords.

Returning to the main road, the **Shusen no Mori** tourist complex (daily 9am–5pm), 3km to the west, comprises a **winery**, **microbrewery** and *shōchū* and sake **distillery**; visitors can tour the winery and *shōchū* distillery (daily 9.30am–4.30pm) and sample products free of charge. In addition to producing alcohol, Shusen no Mori boasts a posh ryokan (see p.880), a decadent onsen bath fringed by tropical plants (daily 10.30am–10pm; ¥1050) and a number of restaurants and craft shops. The most interesting of these is the **glass showroom** (daily 9am–6pm), which features original pieces by master artisan Kuroki Kuniaki, who employs a technique whereby flakes of gold and platinum are dispersed between layers of glass, creating intricately beautiful pieces. Buses run every hour from Aya to Shusen no Mori, so it's generally quicker to walk or cycle.

Take the main road 7km northwest of Aya to find the **Teruha Suspension Bridge** (daily 8am–5.30pm; ¥300), the highest in the world. A walk out on the bridge affords sweeping views of the surrounding evergreen broadleaf forests and emerald waters of the Aya-gawa, a dizzying 142m below. This region is now part of the **Kyūshū Central Mountain Range National Park** and there are stunning walks of varying lengths from the far side of the bridge through the primeval evergreen forest, the last of its type in Japan and home to numerous plant and wildlife species. There's no public transport here, so a bicycle or taxi (about ¥2000 from town) are your only options. If cycling, be warned that it's a steep 7km up to the suspension bridge.

Practicalities

Buses for Aya leave from Miyazaki roughly every half hour from stand #3 of the Miyakō City bus terminal (1hr; ¥1060) and drop passengers at the Aya Basu Machiaisho in the centre of town. The **tourist information** booth (daily 8.30am–5.30pm) on the second floor of the centrally located Honmono Centre (above the bustling organic fruit and veg market) provides maps of the town (in Japanese only) and folders of English-language information which can be perused on the premises. Because Aya's sites are spread out over a large area, it's best to rent a three-gear **bicycle** (¥410 for 4hr) from the Honmono Centre.

Though Aya is best enjoyed as a day-trip from Miyazaki, it does have a number of **accommodation** choices. *Ryōyōtei* (℡ 0985/77-2222, ℻ 77-2518; ⑨) is a ryokan fit for an emperor housed in the Shusen no Mori complex (see p.879). The capacious rooms have wonderful views of a Japanese garden and carp pond and guests are given a choice of Western and Japanese food. A cheaper option is the *Aya-chō Cycling Terminal* (℡ 0985/77-1227, ℻ 77-0932; ⑤ including meals), 5km northwest of the Honmono Centre, which features basic Japanese rooms. The most convenient place to **eat** is *Izumunu* (Mon–Sat 11am–6pm) located across from the Honmono Centre, where they dish up hearty lunch specials like udon and *champon* starting at ¥650.

Travel details

Trains

The **trains** between the major cities listed below are the fastest, direct services. There are also frequent slower services, run by JR and several private companies, covering the same destinations. It is usually possible, especially on long-distance routes, to get there faster by changing between services.

Aso to: Beppu (2 daily; 2hr); Kumamoto (hourly; 1hr 30min); Miyaji (hourly; 6min); Tateno (hourly; 25min).

Beppu to: Aso (2 daily; 2hr); Fukuoka (1–3 hourly; 2hr–3hr); Kita-Kyūshū (2 hourly; 1hr 20min);

Kumamoto (3 daily; 3hr); Miyazaki (hourly; 3hr 30min); Nobeoka (hourly; 2hr 30min); Ōita (frequent; 15min).

Fukuoka (Hakata Station) to: Arita (hourly; 1hr 20min); Beppu (every 20min–1hr; 2hr–3hr); Dazaifu (every 30min; 40min); Futsukaichi (every 10min; 10–20min); Hiroshima (every 15min; 1hr 10min–1hr 50min); Huis ten Bosch (hourly; 1hr 40min); Kagoshima (every 30min; 2hr 20min–3hr 50min); Kita-Kyūshū (every 10min; 20min–1hr 30min); Kumamoto (every 30min; 1hr 20min); Kyoto (every 30min; 2hr 50min–3hr 40min); Miyazaki (hourly; 6hr); Nagasaki (every

30min–1hr; 2hr 10min); Ōsaka (every 20min; 2hr
30min–4hr 30min); Takeo (hourly; 1hr 10min);
Tokyo (every 30min; 5hr–6hr 15min).
Isahaya to: Shimabara (hourly; 1hr 10min).
Kagoshima to: Fukuoka (every 30min; 2hr
20min–3hr 50min); Ibusuki (every 30min–1hr;
50min–1hr 20min); Kirishima Jingū (7 daily;
40–50min); Kumamoto (hourly; 2hr 30min);
Miyazaki (7 daily; 2hr); Nagasaki (hourly; 5–6hr);
Yatsushiro (every 30min; 35min).
Kita-Kyūshū (Kokura) to: Beppu (every 30min;
1hr 20min); Fukuoka (frequent; 20min–1hr 30min);
Hiroshima (every 20min; 50min–1hr 20min); Kyoto
(every 30min; 2hr 30min–3hr 15min); Miyazaki
(hourly; 5hr); Ōsaka (every 20min; 2hr 15min–4hr);
Tokyo (every 30min; 4hr 45min–6hr); Yahata (every
20min; 15min).
Kita-Kyūshū (Yahata) to: Fukuoka (every 20min;
50min); Kokura (frequent; 15min).
Kumamoto to: Aso (hourly; 1hr–1hr 30min);
Beppu (3 daily; 3hr); Fukuoka (every 30min; 1hr
20min); Kagoshima (hourly; 2hr 30min); Misumi
(hourly; 50min); Miyazaki (3 daily; 5hr); Nagasaki
(every 30min; 3hr).
Misumi to: Kumamoto (hourly; 50mins).
Miyazaki to: Aoshima (hourly; 25min); Beppu
(hourly; 3hr 30min); Fukuoka (hourly; 6hr);
Kagoshima (7 daily; 2hr 10min); Kobayashi (3
daily; 1hr 30min); Kita-Kyūshū (hourly; 5hr);
Kumamoto (3 daily; 4hr 50min); Nobeoka (hourly;
1hr 30min); Obi (every 30min–1hr; 1hr 15min);
Ōsaka (1 daily; 13hr 50min); Tokyo (1 daily; 20hr
30min).
Nagasaki to: Fukuoka (every 30min–1hr; 2hr
10min); Huis ten Bosch (hourly; 1hr 30min);
Isahaya (frequent; 20min); Kagoshima (hourly;
5–6hr); Kumamoto (every 30min; 3hr).
Takachiho to: Nobeoka (hourly; 1hr 30min).
Tateno to: Takamori (hourly; 30min).
Yatsushiro to Kagoshima (every 30min; 35min).

Buses

The **buses** listed below are mainly long-distance
services – often travelling overnight – between the
major cities, and local services where there is no
alternative means of transport. For shorter journeys, however, trains are almost invariably quicker
and often no more expensive.
Aso to: Beppu (4 daily; 2hr 40min); Kumamoto
(hourly; 1hr 30min); Kurokawa Onsen (1 daily;
1hr); Senomoto Kōgen (4 daily; 45min).
Beppu to: Aso (4 daily; 2hr 40min); Fukuoka
(every 30min–1hr; 2hr–2hr 20min); Kumamoto (4
daily; 4hr–7hr); Nagasaki (7 daily; 3hr 30min);
Nagoya (daily; 10hr 35min); Ōita (frequent; 20min).

Ebino Kōgen to: *Kirishima Iwasaki Hotel* (3 daily;
20min); Kagoshima (3 daily; 1hr 35min–3hr
10min); Kobayashi (4 daily; 1hr); Miyazaki (4 daily;
2hr 15min–3hr 15min).
Fukuoka to: Beppu (every 20min–1hr; 2hr
15min–3hr 20min); Huis ten Bosch (3 daily; 2hr);
Kagoshima (every 30min–1hr; 3hr 30min); Kita-
Kyūshū (frequent; 1hr 40min); Kumamoto (frequent; 1hr 45min–2hr 25min); Kyoto (daily; 9hr
30min); Miyazaki (every 30min–1hr; 4hr);
Nagasaki (every 20–30min; 2hr 30min–3hr
10min); Ōsaka (daily; 9hr); Tokyo (daily; 14hr
35min).
Isahaya to: Unzen (every 20min–1hr; 1hr 20min).
Kagoshima to: Chiran (10–12 daily; 1hr 20min);
Ebino Kōgen (3 daily; 1hr 45min–3hr); Fukuoka
(every 30min–1hr; 3hr 30min); Ibusuki (every
20min; 1hr 30min); Kumamoto (10 daily; 3hr
30min); Kyoto (daily; 13hr 20min); Miyazaki
(hourly; 2hr 40min); Nagoya (daily; 14hr 20min);
Ōsaka (3 daily; 11hr 40min).
Kirishima Jingū Station to: *Hayashida Onsen
Hotel* (12 daily; 35min); Kirishima Jingū-mae (12
daily; 15min).
Kita-Kyūshū (Kokura) to: Fukuoka (frequent; 1hr
40min); Kumamoto (9 daily; 2hr 35min); Nagasaki
(9 daily; 3hr).
Kumamoto to: Aso (hourly; 1hr 30min); Aso-san
Nishi-guchi (2 daily; 2hr); Beppu (4 daily; 4hr–7hr);
Fukuoka (frequent; 1hr 45min–2hr 25min);
Kagoshima (10 daily; 3hr 30min); Kumamoto Shin-
kō (hourly; 35min); Miyazaki (10 daily; 2hr
10min–3hr 30min); Nagasaki (10 daily; 3hr).
Miyazaki to: Aoshima (3–4 daily; 40–55min);
Ebino Kōgen (3–4 daily; 2hr 15min); Fukuoka (1–2
hourly; 4hr); Kagoshima (10 daily; 2hr 40min);
Kumamoto (hourly; 3hr–3hr 30min); Ōsaka (daily;
12hr 30min); Udo-jingū (hourly; 1hr 30min).
Nagasaki to: Beppu (7 daily; 3hr 30min); Huis ten
Bosch (10 daily; 1hr 15min); Kumamoto (9 daily;
3hr); Unzen (6 daily; 1hr 50min).
Takamori to: Takachiho (5 daily; 1hr 30min).
Unzen to: Shimabara (8 daily; 45min).

Ferries

Beppu to: Hiroshima (daily, 3hr 10min); Kōbe (2
daily; 11hr 35min–12hr 30min); Matsuyama (daily;
2hr 15min); Misaki (4 daily; 2hr 10min); Ōsaka (2
daily; 14hr); Yawatahama (5 daily; 2hr 45min).
Fukuoka to: Naha (1–2 weekly; 25hr); Pusan
(South Korea) by hydrofoil (3 daily; 2hr 55min), by
ferry (3 weekly; 13hr 40min).
Ibusuki to: Kagoshima (1 daily; 40min);
Yakushima (1 daily; 1hr 15min).
Kagoshima to: Ibusuki (1 daily; 40min); Naha

(4–6 weekly; 18hr 30min–24hr); Yakushima (5 daily; 2hr–3hr 45min).

Kita-Kyūshū (Kokura) to: Matsuyama (1 daily; 6hr 30min).

Kita-Kyūshū (Shin-Moji-kō) to: Kōbe (1 daily; 12hr 30min); Ōsaka (2 daily; 13hr); Tokushima (1 daily; 17hr).

Kumamoto to: Shimabara (hourly; 1hr).

Miyazaki to: Kawasaki (6 weekly; 20hr 30min); Ōsaka (1 daily; 12hr 30min).

Nagasaki to: Amakusa (3 daily; 40min).

Shimabara to: Kumamoto (hourly; 1hr); Misumi (6 daily; 1hr).

Yakushima to: Ibusuki (1 daily; 2hr); Kagoshima (5 daily; 2hr–3hr 45min).

Flights

Fukuoka to: Auckland (1 weekly; 15hr 45min); Bangkok (3 weekly; 3hr 35min); Beijing (1 daily; 1hr 30min); Hong Kong (1 daily; 3hr); Jakarta (3 weekly; 7hr 15min); Kansai International (6–7 daily; 1hr); Kuala Lumpur (3 weekly; 5hr 25min–7hr 20min); Melbourne (2 weekly; 14hr 20min); Naha (8 daily; 1hr 40min); Ōsaka (Itami; 5

daily; 1hr); Sapporo (4 daily; 2hr 10min); Seoul (1 daily; 1hr 20min); Tokyo (1–3 hourly; 1hr 30min).

Kagoshima to: Kansai International (2 daily; 1hr 10min); Nagoya (4 daily; 1hr 25min); Naha (3 daily; 1hr 20min); Ōsaka (Itami; 9 daily; 1hr 10min); Sapporo (1 daily; 2hr 25min); Seoul (3 weekly; 1hr 35min); Shanghai (2 weekly, 1hr 30min); Tokyo (9 daily; 1hr 50min); Yakushima (4–5 daily; 40min).

Kumamoto to: Kansai International (2 daily; 1hr 5min); Naha (1 daily; 1hr 35min); Ōsaka (Itami; 6 daily; 1hr 5min); Seoul (2 weekly; 1hr 30min); Tokyo (8 daily; 1hr 30min).

Miyazaki to: Fukuoka (7 daily; 45min); Kansai International (2 daily; 1hr); Nagoya (3 daily; 1hr 10min); Naha (1 daily; 1hr 35min); Ōsaka (Itami; 8 daily; 1hr); Tokyo (15 daily; 1hr 30min).

Nagasaki to: Kansai International (2–3 daily; 1hr 5min); Naha (1 daily; 1hr 35min); Ōsaka (Itami; 6–7daily; 1hr 10min); Sapporo (2 daily; 2hr 20min); Seoul (2 weekly; 1hr 30min); Shanghai (2 weekly; 40min); Tokyo (9 daily; 1hr 35min).

Ōita to: Kansai International (2–3 daily; 1hr); Naha (1 daily; 1hr 35min); Ōsaka (Itami; 5 daily; 50min); Tokyo (8 daily; 1hr 30min).

Okinawa

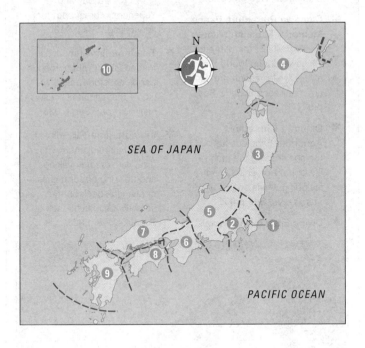

N

SEA OF JAPAN

PACIFIC OCEAN

CHAPTER 10

Highlights

* **Shuri-jō** This World Heritage-listed recreation of the Ryūkyū kingdom's most important castle is Naha's crowning glory. **See p.895**

* **Kokusai-dōri** Experience the cultural mélange of modern-day Okinawa in a stroll along Naha's premier shopping street. **See p.895**

* **Okinawa Prefecture Peace Memorial Museum** Witness the brutality of the battle for Okinawa during World War II at this well-presented museum in a peaceful park. **See p.901**

* **Okinawa Churaumi Aquarium** Fabulous aquarium showcasing the marine life of the Kuroshio Current, including whale sharks and manta rays. **See p.905**

* **Diving** From the soft corals and tropical fish around the Kerama islands to the enigmatic rocks near Yonaguni-jima, Okinawa offers a wealth of outstanding diving experiences. **See p.909**

* **Ishigaki-jima** Soak up the scenic delights of the Yaeyama Islands at Ishigaki-jima's Kabira Bay and Yonehara, a great spot for snorkelling. **See p.919**

* **Taketomi-jima** Tiny beach-fringed island with gorgeous traditional stonewalled village – the ultimate Okinawan chill-out spot. **See p.923**

* **Iriomote-jima** This wild island is an adventure paradise, with great kayaking and trekking opportunities – or just kick back on the serenely beautiful beach at Funauki. **See p.925**

△ Miyako-jima

Okinawa

The prefecture of Okinawa comprises more than one hundred islands, stretching over 700km of ocean from Kyūshū southwest to Yonaguni-jima, almost within sight of Taiwan. Collectively known as the Ryūkyū Shotō, this chain of subtropical islands, with their lush vegetation, paradise beaches and superb coral reefs, has become a popular destination for Japanese holiday-makers and foreign residents alike. Few other tourists make it down here, partly because of the time and cost involved, but if you've had your fill of shrines and temples and want to check out some of Japan's best beaches and dive sites (see box p.909), or simply fancy a spot of winter sun, then Okinawa is well worth a visit.

The largest island in the group, **Okinawa-Hontō**, usually referred to simply as Okinawa, is the region's transport hub and home to its prefectural capital, **Naha**. It's also the most heavily populated and developed of the Ryūkyū chain, thanks largely to the controversial presence of **American military bases** (see box p.902). Okinawa-Hontō boasts a number of historical sights, many of them associated with the **Battle of Okinawa** at the end of the Pacific War (see p.888). But the island has more to offer than battle sites, particularly in its northern region, where the old way of life still survives among the isolated villages.

To see the best of the region, though, you'll have to hop on a plane or ferry and explore the dozens of **outer islands** away from Okinawa-Hontō, many of them uninhabited. Even quite close to Naha, you'll find gorgeous beaches and fantastic dive spots around the **Kerama islands**, just 30km off Okinawa-Hontō. Divers and beach connoisseurs will want to visit **Miyako-jima** and **Ishigaki-jima**, way down the Ryūkyū chain. If you're looking for an idyllic retreat, **Taketomi-jima** can't be beaten, while the adventurous will want to explore **Iriomote-jima**, coated in thick groves of mangrove and steamy rainforest, and home to the elusive Iriomote lynx.

It's on these outer islands that you'll also find the strongest evidence of the much-vaunted **Ryūkyū culture**, born of contact with Taiwan and China, as well as the rest of Japan. The most obvious expressions of this culture are found in the islands' cuisine (see box on p.887) and in a vibrant use of colour and bold tropical patterns, while the Chinese influence is clearly visible in the region's architecture, traditional dress and the martial art of karate – the Ryūkyū warriors' preferred mode of protection. Ancient religious beliefs are kept alive by shamen (called *yuta*) and, on Okinawa-Hontō, there are sumo bouts between bulls. There's also a Ryūkyū dialect, with dozens of variations between the different islands, unique musical instruments, and a distinctive musical style which has reached an international audience through bands such as Nēnēs, Diamantes and Champloose (see p.897). If you're lucky, you'll

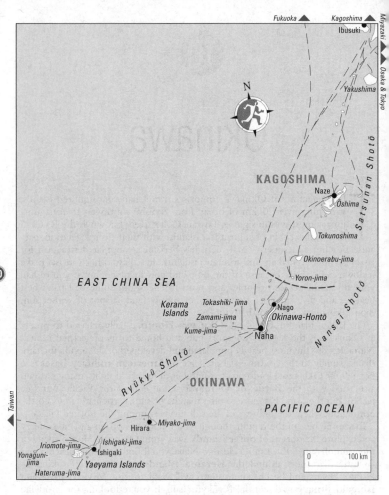

Fukuoka ▲   Kagoshima ▲

Ibusuki

Miyazaki ▲

Osaka & Tokyo ▲

Yakushima

KAGOSHIMA

Naze

Ōshima

Satsunan Shotō

Tokunoshima

Okinoerabu-jima

Yoron-jima

EAST CHINA SEA

Kerama
Islands

Tokashiki-jima

Zamami-jima

Kume-jima

Nago

Okinawa-Hontō

Naha

Nansei Shotō

Ryūkyū Shotō

OKINAWA

PACIFIC OCEAN

Taiwan ◀

Hirara   Miyako-jima

Iriomote-jima   Ishigaki-jima

Yonaguni-
jima   Ishigaki

Yaeyama Islands

Hateruma-jima

0   100 km

stumble on a local festival, such as giant rope tug-of-war contests or dragon-boat races, while the biggest annual event is the *Eisā* festival (15th day of the seventh lunar month) when everyone downs tools and dances to the incessant rhythms of drums, flutes and the three-stringed *sanshin*.

Those in search of local **crafts** will find beautiful *bingata* textiles the most appealing. Originally reserved for court ladies, *bingata* fabrics are hand-dyed with natural pigments from hibiscus flowers and various vegetables, in simple but striking patterns. Also worth searching out are the fine *jofu* cloths of Miyako-jima and the Yaeyama Islands, once gifted in tribute to the local monarchs. Ceramics are thought to have been introduced to the region from Spain and Portugal in the fifteenth century, but Ryūkyū potters concentrated on roof tiles and fairly rustic utensils. Nowadays, they churn out thousands of sake flasks and *shiisā* – the ferocious lion figures that glare down at you from every rooftop. The exquisite local lacquerware has a long history in the islands, too, having been introduced over 500 years ago from China, but the glassware you'll find is much more recent: it's said production took off in the postwar years when Okinawans set about recycling the drinks bottles of the occupying US forces.

Besides Hokkaidō, Okinawa contains Japan's largest areas of unspoilt natural environment and its greatest biodiversity. Much of this wealth of **wildlife** is underwater, spawned by the warm Kuroshio Current that sweeps up the east coast and allows coral reefs to flourish. But there are a number of unique species on land too, including turtles, a crested eagle and the noguchigera (Pryer's woodpecker), in addition to Iriomote's wild cat, the yamaneko. A less welcome local resident is the highly poisonous **habu snake**. It measures around 2m in length, is dark green with a yellow head, and usually lurks in dense vegetation or on roadsides, though rarely ventures into urban areas. As long as you're careful – especially during spring and autumn – you should have no problems; if you are bitten, make for the nearest hospital where they should have anti-venin.

With its subtropical **climate**, Okinawa stays warm throughout the year. Average annual temperatures are around 23°C, with a winter average of 17°C and a minimum of 10°C. Winter lasts from December through February, while the hot, humid summer starts in April and continues into September. Temperatures at this time hover around 34°C and the sun can be pretty intense, though the sea breezes help. The **best time to visit** is in spring or autumn (roughly March to early May and late September to December). The rainy season lasts from early May to early June, while typhoons can be a problem in July and August, and occasionally into October.

Taste of the tropics

It's claimed that one of the reasons Okinawa has Japan's highest percentage of centenarians (28 per every 100,000 population) is its healthy diet. Regardless of whether eating in the islands is good for you, one of the pleasures of a visit to Okinawa is the opportunity to indulge in the distinctly different **Ryūkyū cuisine**, combining Chinese and Japanese cooking styles, with plenty of tropical ingredients and liberal use of pork and fresh seafood.

Among the most common dishes are *Okinawa soba*, a filling bowl of thick wheat noodles and pork chunks, and *champurū* combining stir-fried vegetables in a thicker stew. It comes in many varieties, depending on the principal ingredient; look out for *chanpuru* made with sponge gourd (*nābera*), bitter melon (*gōyā*), wheat gluten (*fu*) and wheat noodle (*sōmen*). The tempura here is also different, the batter being thicker and moister.

Practically every part of the pig is used in local cooking, from the head to the trotters (*tibichi*). Their blood is sautéed with vegetables for *chii-irichii*, their stomach and intestines go into *nakami* soup. Goat stew (*yagijiru*) is a rustic dish particularly popular in the Miyako Islands and you could also try *irabū-jiru*: sea snake stew. Other local fish that may end up on your plate include *irabuchā* (parrot fish) and *miibai* (grouper), as well as plenty of dishes incorporating the squid (*ika*) and its black ink. Vegetarians get a look-in, too, with Okinawa producing many different types of tofu, including the delicious, silky-smooth *jimamedōfu*, made from peanuts.

The most refined Ryūkyū food is **tundā-bun**, the medicinally balanced court cuisine, beautifully displayed and served in small morsels like the mainland's *kaiseki ryōri*. Some of the dishes are an acquired taste though, particularly the blue cheese-like *tōfuyō*, tofu fermented in Okinawa's pungent rice liquor, **awamori**. Like wine, *awamori* improves with age – don't pass up the chance to sample some of this warming and very palatable beverage while travelling in the islands, but take care since it can have an alcohol content of up to sixty percent.

One of the more unusual ways of **getting to Okinawa** – and Japan – is to take the **international ferry** from Taiwan via Ishigaki and Miyako islands to Naha (see p.892 for details). By far the majority of visitors, however, arrive by plane. Most come from the Japanese mainland, though there are **international flights** to Naha from Hong Kong, Korea, Manila, Shanghai and Taiwan. **Domestic airlines** operate between Naha and Tokyo, Ōsaka and a number of other Japanese cities (see "Travel details", p.928), while a few fly direct to Ishigaki and Miyako. Though flying can be expensive, discounts are becoming increasingly common, so it's always worth asking the airlines and travel agents. Overseas visitors can also take advantage of the airpasses offered by JAL and ANA.

The other option is a **local ferry** from Tokyo, Ōsaka, Kōbe or one of several cities on Kyūshū. All of these services stop in Naha, from where some continue to Miyako and Ishigaki (see p.914 for details). These ferries can be a great way to travel if you're not in a hurry, though horribly crowded in the peak summer season.

Getting around between islands presents a similar choice between air and sea, with Naha as the main hub. Inter-island **flights** are operated by Japan Transocean Air (JTA), Ryūkyū Air Commuter (RAC) and Air Nippon (ANK), with connections to all the major islands. The **ferry** network, on the other hand, fans out from Naha's three terminals to every corner of the prefecture, allowing you to island-hop at your leisure. See individual island accounts for more about these sailings.

Some history

In the fifteenth century, the islands that now make up Okinawa were united for the first time into the **Ryūkyū kingdom**, governed from Shuri Castle in present-day Naha. This period is seen as the golden era of Ryūkyū culture. Trade with China, the rest of Japan and other Southeast Asian countries flourished, while the traditionally non-militarized kingdom maintained its independence by paying **tribute to China**. But then, in 1609, the **Shimazu** clan of Kagoshima (southern Kyūshū) invaded. The Ryūkyū kings became **vassals** to the Shimazu, who imposed punitive taxes and ruled with an iron hand for the next two hundred years, using the islands as a gateway for trade with China when such contact was theoretically outlawed by the Togukawa Shogunate. When the Japanese feudal system was abolished in the 1870s, the islands were simply annexed to the mainland as **Okinawa Prefecture**. Against much local opposition, the Meiji government established a military base and tried to eradicate local culture by forcing people to speak Japanese and swear allegiance to the emperor, forbidding schools to teach Ryūkyū history.

By the early twentieth century, Okinawa had been fairly successfully absorbed into Japan and became a key pawn in Japan's last line of defence during the **Pacific War**. Following the battle of Iwō-jima in March 1945, the American fleet advanced on Okinawa and, after an extensive preliminary bombardment, referred to locally as a "typhoon of steel", the Americans invaded on **April 1, 1945**. It took nearly three months of bitter fighting before General Ushijima, the Japanese commander, committed suicide and the island surrendered. The **Battle of Okinawa** left 12,500 American troops dead (plus 37,000 injured) and an estimated 250,000 on the Japanese side, nearly half of whom were local civilians.

It's estimated that one third of the population of Okinawa died in the war, many in **mass suicides** that preceded the surrender, and others from disease and starvation. But the islanders' subsequent anger has been directed at the Japanese government rather than America. Most people feel that Okinawa was sacrificed to save the mainland – this was the only major battle fought on Japanese soil – and that they were misled by Japanese assurances that they were luring the American fleet into a trap. Compounding this was the behaviour of Japanese troops, who are accused of denying locals shelter and medical treatment, and ultimately of abandoning them to the Americans.

By comparison, the American invaders were a welcome relief, despite the islanders' worst fears. They brought in much-needed food supplies – Spam was an instant hit in this pork-loving country – and gradually helped restore the local economy. This wasn't wholly altruistic, of course, since Okinawa was ideally placed for monitoring events in Southeast Asia. As the 1950s Korean War merged into the Vietnam War, so the **American bases** became a permanent feature of the Okinawa landscape (see box on p.902).

In fact, Okinawa remained under **American jurisdiction** until 1972, when local protests led to the restoration of **Japanese sovereignty**. Since then, the two governments have colluded to maintain an American military presence on the island despite growing opposition, which reached a peak when three American servicemen were found guilty of raping a 12-year-old schoolgirl in 1995. In response to this and other incidents, local leader **Governor Ōta** made vociferous demands for a complete withdrawal of the military. However, in a five-year bilateral agreement drawn in 1996, the immediate future of the bases was secured and local wishes largely ignored.

In November 1998, Ōta was beaten in local elections by **Inamine Keiichi**, a pro-development politician eager to embrace the billion dollar cash injections from Tokyo for the bases that keep Okinawa's otherwise impoverished economy afloat. Indeed, the hosting of the **G8 Summit** in Okinawa in July 2000 was seen as a financial reward to the islands that constitute Japan's poorest prefecture and which have the nation's highest unemployment rate.

Okinawa-Hontō

Once the centre of the Ryūkyū kingdom, **Okinawa-Hontō**, or Okinawa Main Island, is a strangely ambivalent place. Locals are fiercely proud of their Ryūkyū heritage, and yet the competing cultures of Japan and America are far more prevalent. To some extent, the island still feels like occupied territory, especially central Okinawa, where the **American bases** and the nearby "American" towns, with their drive-ins and shopping malls, have become a bizarre tourist attraction for mainland Japanese, who come to soak up a bit of American culture.

Fascinating though all this is, it doesn't make Okinawa the most obvious holiday destination. However, if you're drawn by the more appealing outer islands (see p.908), the chances are you'll spend some time on the main island waiting for plane or ferry connections. Okinawa's chief city and the former Ryūkyū capital is **Naha**, whose prime attraction is its reconstructed castle, **Shuri-jō**, the ruins of which have recently been awarded World Heritage status. There are also some interesting market streets and a pottery village to explore, and you'll want to take advantage of its banks – not to mention excellent bars and restaurants – before heading off to remoter regions.

Southern Okinawa saw the worst fighting in 1945, and the scrubby hills are littered with **war memorials**, particularly around Mabuni Hill, where the final battles took place. North of Naha, the island's central district has little to recommend it, but beyond Kadena the buildings start to thin out. Here you'll find one of the better "Ryūkyū culture villages", **Ryūkyū-mura**, and the island's best beaches. The largest settlement in northern Okinawa, **Nago** is an appealing town which provides a base for visiting the stunning Okinawa Churaumi Aquarium and exploring the scenic coastline and mountainous tip of the island culminating in the dramatic cape of **Hedo Misaki**.

Long and thin, Okinawa measures just 135km from tip to toe, so you can drive the whole length in a matter of hours. The best way to get around is to rent your own car or motorbike, particularly if you want to explore the northern hills. Otherwise most places are accessible by local bus – eventually.

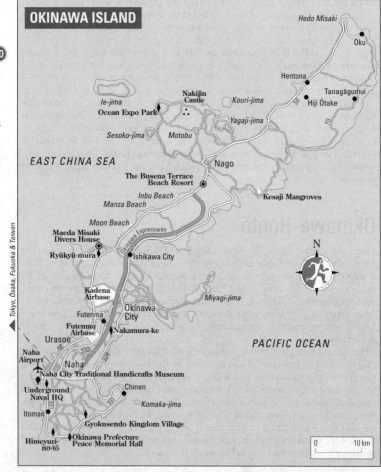

Tokyo, Ōsaka, Fukuoka & Taiwan

Naha

Most people find themselves passing through **NAHA** at some time on their visit to the islands, and though its mix of municipal blocks and parades of tacky souvenir shops catering to the constant stream of Japanese holiday-makers isn't overly attractive, there are a couple of sights to aim for. For more than four centuries Naha was the capital of the Ryūkyū kingdom, and makes much of its royal heritage, though virtually everything was destroyed during the war. The beautifully reconstructed **Shuri-jō**, the king's small, solid castle, constitutes the city's major sight and is well worth visiting, while the Shuri area also contains a moderately informative prefectural museum, as well as some original royal graves and stone-paved lanes. After exploring the central **Tsuboya** pottery district, however, there's not a lot else to detain you.

Naha		
Naha	*Naha*	那覇
Kokusai-dōri	*Kokusai-dōri*	国際通り
Naha Bus Terminal	*Naha Basu Tāminaru*	那覇バスターミナル
Naha Port	*Naha Futō*	那覇埠頭
Naha Shin-kō	*Naha Shin-kō*	那覇新港
Okinawa Prefectural Museum	*Okinawa Kenritsu Hakubutsukan*	沖縄県立博物館
Shuri-jō	*Shuri-jō*	首里城
Tsuboya	*Tsuboya*	壺屋
Tsuboya Pottery Association	*Tsuboya Tōki Kaikan*	壺屋陶器会館
Tsuboya Ceramics Museum	*Tsuboya Tōki Hakubutsukan*	壺屋陶器博物館
Accommodation		
Capsule Inn Okinawa	*Kapuseru In Okinawa*	カプセルイン沖縄
Hakusei-sō	*Hakusei-sō*	栢ﾗ荘
Harumi Youth Hostel	*Harumi Yūsu Hosuteru*	春海ユースホステル
Naha Central Hotel	*Naha Sentoraru Hoteru*	那覇セントラルホテル
Naha Dai-ichi Hotel	*Naha Dai-ichi Hoteru*	那覇第一ホテル
Nansei Kankō Hotel	*Nansei Kankō Hoteru*	南西観光ホテル
Okinawa Guest House	*Okinawa Gesuto Hausu*	沖縄ゲストハウス
Okinawa International Youth Hostel	*Okinawa Kokusai Yūsu Hosuteru*	沖縄国際ユースホステル
Shinkinichi Ryokan	*Shinkinichi Ryokan*	新金一旅館
Hotel Sun Palace	*Hoteru San Paresu*	ホテルサンパレス
Tōyoko Inn Naha Izumisaki Kōsaten	*Tōyoko In Naha Izumisaki Kōsaten*	東横イン那覇泉崎交差点
Hotel Yagi	*Hoteru Yagi*	ホテルやぎ
Hotel Yamaichi	*Hoteru Yamaichi*	ホテル山市
Restaurants		
Bindunchi	*Bindunchi*	びん殿内
Dai-ichi Kōsetsu Ichiba	*Dai-ichi Kōsetsu Ichiba*	第一公設市場
Kishimiiru	*Kishimiiru*	きしみーる
Naha Soba	*Naha Soba*	那覇そば
Oni-san	*Oni-san*	鬼さん
Yotsu-dake	*Yotsu-dake*	四つ竹
Yūnangii	*Yūnangii*	ゆうなんぎい

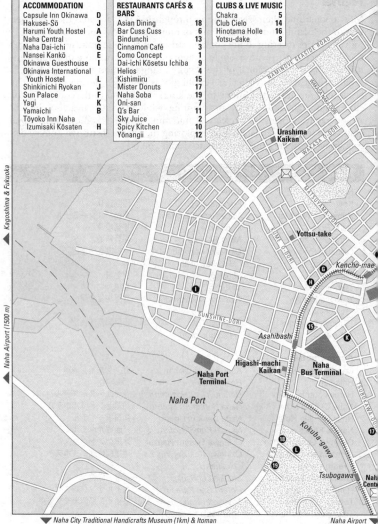

ACCOMMODATION

Capsule Inn Okinawa	D
Hakusei-Sō	J
Harumi Youth Hostel	A
Naha Central	C
Naha Dai-ichi	G
Nansei Kankō	E
Okinawa Guesthouse	I
Okinawa International Youth Hostel	L
Shinkinichi Ryokan	J
Sun Palace	F
Yagi	K
Yamaichi	B
Tōyoko Inn Naha Izumisaki Kōsaten	H

RESTAURANTS CAFÉS & BARS

Asian Dining	18
Bar Cuss Cuss	6
Bindunchi	13
Cinnamon Café	3
Como Concept	1
Dai-ichi Kōsetsu Ichiba	9
Helios	4
Kishimiiru	15
Mister Donuts	17
Naha Soba	19
Oni-san	7
Q's Bar	11
Sky Juice	2
Spicy Kitchen	10
Yōnangii	12

CLUBS & LIVE MUSIC

Chakra	5
Club Cielo	14
Hinotama Holle	16
Yotsu-dake	8

Urashima Kaikan

Yottsu-take

Kenchō-mae

SUNSHINE-DŌRI

Asahibashi

Higashi-machi Kaikan

Naha Port Terminal

Naha Bus Terminal

Naha Port

Kokuba-gawa

Tsubogawa

Naha Cent...

Arrival, information and city transport

Naha **airport** occupies a promontory some 3km southwest of the city centre. The new domestic terminal handles flights from mainland Japan and to Okinawa's outer islands, while the adjacent terminal is for overseas flights. From the airport you can either take a taxi (around ¥800) for the ten-minute journey into central Naha, the monorail (¥230) or one of several frequent local buses (#23, #99, #113, #120, #123, #124 and #125) departing from outside the terminal buildings (¥200).

The new **ferry port**, Naha Shin-kō, lies north of the city. Most ferries, including those from Fukuoka, Ōsaka, Kōbe, Nagoya, Tokyo and Taiwan, dock

NAHA

N

Tomari Port

Tomarin

Ⓐ

MATAYOSHI DORI

ROUTE 58

Miebashi

Okinawa City ▶

Shuri-jō (2.9 km) ▶

Ⓑ Ⓒ
Mitsukoshi
Department
Store

Ⓓ

❶ *Makishi*

Ⓔ

Asato

❷

❸

KUMOJI

❺❹

KOKUSAI-DORI

❻

❼

❽

❾

❿

Ⓙ

Palette
Kumoji

⓫ ⓬ ⓭

⓮

Prefectural
Assembly
Hall

Tsuboya
Pottery
Museum

Kiln

Takaesu
Pottery

Kiln

TSUBOYA

Tsuboya
Pottery
Association

⓰

Naha
Immigration
Office

Prefectural

0   500 m

🔟

OKINAWA | Okinawa-Hontō

here, while slow boats from Kagoshima pull in further south at the old Naha Port. Naha Shin-kō is on the #101 bus route into central Naha (1–3 hourly; 25min; ¥200), while Naha Port is more conveniently located only about fifteen minutes' walk from the main Naha Bus Terminal (see p.894).

Naha's **tourist information** service has desks in both the domestic terminal (daily 9am–9pm; ☎098/857-6884) and the international terminal (daily 10.30am–7.30pm; ☎098/859-0742). Both have English-speaking staff, plentiful maps and brochures, and can help with hotel reservations. There are separate **car rental** desks at both terminals. In downtown Naha, the only other information office is located on the upper floor of the Dai-ichi Kōsetsu Ichiba (see p.896; daily 11am–5pm; ☎098/967-6560), where you may be lucky and find an English-speaker.

The smart new **monorail** (6am–11.30pm daily; ¥200 minimum fare) linking the airport with Shuri 13km away, is a useful way to get around. There are stops at either end of Kokusai-dōri (Kencho-mai and Makishi). Otherwise, there are plenty of **local buses**, with frequent services on the main routes, but traffic often gridlocks at peak times, so don't expect to zip around. Nearly all buses, including long-distance services, start from or pass by Naha Bus Terminal, on the south side of the city. Buses show the route number on the front, with the destination in *kanji*. Lines #1 to #17 operate within the city, while #20 and above go further afield. There's a flat fare of ¥200 within the city, but on other buses take a numbered ticket on entry and pay at your destination. If you plan to use the buses a lot, pick up the island-wide English *Naha City Bus Route Map* from the tourist information offices. Taxi fares start from around ¥550.

Accommodation

Naha has a good range of accommodation, including a plush youth hostel and some excellent-value cheap hotels. Rooms are hard to come by in the peak holiday seasons – Golden Week, August and New Year – when rates may rise by up to forty percent.

Capsule Inn Okinawa Asato, Kokusai-dōri ☎ & ℻ 098/867-6017. Capsule hotel for both men and women, at the north end of Kokusai-dōri. Women always get the spacious deluxe capsules for ¥3500; for men they cost ¥4300. Check in from 3pm.

Hakusei-sō 2-12-7 Nahashimatsuo ☎098/866-5757, ℮ hakusei.hoops.ne.jp. Great-value tatami rooms on the third floor of this block behind the Ichiba food market. ❸

Harumi Youth Hostel 2-22-10 Tomari ☎098/867-3218. The older, smaller and slightly cheaper of Naha's two youth hostels, on the north-west edge of town near the Tomari ferry port, though still a good hike from the centre. It's on bus route #124 from the airport, #101 from Naha Shin-kō and #3 from Naha Port; get off at the Tomari Takahashi stop. Dorm beds ¥3000 per person.

Naha Central Hotel 2-16-36 Makishi ☎098/862-6070, ⓦ www.nahacen.jp. This good-value hotel lies just off Kokusai-dōri behind Mitsukoshi department store. Rooms are on the small side, but nicely decorated and a notch above the competition. ❺

Naha Dai-ichi Hotel 2-2-7 Kume ☎098/868-0111, ℻ 868-0555. One of the cheaper options in central Naha, this no-frills business hotel with boxy, en-suite rooms gets booked up quickly. Rates include a self-service breakfast, and there's also a coin laundry. ❹–❺

Nansei Kankō Hotel 3-13-23 Makishi ☎098/862-7144, ℮ nansei@ona.att.ne.jp. Another decent, mid-range hotel towards the north end of Kokusai-dōri. The bright, comfortable rooms have TV, phone and bath as standard. ❺

Okinawa Guest House 2-6-13 Nishi ☎090-9782-9696. Tucked away in a grimy block behind the Sango Sentā (Coral Centre), this is Naha's cheapest accommodation (just ¥1500 a dorm bed) and as close to a backpacker flophouse as you're likely to find in Japan, although the rooms are much cleaner than those of its Southeast Asian equivalents.

Okinawa International Youth Hostel 51 Ōnoyama ☎098/857-0073, ℻ 859-3567. A swish hostel offering bunk-bed dorms (¥3150 per person), each with its own TV, sofa and wash basin, as well as very comfy three-bed family rooms (¥10,000). They also have a coin laundry and can arrange diving and kayak trips. It's about ten minutes' walk from Naha Bus Terminal, on the south side of the Kokuba-gawa, or on all bus routes from the airport. From the Kōen-mae stop, walk north and turn right beside *KFC*.

Shinkinichi Ryokan ☎098/869-1010. In the same building as the *Hakusei-sō* (see above), this is an equally appealing place, with friendly, English-speaking staff and spotless rooms. ❸

Hotel Sun Palace 2-5-1 Kumoji ☎098/863-4181, ℻ 861-1313. The small balconies overflowing with greenery add a nice flourish on this pleasant hotel, beside a canal to the north of Palette Kumoji. Rooms are light and airy, though it's worth upgrading to the more spacious double or standard twins. They also have Internet access (see "Listings" on p.8998). ❺

Toyoko Inn Naha Izumisaki Kōsaten 2-1-20 Kume ☎098/951-1045, ⓦ www.toyoko-inn.com. New branch of the great budget hotel chain – most of the rooms are good-value singles (from

¥5500). It's a short walk from the south end of Kokusai-dōri. ④

Hotel Yagi 1-16-10 Izumizaki ☎098/862-3008, ⓕ862-3028. Handily placed for Naha Bus Terminal, this budget hotel offers a warm welcome and cheery Western-style rooms with TV, telephone and a small bathroom. Rates include breakfast. ④

Hotel Yamaichi 2-16-13 Makishi ☎098/866-5421, ⓕ867-3713. Though rather aged, the rooms in this small, family-run hotel aren't bad for the location, west of Kokusai-dōri behind the Mitsukoshi store. There's a choice of Western or tatami rooms, some with bathroom. ④

The City

Central Naha is bordered to the south by the Kokuba-gawa, which flows into Naha Port, and to the west by Highway 58. About 500m north of the river, **Kokusai-dōri** cuts northeast from the highway, past the Palette Kumoji department store and Prefectural Assembly Hall. The city's main thoroughfare, nearly 2km long, Kokusai-dōri is lined with a strange mix of classy boutiques, souvenir stalls and army-surplus outlets selling American military leftovers. Follow the road northeast and it eventually leads uphill to **Shuri-jō**, where the castle lies hidden behind stout walls. Alternatively, head east from Kokusai-dōri through the backstreets to the **Tsuboya** district, a pleasing area of little workshops and dusty galleries which is famous for its pottery kilns.

Shuri-jō and around

Perched on a hill 3km northeast of central Naha, **Shuri-jō** (daily 9am–5.30/6.30pm; ¥800) served as the royal residence of the Ryūkyū kings from the early fifteenth century until 1879. Elaborate ceremonies took place in the castle's opulent throne room, on occasion attended by envoys from China and, later, from Kyūshū. Very little of the original remains, but the present buildings, painstakingly restored in the early 1990s, are certainly worth seeing for their distinctive blend of Chinese and Japanese architecture. To reach the castle, take bus #7 from Naha Bus Terminal or Kokusai-dōri (every 15–20min; 30min). It terminates underneath the modern **Suimuikan** information and shopping centre, where you can get a fairly sketchy English-language map of the area. It's also worth popping into the small exhibition room for the short video about Shuri-jō and Ryūkyū culture (every 20min; free).

The castle's main entrance lies across the road from the Suimuikan, through the decorative **Shurei-mon**. This outer gate is a popular spot for group photos, but the inner **Kankai-mon** is a far more impressive structure, its no-nonsense guard tower flanked by sun-baked limestone walls. Inside there's yet another defensive wall and no less than three more gates – the last now housing the ticket office – before you reach the central courtyard. Pride of place goes to the **Seiden**, a double-roofed palace with an immense, colourful porch and two throne halls. From the more elaborate upper throne room, the king, surrounded by gilded dragons writhing against lustrous red and black lacquer, would review his troops or watch ceremonies in the courtyard below. Other buildings house remnants of the dynasty and details of the restoration work, though with only a smattering of English explanations to bring them alive.

Exiting Shuri-jō, a quiet park featuring a stone-walled pond and old trees lies across the road. The pond's pretty, island pavilion once belonged to **Enkaku-ji**, which was built in 1492 as the local headquarters of the Rinzai sect; it was said to have been the most impressive structure in the kingdom. Nowadays only a few shell-pocked walls remain of the original temple, east of the pond. Heading northwest, along the banks of an elongated lake, you soon reach the **Okinawa Prefectural Museum** (Tues–Sun 9am–5pm; ¥210), which provides a good overview of local history and culture.

Buses back into central Naha (#1, #12, #13 and #17) stop outside the museum. If you've got time to kill, walk back to the main road west of Shuri-jō, where the sixteenth-century **mausoleum** of King Shō En survives in a walled compound known as the **Tama-udun** (daily 9am–5.30pm; ¥200). More like a fortress than a grave, the burial chambers stand across a dirt forecourt, with the easternmost reserved for the kings; unfortunately, you can't go inside. Instead, you can continue downhill (west) from the mausoleum and take the next lane left, working your way round to the south of the castle through the attractive residential area of **Kinjō-chō**, whose stone-paved lanes were laid in 1522 to link Naha town with its castle. You can follow them all the way down and catch a bus at the bottom, but services are few and far between; it's better to hike back up to the castle bus stops.

Ichiba-dōri and Tsuboya

Roughly halfway up central Naha's Kokusai-dōri, near Mitsukoshi department store, look out for the **Ichiba-dōri** and **Heiwa-dōri** shopping arcades. Among the souvenir stalls and discount outlets, these streets host a number of lively **markets**, of which the best is Ichiba's food market, **Dai-ichi Kōsetsu Ichiba** (daily 9am–8pm; closed every fourth Sunday of the month) – its narrow entrance is marked by festive international flags. The ground-floor stalls are piled high with sweet-smelling tropical fruits, ice-packed arrays of multi-coloured fish and mysterious, spiny crabs. You'll see fishmongers deftly slicing sashimi, some of it destined for the **food stalls** upstairs (see opposite).

From the market, walk north onto Heiwa-dōri and follow it east. After a few minutes you'll emerge in the pottery district of **Tsuboya**. This compact area has been the centre of local ceramics production since 1682, when the government gathered a number of workshops together, of which around ten are still in operation. Traditionally, the potters here produced large jars for storing the local liquor (*awamori*) and miso paste, but nowadays they concentrate on smaller items for the tourist market, typically half-moon-shaped sake flasks and snarling *shiisā* lions.

To get an overview of the area's history, drop into the **Tsuboya Ceramics Museum** (Tues–Sun 10am–6pm; ¥300), less than 100m from the end of the covered arcade. All the labelling at this nicely designed facility is in Japanese – there's a comprehensive English guidebook (¥630) if you want it, although the reconstruction of a typical Tsuboya prewar home, the slick slide show and the classy pottery exhibits pretty much speak for themselves. Next to the museum, on the embankment above the main road on your left, is a traditional climbing kiln dating from the 1880s, one of the oldest still intact. Of the several **showrooms** along the main road, the biggest is the **Tsuboya Pottery Association** (daily 9am–6pm), at the far east end, displaying a range of different styles.

Wander the back lanes and you'll also stumble across working **potteries**. Take the lane heading north in front of the Pottery Association shop, for example, turn right at the next junction and then into what looks like a private gateway immediately on your left; to the right of the lovely old house you'll see an old climbing kiln. Back at the junction, follow the lane north and then west, past the **Takaesu Pottery**, and keep going along the hillside for an attractive route looping back down to the main street.

Eating, drinking and entertainment

Naha undoubtedly has Okinawa's widest choice of **restaurants**, offering the best local-style *Ryūkyū ryōri* dishes, as well as a fair range of international cuisines. Kokusai-dōri is the best single area to trawl for eating places, particularly in the Kumoji and Makishi districts, north of the Palette Kumoji building, which are full of atmospheric bars, restaurants and *izakaya*. Palette itself has a wide choice of outlets on the ninth floor, plus a decent basement food hall, though not as good as the Mitsukoshi department store.

As you'd expect, with plenty of off-duty GIs and footloose young Japanese tourists and locals, Naha's entertainment scene is far from dull. If you want to hear **live music**, especially funky Okinawan pop and traditional sounds, head to *Chakra* on Kokusai-dōri (daily 7pm–2am; ¥2500–3000; ☎098/869-0283), owned by local music legend Kina Shoukichi. Also worth checking out – although it's 15km north of Naha in neighbouring Ginowan city – is *Live House Shima Uta* (Tues–Sun 8pm–midnight; ¥1500), on Route 58 near Ginowan Kaihin Park. This is run by another local music luminary, China Sadao, who brought the all-female group Nēnēs to world attention, and the concerts here get rave reviews.

Late-night dance **clubs** include the super cool *Hinotama Holle*, at 2-1-35 Higawa (☎098/831-6101), serving up Latin acid jazz, hip hop and hot local bands such as Ryūkyū Underground; and the smart and expensive *Club Cielo*, on the seventh floor at the western end of Kokusai-dōri (the entrance is just up the hill opposite the prefectural assembly hall).

Naha is also a good place to catch performances of traditional **Ryūkyū court dance**, particularly if you coincide with the weekly show in the Higashi-machi Kaikan, just north of the Kokuba-gawa. Performances are usually on Tuesday evening (8pm; ¥2500), but check with the tourist office for the current schedule, and note that there's ¥500 discount on advance tickets. The alternative is a more expensive dinner show where you'll pay from ¥3000 for a meal, sometimes including *tūndā-bun* – beautifully presented royal hors d'oeuvres (see box on p.887). Although somewhat touristy, *Yotsu-dake* on Kokusai-dōri (☎098/863-4444; two shows nightly at 6.30pm & 8pm; 40min) provides an enjoyable night out and the food isn't bad. The staff are friendly and they have a printed English explanation of the food and dances. Other dinner-dance venues include another *Yotsu-dake*, 2-22-1 Kume (☎098/866-3333), and *Urashima Kaikan*, 14-8 Wakasa (☎098/861-1769), both in the backstreets west of Highway 58.

Restaurants

Asian Dining Banyan Town, Ōnoyama. Part of the colourful complex of fast-food restaurants beside the Kokuba-gawa, and housed inside a towering fake banyan tree twinkling with fairy lights at night. Serves decent Southeast Asian cuisine and is best visited for lunch, when it does a couple of set menus for ¥800.

Bindunchi Bl Koramu Biru, 1-4-1 Matsuo, Kokusai-dōri. Cheap and central, the cosy and rustic basement here is one of the best places to sample Okinawan cuisine, with set meals for ¥1000 and *awamori* ice cream.

Cinnamon Café 1-4-59 Makishi. Great spot to while away a quiet afternoon over a good coffee and the best chocolate cake in Naha. They do a mean curry, too.

Como Concept Kokusai-dōri ☎098/861-8071. Stylish café-bar attached to a funky furniture store

with (as you'd expect) very comfy chairs. The food is Japanese-style Italian – nothing great, but the prices are reasonable and there's sometimes live music in the evenings.

Dai-ichi Kōsetsu Ichiba Selection of small, atmospheric restaurants tucked away above the food market off Ichiba-dōri. Choose from the menu or hunt around in the market downstairs for the fish of your choice, which is then prepared and sent upstairs for you to eat. If you're a sashimi fan, the prices are reasonable and the fish doesn't come much fresher. Daily 10am–8pm.

Naha Soba Highway 331, Ōnoyama. No prizes for guessing the house speciality at this rustic noodle house near the *International Youth Hostel*. The *Naha soba* is laced with pork, ginger and spring onion, and they also offer a variety of reasonably priced set meals. From the hostel turning, walk south along the highway, then turn left just before the footbridge.

Spicy Kitchen Sakurazaka-dōri, Makishi 3-chōme. Look out for the chilli-pepper mural on this cheery Indian restaurant up a lane near the east end of Heiwa-dōri. The simple menu includes chicken, mutton and seafood curries from ¥1200, plus a range of vegetarian dishes and a good lunch deal for ¥800.

Suimui Suimuikan, Shuri-jō. Surprisingly good

restaurant in the Shuri-jō information centre (see p.895), serving Okinawa dishes as well as mainstream Japanese and Western meals. Not to be confused with the castle's noisy snack bar. Daily 9am–4.30pm.

Yūnangii 3-3-3 Kumoji. Country-style restaurant, offering a warm welcome and serving Okinawa cuisine, including *Okinawa soba*, *chanpuru* and various pork dishes. Set meals go from around ¥1300, with free rice refills. Closed Sun.

Bars and izakaya

Bar Cuss Cuss 3-9-29 Makishi ☎098/863-4328. It's easy to miss the low door into this hide-away trance/reggae bar with cosy booths and a welcoming vibe. There are monthly dance parties at the upstairs bar.

Helios 2 Matsuo, Kokusai-dōri ☎098/863-7227. Stylish "craft beer pub" belonging to a local microbrewery and offering several types of home brew including pale ale, Weissen, Pilsner and porter. A small taste of three is ¥700. Also serves bar snacks.

Kishimiiru 1-22-1 Izumizaki. Relaxed *izakaya*, with fun decor and a range of tasty dishes. You'll

eat well for under ¥2000 a head.

Oni-san B1, 3-12-4 Kumoji. Noisy, upbeat *izakaya* with a goofy devil on the *noren* curtain. The food's good, prices are reasonable and there's always a free sweet on the way out.

Q's Bar B1, 3-9-3 Kumoji ☎098/866-5641. Wind down the yellow spiral staircase to find this mellow jazz bar decked out with primitive art and big vats of *awamori*. Cover charge ¥350.

Sky Juice 1-3-32 Makishi ☎098/951-3923. Spacious, laid-back "new retro" bar, with a DJ playing appropriately chilled music. From 8am; closed Sun.

Listings

Airlines ANA & ANK ☎0120-029222; Asiana Airlines ☎098/869-7701; China Airlines ☎098/863-1013; China Eastern Airlines ☎098/860-6881; JAL ☎0120-255971 (domestic), ☎0120-255931 (international); JAS ☎0120-511283; Japan Asia Airlines ☎0120-747801; Ryūkyū Air Commuter ☎0120-255971; Philippine Airlines ☎098/951-1933.

Banks and exchange The Ryūkyū Bank branch in the airport arrival lobby (Mon–Fri 9am–4pm) exchanges several major currencies (cash or travellers' cheques); when they're closed the central information counter can change up to US$50 cash. The post office cash machine (Mon–Fri 9am–9pm, Sat & Sun 9am–5pm) in the airport also accepts foreign cash and credit cards, as does the one at the central post office (see opposite), where you can exchange money over the counter, from 9am to 4pm on weekdays only. Also in Naha itself, banks along Kokusai-dōri have foreign exchange desks, or try the main branch of the Okinawa Bank (north of Palette Kumoji), or the Ryūkyū Bank (west on the same road). To withdraw cash on a Visa card apply to the Ryūkyū Bank or Okinawa Bank; Kaihō Bank handles Mastercard transactions.

Bookshops *Bunkyō Tosho* on the seventh floor of Palette Kumoji has a limited selection of English-language books and magazines. You can also try Kokusai-dōri's *Tower Records* in the OPA building

where you'll find a few English-language magazines.

Car and bike rental Nippon Rent-a-Car (☎098/868-4554), Japaren (☎098/858-3911) and Toyota (☎098/857-0100) all have representatives in both Naha airport and the city centre. You can rent motorbikes and scooters at Helmet Shop SEA, 3-15-50 Makishi (☎098/864-5116), west of Kokusai-dōri, from ¥1700 for 3hr.

Consulates United States, 2564 Nishihara, Urasoe City (☎098/876-4211).

Ferries The RKK Line (☎098/868-1126) operates ferries to Ōsaka, Fukuoka and Kagoshima. Ōshima Un'yu (☎098/861-1886) sails to Tokyo, Ōsaka, Kōbe, Miyazaki, Kagoshima and islands in the Satsunan chain. Marix Line (☎098/862-8774) specializes in slow boats through the Satsunan islands to Kagoshima. Arimura Sangyō (☎098/860-1980) boats stop in Naha on their way from Ōsaka to Taiwan, and also call at Miyako and Ishigaki. Most of these ferries depart from Naha Shin-kō, north of town on the #101 bus route, but a few use Naha Port (bus #24), so check when you buy your tickets. For details of ferries to other Okinawa islands, see the individual accounts later in this chapter.

Festivals Shuri-jō is the venue for traditional Ryūkyū New Year celebrations (Jan 2–3) and the Shuri-jō Festival (Nov 1–3), featuring a parade of

Ryūkyū-dynasty clothing, dance displays and other performing arts. The Naha Festival (Oct 10) includes the world's largest tug-of-war – using a rope 180m long and 1.5m in diameter – as well as a 10,000-strong Eisā folk dance parade down Kokusai-dōri.

Hospitals and medical care Izumizaki Hospital, 1-11-2 Kumoji ☎098/867-2116. If you need an English-speaking doctor your best bet is the Adventist Medical Centre, 4-11-1 Kohagura, on Route 29 northeast of Naha ☎098/946-2833.

Internet *Netbox*, Tsubokawa-dōri (☎098/833-6603), on the third floor of the complex housing *Mister Donuts* and the Tsutaya video/CD rental shop, close to the Tsubogawa monorail station, is open daily 24 hours and charges ¥395 for the first hour including free drinks. There's also a Net café on Kokusai-dōri above *Mister Donuts*, and terminals at the airport.

Immigration office To renew your visa apply to the Naha Immigration Office, 1-15-15 Higawa (☎098/832-4185), on Route 221 southeast of Kokusai-dōri.

Police 1-2-9 Izumizaki (☎098/836-0110).

Emergency numbers are listed in "Basics" on p.81.

Post offices Naha Central Post Office, located on the south side of town around 500m down Naha Higashi Bypass from the Meiji Bridge across the Kokuba-gawa, accepts poste restante. For ordinary services, you'll find a sub-post office in Palette Kumoji and another at the north end of Kokusai-dōri beside the *Nansei Kankō Hotel*.

Shopping Kokusai-dōri and the Ichiba-dōri arcades are the places to trawl for souvenirs. Shops specializing in local crafts include the high-quality Okinawa Bussan Centre (daily 9am–7pm), northeast of Palette Kumoji, and the smaller Okinawa Craft Shop (daily 10am–8pm), behind Mitsukoshi. Shuri-jō's Suimuikan also has a decent craft shop.

Taxis Okitō Kōtsū (☎098/946-5654) has English-speaking drivers, or try the Okinawa-ken Taxi Association (☎098/855-1344).

Travel agents For domestic travel, phone JTB on ☎098/864-1321 or Okinawa Tourist ☎098/862-1111. The latter can also help with international tickets, as can HIS on ☎098/868-1133.

 10

OKINAWA

Okinawa-Hontō

Southern Okinawa-Hontō

During the long-drawn-out Battle of Okinawa (see p.888), it was the area **south of Naha** that saw the worst fighting and received the heaviest bombardment. Not only was the **Japanese Naval Headquarters** dug deep into the hills here, but the region's many limestone caves also provided shelter for hundreds of Japanese troops and local civilians, many of whom committed suicide rather than be taken prisoner. One of these caves has been preserved as a memorial to the young **Himeyuri** nurses who died there, and the area is dotted with peace parks and prayer halls. It's not completely devoted to war sights, however. **Gyokusendō Kingdom Village**, over on the southeast coast, combines a stalactite-filled cave with a rather dubious tourist village dedicated to Ryūkyū culture. There's also the lovely inhabited **Komaka Island**, a great spot for snorkelling.

By far the best way of **getting around** this area is by car, allowing you the freedom to explore some of the coves and beaches on the east coast. Exploring by bus involves a lot of waiting for connections. The alternative is to join one of the organized bus tours out of Naha, which pack a lot into a short time at a reasonable price, and come with a practically nonstop Japanese commentary. Four companies offer almost identical southern tours, of which Naha Kōtsū (☎098/868-3750) has the widest choice, running full-day and half-day tours starting from Naha's bus terminal. Both cost ¥4800 and cover the same sights, though on the one-day tour you also visit Naha's Shuri-jō (see p.895; entrance ticket extra) and stop for lunch (included in the price). You can buy tickets at Naha Kōtsū's main office, 3-8-1 Nishi (☎098/868-3750), or from their counter in the airport's domestic terminal.

Underground Naval Headquarters and Naha City Traditional Handicrafts Museum

For centuries, Tomigusuku-jō has stood on the low hills looking north over Naha. During the Pacific War the spot was chosen for the headquarters of the Japanese navy, but, instead of using the old fortifications, they tunnelled 20m down into the soft limestone. The complex, consisting of Rear Admiral Ōta's command room and various operations rooms, is now preserved as the **Underground Naval Headquarters** (daily 8.30am–5pm; ¥420). If you're travelling by bus, take #33, #46 or #101 from central Naha to the Tomigusuku Jōshi Kōen-mae stop (1–2 hourly; 25min; ¥240), from where it's a ten-minute

Around Okinawa-hontō

Southern Okinawa

Gyokusendō Kingdom Village	Gyokusendō Ōkoku-mura	玉泉洞王国村
Himeyuri-no-tō	Himeyuri-no-tō	ひめゆりの塔
Komaka-jima	Komaka-jima	コマカ島
Mabuni Hill	Mabuni-no-oka	摩文仁の丘
Naha City Traditional Handicrafts Museum	Naha-shi Dentō Kōgei-kan	那覇市伝統工芸館
Okinawa Prefecture Peace Memorial Museum	Okinawa-kenritsu Heiwa Kinen Shiryōkan	沖縄県立平和記念資料館
Peace Memorial Hall	Heiwa Kinendō	平和記念堂
Underground Naval Headquarters	Kyū Kaigun Shireibugō	旧海軍司令部壕

Central Okinawa

Hotel City Plaza	Hoteru Shitii Puraza	ホテルシティープラザ
Maeda Misaki Divers House	Maeda Misaki Daibāzu Hausu	真栄田岬ダイバーズハウス
Nakamura-ke	Nakamura-ke	中村家
Nakagusuku-jō ruins	Nakagusuku-jō-seki	中城城跡
Okinawa City	Okinawa-shi	沖縄市
Ryūkyū-mura	Ryūkyū-mura	琉球村
Sunrise Hotel	Sanraizu Hoteru	サンライズホテル

Northern Okinawa

Nago	Nago	名護
Akachōchin	Akachōchin	名護
Busena Terrace Beach Resort	Busena Terasu Biichi Rizōto	ブセナテラスビーチリゾート
Hedo Misaki	Hedo Misaki	辺戸岬
Hentona	Hentona	辺土名
Hiji Ōtaki	Hiji Ōtaki	比地大滝
Jidoriya	Jidoriya	地鶏屋
Kesaji mangroves	Kesaji mangurōbu	慶佐次マングローブ
Kunigami	Kunigami	くにがみ
Minshuku Miyagi	Minshuku Miyagi	民宿みやぎ
Nago Business Hotel	Nago Bijinesu Hoteru	名護ビジネスホテル
Nago Museum	Nago Hakubutsukan	名護博物館
Nakijin-jō ruins	Nakijin-jō-seki	今帰仁城跡
Ocean Expo Park	Kaiyō Haku Kōen	海洋博公園
Oku	Oku	奥
Ōkuni-rindō	Ōkuni-rindō	大国林道
Tanagāgumui	Tanagāgumui	タナガーグムイ
Hotel Tōwa	Hoteru Tōwa	ホテル東和
Yamabuki	Yamabuki	山吹
Yamada-sō	Yamada-sō	山田荘

walk uphill to the ticket gate. Inside, there are a few photos of the 1945 battle, but little else to see beyond holes gouged in the plaster walls; they're said to be where Ōta and 175 of his men killed themselves with hand grenades on June 13 as the Americans closed in. Beside the tunnel entrance there's a small museum and a monument to the four thousand Japanese troops who died in this area.

If you have some more time, or are interested in local crafts, drop by the **Naha City Traditional Handicrafts Museum** (daily except Tues 9am–6pm; ¥300) in the dour concrete building beside Route 331 back near the airport. There's a decent display area with prime examples of fabrics, ceramics, glass and lacquerware, but more interestingly you can watch artisans fashion these objects in the adjoining workshops and studios. If you give them a call it's possible to take lessons here, and there's also a well stocked gift shop. The museum is on bus route #89.

Himeyuri-no-tō

Heading south down the coast, Highway 331 passes through **ITOMAN** town and then cuts inland across the peninsula to **Himeyuri-no-tō** (daily 9am–5pm; ¥300). From the naval headquarters, bus #33 continues to Itoman (1–2 hourly; 40min; ¥370), where you might have to wait a while for the #108, which runs mostly in the morning and late afternoon (20min; ¥200). Himeyuri-no-tō is another war memorial, this time dedicated to more than two hundred schoolgirls and their teachers who committed suicide here in a shallow cave. The nearby **museum** describes how the high-school students, like many others on Okinawa, were conscripted as trainee nurses by the Japanese army in the spring of 1945. As the fighting became more desperate the girls were sent to a Field Hospital, gradually retreating south from cave to cave, and were then abandoned altogether as the Japanese army disintegrated. Terrified that they would be raped and tortured by the Americans, the women and girls killed themselves rather than be captured.

Mabuni hill, Gyokusendō Kingdom Village and Komaka-jima

The final battle for Okinawa took place on **Mabuni hill**, on the island's southeast coast. The site is now occupied by a cemetery and grassy park containing monuments to the more than 200,000 troops – both Japanese and American – and civilians who died on the islands during the war. A distinctive white tower crowns the **Peace Memorial Hall** (daily 9am–5/5.30pm; ¥500; ☎098/997-3011), which contains a 12-metre-high lacquered Buddha and small museum. You'll learn more (though not the full story) if you visit the **Okinawa Prefecture Peace Memorial Museum** (Tues–Sun 9am–4.30pm; ¥300), which has full English translations throughout. This interesting museum, planned under the anti-establishment regime of Governor Ōta, but completed by the more conservative Governor Inamine, doesn't shirk the uncomfortable fact that Japanese soldiers ruthlessly killed Okinawan civilians. Generally, however, the whole build-up to the war is treated in the usual euphemistic way and the exhibition ends on an upbeat note with displays on the postwar history of Okinawa to the present day. The entrance to the park lies on bus route #82 from Itoman (9 daily; 30min; ¥220).

Bus #82 will also take you on to **Gyokusendō Kingdom Village** (daily: April–Oct 9am–5.30pm; Nov–March 9am–5pm; ¥600 for the village, ¥1200 for the village and cave, or ¥1600 including Habu Park). This recently created "village" showcases local crafts and culture, including *Bingata* dyeing, *awamori* brewing and performances of Eisā dances (11am & 12.30pm). It's built over an

The American question

Twenty percent of Okinawa-Hontō and a small number of outer islands are covered by American military bases, employing 27,000 American military personnel. This in itself has fuelled local anger, but what rankles most is that Okinawa makes up less than one percent of the Japanese land mass, yet contains 75 percent of the country's American bases.

Most of the bases are concentrated in central and south Okinawa, on land that was seized in the 1950s. Nowadays the land is leased from the owners by the Japanese government who sublet it to the US military under the Security Treaty. Though the leases are renewed every five years, the landowners have no choice in the matter, since the governor of Okinawa is authorized to sign on behalf of anyone who objects. This worked reasonably well until Governor Ōta Masahide was voted in to power in 1995 – the year the schoolgirl was raped (see p.889) – on a pledge to end the American military occupation. His refusal to cooperate on the leases was eventually overruled by Japan's supreme court, but not before he'd won agreement to relocate a number of artillery ranges and Futenma Airbase away from the main urban areas; the current proposal is for Futenma to be replaced with a floating heliport in Henoko Matsuda Cove, on the east coast of the island up near the northern town of Nago. The 8000 locals are predictably opposed, particularly since the plan will destroy a reef which is home to the shy dugong, sea creatures branded a Japanese national treasure.

The question of the American bases, however, is a thorny one for the islanders, since the Americans contribute vast sums to the local economy and the bases provide thousands of jobs. Despite that, Okinawa remains the poorest of Japan's prefectures, with unemployment twice the national average, and people are beginning to argue for more investment in local industry. Making Okinawa a free-trade zone has been suggested, and Governor Inamine is all for cooperating with Tokyo to get the prefecture more money, as shown with the effort poured into the G8 Summit.

In recent years, public opinion has gradually hardened against the bases, though not against Americans as such; younger Okinawans in particular relish the peculiar hybrid cultural atmosphere that this large number of foreigners brings to the islands. A 1995 poll revealed a majority in favour of a continued American presence but with a more even distribution throughout Japan. At that time, only twenty percent of the population wanted a complete withdrawal, but by 1996 the figure had increased to a convincing ninety percent. Even Governor Inamine's pro-American regime is insisting that the new Henoko base has a fifteen-year limit on its operation as well as be run on a joint military-civilian basis – demands that the US has ruled out.

890–metre-long cave with an impressive array of rock formations along an underground river, but the most popular attraction is the Habu Park (¥600), where you can mug for the cameras with a python wrapped around your shoulders. Afterwards, bus #83 will take you back to central Naha in around one hour (8 daily; ¥490). If you're thinking of heading out this way, you may prefer to take a high-speed boat from the Chinen Kaiyo Leisure Centre to tiny **Komaka-jima**, an uninhabited island surrounded by golden sands and a coral reef, 3km off the Chinen Peninsula; it's an ideal snorkelling spot. To get here take bus #39 from Naha terminal.

Central Okinawa-Hontō

North of Naha, traffic on Highway 58 crawls up the coast of **central Okinawa** between a strip of *McDonald's*, *Shakey's Pizza* and used car lots on one side, and neat rows of artillery on the other. This is army country, with huge tracts of land occupied by the **American military** (see box above).

Kinser, Hoster and Lester camps, and the vast Kadena Airbase, extend along the coast as far north as the Maeda peninsula, where beach resorts take over. You can avoid the coastal strip by taking the expressway or Highway 330 up the island's less crowded centre past **Okinawa City** – this is the best way to reach the north of the island quickly, although a trip on the expressway from end to end costs ¥1000. A bizarre mix of American and Japanese life, Okinawa City is the region's main urban centre, but even here there's little reason to stop. If you do want a break on the journey north, there are a couple of moderately interesting sights in the area. Though it's difficult to get to, **Nakamura-ke** is one of the few genuinely old buildings still standing on Okinawa, and the nearby ruins of **Nakagusuku Castle** offer commanding views. On the district's northern fringes lies **Ryūkyū-mura**, a quieter, more interesting culture village than Gyokusendō (see p.901).

Kita-Nakagusuku

About 10km north of Naha, Highway 330 skirts east of Futenma Airbase before hitting a major junction. A little further north, a road cuts east through the hills to **KITA-NAKAGUSUKU** village where, in the early fifteenth century, Nakamura Gashi served as a teacher to Lord Gosamaru. In the early eighteenth century, after a rocky patch, one of Gashi's descendants was appointed village leader and started building his family's large, beautifully solid residence, **Nakamura-ke** (daily 9.30am–5.30pm; ¥300 including tea; ☎098/935-3500). Protected by limestone walls, a thick belt of trees and a growling *shiisa* perched on the red-tile roof, the house is typical of a wealthy landowner's residence, with its barns, a lovely grain store and the inevitable rows of pigsties. Inside, there are a few family heirlooms, and the enterprising owners have set up a small shop and restaurant next door.

To reach Nakamura-ke by public transport, take one of the many buses from Naha north to Okinawa City (#23, #25, #31 and #90 are all fairly frequent) for the hour's ride to the Futenma junction. Then hop on the next #59 bus heading north (hourly; 15min; ¥140) and ask the driver to let you off at the Nakamura-ke turning, from where it's a 1500-metre walk uphill. Alternatively, a taxi from Futenma costs about ¥700 one way.

While you're up here, it's worth walking five minutes west to where the limestone cliffs merge into the crumbling walls of **Nakagusuku-jō** (daily 9am–5pm; ¥300). These impressive fortifications, consisting of six citadels on a spectacular promontory, were originally built in the early fifteenth century by a local lord, Gosamaru. They weren't enough to withstand his rival, Lord Amawari, however, who ransacked the castle in 1458 and then abandoned the site. Nowadays you can walk through the grassy, tree-filled park and scramble among the ruins to admire the views clear across the island. Taxis usually hang around the castle entrance to whisk visitors back down to Futenma.

Okinawa City

Local tourist literature makes much of the international feel of **OKINAWA CITY**, roughly 20km north of Naha. With the Kadena Base just up the road, it's not surprising that the streets are full of American adverts, chain restaurants and 24-hour shops. But it's all rather tacky and, apart from its hotels, restaurants and Western-style bars (including Okinawa's only Irish pub), the city doesn't really have anything to offer the majority of tourists.

The city centre is the **Goya crossroads**, where Highway 330 and Kūkō-dōri meet. There's a branch of Ryūkyū Bank on its northwest corner. If you need a place to stay, try one of the **hotels** just south on the highway. Of these, the friendly *Sunrise Hotel* (☏098/933-0171, Ⓕ932-6221; ❹) offers the cheapest rooms, but is still comfortably furnished with TV, fridge and large bathrooms. The next-door *Hotel City Plaza* (☏098/933-5599, Ⓕ932-5944; ❺), on the other hand, is a more modern establishment that's only a touch pricier. **Eating** options are more limited. Across the highway from the hotels, the Nakanomachi nightlife district has a number of snack bars and steak houses. There's more of the same on the city's main shopping street, Chūō Park Avenue, to the left of Highway 330 a few blocks north from the Goya crossing.

Ryūkyū-mura

The final sight in Okinawa's central region lies on the west coast, where **Ryūkyū-mura** (daily 8.30am–5.30pm; ¥840) preserves several old Okinawa farmhouses and the remnants of Ryūkyū culture. Though some will find it too touristy, the village provides a hint of what Okinawa was like before the war. In addition to performances of Eisā dances and traditional music, you can see people weaving, dyeing textiles and milling sugar cane for molasses – try the freshly fried local doughnuts. Ryūkyū-mura occupies a wooded hillside west of Highway 58 some 30km north of Naha. Bus #20 takes you right to the door (every 15–20min; 1hr 20min; ¥970); coming from Okinawa City, take bus #62 to Kadena (every 15–30min; 30min; ¥400), then change to the #20 northbound.

Fifteen minutes' walk northwest of Ryūkyū-mura, in Onna village, the *Maeda Misaki Divers House* (☏098/964-2497, Ⓔseaweeds@maedamisaki.com) is a great place to stay, particularly if you've come to Okinawa to dive. The building – an old youth hostel – is a bit run-down, but it's in a quiet location, with walks along the cliffs and down to the white, sweeping curve of Moon beach. Accommodation is in bunk-bed dorms (¥3000 per person) and they do good meals. You can rent bikes (¥1000 per day) and they run diving courses, from ¥9500 for an introductory dive, including all equipment. Beginners' PADI courses are ¥45,000. The nearest bus stop is Kuraha, on bus route #20, from where the hostel is ten minutes' walk northwest.

Northern Okinawa-Hontō

North of Okinawa's pinched waist, the scenery begins to improve as classy resort hotels line the western beaches. Bleached-white, coral-fringed Moon beach merges into Tiger beach and then there's the rocky, wild Onna promontory before you rejoin the sands at Manza. Beyond this strip, **northern Okinawa**'s only major settlement, **Nago**, sits at the base of the knobbly **Motobu peninsula**. A generally quiet, workaday place, there's not a lot to see in Nago, but the small city makes a good base for exploring Okinawa's mountainous north and visiting the impressive **Okinawa Churaumi Aquarium** at the far western tip of the peninsula. The district boasts the island's most attractive scenery, particularly around **Hedo Misaki**, the northern cape, and on through sleepy **Oku** village down the rugged northeast coast. It's possible to travel up the west coast by slow local bus, but you're on your own after Oku.

Nago and the Motobu peninsula

Apart from weekends, when off-duty soldiers come up from the bases, **NAGO** sees few foreigners. If the proposed heliport goes ahead (see box on p.902) all this will change, but for the moment Nago is a slow-moving, fairly pleasant city – more a large town – best-known for its huge banyan tree and a spectacular display of spring cherry blossoms. Its other sights consist of a marginally interesting local museum and views from the former castle hill.

Nago curves round a south-facing bay. Highway 58 runs along the seafront and then turns north again on the west side of town, while behind the harbour a road strikes inland to the central **Nago crossroads**, where it cuts across the city's main shopping street. A short walk south along this street, past the three-hundred-year-old **banyan tree** in the middle of the road and across the river brings you to the small **Nago Museum** (Tues–Sun 10am–6pm; closed fourth Thurs of the month; ¥150). It's worth a quick look, though the displays of rice planting, farming and whale hunting are aimed primarily at showing local youngsters a disappearing way of life. Perhaps more appealing is the next-door **Orion Brewery** (℡0980/54-4103) – phone to arrange a free factory tour and tasting of Okinawa's very drinkable homebrew. To reach **Nago Castle Hill** follow the road northeast from the brewery, along the river and up a long flight of stairs. Nothing remains of the castle, but turn left at the top for an attractively landscaped children's park and views over Nago bay.

Some 10km southeast at the tip of the promontory occupied by the *Busena Terrace Beach Resort* (see p.906) there's an **Underwater Observatory** (daily 9am–6pm; ¥1000), a good way to see some of the area's marine life, if you're not going diving, but not as good as a visit out to **Ocean Expo Park**, on the northwestern tip of the hilly, mushroom-shaped **Motobu peninsula**. The highlight here is the new **Okinawa Churaumi Aquarium** (daily: March to mid-July & Sept–Nov 9.30am–5.30pm; mid-July & Aug 9.30am–6.30pm; Jan, Feb & Dec 9.30am–5pm; last admission one hour before closing; ¥1800), a spectacular facility showcasing the marine life of the Kuroshio Current. The main tank holds 7500 tons of water and is home to several whale sharks, the largest sharks in the world, as well as shoals of manta ray and many other fish; the cinema-scope view will hold you entranced. All explanations are in English and there's an informative section on sharks that dispels many myths about these extraordinary creatures. There are other things to do around the sprawling park, several of them free, including dolphin shows, an ocean nursery and a tank for manatee, and a good beach at the north end. In the middle of the park you'll find the Tropical Dream Centre (¥670), containing two thousand types of orchids and flowers, while at the south end there's the Tropical and Subtropical Arboretum. All these places are connected by an electric bus (¥200 for a day-long ticket). Naturally, it's all hugely popular.

To escape the crowds, continue clockwise around the coast and up into the hills to the **Nakijin-jō ruins** (daily 8.30am–6.30pm; ¥150). Though even more gutted than Nakagusuku (see p.903), the castle's outer walls are slowly being rebuilt, and it's a lovely, peaceful spot with good views north to Hentona and Iheya. There's also a small **museum** (Tues–Sun 9am–5pm; ¥200) if you want to find out more about the history of the hamlet and castle. Buses #65 and #66 circle Motobu clockwise and anticlockwise respectively in roughly two hours, with departures every hour or so from central Nago. These buses stop at the Ocean Expo Park and on the main highway, from where the castle is a gentle one-kilometre climb up a quiet, country road.

Practicalities

Arriving by bus, most services stop near Nago's central crossing before terminating at the **bus terminal** on the main highway to the west of town. However, some stop on the seafront, notably the Express Bus from Naha airport, via Naha Bus Terminal (hourly; 1hr 40min; ¥2000), which ends up outside Nago's Lego-block City Hall, roughly 500m from the centre. You'll find the **tourist information office** (Mon–Fri 8.30am–5.30pm, Sat & Sun 10am–5pm; ℡0980/53-7755) on the main shopping street between the banyan tree and Nago crossroads; staff here speak a modicum of English and they have good English-language maps and pamphlets on the area. The Ryūkyū Bank, just north of the central junction, can **exchange** dollar and sterling cash and travellers' cheques, and there's a small post office a couple of blocks to the west.

Two of the best **places to stay** in Nago are the *Hotel Tōwa* (℡0980/52-3793; ❸) and the *Yamada-sō* (℡0980/52-2272; ❹), opposite each other in the backstreets northeast of Nago crossroads; you'll find them by walking east along the main street and taking the second left. They're both clean and friendly, but the *Hotel Tōwa* wins out for slightly bigger rooms and lower prices. If these are full, try the modern *Nago Business Hotel* (℡0980/54-5557; ❹), which is also nearby. For total luxury, *The Busena Terrace Beach Resort* (℡0980/51-1333, Ⓦwww.terrace.co.jp; ❾), location of the G8 Summit in 2000, has very spacious, tastefully decorated rooms, charming staff and impressive facilities, including six restaurants and an enormous landscaped pool. The beach here, as you'd expect, is pretty nice.

Recommended **restaurants** include *Shinzan Soba*, an unlikely looking shack behind the tourist office which draws many plaudits for its noodles; buy a ticket from the machine – their ¥750 set lunch is a deal. *Ōkuni-rindo* (Mon–Sat

△ Buffalo cart, Taketomi-jima

OKINAWA | Okinawa-Hontō

10

906

5pm to midnight) is a rustic *izakaya* diagonally across from the tourist office at the main crossroads; the European-style food here is reasonably priced. Going more upmarket, *Yamabuki* (Mon–Sat 11am–10pm; ☎0980/52-2143) is in a grey, modern building one block northeast of *Hotel Tōwa*, where they serve an Okinawa set meal, *chanpuru* and other local dishes. Prices are reasonable and there's a selective picture menu, but you'll need to arrive before 7.30pm or make a reservation. Head down towards the harbour from *Hotel Tōwa* and you can't miss the cheerful red lanterns of *Akachōchin* (daily 5pm–1am), a lively *izakaya* offering cheap, filling food on the far side of the shopping street.

Hiji Ōtake, Hedo Misaki and the east coast

North of Nago, Highway 58 hugs the mountainside as the cliffs rise higher, and the only settlements are a few weather-beaten villages in sheltered coves. If you're feeling peckish, a good place for a snack is *Jidoriya*, an unprepossessing shack shortly before Shioya Bay, which serves tasty free-range chicken with soba or rice. At the village of **Kunigami**, head inland along the road that follows the river to reach the start of the walk to **Hiji Ōtaki**, a picturesque 25.7-metre waterfall. The undulating 1.5-kilometre trail here (entry ¥200) starts from the campsite (☎0980/41-3636; ¥2000), which has good washing and cooking facilities plus a small restaurant-cum-shop. About halfway along the trail you'll cross a seventeen-metre suspension bridge, with lovely views across the river; further up and at the falls are excellent swimming spots.

From Kunigami it's another 20km to Okinawa's northern cape, **Hedo Misaki**. Ignoring the unsightly restaurant block and cigarette butts, this is a good spot to stretch your legs, wandering over the headland's dimpled limestone rocks while the waves pound the cliffs below. On clear days you can see northerly Yoron-jima, the first island in Kagoshima Prefecture, and lumpy Iheya-jima to the west, over a churning sea where the currents sweeping round Okinawa collide. If you're travelling by **bus**, take #67 from a stop near central Nago's Ryūkyū Bank to Hentona (1–2 hourly; 1hr; ¥880), then change to #69 for the last leg to Hedo Misaki iriguchi (8 daily; 45min; ¥670); it's a twenty-minute walk out to the point from where the bus drops you.

Six kilometres east of Hedo Misaki, the bus terminates in a large fishing village, **OKU** (15min; ¥330), with an attractive array of traditional Okinawa houses skulking under their low, tiled roofs. A quiet, seemingly deserted place, there's nothing to do but wander the lanes and peer at the neat, walled gardens protected to the seaward side by thick stands of trees. In early spring (Jan & Feb) the surrounding hills are clothed in bright cherry blossoms – and in early April you can feast on the ripened fruit. Most of Oku's inhabitants are elderly, but one young couple run the delightful *Minshuku Miyagi* (☎ & ℻0980/41-8383; ❺ including two meals) beside the river mouth; there are only three rooms, two tatami and one Western, so make sure you book early. From the bus terminus, outside the wonderful village shop, the minshuku's red roof is clearly visible beside the bridge, a few minutes' walk down a sandy track.

Route 70 snakes its way along the east coast, through forests and pineapple groves, with the occasional sea view, making for a pleasant drive. There are few sights here, but one place to aim for is **Tanagāgumui**, a gorgeous swimming hole and small waterfall in a glade reached by a perilous scramble down a 200-metre clay slope. There are ropes strung down the slope to help, but you still need to be sure-footed. Further south just beyond Tairawan Bay is the **Kesaji mangrove forest**, where a boardwalk runs along side the river. This is a good spot to arrange a kayak trip – the *Okinawa International Youth Hostel* in Naha (see p.894) should be able to help.

The outer islands

The beaches on Okinawa-Hontō can't compare with the gems lying offshore among the dozens of **outer islands** that make up the rest of the prefecture. Here, you'll find superb white sands, limpid water and some of the best **diving** in Asia (see the box opposite). Most of these islands also escaped damage during the battles of 1945, and there are no American bases here, so you'll see much more evidence of Ryūkyū culture and the old traditions. Not that they're completely unspoilt; even here the paradise image is punctured by eyesore developments and a good deal of rubbish along the shore, while July and August brings plane-loads of holidaymakers.

Fortunately, there's plenty of choice and, outside the main holiday season, few tourists. One of the most accessible places to head for is **Zamami-jima**, part of the **Kerama Islands** and just a short ferry ride west of Naha, which offers great beaches and diving and has recently become a centre for whale-watching. For a real sense of escape, however, you need to head further south, to **Miyako-jima** and the **Yaeyama Islands**, including the emptier, more mountainous **Ishigaki-jima** and nearby **Iriomote-jima**, often described as Japan's last wilderness. In all these islands, it's the scenery and water sports that provide the main attractions, but Iriomote has the added distinction of its unique wildlife population and lush, almost tropical rainforest.

The Kerama islands

The **KERAMA ISLANDS** are the closest group to Naha, lying some 30km offshore. A knot of three large, inhabited islands and numerous pinpricks of sand and coral, the Keramas offer some of the most beautiful and unspoilt beaches in Okinawa and superb diving among the offshore reefs. **Tokashiki-jima**, the largest island and the closest to Naha, attracts the greatest number of tourists, but all the islands are surprisingly quiet outside the summer peak (July & Aug). This might not last much longer, however. **Zamami-jima**, the most interesting of the group, and nearby **Aka-jima** are busy upgrading their ports, hotels and roads, mainly in response to the the recent boom in winter **whale-watching**.

Historically, **whaling** was an important part of the local economy, but in the 1960s the whales simply disappeared and the industry died. Then, about ten years ago, the humpbacks started coming back to their winter breeding grounds – which the locals have been quick to exploit, though this time for tourism rather than hunting. Several decades earlier, the islanders were faced with less welcome arrivals, when the **US Navy** chose these deep, sheltered

The Kerama Islands		
Zamami-jima	*Zamami-jima*	座間味島
Furuzamami Beach	*Furuzamami Biichi*	古座間味ビーチ
Joy Joy	*Joi Joi*	ジョイジョイ
Marumiya	*Marumiya*	まるみや
Minshuku Sendōron	*Minshuku Sendōron*	民宿船頭殿
Pension Hoshizuma	*Penshon Hoshizuna*	ペンション星砂
Shirahama Islands Resort	*Shirahama Airanzu Rizōto*	シラハマアイランズリゾート
Urizun	*Urizun*	うりずん
Aka-jima	*Aka-jima*	阿嘉島
Kerama airport	*Kerama Kūkō*	ケラマ空港
Tokashiki-jima	*Tokashiki-jima*	渡嘉敷島

With scores of dive sites around Okinawa-Hontō – and many more around the outer islands – one of the best reasons for visiting Okinawa is to go **diving**. There are plenty of dive shops, but only at a few will you find instructors who speak English. A useful website is ⓦwww.okinawascuba.com, which includes an online book store, chatroom, dive-site maps and photo gallery.

Apart from *Maeda Misaki Divers House* (see p.904), one of the most reputable operations is the American-*run Fathoms Diving* (☎090-8766-0868, ⓦwww.fathoms.net) at 1-64 Miyagi, Chatan-chō, around 30km north of Naha. Fathoms charge ¥33,500 for a three-day package, which includes three nights' accommodation, one day of beach diving and one day of boat diving in the Kerama Islands. Rental gear costs ¥2500 per day. For a day beach-dive they charge ¥6500 and for a boat dive ¥12,000. Another reliable local operator is Doug Bennett (☎098/968-4442).

Plenty of sites suitable for beginners lie within close reach of Okinawa-Hontō. Among the best sites are **Sunabe seawall**, where you'll find great soft corals, and **Onna point**, known for its hard corals and fish life. The nearby **Kerama Islands** (see opposite) offer fantastic hard corals, more reef fish than you could count in a week and lots of big fan corals: head to Zamami-jima (see p.910), a particularly laid-back spot from which to organize a dive with the instructors at *Joy Joy* (see p.911).

Experienced divers will want to take off for the islands further south, which provide some unsurpassed locations. Note that here you must speak Japanese if you wish to get detailed instruction. There are over fifty different dive spots to choose from around **Miyako-jima** (see p.911) with cave dives being particularly popular: start off by hooking up with Good Fellas Club (☎0980/73-5483, *fellas@cosmos.ne.jp*) or Sugar Cane (☎0980/72-6259), where Matsumoto Fujio speaks some English.

Around the **Yaeyama Islands** are dotted 360 species of corals and sea anemones, including the rare Ao (blue) and Hama coral reefs off Shirahonoumi on Ishigaki-jima (see p.919). Among the thousand-odd species of fish you can expect to swim with are barracuda, butterfly fish, redfin fusiliers, spadefish and manta rays in the waters between Iriomote-jima and Kohama-jima. Try Aqua Marine Ishigaki (☎0980/83-1558) in Ishigaki City or Diving School Umi-Kōza (☎0980/88-2434) in Kabira. On Iriomote (see p.925), the diving operations attached to both the youth hostels are reputable.

For the ultimate dive experience consider lugging your gear out to **Yonaguni-jima** (see p.927) to see sea turtles and hammerhead sharks and to explore the enigmatic rocks that some claim are the remains of a sunken civilization. Fathoms, on Okinawa-Hontō, organize trips to this distant island.

waters as a base for attacking Okinawa Island. Here, as on Okinawa, there were several mass suicides, including Zamami-jima's whole town council. However, most young Japanese associate the Keramas not with the war but with a cutesy 1988 **film** called *I Want to See Marilyn*. Based on a true story, it tells of a romance between two dogs on neighbouring islands: Shiro on Aka-jima, and Marilyn some 3km away on Zamami. They met when Shiro travelled to Zamami in his owner's boat, but the passion was such that he started swimming over every day to rendezvous with Marilyn on Zamami's Ama beach – or so the story goes.

Fortunately, there are other ways of **getting to the islands**, which are served by **Kerama airport**, on southerly Fukaji-jima, with daily flights from Naha by Ryūkyū Air Commuter (2 daily; 20min; ¥7640/¥13,860 return); boats wait to shuttle passengers from the airport to the islands (¥620–820). The alternative is a **ferry** from Naha's Tomari Port. The high-speed *Queen Zamami* departs twice daily for Zamami, calling at Aka-jima either on the outward or return journey (55min–1hr 15min; ¥2750/¥5230 return; ☎098/868-4567); alternatively, there's the slower *Zamami-maru* (daily; 2hr 15min; ¥1860/¥3540 return; same phone number). For Tokashiki-jima, ferries also go from Tomari Port (2 daily; 1hr 35min; ¥2200/¥4200 return; ☎098/868-7541).

Zamami-jima

A frolicking whale statue greets ferries pulling in to **Zamami-jima**'s new harbour, behind which lies tiny **ZAMAMI village**, the only settlement of any size on the island, with 700 inhabitants out of a total population of 1000. They speak their own dialect and maintain a fierce rivalry with the much larger Tokashiki-jima a couple of kilometres away to the east. A fine place to get away from it all, Zamami-jima has spectacular **beaches**, both on the island itself or a short boat ride away. You can **dive** year-round, but the best time to visit is in autumn, when most tourists have gone and while the water is still warm enough for swimming and snorkelling.

From late January through March, Zamami is the main centre for **whale-watching**. The Whale-Watching Association (☎098/987-2277) arranges **boat trips** from Zamami port every day at 10.30am depending on the weather (2hr; ¥5000). Reservations are essential, and you should bring rain gear and a cagoule as you'll be out in the open sea. The tourist office at the harbour (see below) has an informative leaflet – *Zamami Whale Watching Guide* – with information in English.

With a good pair of binoculars you can often spot humpbacks spouting and cavorting off Zamami's north coast. There's a special **whale observatory** about 3.5km northwest of Zamami village, one of several lookout points scattered round the cliffs and on the island's highest peak, **Takatsuki-yama**. Even allowing for stops it only takes a couple of hours to explore every road on Zamami, after which there's nothing for it but to head to the beach. Roughly 1km southeast of the village, **Furuzamami beach** is the best on the island, with excellent coral and troops of multicoloured fish. In season, you can rent snorkels at the small shop, and there's also a restaurant and showers. However, the beaches get even better on the tiny, **offshore islands**, such as Gahi-jima and Agenashiku-jima, just south of Zamami. In summer (June to mid-Sept) small boats take day-trippers out to these islands (around ¥1000), but out of season you'll have to charter your own boat.

Practicalities

Zamami village faces southwest and is ringed by low hills. Its main street heads inland from the harbour jetty, across a small river to the **Village Office** (☎098/987-2311), **post office** and general store. Coming off the ferry, the new buildings on the left contain the ferry booking office, **tourist information office** (daily 8.30am–5pm; ☎098/987-2277), where you can pick up a good English map of the island, and the Whale-Watching Association office.

There's one **car rental** outlet, Zamami Rent-a-Car (daily 9am–6/7pm; ☎098/987-3250), in the sandy lanes on the village's eastern edge. Prices start at ¥3000 for an hour, or ¥8000 per day, but they only have five vehicles, so it's a good idea to reserve. You can rent **scooters** (¥3000 per day) and **pedal bikes** (¥500 per hour) at a shop (☎098/987-2005) on the road to the Village Office. There are dozens of places offering **diving** trips and courses, but *Joy Joy* (see opposite) and Diving NO-Y (☎098/987-3262), north of the Village Office, are recommended for their friendly, reliable service.

Accommodation on Zamami comprises a reasonable choice of family-run minshuku with a few simple Japanese- and Western-style rooms. It's wise to book ahead at any time of year, particularly if you want to stay at the popular *Pension Hoshizuna* (☎098/987-2253; ❺) or *Minshuku Sendōron* (☎098/987-2016; ❹), both offering clean, bright rooms on the main street. The very friendly *Joy Joy* (☎098/987-2445; ❻ including two meals), on the northwest edge of the village, has a handful of decent rooms and a small garden. If you get stuck, try the grandly named *Shirahama Islands Resort* (☎098/987-3111, ℻987-2655; ❺), on the road out to Furuzamami — while this is Zamami's biggest, smartest hotel, it's a baby compared to the main island's outsized complexes and nothing to rave about. Finally, there's a good **campsite** (☎098/987-3259) behind Ama beach, twenty minutes' walk east along the coast road. A pitch costs ¥300 per person, you can rent tents (¥500) and other equipment, and there are also six-berth cabins (¥21,000).

It's best to arrange **meals** at your accommodation, though Zamami does have one decent restaurant, the *Marumiya* (closed Wed), next door to *Joy Joy*, which does a ¥650 lunch special and reasonable evening meals. The alternatives are a cheap cafeteria upstairs in the old information office building facing the harbour, serving basic noodle and rice dishes, and the snack bar at Furuzamami beach. At night, you can repair to the friendly *Urizun* bar, opposite *Shirayama Islands Resort*.

The Miyako Islands

There's a gap of nearly 300km between Okinawa-Hontō and the next link in the chain, the eight **MIYAKO ISLANDS** centred around **Miyako-jima**, the largest and most interesting of the group. In late April, you'll find Miyako swarming with athletes competing in the All-Japan Triathlon, a combination of swimming, cycling and running, and in July the Miyako Matsuri, the island's main festival, runs for three days, but otherwise the prime attractions are pretty coastal scenery, quiet beaches and watersports. Anyone afraid of snakes will be glad to hear that the Miyako Islands are the only ones in Okinawa free from habu — the snakes were all wiped out in prehistoric times when the oceans engulfed the low-lying land. Having said all this, Miyako-jima — too big and flat to have the desert-island intimacy of Zamami-jima, not quite as exotic or picturesque as Taketomi-jima and Iriomote-jima further south in the Yaeyamas (see p.917) — is something of an also-ran in the Okinawan island stakes.

Miyako-jima

The flat triangular-shaped island of **Miyako-jima** is roughly 35km from tip to tip — its most immediately notable aspect is its extensively cultivated sugar cane. **HIRARA**, the main town, lies on the island's northwest coast, from where roads fan out through the fields. The lack of hills may tempt you to consider cycling here, but you'll need to be prepared for the heat — a better option is to hire a moped or motorbike since public buses are few and far between. A **cash machine** accepting foreign cards can be found at Hirara's post office (Mon–Sat 8.45am–7pm, Sun 9am–5pm) and **Internet** access at both *Jammin'* (see p.917) and *Jazz Bar St Louis* in the backstreets of the Izato district.

It won't take you more than thirty minutes to tick off Hirara's paltry collection of sights. Around 1km north of the harbour along the coast road you'll find the **Nintō Zeiseki** (also called the Fukeiseki), a crumbling, 1.4-metre pinnacle of stone. It stands as a monument to the heavy burden of taxes imposed when Kagoshima's Shimazu clan ruled Okinawa (see p.888) — tax was levied on anyone taller than the stone. Returning to town along the same road,

The Miyako islands

Miyako-jima	*Miyako-jima*	宮古島
Aragusuku	*Aragusuku*	新城
Boraga Beach	*Boraga Biichi*	保良泉ビーチ
Higashi Henna-zaki	*Higashi Henna-zaki*	東平安名岬
Hirara	*Hirara*	平良
Ikema-jima	*Ikema-jima*	池間島
Maehama Beach	*Maehama Biichi*	前浜ビーチ
Miyako Traditional Arts and Crafts Centre	*Miyako-jima Dentō Kōgeihin Sentā*	宮古島伝統工芸品センター
Nintō Zeiseki	*Nintō Zeiseki*	人頭税石
Painagama Beach	*Painagama Biichi*	パイナガマビーチ
Sunayama Beach	*Sunayama Biichi*	砂山ビーチ
Ueno German Culture Village	*Ueno Doitsu Bunka-mura*	うえのドイツ文化村
Yoshino	*Yoshino*	吉野

Accommodation		
Hotel Atoll Emerald	*Hoteru Atōru Emirarudo*	ホテルアトールエメラルド
Hotel Kyowa	*Hoteru Kyowa*	ホテル共和
Miyako-jima Tōkyū Resort	*Miyako-jima Tōkyū Rizōto*	宮古島東急リゾート
Pension Tagaragai	*Penshon Tagaragai*	ペンションタガラガイ
Rasa Cosmica Tourist Home	*Rasa Kosumika Tsūrisuto Hōmu*	ラサコスミカツーリストホテル
Ryūkyū Ryokan Tsurumisō	*Ryūkyū Ryokan Tsurumisō*	琉球旅館つるみ荘
Hotel Sail Inn	*Hoteru Seiru In*	ホテルセイルイン
Yatsushiro Ryokan	*Yatsushiro Ryokan*	八城旅館

Eating		
Banana Kitchen	*Banana Kichin*	バナナキッチン
Chūzan	*Chūzan*	中山
Gaka Goya	*Gaka Goya*	雅歌小屋
Kushiya	*Kushiya*	串屋
Nomura	*Nomura*	のむら

you'll pass the small shrine **Harumizu Utaki**, nestling atmospherically amid the foliage. Up the hill from here, beside another shrine, is the **Miyako Traditional Arts and Crafts Centre**, where you can watch women weaving the delicate *Miyako-jofu* fabric, designated an Important Intangible Cultural Asset. Finally, tucked away in the side streets back towards the harbour is the weatherworn **Hakuai Monument**, presented to Hirara by Kaiser Wilhelm of Germany in 1878 in appreciation of the islanders' rescue of sailors from the German ship *Robertson*, wrecked in a typhoon off Miyako's coast in July 1873. Much more is made of this seminal event in Miyako's history of international relations at the Ueno German Culture Village (see opposite) on the island's southern coast.

Hirara has its own beach, **Painagama**, immediately south of the harbour, but there are much better ones around the island. Top of the list is **Maehama**, around 10km south of Hirara, a long and remarkably pristine strip of soft white sand that is hailed as Japan's best beach. Naturally, a prime chunk of it has been requisitioned by the swanky *Miyako-jima Tōkyū Resort* (☎0980/76-2109,

@www.tokyuhotels.co.jp; 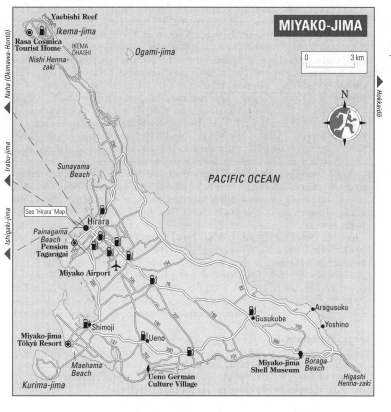❼–❾). Rates are slightly cheaper if you opt for the rooms in the older of the two blocks here, and water-sports enthusiasts won't be disappointed by the range of activities on offer.

Continuing in an anticlockwise direction around the coast, the next place of note you'll hit is the Disneyland-like **Ueno German Cultural Village**. It was here that eight German sailors were saved from the wreck of the *Robertson*, and this kitsch mini-theme park is dominated by replicas of Marksburg castle and a Baroque palace (the annexe of the inevitable attached resort hotel) that stand in their memory. Inside the castle is a **museum** (Tues–Sun 9am–4pm; ¥300), which strives to make the most of Miyako's connections with Germany. The best that can be said about the village is that there's a shop selling a wide range of premium bottled beers from Germany.

The next beach of note is **Boraga**, reached by a steep, twisting road from Route 390. It's a good spot for snorkelling and kayaking, and equipment for both is available from the attractive beachside complex that includes a refreshment hut and a freshwater swimming pool. If you fancy a more substantial lunch, the restaurant next to the missable shell museum on the cliffs above does hearty set menus for under ¥1000. Just east of here lies beautiful **Higashi Henna-zaki**, a two-kilometre-long peninsula renowned for its wild flowers and panoramic views. A trip out to the lighthouse at the very tip is recommended.

Heading north up the east side of the island, duck off the coastal road to find the quiet beaches at **Aragusuki** and **Yoshino**, both excellent snorkelling spots with corals and a plethora of tropical fish. After this there's little to linger for until you reach the bridge at the far north of the island which connects Miyako with tiny **Ikema-jima**. Ikema has a lazy fishing port and more deserted beaches and good coral reefs, including the extensive Yaebishi reef exposed annually during the low spring tides. The best reason, however, for detouring here is the *Rasa Cosmica Tourist Home* (T & F 0980/75-2020; ❼), a delightful pension run by the friendly Nakajima family. There's a hippy feel to the beige adobe building, tastefully decorated inside with pieces picked up from the owner's trips around the Indian subcontinent. The five guest rooms are Western style, rates include two organic vegetarian meals, and snorkelling equipment and bikes are available for free. It's popular, so booking well in advance is essential.

On the way back to Hirara you may well want to pause for yet another lovely beach, **Sunayama**, 2.5km north of the town. You'll need to climb over several dunes to reach the sea, and it's a good spot to come for sunset, which you can view through a naturally eroded stone arch.

Arrival, information and local transport

There are direct **flights** to Miyako from Tokyo, Ōsaka's Kansai International airport and Fukuoka, though the major jumping-off point is Naha (see p.891). Japan Transocean Air (JTA; T 0120-255971) and Air Nippon (ANK; T 0120-029222) both have several departures daily from Naha (¥12,400), while JTA also flies between Miyako and Ishigaki (¥8250). A **taxi** into town from the airport, some 3km from central Hirara, costs about ¥1300 (there are no buses), but if you arrange **motorbike** or **scooter hire** at the airport, the agents will ferry you to your hotel in Hirara for free first, before you pick up your chosen mode of transport. The reliable local operators Okinawa Rent-a-Car (T 0980/73-2774), Nippon (T 0980/72-0919) and Toyota Rent-a-Car (T 0980/72-0100) offer both bikes and **cars** – expect to pay around ¥4000 per day for a bike, including insurance, and ¥5500 for a car. Arimura Sangyō (T 098/860-1980) and RKK Line (T 098/868-1126) between them run two to three **ferries** a week from Naha's Shin-kō or Naha Port to Miyako (from ¥3810 one way; 11hr). Note that these ferries sail overnight and that you need to reserve at least two weeks in advance in July and August.

On the fourth floor of Hirara's **ferry terminal** you'll find the **tourist information office** (Mon–Fri 9am–5.30pm, Sat 9am–noon; T 0980/73-1881), where you can pick up an English pamphlet and map of the island. There's also a helpful information desk (daily except Tues 9am–5.30pm; T 0980/72-0899) at the airport.

Irregular **buses** for the north of the island depart from Yachiyo terminal, a few blocks north of the central post office, while buses south to Maehama and Higashi Henna-zaki leave from Miyako Kyoei terminal on Makuramu-dōri, around 1km east of the post office. If you want to rent a **bicycle**, head to *Ryokan Tsurumi-sō* (see opposite), which charges ¥500 for a day. If you want a **car**, Miyako Taxi (T 0980/72-4123) has a number of English-speaking drivers. Most hotels will be able to hook you up with a **dive operator**; for more details see the box on p.909.

Accommodation

Hirara boasts a good range of **accommodation**, including plenty of cheap minshuku, with prices typically around ¥4000 without meals. If you fancy staying out of town, try the *Miyako-jima Tokyū Resort* at Maehama (see p.912) or the *Rasa Cosmica Tourist Home* on Ikema-jima (see above).

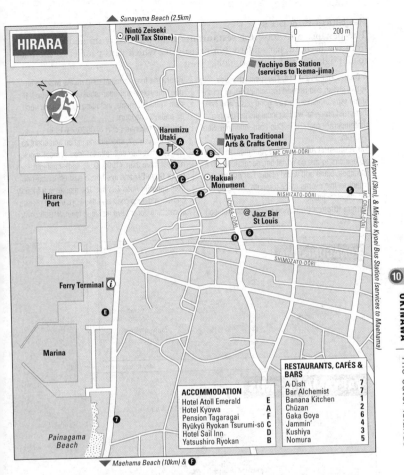

HIRARA

Sunayama Beach (2.5km)

Nintō Zeiseki (Poll Tax Stone)

Yachiyo Bus Station (services to Ikema-jima)

0   200 m

Harumizu Utaki **A**
①   **②** **B**

Miyako Traditional Arts & Crafts Centre

MC CRUM-DŌRI

Airport (3km), & Miyako Kyoei Bus Station (services to Maehama)

③

C

Hakuai Monument

④

NISHIZATO-DŌRI

⑤

Hirara Port

@ Jazz Bar St Louis

D   **⑥**

SHIMOZATO-DŌRI

MC CRUM-DŌRI

CHŪŌ-DŌRI

10

OKINAWA | The outer islands

Ferry Terminal *i*

E

Marina

RESTAURANTS, CAFÉS & BARS

A Dish	7
Bar Alchemist	7
Banana Kitchen	1
Chūzan	2
Gaka Goya	6
Jammin'	4
Kushiya	3
Nomura	5

ACCOMMODATION

Hotel Atoll Emerald	E
Hotel Kyowa	A
Pension Tagaragai	F
Ryūkyū Ryokan Tsurumi-sō	C
Hotel Sail Inn	D
Yatsushiro Ryokan	B

⑦

Painagama Beach

Maehama Beach (10km) & **F**

Hotel Atoll Emerald ☎0980/73-9800, ⒲www.atollemerald.jp. Right beside the ferry terminal, this upmarket option is the classiest place in downtown Hirara, with spacious rooms, a smart Japanese restaurant with waitresses in kimono, and a pool. **⑦**

Hotel Kyowa ☎0980/73-2288, ⒡73-2285. Tucked behind the Harimizu Utaki shrine, this mid-range hotel has friendly staff and a range of decent, Western-style rooms, with the slightly cheaper ones being in the older Honkan building. **⑤**

Pension Tagaragai ☎0980/73-1331. On the main road less than 1km south of the ferry terminal, this pleasant family-run place has mostly Western-style rooms with their own bathrooms, air-con and TV. They can arrange diving trips and have a fine collection of shells in their communal dining room. **④**–**⑤**

Ryūkyū Ryokan Tsurumi-sō ☎0980/73-9314. Hirara's cheapest option has bunk-bed dorm rooms (¥2000 per person) or tatami rooms (¥2500 per person). It's nothing fancy, but well set up, with a communal lounge with hot water, toaster and fridge for self-catering and cheap daily bike and snorkel rental. Look for the pale-blue painted wooden house tucked away back from the harbour.

Hotel Sail Inn ☎0980/74-3854, ⒡72-2308. Business hotel close by Hirara's entertainment district with high-standard Western and tatami rooms. **⑤**

Yatsushiro Ryokan ☎0980/72-1950, ⒡73-1735. Japanese-style accommodation in huge tatami rooms with their own spacious bathrooms, TV and air-con. Good value, as the rates include two very tasty meals. **④**

Restaurants & bars

The best place to look for **restaurants** is in the streets immediately inland from the harbour, particularly Nishizato–dōri, which runs parallel to the main road, Highway 390, but two blocks west.

A Dish ☎0980/72-7114. The menu changes daily at this stylish and relaxed restaurant 500m south of the ferry terminal. There's good pasta and fine thin-crust pizza, as well as local dishes given a contemporary spin. Tues–Sun 6pm–midnight, Sun 5–11pm.

Bar Alchemist After finishing your meal at *A Dish*, nip upstairs to this convivial bar, decorated with a telescope, piano and world globe. The master organizes live events twice a month, including folk and classical music.

Banana Kitchen Occupying a prominent position

where the ferry terminal road meets Makuramu-dōri, this spick-and-span *shokudō* serves up bargain ¥500 set meals, including local dishes such as papaya *chanpuru*.

Chūzan Makuramu-dōri ☎0980/73-1959. Authentic *izakaya*, specializing in fish and sushi as well as what they call "ethnic" food. A meal shouldn't cost more than ¥1000. Daily 4pm–midnight.

Gaka Goya Bar and live house east off Ichiba-dōri from opposite *Hotel Sail Inn*. The master is a friendly English-speaking chap and this is your best chance of catching decent live music in town. ¥1000 cover

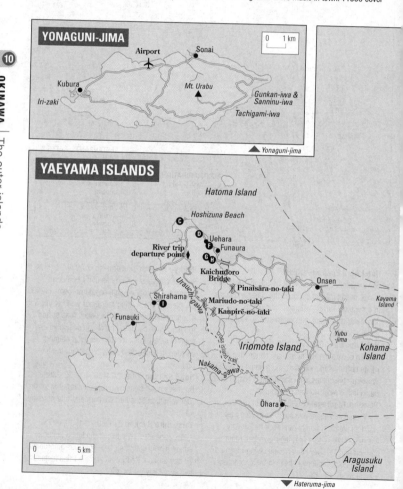

charge. Daily except Wed from 9.30pm.

Jammin' Hirara's obligatory reggae bar, a short stroll away from the west end of Nishizato-dōri, is a cut above the average, conjuring an appropriately tropical vibe. Also offers Internet access, plus decent food, such as spicy jack chicken for ¥800. The master's partner Yamada Yuko is also a diving instructor (©yuko02@hotmail.com). Daily 8pm–3am.

Kushiya ☎0980/72-0734. You'll find this rustic

yakitori-ya just off the west end of Makuramu-dōri; they charge from ¥130 for a stick of grilled chicken. Beer is cheap at ¥500 and you can take your pick from seats or a tatami area. Mon–Sat 6pm–midnight.

Nomura 309 Nishizato-dōri ☎0980/72-2630. Rather plastic decor, but there's a good range of set menus including tempura for ¥1500 and giant prawns for ¥2500.

The Yaeyama Islands

Edging ever closer to the Tropic of Cancer, a further 100km southwest of Miyako-jima and 430km south of Okinawa-Hontō, is a cluster of coral reefs and forested mountains which make up the **YAEYAMA ISLANDS**. The main base for exploring the nine inhabited islands is **Ishigaki-jima**, though you can also stay on nearby **Iriomote-jima**, famous for its wild, wooded

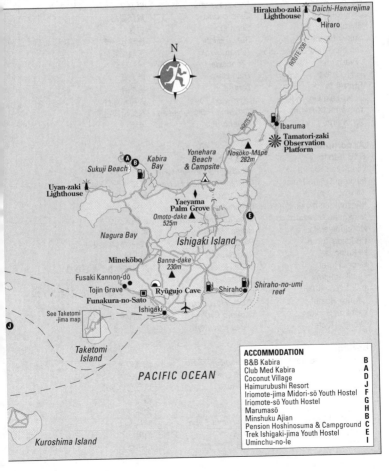

ACCOMMODATION	
B&B Kabira	B
Club Med Kabira	A
Coconut Village	D
Haimurubushi Resort	J
Iriomote-jima Midori-sō Youth Hostel	F
Iriomote-sō Youth Hostel	G
Marumasō	H
Minshuku Ajian	B
Pension Hoshinosuma & Campground	C
Trek Ishigaki-jima Youth Hostel	E
Uminchu-no-le	I

interior and unique wildlife population, or the delightful **Taketomi-jima** where a traditional Ryūkyū way of life is most in evidence. Stuck out on its own, around 100km west of Ishikagi-jima, **Yonaguni-jima** marks Japan's most westerly point, from where it's only another 125km to Taiwan. As with the Miyako Islands, the main reason for coming here is the spectacular **diving** and **snorkelling** opportunities, although trekkers and kayakers will also be inspired by the forest trails, rivers and indented coastline of Iriomote.

Ishigaki-jima

Ishigaki-jima	Ishigaki-jima	石垣島
Ishigaki	Ishigaki	石垣
Fusaki Kannon-dō	Fusaki Kannon-dō	富崎観音堂
Hirakubo-zaki	Hirakubo-zaki	平久保岬
Ishigaki-jima Cave	Ishigaki-jima Shōnyūdō	石垣島鐘乳洞
Kabira Bay	Kabira-wan	川平湾
Minekōbō	Minekōbō	みね屋工房
Miyara Donchi	Miyara Donchi	宮良殿内
Nosoko-māpē	Nosoko-māpē	野底マーペー
Omoto-dake	Omoto-dake	於茂登岳
Shiraho	Shiraho	白保
Sukuji Beach	Sukuji Biichi	底地ビーチ
Tamatori-zaki Observation Platform	Tamatori-zaki Tenbōdai	玉取崎展望台
Tōjin Grave	Tōjin Baka	唐人墓
Tōrin-ji	Tōrin-ji	桃林寺
Ugan-zaki Lighthouse	Ugan-zaki Tōdai	御神崎灯台
Yaeyama Museum	Yaeyama Hakubutsukan	八重山博物館
Yonehara	Yonehara	米原

Accommodation

B&B Kabira	B&B Kabira	川平
Club Med Kabira	Kurabu Meddo Kabira	クラブメッドカビラ
Ishikagi Grand Hotel	Ishikagi Gurando Hoteru	石垣グランドホテル
Minshuku Ajian	Minshuku Ajian	民宿味庵
Minshuku Ishigaki-jima	Minshuku Ishigaki-jima	民宿石垣島
Minshuku Maezato	Minshuku Maezato	民宿まえざと
Hotel Miyahira	Hoteru Miyahira	ホテルミヤヒラ
Parkside Tomo	Pākusaido Tomo	パークサイドトモ
Rakutenya	Rakutenya	楽天屋
Super Hotel Ishikagi-jima	Sūpā Hoteru Ishigaki-jima	スーパーホテル石垣島
Trek Ishigaki-jima Youth Hostel	Torekku Ishigaki-jima Yūsu Hosuteru	トレック石垣島ユースホステル
Yashima Ryokan Youth Hostel	Yashima Ryokan Yūsu Hosuteru	八洲旅館ユースホステル

Eating

Funakura-no-Sato	Funakura-no-Sato	船蔵の里
Genoa	Jenoa	ジェノア
Hōraikaku	Hōraikaku	ほうらいかく
Iso	Iso	磯
Kinjō	Kinjō	金城
Maru Hachi Soba	Maru Hachi Soba	丸八そば
Paikaji	Paikaji	南風
Yunta	Yunta	ゆんた

ISHIGAKI

Kabira Bay

Torin-ji

Miyara Donchi

0   100 m

N

Covered Arcades &
Ishigaki Market

Ai Ai
Bike Rental

Ishigaki
City Hall

Shin'ei-kōen

Yaeyama
Museum

Honda Wing
Bike Rental

Ishigaki City
Tourism
Association

Bus
Terminal

City Library

Ferry
Booking
Offices

**RESTAURANTS,
CAFÉS & BARS**

Asian Kitchen KAPI   2
Blue Café   8
Dachsbrau   1
Genoa   9
Hōraikaku   7
Iso   5
Kinjō   12
La Vie   11
Maru Hachi Soba   3
Paikaji   6
Premier   4
Yunta   10

ACCOMMODATION

Ishigaki Grand Hotel   F
Minshuku Ishigaki-jima   B
Hotel Miyahira   G
Parkside Tomo   E
Rakutenya   C
Super Hotel Ishigaki-jima A
Yashima Ryokan Youth Hostel D

Ferry Terminal for
Hateruma & Yonaguni

Ferry Terminal
for Miyako,
Naha & Taiwan

Iriomote-jima ▼   ▼ Taketomi-jima

OKINAWA | The outer islands

Ishigaki-jima

The third largest island in the Ryūkyū chain, **Ishigaki-jima** is also the administrative centre of the Yaeyama Islands and home to some eighty percent of the the islands' population. Yet outside of the main town **ISHIGAKI**, located on the southwest coast, it's a predominantly rural and mountainous landscape, dominated by the prefecture's tallest peak, Omoto-dake (526m) and fringed with rocky peninsulas, stunning beaches and easily accessible reefs. Indeed, flying into Ishigaki's decidedly homely airport you feel more like you've arrived in some South Seas banana republic rather than the last outpost of one of the wealthiest nations on earth. This could well change if the authorities ever manage to overcome long-standing local opposition to the construction of a new airport – the current proposed location would destroy a precious reef.

Ishigaki is a compact town easily negotiated on foot. **Guided bus tours** (4hr 30min; ¥4350) in Japanese visit all the island's main sights, departing from the bus terminal daily at 9am, but you'll find it easier to use either the buses (see p.922) or, better still, to hire your own transport. **Car rental** is available at roughly the same rates as on Miyako (see p.914) through the Nissan (☎0980/83-0024), Toyota (☎0980/88-0202) and Nippon (☎0980/82-3629) agencies. Good-value **bike and scooter rental** is available at *Ai Ai* (☎0980/82-9530), diagonally opposite the post office, and *Honda Wing* (☎0980/82-3255), opposite the city hall. If you'd rather go by **taxi**, call Tokai Kōtsū (☎0980/82-3585) or Shirayuri Kōtsū (☎0980/83-1688). Note that on Sunday most of the island's petrol stations are closed except for those in Ishigaki; make sure you fill up before setting off around the island.

Apart from hosting the Yaeyamas' best range of tourist facilities, Ishigaki town has a number of minor sights that shouldn't delay you more than an hour before hitting the beaches. The first of these, the small **Yaeyama Museum** (Tues–Sun 9am–4.30pm; ¥200), lies five minutes' walk inland from the harbour, and contains a moderately interesting collection of local artefacts, including a pile of traditional canoes, shaggy *shiisā* masks used in local festivals, and a rather gruesome scroll depicting the tortures of hell. Ten minutes' walk northwest, **Miyara Donchi** (daily except Tues 9am–5pm; ¥200) was built in 1819 and modelled on a traditional *samurai* residence; it's surrounded by a coral rock garden, designated a National Scenic Beauty. On the town's northwest outskirts is **Torin-ji**, an attractive Zen temple founded in 1614 where meditation is still practised. Its two Deva king statues (called *Niōzo*) are now worshipped as the island's protectors.

Although there are buses, the best way to appreciate the island is to get your own transport (see p.919) and start exploring. The tourist literature and locals will urge you to head straight to **KABIRA BAY**, home of cultured black pearls and gorgeous emerald waters, but there are places worth stopping off en route. Around 2km northwest of the town centre along the coastal road is the striking **Tōjin Grave**, a highly decorative monument erected in 1971 to the several hundred Chinese labourers who died off the shores of Ishigaki in 1852. They were being shipped to California from Amoi in China but during the voyage rebelled against their cruel treatment. Unfortunately, their boat was wrecked and many of those who tried to escape were shot by their American and British taskmasters. Nearby **Fusaki Kannon-dō** is a temple originally built in 1701 with good views of Taketomi and Iriomote from its hillside perch. On the way here you'll pass *Funakura-no-Sato* (☎0980/82-8108), a lovely complex of Okinawan houses containing a restaurant, café and gift shop; menu courses of local dishes start from a reasonable ¥2000 and sometimes there are traditional dance shows.

Following the main Route 79 out northwards from Ishigaki will take you past **Minekōbō** (daily 8.30am–6pm) a large gift shop where you can watch weavers make colourful *Yaeyama Jofu* cloth. The road hugs the coast sweeping round Nagura Bay; as you rise up the hill over to Sakieda Bay, consider heading out east along the side road to the picturesque **Ugan-zaki Lighthouse**, commanding an impressive view across the island and, sadly, a favoured sight for suicides. Pack a picnic and enjoy it in peace here or at one of the secluded nearby beaches, scattered with giant shells; the sunsets are often spectacular.

Heading back to the main road, you'll soon hit the turn-off to **KABIRA BAY**, which can also easily be reached by bus from Ishigaki station. Ignore the tourist gift shops, restaurants and dubious Habu snake park and head straight to the viewing platform over the bay, tucked in the trees behind the shrine, to see what all the fuss is about. It's a look-only experience, though: bathing in this placid island-dotted bay is frowned upon because of the nearby pearl farms. You'll be mildly hassled to take a **glass-bottom boat tour** (daily 9.15am–5pm; ¥1000), but don't feel you have to. There are better ways of spending half an hour, not to mention the cash, especially since the scenic wonder of Yonehara (see below) lies immediately east around the bay. There are a couple of good places to stay at Kabira (see "Accommodation", p.922) and nearby **Sukuji beach**, one of the nicest on Ishigaki.

By far Ishigaki's most rewarding beach experience lies some 5km up the coast back along Route 79 at **YONEHARA**. Here you can wade out across a broad expanse of dead coral (make sure you're wearing some foot protection) teeming with sea life to the very edge of the reef, which drops off to the sea floor and is also a mecca for tropical fish. You'll need to be wary of jellyfish here, which can pack a fatal sting. Snorkelling gear can be rented from a shop on the main road, and there's a **campsite**, with basic toilet facilities, in the trees beside the beach. You also won't fail to notice the colourfully painted giant *shiisā* statues outside *Yonego Yaki Kōbō* (daily 9am–6pm), a delightful cottage industry factory and shop churning out the traditional Okinawan guardians in a range of cartoon-like styles.

Behind Yonehara, Ishigaki's mountainous interior holds several **trekking** possibilities, including the hike up **Omoto-dake**; not far north of Yonehara is the turn-off to a grove of Yaeyama palms from where a trail runs up the slopes of the mountain to an observation platform. Locals, however, sing the praises of **Nosoke-māpe** (282m), a couple of kilometres further north along the coast road. This attractive but rather steep peak has a commanding view of the Hirakubo peninsula. Legend has it that a woman pining to see her lover on Iriomote continually climbed Nosoke-māpe and became so sad that she turned to stone at the summit – see if you can find her among the rock outcrops.

At Ibaruma Bay, Route 79 swings east to the opposite side of the island. At the fork you have a choice. Head north through a pastoral landscape and you'll eventually hit the pretty viewpoint of **Hirakubo-zaki**, the end of the line on Ishigaki-jima, punctuated by a dazzling white lighthouse overlooking the tiny island, Daichi Hanare-jima. Otherwise turn south on Route 390 and take the turn-off for the **Tamatori-zaki Observation Platform**. The views from here are splendid and the landscaped grounds burst with crimson hibiscus blooms. Naturally, it's a favourite stop for tour buses. If you're heading up here by public transport, the infrequent bus #9 from Ishigaki will drop you at the foot of the hill at the Tamatori stop.

The main attraction on the way back down the coast to Ishigaki town lies offshore. **Shiraho-no-umi** is a patch of reef containing the rare Ao (blue) and Hama corals. The village of **SHIRAHO** has several minshuku where you can stay and arrange boat trips (around ¥2000) at high tide to snorkel over the reef, one recommendation being *Minshuku Maezato* (☎0980/86-8065; ❹ including two meals), next to the post office; if you're coming here by bus, get off at the Shōgaku-mae stop. Less convenient is the *Trek Ishigaki-jima Youth Hostel* (☎0980/86-8257; dorm beds ¥2700 per person) in Hoshino village, midway between Shiraho and Tamatori-zaki, which has Western-style dorm rooms and is close to the beach.

Finally, back in Ishigaki and turning inland heading up to the Banadake Forest Park, you'll hit the entrance to a minor attraction, the **Ishigaki-jima Cave** (daily 9am–10pm; ¥1000). Only 400m of this 3200-metre cave are open to the public and it has the usual stalactite and stalagmite formations, bats and fossilized coral, evidence that the area was once underwater.

Arrival and information

Direct daily **flights** connect Ishigaki-jima with Tokyo, Ōsaka (Kansai International) and Fukuoka, but there are many more services from Naha (¥16,250); contact Japan Transocean Air (JTA: ☎0120-255971) and Air Nippon (ANK: ☎0120-029222) for details. In addition, a handful of daily flights leave from Miyako-jima (¥8250). Arimura Sangyō (☎0980/82-3844) and RKK Line (☎0980/82-2050) run two to three **ferries** a week between them (13hr; from ¥5350) via Miyako-jima. From Miyako-jima to Ishigaki-jima by ferry (¥1890) takes around five hours. Some services go on to Taiwan (see Naha listings, p.898).

The **Ishigaki Port Terminal**, where boats from Naha, Miyako and Taiwan dock, is around 500m southeast of the central bus terminal; the **ferry wharves** for Taketomi-jima, Iriomote-jima and other Yaeyama islands are across the road from the bus terminal. The **airport** lies a few kilometres east of the town centre; reasonably frequent buses from here into Ishigaki cost ¥200, a taxi around ¥800. If you're planning on getting around the island by bus it's worth investing in one of the two **Free Passes** (¥1000 & ¥2000), both valid for five days; the cheaper one allows as many round trips as you like between the airport, Kabira Bay and the resorts at Sukuji beach; the more expensive covers all of the island's buses.

The **Ishigaki City Tourism Association** (Mon–Fri 8.30am–5.30pm; ⓣ0980/82-2809), in the civic buildings opposite Shinei-kōen five minutes' stroll west of the bus terminal, has maps and a useful English booklet on the Yaeyamas. Next door is the excellent city library, with free **Internet** access (Tues–Fri 10am–7pm, Sat & Sun 10am–5pm); other Internet cafés around town come and go – at the time of research there was one at the west end of the covered shopping arcade. The **cash machines** at the post office (Mon–Fri 8.45am–7pm, Sat & Sun 9am–5pm), a minute north of the bus terminal, accept foreign cards.

Accommodation

Most **accommodation** is located in Ishigaki town, where you'll find one of the island's two youth hostels and several other cheap options, as well as decent mid-range hotels. The upper-end accommodation is at the resorts, the best of which is *Club Med Kabira*. Rates can rise significantly during the main holiday periods.

B&B Kabira 934-4 Kabira Bay ⓣ0980/88-2229, ⓦwww.niki-group.com. Classy boutique hotel with contemporary-style Western rooms and a pleasant restaurant-bar, all with fabulous views of Kabira Bay. Rates include breakfast. ❺

Club Med Kabira Kabira Bay ⓣ0980/84-4600, ⓦwww.clubmed.com. If you're thinking of staying at a resort, then this is the one to go for – although the all-inclusive packages are expensive. The architecture is low-rise and traditionally inspired, all the staff speak English or French and there are excellent facilities, including a trapeze artist on hand to teach you the ropes. They've also hogged one of the best beaches on the island. ❽

Ishigaki Grand Hotel 1 Tonoshiro ⓣ0980/82-6161, ⓦwww.Ishigaki-grand-hotel.com. Mid-range hotel with a convenient location and nicely furnished rooms. Also has a large communal bath and sauna. ❻–❼

Minshuku Ajian 934 Kabira Bay ⓣ0980/88-2251, 88-2473. Run by the English-speaking Tatsu-san, this delightful minshuku offers good tatami rooms with shared facilities, tasty Asian meals and a beautiful view of the famed bay from its spacious wooden deck. ❺ including two meals.

Minshuku Ishigaki-jima 291 Ōkawa ⓣ0980/82-6066, ⓕ83-0637. Three old houses have been joined together to provide the accommodation at this minshuku, one of Ishigaki's most traditional. Regular rates include a small breakfast of coffee and toast; if you want two full meals it's ¥6000 per person. ❹

Hotel Miyahira Misaki-chō ⓣ0980/82-6111, ⓦwww.miyahira.co.jp. Reasonably comfortable, mostly Western-style twin rooms at this upmarket hotel within easy walking distance of the ferry and bus terminals. Rates include breakfast. ❻–❼

Parkside Tomo 6-4 Shinei-chō ⓣ0980/88-8388. Ishigaki's most inexpensive accommodation, charging just ¥2000 for a dorm bed, is a clean, no-fuss place on the west side of Shinei Park. All rooms are tatami; singles (¥2500) have their own TV and air-con. The friendly owner also rents out bikes and scooters for reasonable rates. ❷

Rakutenya 291 Ōkawa ⓣ & ⓕ0980/83-8713. English-speaking hosts Ren and Miyako have created a cosy guesthouse with both tatami and Western-style rooms. Booking is essential since it's small and popular. Ren's mum runs the minshuku next door if this place is full. ❸

Super Hotel Ishigaki-jima 36 Ishigaki ⓣ0980/83-9000, ⓦwww.infinix.co.jp/sh. Single rooms only (¥6000) at this fully automated business hotel. All have TV, air-con and small bathrooms, and there's a free light breakfast served in the lobby.

Yashima Ryokan Youth Hostel 117 Tonoshiro ⓣ0980/82-3157, ⓕ82-4546. This small hostel is located in a traditional house in the backstreets north of the Yaeyama Museum. It's fine, but the hostel has the usual rules and there are better cheap options. Dorm beds ¥2600 per person.

Eating and drinking

Ishigaki is well served with **restaurants**, some of them surprisingly smart for such an out-of-the-way place. For self-catering and local colour, check out the market in the covered arcade just north of the central Shiyakosho-dōri. There are also a few decent **bars**, including the hip reggae bar *Blue Café* (daily from 9pm), just around the corner from the Hot Spar convenience store near the bus terminal; and *Paikaji*, a bustling *izakaya*, just off Shiyakushō-dōri.

Asian Kitchen KAPI Yui Road. Tasty Southeast Asian platters served at this rustic restaurant with a photo-menu. Lunch is a good deal for ¥800–1000. Closed Tues.

Dachsbrau. On Route 79 heading out of Ishigaki towards Kabira, this German-style ale house features Ishigaki's range of homebrews and serves steak dishes. *Premier* in Ishigaki's covered arcade also serves their beer.

Genoa Sanbashi-dōri. Specializes in pizza and crêpes with all kinds of fruit and ice cream – there's even one with a hot dog. Closed Thurs.

Hōraikaku Shiminkaikan-dōri ☎0980/82 3158. Easily spotted Chinese restaurant opposite the Civic Hall. Has a picture menu; meals cost around ¥1500.

Iso 9 Ōkawa. Behind the post office, this is one of the best places for traditional Yaeyama cuisine. Has a photo-menu and dishes start at ¥700. Daily 11am–10.30pm.

Kinjō 2-3-4 Hamizaki-chō. Popular Korean barbecue joint. The ¥1500 deal gets you a plate of marinated beef, cabbage and more veggies, soup, pickles and the Korean rice dish *bibinba*. Wash it down with the local beer.

La Vie 1-2-6 Hamazaki-chō ☎0980/83-3402. Stylish contemporary restaurant specializing in European dishes, with good set lunches and live jazz some evenings. Closed Tues & Sun lunch.

Maru Hachi Soba 402-2 Tonoshiro. A short walk northeast of the youth hostel, and run by no-nonsense ladies, this is *the* place for noodles. Commendations plaster the walls and you can sit at tables or on tatami. A small bowl of noodles costs ¥300, a large one ¥500, and a set with pickles and rice is ¥800.

Yunta 9-2 Misaki-chō ☎0980/82-7118. Popular fish restaurant on Ishigaki's main street. The set lunch for ¥700 is a good deal, while the sushi platters are the thing to go for in the evening.

Taketomi-jima

Many people make the ten-minute ferry crossing from Ishigaki to **Taketomi-jima** (every 15min; ¥1100 return); indeed, this flat island – just 1500m at its widest point and home to less than 300 people – gets inundated with day-trippers eager to see its traditional houses, ride on its buffalo-drawn carts and search lovely sandy beaches for the famous minuscule star-shaped shells. The trick is to stay on after the masses have left, which is when Taketomi really begins to weave its magical spell. The frequent ferries make it feasible to use Taketomi as a base for visiting Ishigaki, but note that the last service back is at 5pm.

There's only one village on Taketomi – also called **TAKETOMI** – and it's a beauty. Practically all the houses are built in traditional bungalow style with low-slung terracotta-tiled roofs, crowned with bug-eyed *shiisa*. Surrounding them are rocky walls, draped with hibiscus and bougainvillea. The popular way of getting around the island's sandy lanes is on rickety **bikes**; touts for the two rental operations (both charge ¥300 per hour) meet all the ferries and, if you're not staying the night, you'd do well to hook up with one for the short ride into the village. The alternative is to take a ride in a *suigyūsha*, the cart pulled by a buffalo (¥1000 per person for 30min), while being serenaded by a *sanshin*-plucking local.

Apart from soaking up the atmosphere, the main thing to see in the village is the **Kohōin Shūshūkan** (daily 9am–5pm; ¥300), a small museum with an attached gift shop. There are over two thousand items on display here, including old cigarette packets, rusting samurai swords, an ornate shrine and expressive festival masks. Punctuating the tiny landscaped garden a few blocks east of the museum is an ugly concrete **lookout tower**. Although it provides a

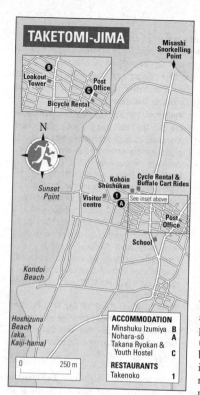

TAKETOMI-JIMA

Misashi Snorkelling Point

Lookout Tower

Post Office

Bicycle Rental

N

Sunset Point

Kohōin Shūshūkan

Cycle Rental & Buffalo Cart Rides

Visitor centre

See inset above

Post Office

School

Kondoi Beach

Hoshizuna Beach (aka. Kaiji-hama)

0   250 m

ACCOMMODATION
Minshuku Izumiya   B
Nohara-sō   A
Takana Ryokan &
Youth Hostel   C

RESTAURANTS
Takenoko   1

picturesque view across the rooftops, the village would do well to pull it down. A nicer ocean scene is provided from the pier on the west side of the village, past the visitor centre – the best spot from which to view sunset. The star-sand beaches, **Kondoi**, **Hoshizuna** and **Kaji**, are a short pedal south of here, also on the west side of the island. Swimming is possible at both, but at low tide you'll have to wade a long way out. The best snorkelling spot is at **Misashi**, on the northern coast, where three rocky islets and their surrounding reefs provide a home to a multitude of colourful sea life.

Make a booking with any of Taketomi's minshuku and you'll be met at the port and driven into the village. Rates at all, except the youth hostel, include breakfast and dinner. The cheapest **accommodation** is at the youth hostel, which shares premises with *Takana Ryokan* (T0980/85-2151, F85-2129; dorm beds ¥2600 per person, rooms ⑤ including meals). The youth hostel rooms are simple tatami ones – the ryokan side of the building is slightly fancier and you get served a better standard of meal. It's one of the few two-storey buildings in the village, near the post office. On the east side of the village, you'll find *Minshuku Izumiya* (T0980/85-2250; ⑤), famous locally for its lovely garden. They also own the thatched house opposite, where it's also possible to stay. Alternatively, *Nohara-sō* (T0980/85-2252; ④) is a fantastic place to stay, with a very laid-back atmosphere, excellent food and free snorkelling gear. Come sundown, a bottle of *awamori* is likely to appear, the *shansin* comes out and an Okinawan singsong begins.

Taketomi-jima		
Taketomi-jima	*Taketomi-jima*	竹富島
Hoshizuna beach	*Hoshizuna biichi*	星砂ビーチ
Kaji beach	*Kaji biichi*	ガイジビーチ
Kohōin Shūshūkan	*Kohōin Shūshūkan*	喜宝院蒐集館
Kondoi beach	*Kondoi biichi*	コンドイビーチ
Minshuku Izumiya	*Minshuku Izumiya*	民宿泉屋
Misashi	*Misashi*	ミサシ
Nohara-sō	*Nohara-sō*	のはら荘
Takana Ryokan	*Takana Ryokan*	高那旅館
Takenoko	*Takenoko*	竹の子

If you're just visiting for the day and want lunch, the village offers a couple of **eating** options, including *Takenoko* on the west side near the museum, known for its noodle and pork dishes. It's also open every evening, save Sunday, until 9pm and is a good spot for a beer.

Iriomote-jima

Brooding darkly some 20km west of Ishigaki, **Iriomote-jima** is an extraordinarily wild place for Japan. Rising sharply out of the ocean, some ninety percent of its uncharted, mountainous interior is covered with dense subtropical rainforest, much of it protected as the **Iriomote National Park**. The island harbours a unique population of wildlife including one of the world's rarest species, the *yamaneko* or **Iriomote lynx**, and although there's little chance of encountering this nocturnal, cat-like animal, the island and its surrounding waters are also home to a splendid array of flora and coral reefs shimmering with tropical fish, and there are plenty of opportunities for snorkelling, diving, kayaking and hiking through the rainforest.

Although it's Okinawa's second largest island, less than two thousand people live here, most of them along a barely developed strip on the north and south coasts. Ferries from Ishigaki sail to two ports on the island: **ŌHARA** in the south and **FUNAURA** in the north. The latter is the better place to head for since it's closer to Iriomote's main scenic attractions and offers the widest range of accommodation at nearby **Uehara**. As on Taketomi, the vast majority of visitors come only for the day, heading straight to the **Urauchi-gawa**, a broad, Amazon-like river, where they hop on boat tours (¥1500; 3hr round trip including hike) up the trail to the scenic waterfalls **Kanpire-no-taki** and **Maryudo-no-taki**. Boats make the eight-kilometre run from 9am to 4pm daily and it's best to get there early and catch the tour groups, since they won't depart with less than four passengers. The touristy nature of this excursion (even cardigan-wearing grannies can easily negotiate the gentle 1.5-kilometre trail through the rainforest up to the falls) is undeniable, yet it's still enjoyable and offers several options for more adventurous trips. One is to hike some 15km across the island from the head of the Kanpire Falls to the **Nakama-gawa**, Iriomote's second largest waterway, and Ōhara. This far from clear route takes at least six hours – get local advice before tackling it, be prepared to camp out and let the authorities know your plans (call ☎0980/85-6510). The other option is to paddle back from the falls in a **kayak**, a great way to view the rainforest at close quarters. Kayak trips can be arranged at the youth hostels or at the river trip departure point and cost around ¥8400 including lunch for a full day. To hire a kayak and paddle on your own, go to Kōto Sharē Puraza (☎0980/85-6723), the café opposite where the tour buses stop for the Kanpire falls; they charge ¥3900 a day. If you're staying at *Irumote-sō Youth Hostel* they organize a daily drop-off at the Urauchi-gawa and Hoshizuna beach (see p.926). Otherwise, both ferry companies run service buses here from Funaura.

Kayaking can also be combined with a trek up to **Pinaisāra-no-taki**, the tallest waterfall in Okinawa, which you can clearly see from the Kaichudoro bridge that spans the bay immediately south of Funaura. An excellent guide to arrange this through is Murata Susumu (☎ & ☎0980/85-6425), aka Hige-san, a wildlife photographer who runs a variety of eco-trips. At low tide you may well find yourself dragging your kayak across the shallows to the Hine-gawa before paddling to the start of the trek. This will give you a chance to closely inspect the mangrove forests and see armies of purple soldier crabs scuttling across the sandbanks. On the climb to the head of the falls, keep a lookout for snakes and be prepared for leeches, especially in the wet season. At the foot of the trail you'll also pass many of the distinctive **sakishima suōnoki** trees, with huge, billowing buttress roots. You'll also notice lumps of coal sparkling in the ground – this was one of Iriomote's riches that Commodore Perry (see "Contexts", p.939) had his eye on when he forced the opening up of Japan in the mid-nineteenth century. The youth hostels can also provide details of hiking trails from Funaura to the falls if you don't fancy kayaking.

Iriomote is a **divers' paradise**, with the Manta Way between the island's eastern coast and **Kohama-jima** (see opposite) being particularly famous for its shoals of manta rays; you're most likely to sight them between April and June. The youth hostels and all minshuku can put you in touch with the island's several dive operations (see box on p.909 for more on diving). **Snorkelling** is particularly good at **Hoshizuna beach**, around 4km northwest of Funaura, where you'll also find a **campsite**, a decent restaurant and snorkelling gear for rent – all of which makes it popular. If you're looking to escape the crowds, head to **Funauki**, reached by three ferries a day (¥410) from **Shirahama**, at the far west end of the coastal road; the beach here, a short trek through the jungle, is one of the most beautiful in all of Japan. If the weather puts paid to outdoor activities (and it does rain a lot on Iriomote), then the best option is to head to the **onsen** (daily 11am–9pm; ¥1200), around 5km east of Funaura.

Arrival, information and local transport

Yaeyama Kankō and Anei Kankō both run several high-speed **ferries** from Ishigaki to Funaura (45min; ¥2000 oneway, ¥3800 return) and Ōhara (35min; ¥1540 one way, ¥2980 return). Buses meet all arrivals and transport passengers to their accommodation and the main tourist locations such as Hoshizuna beach and the Urauchi river. Use these buses, which are free, to get around, but make sure you're aware of the timetables or you may get stuck.

Iriomote-jima		
Iriomote-jima	*Iriomote-jima*	西表島
Funaura	*Funaura*	船浦
Ōhara	*Ōhara*	大原
Shirahama	*Shirahama*	白浜
Funauki	*Funauki*	船浮
Hoshizuna beach	*Hishizuna-no-hama*	星砂の浜
Kanpire-no-taki	*Kanpirī-no-taki*	カンピレーの滝
Mariudo-no-taki	*Mariudo-no-taki*	マリュドの滝
Nakama-gawa	*Nakama-gawa*	仲間川
Pinaisāra-no-taki	*Pinaisāra-no-taki*	ピナイサーラの滝
Ranchhouse Tamago	*Ranchihausu Tamago*	ランチハウスたまご
Shinpachi Shokudō	*Shinpachi Shokudō*	新八食堂
Uehara	*Uehara*	上原
Urauchi-gawa	*Urauchi-gawa*	ウラウチ川
Accommodation		
Coconut Village	*Kokonattsu Birejji*	ココナッツビレッジ
Iriomote-jima Midori-sō Youth Hostel	*Iriomote-jima Midori-sō Yūsu Hosuteru*	西表島みどり荘ユースホステル
Irumote-sō Youth Hostel	*Irumote-sō Yūsu Hosuteru*	いるもて荘ユースホステル
Minshuku Mariudo	*Minshuku Mariudo*	民宿まりゅど
Marumasō	*Marumasō*	まるま荘
Pension Hoshinosuna	*Penshon Hoshinosuna*	ペンション星砂
Uminchu-no-Ie	*Uminchu-no-Ie*	海人の家

There's an **information office** (☏0980/82-9836) in Funaura beside the ferry terminal, but don't count on anyone being there. Iriomote's only road runs along the coast from Ōhara via Funaura and Uehara – where you'll find most of Iriomote's accommodation – to Shirahama in the west; all these villages are linked by infrequent public buses. To really explore the island you'll need to **rent a bike** or **car**. This can be arranged at both the youth hostels; count on around ¥800 per day for a pedal bike, ¥2800 for a motorbike and ¥6000 for a car. Bring plenty of cash with you since there are no convenient exchange facilities.

Accommodation and eating

It's certainly worth **staying** at least one night on the island and it's best to opt for a deal that includes two meals, since **eating** options are very thin on the ground. If you're stuck, or need a snack lunch, try *Shinpachi Shokudō* opposite the Midori-sō youth hostel or *Ranchhouse Tamago* further west along the road. The restaurant at *Pension Hoshinosuna* (see below) does very good set lunches for around ¥1000. A small supermarket in Uehara provides picnic supplies.

Coconut Village ☏0980/85-6045, ℱ85-6308. On the outskirts of Uehara, around 3km north of the Funaura, this modern beachside complex has both small tatami and Western-style rooms (with very low beds), a restaurant and freshwater pool. ❺

Iriomote-jima Midori-sō Youth Hostel ☏0980/85-6526. On the coastal road in Uehara, five minutes by bus from Funaura, this spartan but clean hostel also has good-value minshuku accommodation for ¥4500 per person including two meals, and dorm beds (¥2500 per person). Can arrange transport hire and the full range of Iriomote adventure activities.

Irumote-sō Youth Hostel ☏0980/85-6255, ⓦhttp://ishigaki.com/irumote/index.html. Ten minutes' walk uphill west from the Funaura port, this is the best place to stay on the island, with a stunning hilltop location and a very relaxed atmosphere. Serves excellent meals, has bikes and scooters for rent and a dive club. Dorm beds ¥2800 per person.

Minshuku Mariudo ☏0980/85-6578. Turn left at the top of the hill from Funaura to reach this minshuku with a small grocery shop and garden overlooking the bay. The rooms (with shared bathrooms) have wooden floors and you sleep on a futon. ❹

Maruma-sō ☏0980/85-6156. One of Funaura's nicer minshuku, run by a friendly family. Features small tatami rooms, shared bathroom, coin-operated air-con and a spacious garden by the harbour with access to a sandy, but littered, cove. ❹

Pension Hoshinosuna ☏0980/85-6448, ⓔbluehaven@soleil.ocn.ne.jp. Tastefully furnished Western-style rooms and spacious tatami rooms with attached bathrooms at this small beachside complex, with restaurant, shop and diving centre on hand. Also has a good camping ground (¥300 per pitch; tent rental for ¥525). ❺–❻

Uminchu-no-Ie ☏0980/85-6119, ℱ84-8321. Simple Japanese-style accommodation in a large municipal building at Shirohama – useful if you want to get away from what constitutes crowds on Iriomote and spend time exploring the beautiful coastline here by kayak, which can be rented from the local store at ¥4000 per day. Rates include a breakfast of coffee and bread. ❷

Yonaguni-jima and other islands

If you've really got time on your hands, or a burning desire to get to the far reaches of Japan, the Yaeyama group includes several more islands to visit. **Hateruma-jima**, 56km from Ishigaki, marks Japan's southernmost point and sports beautiful Nishi beach. **Kohama-jima**, 18km west of Ishigaki, is home to the ritzy *Haimurubushi Resort* (☏0980/85-3111, ⓦwww.haimurubushi .co.jp; ❺–❽). Both of these are served by regular ferries, but if you want to get to tiny **Hatoma-jima**, north of Iriomote, or **Aragusku-jima**, 24km southwest of Ishigaki, you'll need to charter a boat.

The island with the most appeal, though, is **Yonaguni-jima**, 127km northwest of Ishigaki and the furthest west you can go and still be in Japan; on a clear day you can see Taiwan, some 125km away, from Yonaguni's high point **Mount**

Urabu. In the past, the island was called Dunan from the word *tonan*, meaning hard to reach; these days getting there is no problem with twice-daily **flights** (45 min; ¥6400) and twice-weekly **ferries** (4hr; ¥3460). Yonaguni is also famous for its Atlas moth (the largest in the world), giant marlin fish, the potent 120°-proof *awamori* liquor *Hanazake* and enigmatic seabed rocks.

Just 11km long, it won't take you long to tour this predominantly rural but hilly island. **SONAI** on the north coast is the main community; ferries dock in its port and the **airport** is a couple of kilometres west. The best way to get around is by rented **bike or car**, which can be arranged in town or at the airport. A circuit of the island shouldn't take you more than half a day, although you'd be mad to pass up the chance to linger at some of the most gorgeous and deserted beaches in the Yaeyamas. Head first west towards the tiny port of **Kubura**, the base for marlin fishing, and out to **Iri-zaki**, where you'll find a simple monument marking Japan's westernmost point, atop sheer cliffs.

Much more interesting is what lies on the seabed beneath. In 1986 local divers came across what looked like a giant rock-carved staircase, or possibly part of a pyramid, 80m long, 50m wide and 20m high. Researchers have flocked to what are now being described as the **deep ocean ruins** ever since. Some claim the rocks are part of the legendary ancient civilization of Mu, an Asian Atlantis; others say they were carved by natural forces, although on photographic evidence alone this seems unlikely. Another diving highlight here is the sight of schools of hammerhead sharks, particularly in the winter months.

More intriguing rock formations can be found above water on Yonaguni's east coast. **Tachigami-iwa** is a stout pillar of rock dusted with greenery, and **Gunkan-iwa** is said to resemble a battleship, although it actually looks more like a submarine rising to the surface. There's little debate over what the **Sanninu-dai** outcrop resembles – it's worshipped by locals as a symbol of virility. On the nearby hillsides, wild Yonaguni horses roam.

Sonai has a handful of **hotels**, among which *Hotel Irifune* (☎0980/87-2311; ❻ including two meals) is small, scruffy, but clean. The owners can arrange diving trips. You can also find more information in Japanese about the island on ⓦwww.yonaguni.jp.

Travel details

Ferries

Naha to: Hakata (1 weekly; 27hr); Ishigaki-jima (2–3 weekly; 12–18hr); Kagoshima (1 daily; 25hr); Kōbe (1 weekly; 44hr); Miyako-jima (2–3 weekly; 8–10hr 30min); Miyazaki (1 weekly; 24hr); Ōsaka (1 weekly; 33hr); Taiwan (1 weekly; 22hr); Tokyo (1–2 weekly; 54hr); Zamami-jima (3 daily; 55min–2hr 15min).

Flights

Ishigaki to: Fukuoka (1 daily; 2hr); Kansai International (1 daily; 2hr 15min); Miyako (3 daily; 30min); Nagoya (1 daily; 2hr 40min); Tokyo (1 daily; 3hr 15min); Yonaguni (2 daily; 30min).
Miyako to: Kansai International (2 daily; 1hr 55min); Tokyo (1 daily; 2hr 35min).
Naha to: Fukuoka (12 daily; 1hr 40min); Hiroshima (1 daily; 1hr 40min); Hong Kong (2 weekly; 3hr 10min); Ishigaki (11 daily; 1hr); Kagoshima (2 daily; 1hr 25min); Kansai International (7 daily; 2hr 10min); Kerama (4–7 daily; 15min); Kōchi (1 daily; 1hr 40min); Kumamoto (1 daily; 1hr 35min); Matsuyama (1 daily; 1hr 35min); Miyako (9–11 daily; 45min); Miyazaki (1 daily; 1hr 35min); Nagasaki (1 daily; 1hr 35min); Nagoya (6 daily; 2hr 30min); Niigata (1 daily; 2hr 40min); Oita (1 daily; 1hr 35min); Okayama (1 daily; 1hr 50min); Sapporo (2 daily; 3hr 35min); Sendai (1 daily; 2hr 55min); Seoul (2 weekly; 2hr 15min); Taipei (2–3 daily; 30min); Takamatsu (1 daily; 1hr 50min); Tokyo (10 daily; 2hr 30min).

10

OKINAWA | Travel details

Contexts

Contexts

History

Thanks largely to its geographical isolation and social cohesion, Japan is among the world's most enduring and stable nations. Though the country has had its share of violent civil wars, coups and one revolution (albeit fairly gentle), Japan has rarely been invaded and never truly colonized. Indeed, according to tradition, it boasts the longest-reigning dynasty in the world, with the present monarch, Emperor Akihito, 125th in an unbroken line stretching back to the first century BC. The reality is, of course, far more complicated.

During the seventeenth century, Japan cut itself off almost completely from outside influence for a period of more than two hundred years. It then did an about-turn, embraced Western technology and in no time possessed one of the world's most powerful economies. Modern Japan initially seems like so many other developed, industrial countries, but scratch the surface and you'll find a society deeply layered in ancient legends and a vibrant history.

The beginnings

It is believed that the Japanese people are descended from immigrants from mainland Asia and possibly Polynesians who moved north along the east Asian coast. This migration is estimated to have taken place over a period prior to 10,000 BC, from when pottery remains have been found. The earliest wave of migrants, known as the **Ainu**, were gradually pushed north by succeeding groups, until today only a few remain in the interior of Hokkaidō (see p.361).

The first migrants lived as fishers and hunters in what is now known as the **Jōmon** era (10,000 BC–300 BC), named after the rope markings on pottery made at that time (see p.962). The **Yayoi** era which followed saw the development of wet-rice cultivation and the use of bronze and iron implements. Then came the **Kofun** era (300 AD–710 AD), whose main legacy is many thousands of burial mounds, mainly in central and western Japan.

It's not surprising that much of this early history is the stuff of myth and legend, first recorded in the **Kojiki**, "Record of Ancient Matters", and the **Nihon-shoki**, "Chronicles of Japan". These are Japan's oldest surviving historical documents, completed in 712 AD and 720 AD respectively. Though they don't always agree, the accounts tell of a land peopled by semi-gods engaged in fabulous adventures. One of these was the sun goddess Amaterasu, from whom all Japan's emperors were once believed to be descended, starting with her great-great-grandson, **Emperor Jimmu**.

The major historical eras

Jōmon	10,000–300 BC	Momoyama	1573–1600
Yayoi	300 BC–300 AD	Edo (or Tokugawa)	1600–1868
Kofun	300–710	Meiji	1868–1912
Nara	710–784	Taishō	1912–1926
Heian	794–1185	Shōwa	1926–1989
Kamakura	1185–1333	Heisei	1989–present day
Muromachi	1333–1573		

According to common belief, Jimmu founded the dynasty about 660 BC and died at well over 100 years of age. Modern historians consider that the legendary figure was in fact based on a successful local chieftain who probably lived about six hundred years later. He is thought to have established his capital at Kashiwabara, between present-day Ōsaka and Nara, and gave the name Yamato to what is now Japan. The country's subsequent political history up to the modern era is the story of the rise and fall of a succession of powerful clans who preserved the monarchy largely as mere figureheads.

Relations with Korea and China

From the earliest days of reliable history, Japan has had close links with **Korea**. Though these were not always amicable – according to the chronicles, Empress Jingō led an invasion force to the peninsula in 200 AD – a significant number of Japan's ruling class are believed to have had Korean connections. It was thus Korean scholars who, in 405, first introduced the **Chinese script** to Japan, which until then had no written language of its own. Then, in 552, the king of Paekche sent an image of Buddha and some Buddhist scriptures to Japan, extolling the virtues of the new belief. By the mid-sixth century the first of Japan's non-imperial ruling dynasties, the Soga clan, had risen to power and taken **Buddhism** to heart. At the same time one of the most revered names of Japanese history appeared on the scene. This was **Prince Shōtoku**, who was installed as heir apparent and regent to Empress Suiko around 592 AD. A zealous Buddhist and great patron of the arts and sciences, Shōtoku also fostered an exchange of scholars with China and Korea, framed a legal code and was responsible for introducing the Chinese calendar.

As the Soga became increasingly arrogant and high-handed during the seventh century, so their power gradually waned. In 645 the Nakatomi clan staged a successful coup, and then, having changed their name to **Fujiwara**, rose to become the most influential and aristocratic family in Japan's history. In the late seventh century, Emperor Mommu chose a Fujiwara lady as his consort, starting a trend that continued until the reign of Emperor Taishō in 1921.

As early as 646, the Fujiwara introduced a series of reforms, the **Taika**, or Great Reforms, reorganizing the government on Chinese lines in order to strengthen the throne. The Chinese system of land tenure and taxation was adopted, and an attempt was made to decentralize the government, though this was hampered by Japan's difficult, mountainous terrain. In 702 further reforms saw the nationalization of land and the founding of a university to teach Chinese history and philosophy. Confucian principles, which espoused filial piety and the subordination of women, were encouraged. For a while it also became the custom to relocate the royal palace after the death of each emperor, until Japan's first permanent capital, **Nara**, was founded in 710.

The Heian Era 794–1185

Nara, however, only survived as the capital until 784, when the Fujiwara decided they needed to escape from the monks and priests who were meddling too much in politics. After a short spell in nearby Nagaoka, the court eventually moved to **Heian-kyō** (Capital of Peace) in 794. Later known as Kyoto, the city remained the official, if not the de facto, capital of Japan until 1869. Thus commenced one of the most stable and long-lasting epochs in Japan's history, an era in which the political influence of the Fujiwara flourished, at least initially, and which saw a blossoming of religion, literature, and other artistic pursuits.

In 760 the **Man'yōshū**, the first great anthology of Japanese poetry, was written in a transliterated form of Chinese. Towards the end of the eighth century Dengyō Daishi, who had spent some years in China, founded the **Tendai sect** of Buddhism, and a few years later, Kōbō Daishi established the **Shingon sect**. According to tradition, it was Kōbō Daishi who developed the simplified *hiragana* syllabary, which Lady Murasaki later used to write the world's first novel, **The Tale of Genji** (see p.1019), some time around 1000 AD. Another work from this period which is still popular today is *The Pillow Book*, a diary of often acid observations on court life by a lady-in-waiting, Sei Shōnagon.

For a while the Fujiwara steadily increased their grip on power. In 866 Fujiwara Yoshifusa was the first person of non-royal blood to be appointed regent, to rule on behalf of the emperor, and his successors held this position virtually continuously for the next three hundred years. The clan's power reached its zenith under **Regent Fujiwara Michinaga**, who held control for thirty years after 967 AD, partly by marrying his daughters to four successive emperors.

The Genpei Wars

During the eleventh century, Buddhist monks were again meddling in secular affairs. The Fujiwaras, whose lives were now dedicated to courtly pursuits, had no option but to invite more militaristic clans, such as the **Minamoto** and **Taira** (also known as the Genji and Heike respectively), to act on their behalf. These clans naturally used the opportunity to advance their own status and thus began the great struggle for power which culminated in the **Genpei Wars** (1180–1185).

The Taira were the first to gain the upper hand, under the leadership of Lord Kiyomori, whose great mistake was to spare the lives of the Minamoto brothers **Yoritomo** and **Yoshitsune**. This pair have achieved an almost legendary status in Japanese history, Yoritomo as the great statesman – despite an unpleasant degree of cruelty and paranoia – and Yoshitsune as the dashing young general. With Yoshitsune commanding the Minamoto fleet, the Taira were finally defeated at the **Battle of Dannoura** (1185), in the straits of Shimonoseki between Honshū and Kyūshū, in one of the most decisive moments of Japanese history.

Dannoura was not to be the end of conflict, however. Yoritomo feared his brother might stage a coup, and this suspicion sparked off a period of internecine strife. A popular story, portrayed in a later Kabuki drama, is that of Yoshitsune defeating a common soldier, Benkei, in single combat. Subsequently Benkei became the most loyal of Yoshitsune's retainers and the two heroes died together near Hiraizumi in 1189, outnumbered by Yoritomo's superior forces.

The Kamakura Era 1185–1333

Yoritomo established his *Bakufu*, or "tent government", at **Kamakura** (near present-day Yokohama), in 1192. The term Tent Government was symbolic of the spartan, military character of the new regime. Yoritomo styled himself Sei-i Tai Shogun, the "Barbarian-subduing Great General", a title which had previously been used on appropriate occasions but which now became permanent. To drive home the martial emphasis of the new government, military governors were appointed to work alongside the civil administrators, and taxes were levied to cover military expenditure. More generally, Japan settled in to a period of **semi-feudalism**, with the peasants being allowed tenure of land in return for service to their local lord.

The Kamakura *Bakufu* did not survive long after the death of Yoritomo in 1199, since his successors lacked his strong character and organizational skills. During the latter part of his administration he had been ably and loyally supported by **Hōjō Tokimasa** who, in partnership with Yoritomo's widow Masa, now took the helm. Tokimasa quickly assumed the combined roles of military and civil governor, ushering in the century-long era of the **Hōjō regents**. By the late thirteenth century, therefore, the government had evolved into a multi-layered entity. A cloistered retired emperor presided over his successor in Kyoto, who had ceded power to the shogun in Kamakura, who in turn had been rendered powerless by the Hōjō regent, who by then had also handed over power to a new generation of front men.

The thirteenth and fourteenth centuries saw the **rise of the merchant class**. Trade and commerce were encouraged by monks travelling to China and Korea, and by a demand for military supplies. The ports of **Hyōgo** (now Kōbe) and **Ōsaka** developed to handle this trade, while towns and markets grew under the patronage of feudal lords and monasteries. On the political front, Regent Yasutoki formulated the **Jōei Code** in 1232, which provided guidelines on behaviour for the samurai class (see box on p.938) as well as rules on land tenure and the maintenance of religious buildings. It was during this period that the class distinctions were demarcated: warriors at the top, then farmers, artisans and, finally, merchants.

This fairly stable state of affairs was shattered in 1268 when the great Mongol leader, **Kublai Khan**, sent six envoys to demand that Japan pay tribute to China. Japan's rejection provoked the Khan to invade in 1274, when the **Mongol army** landed at Hakata (north Kyūshū) but had to withdraw when a storm threatened their fleet. After the Japanese executed further envoys, in 1281 the Khan dispatched a huge punitive expedition, believed to number about 100,000 men. The invaders gained a foothold and fought fiercely for seven weeks, but their fleet was again scattered by a typhoon. The grateful Japanese dubbed it the **kamikaze**, or "Divine Wind", a name which later reappeared during the Pacific War (see p.942).

The Muromachi Era 1333–1573

The demands of war, a generally deteriorating economy and an ineffectual government eventually led to the collapse of the Hōjō in 1333. This coincided with the accession to the throne of the **emperor Go-Daigo**, who, being older than earlier incumbents, was less easy to manipulate. After Go-Daigo's commander defeated the Hōjō, the Kamakura *Bakufu* dispatched **Ashikaga Takauji** to bring Go-Daigo to heel. Seeing his chance to seize power, the wily Takauji switched allegiance to the emperor. When Go-Daigo uncovered Takauji's plot, the two sides clashed briefly before the emperor was forced to retreat to the mountains of Yoshino. Takauji set up a rival emperor in Kyoto and for sixty years Japan had two courts, until they were reconciled in 1392. By this time, the **Ashikaga Shogunate** had established its headquarters in Kyoto's **Muromachi** district, from where they ruled for more than two centuries.

Over the years, the Ashikaga, too, began to lose their grip on power. The shoguns and their retinues were inclined to lives of extravagance. It was during this period that **Kinkaku-ji** and **Ginkaku-ji** (Kyoto's Gold and Silver pavilions) were built, while the decorative arts reached new heights of perfection and Nō theatre was developed. The result of such profligacy was, predictably, increasing exactions on the peasants, and a spate of **peasant revolts**. At the same time, local power bases were re-consolidating, so that by the end of the fifteenth century virtually all central authority had disappeared. In the absence of a strong government, festering inter-clan enmities culminated in the **Ōnin Wars** (1467–78), which took place mainly in and around Kyoto. These marked the start of a period of civil wars which lasted until the early seventeenth century.

In 1549, towards the end of the Muromachi era, the Portuguese missionary **Saint Francis Xavier** arrived on the shores of Kyūshū. Initially the **Christian** newcomers were treated with tolerance, partly out of curiosity, but mainly because they carried valuable new technology. Not surprisingly in a country embroiled in civil war, the Europeans' **firearms** attracted much envious attention. Japan's warlords were quick to master the new weapons and eventually developed tactical use of massed musketry unsurpassed even in Europe.

At the same time, this eastward advancement of the Europeans was counteracted by explorations to the west by **Japanese seafarers**, many of whom were privateers, if not actually pirates. They reached as far as the Indian Ocean, and it is one of the interesting conundrums of history as to what would have happened if these adventurers had not been recalled by the somewhat paranoid Tokugawa regime.

Reunification

The civil wars ended with the **reunification of Japan** under a triumvirate of generals of outstanding ability. The first, **Oda Nobunaga**, had the initial advantage of hailing from Owari, one of Japan's strategically placed central districts. Having achieved dominance of the Kyoto region, however, he was promptly assassinated. His successor was **Toyotomi Hideyoshi**, who had risen from obscurity to be one of Nobunaga's most trusted generals. Hideyoshi avenged Nobunaga's death and managed to outmanoeuvre all rivals with a shrewd mix of force and diplomacy. Success went to his head, however, and he embarked on costly excursions into Korea, which eventually had to be abandoned.

Shortly before his death in 1598, Hideyoshi persuaded **Tokugawa Ieyasu**, now an ally after a period of circumspect confrontation, to support the succession of his son **Hideyori**. This trust was misplaced. After defeating the remaining western clans at the **Battle of Sekigahara** in 1600, the ambitious Ieyasu decided to seize power, and sacked Ōsaka castle, Hideyori's stronghold, in 1615. The western clans retreated to their fiefdoms to brood on their grievances for the next 250 years, when they emerged to exact a sort of revenge against the Tokugawa Shogunate (see p.938).

The rise and fall of the samurai

The origins of the **samurai**, Japan's warrior caste, go back to the ninth century, when the feudal lords began to maintain regular forces. Gradually, they evolved into an elite group of hereditary warriors, their lives governed by an unwritten code of behaviour which came to be known as *bushidō*, **the way of the warrior**. Though practice was often far from the ideal, *bushidō* encouraged rigorous self-discipline, the observance of strict laws of etiquette and, most importantly, unquestioning loyalty.

According to this code, the samurai, his wife and children were expected to die willingly to protect the life and honour of their feudal lord. If they failed in this duty, or were about to be taken prisoner on a battlefield, then suicide was the only fitting response. The traditional, and excruciatingly painful, method of **ritual suicide** was disembowelment with a sword or dagger (*seppuku*), though in later years an accomplice would stand by to cut off the victim's head. However, there were many variations on the theme; one particularly gruesome legend tells of a warrior who had himself buried alive, in full armour, astride his poor horse.

The samurai creed reached full bloom in the early Tokugawa era (see below), when class distinctions were officially delineated. The samurai were deemed "the masters of the four classes" – above farmers, artisans and merchants – and they alone were permitted to carry swords. They even had the right to kill any member of the lower orders for disrespectful behaviour, real or imagined. This privilege was graphically known as *kirisute-gomen*, literally "cut, throw away, pardon".

During the more peaceful seventeenth and eighteenth centuries, many samurai found themselves out of work as their lords were dispossessed and fiefdoms redistributed. Many became **rōnin**, or masterless samurai, whose lives were romanticized in such films as *The Seven Samurai* (see p.992). Among the most celebrated were the 47 *rōnin* (see p.157) and an individual called Musashi, who reputedly prevailed in 66 sword fights, several against heavy odds, and then went to live in a cave since there was no one else worthy of the challenge.

As their fighting skills were no longer required, the samurai grew increasingly impoverished and demoralized. Some found alternative ways to earn a living, while others were encouraged to study and later proved invaluable administrators in the post-1868 Meiji administration. At the same time the government formally abolished the **samurai** system, and only allowed members of the new imperial army to wear swords. All this was too much for some of the old guard, the most famous of which was Saigō Takamori. A larger-than-life hero, Saigō led a rebellion against the Meiji government in 1877 (see p.940) and died on the battlefield in true samurai spirit, fighting to the end against desperate odds.

The Tokugawa Shogunate 1600–1868

Ieyasu established his administrative capital at **Edo**, now Tokyo, and set about guaranteeing the security of the **Tokugawa Shogunate**. The three Tokugawa-related clans were given estates in the most strategically important areas, followed by the lords who had fought on the Tokugawa side. Last came the "outside lords", whose loyalty was questionable; they were allocated fiefdoms in the remotest regions. To keep all these *daimyō* in check they were required to reside part of the year in Edo, thus forcing them into expensive, time-consuming journeys, and to surrender family hostages who lived permanently under the eyes of the authorities in Edo Castle. A sophisticated network of inspectors and spies was set up, and any significant rebuilding of local castles had to be reported.

In its early years, the Tokugawa Shogunate exhibited a high degree of ambivalence towards the European arrivals. As **Christianity** increasingly appeared to threaten state security, more and more strictures were placed on all foreigners and harsh **persecutions** were conducted against the missionaries and Christian converts. By 1638, the year of final exclusion of foreigners, an estimated 250,000 Japanese Christians had been executed, imprisoned or forced to apostatize. The final stand took place in 1637 at **Shimabara**, near Nagasaki, when a Christian-led rebel army was annihilated (see box, p.824). Thus began the period of *sakoku*, or the **closed country**, which lasted more or less continuously until 1853. The only legitimate exceptions to the edicts were Korean diplomats and a handful of Dutch and Chinese traders allowed to operate out of Nagasaki.

The long period of stability under the Tokugawa, interrupted only by a few peasant rebellions, brought steady **economic development**. Several towns grew to a considerable size, and by the late eighteenth century Edo had become the world's largest city, with a population of roughly one million. The arts also flourished, especially during the Genroku Period (1688–1703), which saw the first mention of *ukiyo*, the "**floating world**" of fleeting pleasures. Artists churned out **woodblock prints** (*ukiyo-e*) popularizing the puppet plays of Chikamatsu (see p.971) and novels of Saikaku; **Hokusai** alone is said to have produced 35,000 paintings and illustrated 437 volumes (see p.968).

A chink in the door

During Japan's period of seclusion, a small number of Westerners managed to breach the barriers. Of these, perhaps the most famous were two academics: **Kaempfer**, a Dutchman who wrote the first European-language history of Japan in the late seventeenth century, and the German physician **Siebold** who arrived in 1823. Somewhat surprisingly, Japan also became briefly embroiled in the Napoleonic Wars, when Captain Pellew of the British Royal Navy pursued two Dutch merchantmen, then the enemy, into Nagasaki harbour in 1808. Various British survey vessels and Russian envoys also visited Japan in the early nineteenth century, but the greatest pressure came from the **US**, whose trading and whaling routes passed to the south of the country.

The American government's initial aim was merely to secure victualling stations and guaranteed protection for shipwrecked sailors. With this in mind, **Commodore Matthew Perry** was sent with a small fleet to persuade the Japanese to open at least some ports to foreigners. On his first visit in 1853 he outlined his requirements and promised he would return after the authorities had been given due time to consider them. He also made it clear that refusal was not an option.

His visit threw Japan into turmoil. The shogunate was already fearful of foreign incursions following the British defeat of China in the Opium Wars. Lines were quickly drawn between those for and against acceding to Perry's demands, while the weakness of the shogunate was thrown into clear relief when the emperor demanded that the foreigners be rebuffed – Japan's military was no longer up to the task.

There followed a decade of jockeying for power between the Japanese factions, and for influence by the foreign envoys. The first of these was the American **Townsend Harris** (see p.233), who managed to extract concessions in the form of the pioneering **Treaty of Commerce and Navigation** in 1858. This was followed by a flurry of similar agreements with other Western countries, which were known locally as the "**unequal treaties**". They opened the **treaty ports** of Yokohama, Hakodate, Nagasaki and, later, Kōbe and Ōsaka to trade, forbade the Japanese to impose protective tariffs and allowed foreigners the right of residence and certain judicial rights in the enclaves. Opponents of such shameful appeasement by the shogunate took up the slogan "Revere the emperor! Expel the barbarians!". Other, less reactionary factions could see that Japan was in no state to do this, and their only hope of remaining independent was to learn from the more powerful nations.

During the 1860s there were several murderous attacks on foreign residents, but these paled into insignificance compared to the opposing forces now gathering among the Japanese factions. The great **western clans**, the Satsuma, Chōshū, Tosa and Hizen, lately at each other's throats, combined under the banner of the **emperor** to exact revenge against the Tokugawa, whom they had seen as usurpers of the throne ever since Sekigahara (see p.937). Evidence of the shift in power came in 1863 when the emperor ordered Shogun Iemochi to Kyoto to explain his conciliatory actions – it was the first visit by a shogun to the imperial capital since 1634. To add to the humiliation, he could muster a mere 3,000 retainers, compared with the 300,000 who accompanied Ieyasu to Kyoto on that earlier occasion.

In 1866, seeing the writing on the wall, the fifteenth and final shogun, **Tokugawa Yoshinobu**, formally applied to the emperor to have imperial power restored, and in January 1867 the shogunate was terminated. In December of the same year the **Imperial Restoration** was formally proclaimed and the fifteen-year-old Mutsuhito acceded to the throne, ushering in a period optimistically dubbed **Meiji** or "enlightened rule". In 1869, the young emperor shifted his court from Kyoto to Edo, and renamed it **Tokyo** (Eastern Capital), the first official, administrative and commercial capital of Japan.

The Meiji Era 1868–1912

The reign of **Emperor Meiji**, as Mutsuhito was posthumously known, saw vast changes taking place in Japan. A policy of **modernization**, termed *fukoku kyōhei* (enrich the country, strengthen the military), was adopted. Railways were built, compulsory education and military service introduced, the solar calendar adopted and the feudal fiefs and the class system abolished. Such rapid changes were bound to create resistance and in 1877, **Saigō Takamori**, a hero of the restoration, led an army of 40,000 in the **Satsuma Rebellion**, named after the area of Kyūshū in which it erupted (see p.850).

In the 1880s, even more changes were rubber-stamped by the ruling oligarchy of Meiji Restoration leaders, who imported thousands of foreign advisers (*yatoi*) for assistance. As a craze for Japanese *objets d'art* swept Europe, Western architecture, fashions, food (such as beef, referred to as "mountain whale") and pastimes were *de rigueur* in Japan. But as Japan adopted a Western-style constitution in 1889, drawn up by the emperor's trusted adviser **Itō Hirobumi**, the seeds of the country's later troubles were being sown.

The **Meiji Constitution**, modelled after Germany's, created a weak parliament (the Diet), the lower house of which less than twenty percent of the population were entitled to vote for. In effect the oligarchy, and in particular the military, was still in charge, a situation enforced with the Imperial Rescript on Education in 1890, which enshrined almost as law loyalty to the emperor, family and state. Shinto, which emphasized emperor-worship, became the state religion, while Buddhism, associated too closely with the previous order, was disestablished.

Having taken their lead from the West in terms of material change, Japan's rulers began to copy their territorial ambitions. The island of Hokkaidō, previously left pretty much to the native Ainu, was actively colonized, partly to ward off a rival takeover by Russia. Territorial spats with the ailing empire of China developed into the **Sino-Japanese War** in 1894, over the Chinese tributary state of Korea. The fighting lasted less than a year, with a treaty being signed in Shimonoseki in 1895 which granted Korea independence, and indemnities, economic concessions and territory to Japan, including Taiwan, then called Formosa.

This unexpected victory brought Japan into conflict with the colony-hungry Western powers, and in particular Russia who had her eye on China's Liaodong peninsula for a naval base at Port Arthur. After cordial relations with Britain were cemented in the 1902 Anglo-Japanese Alliance, Japan felt bold enough to launch her navy on a successful rout of the Russian fleet in February 1904. The land battles of the **Russo-Japanese War** were less decisive, but in a US-mediated treaty in September 1905, Russia was forced to make many territorial concessions to Japan.

In 1909, the assassination of Itō Hirobumi, the newly appointed "resident general" of Korea, gave Japan the excuse it was seeking to fully annexe the country the following year. With the military in control, and a plot against the emperor's life uncovered in 1911, any domestic left-wing dissent was quashed. Meanwhile, the Western powers' admiration of plucky Japan tempered any qualms they might have had about its increasingly aggressive territorial behaviour.

The Taishō Era 1912–1926

The sudden death of Emperor Meiji in 1912 ushered in the relatively brief **Taishō** (Great Righteousness) **era**. Meiji's son Yoshihito, the only surviving male out of his fourteen children, suffered hereditary mental illness and by 1921 was so incapacitated that his own son Hirohito was declared regent.

Britain had sent 500 sailors from the Royal Navy to march in Emperor Meiji's funeral parade, and when **World War I** broke out two years later, this was the country Japan chose to ally itself with. Despite gaining more territory in Asia after the war and being one of the "Big Five" at the Paris Peace Conference and a founder member of the League of Nations in 1920, Japan was frustrated by Australia, Britain and the US in its attempts to get a declaration of racial equality inserted as part of the Charter of the League.

This snub didn't stand in the way of continued friendly relations between Japan and the West, though. In 1921 Crown Prince Hirohito was a guest of King George V at Buckingham Palace, while the following year the Prince of Wales spent a month touring Japan.

In many ways, the Roaring Twenties were no different in Japan (at least in the cities) than anywhere else in the industrialized world. Jazz, Marxism, modern arts and café society all caught on. Levelling Yokohama and much of Tokyo, and leaving 140,000 dead or missing, the 1923 **Great Kantō Earthquake** was a significant blow, but the country was quickly back on its feet and celebrating the inauguration of **Emperor Hirohito** in 1926, who chose the name **Shōwa** (Enlightened Peace) for his reign.

The slide to war

Sadly, peace is the last thing that Hirohito's reign is remembered for. Economic and political turmoil in the early 1930s provided the military with the opportunity it needed to seize full control. Japan's politicians stood by helplessly during the **Manchurian Incident** of 1931, when army officers unilaterally cooked up an excuse for attacking and occupying the Manchurian region of northern China. Japan installed **P'u Yi**, the last emperor of China's Manchu dynasty, as the head of their puppet state, Manchukuo, and responded to Western condemnation of its actions by pulling out of the League of Nations.

At home, the military increased its grip on power in the wake of **assassinations** in 1932 of both the finance and prime ministers, and a confused, short-lived **coup** by 1400 dissident army officers in February 1936. At the same time, **rapid industrialization** was laying the foundations for some of the most famous Japanese firms of the twentieth century, including the automobile makers Mazda, Toyota and Nissan, the film company Fuji and the electronics giant Matsushita.

In 1936, Japan nailed its colours to the mast by joining with Nazi Germany and Fascist Italy in the **Anti-Comintern Pact**, and the following year launched a full-scale invasion of China. In December 1937, the infamous **Rape of Nanking** occurred when appalling atrocities and massacres were committed against hundreds of thousands of unarmed Chinese soldiers and civilians.

As **World War II** began in Europe, Japan initially held off attacking Allied colonies in the Far East, but when France and Holland fell to Germany their qualms disappeared. Sanctions were imposed by Britain and the US as Japan's army moved into Indo-China, threatening Malaya and the East Indies. War between the Allies and Japan was becoming inevitable.

The Pacific War

On December 7, 1941, the Japanese launched a surprise attack on the US naval base at Hawaii's **Pearl Harbor**, starting the **Pacific War**. In rapid succession, the Philippines, Indonesia, Malaya and Burma fell to the seemingly unstoppable Japanese forces. However, the tide was stemmed in New Guinea and, in June 1942, the US Navy won a decisive victory at the **Battle of Midway** by sinking four Japanese aircraft carriers.

Although Japan had launched her campaign to secure the "Greater East Asia Co-Prosperity Sphere", in which she would free her neighbours from colonization and help them develop like the West, the brutal, racist and exploitative reality of Japanese occupation meant there was no support from these potential Southeast Asian allies. Nor was there a likelihood of military cooperation between Japan and Germany, who both eyed each other suspiciously despite their pact.

By 1944, with the US capture of the Pacific island of Saipan, Japan was clearly heading for **defeat**. The country was now within range of US heavy bombers, but there was a determination to fight to the bitter end, as exemplified by suicidal kamikaze pilots (see p.861) and the defending forces on the islands of Iwō-jima and Okinawa who fought to the last man.

In March 1945, Tokyo was in ashes and 100,000 were dead following three days of fire bombings. The government insisted that the emperor system remain inviolate when they put down arms, but no such assurances were offered in July 1945 when the Allies called for Japan's unconditional surrender in the Potsdam Declaration. Japan failed to respond, providing the Allies with the excuse they needed to drop the **Atomic bomb** on **Hirōshima** on August 6. Two days later, the USSR declared war on Japan, while the next day, the second A-bomb exploded over **Nagasaki**.

With millions homeless and starving, and the country brought to its knees, it was a breathtaking understatement for Emperor Hirohito to broadcast, on August 15, 1945, that the war had "developed not necessarily to Japan's advantage". For his subjects, gathered at wireless sets around the country, the realization of defeat was tempered by their amazement at hearing, for the first time, the voice of a living god.

The American occupation 1945–1952

Having never lost a war, let alone been occupied, Japan little knew what to expect from the arrival of the "American Shogun" **General Douglas MacArthur**, designated the Supreme Commander of the Allied Forces (SCAP). Some 500 soldiers committed suicide, but for the rest of the population the **Occupation** was a welcome relief from the privations of war and an opportunity to start again.

MacArthur wasted no time in instituting **political and social reform**. The country was demilitarized, the bureaucracy purged of military supporters and war trials held, resulting in seven hangings, including that of the ex-prime minister, Tōjō Hideki. The emperor, whose support for the new regime was seen as crucial, was spared although he had to publicly renounce his divinity to become a symbolic head of state.

In 1946, the Americans took a week to draft a **new constitution**, which, ironically, proclaimed that sovereignty resided in the Japanese people, and contained the unique provision renouncing war and "the threat or use of force as a means of settling international disputes". Land and educational reform followed.

The **peace treaty** signed in San Francisco on September 8, 1951, resolved all issues with the Allies, leaving only the USSR as a threatening communist force. The outbreak of the **Korean War** in 1950 gave a further boost to Japan's economy as the country became the main supplier of food and arms for the US forces.

The Occupation officially ended on April 28, 1952, but with the Korean War continuing and the **Treaty of Mutual Cooperation and Security** guaranteeing the US the right to maintain bases on Japanese soil, a strong American presence remained for many years to come. The island of Okinawa was, in fact, only returned to Japan in 1972.

The 1960s economic miracle

In 1955, in the face of rising left-wing antagonism to the continued security pact with the US, America's CIA provided funding for the right-wing Liberal and Democrat parties to join forces. The **Liberal Democratic Party** (LDP), a tight coalition of power-hungry factions, governed Japan uninterrupted for close on the next forty years, creating the stable political conditions for an incredible economic recovery. The term **Japan Inc** was coined for the close cooperation that developed between government, bureaucracy and business, with the civil service bodies such as the Ministry for International Trade and Industry (MITI) calling many of the shots.

In 1959, **Crown Prince Akihito** married Shōda Michiko, a commoner he had met on the tennis courts of the summer resort Karuizawa, a far cry from the marriage of his own father, arranged by the court without Hirohito even setting eyes on his prospective bride. As the decade closed, the economy had grown at twice the rate expected, and during the 1960s, under a ten-year plan drawn up by **Prime Minister Ikeda Hayato**, it continued to boom. A key year was 1964: Japan joined the rich nations "club", the Organization for Economic Cooperation and Development, inaugurated the high-speed bullet train and hosted the Summer Olympic Games.

During this time Japanese **exports** grew twice as fast as world trade, an incredible reversal of events for a country whose products, only a couple of decades earlier, had been the last word in unreliability. At the same time, Japan protected its home markets by subjecting imports to quotas, a mass of regulations or outright bans. However, there was a price to pay for this economic miracle. Not only did rapid industrialization physically scar the country, but **pollution** wrecked lives. In 1971, Tokyo's metropolitan government officially declared that the capital's residents breathed polluted air, drank contaminated water and were "subjected to noise levels that strain the nerves".

By the 1970s, the ingrained **corruption** festering at the heart of Japanese politics was also becoming clear. The conservative LDP had continued to hold power partly by astutely hijacking its rivals' policies, but mainly by entering into cosy financial relationships with supporters in industry and commerce. Prime Minister **Tanaka Kakuei**, a self-made politician from Niigata, had already attracted criticism for pushing through the needless construction of a Shinkansen line to his home town, when his abuse of party funds in the Upper House elections of July 1974 caused fellow LDP grandees to quit the Cabinet in protest. Takeda rode the scandal out, but couldn't survive the bribery charges, brought in February 1976, in connection with the purchase of aircraft from America's Lockheed Corporation.

The bubble economy

Attention was swiftly diverted from other problems, however, by the **Middle East oil embargo** of 1973. Three-quarters of Japan's energy needs were met by imported fuel, so the overnight quadrupling of oil prices was a severe shock to the country, which rapidly had to introduce measures to tackle inflation, reduce energy consumption and stem growth. The economy suffered, but, as ever, Japan learnt lessons, improved its processes and emerged in the next decade fitter and more vigorous than ever.

A buzzword of the booming 1980s was **kokusaika** (internationalization), even if nobody seemed to know quite what it meant. Yet, at the same time as the Japanese were being urged to take a global view, the world was increasingly complaining about Japan's insular ways. The country's huge **balance of payments surplus** and restrictive trade practices set it at odds with the international community, and particularly the US. The tense situation wasn't eased as cash-rich Japanese companies snapped up American firms and assets, such as the Rockefeller Center in New York, and the trade surplus with the US totalled over $30 billion.

This overseas spending spree was made possible by what would later be known as the **bubble economy** – a period when low interest rates fuelled booming land prices and a runaway stock market. Construction, long the bedrock of the economy, continued apace, with skyscrapers shooting up across the country along with mammoth engineering projects, such as the Seto Ōhashi, the bridge linking the main island of Honshū with Shikoku.

Despite the factional infighting and jockeying for power that continued within the LDP, the party clung on to power by providing voters with a continually rising standard of living and because of weak opposition parties. The country, however, ran through a succession of **scandal-prone prime ministers**, who slipped quickly in and out of office in the wake of bribery allegations and sexual shenanigans.

The 1980s weren't all about conspicuous domestic consumption, however. By the time of the death of Emperor Hirohito in January 1989, Japan was the world's second largest donor of **overseas aid**. But as the Shōwa era came to an end, ushering in the **Heisei** (Accomplished Peace) **era**, the omens for the country were far from auspicious as the overheated bubble economy reached bursting point.

The 1990s: the bubble bursts

The 1990s kicked off with the coronation of Emperor Akihito and a political crisis surrounding the **Gulf War**. Japan was under pressure to send its Self Defence Forces (SDF) overseas, something expressly forbidden by the constitution. As a member of the United Nations and an aspirant for a seat on the Security Council, Japan knew it had to respond to the international call to arms. The compromise of $17.3 billion in financial aid satisfied no one, not least the more hawkish factions of the splintering LDP. In 1992, after protracted debate and amid public demonstrations, the Diet passed a controversial bill allowing Japanese troops to join **UN peacekeeping missions** abroad.

The main reason for continued squeamishness about an overseas military role is the haunting presence of Japan's actions during World War II. The San Francisco treaty did little to satisfy those who had experienced first-hand brutal treatment by the Japanese army during the war, not least the former colonies in Southeast Asia. Old wounds were reopened as the covered-up issue of forced prostitution, or "comfort women", as they were euphemistically dubbed, was blasted across the media in the early 1990s.

Some light relief was supplied in 1993 when Crown Prince Naruhito married Owada Masako, a high-flying career diplomat. But even this happy occasion was marred for some by the fact that Owada, a shining symbol of improved opportunities for women in what remains a highly male-dominated country, appeared to have been pressured into the deeply conservative role of empress-in-waiting.

Despite a growing recognition that the boom years were well and truly over, the mass of the population continued to enjoy the affluent good life. Particularly noticeable were Princess Masako's less fettered contemporaries, the army of **office ladies** (OLs), who with their spending power kick-started many a fashion fad, from a taste for the Italian sweet tiramisu to the G-string panties favoured by podium dancers at mega-discos, such as Tokyo's *Julianna's*.

As the recession gripped and fashions changed, it also seemed that the days of the ruling LDP were finally numbered. Rival LDP factions made independent bids for power rather than brokering yet more deals in smoke-filled rooms. Leading the most influential faction was **Ozawa Ichirō**, one of Japan's powerful politicians, either loathed or loved for his outspoken views and radical policies. A successful no-confidence motion in June 1993 forced Prime Minister Miyazawa Kiichi's shaky government into a hasty **general election**. Although the LDP actually gained one seat, the overall balance of power passed to a coalition of opposition parties, who formed the first non-LDP government in 38 years under leadership of the populist, reforming politician **Hosokawa Morihiro**.

However, hopes of a new beginning for Japanese politics faded as the charismatic Hosokawa, who had stood on an anti-corruption ticket and had relied on Ozawa's support to become prime minister, lasted less than a year. A plan to double the hated consumption tax went down like a lead balloon, and when a story broke about Hosokawa's chequered past with regard to election funding, it was clear he had to go. His successor **Hata Tsutomu**, another ally of Ozawa, saw the Socialists walk out on the coalition on his first day of office, and his premiership went down in history as the shortest since World War II, at just two months.

The Socialists, already decimated in numbers at the last election, did themselves no favours by siding with their old foes, the LDP, to form the next government. This cynical alliance put the LDP back in the control seat, just over a year since it had lost power and forced new premier **Murayama Tomiichi**, a Socialist elder statesman, to have his party drop long-held pacifist policies (much to the disgust of voters).

The political paralysis at the heart of the LDP/Socialist coalition became all too apparent in the sluggish response to the massive **Great Hanshin Earthquake** of January 1995, which devastated Kōbe. Immediate offers of foreign help were rebuffed and the local *yakuza* further shamed the government by organizing food supplies to the thousands of homeless. The nation's self-confidence took a further battering less than a couple of months later when members of a religious cult, **AUM Shinrikyō** (see box opposite), killed 12 and poisoned 5500 when they released sarin nerve gas on the Tokyo subway. Japan went into introspective shock.

In 1996, the LDP returned to full power, under the leadership of former tough-talking trade negotiator **Hashimoto Ryūtarō**, but economic woes continued. No longer were Japan's government and bureaucrats willing – or able – to support enterprises with billions of yen of bad debts spawned by the dubious financial practices of the previous decade. The dead hand of the market had finally caught up with Japan, and the one-time wonder economy that had been the envy of the world appeared on the brink of collapse.

AUM and the sarin gas attack

On March 20, 1995, members of the New Age cult **AUM Shinrikyō** planted bags of the deadly nerve gas sarin on the Tokyo subway. Twelve people died and 5500 others were injured in Japan's worst terrorist attack. In what has been one of Japan's longest trials ever, 11 of the cult's key figures have been sentenced to death, including supreme leader, **Asahara Shōkō.**

Born Matsumoto Chizuo, the virtually blind guru began the "Supreme Truth" cult in the late 1980s – a period dubbed "rush hour of the gods" because of the proliferation of new religions in Japan at the time. At its height in the early 1990s, AUM had 40,000 members in several countries and nearly a billion dollars in assets, earned from, among other things, one-million-yen fees for rituals involving potions made of Asahara's dirty bathwater (called Miracle Pond), his blood, and even his beard clippings.

When AUM failed to get its members elected to the Diet in 1990, Asahara began to use his wealth and power for far more sinister aims. Suspicion had long been mounting against AUM before the tragic events of March 1995, but even after the Tokyo attack it took the authorities two months to arrest the elusive Asahara. In the meantime, the National Police Agency chief was the victim of an attempted assassination, in broad daylight, by an AUM member who escaped on a bicycle. Most of AUM's top dogs were eventually arrested, several immediately confessing their part in the terrorist attack. When the cult's compound near Mount Fuji was raided, a vast arsenal of weapons and chemicals was discovered, as well as Asahara calmly meditating in his pyjamas.

Asahara pleaded not guilty. He never testified and didn't even speak during the eight-year trial except to make a few incoherent, babbling statements – no one is the wiser as to why he ordered the sarin attack now than they were in 1995. Most alarmingly, AUM, now renamed **Aleph**, has survived and continues to grow, its membership being around 1600.

C

CONTEXTS | History

Into the millennium

The official announcement of **recession** in June 1998, coupled with the plummeting value of the yen and rising unemployment, saw the LDP take a drubbing in the August 1998 upper-house **elections**. Hashimoto resigned and was replaced by the genial but lacklustre **Obuchi Keizō**. In July 1999, the Buddhist-backed **Kōmeitō** party joined the LDP right-wing coalition, somewhat undermining its aim to purify Japan's corrupt political system. A major **nuclear accident** in September (see "Environmental Issues", p.987) caused pause for thought, but no cancellation of Japan's increased reliance on this form of energy.

In April 2000, Prime Minister Obuchi suffered a major stroke, dying on May 14 without recovering consciousness. Major bankruptcies continued, with department-store chain Sogō going under with almost ¥2 trillion in debts in July. There were natural disasters aplenty, too, with volcanic eruptions and earthquakes at Mount Usu in Hokkaidō and on the Ogasawara Islands, 200km south of Tokyo, causing thousands to be evacuated.

In April 2001, the gaff-prone and much disliked Prime Minister Mori Yoshiro was replaced by the reform-minded **Koizumi Junichiro**. In December, after many years of trying, Crown Princess Masako and Crown Prince Naruhito gave birth to a baby girl **Princess Akiko**. Although the population were overjoyed at this happy event, it is causing Japan's courtiers and politicians to examine carefully the current rules that allow only a male to become emperor (see box on p.112).

With a highly popular, reform-minded prime minister in place and the economy finally showing some signs of recovery, **Japanese–Korean relations** also took a turn for the better with the countries' successful joint hosting of the 2002 **FIFA World Cup**. However, the diplomatic situation turned nasty again later in the year when it was confirmed, after decades of denials, that North Korea had abducted thirteen Japanese citizens in the 1970s and 1980s and forced them to train North Korean spies in Japanese language and culture.

Initially a phenomenally popular politician, Koizumi's sheen has dimmed over the last few years due to his inability to push through necessary structural changes in the economy. He led the LDP to victory in the November 2003 general elections, but the party lost much ground to the Democratic Party of Japan, causing commentators to hail the results as a political watershed. After decades of one-party rule, Japan now has a true **two-party system**.

Religion, belief and ritual

The indigenous religion of Japan is Shinto, and all Japanese people belong to it by default. From a population of roughly 126 million, 96 million people are also Buddhist and around 1.5 million Christian. The idea of combining religions may seem strange, but a mixture of philosophy, politics and a bit of creative interpretation has, over time, enabled this to happen.

The most important factor that allowed faiths to combine is that Shinto, a naturalistic religion, does not possess one all-powerful deity, sacred scriptures or a particular philosophy or moral code. It holds that its followers must live their lives according to the way or mind of the **kami** (gods), and that the *kami* favour harmony and cooperation. Therefore, Shinto tolerates its worshippers following other religions, and they find it an easy step to combine Shinto's nature worship with the worship of an almighty deity, such as that in Christianity, or with the philosophical moral code of Buddhism.

According to Shinto, the relationship between people and their tutelary *kami* is like that between parent and child. Generations have been born and lived under the protection of the *kami*. When they die, the Japanese become *kami*, so not only are their ancestors *kami*, but they themselves will become so, creating, in theory, an inherent and unbreakable relationship down the generations.

Festivals are a common sight in Japan and many Shinto customs are still manifest in everyday life, from marriage ceremonies to purifying building plots and new cars. Nevertheless, few Japanese today are aware of anything other than the basic tenets of either Shinto or Buddhism and many would not consider themselves "religious" as such. Instead, Shinto and Buddhist ideas are so deeply

The birth of Japan

Japan's mythological origins could have come from the pen of J.R.R. Tolkien. According to the oldest written records, the *Kojiki* and the *Nihon-shoki*, the god Izanagi-no-Mikoto and goddess Izanami-no-Mikoto leant down from the Floating Bridge of Heaven and stirred the ocean with a jewelled spear. Drops of brine falling from the spear created the first island of Japan, Onogoro-jima, where the couple gave birth to an "eight-island country", complete with *kami*. Amaterasu, the sun goddess and ultimate ancestress of the imperial family, was created out of a bronze mirror held in Izanagi's left hand and sent to rule the heavens. Her younger brother, Susanoo, was put in charge of the earth. Unhappy with this situation, he started causing turmoil in the heavens, and so upset Amaterasu that she hid herself in a celestial cave, plunging the world into darkness.

The other gods banished Susanoo to the underworld. Then, in an effort to coax Amaterasu out of the cave, they performed a comical dance involving a spear. Upon hearing the somewhat ribald laughter, Amaterasu's curiosity got the better of her and she poked her head out to see the fun. Enticed out a little further by a beautiful jewel, Amaterasu was then captivated by a bronze mirror. While she was preoccupied, the gods quickly sealed the cave entrance and sunlight returned to the world.

In time, Amaterasu's grandson, Ninigi, was sent down to rule Japan. She gave him three gifts which were to be his imperial regalia: a bronze mirror, a sword and a curved jewel. Here myth finally merges into proto-history, when Jimmu, said to be Ninigi's great grandson, became the first emperor of Japan on the first day of spring 660 BC.

ingrained in everyday life that, in general, there is little sense of conscious involvement. This means that, while many people do not practise any faith on a daily basis, they find it quite natural to pray at a shrine or temple during annual festivals or on a sightseeing trip. And, as elsewhere, people tend to become more involved in religion, particularly Buddhism, during their later years.

Shinto

Shinto, or "the way of the gods", only received its name in the sixth century to distinguish it from the newly arrived Buddhism. Gods are felt to be present in natural phenomena, for example mountains, trees, waterfalls, strangely shaped rocks, even in sounds. But Shinto is more than just a nature-worshipping faith; it is an amalgam of attitudes, ideas and ways of doing things that for more than 2000 years has become an integral part of what it is to be Japanese. Shinto is a personal faith in the *kami*, a communal way of life in accordance with the mind of the *kami* and a spiritual life attained through worship of and communion with the *kami*. People are believed to be the children of both their parents and *kami* and therefore owe their lives to both society and nature. In return for the love and protection they receive, they are obliged to treat both of them with loyalty and honesty, and to continue the family line showing kindness and guidance to their descendants.

Throughout most of Japanese history, Shinto did not play a particularly important role in state politics. This all changed, however, after the Meiji Restoration of 1868 when Shinto was revived as the dominant religion, largely to re-establish the cult of the emperor, while Buddhism was suppressed. Thus started the most sinister episode of Japan's religious and political life: **State Shinto**.

State Shinto ushered in a period of **extreme nationalism** which lasted from around 1890 to 1945. During this period, Japan's mythological origins (see box on p.949) were taught as historical fact and people were encouraged to believe that all Japanese were descended from the imperial line. At the same time, the traditional values of loyalty, inner strength and self-denial expressed in *bushidō* (the way of the warrior) were promoted as desirable personal qualities. Such sentiments were milked by the 1930s military regime to foster a national sense of superiority. Ultimately, this potent cocktail created a highly dedicated nation on the eve of World War II. After the war, Emperor Hirohito was forced to renounce his divinity, to become a merely titular head of state, and the State branch of Shinto was abolished.

Shinto shrines

Shinto shrines are called **jinja** (*kami*-dwelling), although you will also see the suffixes *-jingū* and *-gū*. These terms, and the *torii* gates (see opposite), are the easiest ways to distinguish between Shinto shrines and Buddhist temples. The shrine provides a dwelling for the *kami*, who are felt to be present in the surrounding nature, and it is also a place to serve and worship them. Though there are many styles of **shrine architecture**, they are traditionally built from unpainted cypress wood with a grass-thatch roof. Look out for the *chigi*, extensions of the end beams which form a cross at each end of the roof ridge, and *katsuogi*, short logs lying horizontally on top of the ridge. The best examples of such traditional architecture are the Grand Shrine of Ise, Izumo Taisha (near

Matsue), and Tokyo's Meiji-jingū. Later designs show Chinese or Korean influences, such as the use of red and white paint or other ornamentation.

Perhaps the most distinctive feature of a shrine is the **torii** which marks the gateway between the secular and the spiritual world. Traditionally, these were plain and simple wooden constructions consisting of two upright pillars and two crossbeams. Gradually various styles, such as the distinctive red paint, evolved on the same basic design until there were over twenty different types of *torii*. Nowadays, they are also made of stone, metal and concrete, in which case they tend to remain unpainted. Though the origins are obscure, *torii* means "bird perch" and they were a common form of secular gateway before 1884, after which their use was restricted to shrines.

Inside the compound, you often find pairs of human or animal **statues** on the approach to the shrine building: austere dignitaries in ancient court costume laden with weapons are the traditional Japanese guardians, though you'll also find lion-dogs (*koma-inu*), or large, ferocious-looking *Niō* borrowed from Buddhist temples. Others may be animal-messengers of the *kami*, such as the fox-messenger of Inari, the deity of good harvests.

Somewhere in the compound you'll often see a **sacred tree**, denoted by a twisted straw rope, *shimenawa*, sporting zigzags of white paper tied around it. In the past these trees were believed to be the special abode of some *kami*. Now they're just an expression of divine consciousness which, like other aspects of the surrounding nature, help to bring people's minds out of the mundane world and enter into that of the *kami*.

Finally, you come to the **shrine building** itself. At the entrance there's a slotted box for donations and a rope with a bell or gong at the top. Some say the bell is rung as a purification rite to ward off evil spirits, others that it's to attract the *kami*'s attention. You'll also notice another *shimenawa* delineating the *kami*'s sacred dwelling place. Inside each shrine there's an **inner chamber** containing the *shintai* (divine body). This is a sacred object which symbolizes the presence of the *kami* and is kept under lock and key – if ever seen, it loses its religious power. The sacred objects of some shrines are known to be mirrors (see below). In front of the chamber an **offering table** holds the *gohei*, a symbolic offering consisting of a stick with more white-paper zigzags attached, and the purification wand (*haraigushi*). This is either a wand of thin paper strips and flax, or a sprig of the sacred *sakaki*, an evergreen tree. Sometimes there's also a **mirror** between the table and the inner chamber. The mirror is of great mythological and religious importance since it symbolizes not only the stainless mind of the *kami*, but also the fidelity of the worshipper since it reflects everything truthfully. In some cases the mirror itself can be the sacred object; for example, the mirror that Amaterasu gave Ninigi is supposedly held in the inner chamber of Ise-jingū – Japan's most sacred shrine.

A large shrine may also comprise many other buildings, such as subordinate shrines, an oratory, ablution pavilion, offering hall, shrine office and shop, priests' living quarters, treasure house and sometimes even a platform for sacred dances, a *Nō* drama stage or a sumo arena. It's worth noting that in some cases there will be no shrine building as such, but simply a *torii* and a straw rope around a tree or rock to indicate a *kami*'s dwelling place. At its most extreme, whole mountains are considered to be sacred. This meant that, until the last century, women were not allowed on certain mountains. Now only two are out of bounds to women throughout the year: Ushiro-yama in Okayama-ken and the summit of Sanjō-ga-Take, near Nara, both under the preserve of the Shugendō sect (see p.956).

Shinto rites and festivals

The Japanese pray at shrines for many different reasons, and this may determine which shrine they go to. It may be just to offer thanks to their local or clan *kami* for their protection and blessing, or it may be to pray for something special, for example a successful childbirth. *Kami* are sometimes specialists in a certain type of blessing, so it's no use going to a *kami* who specializes in health if you want to pray for success in a forthcoming exam.

When **visiting a shrine** you should try to fulfil at least three of the four elements of worship. Of these, **purification** is perhaps the most important as it indicates respect for the *kami*. Traditionally, anyone suffering from an illness or open wound, menstruating women or those in mourning are considered impure and are not supposed to enter the shrine. At the ablution pavilion (a water trough near the entrance), ladle some water over your fingertips and then pour a little into your cupped hand and rinse your mouth with it; afterwards, spit the water out into the gutter below. Now purified, you can proceed to the shrine itself and the **offering**. This normally consists of throwing a coin in the box – a five yen coin is considered luckiest – though a special service warrants a larger sum wrapped in formal paper. Depending on the occasion, food, drink, material goods or even sacred dances (*kagura*, performed by female shrine attendants) or sumo contests are offered to the *kami*.

The third element is **prayer**. Pull the rope to ring the bell, bow slightly once, then deeply twice, pray, bow deeply two more times, clap your hands twice at chest level and end with two last bows, deep and then slight. The final element of worship is the **sacred feast**, which usually only follows a special service or a festival. It sometimes takes the form of consuming the food or drink offered to the *kami* – once the *kami's* had its symbolic share. The feast starts with a formal toast of sake and often ends up in great merriment and karaoke.

At the shrine shop you can buy charms (*omamori*) against all manner of ills, fortune papers (*omikuji*), which people then twist round tree branches to make them come true, and wooden votive tablets (*ema*) – write your wishes on the tablet and tie it up alongside the others.

Perhaps the most interesting aspect of Shinto for the visitor is its lively and colourful **festivals**. All shrines have at least one annual festival which is well worth hunting out. During the festival, the *kami* is symbolically transferred from the inner chamber to an ornate palanquin or portable shrine, called a *mikoshi*. This is its temporary home while young men hurtle around the local area with it so that the *kami* can bless the homes of the faithful. The passion with which they run, turning it this way and that, jostling it up and down shouting "*wasshoi, wasshoi*", has to be seen to be believed, especially in rural towns where festivals are usually conducted with more gusto. All this frantic action is said to make the *kami* happy, and it is highly contagious: long after the palanquin has returned to the shrine the merriment continues with the help of copious amounts of alcohol and the odd karaoke machine or two.

Buddhism

The vast majority of Japanese people are followers of **Buddhism** as well as Shinto. Buddhism originated in India with a wealthy Hindu prince called **Siddhartha Gautama** who, dissatisfied with Hinduism's explanation of worldly suffering, rejected asceticism as the way to spiritual realization and turned instead to meditation. After several nomadic years he achieved enlightenment (*nirvana*) while meditating one night under a *bodhi* tree, and devoted the rest of his life to teaching that "right thoughts" and "right actions" must be followed to reduce all material and emotional attachments in order to increase awareness and ultimately to attain *nirvana*.

The **Mahayana** (Greater Vehicle) school of Buddhism, which believes in salvation for all beings jointly rather than the individual pursuit of *nirvana*, was introduced to Japan from China in the mid-sixth century. As with many things, Japan adapted this foreign import to suit its own culture and values. Buddha was accepted as a *kami* and, over the years, certain religious aspects were dropped or played down, for example celibacy and the emphasis on private contemplation.

But Buddhism did not travel alone to Japan; it brought with it Chinese culture. Over the next two centuries, monks, artists and scholars went to China to study religion, art, music, literature and politics, all of which brought great advances to Japanese culture. As a result, Buddhism became embroiled in the **political struggles** of the Nara and Heian eras, when weak emperors used Buddhist and Chinese culture to enhance their own power and level of cultural sophistication and to reduce the influence of their Shintoist rivals. The balance of power between Buddhas and *kami* also shifted: *kami* were regarded as being prone to rebirth, from which they could be released by Buddhist sutras. To this end, Buddhist temples were built next to Shinto shrines, and statues and regalia placed on Shinto altars to help raise the *kami* to the level of Buddhas. Eventually, some *kami* became the guardians of temples, while Buddhas were regarded as the prime spiritual beings.

Up until the end of the twelfth century, Japanese Buddhism was largely restricted to a small, generally aristocratic minority who had been initiated into the faith. However, at this time the dominant sect, **Tendai**, split into various **new sects**, notably Jōdo, Jōdo Shinshū, Nichiren and Zen Buddhism, which each appealed to different sections of the population. The first two in particular were simple forms of the faith which enabled Buddhism to evolve from a religion of the elite to one which also appealed to the population en masse. The Nichiren sect had a more scholastic approach, while Zen's concern for ritual, form and practice attracted the samurai classes and had a great influence on Japan's traditional arts. Almost all contemporary Japanese Buddhism developed from these sects, which are still very much in existence today (see below for more on their basic tenets).

From the fifteenth century, however, Shinto started making a comeback. In reaction to the absorption of the indigenous faith into this foreign religion, various Shinto sects revived the ascendancy of *kami* over Buddhas, ending the idea that they were merely Japanese manifestations of Buddhas. This process came to a head after the 1868 Meiji Restoration, when Shinto was declared the national faith. Most Buddhist elements were removed from Shinto shrines and destroyed, and Buddhism was suppressed until the end of World War II when religious freedom returned to Japan. Nowadays, Buddhism and Shinto coexist peaceably once again and share the vast majority of their followers.

The principal Buddhist sects

The Tendai and Shingon sects were founded in the early ninth century, and were both based on Chinese esoteric Buddhism. Involving meditation and tantric rituals, they were established on mountains and had some similarities to the Shugendō faith of mountain asceticism (see p.956). The **Tendai** (Heavenly Terrace) sect was founded by the monk **Saichō** (767–822) on Hiei-zan near Kyoto, where it is still very much alive. Based on the supremacy of the "Lotus Sutra", which expresses the Buddha's ultimate truth, Tendai recognized other beliefs – including Shinto – as different aspects of the one universal force. Similarly, the **Shingon** (True Word) sect, founded by **Kōbō Daishi** (774–835) and based on Kōya-san, south of Nara, sought to reconcile various faiths around the central image of Dainichi Nyorai, the Cosmic Buddha who embodies the essence of the universe. Shingon emphasizes the idea of mutual interdependence as expressed by mandalas (graphic representations of the Buddhist universe), and asserts that enlightenment can be achieved in one lifetime through chanting and meditation. For centuries, followers of Shingon have also been seeking spiritual purification by completing the 88-temple pilgrimage around Shikoku (see p.714).

Jōdoshū, the Pure Land sect, was founded in 1133 by the monk **Hōnen** during a period of famine, treachery and clan warfare. He asserted that the world was inherently evil and that, as it was impossible to achieve Buddhahood in this life, people should concentrate on salvation in the afterlife. Faith in Amida Buddha (the Buddha of the Western Paradise) would lead to bliss in the next world. Scholastic study and religious ritual were unnecessary, making this sect popular with the uneducated masses. Instead, all that was necessary was daily prayer to Amida, often by chanting the *nembutsu* "*Namu Amida Butsu*" ("Praise to Amida Buddha"). To set the pace, Hōnen would sometimes recite the *nembutsu* 60,000 times a day.

The **Jōdo Shinshū**, "True Pure Land" sect, evolved after the radical philosopher-monk **Shinran** broke away from the Jōdo sect around 1224. He believed that salvation was not just limited to the afterlife, but that by praying to Amida one could be saved in the present life, too. He rejected all religious ritual except prayer and held that saying the *nembutsu* just once was enough if said with sufficient sincerity. He also enraged the monks of other sects by dropping celibacy and meat-eating laws. This inevitably made Jōdo Shinshū even more popular among ordinary folk, and it is one of the biggest Buddhist sects in Japan today.

By contrast, the **Nichiren** sect, named after its founder, had a very scholastic approach. Nichiren (1222–82) believed that truth, enlightenment and salvation can only come from studying Buddhist scriptures, particularly the "Lotus Sutra". He considered all other teachings and sects to be heretical. With their battle cry "*Namu Myōhō Renge Kyō*" ("Hail to the Lotus of Divine Law"), his fanatical followers crusaded their cause almost to the point of violence. Nichiren, however, was also an astute observer of the political situation in mainland Asia. With masterful timing, he warned that unless people repented their sins and followed his sect they would suffer the wrath of the heavens in the form of a foreign invasion – the Mongol hordes attacked soon after (see "History", p.936). Never one to go quietly, Nichiren upset too many people with his fanatical preaching and was exiled on several occasions. At one point he was even sentenced to execution but, according to legend, won a reprieve – no doubt due to divine intervention – when the sword shattered on his neck.

More elaborate than its rivals, **Zen Buddhism** is far more concerned with ritual, form and practice than scholastic study. Instead, enlightenment and salvation can only come from within, and followers of the Sōtō school of Zen try to achieve this by meditating in the lotus position (*zazen*), attempting to empty the mind of all worldly thoughts and desires. Alternatively, followers of the Rinzai school try to achieve this by meditating on enigmatic riddles (*kōan*), whose only answer is enlightenment; perhaps the most famous *kōan* is "What is the sound of one hand?". Both methods serve the same purpose of taking the believer out of the material world and onto a higher plane where they can learn the nature of the Buddha.

Zen was first imported from China in the seventh century, though it didn't really get going until after 1192 when it was reintroduced by the monk **Eisai**. This time it found more success among the new military rulers, now based in Kamakura. Zen's austere practices, demanding individual action, strong self-discipline and a spartan lifestyle, struck a chord with the samurai, who supported the great Zen temples of Kamakura and, later, Kyoto. Zen's minimalist approach to life, coupled with Shinto's appreciation of nature, had a profound influence on Japan's traditional arts (see p.963) and gardens. The **Zen rock gardens**, consisting of rocks placed in a "sea" of white rippled gravel, are designed to aid contemplation about everything and nothing: the whole universe and the tiny grain of sand that is an insignificant part of it. Although the individual rocks sometimes symbolize specific things – a tiger, tortoise, mountain or a crane, for example – Zen rock gardens are meant to be viewed many times without lending themselves to any one particular meaning. (See p.966 for more about Japanese gardens.)

Buddhist temples and worship

As with Shinto shrines, **Buddhist temples** (called *-tera*, *-dera* or *-ji*) come in many different styles, depending on the sect and the date they were built, but the foremost architectural influences are Chinese and Korean. The temple's **main hall** is called the *kon-dō* or *hon-dō*; this is where you will find the principal image of Buddha and a table for offerings. Sometimes the entry **gate** (*San-mon*) is as imposing as the temple itself, consisting of a two-storey wooden structure with perhaps a pair of brightly coloured, fearsome guardians called *Niō*, or *Kongō Rikishi*. Despite their looks, the *Niō* are actually quite good-natured – except to evil spirits.

Some temples also have a pagoda in their compound. **Pagodas** are usually either three or five storeys high with a roof dividing each storey and a metal spire on top. They are Chinese versions of stupas, the Indian structures built to enshrine a relic of the Buddha, and historically used to be the main focus of Buddhist worship. Depending on the temple's size, you might also see other buildings such as a study hall (*kō-dō*), scripture or treasure houses, living quarters and a temple shop. Zen temples, especially the colourful temples of Kyoto, are also famous for their stunningly beautiful rock and landscape gardens, which are designed to aid meditation (see above and p.966).

Buddhism has no festivals or rites to match Shinto, preferring instead simple prayer and chants, the unforgettable smell of smouldering incense, and offerings of food, flowers or money. Its mystic forte is the Zen monks meditating in a lotus position, breathing slowly, emptying their minds and being periodically hit with bamboo sticks to stop them from falling asleep – for which they thank their aggressors.

The most important occasion in Japan's Buddhist calendar is **Obon** (late July to mid-August) when spirits return to earth and families traditionally gather to welcome them back to the ancestral home. *O-higan*, which falls on the spring and autumn equinox (usually March 21 and Sept 23), is again a time to visit ancestors' graves. But probably the biggest celebration is **Shōgatsu** (New Year), though it's as much a Shinto event as a Buddhist one. A long public holiday enables plenty of time for merriment and sake drinking, though remember to remain sober enough to visit the local temple or shrine to pray for good fortune in the coming year.

Shugendō

Shugendō is a colourful blend of Buddhist esoteric and tantric concepts, Chinese Taoist magic and Shinto shamanism. Based on mountain asceticism, the religion was formalized in the eighth century by the monk **En-no-Gyōja**, who was famous for his mystic powers.

Following Shinto practice, Shugendō's mountain priests, **yamabushi**, believe that the mountains are centres of sacred power. They go through elaborate initiation rites, austerities and self-denial to acquire this sacred power which they can then use to heal and bless common people. Their practices include meditation, mountain hiking, sitting in smoke-filled rooms, sumo wrestling, and partial denial of food, sleep and daily ablutions. These are designed to train both body and spirit, and are a metaphor for the soul's uncomfortable journey from death to rebirth.

Shugendō was quite popular until the 1868 Meiji Restoration, when it, along with other forms of Buddhism, was suppressed. Nevertheless, pockets of this mysterious faith can still be found, notably on **Dewa-sanzan** in north Honshū where some of the ancient practices survive. One of the most lively events is the **Shōreisai** (Pine Festival), held on the night of New Year's Eve. Two groups of priests hurl abuse at each other (made all the more colourful by large quantities of sake) and engage in various contests to divine whether the coming year will bring good harvests.

Folk religion

Japanese **folk religion** draws on ideas from Shinto, Buddhism and Chinese Taoism, which added shamanism, spirit possession and magico-religious practices to the pot. The "holy men" (or women) of folk religion may be specialists in, among other things, geomancy, divination, healing, exorcism and communicating with the gods. They offer various rites and advice, for example explaining why misfortunes have occurred or recommending auspicious times for weddings, long journeys and other important events.

One manifestation of such beliefs is the **six-day calendar** (sometimes incorporated into normal calendars) in which one day is considered good for all endeavours, another day is considered bad, and the other days are either good or bad at certain times for certain things. Similar notions govern the **naming of children**. Not only the time and place of birth affects the character and destiny of a person, but also their name. Before deciding on a given name, therefore, parents may consult a *hiriji* (holy man, or priest) about the number of pen strokes required to write the chosen characters. A bad combination of name, time and place of birth may result in a life of persistent misfortune.

There is also a more mythological side to Japanese folk religion involving a whole host of **gods, guardians and demons**. The ones to have on your side are the **Seven Lucky Gods**, *Shichi Fuku-jin*, often seen sailing in a boat on New Year greetings cards to wish good fortune for the coming year. Of these, the best-loved are **Ebisu**, the god of prosperity, identified by his fishing rod and sea-bream; **Daikoku**, the god of wealth, who carries a treasure-sack over one shoulder and a lucky hammer; the squat **Fukurokuju**, god of longevity, marked by a bald, egg-shaped head; while the jovial god of happiness, **Hotei**, sports a generous belly and a beaming smile.

Characters to avoid, on the other hand, are the **oni**, a general term for demons and ogres, though *oni* aren't always bad. At *Setsubun* (Feb 3 or 4) children can be seen running round throwing soya beans all over the place, shouting "*oni wa soto, fuku wa uchi*", meaning "out with the demons, in with good luck". *Tengu* are mischievous mountain goblins with red faces and very long noses, while *kappa* are a bit like a small troll and live under bridges. If anything goes missing while you're hiking, you can probably blame one of these, as they both like to steal things, including animals and children. If it's your liver that's missing, however, it will definitely be a *kappa*; he likes to extract them from people's bodies through the anus, so watch out.

Christianity

Shipwrecked Portuguese traders were the first Christians to set foot in Japan, in Tanegashima, an island off Kyūshū, in 1543. As far as **Christianity** is concerned though, it was not until **Saint Francis Xavier** and his Jesuit missionaries landed in Kagoshima, southwest Kyūshū, in 1549 that things really took off. Initially, the local *daimyō* were eager to convert, largely in order to acquire firearms and other advanced European technologies, while often also maintaining their original religious belief and practices. It wasn't only about trade, though; many feudal lords were also attracted by Jesuit austerity, which accorded with their *bushidō* values, while the poor were attracted by social programmes which helped raise their standard of living.

The port of **Nagasaki** was created in 1571 to trade with the Portuguese. It soon became a centre of Jesuit missionary activity, from where Catholicism spread rapidly throughout Kyūshū. At first, the converts were tolerated by the authorities, and in the late 1570s the then ruler of Japan, the great, unifying general **Oda Nobunaga**, used Christianity, with all its material benefits, to win over his remaining influential opponents against the troublesome Buddhists. In 1582 he was succeeded by **Toyotomi Hideyoshi**, who completed the unification of Japan. To Hideyoshi's mind the Christians had now served their purpose, and their increasing stranglehold on trade, coupled with a growing influence in secular affairs, was beginning to pose a threat. **Persecution** began in 1587 when Hideyoshi ordered the expulsion of all missionaries, though there was little immediate action; in fact the number of foreign missionaries increased temporarily with the arrival of Spanish Franciscan friars. In 1597, however, Hideyoshi struck again: six Franciscan priests and twenty local converts were crucified upside-down in Nagasaki.

Shogun Tokugawa Ieyasu succeeded Hideyoshi in 1598. Though generally more tolerant of the Christian Europeans – principally in the interests of maintaining good trade relations – Ieyasu passed several edicts prohibiting Christianity after 1612. It was a short reprieve. Ieyasu's son, **Hidetada**, turned persecution into an art form when he came to power in 1618. Suspected Christians were forced to trample on pictures of Christ or the Virgin Mary to prove their innocence. If they refused, they were tortured, burnt at the stake or thrown into boiling sulphur; over three thousand local converts were martyred between 1597 and 1660.

Things came to a head with the **Battle of Shimabara** in 1637, when a Christian-led army rebelled against the local *daimyō* (see box, p.824). Japan had been gradually closing itself off from the world during the 1620s, but this was the final straw. Christian worship in Japan was forbidden and the edicts were only finally repealed in the late nineteenth century. Amazingly, a sizeable number of converts in Kyūshū continued to uphold their faith, disguised as *onando buppō* "back-room Buddhism", throughout this time. When foreign missionaries again appeared in Nagasaki in the mid-1860s, they were astonished to discover some 20,000 of these "hidden Christians".

Today, Christians represent less than two percent of Japan's population. Though churches can be found even in small rural towns, Christmas is only celebrated as a brief commercial fling. Christianity – however superficially – has also had an impact on Japanese **weddings**. It is currently fashionable to get married in Western-style chapels, created solely for that purpose, partly because it appears exotic, and partly because it's less complex than the traditional Shinto ceremony.

The new religions

Several **new religions** appeared in Japan during the nineteenth and twentieth centuries, many of them offshoots of Nichiren Buddhism. Their basic beliefs and practices are generally a mix of Shinto, Buddhism and Confucianism, incorporating loyalty to work and the family with teachings of karma, reincarnation and the coming of a new age. Most tend to have charismatic leaders, often of a shamanistic tradition, and grand headquarters. They also tend to appeal to the poorer classes, to whom they offer sympathy, a sense of belonging and importance, and help in adjusting to modern life. Considering the extremely rapid modernization of Japan during the last two centuries, the success of these organizations is perhaps not so surprising.

The biggest such organization is **Sōka Gakkai** (Value Creation Society). It was founded in 1937 by schoolteacher Makiguchi Tsunesaburō, who emphasized the importance of educational philosophy alongside the day-to-day benefits of religion. Under the umbrella of Nichiren Buddhism, Sōka Gakkai's structure was formalized after World War II, focusing on tightly knit groups engaged in educational work, social activities and large-scale jamborees aimed at finding fulfilment in the present. With its proselytizing mission and broad appeal to people of all ages and classes, Sōka Gakkai now claims around twenty million members. The movement also has a nominally independent political branch, the Kōmeitō or "Clean Government Party", founded in 1964 as a backlash to corruption in Japanese politics. With its vast and effective grass-roots network, Kōmeitō has long been a significant group within Japan's opposition parties and since October 1999 has formed part of the ruling LDP-Conservative coalition government.

At the other end of the scale, **AUM Shinrikyō** (AUM Supreme Truth), now officially known as Aleph, was founded in 1986 by a blind yoga teacher, **Asahara Shōkō**. Claiming to be a Buddhist sect, adherents believed that the world would end in 1997 and that only AUM members would survive. At its height, the cult boasted 10,000 members in Japan and 30,000 abroad, mainly in Russia. Little known to most of his followers, however, Asahara's prime goal was world domination, but the truth started to emerge after the 1995 sarin gas attack on the Tokyo subway. Fortunately, the police stopped AUM before Asahara could carry out his plans, but the group's activities stunned the Japanese population and raised fears that Japan may no longer be the safe and harmonious country it once was. See the box on p.947 for more about AUM.

Religion, ritual and culture

It's often said that Shinto and Buddhism have given the Japanese a unique appreciation for ritual, nature and art. Various aspects of Japanese culture have developed from religious ritual and values, such as the Nō drama which evolved out of Shinto's ancient sacred dances (see p.970 for more on Nō). In addition, sumo wrestling, traditional gardens, the tea ceremony and flower arranging all stem from ritualistic aspects of Japanese religions.

Sumo

Japanese mythology teaches that the gods used to wrestle each other. This was adopted in ancient times as a form of divination, and became an important part of New Year festivals to predict the fortunes of the coming year. **Sumo** became a spectator sport as early as the sixth century and is probably the most popular sport in Japan today.

Sumo's connections to its religious past are easy to see. For example, the referee's elaborate **costume** is strikingly similar to that worn by Shinto priests, while the wrestlers' *mawashi* belt, with its tassels reminiscent of Shinto's purification wand, developed from the loincloth, *fundoshi*, worn at Shinto festivals. **The bout** itself is almost all ritual ceremony, with the actual wrestling often lasting only a matter of seconds. As soon as they enter the ring, the wrestlers (*dohyō*) purify themselves by rinsing their mouths with water, in the Shinto manner, and throwing salt into the ring to ward off evil. They usually do the latter three or four times, stamping their feet on the floor and psyching each other out in-between. Sumo wrestlers are highly respected in Japan and are expected to behave with the decorum befitting a religious event. So, despite the evil looks they exchange before lunging at each other, it's very bad form for a wrestler to display emotions of anger or frustration at losing – the gods may still be watching.

Gardens

Japanese **gardens** developed out of the sacred grounds surrounding Shinto shrines and imperial palaces. The earliest gardens, dating from the Nara and Heian eras (eighth to twelfth centuries), took the form of a **pond and island** representing the mythical land of the gods, Tokoyo. Both the turtle and crane, animals alluding to the Chinese isle of the immortals and symbolizing longevity, were associated with Tokoyo and appear frequently in garden design, usually in the form of islands or rock groupings.

Later the rocks, ponds and islands largely lost their religious symbolism, but were used instead to evoke famous Japanese beauty spots or scenes from literary masterpieces. At first these idealized landscapes provided the venue for elegant boating parties as depicted in *The Tale of Genji* (see p.1019), but, as the gardens and their ponds became smaller, evolved into the classic **stroll-gardens**. Designed to be appreciated on foot, these secular, Edo-period gardens comprise various tableaux which unfold as the viewer progresses through the garden, and often "borrow" the surrounding scenery to enlarge the space. Many superb stroll-gardens still exist in Japan; among the most stunning are Takamatsu's Ritsurin-kōen, Suizenji-kōen in Kumamoto and Kōraku-en near Okayama.

Back in the ninth century, Shingon Esoteric Buddhism (see p.954) promoted the idea that paradise could be achieved on earth, by the grace of Amida Buddha. Thus were **paradise gardens** born, in which temples strove to create their own version of Amida's Pure Land, or Jōdo, featuring a pond, islands and rocks in a completely manufactured "natural" setting, such as Uji's magnificent Byōdō-in. By contrast, in the fifteenth century the severe precepts of Zen Buddhism favoured highly austere **"dry gardens"** (*kare-sansui*), in which the entire universe is reduced to a few rocks, white-rippled gravel and one or two judiciously placed shrubs (see p.966). Kyoto's Daisen-in and Ryōan-ji are magnificent examples of this type of garden, which were designed solely to facilitate meditation and lead the viewer to enlightenment.

The tea ceremony

Tea was introduced to Japan from China in the ninth century. Tea drinking, however, didn't really catch on until after the twelfth century, particularly among Zen Buddhists, who appreciated the tea's caffeine kick during their long meditation sessions. Zen Buddhists believe that all actions have a religious significance and the very act of tea-making gradually evolved into part of the meditation process. The highly ritualistic **tea ceremony**, *cha-no-yu*, however, didn't develop until the late sixteenth century under a gifted tea master, samurai and garden designer called **Sen no Rikyū** (1521–1591).

Influenced by the culture of the samurai and *nō*, the most important aspect of the tea ceremony is the **etiquette** with which it is performed. Central to this is the selfless manner in which the host serves the tea and the humble manner in which the guests accept it. Indeed, the inner spirit of the participants during the ceremony is considered more important than its ritual form. Guests are expected to admire the hanging scroll and flower arrangement decorating the tea room, and the cup from which they drink – all are valued for the skill of the craftsmen and their seasonal note or rustic simplicity. Today, the tea ceremony is popular mostly among young women; as with *ikebana*, it's deemed a desirable quality for a woman of marriageable age to acquire.

Ikebana

Ikebana, or the art of flower arranging, also has its roots in ancient Shinto rituals, Buddhist practice and a Japanese aesthetic that balances three components to create a dynamic image. Again, however, *ikebana* reached its peak in the sixteenth century, largely on the coat-tails of the tea ceremony, when several distinct schools emerged.

Originally, the emphasis was on presenting materials and forms in ways which imitated their natural state. While the materials remained natural, the ideology evolved to employ three leading sprays which signify the sky, earth and humankind; the sprays are arranged to express the harmonic balance of these elements in nature. The four main styles of *ikebana* are the self-explanatory *shōkai* (living flowers), the formal *rikka* (standing flowers), *noribana* (heaped flowers), and the more naturalistic *nage-ire* (thrown in). Within each of these there are many schools, such as Ikenobō in Kyoto and Tokyo's Sōgetsu, as well as avant-garde groups which use non-natural materials (iron, glass and so on) to the same harmonious effect.

Peter Grimshaw

Art and architecture

n the mid-nineteenth century an exotic array of pictures, crafts and curios came flooding out of Japan as this virtually unknown country re-established trade with the outside world. Western collectors eagerly snapped up exquisite ink-painted landscapes, boldly colourful *ukiyo-e* pictures, samurai swords, porcelain, inlaid lacquerware, bamboo utensils and ivory carvings – even artists such as van Gogh and Whistler were influenced by the contemporary vogue for things Japanese. From these collections came our first detailed knowledge of the diversity of Japanese arts, ranging from expressions of the most refined spiritual sensibilities to the bric-a-brac of ordinary life.

This enormous artistic range reflects a wide variety of sources of inspiration and patronage over the centuries. Periods of aristocratic rule, military supremacy and merchant wealth all left their mark on Japanese arts, building on a rich legacy of religious art, folk traditions and the assimilated cultural influences of China and Korea. More recently, the West became a model for artists seeking to join the ranks of the avant-garde. Today it's difficult to speak of prevailing tendencies, as Japanese artists both draw on traditional sources and take their place amongst international trends.

What does span the centuries, however, is a love of nature, respect for the highest standards of craftsmanship and the potential for finding beauty in the simplest of things. These qualities pervade the visual arts of Japan but are also reflected in aspects of the performing arts, where the actor's craft, costume and make-up combine with the stage setting to unique dramatic effect. The official designation of valued objects and individuals as "National Treasures" and "Living National Treasures" acknowledges the extent to which the arts and artists of Japan are revered.

One of the joys of visiting Japan, however, is in experiencing the ordinary ways in which the Japanese aesthetic enters into everyday life. The presentation of food, a window display or the simplest flower arrangement can convey, beyond the walls of any museum, the essential nature of Japanese art.

The beginnings

The earliest artefacts excavated in Japan date back to 10,000 BC, when the **Jōmon culture** (10,000–300 BC), a society of hunters, fishers and gatherers, inhabited small settlements throughout the country. The name Jōmon, meaning "cord pattern", refers to the impression made by twisted cord on the surface of clay. Early Jōmon pots were built up from coils of clay pressed together, to which cord markings were applied as a form of decoration, and shells added for further embellishment. Increasingly elaborate variations in the size and type of Jōmon pottery suggest its religious or ceremonial significance. Certainly, by the Middle Jōmon, the production of female pottery figurines and stone phalli point to the association of such items with basic fertility rites. Fired-clay *dogū* are typical of Late Jōmon sculpture; these stiffly posed figures with female attributes, staring out of large oval eyes, mainly occur in sites in eastern Japan.

The more sophisticated **Yayoi culture** (300 BC–300 AD), which displaced the Jōmon, is characterized by a finer-quality, reddish-brown wheel-turned pottery which was first discovered at Yayoi, near today's Tokyo. Their pots were more diverse in shape and function but simpler in decoration, with the incision of straight, curved and zigzagged lines and combed wave patterns. Yayoi also saw the introduction of iron and bronze to Japan, which led to the production of iron tools, while bronze was reserved for ritual objects. The most distinctive Yayoi bronze objects are the *dōtaku*, or straight-sided bells, which have been linked with agricultural rituals and burial practices.

The following **Kofun era** (300–710 AD) is defined by the number of huge burial mounds (*kofun*) built during the period. The tombs were generally bordered by a series of low-fired clay cylinders, or *haniwa*, topped with delightful representations of animals, people, boats and houses. Though probably related to ancient Chinese burial practices, the *haniwa* show a distinctively Japanese artistic form.

The religious influence

Shinto and Buddhism, Japan's two core religions, have both made vital contributions to the art and architecture of Japan. In the case of **Shinto**, the influence is extremely subtle and difficult to define, but is apparent in the Japanese love of simplicity, understatement and a deep affinity with the natural environment. The architecture of Shinto **shrines** captures the essence of these ideals, as well as expressing the sense of awe and mystery which is central to the religion. Their plain wooden surfaces, together with their very human scale, gradually evolved into a native approach to architectural design in which buildings, even important religious edifices, strove to be in harmony with their surroundings (for more about Shinto shrines, see p.950).

The introduction of **Buddhism** into Japan from China in the sixth century had a profound effect on Japanese arts. The process of transmitting this foreign religion to Japan led to the copying of Buddhist sutras, the construction of temples as places of worship and study, and the production of Buddhist paintings and sculptures. The **temples** themselves, with their red-lacquered exteriors, tiled roofs supported by elaborate bracketing and tall pagodas, were in stark stylistic contrast to the architecture of Shinto. They represented visually the superimposition upon Japan's native traditions of a different set of beliefs and values.

Some of Japan's earliest **Buddhist sculptures** can be found at Hōryū-ji (near Nara) and take their inspiration from Chinese and Korean sculpture of an earlier period. Though many statues have been moved to Tokyo's National Museum, the temple is still a magnificent museum of early Buddhist art. Its bronze Shaka (the Historic Buddha) Triad by Tori Bushii, a Korean-Chinese immigrant, dates back to 623 and reflects the stiff frontal poses, archaic smiles and waterfall drapery patterns of fourth-century Chinese sculpture. At the same time, Hōryū-ji's standing wooden Kudara Kannon, depicting the most compassionate of the Bodhisattvas, is delicately and sensitively carved to emphasize its spirituality. Another contemporary example of Buddhist sculpture, possibly also by a Korean immigrant, is the seated Miroku Bosatsu (Future Buddha) at Chūgū-ji, within the Hōryū-ji complex. With one leg crossed and his head resting pensively on one hand, it is a model of the grace and serenity associated with Asuka-era (552–650) sculpture.

As with Christian art, Buddhist **iconography** draws on a wealth of historic and symbolic references. The legends associated with Buddhism and the attributes of Buddhahood are represented in the *mudra*, the hand gestures of the Buddha, his poses and in the objects he holds. Similarly, as with the heightened spirituality of the Bodhisattvas which often flank the Buddha and the exaggerated realism of the fearsome-looking guardian figures at the entrance to the temple compound, the style in which such sculptures are rendered is frequently an aspect of their function. While the sweetness and calm of the Bodhisattvas may direct thoughts heavenwards, the bulging eyes, tensed muscles and aggressive poses of the guardian figures are intended to ward off evil and to protect both the Buddha and the temple.

During the early years of Buddhism in Japan and the periods of closest contact with China (the seventh to tenth centuries), Japanese styles of Buddhist art mimicked those current in China or from her recent past. However, a gradual process of assimilation took place in both painting and sculpture until during the Kamakura era (see p.935) the adaptation of a distinctly Japanese model can be observed in Buddhist art.

The Heian era 794–1185

In 794 the Japanese capital was moved from Nara to Heian-kyō (present-day Kyoto), heralding the start of the **Heian era**. A more significant transitional date, however, is 898, when the Japanese stopped sending embassies to the Chinese T'ang court. The abrupt ending of centuries of close relations with China was to have a significant impact upon artistic developments in Japan. Gradually the cloistered and leisured lifestyle of the Heian aristocracy, combined with a diminishing Chinese influence, spawned a uniquely Japanese cultural identity.

Court life in Heian Japan revolved around worldly pleasures and aesthetic pastimes, and the period is renowned for its artistic and cultural innovation. *Kana*, or the phonetic syllabary, was developed during this time and was employed in the composition of one of Japan's greatest literary masterpieces, **The Tale of Genji**, or *Genji Monogatari*. Lady Murasaki's portrayal of the effeteness and insularity of the Heian-court nobility eloquently described the artistic pursuits which dominated their daily life. The poetry and incense competitions, the arts of painting, calligraphy and gardening, and the elaborate rituals of court dress were all aspects of Heian aesthetic refinement.

A new painting format, the *emaki* or **picture scroll**, also evolved during the Heian era. The narrative hand-scroll allowed for the picture and story to unfold as the viewer unrolled and observed its contents. *Emaki* depicted romances, legends and historical tales, of which the most famous is an illustrated edition of *The Tale of Genji*, published around 1130. The painting technique used, known as *Yamato-e*, employs flat blocks of colour with a strong linear focus and boldness of style which was uniquely Japanese. At the same time, the **decorative arts** reached a similarly high level of sophistication. Inlaid lacquerware, using the *maki-e* technique (sprinkling the surface with gold or silver powder) and finely crafted bronze mirrors employed surface designs to equally dramatic effect.

The lavishness of Heian taste is reflected in **Buddhist painting and sculpture** of this period. New sects of Buddhism gave rise to the diagrammatic mandalas, schematic depictions of the Buddhist universe, while religious sculpture became more graceful and sensual, with gilded, delicately featured deities marking the transition to an aristocratic form of Buddhist art. The large, gilded wooden image of Amida in Uji's Byōdō-in (near Kyoto) is a representative example. Here the serene, seated Buddha is set against a backdrop of elaborate openwork carving with gilded angels and swirling cloud patterns animating the scene. The overall effect is one of splendid sumptuousness.

Samurai culture

Japan's medieval age began in 1185 with the establishment of the Kamakura Shogunate. While Kyoto remained the imperial capital and the cultural heartland of Japan, the rise to power of a military elite generated an alternative artistic taste. *Bushidō*, "the way of the warrior", was the guiding spirit of the samurai class. This spirit gave rise to a demand for art forms that were more in keeping with the simplicity, discipline and rigour of the military lifestyle.

This new realism made itself felt in the portrait painting and picture scrolls of the **Kamakura era** (1185–1333), most graphically in the *Handbook on Hungry Ghosts*, now held in Tokyo's National Museum. Highly individualized portraits of military figures and Zen masters also became popular, as did lively narrative tales focusing on the cult of war and Buddhist legends. Kamakura sculpture similarly combined a high degree of realism with a dynamic energy, reflecting the emergence of popular Buddhist sects which appealed more directly to the common people. The two giant guardian figures at Nara's Tōdai-ji, fashioned by the sculptors Unkei and Kaikei in 1203, are outstanding examples of this vigorous new style.

However, samurai culture had a more direct impact on the development of the decorative arts. Military armour was made in quantity during the Kamakura era and the **art of the sword** became an important area of artistic production for centuries to follow. The long and short sword of the samurai, the sword guard (*tsuba*), scabbard and elaborate fittings and ornaments are all considered achievements of Japanese metalwork design. While sword production in the fifteenth and sixteenth centuries was concentrated in the provinces of Bizen and Mino (today's Okayama and Gifu), by the Edo era (1600–1868), Edo and Ōsaka had become leading centres of sword-making. Sword smiths were noted for their skill in forging and for the meticulousness of finish which they applied to the blades. Through the peaceful years of the Edo era, however, sword fittings came to be associated with the decorative rather than the practical. Sword furniture from this time might be either simple and abstract, or draw on representational themes from nature, religion and everyday life.

The arts of Zen

With the spread of **Zen Buddhism** in the thirteenth century, the arts of Japan acquired a new focus. Here was a religion which cultivated self-discipline and austerity as the path to enlightenment. Not surprisingly, it was taken up with enthusiasm by the samurai class. Meditation is at the centre of Zen practice and many Zen art forms can be seen as vehicles for inward reflection or as visualizations of the sudden and spontaneous nature of enlightenment.

Monochromatic **ink painting**, known as *suiboku-ga* or *sumi-e*, portrayed meditative landscapes and other subjects in a variety of formats including screens, hanging scrolls and hand-scrolls, with a free and expressive style of brushwork that was both speedily and skilfully rendered. *Haboku*, or "flung-ink" landscapes, took this technique to its logical extreme by building up (barely) recognizable imagery from the arbitrary patterns formed by wet ink splashed onto highly absorbent paper. Sesshū (1420–1506), a Zen priest, was Japan's foremost practitioner of this technique.

Zen **calligraphy** similarly moved beyond the descriptive to emphasize spontaneity of expression in a style of writing that captured the essence of its subject matter, frequently based on poems and Zen sayings. Calligraphy of this type can be so expressively rendered as to be almost unreadable except to the practised eye. One of the most striking examples, by the monk Ryōkan Daigu (1757–1831), is a hanging scroll with the intertwined symbols for heaven and earth. Ryōkan's bold brushwork dramatically links the symbols of these two aspects of the cosmos to portray them as one sweeping and continuous force. Both the symbolism of this literal union and the unconventionality of the style in which the characters are rendered encapsulate the spirit of Zen.

A love of nature also lies at the very core of Zen. The qualities of abstraction and suggestion which characterized *suiboku-ga* were fittingly applied to the design of **Zen gardens**. Japanese gardens employ artifice to create an environment that appears more natural than nature itself. Trees and bushes are carefully pruned, colour is restricted and water channelled to convey, in one setting, the essence of the natural landscape. The word for landscape in Japanese is *sansui*, meaning "mountain and water". In Zen-inspired *kare-sansui* or "dry landscape" gardens, such as that of Ryōan-ji in Kyoto, these two elements are symbolically combined. *Kare-sansui* gardens consist only of carefully selected and positioned rocks in a bed of sand or gravel which is raked into water-like patterns. As vehicles for contemplation, such gardens convey the vastness of nature through the power of suggestion.

Cha-no-yu, or "the way of tea", also evolved out of Zen meditation techniques and draws on the love of nature in its architectural setting and utensils. The spirit of *wabi*, sometimes described as "rustic simplicity", pervades the Japanese **tea ceremony**. The traditional teahouse is positioned in a suitably understated garden, and naturalness is emphasized in all aspects of its architecture: in the unpainted wooden surfaces, the thatched roof, tatami-covered floors and the sliding-screen doors (*fusuma*) which open directly out onto a rustic scene. As with the garden itself, colour and ostentation are avoided. Instead, the corner alcove, or *tokonoma*, becomes the focal point for a single object of adornment, a simple flower arrangement or a seasonal hanging scroll.

Tea ceremony **utensils** contribute to the mood of this refined ritual. Raku, Shino and many other varieties of roughcast tea bowls are admired for the accidental effects produced by the firing of the pottery. Water containers, tea caddies and bamboo ladles and whisks complement the tea wares and are themselves much prized for their natural qualities. The guiding light behind all this mannered simplicity was the great tea-master Sen no Rikyū (1521–91), whose "worship of the imperfect" had a long-lasting influence on Japanese artistic tastes.

Feudal arts and architecture

Zen arts flourished during the **Muromachi era** (1333–1573), and close links with China once again dominated cultural life. The Ashikaga shoguns, now headquartered in Kyoto alongside the imperial court, indulged their love of the arts and landscape gardening in grand style. While many of Kyoto's Muromachi palaces and temples were destroyed during the late-fifteenth-century Ōnin Wars, two magnificent monuments still survive in the Kinkaku-ji and Gingaku-ji, the Golden and Silver pavilions. Built as country villas for the shoguns, both these buildings are modest in scale and combine simplicity of design with luxuriousness of finish – particularly the gold-leaf exterior of Kinkaku-ji. The Japanese style of domestic architecture was thus adapted to the requirements and tastes of the military elite.

Some of the most notable emblems of the power and wealth of the feudal lords (*daimyō*) were their **castles**. These reached their apogee in the sixteenth century as the warlords jockeyed for power. The castles were large in scale, surrounded by moats and elaborate defence works, and were constructed of wood on top of monumental stone foundations. Though obviously built for defence, their uncompromising solidity is offset by multistorey watchtowers looking like so many layers of an elaborate wedding cake with their fanciful, multiple roofs. Himeji-jō (White Egret Castle), west of Ōsaka, is an outstanding example of Japan's unique style of castle architecture.

Under the patronage of the feudal hierarchy, Japanese art reached its most opulent during the **Momoyama era** (1573–1600). The scale of feudal architecture created a new demand for decorative **screen paintings**, which were used to adorn every storey and were either fixed on walls, *fusuma* or folding screens (*byōbu*). From the late sixteenth century, the Kyoto-based **Kanō School** of artists came to dominate official taste. Their screens combined the bright colours and decorative boldness of *Yamato-e* with the more subtle compositional features of *suiboku-ga*. Subjects were mainly drawn from nature and from Japanese history and legend, while the extensive use of gold leaf added a shimmering brightness to the dark interior spaces of the great Momoyama castles, palaces and temples. Kanō Eitoku and his grandson, Kanō Tan'yū, were the school's most famous exponents and their works can still be seen in Kyoto's Daitoku-ji and Nijō-jō. This latter is the only surviving palace from the Momoyama era. Originally part of a castle complex, its sweeping roof lines and intricately carved and ornamented gables show a lavishness and boldness of style appropriate to its subsequent use as the Tokugawa shoguns' Kyoto base.

The Edo era 1600–1868

After 1603, the Tokugawa Shogunate was established at **Edo** (modern-day Tokyo) where it remained in power for the next 250 years. These were years of peace and stability in Japan, marked by isolation from the outside world, the growth of cities, economic development and social mobility. To begin with, the merchant class were at the bottom of the feudal social ladder while the samurai remained the ruling elite. As their wealth increased, however, the position and influence of the merchants rose accordingly.

Edo-era arts flourished under these new patrons. In **painting**, while the Kanō school continued to receive official support from the shoguns, other schools explored different styles and found different masters. Artists such as Tawaraya Sōtatsu (died around 1643) and Ogata Kōrin (1658–1716) stand out for reviving aspects of the *Yamato-e* tradition and injecting new decorative life into Japanese painting. Sōtatsu's famous golden screen paintings based on *The Tale of Genji* dramatically adapt the subject matter and style of Heian-era *emaki* to this larger format. Kōrin's most noted works include the "Irises" screens, now held in Tokyo's Nezu Museum, which take an episode from a Heian-era novel, *The Tale of Ise*, and reduce its content to the striking patterns of flatly conceived blue irises and green leaves against a shimmering gold background.

In patronizing the arts, merchants sought not only reflections of their own affluence but also of their lifestyle. Paintings which depicted the often bawdy pleasures of city life came into vogue. The lively entertainment districts of Edo, Osaka and Kyoto, with their brothels, teahouses and Kabuki theatres, were depicted in painted screens and scrolls. This new genre of painting, **ukiyo-e**, or "pictures of the floating world", devoted itself to the hedonistic pastimes of the new rich. By the early eighteenth century, *ukiyo-e* were most commonly produced as hand-coloured woodblock prints which became gradually more sophisticated in their subtle use of line and colour as mass-printing techniques developed.

Catering to popular taste, late-eighteenth-century artists such as Harunobu, Utamaro and Sharaku portrayed famous beauties of the day and Kabuki actors in dramatic poses. Explicitly erotic prints known as *shunga* (spring pictures) were also big sellers, as were humorous scenes of daily life (*manga*), the forerunners of today's comics. **Hokusai** (1760–1849), perhaps the most internationally famous *ukiyo-e* artist, was originally known for his *manga*, but went on to create one of the most enduring images of Japan, "The Great Wave", as part of his series the *Thirty-Six Views of Mount Fuji*. Followed by the equally popular *Fifty-Three Stages of the Tōkaidō*, by Hiroshige (1797–1858), these later landscape prints were instantly popular at a time when travel was both difficult and restricted.

The **decorative arts** reached new heights of elegance and craftsmanship during the Edo era. Varieties of Imari- and Kutani-ware **porcelain** (from Kyūshū and Ishikawa-ken) were made in large quantities for domestic consumption and later for export. Inlaid **lacquerware** was executed in bold and simple designs. Honami Kōetsu (1558–1637) and Ogata Kōrin (1658–1716) were leading lacquer artists of the period, as well as celebrated painters and calligraphers – their design skills translated readily across different materials and craft forms. One of Kōetsu's most famous lacquer works, an inkstone box in the Tokyo National Museum, reflects these combined talents with its inlaid-lead bridge and silver calligraphy forming integral parts of the overall design. Kōrin carried on this tradition with his own black-lacquer, inkstone box; its jagged, lead and silver bridge across a bed of inlaid gold and shell irises translates his earlier "Irises" screens (see p.967) into a three-dimensional format.

Textile production, meanwhile, was centred in the Nishijin district of Kyoto where silk cloth was made both for the Shogunate and the imperial court. Luxurious effects were achieved using elaborate embroidery and weaving techniques, which became works of art in themselves. Paste-resistant **yūzen** dyeing developed in Kyoto in the late seventeenth century. This complicated process involved multiple applications of rice-starch paste and dyes by hand to capture subtle, multicolour painted effects. The resulting patterns were often embellished with embroidery or gold and silver foil. Fine examples of kimono of the period can be seen in Japan's museums, while *ukiyo-e* provide numerous illustrations of this aspect of "the floating world".

Western influences

Episodes of **Western contact** prior to the Edo era resulted in some specific examples of artistic exchange. The *Namban* (southern barbarian) golden-screen paintings of the Momoyama era show Portuguese merchants and missionaries at Nagasaki before they were expelled. The continued Dutch presence similarly gave rise to paintings and prints which portrayed the Dutch settlement at Nagasaki's Dejima. Later, this was also the route for stylistic change generated by imported Western art.

The reopening of Japan by Commodore Perry in 1854 and the fall of the Tokugawa Shogunate in 1867 launched a period of massive social and cultural change. With the restoration of the emperor Meiji to power and a new government in place in Tokyo from 1868, a process of **modernization and westernization** was embarked upon which transformed the face of Japan and of the visual arts.

The opening of the treaty ports furnished a new subject matter for woodblock print artists who produced marvellous portraits of big-nosed Westerners in Yokohama and other ports. Meiji modernization provided additional themes as the opening of the first railway, spinning factory and many other advances were recorded for posterity. Western advisers assisted in the design and construction of **European-style buildings**, some of which can still be found scattered around Japanese cities, while others have been relocated to the Meiji Mura Open-Air Museum near Nagoya.

In the early years of the Meiji era (1868–1912), traditional Japanese and Chinese styles of painting were rejected by many artists in favour of Western styles and techniques. Artists such as Kuroda Seiki (1866–1924) and Fujishima Takeji (1867–1943) studied in Paris and returned to become leaders of **Western-style painting** (*Yōga*) in Japan. Realism, Impressionism and other Western art movements were directly transplanted to the Tokyo art scene. More conservative painters, such as Yokoyama Taikan (1868–1958) worked to establish *Nihon-ga*, a modern style of Japanese painting, drawing on a mixture of Chinese, Japanese and Western techniques.

Western influence on the arts expanded greatly in the Taishō era (1912–1926) with **sculpture**, as well as painting, closely following current trends. In the postwar period, Japanese artists looked again to Europe and America but more selectively took their inspiration from a range of avant-garde developments in the West. Art in Japan today can be seen as a blend of Japanese and international currents. Sources of tradition can no longer be identified purely with the East or the West.

Mingei: the folk craft tradition

It is in the area of the folk crafts that Japan has maintained a distinctive tradition and one that delights in the simplicity and utilitarian aspects of ordinary everyday objects. **Mingei** really is "people's art", the works of unknown craftsmen from all regions of Japan that are revered for their natural and unpretentious qualities.

While Japanese folk crafts flourished during the Edo era, the mass production techniques of the machine age led to a fall in the quality of textiles, ceramics, lacquer and other craft forms. The art critic and philosopher Yanagi Sōetsu (1889–1961) worked from the 1920s to stem this tide and to preserve the craft products of the pre-industrial age. Yanagi established the **Mingei-kan**, or Japanese Folk Crafts Museum, in Tokyo in 1936 to display Japanese folk crafts of every description. But the revival of the *mingei* tradition also celebrated works by living artist-craftsmen as well as regional differences in style and technique. The potters Hamada Shōji (1894–1978), Kawai Kanjirō (1890–1966) and the Englishman Bernard Leach (1887–1979) were most famously associated with the Mingei movement, as was the woodblock artist, Munakata Shiko (1903–1975), and the textile designer Kiesuke Serizawa (1895–1976).

A wide range of traditional handicrafts are still being produced today all over Japan. *Yūzen*-style kimono dyeing and *kumihimo* braid craft are associated with Kyoto; *shuri* weaving techniques with Okinawa; *Hakata ningyō*, or earthenware dolls, with Fukuoka; and Kumano brushes with Hiroshima. Pottery, lacquerware, wood, bamboo and handmade paper products of every description continue to preserve the spirit of *mingei* in contemporary Japan.

The performing arts

The traditional theatre arts evolved in the context of broader cultural developments during different periods of Japan's history. **Nō** (or Noh) is the classic theatre of Japan, a form of masked drama which has its roots in sacred Shinto dances, but was formalized 600 years ago under the patronage of the Ashikaga shoguns and the aesthetic influence of Zen. The bare wooden stage with its painted backdrop of an ancient pine tree, the actors' stylized robes and the elusive expressions of the finely crafted masks create an atmosphere that is both understated and refined. The dramatic contrasts of stillness and sudden rushes of movement, and of periods of silence punctuated by sound, conjure up the essence of the Zen aesthetic. The **kyōgen** interludes inject an element of comic relief into this otherwise stately ceremonial entertainment.

The 240 plays of the **Nō repertoire** are divided into five categories. *Waki-nō* (or *kami-nō*) depict deities in stories of rejoicing; *shura-mono* portray famous warriors in tales of suffering and torment; and *kazura-mono* depict young and beautiful women in a gentle setting. The fourth group comprises *kyōjo-mono* (mad-women pieces) and *genzai-mono*, depicting mad men or obsessed women. In the final category, *kiri-nō* are fast-paced plays featuring supernatural beings, gods or demons. Though a traditional programme contains a selection from each group, with three or four *kyōgen* interludes, most programmes nowadays consist of only two Nō plays and one *kyōgen*.

The principal character in Nō plays is known as the *shite*, and may be either a ghost, mad person, or a superhuman or animal creature. The secondary character, the *waki*, on the other hand, always represents people living in the present. *Shite* characters generally wear a mask, of male, female or demon type, which conceals the actor's presence and allows the characterization to dominate. The actor's skill lies in transcending the conventions of archaic language, mask and formalized costume to convey the dramatic tensions inherent in the play. Dance elements and musical effects aid directly in this process and draw on the folk entertainment tradition from which Nō is derived. Famously inaccessible to some, Nō is capable of achieving tremendously subtle and evocative effects.

By comparison, the **kyōgen** interludes primarily aim at amusement and providing a counterpoint to the Nō drama. As with Nō, *kyōgen* performers are all male and assume a variety of roles, some of which are completely independent of the Nō play, while others comment on the development of the main story. The language used is colloquial (though of sixteenth-century origin) and, compared to the esoteric poetry of Nō, far more accessible to a contemporary audience. There is a greater emphasis on realistic portrayal in *kyōgen* and the actors only occasionally wear masks. Humour is achieved through exaggerated speech and formalized acting techniques and movements. Essentially a dialogue play between two characters or groups of actors, *kyōgen* makes use of wit and satire to balance the mood of Nō.

While Nō is classical and restrained, **Kabuki**, Japan's popular theatre, is colourful, exuberant and full of larger-than-life characters, a highly stylized theatrical form which delights in flamboyant gestures and elaborate costumes, make-up and staging effects. While the language may still be incomprehensible, the plots themselves deal with easily understandable, often tragic themes of love and betrayal, commonly taken from famous historical episodes.

Kabuki originated in the early 1600s as rather risqué dances performed by all-female troupes. The shogun eventually banned women because of Kabuki's association with prostitution, but their replacement – young men – was no more successful and in the end Kabuki actors were predominantly older men, some of whom specialize in female roles (*onnagata*). It developed as a more serious form of theatre in the late sixteenth century when Kabuki was cultivated chiefly by the merchant class. It gave theatrical expression to the vitality of city life and to the class tensions between samurai, merchants and peasants which informed the plots of so many plays. As an indication of the popularity of Kabuki, powerful images of famous actors were a favourite theme of Edo-era *ukiyo-e* prints.

Bunraku, Japan's puppet theatre, was another product of Edo-era culture and exerted a strong influence on Kabuki, even providing many of its plots. Bunraku developed out of the *jōruri* storytelling tradition, in which travelling minstrels recited popular tales of famous heroes and legends, accompanied by the biwa (Japanese lute) or *shamisen* (three-stringed guitar). Adapted to the stage in the early seventeenth century, Bunraku made use of stylized puppets, one-half to one-third the size of humans, to enact the various roles. The great Ōsaka playwright **Chikamatsu Monzaemon** (1653–1724), often referred to as "the Shakespeare of Japan", is responsible for around one hundred Bunraku plays, many of which are still performed in Japan today. The most famous plays in the Bunraku repertoire include Chikamatsu's *Sonezaki Shinjū* (The Love Suicides at Sonezaki), based on a true story, and *Kokusen'ya Kassen* (The Battles of Coxinga), about a legendary pirate.

Three operators take part in a **Bunraku performance**, while a chanter, using a varied vocal range, tells the story to the accompaniment of *shamisen* music. The main puppeteer is in full view of the audience and uses his left hand to manipulate the face and head, with his right controlling the puppet's right arm. One assistant operates the left arm while another moves the puppet's legs; both dressed in black, these moving shadows simply disappear into the background. The skill of the puppeteers – the result of lengthy apprenticeships – contributes to the high degree of realism in the performance, and the stylized movements can result in great drama. Indeed, Kabuki actors employed some puppet-like gestures from Bunraku to enhance and enliven their own acting techniques.

Contemporary theatre

As with the visual arts, there are many different types of contemporary theatre in Japan. **Shingeki** (meaning "new theatre") is the term applied to a type of modern theatre which first developed during the Meiji era. Essentially a theatre of realism, it arose through the influence of Shakespeare and the European naturalists and plays in this representational genre continue to be produced. *Shingeki* is very much the literary product of a playwright and can therefore be distinguished from more spectacle-oriented, home-grown drama forms.

The contemporary theatre scene also embraces the diverse spectacles of **Takarazuka**, a Rockettes-like all-female musical review company originating from Ōsaka in the early 1900s (see box, p.511), and **Butō** (or Butoh), the abstract and improvisational dance form established in the 1950s; the name derives from *ankoku butō*, meaning "dance of utter darkness". Butō developed from the work of dancers Hijikata Tatsumi and Ōno Kazuo, drawing on the traditions of Kabuki and Nō as well as contemporary American dancers such as Martha Graham. It jolted the establishment with the performers' stark white make-up and the spectacle of aggressive eroticism born of instinctive gestures and movements. Though it remains a marginal art form in Japan, Butō's haunting beauty has recently found greater appreciation in Europe and America.

Formerly known as *angura* (underground theatre), the **experimental theatre** of the 1960s has had an ongoing impact through the wide range of *shōgeki-ijō-engeki* (small-theatre drama) companies which cater to the interests and tastes of Japan's younger generation. Drama students from the University of Tokyo led by Hideki Noda (see below) founded *Yume no Yūmin-sha* in 1976, while their counterparts at Waseda University established *Daisan Butai* in 1981. Both young theatre groups focus on the preoccupations and social problems of the *shin-jinrui*, Japan's materially privileged postwar generation. Outside of Tokyo, another more experimental group, *Dumb Type*, was founded in 1984 by Fine Art students from Kyoto City University of Arts. Their multi-media performances make use of installations and video and computer art to explore aspects of human behaviour.

Hideki Noda is still a prominent figure in Japanese contemporary theatre and has been involved in projects ranging from new Kabuki writing and working with his theatre company, Noda Map, to recent forays into opera: in 2004 he directed an innovative version of Verdi's *Macbeth* at the New National Theatre in Tokyo – the first national theatre in Japan dedicated to promoting contemporary performing arts (opera, ballet, and contemporary dance and drama). There are many other theatre groups in Japan creating original works, neo-Kabuki productions and adaptations of Western musicals. At the same time, the more mainstream work of the director **Ninagawa Yukio** has won a considerable following outside Japan. Ninagawa has directed both traditional Japanese plays and Western productions at home and abroad, and in a sense bridges the theatrical conventions of East and West. Another theatre company which has won acclaim abroad is the **Setagaya Public Theatre**, whose members have worked with foreign producers on international productions such as a stage adaptation of Haruki Murakami's collection of short stories, *The Elephant Vanishes*.

Marie Conte-Helm

Music

With a value of well over six billion dollars, Japan has the second-largest music market in the world, after the USA. The advent of satellite TV, with its many music channels, has fuelled music mania among young Asians, and karaoke in particular is wildly popular. The country produces sugary sweet bubblegum **pop** par excellence, which is increasingly popular throughout East and Southeast Asia, but the thriving **roots scene** is more nourishing – fuelled by the dynamic music of the islands of Okinawa. It is these sounds of Japan's "deep south" which have recently been making waves at home and abroad. Otherwise, Japan's bewildering variety of **popular and traditional music** is little known in the West.

Unfortunately, the overriding image of Japanese contemporary music is one of instantly forgettable pop. Teenagers are trained, manufactured and recorded as *idoru kashu*, or idol singers. Boy bands like Smap or Da Pump and cutesy female singers like duo Wink offer watered-down Western pop with Japanese lyrics, their hooklines often sung in meaningless English. Such surface noise aside, nowhere in Asia can you find such a wide range of music: from ancient Buddhist chanting and court music to folk and old urban styles, from localized popular forms such as *kayokyoku* and *enka* to Western classical and jazz – plus every kind of pop you'd find in the West.

Traditional instruments

Shakuhachi
A bamboo flute with five finger-holes – four on the front and one on the back – the *shakuhachi* has a full range of chromatic notes, obtained by adjusting the position of the flute and partially covering the holes. The colour of its tone, while always soft and pure, depends on the bamboo used. During the Edo period, it was played primarily in chamber ensembles with *koto* and *shamizen*, although more recently there's been a revival of the more ancient solo repertoire as an aid to meditation.

Biwa and Shamisen
A pear-shaped plucked lute with four or five strings, the *biwa* originated in China. It was played both in *gagaku* ensembles and solo, but had almost fallen out of use by the end of World War II, until Toru Takemitsu, Japan's most famous contemporary composer, started writing for it, precipitating a revival.

A three-stringed lute, the *shamisen* also came to Japan from China, via Okinawa, where it's known as a *shansin*. The earliest *shamisen*, music is credited to *biwa* players in the early seventeenth century and it has become one of the most popular instruments in Japanese music.

Koto
The Japanese long zither, or *koto*, usually has thirteen strings with moveable bridges and is played with fingerpicks. It is thought to have originated from the Chinese *zheng* and to have arrived in Japan in the eighth century. Similar instruments are found in Korea (*kayagūm*) and Vietnam (*dan tranh*). Found in *gagaku* ensembles, it has developed a rich solo tradition. It is also used to accompany songs and in small "chamber music" ensembles, together with a second *koto*, a *shamisen*, or a *shakuhachi*.

Classical and theatrical music

Classical music can be divided into **gagaku** (court orchestral music) and **shōmyō** (Buddhist chanting). *Gagaku* came from China 1500 years ago as Confucian cere-monial music of the Chinese court. Similar to a chamber orchestra, *gagaku* ensem-bles include as many as twenty instruments, with flutes, oboes, zithers, lutes, gongs and drums. *Gagaku* is now played only as *bugaku* (dance music) or *kangen* (instru-mental music), at the Imperial court and at a few Shinto shrines and Buddhist tem-ples. Unlike Western classical music, themes aren't stated and repeated. Instead, the rhythms are based on breathing and the result is a form that sounds avant-garde – sometimes discordant, sometimes meditative.

Japan's most famous theatrical form, **Nō**, was synthesized in the fourteenth centu-ry from religious pantomimes, folk theatre and court music. Nō, which combines ora-tory, dance and singing in a highly stylized manner, is still performed and continues to influence both Japanese and foreign theatre and music. There are solo singers, small choruses singing in unison and an instrumental ensemble of *fue* (bamboo flute), the only melodic instrument other than the voice, two hourglass drums and a barrel drum.

Bunraku puppetry came after Nō, and was one of the sources of the colourful and sensual **Kabuki** theatre, which emerged in the early seventeenth century. Its combi-nation of Nō narratives, chanting and music based on the *shamisen* (three-string lute), flute and drums led to a more lively and popular musical style. This boosted the popularity of the new *nagauta* style of *shamisen* playing, which in turn influenced popular styles to come, including folk music.

Ancient roots

The many musical styles found in Japan have their roots in Japan's particular historical circumstances – China, Korea, Central and Southeast Asia all exerted considerable influence on the early development of music. The history of music in Japan dates back to the third century BC, but the arrival of eighty Korean musicians in 453 AD and the introduction of Buddhism in the mid-sixth century are the key events. **Gagaku**, court music and religious music (see box above) survive from this period, and Buddhist chanting, **shōmyō**, can still be heard in temples today.

Japanese scholars tend to say all music prior to the Meiji reformation of 1868 is traditional, but within that definition there are different styles from each epoch. Early history (400–1200) produced religious and court styles. In the years to 1500, as society became more militarized, theatrical genres like Nō drama developed (see box above) and itinerant monks chanted long historical narratives to the *biwa*, a Japanese lute whose origins can be traced back to the Silk Road in Central Asia.

Between 1500 and 1868, Japanese rulers imposed a period of near total iso-lation (see p.939), and outside influences were minimized. Old instruments like the *koto* (a kind of zither) continued to develop repertoire, as did the *shakuhachi* bamboo flute. However, it was the three-stringed plucked lute, the *shamisen*, that came to represent new styles, reflecting the development of a sophisticat-ed pre-modern urban culture.

The **shamisen** provided the perfect musical accompaniment for popular styles, dance and drama, as well as the narrative folk styles often called *min'yō* (see opposite). The *nagauta shamisen* style for Kabuki theatre also developed at

this time, as did the *sankyoku*, the typical instrumental ensemble of the time –
koto, *shamisen*, *shakuhachi* and *kokyu* (a bowed fiddle). Very popular during the
Edo period (1600–1868) were the many kinds of folk songs about work, love
and so on. Singers were accompanied by *shamisen*, *shakuhachi*, drums and flutes.

Min'yō – folk music

Japan's **min'yō** (folk) tradition is long and rich. Each region has its own style,
perhaps the most famous of all being the instrumental *shamisen* style from
Tsugaru in Tōhoku. The continued popularity of *min'yō* is partly due to the
nostalgia felt by urbanites for their home towns and villages, and many Japanese
not only listen to *min'yō* but are able to sing a song or two, particularly one
from their home region.

Like many traditional types of music, the form is tightly controlled by various
guilds, a system called **iemoto**. Long apprenticeships are the norm for musicians,
and family-based teaching systems guarantee something is passed on to the next
generation. *Shamisen* master and singer Kiyohide Umewaka, whose father started
a key guild in the 1950s, says the dedication required to master the form means
that there are few professional players. His father taught top *min'yō* singer Sanae
Asano and the spellbinding young *shamisen* player Shin'ichi Kinoshita, the latter
having played a major part in the *shin-min'yo* (new *min'yō*) wave led by singer Ito
Takio, well known for his passionate singing style and willingness to experiment.

Traditional **drumming** from Sado island (see p.349) has now become
famous internationally. Ondekoza, the original group of drummers, and its offshoot, Kodō, are capable of playing very powerful, rootsy gigs with just the various Japanese drums (from the big *daiko* to small hand-drums).

One of the very best places to catch traditional music in action in Japan is at a
local festival, or *matsuri*. At Obon, an ancient Buddhist festival to celebrate the
ancestors, locals get down to a *Bon odori* (Bon dance). Check out the music of
Shang Shang Typhoon, which incorporates various kinds of festival music into its
shows and even has its own festival every year, held just outside Tokyo. Wherever
you go, you'll be dancing, and you'll be dragged up by the local granny if you
try to sit it out. Dances are often centred around a bamboo tower with a big
drum in the centre, moving to either tapes or live *min'yō* of classic *Bon* dances.
You may catch the *mikoshi* procession, where young men dressed in what look
like jockstraps struggle to carry a portable shrine. Such festivals are all about
music, cementing community bonds and having a good time, Japan-style.

Developing modern styles

As Japan began the process of **modernization** under the Meiji Reformation
of 1868, there was already a large pool of traditional music – classical, folk and
urban – available for development or incorporation into newer styles. Another
influence came into the mix in the mid-nineteenth century with the arrival of
Western military bands. These laid the foundations for the Western music that
followed, from classical to popular genres like jazz and chanson.

Two short song forms – **shoka** and **gunka** – developed during the Meiji
period. *Shoka* are songs composed to introduce Western music and singing to

schools. *Gunka* are military songs with strong Japanese elements, acting as a prototype for later Japanese-Western syntheses like *enka*. Popular from the Sino-Japanese war to World War II – when Western forms like jazz were banned – you can still hear these patriotic songs blaring from the trucks of right-wing activists in Tokyo.

At the turn of the century, another immensely popular song form was **ryukoka** ("songs that are popular"), which developed from street entertainers in the Ōsaka region, and was set to a *shamisen* backing. Japan's first recording stars, Kumoemon Tochuken and Naramuru Yoshida, were *ryukoka* performers, and their throbbing vocal styles prefigured important popular forms to come.

With Western culture – movies and music – now flooding Japan, local musicians started to catch on. The first Japanese to play **jazz** were the Hatano Jazz Band, following a trip to the USA in 1912. Tango, foxtrot, rumba, Tin Pan Alley, blues and Hawaiian all followed. The potential for a fusion between Japanese and Western music was most fully realized by two composers, **Nakayama Shimpei** and **Koga Masao**. Sometimes using the Japanese *yonanuki* pentatonic scale with Western arrangements, Shimpei hit the big time with *Kachusha no uta* ("Katherine's Song"), while Koga pioneered the use of single-line guitar accompaniment (standard for many *enka* songs) in the 1931 hit *Sake wa Namida ka Tameiki ka* ("Sake is a tear or a sigh"). Koga also used the *yuri* ornamentation from traditional music in this song.

The resultant style became known as **kayokyoku**, a catch-all term for Japanese popular songs that originated in the 1930s but only came into use after World War II. Roots bands like Shang Shang Typhoon that emerged in the late 1980s use a similar approach to create songs from a mixture of Japanese pop and traditional, Latin, reggae and Asian styles.

Postwar pop

After the famine and devastation that followed the end of World War II, people turned for solace to songs like the influential 1945 hit *Ringo No Uta* ("The Apple Song"), sung by Namiki Michiko and Kirishima Noboru. Despite the arrival of more Western styles like R&B and boogie-woogie, some artists emerged singing *kayokyoku* in a Japanese style. In 1949, at the tender age of 12, **Hibari Misora**, the greatest popular singer of the modern era, made her debut.

Hibari, a precocious child who could memorize long poems and mimic adult singers, was versatile. Her voice could handle the natural voice singing style or *jigoe*, as well as the wavering folk style or *yuri*. Her powerful, sobbing *kobushi* vocal technique created a highly charged atmosphere, but she was also talented enough to cover jazz, *min'yō*, Latin, chanson and torch songs in the thousand recordings she made before her death at 52 in 1989. In many ways, she was Japan's best-known and loved popular cultural icon of the twentieth century: not only did she appear in 160 films, she was also the undisputed queen of **enka** (see box opposite).

Meanwhile, as Hibari was starting her career, **American songs** were spreading across Japan, helped by the Allied occupying forces. Japanese composers like Ryuchi Hattori picked up on the trends with the shuffle-rhythm inspired *Tokyo Boogie Woogie*, even managing a *shamisen* version. Other styles like bluegrass, rockabilly, Hawaiian (a second boom), doowop, R&B and jazz all developed quickly.

In the 1950s, **Japanese Latin** music was established, although its roots were laid down at least twenty years previously. During the Fifties and early Sixties,

Enka has been described as the *"Nihonjin no kokoro"*, the soul of the Japanese. It's about lost love, homesickness or simply drowning the sorrows of a broken heart with sake. The songs feature fog or rain, a smouldering cigarette that means loss, the sad, unbearable farewell at a desolate port, somewhere far from home. This is the world of *enka*.

Enka (from *enzetsu*, meaning public speech, and *ka*, meaning a song) is more than 100 years old and, despite what some younger Japanese say, it is still enormously popular in Japan. Originally it was a form of political dissent, disseminated by song sheets, but it quickly changed in the early twentieth century as it became the first style to truly synthesize Western scales and Japanese modes. Nakayama Shimpei and Koga Masaowere were the trailblazing composers. Koga's first hit in 1931, *Kage Wo Shitaite* ("Longing For Your Memory"), remains a much-loved classic.

Enka seems to be everywhere in Japan. Special television programmes like *Enka no Hanamichi* pump it out, and you'll hear it in restaurants and bars. And, of course, it received a major boost with the invention of karaoke, which helped to spread the genre's popularity both with younger Japanese and foreigners. The classic image is of *enka* queen **Hibari Misora** (see opposite) decked out in a kimono, tears streaming down her face as she sobs through Koga's *Kanashi Sake* ("Sad Sake"), with typically understated backing and single-line guitar. Hibari had the *nakibushi* (crying melody) technique and a stunning vibrato-like *kobushi* which makes the listener's hair stand on end.

When Hibari died in 1989, **Harumi Miyako** inherited her position as the top singer. She is famed for her growling attack and the song *Sayonara*. Many *enka* stars have long careers, and veterans like Kitajima Suburoare are still going strong, but there's a new generation led by Mori Shin'ichi, Yashiro Aki, Kobayashi Sachiko and the multi-talented Itsuki Hiroshi. Recently, a number of upcoming Korean singers have been making waves (Hibari was of Japanese/Korean ancestry). Watch out for Gill Jehee as the next big star.

No *enka* fan can pass up a visit to Rizumu (Rhythm), Kobayashi Kazuhiko's ancient record shop in Ueno, Tokyo. Located under a railway arch in the Ameyoko market, the brightly displayed shop is a treasure trove of memorabilia with music stacked floor to ceiling. Kobayashi-san, quick to notice foreigners' growing interest, has even romanized the titles so you can find that haunting *enka* number you can't get out of your head.

many Cuban-style bands like the Tokyo Cuban Boys were formed; tango and Latin singer Fujisawa Ranko is still remembered for her South American tours. Tango remains popular in Japan and there is even an original Latin rhythm, the *dodompa*. The tradition has been kept strong with the recent success of Orquesta de la Luz.

Kayokyoku gradually became associated with styles that used traditional scales, like *enka*, while the more Western-sounding pop became known as Japanese pops. This latter form was defined by songs like *Sukiyaki* and by the many Western-style groups that developed in the 1960s, known as Group Sounds. **Japanese pops** mirrored all the Western moves – Beatles imitators, rock, folk-rock, folk and psychedelia were all flavour of the day.

Japanese rock

By the late 1960s, musicians were starting to create **Japanese-language rock**. Many pop bands at the time sang in English, but some underground groups tried splicing Japanese into the rock mix. Seminal band Happy End were pioneers. Led by composer Haruomi Hosono and lyricist Matsumoto Takashi, the band tried to mesh folk-rock with Japanese lyrics about love and politics, and in the process inspired an entire generation of rockers.

Rock blossomed as the 1970s advanced. A new generation was about to be turned upside down by **Kina Shoukichi**, a little-known Okinawan musician, with his band **Champloose** (the name comes from the name of a traditional Okinawan stir-fry). Kina (see box on p.980), the son of legendary *min'yō* singer and *sanshin* player Shouei, combined Okinawan *min'yō* and rock on his song *Haisai Oji-san* ("Hey, Man"), which became so famous that it is used today as a drill song for high-school baseball games.

The Asian rock sound, as defined by Champloose, was further developed by bands like Carol, Harada Shinji and RC Succession. **The Southern All Stars**, whose way of singing Japanese as if it were English helped them to become Japan's biggest-selling band in the late 1980s, were another influential group.

But the most successful international and domestic band of the late 1970s and early 1980s has to be **Yellow Magic Orchestra** (YMO), formed by Haruomi Hosono, Sakamoto Ryuchi and Takahashi Yukihiro. Heavily influenced by German band Kraftwerk and computer game ditties, YMO's brand of technopop inspired many followers, notably The Plastics and Melon. Sakamoto went on to a highly visible and successful international career, both as a soloist and as an Oscar-winning film-score composer. Haruomi, certainly regarded in Japan as a pioneer in searching for exotic sounds to incorporate into his music, has been working in diverse fields – soundtracks, songwriting for idol singers, music documentaries for TV and work with artists from James Brown and Ry Cooder to Tunisian singer Amina Annabi. His massive influence on the new roots generation in Japan cannot be overestimated.

What informs Haruomi's work – the search for an identity – is a major preoccupation of roots bands like Shang Shang Typhoon and The Boom. Haruomi became one of the first Japanese musicians to look south to the islands of Okinawa for inspiration: in 1980 both Haruomi and Ry Cooder performed on Kina Shoukichi's second, Okinawan-influenced album, *Bloodline*. Since then, he has worked with noted American producer Bill Laswell, as well as on albums with singers like Koshi Miharu and Moritaka Chisato.

Sandii and the Sunsetz were another band that savoured international success in the 1980s. Led by powerful singer Sandii and composer/producer Kubota Makoto, the band blended reggae and Okinawan music into its mix. But shortly after the band split up, Kubota turned his attention to producing Asian popular music, working with Indonesians like Elvy Sukaesih and Detty Kurnia, as well as Singaporean comedian/singer Dick Lee. Kubota's most recent work has been with dance star Monday Michiru, The Boom and, on his own label, Sushi, with the Madagascan band Njava.

Since her debut in 1980 (*Eating Pleasure*, with Hosono Haruomi), Sandii has moved easily across a broad range of styles. Kubota's interest in creating "an Asian pop style for the 1990s" is in strong evidence on Sandii's albums of that period, which feature the *champur*-style *dangdut* dance form (with house and dance beats in the mix), lots of Asia-Pacific and Brazilian songs and a voice that can carry anything from torch songs to reggae and Japanese pop. Since then Sandii has returned to her roots with several superb Hawaiian albums, one of which featured the outstanding American guitarist Bob Brozman.

Japan's underground and avant-garde music scenes have a long history, with roots in the radical student movement of the late 1960s. **Punk** and **new wave** music had a big impact in Japan, and plenty of enthusiastic young Japanese reacted to the clarion call. Outfits with worldwide cult followings, like all-female indie-poppers Shonen Knife, and the incendiary avant-punk Boredoms, can trace their roots directly back to this scene.

The roots boom

The Japanese genius for assimilating foreign sounds into a new form is well known, and the invasion of **world music** has had a significant effect. Reggae, for example, was considered "underground" for years, but the rise of Japanese outfits like Jamaican-style toaster Rankin' Taxi and ska band Tokyo Ska Paradise Orchestra, playing at events like the annual reggae fest Japansplash, has given the genre a mainstream profile, and ska in particular remains hugely popular, especially in the Kansai region. Visits by Africans like Papa Wemba (whose global management is located in Japan) have created local *lingala* (*soukous*) bands. **Latin music** has also had a big effect, propelling the talented Orquesta de la Luz to the top of the Latin chart in the early 1990s and seeing a plethora of salsa and Latin dance nights spring up at clubs across the country.

But the most significant development has been the rise of **local roots bands** since the late 1980s, when bands like Shang Shang Typhoon (SST), The Boom, and Okinawan artists and bands such as Rinken Band, Nenes, Kina, Daiko Tetsuhiro and Amuro Namie broke onto the scene. Inspiration came from both within Japan (Okinawa and local popular culture) and outside (World Music).

The second coming of the Okinawans (see box on p.980) was heralded by frenetic sell-out gigs of the **Rinken Band** in 1990, and a short time later by the ecstatic comeback of Kina and Champloose. Okinawan traditional music blended with bright pop caught everyone's attention. Okinawans' relationship to mainstream Japanese culture could be compared to the "Celtic" movement in Europe: they have a keen sense of their own identity and, in an increasingly homogenized Japan, a lively folk culture.

The Okinawan method of taking local traditions and updating them with other forms of music was reflected in a wave of bands in the 1990s, foremost amongst them rootsy-rockers **Soul Flower Union**, led by Nakagawa Takashi. Soul Flower Union also have an appealing alter ego, **Soul Flower Mononoke Summit**, where the band blend acoustic guitars, Okinawan and *chindon* (street) music, which advertises products or shops, with drums and various brass instruments. The band's debut, *Asyl Ching-Dong*, features prewar tunes and is strongly influenced by Okinawan master Daiku Tetsuhiro. Recent work has included gigs with the Irish musician Donal Lunny.

Another updated local form is **kawachi ondo**, an old narrative folk style from the central Kansai region. Its rapid-fire, rap-like vocal delivery is somewhat similar to Thailand and Laos' *mor lam*. Traditionally, *kawachi ondo's* wild men, dressed in colourful kimono, perform at local *bon odori* (summer festivals) around the country. The leading modern exponent, **Kawachiya Kikusuimaru**, burst onto the scene with a hit single for a TV commercial about part-time workers (known as "freeters"). He released several classy albums that included Indonesian, reggae and rock elements. He has been quiet of late, releasing only a wonderful (but long-deleted) collection of reggae covers – a tribute to Bob Marley called *Bob Marley Ondo 97*.

The sound of the deep, deep south

Be it at a *min'yō* performance in a small club or among the massed troupes of the annual *Eisa* festival, you'll find graceful dancing, haunting vocals, all kinds of drumming and stunning playing on the three-stringed *sanshin* in the islands of **Okinawa**.

Music has been integral to the island's culture and social life for centuries; it's said that peasants carried their musical instruments into the rice fields, ready for a jam session after work. The folk tradition is very much alive, and in some villages *umui* (religious songs) are still sung at festivals to honour ancestors. Work songs that reflect communal agriculture techniques can still be heard, and various kinds of group and circle dances, some performed exclusively by women, can be found in the smaller islands.

Popular entertainment is known by the general term *zo odori* (common dance), though everyone calls these songs *shima uta* (island songs). The best-known style, one no wedding would be complete without, is called *katcharsee*. Set to lively rhythms laid down by the *sanshin*, which plays both melody and rhythm, and various drums, the dance is performed with the upper body motionless and the lower body swaying sensuously, accompanied by graceful hand movements that echo similar dances in Thailand and Indonesia.

The Asian connection can be clearly seen in the history of the *sanshin*. This three-stringed lute began life in China as the long-necked *sanxian* and was introduced to Okinawa around 1392. Local materials were quickly exhausted so that Thai snake-skin was used for the soundbox and Filipino hardwood for the shorter neck of the altered instrument, which became known as the *sanshin*. Once introduced to mainland Japan, the *sanshin* became bigger, produced a harder sound and was renamed the *shamisen*, one of the quintessential Japanese instruments.

A more recent influence on Okinawan music has come via the US military presence. Local musicians started to copy American pop styles in the 1950s, sometimes mixing in folk music. One major star whose music developed in this way was **Kina Shoukichi** who formed the band Champloose (see p.978) while still at high school, thus opening the way for a new generation of Okinawan rockers, including ex-band members **Nagama Takao**, famous for his fast-action *sanshin* playing and for his work with the now defunct Ayame Band, and **Hirayasu Takashi**.

Another contemporary Okinawan musician to watch out for is **China Sadao**, who records his own solo *min'yō*, as well as reggae-rock with an Okinawan flavour, and brought the all-female group **Nēnēs** to international fame. Nēnēs have played with Ry Cooder, Michael Nyman and George Winston, among others. China has a club, *Shima Uta Live House*, in Ginowan (see p.897), which is one of the best places in the islands to see Okinawan roots music. Other hot acts include **Parsha Club**, led by Ara Yukito, who mix jazz funk, rock and dance with Okinawan *min'yō*, and the former child prodigy **Nakano Ritsuki** (aka Rikki).

None of these bands, however, has had the pop chart success of **The Boom**, one of the earliest roots bands, who have been on the go since the mid-1980s. Led by **Miyazawa Kazufumi**, or Miya, The Boom started off as a ska/two-tone band, but quickly moved onto other styles and incorporated them into a heady brew. In 1993, they had the biggest-selling single in the country (1.5 million copies) with *Shima Uta* ("Island Songs"). It used an Okinawan melody and *sanshin* riffs, set to hard drums and rock guitar. The Boom subsequently moved into Indonesian music, giving it a similar treatment. Brazilian and Latin featured on the albums *Far East Samba* and *Tropicalism*. The latter disc saw the various elements from previous albums blending and maturing. Miya also has a blossoming solo career as well as writing for Sakamoto, Kina, Dick Lee and even reggae singer Yami Bolo.

C

CONTEXTS | Music

Contemporary pop

With the backing of the big music labels, the **J-pop** phenomenon continues unabated. The likes of Ayumi Hamasaki, Hitomi and Hikaru Utada have recently followed in the platform-booted footsteps of Namie Amuro, while boy bands are equally popular – **SMAP** continue to reign supreme after countless years (though they hardly count as a boy band anymore), while the hip hop-influenced **Dragonash** helped propel rap, long popular on the streets and in the clubs, into the national mainstream. In a different league is the more serious rocker and tunesmith **Ringo Sheena**: her 2003 *Karuki, Zamen, Kuri no Hana* (Chlorine, Semen, Chestnut Flowers) is an impressive concept album embracing everything from big-band swing to traditional *koto*, *shamisen* and flute music.

Indie bands and singers have become increasingly popular since the mid-1990s: witness the success of jazz singer **Chie Ayado** and **HY**, one of the country's hottest rock bands, unsurprisingly hailing from Okinawa – their album *Street Story* comfortably shifted half a million copies. Techno DJs **Ken Ishii** and **Ishino Takkyu** (of Denki Groove fame) and electronica outfits such as Ryukyu Underground, who mix up the sounds of Okinawa with dub beats and the occasional lounge-style tempo, are also finding an audience outside Japan. Though they have now unfortunately disbanded, lounge-pop stars **Pizzicato Five** and electro-pop duo **Denki Groove** were two other names hipsters in the West liked to drop throughout the 1990s. Progressive pop-rock act **Cornelius** (actually the alter ego of one Oyamada Keigo), though much-fêted abroad, was never as popular on the home front as many might have thought.

Reggae, and especially ska, is no longer merely copied, and bands like roots revivalists **Dry and Heavy**, techno-dub pioneers **Audio Active**, and the exciting dub-ska Kansai collective **The Determinations**, are all making music which can hold its own around the world.

Japan has long had an important avant-garde music scene. Its best-known practitioners might be Ōsaka's **Boredoms**, but others like **Haco** (herself once the leader of an influential 1980s post-punk outfit, After Dinner) and **Yamamoto Sei'ichi** continue to push back the boundaries of musical improvisation, and many members of this wide-ranging community regularly perform overseas, especially in Europe. The Improvised Music from Japan website (Ⓦ www.japanimprov.com) has extensive biographies and details.

Out-and-out rock is still hugely popular in Japan. On the fringes of this scene lies the heavy psych-rock of the extremely hairy **Acid Mothers Temple**, who hail from Nagoya and are influenced by Black Sabbath and Blue Cheer. More in the mainstream is the driving, punk-influenced rock'n'roll of **The High-Lows** and the angsty blues-rock of **Yura Yura Teikoku**.

If you want to hear work by some of the artists mentioned above, the Rough Guide CDs to the music of Japan and Okinawa (World Music Network) offer a fine introduction to the nation's music scene.

John Clewley, Simon Richmond and Dominic Al-Badri

CONTEXTS | Music

Environmental issues

First impressions of Japan's **natural environment** tend not to be very positive. In the postwar era there has been a massive shift towards an urbanized society, a society where successful people move to the city, not away from it, and where, for the younger generation in particular, contact with nature can be limited to walks in the park with the dog. Cities sprawl in all directions, a confusing mess of power cables and pulsing neon, with little evidence of planning controls. When you do reach the countryside, electricity pylons march across every view, cliffs are shored up with concrete and the coastline consists of nothing but sea walls and offshore breakwaters.

This can partly be explained by the desire to control, or attempt to control, the violent natural forces at play – devastating earthquakes, tidal waves, monsoons, volcanoes – and partly the economic and political might of the construction industry. In the words of one of Japan's leading activists, Yamashita Hirofumi, "Japan's postwar development has had a disastrous impact on the natural environment". Whatever the reason, it comes as something of a shock. After all, this is the nation justly famous for its cherry blossom and fiery autumn colours, which announces the changing seasons on the national news and which prides itself on its heightened aesthetic awareness.

However, nature does still play a pivotal role in Japanese life, as well as its literature, art and religion. Spectacular areas of unspoilt natural beauty are still to be found and there's a growing awareness of the need to safeguard them. The best require a little effort to reach, but even the largest cities contain important havens in their parks and shrine gardens.

Fauna and flora

Japan has an extremely complex zoogeographical history due to the continuous rise and fall of the sea level that repeatedly connected and severed the islands from the Chinese mainland. Generally speaking, the fauna and flora of the Japanese archipelago can be divided into three categories: that of the Southeast Asiatic tropical zone, the Korean and Chinese temperate zone and the Siberian subarctic zone.

The **Southeast Asiatic tropical zone** extends from Taiwan up into the Ryūkyū island chain (Okinawa). Wildlife typically associated with this zone includes the flying fox, crested serpent eagle, variable lizard and butterflies of the Danaidae family. Animals that belong to the **Korean and Chinese temperate zone** inhabit the deciduous forests of Honshū, Shikoku and Kyūshū, the most common of which are the racoon dog, sika deer and mandarin duck. If you're lucky, you'll see the rarer yellow marten, badger and flying squirrel, while – looking out to sea in central Honshū – you may also spot sea lions and fur seals. **The Siberian subarctic zone** covers the coniferous forests of Hokkaidō, inhabited by the brown bear, rabbit-like pika, hazel grouse, common lizard, arctic hare and nine-spined stickleback, amongst others.

In addition, the archipelago contains a number of **endemic species** such as the Japanese macaque, Japanese dormouse, copper pheasant, giant salamander, primitive dragonfly, Pryer's woodpecker and Amami spiny mouse, all of which are now relatively rare. Japan is also home to a number of "living fossils", animals whose characteristics differ from more developed species– such as the critically endangered Amami rabbit and Iriomote wild cat (both native to the Ryūkyū Islands), the frilled shark and the horseshoe crab of Sagami Bay, off Kamakura. Another animal worthy of mention is the freshwater spider crab, the world's largest crustacean, with an awe-inspiring clawspan of up to 3.7m.

Unless you get off the beaten track, contact with wildlife may well be limited to a less inspiring selection of English sparrows, pigeons, cockroaches and the ubiquitous crow. Smaller urban areas (and indeed the suburbs of the larger ones) do, however, offer plenty of hidden treasures for the wildlife enthusiast. **Racoon dogs**, or *tanuki*, with their waddling gait, come out at night to forage for food. These dogs are an integral part of Japanese folklore and are believed to have supernatural powers and cause all sorts of mischief; they are always depicted as big-bellied, with huge testicles and a bottle of sake. Foxes, too, are widespread and were believed to possess people – fox (or *Inari*) shrines are found across the country.

Monkeys are also common in some areas, such as Wakinosawa and Shiga Kōgen, while **wild boar** occasionally make an appearance in outer urban areas, though fortunately these forbidding-looking creatures avoid human contact and are generally heard but not seen. Kites, cranes, herons, cormorants and migratory seagulls can often be seen around lakes and rivers, while the steamy summer brings an onslaught of insects, none more so than the *semi*, or **cicada**, whose wailing provides a constant background symphony.

Tokyo's crows

The incessant cawing of big, black **jungle crows** is one of the most familiar sounds of many Japanese cities, but particularly in Tokyo where, according to one recent survey, the population has quadrupled over the last fifteen years to around 37,000 birds. In recent years the Tokyo Metropolitan Government has received hundreds of complaints about the birds' behaviour. Their most common offence is scavenging among garbage bags and creating an unsightly mess, but they can also get pretty aggressive, especially during the March–June breeding season. Young animals in Ueno zoo have been killed, children have been pecked on the head, but the most famous victim so far is Tokyo Governor Ishihara Shintarō, who was attacked while out golfing. He has since waged a campaign against the birds, culminating in an emergency task force sent into action over the summers of 2000 and 2001 to tear down nests and destroy young chicks. Even these culls, however, failed to work, and big bird traps are now set in the city's parks.

The real answer, of course, is to get rid of the rubbish that attracts the crows to the city in the first place. Since 1994 the authorities in Sapporo have been collecting garbage bags before dawn and then protecting the town's dumps with strong netting. It seems to be working – a recent study of crow droppings suggested that the birds were returning to a more natural diet of insects, small rodents and fruit. A number of Tokyo wards have begun to experiment with similar schemes, but until they introduce a city-wide policy, the crows will just descend in ever larger numbers wherever they find easy pickings.

Marine life

Japan's seas and rivers contain around three thousand species of fish. The waters around the Ryūkyū Islands are home to subtropical anemone fish, parrot fish, wrass and spiny lobster as well as numerous species of shark, turtle and whale. The ocean south of Shikoku and Honshū teems with life, from loggerhead turtles and butterfly fish to dugongs and porpoises, while the colder waters around Hokkaidō bring with them some of the larger whale species – humpback, grey and blue whale – from the Bering Sea and north Pacific.

Ocean currents play a crucial role in this diversity. Warm water flowing round Taiwan and up through the Ryūkyū island chain splits into two upon reaching the island of Kyūshū. The branch flowing north into the Sea of Japan, between Japan and China, is known as the Tsushima-shio, while the Kuro-shio or "Black current" follows the more easterly route. Bearing down from the north, hitting Hokkaidō's northern and eastern shores, comes the cold, nutrient-rich Oya-shio or Kuril current. Where it meets the Kuro-shio off northeastern Honshū, abundant plankton and the mingling of cold- and warm-water species create one of the richest fishing grounds in the entire world.

The United Nations Food and Agriculture Organization estimates that Japan consumes thirty percent of the world's fresh fish. To offset problems caused by **over-fishing**, the Japanese fishing fleet has been cut by a quarter in recent years. This has not, however, stopped the import of fish into Japan from other Southeast Asian countries which, for their own economic reasons, are less concerned about protecting fish stocks.

Forests

Forests of beech, silver fir, broad-leaf evergreens and mangroves once carpeted Japan. However, the postwar economic boom and in particular the massive increase in construction led to the decimation of many of these natural forests. They were replanted with quick-growing Japanese cedar and cypress, but then, as cheaper timber flooded in from Southeast Asia, Canada and South America in the 1970s, local demand slumped, leaving a large proportion of Japan's domestic plantations unused and untended.

While around 67 percent of Japan is still forested, about forty percent of this comprises commercial plantations and the country has come precariously close to losing some of its most spectacular areas of natural forest. The "old-growth" **beech forests** (that is, stands of ancient trees, but not necessarily untouched virgin forest) of the Shirakami Mountains in northwest Honshū, for example, came under direct threat in the 1980s from a government proposal to build a logging road right through them. Citizens' groups, together with the Nature Conservation Society of Japan (NCSJ), mounted a huge campaign to demonstrate the forest's immeasurable ecological and national value. As a result, the government reconsidered the plan and the forest is now designated a UNESCO World Heritage site.

The activities of Japanese paper and timber companies in the old-growth and primary forests (those subjected to only minimal human disturbance) of neighbouring countries is a huge concern for environmentalists worldwide. In Australia, for example, one such company operates a wood-chipping mill that is fed by old-growth eucalyptus trees at a rate of several football fields a day under a twenty-year licence granted by the Australian government. The wood is sold for twenty cents a tonne to make tissues, fax paper and newspapers for the Japanese market. Various Australian environmental groups – Chipstop, Friends of the Earth and The Wilderness Society – have joined forces with the Japan Tropical Forest Action Network (JATAN) among others to petition the Australian government and the Japanese paper industry to use wood chips from sustainable sources instead.

Conservation efforts

The explosion of recreational activities such as mountaineering in the early twentieth century provided the spur to the creation of Japan's first national parks in 1931 (see box on p.986). Indeed, the Physical Fitness Bureau controlled the twelve newly established **national parks** until the military started using them for manoeuvres in the war years. The **Environment Agency**, formed in 1971 and upgraded to a ministry in January 2001, is officially responsible for the national parks and protection of the country's flora and fauna in general, though its scope and successes have been limited.

Endangered species, of which there are 206, are listed in the *Red Data Book of Japan*, which was compiled in 1991 due to direct threats to population numbers from hunting, habitat degradation and environmental pollution. The list includes the Iriomote wild cat (*Felis iriomotensis*), endemic to Okinawa's Iriomote-jima, of which only an estimated one hundred remain, the short-tailed albatross (*Diomedea albatrus*) and the Japanese otter (*Lupus*

Land under protection is classified into numerous categories, of which the most important are the national parks (*kokuritsu-kōen*), covering 5.4 percent of Japan's land mass, quasi-national parks (*kokutei-kōen*; 3.5 percent) and prefectural national parks (5.1 percent). There are now 28 national parks and 55 quasi-national parks and it is estimated that between them they receive a staggering 900 million visitors each year. While for the most part national parks are thought of in terms of recreation, their establishment has been a lifesaver for ecological preservation. Below we give a rundown of some of the most important.

A recent development has been the growth in **eco-tourism** initiatives in and around the national parks, from whale-watching, white-water rafting and hiking to volunteering at nature reserves. Most of the tours and facilities are run by either local community members or otherwise dedicated individuals who act as "interpreters" of the ecological and cultural landscapes of the local area.

Akan National Park, Hokkaidō (p.407). Contains three vast volcanic craters surrounded by primeval forests of silver fir. Lake Akan is home to the unique *marimo* weedballs, which float beneath the surface of the lake on sunny days.

Aso-Kujū National Park, Kyūshū (p.832). Home to the world's largest volcanic crater, part of which is still active, complete with lunar landscapes. Two-thirds of Kyūshū is covered with lava from this huge volcano.

Chichibu-Tama National Park, Honshū Only three hours west of Tokyo, this is a haven for city dwellers. Its hills, gorges and valleys give rise to the Tama river that flows through Tokyo.

Iriomote National Park, Okinawa (p.925). Features lush, virgin jungle, cascading waterfalls, white beaches and spectacular underwater life, and is also home to the rare Iriomote wild cat. The dense jungle has served to resist human encroachment.

Kushiro and Shiretoko National Parks, Hokkaidō (p.410 & p.404). Protected under the Ramsar agreement, Kushiro's wetlands are of massive ecological importance. Shiretoko is home to the Japanese crane and Steller's sea eagle.

Rikuchū Kaigan National Park, Honshū Comprises a narrow strip of Japan's northeast coast, famous for its stretch of white trachyte quartz sand known as Jōdogahama, or Paradise Beach, and rugged cliffs. A bird-watchers' heaven.

Yakushima National Park (see p.985). A World Heritage site protected for its primary and old-growth forests. Part of the Kirishima-Yaku National Park.

lupus) of Shikoku, both of which were once thought to be extinct. Recently, an animal very similar to a Japanese wolf, thought to have been extinct since 1905, was photographed in central Kyūshū.

Conservation efforts come in the form of breeding and feeding programmes, habitat improvement and research projects. In an example of Russo-Japanese cooperation, researchers from both countries attached transmitters to fourteen sea eagles and tracked them by satellite to discover their migratory routes and feeding grounds. Unfortunately, however, many such conservation programmes fall far short of their goals, largely due to an ineffective government system. According to the Mammalogical Society of Japan, over half of the endangered mammals on the list are close to extinction.

At a grass roots level, volunteer groups and non-governmental organizations (NGOs) play a key role both in campaigning and in carrying out government projects, one arena in Japan where women are extremely active. These programmes have brought some success. The **Japanese crane** (*Grus japonensis*), a magnificent tall-standing bird highly celebrated in Japan for its grace and beauty and as a symbol of longevity, has benefited from volunteer-based feeding programmes in the Shiretoko region of Hokkaidō. As a result, the numbers have increased from a mere 33 birds in the 1950s to a stable population of around six hundred today. Ironically, the Japanese crane is one of the birds most commonly seen in Japan – on the back of the thousand yen note.

Environmental concerns

With very few **natural resources** of its own, Japan imports vast quantities of coal, tropical timber, plutonium, oil and natural gas – indeed its per capita resource consumption ranks as one of the highest in the world. While the government, financial institutions and industries push for further economic growth, environmentalists are increasingly asking at what price this is to be achieved. They cite examples of uranium mining on indigenous people's sacred lands to feed Japanese nuclear reactors, the decimation of Australia's and Southeast Asia's old-growth forests to feed Japanese pulp mills, and dangerously high dioxin and carbon dioxide levels.

One major by-product of any such heavily industrialized consumer society is **waste**, of which the country produces a staggering 440 million tons a year. Waste disposal costs the taxpayer a small fortune. Burning it releases poisonous dioxins and working out where to dump it is a logistical nightmare in such a densely populated country. A common "solution" is to use garbage for land reclamation and landfill, often with disastrous results. One such project, completed in 1997, destroyed part of Japan's largest **wetland area** in Isahaya, Nagasaki Prefecture. Fortunately, the protests surrounding Isahaya saved Japan's second-largest and most important wetland area at Fujimae near Nagoya. Despite the city authorities stating that there would be no impact should the area be used for garbage disposal, this time the Environment Agency stepped in with a landmark move to disapprove of the plan, which was promptly cancelled.

Japan is a technologically advanced and therefore energy-efficient country, exemplified by Toyota and Honda's "hybrid" cars, which run off a more efficient and less polluting combination of electric and internal combustion motors. Furthermore, government tax incentives and subsidies supporting the use of solar power have led directly to a forty-percent growth within the industry. Nevertheless, Japan consumes an estimated 5.6 percent of the world's total **energy**, of which over half comes from coal, a by-product of which is carbon dioxide. Under the Kyoto protocol agreed at the 1997 meeting on climate change (COP3), Japan is required to reduce its carbon dioxide emissions by six percent by the year 2010.

Nuclear power

To meet this target, the government intends to increase its use of nuclear power in place of coal – the country currently has 53 reactors including the world's biggest nuclear plant, near Kariwa on the western Sea of Japan coast. Environmentalists are extremely worried about this strategy, particularly given the recent string of serious accidents in the industry. In 1999, two workers at a fuel reprocessing plant in the village of Tōkai, Ibaraki Prefecture, were mixing vastly over-concentrated uranium in steel buckets when they set off a chain reaction causing a "criticality" incident – the most dangerous there is. Subsequent investigation discovered that the workers' manual they were following had been modified by the management in the interest of cutting costs, and that the radiation leaked for a full seventeen hours before the surrounding villagers were evacuated. The two workers later died from radiation exposure and, needless to say, public confidence in the nuclear industry nosedived. Ever since, full-page advertisements and editorials have filled the mainstream newspapers in an effort to regain public support. Further revelations that the Tokyo Electric Power Company covered up the discovery of cracks in thirteen of its reactors during the 1980s and 1990s haven't helped matters.

Pollution

The gradual shift from heavy to hi-tech industry in Japan has led to apparently cleaner rivers and air; many people remark that there are more birds than before and statistics show that Mount Fuji is visible more often these days from Tokyo. However, **chemical pollution** – from agriculture and domestic use, as well as the industrial sector – still remains a serious problem and scientists are beginning to warn of the adverse effects to come from this ever-increasing cocktail of toxicity. The Minamata tragedy (see p.831) was a landmark case that brought to public attention the hazards of industrial waste.

More recently, victims of **air pollution** from factories, power plants and national highways have won important lawsuits or reached out-of-court settlements

Further contacts and informational resources

Friends of the Earth Japan 3-17-24 Mejiro, Toshima-ku, Tokyo 171 ☎03/3951-1081, ⓦwww.foejapan.org/en.

Global Village c/o People Tree, 2-16-29 Jiyugaoka, Meguro-ku, Tokyo 152 ☎03/5731-6671, ⓦwww.globalvillage.or.jp.

Green Action Suite 103, 23-75 Tanaka Sekidenchô, Sakyō-ku, Kyoto 60 ☎075/701-7223, ⓔamsmith@gol.com.

Japan Eco Tourism Society 4-6-4 Shibaura, Minato-ku, Tokyo 108 ☎03/5289-7561, ⓦwww.ecotourism.gr.jp.

Japan Environmental Exchange 6-30-2 Higashi-machi, Jindaiji, Chōfu-shi, Tokyo 182 ☎0424/88-8943, ⓔwagtail@alles.co.jp.

Japan Tropical Forest Action Network (JATAN), Dorumi 801, 5-29-7 Sendagaya, Shibuya-ku, Tokyo 151 ☎03/5367-2865, ⓦwww.jca.apc.org/jatan.

Nature Conservation Society of Japan 3F Yamaji-sanbanchô Building, 5-24 Sanbanchô, Chiyoda-ku, Tokyo 102 ☎03/3265-0521, ⓦwww.nacsj.or.jp.

Wild Bird Society of Japan 2-35-2, Minamidaira, Hino, Tokyo 191 ☎042/593-6871, ⓦwww.wing-wbsj.or.jp.

WWF Japan 6F Nihon Seimei Akabanebashi Building, 3-1-14 Shiba, Minato-ku, Tokyo 105 ☎03/3769-1711, ⓦwww.wwf.or.jp.

Additional websites

ⓦwww.env.go.jp/en/index.html

The Ministry of Environment's site is predictably dry, but contains masses of detail on the legal framework, projects, reports and statistics as well as a decent range of official links.

ⓦwww.jca.apc.org/janic

The Japanese NGO Center for International Cooperation (JANIC) provides a run-down of NGOs working in Japan.

ⓦwww.wdcs.org

The site of the Whale and Dolphin Conservation Society – a good place to check for the latest on whaling issues.

against local authorities and industrial corporations. In November 2000, for example, the Nagoya District Court ordered the state and ten enterprises to pay a total of nearly 300 million yen in compensation to pollution victims and ordered that emissions along a stretch of national highway should be substantially reduced.

Whaling

Japanese **whaling** is one particularly controversial issue that tends to get plenty of international news coverage. The Japanese have traditionally caught whale for oil and meat, but it wasn't until the import of more efficient ships from Norway in the early 1900s that whaling reached unsustainable levels. Japan continues to catch some five hundred whales a year, despite an international ban, exploiting a loophole which allows a quota for scientific research – though this is widely regarded as a cover for commercial whaling. Ironically, scientists have begun voicing their concerns over the high levels of toxins found in dolphin and whale meat available in Japanese stores – which may yet cause a rethink on whaling by the government. Already the level of popular support in Japan for whaling has been falling – one recent survey showed only ten percent in favour – at the same time as an interest in whale-watching has been on the increase. It is becoming abundantly clear that there's more money to be made from whales through tourism than from killing them.

The future

While **environmental awareness** is slowly growing among the general public in Japan, it is still painfully limited. Anyone will tell you their concerns about global warming or dioxin levels, but when it comes down to making certain changes in lifestyle, habits die hard. Recycling rates are high, but then so is demand for packaged goods and plastic-bottled drinks. It will be a long time before the message really sinks in, partially due to a lack of real direction from the government, torn between encouraging consumption to boost the economy and discouraging consumption to reduce pollution and environmental degradation.

Local groups have achieved successes such as the rehabilitation of the Japanese cranes mentioned on p.986, and have also initiated clean-up campaigns, fought for lower dioxin emissions, monitored the activities of local government and challenged the giants of the nuclear industry. A nationwide coalition of various animal-rights groups, spearheaded by the group ALIVE, recently managed to pressure the government to modify the law regarding cruelty to animals by joining forces and creating a huge amount of publicity in support of their cause. The case marks an important shift in attitude towards the protection of animals, and the environment in general, in much the same way as the Fujimae wetlands case did in 1997.

Activism in Japan, strong though it is, is approached in an entirely different way from in the West; the Japanese do not respond well to direct action. To cite one example, the Kyoto based anti-nuclear group Green Action, after failing to drum up much interest for a campaign against the British Sellafield plant, which sends reprocessed nuclear fuel to Japan, started the "Save Peter Rabbit's Homeland" campaign. They were inundated with support – it was nothing less than a stroke of genius.

Global awareness is also increasing as groups monitor and negotiate with companies operating abroad. Among one of the success stories, the Tokyo group Rain Forest Action Network (RAN) successfully campaigned against two subsidiaries of the Mitsubishi industrial giant practising unsustainable logging in Sarawak, Malaysia. After extensive negotiations the subsidiaries involved finally agreed to stop using old-growth pulp or products and change to existing plantation timber.

Film

I f you thought Godzilla and samurai flicks are all there is to Japanese film, think again. The history of cinema in Japan extends over a century, with the first Western-made moving images being shown to rapt audiences in 1896. Within a couple of years, the Japanese had imported equipment and established their own movie industry, which flourished with all things Western in the early decades of the twentieth century. Recovering quickly after World War II, Japanese film burst onto the international scene with the innovative *Rashōmon*, directed by Kurosawa Akira, who, along with Ozu Yasujirō, director of the highly respected *Tōkyō Monogatari* (Tokyo Story), is the country's best-known cinema auteur.

Apart from the scandal surrounding Ōshima Nagisa's explicit *Ai-no-Corrida*, the movie scene generally languished during the 1970s, while in the 1980s, Japanese corporations were more intent on ploughing bubble-era profits and investment into Hollywood production companies rather than home-grown talent. In the 1990s, however, the popularity both at home and abroad of the films of Itami Jūzō and Kitano Takeshi recaptured international attention, while in the new millennium the huge success of horror flicks such as *Ring* and the Oscar-winning animated movie *Spirited Away* has heralded a new and exciting era for Japanese film.

Pre-World War II

Japan got its first taste of cinema at Kōbe's **Shinko Club** in 1896, and by the end of the following year, the crown prince had put in an appearance at Tokyo's Kabuki-za theatre to be entertained by the latest Western wonder. From the very beginning, theatrical embellishments were considered a vital part of the cinema experience; one theatre had a mock-up of a valley in front of the screen, complete with fish-filled ponds, rocks and fan-generated breeze, to increase the sense of realism. Additionally, the story and dialogue were acted out to the audience by a *benshi*, playing a similar role to the theatrical interpreters in traditional Japanese performing arts. Thus when "talkies" arrived in Japan in the 1930s, they were less of a sensation because sound had been part of the movie experience from the very beginning.

The **earliest Japanese films** also looked towards the traditional performing arts, such as classical dance and Kabuki, for their subject matter, although in 1905 cameras were sent to the Asian mainland to record the Russo-Japanese War. By the outbreak of World War I in Europe, there were nine film-production companies in Japan, the largest being Nikkatsu, which released fourteen films a month from its two studios. Western ways of film-making were catching on, and it became increasingly common for actresses to take roles previously played by *oyama* (female impersonators).

The contemporary landscape of **Tokyo** was a popular choice for films which adopted modern, realistic themes (*gendaigeki*). However, the Great Kantō Earthquake of 1923 shifted movie production for a time to **Kyoto**, which with its old architecture was the perfect backdrop for *jidaigeki*, or period dramas.

Both forms were in turn influenced by the art of Western film-making, in particular German Expressionism, while at the same time retaining a quintessential Japanese style.

The **1930s** were the boom years for early Japanese cinema with some five hundred features being churned out a year, second only in production to the United States. One of the era's top directors, though he didn't gain international recognition until the mid-1950s, was **Mizoguchi Kenji** (1898–1956). His initial speciality was the *jidaigeki* melodramas, based in Meiji-era Japan, but he is best known in the West for his later lyrical medieval samurai dramas, such as *Ugetsu Monogatari* (1954). During the 1920s and 1930s, however, Mizoguchi also turned his hand to detective, expressionist, war, ghost and comedy films, becoming the best-known director of realist *gendaigeki*. As Japan fell deeper into the ugliness of nationalism and war, Mizoguchi embraced traditional concepts of stylized beauty in films such as 1939's *Zangiku Monogatari* (*The Story of the Last Chrysanthemums*).

Also developing his reputation during the pre-World War II period was perhaps Japan's greatest film director **Ozu Yasujirō**, whose *Tokyo Monogatari* (*Tokyo Story*) is a permanent fixture on many critic's best-film lists. In the 1930s, Ozu was taking his cues from the West, making films such as *Dragnet Girl*, about rebellious youths. By the time he made his first talking film, *The Only Son*, in 1936 – the story of a country woman who visits her feckless son in Tokyo – Ozu was considered one of Japan's leading directors.

The 1950s and 1960s

Japanese cinema undoubtedly suffered in the authoritarian years surrounding World War II. In 1945 only 26 films were made and the future didn't look any brighter when the Allied Occupation Forces took over, drew up a list of thirteen banned subjects for films, including "feudal loyalty", and burned movies considered unsuitable. However, the occupation authorities were more than happy to encourage "American-style" *gendaigeki*, which led to Japan's first screen kiss, a previously taboo activity, in 1946.

Local talent broke through in 1950 when **Kurosawa Akira**'s brilliant *Rashōmon* hit the screen, subsequently garnering a Golden Lion at the following year's Venice Film Festival and an honorary Oscar. This story of a rape and murder told from four different points of view – including (most ingeniously) from the dead nobleman via a medium – made a star of lead actor Mifune Toshirō and ushered in a decade considered to be the golden age of Japanese film.

In 1954 Kurosawa again teamed up with Mifune to make the classic *Shichinin-no-Samurai* (*The Seven Samurai*), about a band of *rōnin* (masterless samurai) coming to the rescue of a village community plagued by bandits. If the story sounds familiar that's because it was copied by Hollywood in *The Magnificent Seven* (1960), just as another of Kurosawa's samurai dramas, *Yōjimbō* (1961), was the basis for Sergio Leone's *A Fistful of Dollars*. The story snatching was not all one-way. Kurosawa borrowed themes and plots from Dostoevsky, Gorky and Shakespeare, *Throne of Blood* (1957) being based on *Macbeth* and *Ran* (1985) on *King Lear*.

Ozu's masterpiece, *Tokyo Monogatari*, was another highlight of the 1950s. This simply told, yet quietly emotional tale of an elderly couple's visit to Tokyo to see their grown-up children and the cold reception they receive from everyone except their widowed daughter-in-law, has become a classic of world cinema.

At the other end of the artistic spectrum, the 1950s saw the birth of one of Japan's best-known cinema icons, **Godzilla** – or *Gojira* as he was known on initial release in 1954. The giant mutant, whose Japanese name combined gorilla (*gorira*) and whale (*kujira*), was very much a product of fears surrounding nuclear proliferation, rather than the camp monster megastar he would later become. At ¥60 million *Gojira* was one of the most expensive films of its time, with an all-star cast headed by Shimura Takeshi, who went on to star in Kurosawa's *Shichinin-no-Samurai*. Despite the monster being killed off in the grand finale, the movie's success led to an American release, with added footage, in 1956 under the title *Godzilla, King of the Monsters*. Over the next four decades Godzilla kept on returning to do battle with, among others, King Kong, giant shrimps, cockroaches and moths, and a smog monster.

Gangster movies also gained popularity in the 1960s as Japanese studios began pumping out violent yet highly romanticized films about the *yakuza*. Known as *ninkyō eiga* (chivalry films), these movies were usually played like modern-day samurai sagas, the tough, fair *yakuza* being driven by a code of loyalty or honour. One of the major actors to emerge from these movies is Takakura Ken, who has since starred in Western films including Ridley Scott's *Black Rain*.

The 1970s and 1980s

The most successful movie development of the next two decades was the **Tora-san** series, which began with *Otoko wa Tsurai Yo* (*It's Tough Being a Man*) at the tail end of the 1960s. Tora-san, or Kuruma Torajirō, a loveable itinerant peddler from Tokyo's Shitamachi, was played by Atsumi Kiyoshi in 48 films up until the actor's death in 1996, making it the most prolific movie series in the world. The format of the films is invariably the same, with Tora-san chasing after his latest love, or "Madonna", in various scenic areas of Japan, before returning to his exasperated family.

Tora-san was only a hit in Japan, but *Ai-no-Corrida* (*In the Realm of the Senses*; 1976) by rebel filmmaker **Ōshima Nagisa** created an international stir with its explicit sex scenes and violent content. Based on a true story, the film was about an intense sexual relationship between a woman servant and her master which culminates in murder and a chopped-off penis. The censor demanded other kinds of cuts, which forced the director into a lengthy and ultimately unsuccessful legal battle. This was all the more galling for Ōshima, whose film gathered critical plaudits abroad, but remained unseen in its full version at home, at the same time as the major Japanese studios made their money from increasingly violent films and soft-core porn, called *roman poruno*.

By the **late 1970s**, Japanese cinema was in the doldrums. Entrance fees at the cinema were the highest in the world (they're still expensive), leaving the public less willing to try out offbeat local movies when they could see sure-fire Hollywood hits instead. The art-house filmmaker Ōshima turned in the prisoner-of-war drama *Merry Christmas Mr Lawrence* in 1983 and the decidedly quirky *Max Mon Amour* three years later before retiring, content to build his reputation as TV pundit. Instead of investing money at home, Japanese companies, like Sony, went on a spending spree in Hollywood, buying up major American studios and film rights, thus securing software for video releases.

By the end of the 1980s, the one light on the horizon was **Itami Jūzō**, an actor who turned director with the mildly satirical *Osōshiki* (*The Funeral*) in 1984. His follow-up, *Tampopo* (1986), a comedy about the attempts of a proprietress of a noodle bar to serve up the perfect bowl of ramen, set against the background of Japan's gourmet boom, was an international success, as was his *Marusa no Onna* (*A Taxing Woman*) in 1988. The female star of all Itami's movies, which poke gentle fun at Japanese behaviour and society, was his wife, the comic actress Miyamoto Nobuko.

The 1990s

Itami's success was consolidated by a string of hits in the 1990s, but his satirical approach went too far for some with 1992's *Minbō-no-Onna* (*The Gentle Art of Japanese Extortion*), which sent up the *yakuza*. Soon after its release, Itami was severely wounded in a knife attack by mob thugs. Undaunted, he recovered and went on to direct more challenging comedies, such as *Daibyōnin* (1993), about the way cancer is treated in Japanese hospitals, and *Sūpā-no-Onna* (1995), which revealed the shady practices of supermarkets. Itami's career ended abruptly in 1997, when he committed suicide before the publication of an exposé of his love life in a scandal magazine.

Stepping into Itami's shoes as the darling of Japan's contemporary cinema scene is **Kitano Takeshi**, better known locally as Beat Takeshi after his old comedy double act with Beat Kiyoshi in the Two Beats. Kitano had already taken on a serious role in Ōshima's *Merry Christmas Mr Lawrence* when he starred in and also directed *Sono Otoko, Kyōbō ni Tsuki* (*Violent Cop*) in 1989. His next film *3-4 x 10 Gatsu* (*Boiling Point*) was an equally bloody outing, but it was his more reflective and comic *Sonatine* (1993), about a gang war in sunny Okinawa, that had foreign critics hailing him as Japan's Quentin Tarantino. Surviving a near-fatal motorbike accident in 1994, Kitano broadened his movie range with the badly received comedy *Minna Yatteruka* (*Getting Any?*) and *Kid's Return*, a drama about high-school dropouts. 1997's *Hanabi* saw him back on form, scooping up a Golden Lion at the Venice Festival in 1997, just as Kurosawa's *Rashōmon* had done nearly fifty years previously.

Kurosawa himself received a lifetime achievement Academy Award in 1990, the same year as he teamed up with George Lucas and Steven Spielberg to make the semi-autobiographical *Yume* (*Dreams*). His anti-war film *Hachigatsu-no-Kyōshikyoku* (*Rhapsody in August*; 1991), however, attracted criticism abroad for its somewhat one-sided treatment of the subject. Referred to respectfully as "Sensei" (teacher) by all in the industry, Kurosawa's final film before his death, aged 88, on September 6, 1998, was the low-key drama *Mādadayo* (1993) about an elderly academic.

Meanwhile, the prolific **Kurusawa Kiyoshi** has begun to make waves with his quirky genre pictures, such as *The Excitement of the Do-Re-Mi-Fa Girls* (1985), *The Serpent Path* (1998) and its sequel *Eyes of the Spider* (1998). Kurusawa also made *Licence to Live* in 1998, a poignant account of a 24-year-old man waking from a decade-long coma. Other **independent filmmakers** making their mark with more daring subject matter include Tsukamoto Shin'ya, who had an art-house hit with the sci-fi horror movie *Tetsuo* about a man turning into a machine; and Yazaki Hitoshi, who took a cool look at incest in *Sangatsu-no-Raion* (*March Comes in Like a Lion*).

The biggest film of the 1990s was *Princess Mononoke*, still the nation's all-time domestic box-office champ, proving the continued importance and popularity of **animated films** (*anime*; see box, below) in Japan. The film was an international success too, following in the dancesteps of *Shall We Dance?*, director Suo Masayuki's charming ballroom dancing comedy–drama which swept up all thirteen of Japan's Academy Awards in 1996.

The new millennium

Kitano continues to be one of Japan's most internationally popular filmmakers. The low-key charmer *Kikujiro*, which wowed audiences at Cannes in 1999, was followed up in 2000 by the US-based *yakuza* thriller *Brother*. Ever the innovator, *Dolls* (2002) saw Kitano collaborate with fashion designer Yohji

Anime

Anime, which commands an enthusiastic worldwide audience, is a staple of the Japanese film industry, where cutting-edge technology is increasingly being used to bring to life tales of such sophistication and imagination that they leave the sugar-coated works of Disney and other animation studios standing. In recent releases you're likely to come across samurai-sword wielding, teenage vampire slayers, renegade surgeons battling for human rights and anti-government guerrillas.

Although Japan's first animated film was a cartoon short made in 1917, it wasn't until the 1960s and the success of the "god of manga" Tezuka Osamu's *Astroboy* and *Kimba, the White Lion* that the industry began to take off. By the time international attention was grabbed in 1988 by Ōtomo Katsuhiro's dark sci-fi fantasy *Akira*, anime was firmly established, particularly on TV with series such as *Mazinger Z* and *Bubblegum Crisis*. Today the TV big hits such as *Pokemon*, *Dragonball Z* and *Neon Genesis Evangelion* are bolstered not just by spin-off movies and other products but also juggernaut marketing campaigns.

The film *Ghost in the Shell* (Kokaku Kidōtai) in 1995 – including cyborgs with jacks in their heads, bodies transferring down the telephone line, martial arts and a master terrorist called the Puppet Master – was the next overseas success and a strong influence on the Keanu Reeves flick *The Matrix*.

At the softer end of the scale, animators Miyazaki Hayao and Takahata Isao teamed up under the banner of Studio Ghibli, which has spawned a string of charming family-oriented films including *My Neighbour Totoro* (1988), *Kiki's Delivery Service* (1989) and *Porco Rosso* (1992), about a swashbuckling pig who literally flies. Miyazaki's 1997 feature *Mononoke-hime* (*Princess Mononoke*), a violent fable with a strong environmental message, not only became Japan's number-one grossing film, but also cleaned up in a dubbed version in the all-important US market. The studio's pre-eminence in the field of *anime* was crowned in 2003 when *Spirited Away* won an Oscar for best animated feature.

Another of Japan's hottest *anime* studios is Production IG, who produced the animation sequences in Quentin Tarantino's *Kill Bill Part 1*. They also used digital technology, a recent innovation in *anime*, to make *Blood: The Last Vampire*, set in a US army base in Japan on the brink of the Vietnam War, which has plenty of dialogue in English and is squarely aimed at the international market. The film's amazing visuals are a sign of how *anime* is developing, but the same company's *Jin Roh*, a tale of government conspiracy, blending sci-fi, thriller and romance themes, was created using traditional methods and still looks fantastic.

Yamamoto in a visually ravishing tale based on the plots of *bunraku* puppet plays, while 2003's *Zatoichi* served up a bleached blonde Kitano as the blind swordsman, a jolly tap-dancing finale and enough blood and severed limbs to give Quentin Tarantino's *Kill Bill* movies a run for their money. Another master of the gleeful splatterfest is the prolific **Miike Takashi**, who has jumped around from the stylized gangster violence of *Ichi the Killer* to the sci-fi action of his *Dead or Alive* trilogy, via the musical horror comedy of *The Happiness of the Katakuris*. His 2003 effort, *You've Got a Call*, brings horror to the mobile phone.

In the wake of a sad spate of child killer tragedies in Japan, **Fukasaku Kinji**'s *Battle Royal* (in which Kitano Takeshi pops up yet again in a cameo role) – a manga-style interpretation of *Lord of the Flies* – was sure to cause controversy. Stalwart of Tokyo's Toei Studios and revered by the likes of Tarantino and John Woo for his hard-boiled *yakuza* movies, Fukasaku died in 2002, leaving his son Kenta to take over the reigns of *Battle Royal II*, released in 2003.

The most exciting news of recent Japanese cinema, though, has been its reinterpretation of the horror genre, as typified by the international success of the *Ring* movies of **Nakata Hideo**, who hit pay dirt when the original *Ring* got a big-budget Hollywood makeover in 2002. Another welcome boost for the ailing local industry is the continued success of master animator **Miyazaki Hayoa**, whose Studio Ghibli is the Japanese equivalent of Disney; they even have their own mini-theme park (see p.217). *Sen to Chihiro no Kami-Kakushi* (*Spirited Away*) won Japan's first Oscar for an animated feature in 2003.

Films to look out for

Japanese classics

Ai-no-Corrida (*In the Realm of the Senses*; Ōshima Nagisa; 1976). Judge for yourself whether this *cause-célèbre* film is art or pornography. Based on the true story of servant girl Sada Abe and her intensely violent sexual relationship with her master Kichi. A sex game results in Kichi's death and Sada slices off his penis as a keepsake. The real Sada was shown pity and spent just six years in prison. Ōshima followed this film up with the equally erotic *Ai-no-Bōrei* (Empire of Passion), which won him best-director award at the 1979 Cannes Film Festival.

Black Rain (Imamura Shohei; 1989). Not to be confused with the US *yakuza* flick, this serious drama traces the strains put on family life in a country village after the Bomb is dropped on Hiroshima.

Godzilla, King of the Monsters (1956). Originally released two years earlier in Japan as *Gojira*, the giant mutant lizard, born after a US hydrogen bomb test in the Bikini Atoll, was such a hit that previously cut scenes were added for the American market. Raymond Burr plays the journalist telling in flashback the event that led to Godzilla running amok in Tokyo. The 27th tackily enjoyable Godzilla film was released in Japan in 2003; the whole series most likely cost less than the 1998 US remake.

Nijūshi-no-Hitomi (*Twenty Four Eyes*; Kinoshita Keisuke; 1954). One of Japan's most-loved films about the events leading up to, during and after World War II, as seen through the eyes of a first-grade female teacher and pacifist on the island of Shōdo-shima. The twelve cute children in Ōishi-san's class make up the 24 eyes. Shamefully sentimental, the film is ultimately touching and memorable for the luminous performance of Takahime Hideko as the teacher.

Tōkyō Monogatari (*Tokyo Story*; Ozu Yasujirō; 1954*)*. The most popular of Ozu Yasujirō's films, although it may appear laborious to audiences brought up on fast-moving MTV images. An elderly couple travel to Tokyo from their seaside home in western Japan to visit their children and grandchildren. The only person who has any time for them is Noriko, the widow of their son Shōji killed in the war. On their return, the mother falls ill and dies. Ozu's themes of loneliness and the breakdown of tradition are grim, but his simple approach and the sincerity of the acting make the film a genuine classic.

Kurosawa Akira

Kagemusha (1980). Nominated for an Academy Award and co-winner of the Grand Prize at Cannes, Kurosawa showed he was still on form with this sweeping historical epic. A poor actor is recruited to impersonate a powerful warlord who has inconveniently died mid-campaign. The ruse is eventually discovered, but not before many a colourful battle.

Ran (1985). This loose but much-lauded adaptation of *King Lear* is a true epic, with thousands of extras and giant battle scenes. The daughters become sons, although the Regan and Goneril characters survive in the form of the gleefully vengeful wives Lady Kaede and Lady Sue.

Rhapsody in August (*Hachigatsu-no-Kyōshikyoku*; 1991). One of Kurosawa's more recent films is notable for an unlikely performance by Richard Gere as a Japanese-American visiting relations in Nagasaki and feeling sorry for the Atomic bombing.

Rashōmon (1950). The film that established Kurosawa's reputation in the West and brought Japanese cinema to worldwide attention. A notorious bandit, the wife he perhaps rapes, the man he perhaps murders and the woodcutter who perhaps witnesses the events each tell their different story of what happened in the woods. Fascinatingly open-ended narrative and a memorable performance by Mifune Toshirō as the restless bandit make this a must-see movie.

The Seven Samurai (*Shichinin-no-Samurai*; 1954). A small village in sixteenth-century Japan is fed up of being raided each year by bandits so it hires a band of samurai warriors for protection. There's little else to the plot of Kurosawa's entertaining period drama, later remade in Hollywood as *The Magnificent Seven*.

Yōjimbō (1961). Mifune Toshirō stars in one of Kurosawa's best-known samurai sagas as a *rōnin* who arrives in a dusty town, is greeted by a dog carrying a human hand, and discovers he's walked in on a bloody feud. The *rōnin* pits both sides against each other, kills off the bad guys and restores peace to the town.

Kitano Takeshi

Dolls (2003). This reworking of three traditional *bunraku* tales of love and loss is ponderous but frequently gorgeous to look at, with beautifully framed shots of the Japanese countryside through the seasons and actors garbed in ultra-cool Yohji Yamamoto clobber.

Hanabi (1997). Surprisingly introspective Venice Festival winner with Kitano directing himself as a detective pushed to breaking point by a stake-out that went wrong, a seriously ill wife and outstanding loans to the *yakuza*. The artwork that appears in the film was also painted by the multi-talented Kitano.

Kid's Return (1996). In one of his less violent offerings, Kitano turns his attention to a couple of high-school dropouts in Tokyo, one of whom becomes a boxer while the other joins the *yakuza*. Although it supposedly has autobiographical elements, Kitano remains behind the camera for this one.

Kikujirō no Natsū (1999). This comedy (known simply as *Kikujirō* in the West) sees the director star as the eponymous hero, a gruff gangster with a heart of gold, befriended by an eight-year-old boy in search of his missing mother.

Sonatine (1993). One of Kitano's most accomplished films, and one that led to comparisons with Quentin Tarantino. Here he plays a tired gangster, hightailing it to the sunny isles of Okinawa and getting mixed up in mob feuds, before it all turns nasty on the beach.

Violent Cop (1989). Kitano's first film as a director sees him starring as a cop in the *Dirty Harry* mould, bent on revenge. As the title suggests, no punches are pulled in the violence department.

Zatoichi (2003). A classic of Japanese TV remade with an assured, modern touch by Kitano, who also stars as the eponymous hero, a blind master swordsman whom you really don't want to tangle with. The movie's quirky factor is assisted by Kitano's bleach blonde hair job and a finale that has the cast doing a tap-dancing number in *geta* (wooden sandals).

Modern Japanese cinema

Appleseed (Aramaki Shinji; 2004). One of the most technically innovative *anime* films of recent times, blending traditional 2D drawings with 3D computer-generated graphics. The ultra-violent sci-fi plot, based on a cult *manga* comic, is somewhat ho-hum, but the lead character – a doe-eyed but ballsy female warrior, will capture your attention.

Battle Royal (Fukasaku Kinji; 2000). Graphically violent satire that pits school kids against each other to the death on a desert island. Kitano Takeshi features as the kids' teacher in both this and the 2003 follow-up, *Battle Royal II*, where the action shifts to the big city and includes a 9/11-style terrorist destruction of skyscrapers.

Dark Water (*Honogurai Mizu no Soko Kara*; Nakata Hideo; 2002). Stylish tale of everyday terror told by the new master of the genre. Yoshimi is going through a messy, emotionally distressing divorce when she moves with her daughter into a creepy apartment. Water starts dripping through the ceiling and things get worse from there.

Ichi the Killer (Miike Takashi; 2001). Blood, more blood and an ample helping of gore sums up the plot of this *yakuza* tale set in Tokyo's Kabukichō, as told by the *enfant terrible* of Japanese cinema. Not for the squeamish.

Kamikaze Taxi (Masato Harada; 1995). A gangster flick with a twist; it also deals with the issue of ethnic Japanese returning to Japan from South America and being discriminated against as foreigners. Watch out for Yakusho Kōji in a very different role from his ballroom-dancing salaryman in *Shall We Dance?*

Merry Christmas Mr Lawrence (Ōshima Nagisa; 1982). Pop stars David Bowie and Sakamoto Ryūichi, as well as thesps Tom Conti and Jack Thompson, star in this powerful POW drama based on Sir Laurens van der Post's book *The Seed and the Sower*. The art-house version of *Bridge on the River Kwai* just about sums it up. Look out for Kitano Takeshi in his first major role as a brutal camp sergeant.

Minbō-no-Onna (*The Gentle Art of Japanese Extortion*; Itami Jūzō; 1992). A grand Tokyo hotel, hoping to host an international summit meeting, has to deal with the *yakuza* first. Enter the director's wife, Miyamoto Nobuko, playing a feisty lawyer, who's more than a match for the preening gangsters.

Marusa-no Onna (*A Taxing Woman*; Itami Jūzō; 1988). Fascinating comedy about the battle of wills and wiles between a scrupulous tax collector (Miyamoto Nobuko) and her quarry, a love-hotel owner with two sets of books. The follow-up *Murasa-no-Onna II* (*A Taxing Woman's Return*) is a darker, more prescient tale of the links between politicians, developers and a creepy religious cult.

Ōsaka Story (Nakata Toichi; 1994). Nakata Toichi ticks off many difficult contemporary issues in his film, which follows the homecoming of a gay, Korean-Japanese film student to his Ōsaka-based family. His staunchly Korean father expects him to take over the business and get married, but the son has other ideas.

Osōshiki (*The Funeral*; Itami Jūzō; 1984). Itami's first film as a director is a wry comedy about a grieving family bumbling their way through the obscure conventions of a proper Japanese funeral. The young couple learn the "rules" by watching a video and the Buddhist priest turns up in a white Rolls Royce. Like most of his films, *Osōshiki* springs from Itami's personal experience and is all the funnier and more telling for that.

Ring (Nakata; 1998). Remade by Hollywood in 2002 as *The Ring*, this is the original and far superior spine-chiller about a videotape that kills everyone who sees it exactly one week after viewing. The sequel *Ring 2* has a similar plot, but will be confusing to those who didn't see part 1.

Shall We Dance? (Suo Masayuki; 1996). More than just a Japanese version of the Aussie hit *Strictly Ballroom*, Suo's film is firmly set in the reality of everyday lives. Yakusho Kōji plays a quietly frustrated middle-aged salaryman whose spark returns when he takes up ballroom dancing. He has to keep it secret from his family and work colleagues, though, because of the social stigma attached. At turns touching and hilarious, *Shall We Dance?* also makes Blackpool, the ballroom dancer's far-off mecca, appear glamorous.

Spirited Away (*Sen to Chihiro no Kamikaskushi*; Miyazaki Hayao; 2001). This Oscar-winning *anime* is a Japanese *Alice in Wonderland*-style adventure. When her parents take a wrong turn into a mysteriously deserted theme park, spunky kid Chihiro finds she has to negotiate her way around the strange creatures she meets at a huge bathhouse before finding a way home.

Tampopo (Itami Jūzō; 1985). Tampopo, the proprietress of a noodle bar, is taught how to prepare ramen that has both sincerity and guts, in this comedy about Japan's gourmet boom. From the old woman squishing fruit in a supermarket to the gangster and his moll passing a raw egg sexily between their mouths, this is a film packed with memorable scenes, and is guaranteed to get the tummy rumbling.

Foreign films featuring Japan and the Japanese

Black Rain (Ridley Scott; 1989). Gruff Michael Douglas and younger sidekick Andy Garcia team up with stoic local policeman Takakura Ken to deal with the *yakuza*. Notable in that it's set in Ōsaka, providing a different cityscape from Tokyo.

Bladerunner (Ridley Scott; 1982).

Although it's set in the Los Angeles of the future rather than Tokyo, this seminal sci-fi thriller takes its cues directly from contemporary Japan; the sets are practically indistinguishable from a rainy night in Shinjuku's Kabukichō, from the blazing neon to the giant video screens.

Bridge on the River Kwai (David Lean; 1957). Famous prisoner-of-war movie with army major Alec Guinness going bonkers as the Japanese extract blood, sweat and tears from the plucky Brits building a bridge in Thailand's jungle.

Empire of the Sun (Stephen Spielberg; 1987). Based on the J.G. Ballard book, Spielberg's serious film explores the Japanese occupation of Shanghai through the eyes of a young boy. An impressive cast, including John Malkovich and Miranda Richardson, only partly distract from the leaden storytelling.

Kill Bill Part 1 (Quentin Tarantino; 2003). The maverick Hollywood auteur's fourth movie pays homage to his love of *yakuza* gangster flicks and samurai epics. Much super-stylised violence and chop-socky kung fu action as Uma Thurman kicks ass and waves a lethally big sword in Tokyo.

The Last Samurai (Edward Zwick; 2003). Tom Cruise teams up with Billy Connolly and some of Japan's top acting talent in this tale of a US Civil War vet who comes to train the Emperor Meiji's troops in modern warfare, but finds much to learn himself in the samurai code of honour.

Lost in Translation (Sofia Coppola; 2003). Stand-out performances from Bill Murray and Scarlett Johansson in this stylish comedy drama set in and around Shinjuku's Park Hyatt hotel. Brilliantly captures what it's like to be a *gaijin* adrift in Tokyo.

Mishima (Paul Schrader; 1985). Art-house take on the bizarre and fascinating life of Japan's contemporary literary giant Mishima Yukio, who committed ritual suicide after lead-

ing a failed military coup in 1970.

Paradise Road (Bruce Beresford; 1997). Respectable addition to the POW drama genre, this time told from the female point of view. A starry cast, including Glenn Close, Pauline Collins, Cate Blanchett and Juliana Marguiles, forms a vocal orchestra to keep their flagging spirits up in the face of multiple indignities. Based on a true story.

The Pillow Book (Peter Greenaway; 1996). In this dazzling hi-tech adaptation of the Sei Shōnagon classic, the action is updated to contemporary Hong Kong. The beautiful images capture the essence of the book, even if the story of a woman who gets her kicks by writing on the bodies of her lovers flags at times.

Rising Sun (Peter Kaufman; 1993). Based on Michael Crichton's rabble-rousing book about murder and corporate skullduggery, this slick thriller has its moments, most of which involve Sean Connery as the Zen-like detective teamed up with Wesley Snipes' LA cop to crack the case of the dead blonde on the boardroom table. Ultimately simplistic tale of Japanese business practices and manners.

Until the End of the World (Wim Wenders; 1993). Rambling millennium angst road movie with an interesting premise, but gets bogged down during its Australian Outback section. The Japan scenes, contrasting frantic Tokyo and the soothing countryside, are among the best. Also stars the great actor Ryū Chishū, who played the father in Ozu's *Tokyo Story*.

You Only Live Twice (Lewis Gilbert; 1967). Sean Connery's fifth outing as 007 has Bondo-san grappling with arch-enemy Blofeld and sundry Oriental villains in Tokyo and the countryside. Fun escapism, packed with glamorous girls and cool gadgets, including a mini-helicopter in a suitcase (with rocket launchers, of course).

Pop culture

Relatively few Japanese will be able to recommend a Nō play or tell you how to create an ikebana flower display. Ask them to name their favourite comedian or karaoke song, however, and the response will be instant. Popular culture rules in Japan, and with 126 million avid consumers to draw upon, its products and buzzwords are all-pervasive.

The West's familiarity with contemporary Japan – Muji's chic "no-brand" products, Sony's electronic gadgets, Godzilla movies, Yoko Ono – is very slender compared to the thousands of other goods, cultural phenomena and people that are unknown and totally mystifying to the average *nama-gaijin* (raw foreigner). The following is a general A to Z primer for the visitor who would like to appear clued up. More serious students should avail themselves of the wit and wisdom in Mark Schilling's illuminating *The Encyclopedia of Japanese Pop Culture* (Weatherhill).

A: Aribi-ya

One business that has taken off during Japan's recent recession is that of the **Aribi-ya** – or those who sell alibis. In a society obsessed with appearances, *aribi-ya* provide all that's necessary if you want to be seen as someone else. For example, if you need a fake business card, pay stubs, receptionist to answer your nonexistent business phone, even a fictitious boss to make a speech at your wedding, the *aribi-ya* can do it. The idea is nothing new; for years cable-radio stations have been providing alibi channels that, among other background noises, broadcast the buzz of traffic so you can make believe you're calling from a street telephone rather than a love hotel to tell the wife you'll be home late. And if you forget the all-important *omiyage* (present) from that out-of-town business trip you were supposed to have taken, then there's always the gift shop at the major railway station stocking suitable souvenirs from all over the country.

B: Brutus

In a very crowded and competitive market, **Brutus**, and its sister publication *Casa Brutus*, are about the trendiest Japanese magazines around. *Brutus* has stayed ahead of the field thanks to its innovative design and content, with each issue tending to focus, often in documentary-style detail, on a particular topic, be it ramen shops or New York. Magazine fanatics and graphic designers swoon over their special editions, such as the one on Concorde (with its own CD), issued to commemorate the supersonic aircraft's final commercial flight. Handily, for those for whom gorgeous photos and graphics aren't enough, some issues come with English translation inserts.

C: Comedy and Cosu-play

Spend one night watching Japanese television and you'll realize that the stereotype view of the locals being a dour, unfunny lot is rubbish. The Japanese love a laugh and have long enjoyed the skilfully told monologues of *rakugoka*, traditional **comedy** performers. Even more popular is the contemporary format *manzai* – a two-man team of comic (*boke*) and foil (*tsukkomi*). The Kansai area around Ōsaka has traditionally produced the nation's best comics (see box on Manzai, p.508). Beat Takeshi, better known overseas as the art-house movie director and star Kitano Takeshi (see "Film", p.997), was one half of the old *manzai* act The Two Beats, and is still a regular host and guest on quiz and light entertainment shows. The current top performers are Ishibashi Taka-aki and Kinashi Noritake, aka the Tunnels, and U-chan and Nan-chan.

One of Japan's most popular current trends is **Cosu-play**, short for "costume play", where women (mainly) dress up as their favourite character from *anime, manga*, video games or rock bands. There are shops that cater to Cosu-players, stocked with fantasy costumes (although many devotees make their own), and even a magazine devoted to the subject, called *Cosmo* (as in COStume MOdel). Tokyo's Harajuku on a Sunday is the main place to see Cosu-players. The phenomenon also has its dark side. *Gosurori* are Cosu-play girls who dress up like Gothic Lolitas, and they and their provocatively clad brethren attract a host of geeky male admirers, some of whom are basically just peeping toms.

D: Doraemon and Dangō

One of Japan's most famous cartoon characters is **Doraemon**, a time-travelling blue robot cat, and Nobita, his ten-year-old pal from suburban Tokyo, both born in December 1969 in a series of educational magazines. Nobita is always getting into scrapes and it's Doraemon who helps him out, usually by producing a twenty-first-century gadget, such as a helicopter hat to help them fly around, or the *doko-de-mo* door, a pink wood gateway to anywhere in the world. Doraemon has since gone on to star in many comic books, a string of animated films and a TV series, as well as featuring on a host of products.

Construction is one of Japan's biggest businesses and has become a major tool in economic planning since World War II, supervised by the Ministry of Construction. So much public money is available for work that the practice of **dangō**, or bid rigging, is rife. Contracts are often carved up within the industry with bribes to smooth the way. Even though the Fair Trade Commission has tried on many occasions to stop the practice, there have been very few prosecutions.

E: Enjo kōsai

"Subsidized dating", or **enjo kōsai**, is the euphemism for the phenomenon of teenage prostitution, whereby high-school girls date older men for financial compensation. Held up as an example of declining moral values in Japan, *enjo kōsai* has been fuelled by the increase in "telephone clubs" where men pay to wait in a cubicle for a call from a potential date. Female callers ring in on the free-dial numbers often advertised on the free packs of tissues distributed outside stations and on busy streets – though the extent of the problem is probably nowhere near as large as reported in the media.

F: Friday, Flash and Fruits

For a weekly dose of high-gloss scandal-mongering pick up a copy of **Friday** or **Flash**. A combination of *News of the World* and *Life*, these magazines are the antithesis of *Hello*, but equally addictive, offering a regular menu of candid shots of the famous and not so famous. Although they kowtow to Japan's strict laws when it comes to photographs of naked bodies, masking over pubic hair, other shots generally leave nothing to the imagination. There's certainly no squeamishness about shots of dead bodies, or parts of them, as one famous photograph of a railway employee carrying the head of a suicide victim away from the tracks showed.

Fruits magazine also zooms in on images – not of celebrities, but of the young, trendy and everyday folk on the streets. Month by month you can catch the latest street fashions here – like *Brutus* (see p.1001), it's beloved by global media junkies and the image-conscious.

G: Games

Golf was the sport of the boom decade, but is in the bunker now that recession is biting and casual players can no longer afford the ultra-expensive membership and green fees. When Japan's corporate warriors retire, as often as not they can be found down at the neighbourhood park, mallet in hand, enjoying a round of **gateball**, a form of croquet and a favourite pastime of senior citizens.

Japan's most popular game is **baseball** (see p.76). While you'll hear a lot about Ō Sadaharu, the Yomuri Giants player who broke the home-run record of America's Hank Aaron, it's his old team-mate Nagashima Shigeo who still hogs the limelight and has earned the nickname "Mr Giants". Nagashima had clocked up seventeen years as a star player by the time he retired in 1974; he has since made his mark as the Giants' manager, a sports commentator and all-round media personality.

H: Hello Kitty and Hanako

The Japanese have a fatal attraction for cuteness, which manifests itself in a menagerie of cuddly toys and cartoon characters on everything from bank cards to the side of jumbo jets. One design that has made an impact on overseas markets is **Hello Kitty**, a white kitten with a jaunty red hair ribbon. According to the official biography, concocted by parent company Sanrio, Kitty was born in London, where she lives with her parents and twin sister Mimi. The cartoon character, whose image graces an astonishing 12,000 new products a year, also has her own theme park, Sanrio Puroland, in the suburbs of Tokyo.

More trendy than cute is **Hanako**, the phenomenally successful style-bible magazine for young urban women. The popularity of the Australian pop artist Ken Donne in Japan is almost exclusively down to his work being featured regularly on the cover of *Hanako*, whose articles have whipped up a storm for many a consumer product or passing fashion.

I: Idols and iMode

Japanese **idols** (*aidoru*) are a polymorphous bunch, switching between singing, acting and modelling careers, regardless of where they got their start. An idol's time in the sun is usually brief but blazing, their image staring down from a multitude of billboards as well as out from countless magazines and a range of other media. Not to be confused with TV personalities (*tarento*), idols are usually picked for their looks rather than talent, although the best of them do have both.

The top male heart-throb is **Kimura Takuya**, the perennially fresh-faced member of the boy-band SMAP, who has starred in many a *trendy drama* (see p.1008). It's hard to escape J-Pop queen **Hamasaki Ayumi** whose much-photographed face is used to sell everything from cellphones to doughnuts. The one true idol-survivor is Matsuda Seiko, a pop star of the 1980s who refused to give up her career when she married and has since survived a high-profile divorce, becoming a role model for many downtrodden housewives.

If you see people fiddling with their *ketai* (mobile phone), chances are that they're using **iMode**. This service, offered by Japan's largest mobile phone company NTT DoCoMo, is an ultra-sophisticated WAP Internet connection; once the phone is on, you're online. There are over 4000 dedicated iMode services (including ones in English), covering email, games, shopping, horoscopes, restaurant guides and much more.

J: Juku

Japan has one of the most highly educated populations in the world, but its educational system is not without its faults. The pressure-cooker atmosphere created by the need to get good grades to attend the best schools and colleges has led to the development of a parallel education system of **juku**, or "cram schools".

It's estimated that some forty percent of children go to *juku* at some stage, with attendance pretty much compulsory for those who wish to get into the country's top universities. Kids start as young as five years old at these cram schools, prepping for the "examination hell" to be endured at each stage of their education until they reach university, where they can finally relax (degree study is often treated like a three-year holiday between school and career).

The pressure put on kids to get good results and to fit into the homogenized society nurtured by the education system has led to the disturbing phenomenon of *ijime*, or bullying, which results in several deaths a year, often from suicide. There's also been a sharp increase in incidents of violence at schools, and although the figures are low compared to other industrialized countries, they're worrying enough for the government to have made educational reform – emphasizing creativity and respect for the individual – a priority.

K: Karaoke and Kaikai Kiki

The Japanese were partial to a good singsong long before **karaoke**, literally meaning "empty orchestra", was invented, possibly by an Ōsaka record-store manager in the early 1970s. The machines, originally clunky eight-track tape players with a heavy duty microphone, have come a long way since and are now linked up to videos, screening the lyrics crooned along to, and featuring a range of effects to flatter the singer into thinking their caterwauling is harmonious. Not for nothing have karaoke machines been dubbed the "electronic *geisha*".

In the mid-1980s, the whole industry, which earns ¥1 trillion a year, was boosted by the debut of the **karaoke box**, a booth kitted out with a karaoke system and rented out by groups or individuals wanting to brush up on their singing technique. These boxes have proved particularly popular with youngsters, women and families who shied away from the smoky small bars frequented by salarymen that were the original preserve of karaoke. Amazingly, research has shown that the introduction of karaoke has coincided with a significant drop in the number of drunks taken into protective custody by the police, salarymen drinking less, rather than more, as they relax over a rousing rendition of *My Way*.

Kaikai Kiki (@www.kaikaikiki.co.jp) is an ultra-trendy design collective headed up by contemporary artist of the moment, Murakami Takashi, whose colourful, cartoon-like designs have been adopted by Louis Vuitton and Tokyo's Roppongi Hills development. One of Murakami's works (Miss Ko2) sold for $500,000 at an auction in New York, but it's possible to pick up his cute handiwork for a fraction of that cost in the Superflat Museum collection. These free plastic tiny "snack toys", free with packs of chewing gum, have become collectors' items.

L: Love hotels and Louis Vuitton

There are around 35,000 **love hotels** (see p.47) in Japan, which rent rooms by the hour to couples, often married, seeking a little privacy. Once called *tsurekomi ryokan* (drag her/him in hotels), there's now a trend to call them fashion hotels, in acknowledgement of the fact that it's usually the more discerning, trend-conscious woman who makes the room choice. All kinds of tastes can be indulged at love hotels, with rotating beds in mirror-lined rooms being almost passé in comparison to some of the fantasy creations on offer. Some rooms even come equipped with video cameras so you can take home a souvenir of your stay.

Japan is one of the world's most massively brand-conscious nations, and wherever you go you'll seldom be far from a woman with a **Louis Vuitton** bag. The country snaps up over a third of the company's products each year, with some lines being made exclusively for the Japanese market, and the Vuitton shops along Omotesandō and at Roppongi Hills in Tokyo are glitzy shrines to consumerism. Vuitton have even brought in top contemporary artist Murakami Takashi (see "Kaikai Kiki" above) to design their cute new logo.

M: Manga and Muji

All types of drawn cartoons, from comic strips to magazines, are known as **manga**, and together they constitute a multi-billion yen business that accounts for around a third of all published material in Japan. The bestseller is *Shukan Shōnen Jump*, a weekly comic for boys (but read by all ages and sexes), that regularly shifts five million copies, but there are hundreds of other titles, not to mention the popular daily strips in newspapers such as *Chibi Maruko-chan*, about the daily life of schoolgirl Maruko and her family.

Although there are plenty of *manga* that cater to less wholesome tastes, with sexual violence against women being top of the perversions list, comic books are frequently used to explain complicated current affairs topics, such as trade friction problems between the US and Japan, and to teach high-school subjects. *Manga* are targeted at all age groups and it's common to see a cross-section of society reading them.

More than big business, *manga* have become a recognized art form, many incorporating a startling quasi-cinematic style of close-ups and jump cuts. Top artists are respected the world over. The "god of *manga*" was Tezuka Osamu (see p.510), creator of *Astro Boy* and *Kimba, the White Lion* in the 1960s, who went on to pen more challenging fare such as the adventures of the mysterious renegade surgeon Black Jack and the epic wartime saga *Adorufu ni Tsugu* (*Tell Adolf*). Successful *manga* artists, such as Miyazaki Hayao, have also helped boost the enormous popularity of animated movies (*anime*; see box on p.995). Miyazaki's biggest hit has been *Nausicaä*, a sci-fi series set in a post-nuclear holocaust world.

One of Japan's top retail success stories is **Muji**, short for Mujirushi Ryōhin (No-brand quality goods), an offshoot of the giant Seiyu supermarket group, with over 200 branches now around Japan and Europe. Launched in 1980, the stores, which stock practical household goods, clothes, stationery and foods in simple packaging and monotone colours, prospered from the backlash against the designer-label craze that gripped Japan during the boom years of the 1980s. The irony is that the starker economic realities of the following decade, plus a rediscovery of the beauty of simple design, have made Muji's goods desirable commodities in their own right.

N:Nihonjinron and Nampa

Nihonjinron is a bizarre nationwide phenomenon in which the study of the specialness of Japan has been elevated to a high art. It has led to a host of ludicrous pronouncements that wouldn't be given the time of day anywhere else in the world, such as politicians justifying import bans for certain foods and skis because Japanese intestines and snow are, apparently, uniquely different. The fad for books analyzing Japan was sparked in the 1970s by a slim volume *The Japanese and The Jews*, written by a local scholar under the pseudonym Isaiah Ben Dassan. Since then, real *gaijin* experts have climbed on the bandwagon of telling the Japanese about themselves, and some, who've taken the trouble to master the language, have made TV careers out of it.

Nampa refers to the Japanese art of "girl hunting" and is often associated with sleazy-looking guys in sharp suits and savage haircuts who hang around major train station and shopping districts and hassle girls for dates. In a society where shyness is practically obligatory and arranged marriages still very common, such behaviour can be seen, depending on your perspective, either as a liberation from the stifling norms imposed by Japanese society or as outrageously pushy.

O: Otaku and OLS

Nerdish characters who become obsessive about a particular subject are known as **otaku** and Japan has millions of them, highly knowledgeable about their chosen field, be it a particular cartoon character or computer game. Mostly harmless, *otaku* were tarnished by the brutal child murders perpetrated in 1988 by Miyazaki Tsutomu, a young printer whose cruel behaviour had been fed by his vast collection of porn *manga* and videos.

OL is short for office lady, the female clerical workers considered "flowers of the workplace" by their sexist bosses, who need them around to make tea and generally brighten the place up for dull salarymen. If unmarried by the age of 25 and not safely tucked up at home, then an OL is said to be like a Christmas cake – of diminishing value the further from the holiday you get. It's not quite as grim as this for career-minded women today, but the recession hasn't helped increase their chances of promotion as businesses have chopped back on hiring women in the first place.

P: Pachinko, Purikura and Pokemon

One of Japan's top pastimes and major industries, raking in a staggering ¥26.3 trillion a year, is **pachinko**, a pinball game of limited skill. It's not difficult to spot *pachinko* parlours – they look like mini-Las Vegas casinos on steroids, all flashing lights and big neon signs. Inside, the atmosphere is no less in your face.

The noise of thousands of steel balls clattering through the upright electronic bagatelles is deafening, yet rows of players sit mesmerized as they control the speed with which the balls fall through the machine.

The aim of *pachinko* is for the balls to fall into the right holes so more balls can be won. These are traded in for prizes, such as cigarette lighters and calculators. Although it's illegal for the parlours to pay out cash, there's always a cubbyhole close by where prizes can be exchanged for money, a charade that the authorities have long turned a blind eye to. The initial cost of indulging in this mechanized mayhem can be as little as ¥100 for 25 ball bearings; just remember to take your earplugs, too.

Purikura (print club) – digital photo booths which combine your mug shot with a vast selection of designs on a sheet of sixteen mini-stickers – have been a huge success over recent years. Launched by Sega Corp in 1995, there are now tens of thousands of booths around Japan, and no self-respecting teenager is without their album of swapped stickers, with many adults getting in on the act, too, jazzing up their business cards with the personalized *purikura*. At the seedier end of scale, there's a trend for young women to create **ero–pura** (erotic *purakura*). The machines, found in all major shopping areas, are well worth searching out; for a couple of hundred yen you'll have a neat pop-art souvenir of Japan.

Need we say anything about **Pokemon**? The name stands for *poketto monsty* (pocket monster) and as any eight-year-old can tell you there are some 150 of them, all with fantastic powers and silly names like Polywig and Wigglytuffs.

Q: Quiz shows

The combined travel and general knowledge **quiz show** *Naruhodo za Wārudo* (*I Understand the World*), which began on Fuji TV in October 1981, revolutionized the quiz show genre in Japan, with its lively presentation and use of celebrity contestants rather than the general public. Although the show was laid to rest after fifteen seasons in 1996, it has since set the format for a host of copy-cat quizzes packed with bantering celebrities.

R: Rūsu sokkusu and robo-pets

On the wane now as a style statement, but you'll still see plenty of high-school girls in **rūsu sokkusu** (loose socks), baggy white legwarmer socks, worn as only the most dishevelled granny would do. The socks, which are held up by special glue, are believed to present plump calves in a more flattering light. What they're actually about is a form of rebellion from the strict uniform rules that students must keep to at school.

Much more trendy are **robo-pets**, such as Sony's Aibo (🌐www.aibo.com) and Sega's Puchii. This logical extension of the Tamagotchi craze (see p.1008) combines the latest artificial intelligence software with a cute robot animal which interacts emotionally with its owner – just like a real pet, but without the mess and only the occasional battery for food. The latest model of Aibo can recognize its own name and up to fifty simple words, and even take photographs through a camera in its nose.

S: Salarymen and soaplands

The dark-suited **salaryman** is generally a clerical office worker, although the term is applied to many other types of jobs. Guaranteed lifetime employment and steady promotion, Japan's corporate warriors during the boom years of the 1960s through to the 1980s only had to watch out for *karōshi*: death from overwork. Nowadays, the fear is more of their company announcing a "restructuring", a polite way of saying there will be redundancies.

Although it's perhaps not discussed as openly in Japan as in the West, sex generally comes with less hang-ups for the Japanese. One place a frisky salaryman might turn to for relief is a **soapland**, or massage parlour where the rubbing and other services are carried out by women under the guise of a Turkish bath. Soaplands were once called Turkish baths until the Turkish embassy complained that this was insulting to their wholly honourable bathing practices.

T: Taiga and trendy dramas

Long-running soap operas are very unusual in Japan, the exception being the public broadcaster NHK's **taiga dramas**. These epic historical sagas, which screen every Sunday night for a year, began in 1963 and have fallen in and out of popularity ever since. Usually concerning some great warrior figure of the past, *taiga* dramas are pretty much a national institution.

The antithesis of these samurai epics is the even more popular **trendy dramas**, which run for a strict twelve-week season and concern themselves with contemporary issues, such as the trials and tribulations of modern career women or the risky (for Japan) topic of single mothers. One of the most daring and popular, racking up a third of the viewing audience when screened in 1992, was *I Have Been in Love With You For a Long Time*, whose plot revolved around the complex emotional triangle between uptight yuppie Fuyuhiko, his overbearing mother and Fuyuhiko's arranged-marriage (yes, they still happen) bride Miwa.

U: Uyoku

The loudspeaker-mounted trucks of the **uyoku**, or ultra-nationalists, are an inescapable and noisy feature on the streets of every Japanese city. These mobile ghetto blasters, decorated with Rising Sun flags and screaming slogans, blare out distasteful right-wing messages or stop outside large companies and banks, broadcasting embarrassing statements about them.

There are estimated to be around a thousand such ultra-nationalist groups in Japan, and to a startling extent the police turn a blind eye (and deaf ear) to their activities. Politicians and the media who openly criticize the ideals and institutions they hold dear, such as the imperial household, set themselves up for some kind of nasty retribution. To most people, though, *uyoku* are an embarrassment best ignored.

V: Virtual pets and pop stars

The **virtual pet** game Tamagotchi is one of the most successful gizmos of recent years, selling some twenty million units worldwide. Meaning "loveable egg", the pocket game is an egg-shaped key ring with an LCD screen. The aim is to hatch the chick that appears on the screen, feed and nurture it – just like a real pet – over its life span of thirty days so that it rises to heaven and turns into an angel. Now somewhat eclipsed by robo-pets (see p.1007), the Tamagotchi still has its own website (ⓦhttp://travel.teglet.co.jp).

Death or ageing is not something that Japan's first **virtual pop star**, Date Kyōko, has to worry about. The computer-animated character was created in

1996 to fit a precise marketing profile and had an instant hit with her first CD. Although no more enduring than other bubble-gum pop singers, Date's "talents" are an ironic comment on her flesh and blood counterparts, whose voices are just as electronically altered and images as carefully packaged as those of the cyber-songstress.

To confirm the craze, Date has been joined by a bevy of other cyber-idols, including Ai, Shizuru and Yuki Terai.

W: Worlds

The length of Japan it's possible to visit many other **worlds** than the one you're actually travelling in. These theme-park facsimiles of other countries range from Canada World in Hokkaidō through to Huis ten Bosch in Kyūshū, a painstakingly accurate replica of the Netherlands. Along the way, you can also discover many other mini-nations, including theme parks of old Japan, such as Meiji Mura near Nagoya. The popularity of these parks lies in the safely packaged exotic escape they provide from home without the inconvenience of long-distance travel, language barriers and nasty shocks, such as crime and disease.

Y: Yakuza and Yamamba

With membership estimated at around 80,000, the **yakuza** is believed to be a far bigger criminal organization than America's Mafia. Organized crime in Japan is exactly that: a highly stratified, efficient and surprisingly tolerated everyday operation, raking in trillions of yen from extortion, protection rackets, prostitution, gambling and drug peddling.

Part of the reason that the seven major *yakuza* syndicates (who keep offices, like regular companies) have prospered is that they have acted as an alternative police force, containing petty crime and keeping violence within their own ranks. Favours, financial and otherwise, granted to high-ranking politicians and businesses have also gained the *yakuza* protection, and their romantic, samurai-value image has been boosted by countless movies.

It's highly unlikely that your path will cross with a *yakuza*, unless you take to hanging out in the dodgier areas of cities like Tokyo and Ōsaka. Younger gang members, called *chimpira*, can often be spotted by their tight perm hairdos, dark glasses and appalling dress sense. Other giveaway signs to look for are missing digits (amputation of fingers, joint by joint, is the traditional form of punishment for breaking the *yakuza* code) and full body tattoos.

Just as easy to spot, and not that much less scary, are the **yamamba**, teenage girls who have adopted the Japanese witch-like look of bleached hair, white face make-up and funky gear. Though the look isn't nearly so trendy these days, it can still occasionally be seen on the streets of Tokyo's Shibuya. These same slaves to fashion might also have a baby in tow, in which case they're referred to as *yan-mama* (young mothers).

Z: Zoku and Zodiac

Prior to the mid-1980s, Japan's media often reported the latest youth subculture sweeping the country under the tag line of **zoku** (tribe). The most enduring of these was the **bōsōzoku** ("wild speed tribe") of the 1970s, originally a mild version of the Hell's Angels, greased-hair bikers out for a loud time. Now, the term is more commonly used for rebel teenagers.

Dobutsu Uranai (zoological fortune-telling) is the latest manifestation of Japan's fascination with the **zodiac** and superstition. This twist on the traditional zodiac symbols consists of twelve cute animal designs by popular cartoonist Kubo Kiriko. Her book has sold millions of copies and been translated for markets in Taiwan, Hong Kong and Korea. If you read Japanese you can find out which animal you are and have your fortune predicted on the official website (Ⓦ www.animarhythm.com).

Books

The one thing the world is not short of is books about Japan. Virtually every foreign writer and journalist who has passed through the country has felt compelled to commit to paper their thoughts and experiences. Many of these accounts are hopelessly out of date (or just plain hopeless), but we've picked out a personal selection of the best that provide a deeper understanding of what is too easily assumed to be the world's most enigmatic country. As throughout this guide, for Japanese names we have given the family name first. This may not always be the order in which it is printed on the English translation.

Drawing on over a thousand years of literature and navel-gazing, the Japanese also love writing about their own country and culture. The vast bulk of translated works widely available in Britain and the US are novels, spanning from the courtly elegance of *Genji Monogatari* (*The Tale of Genji*) to the contemporary fiction of Nobel Prize winner Ōe Kenzaburō and the Generation-Y author Yoshimoto Banana. Such books are often released by Kodansha (Ⓦwww.kodansha-intl.com), one of the world's biggest publishers, and Charles E. Tuttle (Ⓦwww.tuttlepublishing.com), a long-established imprint for specialist books on Japan. Both have an excellent range of reference and coffee-table books on all aspects of Japanese culture, from architecture and gardens to food and martial arts, which are best bought at major bookstores in Japan, such as Kinokuniya and Maruzen. Look out also for the series of pocket-size booklets by JTB on many different aspects of Japanese culture. Books published by Kodansha, Tuttle and JTB are usually cheaper in Japan, but other books won't be, so buy them before your journey.

A geisha scorned

The phenomenal success of Arthur Golden's *Memoirs of a Geisha* has caused publishers to raid their back catalogues for related titles. *Geisha*, by Liza Dalby (the only foreign woman ever to train as a geisha) is one true-life memoir that has come back for a second round of attention, while another respected cultural observer of Japan, Leslie Downer, has weighed in with *Geisha: the Secret Life of a Vanishing World* and *Madame Sadayakko*. The latter is a biography of Japan's first internationally famous geisha, who charmed the world at the beginning of the twentieth century.

Now comes Iwasaki Mineko, a *grande dame* of Kyoto's Gion geisha district and acknowledged inspiration for Golden's *Memoirs*. Her *Geisha of Gion* aims to set straight a story which Iwasaki claims was grossly distorted by Golden. Iwasaki is particularly miffed at Golden's exposure of the custom of *mizuage*, when a geisha has her virginity auctioned off to the highest bidder. Iwasaki claims she would never have done such a thing, although Golden, rather ungallantly, has gone on record saying that Iwasaki told him that her *mizuage* had been sold for ¥100 million, and that he has the taped conversations to prove it.

Threats of legal action swirled for a while, but now that Iwasaki has had her say in print, they have been quietly forgotten, leaving some to conclude that what really upset the former geisha was how much money Golden had made from her story.

History

Pat Barr *The Coming of the Barbarians*. Entertaining and very readable tales of how Japan opened up to the West at the beginning of the Meiji Restoration.

★ **Ian Buruma** *The Wages of Guilt*. Buruma's skilful comparison and explanation of how and why Germany and Japan have come to terms so differently with their roles in World War II. His *Inventing Japan* looks at the country's history between 1853 and 1964, the period which saw the country transformed from an isolated feudal state to a global economic powerhouse.

★ **John Dower** *Embracing Defeat: Japan in the Aftermath of World War II*. Accessible look by a Pulitzer Prize winner at the impact of the American occupation on Japan. First-person accounts and snappy writing bring the book alive.

John Hersey *Hiroshima*. Classic account of the devastation and suffering wrought by the first A-bomb to be used in war.

George Hicks *The Comfort Women*. The story of one of the more shameful episodes of World War II, when the Japanese forced women to become prostitutes (euphemistically known as "comfort women") for the army.

Richard Hughes *Foreign Devil*. The veteran Australian journalist arrived in Japan in 1940, eighteen months before Pearl Harbor, and came back in 1945 to turn his enormous talent (and wit) to commenting on postwar Japan and the Far East, as well as going behind the scenes with Ian Fleming to research *You Only Live Twice* (see p.1000).

Mishima Akio *Bitter Sea*. The Kyūshū port of Minamata is now a byword in Japan for the devastating impact of industrial pollution. This dramatic account of the poisoning of Minamata's citizens and their long, painful battle for compensation, was penned by a former journalist turned environmentalist.

Sir George Samson *Japan: A Short Cultural History*. One of the standard texts on Japan's past, condensed from the former diplomat's scholarly three-volume epic – though it's still by no means concise.

Edward Seidensticker *Low City, High City* and *Tokyo Rising: The City Since the Great Earthquake*. Seidensticker, a top translator of Japanese literature, tackles Tokyo's history from its humble beginnings to the Great Kantō quake of 1923 in the first book and follows up well with a second volume focusing on the capital's postwar experiences.

Oliver Statler *Japanese Inn* and *Japanese Pilgrimage*. In the first book, a ryokan on the Tōkaidō road provides the focus for an entertaining account of over four hundred years of Japanese history. In *Japanese Pilgrimage*, Statler applies his talents to bringing alive the history of the 88-temple hike around Shikoku.

Richard Storry *A History of Modern Japan*. Ideal primer for basics and themes of Japanese history.

Kenneth Strong *Ox Against the Storm*. The revealing story of Tanaka Shozo's fight against the Meiji Government on behalf of peasants affected by copper pollution. A larger-than-life character, Tanaka was a fierce champion of democracy and people's rights, as well as one of Japan's first conservationists.

Richard Tames *A Traveller's History of Japan*. This clearly written and succinct volume romps through Japan's history and provides useful cultural descriptions and essays.

Marvin Tokayer and **Mary Swartz** *The Fugu Plan*. Semi-fictionalized tale, based on incredible true-life events, which saw over 5000 Jews being allowed into Japan during World War II and protected first in Kōbe and later in Japanese-occupied Shanghai.

Paul Waley *Tokyo: City of Stories*. Intimate, anecdotal history of the capital which delves into Tokyo's neighbourhoods and uncovers some fascinating stories in the process.
Mark Weston *Giants of Japan*. Mark Weston puts flesh on the bones of history with these short, lively biographies of the movers and shakers who helped create the Japan of today. The 37 portraits – including a handful of women – range from emperors to industrialists and poets to film directors.

Business, economics and politics

Geoffrey Bownas, David Powers and **Christopher P. Hood** *Doing Business with the Japanese*. Highly readable and up-to-date guide to approaching and succeeding in this challenging but potentially lucrative market.

Peter Hadfield *Sixty Seconds That Will Change The World*. The main theme – the terrible threat hanging over Tokyo by a coming earthquake – allows Hadfield to reveal much about Japanese attitudes, bureaucracy and politics.

⭐ **Robert M. March** *Working for a Japanese Company*. One of the best studies on what it's really like inside Japan's corporate powerhouses by an Aussie management consultant who's done thorough research.

Miyamoto Masao *Straitjacket Society*. As the subtitle hints, this "insider's irreverent view of bureaucratic Japan" is quite an eye-opener. Unsurprisingly, Miyamoto was fired from the Ministry of Health and Welfare, but his book sold over 400,000 copies.

Ōmae Ken'ichi *The Borderless World*. One of Japan's top management consultants airs his free-market theories of how national economic borders are melting away in the wake of multinational business success. A useful insight into the thoughts of a man whose views have influenced many important businesses and political leaders.

Jacob M. Schlesinger *Shadow Shoguns*. Cracking crash course in Japan's political scene, scandals and all, from *Wall Street Journal* reporter Schlesinger, who spent five years at the newspaper's Tokyo bureau and whose wife was an aide to current top politician Ozawa Ichiro.

Peter Tasker *Inside Japan*. Written by a British financial analyst who has made Japan his home since 1977, this highly readable and intelligent examination of Japanese business and society was first published in 1987, at the height of the boom years, but is still recommended reading.

⭐ **Karel Van Wolferen** *The Enigma of Japanese Power*. Standard text on the triad of Japan's bureaucracy, politicians and business, and the power gulf between them. A weighty, thought-provoking tome, worth wading through.

Arts, culture and society

Ruth Benedict *The Chrysanthemum and the Sword*. Classic study of the hierarchical order of Japanese society, first published in 1946. It's still relevant now for its intriguing insight into the psychology of a nation that had just suffered defeat in World War II.

Alexandra Black *The Japanese House*. A beautifully illustrated study of Japanese architecture and interior aesthetics, tracing their history from the traditional teahouse to modern home design.

Shirley Booth *Food of Japan*. More than a series of recipes, this nicely illustrated book also gives lots of background detail and history of

Japanese food. Also has a useful list of suppliers of Japanese and macrobiotic food in the UK.

Nicholas Bornoff *Pink Samurai*. Everything you ever wanted to know about the history and current sexual practices and mores in Japan, plus – at seven hundred-odd pages – plenty you'd rather not have known.

Ian Buruma *A Japanese Mirror* and *The Missionary and the Libertine*. The first book is an intelligent, erudite examination of Japan's popular culture, while *The Missionary and the Libertine* collects together a range of essays including pieces on Japan-bashing, Hiroshima, Pearl Harbor, the authors Mishima Yukio, Tanizaki Junichirō and Yoshimoto Banana and the film director Ōshima Nagisa.

Kittredge Cherry *Womansword*. Slightly dated but fascinating portrait of women in Japanese society as revealed through language. From "Christmas cake" (an unmarried woman) to "giant garbage" (a retired husband), *Womansword* makes linguistics both fun and thought-provoking.

Mark Coutts-Smith *Children of the Drum*. The life of Sado Island's Kodō drummers captured in powerful black-and-white images by a photographer who spent five years studying and working with the group.

★ **Lisa Dalby** *Geisha*. The real-life *Memoirs of a Geisha*. In the 1970s, anthropologist Dalby immersed herself in this fast-disappearing world and became a geisha. This is the fascinating account of her experience and those of her teachers and fellow pupils. *Kimono*, her history of the most Japanese of garments, is also worth a look.

Lesley Downer *The Brothers*. The Tsutsumi family are the Kennedys of Japan, and their saga of wealth, illegitimacy and the fabled hatred of the two half-brothers is turned into a gripping read by Downer. Also look out for *On the Narrow Road to the*

Deep North, her book following in the footsteps of the poet Bashō, and her books on geisha (see box on p.1011).

Bruce S. Feiler *Learning to Bow*. An enlightening and entertaining read, especially for anyone contemplating teaching English in Japan. This book recounts the experiences of a young American on the JET programme, plonked into a high school in rural Tochigi-ken.

Norma Field *In the Realm of a Dying Emperor*. Field paints a vivid alternative portrait of contemporary Japan, as seen through the experiences of three people who broke ranks: Chibana Shoichi, who hauled down the Rising Sun flag in Okinawa; Nakaya Yasuko, a housewife who tried to stop the burial of her husband, a former Self-Defence Forces member, at a Shinto shrine; and Motōshima Hitoshi, ex-mayor of Nagasaki, who criticized Emperor Hirohito's role during World War II.

Edward Fowler *San'ya Blues*. Fowler's experiences living and working among the casual labourers of Tokyo's San'ya district make fascinating reading. He reveals the dark underbelly of Japan's economic miracle and blows apart a few myths and misconceptions on the way.

Robin Gerster *Legless in Ginza*. A funny and spot-on account of the writer's two-year residence at Japan's most prestigious university, Tokyo's Todai. Gerster writes with a larrikin Aussie verve and notices things that many other expat commentators ignore.

Gunji Masakatsu *Kabuki*. Excellent, highly readable introduction to Kabuki by one of the leading connoisseurs of Japanese drama. Illustrated with copious annotated photos of the great actors and most dramatic moments in Kabuki theatre.

Joe Joseph *The Japanese*. Former *Times* correspondent sets down some thoughts on the nation, mainly gathered during the madly extravagant and unrepresentative bubble years of the late 1980s.

David Kaplan and **Andrew Marshall** *The Cult at the End of the World*. Chilling account of the nerve gas attack on the Tokyo subway by the AUM cult in 1995. The gripping, pulp fiction-like prose belies formidable research by the authors into the shocking history of this killer cult and their crazed leader Asahara Shōkō.

Donald Keene *The Blue-Eyed Tarōkaja*. Wide-ranging anthology of literary essays, interviews and travel pieces by Donald Keene, one of the foremost authorities on Japanese literature.

★ **Alex Kerr** *Lost Japan*. Kerr, the son of a US naval officer, first came to Japan as a child in the 1960s and has been fascinated by it ever since. This beautifully written and thoughtfully observed set of essays covers aspects of his life and passions, including Kabuki, art collecting and cities such as Kyoto and Ōsaka. His follow-up *Dogs and Demons* is a scathing and thought-provoking attack on Japan's economic, environmental and social policies of the past decades.

Richard McGregor *Japan Swings*. One of the more intelligent books penned by a former Tokyo correspondent. McGregor sets politics, culture and sex in 1990s post-bubble Japan in his sights, revealing a fascinating world of ingrained money politics and shifting sexual attitudes.

Brian Moeran *A Far Valley: Four Years in a Japanese Village*. An affectionate though far from rose-tinted view into the daily life of a Japanese village by a cultural anthropologist. Moeran spent four years with his family in a community of potters in deepest Kyūshū, before their dreams were shattered in a totally unexpected and harrowing way.

Patricia Morely *The Mountain is Moving*. Though a bit heavy going in places, this study of the changing role of women in Japanese society is best for its interviews with and portraits of women who have broken with tradition.

John K. Nelson *A Year in the Life of a Shinto Shrine*. Fascinating insight into Japan's native animist religion based on this American ethnologist's research at Suwa-jinja in Nagasaki. Amid all the detail, Nelson also catches gossipy asides such as a trainee priest being told to be "careful not to fart during the ritual".

Gunter Nitschke *Japanese Gardens*. A far less lavish book on gardens than Itoh Teiji's seminal work (see p.1018), but nonetheless informative, wide-ranging and beautifully illustrated.

★ **Donald Richie** *Public People, Private People, A Lateral View* and *Partial Views*. These three books, all collections of essays by a man whose love affair with Japan began when he arrived with the US occupying forces in 1947, set a standard other expat commentators can only aspire to. *Public People* is a set of sketches of famous and unknown Japanese, including profiles of novelist Mishima and the actor Mifune Toshiro. In *A Lateral View* and *Partial Views*, Richie tackles Tokyo style, avant-garde theatre, *pachinko*, the Japanese kiss and the Zen rock garden at Kyoto's Ryōan-ji temple, among many other things.

Saga Junichi *Confessions of a Yakuza*. This life story of a former *yakuza* boss, beautifully retold by a doctor whose clinic he just happened to walk into, gives a rare insight into a secret world. Saga also wrote the award-winning *Memories of Silk and Straw*, a collection of reminiscences about village life in pre-modern Japan.

★ **Mark Schilling** *The Encyclopedia of Japanese Pop Culture*. Forget sumo, samurai and *ikebana*. Godzilla, pop idols and instant ramen are really where

Japan's culture's at. Schilling's book is an indispensable, spot-on guide to late-twentieth-century Japan. Don't leave home without it.

Frederik L. Schodt *Dreamland Japan: Writings on Modern Manga.* A series of entertaining and informative essays on the art of Japanese comic books, profiling the top publications, artists, animated films and English-language *manga*.

Joan Stanley-Baker *Japanese Art.* Highly readable introduction to the broad range of Japan's artistic traditions (though excluding theatre and music), tracing their development from prehistoric to modern times.

★ **David Suzuki** and **Oiwa Keibo** *The Japan We Never Knew.* Canadian broadcaster and writer Suzuki teamed up with half-Japanese anthropologist Oiwa to tour the country and interview an extraordinary range of people, from the Ainu of Hokkaidō to descendants of the "untouchable" caste, the Burakumin. The result is an excellent riposte to the idea of a monocultural, conformist Japan.

Robert Twigger *Angry White Pyjamas.* The subtitle "An Oxford poet trains with the Tokyo riot police" gives you the gist, and although Twigger's writing is more prose than poetry, he provides an intense forensic account of the daily trials, humiliations and triumphs of becoming a master of Aikido. Even if you're not into martial arts, it's worth picking up.

Rey Ventura *Underground in Japan.* The non-Caucasian *gaijin* experience in Japan is brilliantly essayed by Ventura, who lived and worked with fellow Filipino illegal immigrants in the dockyards of Yokohama.

Travel writing

Dave Barry *Dave Barry Does Japan.* Hilarious spoof travel book by top American satirist.

Isabella Bird *Unbeaten Tracks in Japan.* After a brief stop in Meiji-era Tokyo, intrepid Victorian adventurer Bird is determined to reach parts of Japan not trampled by tourists. She heads north to Hokkaidō, taking the time to make acute, vivid observations along the way.

★ **Alan Booth** *The Roads to Sata* and *Looking for the Lost.* Two classics by one of the most insightful and entertaining modern writers on Japan, whose talents were tragically cut short by his death in 1993. The first book sees Booth, an avid long-distance walker, hike (with the aid of many a beer) from the far north of Hokkaidō to the southern tip of Kyūshū, while *Looking for the Lost*, a trio of walking tales, is by turns hilarious and heartbreakingly poignant.

Josie Drew *A Ride in the Neon Sun.* At nearly 700 pages, this isn't a book to pop in your panniers, but full of useful tips for anyone planning to tour Japan by bike. She has subsequently put out a sequel, *The Sun in My Eyes.*

★ **Will Ferguson** *Hokkaido Highway Blues.* Humorist Ferguson decides to hitch from one end of Japan to the other, with the aim of travelling with the Japanese, not among them. He succeeds (despite everyone telling him – even those who stop to pick him up – that Japanese never stop for hitch-hikers), and in the process turns out one of the best ever books of travel writing about the country. Funny and ultimately moving.

Donald W. George and **Amy Greimann Carslon** (eds) *Travelers' Tales Guides: Japan.* A necessarily selective sampler of the best writers who ever penned a Japan travel piece, with contributions from Lafcadio Hearn to Donald Richie, Alan Booth and Pico Iyer.

Pico Iyer *Video Nights in Katmandu*

and *The Lady and the Monk*. The first book, by this former *Time* correspondent, has a brilliant essay on baseball and the incongruities of modern Japan. Iyer obviously fell in love with Japan, a fact reflected in the beautifully written *The Lady and the Monk*, devoted to a year he spent studying Zen Buddhism and dallying with a married woman in Kyoto. It's a rose-tinted, dreamy view of the country, which he has since followed up, in a more realistic way, with his excellent and thought-provoking *The Global Soul* (Bloomsbury).

★ **Donald Richie** *The Inland Sea*. Showing long-time Japan resident Richie's writing at its very best, this subtle, elegiac travelogue, first published in 1971, totally captures the timeless beauty of the island-studded Inland Sea. Richie has often been compared to the nineteenth-century writer Lafcadio Hearn (see box on p.693), so it's appropriate that he serves as editor on *Lafcadio Hearn's Japan*, which includes sections from the classic *Glimpses of Unfamiliar Japan*, among Hearn's other works. In *Tokyo*, Richie captures the essence of the city he has lived in for more than fifty years. One of the best introductions you could read.

Guides and reference books

Mark Brazil *A Birdwatcher's Guide to Japan*. Essential (though hard to find) guide for birdwatchers – it's particularly good for those looking for birds and other wildlife in Okinawa, Western Kyūshū, around Tokyo, and especially eastern Hokkaidō.

Jan Brown *Exploring Tōhoku*. Detailed and well-written guide to Japan's back country by a long-term resident and obvious enthusiast. Provides plenty of historical and cultural information as well as practical snippets.

John Carroll *Trails of Two Cities*. Enjoyable and informative walking guide to Yokohama and Kamakura by a long-time resident. Full of fascinating historical detail and local insights.

Judith Clancy *Exploring Kyoto*. One of the better Kyoto guides, whose thirty well-researched walking tours (each with an accompanying map) cover both the famous sights and the less well-known byways of this ancient city.

★ **Diane Durston** *Old Kyoto* and *Kyoto: Seven Paths to the Heart of the City* (Mitsumura Suko Shoin). Few people can get under the skin of this enigmatic city as well as Diane Durston. In *Old Kyoto* she seeks out the best traditional craft shops, restaurants and ryokan, while her more recent book explores seven neighbourhoods where Kyoto's special magic still survives.

Enbutsu Sumiko *Old Tokyo: Walks in the City of the Shogun*. Tokyo's old Shitamachi area is best explored on foot and Enbutsu's guide, illustrated with characterful block prints, helps bring the city's history alive.

Harry Guest *Traveller's Literary Companion to Japan*. Explore Japan in the company of the country's literary greats and a host of foreign writers. Regional essays with selected extracts are backed up by author bios, booklists and a brief romp through the historical and cultural background.

Brian Harrel (ed) *Cycling Japan*. This highly practical guide tells you everything you need to know for a biking trip around the country, with plenty of personal accounts. If nothing else, try the Yamanote Countryside Ride, a 45-kilometre loop around Tokyo, which is guaranteed to reveal many of the city's forgotten gems.

Anne Hotta and **Ishiguro Yoko** *A Guide to Japanese Hot Springs*. Over

160 onsen, including 25 within easy reach of Tokyo, are detailed in this indispensable guide for bath lovers, as well as the cultural history of natural hot-water pursuits in Japan.

Paul Hunt *Hiking in Japan.* Hunt demonstrates that there's far more to mountain climbing in Japan than scaling Fuji-san. His detailed hikes cover all the top destinations from Kirishima in Kyūshū to Daisetsu-zan in Hokkaidō, by way of the fabulous Japan Alps.

Itoh Teiji *The Gardens of Japan.* This huge coffee-table book offers comprehensive coverage and splendid photos of all Japan's great historical gardens, including many not generally open to the public, as well as contemporary examples.

Thomas F. Judge and **Tomita Hiroyuki** *Edo Craftsmen.* Beautifully produced portraits of some of Shitamachi's traditional craftsmen, who can still be found working in the backstreets of Tokyo. A timely insight into a disappearing world.

Rick Kennedy *Good Tokyo Restaurants.* The author has sampled thousands of restaurants during his many years in Tokyo, so he knows what he's talking about. Not as wide-ranging, or as up-to-date, as other guides, but very reliable.

John Martin and **Phyllis Martin** *Tokyo: A Cultural Guide to Japan's Capital City, Kyoto: A Cultural Guide to Japan's Ancient Imperial City* and *Nara: A Cultural Guide to Japan's Ancient Capital.* Three excellent books designed around walking tours of Japan's most historic cities, which go well beyond the usual sights.

Caroline Pover *Being a Broad in Japan.* The subtitle – "Everything a Western woman needs to thrive and survive" – sums it up, and Pover proves a sassy guide to the various perils and pitfalls of life in Japan from a female perspective, covering everything from finding day care to getting divorced.

Ed Readicker-Henderson *The Traveller's Guide to Japanese Pilgrimages.* A practical guide to Japan's top three pilgrim routes: Hiei-zan (near Kyoto); the 33 Kannon of Saigoku (a broad sweep from the Kii peninsula to Lake Biwa); and following the steps of Kōbō Daishi round Shikoku's 88 temples.

T.R. Reid *Ski Japan!* This witty and informative guide profiles 93 of the best resorts in the country, though ski-mad Reid prefers to be on rather than off the slopes, so don't expect much in the way of accommodation or après-ski recommendations.

Robb Satterwhite *What's What in Japanese Restaurants.* Written by a Tokyo-based epicure, this handy guide covers all the types of Japanese food and drink you're likely to encounter, and the menus annotated with Japanese characters are particularly useful.

Mary Sutherland and **Dorothy Britton** *National Parks of Japan.* With gorgeous photos and a thoroughly researched text, this inspirational book is the essential guide to all 28 of Japan's national parks, covering wildlife, plants, and natural and cultural history.

Tajima Noriyuki *Tokyo: A Guide to Recent Architecture.* A compact, expertly written and nicely illustrated book that's an essential accompaniment on any modern architectural tour of the capital.

TokyoQ *2002 Annual Guide to the City.* Spin-off from the fine website, this handy slim volume is worth picking up for those extra titbits of information that only living in the city provides.

Marc Treib and **Ron Herman** *A Guide to the Gardens of Kyoto.* Handy, pocket-sized guide to more than fifty of the city's gardens, with concise historical details and step-by-step descriptions of each garden.

Gary D'A Walters *Day Walks Near Tokyo.* If you want help getting off

the beaten tourist path, this slim volume describes various strolls and hikes within easy reach of the capital, with clear maps and practical details and directions.
Diane Wiltshire Kanagawa and **Jeanne Huey Erickson** *Japan for*

Kids. Immensely practical guide covering everything from vocabulary for the labour ward, to where to rent a Santa. Aimed mainly at expat parents living in Tokyo, but also full of practical tips and recommendations for visitors with kids.

Classic literature

★ **Kawabata Yasunari** *Snow Country*, *The Izu Dancer*, and other titles. Japan's first Nobel Prize winner for fiction writes intense tales of passion – usually about a sophisticated urban man falling for a simple country girl.
Matsuo Bashō *The Narrow Road to the Deep North*. The seventeenth-century haiku poetry master chronicles his journey through northern Japan, pausing to compose his thoughts along the way.
Murasaki Shikibu *The Tale of Genji*. Claimed as the world's first novel, this lyrical epic about the lives and loves of a nobleman was spun by a lady of the Heian court around 1000 AD.
Natsume Sōseki *Botchan*, *Kokoro* and *I am a Cat*. In his comic novel *Botchan*, Sōseki draws on his own experiences as an English teacher in

turn-of-the-twentieth-century Matsuyama. The three volumes of *I am a Cat* sees the humorist adopting a wry feline point of view on the world. *Kokoro* – about an ageing *sensei* (teacher) trying to come to terms with the modern era – is considered his best book.
Sei Shōnagon *The Pillow Book*. Fascinating insight into the daily life and artful thoughts of a tenth-century noblewoman.
Tanizaki Jun'ichirō *Some Prefer Nettles* and *The Makioka Sisters*. One of the great stylists of Japanese prose, Tanizaki's finest book is often considered to be *Some Prefer Nettles*, about a romantic liaison between a Japanese man and a Eurasian woman. However, there's an epic sweep to *The Makioka Sisters*, which documents the decline of a wealthy merchant family in Ōsaka.

Contemporary fiction

Alfred Birnbaum ed. *Monkey Brain Sushi*. A good introduction to modern Japanese prose, with eleven often quirky short stories by contemporary authors.
Van C. Gessel and **Tomone Matsumoto** (eds) *The Shōwa Anthology*. This collection of short stories is essential reading if you want to get up to speed with the best in contemporary Japanese fiction. The anthology covers the Shōwa era (1926–1989) and includes a number of stories not previously translated into English.
Ishiguro Kazuo *An Artist of the Floating World* and *A Pale View of the*

Hills. Nagasaki-born author who's lived in Britain since 1960. *A Pale View*, his first novel, is a haunting tale set in Nagasaki which unravels the vaguely expressed horrors of the atomic bombing against the backdrop of a dislocated postwar society. *An Artist of the Floating World* takes a look at the rise of Japanese militarism in the twentieth century through the eyes of an ageing painter.
Maruya Saiichi *Singular Rebellion*. Comedy of manners about a middle-aged salaryman who shacks up with a bimbo model, only to find himself also sharing house with granny, just out of jail for murder.

Mishima Yukio *After the Banquet, Confessions of Mask, Forbidden Colours, The Sea of Fertility*. Novelist Mishima sealed his notoriety by committing ritual suicide after leading a failed military coup in 1970. He left behind a highly respectable, if at times melodramatic, body of literature, including some of Japan's finest postwar novels. Themes of tradition, sexuality and militarism run through many of his works.

Miyabe Miyuki *All She Was Worth*. When a young man's fiancé goes missing, a trail of credit-card debts and worse turns up. There's more to this clever whodunnit set in contemporary Tokyo than immediately meets the eye.

Murakami Ryū *Almost Transparent Blue, Sixty-nine, Coin Locker Babies* and *In the Miso Soup*. Murakami burst onto Japan's literary scene in the mid-1980s with *Almost Transparent Blue*, a hip tale of student life mixing reality and fantasy. *Sixty-nine* is his semi-autobiographical account of a 17-year-old stirred by the rebellious passions of the late 1960s, set in Sasebo, Kyūshū. *Coin Locker Babies* is his most ambitious work, spinning a revenger's tragedy about the lives of two boys dumped in adjacent coin lockers as babies. His most recently translated novel, *In the Miso Soup*, is a taut thriller taking a wry look at the underbelly of Tokyo society.

Ōe Kenzaburō *Nip the Buds, Shoot the Kids, A Personal Matter* and *A Healing Family*. Ōe won Japan's second Nobel Prize for literature in 1994 and is a writer who aims, in his own words, to "push back the rising tide of conformity". *Nip the Buds*, his first full-length novel, published in 1958, is a tale of lost innocence concerning fifteen reformatory school boys evacuated in wartime to a remote mountain village and left to

Murakami Haruki

Murakami Haruki is one of the most entertaining Japanese writers around and is hailed as a postwar successor to the great novelists Mishima, Kawabata and Tanizaki. His books, which are wildly popular in Japan, are about conspiracies, suicidal women, futile love, disappearing elephants and talking sheep. In 21 years he has published over a dozen novels and *Underground*, a study of the 1995 Tokyo subway gas attack by the AUM Shinrikyo cult. Translated into some thirty languages, Murakami is being talked of as a future Nobel Prize laureate, though the 54-year-old writer and marathon runner (he's run one a year for the past eighteen years, with a personal best of 3 hours 34 minutes, and is planning a book on the subject) shuns the media spotlight and is happy that few people recognize him.

Many of Murakami's books are set in Tokyo, drawing on his time studying at Waseda University in the early 1970s and running his own jazz bar in Kokubunji, a place that became a haunt for literary types and, no doubt, provided inspiration for his jazz-bar-running hero in the bittersweet novella *South of the Border, West of the Sun*. He's back living in Tokyo now, but has spent large parts of his career abroad, including five years teaching in the US, at both Princeton University and Boston's Tufts University. The contemporary edge to Murakami's writing, which eschews the traditional clichés of Japanese literature, has been fuelled by his work as a translator of books by John Irving, Raymond Carver, Truman Capote and Paul Theroux among others.

A good introduction to Murakami is *Norwegian Wood*, a tender coming-of-age love story between two students, that has sold over five million copies in both of its volumes. The truly bizarre *A Wild Sheep Chase* and its follow-up *Dance Dance Dance*, are funny but disturbing modern-day fables, dressed up as detective novels. His best book is considered to be *The Wind-Up Bird Chronicle*, a hefty yet dazzling cocktail of mystery, war reportage and philosophy.

fend for themselves when a threatening plague frightens away the villagers. *A Personal Matter* sees Ōe tackling the trauma of his handicapped son Hikari's birth, while *A Healing Family* catches up with Hikari thirty years later, documenting his trials and triumphs. Never an easy read, but always startlingly honest.

Yoshimoto Banana *Kitchen*, *Lizard* and *Amrita*. Trendy thirty-something novelist whose quirky, lyrical style and odd stories have struck a chord with modern Japanese youth and overseas readers.

Japan in foreign fiction

★ **Alan Brown** *Audrey Hepburn's Neck*. Beneath this rib-tickling, acutely observed tale of a young guy from the sticks adrift in big-city Tokyo, Brown weaves several important themes, including the continuing impact of World War II and the confused relationships between the Japanese and *gaijin*. An evocative, enchanting fable of contemporary Japan.

James Clavell *Shogun*. Blockbuster fictionalized account of Englishman Will Adams' life in seventeenth-century Japan as an adviser to Shogun Tokugawa Ieyasu.

Lisa Dalby *The Tale of Murasaki*. The eleventh-century Japanese author Murasaki Shikibu and her *Tale of Genji* inspire this imaginative novel that takes the reader inside Kyoto's ancient imperial court.

Ian Fleming *You Only Live Twice*. Bondo-san on the trail of arch-enemy Blofeld in trendy mid-sixties Tokyo and the wilds of Kyūshū, assisted by Tiger Tanaka and Kissy Suzuki.

William Gibson *Idoru* and *Pattern Recognition*. Love in the age of the computer chip. Cyberpunk novelist Gibson's sci-fi vision of Tokyo's hi-tech future – a world of non-intrusive DNA checks at airports and computerized pop icons (the *idoru* of the title) – rings disturbingly true. His latest book, the hip thriller *Pattern Recognition*, also has scenes in Tokyo including ones at the ever-popular Park Hyatt hotel in Shinjuku.

Arthur Golden *Memoirs of a Geisha*. Rags to riches potboiler following the progress of Chiyo from her humble beginnings in a Japanese fishing village through training as a *geisha* in Kyoto to setting up her own teahouse in New York. Full of accurate details and colourful characters – impressively so, given that Golden has spent so little time in Japan itself.

Lian Hearn *Across the Nightingale Floor* and *Grass For His Pillow*. The first two books in a historical fantasy trilogy set in an imaginary world not unlike Japan. Hearn's plotting, mastery of characters and scene have seen these hugely successful books hailed as modern classics.

Steven Heighton *Flightpaths of the Emperor*. Entertaining and thought-provoking collection of short stories by a young award-winning Canadian writer, most based in downtown Ōsaka where Heighton once taught English like the character in some of the tales.

Dianne Highbridge *In the Empire of Dreams*. In this series of loosely connected short stories, Australian expat Highbridge focuses on the experiences of young women – all, bar one, expats – attempting to make a life in Japan. Evocative descriptions and some insights, but few surprises as Highbridge ticks off the issues, from mixed marriages to the *gaijin* who find it impossible to leave.

Gavin Kramer *Shopping*. British lawyer Kramer's zippy first novel is on the bleak side, but captures the turn-of-the-millennium zeitgeist of Tokyo, where schoolgirls trade sex for designer labels and *gaijin* flounder in a sea of misunderstanding.

⭐ **David Mitchell** *Ghostwritten* and *number9dream*. The Hiroshima-based British writer made a splash with his debut *Ghostwritten*, a dazzling collection of interlocked short stories, a couple set in Japan. *number9dream*, shortlisted for the Booker prize in 2001, conjures up a postmodern Japan of computer hackers, video games, gangsters and violence. A demanding, dark read, but unputdownable nonetheless.

John David Morley *Pictures from the Water Trade*. The subtitle, "An Englishman in Japan", says it all as Morley's alter-ego, Boon, crashes headlong into an intense relationship with demure yet sultry Mariko in an oh-so-foreign world. Along the way, some imaginative observations and descriptions are made.

Ruri Pilgrim *Fish of the Seto Island Sea*. Account of three generations of the author's family, starting with her great-grandparents in the 1870s. The book's greatest interest lies in its dramatic backdrop of the war – which the family comes through remarkably intact, albeit in very straitened circumstances – and the deep-seated changes taking place in Japanese society as a result of both the war and the subsequent American occupation.

Peter Tasker *Silent Thunder, Buddha Kiss* and *Samurai Boogie*. Tasker, a British financial analyst, has created a trio of fun, throwaway thrillers, with Bond-like set pieces and lively Japanese characters, especially Mori, his down-at-heel gumshoe.

Language

Language

Language

First the good news. Picking up a few words of Japanese, even managing a sentence or two, is not difficult. **Pronunciation** is simple and standard and there are few exceptions to the straightforward **grammar** rules. With a couple of weeks' effort you should be able to read the words spelled out in **hiragana** and **katakana**, Japanese phonetic characters, even if you can't understand them. And any time spent learning Japanese will be amply rewarded by the thrilled response you'll elicit from the locals, who'll always politely comment on your fine linguistic ability.

The bad news is that it takes a very great effort indeed to become halfway proficient in Japanese, let alone master the language. One of the main stumbling blocks is the thousands of **kanji** characters that need to be memorized, most of which have at least two pronunciations, depending on the sentence and their combination with other characters. Another major difficulty is the multiple levels of **politeness** embodied in Japanese, married with different sets of words used by men and women (although this is less of a problem). Finally, as you move around Japan there are different **dialects** to deal with, such as Ōsaka-ben, the dialect of the Kansai area, involving whole new vocabularies.

English-Japanese language boxes

To help you find your way around, in the guide we've included **language boxes** giving the names of sights, hotels and restaurants in English, *rōmaji* (for pronunciation) and Japanese characters. Using these you will be able to identify the place when you get there, to ask for directions and to cross-reference against a Japanese map. All hotels are listed, but in the case of restaurants and bars we do not include those that have a clearly visible sign in English or *rōmaji*.

Japanese characters

The exact origins of Japanese are a mystery, and until the sixth century it only existed in the spoken form. Once the Japanese imported Chinese characters, known as *kanji*, they began to develop their own forms of written language.

Japanese is now written in a combination of three systems. The most difficult of the three to master is **kanji** (Chinese ideograms), which originally developed as mini-pictures of the word they stand for. To be able to read a newspaper, you'll need to know around two thousand *kanji*, much more difficult than it sounds since what each one means varies with its context.

The easier writing systems to pick up are the phonetic syllabaries, **hiragana** and **katakana**. Both have 45 regular characters (see box, p.1026) and can be learned within a couple of weeks. *Hiragana* is used for Japanese words, while *katakana*, with the squarer characters, is used mainly for loan words from Western languages (especially English) and technical names. Increasingly, **rōmaji** (see opposite), the roman script used to spell out Japanese words, is also used in advertisements and magazines. Good places to practise reading *hiragana* and *katakana* are on the advertisements plastered in train carriages and on restaurant menus.

The first five letters in *hiragana* and *katakana* (**a, i, u, e, o**) are the vowel sounds (see "Pronunciation", opposite). The remainder are a combination of a consonant and a vowel (eg. **ka, ki, ku, ke, ko**), with the exception of **n**, the only consonant that exists on its own. While *hiragana* provides an exact phonetic reading of all Japanese words, it's a mistake to think that *katakana* does the same for foreign loan words. Often words are shortened, hence television becomes *terebi* and sexual harassment *sekuhara*. Sometimes, they become almost unrecognizable, as with *kakuteru*, which is cocktail.

Traditionally, Japanese is written in vertical columns and read right to left. However, the Western way of writing from left to right, horizontally from top to bottom is increasingly being used. In the media and on signs you'll see a mixture of the two ways of writing.

Hiragana and Katakana

The Japanese script consists of **hiragana**, **katakana** and ideograms based on Chinese characters (*kanji*). *Hiragana* and *katakana* are two phonetic syllabaries represented by the characters shown below. *Katakana*, the squarer characters in the table immediately below, are used for writing foreign "loan words". The rounder characters in the bottom table, *hiragana*, are used for Japanese words, in combination with, or as substitues for, *kanji*.

Katakana

a	ア	i	イ	u	ウ	e	エ	o	オ
ka	カ	ki	キ	ku	ク	ke	ケ	ko	コ
sa	サ	shi	シ	su	ス	se	セ	so	ソ
ta	タ	chi	チ	tsu	ツ	te	テ	to	ト
na	ナ	ni	ニ	nu	ヌ	ne	ネ	no	ノ
ha	ハ	hi	ヒ	fu	フ	he	ヘ	ho	ホ
ma	マ	mi	ミ	mu	ム	me	メ	mo	モ
ya	ヤ			yu	ユ			yo	ヨ
ra	ラ	ri	リ	ru	ル	re	レ	ro	ロ
wa	ワ								
n	ン								

Hiragana

a	あ	i	い	u	う	e	え	o	お
ka	か	ki	き	ku	く	ke	け	ko	こ
sa	さ	shi	し	su	す	se	せ	so	そ
ta	た	chi	ち	tsu	つ	te	て	to	と
na	な	ni	に	nu	ぬ	ne	ね	no	の
ha	は	hi	ひ	fu	ふ	he	へ	ho	ほ
ma	ま	mi	み	mu	む	me	め	mo	も
ya	や			yu	ゆ			yo	よ
ra	ら	ri	り	ru	る	re	れ	ro	ろ
wa	わ								
n	ん								

Grammar

There are several significant **grammar** differences between Japanese and European languages. **Verbs** do not change according to the person or number, so that *ikimasu* can mean "I go", "he/she/it goes", or "we/they go". **Pronouns**, such as I and they, are usually omitted, since it's clear from the context who or what the speaker is referring to. There are no **definite articles**, and **nouns** stay the same whether they refer to singular or plural words.

From the point of view of English grammar, Japanese **sentences** are structured back to front. An English speaker would say "I am going to Tokyo" which in Japanese would translate directly as "Tokyo to going". Placing the sound "ka" at the end of a verb indicates a **question**, hence *Tokyo e ikimasu-ka* means "Are you going to Tokyo?". There are also levels of **politeness** to contend with, which alter the way the verb is conjugated, and sometimes change the word entirely. For the most part, stick to the polite **masu** form of verbs and you'll be fine.

If you want to learn more about the language and have a wider range of expressions and vocabulary at your command than those listed below, invest in a phrasebook or dictionary. *Japanese: A Rough Guide Phrasebook* is user-friendly and combines essential phrases and expressions with a dictionary section and menu reader. The phonetic translations in this phrasebook are rendered slightly differently from the standard way rōmaji is written in this book, as an aid to pronunciation. One of the best books for learning Japanese more thoroughly is *Japanese For Busy People* (Kodansha), which comes in three parts and is often used as a set text in Japanese-language classes. A worthy alternative, although more difficult to buy outside of Japan, is *Communicative Japanese for Time Pressed People* (Aratake Publishing).

Pronunciation

Throughout this book, Japanese words have been transliterated into the standard Hepburn system of romanization, called **rōmaji**. Pronunciation is as follows:

a as in rather
i as in macaroni, or ee
u as in put, or oo
e as in bed; e is always pronounced, even at the end of a word
o as in not
ae as in the two separate sounds, ah-eh
ai as in Thai
ei as in weight
ie as in two separate sounds, ee-eh
ue as in two separate sounds, oo-eh
g, a hard sound as in girl
s as in mass (never z)
y as in yet

A bar over a vowel or "ii" means that the vowel sound is twice as long as a vowel without a bar. Only where words are well known in English, such as Tokyo, Kyoto, judo and shogun, have we not used a bar to indicate long vowel sounds. Sometimes, vowel sounds are shortened or softened, for example, the verb *desu* sounds more like *des* when pronounced, and *sukiyaki* like *skiyaki*. Apart from this, all syllables in Japanese words are evenly stressed and pronounced in full. For example, Nagano is Na-ga-no, not Na-GA-no.

Useful words and phrases

Basics

Yes	*hai*	はい
No	*iie/chigaimasu*	いいえ／違います
OK	*daijōbu/ōkē*	だいじょうぶ／オーケー
Well . . . (as in making things less definite)	*chotto*	ちょっと
Please (offering something)	*dōzo*	どうぞ
Please (asking for something)	*onegai shimasu*	お願いします
Excuse me	*sumimasen/shitsurei shimasu*	すみません／失礼します
I'm sorry	*gomen nasai/sumimasen*	ごめんなさい／すみません
Thanks (informal)	*dōmo*	どうも
Thank you	*dōmo arigatō*	どうもありがとう
Thank you very much	*dōmo arigatō gozaimasu*	どうもありがとうございます
What?	*nani?*	なに？
When?	*itsu?*	いつ？
Where?	*doko?*	どこ？
Who?	*dare?*	だれ？
This	*kore*	これ
That	*sore*	それ
That (over there)	*are*	あれ
How many?	*ikutsu?*	いくつ？
How much?	*ikura?*	いくら？
I want (x)	*Watashi wa (x) ga hoshii desu*	私は（x）がほしいです
I don't want (x)	*Watashi wa (x) ga irimasen*	私は（x）がいりません
Is it possible . . . ?	*. . . koto ga dekimasu ka*	。。。ことができますか
It is not possible	*. . . koto ga dekimasen*	。。。ことができません
Is it . . . ?	*. . . desu ka*	。。。ですか
Can you please help me	*Tetsudatte kuremasen ka*	手伝ってくれませんか

Personal pronouns

I	*watashi*	私
I (familiar, men only)	*boku*	ぼく
I (polite)	*watakushi*	わたくし
You	*anata*	あなた
You (familiar)	*kimi*	きみ
He	*kare*	彼
She	*kanojo*	彼女
We	*watashi-tachi*	わたしたち
You (plural)	*anata-tachi*	あなたたち
They (male/female)	*karera/kanojo-tachi*	かれら／かのじょたち
They (objects)	*sorera*	それら

Communicating

I don't speak Japanese	Nihongo wa hanashimasen	日本語は話しません
I don't read Japanese	Nihongo wa yomimasen	日本語は読みません
Can you speak English?	Eigo ga dekimasu ka	英語ができますか？
Is there someone who can interpret?	Tsūyaku wa imasu ka	通訳はいますか？
Could you please speak slowly	Motto yukkuri hanashite kuremasu ka	もっとゆっくり話してくれませんか？
Please say that again	Mō ichido itte kuremasen ka	もう一度言ってくれませんか？
I understand/I see	Wakarimasu/Naruhodo	わかります／なるほど
I don't understand	Wakarimasen	わかりません
What does this mean?	Imi wa nan desu ka	意味は何ですか？
How do you say (x) in Japanese?	Nihongo de (x) o nan-te iimasu ka	日本語で（x）を何て言いますか？
What's this called?	Kore wa nan-to iimasu ka	これは何と言いますか？
How do you pronounce this character?	Kono kanji wa nan-te iimasu ka	この漢字は何て言いますか？
Please write in English/Japanese	Eigo/Nihongo de kaite kudasai	英語／日本語で書いてください

Greetings and basic courtesies

Hello/Good day	Konnichiwa	こんにちは
Good morning	Ohayō gozaimasu	おはようございます
Good evening	Konbanwa	こんばんは
Good night (when leaving)	Osaki ni	お先に
Good night (when going to bed)	Oyasuminasai	おやすみなさい
How are you?	O-genki desu ka	お元気ですか
I'm fine (informal)	Genki desu	元気です
I'm fine, thanks	Okagesama de	おかげさまで
How do you do/Nice to meet you	Hajimemashite	はじめまして
Don't mention it/you're welcome	Dō itashimashite	どういたしまして
I'm sorry	Gomen nasai	ごめんなさい
Just a minute please	Chotto matte kudasai	ちょっと待ってください
Goodbye	Sayonara	さよなら
Goodbye (informal)	Dewa mata/Jā ne	では又／じゃあね

Chitchat

What's your name?	Shitsurei desu ga o-namae wa	失礼ですがお名前は？
My name is (x)	Watashi no namae wa (x) desu	私の名前は（x）です
Where are you from?	O-kuni wa doko desu ka	おくにはどこですか？
Britain	Eikoku/Igirisu	英国／イギリス
Ireland	Airurando	アイルランド
America	Amerika	アメリカ
Australia	Ōsutoraria	オーストラリア
Canada	Kanada	カナダ
France	Furansu	フランス
Germany	Doitsu	ドイツ
Japan	Nihon	日本
Outside Japan	Gaikoku	外国
New Zealand	Nyū Jiirando	ニュージーランド
How old are you?	Ikutsu desu ka	いくつですか？
I am (age)	(age) sai desu	（age）才です

Are you married?	*Kekkon shite imasu ka*	結婚していますか？
I am married/not married	*Kekkon shite imasu/imasen*	結婚しています／いません
Do you like . . . ?	*. . . suki desu ka*	。。。好きですか？
I do like	*. . . suki desu*	。。。好きです
I don't like	*. . . suki dewa arimasen*	。。。好きではありません
What's your job?	*O-shigoto wa nan desu ka*	お仕事は何ですか？
I'm a student	*Gakusei desu*	学生です
I'm a teacher	*Sensei desu*	先生です
I work for a company	*Kaisha-in desu*	会社員です
I'm a tourist	*Kankō kyaku desu*	観光客です
Really?	*hontō*	本当？
That's a shame	*zannen desu*	残念です
It can't be helped	*shikata ga nai/shō ga nai* (informal)	仕方がない／しょうがない

Adjectives

Clean/dirty	*kirei/kitanai*	きれい／きたない
Hot/cold	*atsui/samui*	あつい／さむい
Fast/slow	*hayai/osoi*	はやい／おそい
Pretty/ugly	*kirei/minikui*	きれい／みにくい
Interesting/boring	*omoshiroi/tsumaranai*	おもしろい／つまらない

Numbers

There are special ways of **counting** different things in Japanese. The safest option is to stick to the most common first translation, used when counting time and quantities and measurements, with added qualifiers such as minutes (*pun/fun*) or yen (*en*). The second translations are sometimes used for counting objects, as in *biiru futatsu, onegai shimasu* (two beers please). Above ten, there is only one set of numbers. For four, seven and nine there are alternatives to the first translation used in some circumstances.

Zero	*zero*	ゼロ		
One	*ichi*	一	*hitotsu*	ひとつ
Two	*ni*	二	*futatsu*	ふたつ
Three	*san*	三	*mittsu*	みっつ
Four	*yon/shi*	四	*yottsu*	よっつ
Five	*go*	五	*itsutsu*	いつつ
Six	*roku*	六	*muttsu*	むっつ
Seven	*shichi/nana*	七	*nanatsu*	ななつ
Eight	*hachi*	八	*yattsu*	やっつ
Nine	*ku/kyū*	九	*kokonotsu*	ここのつ
Ten	*jū*	十	*tō*	とう
Eleven	*jū-ichi*	十一		
Twelve	*jū-ni*	十二		
Twenty	*ni-jū*	二十		
Twenty-one	*ni-jū-ichi*	二十一		
Thirty	*san-jū*	三十		
One hundred	*hyaku*	百		
Two hundred	*ni-hyaku*	二百		
Thousand	*sen*	千		
Ten thousand	*ichi-man*	一万		
One hundred thousand	*jū-man*	十万		
One million	*hyaku-man*	百万		
One hundred million	*ichi-oku*	一億		

Time and dates

Now	*ima*	今
Today	*kyō*	今日
Morning	*asa*	朝
Evening	*yūgata*	夕方
Night	*yoru*	夜
Tomorrow	*ashita*	明日
The day after tomorrow	*asatte*	あさって
Yesterday	*kinō*	昨日
Week	*shūkan*	週間
Month	*gatsu*	月
Year	*nen/toshi*	年
Monday	*Getsuyōbi*	月曜日
Tuesday	*Kayōbi*	火曜日
Wednesday	*Suiyōbi*	水曜日
Thursday	*Mokuyōbi*	木曜日
Friday	*Kin'yōbi*	金曜日
Saturday	*Doyōbi*	土曜日
Sunday	*Nichiyōbi*	日曜日

What time is it?	*Ima nan-ji desu ka*	今何時ですか
It's 10 o'clock	*Jū-ji desu*	十時です
10.20	*Jū-ji ni-juppun*	十時二十分
10.30	*Jū-ji han*	十時半
10.50	*Jū-ichi-ji juppun mae*	十一時十分前
AM	*gozen*	午前
PM	*gogo*	午後

January	*Ichigatsu*	一月
February	*Nigatsu*	二月
March	*Sangatsu*	三月
April	*Shigatsu*	四月
May	*Gogatsu*	五月
June	*Rokugatsu*	六月
July	*Shichigatsu*	七月
August	*Hachigatsu*	八月
September	*Kugatsu*	九月
October	*Jūgatsu*	十月
November	*Jūichigatsu*	十一月
December	*Jūnigatsu*	十二月

1st (day)	*tsuitachi*	一日
2nd (day)	*futsuka*	二日
3rd (day)	*mikka*	三日
4th (day)	*yokka*	四日
5th (day)	*itsuka*	五日
6th (day)	*muika*	六日
7th (day)	*nanoka*	七日
8th (day)	*yōka*	八日
9th (day)	*kokonoka*	九日
10th (day)	*tōka*	十日
11th (day)	*jū-ichi-nichi*	十一日
12th (day)	*jū-ni-nichi*	十二日
20th (day)	*hatsuka*	二十日
21st (day)	*ni-jū-ichi nichi*	二十一日
30th (day)	*san-jū-nichi*	三十日

Transport and travelling

Aeroplane	*hikōki*	飛行機
Airport	*kūkō*	空港
Bus	*basu*	バス
Long-distance bus	*chōkyori basu*	長距離バス
Bus stop	*basu tei*	バス亭
Train	*densha*	電車
Station	*eki*	駅
Subway	*chikatetsu*	地下鉄
Ferry	*ferii*	フェリー
Left-luggage office	*ichiji azukarijo*	一時預かり所
Coin locker	*koin rokkā*	コインロッカー
Ticket office	*kippu uriba*	切符売り場
Ticket	*kippu*	切符
One-way	*kata-michi*	片道
Return	*ōfuku*	往復
Non-smoking seat	*kin'en seki*	禁煙席
Window seat	*mado-gawa no seki*	窓側の席
Platform	*hōmu*	ホーム
Bicycle	*jitensha*	自転車
Taxi	*takushii*	タクシー

Directions and general places

Map	*chizu*	地図
Where is (x)?	*(x) wa doko desu ka*	(x) はどこですか
Straight ahead	*massugu*	まっすぐ
In front of	*mae*	前
Right	*migi*	右
Left	*hidari*	左
North	*kita*	北
South	*minami*	南
East	*higashi*	東
West	*nishi*	西
Temple	*otera/odera/-ji/-in*	お寺／一寺／一院
Shrine	*jinja/jingū/-gū/-taisha*	神社／神宮／一宮／一大社
Castle	*-jō*	一城
Park	*kōen*	公園
River	*kawa/gawa*	川
Bridge	*hashi/bashi*	橋
Museum	*hakubutsukan*	博物館
Art gallery	*bijutsukan*	美術館
Zoo	*dōbutsuen*	動物園
Garden	*niwa/teien/-en*	庭／庭園／一園
Island	*shima/jima/tō*	島
Slope	*saka/zaka*	坂
Hill	*oka*	岡
Mountain	*yama/-san/-take*	山／岳
Hot spring spa	*onsen*	温泉
Lake	*-ko*	一湖
Bay	*-wan*	一湾
Peninsula	*hantō*	半島
Cape	*misaki/saki*	岬
Sea	*umi/kai/nada*	海／灘
Gorge	*kyō*	峡

Plateau	kōgen	高原
Train line	sen	線
Prefecture	-ken/-fu	一県／一府
Ward	-ku	一区
Entrance	iriguchi	入口
Exit	deguchi/-guchi	出口／一口
Street	tōri/dōri/michi	通り／道
Highway	kaidō	街道
Shop	mise/-ten/-ya	店／屋

Accommodation

Hotel	hoteru	ホテル
Traditional-style inn	ryokan	旅館
Guesthouse	minshuku	民宿
Youth hostel	yūsu hosuteru	ユースホステル
Single room	shinguru rūmu	シングルルーム
Double room	daburu rūmu	ダブルルーム
Twin room	tsuin rūmu	ツインルーム
Dormitory	kyōdō/ōbeya	共同／大部屋
Japanese-style room	washitsu	和室
Western-style room	yōshitsu	洋室
Western-style bed	beddo	ベッド
Bath	o-furo	お風呂

Do you have any vacancies?	Aita heya wa arimasu ka	空いた部屋はありますか
I'd like to make a reservation	Yoyaku o shitai no desu ga	予約をしたいのですが
I have a reservation	Yoyaku shimashita	予約しました
I don't have a reservation	Yoyaku shimasen deshita	予約しませんでした
How much is it per person?	Hitori ikura desu ka	一人いくらですか
Does that include meals?	Shokuji wa tsuite imasu ka	食事はついていますか
I would like to stay one night/two nights	Hitoban/futaban tomarimasu	一晩／二晩泊まります
I would like to see the room	Heya o misete kudasaimasen ka	部屋を見せてくださいませんか
Key	kagi	鍵
Passport	pasupōto	パスポート

Shopping, money and banks

How much is it?	Kore wa ikura desu ka	これはいくらですか
It's too expensive	Taka-sugimasu	高すぎます
Is there anything cheaper?	Mō sukoshi yasui mono wa arimasu ka	もう少し安いものはありますか
Do you accept credit cards?	Kurejitto kādo wa tsukaemasu ka	クレジットカードは使えますか
I'm just looking	Miru dake desu	見るだけです
Yen	Yen/-en	円
UK pounds	pondo	ポンド
Dollars	doru	ドル
Foreign exchange	gaikoku-kawase	外国為替
Bank	ginkō	銀行
Travellers' cheque	toraberāzu chekku	トラベラーズチェック

Post and telephones

Post office	yūbinkyoku	郵便局
Envelope	fūtō	封筒
Letter	tegami	手紙

LANGUAGE | Useful words and phrases

Postcard	hagaki	葉書
Stamp	kitte	切手
Airmail	kōkūbin	航空便
Surface mail	sarubin	サル便
Sea mail	funabin	船便
Poste restante	tomeoki	留置
Telephone	denwa	電話
International telephone call	kokusai-denwa	国際電話
Reverse charge/collect call	Korekuto-kōru	コレクトコール
Fax	Fakkusu	ファックス
Telephone card	Terefon kādo	テレフォンカード
I would like to call (place)	(place) e denwa o kaketai no desu	(ｐｌａｃｅ)へ電話をかけたいのです
I would like to send a fax to (place)	(place) e fakkusu shitai no desu	(ｐｌａｃｅ)へファックスしたいのです

Health

Hospital	byōin	病院
Pharmacy	yakkyoku	薬局
Medicine	kusuri	薬
Doctor	isha	医者
Dentist	haisha	歯医者
Diarrhoea	geri	下痢
Nausea	hakike	はきけ
Fever	netsu	熱
Food poisoning	shoku chūdoku	食中毒
I'm ill	byōki desu	病気です
I've got a cold/flu	kaze o hikimashita	風邪をひきました
I'm allergic to (x)	(x) arerugii desu	(x) アレルギーです
Antibiotics	kōsei busshitsu	抗生物質
Antiseptic	shōdoku	消毒
Condom	kondōmu	コンドーム
Mosquito repellent	kayoke-supurē	蚊よけスプレー

Food and drink

Places to eat and drink

Bar	nomiya	飲み屋
Café/coffee shop	kissaten	喫茶店
Cafeteria	shokudō	食堂
Pub	pabu	パブ
Pub-style restaurant	izakaya	居酒屋
Restaurant	resutoran	レストラン
Restaurant specializing in charcoal-grilled foods	robatayaki	炉端焼

Ordering

Breakfast	asa-gohan	朝ご飯
Lunch	hiru-gohan	昼ご飯
Dinner	ban-gohan	晩ご飯
Boxed meal	bentō	弁当

Chopsticks	hashi	はし
Fork	fōku	フォーク
Knife	naifu	ナイフ
Spoon	supūn	スプーン
Set meal	teishoku	定食
Daily special set meal	higawari-teishoku	日変わり定食
Menu	menyū	メニュー
How much is that?	ikura desu ka	いくらですか？
I would like (a) . . .	(a) o onegai shimasu . . .	（a）をお願いします
May I have the bill?	okanjō o onegai shimasu	お勘定をお願いします

Staple foods

Bean curd tofu	tōfu	豆腐
Butter	batā	バター
Bread	pan	パン
Dried seaweed	nori	のり
Egg	tamago	卵
Fermented soyabean paste	miso	味噌
Garlic	ninniku	にんにく
Oil	abura	油
Pepper	koshō	こしょう
Rice	gohan	ご飯
Salt	shio	塩
Soy sauce	shōyu	しょうゆ
Sugar	satō	砂糖

Fish and seafood dishes

Fish	sakana	魚
Shellfish	kai	貝
Raw fish	sashimi	さしみ
Sushi	sushi	寿司
Sushi mixed selection	nigiri-zushi	にぎり寿司
Sushi rolled in crisp seaweed	maki-zushi	まき寿司
Sushi topped with fish, egg and vegetables	chirashi-zushi	ちらし寿司
Abalone	awabi	あわび
Blowfish	fugu	ふぐ
Cod	tara	たら
Crab	kani	かに
Eel	unagi	うなぎ
Herring	nishin	にしん
Horse mackerel	aji	あじ
Lobster	ise-ebi	伊勢海老
Octopus	tako	たこ
Oyster	kaki	かき
Prawn	ebi	えび
Sea bream	tai	たい
Sea urchin	uni	うに
Squid	ika	いか
Sweet smelt	ayu	あゆ
Tuna	maguro	まぐろ
Yellowtail	buri	ぶり

Fruit

Fruit	*kudamono*	果物
Apple	*ringo*	りんご
Banana	*banana*	バナナ
Grapefruit	*gurēpufurūtsu*	グレープフルーツ
Grapes	*budō*	ぶどう
Japanese plum	*ume*	うめ
Lemon	*remon*	レモン
Melon	*meron*	メロン
Orange	*orenji*	オレンジ
Peach	*momo*	桃
Pear	*nashi*	なし
Persimmon	*kaki*	柿
Pineapple	*painappuru*	パイナップル
Strawberry	*ichigo*	いちご
Tangerine	*mikan*	みかん
Watermelon	*suika*	すいか

Vegetables and salads

Vegetables	*yasai*	野菜
Salad	*sarada*	サラダ
Aubergine	*nasu*	なす
Beans	*mame*	豆
Beansprouts	*moyashi*	もやし
Carrot	*ninjin*	にんじん
Cauliflower	*karifurawā*	カリフラワー
Green pepper	*piiman*	ピーマン
Green horseradish	*wasabi*	わさび
Leek	*negi*	ねぎ
Mushroom	*kinoko*	きのこ
Onion	*tamanegi*	たまねぎ
Potato	*poteto*	ポテト
Radish	*daikon*	だいこん
Sweetcorn	*kōn*	コーン
Tomato	*tomato*	トマト

Meat and meat dishes

Meat	*niku*	肉
Beef	*gyūniku*	牛肉
Chicken	*toriniku*	鳥肉
Lamb	*ramu*	ラム
Pork	*butaniku*	豚肉
Breaded, deep-fried slice of pork	*tonkatsu*	とんかつ
Chicken, other meat and vegetables grilled on skewers	*yakitori*	焼き鳥
Skewers of food dipped in breadcrumbs and deep-fried	*kushiage*	串揚げ
Stew including meat (or seafood), vegetables and noodles	*nabe*	鍋
Thin beef slices cooked in broth	*shabu-shabu*	しゃぶしゃぶ
Thin beef slices braised in a sauce	*sukiyaki*	すきやき

Vegetarian and noodle dishes

Buddhist-style vegetarian cuisine	*shōjin-ryōri*	精進料理
Chinese-style noodles	*rāmen*	ラーメン
Chinese-style dumplings	*gyōza*	ぎょうざ
Fried noodles	*yakisoba/udon*	焼そば／うどん
Stewed chunks of tofu, vegetables and fish on skewers	*oden*	おでん
Thin buckwheat noodles	*soba*	そば
Soba in a hot soup	*kake-soba*	かけそば
Cold soba for dipping in a sauce	*zaru-soba/mori-soba*	ざるそば／もりそば
Thick wheat noodles	*udon*	うどん

Other dishes

Fried rice	*chāhan*	チャーハン
Lightly battered seafood and vegetables	*tempura*	天ぷら
Meat, vegetable and fish cooked in soy sauce and sweet sake	*teriyaki*	照り焼き
Mild curry served with rice	*karē raisu*	カレーライス
Octopus in balls of batter	*takoyaki*	たこやき
Pounded rice cakes	*mochi*	もち
Rice topped with fish, meat or vegetable	*donburi*	どんぶり
Rice triangles wrapped in crisp seaweed	*onigiri*	おにぎり
Savoury pancakes	*okonomiyaki*	お好み焼
Chinese food	*Chūka-/Chūgoku-ryōri*	中華／中国料理
French food	*Furansu-ryōri*	フランス料理
Italian food	*Itaria-ryōri*	イタリア料理
Japanese-style food	*washoku*	和食
Japanese haute cuisine	*kaiseki-ryōri*	懐石料理
Korean food	*Kankoku-ryōri*	韓国料理
"No-nationality" food	*mukokuseki-ryōri*	無国籍料理
Thai food	*Tai-ryōri*	タイ料理
Western-style food	*yōshoku*	洋食

Drinks

Beer	*biiru*	ビール
Black tea	*kōcha*	紅茶
Coffee	*kōhii*	コーヒー
Fruit juice	*jūsu*	ジュース
Green tea	*sencha*	煎茶
Milk	*miruku*	ミルク
Oolong tea	*ūron-cha*	ウーロン茶
Powdered green tea	*matcha*	抹茶
Water	*mizu*	水
Whisky	*uisukii*	ウイスキー
Whisky and water	*mizu-wari*	水割り
Sake (rice wine)	*sake/nihon-shu*	酒／日本酒
Wine	*wain*	ワイン

Glossary

aikido "The way of harmonious spirit". A form of self-defence performed without weapons, now recognized as a sport.

Amida Nyorai Amida Buddha will lead worthy souls to the Western Paradise (the Pure Land).

banzai The traditional Japanese cheer, meaning "10,000 years".

basho Sumo tournament.

Benten or Benzai-ten One of the most popular folk-goddesses, usually associated with water.

bodhisattva or bosatsu A Buddhist intermediary who has forsaken nirvana to work for the salvation of all humanity.

Bunraku Traditional puppet theatre.

Butō or Butoh Highly expressive contemporary performance art.

cha-no-yu, chadō or sadō The tea ceremony. Ritual tea drinking raised to an art form.

-chō or -machi Subdivision of a city, smaller than a -ku.

-chōme Area of the city consisting of a few blocks.

daimyō Feudal lords.

-dake Mountain peak, usually volcanic.

Dainichi Nyorai or Rushana Butsu The Cosmic Buddha in whom all Buddhas are unified.

donjon Castle keep.

-dōri Main road.

Edo Pre-1868 name for Tokyo.

ema Small wooden boards found at shrines, on which people write their wishes or thanks.

fusuma Paper-covered sliding doors, more substantial than *shōji*, used to separate rooms or for cupboards.

futon Padded quilt used for bedding.

gagaku Traditional Japanese music used for court ceremonies and religious rites.

gaijin Foreigner.

geisha Traditional female entertainer accomplished in the arts.

genkan Foyer or entrance hall of a house, ryokan and so forth, for changing from outdoor shoes into slippers.

geta Traditional wooden sandals.

genki A useful (and often used) Japanese word meaning friendly, lively and healthy.

haiku Seventeen-syllable verse form, arranged in three lines of five, seven and five syllables.

hanami "Flower-viewing", most commonly associated with spring outings to admire the cherry blossom.

-hashi or -bashi Bridge.

hiragana Phonetic script used for writing Japanese in combination with kanji.

ijinkan Western-style brick and clapboard houses.

ikebana Traditional art of flower arranging.

Inari Shinto god of harvests, often represented by his fox-messenger.

-ji Buddhist temple.

jigoku The word for Buddhist "hell", also applied to volcanic mud pools and steam vents.

-jinja or -jingū Shinto shrine.

Jizō Buddhist protector of children, travellers and the dead.

-jō Castle.

Kabuki Popular theatre of the Edo period.

kami Shinto deities residing in trees, rocks and other natural phenomena.

kamikaze The "Divine Wind" which saved Japan from the Mongol invaders (see p.861). During World War II the name was applied to Japan's suicide bombers.

kanji Japanese script derived from Chinese characters.

Kannon Buddhist goddess of mercy. A bodhisattva who appears in many different forms.

katakana Phonetic script used mainly for writing foreign words in Japanese.

-kawa or -gawa River.

-ken Prefecture. The principal administrative region, similar to a state or county.

kendo The "way of the sword". Japan's oldest martial art, using wooden staves, with its roots in samurai training exercises.

kimono Literally "clothes", though usually referring to women's traditional dress.

-ko Lake.

kōban Neighbourhood police box.

kōen or gyoen Public park.

Kōgen Plateau.

-ku Principal administrative division of the city, usually translated as "ward".

kura Traditional storehouse built with thick mudwalls as protection against fire, for keeping produce and family treasures.

kyōgen Short, satirical plays, providing comic interludes in Nō drama.

-machi Town or area of a city.

maiko Apprentice geisha.

manga Japanese comics.

matcha Powdered green tea used in the tea ceremony.

matsuri Festival.

Meiji Period named after Emperor Meiji (1868–1912), meaning "enlightened rule".

Meiji Restoration The Restoration (1868) marked the end of the Tokugawa Shogunate, when power was fully restored to the emperor.

mikoshi Portable shrine used in festivals.

minshuku Family-run lodgings, similar to bed-and-breakfast, which are cheaper than ryokan.

mon Gate, usually to a castle, temple or palace.

mura Village.

netsuke Small, intricately carved toggles for fastening the cords of cloth bags.

ningyō Japanese doll.

Niō or **Kongō Rikishi** Two muscular, fearsome Buddhist kings (*ten*) who stand guard at temple gates, usually one open-mouthed and one closed.

Nō Highly stylized dance-drama, using masks and elaborate costumes.

noren Split curtain hanging in shop and restaurant doorways to indicate they're open.

notemburo Outdoor hot-spring pool, usually in natural surroundings.

obi Wide sash worn with kimono.

odori Traditional dances performed in the streets during the summer Obon festival. The most famous is Tokushima's Awa Odori (see p.736).

onsen Hot spring, generally developed for bathing.

pachinko Vertical pinball machines.

pond-garden Classic form of garden design focused around a pond.

rōmaji System of transliterating Japanese words using the roman alphabet.

rōnin Masterless *samurai* (see p.157).

rotemburo Outdoor hot-spring pool, often in the grounds of a ryokan.

ryokan Traditional Japanese inn.

salarymen The thousands of suited office-workers who keep Japan's companies and ministries ticking over.

samurai Warrior class who were retainers of the *daimyō*.

-san or **-zan** Mountain.

sensei Teacher.

sentō Neighbourhood public bath.

seppuku Ritual suicide by disembowelment, often referred to as *hara-kiri* in English.

Shaka Nyorai The historical Buddha, Sakyamuni.

shamisen Traditional, three-stringed instrument played with a plectrum.

-shima or **-jima** Island.

Shinkansen Bullet train.

Shinto Japan's indigenous religion, based on the premise that gods inhabit all natural things, both animate and inanimate.

Shitamachi Low-lying, working-class districts of east Tokyo, nowadays usually referring to Asakusa and Ueno.

shōji Paper-covered sliding screens used to divide rooms or cover windows.

shogun The military rulers of Japan before 1868, nominally subordinate to the emperor.

shukubō Temple lodgings.

soaplands Euphemistic name for bathhouses offering massages and, frequently, sexual services.

stroll-garden Style of garden design popular in the Edo period (1600–1868), comprising a series of tableaux which unfold as the viewer walks through the garden.

sumi-e Ink paintings, traditionally using black ink.

sumo Japan's national sport, a form of heavy-weight wrestling which evolved from ancient Shinto divination rites.

taiko Drums.

tatami Rice-straw matting, the traditional covering for floors.

-tera, o-tera or **-dera** Buddhist temple.

tokonoma Alcove in a room where flowers or a scroll are displayed.

torii Gate to a Shinto shrine.

ukiyo-e Colourful woodblock prints or paintings which became particularly popular in the late eighteenth century.

waka Thirty-one syllable poem, arranged in five lines of five, seven, five, seven and seven syllables.

washi Traditional handmade paper.

Yakushi Nyorai The Buddha in charge of physical and spiritual healing.

yakuza Professional criminal gangs, somewhat akin to the Mafia.

yama Mountain.

yamabushi Ascetic mountain priests.

yokuzuna Champion sumo wrestler.

yukata Loose cotton robe worn as a dressing gown in ryokan.

Organizations

ANA All Nippon Airways

JAL Japan Airlines

JAS Japan Air System

JNTO Japan National Tourist Organization, the government's overseas tourist office.

JR Japan Railways.

JTB Japan Travel Bureau.

SDF (Self-Defence Forces) Japan's army, navy and airforce, established in 1954 purely for national defence, though now also used for international peacekeeping operations.

TIC Tourist Information Centre with English-speaking staff.

small print and
Index

A Rough Guide to Rough Guides

In the summer of 1981, Mark Ellingham, a recent graduate from Bristol University, was travelling round Greece and couldn't find a guidebook that really met his needs. On the one hand there were the student guides, insistent on saving every last cent, and on the other the heavyweight cultural tomes whose authors seemed to have spent more time in a research library than lounging away the afternoon at a taverna or on the beach.

In a bid to avoid getting a job, Mark and a small group of writers set about creating their own guidebook. It was a guide to Greece that aimed to combine a journalistic approach to description with a thoroughly practical approach to travellers' needs – a guide that would incorporate culture, history and contemporary insights with a critical edge, together with up-to-date, value-for-money listings. Back in London, Mark and the team finished their Rough Guide, as they called it, and talked Routledge into publishing the book.

That first *Rough Guide to Greece*, published in 1982, was a student scheme that became a publishing phenomenon. The immediate success of the book – with numerous reprints and a Thomas Cook prize shortlisting – spawned a series that rapidly covered dozens of destinations. Rough Guides had a ready market among low-budget backpackers, but soon also acquired a much broader and older readership that relished Rough Guides' wit and inquisitiveness as much as their enthusiastic, critical approach. Everyone wants value for money, but not at any price.

Rough Guides soon began supplementing the "rougher" information about hostels and low-budget listings with the kind of detail on restaurants and quality hotels that independent-minded visitors on any budget might expect, whether on business in New York or trekking in Thailand.

These days the guides – distributed worldwide by the Penguin group – offer recommendations from shoestring to luxury and cover more than 200 destinations around the globe, including almost every country in the Americas and Europe, more than half of Africa and most of Asia and Australasia. Our ever-growing team of authors and photographers is spread all over the world, particularly in Europe, the USA and Australia.

In 1994, we published the *Rough Guide to World Music* and *Rough Guide to Classical Music*; and a year later the *Rough Guide to the Internet*. All three books have become benchmark titles in their fields – which encouraged us to expand into other areas of publishing, mainly around popular culture. Rough Guides now publish:

- Travel guides to more than 200 worldwide destinations
- Dictionary phrasebooks to 22 major languages
- History guides ranging from Ireland to Islam
- Maps printed on rip-proof and waterproof Polyart™ paper
- Music guides running the gamut from Opera to Elvis
- Restaurant guides to London, New York and San Francisco
- Reference books on topics as diverse as the Weather and Shakespeare
- Sports guides from Formula 1 to Man Utd
- Pop culture books from *Lord of the Rings* to Cult TV
- World Music CDs in association with World Music Network

Visit **www.roughguides.com** to see our latest publications.

Rough Guide Credits

Text editor: Gavin Thomas
Layout: Link Hall
Cartography: Manish Chandra, Karobi Gogoi, Rajesh Chhibber
Picture research: Harriet Mills
Proofreader: Jan Wiltshire
Production: John McKay
Editorial: London Martin Dunford, Kate Berens, Helena Smith, Claire Saunders, Geoff Howard, Ruth Blackmore, Gavin Thomas, Polly Thomas, Richard Lim, Lucy Ratcliffe, Clifton Wilkinson, Alison Murchie, Fran Sandham, Sally Schafer, Alexander Mark Rogers, Karoline Densley, Andy Turner, Ella O'Donnell, Keith Drew, Andrew Lockett, Joe Staines, Duncan Clark, Peter Buckley, Matthew Milton; **New York** Andrew Rosenberg, Richard Koss, Yuki Takagaki, Hunter Slaton, Chris Barsanti, Steven Horak
Design & Pictures: London Simon Bracken, Dan May, Diana Jarvis, Mark Thomas, Jj Luck, Harriet Mills; **Delhi** Madhulita Mohapatra, Umesh Aggarwal, Ajay Verma,

Jessica Subramanian
Production: Julia Bovis, John McKay, Sophie Hewat
Cartography: London Maxine Repath, Ed Wright, Katie Lloyd-Jones, Miles Irving; **Delhi** Manish Chandra, Rajesh Chhibber, Jai Prakash Mishra, Ashutosh Bharti, Rajesh Mishra, Animesh Pathak, Jasbir Sandhu, Karobi Gogoi
Cover art direction: Louise Boulton
Online: New York Jennifer Gold, Cree Lawson, Suzanne Welles, Benjamin Ross; **Delhi** Manik Chauhan, Narender Kumar, Shekhar Jha, Rakesh Kumar
Marketing & Publicity: London Richard Trillo, Niki Smith, David Wearn, Chloë Roberts, Demelza Dallow, Kristina Pentland; **New York** Geoff Colquitt, Megan Kennedy
Finance: Gary Singh
Manager India: Punita Singh
Series editor: Mark Ellingham
PA to Managing Director: Julie Sanderson
Managing Director: Kevin Fitzgerald

Publishing Information

This third edition published January 2005 by **Rough Guides Ltd**,
80 Strand, London WC2R 0RL.
345 Hudson St, 4th Floor,
New York, NY 10014, USA.
Distributed by the Penguin Group
Penguin Books Ltd,
80 Strand, London WC2R 0RL
Penguin Putnam, Inc.
375 Hudson Street, NY 10014, USA
Penguin Books Australia Ltd,
487 Maroondah Highway, PO Box 257,
Ringwood, Victoria 3134, Australia
Penguin Books Canada Ltd,
10 Alcorn Avenue, Toronto, Ontario,
Canada M4V 1E4
Penguin Books (NZ) Ltd,
182–190 Wairau Road, Auckland 10,
New Zealand
Typeset in Bembo and Helvetica to an original design by Henry Iles.

Printed and bound in China

1056pp includes index
A catalogue record for this book is available from the British Library

ISBN 10: 1-84353-272-7
ISBN 13: 9781843532729

The publishers and authors have done their best to ensure the accuracy and currency of all the information in **The Rough Guide to Japan** however, they can accept no responsibility for any loss, injury, or inconvenience sustained by any traveller as a result of information or advice contained in the guide.

5 7 9 8 6 4

Help us update

We've gone to a lot of effort to ensure that the third edition of **The Rough Guide to Japan** is accurate and up-to-date. However, things change – places get "discovered", opening hours are notoriously fickle, restaurants and rooms raise prices or lower standards. If you feel we've got it wrong or left something out, we'd like to know, and if you can remember the address, the price, the time, the phone number, so much the better.

We'll credit all contributions, and send a copy of the next edition (or any other Rough Guide if you prefer) for the best letters. Everyone who writes to us and isn't already a subscriber will receive a copy of our full-colour thrice-yearly newsletter. Please mark letters: "**Rough Guide Japan Update**" and send to: Rough Guides, 80 Strand, London WC2R 0RL, or Rough Guides, 4th Floor, 345 Hudson St, New York, NY 10014. Or send an email to **mail@roughguides.com**

Have your questions answered and tell others about your trip at **www.roughguides.atinfopop.com**

SMALL PRINT

Acknowledgements

Simon: I'd like to thank my co-authors Sophie, Mark and Dominic for their hard work and commitment to this new edition and Gavin Thomas back at base. The folks at JNTO in London and Australia were, as ever, very helpful. Also much appreciated were the support of Sophie Hemmel, who arranged my stay at the Four Seasons Marunouchi, Nico Jayawardena, for doing the same at the New Otani, and Mark Kobayashi for the Grand Hyatt, Tokyo. Many thanks to Hisayoshi Ataka for taking the hard work out of arranging all our youth hostel stays. A huge thanks goes to Toshiko from Andon Ryokan who not only showed me great hospitality and some wonderful places to eat, but also became my friend. Cheers to Robb Satterwhite, Gardner Robinson, Dan Riney and Gia Payne for fun nights out in Tokyo; to all the cool JETS and CIRS I met along the way, especially the partying guys from Kanazawa; and to Daniel Rosen and all behind the scenes at Kodô who made my trip to Sado truly memorable – *domo arigato gozaimasu*. As always, Tada Taku did a fine job fact-checking and feeding us incredibly useful information. Finally, this book is dedicated to the amazing, adorable and endlessly patient and supportive Twanda.

Dominic: Thanks and praise to the following: David Jack and Matsunaga Sachiko at KTO HQ (for letting me run wild through Shikoku), Christopher Stephens (for all sorts of tasty tidbits), Shimizu Keiji at Tour Club (for some very useful Kyoto updates), Aaron Miller (for showing me that hip-hop exists even in Uwajima), the very kind British girl in Kōchi whose name I forgot to note (for the lowdown on the city's clubs), Sun Ra (for his cosmic space-jazz), Yamazawa Yuri (for not minding while I wasted too much time rummaging around in Takamatsu's second-hand record shops), the entire island of Jamaica (for providing the righteous music I wrote the update to), Justin Ellis & Sally McLaren (for a tip or two on where to dine fine in Kyoto), Shimizu Naoko (for a tip or two on where to nosh posh in Ōsaka), Kyle Barrow, Aidan O'Connor & Simon Moran (for the good times), John Potter (for his lowdown on the Okinawan music scene), Akizuki Keiko and Tsuda Chiaki (for holding one fort), and my momma (for holding the other).

Sophie: I'm indebted to all my friends in Kurayoshi who introduced me to Japan in the first place. Thanks to Nakamoto Bed & Bicycle, Jules and Kie in Amakusa and Minshuku al-Badri for their hospitality over the years, and to all I met along the way – old friends and new. Thanks also to Simon for the gig, and to Chris and Grant for not burning the house down while I was gone.

Mark: Thanks to Emma Kelly and Shigeo Kimura at JNTO Sydney and Hisayoshi Ataka of Japan Youth Hostels for their assistance. Thanks to Masako Suzuki for providing me with a base in Tokyo, to Danola in Sendai and to all those who went out of their way to help me on my travels.

The editor would also like to thank Kylie Clark at JNTO in London for all her help; Katie Lloyd-Jones for keeping a steady eye on many maps; Harriet Mills for perfect pictures; Tanya Hall for last-minute layout; and Sophie Branscombe for all her help and patience over many months.

Readers' letters

Thanks to all who wrote in with comments and suggestions (and apologies to anyone whose name we've misspellt or omitted).

Frank Arnold, Keith Bailey, Laura Barlow, K. Behr, Henk & Vicky Bekker, Misty Bliss-Ikeda, Brenda Bogaert, Brodie, Alice Brotherton, Patricia Buonocore, Mischa Burrows, Gerardo Celis, Brian Cheves, David Cook, Laura Coulter, Pam Courtenay, Lynn Cullivan, Jane Davey, Julian Diggle, Philip S. Dodds, Marc Ernzer, Philippa Fogarty, James Fraser, Helene B. Gagnon, Tenniel Garwes, Willi Gasser, Maria Gilles, John Gregory, M.W. Griffiths, Guy Hanke, Beverly Hasegawa, David Haseldine, Pippa Hector, Tony Helies, Louise Hirasawa, Jim Hodgeon, Darren Hood, Wilfrid Horace, Kar Hughes, Rhidian Hughes, Kim Jardine, J. Johnson, C.M. Jones, Danielle Joseph, Christoph Kappler, Nicolas Karman, Jamie Kelly, Megan Kelly, Aleesha Khan, Teresa Kludt , Brian Knox, R.

Kungel, Michio Kitahara, Bhavin Lakhani, Winni Liang, Raymond Lloyd, David Long, Chris Lowe, Stuart Mace , J. Callum Makkai, Bill & Sandra Martin, Nicola Martin, Annerose Matsushita, Aoife McLysaght, John Moran, Marc Niemann, Megs O'Brien, Naoki Peter, Tom Petch, Emma Phillips, Maegan Plagge, Dominika Plümpe, Tony Power, Sarah Riches, Dave Roberts, Umut Sarpel, Walt Schafer , Phil Scowen, Linda Senior, Caroline Shaw, Mark Smith, Sylvia Squirrel, Matt Staver, Sven Steinmo, Dennis Stern, Alberto Striolo, Teresa Sullivan, Simon Sweeney, Perry Swirsky, Harry Teale, Pimpicha Thanatavee, Otto Tromm, Marina Trowell, Benoit d'Udekem, Tracy Vap, Rob Wakulat, Chris Walker, Jayne West, Kate Williamson, Paul Whitfield, Maxine Winter.

Photo Credits

SMALL PRINT

SMALL PRINT

Index

Map entries are in **colour**.

INDEX

INDEX

1053

Kyoto Royal Hotel
Sanio Agaru kawara-
machi

Nakagyo - ku

kyoto 604

Map symbols

maps are listed in the full index using coloured text

− − −	Chapter division boundary		@	Internet
▬ ··	Provincial boundary		ⓘ	Tourist office
▬▬▬	Motorway		▣	Restaurant
═══	Major road		◉	Accommodation
═══	Minor road		Ⓢ	Subway station
▬▬▬	Pedestrianised street		★	Bus Stop
··········	Road under construction		🛢	Fuel station
− − − − −	Path		⊠	Gate
────	River		⊞	Hospital
− −	Ferry route		⊠	Post office
●·−−·●	Cable car and stations		✈	Airport
═▬═	JR line		🌴	Gardens
▬▬▬	Shinkenson line		‿	Bridge
┤┤┤┤┤┤	Private rail line		⚘	Viewpoint
− − −	Subway line		✳	Observation Platform
− − − − −	Tram line		🌲	Jōmon-sugi
★−−−★	New Tram line		⚵	Five-storied Pagoda
────	Ropeway		⚖	Market
− − − − −	Pedestrian tunnel		⛷	Skiing
⌐⌐⌐⌐⌐	Rocks		♛	Castle
⋃⋃⋃⋃	Reef		🗼	Lighthouse
▮▮▮▮	Escarpment		⬠	Mountain Refuge
▲	Peak		ᚿ	Shrine
⩰	Mountain pass		♠	Buddhist Temple
◓	Cave		▬	Building
🕉	Waterfall		⊟	Church
♦	Place of interest		◯	Stadium
⊙	Statue		⁺₊⁺	Christian Cemetery
♥	Museum		▦	Park
∴	Ruin		▒	Beach
⚊	Campsite			